Ireland

a Lonely Planet travel survival kit

Tom Smallman
Sean Sheehan
Pat Yale
John Murray
Tony Wheeler

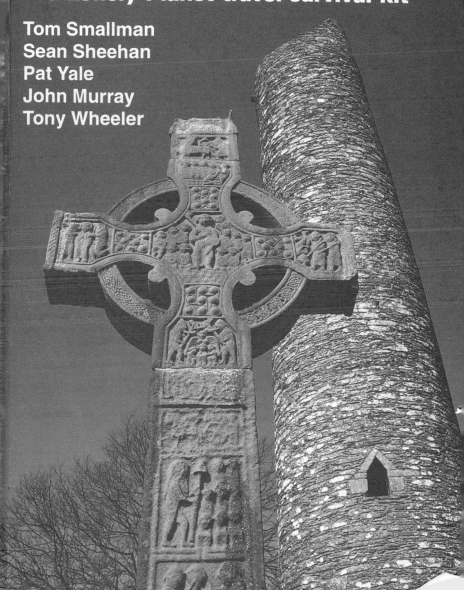

Ireland

2nd edition

Published by
Lonely Planet Publications
Head Office: PO Box 617, Hawthorn, Vic 3122, Australia
Branches: 155 Filbert St, Suite 251, Oakland, CA 94607, USA
               10 Barley Mow Passage, Chiswick, London W4 4PH, UK
               71 bis rue du Cardinal Lemoine, 75005 Paris, France

Printed by
Colorcraft Ltd, Hong Kong
Printed in China

Photographs by
Tom Smallman
Sean Sheehan
Pat Yale
John Murray
Tony Wheeler
Richard Stewart

Front cover & spine: Dublin shop sign (Pat Yale)

First Published
January 1994

This Edition
February 1996

**Although the authors and publisher have tried to make the information as
accurate as possible, they accept no responsibility for any loss, injury or
inconvenience sustained by any person using this book.**

National Library of Australia Cataloguing in Publication Data

Smallman, Tom
Ireland

2nd ed.
Includes index.
ISBN 0 86442 352 7

1. Ireland – Guidebooks. I. Murray, John. Ireland II. Sheehan, Sean,1951-. III. Yale, Pat, 1954-. IV. Title.
(Series: Lonely Planet travel survival kit)

914.1704824

text & maps © Lonely Planet 1996
photos © photographers as indicated 1996
climate charts compiled from information supplied by Patrick J Tyson, © Patrick J Tyson, 1996

Tom Smallman

Tom was born and raised in the UK and now lives in Melbourne, Australia. He had a number of jobs before joining Lonely Planet as an editor and is now working full time as an author. He has worked as co-author on Lonely Planet's travel survival kit to *Canada* and helped to update the 2nd edition of the *Dublin* city guide.

Sean Sheehan

Despite what his name suggests, Sean was born and brought up in London. After teaching for a number of years he took an escape route to South-east Asia where he lived and worked for six years. During that time, alongside acquiring a thirst for travel, he wrote a travel guide to Malaysia and Singapore, edited Shakespeare, ran a computer column for a British publication and worked for a Japanese magazine. His home is now in West Cork in Ireland although he is presently working in Hong Kong and will soon be returning to live in London.

Pat Yale

Way back in 1974, Pat Yale got as far as Turkey in an old van that didn't look as if it would make it past Dover. After graduating, she spent several years selling holidays before throwing up sensible careerdom to head overland from Egypt to Zimbabwe on her own. Returning home, she mixed teaching with extensive travelling in Europe, Asia, and Central and South America. As well as having several books and many articles under her belt, Pat updated the Turkey section for Lonely Planet's *Mediterranean Europe* on a shoestring, helped to update the 2nd edition of the *Dublin* city guide and is currently updating the 5th edition of the travel survival kit to *Turkey*.

John Murray

A native Irishman, John Murray graduated in marine zoology from Trinity College Dublin in 1986. He headed off to the South Pacific and Australia working as a scuba instructor and underwater archaeologist. Flat broke, he earned a ticket home with an article for the Qantas inflight magazine – his first journalistic venture. As well as being one of the author's of the 1st edition of the *Ireland* guide, John has worked as an adventure-film-maker, TV reporter and photo-journalist. His career has taken him to North and South America, Africa and Asia, and he has made a film of the first successful Irish ascent of Mt Everest.

Tony Wheeler

For the 1st edition of the *Ireland* guide, Tony wrote the chapter on Dublin and made a large contribution to the Belfast chapter. He was born in England but grew up in Pakistan, the Bahamas and the USA. He returned to England to do a degree in engineering at Warwick University, worked as an automotive design engineer, returned to university to complete an MBA in London, then dropped out on the Asian overland trail with his wife Maureen. Eventually settling down in Australia, they've been travelling, writing and publishing guidebooks ever since, having set up Lonely Planet Publications in the mid-1970s. Travel for the Wheelers is considerably enlivened by their daughter Tashi and their son Kieran.

From the Authors

Tom Smallman My thanks to Sue Graefe for her patience and support; to the Ryan family – Kathleen, Christy, Kathleen, Roger and Christy – for their hospitality; to Christy senior for helping me sort out my computer problems; to Pat and John for not asking me to help get the maggots out of their car; to Brian Frost for his company and showing me how easy it is to open a car boot, and to Tricia for encouraging him to make the trip; to Arthur for the bed and board; to Narelle Graefe for the huge amounts of background information she was able to supply me with; to Lindy Mark for being so efficient; to the people in the tourist offices who answered my queries especially Mary Neville of Bord Fáilte; to Shamrock Travel in Melbourne; to the Lonely Planet staff in the London, Paris and especially Melbourne offices; and to those readers who wrote in with comments on the first edition.

Sean Sheehan Sean would like to thank the invariably helpful members of tourist offices he met in Ireland. Special thanks to Pat & Irene in Kinsale, Tony Daly and Mrs O'Sullivan in Kenmare, Conal O'Neil in Cork, Darrer Michi in Waterford and Michael Mannix in Tralee.

Pat Yale In my months on the road I experienced much traditional hospitality firsthand, but particular thanks for help with the Northern Ireland section are due to Noreen Mikael of the NITB, to Patricia Moorehead of Belfast's Economic Development Unit, to Maureen Grant in Newry and to Harry Bryson for showing me around Derry. In Belfast, Paul and the staff of the youth hostel made sure I was never bedless, while in Dublin, Robin, Mary, Martin, Patricia, Joe and the cheery breakfast staff of Globetrotter's Tourist Hostel were ever ready with tea and sympathy. In Donegal, Dr Ciaran O'Keeffe of Glenveagh National Park and Michael Gilvarry of the Dunlewey Centre were generous with their time and information. In Dublin, Mary Gibbons offered some fascinating insights into Irish culture, while in Donegal, Becky Garcia introduced me unexpectedly to the Screamers. For help in getting to grips with Irish music, I am indebted to Eddy Gallagher at Finn Farm, Eamon at Screag an Iolair, Eilis Moore, Kieran Gallagher, Paul McGill, Wayne Ford and Eithne Bale, and to the staff of Claddagh Records in Dublin and of Soundsaround in Derry. My tape collection has been enriched accordingly. Finally, thanks to Tony and Sharon for help with ironing out the technical glitches and for home-based tea and sympathy.

From the Publisher

This book was edited in Lonely Planet, Melbourne, by Chris Wyness. Liz Filleul's contribution as an editor and a proofreader was invaluable, as was the help given by Ian Ward, Jane Fitzpatrick, Lyn McGaurr, Anne Mulvaney and Mary Neighbour. Many thanks to Steve Womersley for his help with the computer 'stuff'. Rachel Black did a fabulous job getting the maps right, creating new illustrations and doing the layout. Simon Bracken and Andrew Tudor designed a splendid cover. And finally, a special thanks from the editor to Guinness, Van Morrison, the Pogues and all things Irish which, over the years, have contributed to his well being.

Warning & Request

Things change – prices go up, schedules change, good places go bad and bad places go bankrupt – nothing stays the same. So if you find things better or worse, recently opened or long since closed, please write and tell us and help make the next edition better. Your letters will be used to help update future editions and, where possible, important changes will also be included in a Stop Press section in reprints.

We greatly appreciate all information that is sent to us by travellers. Back at Lonely Planet we employ a hard-working readers' letters team to sort through the many letters we receive. The best ones will be rewarded with a free copy of the next edition or another Lonely Planet guide if you prefer. We give away lots of books, but, unfortunately, not every letter/postcard receives one.

Contents

Map Legend

BOUNDARIES

.... International Boundary

.... Regional Boundary

ROUTES

.... Freeway

.... Highway

.... Major Road

.... Unsealed Road or Track

.... City Road

.... City Street

.... Railway

.... Underground Railway

.... Tram

.... Walking Track

.... Walking Tour

.... Ferry Route

.... Cable Car or Chairlift

AREA FEATURES

.... Parks

.... Built-Up Area

.... Pedestrian Mall

.... Market

.... Cemetery

.... Reef

.... Beach or Desert

.... Rocks

HYDROGRAPHIC FEATURES

.... Coastline

.... River, Creek

.... Intermittent River or Creek

.... Rapids, Waterfalls

.... Lake, Intermittent Lake

.... Canal

.... Swamp

SYMBOLS

❂ CAPITAL		National Capital
◉ Capital		Regional Capital
⬤ CITY		Major City
● City		City
● Town		Town
● Village		Village
■	▼	Place to Stay, Place to Eat
☕	☗	Cafe, Pub or Bar
✉	☎	Post Office, Telephone
❶	❸	Tourist Information, Bank
◗	℗	Transport, Parking
⛪	⌂	Museum, Youth Hostel
⛺	⛢	Caravan Park, Camping Ground
✝	✚	Church, Cathedral
☪	✡	Mosque, Synagogue
卍	卐	Buddhist Temple, Hindu Temple
✛	★	Hospital, Police Station

☯	⛽	Embassy, Petrol Station
✈	✠	Airport, Airfield
▭	✿	Swimming Pool, Gardens
❖	🐘	Shopping Centre, Zoo
☘	⛼	Winery or Vineyard, Picnic Site
←	A25	One Way Street, Route Number
🏛	⚱	Stately Home, Monument
♜	▣	Castle, Tomb
⌒	⌂	Cave, Hut or Chalet
▲	※	Mountain or Hill, Lookout
⛴	⚓	Lighthouse, Shipwreck
)(	◎	Pass, Spring
⚑	⚐	Beach, Surf Beach
∴		Archaeological Site or Ruins
		Ancient or City Wall
		Cliff or Escarpment, Tunnel
		Railway Station

Note: not all symbols displayed above appear in this book

Introduction

Ireland is one of Western Europe's most lightly populated, least industrialised and, in a word, least 'spoilt' countries. It also has one of the longest and most tragic histories in Europe.

That long history is easy to trace, from Stone Age passage tombs and ring forts, through ancient monasteries and castles, down to the great houses and splendid Georgian architecture of the 18th and 19th centuries. The tragic side of that history is equally easy to unearth. The destruction wrought by the Vikings from the end of the 8th century AD onwards is still visible in the ruins of once-great monasteries. The country's history since the arrival of the English in the 12th century is punctuated with rebellion and repression. Oliver Cromwell's visit in 1649-50 is still remembered with horror; and the Irish population has still not recovered from the mass starvation and emigration resulting from the potato famine in the mid-19th century. The 20th century has been no less turbulent, and the Troubles have continued in Northern Ireland up to today. There are, however, hopeful signs of a permanent, though still fragile, peace.

Travellers could be forgiven for forgetting this sad history when facing the peaceful green landscape of the centre, with its lakes and mountains, or the magnificent cliffs of the wild Atlantic coast, and the offshore islands which have been inhabited for millennia. Many traces of traditional culture survive in these remote western areas, and there are still communities in which Irish is the first language.

In cities like Dublin, Cork and Galway, narrow, medieval streets can still be found – a traffic planner's nightmare. Dublin was at its architectural peak in the 18th century, and many of those fine buildings have lasted for over 200 years almost unchanged. But these are not museum cities: they are friendly places with great pubs, live music, good theatres and – when it's not raining – cheerful

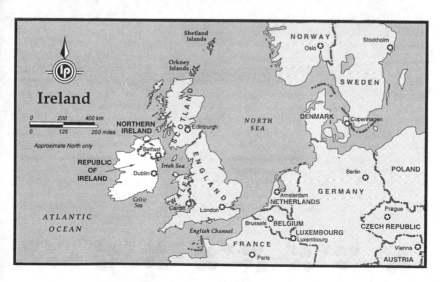

street life. In the North, Belfast and Derry are also remarkably welcoming places, especially now the military conflict may be coming to an end. It's worth emphasising that they are probably safer for visitors than most other European cities!

When the distinction between Ireland the island and Ireland the state needs to be made in this book, the state is referred to as the Republic of Ireland, the Republic or 'the South'. You may also hear Ireland (the state) referred to as Eire, Southern Ireland or the Free State. In this book Northern Ireland is either referred to as such or as 'the North'. You may also hear it dubbed Ulster or 'the six counties'. Prior to the division of Ireland, the old province of Ulster actually comprised nine counties. Six of these went into Northern Ireland and the other three into the Republic of Ireland.

Facts about Ireland

HISTORY
First Settlers

Ireland was probably first settled by humans about 10,000 years ago, at the end of the last Ice Age. This is relatively late in European prehistory, as Palaeolithic or Old Stone Age people were living in southern England 400,000 years ago and in Wales 250,000 years ago.

With the low sea levels of the last Ice Age, there were land or ice bridges between Ireland and Britain and between Britain and mainland Europe. But conditions in Ireland would have been hostile until the glaciers receded between 12,000 and 10,000 years ago, and prey animals such as deer and boar would have been scarce. These increased in numbers as the weather improved. Around 12,000 years ago, the Irish giant elk flourished, and there were probably no humans around to hunt it.

As the ice caps melted, there was an enormous rise in the sea level, and about 9000 years ago Ireland was cut off from Britain. It was around this time that the first humans seem to have reached Ireland (landing in the north-east near the modern-day town of Larne) from Britain, possibly across the land bridge or in small hide-covered boats. These people were Middle Stone Age (Mesolithic) hunter-gatherers. They would have lived in small family or tribal groups collecting fruit and nuts and hunting any animals they could tackle. Their lifestyle would have been similar to that of the Australian Aborigines or the Kalahari Bushpeople.

The traces of these first Irish men and women are faint: a few scattered rubbish dumps or middens, containing shells and the bones of small animals. Their weapons and tools included flint axes and slivers of flint called microliths, which were used as blades set in a bone or wooden handle. They hunted boar, kept dogs and had a fondness for eels and salmon. The richest concentration of these early sites are in northern Ireland, including one at Mt Sandel near Coleraine, and date from around 8000 to 6000 BC.

First Farmers

While the first settlers were busy discovering Ireland, the greatest revolution in human history had already taken place in the fertile crescent of the Middle East. It was another 2000 or 3000 years before farming reached Ireland, around 4000 BC. Farming marked the arrival of New Stone Age or Neolithic times, and archaeologists cannot be certain whether a new wave of farmers colonised Ireland or whether the concept of farming filtered through with just a few immigrants.

A settlement from this era was discovered near Lough Gur in County Limerick, the traces of pottery, wooden houses and implements indicating a much more prosperous and settled way of life than before. Near Ballycastle in north Mayo, a remarkable complex of intact stone field walls dating from these times was discovered hidden under a vast blanket of bog. Also around this time was born one of the first Irish exports. Tievebulliagh Mountain near Cushendall in County Antrim has an outcrop of remarkable hard stone called porcellanite, and it formed the basis of a thriving stone-axe industry. Tievebulliagh stone axes have been found as far away as the south of England.

These farmers had enormous respect for the dead and, from about 3000 BC, built the extraordinary passage graves at Newgrange, Knowth and Dowth in the Boyne Valley. Over 1000 megalithic tombs survive from the Neolithic period, and two large Neolithic settlements have been discovered in the Six Mile Water Valley in County Antrim.

The Bronze Age

The next great human revolution was the ability to work metal and track down the tin and copper ores which could be amalgamated to produce bronze. This heralded the Bronze Age, which in Ireland is characterised by a reduction in the scale and number of stone tombs, but which produced a wonderful legacy of gold and bronze metalwork.

The Bronze Age started in Ireland about 2500 BC, and the early prospectors were amazingly astute at tracking down sources of metal. Almost everywhere that modern geologists have discovered traces of copper and other metals, they have also discovered that someone else had got there some 4000 years previously, without the help of modern equipment and mapping. Bronze Age mine workings can still be seen on Mt Gabriel near Schull in County Cork, and St Kevin's Bed or Cave in Glendalough is thought by many to be an early mine.

Gold-working flourished during the Bronze Age, and the quality of the craftwork and the quantity of metal used say something about the wealth of Ireland at this time. The National Museum in Dublin contains the finest collection of prehistoric goldwork in Europe. Some of the gold may have come from the Wicklow Mountains. (A gold rush took place in the area much later, in 1795.)

Through the Bronze and Iron Ages, the tentacles of trade spread farther and farther out from Ireland. Blue faience beads manufactured in Egypt have turned up in graves on the Hill of Tara in County Meath, as did amber from Scandinavia. The skeleton of a Barbary ape from Spain or Portugal was discovered in a site dating from 200 BC on Eamhain Macha or Navan Fort in County Armagh.

The Celts

The Celts were Iron Age warrior tribes from eastern Europe who conquered large sections of central and southern Europe between 800 and 300 BC. The Romans called them 'Galli' or Gauls and the Greeks used the term 'Keltoi' or Celts. Both societies had cause to fear the Celts, who plundered Rome in the 4th century AD and were described by contemporary scholars as fierce and dashing warriors. The use of iron was by now widespread throughout Europe, although bronze weapons also continued to be used for some time.

Celtic warriors and adventurers probably reached Ireland around 300 BC, and they were certainly well ensconced by 100 BC. In relatively small numbers, they moved in, controlled the country for 1000 years, and left a legacy of language and culture that survives today. The Celts also had a common code of law called the Brehon Law and their religion was druidism. They had a distinctive style of design, and its swirls and loops are seen on many Irish artefacts from the 2nd and 1st centuries BC. Good examples are the Broighter Collar in the National Museum and the Turoe Standing Stone near Loughrea in County Galway. The Irish language is Celtic in origin.

There are no written records for the early Celtic period. Chieftains ensured their immortality through heroic deeds and actions, which would be passed down the generations in songs and stories. The epic tales of *Cúchulainn* and the *Táin Bó Cuailnge* are believed to have come from this period. Cúchulainn is the consummate Celtic hero warrior; similar figures appear in Homer's *Iliad* and in the *Mahabharata* poem from India. The *Táin Bó Cuailnge* may not be historically accurate, but the stories may give some idea of Irish society in the first couple of centuries AD.

The country was divided into five provinces: Leinster, Meath, Connaught, Ulster and Munster. Meath later merged with Leinster. The principal struggle for power as reflected in the *Táin Bó Cuailnge* was between Connaught and Ulster. Eamhain Macha (now called Navan Fort) in County Armagh, mentioned in the *Táin Bó Cuailnge*, is recorded in the map of Ireland drawn in the 2nd century AD by the Egyptian scholar Ptolemy. Within the provinces there were perhaps 100 or more minor kings and chieftains controlling sections of the country (which were called *Tuatha*), and Tara in County Meath became the base for some of the most powerful leaders.

St Patrick & Christianity

The westward march of the Roman empire came to a halt in England. As the empire declined and the Dark Ages began to engulf much of Europe, Ireland became an outpost of European civilisation.

Christianity arrived sometime between the 3rd and 5th centuries, and while St Patrick is given the credit for proselytising the native Irish, there were certainly earlier missionaries. Some scholars dispute that there was a St Patrick at all, and claim the stories about him are really about these early clerics, or later inventions. However, the evidence suggests that there was a St Patrick who lived in the 5th century, and that at the age of 16 he was kidnapped from Britain by Irish pirates. During six years in Ireland as a slave tending sheep, Patrick found religion. After escaping back to Britain, he was instructed to return to Ireland by powerful visions. Patrick first went to Europe to train as a cleric, and from around 432 AD spent the rest of his life converting the Irish to Christianity. His base was Armagh in County Down, probably chosen because of the symbolic pagan significance of nearby Eamhain Macha (Navan Fort).

Much of our knowledge of Patrick comes from his own writings. St Patrick's *Confession* is a copy of one such account from the 9th-century 'Book of Armagh' (held in Trinity College, Dublin).

As Europe sank into the Dark Ages, Ireland in the 7th and 8th centuries became a 'land of saints and scholars', with thriving monasteries where monks wrote in Latin and illuminated manuscripts, including the world-famous 'Book of Kells' (also in Trinity College). Outstanding among the monasteries were Clonmacnois in County Offaly and Glendalough in County Wicklow. Monks such as Colmcille and Columbanus founded monasteries abroad.

The Vikings

During the 8th century, however, Vikings in their slim powerful boats began to appear off the north and east coasts of Ireland attacking settlements, plundering monasteries and ushering in a new, more turbulent period of Irish history. In passing, it must be said that the local Irish clans were just as fond of raiding the monasteries as the Vikings were. Monasteries were places of wealth and power, and were often caught up in inter-tribal squabbles. But the increasingly frequent Viking raids burned into the consciousness of Irish monks, and into their accounts of these times. Round towers were built to act as lookout posts and places of refuge in the event of an attack.

In 795 AD, a Viking fleet sailed down the west coast of Scotland, raiding St Colmcille's monastery on Iona before turning their attentions to the east coast of Ireland. They came ashore either at Rathlin Island off the Antrim coast or Lambay Island near Dublin. Irish weapons and soldiers were no match for the superbly armed and ferocious Norsemen. During the 9th century the Vikings started to settle in Ireland and form alliances with native families and chieftains. They established many settlements which bear Viking names today including Wicklow, Waterford and Wexford. They founded Dublin, which in the 10th century was a small Viking kingdom.

The struggles continued between the Vikings and the native Irish, who learned many lessons in the art of warfare. The most decisive defeat for Viking ambitions was at the Battle of Clontarf in 1014, by Irish forces led by Brian Ború, king of Munster, who was aided in the fight by other Vikings from Waterford and Limerick. The elderly Brian Ború was killed by retreating Vikings and subsequent divisions among his chieftains meant the victory wasn't consolidated, but Viking military power in Ireland had been broken. Large numbers of Vikings, however, remained in Ireland, marrying with the native Irish, converting to Christianity and joining in the struggle against the next wave of invaders – the Normans.

The Norman Conquest

In 1066 the Normans under William the Conqueror invaded and conquered England. They were former Vikings themselves, who had settled in northern France 150 years previously, had come to terms with the French king, and had adopted the language, religion and military technology. They made no immediate effort to involve themselves in Ireland, but this could only be a matter of time. When they did come over, they were, ironically, responding to an invitation by an Irish chief.

This came about because the king of Leinster, Dermot MacMurrough, and the king of Connaught, Tiernan O'Rourke, were arch rivals. Their relationship was not improved by MacMurrough's kidnapping of O'Rourke's wife in 1152 (although it appears she went willingly). O'Rourke defeated MacMurrough, who fled abroad in 1166 to search for foreign allies. After arguing his case in France, MacMurrough obtained a hearing with the astute Henry II of England, who at first was too busy to get involved himself, but encouraged MacMurrough to seek help elsewhere among his subjects.

MacMurrough went to Wales, where he met Richard FitzGilbert de Clare, earl of Pembroke, better known as Strongbow, who agreed to muster an army and return to Ireland with MacMurrough. In return he demanded MacMurrough's daughter in marriage and the inheritance of the kingship of Leinster once MacMurrough was dead. MacMurrough agreed, and the stage was set for more than 800 years of English involvement in Ireland.

In May 1169, the first Norman forces arrived in Bannow Bay, County Wexford. MacMurrough joined them, and they took Wexford Town and Dublin with ease. The next group of Normans arrived in Bannow Bay in 1170, led by his lieutenant Raymond le Gros, and defeated a considerably larger Irish and Viking army at Baginbun Head on the Hook Peninsula.

In August 1170, Strongbow himself arrived, and with le Gros took Waterford after a fierce battle. A few days later MacMurrough arrived and handed over his daughter Aoife to Strongbow. After MacMurrough's death the following year, Strongbow set about consolidating his new position as king of Leinster.

Meanwhile in England, Henry II was watching events in Ireland with growing unease. In 1754 Henry II had been recognised by the pope as Lord of Ireland and technically Strongbow was one of his subjects. But Strongbow's independence of mind and action was worrying him. In 1171, Henry II sailed from England with a huge naval force, landed at Waterford and declared the place a royal city. He took a semblance of control, but the new Norman lords still did pretty much as they pleased.

Just as the Vikings first settled and were then absorbed so were the new Anglo-Norman intruders. Barons like de Courcy and de Lacy set up power bases very similar to native Irish kingdoms, outside the control of the English king. Over the next two hundred years integration between the Anglo-Normans and native Irish was so successful that in 1336 the English crown introduced the Statutes of Kilkenny which made intermarriage and the use of Irish language and customs illegal. It was too late, and assimilation had gone too far. Over the centuries English control gradually retreated to an area around Dublin known as 'the Pale'. Hence the expression 'beyond the Pale' for an area beyond control.

Henry VIII

In the 16th century, Henry VIII moved to reinforce English control over his unruly neighbour. He was particularly worried that France or Spain might use Ireland as a base from which to attack England. The principal power brokers in Ireland, the Anglo-Norman Fitzgeralds, earls of Kildare, and nominally the representatives of the English crown in Ireland, were in open rebellion. Henry sought their downfall.

In 1534, Garret Óg, the reigning earl, was meeting with Henry in London. The story goes that his 27-year-old son Silken Thomas heard rumours that his father had been executed. Silken Thomas gathered his father's forces and attacked Dublin and the English garrisons. In London, Garret Óg was, however, very much alive and well, and Henry packed off a large army to Ireland which easily crushed Silken Thomas's rebellion. The Fitzgeralds may have been trying

TONY WHEELER

TONY WHEELER

TONY WHEELER

TONY WHEELER

TONY WHEELER

TONY WHEELER

TONY WHEELER

PAT YALE

TONY WHEELER

Some of the many door knockers and brightly painted doors found in Dublin

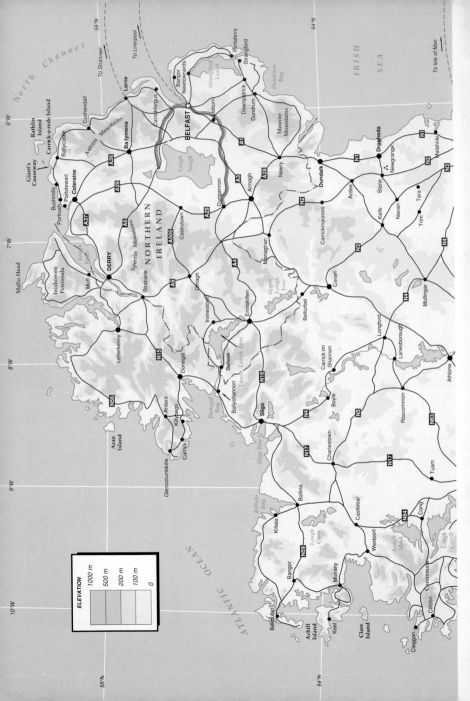

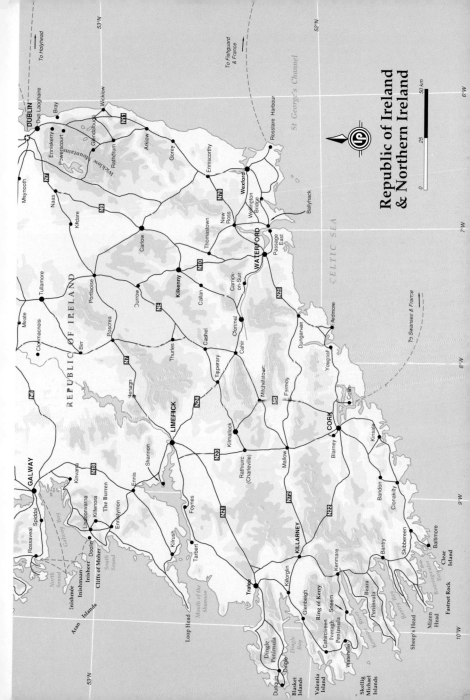

Republic of Ireland & Northern Ireland

TONY WHEELER

PAT YALE

PAT YALE

Busking in Grafton Street, Dublin

to prove they were still a force to be reckoned with in Ireland.

Thomas and his followers surrendered, but they were subsequently executed in what became known as the 'pardon of Maynooth'. This pattern of retribution was to become familiar in following centuries. The Fitzgerald estates were divided among English settlers, and an English viceroy was appointed.

Meanwhile Henry was involved in a separate battle – with the pope, over the difficult matter of his divorce from Catherine of Aragon. In 1532 he broke with the Catholic Church. With the downfall of the earls of Kildare in 1535, Henry was also able to launch an assault on the property of the Catholic Church in Ireland, which had encouraged rebellion. The wealthy Irish monasteries were dissolved – at considerable profit to the crown – over the next few years. In 1541 Henry ensured that the Irish Parliament declared him king of Ireland.

Elizabeth I

Under Elizabeth I, the English consolidated their power in Ireland. The forests of Ireland were proving invaluable as a source of wood for shipbuilding, and oak was turned into charcoal for smelting ores. Strategically, too, Ireland was important as a possible back door for an invasion from England's enemies in mainland Europe.

English jurisdiction was established in Connaught and Munster despite a number of rebellions by the local ruling families. The success of Elizabeth's policies was borne out when survivors of the 1588 Spanish Armada were washed up on the west coast of Ireland and were mostly massacred by the local sheriffs and their forces.

The thorn in Elizabeth's side was Ulster, the last outpost of the Irish chiefs. Hugh O'Neill, earl of Tyrone, was the prime mover in the last serious assault on English power in Ireland. O'Neill had been educated in London, and Elizabeth believed that he would be loyal. A story is told of O'Neill ordering lead from England to reroof his castle; in reality the lead was for bullets. From 1594, O'Neill moved into open con-

Hugh O'Neill, earl of Tyrone

flict with the English and thus began the Nine Years War (1594-1603). He proved a courageous and crafty foe, and the English forces stepped up their campaign against him but met with little success until 1601.

In September of that year, a Spanish force landed in Ireland to join O'Neill. Unfortunately, the Spanish disembarked at Kinsale in County Cork, almost 480 km from O'Neill's territory. O'Neill was forced to march south to join them, and after an exhausting journey ended up fighting the Battle of Kinsale near Cork in unfamiliar country. The Irish were defeated by the English forces under Lord Mountjoy, while the Spanish army was pinned down in Kinsale.

Kinsale was the end for O'Neill and for Ulster. Although O'Neill and his forces made it back to Ulster, their power was broken, and 15 months later in 1603 he surrendered and signed the Treaty of Mellifont, handing over power and authority to the English crown. O'Neill was allowed to stay on in Ulster on condition that he pledge allegiance to the crown, which he did. But, in 1607, after a number of frustrating years of subjugation and harassment, O'Neill and 90 other Ulster chiefs boarded a ship in Lough Swilly for Europe, leaving Ireland for ever. This was the 'Flight of the Earls', and it left Ulster leaderless and open to English rule.

With the native chiefs gone, Elizabeth and her successor, James I, pursued a policy of colonisation known as 'plantation' – an organised and ambitious expropriation of land which sowed the seeds for the division of Ulster that we see today. Huge swathes of land were confiscated from the Irish and large numbers of new settlers came from Scotland and England. They brought a new way of life and a different religion. Unlike most previous invaders, they didn't intermarry with the native Irish, and kept their culture and religion very much to themselves. And so, living among these new Protestant landowners was an impoverished and very angry population of native Irish and Old English Catholics.

Oliver Cromwell

In 1641, worried by developments in England and Ireland and believing Charles I to be pro-Catholic, these Irish and Old English Catholics took up arms. What happened subsequently is a matter of debate: certainly a considerable number of the new settlers were killed, but modern historians have revised the likely number of deaths down to perhaps 2000, from earlier widely exaggerated estimates; and many Catholics were also killed, in revenge. Stories of the 1641 atrocities have been used in anti-Catholic propaganda ever since.

The English Civil War kept most of the English busy at home for much of the 1640s. In Ireland, the native Irish and Old English Catholics, allied under the 1641 Confederation of Kilkenny, supported Charles I against the Protestant parliamentarians in the hope of restoring Catholic power in the country. After Charles' execution, the victorious Oliver Cromwell, leader of the parliamentarians, decided to go to Ireland and sort them out.

He arrived in 1649, and rampaged through the country, leaving a trail of death behind him and shipping many of the defeated as slaves to the Caribbean. Under the Act of Settlement (1652) others were dispossessed and exiled to the harsh and infertile lands in the west of Ireland, in the province of Connaught. Two million hectares of land were confiscated – more than a quarter of the country – and handed over to Cromwell's supporters many of whom remained to settle the land. Cromwell's tour of Ireland has never been forgotten.

Battle of the Boyne

The 1660 Restoration saw Charles II on the English throne. He kept his Catholic sympathies firmly in check. In 1685 his brother James succeeded him. James II's more open Catholicism raised English ire, and he was forced to flee the country at the beginning of 1689, intending to raise an army in Ireland and regain his throne from the Protestant William of Orange who had been invited to sit on the English throne by Parliament.

In late 1688, with rumours spreading among Irish Protestants that Irish Catholics were about to rise in support of James II, the Protestant citizens of Derry heard that a Catholic regiment was to be stationed in their city. After furious debate among the local worthies, 13 apprentice boys purloined the keys to the city and slammed the gates in the face of James's soldiers.

In March 1689 James II himself arrived from France at Kinsale, and marched north to Dublin, where the Irish parliament recognised him as king and began to organise the return of expropriated land to Catholic landowners. The siege of Derry began in earnest in April, and ended after mass starvation with the arrival of William's ships in July. The Protestant slogan 'No Surrender!' dates from the siege, which acquired mythical status among Irish Protestants over the following centuries.

William of Orange landed in 1690 at Carrickfergus, just north of Belfast, with an army of up to 36,000 men, and the Battle of the Boyne took place on 12 July. It was fought between Irish Catholics (led by James II who was a Scot) and English Protestants (led by William of Orange who was a Dutchman). To make things more complicated, James was William's uncle and his father-in-law. James II's principal supporter was Louis XIV of France, and fear of growing French power led both the Catholic king of Spain and the pope himself to back William and the Protestant side!

William's victory was a turning point, and is commemorated to this day by northern Protestants as a pivotal victory over 'popes and popery'. The final surrender of the Irish came in 1691, when the Catholic leader Patrick Sarsfield signed the Treaty of Limerick. He and thousands of his troops went into exile in France where they served in the French army.

Penal Times

The Treaty of Limerick contained quite generous terms of surrender for the Catholics, but these were largely ignored, and replaced by a harsh regime of penal laws a few years later in 1695. They were passed by a Protestant gentry anxious to consolidate their powers and worried that Louis XIV of France might attempt an invasion of Ireland. Also known as a 'popery code', these laws forbade Catholics from buying land, bringing their children up in their own religion, and from entering the army, navy or legal profession. All Irish culture, music and education was banned. There were also lesser restrictions imposed on Presbyterians and other nonconformists.

The Catholics organised open-air masses at secret locations usually marked by a 'mass rock', and illegal outdoor schools known as 'hedge schools' continued to teach the Irish language and culture. Among the educated classes, many Catholics converted to Protestantism to preserve their careers and wealth.

From around 1715, strict enforcement of the religious sections of the penal laws eased off, although many of the restrictions to do with employment and public office still held. A significant majority of the Catholic population were now tenants living in wretched conditions. By the mid-18th century, Catholics held less than 15% of the land in Ireland, and by 1778 barely 5%. Many middle-class Catholics went into trade.

The 18th Century

Meanwhile Dublin thrived, ranking as Europe's fifth-largest city. The Irish ruling class were members of the established Protestant Episcopalian Church, and were descendants of Cromwellian soldiers, Norman nobles and Elizabethan settlers. They formed a new and prosperous upper class known as the Protestant Ascendancy. There was a Protestant-only parliament, but laws still had to be approved by the British crown and parliament. It was from these Protestants that pressure first came for Ireland to be treated on an equal footing with Britain.

A strong 'Patriot' party calling for independence developed under the leadership of Henry Grattan and Henry Flood. When the American War of Independence broke out, Britain was in a difficult position. The majority of her forces had to be withdrawn from Ireland to fight in the colonies, leaving security in Ireland largely at the hands of Protestant 'volunteer' forces under the control of the landowners and merchant classes. To avoid further clashes with the increasingly independent Irish parliament, the British government in 1782 allowed the Irish what it considered to be complete freedom of legislation. The new Irish governing body was known as Grattan's parliament. However, London still controlled much of what went on in Ireland through royal patronage and favours and the crown still had the power of veto.

To achieve prosperity in Ireland, Grattan had espoused improved conditions and rights for Catholics. Henry Flood and the majority of other Protestant members were not as sympathetic, and in the life of the parliament – nearly 20 years – little progress was made.

The French Revolution

In the late 18th century, revolution was in the air, with the American War of Independence and – much more shocking to Britain – the French Revolution of 1789. No longer could the aristocracy and entrenched politicians be complacent about the poverty-stricken masses. In Ireland, an organisation known as the United Irishmen had been formed, and its most prominent leader was a young Dublin

Theobald Wolfe Tone

Protestant and republican, Theobald Wolfe Tone (1763-98).

The United Irishmen had been founded by Belfast Presbyterians and started out with high ideals of bringing together men of all creeds to reform and reduce England's power in Ireland. Their attempts at gaining power through straightforward politics were fruitless, and when war broke out between Britain and France the United Irishmen found they were no longer being tolerated by the establishment. They reformed themselves as an underground organisation committed to bring about change by any means, violent or otherwise. Tone was keen to enlist the help of the French, who, fresh from their European victories, were easily persuaded. At the same time, Protestants were worried by the turn of events and prepared for possible conflict by forming the Protestant Orange Society, which later became known as the Orange Order.

In 1796, a French invasion fleet with thousands of troops approached Bantry Bay in County Cork. On shore the local militia were ill-equipped to repel them. On board one of the French ships was Wolfe Tone, decked out in a French uniform and itching to get into action. However, a strong offshore wind repelled every attempt by the fleet to get up the bay to a safe landing spot. A few attempted to drop anchor but as the wind strengthened into a full gale, the ships were forced to head for the open Atlantic and back to France. A disappointed Wolfe Tone went back with them.

Saved by the weather, the government in Ireland woke up to the serious threat posed by the United Irishmen and similar groups. A nationwide campaign got underway to hunt them out and it proved extremely effective. Meanwhile another group of United Irishmen led by Lord Edward Fitzgerald tried to mount a rebellion, which also failed because of informers and poor communications between the rebels. After uncovering this attempted rebellion, the government and army really got stuck into the population in search of arms and rebels. Floggings and indiscriminate torture sent a wave of panic through the country and sparked off the only really serious fighting of the year, which became known as the 1798 Rising. Wexford, a county not noted for its rebellious tendencies, saw the fiercest fighting, with Father John Murphy leading the resistance. After a number of minor victories the rebels were finally and decisively defeated at Vinegar Hill just outside Enniscorthy.

Meanwhile the French had been planning another invasion, and a few months after Vinegar Hill a small fleet landed in County Mayo and achieved some minor successes but was soon defeated. Wolfe Tone himself arrived later in the year with another French fleet which was defeated at sea. Wolfe Tone was captured and brought to Dublin where he committed suicide in his prison cell. It was the end for the United Irishmen and ironically led to the demise of the independent Irish parliament.

The Protestant gentry, alarmed at the level of unrest, was much inclined to cuddle back up to the security of Great Britain. In 1800, the Act of Union, uniting Ireland politically with Britain, was passed, taking effect from 1 January 1801. Many of the wealthier Irish Catholics supported the Act; the British prime minister, William Pitt, had promised to remove the last of the penal laws, most of which had been repealed by 1793. The Irish parliament voted itself out of existence, and around 100 of the MPs moved to the House of Commons in London.

As if to remind them of the rebellious nature of the country, a tiny and completely ineffectual rebellion was staged in Dublin in 1803, led by a former United Irishman, Robert Emmet (1778-1803). Less than 100 men took part and Emmet was caught, tried and executed. He gave a famous speech from the dock which included the oft-quoted words: 'Let no man write my epitaph...When my country takes her place among the nations of the earth, then and not till then let my epitaph be written'.

The Great Liberator
While Emmet was swinging from the gallows, a 28-year-old Kerry man called Daniel O'Connell (1775-1847) was set on a course that would make him one of Ireland's greatest leaders. The O'Connell family were from Caherdaniel in County Kerry and had made their money from smuggling. Remarkably, the family managed to hang onto their house and lands through penal times.

In 1823, O'Connell founded the Catholic Association with the aim of achieving political equality for Catholics. The association soon became a vehicle for peaceful mass protest and action, and in an 1826 general election it first showed its muscle by backing Protestant candidates in favour of Catholic emancipation. The high point was in the election of 1828 when O'Connell himself stood for a seat in County Clare, even though being a Catholic he could not take the seat. O'Connell won easily, putting the British parliament in a quandary. If they didn't allow O'Connell to take his seat, there might be a popular uprising. Many in the House of Commons favoured emancipation, and the combination of circumstances led them to pass the 1829 Act of Catholic Emancipation allowing Catholics limited voting rights and the right to be elected as MPs.

Although William Pitt had promised to repeal the last of the penal laws after the Act of Union, it hadn't happened. The remaining laws had denied Catholics the right to sit in parliament and take important offices. Emancipation was the removal of these last few hurdles.

After this great victory, O'Connell settled down to the business of securing further reforms. Ten years later he turned his attentions to repeal of the Act of Union and re-establishing an Irish parliament. Now that Catholics could become MPs, such a body would be very different to the old Protestant-dominated Irish parliaments.

In 1843 the campaign really took off, with O'Connell working alongside the young Thomas Davis. His 'monster meetings' attracted up to half a million supporters, and took place all over Ireland. O'Connell exploited the threat that such gatherings represented to the establishment, but he baulked at the idea of a genuinely radical confrontation with the British. His bluff was called when a monster meeting at Clontarf was prohibited and O'Connell called it off.

He was arrested in 1844 but went out of his way to avoid any kind of violent clash. 'Be you, therefore, perfectly quiet', he told a meeting in Dublin. After serving a short spell in prison, O'Connell returned to Derrynane. He quarrelled with the Young Ireland movement (which, having seen pacifism fail, favoured the use of violence) and never again posed a threat to the British. He died four years later in 1847, as his country was being devoured by famine.

The Great Famine
Ireland suffered its greatest tragedy in the years 1845-51. The potato was the staple food of a rapidly growing but desperately poor population. From 1800 to 1840 the population had rocketed from four to eight million, putting even greater pressure on the land. Then between 1845 and 1851 a succession of almost complete failures of the potato crop resulted in mass starvation, emigration and death.

During this time, there were excellent harvests of other crops such as wheat, but these were too expensive for the poor to purchase.

While millions of its citizens were starving, Ireland continued to export food. Some landlords did their best for their tenants, but many others ignored the situation from their homes in Britain.

As a result of the famine about one million people died, many of disease rather than straight starvation, and about another million emigrated. Emigration continued to reduce the population during the next 100 years. Huge numbers of Irish settlers who found their way abroad, particularly to the USA, carried with them a lasting bitterness. Irish-American wealth would later find its way back to Ireland to finance the independence struggle.

Parnell & the Land League

In spite of the bitterness aroused by the famine, there was hardly any challenge to Britain's control of Ireland for quite some time. The abortive Fenian rising in March 1867 had its most publicised action in Manchester when 30 Irishmen attempted to free two of their leaders. In so doing they killed an English policeman, either by accident or design. Three of them were executed and became known in nationalist circles as the 'Manchester Martyrs.

In the 1870s and 1880s a man called Charles Stewart Parnell (1846-91) appeared on the political scene. The son of a Protestant landowner from Avondale in County Wicklow, he had much in common with other members of the Anglo-Irish ascendancy. But there were differences. Parnell's mother was American, and her father had fought the British in America. Parnell's family supported the principle of Irish independence from Britain.

Charles was a boisterous young man, educated in England, and he attended Cambridge before becoming an MP for County Meath. He quickly became noticed in the House of Commons as a passionate and difficult member who asked all the wrong questions.

In 1879 Ireland appeared to be facing another famine as potato crops were failing once again and evictions were becoming widespread. Cheap corn from America had pushed grain prices through the floor and with it the earnings of the tenants who paid their rent from grain they grew on their plots. A Fenian called Michael Davitt began to organise the tenants, and early on found a sympathetic ear in the unlikely person of Parnell. This odd pair were the brains behind the Land League, which initiated widespread agitation for reduced rents and improved working conditions. The conflict heated up and there was violence on both sides. Parnell instigated the strategy known as 'boycotting' against tenants, agents and landlords who went against the Land League's aims and were thus treated as lepers by the local population. Charles Boycott was a land agent in County Mayo and one of the first people the new strategy was used against.

The 'land war', as it became known, lasted from 1879 to 1882 and was a momentous period. For the first time, tenants were defying their landlords en masse. An election in 1880 brought William Gladstone to power in Britain. In the face of the situation in Ireland, he introduced his Land Act of 1881, which improved life immeasurably for tenants, creating fair rents and the possibility of tenants owning their land.

A crisis threatened in 1882 when two of the crown's leading figures in Ireland were murdered in Phoenix Park, Dublin. However, reform had been achieved, and Parnell now turned his attentions to achieving a limited form of autonomy for Ireland called Home Rule. Parnell had an extraordinary ally in William Gladstone, who in 1886 became prime minister for the third time and was dependent on Parnell for crucial support in parliament. But Gladstone and Parnell were defeated partly as a result of defections from Gladstone's own party.

The end was drawing near for Parnell. For 10 years he had been having an affair with Kitty O'Shea, who was married to a member of his own party. When the relationship was exposed in 1890, Parnell refused to resign as party leader, and the party split. Parnell was deposed as leader and the Catholic Church in Ireland quickly turned against him. The 'Uncrowned king of Ireland' was no longer welcome. Parnell's health deteriorated rapidly and he died less than a year later, aged just 45.

Home Rule Beckons

Gladstone was elected as prime minister for the fourth time in 1892 and this time managed to get his 'Home Rule for Ireland' bill through the House of Commons, but it was thrown out by the House of Lords. The Protestant community in Ireland, most numerous in the north-east, were becoming more and more alarmed at Gladstone's support for Home Rule, which might threaten their status and privileges.

By now eastern Ulster was quite a prosperous place. It had been spared the worst effects of the famine, and heavy industrialisation meant the Protestant ruling class was doing nicely.

While Gladstone had failed for the time being, the Ulster Unionists (the Unionist party had been formed in 1885) were now acutely aware that Home Rule could surface again, and they were determined to resist it, at least as far as Ulster was concerned. The unionists, led by Sir Edward Carson, a Dublin lawyer, formed a Protestant vigilante brigade called the Ulster Volunteer Force (UVF), and it held a series of mass paramilitary rallies. The UVF was formed to fight should Home Rule become law and in 1911 their worst nightmare seemed ready to unfold.

In Britain a new Liberal government under Prime Minister Asquith had removed the House of Lords' power to veto bills, and

Edward Carson

It was Edward Carson (1854-1935), a Protestant lawyer from Dublin, who spearheaded the Ulster opposition to Home Rule and led the movement which eventually resulted in Ireland's partition. Carson's career in law included numerous successful prosecutions of Irish tenants on behalf of British absentee landlords, and he played a leading role in the conviction of Oscar Wilde for homosexuality in 1895.

Carson was elected to the British House of Commons in 1892 and was solicitor general for Britain from 1900 to 1905. He was in line for the leadership of the Conservative Party until, in 1910, his fervent distaste for Home Rule and Irish independence led him to take the leadership of the Irish Unionists. Carson believed that without Belfast's heavy industries an independent Ireland would be economically unviable, and that he could frustrate Irish independence simply by keeping the North separate. The British Liberal government's determination to enact Home Rule was frustrated by Carson's parliamentary manoeuvres in 1912, and a year later he actually established a provisional government for the North in Belfast.

Carson threatened an armed struggle for a separate Northern Ireland if independence was granted to Ireland. By 1913 he had established a private Ulster army, and weapons were landed from Germany at Larne in 1914, shortly before the outbreak of WW I. The British began to bend before this Ulster opposition and, in July 1914 Carson agreed that Home Rule could go through for Ireland, so long as Ulster was kept separate. The events of WW I and the Easter Rising in Dublin in 1916 shifted the whole question from Home Rule to complete independence. By 1921, however, the Ulster opposition which Carson had nurtured was so strong that the country was carved up.

A statue of Carson defiantly fronts Stormont, the now unused parliament building which remains a symbol of Northern opposition to a united Ireland. Carson himself is buried in St Anne's Cathedral in central Belfast. ■

began to put another Home Rule for Ireland bill through Parliament – the political price being demanded for the support of the Irish Home Rule MPs. The bill was put through in 1912 against strident unionist and conservative British opposition, which mounted in ferocity.

As the UVF grew in strength, a republican group called the Irish Volunteers, led by the academic Eoin MacNeill, was set up in the south to defend Home Rule for the whole of Ireland. They lacked the weapons and organisation of the UVF, however, which succeeded in large-scale gun-running in 1914. There was widespread support for the UVF among officers of the British army.

Despite opposition, the Home Rule Act was passed, but suspended at the outbreak of WW I in August 1914. The question of Ulster was left unresolved. Many Irish nationalists believed that Home Rule would come after the war and that by helping out they could influence British opinion in their favour. John Redmond, the leader of the Irish Home Rule party, actively encouraged people to join the British forces to fight Germany.

The Gaelic Revival

While all of these attempts at Home Rule were being shunted about, something of a revolution was taking place in Irish arts, literature and identity. The Anglo-Irish literary revival was one aspect of this, championed by the young William Butler Yeats. The poet had a coterie of literary friends such as Lady Gregory, Douglas Hyde, John Millington Synge and George Russell. They unearthed many of the Celtic tales of Cúchulainn, and wrote with fresh enthusiasm about a romantic Ireland of epic battles and warrior queens. For a country that had suffered centuries of invasion and deprivation, these images presented a much more attractive version of history. Yeats and his friends were decidedly upper-crust themselves, and pursued the new literature and poetry primarily through the English language, aiming at the educated classes. A national theatre, later to become the Abbey Theatre, was born in Dublin from their efforts.

At the same time, people like Douglas Hyde and Eoin MacNeill were doing their best to ensure the survival of the Irish language and the more everyday Irish customs and culture. They formed the Gaelic League in 1893 which among other aims, pushed for the teaching of Irish in schools. The Gaelic League stressed the importance of the Irish language and culture to the Irish identity. In the 1890s it was primarily a cultural outfit and only assumed a nationalistic aura later on.

There were many other forces at work. The Gaelic Athletic Association, initially founded in 1884 to promote Irish sport and culture, was by the turn of the century a thriving and strongly politicised organisation. A small pressure group called *Sinn Féin* (which means 'We Ourselves') was set up under the leadership of Arthur Griffith, founder of the *United Irishmen* newspaper. He proposed that all Irish MPs should abandon the House of Commons in London and set up a parliament in Dublin (a similar strategy to that employed by Hungary in gaining its independence from Austria). Another group, the Fenians, also called the *Irish Republican Brotherhood (IRB)*, believed in independence through violence if necessary.

Socialism was gaining support in Dublin amongst the hungry tenement dwellers who had to put up with some of the worst urban housing conditions in Europe. In 1913 Jim Larkin and James Connolly called the transport workers out on strike. Although the strike ended in a return to work, the employers had failed to break the union and Larkin and Connolly had created the Irish Citizens' Army for self-defence. It now joined forces with the Irish Volunteers.

It must be said, however, that the majority of Dubliners were probably more concerned with WW I, and while some might have believed independence from Britain was a good idea, their passions went no further than that.

The Easter Rising

Many Irishmen with nationalist sympathies went off to the battlefields of Europe believing their sacrifice would ensure that Britain stood by its promise of Home Rule for

Ireland. The Home Rule Act was passed just before war broke out and would in theory be put into action once the war was over. However, a minority of nationalists in Ireland were not so trusting of Britain's resolve. The Irish Volunteers split into two groups, those under John Redmond who adopted this wait-and-see approach and a more radical group which believed in a more revolutionary course of action.

Two small groups – a section of the Irish Volunteers under Patrick Pearse and the Irish Citizens' Army led by James Connolly – staged a rebellion that took the country by surprise. On Easter Monday 1916, they marched into Dublin and took over a number of key positions in the city. Their headquarters was the GPO on O'Connell St, and from its steps Pearse read out to nonplussed passers-by a declaration that Ireland was now a republic and that his band were the provisional government. Less than a week of fighting ensued before the rebels surrendered in the face of superior British forces and firepower. The rebels were not popular, and as they were marched to jail they had to be protected from angry Dubliners.

The leader of the Irish Volunteers was Eoin MacNeill, and the rising had been planned by Pearse and others without his knowledge. When he discovered the plans at the last minute, MacNeill attempted to call the rebellion off, resulting in very few turning up on the day. The Germans were also supposed to arrive in U-boats and this didn't happen. So what might have been a real threat to British authority fizzled out completely. Many have said that Pearse knew they didn't stand a chance, but was preoccupied with a blood sacrifice, a noble gesture by a few brave souls that would galvanise the nation. Whether he believed this or not, a blood sacrifice was on the way.

The Easter Rising would probably have had little impact on the Irish situation, had the British not made martyrs of the leaders of the rebellion. Of the 77 given death sentences, 15 were executed. Pearse was shot three days after the surrender, and nine days later James Connolly was the last to die, shot in a chair because he could not stand on a gangrenous ankle. The deaths provoked a sea change in public attitudes to the republicans, whose support climbed from then on.

Countess Markievicz was one of those not executed, because she was female and there had been a recent outcry in Britain over the execution by the Germans of Edith Cavell, a nurse, in Belgium. Countess Markievicz was later to be the first woman elected to the British parliament (preceding Nancy Astor), but she refused to take up her seat. Eamon de Valera's death sentence was commuted to life imprisonment because of his US citizenship.

In the 1918 general election, the republicans stood under the banner of Sinn Féin and won a large majority of the Irish seats. Ignoring London's parliament, where technically they were supposed to sit, the newly elected Sinn Féin deputies – many of them veterans of the 1916 rising – declared Ireland independent and formed the first *Dáil Éireann* (Irish assembly or lower house), which sat in Dublin's Mansion House under the leadership of Eamon de Valera. While the Irish had declared independence, the British had by no means conceded it, and a confrontation was imminent.

The Anglo-Irish War

The day the Dáil convened in Dublin in January 1919, two policemen were shot dead in County Tipperary. This was the beginning of the bitter Anglo-Irish war, which lasted from 1919 to the middle of 1921. This was the period when Michael Collins came to the fore, a charismatic and ruthless leader who masterminded the campaign of violence against the British while at the same time serving as minister for finance in the new Dáil.

The war quickly became entrenched and bloody. On the Irish side was the Irish Republican Army (IRA), successor to the Irish Volunteers, and on the other a coalition of the Royal Irish Constabulary, regular British-army soldiers and two groups of quasi-military status who rapidly gained a vicious reputation: the Auxiliaries and the

Black & Tans. Their use of violence crystallised resentment against the British and support for the nationalist cause. The death from hunger strike of Terence MacSwiney, the mayor of Cork, further crystallised Irish opinion. The IRA formed 'flying columns', small groups of armed volunteers formed to ambush British forces, and on home ground, they operated successfully. A truce was eventually agreed in July 1921.

After months of negotiations in London, the Irish delegation signed the Anglo-Irish Treaty on 6 December 1921, which gave 26 counties of Ireland independence and allowed six largely Protestant Ulster counties the choice of opting out. If they did (a foregone conclusion), a Boundary Commission would then decide on the final frontiers between north and south. This treaty might have sounded like the answer to all of Ireland's problems. In fact it had quite the opposite effect.

The Civil War

The negotiations on the treaty had been largely carried on the Irish side by Michael Collins and Arthur Griffith. Both men knew that many Dáil members would not accept the loss of the north, or the fact that the British king would still be head of the new Irish Free State and Irish MPs would still have to swear an oath of allegiance to the crown. Under pressure from Britain's Lloyd George and after a spell of exhausting negotiations, they signed the treaty without checking with de Valera in Dublin.

Collins regarded the issue of the monarchy and the oath of allegiance as largely symbolic; he hoped that the north-eastern six counties would not be a viable entity and would eventually become part of the Free State. During the treaty negotiations he had been encouraged to think that the Border Commission would decrease the size of that part of Ireland remaining outside the Free State. He hoped that he could convince the rest of his comrades, but he knew the risks and declared, 'I have signed my death warrant'.

In the end Collins couldn't persuade his colleagues to accept the treaty. De Valera was furious, and it wasn't long before a bitter civil war broke out between comrades who, a year previously, had fought alongside each other.

Ireland Since Partition

For the history of Ireland since partition, see the introductions to the Republic of Ireland and Northern Ireland.

GEOGRAPHY

Ireland is an island lying off the north-western edge of the Eurasian landmass, separated from Britain by the Irish Sea and the St George and North channels. The area of the island is 84,421 sq km: 14,139 sq km in the North and 70,282 sq km in the South. It stretches nearly 500 km north to south and just over 300 km east to west, and the convoluted coastline extends for 5631 km.

Political Geography

Ireland is divided into 32 counties. The Republic of Ireland consists of 26 counties, and Northern Ireland of six. The northernmost point in the South is actually farther north than anywhere in the North! To confuse things further the island has traditionally been divided into four provinces: Leinster, Ulster, Connaught and Munster. Northern Ireland is often loosely referred to as Ulster, but three of the Republic of Ireland's counties – Donegal, Cavan and Monaghan – were also in the old province of Ulster, which with the six counties of Northern Ireland makes a total of nine.

Landscape

It can be as little as 50 km from the heart of one of Ireland's major cities through the midland plains to an isolated sweep of mountains and bogland. Most of the higher ground is close to the coast, while the central regions or midlands are largely flat. Almost the entire western seaboard from Cork to Donegal is a continuous bulwark of cliffs, hills and mountains with few safe anchorages. The only significant breaches in the chain are the Shannon estuary and Galway Bay.

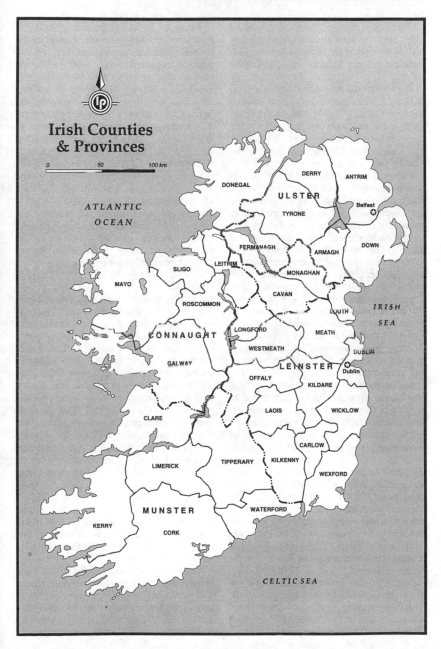

Irish Counties & Provinces

0   50   100 km

ATLANTIC OCEAN

IRISH SEA

CELTIC SEA

ULSTER

DONEGAL
DERRY
ANTRIM
Belfast
TYRONE
FERMANAGH
ARMAGH
DOWN
LEITRIM
MONAGHAN
SLIGO
CAVAN
MAYO
ROSCOMMON
LOUTH
CONNAUGHT
LONGFORD
MEATH
WESTMEATH
GALWAY
LEINSTER
DUBLIN
Dublin
OFFALY
KILDARE
CLARE
LAOIS
WICKLOW
CARLOW
LIMERICK
TIPPERARY
KILKENNY
WEXFORD
WATERFORD
MUNSTER
KERRY
CORK

The western mountain ranges are not particularly high but they are often beautiful. The highest mountains are in the south-west; Carrantuohill in Kerry's Magillicuddy Reeks is the tallest in Ireland – at only 1041 metres.

The Shannon is the longest river in Ireland or Great Britain. It runs for 259 km from its source in Cavan's Cuilcagh Mountains down through the midlands before emptying into the wide Shannon estuary west of Limerick City. Lough Neagh in Northern Ireland is the island's largest lake, covering 396 sq km.

The midlands of Ireland lie above Carboniferous limestone deposited between 300 and 400 million years ago. On the surface, the flat landscape is mostly rich farmland or raised bogs, huge swathes of brown peat rapidly disappearing under the machines of the Irish Turf Board, Bord na Móna.

As you travel west from the midlands, the soil becomes poorer and the fields smaller, and stone walls more numerous. The Cromwellian cry, 'to hell or to Connaught', was not without foundation, as the land west of the Shannon cannot compare with that of fertile counties like Meath and Tipperary. On the western seaboard, small farmers struggle to make a living by raising sheep, potatoes and some cattle.

Before the famine, the pressure on land was enormous; eight million people had to be fed and they farmed in the most inaccessible places. Up the hillsides above today's fields, you may see the faint regular lines of pre-famine potato ridges called 'lazy beds'.

Ice Age The last Ice Age had a huge impact on the Irish landscape. It lasted from 100,000 to just over 10,000 years ago, and most of the country was glaciated. Characteristic U-shaped valleys were carved out by glaciers, as were the small deep-set corrie lakes high on the mountainsides. The receding ice left behind many shallow lakes mainly in the centre of Ireland. Most of the baked sedimentary rocks covering the Wicklow Mountains were stripped away exposing the underlying granite. In County Clare, limestone appeared when a layer of waterproof shale and sandstone was removed.

Many of Ireland's mountains and hills have a round, smooth profile, formed by the abrasive effect of moving ice. The ice also deposited soil in its wake, leaving a layer of boulder clay on many parts of the country. *Drumlins* are small round hills of boulder clay that were dropped and shaped by the passing ice, and there is a large belt of them across the country from County Cavan to Clew Bay in County Mayo. The result is the characteristic 'basket of eggs' topography.

Often pieces of rock were picked up and dropped a long way from their source, and so you find granite 'glacial erratics' as they are called on the limestone desert of Clare's Burren region. Here the ice polished the limestone to mirror smoothness, and in some places you can see deep scratches on the surface of the stone, engraved by harder stones embedded in the moving ice.

CLIMATE

Ireland is farther north than either Newfoundland or Vancouver yet the climate is exceedingly mild with a mean annual temperature of around 10°C. The temperature only drops below freezing intermittently during the winter and snow is scarce – perhaps one or two brief flurries every year. The coldest months of the year are January and February, when daily temperatures range from 4°C to 8°C with 7°C the average. During the summer, temperatures during the day are a comfortable 15°C to 20°C. During the warmest months of July and August the average is 16°C. A hot summer's day in Ireland is 22°C to 24°C although it can sometimes reach 30°C. There are about 18 hours of daylight during July and August, and it's only truly dark after about 11 pm. In May and June Ireland has an average of five to six hours of sunshine a day, while in the south-east during July and August the average is seven hours.

The reason Ireland has such a mild climate is the moderating effect of the Atlantic Ocean and particularly the Gulf Stream. This is an enormous current which moves clockwise around the Atlantic bringing warm water up to Western Europe from the Caribbean.

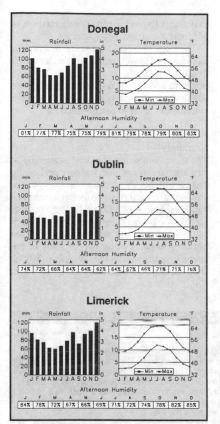

Donegal

Rainfall / Temperature / Afternoon Humidity charts

J	F	M	A	M	J	J	A	S	O	N	D
81%	77%	77%	75%	75%	79%	81%	79%	78%	79%	80%	83%

Dublin

Rainfall / Temperature / Afternoon Humidity charts

J	F	M	A	M	J	J	A	S	O	N	D
74%	72%	66%	64%	64%	62%	64%	67%	66%	71%	71%	76%

Limerick

Rainfall / Temperature / Afternoon Humidity charts

J	F	M	A	M	J	J	A	S	O	N	D
84%	78%	72%	67%	66%	69%	71%	72%	74%	78%	82%	85%

Often the Gulf Stream brings Caribbean sealife with it, and turtles and triggerfish are commonly washed up on the west coast of Ireland.

One thing you can be sure about Irish weather is how little you can be sure of. It may be shirtsleeves and sunglasses in February, winter woollies in March and either during the summer.

And then there's the rain. Ireland does get a lot of rain – about 1000 mm a year, ranging from 750 mm in the midlands to over 1300 mm in the south-west. Certain parts get rain on as many as 270 days of the year. The prevailing winds over Ireland come from the

south-west, and they bring in rainbearing clouds from the Atlantic which dump their loads as soon as they meet high ground.

The heaviest rain usually falls where the scenery is best. The mountains of south-west Kerry are the wettest part of the country. The south-east, particularly Counties Wexford and Waterford, is the driest area, enjoying something like a more southern continental climate.

If you do find the rain getting you down you might find some comfort in the Irish saying: 'It doesn't rain in the pub'!

FLORA

After the end of the last Ice Age 10,000 years ago, a shrubby flora similar to that found in modern Arctic tundra took hold. This was eventually replaced by oak forest, which established itself on most of the island. In the upland regions and on more exposed hill-sides, the oak was mixed with or replaced by birch and pine. In the lower regions where the soil was richer there was also elm, alder, hawthorn and ash. Underneath the oak trees were smaller plants like holly, hazel, ferns, mosses and brambles, which provided a rich habitat for animals.

The Irish landscape and predominant flora that you see today are almost wholly the result of human influence. About 6000 years ago, the first farmers cleared small areas for their crops, the beginning of a long process of deforestation. Substantial tracts of natural oakwood survived until the mid-16th century. The next 200 years saw the country being stripped of its oak for ship timbers, charcoal, tanning and barrels. So extensive was the clearance that by the mid-18th century almost all of the country's timber was being imported, right down to the staves for barrels.

Today only 1% of genuine native oak forest survives. There are remnants in the Killarney National Park and in south Wicklow near Shillelagh, and smaller fragments near Tullamore and Abbeyleix.

The regular dull columns of pine plantations are a now a major feature of the Irish countryside and don't add much in the way of beauty. It's only in the 20th century that such plantations were born, out of the need for local timber and the desire to do something with what many people considered to be wasteland. There are still state subsidies for plantations, although the most widely used species – sitka spruce and lodgepole pine – are so fast growing and so soft as to be unsuitable for high quality wood products. Other pines include Douglas fir, Norway spruce and Scots pine.

Many native plants survive in the hedgerows and in the wilder parts of the country. Because intensive agriculture has only arrived comparatively recently, the range of surviving plant and animal species is much larger than in many other European countries. Irish hedgerows are a blaze of colour in spring and summer.

The Burren limestone region in Clare was covered in light woodland before the early settlers arrived. However, many of the orig-inal plants live on, a remarkable mixture of Mediterranean and alpine species.

The bogs of Ireland are home to a unique flora adapted to wet, acidic and nutrient-poor conditions. Sphagnum moss is the key bogplant and is joined by plants such as the sundew, which uses its long hairs covered in sweet sticky stuff to catch insects.

FAUNA
Mammals

The most common native land mammals of any size are foxes and badgers and while there are plenty about you are unlikely to see any on a casual visit. Smaller mammals include rabbits – introduced by the Normans for food – hares, hedgehogs, red and grey squirrels, shrews and bats. Red deer roam the hillsides in many of the wilder parts of the country, particularly the Wicklow Mountains, and in the Killarney National Park,

Ireland's Bogs

There are two types of bogs – raised bogs and blanket bogs. Raised ones are formed when sphagnum moss gains a foothold in a low-lying, waterlogged area. The moss accumulates as it dies, retaining a lot of water, and the bog starts to form. The centres of these bogs are higher than the edges, hence the term 'raised bog'. These are mostly found in flat areas such as the midlands; the most famous example in Ireland is the Bog of Allen, which once covered as much as 100,000 hectares. The bogs of the midlands have been worked by the Bord na Móna (Irish Turf Board) since 1932. A whole range of enormous machines does the job.

The bogs found covering hills and valleys are known as blanket bogs, and they develop on acid soil in a very wet climate, which usually means 240 days of rain a year or more. There are good examples of blanket bogs still surviving in Wicklow, Sligo, Antrim and the Slieve Bloom Mountains.

About 17% of Ireland's landscape was once made up of bogs, but it is now thought that at the present rate of destruction they could all be gone by the year 2000, wiping out 10,000 years of accumulation. Bog conservation is a recent phenomenon, as bogs have always been seen either as large tracts of potential fuel or as useless and dangerous ground. On top of this they were closely tied to the stereotype of the bog Irishman, so no-one had much affection for them. Now that these great raised bogs have been almost obliterated, there is an urgent need to conserve some of what's left – it has been suggested that 4% should be earmarked for protection. Some argue that it should all be conserved, especially since bogs are home to their own unique family of plants and insects and provide habitation for birdlife.

The preservation properties of bogs are seen as another reason to conserve them. Due to the acidity and lack of oxygen in the peat, fragile organic artefacts are occasionally preserved, which would have disintegrated long ago in any other environment. The countless relics, some of them 5000 years old, include Iron Age wooden highways, preserved bodies and wooden wheels and buckets. Among more recent items found were 300-year-old packets of cheese and butter. ■

which holds the country's only herd of native red deer. Sika deer and other red deer have been introduced from abroad.

Less common in Ireland are the elusive otters, stoats and pine martens which are usually found in remote areas such as the Burren in County Clare or Connemara in County Galway.

Sea mammals include grey and common seals which are found all around the coastline and can often be seen if you keep quiet and know where to look. There are substantial colonies of grey seals living on uninhabited islands off County Mayo and around the shores of Strangford Lough in Northern Ireland. Dolphins often swim close to land, particularly in the bays and inlets off the west coast, and for many years Dingle Harbour has had a famous resident bottle-nosed dolphin called Fungie. There are whales in the sea off Ireland, but they tend to be so dispersed and stay so far out to sea that they are rarely sighted.

Puffins nest in large colonies on seaside cliffs

Birds

Ireland is home to a wide range of migrating and locally breeding birds. Many birds that breed in the Arctic areas of Canada, Greenland, Iceland and elsewhere fly to Ireland to pass the milder winters there, while many others use it as a stopover as they migrate north or south. Brent, barnacle and Greenland white-fronted geese and Bewick's swans, are seasonal visitors. They winter in Ireland in places like the Wexford North and South Slobs, and Dublin's North Bull, Ireland's Eye and Lambay islands, Tyrone's Lough Neagh and Down's Strangford Lough. Also found during the winter are teal, redshanks and curlews. April to May and September to October are the main migration periods.

The coastlines are home to a huge variety of seabirds – kittiwakes, razorbills, puffins, Manx shearwater, storm petrel etc – and most of them breed in the late spring and early summer, the best time to view them. Little Skellig out in the Atlantic Ocean off Kerry is the second largest gannet colony in the world, with some 25,000 pairs breeding

annually on the rock. Other good locations for seabirds are Clear Island in Cork, Hook Head and the Saltee Islands in Wexford, the Burren in Clare, Malin Head in Donegal and Rathlin Island in Antrim.

Birds of prey include hen harriers, sparrow hawks and the odd buzzard. The magnificent peregrine falcon has been making something of a recovery and can be found nesting on cliffs in Wicklow and elsewhere.

One of Ireland's rarer native birds is the corncrake, which used to be common in grasslands and meadows, but has been slowly disappearing. Corncrakes can still be found in some remote and undisturbed areas, such as low-lying flooded grasslands of the Shannon Callows and parts of Donegal. Also rare, choughs – unusual crows with bright red feet and beaks – can be seen in the west, particularly along coastlines with extensive sand-dune complexes.

Fish

The main fish to be found in Ireland are salmon and varieties of trout (brown, rainbow and sea), but there are other species including mackerel and pollack off the coast and pike, bream, perch and roach in lakes and rivers.

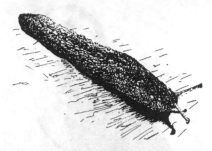

The spotted Kerry slug enjoys the wet climate

Other Fauna

The spotted Kerry slug is found, as the name suggests, in Kerry. So are natterjack toads, Ireland's only species of toad, which live in sandy areas behind Inch Strand and near Castlegregory on the north side of the Dingle Peninsula.

NATIONAL & FOREST PARKS

Ireland has four national parks - Connemara (Galway), Glenveagh (Donegal), Killarney (Kerry) and Wicklow Mountains (Wicklow). These have been developed to protect, preserve and make accessible areas of significant natural heritage and the number is growing. Centred on Mullaghmore near Corofin in County Clare a new park, the Burren National Park, is being developed but has no facilities for visitors yet. Camping is not allowed in any of the parks. The parks are open year round and each one has its own information office, but for general information you can contact the Office of Public Works (☎ 01-661 3111), 51 St Stephen's Green, Dublin 2.

Coillte Teoranta (Irish Forestry Board) administers about 400,000 hectares of forested land which includes designated picnic areas and 12 forest parks. These parks are open all year and feature a range of wildlife and habitats. Some also have chalets and/or caravan parks, shops, cafés and play areas for children. For further information contact Coillte Teoranta (☎ 01-661 5666), Leeson Lane, Dublin 2.

POPULATION

The total population of Ireland is about five million: 3.5 million in the South, 1.5 million in the North. This figure is actually lower than it was 150 years ago. Prior to the potato famines between 1845 and 1851 the population was around eight million. Death and emigration reduced the population to around six million, and emigration continued at a high level for the next 100 years. It was not until the 1960s that Ireland's population finally began to increase again. A high proportion of the population is in the younger age groups with over 50% under the age of 28.

Dublin is the island's largest city and capital of the Republic with up to 1.5 million people living within commuting distance of the city centre. In order of size the Republic's next largest cities are Cork with 136,000, Limerick with 76,500 and Galway with 51,000.

Northern Ireland has a population of about 1.6 million and Belfast, the principal settlement, around 500,000.

PEOPLE

If you can make generalisations about a people, the Irish are a fair-skinned, dark-haired race with quite a number of redhaired and freckled members thrown in for good measure. On the whole they are friendly and accommodating towards foreigners. They are not particularly outgoing. Introductions and conversations are usually low key until some mutual respect is established. If you want to get on with people, don't crash into a B&B or a country pub and make lots of noise. Go quietly, say hello and let conversation arise naturally.

There are few of the class distinctions so prevalent in England, and while advertising and marketing people will divide the population into wealth and class brackets, the boundaries of these are quite fluid. Movement between social classes is common and more to do with personal wealth than birth or background. There are vestiges of an upper class made up of the descendants of the Protestant landed gentry, but their status and their houses are being taken over by the newer business elite.

Though a mixture of many races, genetically the Irish are remarkably homogenous. Invaders such as the Vikings, Normans and British have added to the gene pool, but their characteristics have been diluted through the whole population. Even the Catholics and Protestants of Northern Ireland are more closely related than they might imagine. Settlers from Scotland and England have produced a distinctive Protestant culture which has remained separate to this day. But scholars suggest that Catholics and Protestants are genetically almost identical.

EDUCATION

With such a relatively young population it's not surprising that approximately 25% of Ireland's populace is in full-time education. Attendance at school is compulsory and free up to and including the age of 15. Most of the schools at both primary and secondary levels are run by religious denominations und receive state aid. Secondary schools are for children 12 and over and those who successfully complete their education at this level receive the Leaving Certificate. There are also state-run vocational schools.

At the tertiary level there are four universities. Dublin University is housed in Trinity College; the National University of Ireland (NUI) has colleges in Dublin, Maynooth (Kildare), Cork and Galway: the two other universities are Dublin City University and the University of Limerick. Regional technical colleges provide tertiary vocational training.

Irish is a compulsory subject in primary and secondary schools and the growth of interest in the Irish language and traditional culture has led to the creation of an increasing number of Irish-medium schools (*gaelscoileanna*), mostly at the primary level.

In Northern Ireland, education is modelled on the British system though here, too, many of the schools are operated by religious denominations. There are two universities: Queen's University in Belfast and the University of Ulster with colleges in Belfast, Coleraine, Derry and Jordanstown.

ARTS & CULTURE

Literature

Of all the arts, the Irish have probably had the greatest impact on literature; see the Books & Bookshops section in the Facts for the Visitor chapter for more on the Irish way with words.

Music

The rock band U2 may be Ireland's biggest musical export, but when people talk about Irish music they are generally referring to a much older, more intimate style of traditional/folk music whose most prominent contemporary face belongs to Christy Moore.

For the visitor, the joy of Irish music lies in its sheer accessibility. The biggest names may play the same big venues as the rock stars, but almost every town and village seems to have a pub renowned for its music where you can show up and find a session in progress, even join in if you feel so inclined.

Most traditional music is performed on the fiddle, the tin whistle, the *bodhrán* (a goatskin drum) and the *uileann* pipes. Unaccompanied music fits into five main categories – jigs, reels, hornpipes, polkas and slow airs – while there are two main styles of song – *sean nós*, old-style tunes often sung in Gaelic either unaccompanied or with the backing of a bodhrán, and more familiar ballads. Traditional music has its strongest following in the Republic, but that's not to say you can't find it in Northern Ireland. Nor should it be thought of as the 'possession' of one side of the sectarian divide.

Of the Irish music groups, perhaps the best known is The Chieftains who've been going since the 1960s and have taken their mainly instrumental music as far afield as China. Adding the words come bands like The Dubliners with their notorious drinking songs (like *Seven Drunken Nights)*, the Wolfe Tones who've been described as 'the rabble end of the rebel song tradition', and the Fureys, who have achieved success despite their Traveller origins. Younger groups like Clannad from Donegal, Altan, Dervish and Nomos espouse a quieter, more mystical style of singing, while the London-Irish band The Pogues, led by Shane MacGowan now of The Popes, help keep things wild.

Christy Moore is king of the contemporary singer-songwriter tradition, capable of selling out Dublin's huge Point Depot for six nights in a row. Moore has been singing for decades and his songs traverse the whole range of 'folk' music themes, including controversial political subjects like the H-block prisons and the campaign to free the Birmingham Six, wrongly convicted of two horrific pub bombings. (Dublin-based Elvis Costello was another Irish singer-songwriter to take up this particular cause in song.) Moore's younger brother, Luka Bloom, is now carving out a name for himself too. Other male singer-songwriters to listen out for include Finbar Furey, Mick Hanly, Jimmy MacCarthy, Kieran Goss, Strabane-born Paul Brady, Davy Spillane and Christie Hennessy.

Female singer-songwriters have an equally strong following. The mystical voice of Enya from Donegal has penetrated to a wider audience, as has that of the more controversial Sinéad O'Connor who drew opprobrium by ripping up a picture of the pope before one of her concerts. Amongst the best known contemporary female singers to look out for are sisters Mary and Frances Black, smoky-voiced Mary Coughlan, wild melodian-player Sharon Shannon, Dolores Keane and Eleanor McEvoy. Newcomer Sinéad Lohan's debut album *Who Do You Think I Am?* brought her rave reviews.

If you can't get to hear these singers performing live, it's worth buying either of the two *Women's Heart* albums or *Four for the Road* as general introductions to the singer-songwriter scene. It's also worth listening to Bill Whelan's idiosyncratic *Riverdance* which leapt to fame on the unlikely back of the Eurovision Song Contest.

Of course Ireland also has its rock music scene, exemplified in the 1970s and '80s by bands like Thin Lizzy and the Boomtown Rats and by singers like Bob Geldof, Elvis Costello and Chris de Burgh. U2, whose albums include *Unforgettable Fire, Joshua Tree, Rattle & Hum, Achtung Baby* and *Zooropa*, are the biggest of them all, but in the 1990s The Cranberries were the cutting-edge band to watch out for.

A big influence on U2 was Donegal-born Rory Gallagher, one of the world's great blues guitarists and contemporary of Eric Clapton and John Mayall. He died in 1995.

In a class all of his own is Van Morrison, who seems to have been going forever. In the 1960s he was lead singer with Them whose anthem *Gloria* was a Beatles-era classic. 'Van the Man' moved onto a solo career in the USA, and his *Astral Weeks* is regularly listed by critics as one of the seminal records of the 1960s. Although he has never generated a mass audience, Van Morrison has always attracted a cult following. His continuing relevance was highlighted in 1995 when the wonderful *Brown Eyed Girl* was used as the backing track for peace adverts in Belfast cinemas.

No account of contemporary Irish music could close without reference to the popularity of country music and to Daniel O'Donnell, the Barry Manilow of the Irish music scene, with millions of album sales (mainly to the over-forties) under his belt. Like him or loathe him, he certainly can't be ignored.

Cinema

Ireland and Dublin have made numerous movie appearances and many Irish people have achieved international success in the film industry.

Hollywood came to Ireland in 1952 when John Ford filmed John Wayne as the *The Quiet Man*, wooing Maureen O'Hara in Cong, County Sligo. You can take Quiet Man tours in Cong today. The 1970 David Lean epic *Ryan's Daughter* with Sarah Miles, Robert Mitchum, Trevor Howard and John Mills was filmed on the Dingle Peninsula in County Kerry and the place and the film have been inextricably linked ever since. The Dingle Peninsula has simply become 'Ryan's Daughter country'.

The Field, with Richard Harris, was filmed around Leenane in County Galway. *Hear My Song* about the Irish tenor, Joseph Locke, was a surprise success in the early 90s, as was *Into the West*, a delightful story of two children and a mythical white horse.

The 1992 Tom Cruise and Nicole Kidman vehicle *Far & Away* provided some picturesque views of the west coast region, and Dublin's Temple Bar district stood in for late 19th-century Boston! The 1994 *Secret of Roan Innish* is a mystical tale set off the west coast of Ireland.

Ireland has also been a pure and straightforward backdrop. Youghal in County Cork was Captain Ahab's port in John Huston's 1956 *Moby Dick*. The Irish countryside was used for the WW I aerial epic *The Blue Max* (1966), and *Educating Rita* used Trinity College as its quintessentially English university!

The Powerscourt Estate near Enniskerry in County Wicklow was the setting for films such as Laurence Olivier's 1943 version of *Henry V*, *Barry Lyndon* and John Boorman's *Excalibur*.

Many films have featured Dublin. Joseph Strick attempted the seemingly impossible task of putting *Ulysses* on screen in 1967. The film was promptly banned in Ireland. John Huston's superb final film was *The Dead*, released in 1987 and based on a story from James Joyce's *Dubliners*.

Noel Pearson and Jim Sheridan's *My Left Foot* won Oscars for Daniel Day-Lewis and Brenda Fricker with the true story of Dublin writer Christy Brown, who was crippled with cerebral palsy. The film managed to make some interesting peregrinations around Dublin including visits to John Mulligan's, the pub reputed to pull the best Guinness in Ireland.

The Commitments, by the English director Alan Parker, was a wonderful, bright and energetic 1991 hit about a north Dublin soul band. It accurately records north Dublin's scruffy atmosphere although Dublin audiences (well, north Dublin ones at least) were somewhat amused by some of the geographical jumps around the city which the

characters managed to make! *The Snapper* and *The Van*, the next two of Roddy Doyle's trilogy, were also made into films.

More recently, *A Man of no Importance* starring Albert Finney is set in Dublin in the early 1960s. It tells the story of a gay bus conductor who runs an amateur theatre group and who eventually decides to come 'out'. *Circle of Friends* uses bits of Dublin, especially the interior of the Museum Building of Trinity College. It is based on Maeve Binchy's blockbuster novel of the same name, but changes the book's strong feminist end into Hollywood schlock!

The Troubles in the North have spawned a number of films, including the 1947 film *Odd Man Out*, the 1982 *Angel* and 1984 *Cal*. The IRA featured in the British film *The Long Good Friday* starring Bob Hoskins. Harrison Ford's thriller *Patriot Games* is the story of a man who thwarts an IRA assassination attempt in London and is then hunted by IRA agents seeking revenge. *The Crying Game* is perhaps the most intriguing commercial film to feature the IRA.

In the Name of the Father, filmed in Kilmainham Jail in Dublin, starred Daniel Day-Lewis as Gerry Conlon and Emma Thompson as his lawyer. Beginning with powerful scenes of rioting in Belfast in the early 1970s, it tells the story of the arrest and conviction of the Guildford Four for a pub bombing in England; then of the struggle to clear their names and their subsequent release. Some artistic licence is used in the film: Gerry shares a cell with his father, Guiseppe, who dies in jail, but this didn't happen in real life. However, it doesn't glamourise the IRA – the Balcombe St gang member who later confessed to planting the Guildford bomb is portrayed as a psychopath.

Neil Jordan is one of the most talented writers and directors working today and has built up an impressive body of work. Jordan's films include *Mona Lisa* starring Bob Hoskins, *Cal* starring Stephen Rea, *The Company of Wolves*, *The Miracle* and the multi-Oscar-nominated *The Crying Game* – Jordan won an Oscar for the script. Other

important film-makers are Noel Pearson and
Jim Sheridan who worked together on *My
Left Foot* and *The Field*, and Pat O'Connor
whose first film as director was of Bernard
MacLaverty's *Cal*.

Irish actors like Liam Neeson, Patrick
Bergin, Gabriel Byrne, Pierce Brosnan,
Aidan Quinn and Stephen Rea pursue suc-
cessful careers, following in the footsteps of
Richard Harris, Peter O'Toole and Maureen
O'Hara. Some actors have also had success
in TV. Brenda Fricker appeared in the Aus-
tralian mini-series, *Brides of Christ*, while
Colm Meaney, who played the father in the
Roddy Doyle trilogy, has guaranteed his
immortality by appearing as an officer in
Star Trek: Deep Space Nine.

Architecture
Ireland is packed with prehistoric graves,
ruined monasteries, crumbling fortresses
and many other solid reminders of its long
and often dramatic history. The buildings
used in the country over the last few thousand years fall into a number of groups and
you are likely to come across examples of
some or all of them on your travels.

The simplest structures are standing
stones and stone circles which in Ireland date
from the Stone or Bronze Ages and were
erected all the way up to Christian times.

The earliest settlers built houses of wood
and reeds, of which nothing survives except
the faint traces of post-holes. The principal
surviving structures from Stone Age times
are the graves and monuments the people
built for their dead, usually grouped under
the heading of megalithic tombs, or 'great
stone' tombs.

Megalithic Tombs Among the most easily
recognisable megalithic tombs are *dolmens*,
massive three-legged structures rather like
giant stone stools, in which a number of
bodies were interred before the whole structure was covered in earth. Most are 4000 to
5000 years old. Usually the earth eroded
away leaving the standing stones. There are
good examples at Poulnabrone in Clare,
Proleek near Dundalk, and at Browne's Hill
near Carlow Town; the capstone at Browne's
Hill weighs more than 100 tonnes. Dolmens
are the best known type of chambered tomb
or gallery graves; similar but more complex
are wedge tombs, cist graves and court
cairns.

Passage graves such as Newgrange and
Knowth in Meath are huge mounds with

A typical dolmen, at Kilclooney, north of Ardara in County Donegal

entrances through narrow stone-walled passages leading to burial chambers. They are surrounded by stone circles of unknown significance. Some passage graves were made from piles of stones erected near or on hill tops, sometimes called *cairns*. Good examples are on the Slieve na Calliaghe hills in Meath and Seefin in County Wicklow.

Ogham Stones These are peculiarly Irish standing stones dating from the 4th to 7th centuries AD. *Ogham* (pronounced 'o-am') was an early form of Irish script using a variety of notched strokes placed above, below or across a keyline, usually on stones. The stones mainly indicate graves and are inscribed with the name of the deceased. The majority are found in Counties Cork, Kerry and Waterford, and many have been moved; you may find them incorporated in walls, buildings or gateposts.

Forts Ring forts, 'fairy rings' and raths are all one and the same. The Irish names for forts – *dun*, *rath*, *caiseal/cashel* and *caher* – have ended up in the names of countless towns, villages and townlands. The Irish countryside is peppered with the remains of over 30,000. The earliest known examples date from the Bronze Age, and ring forts have been built and used for many thousands of years since. Some were lived in as late as the 17th century. Wooden and other types of houses were built within the forts' protective confines.

The most common type was the ring fort, with circular earth and stone banks topped by a wooden palisade fence to keep intruders out and surrounded on the outside by a moat-like ditch. Ring forts are found everywhere and were the basic family or tribal enclosure in Ireland for thousands of years. They may have protected anything from one family to the entire court of a tribal chieftain. Ring forts may have up to three earthen ramparts surrounding them; Mooghaun Fort near Dromoland Castle in County Clare is a particularly fine example. Outside Clonakilty in County Cork, Lisnagun ring fort has been reconstructed to give some idea of its original appearance.

Some forts were constructed entirely of stone; Staigue Fort in Kerry and Cathair Dhún Iorais on Clare's Black Head are fine examples. Promontory forts were built on headlands or on cliff edges, which gave natural protection on one side. The Iron Age fort of Dún Aengus on the Aran Islands is a superb example.

The Normans used many ring forts to their advantage by building inside them. A characteristic Norman fort was the motte-and-bailey. The motte was a small flat-topped hill surrounded by a ditch and earthen banks at the base for further protection; attached to and surrounding the motte was the bailey, an enclosure for animals and their keepers. These forts were largely military in purpose, built to protect and secure the Normans' newly conquered territory.

Crannógs Crannógs are artificial islands found in many Irish lakes and are the equivalent of a ring fort on water. Many of them were built completely by humans: wooden piles were driven into the lake floor and the structure built up with wood, stone, earth and anything else the builders could lay their hands on. After the island had been built, the occupants built wooden fences and a house to live in. Craggaunowen Archaeological Centre in Clare has a reconstructed example, and the lake near Fair Head in County Antrim has an easily spotted original.

The midland lakes have many crannógs, which today are usually overgrown with little evidence betraying their artificial origins, except perhaps the too-perfect circular outline. Sometimes they were built in bogs, or the original lake has since become a bog; and many are now hidden below the water level. Estimates put the number in Ireland at over 250. Crannógs date back to the Bronze Age and like the ring forts were used by humans right up to the 16th and 17th centuries. Often there was a secret causeway leading out to the crannóg, just under the surface of the water, and it twisted and turned so that ignorant intruders would have difficulty using it.

Monasteries & Churches The vast majority of early monasteries were built of perishable materials particularly wood. Sometimes the central church or chapel was stone and these are often the only structures that survive. The early stone churches were often very simple, some roofed with timber like Teampall Benen on the Aran Islands or built completely of stone like Gallarus Oratory on the Dingle Peninsula. Early hermitages include the small beehive huts and buildings on the summit of Skellig Michael off County Kerry.

As the monasteries grew in size and stature so too did the architecture. The 'cathedrals' at Glendalough and Clonmacnois are good examples, although they are still tiny when compared with modern cathedrals.

Round towers have become symbols of Ireland, and these tall, stone needle-like structures were built largely as lookout posts and refuges in the event of Viking attacks. The earliest round towers were built in the late 9th or early 10th centuries.

That other great Irish symbol, the Celtic cross, comes from these Christian times. Some suggest that the circle imposed on the arms of the cross represents pagan sun worship being incorporated into the new faith. They developed from simple crosses with rough designs to complex works decorated with high-relief scenes, usually of Biblical characters and tales.

Ireland's early church architecture developed in isolation, as Europe was experiencing the Dark Ages. However, foreign influences began to take effect in the 11th and 12th centuries, and the Cistercians, a European order of monks, established their first Irish monastery at Mellifont, County Louth, in 1141. The strict and formal layout of these new establishments was radically different to the simple and relatively random layout of the traditional Irish monastery as exemplified by nearby Monasterboice, Glendalough in Wicklow and Clonmacnois in Offaly. Cormac's Chapel on the Rock of Cashel shows strong foreign influence, and elements of European Romanesque design became common in Irish monasteries and buildings. Elaborately carved doorways are common, with human and animal heads intricately interwoven into the stone patterns.

With the Normans came the Gothic style of architecture: tall vaulted windows and soaring V-shaped arches were incorporated in the churches and cathedrals of this period.

Castles & Mansions The Normans first built temporary motte-and-bailey forts (see Forts above). Once they had established themselves, however, they built more permanent stone castles. The great castle at Trim, County Meath, is the best example. Castles and cathedrals were built in Dublin and the other large towns.

Many of the castles you see today are the tall, thin tower houses built between the 14th and 17th centuries for local landlords or chieftains. They are often inside a protective wall called a *bawn*. The earliest forms of these are simple, small keeps with few embellishments, while the later forms became more like large, fortified stone houses with sophisticated features, bigger windows, and less emphasis on security.

From the 17th century on, as the established landowning families became wealthier and felt more secure, they built great mansions, particularly in the less rebellious parts of the country around counties Kildare, Meath, Dublin and Wicklow. Castletown House near Celbridge, Russborough House near Blessington and Carton House in Maynooth are good examples.

Georgian Houses In Georgian times, Dublin became one of the architectural glories of Europe, with simple and beautifully built Georgian terraces of red brick, with delicate glass fanlights over large, elegant, curved doorways. Unfortunately, since the 1960s Dublin's Georgian heritage has suffered badly, though you can still see fine examples around Merrion and Fitzwilliam Squares.

Cottages The traditional Irish thatched cottage, built to suit the elements and the landscape, has become rare.

Painting
Although Ireland doesn't have a tradition of painting anything like its literary history, the National Gallery does have an extensive Irish School collection, much of it chronicling the personages and pursuits of the Anglo-Irish aristocracy. Just as W B Yeats played a seminal role in the Celtic literary revival, his younger brother Jack Butler Yeats (1871-1957), inspired an artistic surge of creativity. Their father, John Butler Yeats, was also a noted portrait painter.

Earlier noted portrait painters were Garrett Murphy (1680-1716) and James Latham (1696-1747). Important 18th and 19th-century landscape painters were George Barrett, Robert Carver, William Ashford and Thomas Roberts. James Malton captured 18th-century Dublin on canvas in a number of paintings.

Sport
Gaelic Football & Hurling Ireland has a couple of native games with a large and enthusiastic following – Gaelic football and hurling.

Gaelic football is a fast and exciting spectacle. The ball used is round like a soccer ball, but the players can kick, handle and run with the ball as in rugby. They can pass it in any direction but only by kicking or punching. The goalposts are similar to rugby posts, and a goal, worth three points, is scored by putting the ball below the bar, while a single point is awarded when the ball goes over the bar. Gaelic football is popular in both the South and the North.

Hurling is Ireland's most characteristic sport. It's a ball-and-stick game something like hockey, but much faster and more physical. Visitors are often taken aback by the crash of players wielding what look like ferocious clubs, but injuries are surprisingly infrequent. The goalposts and scoring method are the same as Gaelic football, but the leather ball or *sliotar* is the size of a baseball. A player can pick the ball up on his stick and run with it for a certain distance. Players can handle the ball briefly and pass

Hurling is a fast and physical game

it by palming it. The players' broad wooden sticks are called hurleys.

Hurling has an ancient history and is mentioned in many old Irish tales. Cúchulainn was a legendary exponent of the game. Today hurling is played on a standard field, but in the old days the game might have been played across country between two towns or villages, the only aim being to get the ball to a certain spot or goal.

Both Gaelic football and hurling are played nationwide by a network of town and country clubs and under the auspices of the Gaelic Athletic Association (GAA). The most important competitions are played at county level, and the county winners out of each of the four provinces come together in the autumn for the All-Ireland finals, the climax of Ireland's sporting year. Both finals are played in September at Dublin's Croke Park in front of huge crowds.

Handball Handball is another Irish sport with ancient origins and is also governed by the GAA.

Soccer & Rugby Soccer and rugby union enjoy considerable support all over the country, particularly around Dublin, and soccer is very popular in Northern Ireland.

Big Jack - Ireland's Favourite Englishman
Not many people - let alone anybody English - bring the conversation to a halt in an Irish pub when they appear on the TV, but that's what can happen when 'Big' Jack Charlton is on discussing the Republic of Ireland's soccer team, especially if it has just won an important game.

Jack Charlton, who had had a successful career as a player and was a member of the England team that won the 1966 World Cup, became manager of the Irish Republic in 1986 and immediately set about making it a force in world soccer. In the 1988 European championships it reached the quarter finals, having defeated England along the way. The then Taoiseach, Charles Haughey, paid Big Jack, as he's referred to in the Irish press, the highest tribute possible by making him an honorary Irishman.

In its first World Cup in 1990, the team reached the quarter finals where it was narrowly defeated by Italy, one of the favourites. When the manager and players returned home, 300,000 people appeared on the streets of Dublin to welcome them. There was talk of building a national stadium and naming it Charlton Park or of giving Big Jack, a keen angler, a life-long licence to fish anywhere in Ireland. In 1994 Ireland again qualified for the World Cup (made sweeter by the fact that old rivals, England, didn't), which was held in the USA. In the early stages the team achieved its greatest single victory when it beat Italy 1-0, though this time Ireland didn't quite make the quarter finals.

He resigned following the team's failure to qualify for the 1996 European championships, however, he remains an Irish hero with Irish football fans. ∎

The international rugby team consists of members from the North and the Republic and has a tremendous following. The highlights of the rugby year are the international matches played against England, Scotland, Wales and France between January and March. Home matches are played at Lansdowne Rd in Dublin.

The North and the Republic field separate soccer teams and both have a good record in international competitions. Many of the home players from North and South play professional soccer in Britain and the most successful ones have the status of pop or movie stars. Various British club teams have strong followings in Ireland. Such is the popularity of one, Manchester United, that an opposition organisation has sprung up called ABU – Anyone But United!

Athletics & Boxing Athletics is also popular, and the Republic usually has a few international athletes, particularly in middle and long-distance events. In 1995, Cork athlete, Sonia O'Sullivan, won the 3000 metres final at the World championships in Gothenberg. Boxing has traditionally had a strong working-class following, and Irish boxers are often the only Olympic medal winners or world champions the island produces. Barry McGuigan (former world featherweight champion), Michael Carruth and Wayne MacCullough are some recent heroes.

Golf Golf is enormously popular in Ireland and there are many fine golf courses. Typical fees range from around IR£10 to IR£25 a day; in Ireland fees are usually based on a per day rather than a per round basis. Public courses include Corballs at Donabate (24 km) and Deer Park at Howth (15 km). There are more than 20 private nine-hole and 18-hole club courses in and around Dublin as well as a great many short pitch & putt courses.

If you prefer to spectate rather than participate, the annual Irish Open takes place in June.

RELIGION
The Republic of Ireland is 95% Roman Catholic, 3.4% Protestant and 0.1% Jewish. The remaining 1.5% either have no religious

beliefs or belong to other religious groupings. For years the breakdown in the North was given as 70% Protestant and 30% Catholic, but recent figures suggest it is more like 60% Protestant and 40% Catholic. Most Irish Protestants are members of the Church of Ireland, an offshoot of the Church of England, and the Presbyterian and Methodist churches.

The Catholic Church used to be cited in the Constitution as having a special position in the Republic, but that reference was dropped in 1972. It does still wield considerable influence in the South, and large numbers of the population attend mass every Sunday; it's part of the weekly routine and the social circuit.

The Catholic Church has always taken a strong line on abortion, contraception and divorce, which are forbidden by law, and has opposed attempts to change the present conservative regime on these matters. The Church is treated with a curious mixture of respect and derision by various sections of the community.

Oddly enough, the primates of both the Roman Catholic Church and the Church of Ireland sit in Armagh, the traditional base of St Patrick, which is in Northern Ireland. The country's religious history clearly overrides its current divisions.

LANGUAGE

Although English is the main language of Ireland, it's spoken with a peculiar Irish flavour and lilt. Indeed the Irish accent is one of the most pleasant varieties of English to be heard. Some of the peculiarly Irish sentence constructions in English are closely related to the Irish language; for instance, the usual word order in Irish sentences is verb, subject, object. The present participle is also used more frequently in constructions like 'Would you be wanting a room for the night, then?' Another peculiarity is the use of 'after' as in 'I'm just after going to the shop' meaning 'I have just been to the shop'. The Irish also have a notable bias towards the use of scatological speech.

English is spoken throughout Ireland, but

there are still parts of western and southern Ireland known as *Gaeltacht* areas where Irish is the native language – Kerry, Galway, Mayo, the Aran Islands, Donegal and Ring, County Waterford. The number of native speakers is around 80,000. Irish is a Celtic language, probably first introduced to Ireland by the Celts in the last few centuries BC. Irish is similar to Scottish Gaelic, and has much in common with Welsh and Breton.

Officially the Republic of Ireland is bilingual, and many official documents and roadsigns are printed in both Irish and English. The reality, however, is a little more complex.

Until the time of the plantations in the late 16th and early 17th centuries, successive invaders had been assimilated and adopted the Irish language. From the time of the plantation Irish was seen as the language of the old Irish aristocracy, the poor and dispossessed, and strenuous efforts were made by the English to wipe it out. Social advancement meant giving up Irish. When independence was achieved in 1921 efforts were made to revive the language but progress has been slow.

Irish is compulsory in both primary and secondary schools, and most colleges and universities require prospective students to pass the subject in their school-leaving exams. Despite this – partly because too much emphasis is placed on the complex grammar and too little on speaking the language – most Irish school leavers would be hard pressed to hold a simple conversation in Irish despite having just completed 13 years of daily classes in the subject. Many complain that it's a waste of time studying a difficult language that is not in everyday use.

However, attitudes are changing; it no longer carries a stigma and even in Dublin there is a bit of a revival with several Irish-medium infant and junior schools. There is an Irish-language radio station, Radio na Gaeltachta, broadcasting from Connemara; RTE, the Irish national broadcasting station, has daily news bulletins and programmes in

Irish. An increasing number of people derive intense satisfaction from speaking and keeping alive an ancient aspect of Ireland's culture.

Irish is one of the official languages of the European Union.

Pronunciation

There are three main varieties of pronunciation of Irish in the Gaeltacht areas. These are: Connaught Irish (Galway and north Mayo), Munster Irish (Cork, Kerry, Waterford) and Ulster Irish (Donegal). The pronunciation guidelines given here are an anglicised-spelling version of the 'standard' form, an amalgam of the three dialects.

a   like the 'a' in 'cat'
á   like the 'a' in 'saw'
e   like the 'e' in 'bet'
é   like the 'a' in 'day'
i   like the 'i' in 'sit'
í   like the 'i' in 'fine'
o   like the 'u' in 'sun'
ó   like the 'o' in 'cow'
u   like the 'u' in 'but'
ú   like the 'oo' in 'cook'

c   like the 'k' in 'key'
ch like the 'ch' in the Scottish 'loch'
d   like the 'j' in 'jug' when followed by 'e' or 'i'; like the 'd' in 'door' when followed by 'o' or 'u'
dh like the 'y' in 'young' when followed by 'e' or 'i'; like the 'g' in 'huge' when followed by 'o' or 'u'
t   like the 'ch' in 'church' when followed or preceded by 'e' or 'i'; like the 't' in 'toast' when followed or preceded by 'o' or 'u'
th like the 'h' in 'house'; sometimes at the end of a word it is silent
s   like the 'sh' in 'shirt'

Greetings & Civilities
Hello.
   Dia Dhuit. literally 'God be with you' (dee-a-gwit)
Goodbye.
   Slán Agat. (slawn aguth)
Good night.
   Oiche mhaith. (eeheh woh)
Welcome.
   Fáilte. (fawlta)
Welcome.
   Céad mhíle fáilte. ie a hundred thousand welcomes. (kade meela fawlta)
Thank you.
   Go raibh maith aguth. (goh rev moh aguth)
Thank you very much.
   Gur a mhíle maith agat. (gur a mila moh agut)
   Go raibh mhíle maith agat. (goh rev meela moh aguth)
Please.
   Le do thoil. (le do hull)
Excuse me.
   Gabh mo leiscéil. (gawv mo lesh scale)
How are you?
   Conas a tá tú? (kunas a thaw two)
I am fine.
   Táim go maith. (thawm gohmoh)
What is your name?
   Cad is anim duit? (cod is anim dit)
Sean Sheehan is my name.
   Sean Sheehan is anim dom. (Sean Sheehan iss anim dumb)
another/one more
   ceann eile (keown ella)
good, fine, OK
   go maith (go moh)
nice
   go deas (goh dass)
yes
   tá/sea (thaw/shah)
no/it is not
   níl/ní hea (knee hah)

Questions & Comments
Why?
   Cén fáth? (kane faw)
What is this?
   Cad é seo? (kod ay shawh)
What is that?
   Cad é sin? (kod ay shin)
How much/how many?
   Cé mhéid? (kay vaid)

expensive – very dear
ana dhaor (ana gare)
where is...?
cá bhfuil...? (kaw will)
which way?
cén slí? (kane shlee)
I don't understand.
Ní thuigim. (nee higgim)
this/that
é seo/é sin (ay shoh/ay shin)
big/small
mór/beag (moor/beeugh)
open/closed
oscailte/dúnta (uskulta/doonta)
slowly/quickly
go mall/go tapaidh
(guh mowl/guh top-igg)

Getting Around

I would like to go to...
Ba mhaith liom dul go dtí... (baw woh lum dull go dee)
I would like to buy...
Ba mhaith liom cheannach... (bah woh lumb kyarok)
ticket
ticéid (tickaid)
boat/ship
bád/long (bawd/lung)
car/bus
gluaisteáin/bus (glooshtawn/bus)
here/there
anseo/ansin (anshuh/onshin)
stop/go
stad/ar aghaidh (stod/err eyeg)
town square
lár an baile (lawr an vollyeh)
street/road
sráid/bóthar (sroyed/bowher)
town/city
baile/cathair (bollyeh/kawher)
bank/shop
an banc/siopa (an bonk/shuppa)

Useful Signs

men
fir (fear)
women
mná

toilet
leithreas (lehrass)
police
gardaí (gardee)
post office
oifig an phoist (if-ig on pwist)
telephone
telefón (tay lay foan)
town centre
an lár (an laah)

Accommodation

one night
oíche amháin (eeheh a woin)
one person
aon duine (ayn dinnah)
bed/room
leaba/seomra (leeabah/showmra)
hotel
óstán (oh stahn)
bed & breakfast
loistín oíche (leestin eeheh)

Time & Dates

today/tomorrow
inniu/amárach (innyuv/amawrok)
hour/minute
huair/noiméid (oor/nomade)
week/month
seachtain/mí (shocktin/mee)
What time is it?
Cén tam é? (kane towm ay)
7 o' clock
seacht a chlog (shocked ah klug)

Monday
dé luan (day loon)
Tuesday
dé máirt (day mawrt)
Wednesday
dé céadaoin (day kaydeen)
Thursday
déardaoin (daredeen)
Friday
dé haoine (day heena)
Saturday
dé sathairn (day saheren)
Sunday
dé domhnaigh (day downick)

Numbers

1/2	*leath* (lah)	20	*fiche* (feekh)
1	*aon* (ayn)	21	*fiche aon* (feekh-ayn)
2	*dó* (doe)	30	*tríocha* (chree-okha)
3	*trí* (three)	40	*daichead* (daykh-ayd)
4	*cathar* (kahirr)	50	*caoga* (ka-uga)
5	*cúig* (koo-ig)	60	*seasca* (shay-ska)
6	*sé* (shay)	70	*seachtó* (shocked-ow)
7	*seacht* (shocked)	80	*ochtó* (ukth-ow)
8	*ocht* (ukth)	90	*nócha* (now-kha)
9	*naoi* (nay)		
10	*deich* (jeh)	And so on...	
11	*aon deag* (ayen deeuct)	100	*céad* (kade)
12	*dó deag* (doe dayugg)	1000	*míle* (meal-ah)

Facts for the Visitor

VISAS & EMBASSIES

For citizens of most Western countries no visa is required to visit Ireland. UK nationals born in Great Britain or Northern Ireland do not require a passport to visit the Republic, but you may be asked for some form of identification. Visas are required from Indians, Pakistanis, non-UK passport Hong Kongers and citizens of some African states.

Irish diplomatic offices overseas include:

Australia
    20 Arkana St, Yarralumla, Canberra, ACT 2600 (☎ 06-273 3022)
Canada
    130 Albert St, Ottawa, Ontario K1A 0L6 (☎ 613-233 6281)
Denmark
    Ostbanegade 21, ITH, DK-2100 Copenhagen O (☎ 31-42 32 33)
France
    12 Ave Foch, 75116 Paris (☎ 1-45 00 20 87)
Germany
    Godesberger Allee 119, 5300 Bonn 2 (☎ 228-376937/8/9)
Italy
    Largo del Nazareno 3, 00187 Rome (☎ 6-678 2541/2/3/4/5)
Japan
    Kowa Building, No 25, 8-7 Sanban-cho, Chiyoda-ku, Tokyo 102 (☎ 3-3263 0695)
Netherlands
    Dr Kuyperstraat 9, 2514 BA The Hague (☎ 70-363 0993)
Portugal
    Rua da Imprensa a Estrela, 1-4, 1200 Lisbon (☎ 1-396 1569)
Spain
    Claudio Coello 73, 1st floor, 28001 Madrid (☎ 1-457 0012)
Sweden
    Östermalmsgatan 97, PO Box 10326, 100 55 Stockholm (☎ 8-661 80 05)
Switzerland
    Eigerstrasse 71, 3007 Berne (☎ 31-42353/4)
UK
    17 Grosvenor Place, London SW1X 7HR (☎ 0171-235 2171)
USA
    2234 Massachusetts Ave NW, Washington, DC 20008 (☎ 202-462 3939). In addition there are consulates in the USA in Boston, Chicago, New York and San Francisco.

Foreign Embassies in Ireland

See the Dublin and Belfast chapters for diplomatic offices in that city.

DOCUMENTS

Even if you don't need to bring a passport some form of identification is useful, especially when changing travellers' cheques or hiring a car. To hire a car you'll need a valid driving licence from your country of residence, which you should have had for two years. If you don't have a European licence and you also plan to drive in other parts of Europe, obtain an International Driving Permit (IDP) from your home automobile association before you leave.

A Hostelling International card will give you access to the An Óige and YHANI hostels (see Accommodation later), though you can usually get temporary membership if you just turn up at one of the hostels. With an International Student Identity Card (ISIC) you can get all sorts of discounts on transport, commercial goods and services, and entry to museums and sights. If you're under 26, but not a student, you can apply for a European Youth Card (EYC), also called a Euro26 Card, which offers similar discounts to an ISIC.

CUSTOMS

There is a two-tier system: the first for goods bought duty free, the second for goods bought in an EU country where taxes and duties have been paid.

The second is relevant because a number of products (including alcohol and tobacco) are much cheaper on the continent. Under the rules of the single market, however, as long as taxes have been paid somewhere in the EU there are no additional taxes if the goods are exported within the EU – provided they are for personal consumption. There is no customs inspection apart from those concerned with drugs and national security.

But while you can bring vast quantities of cheap wine purchased, for example, in France to Ireland, wine purchased duty free on board a ferry from France or at an airport remain subject to the normal restrictions. You're allowed to import 200 cigarettes, one litre of spirits, two litres of wine, 60 cc of perfume, 250 cc of toilet water, and other dutiable goods to the value of IR£34.

MONEY
Currency
In Ireland the Irish pound or punt (IR£) is used, and like the British pound sterling it's divided into 100 pence (p). Irish banknotes come in denominations of IR£100, IR£50, IR£20, IR£10 and IR£5. Coins come in the form of IR£1, 50p, 20p, 10p, 5p, 2p and 1p.

The British pound sterling (£) is used in Northern Ireland and comes in the same banknote and coin denominations as the Irish punt. Don't confuse Northern Irish pounds (issued by the First Trust Bank, Ulster Bank, Northern Bank and Bank of England) with Republic of Ireland pounds (issued by the Central Bank of Ireland). 'Sterling' or 'Belfast' are giveaway words on the Northern Irish notes. The Northern Irish pound sterling is worth the same as the British variety. Northern Irish notes are not readily accepted in Britain, but British banks will swap them for normal sterling notes.

The Republic's currency is not legal tender in the North and vice versa, though some businesses may accept the other country's notes at a one-for-one exchange.

Exchange Rates

A$1	=	IR£0.48	=	£0.45
C$1	=	IR£0.56	=	£0.46
NZ$1	=	IR£0.40	=	£0.41
US$1	=	IR£0.72	=	£0.64
IR£1	=		=	£0.98

Changing Money
Most major currencies and brands of travellers' cheques are readily accepted in Ireland, but carrying them in pounds sterling has the advantage that in Northern Ireland or Britain you can change them without exchange loss or commission. American Express and Thomas Cooke travellers' cheques are widely recognised and don't charge commission for cashing their own cheques. Eurocheques can be cashed in Ireland. Travellers' cheques are rarely used for everyday transactions (as in the USA for example) so they will need to be cashed beforehand.

The best exchange rates are obtained at banks. In the Republic they normally open from 10 am to 3 pm, though most also stay open till 5 pm at least one day a week, usually a Thursday or a Friday. In Dublin they stay open until 5 pm on Thursday. In the larger urban centres most banks remain open at lunch time, though in rural areas many close from 12.30 to 1.30 pm. In Northern Ireland banks are open from 10 am to 3.30 pm weekdays and most stay open until 5 pm on Thursday. In the North the Halifax Bank opens on Saturday morning from 9 am to noon.

Bureaux de change and other exchange facilities are usually open longer hours than banks, but the rate and/or commission will be worse. Building societies often handle foreign exchange and are open longer hours than the banks. Many post offices in both the Republic and Northern Ireland have a currency-exchange facility and have the advantage of opening on Saturday mornings.

If you've not obtained some currency in advance there are unofficial money-changers near the border between the North and South, often at petrol stations.

Credit & Charge Cards
Visa, MasterCard, Access and American Express as well as other credit and charge cards are widely accepted, though many B&Bs and some smaller remote petrol stations will only take cash. You can obtain cash advances on your card from a bank and from some automatic teller machines (ATMs) or cash machines, North and South. The Allied Irish Bank (AIB) cash machines are particularly useful.

Costs

Ireland is expensive, but costs vary around the country. A hostel bed in a dormitory will cost IR£4 to IR£10 a night. If you're not staying in a hostel your costs increase dramatically by having to eat out. A meal at lunch time costs IR£3 to IR£5 and in the evening this can easily double. A cheap B&B will cost about IR£12 to IR£20 per person while a more luxurious B&B or guesthouse with attached bathroom would be anything from about IR£15 to as much as IR£40. Dinner in a reasonable restaurant with a glass of wine or a beer will cost from IR£8 to IR£15.

Assuming you stay at a hostel, eat a light pub lunch and cook your own meal in the evening, you could get by on IR£15 a day. In practice you usually spend more and when you move around the country you'll need to factor in transport.

Many places to stay have different high and low season prices. In this book, unless it says otherwise, the prices quoted are for the high season. Some places may have not just a high season but a peak high season price. Entry prices are often lower for children or students than for adults.

At busy times of the year, B&Bs may add a few pounds on to their price. Watch out for the awful practice of charging an extra 50p or IR£1 for a bath. A pint of Guinness is usually at least IR£1.85 and the rounds system – where you take your turn in buying drinks for the assembled company – is a good way of spending a remarkable amount of money in a remarkably short space of time.

Car hire is extremely expensive, and leaded petrol costs about 65p a litre, unleaded three or four pence less.

Sightseeing Discounts

Many parks, monuments and gardens in the Republic of Ireland are operated by the Office of Public Works (OPW). From any of these sites for IR£15 (children and students IR£6) you can get a Heritage Card giving you unlimited access to all these sites for one year – worthwhile if you're planning a serious onslaught on Ireland's plentiful supply of castles, monasteries and other sites. In Northern Ireland the National Trust has a similar deal but it's less useful for most visitors as there are fewer sites. If, however, you are also visiting Britain then National Trust membership (£25, under-23 £11.50, family £46) is worthwhile.

Tipping

Fancy hotels and restaurants usually add a 10% or 12% service charge and no additional tip is required. Simpler places usually do not add service; if you decide to tip, just round up the bill or add at most 10%. Taxi drivers do not have to be tipped, and 10% is fine. Porters should get 50p per bag. Tipping in bars is not expected, but the distinction between pubs and restaurants is blurred by bars becoming more like restaurants at lunch time.

Consumer Taxes

Value-added tax (VAT) is a sales tax that applies to most goods and services in Ireland, excluding books and children's footwear. Residents of the EU are not entitled to VAT refund. Other visitors can claim back the VAT on large purchases which they subsequently export outside the EU. If you buy something from a Cashback Store you will be given a Cashback Voucher which can be refunded at Dublin or Shannon airports, or can be stamped at ferry ports and mailed back for refund.

WHEN TO GO

The weather is warmest in July and August and the daylight hours are long, but the crowds will be greatest, the costs the highest and accommodation harder to come by. In the quieter winter months, however, you may get miserable weather, the days are short and many tourist facilities will be shut. Visiting Ireland in June or September has a number of attractions: the weather can be better than at any other time of the year, it's less crowded and everything is open.

WHAT TO BRING

A travelpack – a combination of backpack and shoulder bag – is the most popular item for carrying gear. A travelpack's straps zip away inside the pack when not needed, making it easy to handle in airports and on crowded public transport. They also look reasonably smart and can be made reasonably thief-proof with small combination locks.

A raincoat or an umbrella is a necessity, as are some warm clothes – even during good summer weather it gets chilly in the evenings. Walkers should be well prepared if they are crossing exposed country. Dress is usually casual, and you are unlikely to come across many coat-and-tie-type regulations.

Bear in mind the strict regulations about birth control in Ireland. Condoms are not always easily available in rural areas, though they are becoming more common in pharmacies and pub-vending machines in the cities.

A minimum packing list could include the following:

- underwear, socks
- two pairs of jeans or trousers
- pair of shorts or a skirt
- a few T-shirts and shirts
- a warm sweater
- a solid, comfortable pair of shoes
- thongs/flip-flops for shared bathrooms
- coat or jacket
- waterproof jacket, in a fabric that breathes
- medical kit and sewing kit
- combination padlock
- Swiss Army knife or equivalent
- small towel
- toothpaste, toothbrush and toiletries
- neck pouch or money belt
- small daypack
- passport photos & copies of important documents

A sleeping bag is useful in hostels and when visiting friends; get one that can be used as a quilt. A sleeping sheet with a pillow cover is necessary if you plan to stay in hostels, though you can buy or hire one if you don't bring your own.

Other possible items include a compass (to help orient yourself on walks), a torch (flashlight), an alarm clock or watch with an alarm function, an adapter plug for electrical appliances, a universal bath/sink plug, sunglasses and an elastic clothesline.

SUGGESTED ITINERARIES

Depending on the length of your stay, you might want to see and do the following things:

Two days:
> Visit Dublin and perhaps a couple of places nearby – Powerscourt and Glendalough to the south, or perhaps Newgrange, Mellifont and Monasterboice to the north.

One week:
> Visit Dublin, then Newgrange, Mellifont, Monasterboice, the Burren and Kilkenny.

Two weeks:
> As above, plus the Ring of Kerry, Killarney and Cork.

One month:
> With your own car you could cover all the main attractions around the coast but you'd be moving quite fast. This would be more difficult to achieve within a month on public transport.

Two months:
> You'd have time to explore Ireland thoroughly with a car or motorcycle, reasonably thoroughly with a bicycle. You could do some walking as well.

TOURIST OFFICES

Bord Fáilte (Irish Tourist Board) and the Northern Ireland Tourist Board operate separate tourist offices but produce some joint brochures and publications.

Local Tourist Offices

Dublin has Bord Fáilte, Dublin Tourism and Northern Ireland Tourist Board offices. Belfast has Northern Ireland and Bord Fáilte offices. Elsewhere in Ireland and Northern Ireland there is a tourist office in almost every town big enough to have half a dozen pubs (it doesn't take much population to justify half a dozen pubs in Ireland). These offices are friendly, helpful and well informed and will find you a place to stay and book it – for a flat IR£1 charge (£1 in the North) if it's local, IR£2 (£2) elsewhere. This a useful service especially in the busy summer months.

In the bigger towns and more touristed

areas opening hours are usually from 9 am to 6 pm Monday to Friday and 9 am to 1 pm on Saturday but the hours are often extended in summer. In other areas the offices may only be open seasonally or for much shorter hours from October to April.

Gulliver

This is the name of a computerised tourist information and reservation service available from many tourist offices and administered by both Bord Fáilte and the Northern Ireland Tourist Board. It provides up-to-date information on events, attractions, transport and accommodation and offers an accommodation booking service. Eventually, anyone intending to visit Ireland will be able to go to a travel agent and access this information and make reservations from anywhere in the world. In Ireland call ☎ 800 600800.

Overseas Representatives

Some of the offices of Bord Fáilte include:

Australia
  5th floor, 36 Carrington St, Sydney, NSW 2000 – also has information on Northern Ireland (☎ 02-299 6177)
Belgium
  Ave de Beaulieu 25, 1160 Bruxelles (☎ 02-673 9940)
Canada
  160 Bloor St East, Suite 934, Toronto, Ontario M4W 1B9 (☎ 416-929 2777)
Denmark
  Box 104, 1004 Kobenhavn K (☎ 033-15 8045)
France
  33 rue de Miromesnil, 75008 Paris (☎ 1-47 42 03 36)
Germany
  Untermainanlage 7, W 6000 Frankfurt Main 1 (☎ 069-23 64 92)
Italy
  Via S Maria Segreta 6, 20123 Milano (☎ 02-8690541)
Netherlands
  Leidsestraat 32, 1017 PB Amsterdam (☎ 020-22 31 01)
New Zealand
  Dingwall Building, 87 Queen St, Auckland 1 (PO Box 279, ☎ 09-379 3708)
Northern Ireland
  53 Castle St, Belfast BT1 1GH (☎ 01232-327888)

Sweden
  Box 5292, 102 46 Stockholm (☎ 08-662 8510)
UK
  Ireland House, 150 New Bond St, London W1Y 0AQ (☎ 0171-493 3201)
USA
  345 Park Ave, New York, NY 10154 (☎ 212-418 0800)

Tourist information for Northern Ireland is handled by the British Tourist Authority, although you may also find offices of the Northern Ireland Tourist Board in some locations:

Canada
  111 Avenue Rd, Suite 450, Toronto, Ontario M5R 3J8 (☎ 416-925 6368)
France
  3 rue de Pontoise, 78100 St Germain-en Laye (☎ 1 39 21 93 80)
Germany
  60329 Frankfurt/Main, Taunusstrasse 52-60 (☎ 069-234 504)
Ireland, Republic of
  16 Nassau St, Dublin 2 (☎ 01-679 1977)
UK
  11 Berkeley St, London W1X 5AD – telephone enquiries only (☎ 0171-493 0601)
  British Travel Centre, 4 Lower Regent St, London SW1Y 4PQ (☎ 0171-839 8416)
USA
  Suite 500, 276 5th Ave, New York, NY 10001 (☎ 212-686 6250)

The head office of the Northern Ireland Tourist Board (☎ 01232-246609) is at St Anne's Court, 59 North St, Belfast BT1 1NB.

USEFUL ORGANISATIONS

The Union of Students in Ireland Travel (USIT) is the Irish youth and student travel association. Their London office is at London Student Travel (☎ 0171-730 3402); 52 Grosvenor Gardens, London SW1W 0AG. In the USA they can be found at the New York Student Center (☎ 212-663 5435), 895 Amsterdam Ave (at West 103rd St), New York, NY 10025. In France the office is USIT Voyages (☎ 1-42 44 14 00), 12 rue Vivienne, 75002 Paris. USIT issue ISIC (International Student Identity Card) cards, and also organise cheap fares to Ireland for students.

For IR£7 full-time students can have a Travelsave stamp affixed to their ISIC card. This gives a 50% discount on Iarnród Éireann (Irish Rail) and Bus Éireann services. For people under 26 there is the European Youth Card (EYC) which entitles holders to discounts on air and rail fares, in restaurants, leisure activities etc. Enquire at the USIT offices in London or New York, or in Dublin (☎ 01-679 8833/677 8117) at 19 Aston Quay, O'Connell Bridge, Dublin 2. They have offices in most major cities in Ireland, including Belfast, Waterford, Cork and Galway.

Membership of Hostelling International entitles you to stay at hostels operated by An Óige in the Republic and by YHANI in the North.

BUSINESS HOURS & HOLIDAYS
Business Hours
Offices are open from 9 am to 5 pm Monday to Friday, shops a little later. On Thursday and/or Friday shops stay open later. Many are also open on Saturday or Sunday. In winter, tourist attractions are often open shorter hours, fewer days per week or may be shut completely.

Outside the cities, shops and businesses often close for one afternoon in the week. It varies from region to region. In small towns most shops are also likely to close for an hour at lunch time.

Pub Hours
In the Republic pubs are open Monday to Saturday from 10.30 am to 11.30 pm between June and September. For the rest of the year closing time is 11 pm. In Dublin, pubs close for a 'holy hour' which may be one or more hours in the afternoon. On Sunday the opening hours are 12.30 to 2 pm and 4 to 11 pm. The only days when pubs are definitely closed are Christmas Day and Good Friday. In the North pubs open from 11.30 am to 11 pm, Monday to Saturday. On Sunday the hours are 12.30 to 2 pm and 7 to 10 pm, but pubs in Protestant areas often stay closed all day.

Public Holidays
Bear in mind that Northern and Southern public holidays (bank holidays) don't always coincide, which can have a bearing on the availability of beds in border resorts like Newcastle. In the North most shops open on Good Friday, but close on the Tuesday following Easter Monday.

Public holidays in the Republic of Ireland (IR), Northern Ireland (NI) or both are:

New Year – 1 January
St Patrick's Day (IR) – 17 March
Good Friday
Easter Monday
May Holiday (IR) – 1 May
May Holiday (NI) – first Monday in May
June Holiday (IR) – first Monday in June
The 12th (NI) – 12 July (next day if 12 July is a
  Sunday)
August Holiday (IR) – first Monday in August
August Holiday (NI) – last Monday in August
October Holiday (IR) – last Monday in October
Christmas Day – 25 December
St Stephen's Day/Boxing Day – 26 December

The St Patrick's Day and St Stephen's Day/Boxing Day holidays are taken on the following Monday should they fall on a weekend.

In Northern Ireland the main thing to remember is that many tourist attractions are closed on Sunday mornings, rarely opening until around 2 pm, well after church finishing time.

EVENTS & FESTIVALS
Many diverse events and festivals are held around the country all year. Following is a list of the more major ones.

January
    There are regular horse races at a number of tracks throughout the country, including Leopardstown in County Dublin and Naas in County Kildare. The international rugby season usually begins in January.
February
    In Dublin the International Film Festival begins at the end of the month. International rugby games for the Five Nations Championship (between Ireland, England, Scotland, Wales and France) take place throughout the month, two of

them being held at Lansdowne Park. In Belfast there's a music festival.

March

New Yorkers may well be disappointed at the celebrations for St Patrick's Day on 17 March. Dublin has a parade as does Armagh and smaller celebrations take place in the other cities, but none of it compares with the razzmatazz in New York. It's a national holiday so shops and businesses close and the day passes off unostentatiously in the countryside, apart from the traditional wearing of a ribbon or shamrock leaf in one's lapel. In Dublin, March also sees the World Irish Dancing Championship take place.

April

Two major sporting events: the Irish Grand National at Fairyhouse, County Meath, and the final of the Gaelic football league competition in Dublin. In Northern Ireland, Easter is the start of the Orange/Protestant marching season culminating on 12 July.

May

At the Royal Dublin Society showgrounds, the Spring Show features agricultural and farming pursuits. At Ennis in County Clare, the Fleadh Nua is a festival of traditional music and dance, while Cork has its own International Choral & Folk Dance Festival. At Bantry, in the same county, there's a Mussel Festival. In Belfast there's a marathon.

June

In Dublin, 16 June is Bloomsday when Leopold Bloom's Joycean journey around the city is reenacted and various readings and dramatisations take place around the city. More bookish events can be found in Listowel in County Cork with its Writers' Week literary festival. Some 48 km from the capital the Irish Derby takes place at the Curragh. Up in Donegal, at Rathmullen, an international fishing festival takes place. From June to the middle of August pilgrims leave from Pettigo in County Donegal for the boat trip to Lough Derg and the penitential Stations of the Cross. Across the border in Belleek there's a small Fiddle Stone festival while in Belfast there's a Jazz & Blues Festival.

July

In the North July is the marching month and every Orangeman in the country hits the streets on the 'Glorious 12th', to celebrate the Protestant victory at the Battle of the Boyne. Because of the possibility of violence at this time the military presence leading up to the 12th is very heavy and security is extremely tight. Fishing events get under way in Athlone and in Mayo, while on the last Sunday of the month there's a mass pilgrimage to the top of Croagh Patrick. The Galway Arts Festival begins in late July.

August

The second week sees the annual Dublin Horse Show at the Royal Dublin Society showgrounds, Ireland's answer to Wimbledon and Ascot when it comes to showing off one's social status. Horseracing takes place in Tralee in County Kerry, and for the last week of the month Tralee has the Rose of Tralee Festival. In the same county at Killorglin the ancient Puck Fair heralds unrestricted drinking for days and nights. Kilkenny has an Arts Week and Clifden in County Galway has the Connemara Pony Show. In Ballycastle in County Antrim the Oul' Lammas Fair occurs over the last weekend of the month and attracts holidaymakers as well as enterprising traders. The August Bank Holiday weekend (the first Monday in August and the Saturday and Sunday that precede it) is the time for Ireland's major annual rock festival known as Féile, at Thurles in County Tipperary. The Belfast Folk Festival takes place this month.

September

The All-Ireland Hurling and Football finals both take place in September. In Lisdoonvarna, County Clare, the Matchmaking Festival gets down to business. Cork has its Film Festival, Sligo its Arts Week, Waterford an International Festival of Light Opera and Dublin a Theatre Festival. Belfast has its own Folk Festival.

October

An International Jazz Festival takes over the city of Cork, with special boat trains bringing audiences from Britain and elsewhere. The Dublin Theatre Festival takes place over two weeks in October. On the last Monday of the month Dublin has its marathon, while Ballinasloe in County Galway hosts the country's biggest cattle and horse fair. Kinsale in County Cork is home to Ireland's gourmet festival.

November

In Wexford the Opera Festival is a prestigious event attracting audiences and participants from all parts of the world. In the North the Belfast Festival takes place at Queen's University.

December

Christmas is a quiet affair in the countryside though on 26 December the ancient practice of Wren Boys is reenacted, when groups of children dress up and expect money at the door after singing a few desultory hymns.

POST & TELECOMMUNICATIONS
Post

Post offices in the South are open from 8.30 am (9.30 am on Wednesday) to 5.30 Monday to Friday, Saturday from 9 am to noon, smaller offices close for lunch. Postcards cost 28p to EU countries, 38p outside Europe, while aerograms cost 45p. An air-mail letter to the USA or Australia costs 52p. All mail to Britain and Europe goes by air so there is no need to use air-mail envelopes or stickers.

Post office hours in the North are from 9 am to 5.30 pm Monday to Friday and 9 am to 1 pm on Saturday. Postal rates are as in Britain – 25p for letters by 1st-class mail, 19p 2nd-class, 25p to EU countries and 39p for letters and postcards to the USA and Australia.

Mail to both the North and the Republic can be addressed to poste restante at post offices but is officially only held for two weeks. Writing 'hold for collection' on the envelope may have some effect.

Over 95% of letters within the country are delivered the next working day. To North America it's about 10 days, the UK and rest of Europe between three and five days and Australia between a week and 10 days.

Telephone

Phones are modern electronic wonders in both North and South. Telecom Éireann has one of the most up-to-date digital telephone systems in the world, with 60% digital exchanges versus 40% in the UK. Phone cards, which save fishing for coins and give you a small discount, are worth having. International calls can be dialled directly from pay phones.

Phone calls between the Republic and the North are classified as international calls.

Calls from Ireland To call a UK number (except for Northern Ireland) from the South dial 0044 plus the area code (minus the 0) plus the number. Thus an 0171 number in London would start 0044-171. To call else-where overseas dial 00 then the international code for that country (1 for the USA or Canada, 61 for Australia, 64 for New Zealand, 65 for Singapore, 852 for Hong Kong, etc) then the area code (dropping any leading 0) and then the number. The one variation is that to call Northern Ireland from Ireland you dial 08 and then the Northern

Irish area code *without* dropping the leading 0. The international operator for enquiries or for making reverse-charge calls is 114, or 10 for help with calls within Ireland and to Britain.

Calls from Northern Ireland From North-ern Ireland dial 00 for international access followed by the country code. The country code for the Republic is 353. Dial 155 for the British Telecom international operator.

Call Costs In the South the standard rate for a five-minute local call is 20p. When making a long-distance phone call from a hotel room bear in mind that the cost will be at least doubled.

The cost of a direct-dialled international call from Ireland varies according to the time of day. Reduced rates are available after 6 pm and before 8 am; between midnight and 8 am and between 2 and 8 pm to Australia and New Zealand. Standard charges for one minute are:

Australia	IR£1.10
France	43p
Germany	43p
North America	83p
New Zealand	IR£1.10
UK	36p

Direct Home Calls Rather than placing reverse charge calls through the operator in Ireland you can dial direct to your home country operator and then reverse charges or charge the call to a local phone credit card. To use the direct home service dial the fol-lowing codes followed by the area code and number you want. Your home country oper-ator will then come on the line before the call goes through:

Australia	1800 5500 61 + number
France	1800 5500 33 + number
New Zealand	1800 5500 64 + number
UK – BT	1800 5500 44 + number
UK – Mercury	1800 5500 04 + number
USA – AT&T	1800 5500 00 + number
USA – MCI	1800 5510 01 + number
USA – Sprint	1800 5520 01 + number

Pay Phones & Phonecards Callcards are available in 10 (IR£2.20), 20 (IR£3.50), 50 (IR£8) and 100 (IR£16) unit versions in the Republic of Ireland. Each unit gives you one local phone call. Cardphones are very useful for making international calls since you do not have to carry a sack of coins to the phonebox. Note that you cannot make international calls via the operator from a cardphone.

Fax & Telegrams Faxes can be sent from post offices or other specialist offices. Phone the operator on 196 in the South to send international telegrams.

TIME
Ireland is on GMT (Greenwich Mean Time) or UTC, the same as London. Without making allowances for daylight-saving time changes, when it is noon in Dublin or London it is 8 pm in Singapore, 10 pm in Sydney or Melbourne, 7 am in New York and 3 am in Los Angeles or Vancouver.

Also as in Britain, clocks are advanced by one hour from mid-March to the end of October. During the summer months it stays light until very late at night, particularly on the west coast where you could still just about read by natural light at 11 pm. In the middle of November it is dark from 5 pm to 8 am.

ELECTRICITY
Electricity is 220 volts, 50 cycles AC, and plugs are usually flat three-pin, as in Britain. Some older buildings may still have the older round-pin plugs, but adapters are available from electrical stores. Apart from shavers, if you have a round two-pin plug bring with you a plastic converter that plugs into the three-pin plug. Many bathrooms have a two-pin 110 to 120-volt AC source for shavers which is useful if you have any 110-volt gadgets.

LAUNDRY
Most hostels have cheap laundry facilities. Irish self-service laundrettes almost all offer a service wash; for IR£4 they'll wash, dry and neatly fold your dirty washing.

WEIGHTS & MEASURES
As in Britain, progress towards metrication in Ireland is slow and piecemeal. On roadsigns distances are measured in miles and km; food in shops is priced and weighed in metric; beer in pubs is still served in pints. There is a conversion table at the back of this book.

BOOKS & BOOKSHOPS
English may be an adopted language but the Irish truly have a way with it! A glance in almost any bookshop in Ireland will reveal huge Irish-interest sections: fiction, history, current events, and numerous local and regional guidebooks. Many larger cities have more than one good bookshop, Waterstone's and Eason's being familiar names, and many small towns will also have a small but well-stocked bookshop. Most, if not all, of the books below should be available in bookshops and libraries across Ireland. They are all paperback unless stated otherwise.

History & Politics
The three volumes that make up *The Green Flag* by Robert Kee (Penguin, London, 1989) offer a useful introduction although the emphasis is more on narrative than analysis. The focus of interest in Kee's books is the 19th and 20th centuries. For an introduction to earlier times try *The Course of Irish History* by Moody and Martin (Mercier Press, Cork, 1987) which has been reprinted many times.

A Concise History of Ireland by Máire & Conor Cruise O'Brien (Thames & Hudson, London, revised 1985) is a readable and comprehensively illustrated short history of Ireland. *Ireland – A History* by Robert Kee (Abacus, London, 1980) covers similar ground in a similar format in a book developed from a BBC/RTE TV series.

The classic study of the 1845-51 famine when some two million Irish either emigrated overseas or perished through lack of food is *The Great Hunger* by Cecil Woodham

Smith (Hamilton, London, 1985). Liam O'Flaherty used the catastrophe as the basis for his novel *Famine* (Wolfhound Press, Dublin, 1988). The most recent novel on the famine is *The Hanging Gale* based on the BBC Northern Ireland/RTE TV series.

The Begrudger's Guide to Irish Politics by Breandán O'hEithir (Poolbeg Books, Dublin, 1986) is a semi-humorous account of the contemporary political scene. He has also written *A Pocket History of Ireland* (O'Brien Press, Dublin, 1989), which gives a concise account of Irish history.

The North
The problem with books about Northern Ireland's recent confused history is that they're in constant need of updating and it is difficult to find a truly impartial account of what has been happening.

A serious and far-reaching attempt to get to grips with Ulster's story is *A History of Ulster* (Blackstaff Press, Belfast, 1992) by Jonathan Bardon. It's a phone directory of a book, which not only goes right back to prehistoric Ulster but also ticks off the Troubles, bomb blast by bomb blast, right up to 1992. Surprisingly it's not just thorough, it's also readable.

German academic Sabine Wichert, a Belfast resident since the early 1970s, manages to bring an outsider's inside view to the question in *Northern Ireland Since 1945* (Longman, Harlow, 1991). Patrick Buckland's *A History of Northern Ireland* (Gill & Macmillan, Dublin, 1981) is concise but somewhat out of date. *The Troubles*, edited by Taylor Downing (Thames Mac-Donald, London, 1980) was written to accompany a TV series on the conflict but also suffers from being over 15 years old. J Bowyer-Bell's *The Troubles – A Generation of Violence* (Gill & MacMillan, Dublin, 1993) is a much more recent account. Gerry Adams, the President of Sinn Féin, gives his account of the Troubles in *The Politics of Irish Freedom* (Brandon Books, Dingle, 1986) and more recently in *Free Ireland: Towards a Lasting Peace* (Brandon Books, 1995), which came out after the ceasefire.

The Dispossessed (Picador, London, 1992) investigates the background and reality of poverty in Britain through the 1980s. Writer Robert Wilson and photographer Donovan Wylie are both Belfast-born and the book concentrates on the story in London, Glasgow and Belfast.

Paisley by Ed Moloney and Andy Pollack (Poolbeg Books, Dublin, 1986) is a compelling account by two Irish journalists of the rise to power of the charismatic leader of the Democratic Unionist Party (not the Unionist Party) and the Free Presbyterian Church of Ulster (not the Presbyterian Church). If nothing else read the introduction with its astonishing Paisley speech.

Despatches from Belfast by David McKittrick (Blackstaff Press, Belfast, 1989), the Irish correspondent for the UK newspaper the *Independent*, covers 1985-89 with well-informed articles from a liberal point of view.

Literature & Fiction
If you took all the Irish writers off the university reading lists for English Literature the degree courses could probably be shortened by a year! Jonathan Swift (1667-1745), William Congreve (1670-1729), George Farquhar (1678-1707), Laurence Sterne (1713-68), Oliver Goldsmith (1728-74), Richard Sheridan (1751-1816), Oscar Wilde (1854-1900), George Bernard Shaw (1856-1950), W B Yeats (1856-1939), John Millington Synge (1871-1909), Sean O'Casey (1880-1964) and James Joyce (1882-1941) are just some of the more famous names born before 1900.

Joyce and Yeats, along with Samuel Beckett (1906-89), have achieved the highest status on the stage of world literature; out of the three Joyce is the most obviously 'Irish' and, despite the awesome difficulty of his last work *Finnegans Wake*, remains accessible as well as rewarding for anyone wanting a window on the Irish soul. *Dubliners* (published in 1914 after 10 years of censorship tangles) is a collection of remarkable short stories, especially the final story *The Dead*, which John Huston turned

James Joyce

Regarded as probably the most significant writer of literature in the 20th century, James Joyce (1882-1941) had a strange and singular life. He was born into a fairly well-off family and at the age of 'half past six' became the youngest-ever pupil at Ireland's most prestigious school – Clongowes Wood School, run by the Jesuits.

By the time he entered University College Dublin, at the age of 16, his family had fallen into hard times and Joyce was a very poor but brilliant student. He paid little attention to the formal syllabus and formed few close relationships. He was downright antagonistic to the increasingly popular Irish cultural nationalism and, while W B Yeats was writing books like *The Cultural Twilight*, Joyce was learning Norwegian so that he could read Henrik Ibsen in the original. He scorned what he later called the 'cultic twalette' of Irish nationalism, but was never really apolitical.

After leaving Ireland with Nora Barnacle he spent the next 10 years in Trieste. Apart from odd jobs in language schools and giving private lessons when strapped for cash, Joyce never worked for anyone else again after leaving his job as a bank clerk in Rome. He lived through WW I in neutral Zurich and after a short return to Trieste spent most of the rest of his life in Paris. When WW II broke out he fled back to Zurich, where he died two years later.

Joyce constantly spurned the idea of returning to live in Ireland. When he first left, his motives were a mixture of economic and ideological ones, but his refusal to return was basically ideological. He certainly didn't lack the money, for Harriet Weaver, editor of the *Egoist* magazine and publisher of *A Portrait of the Artist as a Young Man*, gave him today's equivalent of at least half a million pounds through a series of grants. As well as being an admirer, Weaver also felt sympathetic towards Joyce's problems which included eye diseases. From 1917 to 1930, Joyce underwent a series of 25 operations for glaucoma, iritis and cataracts, which sometimes left him totally blind for short intervals.

Joyce despised the way the Catholic Church maintained its hold over the hearts and minds of his newly independent country and the thought of returning to that conservatism and repression was anathema to him. Joyce was always political in the broad sense of the word and when he moved to Paris in 1920 he left behind in Trieste a library of books that included classic anarchist texts. His refusal to marry was a political statement and when he finally agreed to a registry-office marriage in 1931, it was purely to protect his family.

Joyce was frequently asked why he didn't return to Ireland and one of his few recorded replies was 'Have I ever left it?' All his writing bears this out. Ireland's attitude to Joyce, on the other hand, has been a flagrant case of cultural expropriation, and the benign face that now graces the country's IR£10 note has been craftily doctored to present a kindly old gent, smiling indulgently. It conveys nothing of the man who always refused to change his British passport for an Irish one or the angry young man who left Ireland in 1904 with Nora Barnacle, not to mention the author of a series of thoroughly pornographic letters to his wife. ∎

into an equally memorable film. *A Portrait of the Artist as a Young Man* (published in serial form from 1914) is, for the most part, a semi-autobiographical tale of a young man coming to realise his artistic vocation.

Ulysses (first published 1922) has such topographical realism that it has produced a spate of Dublin guides based on the events in the novel. See the Dublin chapter for suggestions of *Ulysses* walking guides. Although much has changed in 90 years there is still enough left to sustain a steady flow of Joyce admirers, bent on retracing the

events of Bloomsday – 16 June 1904 – which grows in popularity every year.

A recommended read for anyone who wants to know more about Joyce's life is *Nora: A Biography of Nora Joyce* by Brenda Maddox (Hamish Hamilton, 1988). It complements Richard Ellmann's more reverential biography of James Joyce himself (Oxford, 1982).

Samuel Beckett is probably best known for his play *Waiting for Godot* (1956) but his unassailable reputation is based on a number of novels and plays. His writing does not seem so 'Irish' when compared with Joyce or Yeats (which can be a help for the reader new to his work) and a good place to start is with *Murphy* and *Watt*.

A very funny post-Joyce novelist is Flann O'Brien, real name Brian O'Nuallain and second pseudonym Myles na Gopaleen, whose novels include *The Third Policeman*, *At Swim-Two-Birds* and *The Dalkey Archive* (Penguin, London).

Brendan Behan, expelled from school, a member of the IRA, imprisoned in Britain then deported back to Ireland, and an alcoholic, died in a Dublin hospital in 1964 at the height of his fame. His most enduring works are *The Quare Fellow*, *Borstal Boy* and *The Hostage*. John Banville has written a succession of excellent novels including *Long Lankin* and *Book of Evidence*.

Despite (or maybe because of) Ireland's tragic history, the comic vision has always been a characteristic of Irish writers and it features in the work of Roddy Doyle, one of the most successful writers currently achieving fame and fortune because of his way with words. His stories, set in the working class world of north Dublin, won him the Booker prize in 1993 with his *Paddy Clarke Ha Ha Ha*. Earlier, *The Commitments* was made into an internationally successful film. *The Snapper* and *The Van* (Penguin) also trace the trials and tribulations of the Rabbitt family and have been made into films.

Christy Brown's marvellous *Down all the Days* summed up Dublin's back street energy in a slightly earlier era with equal abandon. J P Donleavy's *The Ginger Man* was another high-energy excursion around Dublin, this time from the Trinity College perspective. It received the church's seal of approval by lingering on the Irish banned list for many years.

The legacy of the past – centuries of fighting the British and then a destructive civil war just when victory was at hand – continues to affect Irish writers. *The Informer* (published 1925) by Liam O'Flaherty (1896-1984) was the classic book about the divided sympathies which plagued Ireland throughout its struggle for independence and the ensuing civil war. John McGahern is well worth reading as his fiction is never just narrowly political: *The Barracks* (1963), and especially *Amongst Women* (Faber, 1990), are recommended. Gerry Conlon was one of the Guildford Four who, like the Birmingham Six, suffered years in prison accused of IRA bombings in Britain of which he was completely innocent. His true story *Proved Innocent* (Penguin, 1990) has been made into a film *In the Name of the Father*. Another victim of injustice was Brian Keenan who was one of those held hostage for years in the Middle East and his account, *An Evil Cradling* (Vintage, 1992), relives the ordeal.

John Banville is an important contemporary writer whose novels like *The Book of Evidence*, *Ghosts* and, most recently, *Athena* (Secker & Warburg, 1995) are notable for the quality of their prose. Other new novels by Irish writers appear every month and recent ones in paperback include *Stirfry* by Emma Donoghue (Penguin), dealing with lesbianism, and *Deep End* by Ger Philpott (Poolbeg Press), a novel about AIDS.

A New Book of Dubliners edited by Ben Forkner (Methuen Paperbacks, London, 1988) is a fine collection of Dublin-related short stories, stretching from James Joyce through to stories from the 1980s and including works by Liam O'Flaherty, Samuel Beckett, Oliver St John Gogarty, Flann O'Brien, Sean O'Faolain, Benedict Kiely and others.

Ireland, and Dublin in particular, have produced so many writers that you could easily plan a literary holiday or just a Dublin literary holiday. *A Literary Guide to Dublin* by Vivien Igoe (Methuen, 1995) includes detailed route maps, a guide to cemeteries and an eight-page section on literary and historical pubs.

The Irish way with words applies just as strongly north of the border as south – in fact it's astonishing how many good writers a place as small as Northern Ireland manages to turn out. The Troubles feature in much of their writing.

Bernard MacLaverty's *Cal* (Penguin,

London, 1983) traces a life where the choices are miserable and the consequences terrible and inevitable. *Cal* and McLaverty's other novel, *Lamb*, were both made into films. Those no-win political situations are also seen in Brian Moore's *Lies of Silence* (Vintage, London, 1990), which was shortlisted for the Booker Prize. Moore is a prolific writer; not all his books are about Ireland.

In Glenn Patterson's amusing first novel *Fat Lad* (Minerva, London, 1992) the political situation is a backdrop to a story which captures the feel of life in Belfast today. And the title? It's an Ulster children's mnemonic for learning the names of the six counties: Fermanagah-Armagh-Tyrone (FAT) and Londonderry-Antrim-Down (LAD).

Robert McLiam Wilson's first novel was the award-winning *Ripley Bogle* (Picador, London, 1989) which follows 'the prince of the Pavements...the Parkbench King', a West Belfast tramp, through London, with flashbacks to his youth. The follow-up was *Manfred's Pain* (Picador, London, 1992).

Republished, after 20 years out of print, *Call My Brother Back* (Poolbeg Books, Dublin, 1939) by Michael McLaverty recounts growing up on Rathlin Island and the Falls Rd in the 1920s; much of the feel of his Belfast survives to this day. More recently, Jennifer Johnston's *The Old Jest* (Penguin, London, 1979) also goes back to Ireland between the wars, though here the protagonist is an Anglo-Irish girl growing up in the South at a time when change is about to sweep through the country, with a sense that the Anglo-Irish ascendancy is in its final days.

Ireland has produced its share of women writers. Edna O'Brien enjoyed the accolade of having her *The Country Girls* (1960) being banned. Her latest novel, of 17, *House of Splendid Isolation*, is about the sudden arrival of a hooded gunman on a country doorstep. Iris Murdoch is an internationally recognised author, although she lives in England and isn't noted for using Ireland in her books. Her *The Sea, The Sea* won the Booker Prize.

Clare Boylan's books include *Holy Pictures, Concerning Virgins* and *Black Baby*. Molly Keane wrote several books in the 1920s and 30s under the pseudonym M J Farrell, then had a literary second life in her seventies when *Good Behaviour* and *Time After Time* came out under her real name.

Maeve Binchy, the Jackie Collins of Irish popular fiction, is *the* writer of blockbusters which just rise above the sex and shopping genre. They have lots of Irish settings and *Circle of Friends*, set in Dublin, has been made into a film.

W B Yeats was a playwright and poet, but it is his poetry that has the greatest appeal and, being out of copyright, countless editions are available. His *Love Poems*, edited by Norman Jeffares (Gill & Macmillan, Dublin, 1988) makes a suitable introduction for anyone new to his writing. A collected edition, *The Poems*, in the Everyman series edited by Daniel Albright, is especially good value (IR£11) for a hardback and includes a very useful set of notes.

For a taste of modern Irish poetry try *Contemporary Irish Poetry* edited by Fallon and Mahon (Penguin, London, 1990). Seamus Heaney, winner of the 1995 Nobel Prize for Literature, is there of course, and so are a host of other poets from both the North and the Republic. *A Rage for Order* edited by Frank Ormsby (Blackstaff Press, Belfast, 1992) is a vibrant collection of the poetry of the Northern Ireland crisis.

Tom Paulin writes memorable poetry about the North; try *The Strange Museum*. Other notable contemporary poets are Eavan Boland, Paul Muldoon and Derek Mahon.

Visitors' & Residents' Accounts

To understand the Anglo-Irish read David Thomson's *Woodbrook* (Vintage Books, London, 1990). As a young man Thomson came to the north-west to act as tutor to an Anglo-Irish family and his book charts his gradual awakening to the reality around him.

The nature of life in the North has attracted writers to the region and compelled residents to write about it. *Titanic Town* (Mandarin, London, 1992) is subtitled *Memoirs of a*

Belfast Girlhood, and Mary Costello manages to make growing up in the tough Andersonstown area of West Belfast funny and sad in equal measures. From Sinn Féin president Gerry Adams, *The Street* (Brandon Books, Dingle, 1992) is a collection of stories dealing with life in West Belfast where he grew up.

The Crack – A Belfast Year (Grafton, London, 1987) by Sally Belfrage, is a reporter's accounts from a series of visits to Belfast in the 1980s.

In the mid-1970s Irish travel writer Dervla Murphy jumped on her faithful bicycle Roz, the same one she took to India in the 1960s, and rode off to explore Northern Ireland. The result was *A Place Apart* (Penguin, London, 1978), and despite the fact that it's nearly 20 years since her visit, what strikes you is how little has changed in that time. It's highly readable and so makes an accessible introduction to things like Orangeism, Paisleyism, the problems in South Armagh etc.

In the early 1980s, American travel writer Paul Theroux included Northern Ireland on his round Britain itinerary for *Kingdom by the Sea* (Penguin, London, 1983). Travelling round most of Britain made the famously sour Theroux even more dyspeptic than usual but, surprisingly, he warmed towards the Ulster people. It's no surprise at all that P J O'Rourke gave Belfast a chapter in his book *Holidays in Hell* (Picador, London, 1988). Like many other visitors O'Rourke found Belfast altogether too tame for its reputation. Where are the appalling slums?

For cycling visitors, Eric Newby's *Round Ireland in Low Gear* is another Newby classic of travel masochism complete with lousy weather, steep hills, high winds and predatory trucks.

Guidebooks

Irish Pub Guide (Appletree Press, 1994, 21 Alfred St, Belfast, BT2 8DL) lists and describes a number of pubs across Ireland that are particularly interesting for one reason or another. *The Hidden Gardens of Ireland* by Mariane Heron (Gill & Macmil-

lan, 1994) is an informative guide to its more sober subject.

Culture Shock! Ireland by Patricia Levy (Times Books, 1996) is recommended as an up-to-date introduction to aspects of Irish culture and the book will help the visitor understand the country and its people. *Ireland: Anatomy of a Changing State* by Gemma Hussey (Penguin, London, 1995) is a useful, though perhaps too uncontroversial, guide to various social and political issues that continue to bedevil the country.

See the Activities chapter for details of cycling and walking guidebooks and books on tracing your ancestors. See the previous Literature section for a literary guidebook to Dublin and the Dublin chapter for walking guides to *Ulysses*. An exhaustive listing of courses (Irish language, adventure sports, arts & crafts etc) held in Ireland each summer is available from Perdita Quinlan at 44 Avoca Ave, Blackrock, County Dublin for IR£2.99.

MAPS

There are numerous good-quality maps of Ireland. The Michelin Map of Ireland No 405 (1:400,000) has most of the scenic roads accurately highlighted in green. The four maps – North, South, East and West – that make up the Ordnance Survey Holiday Map series are useful if you want something more detailed than a whole Ireland map. Their scale is 1:250,000.

For greater detail the Ordnance Survey covers the whole island in 25 sheets with a 1:126,720 scale (half an inch to one mile). This series, however, is gradually being replaced by a new series of 89 maps with a 1:50,000 scale (two cm to one km).

The new maps are a pleasure to use and it's always worth checking to see if the area you want is available in the new series. They can be obtained from the Government Publications Sales Office bookshop (☎ 01-661 3111), Sun Alliance House, Molesworth St, Dublin 2.

Special maps for the Kerry Way, Dingle Way and other trails are available from tourist offices, and at a pinch they will suffice. For the Ulster Way, section maps are available from the Sports Council for Northern Ireland (☎ 01232-381222), House of Sport, Upper Malone Rd, Belfast BT9 5LA.

Tim Robinson of Folding Landscapes, Roundstone, County Galway, produces superbly detailed maps of the Burren, the Aran Islands and Connemara and has a detailed map as part of the hill walking guide to Connemara by Joss Lynam (see the County Galway chapter).

MEDIA
Newspapers & Magazines
The Irish Republic has six national daily newspapers and five national Sunday newspapers. The daily *Irish Times* is a bastion of liberal opinion and good journalism and is often mentioned as being up there with the world's best newspapers. The *Irish Press* was founded by Eamon de Valera and for a long time was Republican in orientation and supportive of the Fianna Fáil party, although it has been less so in recent years. At the time of writing it had gone into liquidation as a result of an industrial dispute and its future looked uncertain. The biggest seller is the *Irish Independent* which tends to be lighter in content than the others, with more features and gossip. The *Cork Examiner* has a good journalistic reputation and the *Star* is the country's daily tabloid. On the Sunday front, the *Sunday Tribune* has a liberal approach and claims to be good at investigating and breaking stories. The *Sunday Independent* and *Sunday Press* mirror their daily equivalents, and the biggest seller is the *Sunday World* with plenty of titillation. The *Sunday Business Post* concentrates on financial matters.

In the North you will find the evening *Belfast Telegraph* and the tabloid and staunchly Protestant *News Letter*. British papers and magazines are readily available in both the North and the South. They sell at a slightly higher price in the South than in Britain but still undercut the Irish newspapers.

The main European and US newspapers are sold in the larger newsagents in Dublin and Belfast.

Radio & TV
The Republic of Ireland has two state-controlled TV channels and three radio stations. The state-controlled TV channels are RTE 1 and Network 2. British BBC and independent TV programmes can be picked up in many parts of the country and offer a welcome substitute for the often dreary Irish programming. In its defence, RTE isn't that bad by international standards. It may appear parochial but local topics are always of limited interest to outsiders.

A programme worth watching is *The Late Late Show*, the longest-running chat show in the world, hosted on Friday nights during the winter by Gay Byrne, Ireland's top media personality. The show has a good mix of celebrities and current affairs, and is often an interesting window into Irish life. Current affairs programmes such as *Tuesday File* and *Prime Time* are also worth a look. Watch out for Gaelic football and hurling matches on at weekends. Many hotels and pubs have satellite TV from the European Astra satellite.

Irish radio, AM or FM, varies in quality. Many of the morning programmes consist of phone-ins. RTE Radio One (88-90 FM or 567/729 MW) has a good mix of documentaries, music and talk shows. Broadcasters like Gay Byrne, Pat Kenny and Marion Finucane may give an insight into the country's foibles. RTE's 2FM (92-93 FM or 612/1278 MW) is the national pop music station and does what pop stations do. Mind you, it is a good forum for upcoming Irish rock talent and is where U2 got their first airing. The *Gerry Ryan Show* in the morning is worth listening to. Radio na Gaeltachta (92.5-96 FM or 540/828/963 MW) is the national Irish-language service.

There is a host of regional radio stations, offering good local services. The best of them are LM FM in Counties Louth and Meath broadcasting on 95.8 FM, Radio Kerry on 97.6 FM and Clare FM on 96.4 FM. In Dublin 98 FM and FM 104 stations offer an unending diet of classic international rock and pop tunes. As with TV it is possible to tune into British BBC radio and independent channels, though the further west you go the weaker the signal.

In Northern Ireland, there are two TV stations – BBC NI and Ulster TV, which mix their own programming with input from their parent companies in the UK – BBC and ITV respectively. Channel 4 also broadcasts in Northern Ireland.

Censorship

For many years books and films in Ireland suffered under an absurdly restrictive censorship code. The Censorship of Publications Act of 1929 became more farcical and silly as time went on. At one time Ireland was in the peculiar position of providing taxation advantages to encourage authors to live and work in the country and at the same time banning whatever they wrote. Even between 1960 and 1965, when censorship was definitely on the wane, nearly 2000 books were banned. Films banned in the 1960s included *Ulysses, Paddy* and *Of Human Bondage*, all of them made in Ireland!

The censors seem to have become more liberal although Madonna's opus *Sex* was banned in Ireland – after it had completely sold out! *Basic Instinct*, the controversial 1992 Michael Douglas/Sharon Stone sex and death saga, was shown uncut in Ireland while even in the USA it had to have at least one cut. The censors sometimes seem susceptible to picking on heavily publicised movies: in 1995 *Natural Born Killers* was banned from general release while the violent New Zealand film, *Once Were Warriors* was shown without trouble.

FILM & PHOTOGRAPHY

Ireland has enough spectacular seascapes, ancient ruins, picturesque villages and interesting faces to keep any photographer happy. But almost always it is the mood that makes the shot and Ireland is noted for its rapidly changing and unusual light. In bright sunlight, west coast beaches can look like the tropics, and then a couple of hours and a few clouds later, Arctic Norway. Try and be imaginative with monuments and Celtic

crosses, get the sun behind or at the side of your subject, use fill flash, get low with a wide-angle lens and put some plants or other points of interest in the foreground.

The best times for pictures are early morning and late evening when the sunlight is low and warm. If you are keen and using slide film, the slower the film the better, eg Fuji Velvia 50 ASA or Ektachrome 64 or 100 ASA. However, Irish light can be very dull, so to capture the sombre atmosphere you may need faster film, eg 200 or 400 ASA, and a small tripod will be useful. In good weather a polariser is terrific for cutting out haze and giving punchy primary green fields and blue skies with cotton-puff clouds. A plastic bag is handy to stop your camera getting wet.

Film & Processing

There are plenty of camera shops in the cities and bigger towns, but in smaller towns and villages it is the chemists or pharmacies that stock film and arrange for processing. They will usually have Fuji or Kodak print film. Slide film is usually Fujichrome or Ektachrome, but don't depend on them having any in stock. Kodachrome is becoming increasingly scarce and has to be sent to France for processing. Chemists and many of the smaller camera shops are expensive so stock up beforehand.

In Dublin you can buy very reasonably priced film at LSL Photolabs (☎ 01-478 1078) at 25 Lennox St, Dublin 8, or at Quirke Lynch (☎ 01-496 4666) 41 Lower Rathmines Rd, Dublin 6. Most towns and cities have good quality one-hour processing shops. Developing and printing a 24-exposure print film typically costs around IR£8 for one-hour service or IR£4 to IR£5 for slower turnaround. Slide processing costs about IR£6 a roll and takes a few days, though Quirke Lynch and the Film Bank (☎ 01-660 6082) at 102 Lower Baggot St, Dublin 2, have a same-day service for about IR£15.

Photographing People

You can't generalise about how Irish people will react to having their photographs taken.

As always, being courteous and having a chat beforehand will make things a lot easier for the photographer.

HEALTH

Apart from cholesterol, Ireland poses no serious threats to health. The Catholic distaste for contraception does not prevent condoms being sold through pharmacies, if the pharmacist isn't personally opposed! Condoms are also available from vending machines in some pubs and nightclubs. The pill is available only on prescription.

Citizens of EU countries are eligible for medical care; other visitors should have medical insurance or be prepared to pay. The Eastern Health Board Dublin Area (☎ 01-679 0700; freephone 1800 520 520), 138 Thomas St, Dublin 8, has a Choice of Doctor Scheme which can advise you on a suitable doctor from 9 am to 5 pm, Monday to Friday. Your hotel or your embassy can also suggest a doctor.

Predeparture Preparations

Health Insurance A travel insurance policy to cover theft, loss and medical problems is a wise idea. There are a wide variety of policies and your travel agent will have recommendations. The international student travel policies handled by STA Travel or other student travel organisations are usually good value. Some policies offer lower and higher medical-expense options but the higher one is chiefly for countries like the USA which have extremely high medical costs. Check the small print:

1. Some policies specifically exclude 'dangerous activities' which can include scuba diving, motorcycling, even trekking. If such activities are on your agenda you don't want that sort of policy. A locally acquired motorcycle licence may not be valid under your policy.
2. You may prefer a policy which pays doctors or hospitals direct rather than you having to pay on the spot and claim later.
3. Check if the policy covers ambulances or an emergency flight home. If you have to

stretch out you will need two seats and somebody has to pay for them!

Medical Kit A small, straightforward medical kit is a wise thing to carry. A kit should include:

1. Aspirin or Panadol – for pain or fever.
2. Antihistamine (such as Benadryl) – useful as a decongestant for colds and allergies, to ease the itch from insect bites or stings, and to help prevent motion sickness. Antihistamines may cause sedation and interact with alcohol so care should be taken when using them.
3. Kaolin preparation (Pepto-Bismol), Imodium or Lomotil – for stomach upsets.
4. Antiseptic such as Betadine, which comes as impregnated swabs or ointment, and an antibiotic powder or similar 'dry' spray – for cuts and grazes.
5. Bandages and Band-aids – for minor injuries.
6. Scissors, tweezers and a thermometer (note that mercury thermometers are prohibited by airlines).

Health Preparations If you wear glasses, take a spare pair and your prescription. Losing your glasses can be a real problem, although in many places you can get new spectacles made up quickly, cheaply and competently. If you require a particular medication or a specific oral contraceptive take note of the generic name rather than the brand name as it may not be available locally.

Immunisations These are not necessary for any European country, but they may be necessary if you're stopping over on your way, and could be an entry requirement if you arrive from an infected area. If you're going to Europe with stopovers in Asia, Africa or Latin America, check with your travel agent and doctor. Don't leave it till the last minute, as the vaccinations may have to be spread out a bit.

All vaccinations should be recorded on an International Health Certificate, which is available from your physician or government health department.

Basic Rules

Care in what you eat and drink and maintenance of personal hygiene are the most important health rules, wherever you travel.

Water Don't drink straight from a stream: you can never be certain there are no people or animals upstream. It has been reported that there has been some water pollution in a remote rural area in the north-west.

Water Purification The simplest way of purifying water is to boil it thoroughly. Vigorously boiling for five minutes should be satisfactory; however, at high altitude water boils at a lower temperature, so germs are less likely to be killed.

Filtering will not remove all dangerous organisms, so if you cannot boil water it should be treated chemically. Chlorine tablets (Puritabs, Steritabs or other brand names) will kill many but not all pathogens. Iodine is very effective in purifying water and is available in tablet form (such as Potable Aqua). If you can't find tablets, tincture of iodine (2%) or iodine crystals can be used. Four drops of tincture of iodine per litre or quart of clear water is the recommended dosage; the treated water should be left to stand for 20 to 30 minutes before drinking.

Everyday Health Normal body temperature is 98.6°F or 37°C; more than 2°C higher indicates a 'high' fever. The normal adult pulse rate is 60 to 80 per minute (children 80 to 100, babies 100 to 140). You should know how to take a temperature and a pulse rate. As a general rule the pulse increases about 20 beats per minute for each °C rise in fever.

The breathing rate is also an indicator of illness. Count the number of breaths per minute: between 12 and 20 is normal for adults and older children (up to 30 for younger children, 40 for babies).

Many health problems can be avoided by just taking care of yourself. Wash your hands frequently.

Medical Problems & Treatment

Sunburn Even in Ireland, and even through cloud cover it's possible to get sunburnt surprisingly quickly – especially if you're on water, snow or ice. Use a 15+ sunscreen, wear a hat and cover up with a long-sleeved shirt and trousers.

Heat Exhaustion Dehydration or salt deficiency can cause heat exhaustion. In hot conditions (they do happen!) and if you're exerting yourself make sure you get sufficient nonalcoholic liquids. Salt deficiency is characterised by fatigue, lethargy, headaches, giddiness and muscle cramps. Vomiting or diarrhoea can deplete your liquid and salt levels.

Fungal Infections To prevent fungal infections wear loose, comfortable clothes, avoid artificial fibres, wash frequently and dry carefully. Always wear thongs (flip-flops) in shared bathrooms. If you do get an infection, consult a chemist. Try to expose the infected area to air or sunlight as much as possible and wash all towels and underwear in hot water as well as changing them often.

Cold Hypothermia occurs when the body loses heat faster than it can produce it and the core temperature of the body falls. It is surprisingly easy to progress from very cold to dangerously cold due to a combination of wind, wet clothing, fatigue and hunger, even if the air temperature is above freezing.

Walkers in Ireland should always be prepared for difficult conditions. It is best to dress in layers and a hat is important, as a lot of heat is lost through the head. A strong, waterproof outer layer is essential. Carry basic supplies, including food containing simple sugars to generate heat quickly.

Symptoms of hypothermia are exhaustion, numb skin (particularly toes and fingers), shivering, slurred speech, irrational or violent behaviour, lethargy, stumbling, dizzy spells, muscle cramps and violent bursts of energy.

To treat mild hypothermia, first get the person out of the wind and/or rain, remove their clothing if it's wet and replace it with dry, warm clothing. Give them hot liquids – not alcohol – and some high-kilojoule, easily digestible food. This should be enough to treat the early stages of hypothermia, but if it has gone further, it may be necessary to place victims in warm sleeping bags and get in with them. Do not rub patients, place them near a fire or remove their wet clothes in the wind. If possible, place a sufferer in a warm (not hot) bath.

Diarrhoea A change of water, food or climate can all cause the runs; diarrhoea caused by contaminated food or water is more serious.

A few rushed toilet trips with no other symptoms is not indicative of a serious problem. Moderate diarrhoea, involving half-a-dozen loose movements in a day, is more of a nuisance. Dehydration is the main danger with any diarrhoea, particularly for children where dehydration can occur quite quickly, so fluid replenishment is the main treatment. Weak black tea with a little sugar, soda water, or soft drinks allowed to go flat and diluted 50% with water are all good.

With more severe diarrhoea go straight to the casualty ward of the nearest hospital and have yourself checked. You may need a rehydrating solution to replace minerals and salts. Stick to a bland diet as you recover.

Sexually Transmitted Diseases (STDs)
Sexual contact with an infected sexual partner spreads these diseases. While abstinence is the only 100% preventative, using condoms is also effective. Gonorrhoea and syphilis are the most common of these diseases; sores, blisters or rashes around the genitals, discharges or pain when urinating are common symptoms. Symptoms may be less marked or not observed at all in women. Syphilis symptoms eventually disappear completely, but the disease continues and can cause severe problems in later years. The treatment of gonorrhoea and syphilis is by antibiotics.

There are numerous other sexually transmitted diseases, for most of which effective treatment is available. However, there is no cure for herpes and there is also currently no cure for AIDS.

WOMEN TRAVELLERS
Although women are in some ways second-class citizens in Ireland, they're also generally treated respectfully; pornography keeps a mercifully low profile, and it has even been suggested that sexism in the workplace is less of a problem than in Britain. Occasionally, you'll come across a pub where they still think men should take precedence over women, but this is increasingly unusual.

In many ways Ireland is one of the safest and least harassing countries for women, with the obvious exception of the big towns and cities, especially at night. Many women travellers happily hitch their way around the country without problem, although the usual care should be taken and it goes without saying that anyone can be unlucky. In 1995 a lone woman camper in Northern Ireland was set upon by youths and raped, so it doesn't pay to get complacent.

TRAVEL WITH CHILDREN
Successful travel with young children requires effort, but it can certainly be done. Try not to overdo things and consider using some sort of self-catering accommodation as a base. Include children in the planning process; if they've helped to work out where you'll be going, they will be much more interested when they get there. Include a range of activities – balance a visit to Trinity College for example with one to the National Wax Museum. For more information see Lonely Planet's *Travel with Children* by Maureen Wheeler et al.

DISABLED TRAVELLERS
If you have a physical disability, get in touch with your national support organisation (preferably the travel officer if there is one) and ask about the countries you plan to visit. They often have complete libraries devoted to travel, and can put you in touch with travel

agents who specialise in tours for the disabled.

Guesthouses, hotels and sights in Ireland are increasingly being adapted for people with disabilities though there is still a long way to go. Bord Fáilte's annual *Accommodation Guide* indicates which places are wheelchair accessible. The NITB publishes *Accessible Accommodation in Northern Ireland*. Your travel agent may have access to the most recent details (see Gulliver under Tourist Offices earlier) about facilities available for disabled people. Alternatively, you can obtain information on individual counties in the Republic by writing to the National Rehabilitation Board, Access Department, 25 Clyde Rd, Dublin 4. In Northern Ireland contact Disability Action (☎ 01232-491011), 2 Annadale Ave, Belfast BT7 3UR.

GAY & LESBIAN TRAVELLERS

Gay or lesbian life is simply not acknowledged in most parts of Ireland. Homosexuality for consenting adults was legalised in Northern Ireland in 1982, and in 1993 it was decriminalised in the Republic for consenting adults over the age of 17. In Dublin and Cork there are openly gay and lesbian communities, but in rural areas there's a conspiracy of silence and denial. The magazine *In Dublin* has a section on gay and lesbian services, organisations and entertainment. For more information contact:

National Lesbian & Gay Federation
   Hirschfield Centre, 10 Fownes St, Dublin 2
   (☎ 01-671 0939)
Northern Ireland Gay Rights Association
   Cathedral Buildings, Lower Donegall St, Belfast
   (☎ 01232-664111)

SENIOR TRAVELLERS

Senior citizens are entitled to many discounts in Europe on things like public transport, museum admission fees etc, provided they show proof of their age. In some cases they might need a special pass. The minimum qualifying age is usually 60 to 65 for men, and 55 to 65 for women.

In your home country, a lower age may already entitle you to all sorts of interesting travel packages and discounts (on car hire, for instance) through organisations and travel agents that cater to senior travellers. Start hunting at your local senior citizens' advice bureau.

DANGERS & ANNOYANCES

See also Car & Motorbike in the Getting Around chapter.

Crime

Ireland is probably safer than most countries in Europe but the usual precautions should be observed. Drug-related crime is on the increase and Dublin has its fair share of pickpockets and sneak thieves waiting to relieve the unwary of unwatched bags. See the Dublin chapter for more details.

If you're travelling by car do not leave valuables on view inside when the car is parked. Dublin is particularly notorious for car break-ins, and foreign-registered cars and rent-a-cars are prime targets. Cyclists should always lock their bicycles securely and be cautious about leaving bags on the bike, particularly in larger towns or more touristy locations.

The police in the Republic are called by their Irish name of Garda Síochána, or just garda for one police officer and gardaí (gardee) for more than one. In Northern Ireland the police are called the Royal Ulster Constabulary (RUC) and ☎ 999 is the emergency number in both the North and the South. After dialling ☎ 999 you should specify whether you want the police (gardaí), fire, ambulance or boat or coastal rescue.

Precautions The hassles created by losing your passport can be considerably reduced if you have a record of its number and issue date, or even better, photocopies of the relevant data pages. A photocopy of your birth certificate can also be useful. In addition, add the serial numbers of your travellers' cheques (cross them off as you cash them in) and photocopies of your credit cards, airline ticket and other travel documents.

Keep this emergency material totally separate from your passport, cheques and other cash, and leave extra copies with someone you can rely on back home. Add some emergency money, say IR£50, to this separate stash as well. If you lose your passport, notify the police immediately to get a statement, and contact your nearest consulate.

The Troubles
Obviously there is a certain amount of danger in Northern Ireland but if the cease fire and peace process continue this will diminish. If you confine yourself to the Antrim coast you may well never see the British army, but in Derry or South Armagh, on the other hand, their presence is more obvious. Tourists will be treated with courtesy by the security forces, but you may be asked for some form of identification. Don't leave a bag unattended: apart from the risk of theft it could be the subject of a security alert.

A British accent can be a help or a hindrance, depending on who you're dealing with.

Racism
Most Irish people have little experience of those with different coloured skin, and some prejudice – and curiosity – is inevitable, but it is most unlikely to reach the level of personal hostility that is so common in parts of Britain.

WORK
With unemployment around 15% in the South and well over 10% in the North this is not a good country for casual employment, although there is a great deal of seasonal work in the tourist industry, usually in restaurants and pubs. Without skills, it is very difficult to find a job that pays sufficiently well to enable you to save money. You're almost certainly better off saving in your country of origin.

Ireland is a member of the European Union (EU) so citizens of any other EU country can work in Ireland. If you have an Irish parent or grandparent, it is fairly easy to obtain Irish citizenship without necessarily renouncing your own nationality, and this opens the door to employment throughout the EU. Obtaining citizenship is not an overnight procedure, so enquire about the process at an Irish embassy or consulate in your own country.

HIGHLIGHTS
Scenery, Beaches & Coastline
The scenery is one of Ireland's major attractions, whether it's those soft green fields, awesome cliffs tumbling into a ferocious Atlantic, or rocky and barren areas in the far west. Highlights include the beautiful scenery around the Ring of Kerry and the Dingle Peninsula, the barren stretches of the Burren, the rocky Aran Islands and the beautiful lakeland areas south and north.

Favourite stretches of Ireland's 3200 km of coastline include the wildly beautiful Cliffs of Moher, the Connemara and Donegal coasts and the wonderful Antrim Coast Road of Northern Ireland. There are some fine beaches (and marginally warmer water) around the south-east coast, and some great surfing around the west and north-west coasts.

The EU Blue Flag flies over the cleanest and safest beaches of Ireland. If the beach is not a Blue Flag one it is best to enquire locally before venturing out for a swim.

Museums, Castles & Houses
Trinity College Library with the ancient 'Book of Kells' is on every visitor's must-see list, but Dublin also has the fine National Museum and National Gallery. Belfast has an excellent museum and the extensive Ulster Folk Museum just outside the city.

Ireland is littered with castles and forts of various types and in various stages of ruination. The Stone Age forts on the Aran Islands are of particular interest but there are other ancient ring forts all over Ireland. Castles are numerous and prime examples are Dublin Castle, Charles Fort at Kinsale and Kilkenny Castle, not forgetting Blarney Castle with its famous stone!

The Anglo-Irish aristocracy left a good

selection of fine stately homes, many of them now open to the public like Castletown House, Malahide House, Westport House, Bantry House and Mt Stewart, and the beautiful gardens at Powerscourt.

Religious Sites

Stone rings, portal tombs or dolmens and passage graves are reminders of an earlier pre-Christian Ireland. The massive passage grave at Newgrange is the most impressive relic of that time. Early Christian churches, many well over 1000 years old, are scattered throughout Ireland, and ruined monastic sites, many of them with round towers, are also numerous. Clonmacnois, Glendalough, Mellifont Abbey, Grey Abbey, Inch Abbey and Jerpoint Abbey are particularly interesting monastic sites. The rock-top complex at Cashel is one of Ireland's major tourist attractions, and the beehive huts built by monks on Skellig Michael, off the coast of Kerry, are well worth visiting.

Islands

'Like whales, like castles, like sleeping giants – the islands of Ireland are ranged along the horizon in a host of mysterious shapes.' So goes the tourist board brochure – but, yes, there are all sorts and shapes of islands, inhabited and uninhabited, some of them easily accessible and others requiring the private hire of a boat.

The Aran Islands in County Galway and Achill Island in County Mayo are the most touristy, but it is not difficult to find more isolated ones. The Skelligs have already been mentioned, and their wildlife is fascinating. The Blaskets, off the Dingle Peninsula in County Kerry, are glorious on a fine day and are worth seeing now, before the houses that were inhabited up until 1953 are restored and become part of yet another interpretive centre. Tory Island, off the Donegal coast, is a wild place and is the surprising home of a group of local artists. County Cork has a number of accessible islands, of which Clear Island is famous for its birdlife and scenery and nearby Sherkin Island has sandy and safe beaches.

ACCOMMODATION

The Bord Fáilte's annual *Accommodation Guide* costs IR£5 and has an awesome list of B&Bs, hotels, camp sites, and other accommodation. It far from exhausts the possibilities, however, as there are also a great many places which are not 'tourist-office approved'. This does not necessarily mean they are in any way inferior to the approved places. The Northern Ireland Tourist Board publishes its own *Where to Stay* book (£3.99) which covers the same ground.

If you're travelling on a tight budget, the numerous hostels offer the cheapest accommodation to be found and are also great centres for meeting fellow travellers and exchanging information. In summer and on public holidays they can be heavily booked but so is everything else. Bord Fáilte offices will book local accommodation for a fee of IR£1 or IR£2 in another town. All this really involves is phoning a place on their list; but in high summer, when it may take numerous phone calls to find a free room, that can be a pound or two well spent.

This is especially true in Northern Ireland, where there is a shortage of bed space as a result of the lack of visitors until recently and where the Northern Ireland Tourist Board provides a similar booking service to Bord Fáilte.

Camping

Camp sites are not as common as in Britain or on the continent but there are still plenty of them around Ireland. Some hostels also have camping space and usually offer the use of the kitchen and shower facilities, which often makes them better value than the main camp sites. At commercial sites, costs are typically IR£4 to IR£7 for a tent and many have coin-operated showers. Many sites have different rates depending on the type of tent you have (a two-person tent as opposed to a family tent being the usual distinction) and whether you arrive by bike or car.

Free camping is generally possible as long as you ask permission from the farmer. Around the touristy parts of Kerry and Cork, farmers may ask for a pound or two, but it should never be too difficult to find one who will let you camp for nothing.

Hostels

An Óige and the Youth Hostel Association of Northern Ireland (YHANI) are the two associations that belong to Hostelling International (HI). An Óige has over 40 hostels scattered round the South and YHANI has eight in the North. Annual membership is IR£7.50 (£7.50). Overseas visitors who are not members can stay at the hostels and may join by obtaining a 'guest card' and paying IR£1.25 for a stamp on top of the nightly charge. If they buy six stamps (total IR£7.50) they become a HI member.

To use a hostel you must have or rent a sleeping sheet. Nightly costs vary with the time of year but in June to September are usually IR£5.50 to IR£6.50 except for the more expensive Dublin hostel. Rates are cheaper if you're under 18. Prices quoted are all high season and for those over 18.

An Óige and YHANI hostels have been changing a lot for the better. They operate a fax-a-bed-ahead facility that books accommodation in advance. Bookings can be made by credit card at many of the larger hostels and some hostels have family and smaller rooms. And these days you can take a car to a hostel. Membership enquiries should go to An Óige (☎ 01-830 4555; fax 01-830 5808), 61 Mountjoy St South, Dublin 7, or the Youth Hostel Association of Northern Ireland (☎ 01232-315435; fax 01232-439699) 22-32 Donegall Rd, Belfast BT12 5JN.

Nowhere else in Europe have independent hostels popped up like they have in Ireland. Independent Holiday Hostels (IHH) is a tourist-board approved co-operative group who put out a booklet listing 125 hostels all over Ireland. This is available from IHH Office (☎ 01-836 4700; fax 01-836 4710), 21 Store St, Dublin 1, or from tourist offices. There are no membership requirements and no curfew. There are still more independent hostels which are members of neither group. Independent hostels emphasise their easy-going ambience and lack of rules, and competition from the independents has forced the official hostels to rethink their rule books in recent years.

B&Bs

If you're not staying in hostels you are probably staying in a B&B. It sometimes seems every other house in Ireland is a B&B and you'll stumble upon them in the most unusual and remote locations.

The typical cost is IR£12 to IR£16 a night, and you rarely pay less or more than that, except in the big towns where some luxurious B&Bs can cost IR£25 or more a night. They usually do not have private bathrooms and where they do the cost is usually IR£2 higher. At some places costs are higher for a single room. Prices in the North are similar. Most B&Bs are very small, just two to four rooms, so in summer they can quickly fill up. With so many to try there's bound to be someone with a spare room, however. Outside the big cities, most B&Bs only accept cash.

Breakfast at a B&B is almost inevitably cereal followed by 'a fry', which means fried eggs, bacon and sausages, plus toast and brown bread. A week of B&B breakfasts exceeds every known international guideline for cholesterol intake, but if you decline fried food you're left with cereal and toast. If your bloodstream can take the pressure, you'll have eaten enough food to last you till dinnertime, but it's a shame more places don't offer alternatives like fruit, yoghurt or the delicious variety of Irish breads and scones, which are widely available. In Northern Ireland you may meet the awesome 'Ulster Fry', which adds fried bread, blood sausage, tomatoes and assorted other fried foods to the basic version.

Hotels

Accommodation in a hotel can range from the local pub to a medieval castle. It is often possible to negotiate better deals than the published rates, especially out of season. Ask if any discounts are given and try to think of a reason why you in particular merit one. Out of the main holiday season, hotels often have special deals for certain days of the week, but these are usually quite flexible and can often be extended to whatever days you want. Payment for a night's stay usually includes breakfast.

Other Possibilities

Guesthouses are often just like larger and more expensive B&Bs, but sometimes they are more like small hotels with a restaurant, lounge room and telephone and TV in the rooms. Farmhouse accommodation usually means it's a B&B on a farm; they are sometimes excellent value and you may get a chance to see how the farm works. Country houses are rural B&Bs, usually costing a little more and in a rather grander than usual house.

Self-catering accommodation is often on a weekly basis and usually means an apartment or house where you look after yourself. The rates vary from one region and season to another. A smart cottage around Kinsale in August could be around IR£400 a week, sleeping six people, while the equivalent in Longford in April could be about IR£90.

FOOD

It's frequently said that Irish cooking doesn't match up to the ingredients and traditional Irish cooking tends to imitate English – ie cook it until it's dead, dead, dead. Fortunately, the Irish seem to be doing a better job than the English in kicking that habit and you can generally eat quite well. Of course if you want meat or fish cooked until it's dried and shrivelled and vegetables turned to mush, there are plenty of places that can still perform the feat.

Irish meals are usually meat-based. Beef, lamb and pork chops are the old reliables. A really traditional meal is bacon and cabbage, a delicious combination it makes too, and should be tried at least once.

The curious Irish aversion to seafood probably has, like so many other Irish curiosities, a religious connection. Ireland has always been a meat-eating country but it's also been a strictly, even bizarrely, Catholic one. Until fairly recently the Catholic Friday fasting restrictions were strictly adhered to, so fish became something you were forced to have on Friday and, like long-suffering schoolchildren, if you're forced to eat it you don't like it. As a result Ireland is an island with a remarkably small fishing industry, and fish is still in the process of finding a place on the Irish dining table. Try it – the trout and salmon are delicious.

Irish bread has a wonderful reputation and indeed it can be very good, but, unfortunately, there's a tendency to fall back on the infamous white-sliced bread, *pan* in Irish. B&Bs are often guilty of this crime. Do try some soda bread, made from flour and buttermilk. Irish scones are a delight; tea and scones is a great snack at any time of day. Even pubs will often offer tea and scones.

Traditional foods include:

Bacon & Cabbage
  a stew consisting simply of its two named ingredients: bacon and cabbage
Barm Brack
  an Irish cake-like bread
Boxty
  rather like a filled pancake
Champ
  Northern Irish dish of potatoes mashed with onions
Dublin Coddle
  a semi-thick stew made with sausages, bacon, onions and potatoes
Guinness Cake
  a popular fruitcake flavoured with Guinness beer
Irish Stew
  this quintessential Irish dish is a stew of mutton, potatoes and onions, flavoured with parsley and thyme and simmered slowly
Soda Bread
  Belfast is probably the place in Ireland for bread at its best, but soda bread in particular, white or brown, is found throughout the country

It is common for Irish people to eat their main meal of the day at lunch time, and every town will have at least one hotel or restaurant, offering special three-course meals for around IR£5. A similar meal in the evening may be at least double the cost.

The main alternatives to Irish food are provided by Italian and Chinese restaurants although in the bigger cities like Dublin, Belfast and Cork you'll also find Indian, Middle Eastern, Mexican and other choices.

Fast food is well established, from traditional fish & chips to more recent arrivals like burgers, pizzas, kebabs and tacos. Pubs are often good places to eat, particularly at lunch time when a bowl of the soup of the day (usually vegetable) and some good bread can make a fine and economical meal.

There are some superb vegetarian places and frequently they turn out to be run by British or other Europeans who have settled in Ireland. Hotels and restaurants often feature a vegetarian dish on their menus but you'll soon tire of unimaginative vegetable lasagne or bland vegetable curry. At the more expensive restaurants it is always a good idea to inform them in advance that you want a vegetarian meal. If you are vegetarian then staying at a B&B can be a bad deal. The best excuse for the high prices charged by most B&Bs is the huge breakfast they serve. The vegetarian alternative will usually be just cornflakes and toast, but the charge will be the same. See the B&B section for information on the famous Irish breakfast.

There are several specialist food and restaurant guides to Ireland. The Bridgestone 100 Best Restaurants in Ireland and the Bridgestone Vegetarians' Guide to Ireland (Estragon, 1995) are both by Sally & John McKenna and are practical, independent guides to their subject. Bord Fáilte has its own publication of recommended restaurants but the restaurants concerned simply pay for their entry and submit their own write-up. The Northern Ireland Tourist Board has its own Where to Eat book for £2.50 and covers everything from the very expensive to the local Chinese takeaway.

DRINKS

In Ireland a drink means a beer – either lager or stout. Stout usually means Guinness, the famous black beer of Dublin, although in Cork it can mean a Murphy's or a Beamish. If you don't develop a taste for stout (and you should at least try) a wide variety of lager beers are available including Irish Harp or Smithwicks (the 'w' isn't pronounced) and many locally brewed 'imports' like Budweiser, Fosters or Heineken. Simply asking for a Guinness or a Harp will get you a pint (570 ml, IR£1.85 to IR£2.25 in a pub). If you want a half pint (90p to IR£1.20) ask for a 'glass' or a 'half'. Children are allowed in pubs until 7 or 8 pm and in smaller towns this restriction is treated with customary Irish flexibility.

Irish coffee is something you will see marketed in touristy hotels and restaurants. Sometimes the impression is given that the drink is traditional. Nothing could be further from the truth; it's a modern phenomenon and was considered a bit of a novelty when served to the first trans-Atlantic passengers arriving at Shannon Airport. It's a mixture of coffee and whiskey served in a heated glass and topped with cream.

When ordering a whiskey, Irish people never ask for a Scotch (though Scottish whisky is available); they use the brand name of an Irish whiskey instead: Paddy's, Powers, Bushmills or whatever. It may seem dear but the Irish measure is generous, by law.

Nonalcoholic drinks in pubs and hotels are restricted to the predictable brand-named fizzy ones, and to judge by the prices they charge you might think they were deliberately discouraging customers from drinking them.

Coffee is available in nearly all pubs, from 45p to 80p usually, but don't expect a smile if you order one at 10.30 on a busy night. If you ask for cream with your coffee, cream is what you'll get, a big dollop of it. The Irish drink lots of tea and this is usually served black, in a small teapot, with milk in a separate jug.

ENTERTAINMENT

A Guinness to go with the pub music is the most popular form of entertainment in Ireland. If it's suggested that you visit a particular pub for its 'good crack' (craic in Irish), don't think you've just found the local dope dealer. 'Crack' is Irish for a good time – convivial company, sparkling conversation and rousing music. Pubs offer a variety of music from traditional to rock.

A 'medieval banquet' finds its way on to many tourist itineraries, with the banquet at

Whiskey, Beer & Wine

Apart from imbibing large quantities of alcoholic refreshments, the Irish have also been responsible for some important developments in the field. They were pioneers in the development of distilling whiskey (distilled three times and spelt with an 'e' as opposed to the twice-distilled Scotch whisky) and also adopted the dark British beer known as stout or porter (since it was particularly popular with the porters who worked around Covent Garden market in London). Promoted by the Guinness family, it soon gained an enduring stranglehold on the Irish taste for beer. In neighbouring Britain, lager beers have taken a slice of the market from the traditional British bitter, but in Ireland Guinness still reigns.

In an Irish pub, talk is just as important an ingredient as the beer, though the conversation will often turn to the perfect Guinness. Proximity to the St James's Gate Brewery is one requirement for perfection, for although a Guinness in Kuala Lumpur can still be a fine thing, Guinness is at its best in Ireland. The perfect Guinness also requires expertise in its 'pulling'. If you want a perfect pint, you do not simply hold the glass under the tap and slosh it in. The angle at which the glass is held, the point at which the pouring is halted, the time that then passes while the beer settles and the head subsides and the precision with which the final top-up is completed, are all crucial in ensuring satisfaction. It's worth the wait.

Guinness may still be *the* drink in Ireland, but Irish drinking patterns are changing. The imbibing of ales is in steady decline. On the other hand, even though Ireland doesn't have any vineyards and the Irish are still way behind their continental neighbours in the consumption of wine (a mere 5.7 litres per head per year), recent years have seen a rapid rise in wine sales.

With alcohol such an important social lubricant, it's not surprising that the drink-driving laws introduced in 1994 reducing the permitted blood-alcohol level were met with less-than-strong enthusiasm. The government minister responsible for the legislation even had his home telephone number written up as a 24-hour taxi service in public telephone booths in his Tipperary constituency.

All of this said, however, it is interesting to note that a recent report on health commissioned by the EU found that the per capita consumption of alcohol in Ireland is the lowest in the EU. The Irish drank an average 7.4 litres of alcohol each in 1994 compared with 12.6 litres in France and 10.5 litres in Germany. The EU average is 9.9 litres. An EU official observed that these statistics may be a result of an increasing awareness of health, or it could reflect the fact that Ireland's child population is greater than in other EU countries. ■

Bunratty Castle in County Clare probably being the best known. They tend to be expensive and the food is often disappointing. During the summer, local festivals and concerts are a common event and it is always worth calling in at the local tourist office to check on what's available and coming up.

Theatre is popular, especially in the summer when a number of touring groups travel around the country. Dublin, particu-

larly, is renowned for its excellent theatres and there is always a broad range of plays and shows on. Most famous is the Abbey Theatre, founded by W B Yeats, Lady Gregory and other writers and artists behind the Anglo-Irish literary revival. The Gate Theatre is a much smaller company but has been putting on a remarkable variety of new and unusual work in recent years. Both the Gaiety and Olympia Theatres are beautifully preserved old showhouses which host a mix of plays, pantomimes and shows.

THINGS TO BUY
Clothing
All over the country, but especially in County Galway, it is possible to purchase Aran sweaters. The name derives from the islands where they were first made by the women as working garments for their husbands. Handknitted ones, not unnaturally, are going to cost a lot more than machine-made ones. County Donegal is famous for its tweeds and there are a couple of good stores in Donegal Town with a large selection. It can be purchased in lengths or finished as jackets, skirts or caps. Tweed is also produced in County Wicklow and County Dublin. Handwoven shawls and woollen blankets make lovely presents.

Irish linen is of high quality and comes in the form of everything from blouses to handkerchiefs. The Irish produce some high quality outdoor activities gear – they have plenty of experience with wet weather. Irish lace is another fine product, at its best in Limerick, or Carrickmacross in County Monaghan.

Crystal
Waterford crystal is world famous and is obtainable all over Ireland, although the company has reduced its workforce in Waterford and moved some business overseas. Smaller manufacturers of crystal produce fine work and at prices that are far more attractive. In the North, Tyrone Crystal is based outside Dungannon and the factory can be toured, with no obligation to purchase from the showroom.

Pottery
All over the country there are small potteries turning out unusual and very attractive work. The village of Belleek in County Fermanagh straddles the Northern Ireland border with Donegal and produces delicate bone china. In the South the area around Dingle in County Kerry has superb pottery. Enniscorthy in County Wexford, and Kilkenny and Thomastown in County Kilkenny, also stand out in this regard. Generally, throughout west Cork and Kerry there are countless small workshops that open in the summer with their stocks of pottery and other craftwork.

Food & Drink
Irish whiskey is not just spelt differently; it also has its own distinctive taste. The big names are Paddy, Jameson, Powers, Bushmills and Tullamore Dew, and they are not always readily available in other parts of the world. Two Irish liqueurs are very well established; Irish Mist and Bailey's Irish Cream. Some excellent hand-made cheeses are worth considering as a gift to take home. Two from west Cork are particularly worth mentioning: Gubbeen is a soft cheese from Schull while Milecns is more spicy. Tipperary has its own Cashel Blue and Cooleeny cheeses.

Other Items
Other possibilities include jewellery, especially *Claddagh rings* (see the Glossary for a description of these rings), enamel work and baskets woven of willow or rush. Connemara marble is a natural green stone found in the west of Ireland and is often cunningly fashioned into Celtic designs.

ACTIVITIES

Activities

Ireland is a great place for doing things and, although it's expensive to travel in, many activities not only open up some of the most beautiful and fascinating corners of the island, they are also within the reach of the tightest budget. In fact, those on a shoestring budget may find themselves hiking or cycling out of necessity. Fortunately, a walk or ride in the countryside will almost certainly be a highlight – as well as the cheapest part – of an Irish holiday. For those who have the money, other activities like golf or fishing are available as part of holiday packages that include bed, board and transportation.

Most activities are well organised and have clubs and associations (some of which are listed here) that can give visitors invaluable information and sometimes substantial discounts. Many of these clubs have national or international affiliations, so check with clubs before leaving home.

The tourist boards put out a wide selection of information sheets and brochures covering just about every activity and these can be a starting point for further research.

Walking

There are many superb walks in Ireland and walking has become increasingly popular since the early 1980s when the Wicklow Way, the country's first way-marked trail, was established. There are now well over 20 way-marked trails varying in length from the 26-km Cavan Way to the more than 900 km of the Ulster Way. The network of trails is growing all the time and the eventual aim is to link them all up.

The energetic and the impecunious should definitely consider some long-distance overnight walks. Civilisation is never far away so it's generally easy to follow walks that connect with public transport and link hostels, B&Bs

and villages. Some walkers might opt to walk the entire length of a way, but others might just choose a section that meets the constraints of ability, time or transport.

In most cases, a tent and cooking equipment is not necessary. Warm and waterproof clothing (including a hat and gloves), sturdy footwear, lunch and some high-energy food (for emergencies), a water bottle (with purification tablets), a first-aid kit, a whistle and torch (flashlight), and a map and compass are all that you need.

The countryside can look deceptively gentle but, especially in the hills or on the open moors, the weather can turn nasty very quickly at any time of year. Although Ireland has a relatively mild climate there is one aspect of the weather that will affect the walker and that is the rain. As well as getting you wet, it causes the ground underfoot to be slippery, and low clouds in the hills make navigation problematical. It is vital if you're walking in upland areas to be well equipped and to carry (and know how to use) a compass, good maps and/or a walking guidebook. This is important even though at frequent intervals along the ways there are signposts usually marked with a yellow arrow and walking figure – sometimes the signs are hidden by leafage or simply just missing.

Always leave details of your route with someone trustworthy and let them know when you should be back; never walk alone in isolated areas.

The ways mainly follow old, disused roads, *boreens* (small lanes or roadways) and forest trails. Ireland has a tradition of relatively free access to open country and through privately owned land, but the growth in the number of walkers and the carelessness of a few have made some farmers less obliging. Walkers can help by taking out all litter, not damaging fences or walls and minimising disturbance to farm animals; if you're in doubt ask permission, especially if you plan to pitch a tent.

72

INFORMATION

The maintenance and development of the ways is administered in the South by the Long-Distance Walking Routes Committee (☎ 01-873 4700), Cospóir (National Sports Council), 11th Floor, Hawkins House, Hawkins St, Dublin 2, and in the North by the Sports Council for Northern Ireland (☎ 01232-381222), Upper Malone Rd, Belfast BT9 5LA.

A useful general walking guidebook is *Irish Long Distance Walks* (Gill & Macmillan, Dublin, 1993, IR£7) by Michael Fewer. It is a practical and up-to-date guide for anyone contemplating one or more walks. This guide covers The Aran Ways, the Ballyhoura Way, the Barrow Towpath, the Burren Way, the Cavan Way, the Dingle Way, the Kerry Way, the Kildare Way, the Munster Way, the Slieve Bloom Way, the South Leinster Way, the Táin Way and the Wicklow Way. Joss Lynam has put together a collection of 76 shorter walks in *Best Irish Walks* (Gill & Macmillan, Dublin, 1994). There are also regional and individual-trail walking guidebooks available. A visit to a good bookshop like Eason's in Dublin is recommended or you could contact Gill & Macmillan Publishers (☎ 01-453 1005), Goldenbridge, Inchicore, Dublin 8, for a list of their walking guide titles.

The tourist boards have free information and maps on popular walks, but if you are planning more than one day's walking it is worth investing in one of the route maps available. The Ordnance Survey maps cover the whole island in 25 sheets with a 1:126,720 scale (half an inch to one mile); this series, however, is gradually being replaced by a new series of 89 maps with a 1:50,000 scale (two cm to one km). It's worth checking to see if there's a new map (or maps) available for the walk you're doing. The addresses are:

Ordnance Survey Service
  Phoenix Park, Dublin 8 (☎ 01-820 6100)
Ordnance Survey of Northern Ireland
  Colby House, Stranmillis Court, Belfast BT9 5BJ
  (☎ 01232-661244)

Organised walks are offered by the Irish Walking Holidays Association (☎ 055-27479), Old Rectory, Ballycanew, Gorey, County Wexford. For details of hiking tours in the North contact Mary Doyle (☎ 01232-624289 in the evenings), Ulster Federation of Rambling Clubs, 27 Slievegallion Drive, Belfast BT11 8JN.

For Mountain Rescue, ring ☎ 999.

KERRY WAY

The Kerry Way is 215 km long, making it the longest marked footpath in the Republic. The walk starts and ends in Killarney and stays inland for the first three days, winding through the spectacular Macgillycuddy's Reeks and past 1041-metre Carrantuohill, the highest mountain in Ireland, before winding around the coast through Cahirciveen, Waterville, Caherdaniel, Sneem and Kenmare. It is undoubtedly the best way of seeing the Iveragh Peninsula, rock by rock. One of the glories of this walk is that except at the hostels you are unlikely to come across anyone, least of all tourists.

Direction, Distance & Time

The orthodox route is anti-clockwise from Killarney and all the guides and maps take this for granted, but if you have a good reason the walk could be undertaken in reverse. The 215 km are divided here into nine sections that each require a day's walking. The average daily distance is around 20 km but sometimes you have an extra walk to reach the nearest town.

If you are short of time, you could undertake the first three days of the walk – as far as Glenbeigh – from where a bus or lift could return you to Killarney. This takes in the spectacular Black Valley section and each day's walk is relatively short.

When to Go

The whole walk or parts of it can be undertaken at any time of the year. Some B&Bs and a couple of the hostels close during the winter but there are always alternatives. There are also advantages to walking outside the main June to end of August period: the air is invigorating and fresh, the climate is rarely prohibitive and accommodation places will never be full. During July and August it is definitely advisable to book your accommodation in advance.

Information

There are tourist offices in Killarney (☎ 064-31633) and Kenmare (☎ 064-41233) and they both sell relevant maps and guides.

Guides & Maps The tourist board has its own map guide for IR£2.50 which divides the entire Kerry Way into 12 sections, but far more useful is the new 1:50,000 Ordnance Survey Discovery Series; map No 78 covers the first three days but No 83 – which should be published by the time you read this – is also necessary for completing the whole walk. The Kerry Way is clearly marked on the maps and there are some general notes on the different sections. *New Irish Walk Guides: Southwest* (Gill & Macmillan) also covers the entire way with maps and detailed notes but so does *Irish Long Distance Walks* (Gill & Macmillan) by Michael Fewer and the maps and information in this book are more up-to-date.

Other Preparations

Generally well marked, the route does not require any special skills and can be walked by any reasonably fit person. A compass is advisable, though not essential, because there are places where the odd route sign is missing or tricky to find. Rainwear and waterproof boots are essential, whatever the time of year.

Places to Stay & Eat

Bringing food for lunch is essential for most of the walk. On the first day snacks and coffee are available at Lord Brandon's Cottage. From there it is 2.5 km to the Black Valley Hostel where the hostel shop has a few supplies. During the second day there is nowhere selling or serving food apart from a small shop at the Climber's Inn pub, so a packed lunch is necessary. The third day's walking passes a small shop about halfway along the route, but that's it until you reach Glenbeigh, so a packed lunch is again necessary. This pattern repeats itself for the remainder of the Kerry Way, so always carry a couple of meals in your rucksack.

Accommodation is not a problem – the proviso being the need to book ahead in July

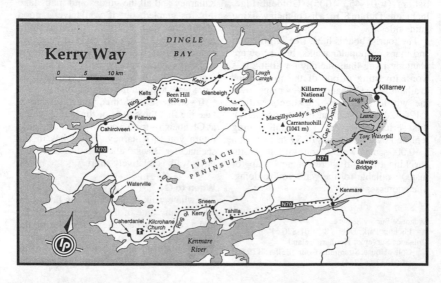

and August – and the relevant hostels and B&Bs are described either in the following sections or in the Kerry chapter under the towns close to or on the Kerry Way.

Getting There & Away

See the Kerry chapter, the Ring of Kerry section in particular, for information on getting to Killarney and the other main towns along the walk. The nearest railway station is at Killarney but the Ring of Kerry bus route cuts across the Kerry Walk at a number of places and this could be used as a shortcut. Pick up a timetable at the Killarney or Kenmare tourist offices or the bus station in Killarney.

Day 1: Killarney to Black Valley

(21 km)

The starting point is the entrance of the Killarney National Park at Muckross. The lakeside road leads to the Torc Waterfall. The total distance can be shortened by starting the walk at the Torc Waterfall – which cuts out the roadside walk – making the journey to the Black Valley easily manageable in one day.

To get to the Torc Waterfall early in the morning, you would need to hitch or drive. There's a car park in front of the tourist information point. (If you're planning to complete the first three days only it's quite safe to leave a car here and pick it up after returning to Killarney from Glenbeigh.)

After the Torc Waterfall, the path goes left, crosses a stone bridge and joins a green road. Turn left here and carry on for a few metres, ignoring a sign that points to a turning on the right. Carry straight on keeping the river on your left. This path, the old Kenmare road, travels across bogland and eventually meets a surfaced road with a sign left for Kenmare. Turn to the right instead, signposted for the Black Valley, and continue until you reach the main N71 road at Galway Bridge, by the side of an old church. A few metres past the church, on the road to Kenmare, the way sign takes you into the wood on the right.

The path leads to Lord Brandon's Cottage and then a short leg takes you to the An Óige *Black Valley Hostel* (☎ 064-34712). You should plan to arrive at the hostel at around 5.30

pm because it is closed before then and very full afterwards. It's best to book in advance. *Hillcrest Farmhouse* (☎ 064-34702) does B&B for IR£20/30. It is reached by a right turn, 750 metres after crossing the Gearhameen River and about two km before the hostel.

Day 2: Black Valley to Glencar

(20 km)

This leg is one of the best on the way. After leaving the hostel, disregard the unsurfaced road going off to the right, which leads to the Gap of Dunloe and back to Killarney. Follow the way ahead to the west down the path that is signposted as a cul-de-sac. It leads through a wood and past houses and rough ground to a small forest of pine trees. Crossing a stile the path goes past a farmhouse and through a gate onto a surfaced road which soon becomes a green road. Keep a careful eye on the tiny signs along this stretch because it is easy to miss some of them.

From here on the path is marked by cairns as it ascends to the summit separating the Black Valley from the Bridia Valley, where you can practise your yodelling. The descent leads to a surfaced road which could be used to reach Glencar if weather makes the right turn to Lack Rd seem unsuitable. Weather permitting, though, turn right at the way sign on the surfaced road and walk uphill. There are more wonderful views from the summit of the Lack Rd pass.

You carry on down to the surfaced road (the one you could have stayed on if the weather is misty), where a left turn leads to Glencar and a well-earned rest at the tastefully refurbished and amenable *Climber's Inn* (☎ 066-60101). *Breda Breen* (☎ 066-60164) and *Rocklands* (☎ 066-60177) are local B&Bs. Alternatively, you can stop walking earlier, after descending from the Black Valley and before ascending the Lack Rd pass, at the *Mountain Lodge* (☎ 066-60173), which does B&B.

Day 3: Glencar to Glenbeigh

(17.5 km)

The first and final stages of this day's walk are the most interesting. The middle part is mainly through planted forests, but the approach to Glenbeigh has exhilarating views.

Leaving the Climber's Inn, the way is marked down a short lane that emerges on a surfaced road. Turn right and at the main junction cross the bridge to the left. Almost immediately the walking sign points to the right, along the river. The path leads through planted forests and comes out on a surfaced road that goes past a shop to a Y-junction. Leave the main road and go left uphill.

There are two routes down to Glenbeigh. To take the shorter route, look for a fading walking sign and turn to the left through a gate. This leads through the Windy Gap at the top of which Glenbeigh and the Dingle Peninsula come into view. It's an easy walk down the other side and along a quiet road into the town.

The other route involves staying on the green road and offers magnificent views of Lough Caragh. Towards the end, though, walking along a surfaced road is necessary. In Glenbeigh there is a hostel, walker-friendly B&Bs and hotels. See the Glenbeigh section in the Kerry chapter for details.

Day 4: Glenbeigh to Foilmore
(20 km)
This leg starts with an exhilarating hill walk overlooking Dingle Bay and then turns inland into the valley of the River Ferta. It can be wet in places but the route around Drung Hill offers the reward of fine views. It then descends through a coniferous wood and across heathland with Been Hill (626 metres) off to the left. There are short stretches of tarmac before the route drops into a broad valley and the townland of Foilmore.

The townland of Foilmore, 20 km from Glenbeigh, marks the end of this stage of the Kerry Way but it's another 6.5 km walk to Cahirciveen (a total of 26.5 km) where there is a hostel, campsite, B&Bs and hotels (see the Kerry chapter).

The day's walk could be kept to 20 km by stopping in Foilmore at *Fransal House* (☎ 066-72997) where B&B is IR£19/28 and

an evening meal IR£11.50. This place is well accustomed to walkers and is worth stopping in. It has a laundry and will prepare a packed lunch for the next day.

Another alternative would be to further shorten the day's walk to around 15 km by turning off the way west of Been Hill and head three km north to Kells where there is a camp site and B&Bs (see Kells in the Kerry chapter). The next day's extra walk on to Cahirciveen via Foilmore would be 16 km.

Day 5: Foilmore to Waterville
(24 km)
This is one of the more demanding day's walks because there are two ridges to climb. The first one takes you into the valley of the River Inney and the second one reaches the townland of Dromod where this day's section of the way ends. The terrain is mostly open heathland with three km on tarmac and a little bit on green roads.

The actual way route from Foilmore to Dromod is only about 17.5 km but you will have to retrace the 6.5 km walk back to Foilmore if you stayed at Cahirciveen. Either way, at the end of the route in Dromond, there is another 6.5 km spur along tarmac to reach Waterville. This makes the Cahirciveen to Waterville route a total of 30.5 km. In Waterville the *Leisure Hostel* (☎ 066-74644) is open May to October. *Cliffords* (☎ 066-74283) in Main St is a walker-friendly B&B and there is also a camp site (see the Kerry chapter). An alternative, before turning off right for Waterville at Dromod, would be to walk 2.5 km to the left to *Beenmore Farmhouse* (☎ 066-74207) where B&B is available.

Day 6: Waterville to Caherdaniel
(27 km)
The walk starts on tarmac, crosses fields and the River Cummeragh, then goes back onto tarmac and then open, rocky fields where the way signs can be difficult to follow. If in doubt, keep heading south and then follow the fence until it reaches a rock face where the way leads on to a small gate. The track climbs up before turning about face and

heading down the other side of this spur. The way then climbs through the Windy Gap (385 metres) and suddenly the southern side of the Iveragh Peninsula appears. Inexperienced walkers might find the gap rather daunting if the weather is very misty.

The end of this day's route is just past the ruins of Kilcrohane Church from where it is 3.25 km to Caherdaniel (see the Kerry chapter) where there are hostels, camp sites and walker-friendly B&Bs. Only one km from Kilcrohane, B&B is available at *Birchgrove Farmhouse* (☎ 066-75106) at Castlecove for IR£13 per person.

Day 7: Caherdaniel to Sneem
(18 km)
This leg of the way follows an old coach road along foothills, roughly following the coast before descending to Sneem. After walking four km you turn onto a green road and cross a stream by a two-arched bridge and from here it is about 1.5 km to the impressive Staigue Fort.

About 10 km of the day's walk is on tarmac, the rest on small country lanes and forestry tracks.

Sneem is the best destination for this day's walk because of its places to stay and eat – hostel, camping, B&Bs and hotels (see the Kerry chapter) – but it does have the disadvantage of making the next day's walk to Kenmare a long one. You could continue on the way past Sneem for seven km to Tahilla where there is B&B at *Hillside Haven* (☎ 064-82065) or the pricier *Tahilla Cove* (☎ 064-45204) at IR£33/56.

Day 8: Sneem to Kenmare
(28 km)
This day's walk hugs the coast for much of the way and the main Ring of Kerry road is never far away. Just over three km is walked along this main road, but the rest of the way is across open land and along small country lanes. There have been minor problems with signposting the second half of this day's walk but by the time you read this the way should be clearly indicated.

Kenmare has a full range of places to stay

and eat (see the Kerry chapter), which is just as well because it's a long walk from Sneem if you didn't press on to Tahilla the night before.

Day 9: Kenmare to Killarney
(24 km)
After leaving town the way has one short descent into a valley and then it's a steep climb through Gowlane Cross and along the old coach road to Killarney. At Windy Gap (the third pass with this name along the Kerry Way) there are splendid views of the Lakes of Killarney and the southern coastline. The way then descends into the Derricunnihy Valley and crosses the river on huge stones. Just past here there is an intersection with the outgoing Kerry Way and about one km further is the main road.

See the Killarney section in the Kerry chapter for details of places to stay and eat.

BEARA WAY
This is one of the more recently established long-distance walks and in its entirety forms a loop around the Beara Peninsula in West Cork. The peninsula itself is relatively unused to mass tourism and makes a dramatic contrast in this respect with the Iveragh Peninsula to the north.

Part of the walk, between Casteltownbere and Glengarriff, follows the route taken by Donal O'Sullivan and his band after the English took his castle following an 11-day siege in 1602. At Glengarriff, O'Sullivan met up with other families and set out on a journey north, hoping to reunite with other remaining pockets of Gaelic life. They set off in winter, over one thousand in all, but only 30 completed the trek.

The walk mostly follows old roads and tracks and rarely goes above 340 metres. It's a moderately easy walk.

Direction, Distance & Time
There is no official start or finish point and the route can be walked in either direction. The total distance is 197 km, divided into nine sections below, but there are opportunities to shorten this by missing out some

sections. The walk could easily be reduced to seven days by skipping Bere Island and Dursey Island, and if you started at Castletownbere you could reach Kenmare in five days or even less.

When to Go
Any time of the year is possible but outside the main April to September season there will be problems finding hostels open. Even B&B places are a little thin on the ground, so between October and March it's essential to ensure your accommodation has been planned for.

Information
The tourist offices in Glengarriff (☎ 027-63084) and Castletownbere (☎ 027-70344) are only open in July and August. The tourist office in Kenmare (☎ 064-41233) is open throughout the summer. If you're planning to include Bere Island it's worth checking the ferry times before you reach Castletownbere.

Guides & Maps The tourist board has its own Beara Way map which would do at a pinch, but best of all would be the new Ordnance Survey 1:50,000 map which hopefully will be available by the time you read this. The old Ordnance Survey 1:126,720 map No 24 covers the Beara Way.

Places to Stay & Eat
There are hostels at Glengarriff, Adrigole, Castletownbere, Allihies, Eyeries, Lauragh and Kenmare and all these places

have B&Bs as well. Day 5 and Day 7 in the sections below only have B&B accommodation. Bere Island only has B&B too, but this day's walk could be completed without needing to stay there overnight. The same is true of Dursey Island where there is no accommodation at all. Free camping should not be a problem as long as you ask permission from the farmer.

A packed lunch is needed for most days of the walk and there are few shops west of Castletownbere so some advance planning is necessary.

Getting There & Away
See the Glengarriff and Kenmare sections in the Cork and Kerry chapters for information on getting to these towns. Apart from the private bus between Bantry and Castletownbere there is no public transport on the peninsula. The nearest railway stations are Killarney and Cork from where there are buses to Kenmare and Glengarriff.

Day 1: Glengarriff to Adrigole
(16 km)
After a short walk along the main road to Castletownbere there is a right turn into a forest and the way climbs to the gap between Gowlbeg (362 metres) on the left and Sugarloaf (581 metres) on the other side of the way. This is the old coach road between Castletownbere and Glengarriff and only local farmers now use this route. Just outside of Adrigole it meets the main road.

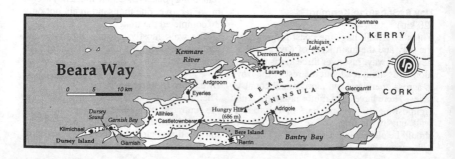

See the Cork chapter for details of places to stay & eat in Glengarriff and Adrigole. The *Adrigole Hostel* is 100 metres west of the road going north to the Healy Pass. Reasonably priced B&Bs (IR£12 per person) in Adrigole are *Beachmount* (☎ 027-60075), open between June and September, and *Ocean View* (☎ 027-60026) which opens in May. There are no restaurants in Adrigole but the B&Bs do an evening meal for IR£11.

Day 2: Adrigole to Castletownbere
(22 km)
The way continues along the old coach road (along this stretch of it Jane Brodrick dies in Daphne du Maurier's *Hungry Hill*), with the main road just below it but out of sight. Hungry Hill (686 metres) dominates your view as the way skirts below it before dropping down alongside a small lake. For the remainder of the journey into Castletownbere the route follows old bog roads.

See the Cork chapter for details of places to stay & eat in Castletownbere. The hostel adds three km onto the day's walk, but there are B&Bs in the town itself. Castletownbere's supermarket is the only one on the Beara Peninsula so stock up here with as much food as your rucksack holds.

Day 3: Bere Island
(21 km)
The island is not often visited by tourists and you could easily be the only walker on the day you choose to follow the Beara Way loop around the island. From the island's ferry point at the village of Rerrin the way first circles the eastern end of Bere Island before returning through the village. This could obviously be skipped, but you miss seeing an impressive wedge tomb on the way. From Rerrin there is the option of taking a 1.6 km spur to a Martello tower, but the main route west of the village passes another tower about one km before a prominent standing stone that marks the middle point of the island.

Turning right near the standing stone allows for a shorter route to the west end ferry point (check the times of service in Castletownbere), but either direction leads to

a loop around the western end of the island before returning to the standing stone and then back to Rerrin for the return ferry to Castletownbere.

There are a couple of pubs and small shops at Rerrin and the *Harbour View* (☎ 027-75011) B&B with doubles for IR£28 and IR£32.

Check the return times for the ferry back to Castletownbere and even if you plan to return the same day allow for the possibility of deciding to stay on the island.

Day 4: Castletownbere to Allihies
(13.6 km)
The walk turns north just outside Castletownbere and then shifts west to head uphill before going through forest, stretches of tarmac and green road and then more forest before reaching Allihies.

The An Óige *Allihies Hostel* is passed on the way before Allihies, and the IHH *The Village Hostel (Bonnie Braes)* is in the village itself. See the Cork chapter for further details of places to stay and eat in the village.

Day 5: Allihies to Dursey Island
(14.4 km)
The route follows the main road out of Allihies for a short distance, as far as the beach at Ballydonegan, before taking an untarred road along the cliffs. Just past Garnish Bay it meets with the outward section of the way and here you can choose a short (to the west) or long (to the south) route to Dursey Sound and the cable car to Dursey Island.

Accommodation and food is scarce at Dursey Island. About one km from Dursey Sound, at Garnish, *Glen Ocean House* (☎ 027-73019) does B&B for IR£14/24. Snacks are available just by the cable car to Dursey Island at *Windy Point House* (☎ 027-73017), and B&B is also available here.

Day 6: Dursey Island
(11 km)
The way runs from near the cable-car station to the western end of the island. About one km west of Kilmichael village take the left bearing and follow the way to the south-west point of

Dursey Head. The route then travels back on itself as far as Tilickafinna where it bears left and heads along the northern side of the island to eventually rejoin the outward route.

There is no accommodation on the island, apart from free camping, and no shops or restaurants so bring everything you need for the day. Check the time of the last cable car back when travelling out to the island.

Day 7: Allihies to Ardgroom
(24 km)
The way heads north-west from Allihies, passing the old copper mines, and meanders across a hillside to the photogenic village of Eyeries. From the village the way follows the coastline then heads inland a bit before dropping down to the village of Ardgroom.

Accommodation is hard to find at Ardgroom, but *O'Brien's* (☎ 027-74019), in the village, does B&B for IR£12 per person. You could stay a night in Eyeries, where there are a couple of B&Bs – *The Shamrock* (☎ 027-74058) charges IR£13/24, and *Cussan House* (☎ 027-74178) IR£15/30 – and the *Ard na Mara Hostel* (☎ 027-74271) at the east end of the village in a family house. Staying in Eyeries means either splitting the day's walking or doubling up the next day and walking 24 km instead of 12 km. Two pubs in Eyeries serve bar food. *The Holly Bar*, which is on the Beara Way in Ardgroom, does soup and sandwiches and there is a small restaurant nearby.

Day 8: Ardgroom to Lauragh
(12 km)
This is a short and easy walk that crosses from Cork into Kerry about halfway along but there are good reasons to stop at Lauragh, at the head of the dramatic Healy Pass that heads down to Adrigole. Derreen Gardens at Lauragh are well worth visiting and there is also the option of a local walk. See the Beara Peninsula section in the Kerry chapter for details of this walk as well as information about the hostel, camping site and B&B. There are no shops or restaurants at Lauragh so plan ahead for your evening meal.

Day 9: Lauragh to Kenmare
(26 km)
The way meets the main Ring of Beara road and travels along it for a mere 200 metres before turning right off it and heading across open country and down to Inchiquin Lake. From there the route heads eastwards and across more open countryside, passing between Dromoughty Lake and a stone circle before turning left for the final stretch into Kenmare. It is a long day's walk, but not a demanding one and Kenmare has lots of creature comforts to make the destination worthwhile.

See Kenmare in the Kerry chapter for details of where to stay and eat in the town.

ULSTER WAY: NORTH-EASTERN SECTION
The Ulster Way makes a circuit right round the six counties of Northern Ireland and Donegal. In total the footpath covers just over 900 km, so walking all of it might take five weeks. However, it can easily be broken down into smaller sections which could more realistically be attempted during a short stay. The scenery along the way varies enormously, encompassing dramatic coastal scenery, gentler lakeside country and the mountainous inland terrain of the Mountains of Mourne. But some of the most spectacular scenery lies along the north-eastern section which follows the Glens of Antrim and then the glorious Causeway Coastline, a UNESCO-recognised World Heritage Site. The stretch of coast immediately surrounding the Giant's Causeway is likely to be busiest, especially in high summer when you should book accommodation well ahead, bearing in mind that it's in fairly short supply in Northern Ireland.

Walking this stretch of coast should not be beyond most averagely fit and sensibly equipped people, but remember that rockfalls along the coast can occasionally obstruct stretches of it. Most – but not all – of the Ulster Way is way-marked with the symbol of a walking man. If you're interested in reading about one man's experiences, look out for

Walking the Ulster Way (Appletree Press, £5.95) by Alan Warner.

Direction, Distance & Time

Since most people are likely to arrive in Northern Ireland via Belfast, the route described follows the coast in an anti-clockwise direction. It covers a distance of 165 km and can be completed in six or seven days. On a good day, the coastal views will be spectacular, but of course Northern Ireland experiences more than its fair share of cold, wet, windy days when mist will blot out the scenery and make walking tough going. Obviously you should be particularly careful when walking on high cliffs in high winds.

When to Go

Northern Ireland's tourist season only really extends from May to September, with a brief burst of activity around Easter. Accommodation is likely to be in particularly short supply over Easter and in July and August when advance booking is essential.

Information

Along this section of the Ulster Way there are tourist offices at Cushendall (☎ 012667 71180), Ballycastle (☎ 012657-62024) and the Giant's Causeway (☎ 012657-31855). You could also get some background information from the Northern Ireland Tourist Board (☎ 01232-246609), St Anne's Court, 59 North St, before setting out. They will certainly be able to supply *An Information Guide to Walking* which includes basic details of 14 walks along the Ulster Way.

Guides & Maps Walking World Ireland (☎ 01-454 5135) publishes *The Ulster Way: A Guide to the Route and its Facilities* (£1.50) by Paddy Dillon, in association with the Environment Service. This gives details of the entire trail together with extracts from the relevant Ordnance Survey maps. You might also look at *Ulster Rambles* by Peter Wright (Greystone Press, £5.99) or *Walking the Ulster Way* (Appletree Press, Belfast, paperback, £6.95) by Alan Warner. The National Trust publishes a good leaflet (45p)

outlining the walks around the Giant's Causeway itself, with information about the geology and botany and drawings of the main rock formations to look out for.

The 1:250,000 Ordnance Survey Holiday Map of Ireland (North) is useful for planning a journey but for actually walking the way you need the more detailed Ordnance Survey of Northern Ireland Discoverer maps. Sheet Nos 5, 9 and 15 cover the North-Eastern Section described below.

Other Preparations

Because Northern Ireland's climate is so unpredictable you need to dress sensibly for this walk; boots would be best even if the forecast is good when you first set out. It's also advisable to carry a spare set of clothes in case you get drenched. As always, it makes sense to let someone know where you're going and when you expect to get back.

Places to Stay & Eat

While some stretches of this walk can seem wonderfully wild, you're never going to be that far from civilisation. Once you get away from Belfast, this is the part of Northern Ireland least affected by 'the Troubles' and with the most developed holiday industry. Tourist offices will happily book your bed ahead for you (and in summer you may be glad to let them take this burden from you!) and you may be able to book an evening meal at the same time – a good idea once you get away from the bigger centres of habitation that have more than one greasy spoon café.

There are several convenient hostels along this route, in Cushendall (YHANI), Ballycastle (IHH) and White Park Bay (YHANI), and they are well used to the needs of walkers. Otherwise, there are a reasonable number of B&Bs, and plenty of camp sites, although some of these are ugly, coast-scarring caravan parks. There are official camp sites at Carnlough, Glenariff, Cushendall, Cushendun, Ballycastle, Ballintoy and Portballintrae. You may also be able to get permission to camp from farmers, but in 1995 a lone woman camper was attacked along this coast, so you should always make sure you've got permission and feel safe.

One or two of the tiniest places along this route may lack a pub, but in general you're unlikely to be starved of a drink. Sunday is likely to be the toughest day to find food and drink as many cafés don't open and pubs either don't serve food at all or stop doing so earlier than on weekdays.

Getting There & Away

The walk starts in Dunmurry, a suburb to the south-west of Belfast. You can get there by train, on the line heading for Lisburn or Portadown (ring ☎ 01232-899411 for details). Alternatively there are frequent buses from the Europa Bus Station (ring ☎ 01232-320011 for details). From Portballintrae you will need to catch a bus to either Portrush or Ballycastle to connect with services back to Belfast. In July and August the Bushmills Bus runs a regular service linking Portballintrae (Hotel Corner) to Portrush, with four buses a day even on Sunday, at 10.23 am, and 12.38, 3.13 and 5.03 pm. Outside these months, services are more sporadic; phone ☎ 01232-333000 to check.

Day 1: Dunmurry to Whiteabbey
(27 km)

The first part of this route, through the West Belfast suburbs, is probably the least promising. You walk along Suffolk Rd and into Colin Glen Forest Park, tracking across it from Hannahstown towards a TV mast, and then climbing up Black Hill (362 metres). From there you must feel your way across the sometimes rough terrain of the Belfast Hills without signs to guide you: climb up Black Mountain (387 metres) and line up another TV mast as a guideline towards Divis (479 metres). From here you head north, crossing a minor road and then the A52, before climbing Squires Hill (377 metres).

You then cross the B95 and head towards Cave Hill, the one that soars above the Belfast suburbs, its curious profile earning it the nickname 'Napoleon's Nose'. Here you can pause to inspect McArt's Fort, the Cave Hill Heritage Centre in Belfast Castle and Belfast's beautifully sited zoo. The Ulster Way is signposted onwards along a riverside walk at Rathcoole and then along the coast at Macedon Point. Unfortunately, you must then follow the busy main road to Whiteabbey where there are pubs and places to eat. There are also two B&Bs: *Iona* (☎ 01232-842256), 161 Antrim Rd, and *Perpetua* (☎ 01232-833041), 57 Collinbridge Park. Both do singles for £18 and doubles for £32. For cheaper beds you'll need to bus back into Belfast city centre.

Day 2: Whiteabbey to Ballynure
(21 km)

You'll be stuck with the North Belfast suburbs until you reach Three Mile Water where the Ulster Way finally meets real countryside. One track will take you up to Knockagh where a prominent obelisk commemorates the men from County Antrim who died in WW I; from here there are panoramic views over Belfast Lough, itself dominated by the twin Harland & Wolff cranes known as Samson & Goliath. From Knockagh, marked paths take the Ulster Way through Woodburn Forest and on to North Carn Forest. The road then traverses fields until it reaches the outskirts of Ballynure. Here, too, you should be able to find B&B and something to eat. Once again, the cheapest accommodation will be a bus ride away in Belfast. Larne, too, is accessible, for a wider range of cheap B&Bs.

Day 3: Ballynure to Glenarm
(32 km)

From Ballynure the path winds steeply upwards, heading towards Ballyboley Forest, the highest point of which is Carninard at 366 metres. After this the way winds across moorland and up Agnew's Hill (474 metres); on a good day you'll be able to see the Antrim Mountains, on a better one the Mourne Mountains way to the south. The path turns mercifully downwards for a while, heading north across more moors, then rising sharply to Sallagh Braes and Robin Young's Hill, with the remains of a prehistoric fort. If you're too tired to go on, a spur runs down to Carncastle. Otherwise you need to follow markers to Scawt Hill (378 metres) and Black Hill (381 metres), thence to Crockandoo and Glenarm. The latter is a sleepy coastal village which has places to stay, including *Margaret's* B&B (☎ 01574-841307), 10 Altmore St, with beds for £14. You can get dinner here too, although there are also pubs in the village.

Day 4: Glenarm to Cushendall
(22 km)

From now on the Ulster Way heads through truly spectacular scenery. At the start of the day you can avoid the busy coast road on a minor road to Straidkelly. Then, unfortunately, you'll be back on the main road as far as Carnlough, a suitable place for a lunch break in the *Harbour House Tea Rooms* overlooking the harbour. After lunch the path climbs up towards (but not past) Cranny Falls and over the humps of Big Trosk (377 metres) and Little Trosk. The next stretch is across moorland where you need to keep an eye out for the marker posts directing you round Denny's Lough, Loughnacally and Lough Natullig. The path then drops down alongside Altmore Burn, past waterfalls and onto Glenariff where there's a camp site in a forest park. Otherwise, continue on past a ruined castle to Cushendall for a YHANI hostel (☎ 012667-71344) and several B&Bs, including the *Riverside Guest House* (☎ 012667-71655) right in the centre at 14 Mill St with beds from £14. There are pubs and places to eat here, too.

Day 5: Cushendall to Ballycastle
(32 km)

From Cushendall the Ulster Way cuts north past the ruins of Layde church and then crosses Cross Slieve, heading for the pretty village of Cushendun with black and white houses designed by Clough Williams-Ellis. There's a small café beside the National Trust information office and several pubs overlooking the harbour. Not all of the route is marked from here, so you should make sure you have a good map before pressing on

along the B92 and then across Cushleake Mountain.

From there you head on uphill again towards Carnanmore (379 metres), which has a burial cairn on the summit. If it's a good day there will be wonderful views as you press on towards the cliffs of Fair Head and Murlough Bay. At this point you're well away from main roads, so the peace is wonderful. From here you follow the coast round to Colliery Bay and down past Bonamargy Friary to Ballycastle with plenty of pubs, restaurants and B&Bs. There's also a good independent hostel (☎ 012657-62337) here

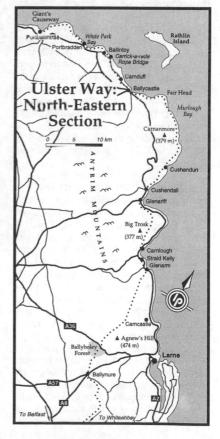

and several camp sites. See the Counties Derry & Antrim chapter for details.

Day 6: Ballycastle to Portballintrae (31 km)

With this stretch of the Ulster Way you hit the most popular – and arguably the most spectacular – part of the coast. Start by following the B15 to Carnduff and tiny Ballintoy, detouring to walk across the hair-raising Carrick-a-rede Rope Bridge to a salmon fishery on the way. The Ulster Way follows the coast as closely as it can, sweeping round to gorgeous White Park Bay (where there's a YHANI hostel), and then to Portbradden, which has Ireland's smallest church. Continuing on you'll past the extensive ruins of Dunsverick Castle, right on the clifftop, and then the exotic rock formations that herald the approach of the Giant's Causeway. You're bound to stop to inspect the famous hexagonal columns and the visitor's centre that inevitably accompanies them. Then the Ulster Way continues its meandering coastal pathway to Portballintrae where there are cafés and B&Bs including the friendly *Keeve-Na* (☎ 012657-32184) in Ballaghmore Rd with beds from £14.

ULSTER WAY: DONEGAL SECTION

The main Ulster Way crosses into Donegal at the small pilgrimage town of Pettigo on Lough Erne, but then circles straight back to Rosscor in Northern Ireland. A spur – also confusingly called the Ulster Way – cuts north across the central moorlands of Donegal to Falcarragh on the north coast. In all, this stretch of walk is only 111 km long which means it can be walked in four or five days. Bear in mind, however, that much of central Donegal is bleak, boggy terrain where walking can be tough going, especially if the weather's bad – which it often is!

This stretch of the Ulster Way is intended for wilderness-lovers, and although the walking-man symbol sometimes appears on markers, in general you'll be looking out for white-painted posts which simply tell you that you're heading in the right general direc-

tion. Places to stay & eat are few and far between, so forward planning is essential. Some of the scenery en route is truly magnificent, as you pass the Blue Stack and Derryveagh Mountains and Errigal Mountain, Donegal's highest at 752 metres. The route also skirts the glorious Glenveagh National Park where you might want to divert and break your journey. There are few dramatic historical remains to distract you, but plenty of minor prehistoric burial sites en route.

Direction, Distance & Time

You could just as easily walk this stretch of the Ulster Way in either direction, but since Pettigo is the link point with the main circuit, it is used here as a base point so that the route described below heads steadily northwards. Since the route out of Falcarragh is not way-marked, it may also be best to start out with assistance and build up to managing without! To walk the full 111 km straight off would take about four days but you may want to break the journey en route. Donegal is notorious for its bleak, blustery weather and you should always remember that visibility can be snuffed out very quickly. The boggy ground can also be pretty treacherous.

When to Go

Donegal has an even shorter tourist season than the rest of northern Ireland, only really getting into its stride from mid-June through to September. Outside those months almost all the tourist offices are closed, although you should still be able to find places to stay. July and August will be the busiest times of year, but this far inland you shouldn't feel crowded out. Bearing in mind the terrain, it's a good idea to give yourself the best chance of decent weather.

Information

Tourist information centres are thin on the ground in this part of the world, and unlikely to be open when you want them anyway. It's best, therefore, to try and get the information you need before setting out. Bord Fáilte has its head office (☎ 01-676 5871) in Dublin at

Baggot St Bridge and this might be a good place to try. In Donegal itself the most reliably open information centre is on the Derry road just outside Letterkenny (☎ 074-21160). Midway along the way the Dunlewey Centre (☎ 075-31699) and Glenveagh National Park Visitor's Centre (☎ 074-37088) are likely to prove more helpful.

Guides & Maps In association with the Environment Service, Walking World Ireland (☎ 01-454 5135) publishes *The Ulster Way: A Guide to the Route and its Facilities* (£1.50) by Paddy Dillon. This gives details of the spur route. The 1:250,000 Ordnance Survey Holiday Map of Ireland (North) is useful for planning the trip, but for actually walking the way you need the more detailed Ordnance Survey 1:50,000 scale Discovery maps, bearing in mind that the route is only sporadically way-marked. Sheet Nos 1, 6 and 11 should do you.

Other Preparations

Since this is a potentially treacherous and very isolated walk, it's imperative to be well equipped before starting out. Stout walking boots are essential for the boggy ground and for fording streams, although carrying a pair of lighter weight runners to wear on the road stretches might be a good idea. Take good, strong waterproofs and a spare set of clothes in case you get soaked. If possible, take a compass – and be sure that you know how to use it!

The paucity of places en route to buy midday meals means you'll need to carry rations. In summer, midges can be a real pain, so it's worthwhile taking repellent with you as well. Since help could be some time coming, it's wise to be prepared with a first-aid kit, a torch, a whistle for attracting attention, a sleeping bag, and loose change for making phone calls. Should the worst come to the worst, ring the gardai on ☎ 999.

Place to Stay & Eat

Places to stay along this route are very limited, although there are two useful

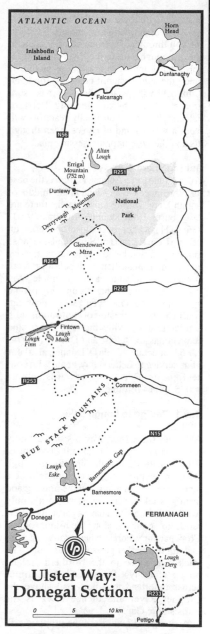

Ulster Way: Donegal Section

hostels, at Fintown and Dunlewey. Otherwise, there are just about enough B&Bs to see you through. There are no official camp sites, although most farmers will probably let you pitch a tent if you ask. The picture is much the same when it comes to food and drink. Even shops are scarce, so make sure you stock up before leaving Pettigo. Falcarragh, when you finally reach it, will seem a wonderland of choice, even though it's an otherwise unprepossessing place.

Getting There & Away

From 1 June to 15 August, Pettigo is the base for pilgrimages to an island in the middle of Lough Derg. During those months there are daily buses from Dublin's Busáras (☎ 01-836 6111). Other buses also converge on Pettigo from Belfast and Sligo. Outside those months you will be able to reach Pettigo by bus from Enniskillen and possibly from Donegal Town but it's a pretty remote spot. If you stick out a thumb it's unlikely people will ignore you. Once you get to Falcarragh you're back in the realms of civilisation, with regular Lough Swilly buses to Derry and connections to Belfast and Dublin (☎ 074-22863 for details). Feda O' Donnell also runs a bus service to Letterkenny, again with connections to Derry and onwards; phone ☎ 075-48114 for times.

Day 1: Pettigo to Lough Eske
(29 km)

Although the Ulster Way doesn't actually reach the lake, you should still head out of Pettigo on the R233 in the direction of Lough Derg. In the pilgrimage season there'll be a lot of coming and going, but the praying and fasting is taken very seriously, so it's only worth diverting if you have a particular interest. If not, continue along the minor road to Crocknacunny Forest where you'll need to look for the marker posts very carefully. The track runs close to the Northern Ireland border at Kelly's Bridge and then climbs across moorland to a bog road above the Clogher River and thence towards the Barnesmore Gap.

Arriving at Lough Eske the problem will be the lack of cheap accommodation unless you've got a tent and fancy free camping. *Harvey's Point* (☎ 073-22208) is a splendid lakeside hotel and restaurant but it's pricey. Your best bet for food and lodging will be to try and flag a bus or passing car into Donegal Town where there's plenty of choice, including an independent hostel (☎ 073-22030) on the Killybegs Rd. Reasonable B&Bs include *Riverside House* (☎ 073-21083) and *Castle View House* (☎ 073-22100), both in Waterloo Place.

Day 2: Lough Eske to Fintown
(36 km)

A minor road follows the east shore of Lough Eske round to the north and then runs uphill to the Doonan Waterfall. The so-called 'Monk's Path' continues through the Corrober Valley, after which the way-markers become infrequent on the way down to the Owendoo River. Fording the river may be difficult if it's been raining, and if you're tired you should head for Commeen from Letterkillew and call it a day. If you're keen to press on to Fintown, follow the track along the Owengrave River to the head of Polldoo Glen and then descend to a group of farms called the Croaghs and follow the farm road along the valley. There are beautiful views of the Blue Stack Mountains but the way-markers are, once again, dodgy and you'll need to pick your way carefully across the R253, round Lough Muck and down the Scraigs above Lough Finn. Typically for Donegal, Fintown has a café, a hostel (☎ 075-46244) and two pubs.

Day 3: Fintown to Dunlewy
(27 km)

This will be another day of picking your way between widely spaced markers on boggy ground, the reward being the wonderful views if the sky is clear. Start by following the R250 out of Fintown and follow the markers to Lough Muck and on to Crockastoller. After that you'll need to climb Moylenanav and Meenbog Hill in the Glendowan Mountains. You should emerge on the R254 on the perimeter of the spectacular Glenveagh National Park. Here the way-markers give up the uneven struggle altogether, so you'll be plotting your own route on to Falcarragh, possibly climbing up into the Derryveagh Mountains and heading for the Ballaghgeeha Gap and the track down into the Poisoned Glen. This stretch of walk is beautiful but difficult, with the ground slippery under foot. Head through the glen for a ruined church and the small village of Dunlewy at the foot of Errigal Mountain (752 metres).

There's the An Óige *An Earagail Hostel* (☎ 075-31180) just outside the village, and the *Dunlewy Centre* has a good café if you get there in opening hours.

Day 4: Dunlewy to Falcarragh
(19 km)
The most straightforward way to get to Falcarragh from Dunlewy is to head east of Errigal Mountain, taking the R251 out of Dunlewy. Anyone with stamina can climb up Errigal Mountain. Otherwise, follow the shores of Altan Lough which lies between Errigal Mountain and Aghla More. You'll need to cross the Tullaghobegly River and then follow the road beside it. A disused railway track should herald the approach to Falcarragh. There you'll find several super-markets, pubs and uninspiring cafés, as well as the IHH *Shamrock Lodge Hostel* (☎ 074-35859) in the high street. Heading out towards Dunfanaghy, *Sea View* (☎ 074-35552) offers more chance of a quiet night to recover from your exertions.

WICKLOW WAY
The popular Wicklow Way was the first trail set up in the country, opening in 1982. At a length of 132 km, it neither starts nor finishes within County Wicklow itself. From its beginnings in Marlay Park, Rathfarnham, in south Dublin, about 13 km from the city centre, the trail quickly leaves the city behind and enters a moun-tain wilderness (the highest point is Mt Mullaghmór at 661 metres) though you're never too far from a public road. Forest walks, sheep paths, bog roads and mountain passes connect up to provide one of the most spectacular walks you could wish for. The walk passes Glencree, Powerscourt, Djouce Mountain, Luggala, Lough Dan, Glenmacnass, Glendalough, Glenmalure and Aghavannagh before heading into County Carlow.

Some sections are desolate, especially south of Laragh, a large part of the trail is above 500 metres and the weather can change quickly. Good hiking boots, outdoor gear and emergency supplies are essential. There are many possible detours: up Glenmacnass to the waterfall, down to the shores of Lough Dan, up to the summit of Lugnaquilla Mountain – all well worth the effort.

Direction, Distance & Time
For the entire trail allow eight to 10 days, plus time for diversions. It's easy to pick up sections and it can be done in either direc-tion, though most walkers start in Dublin. Breaking the journey at Laragh, a bit under half way, would give you the chance to visit the monastic site at Glendalough and do some local walks. The 132-km trail heads south from Dublin and is divided here into eight sections. The distances given include the extra km you'll need to walk to the nearest village off the way.

When to Go
This walk, or parts of it, can be undertaken at any time, but since a good part of the walk is over 500 metres and the weather is change-able it's advisable to check the forecast. The An Óige hostels remain open all year and though some B&Bs close over the winter, others stay open. Because of the way's prox-imity to Dublin and its popularity, walking outside the busy June to the end of August period is worthwhile. In July and August you should book accommodation in advance.

Information
Since the walk starts in Dublin it's worth contacting either the Dublin Tourism office (☎ 01-284 4768), 14 O'Connell St Upper, or Bord Fáilte (☎ 01-676 5871) at Baggot St

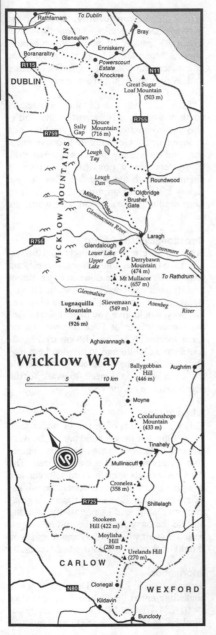

Bridge. From these offices you can get a copy of the Bord Fáilte Information Sheet No 26B. The national park information office (☎ 0404-45425/45338) at the Upper Lake in Glendalough may also be able to help you; it's open daily from late April to late August.

Guides & Maps *The Complete Wicklow Way* by J B Malone or *The Wicklow Way, from Marlay to Glenmalure* by Michael Fewer are good guides to the trail. For other detailed information on walking in the area, check *Hill Walker's Wicklow* or *New Irish Walk Guides, East & South East* both by David Herman. Also useful is *The Wicklow Way – a Natural History Field Guide* (Cospóir, Dublin) by Ken Boyle and Orla Burke.

The Ordnance Survey 1:50,000 Wicklow Way map covers the trail to south of Aghavannagh (about 50 km from the finish). Map No 56, at the same scale, includes much of this section of the way but is newer. The older Ordnance Survey 1:126,720 maps Nos 16 and 19 cover the whole route.

The Wicklow Way Map & Guide contains a series of six strip 1:50,000 maps and is produced by East West Mapping (☎ 054-77835), Ballyredmond, Clonegal, Enniscorthy, County Wexford.

Places to Stay & Eat
There are An Óige hostels at Glencree, Knockree, Glendalough, Glenmalure and Aghavannagh, plus two private hostels in Laragh. Most of the B&Bs are in and around Laragh close to Glendalough, but there are others in Enniskerry, Roundwood, Tinahely, Shillelagh, and in County Wexford at Bunclody a few km south of the end of the walk. South of Laragh accommodation becomes scarcer. Camping is possible along the route but you'll need to ask permission from local farmhouses. Roundwood also has an official camp site.

If you're hostelling you'll need to carry food with you. Enniskerry, Laragh and Roundwood have good places to eat. Stock up with food at Laragh; from there to Clonegal even shops are rare.

Getting There & Away

To get to the start of the walk from Dublin city, take bus No 47, 48A or 48B from Hawkins St or join it later at Glencree by getting bus No 44 to Enniskerry or the DART train to Bray and bus No 85 from there to Enniskerry. The private St Kevin's Bus Service (☎ 01-281 8119) runs twice daily from outside the College of Surgeons off St Stephen's Green in Dublin to Glendalough, passing through Roundwood.

Day 1: Marlay to Knockree
(21 km)

Marlay Park, in Rathfarnham, about 13 km south of central Dublin, is the northern starting point for the Wicklow Way. From the north car park, the path winds through woodland past two lakes before leaving Marlay Park then climbing steeply up Kilmashogue Lane to Kilmashogue Wood. The trail follows the north and east curves of the hillside, coming out onto open moorland with good views of the surrounding mountains, then descends to the edge of Glencullen Forest which it follows to meet the Glencullen road in the valley at Glencullen.

The way follows this road for a time then descends to cross the Glencullen River before ascending to the village of Boranaraltry and up Glencullen Mountain through woodland into County Wicklow. The trail drops again and passes through Curtlestown Wood to cross the public road in Glencree Valley then passes round to the right of the hill to meet the public road once more at Knockree. There's accommodation at the An Óige *Lackan House* hostel (☎ 01-286 4036) in Knockree; it gets busy in summer so you should book ahead.

Day 2: Knockree to Roundwood
(22 km)

From opposite the An Óige hostel in Knockree, the way follows a forest path downhill then turns left into a field and leads to the Glencree River. It follows the river east for about one km to a footbridge which you cross; follow the trail up over a forest road into Crone Wood. When you emerge from the wood there are great views overlooking Powerscourt Deer Park. The trail circles the valley slope toward Powerscourt Waterfall, but turns right into a forest just before you reach the waterfall. Emerging from the forest there are more fine views. After skirting the edge of the forest for a while the trail continues south along the eastern shoulder of Djouce Mountain (716 metres). A half-km side track to the right leads to the summit from which there's a panoramic view.

The main trail continues upward to 633 metres at White Hill then descends along a flat, boggy ridge with a magnificent view of Luggala Lake. The descent toward the valley becomes steeper till it reaches a public road which the way follows downhill until it turns right onto a forest path. Where the forest path meets the public road again there is a lookout point over Lough Dan. Follow the public road to the intersection where you can either continue, or turn left and walk the 1.5 km to Roundwood.

Roundwood Caravan & Camping Park (☎ 01-281 8163) is close to the village, has good facilities and camp sites for IR£6. The *Roundwood Inn* (☎ 01-281 8107) is a popular pub and restaurant on Main St.

Day 3: Roundwood to Laragh
(19 km)

From the intersection, the trail follows the public road south-west downhill, through forest and over the Avonmore River to Oldbridge. To the right by the cross in Oldbridge is a three-km path to the western shore of Lough Dan. Following the Wicklow Way straight on past the cross, you pass Glendalough House Demesne on your left, before descending to a stream, then going up again and turning right into a boreen which leads to Brusher Gate. Turning left (south) at Brusher Gate the way continues to rise through forest before descending again to meet Military Rd. Turn left onto Military Rd for about 300 metres, then take a right turn onto an old pathway and follow it over the Glenmacnass River bridge through woodland to the village of Laragh.

See Glendalough under The Wicklow

ACTIVITIES

Mountains section in the County Wicklow chapter for details of where to stay & eat in the area.

Day 4: Laragh to Glenmalure
(16 km)

Take the Rathdrum road south from Laragh and after about 700 metres turn right onto the Green Rd which runs past the Old Mill Hostel, the Glendalough monastic site, the Lower Lake and the national park information office. Just before Upper Lake the trail turns left, goes over a bridge, climbs up past Poul an Éan Waterfall, then zig-zags its way along the forested shoulder of Derrybawn Mountain (474 metres) and up close to the summit of Mt Mullacor (657 metres). A short path off the way takes you to the summit from which there are more great views of the mountains.

Following the Wicklow Way about 500 metres further you meet a track onto which you should turn left and continue down into Ballinafunshoge Wood. There the path meets a forest road; turn left onto the road and continue along it until you come to the crossroads at Glenmalure.

From Ballinafunshoge Wood there's a steep track off the way down to a public road; from where the track meets the public road the An Óige *Glenmalure Hostel* (no telephone) is about three km to the right over the Avonbeg River. The 16-bed hostel charges IR£5.50, is open daily July to August, weekends only the rest of the year and has no electricity.

Day 5: Glenmalure to Ballygobban Hill
(20 km)

Fewer people walk this section of the Wicklow Way south to Clonegal so the smaller paths are less obvious and you'll need to note the directions on your map and the marker posts more carefully. From here the forest and mountain scenery gradually changes to rolling hills and farmland.

Continue through the crossroads along Military Rd, over the Avonbeg River and past the old barracks, then turn right onto a narrow forest track. The track zig-zags uphill

over Clohernagh Brook and along the slopes of Slievemaan (549 metres) before dropping to meet Military Rd again, which it follows for a short while before turning left onto another forest track. This track heads up over the western shoulder of Carrickashane Mountain (505 metres) and gives great views along the Ow Valley toward Lugnaquilla Mountain (926 metres). The way drops again into the valley to the bridge over the Ow River then heads up Ballygobban Hill (446 metres) to a road junction.

Eight km to the left of the crossroads is the village of Aughrim where you can get B&B at the *Annacurra Inn* (☎ 0402-36430) for IR£19/32 a single/double with bath. The 60-bed An Óige *Aghavannagh Hostel* (☎ 0402-36366), once used by Charles Stewart Parnell as a hunting lodge, is open daily March to November, weekends only over winter, and charges IR£6. To reach the hostel turn right before the bridge and follow the road for nearly 2.5 km.

Day 6: Ballygobban Hill to Tinahely
(22 km)

The first part of this stage passes through the heavily forested Ow Valley. Turn left at the road junction, through Ballygobban Forest. The trail then joins a public road for a short stretch before re-entering woodland to the right over Ballyteigue Bridge. The trail follows the south bank of the Ballyteigue River (a tributary of the Ow River) before climbing the northern slope of Shielstown Hill (536 metres) and bringing Lugnaquilla Mountain into sight again.

After levelling off for a while it begins to descend gently. The route normally curves south-east but because of an access problem it now drops south-west instead, with a couple of sharp turns down to a public road; turn left onto this road and follow it toward the picturesque hamlet of Moyne. You can either take the right turn through Moyne, which eventually rejoins the way near St Colmcille's Well, or continue past the Moyne turn-off to a boreen which drops down to the right toward the well and meets the public road once more.

The road descends steeply, crosses Sandy Ford, turns left and skirts the south-eastern flank of Ballycumber Hill (401 metres). After passing the old Ballycumber school, the way leaves the public road just before the bridge. It heads to the right and over a stream onto a fairly muddy track which curves steeply round Garryhoe Hill (399 metres) through sheep-grazing fields (remember to close the gates) and past a ring fort then a small iron cross. The way loops down and through a wooded valley to meet Coolafunshoge Lane which it follows round the lower slope of Coolafunshoge Mountain (433 metres) to cross the Derry River over a wooden bridge meeting the Tinahely-Hacketstown road. Tinahely is 1.5 km to the left.

Tinahely has a café, shop, pub and several B&Bs including *Murphy's* (☎ 0402-38109) in the town square with rooms at IR£24 with bath. Buses from here connect with Waterford and Dublin.

Day 7: Tinahely to Shillelagh
(16.5 km)
Most of this section is on tarred roads. Turn left after the bridge toward Tinahely then turn sharp right onto a narrow side road. Follow this road for a little over 700 metres then turn left onto the grassy boreen that meanders along the western slope of Muskeagh Hill (401 metres) before dropping down to the right through felled-forest land to meet the public road. Turn left onto this road and follow it to the hamlet of Mullinacuff. Continue past the post office to the crossroads and turn right at the pub. The road heads west and south round Cronelea (358 metres) and over two intersections before meeting a T-junction The way heads left on this road for about one km before heading off to the south. If you want to visit or stay in Shillelagh continue for another two km.

Shillelagh has a shop, pub and a hotel. You can also catch buses from here to Waterford and Dublin.

Day 8: Shillelagh to Clonegal
(19 km)
Return to the Wicklow Way turn-off to the south. This road ascends steeply before

descending again then turning right onto a winding forest track. Emerging from the forest you have good views of the Blackstairs Mountains. The track follows the southern slope of Stookeen Hill (422 metres) to join a public road; the way heads right, then left and left again around the north and west of Moylisha Hill (280 metres) and after passing some cypress trees turns left onto a forest track. This track climbs then descends the western slope of Urelands Hill (270 metres) to meet the public road again after passing Urelands House. The road heads down to the Derry River which it follows into Clonegal in County Carlow.

There are a couple of pubs to have your celebratory drink in, but no accommodation. The nearest public transport is in Bunclody, 6.5 km further south. If you're still feeling fit you can pick up the start of the South Leinster Way a couple of km south-west in Kildavin.

SOUTH LEINSTER WAY
In County Carlow just south-west of Clonegal, on the slopes of Mt Leinster, is the tiny village of Kildavin, the northern starting point of the South Leinster Way. This walking trail through counties Carlow and Kilkenny follows remote mountain roads and river towpaths through the medieval villages of Borris, Graiguenamanagh, Inistioge, Mullinavat, Piltown and on to the finishing post at Carrick-on-Suir just inside the Tipperary border. The southerly section is not as scenic as the rest but the low hills have their own charm, and on a sunny day they offer fine views south over the Suir Valley and Waterford Harbour. The wildlife you might see along the way includes deer, fox, grouse and squirrel.

Direction, Distance & Time
The way heads in a generally south-west direction from Kildavin to Carrick-on-Suir; it could easily be done in the opposite direction. The walk is divided here into five days though it can be done in four if you don't stop over in Graiguenamanagh. The overall distance is 100 km which includes the extra walking to the nearest village to the trail.

ACTIVITIES

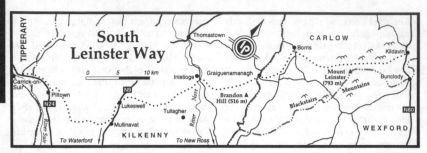

When to Go

This walk can be done at any time of year. Being in the south-east it is relatively dry and the region gets plenty of sunshine between May and September, although the weather can always suddenly change for the worse. In summer the daylight hours are long, especially July and August, but this is also the busiest part of the tourist season so it's a good idea to book accommodation in advance. Many of the B&Bs close over winter, though you should still be able to find some open.

Information

The route is marked so you should have no difficulty finding your way. Ask for the Bord Fáilte Information Sheet No 26D, with details of the route, at the Carlow Town tourist office (☎ 061-317522; open all year), or the one (☎ 056-51500; open all year) in Kilkenny City.

A large part of the trail is above 500 metres and the weather can change quickly. Good hiking boots, outdoor gear and emergency supplies are essential.

Guides & Maps East West Mapping publishes *South Leinster Way – Walkers Guide*. The way is also included in *Irish Long Distance Walks* by Michael Fewer. The Ordnance Survey 1:126,720 maps Nos 19, 22 and 23 cover the whole trail.

Places to Stay & Eat

There are no official camp sites but it is possible to camp on farmland provided you obtain permission. There's an IHH hostel in

Bunclody and, except for Kildavin, plenty of B&Bs in the villages along the route. Food can be had at pubs, while Borris and Inistioge each have a couple of small restaurants. A packed lunch is needed for most days of the walk and you can stock up at grocery stores as you go.

Getting There & Away

The South Leinster Way is reasonably well accessed by public transport. Bunclody, about five km south-west of Kildavin, is served regularly by Bus Éireann buses on the Dublin to Waterford route. J J Kavanagh & Sons' private bus company (☎ 0503-43081) has a service which stops in Borris once daily between Carlow Town and Limerick. Foley's (☎ 0503-24641) private buses stop at Borris and Graiguenamanagh twice daily from Kilkenny City. Neither company operates on Sunday. Thursdays only, a single bus runs between New Ross and Kilkenny City, calling at Inistioge en route in each direction. Carrick-on-Suir is served regularly by train and bus.

Day 1: Kildavin to Borris

(20 km)
The way heads south out of Kildavin on the Bunclody road before turning right after 250 metres onto a boreen. This leads uphill to a track that passes through a wood to a clearing. This clearing gives you a clear view of Mt Leinster ahead. The trail descends gradually to meet a public road east of Corrabut Gap. Turning right onto the road then left shortly afterwards at Carroll's Cross, the way ascends the western slope of Mt Leinster

(793 metres). At the trail's highest point you can make a detour to the top of Mt Leinster or to Slievebawn. The Blackstairs Mountains can be seen to the south. The way now meanders downhill to the village of Borris.

For places to stay and eat see Borris under County Carlow in the Central South chapter.

Day 2: Borris to Graiguenamanagh
(13 km)

The way follows the main street north-west then turns left and down to Ballyteiguelea Bridge over the River Barrow. Turn left onto the towpath just before the bridge. This towpath follows the meanderings of the river for the next 10 km into Graiguenamanagh and County Kilkenny – a relaxed, gentle walk with the Blackstairs Mountains and Brandon Hill (516 metres) visible to the south.

There are several B&Bs in and around Graiguenamanagh. The *Anchor* pub (☎ 0503-24207) has accommodation for IR£15 per person and serves meals.

Day 3: Graiguenamanagh to Inistioge
(13 km)

The way leaves the towpath at Graiguenamanagh and follows the main street onto the Inistioge road then turns left onto a tarred path which rises toward Brandon Hill (516 metres). This path ends at a gateway, but you continue on a track past a house to a road through woodland skirting the western slope of Brandon Hill. When you come out of the forest the way follows a boggy boreen downhill to a tarred road which continues to descend through Kilcross to meet the New Ross road. Turn right onto this road and follow it into the beautiful village of Inistioge on the River Nore.

There are quite a few B&Bs in the Inistioge area and a couple of eateries near the river. The *School House Café* is good for tea, sandwiches and cakes.

Day 4: Inistioge to Mullinavat
(20 km)

The way leaves Inistioge south from the village square along a track beside the river and through a forest, once the demesne

(landed property close to a house or castle) of Woodstock House. After 3.25 km the way forks right then winds uphill to a public road; it turns right onto this road for a short distance before turning left again onto another forest road which climbs Mt Alto. This road meets a gravel boreen where the way turns left towards Curraghmore Hill; the hills of Tipperary can be seen in the distance. After passing through another forest the way crosses a public road then descends to and crosses the Arrigle River, to reach the hamlet of Glenpipe.

From Glenpipe the route heads uphill along a narrow, overgrown boreen, passes through more woodland then, after crossing the public road again, heads downhill to the Derrylacky River and turns left to Lukeswell on the N9. Just past the pub the way turns left, then right and uphill to meet the main road which it follows south into Mullinavat.

See Mullinavat under Southern Kilkenny in the Kilkenny chapter for places to stay and eat.

Day 5, Mullinavat to Carrick-on-Suir
(22.5 km)

The final stretch of the way is mainly over elevated farmland. From the main street in Mullinavat the way turns right, and after crossing a stone bridge over a stream gradually heads uphill past Poulanassy Waterfall and the turn-off to Listrolin. The way follows the road down to the village of Piltown along the southern slopes of the Booley Hills. After passing through Piltown the way crosses the N24 and follows a tarred road to Tibberaghny Castle, then does a loop northward to cross the N24 again 2.5 km east of Carrick-on-Suir. The way then heads along a narrow, winding path to a footbridge over the River Suir, and into the town itself.

See Carrick-on-Suir in the Counties Limerick & Tipperary chapter for details on where to stay and eat, and public transport. Carrick-on-Suir is the starting point for the Munster Way.

OTHER LONG WALKS
Munster Way

This is an 63-km walk that travels along

forestry roads, open moorland, small country roads and a river towpath. The route is clearly laid out with black markers bearing yellow arrows. It could be managed in three days, starting from Carrick-on-Suir in County Tipperary and finishing at Clogheen in County Waterford. The first day of 26 km takes you to Clonmel, the second day of 16 km on to Newcastle and the last day another 21 km to Clogheen which, although five km beyond the official end of the way at the Vee Gap, is where accommodation and transport can be found.

There is a hostel in Clonmel and B&B accommodation elsewhere along the way. The route is covered by the Ordnance Survey 1:126,720 map No 22, or Bord Fáilte Information Sheet No 26J. Check to see if the new Ordnance Survey 1:50,000 series has published the relevant map. The walk is also covered in Michael Fewer's *Irish Long Distance Walks*.

Dingle Way

This 153-km walk in County Kerry is on one of the most beautiful peninsulas in the whole country. It would take eight days to complete the way, beginning and ending in Tralee, with an average daily distance of 22 km. The first three days are the easiest to walk and the first day, from Tralee to Camp, is by far the least interesting. This could be skipped by taking the bus to Camp and starting from there. You could also walk eight km from Camp to the Bog View hostel, and then the next day 15 km on to Lispole and on the third day a mere nine km to Dingle. This would also allow for a lovely 15-km return trip from the Bog View hostel to Lake Annascaul.

See the Dingle Peninsula section of the Kerry chapter for details of where to stay and eat. The route is covered by the Ordnance Survey 1:126,720 map No 20, but map No 83 in the 1:50,000 series is also available. This infinitely better map covers most of the walk but you need map No 78 as well to cover the whole way. The Dingle Way is also covered in *New Irish Walk Guides – South-west* by Seá Ó Súilleabháin and *Irish Long Distance Walks* by Michael Fewer, both pub-

lished by Gill & Macmillan. Bord Fáilte have their own map guide for IR£1.95.

Burren Way

This 45-km walk traverses the limestone plateau in County Clare that presents a strange and unique landscape to the walker. There is very little soil and few trees but a surprising abundance of flora. The way stretches between Ballyvaughan, on the north coast of County Clare, and Liscannor to the south-west and it takes in the village of Doolin, famous as a traditional music centre. The highlight of the route is the track along the dramatic heights of the Cliffs of Moher.

The best time for this walk is late spring or early summer. The route is pretty dry, but walking boots are useful as the limestone is sharp.

The best map will be No 51 (it may be published by the time you need it) in the 1:50,000 Ordnance Survey series. Map No 14 in the old 1:126,720 series is still available but Tim Robinson's Burren map is more useful. Shannon Development, 62 O'Connell St, Limerick, County Limerick, have a leaflet describing the Burren Way. See the Burren Area section of the Clare chapter for information on where to stay and eat and details on some parts of the way.

Royal Canal Way

The Royal Canal was constructed between 1789 and 1801 but became redundant with the coming of the railways. In 1961 it was closed to navigation and its dredging and revival is a very recent affair. It's possible to walk along the towpath of the Royal Canal all the way from Spencer Dock in Dublin to the 40th lock at Mullawomia, a distance of 125 km, without the need to slog up any hills. In future, as work on dredging and rewatering the canal proceeds, it should be possible to continue all the way to Shannon and Longford.

For the first 6.5 km to Reilly's Bridge, the path runs through grotty, run-down urban scenery, but from then on it becomes much more rural and enjoyable (after the interruption of the bridges associated with the M50). There are signposts at every bridge between Clonsilla and Mullingar but not, as yet, all the way along the route. To ensure you don't go wrong you need Ordnance Survey 1:50,000 maps Nos 12, 13 and 16. There's also a good *Guide to the Royal Canal of Ireland* (£5), published by the Office of Public Works, which shows the stretches of the towpath that are overgrown, as well as highlighting important things like pubs! To find out about activities along the Royal Canal, contact the Royal Canal Amenity Group on ☎ 01-831 3731.

Mourne Trail

The Mourne Trail is actually the south-eastern section of the Ulster Way, south of Belfast, and runs from Newry, round the Mourne Mountains, to the seaside resort of Newcastle and then on to Strangford where you can take a ferry across to Portaferry and continue north to Newtownards. From Newry to Strangford is a distance of 106 km and could probably be managed in four days. Route details are given in *The Ulster Way: A Guide to the Route and its Facilities* (£1.50) by Paddy Dillon, published by Walking World Ireland. Ordnance Survey of Northern Ireland Discoverer maps Nos 21 and 29 have all the necessary data for planning a walk. For other information, your best source will be the Mourne Countryside Centre (☎ 013967-24059), 91 Central Promenade, Newcastle, County Down.

There's gorgeous mountain, forest and coastal scenery along the way and, once you've left Newry, not much in the way of built-up towns to spoil the views. Provided you're reasonably fit and well-shod, this is not an especially difficult route to walk although it does climb as high as 559 metres at Slievemoughanmore, the highest point on the Ulster Way. The path is way-marked with the Ulster Way walking-man symbol throughout. Bear in mind that there are not that many B&Bs in this part of Ireland, so it's as well to book ahead. There's a YHANI hostel (☎ 013967-22133) in Newcastle (the biggest accommodation hub in the area) and

another (☎ 012477-29598) in Portaferry if you make it as far as Strangford.

Lough Derg Way

This is a 52-km walking trail that begins in Limerick City and ends in County Tipperary at the village of Dromineer on the eastern shore of Lough Derg, one of three lakes along the Shannon and the Republic's largest lake. The way will eventually extend as far as Portumna in Galway, north of Lough Derg. The 35 km from Limerick to Ballina via O'Brien's Bridge has been fully marked and signposted; it starts outside the Limerick City tourist office and follows the old city canal, the first of the old Shannon navigation canals.

Trail details are given in the *Lough Derg Way* guide and Ordnance Survey 1:126,720 scale maps Nos 15 and 18.

The only drawback to completing the walk is the lack of accommodation along the route. One possibility would be to walk a part of the trail and then catch a local bus back to Limerick City. Enquire at the Limerick City or Killaloe/Ballina tourist office for information and a walk leaflet.

Cavan Way

In the north-west of County Cavan the villages of Blacklion and Dowra are the ends of the 26-km Cavan Way. The way runs in a north-east to south-west direction past a number of Stone Age monuments – court cairns, ring forts, tombs – and this area is said to be one of the last strongholds of druidism. At the midpoint is the Shannon Pot, a pool on the boulder-strewn slopes of the Cuilcagh Mountains and the source of the River Shannon, which from there flows into Lough Allen. The Shannon Pot divides the walk into two parts: from Blacklion it is mainly hill walking; from Shannon Pot to Dowra it's mainly by road. The highest point on the walk is Giant's Grave (260 metres)

The way is covered by Bord Fáilte information sheet No 26I and Ordnance Survey 1: 50,000 map No 26. Blacklion has several B&Bs. A Bus Éireann bus stops once daily in Blacklion between Westport and Belfast; call ☎ 049-31353 in Cavan Town for details.

A new trail, one of several planned, will extend the Cavan Way south along the eastern shores of Lough Allen to Drumshanbo, 25 km south of Dowra in County Leitrim. Dowra also joins up with the Leitrim Way which runs between Manorhamilton and Drumshanbo. Blacklion is also on the Ulster Way.

Wexford Coastal Path

Developed in 1993 the Wexford Coastal Path (Slí Charman) follows the county's coastline for 221 km from Ballyhack in the south-east on Waterford Harbour to Kilmichael Point in the north-east corner near the border with County Wicklow. As well as passing through the main coastal settlements of Kilmore Quay, Rosslare Harbour and Wexford Town, the path also takes you past areas of great natural beauty including the North and South Slobs and the Hook Peninsula. The terrain varies from rocky headlands to sandy beaches.

The path is marked by signs showing a man with a walking stick walking on water. For more information contact the tourist office in Wexford Town.

St Declan's Way

This newly developed 94-km walk, mostly tracing an old pilgrimage way from Ardmore to the Rock of Cashel in Tipperary, traverses the Knockmealdown Mountains. Its highest point is the Bearna Cloch an Bhudeil pass (537 metres) but for the most part the trail is gently undulating. The walk can be done in stages and public transport is available from a number of places along the way – Cappoquin, Ardfinnan, Cahir and Newinn. If you're heading through the pass call the mountain rescue base (☎ 058-54404) at Mt Melleray before and after. A map is available from tourist offices or you can use Ordnance Survey maps – Nos 18 and 22 of the 1:26,720 series or Nos 66, 74, 81 and 82 of the 1:50,000 series. There are B&Bs and hotels along the route; and camping is possible, though to do so you'll need to ask permission from local farmers.

Slieve Bloom Way

Close to the geographical centre of Ireland, the Slieve Bloom Way is a 77-km signposted trail which does a complete circuit of the Slieve Bloom Mountains taking in almost all the major points of interest. The trail follows tracks, forest firebreaks and old roads, and crosses the Mountrath to Kinnitty and Mountrath to Clonaslee roads. Its highest point is at Glendine Gap (460 metres). The recommended starting point is the car park at Glenbarrow, five km from Rosenallis. Bord Fáilte Information Sheet No 26F is available from any tourist office; it's also covered by Ordnance Survey 1:127,00 map No 15 and 1:50,000 map No 54.

It is forbidden to camp in a state forest, but there is plenty of open space outside the forest for tents; otherwise, accommodation en route is almost nonexistent. There is no public transport to the area, though buses do stop in the nearby towns of Mountrath and Rosenallis.

Kildare Way

The 150-km Kildare Way connects a series of canal towpaths in the north of the county. The canals, killed off as transport routes by the advent of the railway, have been revived by people seeking leisure activities like walking, cruising, canoeing and fishing. The walk is mainly flat with few hills and the highest point is at Glenaree Lock (92 metres). At the hub of the Kildare Way is Robertstown from where trails radiate out to Naas, Kildare, Edenderry and Celbridge.

For more information on the Kildare routes ask for the Bord Fáilte Information Sheet No 26E; the Ordnance Survey maps are Nos 16 and 19 in the 1:126,720 series. There is accommodation at the places mentioned above and buses go to most access points.

Cycling

Many visitors explore Ireland by bicycle. The most interesting areas can be hilly, some of the roads have poor surfaces and the weather is often wet, but despite these draw-backs it's a great place for bicycle touring. The facilities are good, distances are relatively short, roads off the main highways have rela-tively little traffic, the scenery is beautiful, and you're never too far from a pub.

INFORMATION
You can either bring your bike with you or rent one in Ireland. Ferries transport bicycles for a small fee and airlines will usually accept them as part of your 20-kg luggage allowance. When buying your ticket check with the ferry company or airline about any regulations or restrictions on the transporta-tion of bicycles.

Bicycles can be transported by bus provided there is room in the luggage compartment. With Bus Éireann the charge varies; on Ulster-bus the cost is half the adult one-way fare with a minimum charge of 70p. By train the cost varies from IR£2 to IR£6 for a one-way journey depending on the distance. Bicycles are not allowed on certain rail routes including the Dublin Area Rapid Transit (DART); check with Iarnród Éireann.

Typical rental costs are IR£7 to IR£10 a day or IR£30 to IR£35 a week plus a deposit of around IR£40 which is refunded when the bicycle is returned. Bags and other equip-ment can also be rented. Raleigh Rent-a-Bike is Ireland's biggest rental dealer and has nine 'Premier' outlets around the country which offer one-way rentals for IR£42 a week. It also has 'Classic' outlets where the bicycle must be returned to the shop it was rented from. For more informa-tion contact Raleigh Ireland (☎ 01-626 1333), Raleigh House, Kylemore Rd, Dublin 10, or pick up one of their leaflets at tourist offices. There are also many local indepen-dent outlets.

Regional and national tour operators orga-nise cycling holidays and the tourist boards can supply you with a list of their names. Irish Cycling Safaris (☎ 01-260 0749), 7 Dartry Park, Dublin 6, organise tours for groups of cyclists in the south-west, the south-east and Connemara, with bikes,

guides, a van that carries luggage, and B&B accommodation.

Numerous tourist-office publications on cycling exist and there are a number of books and guides on the subject. Good maps are available (see Maps in the Facts for the Visitor chapter). You might also want to get in touch with the Irish Federation of Cyclists (☎ 01-855 1522), 619 North Circular Rd, Dublin 1.

WHERE TO CYCLE
South-West
Most of West Cork is ideal cycling territory and examples of local cycling tours for Clonakilty and Schull can be found under those sections in the Cork chapter, but the whole region could be explored on bike. One recommended route is west from Cork City to Kinsale and then on through Timoleague, Butlerstown, Clonakilty, Rosscarbery and down to Baltimore and Clear Island. Another route would be down the Mizen Head Peninsula (starting from Skibbereen where you can hire bikes), looping around the village of Toormore to take in the south and north coasts. A third route would be a circular one of the Sheep's Head Peninsula, starting and finishing in Bantry (where bikes can be hired).

In Kerry, a wonderful tour would be around the starkly beautiful Beara Peninsula from either Kenmare, Glengarriff or Bantry (all with bike hire) and taking in the spectac-ular Healy Pass either down from Lauragh to Adrigole (good brakes are absolutely essen-tial) or with a herculean slog in the other direction. Killarney makes a good base for cycling trips into (but not *around*, unless you want car and coach fumes in your lungs) the Iveragh Peninsula where many of the sights are only accessible by bike or on foot, and examples of two such tours are the 30-km ride via the Gap of Dunloe and the 80-km trip via Lake Acoose and Moll's Gap.

In Clare the Burren region is good for mountain cycling.

North-West
The Lough Gill tour in the Yeats country outside Sligo Town lends itself to cycling.

So, too, do many of the historic and pre-historic sites in the county – as well as other places of interest associated with Yeats – because most of them are in the vicinity of Sligo Town (where you can hire bikes).

Achill Island has largely flat roads which makes cycling an easy way of travelling around the whole island. Bikes can be hired at Achill Sound and returned there after cycling west to Keel, turning north up to Dugort and then back south on another road.

In County Galway, Clifden is the best base for cycling tours of Connemara and takes you through some superb scenery.

In Donegal you can follow the road west of Donegal Town along the coast road via Killybegs to Malin More. North of Killybegs, past Ardara to Dunfanaghy the coast is absolutely superb and there are wonderful cycling tours to be enjoyed around Bloody Foreland and Horn Head. The peninsula that extends west from Ardare is well worth cycling too. North-east of Donegal Town the loop around Lough Eske is a pleasant shorter trip on roads surrounded by the Blue Stack Mountains.

North-East
In County Down, Bangor is a good base from which to cycle the reasonably flat Ards Peninsula: you could follow the coast road south via Donaghdee to Portaferry, from where the A2 heads back north skirting Strangford Lough. Alternatively, Newcastle is a good spot from which to explore the valley routes through the Mourne Mountains in south County Down.

In Antrim the scenic route along the coast north from Belfast to the Giant's Causeway passes through the foothills of the Antrim Mountains. From Enniskillen in Fermanagh you can hire bikes to visit ancient religious sites and antiquities, following roads along the shores of Lower Lough Erne to Belleek on the Donegal border and back.

South-East
Just south of Dublin, the varied scenery of Wicklow – moors, bogs, mountains, lakes, valleys and forests – provides some beautiful

but strenuous cycling. From Wicklow Town south to Wexford the weather is warmer and the landscape flatter. Between Wexford and Waterford, by taking the Ballyhack to Passage East ferry you avoid the longer route north via New Ross.

In Waterford the relatively flat Hook Peninsula – out to the lighthouse at the tip of the head and back along the west side to Duncannon – is a good area to explore by bicycle. In the west of the county the route through the Knockmealdown Mountains offers magnificent views.

Tipperary and Kilkenny have rich, rolling farmland interspersed with ancient monuments like the Rock of Cashel and fine architectural remains. From Kilkenny City there's a beautiful excursion to Kilfane, Jerpoint Abbey, Inistioge and Kells.

Centre
In Westmeath, from Athlone north into Longford east of Lough Rea is Goldsmith Country (named after the 18th-century poet, playwright and novelist, Oliver Goldsmith) and the gentle terrain is great for cycling. A cycle tour of the *drumlins* (a rounded hill formed by retreating glacier) and lakes of Cavan, Monaghan and southern Leitrim along the quiet country roads is very pleasant.

Fishing

Ireland is renowned for its fishing and many visitors come to Ireland for no other reason. Fishing is divided into several categories, topped by dry-fly fishing, where an artificial lure, made to imitate a small insect, is gently dropped on the surface in order to deceive and catch the fish. Fish are described as coarse or game fish, the latter because they vigorously struggle against capture.

In the South, on private stretches of rivers a permit is usually required and the average price is IR£5 a day. In addition a state national licence is required for salmon and sea trout fishing. This costs IR£25 annually,

IR£10 for three weeks, IR£3 for one day and can be purchased from a local tackle shop or direct from the Central Fisheries Board (☎ 01-837 9206), Balngowan House, Mobhi Boreen, Glasnevin, Dublin 9.

It is not necessary to have any licence for brown trout, rainbow trout or coarse fish, nor for general sea angling. However, there is a system of share certificates (issued to help raise funds) for trout and coarse fishing, which you purchase beforehand; in most regions payment is voluntary. The certificates cost IR£12 for a year, IR£5 for three weeks or IR£3 for three days.

In the North a rod licence is required and this is obtainable from the Foyle Fisheries Commission (☎ 01504-42100), 8 Victoria Rd, Derry BT47 2AB, for the Foyle area, and from the Fisheries Conservancy Board (☎ 01762-334666), 1 Mahon Rd, Portadown, Craigavon, County Armagh, for all other regions (£10.65 for 15 days). In addition a permit is required from the owner and this is usually the Department of Agriculture, Fisheries Division (☎ 01232-63939), Stormont, Belfast BT4 3PW which charges £7 a day or £17 for 15 days.

Bord Fáilte and the Northern Ireland Tourist Board produce several information leaflets on fishing. Bord Fáilte annually publishes *The Anglers' Guide*, which lists accommodation, major fishing events and charter-boat operators. Three good books are *Game Angling Guide*, *Coarse Angling Guide* and *Sea Angling Guide* from the Central Fisheries Board and published by Gill & Macmillan (☎ 01-435 1005), Goldenbridge, Inchicore, Dublin 8. They are full of practical information and details of the permits and licences required. The Central Fisheries Board also sells an inexpensive *Angling in Ireland* brochure that sets out what can be caught and where.

Water Sports

Ireland's more than 5630-km coastline, its rivers and numerous lakes provide plenty of opportunities for a range of water sports.

SWIMMING & SURFING

The climate and the water temperature are good reasons why Ireland isn't the first place you'd think of for swimming or surfing. On the other hand, it has some magnificent coastline and some great sandy beaches. Sadly, a number of Irish beaches suffer from pollution, but the cleaner, safer ones have been given the European Blue Flag award and you can get a list of these from An Taisce, The Tailors Hall, Back Lane, Dublin 8.

Following is a list of Ireland's major surfing spots.

North-West
Easkey in the west of County Sligo is known locally as a surfing haunt and is highly regarded by surfers, but by international standards is uncrowded. Achill Island in County Mayo has surfing beaches and there is an Activity Centre on the Keel road where information and equipment is available.

South-West
Barley Cove beach on the Mizen Head Peninsula is the only surfing beach in County Cork, but it is never crowded. In Kerry, around Caherdaniel on the Iveragh Peninsula it is possible to hire equipment at the local beach; the broad, empty beaches around Castlegregory on Castlegregory Peninsula are perfect for surfing; at Inch on the Dingle Peninsula the waves average one to three metres.

West
Spanish Point near Miltown Malby and Lahinch in west Clare are good for surfing.

South-East
In Wexford, equipment is available for hire at Rosslare Strand. In County Waterford, Ballinacourty, Dunmore East, Tramore and Dungarvan are all worth considering for surfing and equipment and advice is available locally.

North
Portrush on the north coast in County Antrim is gaining a name as a surfing centre.

The Irish Surfing Association (☎ 073-21053), Tirchonaill St, Donegal Town, County Donegal can supply you with more details.

SCUBA DIVING

Ireland has some of the best scuba diving in Europe, almost entirely off the west coast; visibility averages over 12 metres but can increase to 30 metres on good days. A number of centres around the country offer equipment and training. Oceantec Diving (☎ 01-280 1083) in Dun Laoghaire, County Dublin, is a five-star PADI centre with a dive shop and school and they can arrange dive vacations on the west coast. For more details about scuba diving in Ireland write to or phone the Irish Underwater Council (☎ 01-284 601), 78A Patrick St, Dun Laoghaire, County Dublin.

Following are some favourite dive sites.

South-West
  Bantry Bay and Dunmanus Bay in County Cork are good sites and they are serviced by a new company that has opened in Glengarriff; the area is just beginning to open up to its scuba diving potential so it's largely virgin territory – a major draw with divers. The Iveragh Peninsula in Kerry has two main bases: Valentia Island with three companies, and Caherdaniel with two companies.
West
  The Connemara coastline and surrounding islands in County Galway are serviced by a local company based at Glassillaun Beach. In County Clare, Kilkee is a popular diving centre and equipment is locally available. Ballyreen, near Lisdoonvarna, is less well known, as are Doolin and Fanore.
South-East
  Around Hook Head in County Wexford is popular and facilities are available.
East
  From Dun Laoghaire scuba divers head for the waters around Dalkey Island.

SAILING

Sailing has a long heritage in Ireland and the country has over 120 yacht and sailing clubs including the Royal Cork Yacht Club at Crosshaven, which, established in 1720, is the world's oldest. The most popular areas for sailing are the west coast especially between Cork Harbour and the Dingle Peninsula, the coastline north and south of Dublin, and some of the larger lakes like Lough Derg, Lough Erne and Lough Gill.

For more information contact the Irish Sailing Association (☎ 01-280 0239), 3 Park Rd, Dun Laoghaire, County Dublin, which is the national body governing the sport. Ireland has a number of professional training schools catering for people of varying degrees of expertise and which operate under the auspices of the Irish Association for Sail Training (☎ 01-677 9801), Confederation House, Kildare St, Dublin 2.

A recommended publication is the *Irish Cruising Club Sailing Directions* available from booksellers or from Mrs Fox-Mills (☎ 01-832 2823), 'The Tansey', Baily, County Dublin. It contains details of port facilities, harbour plans and coast and tidal information.

WINDSURFING

The windsurfer has plenty of locations, along the coast and on rivers and lakes, to indulge this popular sport, with the west coast facing the Atlantic being the most challenging. Even the Grand Canal in Dublin is used by windsurfers. The bay at Rosslare is ideal for windsurfing and you can obtain equipment and tuition there from the Rosslare Windsurfing Centre (☎ 053-32101). The Irish Board Sailing Association (☎ 021-543268), Viaduct House, Castlewhite, Waterfall, County Cork, has details of other centres offering the same.

CANOEING

There are many opportunities for canoeing and it's a great way to travel round the country. The Liffey Descent in September is a major international competition. The type of canoeing in Ireland and degree of difficulty varies from gentle paddling to white-water canoeing and canoe surfing. Information on locations and conditions can be obtained from the Irish Canoe Union (☎ 01-450 1633), House of Sport, Long Mile Rd, Walkinstown, Dublin 12; they also run training courses on the River Liffey. The Tiglin Adventure Centre (☎ 0404-40169), Ashford, County Wicklow, runs courses and organises canoeing trips.

WATER SKIING

There are water-ski clubs all over Ireland offering tuition, equipment and boats. Bord Fáilte provides the names of some of these clubs, but a full list and other details are available from the Irish Water-Ski Federation (☎ 01-624 0526), 29 Hermitage Rd, Lucan, County Dublin.

Birdwatching

Ireland's location on the north-western edge of Europe and the variety and size of the flocks that visit or breed there make it of particular interest to birdwatchers. It is also home to some rare and endangered species. For a description of some of the birds and where to find them see under Fauna in the Facts about the Country chapter.

There are more than 70 reserves and sanctuaries in Ireland, but some are not open to visitors and others are privately owned so you will need to get permission from the proprietors before entering them. It's also illegal to interfere with wild birds, their nests and eggs. Information can be obtained from:

National Parks & Wildlife Service
    Office of Public Works, 51 St Stephen's Green, Dublin 2 (☎ 01-661 3111)
Irish Wildbird Conservancy
    Ruttledge House, 8 Longford Place, Monkstown, County Dublin (☎ 01-284 4407)
Royal Society for the Protection of Birds
    Belvoir Park Forest, Belfast BT8 4QT (☎ 01232 491547)
National Trust
    Rowallane House, Saintfield, County Down BT24 7LH (☎ 01238-510721)

Some useful publications on birdwatching are *Where to Watch Birds in Ireland* (Gill & Macmillan, Dublin, 1994) by C D Hutchinson, *The Birds of Ireland* (Appletree, 1992) by G D'Arcy and *Complete Guide to Ireland's Birds* (Gill & Macmillan, Dublin, 1993) by E Dempsey and M O'Cleary.

Golf

There are 250 golf courses in the South and 80 in the North, often in beautiful settings, and the number seems to be growing all the time. They range from illustrious and expensive ones at Killarney, Portmarnock near Dublin and Royal County Down, to more modest places like the one at Castletownbere on the Beara Peninsula.

Bord Fáilte and the Northern Ireland Tourist Board produce information leaflets, plus brochures on customised golfing holidays with descriptions of courses and local accommodation. You could also try contacting the Golfing Union of Ireland (☎ 01-269 4111), 81 Eglinton Rd, Dublin 4, or the Irish Ladies Golf Union (☎ 01-269 6244), 1 Clonskeagh Square, Clonskeagh Rd, Dublin 4.

Green fees average about IR£10 on weekdays (more on weekends) but the top-notch places will charge more than three times this. Fees are about the same in the North.

Courses are tested for their level of difficulty and many are playable year round. It's always advisable to book in advance. Most clubs give members priority in booking tee-off times; it's usually easier to book a tee-off time on a public course but on weekends, public holidays and days when the weather is good, it's often busy on all courses. You should also check whether there's a dress code, and whether the course has golf clubs for hire (not all do) if you don't have your own.

Hang Gliding

Some of the finest hang gliding can be found at Mt Leinster in Carlow, Great Sugar Loaf Mountain in Wicklow, Benone/Magillan Beach in Derry and Achill Island in Mayo. Contact the Irish Hang-Gliding Association (☎ 01-450 9845), c/o AFAS House of Sport, Longmile Rd, Dublin 12, for general information.

Rock Climbing

Ireland's mountain ranges are not high – Carrantuohill in Kerry's Macgillycuddy's Reeks at only 1041 metres is the tallest in

102 Horse Riding

ACTIVITIES

Ireland – but they are often beautiful and offer some excellent climbing possibilities. For further information get in touch with the Mountaineering Council of Ireland (☎ 01-450 1633), c/o AFAS, House of Sport, Longmile Rd, Dublin 12, which also publishes a number of climbing guides.

The highest mountains are in the south-west. Cork has a number of easy climbs, including Mt Gabriel (407 metres) on the Mizen Head Peninsula, Seefin (528 metres) on the Sheep's Head Peninsula and Sugarloaf Mountain (574 metres) on the Beara Peninsula; Hungry Hill (686 metres), also on the Beara Peninsula is more demanding. The Iveragh Peninsula in County Kerry is the place to head for if you want to be surrounded by mountains just waiting to be climbed. Macgillycuddy's Reeks are here.

In the north-west Knocknarea (328 metres) outside Sligo Town is an easy climb and so, too, is Croagh Patrick (763 metres), in west Mayo, although it takes a lot longer. On Achill Island in Mayo are some of the highest cliffs in Europe. In Galway, Clifden makes a good base for climbing in Connemara, and in Clare there's excellent rock climbing at Ballyreen near Fanore. Errigal Mountain (752 metres) in Donegal is popular with climbers when the weather allows.

At the north end of Lough Tay in the Wicklow Mountains are some spectacular cliffs popular with rock climbers. Also popular are the large crags in Glendalough, at the west end of the valley not far from the Upper Lake. The Tiglin Adventure Centre (☎ 0404-40169), near Ashford, runs rock-climbing courses in the Wicklows.

The Mourne Mountains in County Down, Northern Ireland, have steep, craggy granite peaks including Eagle Mountain, Pigeon Rock Mountain and Slieve Donard which, at 850 metres, is the highest peak in the range. You can base yourself in nearby Newcastle.

Horse Riding

Not surprisingly this is a popular pastime and there are literally dozens of centres throughout Ireland offering horses or ponies for riding along beaches, country lanes, mountain and forest trails and over farmland. Possibilities range from hiring a horse for an hour or so (rates start at around IR£7 or IR£8 an hour) to fully packaged residential equestrian holidays; in some places you can even combine it with English-language tuition. Bord Fáilte and the Northern Irish Tourist Board have full details.

The lovely wooded valleys and heathery mountains of north County Waterford are good for horse riding as are the Wicklow Mountains. Kildare is an equestrian paradise. Other areas include the Dingle Peninsula in Kerry, Connemara in Galway, around Bundoran and the Finn Valley in Donegal and near Clonakilty and Killarney in Cork.

Tracing Your Ancestors

Many visitors to Ireland have ancestors who once lived in this country. Your trip would be a good chance to find out more about them and their lives; you may even find relatives you never even knew about. The Irish diaspora is huge with more than 40 million people of Irish descent in the USA, over five million in Canada, a similar figure in Australia, hundreds of thousands in South America, nobody knows quite how many millions in Britain, plus many in other countries.

To achieve the most success from your visit you should begin researching in your home country, by finding out, if possible, the date and point of arrival of your ancestor(s). If you contact the Genealogical Office (☎ 01-661 8811/4877/1626), 2 Kildare St, Dublin 2, or the Public Record Office of Northern Ireland (PRONI) (☎ 01232-661621), 66 Balmoral Ave, Belfast BT9 6NY, they'll be able to provide you with information on what to do. They can also provide you with a list of local research centres in Ireland, so if you know which county your ancestors came from you can then write to the centres directly. Much of the data of civil and church records is being computerised and many local genealogy centres are connected to a computer network.

If you can't or don't want to undertake the research yourself there are numerous commercial agencies that will do it for you for a fee. For information on these contact the Association of Professional Genealogists in Ireland (APGI), c/o the Genealogical Office in Dublin, and the Association of Ulster Genealogists & Record Agents (AUGRA), Glen Cottage, Glenamchan Rd, Belfast BT4 2NP.

A huge number of books is available on the subject. *The Irish Roots Guide* by Tony McCarthy (Lilliput Press, Dublin, 1991) serves as a useful introduction. Other publications include *Tracing Your Irish Roots* by Christine Kinealy (Blackstaff Press, Belfast, 1990) and recommended is *Tracing Your Irish Ancestors: A Comprehensive Guide* (Gill & Macmillan, Dublin, 1992) by John Grenham. All these publications, and other items of genealogical concern, may be obtained from the Genealogy Bookshop, 3 Nassau St, Dublin 2; in Belfast the place to go is the Familia bookshop, 64 Wellington Place.

Language Courses

IRISH
With the recent revival of the Irish language there is a growing number of courses in the language and culture, particularly in the Gaeltacht-speaking areas.

University College, Galway, runs intensive month-long courses in the summer for IR£580, which includes tuition plus organised social activities and tours. Contact Seamus O'Grady (☎ 091-24411; fax 091-25051), Administrative Director, Summer School, University College Galway, Galway City. In Glencolumbcille, Donegal, weekend and week-long courses in Irish and Irish

culture are provided during the summer by Oideas Gael (☎ 073-30248).

Contact Bord Fáilte for more information.

ENGLISH
Given Ireland's significant contribution to English literature it's probably not surprising that it has increasingly become a centre for the learning of English, particularly for people from other Catholic countries, mainly Spain, Italy, France and Portugal. There are English-language schools all over the country but most are in and around Dublin.

Bord Fáilte publishes a list of schools that have been recognised by the Department of Education for the teaching of English as a foreign language. Some schools run summer programmes and provide specialised courses (eg for business people); the schools can arrange accommodation and organise sporting and cultural activities.

Some of the approved schools in Dublin are:

Academy of English Studies Ireland
    33 Dawson St, Dublin 2 (☎ 01-279 6464; fax 01-279 6465)
Dublin School of English
    10-12 Westmoreland St, Dublin 2 (☎ 01-677 3322; fax 01-626 4692)
English Language Institute
    99 St Stephen's Green, Dublin 2 (☎ 01-475 2965; fax 01-475 2967)
Language Centre
    University College Dublin, Belfield, Dublin 4 (☎ 01-706 8520; fax 01-269 4409)

Scenic Routes

If you're only visiting Ireland for a short time then touring by car or motorcycle will help you to fit in a lot more. Following are some scenic routes, though the list is by no means exhaustive. The west of Ireland has the most dramatic scenery, but there are many other parts of the country where the landscape is also stunningly beautiful.

ACTIVITIES

SOUTH-WEST

The routes that use the main roads to loop around the lush, green peninsulas of Mizen Head and Sheep's Head and the more desolate Beara in West Cork are all very scenic. The north coast of the Beara, the Healy Pass that cuts through the peninsula, and the Goat's Path along the north side of the Sheep's Head are the most spectacular parts of these routes.

The road from Bantry to Kenmare and on to Killarney is a very attractive drive as is the one from Bantry east to Macroom. The Ring of Kerry, the road that loops around the Iveragh Peninsula, is justly famous and attracts a lot of vehicles.

From Tralee in County Clare there are two routes into the Dingle Peninsula, but the more beautiful is the one that follows the northern coastline and crosses over the Slieve Mish Mountains via Connor Pass to the town of Dingle and onto the western headlands.

Following Clare's Atlantic coastline offers dramatic views while the road that follows the south-western shores of Lough Derg passes through gentle countryside and picturesque villages.

WEST & NORTH-WEST

In County Mayo the road between Louisburg and Delphi is one of the most scenic anywhere in the west of Ireland; it works its magic on motorists who all seem unusually willing to slow down. The route in north Mayo that passes Ballycastle has magnificent views.

In Galway the Lough Inagh Valley in Connemara between the Maumturk Mountains and the Twelve Bens is one of the most scenic in the country. There are marvellous views along the road between Recess and Clifden to the south of the Twelve Bens.

Donegal has many scenic routes and one

of the best is the road from Glencolumbcille to Ardara by way of the visually striking Glengesh Pass. From Ballyliffin to Buncrana there is a scenic coastal road via the Gap of Mamore and Dunree.

NORTH-EAST

The A2 road east out of Belfast is a pleasant route to Bangor and the eastern coastline of the Ards Peninsula then south to Portavogie and Portaferry. You can return to Belfast north along the A20 following the eastern shoreline of Strangford Lough.

North of Belfast the A2 will take you to the Giant's Causeway following the magnificent Antrim coast, with the Antrim Mountains to the west; between Cushendun and Ballycastle you can follow an alternative road that loops around the headland and rejoins the A2 at Ballyvoy.

The road that circles Lough Erne from Enniskillen in County Fermanagh is interesting historically as well as visually.

EAST & SOUTH-EAST

South of Dublin there are several routes into the Wicklow Mountains. The most scenic begins at Glencree, leads south over the Sally Gap to Glendalough, continues to Avoca and then on to Arklow on the coast. The Wicklow coast between Greystones and Rathnew has some lovely countryside too.

In southern County Carlow quiet roads connect picturesque villages like Leighlinbridge and Borris, with other villages in neighbouring counties Wexford and Kilkenny. Borris is also one starting point for a scenic drive up to nearby Mt Leinster.

In Waterford the coast road between Tramore and Dungarvan has lots of panoramic views and attractive villages. In the west of the county there are signposted scenic drives round the Knockmealdown Mountains with some terrific views.

Getting There & Away

Whichever way you're travelling to Ireland, make sure you take out travel insurance. This not only covers you for medical expenses and luggage theft or loss, but also for cancellations or delays in your travel arrangements under certain circumstances (you might fall seriously ill two days before departure, for example). Cover depends on your insurance and type of ticket, so ask both your insurer and your ticket-issuing agency to explain where you stand. Ticket loss is also (usually) covered by travel insurance. Make sure you have a separate record of all your ticket details – or better still, a photocopy. Buy travel insurance as early as possible. If you buy it the week before you fly, you may find, for example, that you're not covered for delays to your flight caused by strikes or industrial action.

AIR

Dublin is Ireland's major international airport, and now that flights to or from North America no longer have to operate via Shannon it is possible to fly direct to Dublin. Aer Lingus is the Irish national airline with international connections to other countries in Europe and to the USA. Ryanair is the next largest Irish airline, with routes to Europe and the USA.

There are charter flights between Belfast and overseas centres, but most Belfast connections are to England and Scotland.

Students should contact USIT, the Irish student and youth travel organisation, for cheap air fares to Ireland – see under Useful Organisations in the Facts for the Visitor chapter.

Buying a Ticket

If you're flying to Ireland from outside Europe, the plane ticket will probably be the single most expensive item in your budget, and buying it can be an intimidating business. There is likely to be a multitude of airlines and travel agents hoping to separate you from your money, and

it's always worth putting aside some time to research the current state of the market. Start early: some of the cheapest tickets have to be bought months in advance, and some popular flights sell out early. Talk to other recent travellers – they may be able to stop you making some of the same old mistakes. Look at the ads in newspapers and magazines including any catering specifically to the Irish community in your country, consult reference books and watch for special offers. Then phone round travel agents for bargains. (Airlines can supply information on routes and timetables; however, except at times of inter-airline price wars they don't usually supply the cheapest tickets.) Find out the fare, the route, the duration of the journey and any restrictions on the ticket, then decide which is best for you.

You may discover when you start ringing around that those impossibly cheap flights are 'fully booked', but the agency just happens to know of another one that 'costs a bit more'. Or the flight is on an airline notorious for its poor safety standards and leaves you in the world's least favourite airport in mid-journey for 14 hours (where you're confined to the transit lounge because you do not have a visa). Or the agents may claim to have the last two seats available for Ireland for the whole of July, which they will hold for a maximum of two hours. Don't panic – keep ringing around.

If you're flying to Ireland from the UK, USA or South-East Asia you will probably find that the cheapest flights are being advertised by obscure agencies whose names haven't yet reached the telephone directory – the proverbial 'bucket shops'. Many such firms are honest and solvent, but there are a few rogues who will take your money and disappear, only to reopen elsewhere a month or two later under a new name. If you feel suspicious about a firm, don't give them all the money at once – leave a 20% deposit or so and pay the balance when you get the ticket. If they insist on cash in advance, go

Air Travel Glossary

Apex Apex, or 'advance purchase excursion' is a discounted ticket which must be paid for in advance. There are penalties if you wish to change it.

Baggage Allowance This will be written on your ticket: usually one 20-kg item to go in the hold, plus one item of hand luggage.

Bucket Shop An unbonded travel agency specialising in discounted airline tickets.

Bumped Just because you have a confirmed seat doesn't mean you're going to get on the plane – see Overbooking.

Cancellation Penalties If you have to cancel or change an Apex ticket, there are often heavy penalties involved – insurance can sometimes be taken out against these penalties. Some airlines impose penalties on regular tickets as well, particularly against 'no show' passengers.

Check In Airlines ask you to check in at a certain time ahead of the flight departure (usually 1½ hours on international flights). If you fail to check in on time and the flight is overbooked, the airline can cancel your booking and give your seat to somebody else.

Confirmation Having a ticket written out with the flight and date you want doesn't necessarily mean you have a seat. Until the agent has checked with the airline that your status is 'OK' or confirmed, you could just be 'on request' (RQ), this being the code that would be written in place of OK on your ticket.

Discounted Tickets There are two types of discounted fares – officially discounted (see Promotional Fares) and unofficially discounted. The lowest prices often impose drawbacks like flying with unpopular airlines, inconvenient schedules, or unpleasant routes and connections. A discounted ticket can save you other things than money – you may be able to pay Apex prices without the associated Apex advance booking and other requirements. Discounted tickets only exist where there is fierce competition.

Full Fares Airlines traditionally offer 1st class (coded F), business class (coded J) and economy class (coded Y) tickets. These days, there are so many promotional and discounted fares available from the regular economy class that few passengers pay full economy fare.

Lost Tickets If you lose your ticket an airline will usually treat it like a travellers' cheque and, after inquiries, issue you with another one. Legally, however, an airline is entitled to treat it like cash and if you lose it then it's gone forever. Take good care of your tickets.

No Shows No shows are passengers who fail to show up for their flight, sometimes due to unexpected delays or disasters, sometimes due to simply forgetting, sometimes because they made more than one booking and didn't bother to cancel the one they didn't want. Full fare passengers who fail to turn up are sometimes entitled to travel on a later flight. The rest of us are penalised (see Cancellation Penalties).

On Request An unconfirmed booking for a flight, see Confirmation.

Open Jaws A return ticket where you fly out to one place but return from another. If available, this can save you backtracking to your arrival point.

---

somewhere else or be prepared to take a big risk. Once you have the ticket, ring the airline to confirm that you have a confirmed booking on the flight.

You may decide to pay more than the rock-bottom fare by opting for the safety of a better-known travel agent. Firms such as STA Travel, which has offices worldwide, Council Travel in the USA, or Travel CUTS in Canada offer competitive prices and are unlikely to disappear overnight.

Once you have your ticket, write its number down, together with the flight number and other details, and keep the information somewhere separate. If the ticket is lost or stolen, this will help you get a replacement.

Round-the-World Tickets

Round-the-World (RTW) tickets are often real bargains, and can work out to be no more expensive or even cheaper than an ordinary

Overbooking Airlines hate to fly empty seats and, since every flight has some passengers who fail to show up (see No Shows), they often book more passengers than they have seats. Usually the excess passengers balance those who fail to show up, but occasionally somebody gets bumped. If this happens, guess who it is most likely to be? The passengers who check in late.

Promotional Fares Officially discounted fares like Apex fares which are available from travel agents or direct from the airline.

Reconfirmation At least 72 hours prior to departure time of an onward or return flight you should normally contact the airline and 'reconfirm' that you intend to be on the flight. If you don't do this the airline can delete your name from the passenger list and you could lose your seat. You don't have to reconfirm the first flight on your itinerary or if your stopover is less than 72 hours. It doesn't hurt to reconfirm more than once.

Restrictions Discounted tickets often have various restrictions on them – advance purchase is the most usual one (see Apex). Others are restrictions on the minimum and maximum period you must be away, such as a minimum of 14 days or a maximum of one year. See Cancellation Penalties.

Standby A discounted ticket where you only fly if there is a seat free at the last moment. Standby fares are usually only available on domestic routes.

Tickets Out An entry requirement for many countries is that you have an onward or return ticket, in other words, a ticket out of the country. If you're not sure what you intend to do next, the easiest solution is to buy the cheapest onward ticket to a neighbouring country or a ticket from a reliable airline which can later be refunded if you do not use it.

Transferred Tickets Airline tickets cannot be transferred from one person to another. Travellers sometimes try to sell the return half of their ticket, but officials can ask you to prove that you are the person named on the ticket. This is unlikely to happen on domestic flights, but on international flights tickets may be compared with passports.

Travel Agencies Travel agencies vary widely and you should ensure you use one that suits your needs. Some simply handle tours, while full-service agencies handle everything from tours and tickets to car rental and hotel bookings. A good one will do all these things and can save you a lot of money, but if all you want is a ticket at the lowest possible price, then you really need an agency specialising in discounted tickets. A discounted ticket agency, however, may not be useful for other things, like hotel bookings.

Travel Periods Some officially discounted fares, Apex fares in particular, vary with the time of year. There is often a low (off-peak) season and a high (peak) season. Sometimes there's an intermediate or shoulder season as well. At peak times, when everyone wants to fly, not only will the officially discounted fares be higher, but so will unofficially discounted fares; or there may simply be no discounted tickets available. Usually, the fare depends on your outward flight – if you depart in the high season and return in the low season, you pay the high-season fare. ∎

---

return ticket. Standard fares in the high season are about UK£1550, US$3000, A$3100. An RTW might take you directly to Shannon or Dublin or as a sidetrip from London. Official airline RTW tickets are usually put together by a combination of two or more airlines, and permit you to fly anywhere you want on their route systems so long as you do not backtrack. Other restrictions are that you (usually) must book the first sector in advance and cancellation penalties then apply. There may be restrictions on how many stops you are permitted and usually the tickets are valid for 90 days up to a year from the date of the first outbound flight. An alternative type of RTW ticket is one put together by a travel agent using a combination of discounted tickets.

Travellers with Special Needs

If you've broken a leg, are vegetarian or require a special diet, are travelling in a wheelchair, taking a baby, terrified of flying, or whatever, let the airline staff know as soon as possible so that they can make the necessary arrangements. Remind them when you reconfirm your booking (at least 72 hours before departure) and again when you check in at the airport. It may also be worth ringing round the airlines before you make your booking to find out how they can handle your particular needs.

Airports and airlines can be helpful, but they do need advance warning. Most international airports will provide escorts from the check-in desk to the aeroplane where needed, and there should be ramps, lifts, accessible toilets and reachable phones. Aircraft toilets, on the other hand, are likely to present a problem; travellers should discuss this with the airline at an early stage and, if necessary, with their doctor.

Guide dogs for the blind will often have to travel in a specially pressurised baggage compartment with other animals, away from their owner; smaller guide dogs, however, may be admitted to the cabin. All guide dogs will be subject to the same quarantine laws (six months in isolation etc) as any other animal when entering or returning to countries free of rabies.

Deaf travellers can ask for airport and in-flight announcements to be written down for them.

Children under two travel for 10% of the standard fare (or free on some airlines) as long as they don't occupy a seat. They don't get a baggage allowance either. 'Skycots' should be provided by the airline if requested in advance; these will take a child weighing up to about 10 kg. Children aged between two and 12 years can usually occupy a seat for half to two-thirds of the full fare, and do get a baggage allowance. Pushchairs can often be taken as hand luggage.

To/From the UK

Aer Lingus is the main operator between the UK and the Republic of Ireland. British Airways Express flies to Belfast in Northern Ireland and to Dublin in the South. Dublin is linked by a variety of airlines to several cities in the UK.

Trailfinders (☎ 0171-937 5400), 194 Kensington High St, London W8 (nearest tube station, High St Kensington), produces an illustrated brochure which includes air-fare details. STA Travel (☎ 0171-937 9962), 74 Old Brompton Rd, London SW7 (nearest tube station, South Kensington) has a number of branches in the UK. Look in the listings of magazines like *Time Out*, plus the Sunday papers and *Exchange & Mart* for ads. Also look out for the free magazines widely available in London – start by looking outside the main railway stations and the tube stations.

There is a £5 departure tax from Britain to Ireland (and to other countries in the European Union).

Republic of Ireland There are flights between Dublin and all the major London airports. Aer Lingus and British Midland Airways fly from Heathrow, Aer Lingus and Cityflyer/British Airways Express fly from Gatwick, Ryanair flies from Gatwick, Luton and Stansted, Virgin Atlantic flies from London City Airport, Britannia Airways flies from Luton and Air UK flies from Stansted. Connections are generally frequent; in the summer Aer Lingus has over 15 Heathrow-Dublin services daily and British Midland another seven or eight.

The regular one-way economy fare from London to Dublin is £95, but advance-purchase fares are available offering round-trip tickets for as low as £50 to £75. These should be booked well in advance as seats are often limited.

Heathrow can be reached by airport bus or by the underground. There are regular train services to Gatwick from Victoria Station; there are also regular trains between Stansted and Liverpool St Station. From London City Airport there are shuttlebuses to Liverpool St Station and to Canary Wharf.

UK addresses and London phone numbers are:

Aer Lingus
   228 Regent St, London W1R 5TA (☎ 0181-759 2525)

Air UK
Stansted House, Stansted Airport, Essex
(☎ 01345-666777)
British Airways
Victoria Station Concourse, London SW1V 1JT
156 Regent St, London W1R 5TA
Plus other British Airways Travel Shops in
London and throughout Britain (☎ 0181-897
4000)
British Midland Airways
PO Box 60, Donington Hall, Castle Donington,
Derby DE7 2SB (☎ 0181-745 7321)
Ryanair
235-37 Finchley Rd, London NW3 6LS
(☎ 0171-435 7101)
Virgin Atlantic
London City Airport, Royal Docks, London E16
2PX (☎ 01293-747146)

Other places in the British Isles with flights to Dublin are:

Birmingham:	Aer Lingus, British Midland, Ryanair
Blackpool:	Manx Airlines
Bristol:	Aer Lingus
Cardiff:	Manx Airlines
East Midlands:	Aer Lingus
Edinburgh:	Aer Lingus
Glasgow:	Aer Lingus, Ryanair
Isle of Man:	Manx Airlines
Jersey:	Manx Airlines, Aer Lingus, Jersey European
Leeds/Bradford:	Aer Lingus
Liverpool:	Manx Airlines, Ryanair
Luton:	Ryanair, Britannia Airways
Manchester:	Aer Lingus, Ryanair, Loganair, Manx Airlines
Newcastle-upon-Tyne:	Aer Lingus, Gill Air

Fares between Manchester and Dublin are similar to London-Dublin fares but other connections can be much more expensive.

Other cities in Ireland with air connections from the UK include Cork, Galway, Killarney, Shannon and Sligo.

Northern Ireland There are flights from some regional airports in Britain to the convenient Belfast City Airport (☎ 01232-457745), virtually in the centre of the city, but everything else goes to Belfast International Airport (☎ 01849-422888), in Aldergrove 30 km north of the city.

Belfast has a regular Cityflyer/British Airways Express shuttle service from London Heathrow. Costs on the shuttle range from as low as £74 for a saver off-peak one-way or £125 for an advance-purchase return to as high as £108 for a regular one way with no restrictions.

British Midland Airways offer similar fares, but Britannia Airways (Belfast International) and Manx Airlines/British Airways Express (Belfast City) fly from Luton to Belfast from £43. Luton Airport is only 45 minutes north of London. There are also connections between Belfast and other centres including flights to and from the convenient Belfast City Airport.

To/From Europe
Discount charter flights are often available to full-time students aged under 30 and all young travellers aged under 26 (you need an ISIC or EYC card; see Useful Organisations in the Facts for the Visitor chapter) and are available through large student travel agencies.

Dublin is connected with major centres in Europe. From Paris, the standard return fare to Dublin is FF1440, to Belfast (via London) FF1930. Other places in Europe with connections to Dublin are:

Amsterdam, Netherlands:	Aer Lingus
Barcelona, Spain:	Iberia
Brussels, Belgium:	Aer Lingus, Sabena
Cologne, Germany:	Lufthansa
Copenhagen, Denmark:	Aer Lingus, SAS
Dusseldorf, Germany:	Aer Lingus
Frankfurt, Germany:	Aer Lingus, Lufthansa
Lisbon, Portugal:	TAP
Madrid, Spain:	Aer Lingus, Iberia
Malaga, Spain:	Viva Air
Milan, Italy:	Aer Lingus, Alitalia
Moscow, Russia:	Aeroflot
Munich, Germany:	Lufthansa, Ryanair
Paris, France:	Aer Lingus, Air France
Rome, Italy:	Aer Lingus, Alitalia
Zurich, Switzerland:	Aer Lingus

To/From North America
Flights from North America can now put down in Dublin as well as Shannon, but because competition on flights to London is so much fiercer it will generally be cheaper

to fly to London first. From Ireland to the USA, Virgin Atlantic via London is often the cheapest option.

Aer Lingus connects Dublin (and Shannon) with Baltimore, Boston, Chicago, Cleveland, Detroit, Los Angeles, New Orleans, New York, Orlando, San Francisco and Washington DC. Its New York office (☎ 212-557 1110 or 1-800-223 6537) is at 122 East 42nd St, New York. In Canada Aer Lingus can be contacted by calling ☎ 1-800 223 6537, although it doesn't actually fly to Canada. The only other US operators with direct connections to Ireland are Delta Airlines (☎ 1-800 2414141), which operates Atlanta-Shannon-Dublin, linking into its huge US network, and Aeroflot which flies to Shannon from Washington DC, Miami and Chicago. From Vancouver, Montreal and Toronto in Canada there are direct flights to Ireland on Air Canada and Canadian Airlines.

During the summer high season the round trip between New York and Dublin with Aer Lingus costs US$780 midweek or US$800 at weekends. Usually there are advance-purchase fares offered early in the year which allow you to fly from New York to Dublin for just under US$700 return. In the low season, discount return fares from New York to London will be in the US$450 to US$500 range, in the high season US$600 to US$700. From the west coast fares to London will cost from around US$150 more.

Check the Sunday travel sections of papers like the *New York Times, Los Angeles Times, Chicago Tribune* or *San Francisco Chronicle-Examiner* for the latest fares. The *Toronto Globe & Mail*, the *Toronto Star* or the *Vancouver Sun* will have similar details from Canada. Offices of Council Travel or STA Travel in the USA or Travel CUTS in Canada are good sources of reliable discounted tickets. The magazine *Travel Unlimited* (PO Box 1058, Allston, Massachusetts 02134) publishes details of the cheapest air fares and courier possibilities for destinations all over the world from the USA.

To/From Australia & New Zealand

Excursion or Apex fares from Australia or New Zealand to Britain can have a return flight to Dublin tagged on at no extra cost. Return fares from Australia vary from around A$1600 (low season) to A$2900 (high season) but there are often short-term special deals available. STA Travel and Flight Centres International are good sources of reliable discounted tickets in Australia or New Zealand. The cheapest fares from New Zealand will probably take the eastbound route via the USA but a Round-the-World ticket may be cheaper than a return. Aer Lingus (☎ 02-321 9123) has an office in Sydney at 64 York St, Sydney 2000. In New Zealand call World Aviation Systems (☎ 09-3794 455), Auckland.

SEA

There is a great variety of services from France and Britain to Ireland using modern car ferries. There are often special deals, return fares and other money-savers worth investigating.

Want to travel free? On some routes the cost for a car includes up to four or five passengers at no additional cost. If you can hitch a ride in a less than full car, it costs the driver nothing extra.

To/From the UK

The Britrail Seapass is an extension of a normal Britrail Pass and permits a return sea crossing to Ireland on top of unlimited use of British Rail services. This pass can only be purchased outside the UK. The Inter-Rail pass gives a reduction on services from Holyhead or Fishguard in Wales to Dun Laoghaire or Rosslare in Ireland. Irish Ferries offer a 50% discount to travellers with a Travelsave stamp in their ISIC card (see the Facts for the Visitor chapter).

There are services from eight ports in England, Scotland and Wales (and from the Isle of Man) to six ports in Ireland. The shipping lines are as follows:

Hoverspeed SeaCat
> Sea Containers Scotland, 20 Upper Ground, London SE1 9PF – for services from Stranraer to Belfast by catamaran (☎ 01304-240101)

Irish Ferries
> 150 New Bond St, London W1Y 0AQ – for services from Holyhead and Pembroke (☎ 0171-491 8682)

Isle of Man Steam Packet
> Imperial Buildings, Douglas, Isle of Man – for services from Douglas (☎ 01624-661661)

Norse Irish Ferries
> North Brocklebank Dock, Bootle, Merseyside L20 1BY – for services from Liverpool to Belfast (☎ 0151-944 1010)

P&O
> Cairnryan, Stranraer, Wigtownshire DG9 8RF – for services from Cairnryan to Larne (☎ 01581-200276)

Stena Sealink
> Charter House, Park St, Ashford, Kent TN24 8EX – for services from Holyhead, Fishguard and Stranraer (☎ 01233-647047)

Swansea Cork Ferries
> Ferryport, Kings Dock, Swansea, West Glamorgan SA1 8RU – for services from Swansea (☎ 01792-456116)

There are some interesting possibilities for those who are also touring the UK. Figures quoted are one-way fares for a single adult, for two adults with a car and for four adults with a car.

Swansea to Cork The 10-hour crossing costs £27/185/185 at peak times; the ferry doesn't operate in February.

Fishguard & Pembroke to Rosslare These popular short crossings take 3½ hours (from Fishguard) or 4½ hours (from Pembroke) and cost as much as £28/189/189 on peak season weekends; at other times of year the cost can drop as low as £20/79/79. The high-speed catamaran crossing from Fishguard takes just over 1½ hours and costs £34/199/199 on peak-season weekends.

Holyhead to Dublin & Dun Laoghaire The crossing takes 3½ hours and costs £27/184/184 at peak-season weekends, down to £19/84/84 in the off season. The high-speed catamaran crossing from Holyhead to Dun Laoghaire takes a little over 1½ hours and costs from £22/159/159 to £26/189/189.

Liverpool & Heysham to Belfast The Norse Irish Ferries overnight service is not heavily promoted but it's easy to get to Liverpool from London. The trip costs £50/180/220 at peak times. There are also the Isle of Man Steam Packet services from Liverpool and Heysham via Douglas (Isle of Man). A small car costs £75 in the peak season, passengers cost £40 each.

Stranraer to Belfast The SeaCat service uses a high-speed catamaran to race across in just 1½ hours at a cost of £23/179/197 at peak times.

Stranraer & Cairnryan to Larne There are as many as 15 sailings daily on the Stranraer-Larne route which takes about 2½ hours and cost £34/170/170 at peak times, down to as low as £20/115/115 at other times. The Cairnryan-Larne route takes 2¼ hours and costs £44/250/250 at peak times down to £28/90/90.

To/From France

Le Havre to Rosslare takes 20 hours and in the peak season the cost of this trip can range from a low of FF600/2525/2830 to as much as FF1050/4740/5355. Cherbourg to Rosslare is faster at 17½ hours but the cost is the same. From May to September there are ferries from Le Havre to Cork taking 20½ hours, again at the same fare. There are also Roscoff to Cork services June to September, taking 15 hours and once again at the same price.

These services are all operated by Irish Ferries and some can be used by Eurail pass holders. In France contact Transports et Voyages (☎ 1-42 66 90 90), 8 rue Auber, 75009 Paris. Inter-Rail passes also give reductions on these routes.

LAND & SEA

The relatively low cost of air fares from Britain make taking the bus or train hardly worth the hassle. The Bus Éirann buses are old and cramped, and there are frequent delays. Unless you go from London, the train usually involves horrific connections and hanging around in the dead of night too.

Bus Éireann and National Express operate Eurolines and Supabus services direct from London and other UK centres to Dublin, Belfast and other cities. For details in London contact Eurolines (☎ 0171-730 8235), 52 Grosvenor Gardens, Victoria, London SW1W or National Express (☎ 01990-808080), Victoria Coach Station, Buckingham Palace Rd, London SW1W. Slattery's (☎ 0171-730 3666), 28 Elizabeth St, beside Victoria Coach Station, is an Irish bus company with routes from Bristol, Leeds, London, Liverpool, Manchester and north Wales to Dublin, Galway, Limerick, Tipperary, Tralee, Waterford, Ennis and Listowel. It has another office (☎ 0171-482 1604) at 162 Kentish Town Rd, London NW5 2AG.

London to Dublin takes about 12 hours and costs £32 one way or £49 return during the summer and Christmas peak periods.

London to Belfast takes about 13 hours and the standard fare is £40 one way or £59 return but there are discount fares available.

It's also possible to combine a rail and ferry ticket. From London to Dun Laoghaire takes 9½ hours and costs £59 return (or £49 if you do the overnight crossing) at peak times.

TOURS

There are numerous companies offering general or special-interest tours of Ireland. See your travel agent, check the small ads in newspaper travel pages or contact Bord Fáilte (Irish Tourist Board) and the Northern Ireland Tourist Board (or the British Tourist Authority) for the names of tour operators.

In the USA there are a number of companies offering whirlwind coach tours of Ireland. American Express Vacations (☎ 800-446-6234, 404-368 5100) have 10 and 12-day packages and can be contacted at Box 1525, Fort Lauderdale, Florida 33302. Similar deals can be found with TWA Getaway Vacations (☎ 609-985 4100), 10 E Stow Rd, Marlton, New Jersey 08053. More-expensive tours are operated by Abercrombie & Kent (☎ 800-323 7308, 708-954 2944), 1520 Kensington Rd, Illinois 60521, and include accommodation in castles and country houses.

From the UK, CIE Tours International (☎ 0181-667 0011), 185 London Rd, Croydon, London CR0 2RJ, does four-day to eight-day coach tours plus a seven-day tour that includes the North.

LEAVING IRELAND

There is an airport departure tax but it is built into the price of the ticket. There's no departure tax if you leave by ferry. See under Money in the Facts for the Visitor chapter for details of how to reclaim value-added tax (VAT) when you depart.

WARNING

The information in this chapter is particularly vulnerable to change: prices for international travel are volatile, routes are introduced and cancelled, schedules change, special deals come and go, and rules and visa requirements are amended. Airlines and governments seem to take a perverse pleasure in making price structures and regulations as complicated as possible. You should check directly with the airline or a travel agent to

make sure you understand how a fare (and ticket you may buy) works. In addition, the travel industry is highly competitive and there are many lurks and perks.

The upshot of this is that you should get opinions, quotes and advice from as many airlines and travel agents as possible before you part with your hard-earned cash. The details given in this chapter should be regarded as pointers and are not a substitute for your own careful, up-to-date research.

Getting Around

On the map, travelling around Ireland looks simple enough – the distances are short and there's a network of roads and railways – but in practice there are a few problems. In Ireland, from A to B is never a straight line and there are always a great many intriguing diversions to make. Public transport is often expensive (particularly train services), infrequent or both. Plus, public transport simply does not reach many of the interesting places so having your own transport can be a major advantage – though trying to follow the road signs has its own difficulties.

It's worth considering car rental for at least a part of your trip. However, even if you're not driving, with a mix of buses, the occasional taxi, plenty of time, walking and sometimes hiring a bicycle, you can get to just about anywhere.

DISCOUNT PASSES

Eurail passes are valid for train travel in the Republic of Ireland – but not in Northern Ireland – and entitle you to a reduction on Bus Éireann's three-day Irish Rambler ticket (see below). They are also valid on Irish Ferries between France (Cherbourg and Le Havre) and the Republic (Rosslare and Cork). The Eurail pass is only usable by non-Europeans who have been in Europe for less than six months.

Inter-Rail passes offer a 50% reduction on train travel within Ireland and discounts on Irish Ferries and Stena Sealink connecting ferries.

For IR£8.50 full-time students can have a Travelsave Stamp affixed to their ISIC card. This gives a 50% discount on Iarnród Éireann (Irish Rail), and 15% on Bus Éireann services for fares over IR£1. See under Useful Organisations in the Facts for the Visitor chapter.

There is a variety of unlimited-travel tickets for buses and trains, in the North and South.

Irish Rambler tickets are available from Bus Éireann for bus-only travel within the Republic of Ireland. They cost IR£28 (three days), IR£68 (eight days) or IR£98 (15 days). Bus Éireann's Boomerang service allows you to buy a return ticket for the cost of a one-way ticket but you can only travel on Tuesday, Wednesday and Thursday. It's valid for one month.

For train-only travel within the Republic there is the Irish Explorer ticket which costs IR£60 (five days), while the Irish Rover ticket entitles you to travel in the North as well and costs IR£75 (five days). A bus-and-rail version of the Irish Explorer ticket costs IR£90 (eight days).

Finally, the Emerald Card gives you unlimited travel throughout Ireland on all scheduled services of Iarnród Éireann, Northern Ireland Railways, Bus Éireann, Dublinbus, Ulsterbus and Citybus. The card costs IR£105 (or pounds sterling equivalent) for eight days or IR£180 for 15 days. Children under 16 pay half fare on all these passes.

You can buy the passes after you arrive in Ireland, but they only make economic sense if you're planning to travel around Ireland at the speed of light.

If you're going to be staying in hostels then it's worth considering the Slow Coach (☎ 01-679 2684), 1-2 Aston Place, Temple Bar, Dublin 2, which is operated in association with An Óige and Independent Holiday Hostels. For IR£89 you can travel by bus around Ireland from hostel to hostel with no time limit on when you complete your trip.

AIR

Ireland is too small for flying to be necessary, but there are flights between Dublin and Cork, Galway, Knock, Shannon, Sligo, Waterford and other centres. Most journeys within Ireland take between 30 and 40 minutes. The two main companies operating within the country, as well as handling international flights, are Aer Lingus (☎ 01-844 4777) and Ryanair (☎ 01-677 4422). Aer Lingus has offices in Dublin, Cork, Belfast, Limerick and Shannon. Ryanair's head office is in Dublin, with ticket offices at Dublin, Cork, Shannon, Waterford, Galway, Knock and Kerry airports.

One useful air service is the short flight across to the Aran Islands. See the Galway chapter for details.

BUS

Bus Éireann (☎ 01-836 6111), Busáras, Store St, Dublin 1, is the Republic's bus line, with services all over the South and to the North. All services are non smoking. Fares are not much more than one-third the regular railway fares, and special deals are often available such as cheaper midweek return tickets. Bear in mind that the winter bus schedule is often drastically reduced and many routes simply disappear after September The national timetable only costs 50p, but it doesn't include the fares. Details of unlimited-travel Rambler Tickets are given in the Discount Deals section earlier.

Private buses sometimes compete with Bus Éireann, and sometimes run where the national buses are irregular or absent. The larger ones will usually carry bikes free but always check in advance. Some of the private companies are properly licensed and all passengers are insured, but if this is going to worry you then ask beforehand.

Ulsterbus (☎ 01232-333000/320011), Bus Station, Oxford St, Belfast BT1, is the service in the North. An Ulsterbus Freedom of Northern Ireland Ticket gives you unlimited travel on Ulsterbus and Citybus services for one day for £9 or seven consecutive days for £28. There are no private bus companies in the North (partly for fear of possible paramilitary extortion rackets), though this may change if the peace process continues.

Sample one-way bus fares, travelling times and frequency Monday to Saturday (services are fewer on Sunday) are:

Dublin-Cork
    IR£12, 4 hours 40 minutes, 6 daily
Dublin-Limerick
    IR£10, 3 hours, 5 daily
Cork-Limerick
    IR£9, 2 hours, 5 daily

Killarney-Cork
    IR£8.80, 2 hours, 5 daily
Derry-Belfast
    £16, 1 hour 40 minutes, 5 daily
Derry-Cork
    £17.20, 11 hours, 2 daily
Derry-Galway
    £14, 6 hours 30 minutes, 1 daily
Limerick-Killarney
    IR£9.70, 2 hours 25 minutes, 3 daily
Limerick-Rosslare
    IR£13, 4 hours, 3 daily
Limerick-Donegal
    IR£16, 6 hours, 2 daily
Galway-Limerick
    IR£9.30, 2 hours 25 minutes, 3 daily

Local country buses can work out quite expensive, and services are usually infrequent. From Bantry in south-west Cork, for example, there is only one bus a week running the 26-km journey to the last village on the Sheep's Head Peninsula, and the half-hour journey costs over IR£6. The private buses in County Donegal are a notable exception; Feda O'Donnell buses, for example, charge IR£4 for any journey within the county, though these journeys can be very time consuming.

TRAIN

Iarnród Éireann (Irish Rail) (☎ 01-836 6222), Connolly Station, Amiens St, Dublin 1, operates trains on routes which fan out from Dublin. Although trains will get you to the major urban centres faster than buses, the rail system is not as extensive. There are, for example, no direct connections between Waterford and Cork, or Limerick and Galway. Distances, however, are short in Ireland and the longest trip you can make by train from Dublin is just over four hours to Tralee.

Regular one-way fares from Dublin include Belfast IR£14, Cork IR£32 and Galway IR£24. As with buses, special fares are often available and a midweek return ticket is often not much more than the single fare. Travelling by train on a single ticket is expensive, and it's worth considering how to use a return ticket. First-class tickets cost IR£4 to IR£8 more than the standard fare for a single journey. Ordinary seats can be

Irish Railway Routes

0   25   50 km

reserved for IR£1. If you're under 26 you can get a Faircard for IR£8.50 which gives you a 50% discount on regular intercity fares. For people over 26, the Weekender card offers one-third off the price of intercity travel between Friday and Tuesday.

As well as Connolly Station, enquiries can be made at Iarnród Travelcentre, 35 Lower Abbey St, Dublin 1.

Northern Ireland Railways (☎ 01232-899411), Belfast Central Station, East Bridge St, Belfast BT1 3PB, has four routes from Belfast. One of them links with the system in the South via Newry to Dublin; the other three go east to Bangor, north-east to Larne and north-west to Derry (also called Londonderry) via Coleraine.

CAR & MOTORBIKE

As in Britain, driving in the Republic and the North is on the left and you should only overtake on the outside (to the right) of the

vehicle ahead of you. Safety belts must be worn by the driver and front-seat passengers; in the North passengers in the rear must also wear a safety belt. Children under 12 are not allowed to sit on the front seats. Motorcyclists and their passengers must wear helmets. Minor roads may sometimes be potholed and will often be very narrow, but the traffic is rarely heavy except as you go through popular tourist or busy commercial towns.

Speed limits in the North and South are generally the same as in Britain: 70 mph (112 km/h) on motorways, 60 mph (96 km/h) on other roads and 30 mph (48 km/h) or as signposted in towns. These limits tend to be treated with some disdain in the South. On the quiet, narrow, winding rural roads it's advisable to stick to the speed limit: head-on collisions are not unheard of and there may be a person walking or an animal grazing beside the road just around the next bend.

Roadsigns

When you're travelling around Ireland you'll need a good road map because, as you'll soon come to realise, the roadsigns have to be treated with a certain amount of healthy scepticism, particularly once you get off the motorways and main highways into remoter areas.

There are three main kinds of roadsigns. Those with white lettering on a green background are found on all major routes, with distances given clearly in kilometres. Brown signs with white lettering are used to indicate local tourist offices, sights, accommodation and other facilities. Black-on-white signs are the most problematical for visitors – the older ones give distances in miles, while the newer ones give distances in kilometres; you can usually tell which is which because the newer ones have 'km' after the number while the older ones just have the number.

Sometimes you'll see a sign for your destination, then, as you travel further, you'll see signs to other places at road junctions, but not to where you want to go. At some road junctions there may be no sign at all. This is when a good map comes in handy. As you continue, you may see another sign to your destination – or you may not. Assuming you've gone in the right direction, you could arrive at your destination without having seen another sign for it.

Occasionally, when you do find one, it could be pointing in the wrong direction. This is sometimes the work of pranksters, but another explanation given is that these signposts are so close to the road that heavy vehicles hit the signs as they pass and twist them around. ∎

The Irish can't seem to make up their minds on metrication. In the Republic, speed limits are in miles per hour (though from Dublin airport to the city they are in km), distance signs appear in either km or miles, and most car speedometers are still imperial rather than metric. There used to be a useful distinction between the green signposts that gave distances in km as opposed to the older white signs that used miles, but now there are white signs using km as well!

In the North, speed limits and other laws are as in Britain.

There are parking meters in Dublin and a handful of other cities, but usually parking in car parks or other specified areas is regulated by 'pay and display' tickets or disc parking (you have a disc, available from newsagencies, which rotates to display the time you park your car). It is often loosely enforced in the South. Never leave valuables unattended or visible in your parked car in Dublin, and see the Dublin chapter for further car parking warnings.

In the North, beware of Control Zones in town centres, where, in order to avoid bombing of populated areas, cars absolutely must not be left unattended – you may come back to find that it's been blown up. You can also be fined for not locking your car. Double yellow lines by the roadside mean no parking at any time, and single yellow lines warn of restrictions – the only way to establish the exact restrictions is to find the nearby sign that spells them out. Red, white and blue kerbstones mean you're in a Protestant area; green, white and orange mean it's Catholic!

Petrol is a few pence cheaper in the North. Unleaded petrol is available throughout the North and South. Most service stations accept payment by credit card, but some smaller, remote ones will only take cash. The Automobile Association (AA) has offices in Belfast (☎ 01232-328924), Dublin (☎ 01-677 9481) and Cork (☎ 021-276922). The AA breakdown number in the Republic is ☎ 1800-667788; in the North ☎ 0800-887766. Also in the North, for members of the Royal Automobile Club (RAC) the breakdown number is ☎ 0800-828282.

Rental

Car rental in Ireland is expensive so you will often be better off making arrangements in your home country with some sort of package deal, and in high season it's wise to book ahead. Off season some companies simply discount all rates by about 25%; there are often special deals and the longer you hire the car the lower the relative daily rent. Some smaller companies make an extra daily charge if you go across the border, North or South. Most cars are manual; automatically operated ones are available at a greater fee.

In the Republic of Ireland typical weekly high-season (July and August) rental rates with insurance, collision-damage waiver (CDW), value-added tax (VAT) and unlimited distance are around IR£245 for a small car (Ford Fiesta), IR£290 for a medium-sized car (Toyota Corolla 1.3) and IR£340 for a larger car (Ford Mondeo). In the North, similar cars would cost about 10% more. Check that the posted price includes insurance, CDW and VAT. If you are travelling from the Republic into Northern Ireland it's important to be sure that your insurance covers journeys to the North.

People under 21 are not allowed to hire a car; for the majority of rental companies you have to be at least 23 and to have had a valid driving licence for a minimum of 12 months. Some companies will not rent to you if you're over 70 or 75. Your own licence is usually enough to hire a car for stays up to three months.

The international rental companies Avis, Budget, Hertz, Thrifty and the major local operators, Murray's Europcar and Dan Dooley, have offices all over Ireland. There are many smaller and local operators.

Motorbikes or mopeds are not available for rent.

BICYCLE
See under Cycling in the Activities chapter.

HITCHING
While Lonely Planet doesn't recommend hitching – it's never entirely safe in any country, and the local maniac may not carry

an identifying badge – hitching in Ireland is generally easy. The major exceptions are in heavily touristed areas where the competition from other hitchers is severe and the cars are often full with families. In the Republic there are usually large numbers of Irish hitch-hikers on the road who use hitching as an everyday means of travel.

For visitors the usual hitching rules apply. Carry cardboard and a marker pen so you can make a sign showing where you're going. Try to look like a visitor and put your backpack out on view, ideally with a flag on it. Making yourself an obvious tourist is especially important in the North, and if the subject of the Troubles should come up in conversation it's probably best to exercise some diplomatic caution. Hitching between the Republic and the North has become easier since the start of the peace process and the opening of cross-border roads.

Women hitching alone should be extremely careful when choosing lifts – if in doubt, don't. Many local women hitch alone without serious problems, but a tourist is likely to be more at risk.

Sea Legs: Hitch-hiking the Coast of Ireland Alone by Rosita Boland (New Island Books) tells the tale of an Irishwoman's solo (yes, the Irish are always doing things against the rules) exploration of Ireland by thumb.

BOAT

There are many boat services to outlying islands off the west coast and across rivers. Some of the river services, like the ferry across the River Suir between Ballyhack in County Wexford and Passage East in County Waterford, make interesting little short cuts, particularly for cyclists. Cruises on the River Shannon and on the old canals are popular and there are a variety of trips on lakes and loughs.

If you ask at the tourist offices you will not always get the full information on boats because they won't recommend, or sometimes even mention, operators who don't fulfil all their regulations. The various boats to the Skellig Islands, for instance, do not exist as far

as official tourist literature is concerned, and if you ask about visiting Skellig Michael you will be directed to the Skellig Experience boat trip which doesn't actually land on the island. Details of unofficial boat trips are given under the relevant sections.

LOCAL TRANSPORT

There are comprehensive local bus networks in Dublin (Bus Átha Cliath), Belfast (Citybus) and some other larger towns. The Dublin Area Rapid Transport (DART) line in Dublin and the service from Belfast to Bangor are the only local railway lines. Taxis in Ireland tend to be expensive, but in Belfast and Derry there are share-taxi services operating rather like buses. There are metered taxis in Belfast, Cork, Dublin, Galway and Limerick, but in other places you will need to agree on the fare beforehand. If you book a taxi by telephone there may be a small pick-up charge.

TOURS

If your time is limited it might be worth considering an organised tour, though it is cheaper to see things independently and Ireland is small enough that you can get to even the most remote places in a few hours. Tours can be booked through travel agencies, tourist offices in the major cities, or directly through the tour companies themselves.

CIE Tours International (☎ 01-703 1888), 35 Lower Abbey St, Dublin 1, has coach tours of the South and North all departing from Dublin; the tours include accommodation, breakfast, dinner and discounts for people aged 55 and over. Its four-day 'Taste of Ireland' tour takes in Blarney, the Ring of Kerry, Killarney, the Cliffs of Moher and the region around the River Shannon for IR£229 (in the high season). Its other tours are from six to eight days in length.

Bus Éireann (☎ 01-836 6111) has day trips to various parts of the South between March and September, departing from the Busáras in Dublin.

Gray Line Tours (☎ 01-661 9666), 3 Clanwilliam Terrace, Grand Canal Quay, Dublin 2, has half-day, day and extended trips from Dublin and Limerick which can be booked through the tourist offices in those cities.

If you're backpacking, the excellent Slow Coach (☎ 01-679 2684), 1-2 Aston Place, Temple Bar, Dublin 2, provides a unique service. For IR£89 you can travel round Ireland, taking as long as you like and staying in hostels.

Tír na nóg Tours (☎ 01-836 4684), 21 Store St, Dublin 1, offers six-day and 12-day tours of the South and North, in 15-seater minibuses departing from Dublin. Accommodation en route is in hostels and a 12-day tour in the high season costs IR£279.

Emerald Experience (☎ 01-496 1302), 36 Grove Park, Rathmines, Dublin 2, also advertises tours in hostels. It has separate five-day tours of the South and North each costing IR£120; a combined tour costs IR£195. Buses leave from Isaacs, Avalon House or Kinlay House.

Republic of Ireland

The Republic of Ireland

HISTORY

The Irish Free State, as it was known until 1949, was established after the signing in December 1921 of the Anglo-Irish Treaty, between the British government and an Irish delegation led by Michael Collins. Eamon de Valera had been elected president of the new self-proclaimed republic in August, and he remained in Dublin during negotiations. He was not consulted before signing, and he was outraged when the delegates returned with what he and many other republicans regarded as a betrayal of the IRA's principles.

The Treaty was ratified in the *Dáil* (Irish assembly or lower house) in January 1922, and in June the country's first general election resulted in victory for the pro-Treaty forces. Fighting broke out two weeks later.

Amazingly, the Civil War was primarily about the oath of allegiance to the crown, rather than the exclusion of the six counties from the Irish Free State. Of the 400 or more pages of Dáil records on the Treaty debate, only seven deal with the issue of Ulster. The rest focus on the oath and the crown.

Collins was ambushed and shot dead in Cork by anti-Treaty forces, and de Valera was imprisoned by the new Free State government, under its new prime minister William Cosgrave, which went so far as to execute 77 of its former comrades. The Civil War ground to an exhausted halt in 1923.

After boycotting the Dáil for a number of years, de Valera founded a new party called Fianna Fáil (Warriors of Ireland) which won nearly half the seats in the 1927 election. De Valera and the other new *teachta Dála* (TDs, members of the Dáil) managed within weeks to enter the Dáil by the simple expedient of not taking the oath but signing in as if they had.

Fianna Fáil won a majority in the 1932 election, and remained in power for 16 years. De Valera introduced a new constitution in 1937, doing away with the oath and claiming sovereignty over the six counties of the North. In 1938 the UK renounced its right to use certain Irish ports for military purposes, which it had been granted under the Treaty. The South was therefore able to remain neutral in WW II.

In 1948 Fianna Fáil lost the general election to Fine Gael – the direct descendants of the first Free State government – in coalition with the new republican Clann an Poblachta. The new government declared the Free State to be a republic at last. Ireland left the British Commonwealth in 1949. In 1955 it became a member of the United Nations.

When Sean Lamass came to power in 1959 as successor to de Valera he sought to stem the continuing serious emigration by improving the country's economic prospects. By the mid-1960s his policies had been successful enough to reduce emigration to less than half what it had been in the mid-'50s, and many who had left began to return. He also introduced free secondary education.

In 1972 the Republic (along with Northern Ireland) became a member of the European Economic Community (EEC). At first, membership brought some measure of prosperity, but by the early 1980s Ireland was once more in economic difficulties and emigration rose again. By the early 1990s the Irish economy had begun to recover but unemployment has remained high.

The results of referenda in the 1980s on abortion and divorce left both illegal in the South. But socially, things are changing fast. While single mothers might still have a tough time in remote rural areas, in Dublin they're almost as commonplace as in London and no one bats an eyelid. The abortion debate rages on and people get very steamed up about it, but many Irish women quietly go to Britain to terminate their pregnancies every year. Divorce is still prohibited for the time being, but is unlikely to remain so, as more and more Irish families fall apart, especially in the cities.

In 1991 Mary Robinson was elected as president. Although her power is limited she

The Abortion Debate

Ireland continues to do its best to tie itself into knots over the thorny issue of abortion.

Prior to 1983, therapeutic abortions were legal, and doctors could use their discretion as to whether or not a pregnancy was 'life-threatening' for the woman. Abortion for any other reason, including severe malformation or pregnancy due to rape, was, and still is, not permitted.

In 1983, the law was tightened and incorporated into the constitution, but in such woolly terms that things went on much as before, with one remarkable exception: women could no longer be given any information about seeking abortions abroad. British phone books were duly taken out of libraries, and women's magazines were impounded at the airports.

While the trips to Liverpool abortion clinics continued unabated, Ireland held the moral high ground of protecting the unborn child at any cost – until 1992, when parents whose 14-year-old daughter had allegedly been raped by her friend's father took her to England for an abortion. They contacted the gardai to ask if tissue from the foetus could be collected and used in the prosecution of the alleged rapist. They were then issued with an injunction ordering them to bring the girl back, foetus intact, or face prosecution. All hell broke loose. The matter went to the Supreme Court, which fudged the issue by saying that the girl could travel to the UK for an abortion since she was suicidal.

Anti-abortion campaigners demanded that the High Court prevent women leaving the country to seek abortions abroad. The prospect opened up of pregnancy tests at airports. Others interpreted the High Court ruling to mean that abortion was now legal in Ireland if the woman was suicidal.

A referendum took place on the matter in 1992, on the same day as the general election. The right to travel abroad for an abortion was supported by a clear majority. The option of making abortion available to all women in Ireland was not offered.

In 1995 a new law was passed allowing doctors and pregnancy counselling services to give a pregnant woman the names and phone numbers of abortion clinics in Britain. However, they can't make appointments or arrangements with the clinics for the women.

The contentious issue of whether abortion should be allowed in Ireland continues to be debated. In the meantime, as Mary Harney, leader of the Progressive Democrats, once pointed out, though abortion is illegal in Ireland, an Irish woman is more likely to have an abortion than a woman in the Netherlands, where abortion is freely available. ∎

has wielded considerable informal influence on the government's social policies, contributing to a shift in attitudes away from the traditionally conservative positions on issues such as divorce, abortion and gay rights.

In 1994 the Fine Gael party, under the leadership of John Bruton, came to power in coalition with the Labour Party and the Democratic Left, after a crisis over the appointment of president to the High Court had destroyed the previous coalition and forced the resignation of the then Taoiseach, Albert Reynolds.

GOVERNMENT

The Republic has a parliamentary system of government loosely based on the British model. The parliament *(Oireachtas)* has a lower house known as the *Dáil* (pronounced 'doyle') and the prime minister is the *Taoiseach* (pronounced 'teashock'; the plural is *Taosigh*). The Dáil has 166 elected members and sits in Leinster House on Dublin's Kildare St. Members of the Irish parliament are known as *teachta Dála* (TDs). Currently the Dáil has a higher percentage of female members than does the House of Commons in Britain.

The upper house is the Senate or *Seanad* and senators are nominated by the Taoiseach or elected by university graduates and councillors from around the country. The Senate's functions are limited; senators debate on and pass legislation framed in the Dáil, but many critics claim it is merely a happy hunting ground for failed TDs.

The constitutional head of state is the president *(An tUachtaran)*, who is elected by popular vote for a seven-year term, but has little real power. The popular current incumbent is Mary Robinson.

The Republic's electoral system is proportional representation, a complex but fair system where voters mark the electoral candidates in order of preference. As first-preference votes are counted and candidates are elected, the voters' second and third choices are passed on to the various other candidates.

The principal political parties are Fianna Fáil and Fine Gael, although the Labour Party has been making great strides in recent years.

Founded by Eamon de Valera and other notables, Fianna Fáil has been the driving force in Irish politics since the early years of the state. Fianna Fáil has almost always won the greatest number of seats in general elections, and have usually been either in government or barely out of it. Fianna Fáil has always been a catch-all party, claiming to be the voice of the rural populace, urban workers and business community in turn with no apparent difficulty. Many of Ireland's most notable leaders have come from the party's ranks, including Eamon de Valera, Sean Lemass, Jack Lynch, and more recently the colourful and wily Charles Haughey and Albert Reynolds. The current party leader is Bertie Ahern. Fianna Fáil has in the past usually taken an extremely conservative line on social matters, particularly when it came to divorce, abortion and contraception.

Fine Gael's image has been clean cut, worthy, middle-class and university-educated.

Labour has been on the fringes of power for most of their existence, but have shared in various coalition governments with Fine Gael. Recently the Labour Party has moved to occupy the middle ground and attracts support from all classes of voters.

In 1980 a split in Fianna Fáil resulted in the formation of the small Progressive Democrat party led by Dessie O'Malley, which went into coalition with Fianna Fáil to form

Eamon de Valera, a Fianna Fáil founder

a government not long afterwards. The only other party of consequence is the left-wing Democratic Left.

Coalition has been a feature of most recent governments in the Republic, as the once mighty Fianna Fáil has found itself less and less able to muster the parliamentary majorities it used to command.

The national flag is the tricolour of green, white and orange, and the national symbol is the harp.

ECONOMY

While the Republic of Ireland is often regarded as a basically agricultural country, there has been much light industrial investment since the 1970s, and the majority of people today work in manufacturing or service industries. Big-spending governments in the 1970s and 1980s left a huge national debt which present governments are still having to cope with. However, since 1987 spending has been brought under control, and the debt is now at a sustainable level.

Many of the Republic's key economic indicators suggest that Ireland is one of

Europe's most buoyant economies. Inflation is currently low, running at around 3%. Exports continue to reach record levels and completely outstrip imports. In the period 1990-94 real gross domestic product (GDP) grew by an annual average of over 5%. This was among the highest growth rates in the world at a time when some of the world's richest countries were suffering. The average for the EU as a whole over the same period was 1.2%. The trade surplus for the Republic as a percentage of GDP is the largest in the developed world, a not inconsiderable achievement. It also means that Ireland's small open economy is heavily dependent on the state of the world economy. Britain is the main trading partner followed by the EU and the USA. Over the last decade or so the Republic has to some extent reduced its massive dependence on the British economy, which still absorbs 30% of Ireland's exports.

Irish governments have encouraged educational concentration on computers and software, and Irish firms have made imaginative use of new openings in the field. A computer user on the east coast of the USA, making an early morning phone call to a California software support system, may actually find themselves talking to a software specialist in Ireland. It's cheaper to bounce calls back over the Atlantic than to have people on call in Silicon Valley in the wee hours of the morning.

If it holds, the peace process will have a beneficial effect on the economy. Already the number of tourists to Ireland, North and South, has increased.

Despite what seems like a lot of good news, the Republic still has enormous economic problems, principally unemployment, which has been reduced but is still a huge 15% of the workforce. This situation and the incredible costs of social welfare and unemployment payments are problems that look set to continue for some time yet.

To make matters worse, emigration to Britain and the USA has ceased to be an effective safety valve, as these countries' economies have also been going through tough times. Given Ireland's dependence on trade, its unemployment problems almost certainly cannot be solved domestically and are dependent on a sustained international recovery, especially in Britain. Taxes are high in the Republic, and petrol, alcohol, tobacco, cars and luxury items are particularly expensive. Tourism is enormously important, and Ireland attracts visitors from all over Western Europe as well as from the English-speaking nations.

Dublin

Ireland's capital and its largest and most cosmopolitan city, Dublin is a city of great contrasts. Prosperous Georgian squares can quickly give way to areas where any sign of elegance has long since faded into decay. There's little modern architecture of any note. Dublin is a curious and colourful place, an easy city to like and a fine introduction to Ireland.

Since Ireland finally achieved independence in 1921, Dublin has had a new role as the capital of the country. Still one of the smallest European Union (EU) capitals, it's growing and modernising fast in spite of which it manages to remain a place with soul: the city's literary history seems to bump against you at every corner and the pubs are open to all comers. An evening with a succession of pints of Guinness, that noble black brew, is as much a part of the Dublin experience as the Georgian streets and the fine old buildings.

It's not only the pubs which are easily accessible. Dublin is a city on a human scale so it's easy to get around on foot. Accommodation is plentiful and varied, ranging from cheap and cheerful backpacker hostels to elegant five-star hotels. The food is also surprisingly varied, with dishes from every corner of the world as well as down-to-earth local specialities such as Irish stew or Dublin coddle. It's a city which fits comfortably, like a warm old coat; it may not always be fashionable, but it's always a pleasure to put on.

HISTORY

Dublin officially celebrated its millennium in 1988 but there were settlements here long before 988 AD. The first early Celtic habitation was on the banks of the River Liffey, and the city's Irish name, Baile Átha Cliath, 'the Town of the Hurdle Ford', comes from an ancient river crossing that can still be pinpointed today. St Patrick's Cathedral is said to be built on the site of a well used by Ireland's patron saint for early conversions in the 5th century.

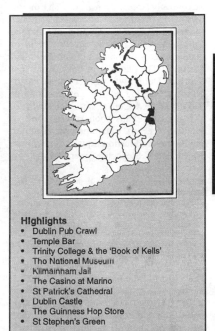

Highlights
- Dublin Pub Crawl
- Temple Bar
- Trinity College & the 'Book of Kells'
- The National Museum
- Kilmainham Jail
- The Casino at Marino
- St Patrick's Cathedral
- Dublin Castle
- The Guinness Hop Store
- St Stephen's Green

It was not until the Vikings turned up that Dublin became a permanent fixture. By the 9th century, raids from the north had become a fact of Irish life, but some of the fierce Danes chose to stay rather than simply rape, pillage and depart. They intermarried with the Irish and established a vigorous trading port at the point where the River Poddle joined the Liffey in a black pool, in Irish a *dubh linn*. Today there's little trace of the Poddle, which has been channelled underground and flows under St Patrick's Cathedral to dribble into the Liffey by the Capel St (or Grattan) Bridge.

Norman and then early English Dublin was still centred around the black pool which gave the city its name. The boom years came with the 18th century, the period of the Protestant Ascendancy when for a time London was the only larger city in the British Empire. As the city expanded, the nouveaux riches abandoned medieval Dublin and moved north across the river to a new Dublin of stately squares surrounded by fine Georgian mansions. The planning of this magnificent Georgian Dublin was assisted by the establishment in 1757 of the Commission for Making Wide & Convenient Streets!

The city's slums soon spread north in pursuit of the rich, who turned back south to new homes in Merrion Square, Fitzwilliam Square and St Stephen's Green.

In 1745 when James Fitzgerald, the earl of Kildare, commenced construction of Leinster House, his magnificent mansion south of the Liffey, he was mocked for this foolish move away from the centre and into the wilds. 'Where I go society will follow,' he confidently predicted and he was soon proved right. Today Leinster House is used as the Irish parliament building and it is right in the centre of modern Dublin.

The Georgian boom years of the 18th century were followed by more trouble and unrest, and the union with Britain in 1801, ending the separate Irish parliament, spelt the end of Dublin's century of dramatic

growth. Dublin entered the 20th century a downtrodden and dispirited place.

The Easter Rising of 1916 caused considerable damage to parts of central Dublin, particularly along O'Connell St where the GPO was gutted. The struggle between British forces and the IRA led to more damage to Dublin including the burning of the Custom House in 1921. A year later Ireland was independent but had tumbled into the Civil War which inflicted still more damage on the city, including the burning of the Four Courts in 1922 and a further bout of destruction for O'Connell St.

Peace finally came to Ireland but Dublin was exhausted – a shadow of its Georgian self. Today, however, Ireland's decline has bottomed out and the country's new role in the European Union holds out the prospect of better times to come. The city's expansion has continued south to Ballsbridge, Dun Laoghaire and beyond but the River Liffey has remained a rough dividing line between southern haves and northern have-nots.

ORIENTATION

Greater Dublin sprawls around the arc of Dublin Bay, bounded to the north by the hills at Howth and to the south by the Dalkey headland.

Dublin in the Movies

Dublin has made numerous movie appearances, particularly successfully in *The Commitments*, a bright and energetic 1991 hit about a north Dublin soul band which neatly captured north Dublin's scruffy atmosphere. The movie *My Left Foot* was as wonderful as the book it came from, *Down all the Days*. It also managed to make some interesting peregrinations around Dublin, including visits to John Mulligan's, the pub reputed to pull the best Guinness in Ireland. Renowned director John Huston's final film, *The Dead*, released in 1987, was based on a James Joyce story from *Dubliners*.

Kilmainham Jail was used as a set for the 1994 film *In the Name of the Father*, about the Guildford Four, wrongly convicted of planting a bomb which killed five people and only acquitted after 15 years in jail. Most recently, Trinity College featured in *Circle of Friends*, based on Maeve Binchy's romantic novel of the same name. *A Man of no Importance* starring Albert Finney is set in the Dublin of the early 1960s. Dublin Castle and Newman House are due to crop up as sets when *Moll Flanders* is released. ■

North of the River Liffey the important streets for visitors are O'Connell St, the major shopping thoroughfare, and Gardiner St, with many B&Bs. Many of the hostels are located in this area. The main bus station or Busáras and one of the two main railway stations are near the southern end of Gardiner St, which becomes rather run down as it continues north. Immediately south of the river is the intriguing old Temple Bar area and the expanse of Trinity College. Nassau St along the southern edge of the campus and pedestrianised Grafton St are the main shopping streets south of the river.

The post codes for central Dublin are Dublin 1 immediately north of the river and Dublin 2 immediately south. The posh Ballsbridge area south-east of the centre is Dublin 4.

Finding Addresses

Finding addresses in Dublin can be complicated by the tendency for street names to change every few blocks and for streets to be subdivided into upper and lower or north and south parts. It doesn't seem to matter if you put the definer in front of or behind the name – thus you can have Lower Baggot St or Baggot St Lower, South Anne St or Anne St South. Street numbering often runs up one side of a street and down the other, rather than having odd numbers on one side and even on the other.

INFORMATION
Tourist Offices

The Dublin Tourism and Bord Fáilte offices offer more-or-less identical services.

If you arrive by air or sea, you will find tourist offices at the airport and on the waterfront at Dun Laoghaire. In the city the Dublin Tourism office, 14 O'Connell St Upper, is open from 8.30 am to 8 pm Monday to Saturday and 10.30 am to 2 pm on Sunday in the summer months, 9 am to 5pm Monday to Saturday in winter, but it can get very crowded, with long queues for accommodation bookings and information. All three offices have the same phone number: ☎ 01-284 4768. Note that Dublin Tourism is due to move into St Andrews

Church in St Andrew's St near Trinity College, and may be there by the time you read this.

The head office of the Irish Tourist Board (☎ 01-676 5871, 01-602 4000) at Baggot St Bridge has an information desk and though it is less conveniently located – well to the south of the city centre, beyond St Stephen's Green – it is also much less crowded. The entrance is in Wilton Terrace.

The new Backpackers' Centre (☎ 01-836 4700), 22 Store St immediately opposite the Busáras, provides information on hostels, public transport, the Slow Coach, etc. It's open Monday to Friday from 10 am to 8 pm and at weekends from noon to 8 pm. It may have to relocate temporarily while building work goes on so if you can't see it, phone to find out where it's gone.

An Óige (☎ 01-830 4555) has its office at the hostel at 61 Mountjoy St, Dublin 7; it's open from 9.30 am to 5.30 pm Monday to Friday and 10 am to 12.30 pm on Saturday from April to September. The AA (☎ 01-677 9481) is at 23 Suffolk St, Dublin 2.

Travellers with disabilities can get help and advice from the National Rehabilitation Board (☎ 01-668 4181), 25 Clyde Road, Ballsbridge, Dublin 4. The Gay Switchboard (☎ 01-872 1055) is in Carmichael House, North Brunswick St, Dublin 7.

Money

The foreign-exchange counter at Dublin Airport is in the baggage collection area and is open for most flight arrivals. There are numerous banks around the centre with exchange facilities; the Bank of Ireland operates a bureau de change in Westmoreland Rd from 9 am to 9 pm Monday to Saturday and from 10 am to 7 pm on Sunday.

American Express and Thomas Cook are across the road from the Bank of Ireland and the Trinity College entrance. Thomas Cook is open from 9 am to 5.30 pm Monday to Saturday, while American Express opens from 9 am to 5 pm Monday to Friday and 9 am to noon on Saturday (the foreign-exchange desk stays open until 5 pm).

DUBLIN

DUBLIN

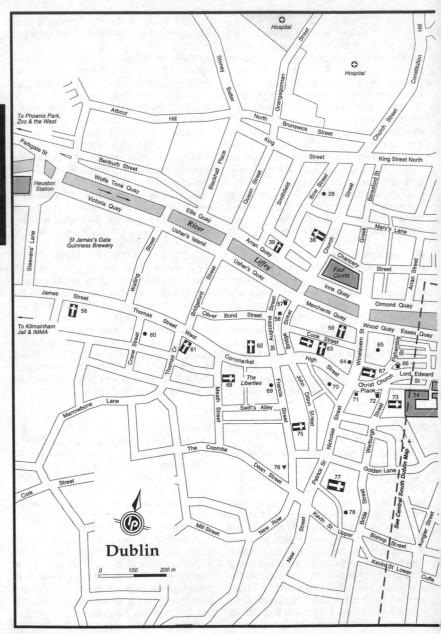

To Phoenix Park,
Zoo & the West

Parkgate St

Heuston
Station

Steevens' Lane

Arbour   Hill

North

Brunswick   Street

Hospital

Hospital

King

Street

King Street North

Constitution   Hill

Church   Street

Beresford St

Benburb Street

Blackhall Place

Queen   Street

Smithfield

Bow   Street

● 28

Greek   Street

Mary's Lane

Wolfe Tone Quay

Victoria Quay

Ellis Quay

River

Arran Quay

39 ✝

38 ✝

Church   Street

Chancery

Four
Courts

Street

Arran Street

Ormond Quay

St James's Gate
Guinness Brewery

Usher's Island

Liffey

Usher's Quay

Inns Quay

Merchants Quay

Wood Quay

Essex Quay

James   Street

To Kilmainham
Jail & IMMA

✝ 56

Watling   Street

Thomas   Street

Bridgefoot   Street

Oliver   Bond   Street

57 ✝
58 ✝

Bridge   St

St Augustine

59 ✝

Winetavern St

65 ●

Fishamble   St

66 ♠

● 60

West   Street

Crane   Street

Thomas   Cr

✝ 61

62 ✝✝

Cornmarket

Cook   Street
63 ✝✝

High   Street

64 ●

67 ●

Lord   Edward   St

Christ Church
Place

71 ●   72 ●

73 ✝

74

The
Liberties

✝ 68

69 ●

Meath   Street

Swift's Alley

Francis   Street

John   Dillon   Street

● 70

Nicholas   Street

Werburgh   Street

Marrowbone   Lane

✝ 75

Cork   Street

The   Coombe

Dean   Street

76 ▼

Golden Lane

Bride   Street

See Central South Dublin Map

Aungier Street

Dublin

0   100   200 m

Mill Street

New Row

Patrick   St

77 ✝

● 78

Kevin   St   Upper

New   Street

Bishop   Street

Kevin St Lower

Cuffe

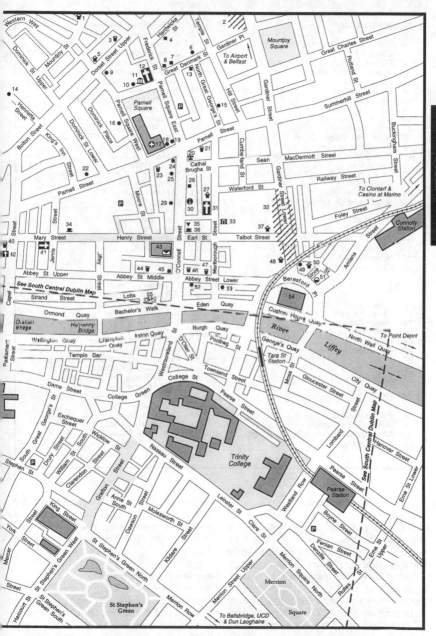

DUBLIN

PLACES TO STAY

1	Dublin International Youth Hostel
2	Cheap B&Bs
4	Waverley House & Sinclair House
5	Young Traveller Hostel
7	Barry's Hotel
8	Castle Hotel
13	Belvedere Hotel
24	Royal Dublin Hotel
26	Gresham Hotel
27	Marlborough Hostel
32	More cheap B&Bs
37	Cardijn Hostel
48	Globetrotters Tourist Hostel/Townhouse Guesthouse
50	Isaac's Hostel (Dublin Tourist Hostel)
58	Conrad Hotel
66	Kinlay House
71	Jurys Christ Church Inn

PLACES TO EAT

34	Bewley's Café
35	Beshoff's Fish & Chips
36	Kylemore Café
76	Old Dublin Restaurant

PUBS

3	Joxer Daly's
21	Fibber Magee's
23	Patrick Conway
40	Slattery's
44	Oval
46	Abbey Mooney's
47	Sean O'Casey's
57	Brazen Head
72	Lord Edward

OTHER

6	Belvedere College
9	National Wax Museum
10	Municipal Gallery of Modern Art (Hugh Lane Gallery)
11	Dublin Writers' Museum
12	Abbey Presbyterian Church
14	King's Inns
15	James Joyce Centre
16	Sinn Féin Bookshop
17	Rotunda Hospital
18	Ambassador Cinema
19	Gate Theatre
20	Telecom Éireann Telecentre
22	Laundry Shop
25	Aer Lingus
28	Irish Whiskey Corner
29	Dublin Bus (Bus Átha Cliath) Office
30	Tourist Office
31	St Mary's Pro-Cathedral
33	Tyrone House
38	St Michan's Church
39	St Paul's Church
41	St Mary's Church
42	St Mary's Abbey
43	GPO
45	Eason's Bookshop
49	Rent-a-Bike (Bike Store)
51	Bus Station (Busáras)
52	Irish Rail
53	Abbey Theatre
54	Custom House
55	C Harding Bicycle Shop
56	St James's Church
59	St Francis' Church (Adam & Eve's Church)
60	Guinness Hop Store
61	St Catherine's Church (Protestant)
62	Church of St John & Augustine
63	St Audoen's Churches
64	Dublinia
65	Dublin Corporation Civic Offices
67	Christ Church Cathedral
68	St Catherine's Church (Catholic)
69	Tivoli Theatre
70	Tailor's Hall
73	St Werburgh's Church
74	Dublin Castle
75	St Nicholas of Myra Church
77	St Patrick's Cathedral
78	Marsh's Library

Post & Telecommunications

Dublin's famed GPO is on O'Connell St, north of the river, and is open from 8 am to 8 pm Monday to Saturday, 10.30 am to 6 pm Sunday and holidays. South of the river the handy post office in Anne St South, just off Grafton St, is well patronised by foreign visitors and used to dealing with their curious requests. The Telecom Éireann Telecentre (☎ 01-661 1111), Findlater House, O'Connell St Upper, has public phones that use cash or phonecards; the staff there will also help you with any queries or problems you may have regarding the phone system and how it works. The telephone area code for Dublin is 01.

Embassies & Consulates

You will find embassies of the following countries in Dublin. For citizens of New Zealand and Singapore, the closest embassies are in London.

Australia
    6th floor, Fitzwilton House, Wilton Terrace, Dublin 2 (☎ 676 1517)
Canada
    65-68 St Stephen's Green, Dublin 2 (☎ 478 1988)
Denmark
    121 St Stephen's Green, Dublin 2 (☎ 475 6404)
France
    36 Ailesbury Rd, Dublin 4 (☎ 260 1666)
Germany
    31 Trimleston Ave, Booterstown, Dublin 4 (☎ 269 3011)
Italy
    63 Northumberland Rd, Dublin 4 (☎ 660 1744)
Japan
    Merrion Shopping Centre, Dublin 4 (☎ 269 4244)
Netherlands
    160 Merrion Rd, Dublin 4 (☎ 269 3444)
New Zealand
    (in London) New Zealand House, Haymarket, London SW1 4QT (☎ 0171-930 8422)

Norway
    44 Molesworth St, Dublin 2 (☎ 662 1800)
Portugal
    Knocksinna House, Foxrock, Dublin 18 (☎ 289 4416)
Singapore
    (in London) 2 Wilton Crescent, London SW1X 8RW (☎ 0171-235 8315)
Spain
    17A Merlyn Park, Dublin 4 (☎ 269 1640)
Sweden
    Sun Alliance House, Dawson St, Dublin 2 (☎ 671 5822)
Switzerland
    6 Ailesbury Rd, Dublin 4 (☎ 671 5822)
UK
    31 Merrion Rd, Dublin 4 (☎ 269 5211)
USA
    42 Elgin Rd, Dublin 4 (☎ 668 8777)

DUBLIN

Bloomsday

Six days after meeting her, the writer James Joyce had his first date with Nora Barnacle, the woman he was to marry, on 16 June 1904. Later, when he came to write his masterpiece *Ulysses*, which describes a single day in the life of Dubliner Leopold Bloom, the date he chose for this latterday odyssey was 16 June 1904. Now Dublin duly celebrates 'Bloomsday' on 16 June each year, with a range of entertainments, some serious, some less so, at venues all round the city. Serious Bloomsdayers don Edwardian costume for the day.

In general, events are designed to follow Bloom's progress round town. You can kick things off with breakfast either at the James Joyce Centre at 35 Great George's St North (☎ 873 1984) or at the *South Bank Restaurant* at 1 Martello Terrace, Dun Laoghaire (☎ 280 8788). In both cases, the 'inner organs of beast and fowl' come accompanied by celebratory readings, a fact reflected in the prices.

In the morning, guided tours of Joycean sites usually leave from the GPO and the James Joyce Centre. Lunch-time activity focuses on *Davy Byrne's*, Joyce's 'moral pub' in Duke St, where Bloom paused to dine on a glass of Burgundy and a slice of Gorgonzola (IR£3.95 at today's prices). Street entertainers are likely to keep you amused as you eat.

In the afternoon, the guided walks are topped up with animated readings from *Ulysses* and Joyce's other books at appropriate sites and times: Ormond Hotel, Ormond Quay, at 4 pm and *Harrison's* restaurant in Westmoreland St later in the day. These performances are given by Balloonatics; ☎041-33946 for details.

Should you have any energy left, you can spin things out to the early hours, perhaps in *Bewley's* in Grafton St where animated performances of Molly Bloom's closing (and at one time controversial) soliloquy take place.

Events also take place in the days leading up to and following Bloomsday. The best source of information about what's on in any particular year is likely to be the James Joyce Centre, although the *Dublin Event Guide* also publishes outline details in advance. Popular events sell out quickly; advance booking, especially for the breakfasts, is essential.

You don't have to know anything about Joyce or his books to enjoy the day, although it certainly helps! ■

Cultural Centres

Dublin has an international selection of cultural centres. The city is a very popular centre for English-language instruction, particularly for students from Spain who flock to Dublin every summer and have become a colourful part of the city scene. The city's cultural centres include:

Alliance Française
    1 Kildare St, Dublin 2 (☎ 676 1732)
British Council
    Newmount House, 22-24 Mount St Lower, Dublin 2 (☎ 676 4088, 676 6943)
Goethe Institute
    37 Merrion Square, Dublin 2 (☎ 661 1155)
Italian Cultural Institute
    11 Fitzwilliam Square, Dublin 2 (☎ 676 6662)
Spanish Cultural Institute
    58 Northumberland Rd, Dublin 4 (☎ 668 2024)

Books & Bookshops

Dublin is the only city in the world which can boast three winners of the Nobel Prize for Literature – George Bernard Shaw in 1925, W B Yeats in 1938 and Samuel Beckett in 1969. The Irish pride in this literary track record is exemplified in the Dublin Writers' Museum in Parnell Square.

James Joyce is, of course, the most Dublin-oriented of Irish writers, and serious Joyce groupies can make their own Bloomsday tour of the city with a number of books which follow the wanderings of *Ulysses's* characters in minute detail. *Joyce's Dublin – A Walking Guide to Ulysses* by Jack McCarthy (Wolfhound Press, Dublin, 1988) traces the events chapter by chapter with very clear maps. *The Ulysses Guide – Tours through Joyce's Dublin* by Robert Nicholson (Mandarin Paperbacks, London, 1988) concentrates on certain areas and follows the events of the various related chapters. Again there are clear and easy-to-follow maps.

Dublin has also featured prominently in more recent books ranging from J P Donleavy's *The Ginger Man* to Roddy Doyle's trilogy *The Commitments, The Snapper* and *The Van*. Stephen Conlin's *Dublin – One Thousand Years* (The O'Brien Press, Dublin, 1988) is an evocative collection of watercolour views recreating Dublin over the centuries. The Irish bookshop chain, Eason, publishes a series of slim booklets on subjects of Irish interest, including several on Dublin.

Directly opposite Trinity College at 27-29 Nassau St is Fred Hanna's (☎ 677 1255) excellent bookshop. Round the corner at 57 Dawson St is the large and well-stocked Hodges Figgis (☎ 677 4754). Facing it across the road at 7 Dawson St is Waterstone's (☎ 679 1415), which also carries a wide range of books. At 24 Grafton St, the Dublin Bookshop (☎ 677 5568) has a particularly good selection of books of Irish interest. North of the Liffey, Eason (☎ 873 3811), 40 O'Connell St, near the post office, has a wide range of books and one of the biggest selections of magazines in Ireland. The Winding Staircase (☎ 873 3292), 40 Lower Ormond Quay, does new and second-hand books and has a café upstairs.

A number of bookshops cater to special interests. Forbidden Planet (☎ 671 0688) at 36 Dawson St, Dublin 2, is a wonderful science fiction and comic book specialist. The Sinn Féin Bookshop (☎ 872 7096) is at 44 Parnell Square West, Dublin 1. An Siopa Leabhar (☎ 478 3814), in Harcourt St, just off St Stephen's Green, has books in Irish. The Irish Museum of Modern Art (IMMA) at the Royal Hospital Kilmainham and the National Gallery in Merrion Square both have bookshops offering a good range of art books. There's an excellent bookshop in the Dublin Writers' Museum on Parnell Square North, Dublin 1. The Library Book Shop at Trinity College has a wide selection of Irish interest books, including, of course, various titles on the 'Book of Kells'. For all kinds of official publications and maps, there's also the Office of Public Works bookshop (☎ 671 0309) in Sun Alliance House, Molesworth St, Dublin 2.

George Webb (☎ 677 7489), 5 Crampton Quay, Dublin 1, has old books of Irish interest as do Green's Bookshop (☎ 873 3149) in Parnell Square, Dublin 1, and Cathach Books (☎ 671 8676) at 10 Duke St, Dublin 2.

Laundry

Convenient laundries in north Dublin include the Laundry Shop (☎ 872 3541) at 191 Parnell St, Dublin 1, off Parnell Square, and the Laundrette at 110 Dorset St Lower near the An Óige Hostel. Near Trinity College and Temple Bar is the cheerful All American Laundrette Co at 40 South Great George St. South of the centre and just north of the Grand Canal is Powders Laundrette (☎ 478-2655) at 42A Richmond St South, Dublin 2. If you're staying north-east of the centre at Clontarf there's the Clothes Line (☎ 833 8480) at 53 Clontarf Rd.

Medical Services

The Eastern Health Board Dublin Area (☎ 671 4711), 138 Thomas St, Dublin 8, has a Choice of Doctor Scheme which can advise you on a suitable doctor from 9 am to 5 pm Monday to Friday. It also provides services for the physically and mentally handicapped. There are Well Women clinics at 35 Lower Liffey St (☎ 872 8095) and 73 Leeson St (☎ 661 0083). Both can help with all female medical problems and can supply contraceptives, including the 'morning-after' pill.

Emergency

For emergency assistance phone ☎ 999 (free call) for police, ambulance or fire brigade. Other useful numbers include:

Poisons Information Service
    Beaumont Hospital, Beaumont Rd, Dublin 9 (☎ 837 9964/9966)
Rape Crisis Centre
    70 Leeson St Lower, Dublin 2 (☎ 661 4911; toll free 1800 778 888)
Drugs Advisory & Treatment Centre
    Trinity Court, 30-31 Pearse St, Dublin 2 (☎ 677 1122)

Dangers & Annoyances

Until recently, Dublin was widely regarded as a very safe city. However, a rising drug problem over the last six years seems to have spawned a mini crime wave. Notices all over town alert you to the risk of pickpockets and sneak thieves, many of them unusually young. If you have a car, don't leave valuables inside it when it's parked; Dublin is notorious for car break-ins, and foreign-registered cars and rental cars are a particular target. Cyclists should always lock their bicycles securely and remove anything removable. Certain areas of Dublin are not safe at night and visitors should avoid run-down, deserted-looking and poorly lit areas. Camping in Phoenix Park would be a very bad idea indeed.

As in other parts of Europe, beggars, some of them alarmingly young, are now commonplace. If you don't want to give them money, but would like to do something to help the homeless and long-term unemployed, you could buy a copy of the magazine *The Big Issues* (IR£1), some of the proceeds of which go to them.

Like all big cities, Dublin is choking on traffic fumes. Nor has smoking died the social death it has in Britain, the USA or other Western countries; cinemas may be smoke-free zones, but not even all the expensive restaurants have designated non-smoking areas. Consequently, after a few days here you may feel your lungs are in need of a burst of fresh air.

ALONG THE LIFFEY

The River Liffey comes down to Dublin from the Wicklow Hills, passing the open expanse of Phoenix Park and flowing under 14 city bridges (one of which is pedestrian and one a railway) before reaching Dublin Harbour and Dublin Bay. As the crow flies it's only about 20 km from its source to the sea, but the Liffey contrives to twist and turn for over 100 km along its route and changes remarkably in that distance. Even well into the city, around Phoenix Park, the Liffey is still a rural-looking stream, and if you're waiting for a train at Heuston Station you can wander over to the river and watch the fish in the remarkably clear water below.

The city doesn't make much of its river, although Joyce immortalised its spirit as 'Anna Livia' who appears in sculpted form in the middle of O'Connell St ('the floozy in the jacuzzi') and on thousands of Dublin doorknockers. The best views are to be had

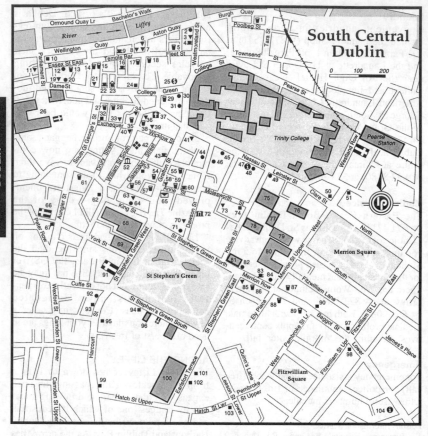

South Central Dublin

from O'Connell Bridge or, just upstream, from the pedestrian Ha'penny Bridge of 1816 which leads to the colourful Temple Bar area.

There have been bridges over the Liffey for nearly 800 years; the oldest currently standing is the Liam Mellows Bridge which was originally built at Queen's Bridge in 1768. It's still popularly known as the Queen St Bridge, for the simple reason that Queen St runs down to it.

The River Poddle originally joined the Liffey near the Grattan Bridge, better known as the Capel St Bridge, which crosses the

river from Capel St. The black pool or *dubh linn* at this point gave the city its name, but today the miserable Poddle runs its final five km in an underground channel and trickles into the Liffey through a grating on the south side of the river just downstream from the bridge.

The Liffey does more than divide Dublin into northern and southern halves – it also marks a psychological and social break between north and south. The movie *The Commitments* played upon this division, with run-down north Dublin as the place with 'soul'.

PLACES TO STAY

10 Clarence Hotel
23 Strollers Hostel
24 Bloom's Hotel
32 Central Hotel
50 Mont Clare Hotel
51 Davenport Hotel
53 Westbury Hotel
62 Grafton Plaza
67 Avalon House
74 Buswell's Hotel
81 Shelbourne Hotel
90 Georgian House
93 Russell Court Hotel
94 Staunton's on the Green
95 Albany House
97 Longfield's
98 Fitzwilliam
99 Harcourt Hotel
101 Latchfords
102 Conrad Hotel
103 Leeson Court

PLACES TO EAT

3 Beshoff's Fish & Chips
4 Bewley's Café
6 Omar Khayyam
7 Gallagher's Boxty House
8 Elephant & Castle
9 Chameleon Café
11 Poco Loco
16 Bad Ass Café
19 Les Fréres Jacques
21 La Mezza Luna
22 Well Fed Café
33 Trattoria Pasta Pasta
34 QV-2
36 Trocadero
39 Cornucopia
40 Munchies
41 Judge Roy Bean
43 Bewley's Oriental Café
58 Eddie Rocket's
60 Cotham Café
63 Pasta Fresca
70 La Stampa
73 Polo One
83 Galligan's Café
85 Pierre Victoire

PUBS

1 John Mulligan's
5 Palace Bar
13 Bad Bob's
14 Norseman

15 Temple Bar
17 Auld Dubliner
18 Oliver St John Gogarty
27 Dame Tavern
28 Stag's Head
29 O'Neill's
35 Old Stand
38 International Bar
54 Bruxelles
55 Davy Byrne's
56 Neary's
57 McDaid's
59 John Kehoe's
61 Break for the Border
86 O'Donohue's
87 Doheny & Nesbitt's
88 James Toner's
89 Baggot Inn

OTHER

2 USIT Travel Office
12 Project Arts Centre
20 Olympia Theatre
25 Bank of Ireland
26 City Hall
30 Thomas Cook
31 American Express
37 St Andrew's Church
42 Powerscourt Townhouse
   Shopping Centre
44 Hodges Figgis Bookshop
45 Fred Hanna's Bookshop
46 Waterstone's Bookshop
47 Northern Ireland Tourist Board
48 Kilkenny Shop
49 Heraldic Museum, Alliance Française &
   Genealogical Office
52 Civic Museum
64 Gaiety Theatre
65 Post Office
66 Whitefriars Carmelite Church
68 St Stephen's Green Shopping Centre
69 Royal College of Surgeons
71 Aer Lingus
72 Mansion House
75 National Library
76 National Gallery
77 Leinster House (Irish Parliament)
78 National Museum
79 Natural History Museum
80 Government Buildings
82 Huguenot cemetery
84 Irish Ferries
91 Unitarian Church
92 An Siopa Leabhar Bookshop
96 Newman House
100 National Concert Hall
104 Bord Fáilte (Irish Tourist Board)

DUBLIN

Although Liffey water was once a vital constituent in Guinness, you may be relieved to hear that this is no longer the case.

Dublin Harbour

In medieval times the River Liffey spread out into a broad estuary as it flowed into the bay. That estuary has long since been reclaimed (Trinity College has stood on it for 400 years) and the Liffey is embanked as far as the sea.

Dublin Harbour first came into existence in 1714, when the Liffey embankments were built. North Wall Quay was then built, and later a five-km breakwater known as the South Wall was added, followed by the North and South Bull Walls. The South Wall starts at Ringsend, where Oliver Cromwell first set foot in Ireland in 1649. From there it runs out to the Pigeon House Fort, built from 1748 and now used as a power station, and from there continues a further two km out to the 1762 Poolbeg Lighthouse at the end of the breakwater. It's a pleasant, though surprisingly long, stroll out to the lighthouse.

Custom House

James Gandon was 18th-century Dublin's pre-eminent architect; the Custom House, the Four Courts building farther up the river, the King's Inns and some elements of the parliament building (now the Bank of Ireland) are among his masterpieces.

The Custom House, his first great building, was constructed between 1781 and 1791 just past Eden Quay, in spite of vociferous local opposition.

In 1921, during the independence struggle, the Custom House was set alight and completely gutted in a fire that burned for five days. The interior was later extensively redesigned, and a further major renovation took place between 1986 and 1988.

The glistening white building stretches for 114 metres along the Liffey and the best complete view is obtained from across the river, though a close-up inspection of its many fine details is also worthwhile. The building is topped by a copper dome with four clocks. Above that stands a five-metre-high statue of Hope.

Four Courts

On Inns Quay beside the river the extensive Four Courts with its 130-metre-long facade was another of James Gandon's masterpieces. Construction of the building, which began in 1786 and soon engulfed the Public Offices (built a short time before at the western end of the same site), continued through to 1802. By then it included a Corinthian-columned central block connected to flanking wings with enclosed quadrangles. The ensemble is topped by a diverse collection of statuary.

There are fine views over the city from the upper rotunda of the central building. The original four courts – Exchequer, Common Pleas, King's Bench and Chancery – branched off this circular central building. The 1224 Dominican Convent of St Saviour formerly stood on the site, but was replaced first by the King's Inns and then by the present building. The last parliament of James II was held here in 1689.

The Four Courts played a brief role in the 1916 Easter Rising, without suffering any damage, but the events of 1922 were not so kind. When anti-Treaty republicans seized the building and refused to leave, it was shelled from across the river; as the occupiers retreated, the building was set on fire and a great many irreplaceable early records were burnt. This event sparked off the Civil War. The building was not restored until 1932.

SOUTH OF THE LIFFEY

South Dublin has the fanciest shops, almost all the restaurants of note and a majority of the hotels, as well as most of the reminders of Dublin's early history and the finest Georgian squares and houses.

Trinity College

Ireland's premier university was founded by Queen Elizabeth I in 1592 on land that had been confiscated from a monastery. By providing an alternative to education on the

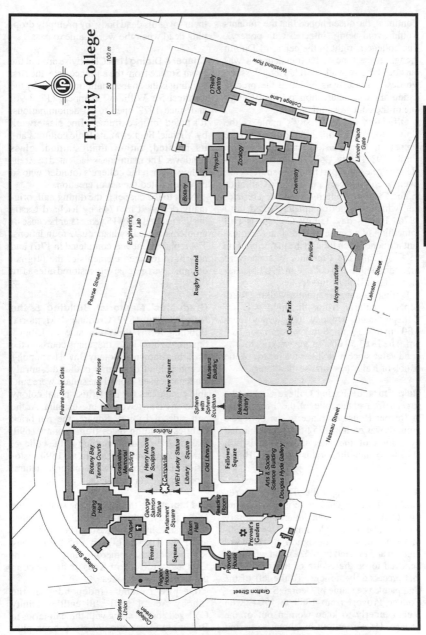

Continent, the queen hoped that the students would avoid being 'infected with popery'. The college is right in the centre of Dublin though at the time of its foundation it was outside the city walls. Archbishop Ussher, whose scientific feats included the precise dating of the act of creation to 4004 BC, was one of the college's founders.

Officially, the university's name is the University of Dublin, but Trinity College happens to be the institution's sole college. Until 1793 Trinity College remained completely Protestant apart from one short break. Even when the Protestants allowed Catholics in, the Catholic Church forbade it, a restriction which was not completely lifted until 1970. To this day Trinity College is still something of a centre of British and Protestant influence even though the majority of its 9500 students are Catholic. Women were first admitted to the college in 1903, earlier than at most British universities.

During the summer months walking tours depart regularly from the main gate on College Green, Monday to Saturday from 9.30 am to 4.30 pm, Sunday from noon to 4 pm. The IR£3.50 cost of the walking tour is good value since it includes the fee to see the 'Book of Kells' (see that section later).

Main Entrance Facing College Green (the street in front of the college), the 'Front Gate' or Regent House entrance to the college's grounds was built in 1752-59 and is guarded by statues of the poet Oliver Goldsmith (1730-74) and the orator Edmund Burke (1729-97).

Around the Campanile The open area reached from Regent House is divided into Front Square, Parliament Square and Library Square. The area is dominated by the 30-metre Campanile, designed by Edward Lanyon and erected in 1852-53 on what was believed to be the centre of the monastery that preceded the college. To the left of the Campanile is a statue of George Salmon, the College Provost from 1888 to 1904, who fought bitterly to keep women out of the college. He carried out his threat to permit

them 'over his dead body' by promptly dropping dead when the worst came to pass.

Chapel & Dining Hall Clockwise around the Front Square from the entrance gate, the first building is the chapel, built from 1798 by the architect Sir William Chambers (1723-96) and since 1972 open to all denominations. It's noted for its extremely fine plasterwork by Michael Stapleton, its Ionic columns and its painted, rather than stained, glass windows. The main one is dedicated to Archbishop Ussher, the college's founder, who so precisely dated the act of creation.

Next to the chapel is the dining hall, originally designed in 1743 by Richard Castle but dismantled only 15 years later because of problems caused by inadequate foundations. The replacement was completed in 1761 and may have retained elements of the original design. It was extensively restored after a fire in 1984.

Graduates' Memorial Building & the Rubrics The 1892 Graduates' Memorial Building forms the north side of Library Square. Behind it are the tennis courts in the open area known as Botany Bay. The popular legend behind this name is that the unruly students housed around the square were suitable candidates for the British penal colony at Botany Bay (Sydney) in Australia. At the east side of Library Square, the red-brick Rubrics Building dates from around 1690, making it the oldest building in the college. It was extensively altered in an 1894 restoration and then underwent major structural modifications in the 1970s.

Old Library To the south of the square is the Old Library, which was built in a rather severe style by Thomas Burgh between 1712 and 1732. The Old Library's 65-metre Long Room contains numerous unique ancient texts and the 'Book of Kells' is displayed in the Library Colonnades.

Despite Ireland's independence, the Library Act of 1801 still entitles Trinity College Library, along with three libraries in Britain, to a free copy of every book pub-

Book of Kells

For visitors, Trinity College's prime attraction is the magnificent 'Book of Kells', an illuminated manuscript dating from around 800 AD – one of the oldest books in the world. Although the book was brought to the college for safekeeping from the monastery at Kells in County Meath in 1654, it undoubtedly predates the monastery itself. It was probably produced by monks at St Columcille's monastery on the remote island of Iona, off the west coast of Scotland. When repeated Viking raids made their monastery untenable, the monks moved to the temporarily greater safety of Kells in Ireland in 806, taking their masterpiece with them. In 1007, the book was stolen and then rediscovered three months later, buried in the ground. Some time before the dissolution of the monastery, the metal shrine or *cumdach* was lost, possibly taken by looting Vikings who would not have valued the text itself. About 30 of the beginning and ending folios have also disappeared.

St John the Eagle, Book of Kells

The 'Book of Kells' contains the four gospels of the New Testament, written in Latin, as well as prefaces, summaries and other text. If it were merely words, the 'Book of Kells' would simply be a very old book – it's the extensive and amazingly complex illustrations which make it so wonderful. The superbly decorated opening initials are only part of the story, for the book also has numerous smaller illustrations between the lines.

The 680-page (340-folio) book was rebound in four calfskin volumes in 1953. Two volumes are usually on display, one showing an illuminated page and the other showing text. The pages are turned over regularly, but you can acquire your own reproduction copy for a mere US$18,000. If that's too steep, the library bookshop has various lesser books, including *The Book of Kells* (paperback, Thames & Hudson, London, 1980) with some attractive colour plates and text for less than IR£10.

The 'Book of Kells' is usually on display in the East Pavilion of the Colonnades library, underneath the actual library. As well as the 'Book of Kells', the 807 'Book of Armagh' and the 675 'Book of Durrow' are on display in the East Pavilion. ∎

lished in the UK. Housing this bounty requires nearly another km of shelving every year and the collection amounts to around three million books. Of course these cannot all be kept at the college library, so there are now additional library storage facilities dotted around Dublin.

The Long Room is mainly used for about 200,000 of the library's oldest volumes. Until 1892 the ground floor Colonnades was an open arcade, but it was enclosed at that time to increase the storage area. A previous attempt to increase the room's storage capacity had been made in 1853, when the Long Room ceiling was raised.

Apart from the world-famous 'Book of Kells', also on display is the so-called harp of Brian Ború, which was definitely not in use when the army of this early Irish hero defeated the Danes at the Battle of Clontarf in 1014. It does, however, date from around 1400, making it one of the oldest harps in Ireland.

Other exhibits in the Long Room include

a rare copy of the Proclamation of the Irish Republic, which was read out by Patrick Pearse at the beginning of the Easter Rising in 1916. The collection of 18th and 19th-century marble busts around the walls features Jonathan Swift, Edmund Burke and Wolfe Tone, all former members of Trinity College.

The Long Room and 'Book of Kells' are open from 9.30 am to 5.30 pm Monday to Friday, noon to 5 pm Sunday. Entry is IR£2.50/2 (children under 12 free). In high season it gets packed out, so try and come out of season. The Colonnades also houses a very busy book and souvenir shop and a temporary exhibition hall.

Reading Room, Exam Hall & Provost's House Continuing clockwise around the Campanile there's the Reading Room and the Public Theatre or Exam Hall, which dates from 1779-91. Like the Chapel building which it faces and closely resembles, it was the work of William Chambers and also has plasterwork by Michael Stapleton. The Exam Hall has an oak chandelier rescued from the Houses of Parliament (now the Bank of Ireland) across College Green and an organ said to have been salvaged from a Spanish ship in 1702, though the evidence indicates otherwise.

Behind the Exam Hall is the 1760 Provost's House, a particularly fine Georgian house where the provost or college head still resides. The house and its adjacent garden are not open to the public.

Berkeley Library To one side of the Old Library is Paul Koralek's 1967 Berkeley Library. This solid square brutalist-style building has been hailed as the best example of modern architecture in Ireland, though it has to be admitted the competition is not great. It's fronted by Arnaldo Pomodoro's 1982-83 sculpture *Sphere with Sphere*.

George Berkeley was born in Kilkenny in 1685, studied at Trinity when he was only 15 years old and went on to a distinguished career in many fields, but particularly in philosophy. His influence spread to the new English colonies in North America where, among other things, he helped to found the University of Pennsylvania. Berkeley in California, and its namesake university, are named after him.

Arts & Social Science Building & Douglas Hyde Gallery South of the old library is the 1978 Arts & Social Science Building, which backs on to Nassau St and forms the alternative main entrance to the college. Like the Berkeley Library it was designed by Paul Koralek; it also houses the Douglas Hyde Gallery of Modern Art (☎ 608 1116). Fellows Square is surrounded on three sides by the two library buildings and the Arts & Social Science Building.

The Dublin Experience After the 'Book of Kells' the college's other big tourist attraction is the Dublin Experience, a 45-minute audiovisual introduction to the city. Shows take place at the back of the Arts & Social Science Building every hour from 10 am to 5 pm daily late May to the beginning of October. Entry is IR£2.75/2.25. Combined tickets to 'The Book of Kells' and the Dublin Experience are available.

Around New Square Behind the Rubrics Building, at the eastern end of Library Square, is New Square. The highly ornate 1853-57 Museum Building has the skeletons of two enormous giant Irish deer just inside the entrance and the Geological Museum upstairs. It's open by prior arrangement only (☎ 608 1477).

The 1734 Printing House, designed by Richard Castle to resemble a Doric temple and now used for the microelectronics and electrical engineering departments, is at the north-west corner of New Square.

At the eastern end of the college grounds are the rugby ground and College Park, where cricket games are often played. There are a number of science buildings at the eastern end of the grounds. The Lincoln Place Gate at this end is usually open and makes a good entrance or exit from the college, especially if you are on a bicycle.

Bank of Ireland

The imposing Bank of Ireland building (☎ 677 6801), on College Green directly opposite Trinity College, was originally built in 1729 to house the Irish Parliament. When the parliament voted itself out of existence by the Act of Union in 1801, it became a building without a role. It was sold with instructions that the interior be altered to prevent it from being used as a debating chamber in the future. Consequently, the large central House of Commons was remodelled but the smaller chamber of the House of Lords survived. After independence the Irish government chose to make Leinster House the new parliamentary building and ignored the possibility of restoring this fine building to its original use.

Over a long period of time a string of architects worked on the building, yet it somehow manages to avoid looking like a hotchpotch of styles. Edward Lovett Pearce designed the circular central part of the building which was constructed between 1729 and 1739, and the east front was designed by James Gandon in 1785. Other architects involved in its construction were Robert Park and Francis Johnston, who converted it from a parliament building to a bank after it was sold in 1803.

Inside, the banking mall occupies what was once the House of Commons, but offers little hint of its former role. The Irish House of Lords is much more interesting with its Irish oak woodwork, late 18th-century Dublin crystal chandelier and 10-kg silver-gilt mace. The tapestries date from the 1730s and depict the Siege of Derry in 1689 and the Battle of the Boyne in 1690, the two great Protestant victories over Catholic Ireland.

The building can be visited during banking hours, Monday to Friday from 10 am to 3 pm, on Thursday to 5 pm. Free talks (as much about Irish history as about the building) take place on Tuesday at 10.30, 11.30 am and 1.45 pm.

Around the Bank of Ireland

The area between the Bank and Trinity College, today a constant tangle of traffic and pedestrians, was once a green swathe and is still known as College Green. In front of the bank stands a statue of Henry Grattan (1746-1820), a distinguished parliamentary orator.

The traffic island where College Green, Westmoreland St and College St meet houses public toilets (no longer in use) and a statue of the poet and composer Thomas Moore (1779-1852), renowned for James Joyce's comment in *Ulysses* that standing atop a public urinal was not a bad place for the man who penned the poem 'The Meeting of the Waters'. At the other end of College St, where it meets Pearse St, another traffic island is topped by a 1986 sculpture known as *Steyne*. It's a copy of the *steyne* (the Viking word for stone), erected on the riverbank in the 9th century to stop ships from grounding, and not removed until 1720.

Temple Bar

West of College Green and the Bank of Ireland, the maze of streets that make up Temple Bar are sandwiched between Dame St and the river. This is one of the oldest areas of Dublin and now has numerous restaurants, pubs and trendy shops.

Dame St, which forms the southern boundary of the Temple Bar area, links new Dublin (centred around Trinity College and Grafton St) and old (stretching from Dublin Castle to encompass the two cathedrals). Along its route Dame St changes name to become Cork Hill, Lord Edward St and Christ Church Place.

Temple Bar Information For information specifically on Temple Bar, the Temple Bar information centre (☎ 671 5717), on Eustace St, publishes a *Temple Bar Guide*. The notice board in the Resource Centre/Well Fed Café on Crow St offers a useful round-up of local goings-on. Morrigan Books' *Heritage Guide to Temple Bar* has an interesting map and description of the area.

Temple Bar History This stretch of prime riverside land was the property of Augustinian friars from 1282 until Henry VIII made his big land grab in 1537 with the dissolution of the monasteries. Temple Lane was known as Hogges Lane at that time and gave access to the friars' house. During its monastic era the Temple Bar area was marshy land that had only recently been reclaimed from the river. Much of the area was outside the city walls and the River Poddle flowed through it, connecting the black pool with the Liffey.

The land was named after a former owner, Sir William Temple (1554-1628). The term 'bar' referred to a riverside walkway.

The narrow lanes and alleys of Temple Bar started to take form in the early 18th century when this was a disreputable area of pubs and brothels. Through the 19th century it developed a commercial character with many small craft and trade businesses, but in the first half of the 20th century it went into decline, along with most of central Dublin.

In the 1960s it was decided to demolish the whole area to build a major bus station, but these plans took a long, long time to develop and meanwhile the area became a thriving countercultural centre. In the 1980s the bus station plan was abandoned and Temple Bar was encouraged to develop as a centre for restaurants, shops and entertainment instead. In its finished version it now boasts two public squares, residential apartments, a student housing centre and a Viking museum on the riverside.

Exploring Temple Bar The western boundary of Temple Bar is formed by Fishamble St, which is the oldest street in Dublin, dating back to Viking times ... not that you'd know that to look at it now. Christ Church Cathedral, originally dating from 1170, stands beside Fishamble St. There was an even earlier Viking church on this site. Brass symbols set into the pavement direct you towards a mosaic laid out to show the ground plan of the sort of Viking dwelling excavated here in 1980-81.

In 1742 Handel conducted the first performance of his *Messiah* in the Dublin Music Hall, which stood at that time behind what is now Kinlay House. The Music Hall, which had opened a year earlier in 1741, was

designed by Richard Castle; the only reminder of it today is the entrance and the original door, which stand to the left of Kennan's engineering works.

Parliament St, which runs straight up from the river to the City Hall and Dublin Castle, has Read's Cutlers at No 4. This is the oldest shop in Dublin, having operated under the same name since 1760. At the bottom of the street, beside the river, the Sunlight Chambers may be filthy but have a beautiful frieze running round the facade. Sunlight was a brand of soap manufactured by the Lever Brothers, who were responsible for the turn-of-the-century building. The frieze shows the Lever Brothers' view of the world and soap: men make clothes dirty, women wash them!

Eustace St is particularly interesting, with the popular Norseman pub at the river end and the 1715 Presbyterian Meeting House. The Dublin branch of the United Irishmen, who set themselves up to campaign for parliamentary reform and equality for Catholics, was first convened in 1791 in the Eagle Tavern, now the Friends Meeting House.

Merchant's Arch leads to the Ha'penny Bridge. If you cross to the north side of the Liffey, pause to look at the statue of two stout Dublin matrons sitting on a park bench with their shopping bags, dubbed 'the hags with the bags'. The Stock Exchange lives on Anglesea St, in a building dating from 1878. The Bank of Ireland also occupies a corner of Temple Bar.

Dublin Castle

Dublin Castle (☎ 677 7129) is more palace than castle. It was originally built on the orders of King John in 1204 and enjoyed a relatively quiet history despite a siege by Silken Thomas Fitzgerald in 1534, a fire which destroyed much of the castle in 1684, and the events of the 1916 Easter Rising. It was so lightly defended in 1916 that it would probably have fallen had the insurrectionists only realised they faced such lightweight opposition. The castle was used as the official residence of the British viceroys of

Ireland, until the Viceregal Lodge was built in Phoenix Park. Earlier it had been used as a prison; Red Hugh O'Donnell, one of the last of the great Gaelic leaders, escaped from the Record Tower in 1591, was recaptured, and escaped again in 1592.

Only the Record Tower, built between 1202 and 1258, survives from the original Norman castle. Parts of the castle's foundations remain, and a visit to the excavations is the most interesting part of the castle tour. The castle moats, now completely covered by more modern developments, were once filled by the River Poddle.

The castle tops Cork Hill, behind the City Hall on Dame St, and, provided it's not in use for important state business, tours are held from 10 am to 12.15 pm and 2 to 5 pm Monday to Friday; afternoons only at weekends. Tours cost IR£1.75/1. Friday morning is not a good time to visit because that's when the Peace & Reconciliation Forum meets. More significantly, the castle will be closed completely during the latter half of 1996 while Ireland holds the presidency of the European Union. The visitor centre contains the Castle Bistro where pleasant lunches are available.

Castle Tour The main Upper Yard of the castle with the entrance underneath the Throne Room is reached either directly from Cork Hill or via the Lower Yard. Starting from the main entrance, the castle tour takes you round the state chambers, which were developed during Dublin's British heyday but are still used for official state occasions. The sequence of rooms the tour takes you through may vary.

From the entrance you ascend the stairs to the Battle-Axe Landing, where the viceroy's guards once stood, armed with battle-axes. To the left is a series of drawing rooms, formerly used as visitors' bedrooms. One contains a Van Dyck painting of Elizabeth, second Viscountess of Southampton at the age of 17, another a book painted on vellum between 1989 and 1991 as a sort of latterday Book of Kells. The castle gardens, visible from the windows of these rooms, end in a

high wall said to have been built for Queen Victoria's visit to block out the distressing sight of the slums on Stephen St. James Connolly was detained in the first of these rooms after the siege of the GPO in 1916. From here he was taken to Kilmainham Jail to face a firing squad, still unable to stand because of a bullet wound to his ankle.

From the long State Corridor you enter the State Drawing Room, which was seriously damaged by a fire in 1941. It has been restored with furniture and paintings dating from 1740. The mirror with Apollo on it at one end was purchased for £5 from a sheep farmer who had painted it black and was using it as a headboard. From there you enter the ornate Throne Room, which was built in 1740.

The long Portrait Gallery, at one time divided into a series of smaller rooms, has portraits of some of the British viceroys. It ends at an anteroom from which you enter George's Hall, tacked on in 1911 for King George V's visit to Ireland. From these rooms you return through the anteroom to the blue Wedgwood Room (yes, the whole room does look like Wedgwood china), which in turn leads to the Bermingham Tower, originally dating from 1411 but rebuilt in 1775-77. The tower was used as a prison on a number of occasions, particularly during the independence struggle from 1918 to 1920.

Leaving the tower you pass through the 25-metre-long St Patrick's Hall. The Knights of St Patrick, an order created in 1783, were invested here and their standards are displayed around the walls. Now Irish presidents are inaugurated here and it is used for receptions. The huge painting on the ceiling shows St Patrick lighting the fire on Slane Hill; the Irish chieftains handing over power to the Anglo-Normans; and the coronation of George III who created the Order of St Patrick.

St Patrick's Hall ends back on the Battle-Axe Landing but the tour now takes you down to the Undercroft where remnants of the earlier Viking fort, the 13th-century Powder Tower and the city wall can be seen.

This excavation of the original moat is now well below street level.

Bedford Tower & Genealogical Office Other points of interest in the castle include the Bedford Tower and the Genealogical Office, directly across the Upper Yard from the main entrance. In 1907 the collection known as the Irish Crown Jewels was stolen from the tower and never recovered.

The entranceway to the castle yard beside the Bedford Tower is topped by a figure of justice which has always been a subject of mirth. She faces the castle and has her back to the city – seen as a sure indicator of how much justice the average Irish citizen could expect from the English. The scales of justice also had a distinct tendency to fill with rain and tilt in one direction or the other, rather than assuming the approved level position. Eventually a hole was drilled in the bottom of each pan so the rainwater could drain out.

Royal Chapel In the Lower Yard is the Church of the Holy Trinity, previously known as the Royal Chapel, which was built in Gothic style by Francis Johnston in 1807-14. Decorating the cold grey exterior are over 90 heads of various Irish personages and assorted saints carved out of Tullamore limestone. The interior is wildly exuberant, with fan vaulting alongside quadripartite vaulting, wooden galleries, stained glass and lots of lively looking sculpted angels.

Record Tower Towering over the chapel is the Record Tower, which was used as a storage facility for official records from 1579 until they were transferred to the Record Office in the Four Courts building in the early 19th century. When the Four Courts was burnt out at the start of the Civil War in 1922, almost all these priceless records were destroyed. Although the tower was rebuilt in 1813 it retains much of its original appearance, including the massive five-metre-thick walls.

City Hall & Municipal Buildings Fronting Dublin Castle on Lord Edward St, the City Hall was built by Thomas Cooley in 1769-79 as the Royal Exchange and later became the offices of the Dublin Corporation. It stands on the site of the Lucas Coffee House and an Eagle Tavern in which Dublin's infamous Hell Fire Club was established in 1735. Parliament St (1762), which leads up from the river to the front of City Hall, was the first of the wide boulevards to be laid out by the Wide Streets Commission.

The 1781 Municipal Buildings, immediately west of the City Hall, were built by Thomas Ivory (1720-86), who was also responsible for the Genealogical Office in Dublin Castle. The Genealogical Office as an institution dates from 1552, but where it is now housed dates from the 18th century and was built by Ivory.

Christ Church Cathedral
Christ Church Cathedral (Church of the Holy Trinity) (☎ 677 8099) is on Christ Church Place, just south of the river and west of the city centre and the Temple Bar district. Dublin's original Viking settlement stood between the cathedral and the river. This was also the centre of medieval Dublin, with Dublin Castle nearby and the *Tholsel* or town hall (demolished in 1809) and the original Four Courts (demolished in 1796) both beside the cathedral. Nearby on Back Lane is the only remaining guildhall in Dublin. The 1706 **Tailor's Hall** was due for demolition in the 1960s, but survived to become the office of An Taisce, the National Trust for Ireland.

Originally built in wood by the Danes in 1038, the cathedral was subsequently rebuilt in stone from 1172, by Richard de Clare, Earl of Pembroke (better known as Strongbow). The archbishop of Dublin, Laurence (Lorcan in Irish) O'Toole, was later to become St Laurence, the patron saint of Dublin. Strongbow died in 1176 and Laurence O'Toole in 1180, before the church was complete. Nor was their cathedral destined to have a long life: the foundations were essentially a peat bog and the south wall collapsed in 1562. It was soon rebuilt, but the central tower was also a replacement for two earlier

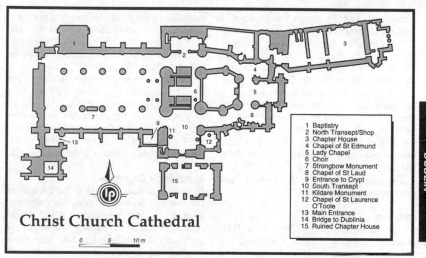

Christ Church Cathedral

0   5   10 m

1 Baptistry
2 North Transept/Shop
3 Chapter House
4 Chapel of St Edmund
5 Lady Chapel
6 Choir
7 Strongbow Monument
8 Chapel of St Laud
9 Entrance to Crypt
10 South Transept
11 Kildare Monument
12 Chapel of St Laurence O'Toole
13 Main Entrance
14 Bridge to Dublinia
15 Ruined Chapter House

DUBLIN

steeples which had burnt down. Most of what you see from the outside dates from architect G E Street's major restoration which took place between 1871 and 1878. Above ground level the north wall, the transepts and the western part of the choir are almost all that remain from the original. Even the flying buttresses date from the 19th-century restoration.

Through much of its history Christ Church vied for supremacy with nearby St Patrick's Cathedral, but like its neighbour it fell on hard times in the 18th and 19th centuries and was virtually derelict by the time restoration took place. Earlier, the nave had been used as a market and the crypt had housed taverns. Today, of course, both these Church of Ireland cathedrals are outsiders in a Catholic nation.

From the south-east entrance to the churchyard you walk past the ruins of the chapter house, dating from 1230. The entrance to the cathedral is at the south-west corner and as you enter you face the north wall. This survived the collapse of its southern counterpart, but has also suffered from subsiding foundations; from the eastern end it leans visibly.

The south aisle has a monument to the legendary Strongbow, but the armoured figure on the tomb is more likely to be of the Earl of Drogheda than Strongbow himself. His internal organs may indeed have been buried here and the half-figure beside the tomb may relate to that burial. A popular legend relates that this half-figure is of Strongbow's son, who was cut in two by his father when his bravery in battle came into question.

The south transept contains the superb Baroque tomb of the 19th earl of Kildare (died 1734). His grandson, Lord Edward Fitzgerald, was a member of the United Irishmen and died in the abortive 1798 rebellion. The entrance to the Chapel of St Laurence is off the south transept and contains two effigies, one of them reputed to be that of either Strongbow's wife or sister. Laurence O'Toole's embalmed heart was placed in the Chapel of St Laud.

At the east end of the cathedral is the Lady Chapel or Chapel of the Blessed Virgin Mary. Also at the east end is the Chapel of St Edmund and the chapter house, the latter closed to visitors. Parts of the choir, in the centre of the church, and the north transept are original, but the baptistry was added at the time of the 1875 restoration.

An entrance by the south transept descends to the unusually large arched crypt which dates back to the original Danish church of 1000 years ago. Curiosities in the crypt include 1670 stocks that once stood in the cathedral yard. A glass display case houses a mummified mouse with a mummified cat in hot pursuit that were trapped inside an organ pipe in the 1860s! From the main entrance a bridge, part of the 1871-78 restoration, leads to Dublinia (see below).

The cathedral is open from 10 am to 5 pm daily and entry is IR£1/50p.

Dublinia

Inside what was once the Synod Hall attached to Christ Church Cathedral, the Medieval Trust has created Dublinia, a lively attempt to bring medieval Dublin to life. The ground floor has models of episodes in Dublin's history which are explained through headsets as you walk around. On the 1st floor, finds from medieval excavations are on display alongside a large model of the city. There are also models of the medieval

quayside and of a cobbler's shop. On the top floor a multi-media show runs every half-hour. Finally you can climb neighbouring St Michael's Tower for panoramic views over the city to the Dublin Hills.

Dublinia is open daily from 10 am to 5 pm April to September. In winter it's open from 11 am to 4 pm Monday to Saturday and 10 am to 4.30 pm on Sunday. There's a souvenir shop and a pleasant café. Admission costs IR£3.95/2.90 which gets you into Christ Church Cathedral free (via the link bridge).

St Patrick's Cathedral

St Patrick himself is said to have baptised converts at a well within the cathedral grounds, so the cathedral (☎ 475 4817) stands on one of the earliest Christian sites in the city. Like Christ Church Cathedral it was built on distinctly unstable ground, with the subterranean River Poddle flowing under its foundations. Because of the high water table St Patrick's does not have a crypt.

Although a church stood on the Patrick St site from as early as the 5th century, the present building dates from 1190 or 1225, opinions differ. The stone Norman construc-

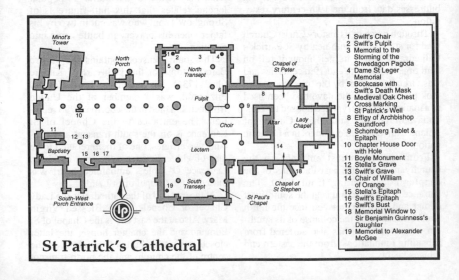

St Patrick's Cathedral

1 Swift's Chair
2 Swift's Pulpit
3 Memorial to the Storming of the Shwedagon Pagoda
4 Dame St Leger Memorial
5 Bookcase with Swift's Death Mask
6 Medieval Oak Chest
7 Cross Marking St Patrick's Well
8 Effigy of Archbishop Saundford
9 Schomberg Tablet & Epitaph
10 Chapter House Door with Hole
11 Boyle Monument
12 Stella's Grave
13 Swift's Grave
14 Chair of William of Orange
15 Stella's Epitaph
16 Swift's Epitaph
17 Swift's Bust
18 Memorial Window to Sir Benjamin Guinness's Daughter
19 Memorial to Alexander McGee

tion was rebuilt in the early 13th century in a style mimicked by the present form.

Like Christ Church Cathedral, it also had a rather dramatic history. A storm brought down the spire in 1316 and soon after the building was badly damaged in a fire. An even more disastrous fire followed in 1362 which required the addition of Archbishop Minot's west tower in 1370. For some reason it was constructed at a slight angle to the rest of the cathedral. In 1560 one of the first clocks in Dublin was added to the 43-metre tower, and a 31-metre spire in 1749. During his 1649 visit to Ireland, Oliver Cromwell converted St Patrick's to a stable for his army's horses, an indignity to which he also subjected numerous other Irish churches. Jonathan Swift was the dean of the cathedral from 1713 to 1745. Prior to its mid 19th-century restoration the cathedral became a ruin, with a collapsed roof and individual chapels walled off as separate churches.

Its current form dates mainly from some rather over-enthusiastic restoration in 1864 which included the addition of the flying buttresses. St Patrick's Park, the expanse of green beside the cathedral, was a crowded slum until it was cleared and its residents evicted in the early years of this century.

On entering the cathedral from the south-west porch you come almost immediately to the graves of Swift and Esther Johnson or Stella, Swift's long-term companion. On the wall are Swift's own Latin epitaphs to the two of them, and a bust of him.

The huge dusty Boyle Monument was erected in 1632 by Richard Boyle, the earl of Cork, and is decorated with numerous painted figures of members of his family. It stood beside the altar until, in 1633, the lord deputy of Ireland, Thomas Wentworth, the future earl of Strafford, complained that worshippers were unable to pray without 'crouching to an earl of Cork and his lady...or to those sea nymphs his daughters, with coronets upon their heads, their hair dishevelled, down upon their shoulders'. This broadside was enough to have it shifted, but although Wentworth won this round of his bitter conflict with the earl of Cork, the latter had the final say when he contributed to the process of Wentworth's impeachment and execution. The figure in the centre on the bottom level is of the earl's five-year-old son, Robert Boyle (1627-91), the future scientist. His contributions to physics include Boyle's Law, which relates the pressure and volume of gases.

In the north-west corner of the church is a cross on a stone slab, which once marked the position of St Patrick's original well. The south transept was formerly a separate chapter house.

During the cathedral's decay in the 18th and 19th centuries the north transept was virtually a separate church. It now contains memorials to the Royal Irish Regiments. The Swift corner in the north transept features Swift's pulpit, his chair and a book-filled glass cabinet containing his death mask.

The Guinness family were noted contributors to the cathedral's restoration and a

---

Chancing One's Arm

Leaning against a column at the west end of the cathedral is an old door with a hole hacked through it, which was once the entry to the chapter house. In 1492, the year in which Columbus was busy landing in the New World, a furious argument took place within the cathedral between the earl of Kildare and the earl of Ormonde. Each was supported by his armed retainers, but when strong words were about to lead to heavy blows, the earl of Ormonde retreated to the chapter house. Fortunately, a peaceful settlement was reached and a hole was chopped through the door so the earls could shake hands on the agreement. In extending his arm through the door, the earl of Kildare added the phrase 'chancing one's arm' to the English language. ■

monument to Sir Benjamin Guinness's daughter stands in the Chapel of St Stephen beneath a window bearing the words 'I was thirsty and ye gave me drink'! The chapel also has a chair used by William of Orange at a service in the cathedral after his victory at the Boyne.

The cathedral is open from 9 am to 6 pm Monday to Friday, 9 am to 5 pm Saturday (to 4 pm November to April), and 10 to 11 am and 12.45 to 3 pm Sunday. Entry is IR£1.20/50p. The cathedral's choir school dates back to 1432 and the choir took part in the first performance of Handel's *Messiah* in 1742. You can hear the choir sing every day except Wednesday in July and August. Bus Nos 50, 50A or 56A from Aston Quay or Nos 54 or 54A from Burgh Quay run to the cathedral.

Marsh's Library

In St Patrick's Close beside St Patrick's Cathedral is Marsh's Library (☎ 454 3511), founded in 1701 by Archbishop Narcissus Marsh (1638-1713) and opened in 1707. It was designed by Sir William Robinson, who was also responsible for the Royal Hospital, Kilmainham. The oldest public library in the country, it contains 25,000 books dating from the 16th to the early 18th centuries, as well as maps, numerous manuscripts and a collection of incunabula, the technical term for books printed before 1500. One of the oldest and finest books in the collection is a volume of Cicero's *Letters to his Friends* printed in Milan in 1472. The manuscript collection includes one in Latin dating back to 1400.

In the virtually unchanged interior, the three alcoves where scholars were once locked in to peruse rare volumes still stand. The skull lurking in the furthest one does not, however, belong to some poor forgotten scholar. Instead it's a cast taken of Swift's Stella's head. A bindery to repair and restore rare old books operates from the library which, hardly surprisingly, makes an appearance in Joyce's *Ulysses*.

Marsh's Library is open Monday and Wednesday to Friday from 10 am to 12.45

pm and 2 to 5 pm, Saturday from 10.30 am to 12.45 pm. An entry donation of IR£1 is requested. You can reach the library by taking bus Nos 50, 50A or 56A from Aston Quay or bus Nos 54 or 54A from Burgh Quay.

St Werburgh's Church

In Werburgh St, just south of Christ Church Cathedral and tucked in beside Dublin Castle, St Werburgh's stands on ancient foundations. Its early history, however, is unknown. It was rebuilt in 1662, in 1715 and again in 1759 (with some elegance) after a fire in 1754. It is linked with the Fitzgerald family; Lord Edward Fitzgerald, who joined the United Irishmen and was a leader of the 1798 Rising, is interred in the vault. In what was an unfortunately frequent theme of Irish uprisings, compatriots gave him away and he died from wounds received while being captured. Major Henry Sirr, his captor, is buried in the graveyard. A Baroque tower was added to the church in 1768, but was demolished in 1810 when Dublin Castle authorities, concerned about its use as a lookout over the castle, had it declared unsafe.

Despite its long history, fine design and interesting interior, the church is rarely used today. A note at the front directs you round the corner to 8 Castle St if you want to have a look inside. If you can't raise anybody there, you could try phoning (☎ 478 3710). Werburgh St was also the location of Dublin's first theatre and Jonathan Swift was born just off the street in Hoey's Court in 1667.

St Audoen's Churches

Lucky St Audoen has two churches to his name, both just west of Christ Church Cathedral. The Church of Ireland church is the older and smaller building, and indeed is the only surviving medieval parish church in the city. Its tower and door date from the 12th century, the aisle from the 15th century and various other bits and pieces from early times, but the church today is mainly a 19th-century restoration. The tower's bells include the three oldest bells in Ireland, all dating from 1423.

The church is entered via an arch beside Cook St, to the north of the church. Part of the old city wall, this arch was built in 1240 and is the only surviving reminder of the city gates. Parts of an even earlier Viking church of St Colmcille may be included in the later constructions. The church is undergoing Office of Public Works restoration.

Joined onto the older Protestant St Audoen's is the newer and larger Catholic St Audoen's, which was completed in 1846. The dome was replaced in 1884 after it collapsed, and the front with its imposing Corinthian columns was added in 1899. Unfortunately, you're unlikely to find either church open.

The National Museum
The National Museum, on Kildare St east of St Stephen's Green, was completed in 1890 to a design by Sir Thomas Newenham Deane; note the lovely zodiac design picked out in mosaic in the hallway. The star attraction is the Treasury, which has two superb collections and an accompanying audiovisual display.

One of the collections is of Bronze and Iron Age gold objects, including a magnificent gold collar and a delicate little gold model of a galley, both from the Broighter Hoard (1st century BC), the Gleninsheen Gorget – another collar from about the 8th century BC – and other hoards discovered by railway workers, ploughmen and peat cutters – rarely by archaeologists.

The other Treasury collection is from medieval times. Outstanding among the objects on display are the 8th-century silver Ardagh Chalice, the 12th-century Cross of Cong, which once enshrined a supposed fragment of the True Cross, and the beautiful 8th-century Tara Brooch, made of gold, enamel and amber.

Upstairs, Viking Age Dublin tells the story, not surprisingly of Dublin's Viking era, with exhibits from the excavations at Wood Quay – the area between Christ Church Cathedral and the river, where

Dublin City Council plonked its new headquarters. Other exhibits focus on the 1916 Easter Rising and the independence struggle between 1900 and 1921. Numerous interesting displays relate to this important period of modern Irish history. Frequent short-term exhibitions are also held.

The museum's collections of Irish decorative arts, ceramics, musical instruments and Japanese decorative arts are being rehoused in the Collins Barracks in Benburb St, off Ellis Quay, and may be viewable by the time you read this; phone ☎ 661 8811 to find out.

The museum is open Tuesday to Saturday from 10 am to 5 pm and Sunday 2 to 5 pm. Entry is free but guided tours are available for IR£1. There's a good café on the ground floor.

The National Gallery
Opened in 1864, the National Gallery (☎ 661 5133) in Merrion Square is particularly strong, of course, in Irish art but also has high-quality collections of every major school of European painting.

On the lawn in front of the gallery is a statue of the Irish railway magnate William Dargan, who organised the 1853 Dublin Industrial Exhibition at this spot; the profits from the exhibition were used to found the gallery. Nearby is a statue of George Bernard Shaw, who was a major benefactor of the gallery. The proceeds from *My Fair Lady* certainly helped the gallery's acquisition programme.

The gallery has three wings: the original Dargan Wing, the Milltown Rooms and the Modern Wing. The Dargan Wing's ground floor has the imposing Shaw Room, lined with full-length portraits and illuminated by a series of spectacular Waterford crystal chandeliers. Upstairs a series of rooms is dedicated to the Italian early and high Renaissance, 16th-century north Italian art and 17th and 18th-century Italian art. Fra Angelico, Titian and Tintoretto are among the artists represented here.

The central Milltown Rooms were added in 1899-1903 to house the art collection of Russborough House which was presented to the gallery in 1902. The ground floor displays the gallery's fine Irish collection plus a smaller British collection, with works by Reynolds, Hogarth, Gainsborough, Landseer and Turner. One of the highlights is the room at the back of the gallery displaying works by Jack B Yeats (1871-1957), the younger brother of W B Yeats. Other rooms relate to specific periods and styles of Irish art, including one room of works by Irish artists painting in France.

Upstairs are works from Germany, the Netherlands and Spain. There are rooms of works by Rembrandt and his circle and by Spanish artists of Seville. The Spanish collection features works by El Greco, Goya and Picasso.

The Modern Wing was added in 1964-68 but has been undergoing extensive refurbishment; it should be open for viewing by the time you read this. The gallery also has an art reference library, a lecture theatre, a good bookshop and an excellent and deservedly popular restaurant. The gallery hours are from 10 am to 5.30 pm Monday to Saturday (to 8.30 pm Thursday), and 2 to 5 pm on Sunday. Entry is free and there are guided tours at 3 pm on Saturday and at 2.30, 3.15 and 4 pm on Sunday.

Leinster House – The Dáil

Both the lower house (Dáil) and the upper house (Seanad) of Ireland's parliament, the Oireachtas na hÉireann, meet in Leinster House on Kildare St. The entrance to Leinster House from Kildare St is flanked by the National Library and the National Museum. Originally built as Kildare House in 1745-48 for the earl of Kildare, the name of the building was changed when he also assumed the title of duke of Leinster in 1766. One of the members of the Fitzgerald family who held the title was Lord Edward Fitzgerald, who died of wounds he received in the abortive 1798 Rising.

Leinster House's Kildare St frontage was designed to look like a town house, whereas the Merrion Square frontage was made to look like a country house. Richard Castle, the house's architect, later built the Rotunda

Hospital in north Dublin to a similar design. The lawn in front of the Merrion Square country-house frontage was the site for railway pioneer William Dargan's 1853 Dublin Industrial Exhibition, which in turn led to the creation of the National Gallery. There's a statue of him at the National Gallery end of the lawn. At the other end of the lawn is a statue of Prince Albert, Queen Victoria's consort. Queen Victoria herself was commemorated in massive form on the Kildare St side from 1908 until the statue was removed in 1948. The obelisk in front of the building is dedicated to Arthur Griffith, Michael Collins and Kevin O'Higgins, architects of independent Ireland.

The Dublin Society, later named the Royal Dublin Society, bought the building in 1814 but moved out in stages between 1922 and 1925, when the first government of independent Ireland decided to establish their parliament there.

The Seanad, or Senate, meets in the north-wing saloon, while the Dáil meets in a less interesting room that was originally a lecture theatre added to the original building in 1897. When parliament is sitting, visitors are admitted to an observation gallery. You get an entry ticket from the Kildare St entrance on production of some form of identification. No bags can be taken in with you or notes or photographs taken. Parliament sits for 90 days a year, usually between November and May, on Tuesday (from 2.30 to 8.30 pm), Wednesday (from 10.30 am to 8.30 pm) and Thursday (from 10.30 am to 5.30pm).

Government Buildings

On Merrion St Upper, on the south side of the Natural History Museum, the domed Government Buildings were opened in 1911, in a rather heavy-handed Edwardian interpretation of the Georgian style. On Saturday 40-minute tours are conducted from 10.30 am to 12.30 pm and 1.30 to 4.50 pm. Tickets are available from the National Gallery ticket office. Only 16 people can join each tour, so if a group has just arrived you may have to wait; although you can't book in advance, you can go along in the morning and put your name down for later in the day. You get to see the Taoiseach's office, the ceremonial staircase with stunning stained-glass window, the cabinet room and innumerable fine examples of Irish arts & crafts on loan from the Arts Council. Bags can't be taken into the building.

Across the road at No 24 is Mornington House, a Georgian mansion thought to be the birthplace of the Duke of Wellington, who was somewhat ashamed of his Irish origins. It's possible that his actual birthplace was Trim in County Meath. The mansion is due to become a hotel.

The National Library

Flanking the Kildare St entrance to Leinster House is the National Library, which was built in 1884-90, at the same time and to a similar design as the National Museum by Sir Thomas Newenham Deane and his son Sir Thomas Manly Deane. Leinster House, the library and museum were all part of the Royal Dublin Society (formed in 1731), which aimed to improve conditions for poor people and to promote the arts and sciences. The library's extensive collection has many valuable early manuscripts, first editions, maps and other items. Temporary displays are often held in the entrance area and the library's reading room featured in *Ulysses*. The library is open Monday from 10 am to 9 pm, Tuesday to Friday 10 am to 5 pm, Thursday and Saturday 10 am to 1 pm.

Heraldic Museum & Genealogical Office

On the corner of Kildare and Nassau Sts, the former home of the Kildare St Club is shared by the Heraldic Museum and Genealogical Office and the Alliance Française. It's a popular destination for visitors intent on tracing their Irish roots. The Kildare St Club was an important right-wing institution during Dublin's Anglo-Irish heyday. Note the whimsical though rather worn stone carvings of animals that decorate the building's windows, including monkeys playing billiards.

The Heraldic Museum's displays follow the story of heraldry in Ireland and Europe.

It's open free on Monday to Wednesday from 10.30 am to 8.30 pm and on Thursday and Friday from 10 am to 4.30 pm.

Natural History Museum

Just as the National Library and the National Museum flank the entrance to Leinster House on the Kildare St side, the National Gallery and Natural History Museum perform the same function on the Merrion St Upper/ Merrion Square side.

The Natural History Museum (☎ 661 8811) has scarcely changed since 1857 when Scottish explorer Dr David Livingstone delivered the opening lecture. It's known as the Dead Zoo, but despite that disheartening appellation it's well worth a visit, for its collection is huge and surprisingly well kept. That moth eaten look which afflicts neglected collections of stuffed animals has been kept well at bay and children in particular are likely to find it fascinating.

The collection of skeletons, stuffed animals and the like covers the full range of Irish fauna and includes three skeletons of the Irish giant elk, which became extinct about 10,000 years ago.

The museum hours are from 10 am to 5 pm Tuesday to Saturday, 2 to 5 pm on Sunday. Entry is free.

Grafton St

Grafton St was the major traffic artery of south Dublin until it was turned into a pedestrian precinct in 1982. It's now Dublin's fanciest and most colourful shopping centre with plenty of street life and the city's most entertaining buskers. The street is equally lively after dark as some of Dublin's most interesting pubs are clustered around it.

Apart from fine shops, like the Brown Thomas (opened in 1848) department store, Grafton St also boasts Bewley's Oriental Café. This branch of the chain has memorabilia relating to the company's history upstairs. At the College Green end of the street look out for the modern statue of Molly Malone of song fame, rendered in such extreme *déshabillée* that she's nicknamed the 'tart with the cart'.

Back from Grafton St on William St South is the elegantly converted Powerscourt Townhouse Shopping Centre. Built between 1771 and 1774, this grand house has a balconied courtyard, and, following its conversion in 1981, now shelters three levels of modern shops and restaurants. The Powerscourt family's principal residence was Powerscourt House in County Wicklow and this city mansion was soon sold for commercial use. It survived that period in remarkably good condition and in its new incarnation forms a convenient link from Grafton St to the South City Market on South Great George's St. The building features plasterwork by Michael Stapleton, who also worked on Belvedere House in north Dublin.

Dublin Civic Museum

Housed in the 18th-century Assembly House beside the Powerscourt Townhouse, the Dublin Civic Museum (☎ 679 4260) is at 58 William St South, just a stone's throw from Grafton St. During 1995 much of the building was temporarily occupied by the city's archivists. However, when they move out you should again be able to see displays relating to the history of the city. In particular, look out for the head from Lord Nelson's Pillar on O'Connell St which was toppled by the IRA in 1966.

The museum is open Tuesday to Saturday from 10 am to 6 pm, Sunday 11 am to 2 pm, and entry is free. It's worth popping in just to see the architecture.

Mansion House

Mansion House on Dawson St was built in 1710 by Joshua Dawson, after whom the street is named. Only five years later the house was bought as a residence for the Lord Mayor of Dublin. The building's original brick Queen Anne style has all but disappeared behind a stucco facade tacked on in the Victorian era. The building was the site for the 1919 Declaration of Independence but is not generally open to the public. Next door is the **Royal Irish Academy**, also generally closed to visitors.

St Stephen's Green

On warm summer days the nine hectares of St Stephen's Green provide a popular lunchtime escape for city office workers. The Green was originally an expanse of open common land where public whippings, burnings and hangings took place. The Green was enclosed by a fence in 1664 when Dublin Corporation sold off the surrounding land for buildings. A stone wall replaced the fence in 1669 and trees and gravel paths soon followed within. By the end of that century restrictions were already in force prohibiting buildings of less than two storeys or those constructed of mud and wattle. At the same time Grafton St, the main route to the Green from what was then central Dublin, was upgraded from a 'foule and out of repaire' laneway to a crown causeway.

The fine Georgian buildings around the square date mainly from Dublin's mid to late 18th-century Georgian prime. At that time the north side was known as the Beaux' Walk and it is still one of Dublin society's most esteemed meeting places. Further improvements were made in 1753, with seats being put in place, but in 1814 railings and locked gates were added and an annual fee of one guinea was charged to use the Green. This private use continued until 1877 when Sir Arthur Edward Guinness, later Lord Ardilaun, pushed an act through parliament which once again made the Green a public place. The gardens and ponds of the central park date from 1880 and were financed by the wealthy brewer.

Across the road from the west side of the Green are the 1863 **Unitarian Church** and the **Royal College of Surgeons**, the latter with one of the finest facades around St Stephen's Green. It was built in 1806 and extended in 1825-27 to the design of William Murray. Forty years later Murray's son, William G Murray, designed the Royal College of Physicians building on Kildare St. In the 1916 Rising, the Royal College of Surgeons was occupied by the colourful Countess Markievicz (1868-1927), an Irish nationalist married to a Polish count. The countess would have handled modern media with aplomb; her first question upon taking the college was the whereabouts of the scalpels, implying they would be useful in hand-to-hand combat with British troops. The columns still bear bullet marks.

At one time the main entrance to the Green was on this side, but now it is through the **Fusiliers' Arch** at the north-west corner of the Green from Grafton St. Modelled on the Arch of Titus in Rome, the arch commemorates the 212 soldiers of the Royal Dublin Fusiliers who died in the Boer War (1899-1902).

A path from the arch passes by the duck pond while around the fountain in the centre of the Green are a number of statues, including a bust of Countess Markievicz. The centre of the park also has a garden for the blind, complete with signs in Braille and plants which can be handled.

On the eastern side of the Green there's a children's play park and to the south is a fine old **bandstand**, erected for Queen Victoria's jubilee in 1887. Concerts often take place here in the summer.

Just inside the Green at the south east corner, near Leeson St, is a statue of the Three Fates, presented to Dublin in 1956 by West Germany in gratitude for Irish aid immediately after WW II. The north-west corner, opposite the Shelbourne Hotel and Merrion Row, is marked by the Wolfe Tone Monument to the leader of the abortive 1796 invasion. The vertical slabs which serve as a backdrop for Wolfe Tone's statue have been dubbed 'Tonehenge'. Just inside the park at this entrance is a memorial to the victims of the potato famines.

Notable buildings around the Green include the imposing old 1867 **Shelbourne Hotel** on the north side, with statues of Nubian princesses and their ankle-fettered slave girls decorating the front. Just beyond the Shelbourne is a small **Huguenot cemetery** dating from 1693, when many French Huguenots fled here from persecution under Louis XIV.

Grafton St runs from the north-west corner of the Green, while Merrion Row, with its popular pubs, runs from the north-

east. At the south-east is Leeson St, the nightclub centre of Dublin. The Hotel Conrad, Dublin's Hilton Hotel, is just off the square from this corner on Earlsfort Terrace, as is the National Concert Hall.

Harcourt St, from the south-west corner, was laid out in 1775. Well-known names associated with the street include Edward Carson, who was born at No 4 in 1854. As the architect of Northern Irish 'unionism' he makes an easy scapegoat for many of the problems caused by Ireland's division. Bram Stoker, author of *Dracula*, lived at No 16 and George Bernard Shaw at No 61. For 99 years from 1859 to 1958 the Dublin-Bray railway line used to terminate at Harcourt St Station, which was then at the bottom of this road.

At No 80-81 on the south side of the Green is **Iveagh House**, where the Guinness family was once domiciled; today the Department of Foreign Affairs lives there. Designed by Richard Castle in 1730, this was his first project in Dublin. He went on to create many more buildings, including Leinster House and the Rotunda Hospital.

At No 85-86 on the south side of the Green is **Newman House**, which is now part of University College Dublin. These buildings have some of the finest plasterwork in the city. No 85 was built between 1736 and 1738 by Richard Castle for Hugh Montgomery MP. The particularly fine plasterwork was by the Swiss stuccodores Paul and Philip Francini (also known as Paolo and Filippo Lafranchi) and can be best appreciated in the wonderfully detailed Apollo Room on the ground floor.

Richard Chapel Whaley MP had taken possession of No 85 in 1765 but decided to display his wealth by constructing a much grander home next door at No 86.

Whaley's son Buck contrived to become an MP while still a teenager and also one of the more notorious members of Dublin's Hell Fire Club. He was also a noted gambler, once walking all the way to Jerusalem to win a bet.

The Catholic University of Ireland, predecessor of University College Dublin, acquired the building in 1865, with the Jesuits following in their footsteps. Some of the plasterwork was a little too detailed for Jesuitical tastes, however, so cover-ups were prescribed. On the ceiling of the upstairs Saloon previously naked female figures were clothed in what can best be described as furry swimsuits. One survives the restoration process.

The Catholic University named Newman House after its first rector, John Henry Newman. Gerard Manley Hopkins, professor of classics at the college from 1884 until his death in 1889, lived upstairs at No 86. It was not until some time after his death that his innovative if rather depressive poetry was published. His room is now preserved as it was during his residence; stories that the one in which he died has been turned into a toilet are probably apocryphal. Among former students of the college are James Joyce, Patrick Pearse, leader of the 1916 Easter Rising, and Eamon de Valera.

The restoration of Newman House (☎ 475 7255) has been going on since 1990 and will continue for some time. The house is open June to September from 10 am to 4.30 pm Tuesday to Friday (no tours between 1.30 and 2.30 pm), Saturday 2 to 4.30 pm and Sunday 11 am to 2 pm. At other times of the year phone for information. The IR£2/1 entry includes a video about the building and a 40-minute guided tour.

Next to Newman House is the **Catholic University Church** or Newman Chapel, built in 1854-56 with a colourful neo-Byzantine interior that attracted a great deal of criticism at the time. Today this is one of the most fashionable churches in Dublin for weddings.

Merrion Square

Merrion Square, with its well-kept central park and elegant Georgian buildings, dates back to 1762 and has the National Gallery on its west side. Around this square you can find some of the best Georgian Dublin entrances, with fine doors and peacock fanlights, ornate door knockers and more than a few foot scrapers where gentlemen would remove

mud from their shoes before venturing indoors. Oscar Wilde's parents, the surgeon Sir William Wilde and the poet Lady Wilde, who wrote under the pseudonym Speranza, lived at 1 Merrion Square North. Oscar was born in 1854 at the now near-derelict 21 Westland Row, just north of the square.

W B Yeats (1865-1939) lived first at 52 Merrion Square East and later, in 1922-28, at 82 Merrion Square South. George (Æ) Russell (1867-1935), the 'poet, mystic, painter and co-operator', worked at No 84. Daniel O'Connell (1775-1847) was a resident of No 58 in his later years. The Austrian Erwin Schrödinger (1887-1961), co-winner of the 1933 Nobel Prize for physics, lived at No 65 between 1940 and 1956. Dublin seems to attract the writers of horror stories: Joseph Sheridan Le Fanu (1814-73), who penned the vampire classic *Carmilla*, was a former resident of No 70. The UK Embassy was at 39 Merrion Square East until it was burnt out in 1972 in protest against Bloody Sunday in Derry, Northern Ireland. The Architectural Association is at 8 Merrion Square North, a few doors down from the Wilde residence. The Leinster Lawn at the western end of the square has the 1791 **Rutland Fountain** and an 18-metre obelisk honouring the founders of independent Ireland.

Merrion Square has not always been merely graceful and affluent, however. During the 1845-51 potato famines, soup kitchens were set up in the gardens, which were crowded with starving rural refugees.

Damage to fine Dublin buildings has not always been the prerogative of vandals, terrorists or protesters. Merrion Square East once continued into Fitzwilliam St Lower in the longest unbroken series of Georgian houses anywhere in Europe. In 1961 the Electricity Supply Board knocked down 26 of them to build an office block. At the south-east corner of Merrion Square it had the decency to preserve one of the fine old Georgian houses at **No 29 Fitzwilliam St Lower** which has been restored to give a good impression of genteel home life in Dublin between 1790 and 1820.

The house is open from 10 am to 5 pm Tuesday to Saturday and 2 to 5 pm on Sunday, and an audiovisual display on its history is followed by a 30-minute guided tour. Entry has been free up till now, but it is likely that a fee will be introduced; phone ☎ 702 6165 to check.

Merrion St Upper & Ely Place

Merrion St Upper was built around 1770, and runs south from Merrion Square towards St Stephen's Green. The Duke of Wellington was probably born at the now rather run-down 24 Merrion St Upper. On the other side of Baggot St, Merrion St becomes Ely (pronounced 'e-lie') Place.

John Philpot Curran (1750-1817), a great advocate of Irish liberty, once lived at No 4, as did the novelist George Moore (1852-1933). The house at No 6 was the residence of the earl of Clare. Better known as Black Jack Fitzgibbon (1749-1802), he was a bitter opponent of Irish political aspirations, and in 1794 a mob attempted to storm the house. Ely House at No 8 is one of the city's best examples of a Georgian mansion. The plasterwork is by Michael Stapleton and the staircase, which illustrates the Labours of Hercules, is one of the finest in the city. At one time the surgeon Sir Thornley Stoker (whose brother Bram Stoker wrote *Dracula)* lived here. Oliver St John Gogarty (1878-1957) lived for a time at No 25, but the art gallery of the Royal Hibernian Academy now occupies that position.

Fitzwilliam Square

South of Merrion Square and east of St Stephen's Green, the original and well-kept Fitzwilliam Square is a centre for the Dublin medical profession. Built between 1791 and 1825, it was the smallest and the last of Dublin's great Georgian squares. It's also the only square where the central garden is still the private domain of residents of the square. William Dargan (1799-1861), the railway pioneer and founder of the National Gallery, lived at No 2, and Jack B Yeats (1871-1957) at No 18. Look out for the attractive 18th and 19th-century coalhole covers.

Other South Dublin Churches

St Andrew's Church The Protestant St Andrew's Church is on St Andrew's St near Trinity College, the Bank of Ireland and Grafton St. Designed by Charles Lanyon, the Gothic-style church was built in 1860-73 on the site of an ancient nunnery. Across the street, on the corner of Church Lane and Suffolk St, there once stood a huge Viking ceremonial mound or *thingmote*. It was levelled in 1661 and used to raise the level of Nassau St, which had previously been subject to flooding.

Whitefriars Carmelite Church Next to the popular Avalon House backpackers hostel on Aungier St, the Carmelite Church stands on the former site of the Whitefriars Carmelite monastery. The monastery was founded in 1278 but, like other monasteries, was suppressed by Henry VIII in 1537 and all its lands and wealth seized by the Crown. Eventually the Carmelites returned to their former church and re-established it, dedicating the new building in 1827.

In the north-east corner of the church the 16th-century Flemish oak statue of the Virgin & Child escaped destruction during the Reformation; it probably once belonged to St Mary's Abbey in north Dublin. The church's altar contains the remains of St Valentine, of St Valentine's Day fame, donated to the church in 1836 by the pope.

St Ann's Church St Ann's on Dawson St near Mansion House was built in 1720 but is now lost behind an 1868 neo-Romanesque facade. There's a fine view of it looking down Anne St South from Grafton St, and it is noted for its lunch-time recitals.

St Stephen's Church Built in 1824 in Greek Revival style, St Stephen's, complete with cupola, is at the far end of Mount St Upper from Merrion Square and has been converted into business units. Because of its appearance, it has been nicknamed the 'Peppercanister Church'. You can get in to see the interior between 12.30 and 3.20 pm Monday to Friday.

South Dublin Theatres

Dublin's famous **Abbey Theatre** is north of the Liffey, but the city's first theatre opened in 1637 on Werburgh St, near Dublin Castle and the two cathedrals. It was closed by the Puritans only four years later, but another theatre, Smock Alley Playhouse or Theatre Royal, opened in 1661 and continued for over a century. Today theatres south of the Liffey include the **Gaiety Theatre** on King St South, just off Grafton St. Built in 1871, this is Dublin's oldest theatre and now hosts a variety of performances.

The 1892 **Olympia Theatre**, on Dame St in Temple Bar, is the city's largest and second-oldest theatre and is a venue for popular performances. It was previously known as the Palace Theatre and Dan Lowry's Music Hall. Also south of the Liffey is the **Tivoli Theatre** on Francis St in the Liberties. A number of other Dublin theatres are listed under Other Theatres in the Other Sights section later.

NORTH OF THE LIFFEY

Though south Dublin has the lion's share of the city's tourist attractions, there are still many reasons to head across the Liffey, starting with Dublin's grandest avenue.

O'Connell St

O'Connell St is the major thoroughfare of north Dublin and probably the most important and imposing street in the whole city, even now that its earlier glory has gone. It started life in the early 18th century as Drogheda St, named after Viscount Henry Moore, the earl of Drogheda. There are still a Henry St, a Moore St and an Earl St nearby. The earl even managed to squeeze in an Of Lane! At that time Capel St, farther to the west, was the main traffic route and Drogheda St, lacking a bridge to connect it with south Dublin, was of little importance.

In the 1740s Luke Gardiner, later Viscount Mountjoy, widened the street to 45 metres to turn it into an elongated promenade bearing his name. However, it was the completion of the Carlisle Bridge across the Liffey in 1794 which quickly made it the city's most important street. In 1880 the Carlisle Bridge was replaced by the much wider O'Connell Bridge which stands today.

Gardiner's Mall soon became Sackville St, but it was renamed again in 1924 after Daniel O'Connell, the Irish nationalist leader whose 1854 bronze statue surveys the avenue from the river end. The bullet marks are a legacy of the Easter Rising in 1916 and the Civil War in 1922.

The street's once most famous monument was a victim of explosive redesign. In 1815 O'Connell St was graced with a Doric column topped by a statue of Nelson, the British naval captain who defeated the French at Trafalgar. It predated his column in Trafalgar Square (London) by 32 years, but in 1966, in an unofficial celebration of the 50th anniversary of the 1916 Rising, this symbol of British imperialism was damaged by an explosion and subsequently demolished. Nelson's demise put an end to the quip that the main street of the capital city of this most piously Catholic of countries had statues honouring three noted adulterers: O'Connell at the bottom of the street, Parnell at the top and Nelson in the middle.

The site of Nelson's demolished column is halfway up the street, between Henry and Earl Sts, opposite the GPO. Nearby, a figure of James Joyce lounges nonchalantly at the top of pedestrianised Earl St North. Just beyond the former site of the column is a fountain figure of Anna Livia, Joyce's spirit of the Liffey – a 1988 addition to the streetscape. It was almost immediately dubbed the 'floozy in the jacuzzi'.

The tourist office and the Gresham Hotel are on the right before the figure of Father Theobald Mathew (1790-1856), the 'apostle of temperance', a hopeless role in Ireland. This quixotic task, however, also resulted in a Liffey bridge bearing his name. The top of the street is completed by the imposing statue of Charles Stewart Parnell (1846-91), Home Rule advocate and victim of Irish morality.

O'Connell St has certainly had its share of drama; its high-speed redevelopment began during the 1916 Easter Rising when the GPO building became the starting point for, and main centre of, the abortive revolt. Only six years later in 1922 the unfortunate avenue suffered another bout of destruction when it became the scene of a Civil War clash that burnt down most of the eastern side of the street.

Poor O'Connell St was to suffer even more damage in the 1960s and 1970s when Dublin went through a period of rampant development under lax government controls. Developers seemed to have a free hand to tear anything down and sling anything up so long as there was money in it and today's tacky fast-food and cheap-office-block atmosphere is a reminder of that era.

Close to O'Connell St is an energetic and colourful open-air market area just to the west on Moore St. The Abbey Theatre and the Catholic St Mary's Pro-Cathedral are to the east. At the top of O'Connell St is Parnell Square.

General Post Office

The GPO building on O'Connell St is an important landmark physically and historically. The building, designed by Francis Johnston and opened in 1818, was the focus for the 1916 Easter Rising when Patrick Pearse, James Connolly and the other leaders read their proclamation from the front steps. In the subsequent siege the building was completely burnt out. The façade with its Ionic portico is still pockmarked from the 1916 clash and from further damage wrought at the start of the Civil War in 1922. The GPO was not reopened until 1929. Its central role in the history of independent Ireland has made it a prime site for everything from official parades to personal protests.

Abbey Theatre

Opened in 1904, the Abbey Theatre (☎ 878 7222) is just north of the Liffey on the corner of Marlborough St and Abbey St Lower. The Irish National Theatre Society soon made a name not only for playwrights like J M Synge and Sean O'Casey but also for Irish acting ability and theatrical presentation. The 1907 premiere of J M Synge's *The Playboy of the Western World* brought a storm of protest from theatregoers, and Sean O'Casey's *The Plough & the Stars* prompted a similar reaction in 1926. On the latter occasion W B Yeats himself came on stage after the performance to tick the audience off!

The original theatre burnt down in 1951. It took 15 years to come up with a replacement and the dull building fails to live up to its famous name or the company's continuing reputation. The smaller Peacock Theatre at the same location presents new and experimental works.

St Mary's Pro-Cathedral

On the corner of Marlborough and Cathedral Sts, just east of O'Connell St, is Dublin's most important Catholic church, built between 1816 and 1825. The Pro-Cathedral was originally intended to be built on O'Connell St, but fears that such a prominent position would provoke anti-Catholic feeling among the English led to its site being comparatively hidden. Unfortunately, the cramped Marlborough St location makes it all but impossible to stand back far enough to admire the front with its six Doric columns, modelled on the Temple of Theseus in Athens.

The 1814 competition for the church's design was won by John Sweetman, a former owner of Sweetman's Brewery. Who organised the competition? Why William Sweetman, John Sweetman's brother. And did John Sweetman design it himself? Well, possibly not. He was living in Paris at the time and may have bought the plans from a French architect who designed the remarkably similar Notre Dame de Lorette in Paris.

Tyrone House

On Marlborough St, opposite the Pro-Cathedral, the sombre Tyrone House, built in 1740-41, is now occupied by the Department of Education. It was designed by Richard Castle and features plasterwork by the Francini brothers. On the lawn is a marble *Pietà* (statue of the Virgin Mary cradling the dead body of Jesus Christ) sculpted in 1930 and given to Ireland by the Italian government in 1948 in thanks for Irish assistance

DUBLIN

immediately after the war. This area was once a busy red-light district known as Monto and featured in Joyce's *Ulysses* as Nighttown.

Parnell Square

The principal squares of north Dublin are poor relations of the great squares south of the Liffey. Parnell Square's north side was built on lands acquired in the mid-18th century by Dr Bartholomew Mosse and was originally named Palace Row. The terrace was laid out in 1755 and Lord Charlemont bought the land for his home at No 22 in 1762. Charlemont's home was designed by Sir William Chambers, who also designed Lord Charlemont's extraordinary Casino at Marino to the north-east of the city centre. Today the building is home to the Municipal Gallery of Modern Art. The street was completed in 1769 and the gardens were renamed Rutland Square in 1786, before acquiring their current name.

In 1966 the northern slice of the square was turned into a Garden of Remembrance for the 50th anniversary of the 1916 Easter Rising. Its centrepiece is a sculpture by Oisin Kelly depicting the myth of the Children of Lir, who were transformed into swans for 900 years. The square also contains the Gate Theatre, the Ambassador Cinema and the Rotunda Hospital.

There are some fine, though generally rather run-down, Georgian houses on the east side of the square. Oliver St John Gogarty, immortalised as Buck Mulligan in Joyce's *Ulysses*, was born at No 5 in 1878. On the other side of the square, at 44 Parnell Square West, you can find the Sinn Féin Bookshop.

Dr Bartholomew Mosse, who originally acquired the land on which Parnell Square is built, opened the **Rotunda Hospital** in 1757. This was the first maternity hospital in Ireland or Britain, built at a time when Dublin's burgeoning urban population suffered horrific levels of infant mortality. The hospital shares its basic design with Leinster House because Richard Castle reused the floorplan as an economy measure.

To his Leinster House design Castle added a three-storey tower which Mosse had intended to use as a lookout to raise funds for the hospital's operation. The Rotunda Assembly Hall, now occupied by the Ambassador Cinema, was built as an adjunct to the hospital as another fundraiser. At one time an adjacent pleasure garden was another money-raising venture. Over the main entrance of the hospital is the Rotunda Chapel, built in 1758 with superb coloured plasterwork by Bartholomew Cramillion.

The Rotunda Hospital still functions as a maternity hospital. The Patrick Conway pub opposite the hospital dates from 1745 and has been hosting expectant fathers since the day the hospital opened.

At the top end of O'Connell St, in the south-east corner of Parnell Square, is the **Gate Theatre**, opened in 1929 by Micheál MacLiammóir and Hilton Edwards. MacLiammóir continued to act at his theatre until 1975, when he retired at the age of 76 after making his 1384th performance of the one-man show *The Importance of Being Oscar* (Oscar being Oscar Wilde, of course). The Gate Theatre was also the stage for Orson Welles's first professional appearance. The building dates from 1784-86 when it was constructed as part of the Rotunda complex of the Rotunda Maternity Hospital.

The **Municipal Gallery of Modern Art** or Hugh Lane Gallery (☎ 874 1903) at 22 Parnell Square North has a fine collection of work by the French Impressionists and of 20th-century Irish art.

The gallery was founded in 1908 and moved to its present location in Charlemont House, formerly the Earl of Charlemont's town house, in 1933. The gallery was established by wealthy Sir Hugh Lane, who died in the 1915 sinking of the *Lusitania*, which was torpedoed off the southern coast of Ireland by a German U-boat. The Lane Bequest pictures, which formed the nucleus of the gallery, were the subject of a dispute over Lane's will between the gallery and the National Gallery in London. A settlement was finally reached in 1959 which split the collection.

The gallery includes a shop and the Gallery Restaurant. In 1995 the gallery was being extensively renovated. It used to be open, free, Tuesday to Friday from 9.30 am to 6 pm, Saturday 9.30 am to 5 pm, Sunday 11 am to 5 pm, but phone to check before visiting.

The **Dublin Writers' Museum** (☎ 872 2077), 18 Parnell Square North next to the Hugh Lanc Gallery, celebrates the city's long and continuing history as a literary centre. The Gallery of Writers upstairs houses busts and portraits of some of Ireland's most famous writers; their letters, photographs and first editions are downstairs. There's a good section on children's authors on the top floor.

The museum also has a bookshop and the Chapter One restaurant.

Entry is IR£2.60/1.10 (students IR£2) and it's open from 10 am to 5 pm Monday to Saturday, 11.30 am to 6 pm Sunday. In June, July and August it stays open until 7 pm on Friday. If you plan to visit the James Joyce Tower and the George Bernard Shaw Museum, bear in mind that combined tickets are cheaper than three separate ones.

While the museum concerns itself primarily with dead authors, next door at No 19 the Irish Writers' Centre provides a meeting and working place for their living successors.

The soaring spire of the **Abbey Presbyterian Church** at the corner of Frederick St and Parnell Square North, overlooking Parnell Square, is a convenient landmark. Dating from 1864 the church was financed by the Scottish grocery and brewery magnate Alex Findlater and is often referred to as Findlater's Church.

National Wax Museum

Every city worth its tourist traps has a wax museum. Dublin's National Wax Museum (☎ 872 6340) is on Granby Row, just north of Parnell Square. Along with the usual fantasy and fairy-tale offerings, the inevitable Chamber of Horrors and a rock music 'megastars' area, there are also figures of Irish heroes like Wolfe Tone, Robert Emmet and Charles Parnell, the leaders of the 1916

Easter Rising, and the Taoisigh (prime ministers, plural of Taoiseach). Prominent figures from the northern Troubles also get a look in – John Hume and Ian Paisley, but no Gerry Adams yet. Recorded commentaries explain each individual's role in Irish history. The museum is open Monday to Saturday from 10 am to 6 pm, Sunday noon to 6 pm. Entry is IR£3.50/2, family IR£10.

Great Denmark St

From the north-east corner of Parnell Square, Great Denmark St runs eastwards to Mountjoy Square, passing by the 1775 Belvedere House which has been used since 1841 as the Jesuit **Belvedere College**. James Joyce was a student there between 1893 and 1898 and describes it in *A Portrait of the Artist as a Young Man*. The building is renowned for its magnificent plasterwork by the master stuccodore Michael Stapleton and for its fireplaces by the Venetian artisan Bossi.

Mountjoy Square

Built between 1792 and 1818, Mountjoy Square was a fashionable and affluent centre at the height of the Protestant Ascendancy, but today it's just a run-down symbol of north Dublin's urban decay. Viscount Mountjoy, after whom the square was named, was that energetic developer Luke Gardiner, who briefly gave his name to Gardiner Mall before it became Sackville St and then O'Connell St. The square was in fact named after him twice, as it started life as Gardiner Square.

Legends relate that this was where Brian Ború pitched his tent at the Battle of Clontarf in 1014. Residents of the square have included Sean O'Casey, who set his play *The Shadow of a Gunman* here, though he referred to it as Hilljoy Square. As a child James Joyce lived just off the square at 14 Fitzgibbon St.

St Francis Xavier Church

Built in 1829-32 on Gardiner St Upper, the Catholic St Francis Xavier Church has a superb Italian altar and coffered ceiling. It was originally intended that the church be built on Great Charles St, behind Mountjoy Square.

St George's Church

St George's Church is on Hardwicke Place off Temple St, but was originally intended to be built in Mountjoy Square. It was built by Francis Johnston from 1802 in Greek Ionic style and has a 60-metre-high steeple modelled after that of St Martin-in-the-Fields in London. The church's bells were added in 1836 and originally hung in a bell tower in Francis Johnston's own back garden in nearby Eccles St. Not surprisingly, neighbours complained about the noise and Johnston eventually willed them to the church. This was one of Johnston's finest works and the Duke of Wellington was married here, but the church is no longer in use.

St Mary's Abbey

Despite the intriguing history of St Mary's Abbey, there is little to see, the opening hours are very restricted and even finding the abbey is tricky; it's just west of Capel St in Meetinghouse Lane, which runs off a street named Mary's Abbey. When the abbey was founded in 1139 this was a rural location, far from the temptations of city life to the south of the Liffey. In 1147, soon after its foundation by the Benedictine monks, it was taken over by the Cistercians. Until its suppression in the mid-16th century this was the most important monastery within English-controlled Ireland. St Mary's property was confiscated by Henry VIII in 1537; it turned out to be the most valuable in all of Ireland, at a total of £537. Mellifont Abbey to the north of Dublin came in second at £352 but no other monastery in the whole country was worth over £100.

The abbey was virtually derelict when the next century rolled around, although at that time Dublin had not started its sprawl north of the river. Records indicate that in 1676 stones from the abbey were used to construct the Essex Bridge and it was not until com-

paratively recently that the remaining fragments were rediscovered.

The chapter house, where the monks used to gather after morning mass, is the only surviving part of the abbey, which in its prime encompassed land stretching as far east as Ballybough. The floor level in the abbey is two metres below street level – a clear indication of the changes wrought over eight centuries. Exhibits in the abbey tell of the destruction of the Reformation in 1540 and the story of the statue from St Mary's which is now in the Whitefriars Carmelite Church on Aungier St in south Dublin.

At the time of writing the abbey was closed indefinitely. You could try phoning ☎ 872 1490 to see if it's reopened. The old opening hours were just mid-June to September and even then only on Wednesday from 10 am to 5 pm. Entry was IR£1/40p.

St Mary's Church

In Mary St, between Capel and Liffey Sts, St Mary's was designed in 1697 by Sir William Robinson, who was also responsible for the Royal Hospital Kilmainham. The church was completed in 1702 and a roll call of famous Dubliners were baptised there. It was in this church that John Wesley, the founder of Methodism, preached for the first time in Ireland in 1747. Nevertheless, like so many other fine old Dublin churches, it is no longer in use. Irish patriot Wolfe Tone was born on the adjacent Wolfe Tone St.

St Michan's Church

Named after a Danish saint, St Michan's Church on Church St Lower, near the Four Courts, dates from its Danish foundation in 1095, though there's barely a trace of that original church to be seen. The battlement tower dates from the 15th century but otherwise it was rebuilt in the late 17th century and considerably restored in the early 19th century and again after suffering damage in the Civil War.

The church contains the organ which Handel may or may not have played for the first-ever performance of his *Messiah*. The organcase is distinguished by a fine oak carving of 17 entwined musical instruments on its front. On one side of the altar a skull on the floor is said to represent Oliver Cromwell, on the other a penitent's chair was for people to make public confessions. The main 'attraction' lies in the subterranean crypt where a group of bodies have been preserved to varying degrees not by mummification but by the constant dry atmosphere. In 1996 a fire lit by vandals caused the crypt to be closed to the public.

Tours are conducted from 10 am to 12.45 pm and 2 to 4.45 pm Monday to Friday, and on Saturday morning only. The cost is IR£1.20/50p.

Irish Whiskey Corner

Just north of St Michan's Church, the Irish Whiskey Corner (☎ 872 5566) is in an old warehouse on Bow St, Dublin 7, and the admission charge of IR£3 includes entry to the museum, a short film and a sample of Irish whiskey. From May to October there are tours Monday to Friday at 11 am, and 2.30 and 3.30 pm; in winter only the afternoon tour operates.

James Joyce Centre

North Great George's St was once a fashionable address in 18th-century Dublin. However, like so much of the north it fell on hard times after the Act of Union turned Dublin into a backwater. After James Joyce's family moved into the north of the city, he would have been familiar with the street; the dancing instructor Denis Maginni who taught in the front room appears several times in *Ulysses*. In the 20th century many of the houses became run-down tenements; No 35 was taken over by Dublin Corporation who wanted to tear it down.

Then in 1982 Senator David Norris, a charismatic Joycean scholar and gay-rights activist, moved into the street and persuaded the Dublin Corporation to let him take over the house. It has now been restored and turned into a centre for the study of James Joyce and his books. A self-guide tour leaflet is available and visitors can see the room where Maginni taught and a collection of pictures of the 17 Dublin addresses occupied at one time or another by Joyce's family and of the real individuals fictionalised in his books. Some of the fine plaster ceilings are restored originals, others careful reproductions of Michael Stapleton's designs.

Admission is IR£2/1.50. The house is open Monday to Saturday from 9.30 am to 5 pm and Sunday from 12.30 to 5 pm. Tours of north Dublin depart from here every day except Sunday (see Walking Tours below).

Incidentally, North Great George's St as a whole has benefited from a facelift and boasts some fine Georgian doorways and fanlights.

King's Inns & Henrietta St

North of the river on Constitution Hill and Henrietta St is King's Inns, home for the Dublin legal fraternity. This classical building is another James Gandon creation though it suffered many delays between its design in 1795 and its final completion in 1817. Along the way a number of other architects lent a hand, including Francis Johnston, who added the cupola. The building is normally open only to members of the Inns.

Henrietta St, leading up to the south side of the building, was Dublin's first Georgian street and has buildings dating from 1720 but is unfortunately now in a state of disrepair. These early Georgian mansions were large and varied in style and for a time Henrietta St rejoiced in the name Primate's Hill, as the archbishop of Armagh and other high church officials lived there. Luke Gardiner, who was responsible for so much of the early development of Georgian north Dublin, lived at 10 Henrietta St.

OTHER SIGHTS

There's still much more to see in Dublin. To the west are the Guinness Brewery in the colourful Liberties area, Kilmainham Jail and Phoenix Park. To the north and northeast are the Royal Canal, Prospect Cemetery, the Botanic Gardens, the Casino at Marino and Clontarf. To the south and south-east are the Grand Canal, Ballsbridge, the Royal

DUBLIN

DUBLIN

Dublin Showground and the Chester Beatty Library.

St Catherine's Church

Westward from St Audoen's Church, towards that more recent Dublin shrine, the Guinness Brewery, is St Catherine's Church, whose huge front faces on to Thomas St. The church was built on the site of St Thomas Abbey, which King Henry II built in honour of Thomas à Becket, the Archbishop of Canterbury, after having him killed. The church was completed in 1769 and, after narrowly escaping redevelopment in the 1960s, is now used as a community centre. After being hanged, the corpse of patriot Robert Emmet was put to the further indignity of being beheaded outside the church in 1803.

Guinness Brewery

Moving west past St Audoen's churches, Thomas St metamorphoses into James's St in the area of Dublin known as the Liberties. Along James's St stretches the historic St James's Gate Guinness Brewery (☎ 453 6700, ext 5155) where 2½ million pints of stout are still brewed daily. From its foundation by Arthur Guinness in 1759, on the site of the earlier Rainsford Brewery, the operation has expanded down to the Liffey and across both sides of the street. It covers 26 hectares and for a time was the largest brewery in the world. The oldest parts of the site are south of James's St; at one time there was a gate spanning the street.

In the Guinness Hop Store on Crane St, visitors can watch a Guinness audiovisual display and inspect an extensive Guinness museum. It may not be a tour of the brewery, but your entry fee includes a glass of the black stuff.

In its early years Guinness was only one of dozens of Dublin breweries but it outgrew and outlasted all of them. At one time a Grand Canal tributary was cut into the brewery to enable special Guinness barges to carry consignments out onto the Irish canal system or to the Dublin port. When the brewery extensions reached the Liffey in 1872, the fleet of Guinness barges became a

familiar sight. There was also a Guinness railway on the site, complete with a spiral tunnel. Guinness still operates its own ships to convey the vital fluid to the British market. Over 50% of all the beer consumed in Ireland is brewed here.

The Guinness family became noted philanthropists. Sir Benjamin Lee Guinness, grandson of the brewery founder, restored St Patrick's Cathedral. Sir Benjamin's son, Lord Ardilaun, opened St Stephen's Green to the public and converted it into a park, and his brother Lord Iveagh helped to build a wing of the Rotunda Hospital.

Opening hours are from 10 am to 4.30 pm (last audiovisual show at 3.50 pm) Monday to Friday. Entry is IR£2/50p. To get there take bus No 21A, 78 or 78A from Fleet St. The upper floors of the building house temporary art exhibits.

Round the corner at No 1 Thomas St, a plaque marks the house where Arthur Guinness (1725-1803) lived. In a yard across the road stands **St Patrick's Tower**, Europe's tallest smock windmill, built about 1757.

IMMA & Royal Hospital Kilmainham

The Irish Museum of Modern Art or IMMA (☎ 671 8666) at the old Royal Hospital Kilmainham is close to Kilmainham Jail. The gallery only opened in 1991 and the exhibits look a bit swamped by their expansive surroundings. Regular temporary exhibition top up the permanent displays.

The Royal Hospital Kilmainham was built in 1680-87 but not as a hospital. It was in fact a home for retired soldiers and continued to fill that role until after Irish independence. It preceded the similar Chelsea Hospital in London and inmates were often referred to as 'Chelsea Pensioners' although there was no connection. At the time of its construction it was one of the finest buildings in Ireland and there was considerable muttering that it was altogether too good a place for its residents. The building was designed by William Robinson, whose other work included Marsh's Library.

There's a good café and bookshop. The IMMA is open from 10 am to 5.30 pm Tuesday to Saturday and noon to 5.30 pm on Sunday. Entry is free and there are guided tours on Sunday, Wednesday and Friday at 2.30 am and Saturday at 11.30 am, with heritage tours on Sunday between 2 and 4.30 pm. You can get there on bus Nos 24, 79 or 90 from Aston Quay outside the Virgin Megastore.

Kilmainham Jail

Built in 1792-95, the threatening old Kilmainham Jail (☎ 453 5984) on Inchicore Rd played a key role in Ireland's struggle for independence and was the site of the executions that followed the 1916 Easter Rising. During each act of Ireland's long and painful path to independence from neighbouring Britain, at least one part of the performance took place at the jail. The uprisings of 1799, 1803, 1848, 1867 and 1916 all ended with the leaders being confined in Kilmainham. Robert Emmet, Thomas Francis Meagher, Charles Stewart Parnell and the 1916 Easter Rising leaders were all visitors, but it was the executions in 1916 which most deeply etched the jail's name into the Irish consciousness. Of the 15 executions that took place between 3 and 12 May after the rising, 14 were conducted here. As a finale, prisoners from the Civil War struggles were held here from 1922. The jail closed for good in 1924.

A visit starts with an excellent audiovisual introduction followed by a tour. Incongru-ously sitting outside in the yard is the *Asgard*, the ship which successfully ran the British blockade to deliver arms to nationalist forces in 1914. The tour finishes in the gloomy yard where the 1916 executions took place. You almost expect to see the gates swing back and a wounded James Connolly brought in to face the firing squad.

Opening hours are from 10 am to 6 pm daily May to September, and 1 to 4 pm Monday to Friday and 1 to 6 pm on Sunday from October to April. Entry is IR£2/1 and you can get there by bus Nos 23, 51, 51A, 78 or 79 from the city centre.

A new visitor's centre is due to open in time for the 80th anniversary of the 1916 Easter Rising.

Kilmainham Gate was designed by Francis Johnston in 1812 and originally stood, as the Richmond Tower, at Watling St Bridge near the Guinness Brewery. It was moved to its current position opposite the jail in 1846 as it obstructed the increasingly heavy traffic to the new Kingsbridge Railway Station, now known as Heuston Station.

Phoenix Park

The 700-plus hectares of Phoenix Park make it one of the world's largest city parks, dwarfing Central Park in New York (a mere 337 hectares) and all the London parks – Hampstead Heath is only 324 hectares. There are gardens and lakes, a host of sporting facilities, the second-oldest public zoo in Europe, a visitor's centre and castle, various government offices, the Garda Síochána (police) Headquarters, the residences of the US ambassador and the Irish president, and even a herd of deer.

The land was originally confiscated from the Kilmainham priory of St John to create a royal deer park. It was turned into a park by Lord Ormonde in 1671 but was not opened to the public until 1747 by Lord Chesterfield. The name Phoenix is actually a corruption of the Irish words for clear water, *fionn uisce*. The park played a crucial role in Irish history, as Lord Cavendish, the British Chief Secretary for Ireland, and his assistant were murdered here in 1882 by an Irish nationalist secret society called the National Invincibles. Lord Cavendish's home is now Deerfield, the US ambassador's residence, and the murder took place outside **Áras an Uachtaráin**, from 1782 until 1922 the viceroy's residence, now occupied by the Irish president. It was built in 1751 and enlarged in 1782 and again in 1816. From 1922 until the final ties with the British crown were cut in 1937 it was the home of Ireland's governor-general.

Near the Parkgate St entrance to the park is the 63-metre-high **Wellington Monument** obelisk. It took from 1817 to 1861 to be built, mainly because the Duke of Wellington fell from public favour during its construction. Nearby are the People's Garden, dating from 1864, the bandstand in the Hollow and the Dublin Zoo. Main Rd separates the Hollow and the zoo from the Phoenix Park Cricket Club of 1830 and from Citadel Pond, usually referred to as the Dog Pond.

Established in 1830, **Dublin Zoo** (☎ 677 1425) is one of the oldest in the world. It's mainly of interest to children although the pets' corner is a depressing sight. The lion-breeding programme dates back to 1857 and produced the lion that roars at the start of MGM films. Entry is IR£5.50/2.90 and it's open from 9.30 am to 6 pm Monday to Saturday, and from 10.30 am on Sunday. The 12-hectare zoo is in the south-east corner of Phoenix Park and can be reached by bus No 10 from O'Connell St or bus No 25 or 26 from Abbey St Middle.

Behind the zoo, on the edge of the park, the Garda Síochána Headquarters has a small **police museum**.

Main Rd runs right through the park past the Irish president's residence on the right. On the left a huge cross marks the site where Pope John Paul II preached to 1¼ million people in 1979. In the centre of the park the **Phoenix Monument**, erected by Lord Chesterfield in 1747, looks very unphoenix-like and is often referred to as the Eagle Monument. North-west of the monument is the **Visitor Centre** housed in what were once the stables of the Papal Nuntiate. A video outlines the history of the park and there are two floors of exhibits. Visitors are taken on a tour of neighbouring **Ashtown Castle**, a 17th-century tower house which had been concealed inside the Papal Nuntiate until its demolition in 1986; box hedges pick out the ground-plan of the old building. The Visitor Centre is open daily in March and October to November from 9.30 am to 5 pm, closing half an hour earlier from December to February. June to September it stays open until 6.30 pm. Admission is IR£2/1.

The southern part of the park is given over to a large number of football and hurling fields, and, though they occupy about 80 hectares (200 acres), the area is known as the Fifteen Acres.

White's Gate, the park exit from its north-west side, leads to Castleknock College and Castleknock Castle. Near White's Gate and Quarry Pond at the north-west end of the park are the offices of the Ordnance Survey, the government mapping department. South of this building is the attractive rural-looking Furry Glen and Glen Pond corner of the park.

Looping back towards the Parkgate entrance, you'll see **Magazine Fort**, which stands on Thomas's Hill. The fort took from 1734 to 1801 to build and never served any discernible purpose although it was a target for the 1916 Easter Rising.

The Royal Canal

Constructed from 1790, by which time the older Grand Canal was already past its prime, the Royal Canal, which encircles Dublin to the north, was a commercial failure, but its story is certainly colourful. It was founded by Long John Binns, a Grand Canal director who quit the board because of a supposed insult over his being a shoemaker. He established the Royal Canal principally for revenge but it never made money and actually became known as the Shoemaker's Canal. In 1840 the canal was sold to a railway company and tracks still run alongside much of the canal's route through the city.

The Royal Canal towpath makes a relaxing walk through the heart of the city. You can join it beside Newcomen Bridge at Strand Rd North, just north of Connolly Station, and follow it to the suburb of Clonsilla and beyond, over 10 km away. The walk is particularly pleasant beyond Binns Bridge in Drumcondra. At the top of Blessington St, near the Dublin International Youth Hostel, a large pond which was used when the canal also supplied drinking water to the city, now attracts waterbirds.

Prospect Cemetery

Prospect or Glasnevin Cemetery, the largest in Ireland, was established in 1832 as a cemetery for Roman Catholics who faced opposition when they conducted burials in the city's Protestant cemeteries. Many of the monuments and memorials have staunchly patriotic overtones with numerous high crosses, shamrocks, harps and other Irish symbols. The single most imposing memorial is the colossal monument to Cardinal McCabe (1837-1921), the Archbishop of Dublin and Primate of Ireland.

A modern replica of a round tower acts as a handy landmark for locating the tomb of Daniel O'Connell, who died in 1847 and was reinterred here in 1869, when the tower was completed. Charles Stewart Parnell's tomb is topped with a huge granite rock. Other notable people buried here include Sir Roger Casement, who was executed for treason by the British in 1916 and whose remains were not returned to Ireland until 1964; the republican leader Michael Collins who died in the Civil War; the docker and trade unionist Jim Larkin, a prime force in the 1913 general strike; and the poet Gerard Manley Hopkins. There's also a poignant 'class' memorial to the men who have starved themselves to death for the cause of Irish freedom over the century, including 10 of them in 1981.

The most interesting parts of the cemetery are at the south-eastern Prospect Square end. The cemetery watchtowers were once used to keep watch for body snatchers. *Ulysses* pauses at the cemetery and there are a number of clues for Joyce enthusiasts to track down.

National Botanic Gardens

Founded in 1795, the National Botanic Gardens, directly north of the centre on Botanic Rd in Glasnevin, were used as a garden before that time, but only the Yew Walk, also known as Addison's Walk, has trees dating back to the first half of the 18th century. Unfortunately, much of the gardens are like a rather dull garden allotment – you start to wonder where the potato beds are.

The gardens cover 19 hectares and are flanked to the north by the River Tolka. The recently restored curvilinear glasshouses date from 1843-69 and were created by Richard Turner who was also responsible for the glasshouse at the Belfast Botanic Gardens and the Palm House in London's Kew Gardens. Dublin's gardens also have a palm house, built in 1884. Among the pioneering botanical work conducted here was the first attempt to raise orchids from seed, back in 1844. Pampas grass and the giant lily were first grown in Europe in these gardens.

The gardens are open Monday to Saturday from 9 am to 6 pm in summer and 10 am to 4.30 pm in winter, Sunday 11 am to 6 pm in summer and 11 am to 4.30 pm in winter. The conservatories have shorter opening hours; in particular, they only open on Sunday afternoon from 2 pm. Entry is free. You can get there on bus Nos 13 or 19 from O'Connell St or Nos 34 or 34A from Abbey St Middle.

Casino at Marino

The Casino at Marino on Malahide Rd in Marino, just north-east of the centre, is not a casino at all but a pleasure house built for the earl of Charlemont in the grounds of Marino House in the mid-18th century. Although Marino House itself was demolished in the 1920s the Casino survives as a wonderful folly.

Externally the building, with its 12 Tuscan columns forming a temple-like facade and its huge entrance doorway, creates the expectation that inside it will be a simple single open space. But inside it's an extravagant convoluted maze: the flights of fancy include chimneys for the central heating which are disguised as roof urns, downpipes hidden in columns, carved draperies, ornate fireplaces, beautiful parquet floors constructed of rare woods and a spacious wine cellar. A variety of statuary adorns the outside but it's the amusing fakes which are most enjoyable. The towering front door is a sham, and a much smaller panel opens to reveal the secret interior. Similarly, the windows have blacked-out panels to hide the fact that the interior is a complex of rooms, not a single chamber.

In 1870 the town house was sold to the government. The Marino estate followed in 1881 and the by then decrepit Casino in 1930. Restoration is continuing and although the Casino grounds are only a tiny fragment of the Marino estate, trees and planting will help to hide the surrounding houses.

The Casino is open daily from 9.30 am to 6.30 pm from early June to September. At other times of the year ring the Casino (☎ 833 1618) or the Office of Public Works

(☎ 661 3111, ext 2386) for details of opening hours. You can only visit the building on a guided tour; entry is IR£2/1. The Casino is just off Malahide Rd, north of the junction with Howth Rd in Clontarf. Bus Nos 20A, 20B, 27, 27A, 27B, 32A, 42 or 42B will take you there from the centre.

Clontarf & North Bull Island

Clontarf, a bayside suburb five km north-east of the centre, has popular cheaper B&Bs. The name was originally *Cluain Tarbh*, the bull's meadow, and it was here in 1014 that Brian Ború defeated the Danes at the Battle of Clontarf. The Irish hero was killed by fleeing Danes who found the old man in his tent, and his son and grandson died in the battle. The Normans later erected a castle here which was handed on to the Knights Templar in 1179, rebuilt in 1835 and later converted into a hotel.

The North Bull Wall, extending from

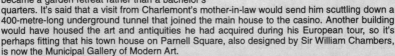

The Earl & the Casino
The somewhat eccentric James Caulfield (1728-99), later to become the earl of Charlemont, set out on a European grand tour at the age of 18 in 1746. The visit was to last nine years, including a four-year spell in Italy, and he returned to Ireland with a huge art collection and a burning ambition to bring Italian style to the estate he acquired in 1756. He commissioned Sir William Chambers to design the casino, a process which started in the late 1750s, continued into the 1770s, and never really came to a conclusion, in part because Lord Charlemont frittered away his fortune.

When Lord Charlemont married, the casino became a garden retreat rather than a bachelor's quarters. It's said that a visit from Charlemont's mother-in-law would send him scuttling down a 400-metre-long underground tunnel that joined the main house to the casino. Another building would have housed the art and antiquities he had acquired during his European tour, so it's perhaps fitting that his town house on Parnell Square, also designed by Sir William Chambers, is now the Municipal Gallery of Modern Art.

Despite his wealth, Charlemont was a comparatively liberal and free-thinking aristocrat. He never fenced in his demesne and allowed the public to use it as an open park.

He was not the only local eccentric; in 1792 a painter named Folliot took a dislike to the lord and built Marino Crescent at the bottom of Malahide Rd purely to block his view of the sea. Bram Stoker (1847-1912), author of *Dracula*, was born at 15 Marino Crescent.

After Charlemont's death his estate, crippled by his debts, collapsed. The art collection was dispersed. ■

Clontarf about a km into Dublin Bay, was built in 1820 at the suggestion of Captain William Bligh of HMS *Bounty* mutiny fame, in order to stop the harbour from silting up. The marshes and dunes of North Bull Island are home to the Royal Dublin and St Anne's golf courses. Many birds migrate here from the Arctic in winter, and at times the bird population can reach 40,000. The interpretive centre is reached via the northern causeway to the island but buses don't run as far as this and it's a good 1.5 km to walk across.

The Grand Canal

Built to connect Dublin with the River Shannon, the Grand Canal makes a graceful six-km loop around south Dublin. At its eastern end the canal forms a harbour connected with the Liffey at Ringsend. True Dubliners, it is said, are born within the confines of the Grand and Royal Canals.

For more information on the canal, look for the book *The Grand Canal* by Conaghan, Gleeson & Maddock (Office of Public Works).

Although Parliament proposed the canal in 1715, work did not commence until 1756. Construction was so slow that in 1775 a visitor commented that 'it bids fair for being completed in three or four centuries'. Nevertheless, in 1779 the first cargo barges started to operate to Sallins, about 35 km west of Dublin. Passenger services commenced a year later, when the terminus of the canal was the James's St Harbour, near the Guinness Brewery. By 1796 it was the longest canal in Britain or Ireland. It extended for 550 km, of which about 250 km was along the Rivers Shannon and Barrow.

Railways started to spread across Ireland from the mid-19th century and the canal went into decline. WW II provided a temporary respite, but the private canal company folded in 1950 and the last barge carried a cargo of Guinness from Dublin in 1960.

The canal fell into disrepair and in the early 1970s the St James's St Harbour and the stretch of canal back from there to the Circular Line were filled in. Recently the canal has enjoyed a modest revival as a tourist attraction. Despite the very limited number of boats that now ply the canal, all the locks are in working order.

The Grand Canal enters the Liffey at **Ringsend**, through locks that were built in 1796. The large **Grand Canal Dock**, flanked by Hanover and Charlotte quays, is now used by windsurfers.

At the north-west corner of the dock is **Misery Hill**, once the site for the public execution of criminals. It was once the practice to bring the corpses of those already hung at Gallows Hill, near Baggot St Upper, to this spot, to be strung up for public display for anything from six to 12 months.

Just upstream from the Grand Canal Dock is the flashy **Waterways Visitors' Centre**, built by the Office of Public Works as an exhibition and interpretation centre on the construction and operation of Irish canals and waterways. From its roof you can get your bearings and try and imagine what the grim surroundings will look like when/if redevelopment plans get into their stride. The centre is open June to September from 9.30 am to 6.30 pm, and from 2.30 to 5 pm in October and May. Admission costs IR£2/1.

A memorial to the events of the 1916 Easter Rising can be seen on the **Mount St Bridge**. A little farther along, Baggot St crosses the canal on the 1791 **Macartney Bridge**. The main office of Bord Fáilte is on the north side of the canal, and Bridge House and Parson's Bookshop are on the south side.

This lovely stretch of the canal with its grassy, tree-lined banks was a favourite haunt of the poet Patrick Kavanagh. Among his compositions is the hauntingly beautiful *On Raglan Road*, a popular song which Van Morrison fans can find on the album *Irish Heartbeat* with the Chieftains. Another Kavanagh poem requested that he be commemorated by 'a canal bank seat for passers-by' and Kavanagh's friends obliged with a seat beside the lock on the south side of the canal. A little farther along on the north side you can sit down by Kavanagh himself, cast in bronze, comfortably lounging on a bench and watching his beloved canal.

DUBLIN

Poet Patrick Kavanagh loved the Grand Canal

The next stretch of the canal has some fine pubs, such as the *Barge* and the *Porto Bello*, both right by the canal. The Porto Bello is a fine old-fashioned place with music on weekend evenings and Sunday mornings. The *Lower Deck* on Richmond St is also near the canal. You could also pause for a meal at the *Locks Restaurant*. The Institute of Education Business College by the Porto Bello was built in 1807 as Portobello House; as the Grand Canal Hotel, it was the Dublin terminus for passenger traffic on the canal. The artist Jack B Yeats lived here for seven years until his death in 1957.

Farther west from here the **Circular Line** is not so interesting and is better appreciated by bicycle rather than on foot. The spur running off the Circular Line alongside Grand Canal Bank to the old St James's St Harbour has been filled in and is now a park and bicycle path.

Ballsbridge & Donnybrook

Just south-east of central Dublin, the suburb of Ballsbridge was principally laid out between 1830 and 1860 and many of the streets have British names with a distinctly military flavour. Many embassies, including the US Embassy, are located in Ballsbridge. It also has some middle-bracket B&Bs and several upper-bracket hotels. If you're not staying in Ballsbridge, the main draws are

the Royal Dublin Showground, the Chester Beatty Library and the Lansdowne Rd rugby stadium.

Adjoining Ballsbridge to the south is Donnybrook, at one time a village on the banks of the River Dodder. For centuries it was famous for the Donnybrook Fair which was first held in 1204. By the 19th century it had become a 15-day event centred around horse dealing, which was such a scene of drunkenness and sexual debauchery that the increasingly sedate residents of Donnybrook had it banned in 1855.

Royal Dublin Society Showground On Merrion Rd in Ballsbridge, south of the centre, the Royal Dublin Society Showground is used for various exhibitions through the year. The society was founded in 1731 and had its headquarters in a number of well-known Dublin buildings, including, from 1814 to 1925, Leinster House. The society was involved in the foundation of the National Museum, Library, Gallery and Botanic Gardens. The most important annual event at the showground is the August Dublin Horse Show which includes an international showjumping contest and attracts the horsey set from all over Ireland and Britain.

Tickets for the horse show can be booked in advance by contacting the Ticket Office (☎ 668 0866), Royal Dublin Society, PO Box 121, Ballsbridge, Dublin 4. Ask at the tourist office or consult a listings magazine for other events.

Chester Beatty Library & Gallery of Oriental Art This library and gallery (☎ 669 2386) houses the collection of the mining engineer Sir Alfred Chester Beatty (1875-1968). It includes over 20,000 manuscripts, numerous rare books, miniature paintings, clay tablets, costumes and other objects, predominantly from the Middle East and Asia.

The gallery includes a reference library and a bookshop, but unfortunately only a tiny fraction of the total can be shown at any one time, a situation which should change when it moves into new premises in the old Barracks of Dublin Castle.

The gallery is south of the centre at 20 Shrewsbury Rd, Dublin 4, just beyond Ballsbridge en route to Dun Laoghaire. Bus Nos 5, 7, 7A, 7X or 8 from Burgh Quay, Nos 46 or 46A from College St or No 10 from O'Connell St will drop you nearby. Alternatively, take the DART to Sandymount Station, Sydney Parade. Opening hours are from 10 am to 5 pm Tuesday to Friday, 2 to 5 pm on Saturday. Entry is free and there are guided tours on Wednesday and Saturday at 2.30 pm.

Pearse Museum

Patrick (or *Padráig* in the Irish he worked so hard to promote) Pearse was a leader of the 1916 Easter Rising and one of the first to be executed by firing squad at Kilmainham Jail. St Enda's, the school he established with his brother Willie to further his ideas of Irish language and culture, is now a museum (☎ 493 4208) and memorial to the brothers.

The Pearse Museum is at the junction of Grange Rd and Taylor's Lane in Rathfarnham, south-west of the city centre. From May to August it's open every day from 10 am to 5.30 pm. From February to April and in September and October it closes half an hour earlier. From November to January it closes at 4 pm. Entry is free and you can get there on bus No 16 from the city centre.

Marlay Park

This park area south of the centre at Rathfarnham in Dublin 16 has numerous attractions, including a model railway with rides for children on Saturday afternoons. The park is the northern starting point for the Wicklow Way walking track.

Other Museums

Apart from the museums described in the north and south Dublin sections, there are a number of other smaller museums or museums of specialist interest.

George Bernard Shaw House (☎ 872 2077) at 33 Synge St, Dublin 2, is open from 10 am to 5 pm Monday to Saturday, 2 to 6 pm Sunday and holidays, May to September. Entry is IR£2/1.10 (students IR£1.60).

The **Irish Traditional Music Archive** (☎ 661 9699), at 63 Merrion Square South, collects, preserves and organises traditional Irish music. It's open to the public by appointment.

The **Geological Survey of Ireland** (☎ 660 9511), at Haddington Rd, Dublin 4, has exhibits on the geology and mineral resources of Ireland. It's open Monday to Friday from 2.30 to 4.30 pm.

The **Irish Jewish Museum** (☎ 453 1797) at 3-4 Walworth Rd, off Victoria St, Portobello, Dublin 8, is housed in what was once a synagogue and relates the history of Ireland's Jewish community. It's open Sunday, Tuesday and Thursday from 11 am to 3.30 pm.

The **Museum of Childhood** (☎ 497 3223) is at The Palms, 20 Palmerston Park, Rathmines, Dublin 6, south of the centre. Its main display is a collection of dolls, some of them nearly 300 years old. The museum is open Sunday from 2 to 5.30 pm although you may be able to make an appointment to visit at other times. Entry is IR£1/75p.

The **Irish Architectural Archive & Architecture Centre** at 73 Merrion Square South, Dublin 2, traces Dublin's architectural history from 1560 to the current day. The archive is housed in a fine 1793 town house. The Royal Institute of the Architects of Ireland has its headquarters across the square at 8 Merrion Square North, and exhibitions and displays are also held there.

The **Plunkett Museum of Irish Education** (☎ 497 0033) is at the Church of Ireland College of Education, Rathmines Rd Upper, Dublin 6, and is open by appointment only.

Other Galleries

As well as the National Gallery and the IMMA south of the river and the Hugh Lane Municipal Gallery of Modern Art north of the river, there are a great many private galleries, arts centres and corporate exhibition areas.

The **Douglas Hyde Gallery** (☎ 608 1116)

is in the Arts Building in Trinity College, and the entrance is on Nassau St. The **City Arts Centre** (☎ 677 0643) at 23-25 Moss St has changing exhibitions in its two galleries which are open free Monday to Saturday from 11 am to 5 pm.

In the **Bank of Ireland** building on Baggot St Lower, just past Fitzwilliam St towards the Bord Fáilte office and Ballsbridge, there are usually changing displays of contemporary Irish art.

ACTIVITIES
Dublin offers plenty of sporting opportunities for both spectators and participants.

Beaches & Swimming
Dublin is hardly the sort of place to work on your suntan and even a hot Irish summer day is unlikely to raise the water temperature much above freezing. However, there are some pleasant beaches and many Joyce fans feel compelled to take a dip in the Forty Foot Pool at Dun Laoghaire. Sandy beaches near the centre include Sutton (11 km), Portmarnock (11 km), Malahide (11 km), Claremount (14 km) and Donabate (21 km). Although the beach at Sandymount is nothing special, it is only five km from central Dublin. There are outdoor public pools at Blackrock, Clontarf and Dun Laoghaire.

Scuba Diving
The Irish Underwater Council (☎ 284 4601), 78A Patrick St in Dun Laoghaire, publish the quarterly magazine *Subsea*. Oceantec (☎ 280 1083) is a dive shop in Dun Laoghaire that organises local dives. See the Dun Laoghaire section for more information.

Sailing & Windsurfing
Howth, Malahide and Dun Laoghaire are the major sailing centres in the Dublin area, but you can also go sailing at Clontarf, Kilbarrack, Rush, Skerries, Sutton and Swords. See the Dun Laoghaire section for details of the sailing clubs there. The Irish Sailing Association (☎ 280 0239) is at 3 Park Rd, Dun Laoghaire.

Dinghy sailing courses are offered by the Irish National Sailing School (☎ 280 6654), 115 George's St Lower, Dun Laoghaire, and by the Fingall Sailing School (☎ 845 1979) Upper Strand Rd, Broadmeadow Estuary, Malahide.

Windsurfing enthusiasts can head to the Surfdock Centre (☎ 668 3945) at the Grand Canal Dock, Dock Rd South, Ringsend, Dublin 4. Surfdock runs windsurfing courses here costing from IR£30 for a three-hour 'taster' session or IR£90 for a 12-hour course. You can also rent sailboards from IR£7 an hour.

Fishing
Fishing tackle shops in Dublin can supply permits, equipment, bait and advice. Check the classified phone directory under Fishing Gear & Tackle. Sea fishing is popular at Howth, Dun Laoghaire and Greystones. The River Liffey has salmon fishing (only fair) and trout fishing (good). Brown trout are found between Celbridge and Millicent Bridge, near Clane, 20 km from the centre. The Dublin Trout Anglers' Association has fishing rights along parts of this stretch of the Liffey and on the River Tolka.

Gliding & Hang-Gliding
Phone ☎ 831 4551 or 088-589245 for information on hang-gliding from the Great Sugar Loaf Mountain in County Wicklow. Contact the Dublin Gliding Club (☎ 298 3994), at Gowtan Grange near Punchestown, for general gliding information.

ORGANISED TOURS
Many Dublin tours operate only during the summer months but at that time you can take bus tours, and walking tours. You can book these tours directly with the operators or through your hotel front desk, at the various city tourist offices or with a travel agent or American Express.

Bus Tours
Gray Line has tours around Dublin and farther afield but only in the summer. Reservations can be made through Dublin Tourism

(☎ 874 4466, 878 7981 & 661 9666 – the latter for Sunday bookings only), 14 O'Connell St Upper. Different morning and afternoon tours are available, each costing IR£14, including any admission charges, and lasting 2¾ hours. There is a variety of half-day tours out of Dublin to Newgrange, Malahide Castle, Powerscourt Gardens or Newbridge House, each costing IR£14. Day-long tours out of Dublin cost IR£27 and include tours to Glendalough and the Wicklow Mountains, to the Boyne Valley and various combinations of the half-day tours.

Gray Line also has nightlife tours to Jury's Irish Cabaret (IR£18.90 with two drinks or IR£31.50 with dinner) or to Doyle's Irish Cabaret (IR£18.90 with two drinks or IR£29.90 with dinner). See the Irish Entertainment section under Entertainment for more details.

Dublin Bus (☎ 872 0000) tours can be booked at their office at 59 O'Connell St Upper or directly across the road at the Bus Éireann counter in the Dublin Tourism office, 14 O'Connell St Upper. The three-hour tour uses an open-top double-decker bus as long as the weather permits and operates twice daily throughout the year. The tour costs IR£7/4.

Dublin Bus also operates a hop-on hop-off Heritage Trail bus which does a city tour, with commentary, 11 times daily from mid-April to late September. There are eight additional daily circuits during the peak summer months. The IR£5/2.50 ticket lets you travel all day, getting on or off at the eight stops. Old Dublin Tours (☎ 458 0054) also does city sightseeing tours.

You can book Bus Éireann tours directly at the Busáras (☎ 836 6111), or through the Bus Éireann desks at the Dublin Bus office, 59 O'Connell St Upper, or the Dublin Tourism office, 14 O'Connell St Upper. During the summer months they operate a Monday to Saturday city tour which takes 3¾ hours and costs IR£9/4.50, including entry to the 'Book of Kells' exhibit.

Bus Éireann also has two tours out of the city which operate daily during the summer

months, take 2¾ hours and cost IR£8/4). The North Coast Tour does a loop via Howth, Malahide, the Casino at Marino and the Botanic Gardens. The South Coast Tour goes via Dun Laoghaire, Bray and Greystones and then returns through the mountains via Enniskerry.

Bus Éireann also has several day tours outside Dublin. Tours to Glendalough and Wicklow are conducted daily from June to mid-September, and daily except Friday for a couple of additional months. The cost is IR£15/8. A full-day tour to the Boyne Valley and Newgrange operates on Sunday, Tuesday and Thursday from mid-May to late September and also costs IR£15/8. In the summer months there are also day tours farther afield to places such as Kilkenny, the River Shannon, Waterford, the Mountains of Mourne, Armagh and Navan, and Lough Erne.

Mary Gibbons Tours (☎ 283 9973) also does half-day Dublin city tours (IR£12) and tours to the Boyne Valley (IR£14) and Powerscourt/Glendalough (R£14). A full-day Dublin and Boyne Valley tour costs IR£23.

Walking Tours

During summer there are various walking tours which are a great way to explore this very walkable city. A Trinity College walking tour departs frequently from Front Square just inside the college and costs IR£3.50/3, including entry to 'The Book of Kells' exhibit. See the Trinity College section under Things to See earlier for more details.

Dublin Footsteps Walking Tours (☎ 496 0641) operates 1½ to two-hour walks for IR£4. The tours start from Bewley's Café on Grafton St, and explore medieval Dublin or 18th-century Dublin and literary Dublin. One-and-a-half-hour walking tours of north Dublin, focusing on sites associated with James Joyce, depart from the James Joyce Centre at 35 North Great George's St at 2.30 pm Monday to Saturday; phone ☎ 873 1984 to check outside the summer months. The cost of a tour of the centre and the walk is IR£5/3.50.

Historical Walking Tours (☎ 845 0241) are conducted by Trinity College history graduates, take two hours and depart from the front gates of Trinity College. The walks take place several times daily from mid-May to September and cost IR£4/3.

The Dublin Literary Pub Crawl (☎ 454 0228) operates seven days a week, starting at 7.30 pm from Davy Byrne's on Duke St, just off Grafton St. From May to September there are also tours at 3 pm (and at noon on Sunday as well). The walk is great fun and costs IR£6/5, though Guinness consumption can quickly add a few pounds to the figure. The two actors who lead the tour put on a theatrical performance appropriate to the various places and pubs along the way. The particular pubs chosen vary from night to night but could include Mulligan's in Poolbeg St, the Palace Bar in Fleet St, the Stag's Head in Dame St, McDaid's in Barry St, Neary's in Chatham St, the Norseman in Eustace St, the Long Hall in George's St or O'Neill's in Suffolk St.

The Dublin Musical Pub Crawl (☎ 478 0191) leaves from upstairs in St John Gogarty's pub in Temple Bar every night except Friday at 7.30 pm. Two musicians take you to McDaids and The Clarendon and put on sample traditional music sessions with a commentary. You wind up in O'Donohue's for a final session around 10 pm. Once again this is great fun and a good intro to traditional music if you're interested but ignorant. Tours cost IR£5.

Carriage Tours
At the junction of Grafton St and St Stephen's Green you can pick up a horse and carriage with a driver/commentator. Half-hour tours cost IR£20 and the carriages can take four or five people. Tours of different lengths can be negotiated with the drivers.

Tour Guides
Bord Fáilte-approved guides can be contacted via the tourist board. The recommended fees for a full-day approved guide in Dublin are

IR£35 to IR£50 in English, IR£45 to IR£65 in a foreign language.

CULTURAL & SPORTING EVENTS
Highlights of the Dublin year include the following events:

March – The St Patrick's Day Parade with an international marching band competition and up to a quarter of a million spectators.
May – The Irish Football Association Cup Final.
June – On the 16th, Dublin celebrates Bloomsday, commemorating the day immortalised in James Joyce's *Ulysses*.
August – The Dublin Horse Show at the Royal Dublin Society Showground.
September – The All Ireland Hurling Final takes place on the first Sunday in September at Dublin's Croke Park and attracts a crowd of 60,000 to 80,000 spectators.
The All Ireland Football Final takes place at Croke Park on the third Sunday in September.
October – The Dublin Theatre Festival.

PLACES TO STAY
Dublin has a wide range of accommodation possibilities, but in summer finding a bed can be difficult in anything from the cheapest hostel to the most expensive five-star hotel. If you can plan ahead and book your room, it will make life easier. The alternative is to head straight for the Backpackers Centre, 21A Store St, for advice on hostels or for one of the tourist offices at the airport, by the harbour in Dun Laoghaire or in Dublin itself and ask them to book you a room. For a flat fee of IR£1 they will find you somewhere in Dublin to stay. If it takes a lot of phoning around this can be a pound very well spent.

Accommodation in central Dublin can be neatly divided into areas north and south of the River Liffey. The south side is generally neater, cleaner and more expensive than the north side. Prices drop as you move away from the centre. The seaside suburbs of Dun Laoghaire, Howth and Bray are also within easy commuting distance of central Dublin on the convenient DART rail service.

Camping
There's no convenient central camp site in Dublin. *Do not* try to camp in Phoenix Park:

a German cyclist camping there was murdered in 1991. At the *Shankill Caravan & Camping Park* (☎ 282 0011), 16 km south of the centre on the N11 Wexford Rd, a site for two costs IR£6 in summer. You can get there on bus No 45 or 46 from Eden Quay. Another site is *Donabate Caravan Park* (☎ 843 6008) near Swords, 16 km north of Dublin.

Hostels

Since there are no conveniently central camp sites in Dublin, budget travellers usually head for one of Dublin's numerous hostels, one operated by An Óige, the national youth hostel association, the others independently. Hostels offer the cheapest accommodation and are also great centres for meeting other travellers and exchanging information. In summer (late June to late September) they can be heavily booked but then so is everything else.

North of the Liffey The An Óige *Dublin International Youth Hostel* (☎ 830 1766) in Mountjoy St is a big, well-equipped hostel in a restored and converted old building. From Dublin Airport, bus No 41A will drop you in Dorset St Upper, a few minutes' walk from the hostel. It's a longer walk from the bus and railway stations but it's well signposted. The hostel is in the run-down northern area of the city centre, and you should keep an eye on your bags in adjacent streets. The nightly cost for Hostelling International members is IR£9, non-members IR£9.50, and there's an overflow hostel for the height of the summer crush.

Just round the corner from the An Óige hostel is the middle-sized *Young Traveller Hostel* (☎ 830 5000) on St Mary's Place, just off Dorset St Upper. All the rooms accommodate four people and have a shower and washbasin but there are no kitchen facilities. The nightly cost is IR£9 including breakfast. It may not be a great idea to walk alone in the streets round here at night.

The IHH *Cardijn House Hostel* (☎ 878 8091), aka 'Goin' My Way', is a smaller, older hostel at 15 Talbot St, east of O'Connell St. The nightly cost is IR£7 plus

50p for a shower. Breakfast is included and there are good, clean cooking facilities. The IHH *Marlborough Hostel* (☎ 878 7629), 81-82 Marlborough St, right behind the Dublin Tourism office and next to the Pro-Cathedral, has dorms accommodating four to 10 people and the nightly cost is IR£7.50 per person irrespective of the dorm size. Double rooms cost IR£11 per person. Cooking facilities are available.

For convenience you can't beat the big IHH *Isaac's Hostel* (☎ 874 9321), 2-5 Frenchman's Lane, a stone's throw from the Busáras or Connolly Railway Station, and not far from the popular restaurants and pubs on either side of the Liffey. This hostel has cooking facilities and a small café, but is run along lines that make old-fashioned An Óige hostels look positively laidback: no one can get into the dorms between 11 am and 5 pm, and baggage put into the locker-room can only be retrieved on the hour and half-hour. Trains also pass so close to some rooms that the line might as well be passing through your pillow. Dorm beds are cheap at IR£5.75 to IR£7.50 and there are singles at IR£14 and doubles at IR£17.25 per person in the adjoining *Isaac's Hotel*.

Nearby at 46-48 Gardiner St Lower is the much more relaxed and welcoming IHH *Globetrotter's Tourist Hostel* (☎ 873 5893) where dorm beds cost IR£10 including continental breakfast. With 10 to a dorm there's bound to be some disturbance, but this is a clean, modern place with good security. The breakfasts, in a pleasant dining room overlooking a small garden, are well worth the few extra pounds. If you arrive midweek out of season a three-nights-for-the-price-of-two may eliminate even that small price difference.

A little further down Gardiner St Lower at No 82-83 is IHH *Abraham House* (☎ 855 0600) where beds in the largest dorms cost IR£7.50 in low season, IR£9.50 in high.

South of the Liffey South of the Liffey, IHH *Kinlay House* (☎ 679 6644) is central, beside Christ Church Cathedral at 2-12 Lord Edward St, but some rooms can suffer from traffic noise. Kinlay House is big and well equipped and costs from IR£11 per person for four-bed dorms, IR£11.50 to IR£13 for the better rooms (some with bathrooms) and IR£17 for a single. Continental breakfast is included and cooking facilities are available. Bus Nos 54A, 68A, 78A and 123 stop outside.

IHH *Avalon House* (☎ 475 0001), in an old building that has been comprehensively renovated at 55 Aungier St, is nicely positioned just west of St Stephen's Green. It's well equipped and some of the cleverly designed rooms have mezzanine levels, which are great for families. The basic nightly cost in dorms accommodating up to 12 is IR£10.50 including a continental breakfast. A bed in a four-bed room with attached bathroom costs IR£11.50; in a two-bed it's IR£13.50. To get there take bus Nos 16, 16A, 19 or 22 right to the door or bus Nos 11, 13 or 46A to nearby St Stephen's Green. From the Dun Laoghaire ferry terminal you can take bus No 46A to St Stephen's Green or the DART to Pearse Station.

Right in the lively (and noisy) Temple Bar area is *Strollers* (☎ 677 5614), 58 Dame St, with prices inclusive of breakfast from IR£10.50 to IR£14.50 a head. There are no cooking facilities, but guests get discounts in the adjoining café.

Further out but with a good range of sleeping set-ups is *Morehampton House* (☎ 668 8866) at 78 Morehampton Rd, Donnybrook, Dublin 4. The cheapest beds, at IR£7.95, are in 10 or eight-bed basement dorms. For bigger, lighter eight and four-bedded rooms you pay IR£9.95; for twins IR£12.50; and for triples IR£11. Breakfast is another IR£1, but there are clean, spacious cooking facilities and a garden for alfresco picnics. Bus Nos 10, 46A and 46B pass by.

Student Accommodation

In the summer months you can stay at Trinity College or University College Dublin (UCD). Trinity College (☎ 608 1177) sometimes has accommodation on campus in the city, but it's expensive at IR£25 per person for B&B. At *Trinity Hall* (☎ 497 1772),

Dartry Rd, Rathmines, rates are IR£15 to IR£25 for singles or IR£14 to IR£25 if you share a twin. If you're under 25 and have a student card, the price may drop. There are some family rooms where children aged under 10 can stay for free with two adults. To get there, take bus No 14 or 14A from D'Olier St beside the O'Connell Bridge.

UCD Village (☎ 269 7696) is six km south of the centre, en route to Dun Laoghaire. Accommodation here is in apartments, with three single rooms sharing a bathroom and a kitchen/meals/living area. It's very modern and well appointed but way out and, at IR£18 (IR£108 a week), rather expensive. For a family a three-room apartment at IR£48 could be good value. If you have a car, the ease of parking may compensate for the distance and the soulless surroundings; if you don't, bus No 10 departs every 10 minutes from O'Connell St/St Stephen's Green and goes direct to the campus. The fare is IR£1.

B&Bs

B&Bs, the backbone of cheap accommodation in Ireland, are well represented in Dublin and typically cost IR£15 to IR£20 per person per night. The cheaper B&Bs usually do not have private bathrooms, but where they do the cost is often just a pound or two more. Dublin also has some more luxuriously equipped B&Bs costing from IR£25 per person, but this category is usually monopolised by the smaller hotels and guesthouses. Most places levy single supplements.

If you arrive when accommodation is tight and don't like the location offered, the best advice is to take it and then try to book something better for subsequent nights. Booking just one or two days ahead can often turn up a much better choice.

If you want something cheap but close to the city, Gardiner St Upper and Lower in Dublin 1 on the north side of the Liffey is the place to look. It's a rather grotty and run-down area, but is cheap and convenient.

Further out you can find a better price and quality combination north of the centre at Clontarf or in the seaside suburbs of Dun

Laoghaire or Howth. The Ballsbridge embassy zone, just south of the centre, offers convenience and quality but you pay more for the combination. Other suburbs to try are Sandymount (immediately east of Ballsbridge) and Drumcondra (north of the centre en route to the airport).

Gardiner St There is a large collection of places on Gardiner St Lower, near the bus and railway stations, and another group on Gardiner St Upper, farther north just past Mountjoy Square. The B&Bs are respectable if rather basic.

At 75 Gardiner St Lower is the *Maple Guest House* (☎ 874 0225/5239) which has singles/doubles for IR£35/50 with attached bathroom.

The plain *Harvey's Guesthouse* (☎ 874 8384), 11 Gardiner St Upper, and *Stella Maris* (☎ 874 0835), next door at No 13, are just north of Mountjoy Square. Rooms are IR£16 per person or IR£18 with bath. There are several more B&Bs in the next few buildings, such as *Flynn's B&B* (☎ 874 1702) at No 15, *Carmel House* (☎ 874 1639) at No 16 and *Fatima House* (☎ 874 5410) at No 17. The cheapest is *Marian Guest House* (☎ 874 4129), at No 21, with rooms from IR£15 per person. Just off Gardiner St Upper from Mountjoy Square at 4 Gardiner Place is the *Dergvale Hotel* (☎ 874 4753). Regular rooms are slightly more expensive, and singles/doubles with attached bathroom cost IR£26/50.

Hardwicke St is only a short walk from these Gardiner St Upper places and has a number of popular B&Bs, such as *Waverley House* (☎ 874 6132), at No 4, or *Sinclair House* (☎ 855 0792), next door at No 3. At these places singles cost IR£20 to IR£22 and doubles IR£30 to IR£34.

Clontarf There are numerous places along Clontarf Rd, about five km from the centre. One of these is the friendly *Ferryview* (☎ 833 5893) at No 96. Farther along there's the slightly more expensive *White House* (☎ 833 3196) at No 125, *San Vista* (☎ 833 9582) at No 237, *Bayview* (☎ 833 9870) at

No 265 and *Sea Breeze* (☎ 833 2787) at No 312. These Clontarf Rd B&Bs typically cost IR£15 to IR£20 for singles, IR£25 to IR£35 for doubles. Bus No 30 from Abbey St will get you there for IR£1.

Ballsbridge & Donnybrook Ballsbridge is not only the embassy quarter and the site for a number of upper bracket hotels but is also the locale for a number of better quality B&Bs, such as *Morehampton Townhouse* (☎ 660 8630) at 46 Morehampton Rd, Donnybrook, directly opposite the Sachs Hotel. Singles/doubles are IR£40/55. All rooms are centrally heated and have bathrooms and the excellent breakfast proves that there can be more to life than just bacon and eggs.

Mrs O'Donoghue's (☎ 668 1105) convivial but signless place at 41 Northumberland Rd costs IR£24/44. Despite its imposing Victorian presence there are only eight rooms in this fine and very traditional B&B.

Middle-Range Guesthouses & Hotels
The line dividing B&Bs from guesthouses and cheaper hotels is often a hazy one. Places in this middle-range bracket usually cost from IR£25 to IR£60 per night per person. Some of the small, central hotels in this category are among the most enjoyable places to stay in Dublin.

These middle-range places are a big jump up from the cheaper B&Bs in facilities and price but still cost a lot less than Dublin's expensive hotels. Breakfast is usually provided (it usually isn't in the top-notch hotels) and it's very good (unlike that offered by some cheap B&Bs). Many of these hotels offer fruit, a choice of cereals, croissants, scones and other morning delights to supplement the inevitable bacon and eggs.

North of the Liffey – Dublin 1 Just north of the Liffey at 35-36 Abbey St Lower is *Wynn's Hotel* (☎ 874 5131, fax 874 1556). Only a few steps away from the Abbey Theatre, this older hotel has 70 rooms, all with attached bathroom, which cost IR£52/83 for singles/doubles with reductions at weekends. Right by the river the *Ormond Hotel*

(☎ 872 1811, fax 872 1909), Ormond Quay Upper, Dublin 1, has 55 rooms with attached bathroom for IR£47/68. A plaque outside notes its role in *Ulysses*.

At 47-48 Gardiner St Lower *The Townhouse* (☎ 878 8808, fax 878 8787), next door to the Globetrotter's Tourist Hostel and sharing a breakfast room with it, has singles for IR£25 and doubles for IR£45 with en-suite facilities and a good breakfast thrown in. This is a pleasingly decorated and safety-conscious guesthouse with a small Japanese garden and a car park – an excellent choice all round.

Farther from the river is the *Castle Hotel* (☎ 874 6949, fax 872 7674) at 34 Gardiner Row with 35 rooms. It's just off Parnell Square, only a few minutes' walk from O'Connell St but on the edge of the better part of north Dublin, before the decline sets in. Rooms cost IR£29.50 single, IR£58 double, IR£75 triple. Further along on the same side of the road is *Barry's Hotel* (☎ 874 9407, fax 874 6508) at 1-2 Great Denmark St. The hotel's 29 rooms cost IR£26.75/45.50 with attached bathroom. Across the road is the *Belvedere Hotel* (☎ 872 8522, fax 872 8631) opposite Belvedere College, which James Joyce attended as a boy. The 45 rooms, all with attached bathroom, cost IR£26.75/45.50 for singles/ doubles.

South of the Liffey – Dublin 2 The *Fitzwilliam* (☎ 660 0448, fax 676 7488), 41 Fitzwilliam St Upper, Dublin 2, is very central, right on the corner of Baggot St Lower, but is still surprisingly quiet at night. There are 12 rooms in this small hotel, all of which have en-suite bathroom, costing IR£39/75 for singles/doubles at the height of summer.

Even more central is *Georgian House* (☎ 661 8832, fax 661 8834) at 20-21 Baggot St Lower, equally close to St Stephen's Green or Merrion Square. Once again this is a fine old Georgian building in excellent condition. Its 47 rooms all have attached bathrooms and cost IR£60/95 in summer. The breakfast is excellent and at night the

restaurant is noted for its seafood. There's also a car park.

At St Stephen's Green South the new *Staunton's on the Green* hotel (☎ 478 2133, fax 478 2263) is in a Georgian house in an excellent position. Singles/doubles cost IR£53/88, including breakfast.

Close to the Green in another magnificent Georgian building at 21-25 Harcourt St is the *Russell Court Hotel* (☎ 478 4991, fax 478 4066) with 42 rooms, all with attached bathroom and costing IR£55/77 a night. Across the road at No 84 the newly opened *Albany House* (☎ 475 1092, fax 475 1093) has singles/doubles for IR£50/59. Further down at No 60 in another Georgian building where George Bernard Shaw lived from 1874 to 1876 is the *Harcourt Hotel* (☎ 478 3677, fax 75 2013) with 40 rooms costing from IR£35/60 to IR£56/100 with bathrooms.

Another place off St Stephen's Green is *Leeson Court* (☎ 676 3380, fax 661 8273), 26-27 Leeson St Lower, at the start of Dublin's nightclub block. The 20 rooms have attached bathrooms and cost IR£45 to IR£50 for singles and IR£75 to IR£85 for doubles. The *Grafton Plaza* (☎ 475 0888, fax 475 0908) in Johnsons Place behind the St Stephen's Green Shopping Centre looks as if it should be more expensive than it actually is. In fact a single/double costs IR£65/85 in high season with continental breakfast an extra IR£4.75.

At 99-100 Baggot St Lower *Latchford's* (☎ 676 0784) offers serviced rooms with self-catering facilities in an impressive Georgian house with fine plaster ceilings in some bedrooms. Prices range from IR£45 single and IR£65 double to IR£60 and IR£85 double in high season, with reductions for week-long stays. There's an excellent bistro attached.

Immediately opposite Christ Church Cathedral in Christ Church Place the big new *Jurys Christ Church Inn* (☎ 475 0111, fax 475 0488) has rooms for IR£49 each. Unfortunately it lacks a car park so you'll need to budget another IR4.80 a day to use the nearest public one.

At 21-22 Wellington Quay, overlooking

the River Liffey and backing on to the fascinating Temple Bar area, the newly renovated *Wellington Hotel* (☎ 677 9315, fax 677 9387) charges IR£35 to IR£45 for a single and IR£68 to IR£80 for a double. Further along at 6-8 Wellington Quay is the *Clarence Hotel* (☎ 662 3066, fax 662 3077), a larger old hotel. In 1992 it was bought by the band U2 and at the time of writing was undergoing extensive renovation. When it reopens, expect super-duper rooms with super-duper prices to match.

Elsewhere in Dublin *Ariel House* (☎ 668 5512, fax 668 5845) is at 52 Lansdowne Rd, Dublin 4, two km south-east of the centre in the Ballsbridge area. It's conveniently close to Lansdowne Rd Station and the big Berkeley Court Hotel. There are 28 en-suite rooms, and the nightly cost is IR£50/100 for singles/doubles, with breakfast extra; out of season you may be able to negotiate a discount.

Further down, Lansdowne Rd changes its name to Herbert Rd, where you will find the *Mt Herbert* (☎ 668 4321, fax 660 7077) at 7 Herbert Rd, Dublin 4, about three km from the centre. This larger hotel was once the Dublin residence of an English lord. There are 155 en-suite rooms, which cost IR£43.50/63 with breakfast thrown in.

The well-equipped *Ashling Hotel* (☎ 677 2324) is on Parkgate St, Dublin 8, 2.5 km from the centre and directly across the river from Heuston Station. Beds in its 54 rooms cost IR£56.50/86 for singles/doubles.

Expensive Hotels
Dublin's top-bracket hotels cost from IR£60 per person or IR£100 for a double. Hotels in this price range are divided into two categories: the city's best hotels, most of them categorised as A* hotels by the Irish Tourist Board and all of them costing well over IR£100 for a double; and the other expensive hotels, which fall just below the top bracket in standards and price but are still more expensive than the middle range.

Almost-but-not-quite Top Bracket At the top end of O'Connell St in north Dublin,

farther up from the Gresham Hotel, is the *Royal Dublin Hotel* (☎ 873 3666, fax 873 3120), with 117 rooms at IR£82/110 for singles/doubles.

Bloom's Hotel (☎ 671 5622, fax 671 5997), on Anglesea St, right behind the Bank of Ireland in the colourful Temple Bar district, has 86 rooms costing IR£90/110 for singles/doubles. Just south of Dame St is the *Central Hotel* (☎ 679 7302, fax 679 7303) at 1-5 Exchequer St, which has 70 rooms at IR£95/140 without breakfast. Though the rooms are rather small it's well located.

Close to the National Museum, *Buswells* (☎ 676 4013 & 661 3888, fax 676 2090), 23-27 Molesworth St, has singles/doubles for IR£60/100 without breakfast. The small *Longfield's* (☎ 676 1367, fax 676 1542) is at 9-10 Fitzwilliam St Lower, between Merrion and Fitzwilliam squares, and has 26 rooms at IR£90/140 for singles/doubles.

Stephen's Hall (☎ 661 0585, fax 661 0606) is just a stone's throw from the south-east corner of St Stephen's Green at 14-17 Leeson St Lower. The 37 rooms, all with attached bathroom, cost IR£95/134, including breakfast.

About three km south-east of the centre in Donnybrook, just beyond Ballsbridge, is the *Sachs Hotel* (☎ 668 0995, fax 668 6147) at 19-29 Morehampton Rd, Dublin 4. This small but elegant and expensive place has 20 rooms, all en suite, costing IR£75/110.

Top Bracket Dublin has seven hotels which have the Irish Tourist Board's A* rating. Even a single room at these hotels can cost IR£100 or more, though most guests will have probably booked through an agency or as part of a package and obtained some sort of discount from the rack (published) rates.

The city's best known hotel is the elegant *Shelbourne*, strategically placed overlooking St Stephen's Green and indubitably the best address to meet at in Dublin. Despite the prices the rooms are a little cramped, but afternoon tea (IR£7.50 a head) at the Shelbourne is something all Dublin visitors should experience, regardless of whether they stay there.

The *Conrad*, a popular business hotel, is run by the Hilton group and is just south of St Stephen's Green. Also close to St Stephen's Green, the modern *Westbury* is in a lane just off Grafton St, south Dublin's pedestrianised main shopping street. Rooms on the upper floors offer views of the Dublin hills. The *Mont Clare* is a classic old hotel on elegant Merrion Square. The *Davenport Hotel*, which opened in mid-1993 opposite the Mont Clare on Westland Row, is housed inside what was once Merrion Hall, built in 1863 for the Plymouth Brethren (a puritanical religious sect). *Berkeley Court*, south-east of the centre in Ballsbridge in a quiet and relaxed location on Lansdowne Rd, offers spacious rooms. Ireland's largest hotel, the modern *Burlington*, is also south of the centre, just beyond the Grand Canal. In the same general area is *Jury's Hotel & Towers*, a large, modern hotel on Pembroke Rd. In the summer months the Irish cabaret here is very popular.

The long-established *Gresham* is on imposing O'Connell St Upper.

Berkeley Court Hotel A*
  Lansdowne Rd, Dublin 4; two km from the centre, 187 rooms, fitness centre, IR£139/155 (☎ 660 1711, fax 661 7238)
Burlington Hotel A*
  Leeson St Upper, Dublin 4; two km from the centre, 451 rooms, IR£102/127 (☎ 660 5222, fax 660 8496)
Conrad Hotel A*
  Earlsfort Terrace, Dublin 2; 191 rooms, IR155/180 (☎ 676 5555, fax 676 5424)
Davenport Hotel
  Westland Row, Dublin 2; 120 rooms, IR£120/150 (☎ 661 6800, fax 661 5663)
Gresham Hotel A*
  O'Connell St Upper, Dublin 1; 208 rooms, IR£80/160 (☎ 874 6881, fax 878 7175)
Jury's Hotel & Towers A*
  Pembroke Rd, Ballsbridge, Dublin 4; 2.5 km from the centre, 394 rooms, swimming pool, IR£110/130 (☎ 660 5000, fax 660 5540)
Mont Clare Hotel A
  Merrion Square, Dublin 2; 74 rooms, from IR£90 to IR£150 (☎ 661 6799, fax 661 5663)
Shelbourne Hotel A*
  St Stephen's Green, Dublin 2; 160 rooms, IR£160 for singles, from IR£180 for doubles (☎ 676 6471, fax 661 6006)

Westbury Hotel A*
  Off Grafton St, Dublin 2; 203 rooms, IR£139/155 (☎ 679 1122, fax 679 7078)

Airport Hotels There are several hotels near Dublin Airport, including the large *Forte Crest Hotel* (☎ 844 4211, fax 842 5874), off the N1 motorway beside the airport. It has 188 rooms costing IR£85/110 for singles/doubles.

PLACES TO EAT
Restaurants are divided into three popular zones. There are limited possibilities north of the Liffey, but the trendy Temple Bar enclave and Dame St along its southern boundary are packed with restaurants of all types. There are also numerous restaurants on both sides of busy Grafton St and along Merrion Row and Baggot St.

North of the Liffey
Dining possibilities north of the Liffey essentially consist of fast food, cheap eats or chains. Which is not to say that you'll eat badly here, just that the choice of restaurants is much better to the south.

Fast Food & Cafés O'Connell St is the fast-food centre of Dublin. At No 34 there's an *Abrakebabra*, at No 9 there's a *Burger King*, at Nos 14 and 52 there are branches of *La Pizza* and at No 62 there's a *McDonald's*.

Isaac's and the *Dublin International Youth Hostel* (see Hostels in the Places to Stay section) both have good cafeteria-style facilities. At 1-2 O'Connell St the *Kylemore Café* is a big, somewhat impersonal fast-food place which is also good for a cup of tea or coffee any time of day. Alternatively, on the 1st floor of *Clerys* department store you can get afternoon tea complete with cucumber sandwiches in stylish surroundings for IR£3.75. Ireland's most famous purveyor of fish & chips from IR£2.95, *Beshoff's* has a branch in O'Connell St with great views from the upstairs windows.

There's a *Bewley's Café* north of the Liffey at 40 Mary St.

If you're around the Corporation Fruit

Market, between Chancery St and Mary's Lane, pop in to *Paddy's Place* (☎ 873 5130) where the food is as staunchly Irish as the name. It's open from 7.30 am to 3 pm Monday to Friday so you can go there for an early breakfast or a filling lunch-time Irish stew or Dublin coddle.

Restaurants Restaurant possibilities north of the Liffey are pretty limited, but *Chapter One* (☎ 873 2266) at the Dublin Writers' Museum on the north side of Parnell Square is worth a look even though the food is resolutely conservative. They serve lunch and dinner and feature a menu for patrons of the Gate Theatre, on the other side of the square.

Closer to the river at 101 Talbot St is *101 Talbot St* (☎ 874 5011), open for lunch Monday to Saturday and dinner Tuesday to Saturday in a brave attempt to bring good food north of the river. The prices are reasonable, the food moderately adventurous and well prepared. Pasta dishes from IR£4.95 are filling.

Residents of the Gardiner St hostels and D&Bs can also eat at *Hamburger Heaven* (☎ 855 2424), 5 Beresford Place, where the price tags on the 25 varieties of burger are somewhat higher than at McDonald's.

Temple Bar
The old, interesting and rapidly revitalising Temple Bar area is Dublin's most concentrated restaurant area. It's bounded by the river to the north, Westmoreland St to the east and Christ Church Cathedral to the west. The southern boundary is Dame St and its extension, Lord Edward St, but for convenience's sake restaurants on both the northern and southern side of Dame St are listed in this section.

Fast Food & Cafés *Abrakebabra* has a branch at the O'Connell Bridge end of Westmoreland St. *Beshoff's* (☎ 677 8026) has a second branch with waiter service upstairs at 14 Westmoreland St, also just south of O'Connell Bridge.

Backpackers staying at *Kinlay House*, at the Christ Church Cathedral end of Lord Edward St (see Hostels in the Places to Stay section), will find good cafeteria-style facilities there. The *Well Fed Café* (☎ 677 2234), 6 Crow St, is a big, busy, alternative-style place with large portions of food. It's great for lunch or a snack and caters particularly well to vegetarians. It's open from noon to 8 pm Monday to Saturday.

The Chameleon (☎ 671 0362), at 1 Fownes St just off Wellington Quay, offers an Indonesian *rijstaffel*. The restaurant section upstairs opens on Thursday to Saturday evenings.

Italian Restaurants Temple Bar has all sorts of restaurants but the Irish passion for pasta and pizza comes through loud and clear.

The very popular *Bad Ass Café* (☎ 671 2596), 9-11 Crown Alley, is a bright, cheerful, warehouse-style place just south of Ha'penny Bridge. It offers pretty good pizzas from IR£7 in a convivial studentish atmosphere with pulleys to whip orders to the kitchen at busy times, but doesn't open for breakfast. One of its claims to fame is that Sinéad O'Connor once worked here as a waitress. A couple of doors down *Garibaldi's* (☎ 671 7288) at 15-16 Crown Alley does burgers and steaks to complement the pizzas and pastas. *Nico's* (☎ 677 3062), 53 Dame St on the corner of Temple Lane, offers conservative Italian food with a strong Irish influence. It's solidly popular, has a piano player, is open for dinner Monday to Saturday, and also for lunch on weekdays. Main dishes are in the IR£7 to IR£10 range. *Pizzeria Italia* (☎ 677 8528), 23 Temple Bar, is another simple pizzeria offering classic pizzas at standard prices. It's open Tuesday to Saturday.

You can also find pizza at the fancier *Da Pino* (☎ 671 9308), 38-40 Parliament St on the corner of Dame St. This spacious and bright restaurant has pizzas at IR£3.50 and IR£6 and a wide international selection of beers at IR£1.80 and IR£2.30. *La Mezza Luna* (☎ 671 2840) is also on Dame St but the entrance is round the corner in Temple Lane. This slightly more upmarket restaurant is enormously popular, and you may have to book a table or be prepared to wait. The pasta dishes are great value at IR£4 to IR£7. It's open Monday to Thursday from 12.30 to 11 pm, Friday and Saturday 12.30 to 11.30 pm and Sunday 4 to 10.30 pm.

Il Pasticcio (☎ 677 6111), 12 Fownes St, does wood-baked pizzas and good pasta in a rather cramped setting with paintings on the walls by up-and-coming artists. Pasta main dishes range from IR£4.50 to IR£6.95, pizzas from IR£4.50 to IR£5.95. In 3-4 Bedford Row, down a side turning and therefore likely to have tables when other places are full, *Café Gertrude* (☎ 677 9043) also does pizza at realistic prices.

Other Restaurants Despite the number of trattorias, ristorantes and pizzerias, there's more to Temple Bar than pasta and pizza. At the *Eamonn Doran Imbibing Emporium* (☎ 679 9773) you can get burger or fish for IR£5 or a four-course meal for IR£15. It's at 3A Crown Alley, directly across from The Bad Ass Café, and has a similar venue in New York City.

Omelettes are a speciality at the popular and bustling, but overpriced, *Elephant & Castle* (☎ 679 3121), 18 Temple Bar; how 'free' are coffee fill-ups when the first cup is IR£1.50? It stays open until midnight on Friday and Saturday, until 11.30 pm on other days. Next door at 20-21 Temple Bar is the equally popular *Gallagher's Boxty House* (☎ 677 2762). A *boxty* is rather like a stuffed pancake and tastes like an extremely bland Indian *masala dosa*. Real Irish food is not something that's widely available in Dublin so it's worth trying. Main dishes are IR£6 to IR£7. Next to that is the *Alamo* (☎ 677 6546) where you can get good reasonably priced Mexican dishes.

On the corner of Wellington Quay and Asdills Row is *Omar Khayyam* (☎ 677 5758), a popular, good Middle Eastern restaurant offering all the usual Lebanese-style dishes; kebabs are IR£9.75 and the menu includes some vegetarian dishes. You can remain in the Arab world at *Le Restaurant Casablanca* (☎ 679 9996), 22 Temple Bar,

where the food is Moroccan and includes such North African specialities as tahini and couscous. The Casablanca is open every day.

Poco Loco (☎ 679 1950), 32 Parliament St, offers straightforward Tex-Mex interpretations of Mexican food but they do have Corona beer (cerveza if you wish!) and their combination plates are great value at IR£6 to IR£9. It's open weekdays for lunch and every day for dinner.

Dame St's international mix of restaurants includes Chinese possibilities like *Fan's Cantonese Restaurant* (☎ 679 4263/73) at No 60. *Les Frères Jacques* (☎ 679 4555) at No 74 is one of Temple Bar's fancier places with set meals for IR£22. The food is as French as the name would indicate, the mood is slightly serious, and the bill can make quite a dent in your budget. It's open Monday to Friday for lunch, Monday to Saturday for dinner.

Turn off Dame St into Crow St where you'll find *Tante Zoé's* (☎ 679 4407) at No 1. It's open Monday to Saturday for lunch, Monday to Sunday for dinner and is yet more proof of how cosmopolitan Dublin dining can be, since Cajun and Creole food is the speciality with starters for IR£2.75 and main dishes from IR£7. The next lane again is Fownes St Upper, where your taste buds can continue their travels to Portugal at the *Little Lisbon* (☎ 671 1274). It's open every day, and Australians will feel right at home here as it has a BYO licence, allowing you to bring your own wine. From noon to 5 pm you can take advantage of a special lunch menu for IR£3.95.

The *Broker's Restaurant* (☎ 679 3534), 25 Dame St, serves up truly traditional Irish fare – you can even have Irish stew and three-course meals for around IR£10.

Around Grafton St

Pedestrianised Grafton St is the No 1 shopping street in south Dublin and notably lacking in restaurants and pubs. The streets to the east and west of Grafton St are more promising. Dame St restaurants are all covered in the Temple Bar section.

Fast Food & Cafés Grafton St is the fast-food centre south of the Liffey with a *McDonald's* at No 9, a *Burger King* at No 39 and *La Pizza* just round the corner at 1 St Stephen's Green North. *Captain America* (☎ 671 5266), 44 Grafton St, has burgers until midnight every night of the week.

There are three branches of Bewley's cafés around the centre. *Bewley's* is a huge cafeteria-style place that offers good-quality food, including breakfast, lunch-time sandwiches (IR£1.50 to IR£3) and complete meals (IR£3.50 to IR£5). It's equally good for a quick cup of tea or coffee and actually offers a choice of teas. Watch the price of cakes though.

The 78 Grafton St branch, Bewley's Oriental Café, is the flagship, with company memorabilia displayed upstairs. It's open from 7.30 am to 1 am Sunday to Thursday and round the clock Friday and Saturday. On Sunday it's open from 9.30 am to 7 pm. The branch at 11-12 Westmoreland St is open from 7.30 am to 9 pm Monday to Saturday and 9.30 am to 8 pm Sunday There's also a branch at 13 South Great George's St.

Round the corner from Dublin Castle at 2 Werburgh St *Leo Burdock's* (☎ 54 0366), next to the Lord Edward Pub, is said to dole out the best fish & chips in Ireland. You can eat them down the road in the park beside St Patrick's Cathedral. It's open until 11 pm Monday to Saturday.

The Grafton St area has office workers, Trinity College students and tourists to feed and there are plenty of cafés and restaurants to keep them happy at lunch time. Backpackers staying at *Avalon House* on Aungier St (see Hostels in the Places to Stay section) can take advantage of the most stylish hostel café in town.

Subway, on Anne St South just off Grafton St, turns out filling sandwiches, baps (a soft Irish version of a bread roll) and rolls for IR£1.80 to IR£3.90. Eat there or even better, if it's a sunny day, have a picnic in nearby St Stephen's Green. At 6 Anne St South is *The Coffee Inn* (☎ 671 9302) with good coffee, outdoor tables (weather permitting) and late opening hours (until 3 am on Friday and Saturday) every night of the week. There are pizzas and pasta dishes to go with the coffee. *Café Java* (☎ 670 7239) at 5 Anne St South does excellent lunches for around IR£3.50; the set IR£3.95 weekday lunch offers soup, a sandwich and tea or coffee. There's a second branch (☎ 660 0675) at 145 Upper Leeson St.

Munchies on the corner of Exchequer St and William St South, just west of Grafton St, claims to produce the best sandwiches in Ireland. For IR£1.80 (sandwiches) or IR£2 (baps) you can check if it's true. A little closer to Grafton St at 19 Wicklow St is *Cornucopia* (☎ 677 7583), a popular wholefood café turning out all sorts of goodies for those trying to escape the Irish cholesterol habit. There's even a hot vegetarian breakfast for IR£2.25 as an alternative to muesli. It's open for lunch Monday to Saturday and until 8 pm on weekday evenings, 9 pm on Thursday. Head the other way along Exchequer St to the *Wed Wose Café* at No 18 which tops up the sandwiches with burgers.

The Powerscourt Townhouse Shopping Centre is stuffed with eating places and makes a great place for lunch. They include *Blazing Salads II* (☎ 671 9552), a very popular vegetarian restaurant on the top level with a variety of salads for 70p each. It's open Monday to Saturday from 9.30 am to 6 pm. *La Piazza* next door does pizzas. On the 1st floor *Chompy's* (☎ 679 4552) boasts a Grand Slam breakfast for IR£5 or salads for IR£4. In the open central area is *Mary Rose*, a good place for breakfast (IR£1.50). On the ground floor would-be lunchers will find the *Whistlestop Café*, *Fair City Sandwich Bar* and *Snappy Snacks*, serving everything from soups to burgers. *Twisted Lemon* does crêpes and pancake pizzas and you can round off with a coffee at *Coffee Roastery*.

For sizeable sandwiches there are branches of *O'Brien's* at 54 Mary St and in the St Stephen's Green Shopping Centre.

Other places to eat in St Stephen's Green Shopping Centre include a branch of *Café Kylemore* on the first floor and the *Pavlova Pantry* on the second. Just beside the centre is a branch of *Chicago Pizza Pie Factory*

DUBLIN

(☎ 478 1233). Nearby in Clarendon Market the new *Café des Artistes* promises great things with its breakfasts and lunch-time baguettes.

The large *Kilkenny Kitchen* (☎ 677 7066) is on the 1st floor of the Kilkenny Shop at 6 Nassau St. The generally excellent food is served cafeteria-style and at times the queues can be discouragingly long. At peak times there's a simpler food counter which can be faster. It's open Monday to Saturday from 9 am to 5 pm, and to 8 pm on Thursday.

Capers (☎ 679 7140) is above the Runner Bean greengrocer's at 4 Nassau St, also opposite Trinity. It's popular with students, and from the upstairs room you can gaze across the college grounds. The food comes in healthy quantities, in healthy style (plenty of vegetarian dishes) and with lots of salads.

Fitzer's slick outlets are great places for lunch or early evening meals on weekdays. There's a Fitzer's (☎ 677 1155) at 52 Dawson St, towards the Trinity College and Nassau St end. The best Fitzer's, however, is in the National Gallery, and is covered in the Merrion Row, Baggot St & Beyond section.

For a really excellent cheap lunch, look for *Marks Bros Café* (☎ 677 0185) at 7 South Great George St. It's been there for over a decade now, turning out big, filling sandwiches, tasty soups and scrumptious carrot cake at prices that leave Bewley's standing.

Restaurants St Andrew's St, just west of Grafton St's northern end, is packed with good restaurant possibilities. The excellent *Trocadero* (☎ 677 5545, 679 9772), 3 St Andrew's St, offers no culinary surprises which is exactly why it's so popular. Simple food, straightforward preparation, large helpings and late opening hours are the selling points. The Troc, as it's locally known, is open past midnight every night except Sunday, when it closes just a little earlier.

Across the road, *QV-2* (☎ 677 3363) at 14-15 St Andrew's St manages to look more expensive than it is. There are good pasta dishes for IR£5.95 to IR£7.95 and main courses for IR£7.25 to IR£12.50, but vegetables cost extra. It offers good, mildly adventurous food, pleasant surroundings and a dessert called Eton Mess (IR£2.75) which should not be missed. It's open every day for lunch and dinner until after midnight.

Still on St Andrew's St the *Cedar Tree* (☎ 677 2121) at No 11A is a Lebanese restaurant with a good selection of vegetarian dishes. Or turn the corner to *La Taverna* (☎ 677 3665) at 33 Wicklow St. It's open daily for lunch and dinner and combines sunny Greek food with an equally sunny atmosphere. At 12A Wicklow St the *Imperial Chinese Restaurant* (☎ 677 2580) is open every day, but is notable for its lunch-time dim sums.

Pasta Fresca (☎ 679 2402) is at 3-4 Chatham St, just off Grafton St's southern end. This modern, cheerful restaurant proves once again that the Irish really like their Italian food. It has very authentic pasta dishes for IR£4.95 to IR£8.50 and is open from 8 am until reasonably late Monday to Saturday. On Sunday it opens from noon to 8.30 pm. Just off Chatham St, *Pizza Stop* (☎ 679 6712) at 6 Chatham Lane is a very popular pizzeria with pizzas for IR£5 to IR£8. Alternatively, at 27 Exchequer St, a bit to the north, there's the popular *Trattoria Pasta Pasta* (☎ 679 2565) with pasta dishes from IR£7.

There are several pubs with good food close to Grafton St. The *Stag's Head* (☎ 679 3701) is on Dame Court, and, apart from being an extremely popular drinking spot during the summer months (see the Entertainment section), also turns out simple, well-prepared and very economical meals. At 37 Exchequer St on the corner of St Andrew's St is the *Old Stand*, another popular place for pub food with meals at about IR£5.

Davy Byrne's, 21 Duke St, has been famous for its food ever since Leopold Bloom dropped in for a sandwich. It's now a swish watering hole but you can still eat there. Farther west the *Lord Edward Seafood Restaurant* (☎ 454 2420), upstairs in the Lord Edward Pub at 23 Christ Church Place opposite Christ Church Cathedral, has pub-style seafood. It's open Monday to Friday for lunch and Monday to Saturday for dinner. Even farther west *The Brazen Head* in Bridge St is always packed at lunch time. It has a variety of menus offering everything from sandwiches to a carvery.

Judge Roy Bean's (☎ 679 7539), 45-47 Nassau St on the corner of Grafton St, serves whopping helpings of tacos and has a very popular bar. *Eddie Rocket's* (☎ 679 7340), 7 Anne St South, is a 1950s-style American diner ready to dish out anything from breakfast at 7.30 am to an excellent late-night burger from IR£2.95. Friday and Saturday nights it's open right through to 4 am. Next door is the trendy, popular *Cotham Café* (☎ 679 5266), 8 Anne St South, with pizzas prepared with some pizzazz. If you can stand the smell, the *Periwinkle Seafood Bar* (☎ 679 4203) in the Powerscourt Townhouse Shopping Centre serves economically priced seafood lunches with the accent on shellfish.

Regular visitors to India may remember Rajdoot as a popular brand of Indian motorcycle; those in search of Indian food in Dublin can scoot down to *Rajdoot Tandoori* (☎ 679 4274) for superb North Indian tandoori dishes. It's at 26-28 Clarendon St in the Westbury Centre, behind the Westbury Hotel. Set lunches cost IR£6.95. Nearby, and with similarly Mogul-style Indian cuisine, is the *Shalimar* (☎ 671 0738), 17 South Great George's St, which offers a wide variety of delectable Indian breads and *baltis* but isn't particularly cheap.

La Stampa (☎ 677 8611), 35 Dawson St, is Dublin's up-market Italian restaurant with a large and very attractive Georgian dining area, liberally festooned with colourful paintings. It's open from lunch time until late every day and main courses are in the IR£9 to IR£14 range.

The very stylish *Polo One* (☎ 676 2233) is at 5-6 Molesworth Place, a smaller lane off Molesworth St, tucked in behind St Ann's Church which fronts on to Dawson St. The emphasis is on seafood and there's a distinct French bias to the cooking. Set lunch menus cost IR£10, but dinner is strictly à la carte. The wines are pricey but the food tastes as good as it looks.

For a French restaurant without the pretentiousness which that sometimes implies, try *Chez Jules* (☎ 677 0499) tucked away at 16A D'Olier St. You eat at long benches with red-and-white check cloths and the food is well cooked and not at all extortionately priced.

In the basement of Newman House at 85-86 St Stephen's Green is *The Commons* (☎ 475 2597), the unexpected first of Dublin's two Michelin-starred restaurants, unexpected because it's only been in business since 1991. As you'd expect, the food here is pricey and it would be as well to book ahead, especially for weekends. Chef Michael Bolster's 'tasting menu' of six courses costs IR£45.

Finally, on Stephen St Lower, behind the big St Stephen's Green Shopping Centre, *Break for the Border* (☎ 478-0300) is a busy, barn-like restaurant, bar-and-entertainment complex serving Tex-Mex food until late. Look for the Western horse and rider statue out front. If it looks a bit too impersonal for you, dive down Clarendon Market to the *Orange Room* (☎ 677 5099) which does tasty, filling modern cooking in much cosier surroundings.

Merrion Row, Baggot St & Beyond

Merrion Row, leading out south-east from St Stephen's Green, and its extension, Baggot St, is a busy boulevard of middle to upper bracket guesthouses, popular pubs and an eclectic selection of restaurants.

Fast Food & Cafés *Fitzer's* (☎ 668 6481), inside the National Gallery in Merrion Square, is a restaurant well worth a detour, particularly at lunch time. The artistic interlude as you walk through makes a pleasant introduction to this slightly pricey but very popular restaurant. It has the same opening hours as the gallery (Thursday until 8.30 pm) and has meals for IR£4.60 to IR£5.25, as well as salads, cakes and wine. There's a *Fitzer's Take-Out* (☎ 660 0644) at 24 Baggot St Upper.

Starting from the Shelbourne Hotel on St Stephen's Green, *Galligan's Café* (☎ 676

5955), 6 Merrion Row, is a great place for breakfast from 7.30 am weekdays or from 9 am on Saturday and for lunch or afternoon snacks. Across the road *Pierre Victoire* (☎ 678 5412) does set lunches for IR£5.90 and set dinners for IR£6.90. Farther along, *Georgian Fare* (☎ 676 7736), 14 Baggot St Lower, has good sandwiches, while *Miller's Pizza Kitchen* (☎ 676 6098), 9-10 Baggot St Lower, is firmly in pastaland.

Restaurants There's an international line-up of restaurants among the colourful Baggot St pubs, one of which is *Ayumi-ya* (☎ 662 0233), in the basement at 132 Baggot St Lower. This is a very Westernised Japanese steakhouse offering good-value set meals comprising a starter, soup, main course, dessert and tea or coffee for IR£13.95. No surprises here but the food is good. There's a second more formal branch of Ayumi-ya in the suburb of Blackrock, serving more traditional Japanese food.

The *Ante Room* (☎ 660 4716), 20 Baggot St Lower, underneath the popular Georgian House guesthouse, is a seafood specialist with main courses from about IR£10 and traditional Irish music on most summer nights.

The Michelin-starred *Restaurant Patrick Guilbaud* (☎ 660 1799) has a reputation as Dublin's best place for French food in the modern idiom and the restaurant itself is equally modern. Don't come here unless your credit card is in A1 condition. The smooth décor and service is backed up by delicious food. There's nothing overpoweringly fancy about anything, it's just good food, beautifully prepared and elegantly presented. There's a set menu for IR£30, but with drinks and service you should count on at least IR£45 per person. Patrick Guilbaud is at 46 James's Place, just off Baggot St Lower beyond Fitzwilliam St. It's open for lunch and dinner Monday to Saturday.

You can slide backwards in time by continuing along Baggot St, across the Grand Canal and on to Pembroke Rd to *Le Coq Hardi* (☎ 668 9070) at No 35. This is the older counterpart of Patrick Guilbaud with

heavier, more traditional French dishes and a superb wine list. The bill is likely to be a little heavier as well. It's open for lunch Monday to Friday and for dinner Monday to Saturday.

Also out from the centre is the *Lobster Pot Restaurant* (☎ 668 0025) at 9 Ballsbridge Terrace, Dublin 4. It's a staunchly old-fashioned place offering substantial and solid dishes in an equally substantial atmosphere. As the name indicates, seafood is the speciality. Prices are fairly high. Right next door is *Roly's Bistro* (☎ 668 2611) at No 7 which receives rave write-ups for its food; advance booking is advisable. Close by at 15-17 Ballsbridge Terrace is *Kites Chinese Restaurant* (☎ 660 7415), where Chinese food with style is the story and the prices are moderate to high.

If you're after real Irish food then the place to go is *Oisin's* (☎ 475 3433), 31 Camden St Upper, to the south-west of St Stephen's Green, a block over from Harcourt St. The menu offers all the traditional Irish dishes, including Irish stew and Dublin coddle for fancy prices. Oisin's is open for dinner Tuesday to Sunday.

The *Old Dublin* restaurant (☎ 454 2028), 90 Francis St, makes an interesting departure from the standard Irish menu, as it specialises in Russian and Scandinavian food. It costs around IR£20 a head but is worth the splash.

ENTERTAINMENT
Dublin has theatres, cinemas, nightclubs and concert halls, but just as in every village throughout the Emerald Isle, the pubs are the real centres of activity. Dublin has hundreds of pubs and they're great for anything from a contemplative pint of Guinness to a rowdy night out with the latest Irish rock band. For what's-on information get the fortnightly magazine *In Dublin* (IR£1.50) or the giveaway *Dublin Event Guide*.

A Pub Crawl
See the Organised Tours section for information on the excellent and highly recommended Literary and Musical Pub

Crawls, which on summer nights make fine introductions to some of Dublin's pubs. Pubs must close at night by 11.30 pm, or by 11 pm in winter.

A visit to the city should properly include a walking tour of some of the best of the old pubs. A traditional Irish pub has *snugs*, partitioned-off tables where you can meet friends in privacy. Some snugs even have their own serving hatches, so drinks can be passed in discreetly should the drinkers not want to be seen ordering 'just the one'.

Even in medieval times the city was well supplied with drinking establishments and in the late 17th century a count revealed that one in every five houses in the city was involved in selling alcohol. A century later another survey counted 52 public houses along Thomas St in the Liberties. There may not be quite so many today but Dublin still has a huge selection of pubs, so there's no possibility of being unable to find a Guinness should you develop a thirst.

A Dublin pub crawl should start at the *Brazen Head* on Bridge St just south of the Liffey beyond Christ Church Cathedral. This is Dublin's oldest pub, though its history is uncertain. Its own sign proclaims that it was founded in 1198, but the earliest reference to it is in 1613 and licensing laws did not come into effect until 1635. Others claim that it was founded in 1666 or 1688, but the present building is thought to date from 1754. The sunken level of the entrance courtyard is a clear indicator of how much street levels have altered since its construction. In the 1790s it was the headquarters of the United Irishmen, who, it would appear, had a tendency to talk too much after a few drinks, leading to numerous arrests being made here. At that time Robert Emmet was a regular visitor. Not surprisingly, James Joyce mentioned it in *Ulysses* with a half-hearted recommendation for the food: 'you get a decent enough do in the Brazen Head'.

From the Brazen Head walk eastward along the Liffey to the trendy Temple Bar district and dive into those narrow lanes for a drink at popular pubs like the *Norseman* and the *Temple Bar*. On summer evenings young visitors to Dublin congregate for a nightly street party that stretches along Temple Bar from one pub to the other.

On Fleet St in Temple Bar, the *Palace Bar*, with its tiled floor and mirrors, is frequently pointed out as a perfect example of an old Dublin pub and is popular with journalists from the nearby *Irish Times*. On the corner of Temple Bar and Anglesea St is the *Auld Dubliner*, and on the opposite corner, at the junction of Fleet and Anglesea Sts, is the restored *Oliver St John Gogarty* where Musical Pub Crawls kick off nightly except Friday at 7.30 pm.

From Temple Bar cross Dame St, itself well supplied with drinking establishments, to the intersection of Dame Court and Dame Lane, where *Dame Tavern* and the *Stag's Head* face each other from opposite corners. Here, too, a street party takes place between the pubs on summer evenings. The *Stag's Head* was built in 1770, then remodelled in 1895 and is sufficiently picturesque to have featured in a postage stamp series on Irish pubs.

With time and energy you could divert down South Great George St to the luxuriant *Long Hall*. Otherwise, continue down Dame Lane past the *Banker's* to *O'Neill's* on Suffolk St. It's only a stone's throw from Trinity College, so this fine old traditional pub has long been a student haunt. A block over on Exchequer St is the *Old Stand*, furnished in hybrid Georgian-Victorian style and renowned for its rugby connections and fine pub food. On the other corner, on Wicklow St, the *International Bar* has entertainment almost every night, including a Comedy Cellar on Wednesday.

Emerge on to Grafton St, which, despite being Dublin's premier shopping street, is completely publess. Fear not – there are numerous interesting establishments just off the street, including *Davy Byrne's* on Duke St. Davy Byrne's was Bloom's 'moral pub' in *Ulysses* and he stopped there for a Gorgonzola cheese sandwich with mustard washed down with a glass of Burgundy. It also featured in *Dubliners*, but after a recent glossy refurbishment has become a yuppie hang-out which Joyce would hardly recognise.

Writer Brendan Behan, who was known to like
a drink or two, frequented McDaid's pub

On Harry St, also off Grafton St, you'll
find *McDaid's*, once Brendan Behan's local,
now a bit of a tourist trap. Across the road
from it is the *Bruxelles*. On Anne St South
there's *John Kehoe's* with its old snugs,
where patrons can still savour their Guinness
in privacy. Chatham St features *Neary's*, a
showy Victorian era pub with a particularly
fine frontage, popular with actors from the
nearby Gaiety Theatre.

From the end of Grafton St turn along the
north side of St Stephen's Green (the 'Beaux'
Walk') and continue on past the Shelbourne
Hotel to Merrion Row for a drink at
O'Donoghue's. In the evening you'll almost
certainly have music to accompany your pint
as this is one of Dublin's most famous music
pubs. The folk group the Dubliners started
out here. On summer evenings a crowd spills
out into the courtyard beside the pub.

Merrion Row changes name to become
Baggot St Lower and facing each other
across the street are two very traditional old
pubs *James Toner's* and *Doheny & Nesbitt's*.
Toner's, with its stone floor, is almost a
country pub in the heart of the city and the
shelves and drawers are reminders that it
once doubled as a grocery store. Doheny &
Nesbitt's is equipped with antique snugs and
is a favourite place for political gossip
among politicians and journalists; Leinster

House is only a short stroll away. *Baggot Inn*,
close to Toner's, is a popular place for rock
music. If you continue farther along Baggot
St you'll come to *Larry Murphy's* and the
Henry Grattan.

Backtrack a few steps to Merrion St Upper
and walk north past Merrion Square to
Kenny's on Lincoln Place, which is tucked in
behind Trinity College and has long been a
Trinity student haunt. It's well known for its
spontaneous traditional music sessions.
Continue round the edge of Trinity College
towards the river where you'll come to *John
Mulligan's* on Poolbeg St, another pub that
has scarcely changed over the years. It featured as the local in the film *My Left Foot* and
is popular with journalists from the nearby
newspaper offices. Mulligan's was established in 1782 and has long been reputed to
have the best Guinness in Ireland as well as
a wonderfully varied crowd of 'regulars'.

South of the centre there are more interesting pubs along the Grand Canal (see the
Grand Canal section).

No thorough pub crawl should be
restricted to pubs south of the Liffey, so head
north to try *Slattery's* at 129 Capel St, on the
corner of Mary's Lane, and *Sean O'Casey's*
at 105 Marlborough St, on the corner of
Abbey St Lower. Both are busy music pubs
where you'll often find traditional Irish
music downstairs and loud rock upstairs.
Other north Dublin pubs to sample are the
Oval on Abbey St Middle, another
journalists' hang-out, and *Abbey Mooney's*
on Abbey St Lower.

Head farther north to the *Patrick Conway*
on Parnell St which has been in operation
since 1745; new fathers have been stopping
in here for a celebratory pint from the day the
Rotunda Maternity Hospital opened across
the road in 1757. *Joxer Daly's* at 103-104
Dorset St Upper is a Victorian-style pub,
conveniently close to the Young Traveller
and An Óige hostels.

Pub Entertainment

There's considerable overlap between music
styles at the various Dublin pubs – some
specialise solely in one type of music, others

switch from night to night. Others may have one band on upstairs and another, of an entirely different style, downstairs.

Rock Music Various pubs specialise in rock music, and some of them charge an entry fee. *Whelan's*, the *Purty Kitchen* and the *Baggot Inn* hold rock sessions almost every night. Other pubs which often serve up rock are *Fibber McGee's*, *The Mean Fiddler* and *Larry O'Rourke's*. During the summer months the *Olympia Theatre* has 'Midnight at the Olympia' performances on Friday and Saturday nights.

Traditional & Folk Music Traditional Irish music and folk music also have big followings in Dublin pubs. Worth trying are *The Auld Dubliner*, *Boss Croker's*, the *Brazen Head*, *Larry O'Rourke's*, *The Mean Fiddler*, *Mother Redcaps*, *O'Donoghue's*, the *Purty Kitchen*, *Slattery's* and *Whelan's*.

Country Music Along with all the other popular music forms in Ireland, there's a real passion for country music, especially at *Bad Bob's* in Temple Bar (see the Discos & Nightclubs section). Pubs where country music is popular include *Barry's Hotel*, the *Lower Deck* and the *Purty Kitchen*. *Break for the Border* in Stephen St Lower also hosts regular country music sessions.

Jazz & Blues Jazz and blues are also played at several pubs, including the *Barge*, *Boss Croker's*, *Harcourt Hotel*, the *International Bar*, *McDaid's*, *Hotel Pierre*, *Slattery's* and *Whelan's*. *Sach's Hotel* and *Jury's Hotel* also have jazz sessions on Sunday.

Comedy Several pubs have comedy acts from time to time, including the *Waterfront* and the *Purty Kitchen*. The *International Bar* has a regular Wednesday night Comedy Cellar, which takes place upstairs, of course.

Venues The phone numbers and locations of the music and entertainment pubs mentioned here are as follows:

The Auld Dubliner
   17 Anglesea St, Dublin 2 (☎ 677 0527)
Bad Bob's Backstage Bar
   East Essex St, Dublin 2 (☎ 677 5482)
The Baggot Inn
   143 Baggot St, Dublin 2 (☎ 676 1430)
The Barge Inn
   42 Charlemont St, Dublin 2 (☎ 475 1869)
Barry's Hotel
   Great Denmark St, Dublin 1 (☎ 874 6943)
Boss Croker's
   39 Arran Quay, Dublin 7 (☎ 872 2400)
The Brazen Head
   Bridge St, Dublin 8 (☎ 677 9549)
Fibber Magee's
   Gate Hotel, Parnell St, Dublin 2 (☎ 874 5253)
The Harcourt Hotel
   60 Harcourt St, Dublin 2 (☎ 778 3677)
Howl at the Moon (O'Dwyer's Pub)
   68 Mount St, Dublin 2 (☎ 676 1717)
The International Bar
   23 Wicklow St, Dublin 2 (☎ 677 9250)
Jury's Hotel
   Ballsbridge, Dublin 4 (☎ 660 5000)
Larry O'Rourke's
   72 Dorset St Upper, Dublin 1 (☎ 475 1423)
The Lower Deck
   Portobello Harbour, Dublin 8 (☎ 475 1423)
McDaid's
   3 Harry St, Dublin 2 (☎ 679 4395)
The Mean Fiddler
   16 Wexford St, Dublin 2 (☎ 478 0391)
Mother Redcaps
   Back Lane, The Liberties, Dublin 8 (☎ 454 0652)
O'Donoghue's
   15 Merrion Row, Dublin 2 (☎ 661 4303)
Hotel Pierre
   Seafront, Dun Laoghaire (☎ 280 0291)
The Purty Kitchen
   Old Dunleary Rd, Dun Laoghaire (☎ 280 1257)
Sach's Hotel
   19-29 Morehampton Rd, Dublin 4 (☎ 668 4829)
Slattery's
   129 Capel St, Dublin 1 (☎ 872 7971)
The Waterfront
   Sir John Rogerson's Quay, Dublin 2 (☎ 677 8466)
Whelan's
   25 Wexford St, Dublin 2 (☎ 478 0766)

Irish Entertainment

There are several places in Dublin where tourists can go for an evening of entertainment, with Irish songs, Irish dancing and probably a few Irish jokes thrown in along the way.

Jury's Irish Cabaret (☎ 660 5000) at

Jury's Hotel, Ballsbridge, Dublin 4, features 2½ hours of Irish music, song and dance. This has been a tourist favourite for 30 years. You can either come for dinner and the show (IR£32.50) from 7.15 pm or just for the show (IR£20, including two drinks) from 8 pm. It operates nightly except Monday from the beginning of May to mid-October.

Similar performances are put on at the *Burlington Hotel* (☎ 660 5222) at Upper Leeson St, Dublin 4. The two-hour performances take place nightly from 8 pm May to October. Dinner starts an hour earlier and the cost for dinner and the show is IR£32.50. The *Clontarf Castle* (☎ 833 2321) at Castle Ave, Clontarf, Dublin 3, also has shows from 7.30 pm Monday to Saturday.

Cinema

Dublin's restaurants are overwhelmingly south of the river, pubs are more evenly spread between north and south, but city cinemas are more heavily concentrated on the north side.

The multi-screen first-run cinemas are the four-screen *Adelphi* (☎ 873 0433), 98 Abbey St Middle, Dublin 1; the one-screen *Ambassador* (☎ 872 7000), Parnell St; and the six-screen *Savoy* (☎ 874 8487), O'Connell St Upper, Dublin 1. The three-screen *Screen* (☎ 671 4988, 872 3922), College St, Dublin 2, is south of the river and is more art house, less big release. Ditto for the *Light House* (☎ 873 0438), Abbey St Middle, Dublin 1. The *Irish Film Centre* (☎ 679 5744) has two screens at 6 Eustace St in Temple Bar. The complex there also has a bar, a café and a bookshop; comedy shows are sometimes staged in the atrium.

Entry prices are generally between IR£3 and IR£5, though there may be reduced prices for afternoon shows. Late-night shows take place from time to time, particularly at the Savoy on Saturday nights.

Theatre

Dublin's theatre scene is small but busy. (See South Dublin Theatres and Abbey Theatre under Things to See earlier for more information about the histories of some of Dublin's best known theatres.) Theatre bookings can usually be made by quoting a credit card number over the phone and the tickets can then be collected just before the performance.

The famous *Abbey Theatre* (☎ 878 7222) is on Abbey St Lower, Dublin 1, near the river. This is Ireland's national theatre and it puts on new Irish works as well as a steady series of revivals of classic Irish works by W B Yeats, J M Synge, Sean O'Casey, Brendan Behan, Samuel Beckett and others. Performances are at 8 pm, with Saturday matinees at 2.30 pm. Tickets cost IR£10 and IR£12.50, but student discounts are available. The smaller *Peacock Theatre* is part of the same complex but ticket prices are lower.

Also north of the Liffey is the *Gate Theatre* (☎ 874 4045) on the south-east corner of Parnell Square, right at the top of O'Connell St. It specialises in international classics and older Irish works with a touch of comedy by playwrights such as Oscar Wilde, George Bernard Shaw and Oliver Goldsmith.

The *Olympia Theatre* (☎ 677 8962), on Dame St, often has rock concerts as well as plays. The *Gaiety Theatre* (☎ 677 1717), on King St South, puts on modern plays and TV shows. Over in the Liberties the *Tivoli Theatre* (☎ 454 4472) is on Francis St, Dublin 8, directly opposite the Iveagh Market.

Experimental and less-commercial performances take place at the *City Arts Centre* (☎ 677 0643) at 23-25 Moss St, Dublin 2, and at the *Project Arts Centre* (☎ 671 2321), 39 Essex St East, Temple Bar, Dublin 1. The *International Bar* (☎ 677 9250), 23 Wicklow St, Dublin 2, sometimes hosts theatrical performances. Puppet performances are put on at the *Lambert Puppet Theatre & Museum* (☎ 280 0974) in Clifton Lane, Monkstown.

Theatrical performances also take place at:

Andrew's Lane Theatre
    9-17 St Andrew's Lane, Dublin 2 (☎ 679 5720)
Eblana Theatre
    Busáras, Dublin 1 (☎ 679 8404)

Focus Theatre
 6 Pembroke Place, Dublin 2 (☎ 676 3071)
Players' Theatre
 Trinity College, Dublin 2 (☎ 677 2941, ext 1239)
Riverbank Theatre
 10 Merchant's Quay, Dublin 8 (☎ 677 3370)

Concerts

Classical concerts are performed at the *National Concert Hall* (☎ 671 1888) in Earlsfort Terrace, Dublin 2, just south of St Stephen's Green. In summer there are usually lunch-time concerts on Tuesdays and Fridays with entry prices of around IR£3. Classical performances may also take place at the *Bank of Ireland Arts Centre* in Foster Place, at the *Hugh Lane Gallery* in Parnell Square or at the *Royal Dublin Showground Concert Hall*.

Big rock concerts are held at the *Point Depot* (☎ 836 3633) at East Link Bridge, North Wall Quay, by the river and originally constructed as a railway terminus in 1878. The *Lansdowne Rd Stadium*, a mecca for rugby enthusiasts, is also used for big rock performances. Smaller performances often take place at the pleasantly tatty *Olympia Theatre* (☎ 677 7744) in Dame St, Temple Bar.

Bookings can be made either directly at the concert venue or through HMV (☎ 679 5334; 24-hour credit-card bookings ☎ 456 9569) at 65 Grafton St, Dublin 2.

Discos & Nightclubs

Leeson St Lower, to the south-east of St Stephen's Green, is the nightclub quarter of Dublin, with a whole string of clubs along this one busy block. They're easily pinpointed by the black-suited bouncers lined up outside, but which clubs are currently in changes from one year (or even one month) to another. It's probably best just to follow the crowds – if it looks busy it's likely to be good. Leeson St clubs usually stay open until around 4 am and there are no admission charges, but the price of drinks certainly makes up for that; count on paying at least IR£15 for a bottle of very basic wine.

Other popular venues usually do have an entry charge. *Lillie's Bordello*, whose entrance is in an alley off Grafton St at the Trinity College end, is usually open to 2 am. Rather different is *Bad Bob's Backstage Bar* (☎ 677 5482) in East Essex St in Temple Bar where there's music every night, except that here it's country music rather than rock. Entry is in the IR£6 to IR£8 bracket. Still in Temple Bar, *Club M* at Bloom's Hotel is very popular.

Break for the Border (☎ 478 0300), on Stephen St Lower, is a huge entertainment complex combining a bar with a Tex-Mex restaurant. You can hardly miss *Howl at the Moon* (☎ 676 1717) in O'Dwyer's in Mount St where the entrance is beneath the stomach of a huge carved wolf. It's open until 2 am every night and admission is IR£2 during the week, IR£5 at weekends. An over-30s club should have opened upstairs by the time you read this.

In Temple Bar the *Eamonn Doran Imbibing Emporium* (☎ 679 9773), 3A Crown Alley, has food, drink and music every night.

Probably Dublin's flashiest nightclub is *The Pod* (☎ 478 0166), in Harcourt St, but don't even think of showing up there unless you've got the clothes to be seen in, and the cash to match.

Shaft, 22 Ely Place, and *Beatroot*, on the 13th floor at 34 O'Connell St Upper, are currently the 'in' gay clubs. For more details look out for the monthly *Gay Community News* available through the Temple Bar Information Service in Eustace St, or in Condom Power (see Things to Buy below).

Buskers

Dublin is well set up for free entertainment in the form of buskers, but contributions are always gratefully accepted. The best of the city's plentiful supply work busy Grafton St, where they are occasionally hassled by shopkeepers (for blocking access to their concerns) and by the police, but are mainly left to get on with it. At the Trinity College end of Grafton St you'll usually trip over pavement artists, some of them distressingly young, busily chalking their pictures around the statue of Molly Malone. Farther along the

DUBLIN

street you're likely to meet crooning folk singers, raucous rock bands, classical string quartets and oddities like the poet who breaks into verse only when paid cash in advance.

Spectator Sports
In Dublin, the Irish love of horse racing can be observed at Leopardstown in Foxrock and in Phoenix Park. (Horses of less-exalted breeds can be found at the Smithfield horse-trading market behind the Four Courts building in central Dublin on the first Sunday of each month.) Greyhound racing takes place at Harold's Cross Park near Rathmines and Shelbourne Park in Ringsend. For current information on horse and greyhound meetings call ☎ 1550 11 22 18 (24 hours).

The rugby season is from October to March and the soccer season is from August to May; matches take place at Lansdowne Rd near Ballsbridge. Hurling and Gaelic football games are held between February and November at Croke Park north of the Royal Canal in Drumcondra. Call ☎ 1550 11 22 15 (24 hours) for the latest details.

THINGS TO BUY
If it's made in Ireland, you can probably buy it in Dublin. Popular purchases include fine Irish knitwear like the renowned Aran sweaters; jewellery with a Celtic influence, including Claddagh rings with two hands clasping a heart; books on Irish topics; crystal from Waterford, Galway, Tyrone and Tipperary; Irish coats of arms; china from Beleek; Royal Tara chinaware; and linen from Donegal. Citizens of non-EU countries can reclaim the VAT (sales tax) paid on purchases made at stores displaying a Cashback sticker; ask for details.

Dublin's main shopping street is pedestrianised Grafton St with the big department stores: long-established Brown Thomas/Switzers and the brand-new Marks & Spencer. At one end of Grafton St is the striking white-balconied St Stephen's Green Shopping Centre, but more interesting is the Powerscourt Townhouse Shopping Centre, a converted 18th-century building, between William St South and Clarendon St, worth visiting for the architecture even if you can't afford the designer wedding dresses. At the Trinity College end of Grafton St is Nassau St, with the House of Ireland and the Kilkenny Shop, both selling a variety of Irish crafts. This is also where you'll find Knobs & Knockers (☎ 671 0288) if you fancy a Dublin doorknocker to grace your home front door.

Grafton St has most of the big, international-name stores, but Temple Bar is the area to head for if you want to find the one-offs. Claddagh Records (☎ 677 0262) in Cecilia St, for example, sells a wide range of Irish traditional and folk music, while China Blue, Eager Beaver and Flip are just a few of the designer clothes shops. Giving the lie to Dublin's squeaky clean image is Condom Power, a sex shop by another name, in the basement of 57 Dame St.

The Colonnades shop in Trinity College has a range of merchandise linked to 'The Book of Kells', while the Guinness Hop Store can kit you (and your fridge) out in Guinness advertising materials. Also worth trying for small gifts and souvenirs is the Irish Celtic Craftshop (☎ 679 9912) at 10-12 Lord Edward St. For woollens, head for the Dublin Woollen Company (☎ 677 5014) at 41 Ormond Quay, The Sweater Shop (☎ 671 3270) at 9 Wicklow St or Blarney Woollen Mills (☎ 671 0068) at 21-23 Nassau St. For bookshops, see Books & Bookshops earlier.

Of Dublin's markets, probably the most promising for visitors, with a good selection of secondhand books, crafts, pictures, jewellery and records, is Mother Redcaps (☎ 454 0652) in Back Lane, near Christ Church Cathedral. It opens on Friday, Saturday and Sunday from 10 am to 5.30 pm.

GETTING THERE & AWAY
The Union of Students in Ireland Travel office(USIT) (☎ 679 8833) in Dublin is at 19 Aston Quay, right by O'Connell Bridge. It's open from 9 am to 6 pm Monday to Friday (until 8 pm on Thursday) and from 11 am to 4 pm on Saturday.

TONY WHEELER

PAT YALE

TOM SMALLMAN

PAT YALE

PAT YALE

PAT YALE

A	B
C	D
E	F

Dublin

A: Dublin Castle yard entrance
B: Sightseeing bus
C: Georgian houses, Fitzwilliam Square

D: Bloomsday busker
E: James Joyce Centre
F: Bloomsday revellers

TOM SMALLMAN

TONY WHEELER

TONY WHEELER

TONY WHEELER

TONY WHEELER

TOM SMALLMAN

A	B
C	D
E	F

Dublin

A: St Stephen's Green
B: *Sphere with Sphere*
C: The Temple Bar
D: O'Neills Pub

E: Christ Church Cathedral
F: Traditional dancing beside Pearse Museum, Rathfarnham

Air

Dublin is Ireland's major international gateway airport with flights from all over Europe, and from North America. See the Getting There & Away chapter for details on flights and fares.

Airline offices in Dublin include:

Aer Lingus
    42 Grafton St, Dublin 2
    40-41 O'Connell St Upper, Dublin 1
    13 St Stephen's Green (on the corner of Dawson St)
    Jury's Hotel, Ballsbridge
    12 George's St Upper, Dun Laoghaire (☎ 844 7777 for UK enquiries, 844 7747 for elsewhere)
Aeroflot
    15 Dawson St, Dublin 2 (☎ 679 1453)
Air France
    29-30 Dawson St, Dublin 2 (☎ 677 8899)
Alitalia
    Norwich Union House, 60-63 Dawson St, Dublin 2 (☎ 677 5171)
British Airways Express (☎ 1800 62 67 47)
British Midland
    Nutley, Merrion Rd, Dublin 4 (☎ 283 8833)
Delta Airlines
    24 Merrion Square, Dublin 2 (☎ 676 8080)
Iberia Airlines
    54 Dawson St, Dublin 2 (☎ 677 9486)
Lufthansa
    Dublin Airport (☎ 844 5544)
Manx Airlines
    c/o British Midland (phone reservations only) (☎ 260-1588)
Qantas
    Dublin Airport (☎ 874 7747)
Ryanair
    3 Dawson St, Dublin 2 (☎ 677 4422)
Sabena: Belgian World Airlines
    Dublin Airport (☎ 844 5454)
Scandinavian Airlines (SAS)
    Dublin Airport (☎ 844 5440)
TAP Air Portugal
    54 Dawson St, Dublin 2 (☎ 679 8844)
Virgin City Jet
    Dublin Airport (☎ 844 5577/66)
Viva Air
    54 Dawson St, Dublin 2 (☎ 677 9486)

Bus

The Busáras, at Store St just north of the Custom House and the River Liffey, is Bus Éireann's central bus station. Information on buses is available there from the Travel Centre (☎ 836 6111) open Monday to Satur-day from 8.30 am to 7 pm, Sunday and public holidays from 10 am to 7 pm.

Standard one-way fares from Dublin include Cork IR£12 (five daily, 3½ hours), Donegal IR£10 (five daily, 4¼ hours), Galway IR£9 (three daily, 3¾ hours), Rosslare Harbour IR£9 (six daily, three hours), Tralee IR£14 (five daily, six hours) and Waterford IR£7 (seven daily, 2¾ hours). These fares are much cheaper than the regular railway fares; return fares are usually only a little more expensive than one way, and special deals are often available.

Buses to Belfast in Northern Ireland depart from the Busáras four times a day Monday to Saturday (three times on Sunday). Services from the Europa Bus Station in Belfast's Glengall St operate with the same frequency. The trip takes about three hours and costs IR£9.50 one way or IR£12 for a return within one month.

Train

Trains fan out from Dublin. Connolly Station (☎ 836 3333), just north of the Liffey and the city centre, is the station for Belfast, Derry, Sligo and other points to the north. Heuston Station (☎ 836 5421), just south of the Liffey and well west of the centre, is the station for Cork, Galway, Killarney, Limerick, Wexford, Waterford and other points to the west, south and south-west. The Iarnród Éireann Travel Centre is at 35 Abbey St Lower. For information about fares and times call ☎ 836 6222.

The longest trip you can make by train from Dublin is about four hours to Tralee in County Kerry. Fares are high: examples of regular one-way fares from Dublin are Belfast IR£14 (six daily, 2¼ hours), Cork IR£32 (up to eight daily, 3¼ hours), Galway IR£24 (four daily, three hours) or Limerick IR£25 (up to 13 daily, 2¼ hours). As with buses, special fares are often available. A same-day return to Belfast can cost as little as IR£13, a pound less than a one-way ticket! First-class tickets cost about IR£4 to IR£8 over the standard fare for a single journey.

DUBLIN

Ferry

There are two direct services from Holyhead on the north-west tip of Wales – one to Dublin, and the other to Dun Laoghaire, the port on the southern side of Dublin Bay. See the Getting There & Away chapter for details.

Bus & Ferry

There are coaches direct from London and other UK centres to Dublin – see the Getting There & Away chapter for details.

GETTING AROUND
To/From Dublin Airport

Dublin Airport (☎ 704 4222) has a currency-exchange counter in the baggage arrivals area; a branch of the Bank of Ireland on level 2 which keeps regular banking hours and also offers currency exchange; a post office (open Monday to Friday from 9 am to 5 pm); an Aer Rianta (the Irish airport authority) desk with information about the airport's facilities; a Bord Fáilte tourist office that also books accommodation; a CIE desk with information on trains and buses; plus shops, restaurants, bars, a hairdresser, a nursery, a church and car-hire counters. In the car park atrium there's a left-luggage office (☎ 704 4633), open daily from 6 am to 10 pm.

The airport is 10 km north of the centre and can be reached from the city by bus or taxi.

Airport Bus Services The Airlink Express Coach, operated by the Dublin Bus company, runs to/from the Busáras (the central bus station just north of the River Liffey in central Dublin) and less frequently to/from Heuston Station for IR£3 (children IR£1.50). It takes about half an hour. Time-tables are available at the airport or in the city. Monday to Saturday, city to airport services go about every 20 to 30 minutes from 7.30 am to 10.40 pm. On Sunday they operate less frequently from 7.35 am to 12.10 pm. Monday to Saturday airport to city services operate from 6.40 am to 11 pm. On Sunday they run from 7.30 am to 10.55 pm. The demand for seats can sometimes exceed

the capacity of the bus, in which case it's worth getting a group together and sharing a taxi.

The alternative service is on the slower bus Nos 41and 41A, which makes a number of useful stops on the way, terminates on Eden Quay near O'Connell St and costs IR£1.10. The trip can take up to one hour, but they operate longer hours and run more frequently than the express bus.

There are direct buses between the airport and Belfast.

Airport Taxi Services Taxis are subject to all sorts of additional charges for baggage, extra passengers and 'unsocial hours'. However, a taxi usually costs about IR£10 between the airport and the centre, so between four people it's unlikely to be more expensive than the express bus. There's a supplementary charge of 80p from the airport to the city, but this charge does not apply from the city to the airport. Make sure the meter is switched on, as some Dublin airport taxi drivers can be as unscrupulous as their brethren anywhere else in the world.

To/From the Ferry Terminals

Buses go to the Busáras from the Dublin Ferryport terminal (☎ 855 2222), Alexandra Rd, after all ferry arrivals from Holyhead. Buses also run from the Busáras to meet ferry departures. For the 9.45 am ferry departure from Dublin, buses leave the Busáras at 8.45 am. For the 9.45 pm departure, buses depart from the Busáras at 8.15 and 9 pm and from Heuston Station at 8.15 pm.

To travel between Dun Laoghaire's Carlisle Terminal (☎ 880 1905) and Dublin, take bus No 46A to St Stephen's Green, or bus Nos 7, 7A or 8 to Burgh Quay; or take the DART (see the Train section later) to Pearse Station (for south Dublin) or Connolly Station (for north Dublin).

To/From Connolly & Heuston Stations

The No 90 Rail Link Bus runs between the two stations up to six times an hour at peak periods and costs a flat 60p. Connolly Station is a short walk north of the Busáras.

Bus

The Dublin Bus company (Bus Atha Cliath) has an information office (☎ 873 4222) at 59 O'Connell St Upper, directly opposite the tourist office. It's open from 9 am to 5.30 pm Tuesday to Friday; from 8.30 am on Monday. On Saturday it closes at 1 pm.

The city centre is divided into a 13-stage Citizone. Within the Citizone the cheapest fare is 55p and the maximum IR£1.10. Ten-ride tickets offer dicounts of between 50p and IR£1.50. One-day passes cost IR£3.30 for the bus, or IR£4.50 for bus and rail. Other passes include a one-week bus pass for IR£10.40 (students IR£8.50), or a bus and rail pass for IR£14.50 (plus IR£2.50 for a photo). Late-night buses run from the College St, Westmoreland St, D'Olier St triangle until 3 am on Friday and Saturday night and go as far as Howth, Dun Laoghaire and Swords.

The central bus station or Busáras is just north of the river, behind the Custom House and has a left-luggage facility (IR£1.50).

Train

The Dublin Area Rapid Transport (DART) provides quick rail access to the coast as far north as Howth and as far south as Bray. Pearse Station is convenient for central Dublin south of the Liffey and Connolly Station for north of the Liffey. Monday to Saturday there are services every 10 to 20 minutes, sometimes even more frequently, from around 6.30 am to midnight. Services are less frequent on Sunday. It takes about 30 minutes from Dublin to Bray at one extreme or Howth at the other. Dublin to Dun Laoghaire only takes about 15 to 20 minutes. There are also Suburban Rail services north as far as Dundalk, inland to Mullingar and south past Bray to Arklow.

A one-way DART ticket from Dublin costs IR£1.10 to Dun Laoghaire or Howth, IR£1.30 to Bray. Within the DART region, a one-day, unlimited-travel ticket costs IR£3.50 for an adult, IR£1.75 for a child or IR£5 for a family. A ticket combining DART and Dublin Bus services costs IR£4, IR£2 and IR£6 respectively, but this ticket cannot be used during Monday to Friday peak hours (7 to 9.45 am, 4.30 to 6.30 pm). A weekly DART and bus ticket costs IR£14 but requires an ID photo. A Dublin Explorer ticket allows you four days DART and bus travel for IR£10.50 but cannot be used until after 9.45 am Monday to Friday.

Bicycles cannot be taken on DART services, but they can be taken on the less-frequent suburban train services, either in the guards' van or in a special compartment at the opposite end of the train from the engine. There is a IR£2 charge for transporting a bicycle up to 56 km.

There are left-luggage facilities at both Heuston and Connolly railway stations (IR£1, backpacks IR£2 at Connolly).

Taxi

Taxis in Dublin are expensive with an IR£1.80 flagfall and the usual rapid increase thereafter. In addition there are a number of extra charges – 40p for each extra passenger, 40p for each piece of luggage, IR£1.20 for telephone bookings and 40p for unsocial hours, which means 8 pm to 8 am and all day Sunday. Public holidays are even more unsocial and require a higher supplement.

Taxis can be hailed on the street and are found at taxi ranks around the city, including on O'Connell St in north Dublin, College Green in front of Trinity College and St Stephen's Green at the end of Grafton St. There are numerous taxi companies that will dispatch taxis by radio. Try City Cabs (☎ 872 7272) or National Radio Cabs (☎ 677 2222).

Phone the Garda Carriage Office on ☎ 873 2222, ext 395/406 for any complaints about taxis.

Car & Motorbike

As in most big cities, having a car in Dublin is as much a millstone as a convenience, though it can be useful for day trips outside the city limits.

There are parking meters around central Dublin and a selection of open and sheltered car parks. You don't have to go far from the centre to find free roadside parking, especially in north Dublin. However, the police warn visitors that it's safer to park in a supervised car park, since cars are often broken into even in broad daylight close to major tourist attractions. Rental cars and cars with foreign number plates, which may contain valuable personal effects, are a prime target. When booking accommodation you may want to check on parking facilities. Some B&Bs which claim to offer private parking, especially in the centre, may have a sharing arrangement with a nearby hotel to use its car park – provided the car park hasn't been filled by the hotel patrons' cars.

Car Rental See the Getting Around chapter for information on car rental. Argus, Avis, Budget, Eurodollar, Hertz and Murrays Europcar have desks at the airport, but numerous other operators are based close to the airport and will deliver cars for airport collection. Typical weekly high-season rental rates with insurance and unlimited km are IR£245 for a small car (Ford Fiesta), IR£290 for a medium-sized car (Toyota Corolla 1.3) and IR£340 for a larger car (Ford Mondeo). Argus has particularly competitive prices. There are many smaller local operators with lower prices.

Some of the main rental companies in Dublin are:

Argus Rent-a-Car
    59 Terenure Rd East, Dublin 6; also has a desk in the O'Connell St tourist office (☎ 490 4444)
Avis Rent-a-Car
    1 Hanover St East, Dublin 2 (☎ 677 4010)
Budget Rent-a-Car
    Dublin Airport, Dublin 9 (☎ 844 5919)
Dan Dooley Car & Van Rentals
    42-43 Westland Row, Dublin 2 (☎ 677 2723)
Hertz Rent-a-Car
    149 Leeson St Upper, Dublin 2 (☎ 660 4504)
Murrays Europcar Car Rental
    Baggot St Bridge, Dublin 4 (☎ 668 1777)
Payless Car Rental
    Dublin Airport, Dublin 9 (☎ 844 4092)
Practical Car Rental
    St Stephen's Green, Dublin 2 (☎ 671 5540)
Thrifty Rent-a-Car
    14 Duke St, Dublin 2 (☎ 679 9420)
Windsor Car Rentals
    Rialto, Dublin 8 (☎ 454 0800)

Bicycle

Dublin is not a bad place to get around by bicycle, as it is small enough and flat enough to make bike travel a breeze, but the absence of cycle lanes is a source of considerable local grievance. Many visitors explore farther afield by bicycle, a popular activity in Ireland despite the often less-than-encouraging weather.

All the hostels seem to offer secure bicycle parking areas, but if you're going to have a bike stolen anywhere in Ireland, Dublin is where it would happen. Lock your bike up well. Surprisingly, considering how popular bicycles are in Dublin, there's a scarcity of suitable bicycle parking facilities. Grafton St and Temple Bar are virtually devoid of places to lock a bike. Elsewhere, there are signs on many likely stretches of railing announcing that bikes must not be parked there. Nevertheless, there are places where you can park your bike, such as the Grafton St corner of St Stephen's Green.

Bicycle Rental You can either bring your bike with you or rent in Dublin, where typical rental costs are IR£7 to IR£10 a day or IR£30 to IR£35 a week. Some of the hostels offer bike rental.

Rent-a-Bike has eight offices around the country and offers one-way rentals between its outlets for an extra IR£5. The head office of Rent-a-Bike is at the Bike Store (☎ 872 5399/5931), 58 Gardiner St Lower, Dublin 1. It's just round the corner from Isaac's Hostel and a stone's throw from the Busáras. They don't offer daily rentals but you can extend a weekly rental by the day.

Raleigh Rent-a-Bike agencies can be found all over Ireland, north and south of the border. Contact them at Raleigh Ireland (☎ 626 1333), Raleigh House, Kylemore Rd, Dublin 10. Raleigh agencies in Dublin include:

Joe Daly
    Main St Lower, Dundrum, Dublin 14 (☎ 298 1485)
C Harding for Bikes, 30 Bachelor's Walk, Dublin 1 (☎ 873 2455)

T Hollingsworth
14/54 Templeogue Rd, Templeogue, Dublin 6
(☎ 490 5094, 492 0026)
Hollingsworth Bikes
1 Drummartin Rd, Stillorgan, Dublin 14 (☎ 296 0255)
Little Sport
3 Marville Ave, Fairview, Dublin 3 (☎ 833 0044)
McDonald's Cycles
38 Wexford St, Dublin 2 (☎ 475 2586)
McDonald's Cycles
1 Orwell Rd, Rathgar, Dublin 6 (☎ 497 9636)
Shankill Cycle Shack
Barbeque Centre, Old Bray Rd, County Dublin (☎ 282 7577)

Around Dublin

Although the centre of Dublin is set back from the bay, there are a number of seaside suburbs around the curve of Dublin Bay. Dun Laoghaire to the south and Howth to the north are historic ports and popular day trips from the city. Connected to central Dublin by the convenient DART rail service, they also make interesting alternatives to staying right in the city. Malahide with its castle, the imposing Anglo-Irish mansion of Newbridge House, and the village of Swords are other Dublin-area attractions.

DUN LAOGHAIRE

Dun Laoghaire (pronounced 'dun leary'), only 13 km south of central Dublin, is both a busy harbour with ferry connections to Britain and a popular resort. From 1821, when King George IV departed from here after a visit to Ireland, until Irish independence in 1922, the port was known as Kingstown. There are many B&Bs in Dun Laoghaire, they're a bit cheaper than in central Dublin and the fast and frequent DART rail connections make it easy to stay out here.

History

There was a coastal settlement at the site of Dun Laoghaire over 1000 years ago, but it was little more than a small fishing village until 1767, when the first pier was con-structed. Dun Laoghaire grew more rapidly after that time and the Sandycove Martello Tower was erected in the early 19th century, as there was great fear of an invasion from Napoleonic France.

Construction of the harbour was proposed in 1815 to provide a refuge for ships unable to reach the safety of Dublin Harbour in inclement weather. Originally, a single pier was proposed, but engineer John Rennie proposed to build two massive piers enclosing a huge 100-hectare artificial harbour. Work commenced in 1817 and by 1823 the workforce comprised 1000 men. However, despite huge expenditure the harbour was not completed until 1842, Carlisle Pier was not added until 1859 and parts of the West Pier stonework have never been finished. The total cost approached £1 million, an astronomical figure in the mid-19th century.

Shipping services began to/from Liverpool and Holyhead, and the completion of a rail link to Dublin in 1834 made this a state-of-the-art transport centre. The line from Dublin was the first railway anywhere in Ireland. It's only just over 100 km from Dun Laoghaire to Holyhead in Wales and a ferry service has operated across the Irish Sea on this route since the mid-19th century.

The first mail steamers took nearly six hours to make the crossing, but by 1860 the crossing time was reduced to less than four hours and on one occasion in 1887 the paddle steamer the *Ireland* made the crossing in less than three hours. Car ferries were introduced in the early 1960s. During WW I the RMS *Leinster* was torpedoed by a German U-boat 25 km from Dun Laoghaire and over 500 lives were lost.

Orientation & Information

George's St Upper and Lower, which runs parallel to the coast, is the main shopping street through Dun Laoghaire. The huge harbour is sheltered by the encircling arms of the East and West Piers. Sandycove with the James Joyce Museum and the Forty Foot Pool is about a km east of central Dun Laoghaire.

The tourist office (☎ 284 4768) is located

DUBLIN

DUBLIN

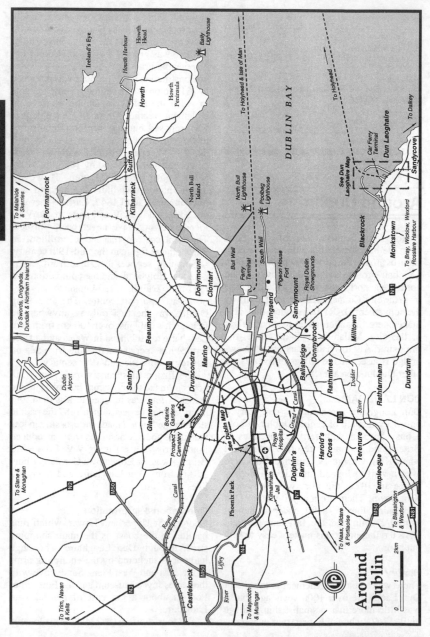

Around Dublin

Bally Lighthouse

Howth Head

Howth Harbour

Ireland's Eye

Howth Peninsula

Howth

Sutton

Kilbarrack

To Holyhead & Isle of Man

To Holyhead

DUBLIN BAY

To Dalkey

Car Ferry Terminal

Dun Laoghaire

Sandycove

See Dun Laoghaire Map

Portmarnock

To Malahide & Skerries

North Bull Island

North Bull Lighthouse

Poolbeg Lighthouse

Blackrock

Monkstown

N11

To Bray, Wicklow, Wexford Rosslare Harbour

Bull Wall

South Wall

Ferry Terminal

Dollymount

Clontarf

Ringsend

Pigeon House Fort

Sandymount

Royal Dublin Showgrounds

To Swords, Drogheda, Dundalk & Northern Ireland

M1

Beaumont

Santry

N1

Marino

Drumcondra

Ballsbridge

Donnybrook

Rathmines

Milltown

N11

Rathfarnham

Dundrum

Dublin Airport

Glasnevin

Botanic Gardens

See Dublin Map

Prospect Cemetery

Royal Hospital

Harold's Cross

Grand Canal

Dodder River

Terenure

Templeogue

M50

N81

N2

To Slane & Monaghan

M50

Royal Canal

Phoenix Park

Kilmainham Jail

Dolphin's Barn

N7

To Naas, Kildare & Portlaoise

To Blessington & Wexford

N4

To Maynooth & Mullingar

N3

To Trim, Navan & Kells

Castleknock

Liffey River

0 1 2km

Around Dublin

in Carlisle Terminal where the ferries arrive and depart. A new ferry terminal and berthing facilies are being built nearby. Pembrey's Bookshop, 78 George's St Lower, almost at the junction with Marine Rd, has a good selection of books. Across the road there's a branch of Eason's, the newsagent and bookshop chain.

The Harbour

The 1290-metre East and 1548-metre West piers, each ending in a lighthouse from the 1850s, have always been popular walking sites (especially the East Pier), bird-watching and fishing (particularly from the end of the West Pier). You can also ride a bicycle out along the piers (bottom level only). In the last century the practice of 'scorching' – riding out along the pier at breakneck speed – became so prevalent that bicycles were banned for some time.

The East Pier has an 1890s bandstand and a memorial to Captain Boyd and the crew of the Dun Laoghaire lifeboat who were drowned in a rescue attempt. Near the end of the pier is the 1852 anemometer, one of the first of these wind-speed measuring devices to be installed anywhere in the world. The East Pier ends at the East Pier Battery with a lighthouse and a gun saluting station, which is useful when visiting VIPs arrive by sea.

The harbour has long been a popular yachting centre and the Royal Irish Yacht Club's building, dating from around 1850, was the first purpose-built yacht club in Ireland. The Royal St George Yacht Club's building dates from 1863 and that of the National Yacht Club from 1876. The world's first one-design sailing boat class started life at Dun Laoghaire with a dinghy design known as the *Water Wag*. A variety of specifically Dublin Bay one-design classes still race here, as do Mirrors and other popular small sailing boats.

Carlisle Pier, opened in 1859, is also known as the Mailboat Pier and was modified to handle drive on/drive off car ferries in 1970. St Michael's Pier, also known as the Car Ferry Pier, was added in 1969. Over on the West Pier side of the harbour are two

anchored lightships which have now been replaced by automatic buoys.

National Maritime Museum

The National Maritime Museum is housed in the Mariner's Church in Adelaide St, built in 1837 'for the benefit of sailors in men-of-war, merchant ships, fishing boats and yachts'. The window in the chancel is a replica of the Five Sisters window at York Minster in England. The museum is open May to September from 2 to 5.30 pm Tuesday to Sunday; entry is IR£1.50/75p.

Exhibits include a French ship's longboat captured at Bantry in 1796 from Wolfe Tone's abortive invasion. The huge clockwork-driven Great Baily Light Optic came from the Baily Lighthouse on Howth Peninsula. It operated from 1902 until 1972, when it was replaced with an electrically powered lens.

There's a model of the *Great Eastern* (1858), the early steam-powered vessel built by English engineer Isambard Kingdom Brunel, which proved a commercial failure as a passenger ship but successfully laid the first transatlantic telegraph cable between Ireland and North America. There are various items from the German submarine U19 which landed Sir Roger Casement in Kerry in 1916 (see the Sandycove section). These were donated 50 years after the event by the U-boat's captain, Raimund Weisbach.

Around the Town

Nothing remains of the *dún* or fort that gave Dun Laoghaire its name, as it was totally destroyed during the construction of the railway line. The railway line from Dun Laoghaire towards Dalkey was built along the route of an earlier line known as the Metals. This line was used to bring stone for the harbour construction from the quarries at Dalkey Hill. By means of a pulley system, the laden trucks trundling down to the harbour pulled the empty ones back up to the quarry.

On the waterfront is a curious monument to King George IV to commemorate his visit in 1821. It consists of an obelisk balanced on

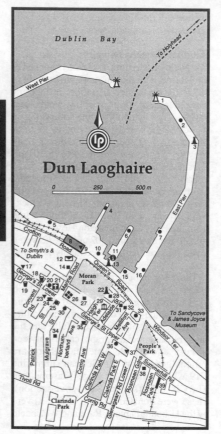

PLACES TO STAY

14 Port View Hotel
27 Royal Marine Hotel
28 Bayside B&B
31 Kingston Hotel
32 Hotel Pierre
34 Innisfree B&B
38 Rosmeen Gardens B&Bs

PLACES TO EAT

9   Restaurant Na Mara
17 Trudi's Bistro
23 Lal Qila
24 Ritz Café (Fish & Chips)
35 The Coffee Bean
37 Outlaws Restaurant

PUBS

18 Cooney's
19 Dunphy's

OTHER

1   Lighthouse
2   Anemometer
3   Lifeboat Memorial
4   Car Ferry/St Michael's Pier
5   Royal Irish Yacht Club
6   Carlisle/Mailboat Pier
7   Bandstand
8   Dun Laoghaire DART Station
10 Royal St George Yacht Club
11 Carlisle Terminal & Tourist Office
12 GPO
13 King George IV Monument
15 National Yacht Club
16 Compass Pointer
20 Pembrey's Bookshop & Ann's Bakery
21 St Michael's Church
22 Christ the King Sculpture
25 Eason's Bookshop
26 Dun Laoghaire Shopping Centre
29 National Maritime Museum
30 Aer Lingus
33 Oceantec Adventures Dive Shop
36 Star Laundry
39 Sandycove & Glasthule DART Station

four stone balls, one of which is missing as a result of an IRA bomb attack. On the other side of the coast road is the *Christ the King* sculpture, which was created in Paris in 1926, bought in 1949 and then put in storage until 1978 because the religious authorities decided they didn't like it.

Sandycove

Only a km south of Dun Laoghaire is Sandycove, with a pretty little beach and the Martello Tower that houses the James Joyce Museum. Sir Roger Casement, who attempted to organise a German-backed Irish

opposition force during WW I, was born here in 1864. He was captured after being landed in County Kerry from a German U-boat and executed by the British as a traitor in 1916.

James Joyce Museum South of Dun Laoghaire in Sandycove is the Martello Tower where the action commences in James

Holiday in Sandycove

In 1904 Oliver St John Gogarty – the 'stately, plump' Buck Mulligan of *Ulysses* – rented the Martello Tower from the army for the princely sum of £8 a year and Joyce stayed there briefly. The stay was actually less than a week, as another guest, Samuel Chenevix Trench (who appears in *Ulysses* as the Englishman, Haines), had a nightmare one night and dealt with it by drawing his revolver and taking a shot at the fireplace. Gogarty took the gun from him, yelled 'Leave him to me' and fired at the saucepans on the shelf above Joyce's bed. Relations between Gogarty and Joyce had been uneasy after Joyce had accused him of snobbery in a poem, so Joyce took this incident as a hint that his presence was not welcome and left the next morning. He was soon to leave Ireland as well, eloping to the Continent with Nora Barnacle in 1904.

Trench's aim did not improve, as just five years later he shot himself, fatally, in the head. ■

Joyce's epic novel *Ulysses*. It now houses a James Joyce Museum with photographs, letters, documents, various editions of Joyce's work and two death masks of Joyce on display. The museum was opened in 1962 by Sylvia Beach, the Paris-based publisher who first dared to put *Ulysses* into print.

A string of Martello towers were built around the coast of Ireland between 1804 and 1815 in case of invasion by Napoleon's forces. The granite tower stands 12 metres high with walls 2.5 metres thick and was copied from a tower at Cape Mortella in Corsica. Originally, the entrance to the tower led straight into what is now the 'upstairs'. Other tower sites included Dalkey Island, Killiney and Bray, all to the south of Dun Laoghaire, and to the north, Howth and Ireland's Eye, the island off Howth.

There are fine views from the tower. To the south-east you can see Dalkey Island with its signal tower and Killiney Hill with its obelisk. Howth Head is visible on the northern side of Dublin Bay. Right next to

the tower is the house of architect Michael Scott, who owned the tower from 1950 until it was turned into a museum. There's another Martello Tower not far to the south near Bullock Harbour.

The tower (☎ 280 9265) is open April to October from 10 am to 1 pm and 2 to 5 pm Monday to Saturday and 2 to 6 pm Sunday. Entry is IR£2/1.10 (students IR£1.60). At other times of the year the tower is only open on weekdays and then only to groups for a flat fee of IR£45. Call Dublin Tourism (☎ 284 4768) for more details.

You can get to the tower by a 30-minute walk along the seafront from Dun Laoghaire Harbour, a 15-minute walk from Sandycove & Glasthule DART Station or a five-minute walk from Sandycove Ave West, which is served by bus No 8.

Forty Foot Pool Just below the Martello Tower is the Forty Foot Pool, an open-air sea water bathing pool that probably took its name from the army regiment, the Fortieth Foot, which was stationed at the tower until it was disbanded in 1904. At the close of the first chapter of *Ulysses*, Buck Mulligan heads off to the Forty Foot Pool for a morning swim. A morning wake-up here is still a Dun Laoghaire tradition, winter or summer. In fact a winter dip is not that much braver than a summer one since the water temperature only varies by about 5°C, winter or summer. Basically, it's always bloody cold.

When it was suggested that in these enlightened times a public stretch of water like this should be open to both sexes, the 'forty foot gentlemen' put up strong opposition. They eventually compromised with the ruling that a 'togs must be worn' sign would now apply after 9 am. Prior to that time nudity prevails and swimmers are still predominantly 'forty foot gentlemen', and the odd brave woman.

Activities

A series of walks in the Dun Laoghaire area make up the signposted Dun Laoghaire Way. The *Heritage Map of Dun Laoghaire* includes a map and notes on the seven separate walks.

Scuba divers head for the waters around Dalkey Island. Oceantec Adventures (☎ 280 1083, fax 284 3885) is a dive shop at 10-11 Marine Terrace in Dun Laoghaire. They rent diving equipment at IR£12.50 for half a day; a local dive costs IR£22.50.

Places to Stay

B&Bs Rosmeen Gardens is packed with B&Bs. To get there, walk south along George's St, the main shopping street; Rosmeen Gardens is the first street after Glenageary Rd Lower, directly opposite People's Park. *Mrs Callanan* (☎ 280 6083) is at No 1, *Rathoe* (☎ 280 8070) is at No 12, *Rosmeen House* (☎ 280 7613) is at No 13, *Mrs McGloughlin* (☎ 280 4333) is at No 27, *Annesgrove* (☎ 280 9801) is at No 28 and *Mrs Dunne* (☎ 280 3360) is at No 30. Prices here are IR£20 to IR£28 for singles, IR£28 to IR£40 for doubles.

There are also some B&Bs on Northumberland Ave, like *Innisfree* (☎ 280 5598) at No 31. Close to the harbour is *Bayside* (☎ 280 4660) at Seafront, 5 Haddington Terrace, which is slightly more expensive with singles for IR£25, doubles from IR£40. Others can be found on Mellifont and Corrig Aves.

Hotels Dun Laoghaire has a number of attractively situated seaside hotels. The port's premier hotel is the A-rated *Royal Marine Hotel* (☎ 280 1911, fax 280 1089) on Marine Rd, only a few minutes' walk from Dun Laoghaire's Carlisle Terminal. There are 104 rooms, all with attached bathroom, costing from IR£65 to IR£160.

Also pleasantly located on Royal Marine Rd is the small *Port View Hotel* (☎ 280 1663, fax 280 0447). About half of the 20 rooms have en suite facilities and these better rooms cost IR£28.50/51 for singles/doubles. The larger *Hotel Pierre* (☎ 280 0291, fax 284 3332), is also close to the waterfront at 3 Victoria Terrace. There are 36 rooms, almost all of them with en-suite facilities at IR£32/70. Close by on Haddington Terrace

is the *Kingston Hotel* (☎ 280 1810, fax 280 1237) with 24 rooms, all with attached bathroom, costing IR£31/48.

Places to Eat

Fast Food & Cafés Branches of *McDonald's, La Pizza* and *Abrakebabra* can all be found on George's St. Just off George's St on Patrick St is the *Ritz Café* for traditional fish & chips.

Ann's Bakery, next to Pembrey's Bookshop, has good tea and snacks during the day. *The Coffee Bean*, on George's St Upper near the corner of Corrig Ave, is popular at lunch times, with good coffee and snacks like baked potatoes and quiches for IR£2 to IR£3.

Restaurants *Outlaws* (☎ 284 2817), 62 George's St Upper, offers steak, burgers (including a vegeburger) and other 'Wild West' fare, and is open in the evenings from 5.30 pm. *Lal Qila* (☎ 280 5623), on Convent Rd just off George's St Lower, has a standard Indian menu; the vegetarian dishes cost IR£4 and the meat ones IR£6.25. Alternatively, there's the *Krishna Indian Restaurant* (☎ 280 1855) on the 1st floor at 47 George's St.

Near the harbour *Restaurant Na Mara* (☎ 280 6787), in what used to be the railway station, offers more expensive food (around IR£20) with the emphasis on seafood. *Trudi's Bistro* (☎ 280 5318), 107 George's St Lower, is another fancier restaurant which offers excellent and slightly adventurous food (like stuffed parsnips). Count on paying around IR£20 to IR£25 per person, including drinks. It's open in the evening from Tuesday to Saturday.

Finally, many Dubliners suggest that a trip beyond Dun Laoghaire to Bray in County Wicklow is worthwhile purely to eat at the *Tree of Idleness* (see the Bray section).

Entertainment

Popular pubs include *Cooney's*, 88 George's St Lower, and *Dunphy's*, right across the road at No 41. Farther out along George's St is *Smyth's*, with its seafaring interior. *Hotel Pierre* is noted for its jazz performances, and the *Purty Kitchen & Bar* on the Old Dunleary Rd often has traditional Irish music or rock.

Getting There & Away
See the introductory Getting There & Away chapter for details of the ferries between Dun Laoghaire and Holyhead in the UK.

Bus Nos 7, 7A, 8, or 46A or the DART rail service will take you from Dublin to Dun Laoghaire. It only takes 15 to 20 minutes to cover the 12 km by DART with a one-way fare of IR£1.10.

DALKEY
South of Sandycove is Dalkey (*Deilginis*), which has the remains of a number of old castles. **Bulloch Castle** overlooking Bullock Harbour was built by St Mary's Abbey in Dublin in the 12th century. On Castle St in Dalkey are two castles – the **Goat Castle** and **Archibold's Castle**. On the same street is the ancient **St Begnet's Church**, dating from the 9th century.

Dalkey Quarry is now a popular site for rock climbers, and originally provided most of the stone for the gigantic piers at Dun Laoghaire Harbour.

Dalkey has several holy wells, including **St Begnet's Holy Well** on Dalkey Island which is reputed to cure rheumatism. The island has an area of nine hectares and lies just a few hundred metres offshore. The waters around the island are popular with local scuba divers. A number of rocky swimming pools are also to be found along the coast at Dalkey.

Dalkey is on the DART suburban line or you can catch bus No 8 from Burgh Quay.

HOWTH
The bulbous Howth Peninsula delineates the northern end of Dublin Bay. Howth (*Binn Éadair*) town is only 15 km from central Dublin and is easily reached by DART train or by simply following the Clontarf Rd out around the north bay shoreline. En route you pass Clontarf, site of the pivotal clash between Celtic and Viking forces at the Battle of Clontarf in 1014. Farther along is North Bull Island, a wildlife sanctuary where

many migratory birds pause in winter. Howth is a popular excursion from Dublin and has developed as a residential suburb.

History
Howth's name (which rhymes with 'both') has Viking origins, and comes from the Danish word *hoved* or head. Howth Harbour dates from 1807-09 and was the main Dublin harbour for the packet boats from England. The Howth Rd was built to ensure rapid transfer of incoming mail and dispatches from the harbour to the city. The replacement of sailing packets with steam packets in 1818 reduced the transit time from Holyhead to seven hours, but Howth's period of importance was short because by 1813 the harbour was already showing signs of silting up. It was superseded by Dun Laoghaire in 1833. Howth's most famous arrival was King George IV, who visited Ireland in 1821 and is chiefly remembered because he staggered off the boat in a highly inebriated state. He did manage to leave his footprint at the point where he stepped ashore on the West Pier.

In 1914 Robert Erskine Childers's yacht, *Asgard*, brought a cargo of 900 rifles in to the port to arm the nationalists. During the Civil War, Childers was court-martialled by his former comrades and executed by firing squad for illegal possession of a revolver. The *Asgard* is now on display at Kilmainham Jail.

Howth Town
Howth is a pretty little town built on steep streets running down to the waterfront. Although the harbour's role as a shipping port has long gone, Howth is now a major fishing centre and yachting harbour.

St Mary's Abbey stands in ruins near the centre and was originally founded in 1042, supposedly by the Viking King Sitric, who also founded the original church on the site of Christ Church Cathedral in Dublin. It was amalgamated with the monastery on Ireland's Eye in 1235. Some parts of the ruins date from that time, but most of it was built in the 15th and 16th centuries. The tomb of Christopher St Lawrence (Lord Howth), in the south-east corner, dates from around 1470. You can walk around the abbey grounds, but to enter the abbey itself you need to obtain the key from the caretaker. There are instructions on the gate explaining where to get the key.

Howth Castle & Demesne

Howth Castle's demesne was acquired by the Norman noble Sir Almeric Tristram in 1177 and has remained in the family ever since, though the unbroken chain of male succession finally came to an end in 1909. The family name was changed to St Lawrence when Sir Almeric won a battle at, so he believed, St Lawrence's behest.

Originally built in 1564, the St Lawrence family's Howth Castle has been much restored and rebuilt over the years, most recently in 1910 by the British architect Sir Edwin Lutyens.

A legend relates that in 1575 Grace O'Malley, the 'Queen' of western Ireland, dropped by the castle on her way back from a visit to England's Queen Elizabeth I. When the family claimed they were busy having dinner and refused her entry, she kidnapped the son and only returned him when Lord Howth promised that in future his doors would always be open at meal times. As a result, so it is claimed, for many years the castle extended an open invitation to hungry passers-by.

Despite Grace O'Malley's actions, the castle is no longer open, but the gardens can be visited in spring and summer and there's a popular golf course beyond the castle.

The castle gardens are noted for their rhododendrons, which bloom in May and June, for their azaleas and for a long stretch of 10-metre-high beech hedges which were planted back in 1710. The castle grounds also have the ruins of 16th-century **Corr Castle** and an ancient dolmen known as **Aideen's Grave**. It is said that Aideen died of a broken heart after her husband was killed at the Battle of Gavra near Tara in 184 AD, but that's probably mere legend as the dolmen is thought to be much older.

The castle is only a short walk from the centre of Howth.

National Transport Museum

The somewhat ramshackle National Transport Museum has a variety of exhibits, including double-decker buses, fire engines and trams including a Hill of Howth tram which operated from 1901 to 1959. It's open on weekends throughout the year from 2 to 6 pm in summer, 2 to 5 pm in winter. Entry is IR£1.50/50p. You can reach the museum by entering the castle gates and turning right just before the castle.

Around the Peninsula

The 171-metre **Summit**, to the south-east of the town, offers views across Dublin Bay to the Wicklow Hills. From the Summit you can walk to the top of the Ben of Howth, which has a cairn said to mark a 2000-year-old Celtic royal grave. The 1814 **Baily Lighthouse** at the south-east corner is on the site of an old stone fort or 'bailey' and can be reached by a dramatic clifftop walk. There was an earlier hilltop beacon here in 1670.

Ireland's Eye

Only a short distance offshore from Howth is Ireland's Eye, a rocky sea-bird sanctuary with the ruins of a 6th-century monastery. There's a **Martello Tower** at the north-west end of the island, where boats from Howth land, while the east end plummets into the sea in a spectacularly sheer rock face. As well as the sea birds wheeling overhead, you can see young birds on the ground during the nesting season. Seals can also be spotted around the island.

Doyle & Sons (☎ 831 4200) take boats out to the island from the East Pier of Howth Harbour during the summer, most frequently on weekend afternoons. The cost is IR£3/1.50 return. Don't wear shorts if you're planning to visit the monastery ruins, as they are surrounded by a thicket of stinging nettles. And do take your garbage away with you – far too many island visitors don't.

Farther north from Ireland's Eye is **Lambay Island**, a more remote and even more important sea-bird sanctuary.

Places to Stay

There are several B&Bs along Thormanby and Nashville Rds with typical overnight costs of IR£15 to IR£16 per person. *Gleanna-Smol* (☎ 832 2936) is on Nashville Rd, while *Hazelwood* (☎ 839 1391) and *Highfield* (☎ 832 3936) are both on Thormanby Rd.

The *St Lawrence Hotel* (☎ 832 2643), on Harbour Rd directly overlooking the harbour, has 11 rooms, all with attached bathroom. Singles/doubles cost IR£27/48 including breakfast. On the Dublin side of Howth village there are good views of Ireland's Eye from the more up-market *Howth Lodge Hotel* (☎ 832 1010) where rooms with attached bathroom cost IR£60 per person. By the golf course in the grounds of Howth Castle is the larger *Deer Park Hotel* (☎ 832 2624), charging IR£60/100 a single/double.

Places to Eat

If you want to buy food and prepare it yourself, Howth has fine seafood and you can buy it, fresh from the trawler, at the string of seafood shops on the West Pier.

Pizza Place (☎ 832 2255), 12 West Pier, has reasonably priced pizzas and pasta dishes from IR£3.25, along with a great selection of Italian ice creams. *Lil's*, on Harbour Rd, has good snacks like a ploughman's sandwich (IR£3) during the day while upstairs *Porto Fino's Ristorante* (☎ 839 3054) serves Italian food in the evenings. Other economical alternatives include Howth's plentiful supply of pubs, like the *Pier House* (☎ 832 4510) on the East Pier. The *Ye Old Abbey Tavern* (☎ 839 0307) by St Mary's Abbey has traditional Irish entertainment in the evenings and is open from 7.30 pm to 12.30 am. The *St Lawrence Hotel* (☎ 832 2643) by the harbour has a carvery restaurant that is open daily.

The King Sitric (☎ 32 5235), near the East Pier, is well known for its fine seafood and is open for lunch and dinner Monday to Saturday. Main dinner courses cost IR£17 to IR£23 or you can have a set dinner menu for IR£25.

Entertainment

Howth's pubs are noted for their jazz performances. You can try *The Cock Tavern* near the entrance to the abbey grounds, the *Baily Court Hotel*, on Thormanby Rd, the *Waterside Inn*, the *Pier House*, both on Harbour Rd, *Ye Old Abbey Tavern*, on Main St, and others – they're all likely to have something on and are all in the centre.

Getting There & Away

The easiest and quickest way to get to Howth from Dublin is by the DART, which will whisk you out there in just over 20 minutes for a fare of IR£1.10.

SWORDS

The village of Swords is 16 km north of Dublin and five km west of Malahide. The Archbishop of Dublin built a fortified palace here in the 12th century, but the castellated walls date from the 15th century and numerous other modifications were made over the centuries. The windows to the right of the main entrance date from around 1250.

Swords also had an ancient monastery, but today only its 23-metre-high round tower remains and that was rebuilt several times between 1400 and 1700. It stands in the grounds of the Church of Ireland. The body of Brian Ború was kept overnight in the monastery after his death in 1014 at the Battle of Clontarf, when his forces defeated the Vikings.

Bus Nos 33 and 33B depart from Dublin's Eden Quay every half-hour or so and take less than an hour to get to Swords.

MALAHIDE

Malahide, on the coast beyond Howth, has virtually been swallowed by Dublin's northward expansion, although it still has its own pretty marina. The well-kept 101 hectares of the Malahide Demesne, which contains Malahide Castle, is the town's principal attraction. The Talbot Botanic Gardens are next to the castle and the extensive Fry Model Railway is in the castle grounds.

DUBLIN

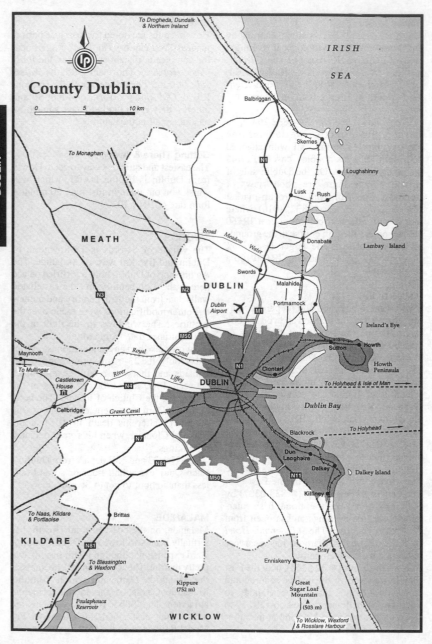

County Dublin

0   5   10 km

To Drogheda, Dundalk & Northern Ireland

IRISH

SEA

Balbriggan

To Monaghan

N1

Skerries

Loughshinny

Lusk   Rush

Broad Meadow Water

Donabate

Lambay Island

MEATH

N3   N2

Swords

DUBLIN

Malahide

Portmarnock

Dublin Airport

M1

Ireland's Eye

M50

Sutton   Howth

Royal   Canal

River   Liffey

N1

Clontarf

Howth
Peninsula

Maynooth

To Mullingar

Castletown
House

N4

DUBLIN

To Holyhead & Isle of Man →

Celbridge

Dublin Bay

Grand Canal

Blackrock

To Holyhead →

N7

Dun
Laoghaire

Dalkey

Dalkey Island

N81

M50

N11

Killiney

KILDARE

N81

*To Naas, Kildare
& Portlaoise*

Brittas

*To Blessington
& Wexford*

Bray

Enniskerry

Kippure
(752 m)

Great
Sugar Loaf
Mountain
(503 m)

Poulaphouca
Reservoir

WICKLOW

*To Wicklow, Wexford
& Rosslare Harbour*

Malahide Castle

Despite the vicissitudes of Irish history, the Talbot family managed to keep Malahide Castle (☎ 846 2184) under their control from 1185 to 1976 apart from a short interlude while Cromwell was around (1649-60). The oldest part of the castle is a three-storey 12th-century tower house; otherwise it's the usual hotchpotch of additions and renovations. The facade is flanked by circular towers which were tacked on in 1765.

The castle is packed with furniture and paintings, and Puck, the family ghost, is still in residence. Highlights include the 16th-century oak room with its decorative carvings and the medieval Great Hall with family portraits, a minstrel's gallery and a gigantic painting of the Battle of the Boyne.

The castle's opening hours vary through the year. All year it's open Monday to Friday from 10 am to 12.45 pm and 2 to 5 pm. November to March it's also open on weekends and holidays from 2 to 5 pm. April to October weekend hours are extended: Saturday, Sunday and holidays from 11.30 am to 6 pm. Entry is IR£2.75/1.40 (students IR£2.15). Combined tickets are available for the castle and railway (see the next section) and for the castle and Newbridge House.

Fry Model Railway

Ireland's biggest model railway layout covers 240 square metres and authentically displays much of Dublin and Ireland's rail and public transport system, including the DART line and Irish Sea ferry services in O-gauge (track width of 32 mm). There's also a separate room exhibiting railway models and other memorabilia.

April to September it's open Monday to Thursday from 10 am to 1 pm and 2 to 6 pm, Saturday 11am to 1pm and 2 to 6 pm, Sunday and holidays 2 to 6 pm. In June, July and August it's also open on Friday from 10 am to 1 pm and 2 to 6 pm. From October to March it's open on weekends and holidays from 2 to 5 pm. Entry is IR£2.35/1.30 (students IR£1.75). You can get combined castle and railway tickets for IR£4.35/2.25 (students IR£3.35).

Getting There & Away

Bus No 42 from Talbot St takes about 45 minutes to get to Malahide. Aternatively, take a Drogheda suburban train to the Malahide town station, only 10 minutes' walk from the park. Malahide is 13 km north of Dublin.

NEWBRIDGE HOUSE

North of Malahide at Donabate is Newbridge House (☎ 843 6534), a historic Georgian mansion with fine plasterwork, a private museum, an impressive kitchen and a large traditional farm with cows, pigs and exotic chickens. In the stables look out for the Lord Chancellor's elaborate coach, built in 1790. It was painted black for Queen Victoria's funeral and it wasn't until 1982 that the paint was scraped off to reveal the glittering masterpiece underneath.

Newbridge House is open April to September from 10 am to 1 pm and 2 to 5 pm Monday to Friday, 11 am to 6 pm Saturday, 2 to 6 pm Sunday and holidays. During November and March it's open only on weekends and holidays from 2 to 5pm. Entry is IR£2.50/1.35 (students IR£2.15). The 144 hectares of Newbridge Demesne surrounding the house are open from 10 am to 5 pm in midwinter and to 9 pm in midsummer.

Getting There & Away

Donabate is 19 km north of Dublin. Bus no 33B runs from Eden Quay to Donabate village. You can also get there on the suburban rail service from Connolly or Pearse stations.

LUSK HERITAGE CENTRE

On the way to Skerries you'll spot the dominating turrets of Lusk church, where a 10th-century round tower stands right beside and joined to a medieval tower. The various floors of the tower are now used to display a selection of medieval and later effigies from churches in the County Dublin area.

The much duller 19th-century nave houses Willie Monks' dusty, somewhat forlorn collection of household and other items. The heritage centre is open mid-June to mid-September only from 2 to 5 pm on

Wednesday and Sunday only. Admission is IR£1/40p. Bus No 33 from Eden Quay takes just under an hour to get there.

SKERRIES

The sleepy seaside resort of Skerries is 30 km north of Dublin. St Patrick is said to have made his arrival in Ireland here at Red Island, now joined to the mainland. There's a good cliff walk south from Skerries to the bay of Loughshinny.

At low tide you can walk to Shenick's, a small island off Skerries. Colt and St Patrick's are two other small islands, the latter with an old church ruin. Farther offshore is Rockabill with a lighthouse. The 7th-century oratory and holy well of St Moibhi and the ruins of Baldongan Castle are all near the town.

Getting There & Away

Bus No 33 departs from Dublin's Eden Quay about every hour and takes just over an hour to reach Skerries. Trains from Connolly Station are less frequent but slightly faster.

County Wicklow

Not all of Ireland's impressive landscapes are in the west of the country. Barely 16 km south of Dublin, you can drive for an hour through wild and desolate scenery, without seeing more than a handful of houses or people. The most beautiful parts of County Wicklow (*Cill Mhantáin*) are within a broad north-south swathe running down the centre of the mountains, beginning at Glencree close to Dublin and ending somewhere around Avoca. At Glendalough are some of the best preserved early Christian remains in the country. The Wicklow Way, which at 132 km is the longest trail in the country, and other trails provide good opportunities for hiking and cycling.

County Wicklow's rolling granite hills are the source of Dublin's River Liffey. Southern Wicklow was one of the last outposts of the Gaelic Irish: using remote valleys like Glenmalure and the Glen of Imaal as hideouts, families like the O'Tooles and the O'Byrnes would grasp any opportunity to harry and attack the English. Such was the crown's concern that they built an access road to the bandits from Dublin through the heart of the mountains. Today, thanks to their efforts, the Military Rd takes you through the finest Wicklow scenery.

In northern Wicklow, the Anglo-Irish gentry felt close enough to the safety of Dublin to build magnificent mansions at Russborough near Blessington and Powerscourt near Enniskerry. Unfortunately the latter was destroyed by fire in 1974, though the exquisite formal gardens are still one of the county's biggest draws and are well worth a visit.

The county's highways and main towns, many of them dormitories for Dublin, lie along the relatively narrow coastal strip south to Wexford. It's a pleasant trip south with seaside resorts and some fine beaches along the way, especially at Brittas Bay, the first of a chain stretching from here to County Waterford.

Highlights

- Fine beaches, especially at Brittas Bay
- Military Rd, which goes through the finest Wicklow scenery
- Russborough House near Blessington, one of the best stately homes in Ireland
- The Wicklow Way, the longest trail in the country
- Glendalough, the site of some of the best preserved early Christian remains
- Powerscourt Estate, near Enniskerry, and its exquisite formal gardens

Wicklow Mountains

From Killakee, a few km north-west of Glencree, you can turn your back on the sprawl of Dublin and travel for 30 km on the Military Rd across vast sweeps of heather-clad moors, bogs and mountains embedded with small corrie lakes.

The Wicklow Mountains are a vast granite intrusion or batholith, a welling up of hot igneous rock which consolidated some 400 million years ago. The heat baked the overlying clays and sedimentary rocks producing shiny mica schists which can be seen across

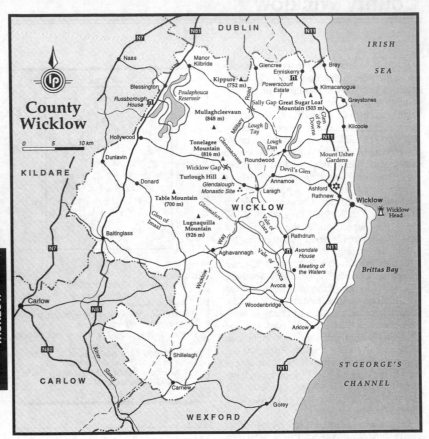

the county, but particularly in the rivers and streams around Glenmalure. The soft metamorphosed rocks have weathered away over the millennia, exposing the granite, but significant traces remain, particularly on top of Lugnaquilla (926 metres), where a cap of schist remains.

The mountains were rounded and shaped during the Ice Ages, producing the smooth profiles you see today. While flattening the peaks, the ice also created deep valleys such as Glenmacnass, Glenmalure and Glendalough. Corrie lakes such as Lough Bray Upper &

Lower were gouged out by ice at the head of glaciers.

Beginning on Dublin's southern fringes, the narrow Military Rd winds down to the remotest parts of Wicklow. The best place to join it is at Glencree via Enniskerry, from which it runs south through the Sally Gap, Glenmacnass, Laragh, Glendalough and on to Glenmalure and Aghavannagh.

The road was built in the first years of the 19th century by the British to get access to the Wicklow rebels, including Michael Dwyer, who were holed up in the southern half of the county, particularly around Glenmalure. Barracks were built at Glencree, Glenmalure and Aghavannagh. The road was a considerable feat of engineering, travelling across open bog and barren mountainscapes for 50 km.

Enniskerry is a good starting point, and on the trip south, there's a diversion east at the Sally Gap to have a look at Lough Tay, Lough Dan and the Luggala Estate. Farther south you pass the great waterfall at Glenmacnass before dropping down into Laragh, with the magnificent valley and monastic ruins of Glendalough nearby. But don't stop there. Continue south over and up the valley of Glenmalure, and if you are fit enough climb Lugnaquilla, Wicklow's highest peak.

There are two principal passes over the mountains from east to west: the Sally Gap at the northern end and the Wicklow Gap farther south, over which you can head west from Glendalough.

The western flanks of the mountains are not as attractive as the centre or the east. The Glen of Imaal, north-west of Aghavannagh, is one of the most remote and scenic spots on the west side.

There are An Óige hostels at Glencree, the Devil's Glen, Blessington, Knockree near Enniskerry, Glendalough, Glenmalure and Aghavannagh.

ENNISKERRY

Enniskerry, south of Dublin on the R117, owes its origin to the adjoining Powerscourt Estate. The landlord built this elegant, picturesque little village to accompany his impressive manor, the entrance to which is just south of the village square. Set round a small triangle, the rows of cottages ooze quiet charm. A number of pleasant little cafés have sprung up and are great places to unwind after a foray into the mountains, for which Enniskerry is an excellent base.

Heading west up the hill takes you through some lovely scenery into Glencree and the hamlet of the same name 10 km up at the head of the valley, which leads to the Military Rd.

Enniskerry is a popular daytrip destination for Dubliners, but the village has so far escaped the blight of modern urban development, though this may change as Dublin expands and the Powerscourt Estate is developed. Don't miss the small detour to Powerscourt Waterfall & Gardens.

Places to Stay

B&Bs *Cherbury* (☎ 01-282 8679) overlooks the valley in Monastery, one km west of Enniskerry, on the Glencree road. Rooms with bathroom cost IR£16 per person. In the village is *Corner House* (☎ 01-286 0149) costing IR£20/30 for singles/doubles.

Hotels The attractive *Enniscree Lodge House* (☎ 01-286 3542) is on the right as you head from Enniskerry up into Glencree, and has wonderful views of the valley. Inside it's cosy with open fires, a snug little bar, and good food. B&B is IR£45/77 a single/double and it's closed from October to January.

The *Powerscourt Arms* (☎ 01-282 8903) is right in Enniskerry village facing the square. It has the potential to be a terrific little country hotel but is currently run-of-the-mill, though reasonably priced. B&B costs IR£19/32 a single/double.

Places to Eat

Enniskerry has several good places to eat. Up the hill past the post office is *Buttercups*, a small deli and bread shop serving delicious takeaway food. *Poppies*, on the square, is a lovely little café-cum-restaurant which is open all day with a selection of pies, quiches, cakes and main courses in the IR£3 to IR£5 range; it also sells home-made bread and jams. Another reasonably priced place similar to Poppies is *Harvest Home*, up the hill past the Glenwood Inn, with meals from IR£4 to IR£5.

For more luxurious surroundings, you have a couple of choices on the road west leading to Glencree. The first is *Curtlestown House Restaurant* (☎ 01-282 5803), an upmarket restaurant in a farmhouse about five km along. It's fairly expensive, with a set menu at IR£18, but the food is delicious.

WICKLOW

It's open for dinner weekdays, lunch only on Sunday and is closed Monday. *Enniscree Lodge House* (☎ 01-286 3542) further up the same road also serves excellent food. A four-course dinner will cost you IR£20.

Getting There & Away

Enniskerry is just three km west of the N11, the main Dublin to Wicklow, Arklow and Wexford road, and you can catch Bus Éireann (☎ 01-836 6111) express buses from the Busáras in Dublin, which will drop you at the turn-off for Enniskerry. Dublin area bus No 44 goes to Enniskerry from Hawkins St in Dublin, or you can take the DART train to Bray and get bus No 85 from the station.

POWERSCOURT ESTATE

This 64-sq-km estate near Enniskerry is a big tourist attraction; its formal gardens have fine views over the surrounding countryside. The main entrance to the house and estate is 500 metres south of the square in Enniskerry. Driving past the entrance, you go around the edge of the estate and eventually towards the famous Powerscourt Waterfall.

The layout of the present estate dates from the 17th and 18th centuries and the 20-hectare formal gardens were laid out in the 19th century, with the magnificent natural backdrop of the Great Sugar Loaf to the east. There are five garden terraces extending for over 500 metres down to Triton Lake. The Italian Gardens took 100 men 12 years to complete.

The wilder parts of the estate were the setting for films such as John Boorman's *Excalibur*, Stanley Kubrick's *Barry Lyndon*, and Laurence Olivier's 1943 *Henry V*.

Powerscourt House (1731) is by Richard Castle, who also designed Dublin's Leinster House and Russborough House in Blessington. Today it is owned by the Slazenger family.

A disastrous fire gutted the interior in 1974 just before the house was due to be opened to the public. There are plans to restore it.

Powerscourt Estate (☎ 01-286 7676) is open March to October, from 9.30 am to 5.30 pm daily, admission is IR£2.80/1.70 (students IR£2) and guided tours are available. There is a teashop and garden centre. A full-length ramble takes just over an hour or there are shorter routes taking in just the highlights.

A longer walk of six km carries you out to a separate part of the estate and a lovely ramble down a track to the **Powerscourt Waterfall**, at 130 metres the highest in Britain or Ireland. It's most impressive after heavy rain. You can also get to the falls by road, following the signs from the estate entrance. The waterfall is open daily all year round from 10.30 am to 7 pm or dusk in winter, and admission is IR£1.50. The road to the waterfall continues along the southern slopes of Glencree and joins up with the Military Rd which goes south to the Sally Gap.

GLENCREE

Just south of the border with Dublin and 10 km west of Enniskerry, is Glencree, a small leafy hamlet set into the side of the valley of the same name. The valley opens east giving a magnificent view down to the Great Sugar Loaf Mountain and the sea.

The valley floor is home to the Glencree Oak Project, an ambitious plan to reforest part of Glencree with native oak vegetation which once covered most of the country, the finest of which grew in the Glencree region. Today Ireland lacks woodlands of deciduous trees and the project is an attempt to restore some of them. It takes 100 years for an oak to mature and the tree is a symbol of strength and endurance. It had special significance in Celtic religion and mythology and the term 'Druid' is derived from 'Daire' (meaning 'oak').

The village has a tiny shop and a hostel, but – remarkably – not one pub. A small grotto to the Virgin Mary, who is said to have appeared here in the 1980s, is set into the hillside. The village is also home to a German cemetery, dedicated to German servicemen who died in Ireland during WW I and WW II, mostly after shipwrecks or plane crashes. The cemetery is a poignant and peaceful place. Just south of the village, the former military barracks are now a sort of retreat house and reconciliation centre for people of different religions in the Republic and the North.

The Military Rd leads on south meeting the Sally Gap, one of the two main east-west routes over the Wicklow Mountains.

Places to Stay

The An Óige *Stone House* hostel (☎ 01-286 4037), right in the middle of the village just up from the German cemetery, has 40 beds costing IR£4 low season and IR£5.50 from June to September. An oak tree was planted at the back of the hostel in 1988 as part of its contribution to raise awareness about Ireland's forests.

The An Óige *Lackan House* hostel (☎ 01-286 4036) is seven km south-west of Enniskerry, in Knockree at the base of Knockree Mountain. It is right by the Wicklow Way in a converted farm. It's open year round, has 42 beds and charges IR£4.50 low season or IR£5.50 from June to September.

These get busy in summer so you should book ahead.

SALLY GAP

The Sally Gap is one of the two main passes across the Wicklow Mountains from east to west. From the turn-off on the lower road between Roundwood and Kilmacanogue just north of Roundwood, the narrow road passes above the dark waters of Lough Tay and Lough Dan and the Luggala Estate. It then heads up to the Sally Gap crossroads where it cuts across the Military Rd and heads north-west for Kilbride and the N11, following the young River Liffey, still only a stream. Just north of the Sally Gap crossroads is Kippure Mountain (752 metres) with its TV transmitter. The surrounding bogs have dark lines cut into them by turfcutters.

LOUGH TAY & LOUGH DAN

Lough Tay lies like a spilt pint of Guinness at the bottom of a spectacular gash in the mountains five km south-east of the Sally Gap crossroads, and about the same distance from Roundwood further off to the south-east. Lough Tay's beauty starred in John Boorman's film *Excalibur*. The lake is part of Luggala, an estate owned by Garech de Brun, a member of the Guinness family and an Irish music enthusiast. At the north end of Lough Tay above a creamy brown beach sits Luggala House, overlooked by some spectacular cliffs on the far side of the valley. These are popular with rock climbers.

Luggala Estate covers almost all of the valley, as far down as Lough Dan, which nestles among lower hills to the south. The road to the Sally Gap skirts the top of the valley on the eastern side and is crossed by the Wicklow Way walking trail, which continues south past Lough Dan.

There are some magnificent walks around the valley. A convenient starting point for any of the walks is just before the road dips over the southern edge of the valley and down towards Roundwood. Here, a small private road heads down into the valley and you are allowed to walk or cycle (but not drive) down. Along the road you pass the private entrance to Luggala House and a small estate cottage with a sign indicating the distance to Lough Dan as '2 Irish Miles'.

The first and easiest option is to walk all the way down to Lough Dan to the south, which from the top of the road is about four km each way. There is a lovely view of the cliffs and Lough Tay from among the trees at the valley floor. If you look carefully along the way, you can make out the traces of the old potato furrows (lazy beds) on the hills, dating from famine times, and there are also ruined cottages. This is part of the Wicklow Way.

Another option is to walk round Lough Tay. As before, follow the private road to the valley floor but then head north-west up the mountain to the cliffs overlooking the lake. This mountain is called Fancy. You can continue north from there, meet the road to the Sally Gap and then return to your starting point.

ROUNDWOOD

Roundwood is widely touted as the highest village in Ireland (238 metres above sea level), though it's hardly Mont Blanc. The village is pleasant, but nondescript: essentially one long main street which leads south to Glendalough and southern Wicklow. In the village there are turn-offs for Ashford to the east and the south shore of Lough Dan to the west. Unfortunately, almost the entire southern shoreline of Lough Dan is private property and you cannot get down to the lake on this side. To the north of the village is the turn-off to Bray.

Roundwood has some nice pubs which are usually packed with tired walkers on weekend afternoons. There are shops, a post office and a thriving country market selling cakes, breads, flowers etc, held every Sunday afternoon March to December from 2 to 5 pm in the small hall on Main St.

North-west of the village you will find some of the best scenery in the county on the road to the Sally Gap, with a tremendous panorama over Lough Tay and the Luggala Estate. From up there you can walk down to Lough Dan through the estate.

Places to Stay & Eat
Roundwood Caravan & Camping Park (☎ 01-281 8163), within walking distance of the village pubs, has good facilities and sites for IR£6. The *Roundwood Inn* (☎ 01-281 8107) is a popular pub and restaurant at the north end of Main St. They do excellent snacks and the restaurant is good but not cheap; Irish stew is IR£5.50. They are open for dinner from 7.30 pm except Monday and for lunch only on Sunday.

Getting There & Away
St Kevin's Bus Service (☎ 01-281 8119) passes through Roundwood on its twice daily run between Dublin and Glendalough (see that section for more details).

GLENMACNASS
The most desolate section of the Military Rd runs between the Sally Gap crossroads and Laragh through wild bogland. Along the way you may catch glimpses of Lough Dan off to the east, and until you reach the top of

Glenmacnass Valley not a single building breaks the sense of isolation.

The highest mountain to the west is Mt Mullaghcleevaun (848 metres), and River Glenmacnass flows south and tumbles over the edge of the mountain plateau into Glenmacnass in a great foaming cascade. The drop marks a boundary between granite and metamorphosed schist.

There is a car park near the top. Be careful when walking on rocks near the Glenmacnass Waterfall, as a number of people have slipped to their deaths. There are fine walks in the area up Mt Mullaghcleevaun or the hills to the east of the waterfall car park.

THE WICKLOW GAP
Between Mt Tonelagee (816 metres) to the north-east and Table Mountain (700 metres) to the south-west, the Wicklow Gap is the second major pass over the mountains. The eastern end of the road begins just to the north of Glendalough (see the following section) and climbs through some lovely scenery north-westward up along the Glendassan Valley. It passes the remains of some old lead and zinc workings before meeting a side road which leads south and up Turlough Hill, the site of Ireland's only pumped storage power station.

A lake was created on the summit and a tunnel was bored down through the hill to the other lake at its base. The water is pumped to the top reservoir at times of low electricity demand and sent down through the turbines in the tunnel at times of high demand. You can walk up the hill to have a look over the top lake and tours of the Turlough Hill Electricity Generating Station (☎ 0404-45113) are available upon request, with one week's notice.

GLENDALOUGH
Glendalough (*Gleann dá Loch*), the 'glen of the two lakes', is a magical place – an ancient monastic settlement tucked beside two dark lakes overshadowed by the sheer walls of a deep valley. It's one of the most picturesque settings in the Wicklow Mountains or for that

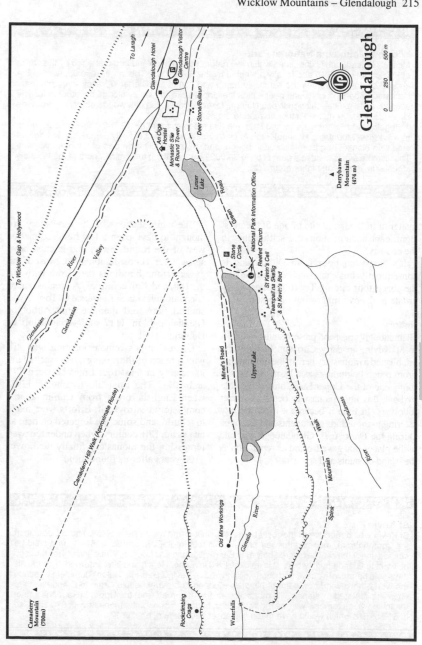

Glendalough

0   250   500 m

To Laragh

Glendalough Hotel

Glendalough Visitor Centre

An Óige Hostel

Monastic Site & Round Tower

Deer Stone/Bullaun

Lower Lake

Green Road

National Park Information Office

Stone Circle

Reefert Church

St Kevin's Cell

Teampall na Skellig & St Kevin's Bed

Derrybawn Mountain (474 m)

To Wicklow Gap & Hollywood

Glendassan River

Valley

Glendassan

Miner's Road

Upper Lake

Camaderry Hill Walk (Approximate Route)

Camaderry Mountain (700m)

Rockclimbing Crags

Old Mine Workings

Waterfalls

Glendalo River

Spink Mountain

Poulanass River

Walk

WICKLOW

Wicklow Mountains National Park

Most of Glendalough is contained within two nature reserves, owned and managed by the Office of Public Works (OPW) and legally protected by the Wildlife Act. The larger reserve, west of the visitors' centre, conserves the extensive heath and bog of the Glenealo Valley – an important habitat for moorland birds and deer – plus the Upper Lake and valley slopes on either side. The second reserve, Glendalough Wood Nature Reserve, conserves oak woods stretching from the Upper Lake as far as the Rathdrum road to the east.

Together with other state-owned land, the two reserves form the 12,700-hectare heart of the new Wicklow Mountains National Park. At Liffey Head, north-east of Sally Gap, 2500 hectares of mountain blanket bog have also been bought and will eventually form part of the national park. The ultimate aim is to have a park of up to 30,000 hectares along the entire length of the Wicklow Mountains, mostly on higher ground. ■

matter in Ireland, and site of one of the most significant ancient monastic settlements in the country.

It's barely an hour from Dublin and is consequently busy and well-established on the coach-tour circuit. Try to get there early or late in the evening or out of season.

History

Glendalough's past and present status is thanks to St Kevin, an early Christian bishop who established a monastery here in the 6th century. From rough beginnings as a hermitage on the south side of the Upper Lake, only accessible by boat, this little monastery began to attract followers. In time it became a monastic city catering to thousands of students and teachers. During the Dark Ages, Glendalough was one of the places that gave Ireland its reputation as the island of saints and scholars.

The main sections of the monastery are thought to have been a few hundred metres west of the round tower, and it must have spread over a considerable area. Most of the present stone buildings date from between the 10th and 12th centuries. A famous son of Glendalough was St Laurence O'Toole, who studied here and then became Abbot of Glendalough in 1117 and Archbishop of Dublin in 1161.

Glendalough's remote location was still within reach of the Vikings, who sacked the monastery at least four times between 775 and 1071. The final blow came in 1398, when English forces from Dublin almost completely destroyed it. Efforts were made to rebuild, and some life lingered on here as late as the 17th century, when under renewed repression the monastery finally died, over 1100 years after its foundation.

St Kevin

St Kevin was a member of the royal house of Leinster and his name is derived from Ceomghan (or Coemhghein), meaning the 'fair one' or 'well featured'. Born around 498 AD, as a child he studied under the charge of three holy men Éanna, Eoghan and Lochan. While under their tutelage he went to Glendalough where, it is said, he lived in a tree. He left and later returned to spend his days as a hermit in the cave that became known as St Kevin's Bed. He couldn't completely escape the world, however; knowledge of his piety widened and many people came to Glendalough to share his isolated existence. His monastic settlement spread from the Upper Lake to the site of the town whose remains we see today. St Kevin became abbot of the monastery in 570 and died in 617 or 618 which would have made him about 120 years of age! ■

Geography

Glendalough Valley was carved out by a series of glaciers, the last one retreating around 12,000 years ago. There was once one long deep lake which was later divided into the two you see today by the delta of the River Poulanass from the southern slopes. The larger Upper Lake is about 35 metres deep and has deep layers of fine silt and ooze on the bottom.

The surrounding mountains are formed mostly of 400-million-year-old granite and schist, the remains of earlier sediments cooked by the welling up granite. The granite has a number of mineral veins in it containing white quartz and ores of lead, silver and zinc. There were extensive mining operations here between 1800 and 1920, with as many as 2000 miners working the mines, some of which were known as Van Diemen's mines because of their remote location (a reference to Van Diemen's Land, the original name for Tasmania, Australia, and one of Britain's former penal colonies).

The remains of the buildings and poisonous grey tailings from the mines are clearly visible at the far end of the Upper Lake and high on the surrounding slopes. Some of the shafts extended north for nearly two km through the mountain into the Glendassan Valley, and you can see the remains there while driving up the Wicklow Gap.

Orientation

It's important to get your bearings in Glendalough as the ruins and sites are spread out all over the valley. Coming from Laragh you first see the visitors' centre, then the Glendalough Hotel which is beside the entrance to the main group of ruins and the round tower. The Lower Lake is a small dark lake just west of the main group of ruins, while farther west up the valley is the much bigger and more impressive Upper Lake which has a large car park with more ruins nearby. Be sure to visit the Upper Lake and take one of the surrounding walks.

Information

At the valley entrance just before the Glendalough Hotel is the Glendalough Visitor Centre (☎ 0404-45325/52), which has a good 20-minute audiovisual presentation on the monasteries in Ireland. It's open daily from 9.30 am to 6 pm year round, and admission is IR£2/1.

At the Upper Lake is an information office (☎ 0404-45425/45338) which has details of activities in the national park. It's open daily from late April to late August from 10 am to 6.30 pm, but if it's closed when you get there it means the staff are out running guided walks. *Exploring the Glendalough Valley* (OPW) is a good booklet on the trails in the area.

The Ruins

The principal remains are of seven churches, a monastic gatehouse (the only one of its kind in existence), a fine round tower, and a monastic graveyard. The bulk of the ruins are east of the Lower Lake by the round tower, and some farther east by the approach road from Laragh.

The more scenic Upper Lake has a smaller group of remains near the car park. The original site of St Kevin's settlement is at the base of the cliffs towering over the south side of the Upper Lake and accessible only by boat; unfortunately, there is no regular boat service to the site.

Upper Lake Sites The earliest sites are thought to be those at **Teampall na Skellig**, where St Kevin first lived as a hermit. It's a small platform at the base of the vertical cliffs on the south side of the Upper Lake. It's directly across the lake from the path that leads down the north shore to the mining village.

The terraced shelf at Teampall na Skellig has the reconstructed ruins of a church and early graveyard. Rough wattle huts once stood on the raised ground nearby. Scattered around are some early graveslabs and simple stone crosses.

Just east of here and 10 metres above the lake waters is a little cave two metres deep called **St Kevin's Bed**, said to be where Kevin lived. There is a local story – more than likely a recent fabrication – about a woman appearing in the cave to tempt old Kevin. The earliest human habitation in the cave was long before St Kevin's era. It may have been the burial chamber of a Bronze Age chief or perhaps even a prehistoric mine, as there is evidence that people lived in the valley for many thousands of years before the monks arrived.

In the green area just south of the car park is a large **stone circle**, thought to be the remains of an early Christian caher or stone fort.

Follow the lakeshore path south-west of the car park and in a quiet leafy clearing you will find the considerable remains of **Reefert Church** above the tiny River Poulanass. This is a small, plain 10th-century Romanesque-style nave-and-chancel church with some reassembled arches and walls. Traditionally, Reefert (which means 'king's burial place') was the burial site of the chiefs of the local O'Toole family, and they probably built the church on the site of an earlier one. The surrounding graveyard has a number of rough stone crosses and slabs, most made of shiny mica schist.

If you follow the lake path to the west, you will find, at the top of a rise overlooking the lake among trees, the scant remains of **St Kevin's Cell**, a small bee-hive hut.

Lower Lake Sites While the Upper Lake has the best scenery, the most fascinating buildings lie in the lower part of the valley east of the Lower Lake.

Just round the bend from the hotel is the stone arch of the monastery **gatehouse**, the only surviving example of a monastic entranceway in the country. There used to be another storey and a containing wall. Just inside the entrance is a large slab with an incised cross.

Inside the entrance is a graveyard which is still used; the gravestones span many centuries. The 10th-century **round tower** is 33 metres tall and 16 metres in circumference at the base. The upper storeys and conical roof were reconstructed in 1876. Near the tower to the south-east is the **Cathedral of St Peter**

The 10th-century round tower is 33 metres tall

& St Paul, the main body or nave of which dates from the 10th century. The chancel and sacristy date from the 12th century. Inside are some good carvings and early gravestones.

At the centre of the graveyard to the south of the round tower is the **Priest's House**. This odd little building dates from 1170 AD and has been heavily reconstructed. It may have been the location of shrines of St Kevin. Later during penal times it became a burial site for local priests – hence the name. The 10th-century **St Mary's Church** is 140 metres south-west of the round tower. It probably stood originally outside the walls of the monastery and belonged to nuns of the valley's convent. It has a lovely western doorway.

A little to the east are the scant remains of **St Kieran's Church**, the smallest of Glendalough's churches, which commemorates St Kieran, the founder of Clonmacnois Monastery in County Offaly.

Glendalough's trademark is **St Kevin's Church** or **Kitchen** at the southern fringes of the enclosure. This little church, with miniature round-tower-like belfry, protruding sacristy and steep stone roof, is a little masterpiece in stone. How it got its name as a kitchen is unknown as there is no indication that it was anything other than a church. The oldest parts of the building and the belfry date from the 11th century and the structure has been remodelled since. But it is still a classic early Irish church. It was used by Catholics up to 1850 and now stores carvings and slabs that are not on public display.

On crossing the river just south of these two churches, at the junction with the green road, is the **Deer Stone** in the middle of a group of rocks. Legend has it that when St Kevin needed some milk for two orphaned babies, a doe stood here waiting to be milked. The stone is what is known as a *bullaun*, and you find them around monastic sites. They were grinding stones for medicines or food. Many are thought to be prehistoric and were widely regarded as having supernatural properties. Women who bathed their faces with the water from the hollow would be beautiful forever. The early churchmen brought them into their monasteries, perhaps hoping to inherit some of the stones' powers.

The road east leads to **St Saviour's Church** with its detailed carvings, and west is a nice woodland trail leading up the valley past the Lower Lake to the Upper Lake.

Glendalough Walks
Numerous fine walks fan out from Glendalough. The first, easiest and most popular option is the gentle but delightful walk along the north shore of the **Upper Lake** to the lead and zinc mine workings which date from 1800. It's about 30 minutes' walk to the mines. The best route is along the lake shore rather than on the road which runs 30 metres in from the shore. You can continue on up the head of the valley if you wish.

Alternatively you can go up **Spink Mountain**, the steep ridge with vertical cliffs running along the south flanks of the Upper Lake. You can go part of the way and turn back, or complete a circuit of the Upper Lake by following the top of the cliff, eventually coming down by the mine workings and back along the north shore. The circuit takes about three hours.

The third option is a hike up **Camaderry**

(700 metres), a mountain hidden behind the hills that flank the northern side of the valley. It starts on the road just 50 metres back towards Glendalough from the entrance to the Upper Lake car park. Head straight up the steep hill to the north and you come out on open mountains with sweeping views in all directions. You can then continue up Camaderry to the north-west or just follow the ridge west looking over the Upper Lake. To the top of Camaderry and back takes about four hours.

If you are intending to go on a serious hike, make sure you take all the usual precautions, have the right equipment and most importantly tell someone where you are going and when you should be back. For Mountain Rescue, ring ☎ 999. For more detailed information on walking in the area, check *Hill Walker's Wicklow* or *New Irish Walk Guides, East & South East* both by David Herman. For walking partners check at the hostels or go on an organised walk with the information office (☎ 0404-45425) or Tiglin Adventure Centre (☎ 0404-40169).

Other Activities
At the west end of the valley beyond the Upper Lake and the mine workings are a couple of large crags, popular with rock climbers. The Mountaineering Council of Ireland publishes a guide to the routes which is available from Joss Lynam (☎ 01-288 4672). Laragh Trekking Centre (☎ 0404-45282), based just outside the village, runs horse trail rides.

Places to Stay
Camping No camping is allowed within the national park. The independent *Old Mill Hostel* (see the following section) will let you pitch a tent for IR£4.50 a night and has the advantage of washing and cooking facilities. The nearest official camping spot is in Roundwood (see that section later).

Hostels There are now a number of hostels in the Glendalough area. The superior An Óige *Glendalough Hostel* (☎ 0404-45143/45342) is about 300 metres west of the round tower. It has good facilities and is open year round. Low season, they charge IR£4.50 a night, and IR£6 a night from June to September. Another An Óige hostel, *Tiglin Hostel* (☎ 0404-40169), in Devil's Glen about 10 km north-east of Laragh via Annamoe, has hostel accommodation at the same rates.

In the village of Laragh, *Wicklow Way Hostel* (☎ 0404-45398), beside Lynham's Bar, charges IR£6 for a dorm bed and is open all year.

The independent *Old Mill Hostel* (☎ 0404-45156) is housed in farm buildings about four km from Glendalough. It's one km south of Laragh on the road to Rathdrum. They charge IR£6.50 a night for a bed in dorms or IR£9 in double rooms. There is a craft centre nearby.

B&Bs Most B&Bs are in or around Laragh, the village three km east of Glendalough, or on the road down into Glendalough itself. *Lilac Cottage* (it has no phone or sign but you can find it by the colour of the house) in Laragh is run by an ex-pat New Zealander and is one of the cheapest; simple but adequate rooms with separate bathroom cost IR£10. *Elizabeth Kenny* (☎ 0404-45236) is next door to the shop-cum-post-office in Laragh. Farther down towards Glendalough opposite Trinity Church, *Valeview* (☎ 0404-45292) has well-kept rooms, a great view of the valley and, as well as the normal cooked breakfast, provides the option of yoghurt and fruit. Both charge IR£14/16 per person without/with bathroom.

Laragh Trekking Centre (☎ 0404-45282) charges IR£27/37 for singles/doubles with bathroom. The house is in Glenmacnass: turn north at the shop-cum-petrol-station in Laragh on the Dublin side of the bridge, and keep going for almost four km. Five km north-east of Glendalough in Annamoe on the main road to Roundwood is *Carmel's* (☎ 0404-45297), which costs IR£25/32 for rooms with bathroom. It's open March to the end of October.

Hotel *Glendalough Hotel* (☎ 0404-45135)

has one of the best locations in the country. The main older block is next to the monastic ruins and the river runs underneath the dining room. A new extension to the hotel is presently being built. B&B is IR£42.50/65.

Country House *Derrybawn House* (☎ 0404-45134) stands in wooded grounds just south of Laragh on the road to Rathdrum. B&B costs IR£32/50 and it's open all year.

Places to Eat
About the best place for anything substantial is the *Wicklow Heather Restaurant* (☎ 0404-45157), beside the post office in Laragh, which does good helpings at reasonable prices. A set lunch will cost IR£6 and it's open for dinner until 9 pm. Nearby, *Lilac Cottage* does teas and snacks during the summer.

During the summer, a little cottage up a lane opposite the Glendalough Hotel does delicious scones, ginger cake and tea or coffee. You can't miss their sign that simply says 'Teas'. The *Glendalough Hotel* (☎ 0404-45135) has a straightforward restaurant where a four-course lunch costs IR£8, and serves food in the bar. It's popular with coach-tour groups.

Getting There & Away
All year round, St Kevin's Bus Service (☎ 01-281 8119) runs to Glendalough from outside the College of Surgeons off St Stephen's Green in Dublin, at 11.30 am and 6 pm daily. The one-way/return fare is IR£5/8.

GLENMALURE
Deep in the mountains, near the southern end of the Military Rd, is Glenmalure, a sombre and majestic blind valley overlooked on its western side by Wicklow's highest peak, Lugnaquilla (926 metres), and flanked farther up by classic scree slopes of loose boulders. After coming over the mountains into Glenmalure you turn north-west at Drumgoff bridge. From there it's about six km up the road beside the Avonbeg River in

Glenmalure to a car park where trails lead off in various directions.

The upper slopes of the hills around Glenmalure have a cap of mica schist, a shiny flat rock which sparkles in the streams. This is the baked remains of the sedimentary rock that used to cover the area before the welling up of hot granite which formed the Wicklow Mountains some 400 million years ago.

For a long time, Glenmalure was a stronghold of resistance against the English. Various clans, particularly the O'Byrnes, made forays up into the Pale, harassing and harrying the crown's forces and loyal subjects. The most famous clan leader was Fiach MacHugh O'Byrne. In Glenmalure in August 1580 he defeated an army of 1000 English soldiers led by the Lord Deputy, Lord Grey de Wilton; over 800 men died in the battle. English control in Ireland was set back for decades. Fiach was captured in 1597 and his head was impaled on the gates of Dublin Castle.

Near Drumgoff is a memorial – Dwyer's or Cullen's Rock, which commemorates both the Glenmalure battle and another rebel who holed up here, Michael Dwyer. Men were hanged from the rock during the 1798 Rising.

Michael Dwyer, a 1798 leader born in the nearby Glen of Imaal, successfully sustained the struggle against the English for five years from this remote outpost before being captured in 1803 and deported to Australia, where he died in 1825. For more details, see the Glen of Imaal section under West Wicklow later in this chapter. There are some ruined barracks from the time of the 1798 Rising at the foot of the valley.

Walks

There are several options. You can walk up Lugnaquilla or head up the blind valley east of the car park, the lovely Fraughan Rock Glen. Or you can go straight up Glenmalure passing the small seasonal An Óige hostel after which the trail divides – heading northeast, the trail takes you over the hills to

Glendalough, while going north-west brings you into the Glen of Imaal.

The head of Glenmalure and parts of the neighbouring Glen of Imaal are off-limits – it's military land, well posted with warning signs. If you hear any loud bangs it's just the army practising in the firing range.

Places to Stay

About one km up from the car park in Glenmalure is the small, 36-bed An Óige *Glenmalure Hostel*. It's open between 1 July and 31 August and on weekends the rest of the year. It has no phone or electricity and dorm beds cost IR£4.50/5.50 in the low/high season. Much bigger is the An Óige *Aghavannagh House* hostel (☎ 0402-36102), 14 km south-west. It's in former barracks built at the time of the 1798 Rising and was once used as a shooting lodge by Charles Stewart Parnell. It charges IR£5/6 in the low/high season. Both hostels make good bases for walking up Lugnaquilla.

WICKLOW WAY

The Wicklow Way was the first trail set up in the country, opening in 1981. It is 132 km long and neither starts nor finishes within County Wicklow itself. See the Activities chapter for details.

West Wicklow

The western slopes of the Wicklow Mountains were less deeply glaciated than the eastern ones, and the landscape isn't as spectacular. From the Sally Gap crossroads to Kilbride, however, you pass the upper reaches of the River Liffey and some lovely wild scenery. It's also a picturesque trip over the Wicklow Gap from Glendalough.

The most interesting features of West Wicklow are the Poulaphouca Reservoir (also known as Blessington Lakes), Russborough House nearby, and farther south the Athgreany Piper's Stones near Donard and the lovely Glen of Imaal.

WICKLOW

BLESSINGTON

Blessington is 35 km south-west of Dublin on the N81and its wide, pleasant main street is lined on both sides by solid 17th and 18th-century town houses. It used to be an important stop on the stage-coach run between Dublin, Carlow, Waterford and Kilkenny, and from 1888 to 1932 a tram ran from here to Terenure in Dublin. It makes a good base from which to explore the surrounding area.

The village is near the shores of Poulaphouca Reservoir, created in 1940 to drive the turbines of the local Electricity Supply Board (ESB) power station to the east of the town and also to supply Dublin with water.

Blessington owes its origins to an archbishop of Dublin, Michael Boyle, who designed the village in the 1670s. Boyle's manor, Downshire House, was destroyed by fire in 1760, but the village soon acquired Russborough House. The village was all but destroyed by rebels in 1798. Connected by the R140, Blessington is only 13 km south-east of Naas, in County Kildare.

Information

There is a seasonal tourist office (☎ 045-65850), in the Blessington Business Centre, open June to August, from 9.30 am to 5 pm Monday to Thursday, to 7 pm on Friday; it closes for lunch between 1 and 2 pm.

Places to Stay & Eat

Hostels The An Óige *Baltyboys Hostel* (☎ 045-67266), on the peninsula opposite Russborough House, is open from March to November and is five km from Blessington. Go along the road south to Poulaphouca then turn east at Burgage Cross heading for Valleymount. In the low season they charge IR£4.50 and in the high season (June to September) IR£5.50. You can go angling for brown trout and perch on the reservoir. Bus No 65 from Dublin passes the hostel.

B&Bs The *Heathers* (☎ 045-64554) is in Poulaphouca, overlooking the reservoir seven km south along the Baltinglass road

from Blessington and only three km from Russborough House. B&B is IR£18.50/30 for singles/doubles. Also in Poulaphouca is the *Conifers* (☎ 045-64298), open all year round and charging IR£20/30.

Hotel The *Downshire House Hotel* (☎ 045-65199), on Main St, has quite a good restaurant and charges IR£30/47 for B&B.

Country Houses The early 19th-century *Manor* (☎ 01-582105) has 18 hectares of gardens with views over the Wicklow Hills. It's about 10 km north-west of Blessington, just south of Manor Kilbride and is open April to October. B&B is a hefty IR£45 per person. Even more pricey is the rambling *Rathsallagh House* (☎ 045-53112), 20 km south of Blessington in Dunlavin. B&B is from IR£170 in the high season, single or double. The excellent dinner will cost you a bit over IR£27 per person.

Getting There & Away

Blessington is regularly serviced daily by Dublin suburban bus No 65 from Eden Quay. The Bus Éireann (☎ 01-836 3111) express bus No 005 going to and from Waterford stops in Blessington two or three times a day; from Dublin it's pick up only, from Waterford it's drop off only.

RUSSBOROUGH HOUSE

Just five km south-west of Blessington is one of the finest houses in Ireland, built for Joseph Leeson later Lord Russborough, whose family were major players in Ireland's 18th-century brewing industry.

Russborough House (☎ 045-65239), a magnificent Palladian villa, was built between 1740 and 1751. It was designed by Richard Castle, at the height of his fame and ability, with the help of another architect, Francis Bindon from County Clare. The front facade is enormous. The granite central building is flanked on each side by two long and elegant wings connected to the main block by curving, pillared colonnades. This 275-metre frontage is further extended by granite walls and Baroque gates, and topped

aeaeaellaeaeaeaeaeaeaeae.,

off with urns and heraldic lions. The interior has many impressive state rooms and remarkable plasterwork by the Francini brothers, Paul and Philip, whose work can also be seen in Celbridge's Castletown House in County Kildare.

Joseph Leeson filled the house with works of art, furniture and other treasures. The house stayed in the family until 1931. In 1952 it was sold again, to Sir Alfred Beit, nephew of another Sir Alfred Beit, co-founder of de Beers. The older Sir Alfred had used his diamond wealth to purchase important works of art. The nephew inherited the lot, and paintings by Velasquez, Vermeer, Goya and Rubens now fit comfortably into their grand surroundings. Lovers of antique silver, furniture and porcelain will have a field day.

The house was closed to the public until 1976, when Sir Alfred set up the Beit Foundation, making the house a centre for the arts. Paintings from the National Gallery of Ireland are sometimes exhibited here. The house is open every day from 10.30 am to 5.30 pm from June to August. In April, May, September and October it is open on Sunday and bank holidays only. Admission is IR£3/1 (students IR£2) for the main 45-minute tour of the house including all the important paintings. An additional 30-minute tour of the bedrooms upstairs containing more silver and furniture costs IR£1.50, children free.

The lake in front of the house is part of Poulaphouca Reservoir.

ATHGREANY PIPER'S STONES

Not far south of Blessington on the minor road to Donard that leaves the N11 just south of Hollywood are the Athgreany Piper's Stones. These make up a prehistoric stone circle of 14 large lumps of granite in verdant surroundings. Another single boulder sits outside the circle. Many stones and stone rings throughout the country are called piper's stones or circles because they are said to be people turned to stone for dancing on or near pagan ground. The circles are said to be the dancers and the odd stone outside is the piper.

GLEN OF IMAAL

Seven km south-east of Donard, the Glen of Imaal is about the only scenery of real consequence on the western flanks of the Wicklow Mountains. And a lovely place it is too, overlooked by Lugnaquilla. The glen is named after Mal, a brother of the 2nd-century king of Ireland Cathal Mór, and is nine km long by six km wide. The north-eastern slopes of the glen are mostly cordoned off by the army for use as a firing range and for manoeuvres. Keep an eye out for red danger signs.

The area's most famous son was Michael Dwyer, who led rebel forces during the 1798 Rising and held out for many years in the hills and glens around here. On the south-east side of the glen at Derrynamuck is a small whitewashed thatched cottage, where Dwyer and three friends were surrounded by 100 English soldiers. One of his companions, Samuel McAllister, ran out the front, drawing fire and meeting his death, while Dwyer escaped into the night. Dwyer was eventually deported to Australia and jailed on Norfolk Island, but he became chief constable of Liverpool near Sydney before he died in 1825. The cottage is now a small folk museum.

Donard is a hamlet in the glen about eight km south-east of Dunlavin. The 40-bed An Óige *Ballinclea Hostel* (☎ 045-404657), four km south-east of Donard on the road to Knockanarrigan and 13 km west of Glenmalure, is open March to November. It charges IR£4.50 low season and IR£5.50 from June to September.

BALTINGLASS

In the far western corner of Wicklow, 27 km south-west of Blessington along the N81, is Baltinglass on the banks of the River Slaney. This small town grew up around the **Abbey of Vallis Salutis**, which was founded in 1148 by Dermot MacMurrough for the Cistercians, as a satellite to Mellifont Monastery in County Louth. It was MacMurrough, as king of Leinster, who 'invited' the Anglo-Normans to Ireland, an offer they gratefully accepted. The rest, as they say, is history. Some locals suggest MacMurrough was laid to rest here in 1171, though he is more than likely buried near his base in Ferns, County Wexford. Records suggest that the parliament of Ireland met for three days in the abbey in 1397.

The abbey ruins lie 350 metres north of the town centre and consist of a long nave with a number of simple Gothic arches and the barest remnants of a cloister. The eastern section of the structure was used as a Protestant church long after the dissolution of the monasteries in 1541. A Gothic-style bell tower was added in 1815.

If the abbey gate is closed you can enter via St Mary's churchyard next door.

A stiff climb to the summit of Baltinglass Hill to the north-east brings you to **Rathcoran**, a large hill fort and a Bronze Age cairn which contains a number of passage graves.

The IHH *Rathcoran House* hostel (☎ 0508-81073), in Baltinglass, has dorm beds for IR£7 and is open from May to mid-September. The town also has several B&Bs.

The Coast

The main N11 road from Dublin to Wexford passes to the west of Bray and runs on south through Wicklow, keeping a few km inland from the sea. South of Kilmacanogue you see the Great Sugar Loaf Mountain (503 metres) to the west and pass through a great glacial rift, the Glen of the Downs, carved out by floodwaters from an Ice Age lake, with its slopes covered in native oak and beech. There is a forest walk up to a ruined teahouse on top of the ridge to the east.

If you are travelling farther south, the coastal route is best, through Greystones, Kilcoole and then some lovely country lanes down to Rathnew before you rejoin the main road again.

Worth seeing in the region of Wicklow Town are the Mount Usher Gardens near Ashford and the fine beaches of Brittas Bay which stretch on south into County Wexford. The inland road from Arklow up into the mountains through Woodenbridge and

Avoca is pleasant, but not as grand as the mountains farther north.

BRAY

Bray is a big, rather grim dormitory town on the coast just 19 km south of Dublin. In Victorian times the arrival of the railway turned it into the 'Brighton' of Ireland, a bustling seaside resort with a long straight promenade, fronted by a beach and backed by hotels and lodging houses, all nicely overshadowed by Bray Head to the south. There even used to be a cable car from the prom up to the summit. The seafront is now home to B&Bs, cheap hotels, fast-food places and amusement arcades, but the heart of Bray is Main St, lined with chain stores, other shops and pubs.

The locals are doing something to improve the look of the town. The impressive red-brick Tudor-style town hall at the top of Main St houses a restaurant, art gallery and museum and heritage centre (☎ 01-286 0987). The promenade, a wonderful construction, is being given a badly needed overhaul.

The seasonal tourist office (☎ 01-286 7128) is in the old courthouse beside the Royal Hotel near the bottom of Main St. The main post office is off the south end of Main St on Quinsboro Rd. The excellent Dubray Books, on Main St, has maps and walking guides to Wicklow and has a branch on Grafton St in Dublin.

Things to See & Do

There is a fine eight-km **cliff walk** around Bray Head to Greystones from the south end of the promenade. From Bray Head there are good views to the south of the Great Sugar Loaf Mountain. Bray Head has many old smuggling caves and rail tunnels including one which is 1.5 km long, the second longest in Ireland, built by the engineer Isambard Kingdom Brunel in 1856. The inland rail route was an easier and more obvious choice, but the local earl didn't want the railway through his land. James Joyce lived in Bray from 1889 to 1891 and, as in Sandycove

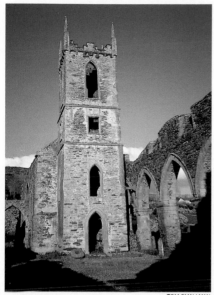

County Wicklow
Top Left: Abbey of Vallis Salutis, Baltinglass
Top Right: North Wicklow
Bottom: Saviour's Church, Glendalough

TOM SMALLMAN

JOHN MURRAY

TOM SMALLMAN

County Wexford

Top Left:	Statue of Commodore John Barry, Wexford Town
Top Right:	The lighthouse, Hook Head
Bottom:	Dual-purpose pub in Wexford Town

near Dun Laoghaire, there is a **Martello Tower**.

The **National Aquarium** (☎ 01-286 4688), on the seafront, contains more than 700 species of fish, including the kissing gourami. Entry is IR£2.50/1.50. **Kilruddery House & Gardens** (☎ 01-286 3405), about three km south of Bray, has been home to the Brabazon family since 1618 and has one of the oldest gardens in Ireland. It's open daily May, June and September from 1 to 5 pm. Entry to the house and gardens is IR£2.50, to the gardens only is IR£1.

Two 18-hole **golf** courses are nearby – Bray Golf Club (☎ 01-286 2484), just north of town, and Woodbrook (☎ 01-282 1838), a championship links.

Places to Eat

The Tree of Idleness (☎ 286 3498, 282 8183), The Strand, is a renowned seafront restaurant with delicious Greek-Cypriot food; mains start from IR£2.50. The *Porter House*, nearby on the seafront, has pub food but its main attraction is the wide variety of beers from around the world.

Things to Buy

The biggest and best local craft shop is Avoca Handweavers (☎ 01-286 7466/3235), a bit south of town in Kilmacanogue on the N11. There's a huge array of hand-made crafts and garments in the showroom, and weavers will answer questions while working away on their looms making tweed. A café serves snacks and lunches. If you're coming from Bray, take the right fork up by the town hall, continue for three km till you come to the N11 then turn left (south) for one km.

They have a shop and mill (☎ 0402-35105) in the village of Avoca in south Wicklow where most of the cloth is woven, but this branch near Bray is more accessible.

Getting There & Away

Bus Dublin suburban bus Nos 45 (from Hawkins St) and 84 (from Eden Quay) run every 45 minutes or so between Dublin and Bray. A good place to catch them in Dublin is outside Trinity College on Nassau St. Both go past Bray's railway station and bus Nos 84 and 84A run on to Greystones and Kilcoole. Bus No 85 runs from the railway station to Enniskerry every 25 to 45 minutes.

St Kevin's Bus Service (☎ 01-281 8119) has two buses from the town hall daily to Dublin at 12.10 pm and 6.40 pm. The return fare is IR£6.

On its Dublin to Rosslare Harbour route Bus Éireann (☎ 01-836 6111) picks up passengers in Bray for destinations south to Rosslare Harbour and drops them off in the reverse direction.

Train Bray's Daly Railway Station (☎ 01-236 3333) is 500 metres east of Main St just before the seafront. There are DART train services into Dublin (Pearse, Tara and Connolly stations) and north to Howth every five minutes at peak times and every 20 or 30 minutes at quiet times.

The station is also on the mainline from Dublin to Wexford and Rosslare Harbour, and there are up to five trains daily in each direction Monday to Saturday, four on Sundays. Some of these stop at Greystones, Wicklow and Arklow.

Getting Around

Taxi If you need a taxi try Bray Cabs 88 (☎ 01-286 1111), 39 Quinsboro Rd, or Bray Taxi Service (☎ 01-282 9826), 5 Main St.

Bicycle E R Harris (☎ 01-286 3357), 87C Greenpark Rd, and Bray Sports Centre (☎ 01-286 3046), 8 Main St, are official Raleigh Rent-a-Bike dealers, with bikes for IR£7/30 a day/week plus deposit.

GREYSTONES TO WICKLOW

Situated eight km south of Bray, the resort of **Greystones** was once a charming fishing village, and the seafront around the little harbour is idyllic, with a broad bay and beach sweeping around north to Bray Head. In summer, the bay is dotted with dinghies and windsurfers. The countryside around the town is now being overrun with housing developments.

Kilcoole, three km south of Greystones,

is noteworthy only as the setting for Ireland's leading TV soap opera, *Glenroe*, broadcast on Sunday night at 8.30.

South of Kilcoole there is a turn-off to Ashford, but if you miss it the road joins the N11 further along at Rathnew where you can take a right (north) turn. In Ashford is the **Mt Usher Gardens** (☎ 0404-40116). This lovely eight-hectare garden is informally laid out around the River Vartry and has rare plants from around the world. Admission is IR£2 (students IR£1.20). There is a seasonal tourist office (☎ 0404-40150) in Ashford during the summer. Bus Éireann (☎ 01-836 6111) buses stop here outside Ashford House on its Dublin to Rosslare Harbour route.

West of Ashford the road leads into the Wicklow Mountains through **Devil's Glen** (beginning three km from Ashford), a deep and lovely wooded glen with a fine walking trail along its length. The **Tiglin Adventure Centre** (☎ 0404-40169), three km further west, runs courses in many different sports including rock climbing and canoeing and organises treks throughout the mountains. The centre also provides hostel accommodation (see Places to Stay under Glendalough earlier).

WICKLOW TOWN & AROUND

Wicklow Town, 27 km south of Bray, is fairly ordinary as county towns go, but does boast a fine big harbour, which hosts the start of the biennial Round Ireland yacht race. The sweep of beach and bay to the north and the bulge of Wicklow Head to the south are the locale's best features.

The name Wicklow comes from 'Vykinglo', a Viking word variously interpreted as lookout, signal point or Viking meadow. The ruined Black Castle on the coast at the south end of town and some narrow streets are about all that remains of Wicklow's Viking and Anglo-Norman past.

The tourist office (☎ 0404-69117/8), in Fitzwilliam Square, is open year round from 9 am to 5.30 pm Monday to Friday; June to August it also opens on Saturday from 9.30 am to 5.30 pm. It closes for lunch between 1 and 2 pm.

Things to See & Do

The few remaining fragments of the **Black Castle** are on the shore at the south end of town, with pleasant views up and down the coast. The castle was built by the Fitzgeralds from Wales in 1169 after they were granted lands in the area by Strongbow. At the time they were under attack from the Wicklow O'Byrne and O'Toole clans. The castle used to be linked to the mainland by a drawbridge, and rumour has it that an escape tunnel ran from the sea cave underneath up into the town. At low tide you can swim or snorkel into the cave.

The walk round to **Wicklow Head** along the cliffs offers great views of the Wicklow Mountains.

Starting just 16 km south of Wicklow is a string of fine **beaches**: Silver Strand, Brittas Bay and Maheramore. With high dunes, safe shallow bathing and white powdery sand, the beaches attract droves of people from Dublin in good weather. Caravan parks lie behind the dunes. Even at busy times there is plenty of room.

Getting There & Away

Up to two Bus Éireann (☎ 01-836 6111) buses a day leave from the Grand Hotel on Main St to Dublin and to Rosslare Harbour. Iarnród Éireann (☎ 1-850 836 6222) trains stop at Wicklow three times daily (four times on Friday) in each direction between Dublin and Rosslare Harbour.

South Wicklow

RATHDRUM

Rathdrum is a quiet country hamlet to the south of Glendalough and the Vale of Clara, the pleasant valley leading north to Laragh. Twisting roads lead down to a stone bridge over the Avonmore River which joins with the Avonbeg River at the Meeting of the Waters farther south in Avoca. There is not much to this peaceful village, just a few old houses and shops – although in the late 19th century it could have claimed to be the unofficial capital of Wicklow, as it had considerable industry and a poorhouse.

In the 18th and 19th centuries, Rathdrum had a healthy flannel industry. In 1861 the railway and the fine aqueduct were built.

The tourist office (☎ 0404-46768) is open Monday to Saturday from 9.30 am to 5.30 pm (closed between 1 and 2 pm).

The Whaley Family

The wealthy Whaley family once resided in Whaley Abbey near Rathdrum. These characters were considered eccentric even by the standards of the 18th-century upper class. Richard Whaley was known as 'Burn Chapel' Whaley for his efforts as a priesthunter. His son was Buck Whaley (1766-1800), a notorious rake and gambler. Once he accepted a wager to walk to Jerusalem and play handball against the Wailing Wall, winning £15,000 in the process. ∎

Avondale House

In 1846 the great Irish politician Charles Stewart Parnell was born in Avondale House (☎ 0404-46111), almost three km south of Rathdrum, just before the Meeting of the Waters. The house dates from 1779 and has a small museum dedicated to Parnell. The rest of the building is home to the Irish Forestry Service, which looks after the estate's 209 hectares of woodland. There is an arboretum and nature walks. The house and forest are open to the public daily year round and admission is IR£2.50/1.50.

Places to Stay

The 33-bed IHH *Old Presbytery* hostel (☎ 0404-46930) in Rathdrum, is open all year. You can camp in the grounds, or sleep in dorm beds for IR£8/10 in the low/high season. It has a laundry and you can rent bikes.

Most of the good B&Bs near Rathdrum are in Corballis, along the road south to Avoca and Arklow. *Beechlawn* (☎ 0404-

46474), 500 metres from Rathdrum on the Avoca road, costs from IR£18.50/27 a single/double. At *The Hawthorns* (☎ 0404-46217), also in Corballis, one km from Rathdrum, B&B is IR£18/26, or IR£20/30 with bathroom. A little farther along the same road is *St Bridget's* (☎ 0404-46477) where B&B is IR£20/30 with separate bathroom.

Getting There & Away

The Bus Éireann (☎ 01-836 6111) Dublin to Wexford and Rosslare Harbour bus stops at Rathdrum twice a day in each direction. Three Iarnród Éireann (☎ 1-850 836 6222) trains stop at Rathdrum daily in each direction between Dublin and Rosslare Harbour.

VALE OF AVOCA

The Avonbeg and Avonmore rivers come together to form the River Avoca at the Meeting of the Waters, a lovely spot made famous by the poem of the same name by Thomas Moore (1779-1852):

There is not in this wide world a valley so sweet
As that vale in whose bosom the bright waters meet;
Oh! the last rays of feeling and life must depart,
Ere the bloom of that valley shall fade from my heart.

The Vale of Avoca meanders through a gentle and darkly wooded valley, charming but not awe-inspiring.

For several hundred years, there were active copper mines in the area which left a section of badly scarred landscape northwest of Avoca village. They also polluted the River Avoca, once famous for its salmon. The last mine closed in 1982.

The village of Avoca (*Abhóca*) has some nice country pubs beside a bridge over the river. Nearby is **Avoca Handweavers** (☎ 0402-35105) selling tweeds and garments of their own making as well as other Irish products. They have a good café open during the day and they run tours of the mill, where you can see people working the looms.

Five km north-east in Cronebane is the **mottie stone** near the Meeting of the Waters. This is described variously as the halfway point between Dublin and Wexford, some sort of Stone Age ritual site, or a hurling stone of the legendary Celtic warrior, Fionn MacCumhaill.

Places to Stay

Camping There are two well-equipped camp sites near the village of Redcross, about seven km north-east of Avoca on the R754 country road. *Johnson's* (☎ 0404-48133) is just north of Redcross and charges IR£5 per tent, while the *River Valley Park* (☎ 0404-41647) is just south of the village and also charges IR£5 per tent.

B&Bs The Georgian *Riverview House* (☎ 0402-35181), in Avoca, is highly recommended. It's open May to October and has singles/doubles with separate bathroom for IR£16/28. The *Arbours* (☎ 0402-35294), in an old farmhouse, has great breakfasts and rooms with separate bathroom for IR£19/28. *Ashdene* (☎ 0402-35327), two km outside Avoca in Knockanree Lower and open April to October, offers B&B for IR£14/28 or IR£19/32 with bathroom. At *Greenhill's* (☎ 0402-35197), also in Knockanree Lower, rates are IR£19/32 with bathroom.

Getting There & Away

The nearest public transport is in Rathdrum or Arklow.

ARKLOW

Besides Bray, Arklow (*An tInbhear Mór*) is probably County Wicklow's busiest town. The name in Irish, *An tInbhear Mór*, means 'great estuary'. It's a thriving commercial shopping centre with some light industry, notably some potteries and a large fertiliser plant north of the town (which has scaled down its operations but still frequently releases some questionable white smoke). You could use Arklow as a base to explore farther into the Wicklow hills, but it is not a particularly attractive place in its own right.

From humble origins as a minor fishing village, Arklow became one of the busiest ports in the country and a well-known boat-building centre. A famous shipyard, Tyrrell

& Sons, continues the tradition and Sir Francis Chichester's *Gypsy Moth IV* (now in Greenwich, London) and the Irish training vessel the *Asgard II* were built here. In 1841 the port had as many as 80 schooners working out of the harbour. It exported ores from the Avoca mines, and during WW I munitions and explosives from a local factory.

During the 1798 Rising, Arklow saw some of the fiercest fighting when some 20,000 of the rebels led by Father Michael Murphy tried to storm the town and were defeated by the better equipped and trained British army. Murphy and 700 men died in the battle, and a monument to them sits near the Catholic church today.

The tourist office (☎ 0402-32484), in a small portable building beside the courthouse, is open Monday to Saturday from 9.30 am to 1 pm, Sunday from 2 to 5 pm.

A small **maritime museum**, on St Mary's Rd, traces the town's sea-going past; it's open daily from 10 am to 5 pm (closed for lunch between 1 and 2 pm) and admission is IR£1.50. There are some reasonable **walks** along the river in town and along the shore north and south of town. Nearby attractions include the Brittas Bay beaches to the north and the Vale of Avoca to the east.

Places to Stay & Eat

There are plenty of B&Bs to choose from especially on the south side of town. You could try *Tara* (☎ 0402-39333), one km from the centre on the Gorey road, which has simple rooms for IR£12/13 per person without/with bathroom. During the summer, the *Riverview Café* down by the river is good for snacks. The best two pubs in town for food and entertainment are *Kitty's* and *Christy's*, both on Main St. Kitty's food (IR£7 for a main course) is excellent and so is the atmosphere. Upstairs, there is music (usually rock) a few times a week. Christy's also has good food, including vegetarian options and a nice and reasonably cheap conservatory restaurant out the back. Lunchtime specials cost IR£3.95.

Getting There & Away

Bus Éireann (☎ 01-836 6111) has regular buses from the Busáras in Dublin to Arklow via Wicklow Town. The bus stop is outside the Chocolate Shop. There are Iarnród Éireann (☎ 1-850 836 6222) trains from Dublin (Connolly or Pearse stations) three times daily Monday to Thursday and Saturday, four times on Friday and twice on Sunday.

Counties Wexford & Waterford

The ferry connection at Rosslare Harbour is what brings a lot of visitors through the counties of Wexford and Waterford, but there are places here to visit and enjoy in their own right. The coastline offers some superb beaches and possibilities for water sports, and the main centres of Wexford Town and Waterford City are lively places well used to visitors. There is a rich historical heritage to this part of Ireland, and the countryside, while it lacks the rugged splendour of the west and south-west, has its own appealing beauty that surprises many visitors.

County Wexford

County Wexford takes up the south-east corner of Ireland and many visitors arrive at Rosslare Harbour on the ferries from Wales and France. Most of them speed through Wexford en route to Dublin, Kilkenny or the west coast, but while Wexford hasn't a huge amount to divert them, there are a few spots worth looking over.

Geographically, the county is almost entirely flat, except near its western borders with Carlow and Kilkenny where the Blackstairs Mountains rise to 796 metres at their highest point, Mt Leinster. There are some pleasant routes through these little-explored hills, particularly west from Enniscorthy and over the Sculleoge Gap. Good flat land and a healthy annual dose of sunshine favour tillage crops like oats and wheat which struggle under damper conditions elsewhere.

Wexford Town itself is pleasant enough, but retains few traces of its Viking past. To its north, a string of fine beaches runs along the coast towards County Wicklow. In the centre, Enniscorthy is an attractive hilly town on the banks of the River Slaney. Farther west, the River Barrow runs right by New Ross, which is a good base to explore the lovely upper reaches of the river.

Highlights
- Walking, cycling or driving along the lovely Hook Peninsula in County Wexford
- Birdwatching on the Saltee Islands
- The historic sights of Waterford city

On the south coast is the fishing village of Kilmore Quay and farther west is the flat and lonely Hook Peninsula, where you will find one of the oldest lighthouses in the world.

WEXFORD TOWN
Wexford (*Loch Garman*) vies with Waterford City for the position of principal settlement in the south-east. It was once a thriving port, but over the centuries the slow-moving River Slaney has deposited so much silt and mud in the estuary as to make the channel almost unusable. Now most commercial sea traffic goes through Waterford and all passenger traffic through Rosslare Harbour, 20 km to the south-east.

A settlement called Menapia appeared on Ptolemy's map of Ireland in the 2nd century AD, where Wexford sits today. The Vikings arrived in the region around 850 AD, attracted by its handy location near the mouth of the River Slaney. The Viking name

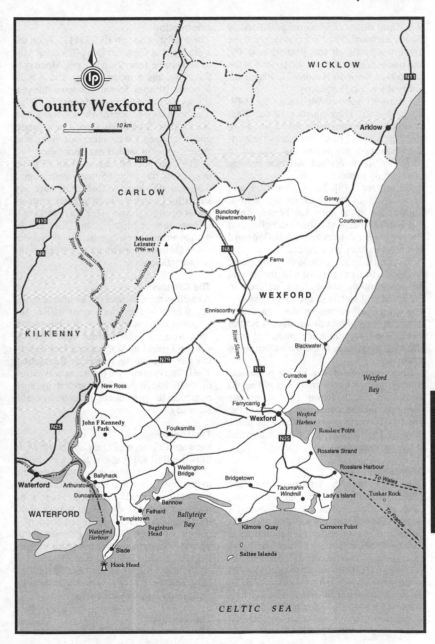

County Wexford

0   5   10 km

WICKLOW

N11

N81

Arklow

CARLOW

N80

Gorey

N10

Bunclody
(Newtownbarry)

Courtown

N9

River Barrow

Mount
Leinster
(796 m)

Blackstairs Mountains

N81

Ferns

WEXFORD

KILKENNY

Enniscorthy

River Slaney

Blackwater

N79

Curracloe

N11

Ferrycarrig

Wexford Bay

New Ross

John F Kennedy
Park

Foulksmills

Wexford

Wexford
Harbour

Rosslare Point

N25

N25

Rosslare Strand

Ballyhack

Wellington
Bridge

Bridgetown

Rosslare Harbour

To Wales

Waterford

Arthurstown

Duncannon

Tacumshin
Windmill

Lady's Island

Tuskar Rock

To France

WATERFORD

Templetown

Fethard

Bannow

Ballyteige
Bay

Kilmore Quay

Carnsore Point

Baginbun
Head

Waterford
Harbour

Slade

Hook Head

Saltee Islands

CELTIC SEA

Waesfjord means 'harbour of mud flats' or 'sandy harbour'. The Normans captured the town just after their first landings in 1169, and traces of their fort can still be seen in the grounds of the Irish National Heritage Park north of town at Ferrycarrig.

Cromwell included Wexford in his 1649-50 Irish tour. Three-quarters of the 2000 inhabitants were put to the sword, including all of the town's Franciscan friars – the standard treatment for towns that refused to surrender. After Wexford, surrender became increasingly popular.

During the 1798 Rising, Wexford was once again in the thick of the action. Enniscorthy to the north saw heavier fighting, but the rebels under their leader Bagenal Harvey made a determined stand in Wexford Town before they were defeated.

Wexford is an attractive town, particularly the approach from the east with the bridge, the quays and the church spires reflected in the broad still waters of the Slaney estuary. The town itself centres on the long waterfront quays and Main St which runs behind them. There are still a few boats but little effort has been made to use the waterfront to advantage.

Little remains of the Viking influence. Among the few traces are pieces of the old town walls near the Rowe St church and the Westgate, and the narrowness of many of the streets. Today, they are packed with pubs, shops and restaurants. The city is renowned for its opera festival.

Orientation

From the bridge at the north end of town, the quays run south-east along the waterfront, first as Commercial Quay, becoming Custom House Quay, through the small kink called the Crescent and on for a short time as Paul Quay before turning inland. The quays are of little interest except as a place for an evening stroll. They are all roughly parallel to the Main Sts which run a block inland. To the north is Selskar St, which runs south as North Main St and then South Main St. Most of the banks, shops and other commercial outlets are along the Main Sts.

Information

The tourist office (☎ 053-23111), is on the waterfront at Crescent Quay. It's open May to September from 9 am to 6 pm, Monday to Saturday, and Sunday in July and August between 10 am and 5 pm. The rest of the year it's open 9 am to 5.15 pm, Monday to Friday. The bookshop called the Book Centre is on North Main St and has French newspapers and magazines. On the other side of the road there's a useful second-hand bookshop.

The main post office is on Anne St and is open every day except Sunday from 9 am to 5.30 pm (Wednesday from 9.30 am). My Beautiful Laundrette is on St Peter's Square and is open six days a week. Disc parking is in operation in the town and discs can be bought in most newsagents. For provisions visit Dunnes supermarket close to the railway station.

The Crescent

As well as the Chamber of Commerce building which houses the tourist office, the Crescent is home to a statue of Commodore John Barry, a local seaman born in 1745, who emigrated to America and founded the US navy during the American Revolution. The US navy presented the statue to Wexford in 1956 and it has been visited by such notables as presidents Eisenhower and Kennedy.

The Bull Ring

Between Commercial Quay and North Main St is the Bull Ring, at one time a centre for bull-baiting and other medieval entertainments but also the site of Cromwell's long-remembered massacre. There's no reminder of that bloody event today and the Bull Ring is merely the intersection of a number of streets. The *Lone Pikeman* statue by Oliver Sheppard commemorates the participants in the 1798 Fenian rebellion.

The town market is right beside the Bull Ring and there is usually a market here on Friday and Saturday mornings.

The Westgate

Some stretches of the town walls remain,

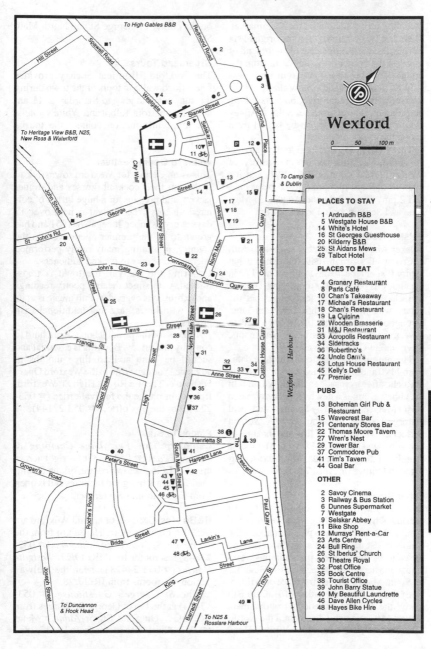

Wexford

0   50   100 m

PLACES TO STAY

1 Ardruadh B&B
5 Westgate House B&B
14 White's Hotel
16 St Georges Guesthouse
20 Kilderry B&B
25 St Aidans Mews
49 Talbot Hotel

PLACES TO EAT

4 Granary Restaurant
8 Paris Café
10 Chan's Takeaway
17 Michael's Restaurant
18 Chan's Restaurant
19 La Cuisine
28 Wooden Brasserie
31 M&J Restaurant
33 Acropolis Restaurant
34 Sidetracks
36 Robertino's
42 Uncle Sam's
43 Lotus House Restaurant
45 Kelly's Deli
47 Premier

PUBS

13 Bohemian Girl Pub &
   Restaurant
15 Wavecrest Bar
21 Centenary Stores Bar
22 Thomas Moore Tavern
27 Wren's Nest
29 Tower Bar
37 Commodore Pub
41 Tim's Tavern
44 Goal Bar

OTHER

2 Savoy Cinema
3 Railway & Bus Station
6 Dunnes Supermarket
7 Westgate
9 Selskar Abbey
11 Bike Shop
12 Murrays' Rent-a-Car
23 Arts Centre
24 Bull Ring
26 St Iberius' Church
30 Theatre Royal
32 Post Office
35 Book Centre
38 Tourist Office
39 John Barry Statue
40 My Beautiful Laundrette
46 Dave Allen Cycles
48 Hayes Bike Hire

WEXFORD & WATERFORD

including a fine section by the Cornmarket. There is only one survivor of the original six town gates: the Westgate, at the north end of town on the corner of Slaney St in from the bridge. The Westgate dates from 1300, was built as a toll gate and is now the focus for Wexford Town's reconstruction of its Viking past. Part of the wall encloses Selskar Abbey just to the south and it can be scaled from inside the abbey grounds.

The Westgate Centre beside the gate has an audiovisual display on the history of Wexford. Admission is IR£1.50/1, and it's open from 9 am to 5 pm (closed between 1 and 2 pm) during July and August. In May, June and September it opens at 11 am.

Selskar Abbey
Selskar Abbey's dilapidated state is a result of Cromwell's visit in 1649. It is claimed that Henry II spent the 40 days of Lent in 1172 in the abbey as penance for murdering Thomas à Becket two years earlier, but in fact the abbey was not built until 20 years later. Strongbow's sister Bascilla is supposed to have married one of his brave lieutenants, Raymond le Gros, in the abbey.

The present red sandstone structure dates from 1190 and was founded by Alexander de la Roche after a crusade to the Holy Land. In the abbey grounds a newly cut gravestone to a Mrs McGee (erected by an interested local historian) states that she was 'A woman perfect in every office of life' and that one of her sons was Thomas D'Arcy McGee 'a founding father of Canada, who was assassinated in Ottowa on April 7th 1868' (sic).

Other Sights
South of the Bull Ring on Main St is **St Iberius' Church** of 1760. Near the corner of King and Barrack Sts is a plaque marking the centre of **St Doologue's Parish**, said by locals to be the smallest parish in the world at just two hectares in size. Near the Goal Bar on South Main St is the birthplace of William Cody Sr, who was the father of Buffalo Bill Cody, the famous American frontiersman. Robert McClure, who discovered the North-West Passage, was born above White's Hotel

on the corner of George St and North Main St.

Organised Tours
The Wexford Historical Society provides free guided walking tours of the town during the summer, Monday to Saturday at 11 am and 2.30 pm from Talbot and White's hotels. For more information contact the tourist office.

Wexford Opera Festival
This is an excuse for Wexford townsfolk to shake out their cocktail dresses and dinner jackets and prepare for a huge influx of cultured visitors. The festival is held over 17 days every October. It began in 1951 and has grown to be the premier opera event in the country, presenting many rarely performed operas and shows to packed audiences.

During the festival, the town is transformed, with street theatre, poetry readings and exhibitions every day. Pub music is at its peak, with blues, jazz and traditional Irish groups.

Tickets for the principal operas are hard to come by and pricey. Booking is essential and should be done at least three months in advance. You can write to the Wexford Opera Festival at Theatre Royal, High St, Wexford, Ireland, or phone the festival office (☎ 053-22240) or the box office (☎ 053-22144).

Places to Stay
Camping The *Ferrybank Camping & Caravan Park* (☎ 053-44378) is right across the river from the town centre, off the Dublin road. The park has good facilities and is open from Easter to mid-September.

B&Bs Most B&Bs in or around Wexford are IR£13 a night or more. Half a km from the centre on St John's Rd, *Kilderry* (☎ 053-23848) has rooms from IR£19/27. *Westgate House* (☎ 053-244281) near the railway station has rooms from IR£17/28.

The *St George's Guesthouse* (☎ 053-43474) at the top of George St charges from IR£18/32. On John St, *St Aidan's Mews* (☎ 053-22691) has rooms from IR£17/28.

Ardruadh (☎ 053-23194) is on Spawell Rd at the north end of town beyond the Westgate and costs from IR£19/33. *McMenamin's Townhouse* (☎ 053-46442) is also in this area at 3 Auburn Terrace, off Redmond Rd, and the IR£22.50/45 rate includes a particularly good breakfast.

Heritage View (☎ 053-45168) is 3.5 km north of town, overlooking the heritage park in Ferrycarrig, and costs from IR£18.50/30.

Hotels *White's Hotel* (☎ 053-22311), on the corner of George St and North Main St, is mostly new but incorporates part of an old coaching inn. It's a friendly and well-run establishment with B&B from IR£45/66 and they do a wide range of food. The *Talbot Hotel* (☎ 053-22566) has a ghastly exterior but the rooms are good. B&B runs from IR£55/82.

The comfortable *Wexford Lodge Hotel* (☎ 053-23611), is just over the bridge on the east bank of the river, and is a little down-market from the others with rooms from IR£35/50. The *Ferrycarrig Hotel* (☎ 053 22999) is beside the Heritage Park on the banks of the River Slaney. This is a top-class modern hotel, charging from IR£49/78.

Country Houses *Clonard House* (☎ 053-47337) is a 1780's farmhouse three km from town off the main Waterford road (N25). B&B is IR£19/32, the rooms have period furniture (three with four-poster beds) and the food is excellent. Dinner is IR£13.

Newbay House (☎ 053-42779) is an 1820's Georgian country house in wooded grounds. More four poster beds but B&B is IR£29 per person. The house is three km north-east in Newbay.

Places to Eat

Cafés & Takeaways *Kelly's Deli* at 80 South Main St do sandwiches and lunches with some vegetarian choices. There are garden seats at the back and a takeaway service. *La Cuisine* is a similar place at 80 North Main St offering lunch specials and home baking. There's also the *Wooden Brasserie* on the corner with Rowe St and the *Chapter Coffee*

Shop under the Book Centre on North Main St is good for a salad lunch and pastries. *Sidetracks* is a small café facing the sea and it's OK for a coffee.

North and South Main Sts have something for most tastes, including fish & chips at the *Premier* at 104 South Main St or fast food at *Uncle Sam's* at 53 South Main St. *Robertino's* at 19 North Main St is a pleasant Italian place with IR£6 lunches and vegetarian choices. Also on North Main St is the *M&J Restaurant*, a modern cafeteria-style place with a large menu and takeaway service but closing around 6 pm, a hour or so later at weekends. Chinese meals are available at *Chan's Takeaway* at 15 Selskar St.

The *Paris Café* at the top of Selskar St does decent coffee and snacks. For a picnic buy some bread here and other items in the supermarket across the road.

Restaurants *Michael's Restaurant* is a good middle-of-the-road place – more of a café really – at 94 North Main St, serving omelettes, steak and fish in the IR£5-10 range. One of the best places in town with a fine selection of local seafood and meat dishes is the *Granary* (☎ 053-23935) at Westgate. The set dinner is IR£16 and for the hour or so after opening at 6 pm there's an 'early bird' set dinner from IR£13. The best place for a lunch around IR£5 is the *Country Kitchen* in White's Hotel, entered on North Main St opposite Chan's Restaurant.

For Chinese food, try the *Lotus House* (☎ 053-24273) at 70 South Main St or, for more upmarket European and Chinese food, it's worth trying *Chan's Restaurant* (☎ 053-22356) at 90 North Main St. The *Acropolis* (☎ 053-22355) is one of the very few Greek restaurants outside of Dublin and it's at 6 Anne St. A two-course meal is about IR£12 in the evening, it's open until midnight and French and German are spoken.

Entertainment

Pubs Even for Ireland Wexford has a lot of pubs, many of them strung along North and South Main Sts where you'll find *Tim's Tavern*, the *Commodore* and the *Bohemian*

WEXFORD & WATERFORD

Girl. The *Goal Bar*, on South Main St, has a beer garden and regular music sessions.

On Cornmarket, towards the abbey ruins, is the atmospheric old *Thomas Moore Tavern*. Music often features at the *Wren's Nest* and the *Tower Bar* on the quay. For the 20s to 30s age group the pub to go to is the *Centenary Stores*, on Charlotte St just off North Main St. It has Irish music on Wednesday night. The *Wavecrest Bar* on Commercial Quay has Irish music almost every night during the summer.

Theatres & Cinema Wexford has a number of theatres and there is almost always a show on somewhere. The *Theatre Royal* (☎ 053-22144) is in High St and the *Wexford Arts Centre* (☎ 053-23764) is in the Cornmarket and caters for exhibitions, displays, theatre, dance and music performances.

The *Savoy* three-screen cineplex is near the railway station.

Getting There & Away
Continue south from the quays for Rosslare and Rosslare Harbour. For Duncannon or Hook Head, turn west either at the Crescent along Harpers Lane or from Paul Quay along King St.

Note the short cut between counties Wexford and Waterford by taking the Ballyhack to Passage East ferry and avoiding the longer route via New Ross. Cyclists in particular will find this easier.

Bus The Wexford office of Bus Éireann (☎ 053-22522) is at the railway station on Redmond Place at the north end of the quays past the main bridge over the river. It's open from 8.30 am to 6 pm. There are buses to Rosslare Harbour (seven daily, 20 minutes, IR£2.50) and also services to Dublin (five daily, 2½ hours IR£7), Killarney (two daily, 5½ hours, IR£15) and other locations.

The Ardcavan Coach Company (☎ 053-22561) operates between Dublin and Rosslare Harbour daily. Their Wexford stop is at Crescent Quay by the tourist office.

Bus Éireann also have limited local services to Gorey via Courtown, Carne and Kilmore Quay. During July and August, they run tours of the surrounding areas.

Train O'Hanrahan Railway Station (☎ 053-22522) is on the north end of town in Redmond Place near the waterfront. Wexford is on the Dublin to Rosslare Harbour line and is serviced by three trains daily in each direction, two on Sunday (2½ hours, IR£10). The train offers a lovely view of the town as it passes along the quays. There are also three trains daily (only two on Sunday) to Rosslare Harbour (25 minutes, IR£3.50).

Getting Around
The Bike Shop (☎ 053-22514) at 9 Selskar St and Hayes (☎ 053-22462) at 108 South Main St both have bikes for IR£7 a day or IR£30 a week. Dave Allen Cycles, next to Kelly's Deli and also at the bottom of South Main St, also hires out bikes. Murrays Rent-a-Car (☎ 053-22122) has an office on Redmond Place up towards the railway station.

AROUND WEXFORD TOWN
Irish National Heritage Park
Four km north of Wexford, beside the Dublin to Rosslare N11 road at Ferrycarrig, is the Irish National Heritage Park (☎ 053-41733). This is an outdoor theme park, which attempts to condense and package a country's entire history in one place. It's moderately interesting and the tour, included in the entry price, is an informative one.

From the entrance you visit recreations of dwelling places, graves and fortifications used in Ireland over many thousands of years. There is a Mesolithic camp site, a Neolithic farmstead, a dolmen, a cyst burial tomb, a stone circle, a rath or ring fort, a monastery, a *crannóg* or lake settlement, a Viking shipyard, a motte-and-bailey, a Norman castle and a couple of other smaller displays. A replica of a Viking longship sits at anchor in the River Slaney just out from the park.

The park has some drawbacks: a major road and a railway line run through it; the

Norman castle is concrete painted white; and there would be a lovely view of the River Slaney and Ferrycarrig Tower but for a large green wire fence in the way.

Entry is IR£3/2, opening hours are 9 am to 7 pm from March to October with last admissions at 5 pm. A bus goes to the park from Wexford Town; ask in the tourist office about times.

Johnstown Castle & Gardens
The former home of the Fitzgerald and Esmonde families is a splendid 19th-century Gothic-style castellated house overlooking a small lake and surrounded by 20 hectares of well-kept, thickly wooded gardens. The castle and its outbuildings now hold an agricultural research centre, the headquarters of the Irish Environmental Protection Agency and an agricultural museum.

The castle interior is off limits, but the grounds and the museum (☎ 053-42888) are open to the public. There is an admission charge of IR£1.75 and the gardens are open every day from 9 am to 5 pm, while the museum is open 9 am to 5 pm Monday to Friday, 2 to 5 pm on weekends. Times vary in winter. The castle is seven km south-west of Wexford on the way to Murntown.

Wexford Wildfowl Reserve
Four to five km north-east of Wexford Town are the North Slobs, a swathe of low-lying land reclaimed from the sea, which is still held back by a long retaining wall. The Slobs are home to half the world's population of Greenland white-fronted geese in winter, some 10,000 birds. It's a great sight on winter evenings to go out to the sea wall and watch the V-shaped formations of geese flying overhead out into the darkness of the bay, where they pass the night on sandbanks and islands.

Wintertime is also good for brent geese from Arctic Canada, and throughout the year you will see mallard, pochard, godwits, mute and bewick swans, redshank, terns, coot, oystercatchers and many more species.

The Wexford Wildfowl Reserve (☎ 053-23129) was set up here to protect the many different species and provide them with feeding grounds. It has shelters, a meeting room and an observation tower.

To get to the Slobs and the nature reserve go out of Wexford on the Dublin road, over the bridge and north for 3.5 km until you see a signpost for the reserve pointing to the right.

The Raven
This nature reserve near Curracloe is a lovely spot. A long walk through forest brings you out on dunes where you may see Greenland white-fronted geese and various waders. To get there take the Dublin road out of town, follow the signposts for Curracloe Beach and watch out for signs for the Raven off to the right.

Curracloe Beach
Curracloe is one of a string of magnificent beaches that line the coast north of Wexford Town and into Wicklow. The beach is over 11 km long. Extensive dunes behind the beach provide some shelter, and you can pitch a tent here if you are discreet. Curracloe Beach is 15 km north-east of Wexford off the Dublin road. There is a camp site nearby.

ROSSLARE STRAND
Rosslare Strand is about eight km north of Rosslare Harbour and 15 km south of Wexford Town. The long golden beaches attract huge crowds in summer and there are also good walks north to Rosslare Point. The long shallow bay is ideal for windsurfing, and boards, wetsuits and tuition are available from Kieran Lambert at the Rosslare Windsurfing Centre (☎ 053-32581).

Places to Stay
Camping The *Burrow Camping & Caravan Park* (☎ 053-32190) is just south of the village and has excellent facilities including laundry, sail boards, tennis courts and money exchange. The cost for all this is a hefty IR£12 per night regardless of tent size or number of people. The nearby *Rosslare Holiday Park* (☎ 053-32291) has the basic facilities and charges IR£8.

B&Bs *Decca House* (☎ 053-32410) is one km from Rosslare Strand, costing from IR£18.50/27. *Grahmorack* (☎ 053-32295) is 3.5 km inland. Go to Tagoat on the main road to the harbour and turn south; the house is signposted and is one km down the road. There are four rooms costing IR£15 per person.

Hotels *Kelly's Resort Hotel* (☎ 053-32114) has every sports and leisure facility in the book and is popular with families. B&B is from IR£50/80. Cheaper places include the *Burrow Park Hotel* (☎ 053-32190) near the centre of the village; it charges from IR£25/46.

Getting There & Away
The trains on the main line between Dublin, Wexford and Rosslare Harbour stop at Rosslare Strand. Bus services are limited. A single daily bus from Wexford at 6 pm to Rosslare Harbour stops at Rosslare Strand.

ROSSLARE HARBOUR
At the south-eastern tip of the country, Rosslare Harbour is 20 km south-east of Wexford Town and has busy ferry connections to Wales and France. The harbour surrounds are not particularly pretty, but there are plenty of places to stay if you have to wait for your boat.

Information
There are two tourist offices. The one in the ferry terminal building (☎ 053-33622) is open year round while the one by the main Wexford road in Kilrane (☎ 053-32232) north of town is open April to September.

Places to Stay
Camping No official camp sites are found in Rosslare Harbour itself, but you could camp on the beach or in a field nearby or stay eight km north in Rosslare Strand (see the previous section).

Hostel The An Óige *Rosslare Harbour Hostel* (☎ 053-33399) is just up the hill from the ferry terminal on Goulding St. The hostel opens early or late for ferry arrivals and departures and will also accept advance credit-card bookings. The nearest independent hostel is near New Ross (see that section later).

B&Bs One of the cheapest places around is *Glenville* (☎ 053-33142) on St Patrick's Rd near the harbour, at IR£14/28. *Laurel Lodge* (☎ 053-33291), IR£18/30, is a km from the ferries. In town, overlooking the harbour, the big *Ailsa Lodge* (☎ 053-33230) has fine-tuned its rates to match demand; from IR£18/28 in August.

Quite a number of the local B&Bs are in Kilrane, a km inland on the Wexford road. *Kilrane House* (☎ 053-33135) is a 19th-century house with open fires and rooms from IR£20/30. *Blantyre* (☎ 053-33536) is 200 metres off the Wexford road and has rooms at IR£18.50/27, with shared bathroom.

Hotels Rosslare Harbour has plenty of modern hotels. The *Hotel Rosslare* (☎ 053-33110) sits on top of the cliff overlooking the ferry port and has plenty of facilities and excellent bar food. B&B costs from IR£21/46. The *Tuskar House Hotel* (☎ 053-33363) is barely 250 metres from the ferry terminal and costs from IR£32/52.

Places to Eat
Rosslare Harbour's hotel bars and restaurants are fine for the short time you are likely to be there. At *Hotel Rosslare* (☎ 053-33110) an excellent lunch costs from IR£7 to IR£12 and they usually have some vegetarian choices. The attractive *Portholes Bar* in Hotel Rosslare offers good bar food, specialising in seafood, with main courses from around IR£5.

Getting There & Away
Ferry Two ferry companies operate to and from Rosslare Harbour and there is a convenient train and bus station by the ferry terminal.

Stena Sealink (☎ 053-33115) has a day and a night connection to Fishguard in Wales from where there are rail connections to London. Irish Ferries (☎ 053-33158) has two daily sailings to Pembroke in Wales (where there are also rail connections to London) with a journey time of around 4½ hours. To France depending on the season, it has one or two sailings a week to Cherbourg, two or three to Le Havre and one or two to Roscoff. Sailing times are around 24 hours.

Bus There are Bus Éireann buses to Wexford (seven daily, 20 minutes IR£2.50) and Dublin, and a single daily service to Galway via Kilkenny in July and August.

The Ardcavan Coach Company (☎ 053-22561) operates between Rosslare Harbour and Dublin daily; it also goes to Wexford, Enniscorthy, Ferns, Gorey and Arklow.

Train Trains (☎ 053-33114) operate from the ferry terminal and there are services to Dublin via Wexford (three daily, two on Sunday, three hours IR£10) and Waterford (two daily, 1¼ hours, IR£9).

Car Rental Budget (☎ 053-33318), Hertz (☎ 053-33238) and Murrays (☎ 053-32181) have car hire desks in the terminal.

SOUTH OF ROSSLARE HARBOUR
Nine km south of Rosslare Harbour is **Carnsore Point**, where Ireland's first nuclear power station was to be built. Fortunately, vociferous opposition – and the cost – killed the project. Carnsore Point was noted as the country's south-easternmost point in the map drawn by Ptolemy in the 2nd century AD. Offshore to the east is Tuskar Rock Lighthouse.

Carne has a fine beach, and the *Carne Beach Caravan & Camping Park* (☎ 053-31131) is near the point. You could also camp along the beach somewhere. There is excellent pub food and seafood in the *Lobster Pot* (☎ 053-31110) bar and restaurant in Carne.

Turning west brings you to **Tacumshin**, where in 1840 Nicholas Moran built the Tacumshin Windmill, one of Ireland's few thatched windmills. The key can be picked up from the little shop where you park; there

may be a charge. Just to the east is **Lady's Island**, the site of an early Augustinian priory and still a centre of devotion. Both Tacumshin and Lady's Island have small brackish lakes which are home to many migrating and breeding **birds** through the year. Lady's Island is best from autumn to spring, and you may see brent geese, shell duck, redshank, godwits, mute swan, teal and various terns.

Bridgetown is 12 km south-west of Wexford Town on the way to lovely Kilmore Quay. This was the first area in Ireland to be colonised by the Anglo-Normans. To the west, en route to Hook Head, the Irish chapter of Hell's Angels meet at **Wellington Bridge** over the June bank holiday weekend! **Hook Head** is well worth a detour and you can save yourself a circuitous trip north by taking a ferry from Ballyhack across to Passage East in Waterford (see Passage East). There is no public transport to this area.

Forth, Bargy & Yola
Faint remnants of a dialect called *yola* still survive in the south-east of County Wexford, which is sometimes called 'Forth & Bargy'. Yola stood for 'ye olde language' and was a mixture of old French, English, Irish, Welsh and Flemish. Examples of the language would be to *curk*, meaning to sit on your thighs or a *chi o' whate* meaning a small amount of straw. To be *hachee* is to be bad-tempered and a *stouk* is a truculent woman. ■

KILMORE QUAY
Peaceful Kilmore Quay is a small fishing village on the east side of Ballyteige Bay, noted for its lobster and deep-sea fishing. The village's Seafood Festival in the second week of July includes all types of seafood tastings, music and dancing.

Lining the attractive main street up from the harbour are a number of whitewashed thatched cottages. The harbour is the

WEXFORD & WATERFORD

jumping-off point for the Saltee Islands, which are clearly visible out to sea. In the harbour the Guillemot Lightship houses a small maritime museum, open during the summer. To the north-west a good sandy beach stretches towards Cullenstown.

Places to Stay & Eat
Killturk Hostel (☎ 053-29883), two km from Kilmore Quay on the main Wexford road, is a good place to stay. It charges IR£5.50 a night in dorms or IR£14 for private rooms, and has a low-priced café.

Coral House (☎ 053-29640) is in Grange, Kilmore, two km along the R739 road, and a bed with a shower is IR£15.

Food and drink possibilities include the *Wooden House Restaurant & Bar*, the *Silver Fox Restaurant* or the *Hotel Saltees* (☎ 053-29601), which has a good-value tourist menu and B&B around IR£36/58.

Getting There & Away
Public transport to Kilmore Quay is very limited. On Wednesday and Saturday only there are two Bus Éireann buses leaving Wexford Town at 10 am and 3.30 pm, returning at 10.35 am and 4.10 pm (4.35 pm on Saturday). Every Friday there is a private bus from Kilmore Quay to Wexford. For details, ask at the post office.

SALTEE ISLANDS
The Saltee Islands are four km offshore from Kilmore Quay and have some of the oldest rocks in Europe, dating back 2000 million years or more.

Once the haunt of privateers and smugglers, the Saltees are one of Ireland's most important bird sanctuaries and home to over 375 recorded species, principally gannets, guillemots, cormorants, kittiwakes, puffins and Manx shearwaters. The best time to visit is in the spring and early summer nesting season, as once the chicks can fly, the birds leave, and by early August it's very quiet.

The Saltees – nicknamed the 'graveyard of a thousand ships' – were touched by the 1798 Rising, for it was here that two of the Wexford rebel leaders, Bagenal Harvey and

Dr John Colclough, were found hiding before they were brought to Wexford, hanged and beheaded. The Saltees were bought in 1943 by Michael Neale who then crowned himself Prince Michael, the 'First Prince of the Saltees'. He even erected a throne and obelisk in his own honour on the Great Saltee. Luckily you don't need his royal consent to venture onto the islands, just the name of someone who can get you there – try the tourist office in Wexford or local boatmen like Declan Bates (☎ 053-29684) or Tom O'Brien (☎ 053-29727). Fares are IR£6 to IR£10 return – bargain with the boatmen. The trip should take about 45 minutes. For more on the islands read *The Saltees, Islands of Birds & Legends* by Richard Roche & Oscar Merne, published by O'Brien Press.

HOOK PENINSULA
The south-west of the county is dominated by the long tapering finger of Hook Peninsula, terminating at Hook Head. Cromwell's statement that Waterford Town would fall 'by Hook or by Crooke', referred to the two possible landing points from which to take the area: here or at Crooke in County Waterford. In good weather, it's a fine journey out to the lighthouse at the tip of the head and back along the west side to Duncannon. On the west side is a car ferry to Passage East in County Waterford saving a detour to the north via New Ross (see the Passage East section later).

On the way out to Hook, **Tintern Abbey** is a 12th-century Cistercian abbey in a lovely rural setting near the village of Saltmills. Currently being restored, it was founded by William Marshall, earl of Pembroke after he nearly perished at sea. Continuing south towards the head, **Fethard-on-Sea** is the largest village in the area.

Just south of Fethard is **Baginbun Head** near Bannow Bay, where the Anglo-Normans made their first landings in Ireland in May 1169. Joining forces with the far larger army of Dermot MacMurrough, they captured Wexford in the same year. Ramparts were built to fortify the headland at

Baginbun, until more Normans arrived in 1170 under Raymond le Gros. Shortly after he landed, 3000 Irish-Norse soldiers set out from Waterford City and attacked Baginbun, outnumbering the defenders seven to one.

Le Gros stampeded a herd of cattle onto them and then taught them a lesson in organised warfare. Seventy of Waterford's citizens and soldiers were captured, had their legs broken and were thrown over the cliffs to their death. So it was to be that:

> At the creek of Baginbun,
> Ireland was lost and won.

After the Norman leader Strongbow had landed at Passage East with another 1200 men, the Anglo-Normans gathered their forces and in August 1170 marched on to Waterford City. This was the beginning of more than 800 years of English involvement in Ireland.

Today at Baginbun, a small road leads down to a battered memorial overlooking Baginbun Beach and the headland out to the right. If you look carefully at the headland, you can make out the overgrown earthen ramparts built by the Normans when they first arrived. The stone **Martello Tower** dates from the early 1800s. Bannow Bay to the east, the first landing area of the Normans, is the site of a lost town – Norman or Viking – which was swamped by sand and sea in the 1600s.

The journey out to **Hook Head** is lovely, the land extremely flat with few houses interrupting the open space. About two km from the head, turning left at a T-junction brings you down to the odd little village of **Slade** with an imposing ruined castle dominating the harbour. There are usually a couple of boats moored here but otherwise it is a sleepy place.

Farther south, Hook Head itself is crowned by Europe's, and possibly the world's, oldest **lighthouse**. It's said that monks lit a beacon on the head from the 5th century and that the first Viking invaders were so happy to have a guiding light that they left the monks alone. In the 12th century

a more solid beacon was erected by the Norman Raymond le Gros, and 800 years later that is largely the structure you see today.

There are lovely walks both sides of the head, a haunting and beautiful place in the evening. Be careful of the numerous blowholes on the west side of the peninsula. The rocks around the lighthouse are carboniferous limestone, rich in fossil remains. If you search carefully, you may find 350-million-year-old shells and tiny disc-like pieces of crinoids, a type of starfish. Hook Head is also a good vantage point for **bird-watching** and over 200 species have been recorded passing through the area.

The village of **Duncannon** is a small holiday resort with a lovely sandy beach and a good view over Waterford Harbour. On the west of the village is Duncannon Fort, one of many structures built on this site since pre-Norman times.

Four km to the north of Duncannon is **Ballyhack** where there is a year-round ferry to Passage East in County Waterford (see the Getting There & Away section under Passage East later). Ballyhack also has a 15th-century **Knights Templar castle** overlooking the estuary. It's open from 10 am to 6 pm daily in July and August, admission IR£1/50p.

Dunbrody Abbey is a beautiful ruin on the west side of Hook Head near the village of Campile and about nine km north of Duncannon. It was built around 1170 AD by the English Cistercian monks from Buildwas in Shropshire, England. Various buttresses and supports had to be added later, to keep it upright. Most of the structure is still there and it is a fine sight among the fields. **Dunbrody Castle** nearby is owned by Lord Patrick Belfast and is open to the public.

Scuba Diving

Hook Head is popular with divers; the best spots are out from the little inlet under the lighthouse or from the rocks at the southwest corner of the head. The underwater scenery is pleasant, with lots of little caves, crevasses and gullies. The depths are no more than 15 metres. If it's too rough try

Churchtown, about one km back from the point just before the road goes inland by the ruincd church. Follow the path west to some gullies and coves. Otherwise try the rocks south of Slade harbour, a popular area. Tanks can be filled at the Naomh Seosamh Hotel in Fethard and in summer there are often local dive groups here.

Places to Stay
Fethard-on-Sea has most of the area's accommodation, but there are a few places on the west side of the peninsula around Duncannon and Ballyhack.

Camping The *Fethard Camping & Caravan Park* (☎ 051-397123) is at the northern end of town, while the *Ocean Island Caravan Park* (☎ 051-397148) is about a km farther north. Both charge around IR£7 per tent. The best bet of all is to stock up and head a farther 12 km out to Hook Head where there is lovely camping along the shore. There is a small petrol station and shop about five km from the headland for replenishing supplies.

Hostel The only hostel in the region is the An Óige *Arthurstown Hostel* (☎ 051-389411), one km from Ballyhack on the west side of the peninsula.

B&Bs In Fethard the *Hotel Naomh Seosamh* (☎ 051-397129), on the main street, is popular and good fun at weekends; it costs from IR£17/34 and has a diving compressor. *Bore a Trae House* (☎ 051-397102), three km south-west of Fethard on the way to the head in Templetown, is a good B&B costing around IR£13/26.

Places to Eat
Fethard's hotels and pubs are the principal eating spots on the peninsula, but nowhere stands out. Restaurants are almost non-existent but on the west side of the peninsula, Ballyhack is home to the *Neptune Bar & Seafood Restaurant* (☎ 051-389284) a terrific little place serving simple but delicious seafood. There's a tourist dinner for

IR£12.50 and your own wine can be brought (IR£3 corkage charge).

Hopetown House in Foulksmills has the *Cellar Restaurant* (☎ 051-63771), with dinner from IR£20 or a midweek special from IR£16.50. The *Moorings Seafood Bar & Restaurant* (☎ 051-389242) in Duncannon has good seafood while the *Templar's Inn* (☎ 051-97162), in Templetown, also specialises in seafood and has main courses around IR£10. The *King's Bay Inn* (☎ 051-89173), in Arthurstown, offers snacks and seafood with main courses from IR£5 to IR£10.

Getting There & Away
Particularly if you're travelling by bike, it's worth taking the 10-minute crossing between County Wexford and County Waterford on the Ballyhack to Passage East ferry. For details on fares and times see under Passage East, County Waterford, later in this chapter. Bus services are virtually non-existent, although on Monday and Thursday a Bus Éireann bus on a run from Wexford to Waterford will drop you in Fethard. It leaves Wexford Town at 2.50 pm.

NEW ROSS
New Ross (*Rhos Mhic Triúin*), 34 km west of Wexford Town, is a sizeable settlement astride the River Barrow. New Ross is not an especially pretty town, with large oil-storage tanks and old warehouses looming over the river banks. The east bank is better than the west, with some small, steep, narrow streets and St Mary's Church.

New Ross was the scene of fierce fighting during the 1798 Rising when a group of rebels under Bagenal Harvey and John Kelly tried to take the town. They were repelled by the defending garrison leaving 3000 people dead and much of the town in ruins.

Information
A tourist office (☎ 051-21857) operates from the refurbished grain store building on the quay during July and August. The post office is on Charles St, just off the quay. The John F Kennedy Trust (☎ 051-25239), is

based in the same old grain store building on the quay as the tourist office. It has a genea-logical database for people wishing to trace their ancestors from the region.

St Mary's Church
St Mary's Church is a roofless ruin on Church Lane and was founded by William and Isabella in the 13th century. Inside is a rough slab with some barely decipherable words, 'Isabel ... Laegn' which can be trans-lated roughly as 'Isabel of Leinster'. She died around 1220 and was buried in England so this may be some sort of memorial to her. The key to the church is available from the caretaker across the road.

Cruises
The Galley Cruising Restaurant (☎ 051-21723) operates out of New Ross. There is a lunch time cruise at 12.30 pm from April to October, which costs IR£11. There is a two-hour cruise including afternoon tea which leaves at 3 pm from June to August and costs IR£5. A dinner cruise takes place between April and September. This costs from IR£17 and departs at 5.30 pm or 7 pm.

Places to Stay & Eat
The IHH *Mac Murrough Hostel* (☎ 051-21383) is three km north-east of town and this is the nearest hostel to Rosslare. It's a farm hostel, sleeping 17, and a bed is IR£5.50.

Katie Pat's (☎ 051-22404) on the quay is good for cheap sandwiches and lunches. It also has a restaurant upstairs and serves dinner from 5 pm to 9 pm, with main courses in the IR£6 to IR£12 range. Across the road from Katie Pat's is *John V's* pub (☎ 051-25188), which does a good lunch in the bar, and has a restaurant upstairs with a good selection of fresh seafood.

For a more formal meal try the hotel res-taurants or the *Galley Cruising Restaurant*; see Cruises.

Getting There & Away
Bus Éireann (☎ 053-22522) have a twice-daily service to Dublin from outside the Mariners Bar, on the quay. They also have services to Rosslare Harbour, Wexford, Waterford and the odd bus down towards Hook Head.

Getting Around
You can hire bikes from Edward Prendergast (☎ 051-21600) at Abbey House, The Quay. Dinghies are available from New Ross Boating Club on the opposite bank from the Galley Restaurant mooring.

AROUND NEW ROSS
Five km south of New Ross, **Dunganstown** was the birthplace of Patrick Kennedy, grandfather of John F Kennedy. Patrick left Ireland for the USA in 1858 and JFK visited the town during his presidency. The original Kennedy house no longer exists but there is a small cottage belonging to the Ryan family who are direct descendants, and a small plaque marks the spot.

A couple of km to the south, the **John F Kennedy Park & Arboretum** (☎ 051-88171) covers 252 hectares of woodlands and gardens with more than 4500 species of trees and shrubs. The park was opened in 1968 in memory of the late US president, and was funded by some prominent Irish-Ameri-cans. There are a couple of km of pleasant shaded walks with rest spots.

Slieve Coillte hill, opposite the park entrance, offers a splendid view of the sur-rounding countryside and out to the Saltee Islands. You can drive or walk to the top and it's not necessary to pay the park entry fee just to go up the hill.

ENNISCORTHY
Enniscorthy (*Inis Coirthaidh*) is an attractive hilly town, on the steep banks of the River Slaney in the heart of County Wexford, 20 km north-west of Wexford Town. It was the site of some of the fiercest fighting of the 1798 Rising and has a good local museum. As if in deference to the past the town has an engaging number of unreconstructed shop fronts that evoke the past – not quite the 1790s but definitely the 1950s.

Information

The tourist office (☎ 054-34699) in the town centre is open July and August only. Brochures and books can be found in the Wexford County Museum when the office is closed. The Book Shop is on Court St while the main post office is at the bottom of Castle Hill on Abbey Square. There is a laundry at the top of Rafter St next to the Chinese restaurant.

Enniscorthy Castle & Wexford County Museum

Enniscorthy's impressive Norman castle dates from 1205 and was a private residence until 1951. It is the town's major attraction: a fine stout building with drum towers at the three corners. The poet Edmund Spenser lived here for a time and it is said locally that he was given the castle as a present by Queen Elizabeth I for the many flattering things he said about her in his great work *The Faerie Queene*.

It was the site of a fierce battle in 1649, and during the 1798 Rising the rebels took control of the town and used the castle as a prison. Today it houses the Wexford County Museum (☎ 054-35926) which includes many different displays covering particularly the 1798 and 1916 risings as well as a collection of pottery, military memorabilia

The 1798 Rising

In the Market Square is a memorial by Oliver Sheppard, commemorating Father John Murphy and his band of rebels who stormed the town and captured the castle in May 1798. One faction marched under the banner MWS, for 'Murder Without Sin'. It was on Vinegar Hill, to the east of the town, where the rebels had set up their headquarters, that the last major battle of the rising took place. On 9 June, a force of 20,000 troops led by generals Lake and Johnson almost completely surrounded the rebels, who held out against huge odds for 30 days. The windmill on the hill, now ruined, was the rebel command post. ■

and policemen's hats and patches from around the world.

The castle and museum are open weekdays in summer from 10 am to 6 pm (closed for lunch) and from 2 to 5.30 pm on Sunday. In winter it just opens 2 to 6 pm. Admission is IR£2/1.

Potteries

Near the town you can find numerous potteries including Hillview and Carley's Bridge potteries, both on the road to New Ross; Badger's Hill Pottery, farther along the same road; and Kiltrea Bridge Pottery, north-west of the town.

Festival

During the first and second weeks in July, Enniscorthy holds its annual Strawberry Fair.

Places to Stay

B&Bs *Murphy's* (☎ 054-33522) at 9 Main St costs from IR£13/26. *Woodville House* (☎ 054-47810), with comfortable rooms from IR£14/28 is eight km south on the Ballyhogue road, a minor road along the west side of the River Slaney.

In Ballycarney, *Oakville House* (☎ 054-88626) overlooks the Slaney Valley. The gardens are particularly nice, and B&B is from IR£18.50/27. The house is nine km away signposted off the N80 road to Bunclody.

The comfortable *Murphy Flood's Hotel* (☎ 054-33413) is conveniently located on Main St just up from Market Square. B&B costs from IR£26/44. *Ballinkeele House* (☎ 053-38105) is a lovely old mansion dating from 1840 and is 10 km south-east from Enniscorthy in Ballymurn. They have four elegant rooms for IR£28 and IR£30 B&B. Dinner is IR£18.

Places to Eat

There is a variety of small restaurants and bistros in the low and moderate price ranges. The *Antique Tavern*, at the bottom of Slaney St, has good and affordable lunches. The *Concorde* at the top of Rafter St serves burger

& chips etc and has a takeaway service. There's a Chinese restaurant on the opposite side of the street. At the monument end of Rafter St the *Paris Café* is good for cakes and bread if you're planning a picnic. *Waffle's Bistro* on Castle Hill has lunches for around IR£5. The *Coffee Shop* is on Court St.

Murphy Flood's Hotel also has a restaurant with dinner at IR£17 a head, or you could try the *Tavern Bar* in Templeshannon, on the east bank of the river, for reasonable pub food.

Getting There & Away
Bus The Bus Éircann bus stop is on the riverfront on the east bank outside the Bus Stop Shop, and is serviced by four daily buses (three on Sundays) to Dublin, as well as services to Rosslare Harbour and Wexford Town.

Train Enniscorthy is on the Dublin to Rosslare Harbour line with three trains daily, two on Sundays in each direction. The station (☎ 054-33488) is on the east bank of the river.

GOREY
The small market town of Gorey is 20 km south of Arklow, on the main Dublin to Wexford road and below the foothills of the Wicklow Mountains. There is a street market on Saturday.

During the 1798 Rising, Gorey was attacked by a group of rebels trying to reach the coast road to Dublin. They camped on Gorey Hill just south-west of the town and there is a small memorial to their efforts at one end of Main St. There is a good ramble out to **Tara Hill** seven km north-east of town. The Church of Ireland parish **church** has some fine stained glass by Michael Healy from around 1904.

The tourist office (☎ 055-21248) on Lower Main St is open July to August only, from 10 am to 6 pm Monday to Saturday.

COURTOWN
Seven km south-east of Gorey along the L31 is the small seaside resort of Courtown at the

mouth of the River Ounavarra. The beach to the north of the village is popular with Irish holidaymakers and there are also the usual amusements, takeaways and seaside caravan parks and guesthouses. The Bayview Hotel dominates the village beachfront. This area has the lowest rainfall in Ireland.

Places to Stay
Camping & Hostel *Courtown Caravan & Camping Park* (☎ 055-25280) is well signposted just inland from Courtown. They charge IR£10 per tent or IR£5.50 if you are hiking or cycling, and have excellent facilities. *Parklands Holiday Park* (☎ 055-25202), just south of Courtown, has only 10 tent pitches and is a little dearer. Otherwise you could find a quiet spot among the dunes and pitch your tent for free. The *Anchorage Hostel* (☎ 055-25335) is a small place some five km south of Courtown at Poulshone. Beds are IR£6 and a double is IR£14.

B&Bs *Riverchapel House* (☎ 055-25120), one km from the harbour costs IR£16/28. *Seamount House* (☎ 055-25128) is in the village and costs from IR£19/30.

Places to Eat
Good restaurants include the *Bosun's Chair* in Ardmine, two km south of Courtown along the coast (☎ 055-25198) and the *Cowhouse Bistro* (☎ 055-25219) at Tomsilla Farm, outside of town on the main road to Gorey. A set five-course dinner here is IR£15, but they don't serve lunch.

FERNS
Ferns is 17 km south-west of Gorey. Most traffic whizzes on south, bound for Wexford and Rosslare Harbour, but this sleepy little village was for several hundred years, up to the 13th century, the administrative capital of Leinster and also an important diocese in the province. It was the base for the MacMurroughs, the kings of Leinster, and in particular for Dermot MacMurrough, the king who brought the Normans to Ireland and died here in 1171.

Ferns Castle

The remains of this castle at the north-west end of the village are thought to be on the site of Dermot MacMurrough's previous castle and they date from around 1220 AD. There are a couple of intact walls, a surviving part of the moat, and one complete tower which can be climbed with a superb view from the top. To the left of the door at the top is a murder hole through which oil or arrows could be dropped on attackers below. The castle was largely destroyed and most of the population of the town put to death in 1649 by Parliamentarians under Sir Charles Coote.

Other Sights

Other antiquities include fragments of the 13th-century **Cathedral of St Aidan** (now part of the modern Church of Ireland cathedral) with a graveyard and the remains of a high cross said to mark the grave of Dermot MacMurrough. Father Redmond, who is buried in the graveyard, is said to have saved the life of a young student in France, one Napoleon Bonaparte. Outside the graveyard is **St Moling's Well**, and there are also some remains of an **Augustinian monastery**, founded by Dermot MacMurrough in the 1150s.

Places to Stay & Eat

The friendly *Clone House* (☎ 054-66113) is a 350-year-old farmhouse three km from Ferns on the Enniscorthy road, with four bedrooms, three with own bathroom, from IR£20/30.

The *Celtic Arms* (☎ 054-66490) at the south end of Main St has a restaurant lunch for IR£7.25 and dinner for IR£14.

Getting There & Away

Bus Éireann buses on the main Dublin to Wexford route stop in Ferns. There are at least five daily in both directions; contact Wexford bus station (☎ 053-22522) for details.

MT LEINSTER

Bunclody, on the border with County Carlow

16 km north-west of Ferns, is a good base from which to climb Mt Leinster, at 796 metres the highest mountain in the Blackstairs. If you want to drive to the top, take the Borris road out of Ferns for eight km, turn left at the sign for the Mt Leinster Scenic Rd, and continue to the radio mast at the top. The last few km are on narrow, exposed roads with steep fall-offs, so drive slowly and watch out for sheep. Mt Leinster also has one of the best locations for **hang-gliding** in the country.

WEXFORD COASTAL WALK

Wexford Coastal Walk (Slí Charman) follows the county's coastline for 221 km from Ballyhack to Kilmichael Point. See the Activities chapter for more details.

County Waterford

Wedged in the south-east corner of Ireland, County Waterford combines low farmland and sandy coastlines rather like those of County Wexford with the more rugged landscape typical of much of County Cork.

WATERFORD CITY

Like Kilkenny, Waterford (*Port Láirge*) has a medieval feel, with narrow alleyways leading off many of the larger streets. Reginald's Tower houses the city museum and marks the Viking heart of the city. The area around the tower is one of the most attractive in the city, and later Georgian times also left a legacy of fine houses and commercial buildings, particularly around The Mall, George's St and O'Connell St.

Waterford, however, is first and foremost a commercial city and port. The estuary of the River Suir is deep enough to allow large modern ships right up to the city's quays. The port has been used since earliest times and is still one of the busiest in Ireland.

Waterford crystal is made here: the hand-blown cut glass is one of Ireland's most famous exports.

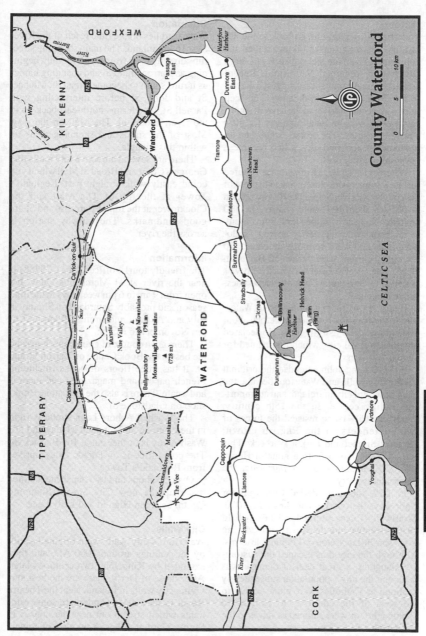

County Waterford

History

Waterford City's origins go back to the 8th century, when a group of Vikings settled at a convenient riverside site called Port Lairge which they renamed Vadrafjord. Recent archaeological excavations suggest a date of 915 AD for the city's foundation. The deep inlet with access upriver to the heart of south-east Ireland was an ideal highway for their sturdy longships. The Norse established an independent fortified city which became a booming trading post.

Waterford's strategic importance ensured that its fortunes were closely linked to those of the country as a whole (see the History section in the Facts about the Country chapter). In 1170 an Irish/Viking army sallied forth from the city to do battle with the newly arrived Anglo-Normans and was roundly defeated: 70 prominent citizens were thrown off Baginbun Head to their deaths. Later that year the city was besieged by Strongbow, who overcame a desperate defence.

Henry II of England turned up in Waterford in October 1171, rather concerned about Strongbow's new assertiveness. He declared the place a royal city, which it remained for almost 500 years.

In 1210 King John extended the original Viking city walls and Waterford became the most powerful city in Ireland, and an important trading centre. In the 15th century, Waterford City twice resisted the forces of two pretenders to the English crown, Lambert Simnel and Perkin Warbeck. This earned it the motto from a grateful Henry VII, *Urbs intacta manet Waterfordia*, the 'unconquered city'.

In 1649 the town defied Cromwell for eight days before he withdrew. In 1650, Cromwell's forces returned and the city held out for over two months, finally surrendering to his son-in-law Ireton on honourable terms. Although the city thus escaped the customary slaughter, a great deal of damage was done and the city's population subsequently declined as Catholics were either exiled to the west of the country, 'to Hell or to Connaught', or were shipped as slaves to the Caribbean.

Orientation

Waterford lies on the tidal reach of the River Suir 16 km inland. The main shopping street runs directly back from the River Suir, beginning as Barronstrand St and changing names as it runs south to become Broad St, Michael St and John St before intersecting with Parnell St, which runs north-east back up to the river, becoming The Mall on the way. Most of the sights and shopping areas lie within this triangle.

There are several attractive tiny malls like George's Court and Broad St Mall which you could easily walk straight past. Reginald's Tower at the top of The Mall and the Clocktower at the top of Barronstrand St are good landmarks. The railway station is across the river.

Information

The friendly tourist office (☎ 051-75788) is near the river at 41 Merchant's Quay. It's open from 9 am to 6 pm weekdays in the high season and probably Saturday and Sunday in July and August, and from 9.30 am to 5.15 pm November to March.

There are a couple of good bookshops and the best is the Book Centre on Barron Strand St. It has three floors of books (including French papers and magazines) and records and a café. There is also the Gladstone Bookshop on Gladstone St.

The Washed Ashore Launderette is right in the centre at 36 Merchant's Quay and D's Wash Away is farther out at 109 Barrack St. The post office is on Parade Quay upriver from Reginald's Tower.

Over 30 shops and two department stores make up the new City Square Shopping Centre between High St and Lady Lane.

City Walls

Waterford's city walls were originally built by the Vikings around 1000 AD, and then extended by King John two centuries later. After those of Derry, these are the best surviving city walls in Ireland. Near the Theatre Royal in the Palace Garden are some remnants which stretch out near the houses in Spring Garden Alley. A number of towers

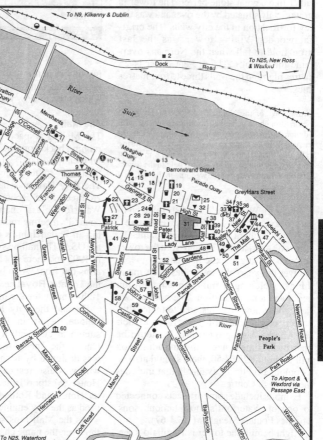

PLACES TO STAY

2 Jury's Hotel
4 Portree Guesthouse
6 Dooley's Hotel
16 Granville Hotel
34 Viking House Hostel
47 Tower Hotel
48 Beechwood B&B
51 Derrynane House
54 Corlea B&B

PLACES TO EAT

3 Dwyer's
8 Maxim House
9 Haricot's Wholefood
15 Chapman's Pantry
29 Bewley's Coffee Shop

32 Happy Garden
36 Sizzlers
38 Opus 1
44 Reginald's
45 Jade Palace
   Restaurant
56 Gino's

PUBS

5 Metropole Bar
18 T & H Doolan's Bar
20 Egan's Pub
30 Lord's Pub
42 Olde Stand Bar
52 Olde Rogue
55 Pulpit
57 Gooff's

OTHER

1 Railway & Bus Station
7 Washed Ashore Laundrette
10 Tourist Office
11 Roxy Theatre Club
12 Garter Lane Arts Centre
13 Clocktower
14 Gladstone Bookshop
17 USIT Travel
19 Holy Trinity Cathedral
21 Blackfriars Abbey
22 Beach Tower
23 St Patrick's Church
24 Book Centre
25 Post Office
26 Ballybricken Green
27 St Patricks
   Presbyterian Church

28 Cinema
31 City Square Shopping
   Centre
33 Wright's Cycle Depot
35 French Church
37 Heritage Centre
39 Christ Church Cathedral
40 St Olaf's Church
41 Half Moon Tower
43 Reginald's Tower
   & Museum
46 City Hall
49 Theatre Royal
50 Bishop's Palace
53 Rapid Express Bus Stop
58 French Tower
59 Double Tower
60 Rice Museum
61 Watch Tower

WEXFORD & WATERFORD

Waterford

0   100   200 m

also remain, including one on Patrick St, another near Railway Square (the Watch Tower), the French Tower at one end of Castle St and Reginald's Tower on The Mall.

Reginald's Tower

The most handsome and historically interesting remnant of the city walls is Reginald's Tower, which was built by the Normans in the 12th century. It stands on the site of the original wooden tower built by the Viking Reginald the Dane in 1003 AD and looks rather like a great stone barrel. The tower is strategically situated by the river and was the key fortification in the city walls. The original wooden Viking tower was the last stronghold to fall when the Normans overcame the Vikings. The present tower is 25 metres high and the walls three to four metres thick.

Within days of the Norman takeover in 1170, the victor, Strongbow, cemented his military success with a diplomatic marriage to the king of Leinster's daughter Aoife – in the upper room of the tower, according to legend. In fact, the wedding took place in Christ Church Cathedral and the feast was held in the tower. There is a fine painting of the wedding in the National Art Gallery in Dublin.

Many of Waterford's English royal visitors stayed here in this 'safe house', including Richard II, Henry II and James II, who took a last look at Ireland from the tower before departing to exile in France.

Over the years the tower has been many things, including a mint, an ammunition depot and a police station. The bottom two floors have now been restored to their 12th-century origins and the top two floors to their late Middle Ages provenance. It should be open by the time you read this and admission will be around IR£2.50; there should also be a combination ticket available that includes the Heritage Centre.

Exhibits include some artefacts connected to one of Waterford's most famous sons, Thomas Francis Meagher (1823-67).

Right behind the tower is Reginald's restaurant and pub which incorporates a section of the old city wall inside the building. The

Thomas Francis Meagher

Born in the Granville Hotel, this Young Ireland leader was captured in Derrynane House (now a B&B) for his part in the 1848 Rising and was shipped to a penal colony in Australia. From there he escaped to the USA, where he was the captain of the 'Fighting 69th' Irish Brigade in Fort Sumter and Fredricksburg in the American Civil War. Meagher later became governor of Montana and died in 1867, while spending the night on a Missouri paddle steamer. He went for a walk on deck, tripped on a coil of rope and fell overboard. His body was never recovered. ■

two arches in this wall were sallyports, from which boats could 'sally forth' on to the inlet which used to flow right by the wall.

The Mall

The Mall is a spacious 18th-century street running back from the riverside. It was built on reclaimed land, which until 1735 was a tidal inlet running alongside the city wall. The **City Hall** was built in 1788 by local architect John Roberts and a remarkable Waterford-glass chandelier hangs in the council's meeting room. There is a replica of this in Philadelphia's Independence Hall in the USA. The hall was completely renovated in 1992 and there is a fine Waterford coat of arms out front. Also built by John Roberts, the **Theatre Royal** nearby is the finest intact 18th-century theatre in the country.

Beyond the City Hall is the **Bishop's Palace**, begun in 1741 and for which a stretch of city wall had to be demolished. One of the finest townhouses in Ireland, it was designed by Richard Castle or Cassels who was also responsible for Powerscourt House, Westport House and Dublin's Leinster House and Rotunda Hospital. It is now used as the city engineering offices.

As the Mall runs south-west away from the river, the name changes to Parnell St and then Manor St where it is flanked by two good stretches of Anglo-Norman wall. On

WEXFORD & WATERFORD

the east side of the road is **Watch Tower** while Castle St runs west by **Double Tower** and **French Tower**.

Christ Church Cathedral
Behind the City Hall is Christ Church Cathedral in Cathedral Square. It was designed by John Roberts and building began between 1770 and 1773 and went on for 20 years.

A Viking church was first built on the site around 1050, and was enlarged, extended and rebuilt numerous times in the following centuries. It suffered at the hands of Cromwell's troops and was eventually demolished to make way for the present building. During demolition, a remarkable collection of 15th-century Italian priest vestments were uncovered, which are now on display in the Waterford Heritage Centre.

The tomb of James Rice, who died in 1469, is well worth a look. It was moved here from a chapel which Rice founded in the earlier Viking church. His body is depicted in a state of decay with worms and frogs crawling out of it, and his right hand has been broken off at the wrist. Rice was Lord Mayor of Waterford on seven occasions.

The building also houses some John Wesley bibles. The cathedral is Church of Ireland and closes at 4 pm.

With the Georgian corporation offices and engineering offices nearby tastefully restored, Cathedral Square provides a pleasant, quiet area in which to sit and relax.

The French Church
The extensive ruins of the French Church, also known as 'Grey Friars' are on Greyfriars St. The church was built in 1240 by Franciscan monks and later Henry III laid on honours and riches. The building was used as a hospital after the 16th century and the suppression of the monasteries by Henry VIII. One of the hospital's last leading doctors was T F Meagher's father, Thomas Meagher Senior, Mayor of Waterford.

The name of the church comes from the French Huguenot refugees who used it in the 17th and 18th centuries, after which it fell into ruins. Among the memorial stones inside is one to the architect John Roberts. You can pick up the key to the church from across the road at 5 Greyfriars St.

Waterford Heritage Centre
Next to the ruins of the French Church on Greyfriars St is the small Waterford Heritage Centre (☎ 051-71277) with an exhibition of original royal charters of the city from 1215 onwards and displays of local Viking artefacts. Entry is IR£1 or a little more to include entrance to Reginald's Tower. It is open April to October inclusive between 10 am and 5 pm on Monday to Friday and between 10 am and 5 pm on Saturday.

Other Buildings
The ruins of the Dominican **Blackfriars Abbey** on Arundel Square date from 1226 and possess an intact square tower. The monks were disbanded in 1541.

Nearby on Barronstrand St is the Catholic **Holy Trinity Cathedral**, built between 1792 and 1796 by John Roberts who also designed the Protestant Christ Church Cathedral and was himself a Protestant. The exterior is – perhaps deliberately – plain but the interior is sumptuous with a fine carved pulpit, painted pillars with Corinthian capitals and Waterford crystal chandeliers. It's a surprising contrast to the austere interior of Roberts' Christ Church Cathedral.

Edmund Ignatius Rice, founder of the Christian Brothers, established his first school at Mt Sion in Waterford. On Barrack St there's a **Rice Museum** at the school site.

At **Ballybricken Green** bull baiting took place from the 15th to 18th century. Nearby is the old city wall's **Half Moon Tower** by Patrick St. **St Patrick's Church** on Jenkins' Lane is an 18th-century Catholic chapel which managed to survive the savage suppression of Catholicism at that time. At the top of Jenkins' Lane is the **Beach Tower**, another remnant of the old city wall.

On Olaf St, **St Olaf's Hall** is named after a favourite Viking saint and was founded by the Norse king, Sitric, around 870 AD during Waterford's earliest years. After falling into ruins it was almost totally rebuilt in 1734 and remains much as you see it today.

The **Chamber of Commerce** building on Great George's St was originally built as a town house by John Roberts and has a magnificent staircase.

Waterford Crystal

The first Waterford glass factory was established at the west end of the riverside quays in 1783. This first phase of the business closed in 1851 due to punitive taxes imposed on the raw materials by the British government. It was not revived until 1947 and it took almost five years before production was up and running. Today, highly skilled workers continue the tradition and produce remarkable work that is sold all over the world. The glass is a heavy lead (over 30%) crystal made up of three basic ingredients: red lead, silica sand and potash.

Tours of the Waterford Crystal plant, two km out of town on the Cork road, are free and officially you're supposed to book in advance (☎ 051-73311) but in practice you can generally just turn up. If you do want to book, then it can be done direct or through the tourist office. The glass blowers and cutters (all men) take about five years to learn their trade. About 80% of the output is exported to the USA.

The full tour takes about 40 minutes and operates daily between April and October for a cost of IR£2.50/1.50. There are tours between 9 am and 4 pm, every 15 minutes, after which you can part with your money in the Crystal Gallery if you so wish. Buses run to the factory from the clocktower on the quays.

Organised Tours

Walking Tours Jack Burtchaell (☎ 051-73711) runs guided historic walking tours of the city from March to October from the Granville Hotel twice daily at noon and 2 pm. The cost is IR£3.

Cruises The Galley Cruising Restaurant (☎ 051-21723) operates out of Waterford during June, July and August. There is a two-hour cruise including afternoon tea which leaves from Meagher Quay at 3 pm and costs IR£5.

Festivals

Waterford has a Light Opera Festival in September/October. Although not as famous as the Wexford Opera Festival, it has cheaper and more easily accessible shows. Booking is still advisable. Much of the city takes part; there are pub singing competitions and late bar extensions. Contact the Theatre Royal (☎ 051-74402), The Mall, Waterford, or Waterford Opera Festival (☎ 051-32001).

Places to Stay

Camping See the Tramore section for details of the nearest camping sites.

Hostels The IHH *Viking House* (☎ 051-53827), is tucked behind the quayside in Coffee House Lane in the ancient heart of the city. It's a modern, clean and efficient hostel that includes a light breakfast in its bed rates. These start at the basic IR£7.50 dorm bed and move up through IR£9-10 en-suite four- and six-bed rooms, to doubles for IR£11-13 per person and IR£13 singles. Family rooms are IR£30. There are lots of facilities including currency exchange, left-luggage facility, bus ticket sales and laundry.

B&Bs *Beechwood* (☎ 051-76677) is central at 7 Cathedral Square and has rooms for IR£15/25. The friendly *Portree Guesthouse* (☎ 051-74574) on Mary St costs from IR£16/25. The Mall and its extension Parnell St are good places to look and you could try *Derrynane House* (☎ 051-75179) at 19 The Mall, with rooms around the same price. Also worth trying is *Corlea* (☎ 051-75764) at 2 New St, which does B&B for IR£14/25.

Knockboy House (☎ 051-74452) is almost five km from Waterford on the Dunmore East road, set back from the road, near the River Suir; you can recognise it by the glass conservatory. Rooms are from IR£18.50/27.

Hotels *Granville Hotel* (☎ 051-55111) is a lovely old building and top-class hotel on

Meagher Quay in the city. B&B runs from IR£50/82. For a bedside view of Reginald's Tower there is the modern *Tower Hotel & Leisure Centre* (☎ 051-75801), at the north end of The Mall, which has an indoor pool, sauna and gymnasium. B&B is IR£60/90. On the other side of the river there's *Jury's Hotel* (☎ 051-32111), part of the well-known chain and they have much the same facilities for similar rates.

Dooley's (☎ 051-73531) is on The Quay and provides the best hotel value. Spacious rooms are from IR£20/60 and it's a friendly place.

Places to Eat

Cafés & Snacks *Sizzlers*, near Reginald's Tower, is open 24 hours at weekends and serves cheapish meals. *Chapman's Pantry* is a terrific little coffee-shop-cum-restaurant behind the deli of the same name on Meagher Quay next to the Granville Hotel. It's open all day from 8 am to 6 pm and the deli downstairs is good too. At 11 O'Connell St *Haricot's Wholefood* has vegetarian and nonvegetarian dishes for around IR£5. Their brown-bread ice cream is a must. They're open Monday to Friday from 10 am to 8 pm, Saturday to 5.45 pm.

Bewley's, the coffee-house chain, has an outlet here in the Broad St mall.

Pub Food All the pubs on Baronstrand St are locked into healthy competition for lunch specials at around IR£3-5. *Egan's* has the most space and serves the food, cafeteria-style, in a separate area at the back.

T & H Doolan on Great George's St is good for lunches, as is the *Olde Stand*, in Michael St; it's a Victorian pub serving good bar food downstairs and a wide range of seafood and steaks upstairs for around IR£10.

McAlpin's Suir Inn (☎ 051-828182), in Cheekpoint five km from Waterford, is a well-known place and the crowds at weekends are testament to the quality of their seafood. They do food in the evenings only from around 6.30 to 9.30 pm, Tuesday to Saturday.

Restaurants Once again the Chinese and the Italians dominate the foreign invasion. *Gino's*, on Applemarket just off Michael St, and *Gianni's* on The Mall do good pizzas. For Chinese meals and takeaways, there is *Maxim House* (☎ 051-75820) on O'Connell St or the *Happy Garden* on Arundel Square. For upmarket Chinese the *Jade Palace* (☎ 051-55611) on The Mall is said to be one of the best (and most expensive) Chinese restaurants in Ireland.

The middle-of-the-road *Reginald's* bar and restaurant (☎ 051-55087) behind Reginald's Tower serves seafood and meat dishes for around IR£10. The popular *Strongbow's* at 124 Parade Quay does chicken, steak and fish. *Poppy's* (☎ 051-70008) in the Book Centre is bright and cheerful with vegetarian specials. *Opus 1* (☎ 051-57766), close to Christ Church Cathedral, is a small, cosy place serving traditional Irish dishes with an international flourish. It has a good reputation locally and main dishes are between IR£10-15, It's open for lunch and dinner, but closed Sunday.

One of the best, if not *the* best place in town is *Dwyer's* (☎ 051-77478), 5 Mary St in an old barracks near the bridge. The food is sophisticated but comes in generous helpings. They have a good special dinner rate of IR£13 between 6 and 7.30 pm; later on a full dinner is in the IR£20 range (closed Sunday and first fortnight in July). The other good place in town is *Prendiville's Restaurant* (☎ 051-78851) in a Gothic lodge out on the main Cork road. A set dinner between 6.30 and 8 pm is IR£15, otherwise it's over IR£20. If you are feeling ostentatious you could make your way the five km east to Ballinakill and *Waterford Castle* (☎ 051-78203) a top-class castle hotel. The restaurant here is very good, and dinner will cost at least IR£30 a head.

Entertainment

Pubs & Clubs There are lots of pubs, many featuring music. The venerable *T & H Doolan* on Great George's St, incorporates a remnant of the 1000-year-old city wall.

WEXFORD & WATERFORD

Sinead O'Connor played here in the early days of her career.

Geoff's and the *Pulpit*, located where John St becomes Michael St, both attract a young and lively drinking crowd. The Pulpit has a nightclub upstairs, the *Preacher's*. Across the road from those two is the *Olde Rogue* while back towards the river is *Lord's*, just off Broad St. *Egan's*, on Barronstrand St, has the odd karaoke night and a fully-fledged nightclub upstairs called *Snags*. Other popular pubs include the *Metropole*, on the corner of Bridge and Mary Sts, with the Metroland Ballroom next to it. *Reginald's* near the tower has a nightclub and occasional jazz sessions. There is also the *Roxy Theatre Club* on O'Connell St with music and discos.

Arts Centres, Theatre & Cinema The *Garter Lane Arts Centres* (☎ 051-55038) at 5 and 22 O'Connell St host films, exhibitions, poetry readings and works from their theatre company, the Red Kettle Theatre Group. They're open Tuesday to Saturday.

The Waterford Show is a new venture that combines music, dancing and wine in a 90-minute programme about the history of the city. It starts at 8.45 pm on Thursday, Friday and Sunday and costs IR£6. The show takes place in the City Hall and tickets can be booked at the tourist office, Waterford Crystal or at the City Hall prior to the show. Enquire here about the tentative plan to incorporate an early dinner into the programme.

The five-screen *cinema* is just off Broad St on Patrick St.

Getting There & Away
USIT Travel (☎ 051-72601), is at 36-37 George's St. If you are heading to or from Wexford see Passage East later for information on the useful short cut using the ferry service there.

Air Waterford Airport (☎ 051-75589) is six km south of the city. There is a daily British Airways Express flight to Stansted, which can cost as little as IR£89 return, and Suckling Airways run two daily flights to Luton.

Bus The Bus Éireann intercity station (☎ 051-73401) is based at Plunkett Railway Station just over the bridge on the north side of the river. There are plenty of buses daily to Dublin, Cork, Limerick and just about everywhere you may want to go. For bus times and fares ring ☎ 051-79000. Rapid Express Coaches (☎ 051-72149) at 32 Michael St run a regular service between Waterford/Tramore and Dublin (seven daily, five on Sunday, IR£5).

Suirway Bus & Coach Service (☎ 051-382209), based in Passage East, provides the most comprehensive local service to the county's outlying towns and villages. Most depart from outside the tourist office on Meagher Quay.

Train From Plunkett Railway Station (☎ 051-73401) on the north side of the river, there are regular train connections to Dublin (four daily, 2½ hours, IR£11), Limerick (one daily, 2½ hours, IR£17), and Rosslare (twice daily, 80 minutes, IR£9).

Getting Around
Wright's Cycle Depot (☎ 051-74411) on Henrietta St is a Raleigh Rent-a-Bike outlet. There is also BnB Cycles (☎ 051-70356) at 22 Ballybricken. Taxis are operated by BBC Cabs (☎ 051-79080) and there is a taxi rank at Plunkett Railway Station and another outside Penny's department store.

PASSAGE EAST
Heading east from Waterford City on the coast road, your first port of call will probably be Passage East, 112 km away, with its little harbour and thatched cottages at the foot of low hills. The Ballyhack to Passage East to Ballyhack ferry is a useful short cut between counties Waterford and Wexford.

Passage East has seen a lot of traffic in its time. Strongbow landed here in 1170 with 1200 men before his march on Waterford City. A year later Henry II arrived with 4000 men, while King James left Ireland from here in 1690 after his defeat at the Battle of the Boyne.

Just south of the village is **Crooke**. Near

Crooke are the remains of the Geneva Barracks. Built in the 18th century as part of a settlement for Swiss refugees, the buildings were turned into barracks after the plan fell through. It was here that a young rebel of the 1798 Rising came to confess his sins. The priest turned out to be an army officer disguised in a cassock, arresting the lad and subsequently hanging him. The story has been immortalised in the song *Croppy Boy*.

Places to Stay & Eat
The village has a couple of cheap B&Bs, *Cos Abhann* and *Harbour Lights*. *Chives* (☎ 051-382646) is a handy little seafood restaurant in Passage East with dinner served from 7 to 10 pm. Main courses are around IR£6.50.

Getting There & Away
If you are heading to or from Wexford, there is a car ferry across the estuary from Passage East to Ballyhack in County Wexford. This can save you an hour's drive via New Ross to the north. The ferry company (☎ 051-382488) is on Barrack St in Passage East and the ferry operates a continuous service from 7.20 am to 10 pm from April to September and 7.20 am to 8 pm the rest of the year. On Sunday first sailings are at 9.30 am. The crossing time is 10 minutes and the cost for a car is IR£3.50 one way, IR£5.50 return, for pedestrians 80p one way and IR£1 return, or cyclists IR£1 one way and IR£1.50 return. Return tickets are valid for an unlimited time.

Suirway Bus & Coach Service (☎ 051-382209) has two buses daily from Waterford City to Passage East.

DUNMORE EAST
Dunmore East is a busy little fishing village on a coastline of low red sandstone cliffs and discreet coves. The most popular beaches are Counsellor's Beach, facing south among the cliffs, and Lawlor's Beach, right in the village. Dunmore East has plenty of neat thatched cottages, many of them summer homes. The attractive stone harbour is overlooked by the unusual Doric lighthouse built in 1823, and is thronged with boats during

the summer when there is a nightly fish market. There is a good view of Hook Head lighthouse across the water in Wexford. The noisy birds nesting in the cliffs above the harbour are kittiwakes.

Dunmore East Adventure Centre (☎ 051-383783) rents equipment for windsurfing, canoeing, surfing and snorkelling and short courses in most of these water sports are also available.

Places to Stay
Camping & Hostel *Dunmore East Caravan & Camping Park* (☎ 051-383174) is just south of the village and the charge is IR£6 per tent. *Dunmore Harbour House* (☎ 051-383218), situated at the pier, has beds for IR£6.50 and IR£8.50 and doubles for IR£21 and IR£28. There is a good restaurant as well as the usual kitchen, and bikes can be hired. The hostel was once a hotel servicing passengers on the mail boat service between Dunmore East and Milford Haven in Wales.

B&Bs *Church Villa* (☎ 051-383390) is one of a row of old cottages in the town opposite the Protestant Church and near the Ship Restaurant. Its cosy rooms, most with showers, cost IR£18/30. *Dunmore Lodge* (☎ 051-383454) is an old country lodge within a few minutes' walk of the village. Rooms cost from IR£20/30. *Foxmount Farm* (☎ 051-74308) is a 17th-century country house on its own farm with good rooms from IR£15/30. The house is six km from Dunmore East.

Hotels The *Candlelight Inn* (☎ 051-383215) is a hotel and restaurant overlooking the estuary. It costs from IR£35/60. The *Haven Hotel* (☎ 051-383150) is a Victorian mansion in extensive grounds overlooking the sea. B&B runs at IR£30/60. The *Ocean Hotel* (☎ 051-383136) in town charges from IR£35/54.

Places to Eat
The *Candlelight Inn* has a good restaurant, with dinners from around IR£14. The *Ship Inn & Restaurant* (☎ 051-383144) is on a

corner overlooking Dunmore Bay. The food, both in the bar and restaurant, is good, particularly the seafood, and there are vegetarian options. It's open daily during the summer season for lunch from 12.30 pm and for dinner from 7 to 10 pm.

The *Strand Inn* (☎ 051-383174) is near the harbour and the food can be imaginative, with vegetarian choices. A full dinner will cost you around IR£16, but the bar food is more than adequate. They are open for lunch between 12.30 and 2.30 pm and dinner from 7 to 10 pm. For regular pub food try any of the hotels or the *Anchor Bar* which is also worth trying for music.

The hostel at the pier has its own *Old Convent Restaurant* specialising in seafood and with an 'early bird' menu between 4-7 pm.

Getting There & Away
There are four daily buses in summer and three in winter between Waterford City tourist office and Dunmore East. Contact the Suirway Bus & Coach Service (☎ 051-382209) for details.

TRAMORE & AROUND
Tramore is 10 km south of Waterford and the busiest of County Waterford's seaside resorts. An enormous five-km beach is backed with 30-metre-high dunes at the east end. Tramore is a fairly tacky resort, with amusements, a boating lake, bumper cars and lines of fast-food outlets down by the promenade.

There are regular race meetings during the summer with the principal gathering in mid-August. The tourist office (☎ 051-381572), on the square, is open June to mid-September, Monday to Saturday, 10 am to 6 pm.

Things to See
Apart from the beach, Tramore's big visitor attraction is **Celtworld** (☎ 051-386166), in an ultra-modern hall by the amusement arcade, where visitors are 'brought back through the centuries to the arrival of ancient tribes to Ireland'. The IR£3.25 admission pays for a mildly interesting half-hour audio-visual presentation of battles, heroes, sorcerers and monsters based on the work of Jim Fitzpatrick, Ireland's leading exponent of a colourful Celtic artistic style. Celtworld is open from 10 am to 10 pm in the summer and to 5 pm at other times.

Great Newtown Head is plainly visible to the south-west with its standing pillars and the **Iron Man**, a huge painted iron figure of an 18th-century sailor in white breeches and blue jacket with his arm pointing seaward to warn approaching ships. The pillars and the corresponding pair on Brownstown Head opposite, were erected by Lloyds of London in 1816; 360 lives had been lost in a shipping disaster when a boat mistook Tramore Bay for Waterford Harbour and was wrecked on the shore.

Eight km north of Tramore and signposted off the L26 are the two **dolmens** of Knockeen and Gaulstown.

Places to Stay
Camping There are three caravan and camp sites near Tramore. The one with the best facilities is *Newtown Cove Caravan & Camping Site* (☎ 058-381979) on the road to Great Newtown Head and Dungarvan. It's open May to September, and costs IR£8 for a tent or caravan or IR£3 per person for hikers and cyclists. Other sites are *Atlantic View Caravan & Camping* (☎ 051-381610) on the seafront, which charges IR£7, and *Fitzmaurice's Caravan & Camping* (☎ 051-381968), near Atlantic View on the inland side of the road, with similar facilities and charging similar rates.

Hostel *The Monkey Puzzle* hostel (☎ 051-386754) is on Upper Branch Rd, not far from the tourist office. Beds are IR£6 and there are two doubles for IR£17. There are also bikes for hire.

B&Bs *Oban House* (☎ 051-381537), *Oban House* (☎ 051-381537) at the north-east end of town at 1 Eastlands, Pond Rd, overlooks the bay and costs around IR£19/27. *Venezia* (☎ 051-381412) is in a cul-de-sac off Church Grove Rd and costs from IR£18.50/27. *Cliff*

House (☎ 051-381497) on Cliff Rd overlooks the bay and costs around IR£19/27.

Mountain View (☎ 051-396107) is in Fennor, seven km west of Tramore on the Dungarvan road. It's one of the few thatched cottage B&Bs in the country and costs from IR£17/24.

Getting There & Away
Bus Éireann (☎ 051-73401) runs more than 15 buses daily between Waterford City and Tramore.

TRAMORE TO DUNGARVAN
The road between Tramore and Dungarvan, 41 km to the west along the coast, is punctuated with numerous small villages set in tidy coves. The route is surprisingly scenic with plenty of places to stop and enjoy the views. **Annestown, Bunmahon** and the picturesque **Stradbally** come in quick succession along a winding road. The *Cove Bar* in Stradbally has reasonable pub food or there is *Ye Olde Bank Restaurant* five km from Stradbally in Kilmacthomas.

Eight km to the west of Stradbally is the popular Blue Flag beach at **Clonea**, with the *Clonea Strand Hotel* (☎ 058-42416) and its 10-pin bowling alley, leisure centre and Turkish baths. There is also a camping site here, *Casey's* (☎ 058-41919), charging IR£9 for a car and tent but IR£3.50 per person for hikers or cyclists. There is a surfing beach farther west in **Ballinacourty**.

DUNGARVAN
Dungarvan (*Dún Garbhán*) is a small port and market town which grew up in the shelter of an Anglo-Norman castle. Old records suggest that in the 3rd century AD, a tribe called the Decies or Deise settled around here and the surrounding area now bears their name.

Today the fairly modern but nondescript town is the administrative centre for County Waterford and has a lovely setting at the foot of forested hills on the wide bay where the River Colligan meets the sea. Until the river was bridged in the last century the shallow crossing was known as 'Dungarvan's

Prospects'; women had to raise their skirts to wade across and the sight was famous among local men.

Abbeyside (the north-east part of town) was the birthplace of Ernest Walton, whose work on nuclear fission won the Nobel Prize for physics in 1951. The town park is named after him.

Dungarvan is 48 km west of Waterford City and makes a convenient base from which to explore western County Waterford and the Monavullagh, Comeragh and Knockmealdown mountains to the north.

Orientation & Information
The town's central shopping area is centred around the neatly laid out Grattan Square on the south side of the river. Greater Dungarvan consists of Dungarvan Town itself and Abbeyside over the bridge in the north-east part of town.

The tourist office (☎ 058-41741) in the town centre is open from April to the end of August.

Things to See & Do
A Norman construction, **King John's Castle** (1185) by the quays, is not in great condition but is being restored. The **Old Market House** has a small heritage museum (admission free). As you drive out Dungarvan to the west, you'll pass a **monument** to the greyhound Master McGrath which won the Waterloo Cup three times in the 1860s.

Places to Stay
The IHH *Dungarven Holiday Hostel* (☎ 058-44340) is opposite the Garda Station and charges IR£6.50 for a bed and IR£15 for a double.

The friendly *Abbey House* (☎ 058-41669) on Friarswalk, Abbeyside is near the church and costs IR£18/26. *Fáilte House* (☎ 058-43216) overlooks the sea from the Youghal road and costs IR£18/32.

The *Old Rectory* (☎ 058-41394) is just out of town on the Waterford road with rooms around IR£18.50/27. Almost eight km west of Dungarvan on the N25 Youghal road,

Seaview (☎ 058-41583) has sweeping views over Dungarvan and the sea and the rooms cost from IR£18/26.

Lawlor's Hotel (☎ 058-41122) on T F Meagher St is just off Grattan Square. B&B is IR£47/74.

Places to Eat

Dining possibilities are limited but the *Ormond Café* in Grattan Square does good snacks during the day. *An Bialann*, in the square does snacks all day, and *Hayes Hot Bread* on Main St has good coffee, buns and pastries. The *Mill* restaurant and wine bar has good inexpensive pizzas. For pub food *Downey's* on Main St is one of the better places. For a more formal dinner try one of the hotels. For straightforward Chinese dinners and takeaways try *Jumbo's* on the causeway. And for a night's music and good food head out to *Seanachie* restaurant (☎ 058-46285), seven km from town on the Cork Rd.

Entertainment

An Gabha is on Main St and attracts a young crowd. The *Buttery Bar*, in Lawlor's Hotel, is one of the trendiest places in town. *Downey's* in Main St and the *Moorings* on the quay have a good atmosphere at weekends. The *Anchor* on the quay has local bands and traditional Irish music. For a genuine Irish music scene head out to Helvick on the Ring peninsula and the pub *Tigh an Cheoil* or to *Seanachie*, a few km out on the Cork road.

Getting There & Away

Bus Éireann services run to Dublin, Waterford, Killarney and Cork from the stop on Davitt's Quay.

Getting Around

Murphy's Toys & Cycles (☎ 058-41376) is the Raleigh bike dealer on Main St and has bikes for IR£7 a day or IR£30 a week.

AN RINN (RING)

An Rinn or Ring, 12 km to the south of Dungarvan on Helvick Head, is a Gaeltacht

– an Irish speaking area, with its own special heritage and culture – one of the most famous in Ireland. Many an Irish teenager has studied the language in Ring College on the Helvick Head road. The school runs *ceilís*, *seisúns* (sessions) of traditional music and dance, most nights during the summer, and there are also evening seisúns in the bar *Tigh an Cheoil* (☎ 058-46209) in an old cottage in Baile Na nGall on the way to Helvick Head. On the road to Youghal, the *Seanchaí* pub is beside the road in the middle of nowhere and they also have frequent music sessions. *Mooney's* pub in Ring has excellent sessions every night during the summer.

Aisling B&B (☎ 058-46134) is six km from Dungarvan at Gurtnadiha and charges IR£10 per person for B&B. It is closed from 24 July to 14 August. *Failoeán* (☎ 058-46127) overlooks the pier at Helvick Head and charges IR£12 for B&B. *Helvick View* (☎ 058-46297) near Helvick Head is the only other B&B around. All households speak Irish and English.

ARDMORE

South of Helvick Head the coast road veers inland and 23 km later brings you back to the sea at Ardmore. A popular seaside resort with a Blue Flag beach, Ardmore (*Ard Mór*) has a main street of pretty, pastel-coloured buildings. Unfortunately, an ugly sprawl of caravan parks spoils the coastal view to the east. However, don't let this put you off: the town is a nice little place and the beach is lovely.

It is claimed locally that St Declan set up shop here between 350 and 420 AD, well before St Patrick turned up from Britain to convert the heathens. The name of the village comes from *ard mór* or 'great hill'.

Information

There is a locally run tourist office (☎ 024-94444) just off Main St beside the amusement arcade. It's open May to September, seven days a week.

St Declan's Church & Oratory

Above the town on the site of St Declan's

original monastery stand the ruins of St Declan's Church and a fine slender round tower. The 30-metre tower dates from the 12th century, relatively late. Each of its four storeys is marked on the exterior wall by a ring of projecting stones.

The outer west gable wall of the 13th-century church has some stone carvings retrieved from an older 9th-century church and placed here. They show the Archangel Michael weighing souls, the Adoration of the Magi and a clear depiction of the Judgement of Solomon. Inside the church are two Ogham stones.

The little building in the compound is the 8th-century St Declan's Oratory or Beannachán, which predates the tower and cathedral. It was restored in the 18th century and is traditionally said to be the resting place of St Declan. The depression in the floor is due to worshippers removing earth from the grave site – it was supposed to protect from disease.

St Declan's Well

Overlooking the sea, St Declan's Well is beyond the Cliff House Hotel to the south of the town. Pilgrims once washed in this holy well. Beside it are the ruins of the Dysert Church. There's a fine cliff walk leading from the well. At the south end of the beach is **St Declan's Stone**, said to have arrived on the waves from Wales following St Declan. Crawling under it on St Declan's day (24 July) is said to be a cure for rheumatism as well as bringing spiritual benefits.

The ruin on the headland south of the village looks promising, but it's only an 1860s coastguard station.

St Declan's Way

This newly developed 94-km walk, mostly traces an old pilgrimage way from Ardmore to the Rock of Cashel in Tipperary. See the Activities chapter for more details.

Places to Stay & Eat

B&Bs *Byron Lodge* (☎ 024-94157) is a 150-year-old house on the edge of town, with rooms from IR£18.50/27. To get there find

the second thatched cottage on the main street in Ardmore and turn up the road beside it passing through a crossroads. Byron Lodge is up on your right. *Paddy Mac's* pub, on Main St, offers good pub snacks and lunches, with dinner on Sunday only. Beside the pub is the small *Beachcombers Restaurant* which serves snacks, soups and spaghetti for from IR£2 to IR£5. Across the road is the *Cup & Saucer Restaurant* for middle-of-the-road quiche, jacket potatoes and fish & chips.

Hotels The *Cliff House* (☎ 024-94106) is a big, white building on the low cliffs overlooking the bay. Rooms cost IR£22/50. In the village the *Round Tower Hotel* (☎ 024-94494) costs IR£20 B&B.

Getting There & Away

The bus stop is at O'Reilly's pub on Main St. There are three buses daily to Cork and two to Waterford, all year round. During July and August there are three daily buses to Dungarvan and two during the rest of the year. All are Bus Éireann services.

NORTH COUNTY WATERFORD

Some of the most scenic parts of County Waterford are in the north of the county around **Ballymacarbry** (or Ballymacarberry) and into the **Nire Valley** which runs through the heart of the rugged Comeragh Mountains. This area is just south of below Clonmel in County Tipperary.

While not as rugged as the west of Ireland, the mountain scenery has a beauty of its own. Most of the hills are of red sandstone from the Devonian period, some 370 million years ago. They form the easternmost extension of a great mass of this rock which underlies most of the scenery of Cork and Kerry.

The lovely wooded valleys and heathery mountains are good for hill walking and pony trekking. Melody's Riding Stables (☎ 052-36147) in Ballymacarbry have horses for half-day or full-day outings and are open from Easter to October. The Nire Valley area forms part of the Munster Way walking trail from Carrick-on-Suir; for information contact any local tourist office.

Touraneena Heritage Centre (☎ 058-47353), 15 km north of Dungarvan on the R672, has displays of bread and butter-making, home-curing bacon and a working forge showing Irish country life of old. It's open from 10 am to 8 pm from mid-May to October, admission is IR£3/2.50.

Places to Stay & Eat
Hanora's Cottage Guesthouse (☎ 052-36134) in the Nire Valley costs from IR£32/44. Their tearoom-cum-restaurant does excellent snacks and lunches. From the main Dungarvan to Clonmel road (R672), head to Ballymacarbry then turn east off the T27 to Nire Church.

Nire Valley Farmhouse (☎ 052-36149) is just north-west of Ballymacarbry and does B&B at around IR£16/26. Farther north on the same road is *Clonanav Farm* (☎ 052-36141), Ballymacarbry, Nire Valley, charging from IR£18/32. Dinner is IR£12.

Getting There & Away
There is a single bus service to and from Dungarvan on Tuesday and to Clonmel on Friday. Contact Waterford bus station (☎ 051-73401) for details.

WEST COUNTY WATERFORD
The small market town of **Cappoquin** is overlooked by the Knockmealdown Mountains. The River Blackwater takes an abrupt turn southwards near the town and the Black-water Valley to the west is picturesque. There is excellent coarse and game fishing locally and Glenshelane Park, just outside the town, has some lovely forest walks and picnic spots. Salmon-fishing permits are available from the Toby Jug Guesthouse (☎ 058-54317). The Blackwater Valley is also where traces of the earliest Irish peoples have been found – mesolithic microliths or small stone blades from around 9000 years ago.

Cappoquin is 17 km north-west of Dungarvan and is of little note except for **Mt Melleray Cistercian Abbey** (☎ 058-54404) just over six km to the north of town. The

abbey was founded in 1832 by a group of Irish monks who had been expelled from a monastery near Melleray in Brittany, France. A fully functioning monastery, Mt Melleray is open to male and female visitors for quiet reflection or those who just wish to see something of the monks' daily routine. They have a guesthouse and don't charge for a bed, but it would be bad manners not to make a contribution.

Getting There & Away
There are two daily Bus Éireann buses (one on Sunday) on a route between Waterford, Dungarvan, Cappoquin and Lismore.

LISMORE
Lismore (from *lios mór* meaning 'round hill') is a small town, beautifully situated on the River Blackwater at the foot of the Knockmealdown Mountains. The river rolls on south to Youghal and the sea. The fertile Blackwater Valley is where some of the earliest traces of the Stone Age inhabitants of Ireland have been found.

Lismore was the location of a great monastic university first founded by St Cartach or Carthage in the 7th century. In the 8th century, with St Colman at the helm, the monastery became a huge centre of learning. From the 10th century on, it was sacked many times by the Vikings but hung on as the religious capital of Deise (Deices).

Information
Lismore has a seasonal tourist office (☎ 058-54975) in the Lismore Heritage Centre, in the old courthouse in the town centre. It's open from April to the end of October between 10 am and 5 pm weekdays, and between 2 pm and 5.30 pm at the weekends (slightly longer hours in the summer months). You'll also find a bureau de change there.

St Carthage's Cathedral
Up to the 17th century, the remains of eight churches were still to be found locally but today little remains of its former greatness. The striking cathedral (1633) sits among

peaceful gardens. Inside are some noteworthy tombs including a MacGrath family
crypt dating from 1557 as well as the small
chapel of St Colmcille.

Lismore Castle
From the Cappoquin road there are fine
glimpses of the majestic Lismore Castle
overlooking the river. In the 12th century
Henry II came through the area and chose
this site for a castle, which was eventually
erected by Prince John, lord of Ireland, in
1185. The castle was the local bishop's residence until 1589, when it was presented to
Sir Walter Raleigh along with some 200 sq
km of the surrounding countryside.

Raleigh, a famous soldier and favourite of
Queen Elizabeth I, later sold it to the earl of
Cork, Richard Boyle. His 14th child, Robert
Boyle (1627-91), was born here and is cred-
ited with being the first methodical modern
scientist.

Boyle's Law is the principle that the pressure of a gas
varies with its volume at a constant temperature, and
it was a discovery fundamental to modern physics.
Boyle also dabbled in alchemy and established that
air has weight. He was deeply interested in religion
and had the Old Testament printed in Irish, Welsh,
Malay and Turkish.

Lismore Castle passed to the duke of
Devonshire in 1753 and his descendants still
own it today. The present castle mostly dates
from the 19th century, but does incorporate
small sections of the earlier buildings. It was
during the rebuilding that the 15th-century
'Book of Lismore' and the Lismore Crozier
(now in the National Museum, Dublin) were
discovered. The book documents the lives of
a number of Irish saints, but also holds an
account of the voyages of Marco Polo. A
more recent occupant of the castle was Adele
Astaire, sister of Fred Astaire.

The castle is closed to day trippers but can
be rented by the week by seriously rich
groups. The Castle Gardens (☎ 058-54424)
are open from May to September, admission
is IR£2.50.

Lismore Heritage Centre
The Lismore Heritage Centre (☎ 058-
54975) is in the old courthouse in the town
centre. There is an audiovisual presentation
of local history and attractions, legends,
follies and walks along the River Blackwater. It's open April to October and has the
same hours as the tourist office. There are
shows every half hour and admission is
IR£2.50.

Places to Stay & Eat
Kilmorna House Hostel (☎ 058-54315) in
Lismore has beds for IR£6. There is no official camp site nearby but you could ask local
farmers about their fields out of town or near
the castle.

Beechcroft (☎ 058-54273) on Deerpark
Rd, about one km from the town centre, costs
IR£16/28. *Ballyrafter House* (☎ 058-54002)
is one km north of town. They charge
IR28/60 and an excellent dinner is around
IR£18. *Lismore Hotel* (☎ 058-54304) is a
straightforward hotel charging IR£25/50 for
B&B.

The cosy *Celtic Kitchen Café* across from
the Heritage Centre on Main St has good
snacks during the day; it also serves dinner.
Rafters on East Main St above the Roche's
supermarket does middle-of-the-road
lunches and dinners from IR£5 to IR£10.
Rose's West End pub on West St offers soup
and toasted sandwiches. Two pubs with food
and atmosphere are *Eamon's* and *Madden's*.

Getting There & Away
The bus stop is at Rose's West End pub on
Main St. There are two buses daily (one on
Sunday) on the Waterford City-Dungarvan-
Cappoquin-Lismore route, in the morning
and evening. There are more than 10 buses
daily between Lismore and Dungarvan. For
details contact Waterford bus station (☎ 051-
73401).

MUNSTER WAY
This walking trail covers some 80 km
between Carrick-on-Suir in County Tipperary and the northern slopes of the
Knockmealdown Mountains. East of the Vee

Gap the Munster Way crosses a path which marks the ancient roadway Rían Bó Phádraig or 'the track of St Patrick's cow'. This was a highway and pilgrimage route connecting Lismore with Ardfinnan and Cashel. Nearby is a modern memorial to Liam Lynch who was killed during the Irish Civil War in 1922-23.

See the Activities chapter for more information and details of maps and guides.

County Cork

County Cork has everything which makes Ireland so attractive and a case could be made for arriving here before visiting Dublin. The city of Cork (*Corcaigh*) is engagingly small and free of urban stress. The northern part of the county is renowned for fishing while the main tourist trail heads down to Kinsale, the gourmet capital of Ireland, and west through the historic towns of Clonakilty and Skibbereen to the peninsulas jutting out into the Atlantic. These underpopulated extremities of land are rich in history and nature and offer wonderful scenery to accompany the excellent walking, climbing and cycling possibilities. The famous highlight of the county is kissing the Blarney Stone but the pleasures of drifting through West Cork may linger in the mind far longer.

The Coast of West Cork (Appletree Press, Belfast, 1991) was first published in 1977, but it keeps its appeal and makes a useful companion for the historically-minded visitor to the south-west.

Cork City

The Irish Republic's second largest city is a surprisingly appealing place, where it's easy to find a day or two drifting away. By day the city centre buzzes in its own unhurried style and at night the pub scene is very lively. There are places of historic interest to visit.

HISTORY

The town dates back to the 7th century and survived Cromwell's visit but fell to King William in 1690. In the 18th century it was an important commercial centre with a major butter market that shipped its produce across the world. A century later the potato famine turned Cork into a sorry place, where disillusioned and dispossessed Irish folk said farewell to their homeland. The port of Cobh

Highlights

- The scenic route to West Cork from Kinsale through Clonakilty and Skibbereen to the Mizen Head
- Walking and birdwatching on Clear Island
- Walking all or part of the Beara Way which loops the desolate Beara Peninsula
- Climbing Hungry Hill on the Beara Peninsula and relaxing afterwards in a pub in Castletownbere
- The town of Clonakilty and the local historical sights
- Visiting the town of Kinsale, for its picture-postcard charm and gastronomic treats
- Kissing the Blarney Stone to 'gain the privilege of telling lies for seven years'
- The interior of Bantry House for its eclectic collection of art and artifacts from around the world

remained the major departure point for Irish emigrants right up to the 1960s.

Cork played a key role in Ireland's independence struggle. Thomas MacCurtain, a mayor of the city, was killed by the Black & Tans in 1920. His successor, Terence MacSwiney, died in Brixton Prison in London after 75 days on hunger strike. The Black & Tans were at their most unpleasant in Cork and much of the town was burnt down during their reign of terror. As a finale,

County Cork

CORK

The Irish Diaspora

Half of the people born in Ireland since 1820 have emigrated. This astonishing statistic accounts for the estimated 60 million people around the world who can claim to be of Irish origin. The most dramatic and tragic period of emigration occurred as a result of the potato famine of 1845-51 – when more than a million left – but the story of Irish emigration goes back a lot longer than this and still continues, albeit on a smaller scale today.

During 1652-53, Oliver Cromwell expelled somewhere in the region of 30,000 soldiers, and many more thousands of civilians were transported. The West Indies was a favourite destination because once there they could be sold as slaves. Later, after the Treaty of Limerick in 1691, some 20,000 men and their families went to France.

In the 18th century, emigration to North America began, especially from Ulster where Presbyterians were fed up with being treated as second-class citizens. The potato famine accelerated a process that was already well established and, between 1855 and 1914, another four million Irish people left for a new life, mostly heading for the USA and Britain.

Once a man or woman – and women often outnumbered men in their determination to leave – had made the decision to book a transatlantic passage it was understood that there was little likelihood of them ever returning. This gave rise to the 'American Wake' when the farewell party was recognised as a final parting between the emigrants and their families and friends.

With a contemporary chronic unemployment rate of around 15%, it is not surprising that young Irish men and women continue to emigrate. A lottery allocates precious US visas with the promise of employment and, for many young people, leaving for a short or long spell overseas is considered a natural move. They no longer queue up at ports like Cobh, but they are still following in the footsteps of their forbears.

Today there are approximately 12 million Americans of Irish origin, with the biggest concentration in New York, Boston and Philadelphia. Some of these people still feel their roots strongly, even contributing financially to the military struggle in Northern Ireland. ■

Cork was also a centre for the Civil War that followed independence, and Irish leader Michael Collins was ambushed and killed outside Cork. Today Cork is noted for its friendly rivalry with Dublin; it has always been a pugnacious town with fiercely proud residents.

ORIENTATION

The town centre is an island between two channels of the Lee River. Oliver Plunkett St and the curve of St Patrick's St are the main central roads. The railway station and several hostels are to the north and east of the city, and MacCurtain St is the main thoroughfare here. On the other side of the city, Washington St leads out to Killarney and West Cork with two more hostels along the way. The Shandon area, rising on a hill to the north of the river, is an interesting older area to wander around.

INFORMATION

The tourist office (☎ 021-273251), on Grand Parade near the western end of Oliver Plunkett St, opens from 9 am to 7 pm and from 2 to 5 pm on Sunday in July and August, and from 9 am to 6 pm six days a week in June. Otherwise, it closes at 5.30 pm and for an hour at lunch. Harbour cruises can be booked here. Cars can be rented from the tourist office and the airport. The South Quay Co-Op on Sullivan's Quay and the Triskel Arts Centre have useful notice boards. The GPO is on Oliver Plunkett St.

Bookshops

Waterstone's big bookshop runs between St Patrick's and Paul Sts. Eason on St Patrick's St has a wide, less academic stock, including French newspapers and magazines. In the Paul St area there are a number of smaller bookshops: Connolly's, next to the shopping centre in Paul St, has a second-hand selection, the Mercier Press have their shop in French Church St, and the Collins Bookshop in Carey's Lane is also good. The Shelf is a useful second-hand bookshop on George's Quay.

Laundry
There's a laundrette at 14 MacCurtain St across from the big Isaac's Hostel, or you could try the College Laundrette on Western Rd opposite the gates of the University College of Cork.

Camping Equipment
The Tent Shop in Rutland St off South Terrace (☎ 021-965582) hires out equipment, while the Scout Shop near Isaac's on MacCurtain St sells cheaper equipment but doesn't hire it out. Around the corner from Isaac's, in York St, Tents & Leisure sells and hires out tents.

Parking
Parking coupons, obtainable at newsagents, should be displayed inside the car window and are needed to park virtually anywhere in the city centre. Alternatively, use the big car

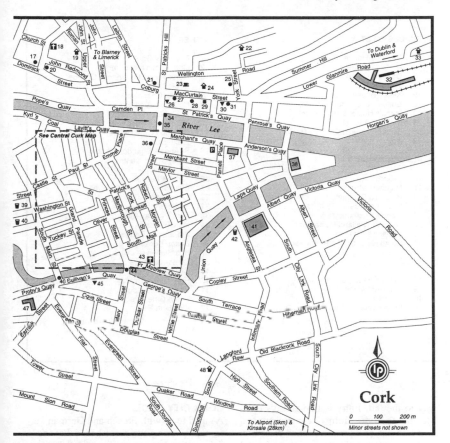

Cork

0   100   200 m

Minor streets not shown

park behind the Merchant Quay shopping centre, or park for free in the Shandon area.

ST FINBARR'S CATHEDRAL

The foundations for this imposing Protestant cathedral were laid in 1865 and construction was completed in 1879. The cathedral was designed by the Victorian architect William Burges, who was also responsible for the restoration of Cardiff Castle and the design of Castell Coch near Cardiff. Two earlier cathedrals stood on the site; one was damaged in the siege of Cork in 1690, and its replacement, built from 1735, was super-

seded by the present construction. Nearby are the fragmentary remains of the 17th-century Elizabeth Fort.

CORK PUBLIC MUSEUM

The ground floor is mostly given over to the nationalist struggle, in which Cork played an important role, while the 1st floor has displays on ancient metallurgy and fossils. Temporary exhibitions are often worth the visit alone. The museum is in Fitzgerald Park behind Western Rd. Bus No 8 stops at the main gates of the university; on the other side of the road there is a brown sign pointing the

PLACES TO STAY

3	Campus House Hostel
4	An Óige Hostel
5	Castlewhite Apartments
14	Jury's Hotel
19	Kinlay House Shandon Hostel
22	Sheila's Cork Tourist Hostel
24	Isaac's Hostel & Restaurant
29	Metropole Hotel
33	Cork International Tourist Hostel
48	Kelly's Hostel

PLACES TO EAT

10	Clifford's Restaurant
11	Michael's Bistro
13	Paradiso Restaurant
23	O'Briens Café
24	Isaac's Restaurant
26	Taste of Thailand Restaurant
30	Luciano's Pizzeria
45	South Quay Co-Op Restaurant

PUBS

12	Reidy's Vault Bar
39	Washington Inn
40	Reardens
42	Lobby, Charlie's, An Phoenix, Donkey's Ears

OTHER

1	Cork City Gaol
2	Cork Public Museum
6	North Wing of University College
7	Boole Library
8	Honan Chapel
9	College Laundrette
15	St Finbarr's Cathedral
16	North Gate Bridge
17	Shandon Craft Centre/Cork Butter Exchange
18	St Anne's Shandon Church
20	Firkin Crane Centre
21	City Limits
25	Tents & Leisure
27	Everyman Palace Theatre
28	Laundrette
31	Scout Shop
32	Kent Railway Station
34	Irish Ferries
35	St Patrick's Bridge
36	Eason Bookshop
37	Bus Station
38	Customs House
41	City Hall
43	Holy Trinity Church
44	Parliament Bridge
46	South Gate Bridge
47	Elizabeth Fort

way to the left. Entry is free and it's open Monday to Friday from 11 am to 1 pm and 2.15 to 5 pm, to 6 pm in summer, closed on Saturday but open Sunday afternoon from 3 to 5 pm.

ST ANNE'S CHURCH, SHANDON
Open from 10 am to 5 pm, the church tower has two walls faced with limestone and two with sandstone. The weathervane in the shape of a salmon was chosen because, it seems, the monks of the city reserved for themselves the right to fish salmon in the river. There is a charge of IR£1.50 for viewing the church, climbing the tower and ringing its famous bells. It costs IR£1 to just view the church interior and its small collection of 17th-century books that includes the letters of John Donne.

CORK CITY GAOL
A taped tour (with French and German versions) covering the furnished cells and a culminating audiovisual display tell the story of this 19th-century prison. Open from 9.30 am, the last tour is at 5 pm and costs IR£3/2. There's also a shop and refreshment area. The gaol is on Sunday's Well Rd, west of the city, over half an hour's walk. Enquire at the tourist office about a bus service departing for the gaol from outside the tourist office; it costs IR£1 return. A taxi costs IR£2.50.

WALKING TOURS
South & West
This tour begins not far from the tourist office and ends at the Cork Public Museum, from where it is a short walk back to the town centre. On Grand Parade between Oliver

Plunkett St and Washington St, is the small Bishop Lucey Park on the Washington St side. Go through the park (if closed, use the alleyway by the side) to the old church in the right end corner. The church now houses the Cork Archive Centre and adjoining is the **Triskel Arts Centre** – an important venue for films, theatre and the like.

Going to the left down South Main St, the Tudor-style Beamish & Crawford brewery is not easily missed. Opposite, the An Cuileg pub is on the corner of Tuckey St. Go down Tuckey St where, at the end on the left, a bollard bears testimony to the days when Grand Parade was an open canal and boats moored by the quayside. Turn to the right and follow Grand Parade past the 18th-century bow-fronted houses, passing on your left an ornate **nationalist monument**. As you continue around to the South Mall there is a smaller monument on the right, just past the public toilets, to the victims of the Hiroshima and Nagasaki atomic bombs.

Down South Mall the **Imperial Hotel** comes into view on the left. The hotel, dating back to 1816, was where Michael Collins, commander-in-chief of the army of the Irish Free State, slept the night before setting out for a journey that would end in ambush and death on 22 August 1922. On the night he arrived at the Imperial the two sentries in the lobby were asleep and Collins literally knocked their heads together out of irritation.

At the end of South Mall the **City Hall** looms across the river. In 1963 President John F Kennedy visited Ireland and gave an address from the steps of City Hall. He had returned as a conquering hero to the land his great-grandfather had left, and the crowd in Cork was the biggest ever to gather in the city.

From the bridge at low tide, cormorants can be seen diving for fish. Across the bridge four pubs come into view on Union Quay, all music venues. Union Quay leads on to George's Quay with **Holy Trinity Church** on the right across the river. On the other side of the road is a colourful display mounted on the wall outside Fitzpatrick's second-hand shop; unfortunately what is on display inside is nowhere near as interesting.

The next bridge on the right is the single-arched **Parliament Bridge** that was built in 1806 to commemorate the Act of Union which six years earlier had seen the end of the Irish parliament and the dispatch of its members to Westminster in London. The next bridge is the **South Gate Bridge** of 1713, which marks the site of the medieval entrance to the city. Bishop St and **St Finbarr's Cathedral** are straight on.

From the cathedral it is a short walk west to **University College Cork** where, in the corridor of the quadrangle building that faces Western Rd, there is a collection of Ogham stones. They are in the corridor of the north wing, which is the one with a tower, directly behind you as you face the main entrance to the Boole Library.

If you face the front of the Boole Library and walk to the left, the Department of Plant Science comes into view; behind this building is the **Honan Chapel**. This small chapel was built in 1915 and is well worth a visit. The stained-glass windows and modernistic use of Celtic designs are intriguing.

Go back to the quadrangle and follow the pathway through the north wing by the tower. Follow the road down to the main gate. As you come out at the main gates the **Cork Public Museum** is close by, on the other side of the road and to the left behind Western Rd in Fitzgerald Park. After visiting the museum, head back to the city along Mardyke Walk, which becomes Dyke Parade, turning right in Mardyke St at the corner with Clifford's restaurant. Then turn left onto Lancaster Quay, which becomes Washington St, before reaching Grand Parade.

North

This circular tour begins and ends at the corner of St Patrick's St and Grand Parade, outside the Queen's Old Castle shopping centre (named after a guard tower on the medieval city walls).

From the shopping centre follow the bend of St Patrick's St (the street was built over a branch of the river). On the left a sign points to the Church of St Peter & St Paul. The street

CORK

River Lee

Coal Quay

Lavitt's Quay

Merchant's Quay

Kyle Street

St Pauls Avenue

Corn Market Street

Castle Street

South Main Street

Washington Street

Grand Parade

Tuckey Street

South Main Street

Paul Street

French Church Street

Academy Street

Careys Lane

Emmet Place

Faulkners Lane

Bowling Green Street

William Street

Drawbridge Street

St Patrick's Street

Merchant Street

Maylor Street

Caroline Street

Winthrop Street

St Patrick's

Cork Street

Robert Street

Oliver Plunkett Street

Phoenix Street

Pembroke Street

Cork Street

Morgan Street

Marlborough Road

Princes Street

Marlborough Road

Oliver Plunkett Street

Princes Street

South Mall

Central Cork

0   50   100 m

ends at St Patrick's Bridge with St Patrick's Quay on the other side to the right. The quayside was once crowded with foreign ships loading up with salted butter, but these days there's only the occasional vessel to be seen.

Cross the three-arched bridge and turn to the left along Camden Place with its late 18th-century Georgian houses. Follow the road round to the right, and then take Dominick St to the left. Once the commercial heart of Cork, this area is now run down, despite the expensive Shandon Craft Centre in what was once the Cork Butter Exchange. The round building nearby, the Firkin Crane building, housed the weighing scales for the butter-casks (firkins) and is now home to a theatre group. At the corner with Church St there is no mistaking St Anne's Church with the famous Shandon Steeple.

Head down Church St and turn left into Shandon St which heads down to the North Gate Bridge. Across the bridge is the beginning of North Main St, looking decidedly shabby. Towards the end of North Main St, on the left, is the back of the Queen's Old Castle shopping centre.

CORK

PLACES TO STAY

29   Imperial Hotel

PLACES TO EAT

3   Bully's Restaurant
5   The Ginger Bread House Café
6   Singapore Gourmet Restaurant
7   Pierre's Restaurant
8   Paddy Garibaldi's Restaurant
9   Thyme Out Café
11 Café Mexicana
14 China Gold Restaurant
15 Oyster Tavern Pub Restaurant
17 Pomodoro Restaurant
19 O'Briens Café
20 English Market
21 Bewley's Café
22 The Long Valley
26 Twomey's Bakery
27 Ivory Tower Restaurant
28 Halpin's Café

PUBS

25 Mollies
30 An Spailpín Fánach Pub

OTHER

1   Cork Opera House
2   Crawford Art Gallery
4   Aer Lingus Office
10 Church of St Peter & St Paul
12 Waterstone's Bookshop
13 Queen's Old Castle Shopping Centre
16 USIT Travel Office
18 Triskel Arts Centre
23 GPO
24 Bishop Lucey Park
31 Beamish & Crawford Brewery
32 Tourist Office
33 Cork to Swansea Ferry
34 Nationalist Monument

Walk through the centre to get back to your starting point.

ORGANISED TOURS

The tourist office organises free walking tours in summer, each Tuesday and Thursday at 7.30 pm. There are also walking tours of the university at 2.30 pm, Monday to Friday, which start at the main gates on Western Rd and cost IR£2/75p.

Cycle tours are handled by Rothar (☎ 021-274143) to Blarney and Cobh for IR£15 and East Cork for IR£20, departing from St Finbarr's at 10 am (Sunday 11 am).

FESTIVALS

The Cork International Jazz Festival takes place in late October and there's an International Film Festival three to four weeks earlier. Tickets for both can sell out quickly, and programmes are available from the Cork Opera House, Emmett Place (☎ 021-270022). A Choral Festival takes place towards the end of May and the International Folk Dance Festival takes place in September in Cobh. The Cork Youth Arts Festival takes place at the end of June; details are available from the Triskel Arts Centre.

PLACES TO STAY
Camping

The *Cork City Caravan & Camping Park* (☎ 021-961866) is on Togher Rd quite close to the centre. It is signposted from the Wilton/city hospital roundabout on the main road to West Cork, and bus No 14 from the centre stops outside. The site is conveniently close both to the Wilton shopping centre and the city. *Bienvenue Caravan & Camping Park* (☎ 021-312711) is on a slip road opposite the entrance to Cork Airport on the R600.

Hostels

The competition between hostels in Cork is fierce. At 48 MacCurtain St, quite close to the centre, IHH *Isaac's* (☎ 021-500011) is popular. A bed costs IR£5.70 in the big dorms, IR£7.50 in the smaller three to seven-bed dorms, IR£31 for private doubles, and IR£17.25 for a single. A light breakfast is included except for the cheapest beds. There's a cafeteria and bicycle hire, but the dorms are closed from 11 am to 5 pm.

Almost as central is *Kinlay House Shandon* (☎ 021-508966) at Bob & Joan Walk in the old Shandon district just north of the river, immediately behind St Anne's Church, Shandon. Dorm beds in rooms for four cost IR£7, twin rooms are IR£21 or

CORK

singles are IR£15, all including a light breakfast. It's a friendly and well-run place.

Beyond Isaac's, towards the railway station and back from MacCurtain St on Belgrave Place, Wellington Rd is *Sheila's Cork Tourist Hotel* (☎ 021-505562) which is neat, clean, tidy and very well equipped. There's even a sauna! Dorm beds are IR£6, private doubles IR£18. They rent bicycles.

The *Cork International Tourist Hostel* (☎ 021-509089) at 100 Lower Glanmire Rd is just beyond the railway station and is small, friendly and engagingly scruffy. The nightly cost is IR£5.

Kellys (☎ 021-315612) at 25 Summerhill South is a new place, south of the river near George's Quay. Beds are from IR£6, there's a laundry, bikes for hire and no afternoon lockout.

On the other side of the centre is the An Óige *Cork International Youth Hostel* (☎ 021-543289) at 1-2 Western Rd. It's a big, well-organised hostel and costs IR£6.50 per night. The rooms are shut between 10 am and 5 pm, although there is access to the sitting room and a small kitchen. There are bikes for rent at IR£7 a day. Take bus No 8 two km out of the centre. *Campus House* (☎ 021-343531) is beyond the An Óige hostel at 3 Woodland View, Western Rd. It's small but tidy and costs IR£6.

B&Bs

Lower Glanmire Rd beyond the railway station is lined with economical B&Bs. *Kent House* (☎ 021-504260) at No 47, *Oakland* (☎ 021-500578) at No 51 and *Tara House* (☎ 021-500294) at No 52 all have singles around IR£18, doubles from IR£28. Tivoli is the area further east with more places, including the 20-bed *Lotamore House* (☎ 021-822344) at IR£30/48.

On the opposite side of town, along Western Rd to West Cork, there are plenty of B&Bs like *St Kilda's* (☎ 021-273095), a big blue house with its own car park out the front, close to the gates of the university. A few doors along is *Antoine House* (☎ 021-273494). Prices range from IR£25/36. If you're coming into Cork from the west, all

these places are on the left after the roundabout at Cork hospital.

Hotels

The biggest in the city is *Jurys* (☎ 021-276622) on the stretch of road between Washington St and Western Rd known as Lancaster Quay. Singles/doubles are IR£90/104, excluding breakfast, and there's a small outdoor swimming pool. The *Imperial* (☎ 021-274040) is more centrally located in South Mall with rooms at IR£75/110.

The *Metropole* (☎ 021-508122) on MacCurtain St, with rooms from IR£45/70, was originally a temperance hotel, a rare institution in Ireland. Its magnificent facade has lasted well.

Good value, especially for families, are two hotels with a fixed room rate for up to three adults or parents and two children. *Jurys Inn* (☎ 021-276444) is in the centre on Anderson's Quay, at IR£45, while *Forte Travelodge* (☎ 021-310722) is near the airport at the Kinsale Rd roundabout, at IR£32. Breakfast is not included but inexpensive restaurants are attached.

PLACES TO EAT
Cafés & Takeaways

The *Farmgate Café* has a gallery setting in the English Market, an indoor food market accessed opposite Bishop Lucy Park on Grand Parade. Alternatively, buy some West Cork cheese from the shop downstairs and fresh bread from *Twomey's* around the corner in Oliver Plunkett St, and head over the road to the park for a picnic.

There are numerous other places around Oliver Plunkett St and the pedestrian-only streets connecting it with St Patrick's St, including several fast-food places. *Bewley's* on Cork St is a popular café, an offshoot of Bewley's in Dublin. *Halpin's* at 14-15 Cork St is similar in style with deli and restaurant.

Try *O'Briens* for tea, scones, sandwiches and good home-made ice cream. There's one on Washington St, near the tourist office and town centre, and one at 39 MacCurtain St near Isaac's and other hostels. If you're out at the museum try the pleasant little *Tea*

Room which has good-value sandwiches and meals for under IR£5.

Between St Patrick's St and the pedestrian area of Paul St are several narrow lanes with good places for a sandwich or meal. Try the *Ginger Bread House* or *Thyme Out* on French Church St for lunch or a coffee or tea. The *Crawford Gallery Restaurant* in Emmet Place offers very good food at reasonable prices. The café at the *Triskel Arts Centre* is also worth a visit.

Reidy's Vault Bar, opposite Jurey's Hotel on Western Rd, is a comfortable pub serving seafood all day in the IR£5-10 range. *The Long Valley* on Winthrop St near the post office is famous for its giant, lunch time sandwiches.

Restaurants

In the pedestrian area between St Patrick's and Paul Sts, *Bully's* at 40 Paul St is a reasonably priced restaurant with pizza and pasta; French Church St has *Pierre's*, a new place offering French-style food with a IR£9 set meal between 6 and 7 pm, Monday to Saturday; a block away in Carey's Lane there's *Café Mexicana* and *Paddy Garibaldi's* (yes it's Irish-Italian). Next door the grandly-named *Singapore Gourmet Restaurant* serves Chinese and Malay dishes for under IR£10.

Gino's at 7 Winthrop St off Oliver Plunkett and *Luciano's* on MacCurtain St are two good pizzerias. *Pomodoro* is a comfortable little mock-Italian place in Cork St with dishes around IR£6.

For vegetarians, *Paradiso* (☎ 021-277939), opposite Jury's Hotel on Western Rd, has an attractive menu. Lunch, around IR£5, is busy with nearby university folk; dinner starts around IR£8. The *South Quay Co-Op*, upstairs at 24 Sullivan's Quay, is well-established and has IR£4 lunch specials and main dishes in the evening for IR£6.

Isaac's Restaurant, not run by the hostel on MacCurtain St where it's located, is popular at night with meals around IR£12 a head. *Taste of Thailand*, just across St Patrick's bridge, has a three-course dinner before 7.30 pm for IR£10.

The *Oyster Tavern* is in Market Lane, an alleyway near Burger King on St Patrick's St. The pub merges into a restaurant with a set dinner around IR£25, lunch IR£10, and bar food is available. There are a few fancy Chinese restaurants on St Patrick's St: *China Gold* is typical, with a set meal for two at IR£27.

The *Ivory Tower* (☎ 021-274665) is at 35 Princes St and serves interesting world food meals, with seafood and vegetarian dishes always available. A set dinner with wine is about IR£25 but lunch, around IR£6, is better value.

Jury's Hotel on Western Rd has two restaurants: the *Glandore* is open all day and costs around IR£19 per head, while the *Fastnet* is open evenings only and is more expensive. Dinner in *Clouds* at the Imperial Hotel or the *Riverview* at the Metropole could be enjoyed for around IR£16.

There are a few non-hotel restaurants offering fine dining and alternatives to the traditional Irish menu. *Clifford's* (☎ 021-275333) on Dyke Parade across from Jury's is highly regarded and, around the corner in Mardyke St, *Michael's Bistro* has the same owner chef but less expensive meals: IR£5 for lunch, dinner dishes from IR£7, open Tuesday to Saturday. Two others are in the suburbs: *Arbutus Lodge* (☎ 021-501237) is west of town in Montenotte while *Lovetts* (☎ 021-294909) is south in Douglas. Reservations are necessary and you can expect to pay at least IR£25 per person.

ENTERTAINMENT
Pubs

Cork's cultural rivalry with Dublin extends to drink. A pint of Murphy's is the stout of choice here, or a Beamish, which is often cheaper. On Union Quay from the corner of Anglesea St, the *Lobby*, *Charlie's*, *An Phoenix* and the *Donkey's Ears* are all side by side, and virtually every night one or other will have music. Check their notice boards.

The *An Spailpín Fánach* on South Main St, which according to the tourist-board pub guide is 'probably the oldest pub in Ireland', has a little loft bar which is easily missed. To the south, at 48 Barrack St, the arty *Nancy Spain's* has good music. *Mollies*, in Tuckey St, has stand-up comedians every Tuesday from about 10 pm, no cover charge. On Coburg St, *City Limits*, next to a small hotel, also has comedy routines on Friday and Saturday.

In Washington St there is a cluster of popular student pubs with music; two of them are near the imposing Court Building – the *Washington Inn* and *Reardens*. The *Half Moon Club* is at the Cork Opera House and has live music Thursday to Saturday.

Theatres & Galleries

Cork prides itself on its cultural pursuits. The mainstream theatre is the *Cork Opera House* (☎ 021-270022) in Emmet Place, but the *Triskel Arts Centre* (☎ 021-272022) is more adventurous. The centre is off South Main St and its notice board advertises all artistic events in the city. The *Everyman Palace* (☎ 501673) is also in MacCurtain St. The *Crawford Art Gallery*, in Emmet Place, is worth a visit and has no admission charge. The *Firkin Crane Centre* (☎ 021-507487) has mid-week sessions of traditional dance and song in the summer.

GETTING THERE & AWAY

USIT (☎ 021-270900) is hidden away at 10-11 Market Parade, an arcade off St Patrick's St near the Grand Parade junction.

Air

Cork Airport has direct flights to Dublin, London, Manchester, Exeter, Jersey, Paris, Rennes and Amsterdam. Other overseas flights go via Dublin. For flight information call ☎ 021-313131 or contact the Aer Lingus office in Academy St (☎ 021-274331). The airport is about eight km south of the city centre on the South City Link Road and takes about 20 minutes to reach by car.

Ferry

There are ferry connections with the UK and France. The Cork to Swansea Ferry has an office at 52 South Mall (☎ 021-271166), and an office at the ferry terminal (☎ 021-

378036) which is open for arrivals and departures only. The return fare in July for a car and passengers ranges from IR£230 (mid-week) to IR£370 (weekend). Before the end of May, fares are around IR£190. The single non-motorist fare ranges from IR£20 before 25 May to IR£27 in August. The ferry does not operate in February.

Brittany Ferries (☎ 021-277801) has an office next to the tourist office; their services to Roscoff (March-October) and St Malo (April-September) cost IR£439 return, high season, IR£141 for a non-motorist.

Irish Ferries (☎ 021-504333) has an office at 9 Bridge St, at the corner of St Patrick's Quay, and operates services to Le Havre, Cherbourg and Roscoff. The July return fare for a vehicle and two passengers ranges from IR£300 to IR£355; single non-motorist fare is IR£67.

The ferry terminal is at Ringaskiddy, about 15 minutes by car from the city centre.

Bus

The bus station (☎ 021-508188) is on the corner of Merchant's Quay and Parnell Place on the central island. You can get to almost anywhere in Ireland from Cork: Dublin, 4½ hours, four daily, IR£12; Killarney, two hours, five daily, IR£8.50; and Wexford, 3½ hours, two daily, IR£12.

Train

The Kent Railway Station (☎ 021-506766) is across the river on Lower Glanmire Rd. There is a direct train connection to Dublin, 2½ hours, eight daily, IR£33; and indirect routes to other towns such as Killarney, two hours, four daily, IR£13.50; and Waterford, 3½ to five hours, four daily, IR£17.

Hitching

Lower Glanmire Rd, beyond the railway station, is not only lined with cheap B&Bs, it's also often lined with hitchhikers, heading out of town to Dublin.

GETTING AROUND
To/From the Airport

A bus operates regularly between the airport

and the bus station (☎ 021-508188), all week.

Bicycle Rental
A number of the hostels rent bicycles at around IR£7.

Two places handle the Raleigh Rent-a-Bike scheme: Cycle Scene (☎ 021-301183) at 396 Blarney St, and the Cycle Repair Centre (☎ 021-276255) at 6/7 Kyle St. If you hire a bike in Limerick at Emerald's Cycles you can drop it off at the Cycle Repair Centre, and vice versa.

Around Cork

BLARNEY CASTLE
Even the most untouristy visitor will probably feel compelled to kiss the Blarney Stone and get the gift of the gab or, as an 18th-century French consul put it, 'gain the privilege of telling lies for seven years'. It was Queen Elizabeth I who invented the term, due to her exasperation with Lord Blarney's ability to talk endlessly without ever actually agreeing to her demands. Bending over backwards to kiss the sacred rock requires a head for heights. The castle itself, a tower house, dates from 1446 and is built on solid limestone.

The castle is open Monday to Saturday from 9 am to 6.30 or 7 pm, or to sundown. Sunday it's open 9.30 am to 5.30 pm or sundown. Entry is IR£3/2. Your enjoyment of a visit to Blarney (*An Bhlarna*) will probably be in inverse relation to the number of coach tours there at the time. Getting there at opening time is one way of beating the crowds.

The adjacent **Blarney House** is open noon to 6 pm from Monday to Saturday, from June to mid-September. It is a late 19th-century baronial house full of Victorian trappings and chandeliers made of Waterford glass. Entry is IR£2.50/1 but a combined castle and house ticket saves 50p.

The **Blarney Woollen Mills** is a giant tourist shop in Blarney village selling every-thing from quality garments to tacky green telephones in the shape of Ireland accompanied by a 'no blarney' guarantee.

Places to Stay
Accommodation is not in short supply and the tourist office (☎ 021-381624), which has a left luggage room, will make bookings.

Camping & Hostel The *Blarney Caravan & Camping Park* (☎ 021-385167) is 2.5 km from town on the R617 and is signposted in Blarney. A couple of km outside of Blarney on the road west to Killarney   there is an unaffiliated hostel (☎ 021-385580) with IR£5 beds and IR£14 for a private double.

B&Bs Blarney has a host of B&Bs, most of them only open from April or May to October or November. Three exceptions, which are open all year, are *Mrs Callaghan* (☎ 021-385035) and *Killarney House* (☎ 021-381841) both on Station Rd and *Knockawn Wood* (☎ 021-870284) at Curraleigh, six km west of Inniscarra.

Hotels There are two big hotels: the *Blarney Park* (☎ 021-385281) and *Christy's* (☎ 021-385011), costing IR£104 and IR£76, respectively, for a double. The Blarney Park has a leisure centre with a pool and a slide.

Places to Eat
The village of Blarney has a number of restaurants and pubs serving food. The *Blarney Stone Restaurant* has food starting at IR£3 and *Mackey's* next door serves meals for around IR£10. Bar food at the *Muskerry Arms* opposite is reasonably priced and at night the pub has a steak and seafood restaurant.

Entertainment
Blair's Inn is six km west of Blarney at Cloghroe but it is worth the trip on a Sunday or Monday when traditional ballad sessions take place. In town itself the *Muskerry Arms* usually has some kind of live music every night of the summer.

Getting There & Away
Blarney is eight km north-west of Cork and buses run regularly from the Cork bus station. There are also private services from some of the hostels.

Getting Around
T McGrath (☎ 021-385658), next to the Blarney Camping Park, has bikes for hire at IR£7 a day.

BALLINCOLLIG
The village of Ballincollig, eight km west of Cork on the main road to Killarney, is home to the Royal Gunpowder Mills. Throughout the 19th century this was one of the largest gunpowder manufacturing plants in Europe. Open from 10 am to 6 pm, admission is IR£2.50/1.50. There's a regular city bus service to the village from the bus station in Cork.

COBH
Cobh (pronounced 'cove') was for many years the port of Cork, and has always had a strong connection with Atlantic crossings. The very first crossing of the Atlantic by a steamship was made from Cobh by the *Sirius* in 1838. The *Titanic* made its last stop here before its fateful Atlantic crossing and it was near Cobh that the *Lusitania* was sunk in 1915. On a more cheerful note, Cobh was home to the world's first yacht club. The Royal Cork Yacht Club was founded here in 1720, but now operates from Crosshaven on the other side of Cork Harbour.

Cobh is actually on Great Island which fills much of Cork Harbour and is joined to the mainland by a causeway. In the British era it was known as Queenstown, because it was the place where Queen Victoria arrived in 1849, on her first visit to Ireland. Today it's a picturesque little port with few reminders of its unhappy history.

St Colman's Cathedral
Cobh is dominated by the massive but comparatively recent St Colman's Cathedral. Construction of the French-Gothic-style cathedral commenced in 1868 but it was not completed until 1915. The Irish communities in Australia and the USA contributed a large part of the construction cost. The cathedral is noted for its 47-bell carillon, the largest in Ireland. The biggest bell weighs in at 3440 kg. St Colman (522-604) is the patron saint of the local diocese of Cloyne.

Lusitania Monument
There's a *Lusitania* monument, depicting two sailors on either side of an angel, by the waterfront of the port. A km north of the town in Clonmel's churchyard there is a communal grave for the bodies retrieved from the sinking.

Cobh Heritage Centre
The Cobh heritage centre has displays on the mass emigrations following the famine, the era of the great liners and the tragedies of the *Titanic* and *Lusitania*. It is at Cobh's old railway station and admission is IR£3.50/2.50. Opening hours are from 10 am to 6 pm, March to October, and there is a craft and coffee shop.

Activities
For sailing activities contact the Sailing Centre (☎ 021-811237) on East Beach. The local riding school (☎ 021-811908) has pony trekking, and Marine Transport (☎ 021-811485) handle harbour cruises.

Festivals
Cobh has an International Folk Dance Festival in July, the Cobh People's Regatta in August and the International Sea Angling Festival in September.

Places to Stay & Eat
Cobh's best B&B is *Westbourne House* (☎ 021-811391) which costs IR£10 and is on the left if you're walking up from the station. If that is full ask their advice or try *Mrs O'Rourke* (☎ 021-812450) at Bellavista in Bishop's Rd, with singles/doubles from IR£20/32.

The *Commodore* (☎ 021-811277) is the premier hotel and features a heated indoor pool. Singles/doubles cost from IR£33/58 in summer. The Commodore is also the most reliable place for a decent meal, with set lunches, bar meals and dinner for IR£19. A couple of cafés in town serve quick meals.

Entertainment
Pub music is never far away in the summer. The *Commodore Hotel* has music on Saturday nights, and other bars like the *Well House* or the *Rotunda* are worth checking out. The oldest bar in town, *Mansworth's* on Midleton St near the cathedral, has music every night of the week in July and August.

Getting There & Away
Cobh is 24 km south-east of Cork, off the main N25 Cork to Rosslare road. There are regular trains and buses and the last bus for Cork leaves at 10.10 pm from outside the post office. Another alternative is to take the small car ferry across Cork Harbour from Glenbrook to Carrigaloe.

FOTA WILDLIFE PARK
Unique in Ireland, the Fota Wildlife Park (☎ 021-812678) is ideal for children of all ages. Giraffes, ostriches, monkeys, kangaroos and penguins wander freely, and lemurs invade the coffee shop. Cheetahs, who can run at nearly 100 km/h, don't have the room to do that here but they are bred and exported to countries like India where they originally came from. Ostriches are also bred. This is not a safari park so cars are left outside and visitors walk around to view the animals. Admission is IR£3.50/2. The car park is another IR£1. It's open from April to October, from 10 am to 5 pm, from 11 am on Sunday.

Getting There & Away
The park is 16 km from Cork, and the Cork to Cobh train stops at the park.

MIDLETON
The Jameson heritage centre whiskey distillery is the only reason to go to Midleton but this alone makes it a worthwhile trip. Whiskey has been distilled here since the early 19th century, and original works were opened to the public after a new distillery was opened in 1975.

Guided tours start with a film show and then a walkabout that covers the whole process, from the storeroom where local farmers had their barley weighed and deposited, to the malting process and on to the milling powered by a superb waterwheel. The original stills remain in position, including the largest one in the world. You will also discover the crucial differences between Irish whiskey and Scotch whisky. This is one of the better heritage places in Ireland for a visitor to get a real sense of the working lives of the people. The tour includes a tipple in the bar, and snacks are available.

Admission is IR£3.50/1.50 and tours are available in French and other languages.

Getting There & Away
A number of buses from Cork stop at Midleton, which is just off the main Cork to Waterford road.

YOUGHAL
Youghal (pronounced 'yawl') is an interesting little town near the border with County Waterford and close to Ardmore, another pleasant coastal resort. In 1588 its mayor was Sir Walter Raleigh and tradition has it that he planted the first potatoes here after bringing them back from the New World.

Orientation & Information
Youghal (*Eochaill*) consists of little more than one north-south main street, appropriately called Main St and carrying one-way traffic for most of its length. If you come through Youghal in the wrong direction (bound from Waterford to Cork) you could easily miss the lot.

The old Clock Gate at the south end of Main St is Youghal's major landmark and nearby is the tourist office (☎ 024-92390) in Market House. Open all year and seven days a week between April and September from 9.30 am to 5.30 pm. The office has a small heritage centre telling the history of the town, charging IR£1.

Youghal's safe beaches stretch away south of town.

Youghal

0   100   200 m

PLACES TO STAY

7   Roseville B&B
24 Hillside B&B
25 Devon View B&B
26 Devonshire Arms Hotel
27 Walter Raleigh Hotel

PLACES TO EAT

1   Aherne's Restaurant
14 Coffee Pot Café
15 Old Well Café

PUBS

4   The Nook
16 Moby Dick's
21 JD's
22 Blackwater Inn

OTHER

2   Bus Depot
3   Myrtle Grove
5   Alms Houses
6   Tynte's Castle
8   Red House
9   St Mary's College
10 St Mary's Church of Ireland
11 Post Office
12 Benedictine Abbey
13 St Mary's Roman Catholic Church
17 Clock Gate
18 Tourist Office
19 Water Gate
20 Challenge Centre
23 Town Hall

Clock Gate

Youghal's landmark is the curious
clocktower which actually bridges Main St.
This was originally the site of the Iron Gate,
a key part of the town's fortifications, but it
was replaced by the present building, a combination of clocktower and jail, in 1777. The
countryside around Youghal was a hotbed of
rural unrest and the new jail soon proved too
small. First of all the jailer's quarters were
moved elsewhere and then an additional
storey was added to the building. Horrific
events took place here with prisoners rou-
tinely tortured, flogged or even hung from

the tower's windows. Steps lead uphill from
the clocktower to Town Wall Rd/Raheen Rd
which runs outside the city walls.

Water Gate

The Water Gate was built in the 13th century
to provide access through the town walls to
the docks. It is still known as Cromwell's
Arch, as this is the place from which Cromwell left Ireland in 1650.

Benedictine Abbey

All that now remains of this 14th-century
abbey is one gable wall with a Gothic doorway

that is easily missed, set into the street with houses either side. Open the door and walk down the narrow passageway which contains the original piscina, a perforated stone basin used for carrying away the water used in rinsing the chalice during a Mass.

Red House & Alms Houses
Continue farther up Main St to Red House which was built in 1706 by a Dutchman and takes its name from its red brickwork. It displays characteristics of Dutch architecture, like the cornerstones positioned under the triangular gable, and a roof in which each face has two slopes, the lower one being steeper than the upper one.

A few doors farther up the street are the Alms Houses, built in 1610 by Richard Boyle, the local lord, to house ex-soldiers.

Tynte's Castle
Across the road from the Alms Houses is Tynte's Castle which dates from the 15th century. It was originally in a defensive riverfront position but the silting up and changing course of the River Blackwater has left it high and dry. About 100 years after it was built the castle was confiscated from its original owners and taken over by Sir Robert Tynte, who married the widow of the poet Edmund Spenser. Today, sadly, the building is decaying.

Myrtle Grove
Scholars dispute whether Sir Walter Raleigh ever lived at Myrtle Grove but that, nevertheless, is the house's chief claim to fame. It was built in the mid-17th century for the warden of nearby St Mary's College. Enquire at the tourist office about possible tours of the house.

St Mary's Church of Ireland
Just uphill from Myrtle Grove is St Mary's Church of Ireland or St Mary's Collegiate Church. A Danish church is said to have stood here in the 11th century, but after its destruction in a storm the present church was built in 1220 incorporating elements of the earlier church. Over the centuries there have been various additions and alterations to the church, not always aesthetically pleasing, but it remains one of the oldest churches in Ireland still in use. Richard Boyle's monument shows himself, his wife and all 16 of his children; those shown lying down died as infants. There is another noted Boyle monument in St Patrick's Cathedral in Dublin. The church also has a 14th-century eight-sided baptismal font and interesting gravestones, some with Norman-French inscriptions.

Town Walls
St Mary's churchyard is bounded by a fine stretch of the old town wall, and by walking up behind the church you can walk along the wall and see one of the remaining turrets. Unless you do a bit of scrambling you'll have to come back the same way. Town Wall Rd running alongside the wall offers a good view of this solid construction and you can continue around the outside of the wall and then take the road and steps down to the Clock Gate.

The walls date back at least to the 15th century although they were strengthened in the following century. They are among the best preserved medieval walls in Ireland.

Activities
The Youghal Challenge Centre (☎ 024-92793) is in Market Square and offers various sport and leisure activities, lasting from half a day to a whole week.

Organised Tours
From May to September walking tours, IR£2.50/1, can be booked from the tourist office. They operate Monday to Saturday at 11 am and 3 pm. Enquire also at the tourist office about river and harbour cruises which, after a change of ownership, may still be running in the afternoons.

Places to Stay
Camping The *Sonas* camp site (☎ 024-98132) is about 15 km to the south, on the sea shore. To get there, take the road off the N25 (west of town) to the village of Ballymacoda, then head west through the

village. The *Summerfield Caravan & Camping Park* (☎ 024-93537) is just over one km west of Youghal off the main Cork road. Both camp sites are open from May to early September.

B&Bs The least expensive accommodation is at *Hillside* (☎ 024-92468), 6 Strand St, on the one-way road leading to Cork. A bed without breakfast is an option here. *Devon View* (☎ 024-92298) is at the Cork end of town, almost opposite the Devonshire Arms, and has singles/doubles from IR£15/27. Coming into town from Waterford, *Roseville* (☎ 024-92571) is in Catherine St near the beginning of the one-way street. Singles/doubles here are IR£18/30.

Hotels The *Devonshire Arms* (☎ 024-92018) is in town, with singles/doubles from IR£30/59. The *Hilltop Hotel* (☎ 024-92911) is out of town in the Cork direction and has more rooms for about the same price. The *Walter Raleigh* (☎ 024-92011), at the Cork end of town, has rooms from IR£20/40.

Places to Eat
The best general menu is to be found at the *Old Well* in the middle of town and the *Coffee Pot* café is next door. The *Cosy Café*, just out of town at the Cork end, is another good-value place serving lunch for IR£4 and dinner for IR£10. The *Devonshire Arms* has a bar menu.

Aherne's (☎ 024-92424), at the Waterford end of town, is an award-winning restaurant/pub famous for its seafood fresh from Youghal Bay or the nearby River Blackwater estuary. Dinner is IR£22.50, and reasonably priced bar food is available throughout the day.

Entertainment
The *Blackwater Inn*, *JD's* and the *Nook* on Main St usually have music. *Moby Dick's* is near the tourist office and has little to recommend it other than being John Huston's port of call during the filming of *Moby Dick* in Youghal in 1954 – the memorabilia on the walls commemorate the fact. The holiday weekend at the end of August is the occasion for Youghal's busking (street music) festival and the pubs are particularly lively at that time.

Getting There & Away
The Tralee to Rosslare bus stops in Youghal connecting the town with Killarney, Cork and Waterford. The Cork to Waterford bus also stops in Youghal.

West Cork

KINSALE
If the Walt Disney team set out to produce a picture-perfect Irish village, they'd end up with Kinsale (*Cionn tSáile*) minus the traffic jams. It is easily reached from Cork by taking the route south to the airport. Partly on account of heavy promotion by Bord Faílte, it attracts more and more visitors each year. An added attraction is its undisputed claim as the gourmet capital of Ireland.

History
As early as the 13th century Kinsale was in the hands of the Anglo-Normans.

In September 1601, a Spanish fleet anchored at Kinsale and was besieged by the English. The Irish army marched the length of the country to attack the English, but were defeated in battle outside Kinsale on Christmas Eve. For the Catholics of Kinsale, the immediate consequence was that they were banned from the town completely, and it was another 100 years before they were allowed to return. Historians now give 1601 as the beginning of the end of Gaelic Ireland.

After 1601 the town developed apace as a ship-building port. In the early 18th century Alexander Selkirk left Kinsale Harbour on a voyage that was to leave him stranded on a desert island for years, providing Daniel Defoe with the idea for *Robinson Crusoe*. Nowadays, the town's nautical tradition is maintained by yacht owners and deep-sea anglers.

Information

The tourist office (☎ 021-772234) is in the centre of town close to where the buses stop. Various tourist-oriented activities start from outside the office. There's a laundrette on Main St.

Museum

There's a small museum in the old courthouse building in Market Square where the enquiry into the sinking of the *Lusitania* in 1915 was held. The most interesting exhibits inside are those dealing with the disaster. Admission is 50/20p.

Charles Fort

Outside Kinsale are the huge ruins of 17th-century Charles Fort, reputedly one of the best preserved star forts in Europe, now an OPW site. It was built in the wake of the events of 1601 and remained in use until 1922 when it was burnt down by anti-Treaty forces of the IRA. Entry is IR£2/1 and it's open 9 am to 6 pm, in summer, closing half an hour earlier on Sunday.

The fort is three km east of town and is signposted in the centre of Kinsale. You can also walk there by following the signposted Scilly Walk.

Desmond Castle

This house on Cork St was built in the 16th century and was occupied by the Spanish in 1601. Since then it has been put to various uses and is now another OPW site. If pressed for time just admire the external masonry, however, the IR£1/40p admission includes a knowledgeable guided tour. It's open from 9 am to 6 pm and closed on Monday before mid-June.

Gourmet Festival

Held annually in early October, this four-day festival is organised by the 12 restaurants that constitute the Good Food Circle of Kinsale. Membership for the four days costs around IR£70 and includes entry to various events and a 10% discount in the restaurants. One-day tickets are also available; details

and booking from Peter Barry, Scilly, Kinsale (☎ 021-774026).

Organised Tours

There are horse-and-carriage tours costing IR£2.50, which take you on a 20-minute jaunt around town with an amusing commentary provided by the chatty driver.

Privately run walking tours also begin from outside the tourist office. Costing IR£3, the tours are available in French, German and Spanish – check the window poster for exact departure times.

Pony trekking tours with guides are run by Ballinadee Stables (☎ 021-778152).

Places to Stay

Camping The official camp site is *Garrettstown House Caravan & Camping Park* (☎ 021-778156) which is 10 km south-west of town near the village of Ballinspittle from where it's signposted.

Hostel The IHH *Dempsey's Hostel* (☎ 021-772124) is a couple of minutes' walk from the centre of town and costs IR£5 a night plus 50p for showers. Two double rooms are IR£12 each.

B&Bs The tourist office has a useful free accommodation list detailing price and amenities at every registered B&B in the town and surrounding area. One of the few less expensive places is *O'Donovan's* (☎ 021-772428), centrally located in Guardwell, at the top end of Main St, and has singles/doubles from IR£14/27.

More characterisic of Kinsale are quality guest houses that have more in common with hotels. *Kieran's Folk House Inn* (☎ 021-772382) is a friendly place, also in Guardwell, and has good rooms from IR£35/50. On Main St itself, *Tierney's Guest House* (☎ 021-772205) has singles/doubles for IR£25/35. Next to the post office in Pearse St the *Old Bank House* (☎ 021-774075) has rooms from IR£40/60 and is under the same ownership as the Vintage restaurant.

All these places can be a little noisy at

Friars Street

🏠 1

Rose Abbey

Fraly Ave

2 🏠

Church St

Cork   Street

Blind Gate

🏠 3

Rampart Lane

4 ▲
5 ▼

Guardwell

6 🏛
Market Square

Newman's   Mall

The   New   Road

7 ■

8 ▲
9 ▲

10 ▲
13 ▼ 14
15 ▼

The   Glen

The

Rampart

11 ▼
17 ▼

12 ▼

16 ■
18 ●
19 ▼

Main

20 ▼
21 ▼

22 ▼

24 ■

Barrack

Hill

23 ▼

25 ▼

Market   Quay

26 ▼

27 ▼

Higher O'Connell St

Street

28 🏠

Emmet Street

Pearse Street

29 ✉

The

31 ℹ

30 ▼

33 ▼
36
37   34 🚲
38 ▼   39 ●

32 ■

35 🚲
40 ■

Ramparts

Winter's Hill

Kinsale

Harbour

Kinsale

0   25   50 m

The Mall

Lower O'Connell Street

St John's

Eastern   Road

To Dempsey's Hostel,
Cork & Airport

Long

Quay

41 ■

The Pier Road

Hill

42 ▼

Dennis Quay

43 ▼

To Trident Hotel,
Millwater House
Guesthouse, Bandon
& West Cork

44 ■
45 ▼
46 ■

River   Road

High

Scilly

Road

To Charles Fort

Kinsale

night. A more sedate atmosphere can be enjoyed at the comfortable *Moorings* (☎ 021-772376), out at Scilly. Rooms are from IR£45/70.

Millwater House (☎ 021-772505) is just over a km from town on the Bandon road and has singles/doubles for IR£20/30.

Hotels First choice for sea views and amenities is the *Trident Hotel* (☎ 021-772301), situated near the harbour, with singles/doubles from IR£61/90 in the summer. A little nearer to town is *Acton's* ☎ 021-772135, with singles/doubles from IR£100

in the summer. At the other end of town in Pearse St is the similarly priced *Blue Haven* ☎ 021-772209. On the same street is the faded *Perryville House* (☎ 021-772731). The huge rooms are ideal for families and cost around IR£45.

Places to Eat

If your budget won't stretch to a meal at one of the dozen or so 'Good Food Circle' restaurants, you can still eat well at many more mundane establishments. Reservations are often advisable so give yourself time to wander around and window shop the menus.

PLACES TO STAY

4   O'Donovan's B&B
7   Kieran's Folk House Inn
16 Tierney's Guest House
24 Blue Haven Hotel
32 Old Bank House
40 Perryville House
41 Acton's Hotel
46 Moorings Guest House

PLACES TO EAT

5   Suki's Restaurant
8   Battered Fish Restaurant
9   Patsy's Corner Café
12 Trotters Restaurant
13 Seasons Restaurant
14 Mother Hubbard's Café
15 White House Restaurant & Pub
19 Wild Geese Restaurant
20 The Shack Restaurant
23 Hoby's Restaurant
24 Blue Haven Restaurant
25 Cottage Loft Restaurant
26 Jim Edwards' Restaurant
27 Copper Grill Restaurant
30 Fisherman Inn Restaurant
33 Vintage Restaurant

36 Max's Wine Bar Restaurant
37 Yello Gallery Café
38 Janey Mac Restaurant
42 Chez Jean-Marc Restaurant
43 Paddy Garibaldi's
45 Man Friday Restaurant

PUBS

10 Greyhound Pub
11 Shanakee
17 An Feadóg
21 Lord Kinsale
22 1601 Pub
44 Spaniard

OTHER

1   St John's Church
2   Desmond Castle
3   St Multose Church
6   Museum
18 Laundry
28 Methodist Church
29 Post Office
31 Tourist Office
34 Deco's Cycles
35 Mylle Murphy, Bike Hire
39 Bus Stop

Bottom End The *Copper Grill*, just down from the Blue Haven in Pearse St, does breakfast and other meals for IR£4-6. The *Wild Geese Restaurant* on Main St is a fraction dearer. *The Shack*, just across the road, serves tasty lasagne and other dishes for under IR£5. The pleasant *Yello Gallery*, at the other end of Main St, is open from breakfast onwards and meals are around IR£7. At the *Battered Fish* on the corner of Guardwell, you can bring your own wine. And if you want to escape from seafood try *Suki's* Asian cuisine on Guardwell, where meals will cost you less than IR£10; it has a takeaway service as well.

A good place for sandwiches and inexpensive meals is *Mother Hubbard's* at the corner of Pearse St or *Patsy's Corner* at Market Square. Tucked away down Lower O'Connell St is *Paddy Garibaldi's* (which has a restaurant in Cork also), serving pizzas and burgers for around IR£5. The upmarket

places that are open during the day serve affordable food at lunch time and *Seasons* near Market Square is worth checking out. Some, like *Max's Wine Bar* (☎ 021-772443) in Main St, have a tourist menu before 8 pm, for around IR£12. *Janey Mac* (☎ 021-774860) on Main St is another wine bar, serving fish dishes in the IR£8-10 range. Less expensive is the *Spinnaker* where dinner costs IR£6-10. It is located at Scilly, a short and pleasant walk in the direction of Fort Charles.

In the centre of Kinsale the *White House* pub (☎ 021-772125) is the oldest in town and the small restaurant is behind the bar. It's rather a functional place but the food is excellent, lunch is good value, and the evening bar menu is worth checking. Other pubs worth a look for a drink and a bite to eat are the *1601* in Pearse St and the old-style *Greyhound* near Market Square.

Another of the Good Food Circle restaurants that is moderately priced is *Jim*

CORK

Edwards' (☎ 021-772541) on Market Quay, probably the best place for a steak in town. The *Fisherman Inn* (☎ 021-772233) on Main St serves dinner dishes for around IR£12, while *Hoby's*, also on Main St, is a small, unpretentious place with a seafood dinner for IR£12.50. *Trotters* (☎ 021-774733), near Market Square, is similarly priced and despite the name serves vegetarian dishes.

Top End Expect to pay at around IR£25 a head for any à la carte dinner at the more expensive places. The *Blue Haven* (☎ 021-772209) pub and restaurant on Pearse St is comfortable. So, too, is the *Vintage Restaurant* (☎ 021-772502) on Main St. A set dinner for IR£16 can be had at the *Cottage Loft* (☎ 021-772803) on Main St.

Man Friday (☎ 021-772260), out at Scilly, is different if only because it isn't rubbing shoulders with other prestigious restaurants. Back in town the *Captain's Table* at Acton's and the *Savannah* at the Trident are both good restaurants. Regarded as one of the best is *Chez Jean-Marc* at the bottom of Lower O'Connell St, where you can have Parisian cuisine with an Irish touch for around IR£25.

Entertainment
Kinsale has a lively pub scene in the summer and music is never difficult to find. The *1601* on Pearse St is always crowded, as are *An Feadóg* and *Lord Kinsale* on Main St and *The Shanakee* around the corner. Just across the road, *Kieran's Folk House Inn* also has a popular bar. Out at Scilly, the *Spaniard* is a cosy pub with character. Nightclubs in town include the *White Lady*, near the Trident hotel on Lower O'Connell St which is popular with younger people. The *Bacchus Brasserie*, attached to Kieran's Folk House Inn, attracts an older crowd.

Getting There & Away
Bus Éireann buses connect Kinsale with Cork three or four times a day. The bus stop is at the Esso garage on The Pier Road near the tourist office.

Getting Around
Bikes, including a few children's ones, can be hired from Mylie Murphy (☎ 021-772703) in Pearse St. There is also *Deco's Cycles* (☎ 021-77884) in Main St. Taxis can be hired locally (☎ 021-772642 or 021-774900).

KINSALE TO CLONAKILTY
Following the quays west out of Kinsale the main R600 road passes through Ballinspittle and Timoleague before joining the main road from Bandon to reach Clonakilty. In Timoleague a detour is possible by going south to Courtmacsherry and continuing on to Clonakilty by way of a small coastal road that goes through Butlerstown.

Ballinspittle
If you've been to Knock in Mayo you'll appreciate knowing that this village narrowly avoided a similar fate. In the summer of 1985 a grotto outside of town with a statue of the Virgin Mary began to attract worshippers after it was reported that the statue had moved. Thousands, and then tens of thousands, of people reported seeing the same phenomenon and Ballinspittle (*Béal Átha an Spidéil*) was on the map. There were similar reports in other parts of the country but the whole thing came to a sudden end. The grotto is by the side of the main road before entering Ballinspittle from the direction of Kinsale.

Timoleague Friary
The friary was probably founded in the 13th century but the buildings date from various periods with alterations still being made in the early 17th century. In 1642 the place was vandalised by the English and all the stained glass was smashed, but the remains are still one of the best preserved Franciscan friaries in Ireland.

The friary is clearly visible from the road approaching Timoleague from Kinsale.

Timoleague Castle Gardens
A moss-covered base is all that remains of the 13th-century castle that once stood here. However, the gardens are attractive and

worth visiting. The palm trees in the two gardens are a reminder of the mild climate, and there is a superb *Callistemon linearis* (bottlebrush) tree. Admission is IR£2/1 from 11 am to 5.30 pm. Follow the signs from the centre of Timoleague village or from the friary.

Places to Stay

Camping *Sexton's* camp site (☎ 023-46347) is signposted off the main road outside of Timoleague on the main road to Clonakilty.

Hostel Outside Timoleague on the right side of the road to Clonakilty, the IHH *Lettercollum House* (☎ 023-46251) was once a convent but is now a hostel and restaurant. There are three doubles and three family rooms from IR£8 per person and dorm beds for IR£6. Bikes can be hired.

B&Bs *Travara Lodge* (☎ 023-46493) in Courtmacsherry is an interesting Georgian house that also opens a restaurant at night. Singles/doubles are from IR£22/36

Hotel The *Courtmacsherry* (☎ 023-46198) has seen better days but it remains a comfortable and friendly place with singles/doubles from IR£26.50/53. There's a self-catering wing and a riding stable attached.

Places to Eat

On the road from Kinsale to Timoleague, the *Pink Elephant* (☎ 023-49608) bar and restaurant cannot easily be missed. Good bar food is available all day, the restaurant opens around 5 pm for high tea and dinner between 7 and 9.30 pm. Prices are reasonable and, compared to some of the Kinsale places, very good value. Also signposted off the main road but on the other side of Timoleague, Lettercollum House has an interesting restaurant that serves easily the best food in the area. Meat and vegetarian à la carte dinners are available and hostellers can enjoy quality meals at affordable prices. In Timoleague village, *Dillon's* pub serves excellent bar food. Dinner at the restaurant in *Traverna Lodge* B&B is IR£14 and mostly features local seafood.

Getting There & Away

The only bus service leaves Cork at 5.45 pm for Timoleague and departs from there, outside Pat Joe's pub, at 8 am bound for Cork.

CLONAKILTY

This small town was founded early in the 17th century by the first earl of Cork who settled it with 100 English families and planned it to be a Protestant town from which Catholics would be excluded. The plan was a failure; Clonakilty is now very Irish and very Catholic – witness the Presbyterian chapel that has been turned into a post office.

From the mid-18th until the mid-19th century the town was a centre for producing linen, employing over 10,000 people. The bakery by the public water pump was once a linen hall, and where the fire station now stands there was a linen market. The town library has been pleasingly converted from a corn mill, which was driven by the nearby river.

Today, Clonakilty is well geared to the tourist market, with a lively pub and music scene and a number of places to visit in the vicinity.

Orientation & Information

The tourist office (☎ 023-33226) is in Asna St but only opens during July and August, between 10 am and 6 pm Monday to Saturday, closing for lunch from 1 to 2 pm. There is a laundry close to O'Donovan's hotel.

Just three km south of town is Inchydoney, one of the best beaches in Cork, but there is a dangerous riptide and when lifeguards are on duty a red warning flag indicates danger. Deep-sea fishing and shore angling is possible at Ring; contact P Houlihan at Blackbird's pub in Connolly St for boat hire.

West Cork Regional Museum

The museum is the best in Cork for material relating to the industrial and social history of the area. It is particularly interesting for its exhibits on the nationalist struggle in the first two decades of this century. It is open from May to October, Monday to Saturday, 10.30

CORK

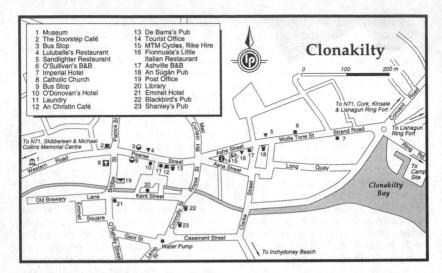

Clonakilty

1 Museum
2 The Doorstep Café
3 Bus Stop
4 Lulubelle's Restaurant
5 Sandlighter Restaurant
6 O'Sullivan's B&B
7 Imperial Hotel
8 Catholic Church
9 Bus Stop
10 O'Donovan's Hotel
11 Laundry
12 An Christin Café
13 De Barra's Pub
14 Tourist Office
15 MTM Cycles, Bike Hire
16 Fionnuala's Little Italian Restaurant
17 Ashville B&B
18 An Súgán Pub
19 Post Office
20 Library
21 Emmet Hotel
22 Blackbird's Pub
23 Shanley's Pub

am to 5.30 pm and 2.30 to 5.30 pm on Sunday. Admission is IR£1/50p.

Horse Riding

The Rosscarbery Riding Centre (☎ 023-48232) is a farm that organises horse trekking. It is 11 km west of Clonakilty on the N71 and is signposted opposite the turn-off for Owinhincha Beach. The Henry Ford Homestead (☎ 023-39117) and the Burgatia Riding Centre (☎ 023-48232) offer similar rates: expect to pay between IR£12-15 for 90 minutes.

Festival

A 10-day festival is held at the beginning of July. Contact the tourist office for details of events. The tourist office will also provide details on a new Model Village and Animal Village, both of which would appeal to children of all ages.

Places to Stay

Camping *Desert House Caravan & Camping Park* (☎ 023-33331) is within walking distance of town on the road to Ring and overlooking the river.

B&Bs *O'Sullivan's* (☎ 023-33011), a town house at 15 Wolfe Tone St, charges from IR£12-15 per person. In Clarke St, *Ashville* (☎ 023-33125) has four doubles for IR£24-26. Within walking distance of town there is *Desert House* (☎ 023-33331), which is also the camp site, on the road to Ring. Singles/doubles start at IR£18.50/27.

For a place with some history, seek out the 17th-century house attached to *Castle Salem* (☎ 023-48381) which is 15 km west of Clonakilty off the main road. B&B is around IR£13; ask for the bed that William Penn (founder of Pennsylvania) slept in.

Hotels The *Imperial* (☎ 023-34185), at the Cork end of Wolfe Tone St, has singles/doubles from IR£16/30. A little more expensive, at IR£17/34, is *O'Donovan's* (☎ 023-33250) in the middle of town on Pearse St. There is also a hotel at the beach, the *Inchydoney* (☎ 023-33143), charging a flat IR£20 per person which drops to IR£15 outside of July and August.

Places to Eat

There is quite a choice and they're all spread along the main street that changes its name four times as it travels through the town.

CORK

Starting at the west end, *The Doorstep* is at the corner of Oliver Plunkett St and Patrick St and includes vegetarian possibilities in its lunch menu. Meals are under IR£5 but it closes at 5.30 pm. Further along in Pearse St, *Lulubelle's* (☎ 023-33801) opens at 7 pm, except Sunday and Monday when it's closed, and offers an interesting mix of Eastern and European dishes. The curries are quite mild and cost IR£8.

Across the road, *O'Donovan's* hotel has a café-style restaurant serving mostly traditional Irish meals during the day. A few doors down, *An Chistin* is a tiny café serving filling sandwiches at lunch time.

Fionnuala's Little Italian Restaurant (☎ 023-34355) on Ashe St serves pizza and pasta from IR£5 for lunch and from IR£8 for dinner. Pub food is not difficult to find and *An Súgán* on Wolfe Tone St is popular for lunch. A set dinner here is IR£19 but there's a tourist dinner for IR£12 before 8 pm. Across the road, the *Sandlighter* has a set dinner for IR£13.50.

Entertainment
Clonakilty has a lively pub scene, especially in July during the festival period. *An Súgán* on Wolfe Tone St and *De Barra's* on Pearse St are crowded at weekends. Other places to try are *Blackbird's* or *Shanley's* in Connolly St. The popular *O'Donovan's* hotel has regular music sessions and the *Emmet* hotel also has musical nights, often attracting well-known bands, and a weekend disco.

Things to Buy
Black pudding, made from the blood of pigs and a common ingredient in the full Irish breakfast, is found throughout Ireland but Clonakilty black pudding is particularly renowned. As such it features on menus in some of the most expensive restaurants in the county, and quite often the source is Twomey's Butchers at 16 Pearse St. The shop has a reputation for making the best black pudding in Cork.

Getting There & Away
From Monday to Saturday the Cork to Killarney bus stops in Clonakilty. It leaves at 10.25 am from outside Spiller's hardware shop in Pearse St, reaching Killarney just after 2 pm. The bus for Cork leaves at 7.10 am and 7.20 pm from outside Blewitt's photography shop, opposite the Bank of Ireland on Pearse St, reaching Cork in 80 minutes. The single fare is IR£5.90.

Getting Around
Bicycles can be hired from MTM Cycles (☎ 023-33584) in Ashe St.

AROUND CLONAKILTY
Cycling Tour
This is a short tour that leads to Castlefreke, just east of Rosscarbery. Take the N71 west, and after five km take the left turn signposted for Rosscarbery, Long Strand, Red Strand and Rathbarry. Continue along this road until reaching a junction that points to Rosscarbery six km and Owenahincha two km. There is a lodge on the right side of the road, the original entrance to the Castlefreke Estate. Follow the road up by the lodge for 600 metres into a car park and ignore the old sign warning against trespassers. The pathway leads to the remains of a castle that was built in 1790 by the Freke family. The story goes that when the last of the line emigrated to Kenya, he stood at the bottom of the stairs and shot out the eyes in a portrait of an early ancestor, before walking out of the house never to return.

The tour can be extended by following the main road down to Inchydoney Beach and then back up to the N71. From there it is a short distance to the causeway at Rosscarbery. A left turn on the other side of the causeway leads to Coppinger's Court and Drombeg Stone Circle. To reach Coppinger's Court follow the road for 1.5 km, ignoring the small turning on the left, and 200 metres after a sign for Vicky's Frames turn left. Cross a bridge and turn right at the T-junction. Coppinger's Court, a four-storey fortified house of the 17th century, is in a field on the right. The house's tall Elizabethan chimneys are extremely well preserved.

The road returns to the main road taken from Rosscarbery and turning left leads to a sign on the left for Drombeg Stone Circle.

The main road carries on to Glandore, which has a small beach, and a bridge over the estuary leads to Union Hall.

Lisnagun Ring Fort

There are over 30,000 ring forts scattered across Ireland, but this is the only one that has been reconstructed in order to give some impression of how they were used. Excavation began in 1987 and the result is a successful restoration of a 10th-century defended farmstead, complete with *souterrain* (an underground chamber) and a central hut that was thatched by someone who spent a month working on it for free in return for his food.

The fort is open daily from 1 to 6 pm; admission is IR£2/1. There is a sign to the fort on the N71 outside of town on the Cork road or, from Clonakilty itself, take a turning at the Fax Bridge roundabout at the end of Strand Rd. The turning is the one between the road to Cork and the road to Ring, but it is only signposted for a local B&B and not the fort. Follow the road for about three km and there is a sign to the right for the fort.

West Cork Heritage Centre

This centre is in the town of Bandon, 20 km to the north-east of Clonakilty and situated on a river of the same name. This was a major Protestant settlement in the 17th century, infamous for excluding Catholics. It bore a notice on the city walls declaring:

> Jew, Turk or atheist
> May enter here, but not a papist.

Under which, so it goes, was scrawled:

> Whoever wrote this wrote it well
> For the same is written in the gates of Hell.

The Centre has various exhibits relating to local life through the ages, the most successful being the recreated country shop and bar. Admission is IR£2.50 and it's open from April to October,

Monday to Saturday from 10 am to 6 pm, and on Sunday from 2 to 6 pm.

Michael Collins Memorial Centre

The centre is a memorial to Michael Collins, who was born here in 1890. The actual old house where he was born and lived for about 10 years is still standing and has been repaired. His family then built a new house where Collins lived until he emigrated to London in 1906. Very little of this home remains for it was burnt down by the Black & Tans in 1921. Despite the meagre remains, the place manages to create an aura of respect for a man who would have been heartbroken at the consequences of the treaty he signed in 1921.

The Memorial Centre is signposted on the N71, five km west of Clonakilty.

Castle Salem

The most surprising aspect of this 15th-century castle is the entrance. In the 17th century a house was built onto one of the three-metre-thick castle walls, and at the top of the house's carpeted staircase an ordinary-looking door opens onto the 1st floor of the castle. There is not that much to see and the castle is slowly crumbling away.

The castle was originally called Benduff Castle. Cromwell confiscated it, and gave it to an English soldier, Major Apollo Morris, who later became a Quaker. He renamed it Shalom, Hebrew for peace, which turned into Salem. An old Quaker churchyard is behind the wall on the right immediately after entering the grounds, and it is said that William Penn visited Morris in the house.

Castle Salem is signposted on the N71, 15 km west of Clonakilty. Entry is IR£2/1.

ROSSCARBERY TO SKIBBEREEN

The main N71 road from Rosscarbery to Skibbereen goes via Leap, but far more interesting is a longer route that begins by turning left at the end of the causeway at Rosscarbery. This travels nearer to the sea and takes in a number of interesting places.

Rosscarbery

This small town, where O'Donovan Rossa,

A	
B	C
D	

County Waterford
A: Red House Inn, Lismore
B: St Carthage's Cathedral, Lismore
C: Rural scene just outside Lismore
D: Lismore Castle

TONY WHEELER

SEAN SHEEHAN

TONY WHEELER

SEAN SHEEHAN

County Cork

Top Left:	Clocktower, Youghal
Top Right:	John J. O'Grady Pub, Clonakilty
Bottom Left:	Old town wall, Youghal
Bottom Right:	An Súgán pub, Clonakilty

Michael Collins

As a young man Michael Collins left Ireland to work as a civil servant in London but returned in 1916, at the age of 26, and took part in the Easter Rising. The experience convinced him that continued armed struggle was the only way to secure independence, and he rose to fame as the leader and organiser of a new type of urban and rural guerilla warfare.

Michael Collins inspired tremendous respect among the Irish and fear among the British, who had offered a high reward for his capture. He became a living legend, not least for the ease with which he evaded arrest at checkpoints.

Collins managed to place infiltrators in various parts of the British civil and military presence in Ireland. On one memorable occasion, he was conducted into the headquarters of the Dublin detective force by a double agent, and spent the night reading secret reports. His 'flying columns' and assassination squads were very successful and helped to drive the British to the negotiating table in 1921.

He did not want to travel to Downing St and negotiate terms and asked that de Valera take his place. De Valera refused, and in London Collins signed a treaty which left the six counties of the North still under British rule. He felt at the time that this was the best deal that could be secured, mainly because he knew military resistance was at breaking point. He prophetically declared, 'I have signed my own death warrant'.

On his return to Ireland, civil war broke out with de Valera heading the anti-Treaty group. Collins was killed in an ambush near Macroom in Cork, five days short of his 31st birthday.

Neil Jordan's film about Michael Collins was filmed in West Cork. ■

founder of the Fenian Movement, was born in 1831, has a 12th-century Romanesque church with an elaborately carved doorway. The town is at the head of a landlocked inlet of Rosscarbery Bay. Turn right, if coming from Clonakilty, at the end of the causeway. The shallow estuary here is wonderful for watching wading birds.

Drombeg Stone Circle

There are scores of stone circles in West Cork but this one, nine metres in diameter and dating to around 100 BC, is one of the best. On the west side is a horizontal stone faced by two stones on the east that are larger than the others in the ring. The axis of these two stones with the recumbent one opposite is aligned to the midwinter sunset.

Nearby is a cooking place with a stone trough where hot stones can bring water to the boil in 15 minutes and keep it hot for hours afterwards.

Travelling from Clonakilty the N71 crosses a causeway at Rosscarbery; at the other end a road is signposted off to the left for Drombeg, Coppinger's Court and B&Bs.

Along this road another sign points to the left which leads to the site.

Glandore

This little fishing village becomes sentient in the summer when well-off boating folk arrive. It would dismay William Thompson (1785-1833) who owned land here and established a commune as a model of his socialist philosophy. Marx refers to him in *Das Kapital*.

Union Hall

Disappointingly there is no union hall in this small village. It was named after the Act of Union in 1801, which abolished the separate Irish parliament. The equally unfortunate Irish name, Brean Traigh, means 'foul beach'. Jonathan Swift came here in 1723 to grieve over the death of his friend Vanessa. Outside Union Hall on the road to Castletownshend is the small **Ceim Hill Museum** (☎ 028-36280) run by Teresa O'Mahony, who practises folk medicine, in her ancient farmhouse. It's recommended for its wonderful mixture of eccentricity and

CORK

genuine artefacts. Admission is IR£2/1 and it's open from 10 am to 7 pm.

Castletownshend

This atypical Irish village developed in the late 17th and early 18th centuries when English families settled here. Edith Somerville and her cousin Violet Martin (whose pen-name was 'Martin Ross') began a literary partnership here, writing their *RM* stories. They are buried in St Barrahane's church which can be reached by turning left at the bottom of the village and climbing the steps.

Places to Stay

Rosscarbery At *Mrs Horrigan's* (☎ 023-48161) in the Post Office House, B&B is a modest IR£11. The *Carbery Arms* (☎ 023-48101) is in the large town square and is a little more expensive.

Glandore The *Meadow Camping Park* (☎ 028-33280) is just outside the village on the road to Rosscarbery. Sites are IR£3 and IR£4. The *Marine Hotel* (☎ 028-33366) attracts anglers. One km from Glandore, *Mrs Mehigan* (☎ 028-33233) does B&B on her Kilfinnan farm, charging from IR£17/28. Across the estuary bridge in Union Hall, *Mr O'Mahony* (no telephone) at Maulicurrane does B&B for IR£11.

Near Leap *Mont Bretia* (☎ 028-33663), seven km from Skibbereen, distinguishes itself in a number of ways. The IR£15 B&B rate includes free use of bicycles, maps and information on cycle/walking routes, and free tea and coffee. An organic kitchen garden provides vegetables, and wholefood evening meals start at IR£6.50; patrons can bring their own drink. It is near Adrigole but they will collect guests from Skibbereen or Leap.

By road from Clonakility, take a right turn signposted for Drinagh off the main road, eight km from Leap and just a couple of km before Skibbereen. After five km look for the Adrigole creamery and take the second left at the fork just past it (signposted for another B&B called Sprucedale). Mont Bretia is up on the left.

Union Hall The IHH *Maria's Schoolhouse* (☎ 028-33002) is a new hostel at Cahergal with beds from IR£7 and doubles from IR£18.

Places to Eat

In Rosscarbery's large square there is a pleasant teashop, *Roisin's*, and *Calnan's* pub just off the square serves inexpensive bar food all day. *Glandore's Marine Hotel* serves bar food at lunch and in the evening. In Castletownsend *Mary Ann's* is an old pub serving local seafood, between IR£5.50 and IR£13, in the bar throughout the day. The pub's restaurant (☎ 028-36146) opens in the evening for a substantial IR£20 dinner.

Getting There & Away

There is no bus service to Glandore or Union Hall, but the Clonakilty to Goleen bus stops in Rosscarbery.

SKIBBEREEN

The market town of Skibbereen should really twin with a town in Algeria, for this West Cork market town owes its existence to the Algerian raiding party which raided nearby Baltimore in 1631. The frightened English settlers moved west and established two settlements which grew into Skibbereen. For a long time the town was associated with its Protestant founders, but during the famine years Skibbereen became known for the sufferings of the local Catholic peasantry. The repercussions were long-lasting: nearly half the area's population emigrated in the first half of the 20th century. Today the town prospers from the weekly market and a steady influx of tourists on the West Cork trail.

Orientation & Information

The town's landmark is the statue dedicated to the heroes of the many Irish rebellions against the British. It stands at the junction of three roads and close to the post office. The road that goes past with the post office on the left leads south to Lough Hyne and Baltimore. The main shopping street, Main St, leads to a junction with Ilen St which

Road Bowling

You are only likely to come across this rare sport on a quiet road on a Sunday afternoon in West Cork or County Armagh in Northern Ireland. It is not played anywhere else in the country. A giveaway sign of a game in progress are small groups of men waiting by the side of the road for your vehicle to pass so that the game can resume. Some distance ahead of the main group will be a smaller group, whose task is to chart the distance that a steel ball has been thrown by the two competing sides. The object of the game – upon which various bets are laid – is to cover a set distance of winding road in as few hurls of the ball as possible. The rules allow for the ball to be lofted over a stretch of field hoping to shortcross a bend in the road. Bets are laid on teams and even individual bowls of the 18-cm 794-gram ball. ■

heads west to Ballydehob and Bantry. North Rd heads towards the main Cork roads and houses the tourist office (☎ 028-21766), which is open all year from 9.15 am to 5.15 pm (often later in the summer) Monday to Saturday.

There is a laundrette on Main St opposite the Eldon Hotel, and another one on Ilen St near the West Cork Hotel, that stays open until 9 pm. There are two small bookshops along North St, one of them selling second-hand books.

Things to See & Do

The weekly **market**, every Wednesday, is worth a visit if only to try and make sense of the machine-gun patter of the auctioneer. Along North Rd, next to the town's church, is the **West Cork Arts Centre**, open from 12.30 pm each day and worth checking out to see what's on. Art exhibitions are hosted regularly and in summer there is often something theatrical or musical in the area. The notice board outside lists useful information regarding local events as does the pleasant library on the opposite side of the road. A few miles out of town, signposted on the road to Baltimore, **Tragumna**, consisting of a pub and a knitwear shop, meets the ocean, and bathing is possible here in fine weather.

Places to Stay

B&Bs The road to Baltimore is lined with places. In town, *Windmill* (☎ 028-21606) at 45 North St is a guesthouse with singles/doubles from IR£16/32.

Hotels The *West Cork Hotel* (☎ 028-21277), opposite the river on Ilen St, is the best at IR£60 a night for two. On Bridge St (the continuation of Main St in the direction of Schull) the *Eldon Hotel* (☎ 028-21300) has a quiet charm and singles/doubles here start at IR£16/32.

Places to Eat

The *Eldon Hotel* has a good bar menu and meals from IR£4 are available until 9 pm. The enterprising *Sables Restaurant* and wine bar is also on Bridge St; lunch is around IR£5 and it opens for dinner. Sables is closed on Sunday.

Also on Bridge St, *Annie May's* pub has above average bar food in the IR£3 to IR£10 price range. For coffee and snacks, try *Ann O'Donovan's* next door, or the *Stove*, by the bridge on Main St, which also serves breakfast all day. *Field's Coffee Shop* is popular with local shoppers.

Restaurant 48, down past the tourist office in North St, is a new French-style establishment serving seafood dinners from 7 pm for IR£12, and you can bring your own wine.

Further down North St, the *Windmill Tavern* has a wide-ranging menu and an IR£11 set dinner. Further down the road again, by the Arts Centre, the similarly-priced *Ivanhoe Wine Bar* is also worth checking out.

Island Cottage (☎ 028-38102) is on Hare Island in Roaring Water Bay. Make a reservation, and arrange transport with John O'Neil (☎ 028-38144) which adds IR£4 per

CORK

person (IR£2 if he's on a mail trip) to the cost of the IR£16 set dinner. It's good value and good fun.

Entertainment

Sean Og's bar in Market St, near the square, has music most weekend nights, as does *Kearney's Well* in North St. *Annie May's* has some interesting musical evenings and the *West Cork Hotel* has a Tuesday cabaret from 4 pm, costing IR£4 per person.

Also worth a visit is the *Stag's Head* at Caheragh on the road to Drimoleague. In the past, when dance halls were unheard of, music and dance sessions were held on a specially surfaced area outside of pubs. The Stag's Head has recreated such a venue and there are regular Sunday afternoon dancing sessions.

Getting There & Away

Bus Éireann information is available from O'Cahalales bar next to the Eldon Hotel on Main St. Buses run daily to Cork, Baltimore, Schull, Drimoleague and Killarney. The bus stop is opposite the Eldon Hotel.

Getting Around

Bicycles can be hired from Roycroft & Son (☎ 028-21235, 21810 after hours) in Ilen St.

LOUGH HYNE

Lough Hyne is a saltwater lake connected to the sea by a narrow channel, and this area is now a nature reserve, with seldom-used small roads. Baltimore could be reached from here. Nearby is **Knockomagh Wood**, an attractive mixture of deciduous and evergreen trees on the right of the road approaching the lough. Lough Hyne is six km due south of Skibbereen, and well signposted from the town statue.

BALTIMORE

Situated 13 km down the River Ilen from Skibbereen, Baltimore has a population of around 200. During the summer months this doubles, with an influx of sailing folk and visitors to Sherkin and Clear islands.

Information

There is a small tourist office at the harbour (☎ 028-20441) which is open from 9.30 am to 5.30 pm, Monday to Saturday, closed between 12.30 and 1.30 pm for lunch. Accommodation on Clear and Sherkin islands can be arranged through this office.

The Algiers Inn (☎ 028-20352) organises sea angling trips, and shorter journeys for mackerel and pollack fishing.

Places to Stay

Rolf's Hostel (☎ 028-20289) has beds for IR£6 and doubles for IR£20. Camping is also possible. The guesthouse *Algiers Inn* (☎ 028-20145) is open all year with beds for IR£15. There are a few B&Bs, *Corner House* (☎ 028-20143) being centrally located, with doubles for IR£32.

Places to Eat

There is a string of restaurants overlooking the harbour. *Harbour Restaurant* has meals for IR£5 to IR£10 and serves breakfast and children's meals. *Chez Youen*, a few doors down, does French-style seafood, with lunch for IR£12.50 and dinner from IR£21 to IR£32.

For light meals try the inexpensive *Lifeboat Restaurant*, open from 9 am to 6 pm. It also manages the post office and a bureau de change. The *Customs House* is a quieter place with a seafood set dinner for IR£15; lunch is IR£8.

Getting There & Away

Buses from Skibbereen travel to Baltimore and back. Check the schedule at the tourist information office in Skibbereen or the information point on the Baltimore pier. Being only 13 km away, it is easily cycled from Skibbereen, and hitching is possible.

A daily summer boat, but not Tuesday or Saturday, runs between Baltimore and Schull (☎ 028-39153) for IR£6. Bikes are free.

CLEAR ISLAND

The boat from Baltimore takes 45 minutes to cover the 11-km journey to this island and it's a stunning trip on a clear day, retracing the route through the harbour that the Algerians took when they launched their attack on the village of Baltimore in 1631.

Clear Island is the most southerly point of Ireland apart from the Fastnet Rock which lies six km to the south-west. It has about 150 Irish-speaking inhabitants, one shop and three pubs. It is a place for country walks and birdwatching; the island is probably the best place in Europe for watching the Manx shearwater and other seabirds.

Orientation & Information

The island is five km long and just over 1.5 km wide at its broadest. It narrows in the middle where the north and south harbours are divided by an isthmus. There is a tourist information post beyond the pier, open from 4 to 6 pm every day in July and August, but if it's closed the useful IR£2 *Walkers' Guide* is available in the nearby coffee shop.

Walking Tour

This is a circular route that takes from one to three hours.

After arriving in North Harbour, turn left at the end of the pier and take the road up the hill, ignoring the path that goes left at the coffee shop with a signpost to the heritage centre. At the shop junction go left across the isthmus; South Harbour soon comes into view. Wild flowers abound on the island; along this stretch of road the hairy birdsfoot trefoil (a yellow pea flower, lying close to the ground and with distinctive hairy leaves) can be found – it only occurs in one other spot in Ireland.

The road leads to the hostel. Turn left just before you reach it and follow the road up past the school and post office. At the T-junction, turn left and head towards the eastern end of the island. There are a couple of turnings on the left that lead down to the sea but there are no beaches to speak of. The lovely sandy beaches in the distance are on Sherkin Island.

Returning to the T-junction, rather than turn left continue straight on to the **heritage centre**. In the summer it is open from 3.30 to 5.30 pm, and it contains exhibits on the history and culture of the island. There are fine views looking north across the water to the Mizen Head Peninsula. From the centre it is a short distance downhill to the shop and pubs.

Birdwatching

The Bird Observatory is a white-fronted two-storey building by the harbour. Turn right at the end of the pier and it's 100 metres along. If you have not booked in to stay here it is still worth calling in and asking about any birdwatching trips that might be planned. Clear Island is famous for its movements of large seabirds, especially in July and August when Manx shearwaters, gannets, fulmars and kittiwakes regularly fly past the south of the island. The guillemot is the only notable seabird that breeds on the island; the others live on the westerly Kerry rocks and fly past the island heading for the Celtic and Irish seas. In the evening they return and the sight is equally amazing; in summer up to 35,000 shearwaters can fly past in an hour, just above the surface of the water.

The best place to view the seabirds is at Blananarragaun, the south-west tip of the island. To reach it from the pier, head up to the shop and turn right, following the sign for the camp site. When the road comes to an end just go due south to the end of the spur of land.

The Bird Observatory has a small library of books but the one to read up beforehand is *The Natural History of Cape Clear Island* edited by Sharrock (London, 1973). The book is no longer in print so only libraries will have copies.

Places to Stay

The camp site (☎ 028-39119) costs IR£2.70 per person and is signposted from the shop. It is open from 1 June to the end of September.

The An Óige *Cape Clear Island Hostel* (☎ 028-39144) costs IR£5.50, is open from Easter until the end of October and is just a short walk from the pier. *The Glen* hostel

028-39121) is open all year and also does B&B. The *Bird Observatory* (no telephone) has limited hostel accommodation; just turn up and see if a bed is available. It's most likely to be full at the beginning of October.

B&B is available at *Cluain Mara* (☎ 028-39153) for IR£15, evening meal IR£10, and is available all year. The house is up behind the last of the three pubs and is signposted.

Places to Eat

Cistin, near the pier, is the only restaurant on the island so consider a picnic. There is one shop near the pier but its stock is limited. The café serves light meals. There are three pubs within staggering distance of each other and at night drinking-up time is generous.

Getting There & Away

The boat office (☎ 028-39119) and the tourist office in Baltimore have boat timetables.

From Baltimore the return cost is IR£7/3.50. There is no extra charge for bikes. From Schull (☎ 028-28138) the return cost is IR£7/IR£2. Boats leave from the pier in Schull during July and August at 10 am, 2.30 and 4.30 pm, and sometimes there's a service in May also.

SHERKIN ISLAND

People tend to visit this small island – it's five km long and about the same wide – for two reasons: the beaches and the two pubs. There are three sandy areas: Trabawn, Cow and Silver strands, all on the far side of the island and reached by road from the pier. All three are safe for swimming and suitable for children. In late August each year a regatta is held and the pubs stay open even longer than usual. The best place for general information is the post office (☎ 028-20181), which is beside the road running across the island from the pier to the beaches.

Places to Stay & Eat

Camping is free; ask permission from the farmer first.

B&Bs on the island includes *Garrison House* (☎ 028-20185), *Island House*

(☎ 028-20314), *Cuina* (☎ 028-20384), the *Jolly Roger Tavern* (☎ 028-20379) and *Buggy's* (☎ 028-20384). These all charge about IR£15 per person.

The two pubs, at Garrison House and the Jolly Roger, both serve bar food. The Jolly Roger is the older of the two and near the remains of the old O'Driscoll Castle; to get to either pub, turn right just before the post office.

Getting There & Away

There is a regular boat service from Baltimore (☎ 028-20125) and the journey takes less than 10 minutes. The boat service runs seven times a day, starting at 10.30 am; the last boat leaves Sherkin at 8.45 pm. The fare is IR£4 return.

The Mizen Head Peninsula

From Skibbereen the road winds west to Ballydehob. Expatriates from Britain and north European countries are scattered across West Cork, and while Kinsale attracts the well-heeled, others such as the less economically advantaged, or blow-ins as they are semi-affectionately called, have discovered the land around Ballydehob. From the town the road goes west to Schull, with Mt Gabriel (407 metres) in view most of the time, easily identified by the two tracking spheres perched on the summit. They are part of an air-and-sea monitoring system, and some years ago the IRA tried to bomb the installation claiming it was part of NATO (Ireland is not a member of NATO). Around 1500 BC the lower slopes of the mountain were extensively mined for copper. The mountain's summit can be reached by road.

From the top of Mt Gabriel, and most high ground on the peninsula, there are views of the Fastnet Lighthouse on a rock 11 km off the coast. The first lighthouse was built there in 1854 and was replaced in 1906 by a sturdier one which is now fully automated.

The next stop west is Goleen, a small village passed through on the way to Crookhaven, Barleycove and Three Castle Head. The end of the peninsula offers history, nature and the best beach in West Cork.

Returning from Mizen Head you can take a coastal road that keeps Dunmanus Bay on the left for most of the way to Durrus. At Durrus one road leads on to Bantry and the other goes out west to the Sheep's Head Peninsula.

BALLYDEHOB

The name of this picturesque village comes from the Irish Beal Atha an dha Chab, meaning 'the ford at the mouth of two rivers'. Coming into the village from the east, look out for the old 12-arched tramway viaduct.

Places to Stay

There is a small but cosy camp site (☎ 028-37232) about 200 metres from the village on the road to Durrus. Charges are IR£2.50 per person. B&B in Ballydehob is available at the *Ballydehob Inn* (☎ 028-37139) from IR£15/26. On the road to Schull, *Lynwood* (☎ 028-37124) has three beds for IR£20/30.

Places to Eat

The *Ballydehob Inn*, on the corner of the road to Durrus, serves bar food and has a restaurant. *Duggan's* is in the centre of the village opposite the garage and is the least expensive place for light meals and takeaways. *Annie's*, a few doors down, does dinner for IR£20. The menu is seafood and steaks. A similar menu can be found at the *Teach Dearg Restaurant* (☎ 028-37282) to the north-east of Ballydehob at Scarteenakilleen, reached by turning right off the road to Bantry.

Getting There & Away

The twice-daily bus between Clonakilty and Schull stops in Ballydehob.

SCHULL

A small village at the foot of Mt Gabriel, Schull in summer is as touristy as anywhere

on the Ring of Kerry. For the best view of its harbour and Fastnet Rock, take the road from Ballydehob to Durrus and Goleen, and turn off for Schull after five km.

Information

A free tourist information booklet, which includes local walks, is available from The Courtyard and other pubs. O'Keeffe's at 48 Main St has a bureau de change.

Mizen Books and Fuschia Books are both on the main street and both sell second-hand books.

The Planetarium

The only planetarium (☎ 028-28552) in the Republic has an eight-metre dome and a video and slide show. In July and August it's open from Tuesday to Saturday from 2 to 5 pm and 7 to 9 pm, with Star Shows at 8 pm on Tuesday, Thursday and Saturday; check the days and times for other months. Admission is IR£1/50p and IR£2.50/1.50 for the Star Show.

At the Goleen end of the village there is a sign pointing the way to the left to the planetarium.

Cycling Tour

This is a circular trip of 31 km. Leave Schull on the road to Goleen but take the left turning signposted 'Coastal Route'. Follow this small road straight across two small junctions and look for an old tower on the left after about five km as the road climbs gently. The main Schull-Goleen road is met at a T-junction. Turn left and after 2.3 km a church is passed on the right and just after this, at Toormore, there is a right turning signposted for Durrus. Ignore this and carry straight on for six km until Goleen is reached after passing a knitwear shop and café. From Goleen you could continue on for another eight km to Crookhaven, or return to Schull on the main R591 road to Toormore and then the R592 back to Schull.

Places to Stay

Hostel & Camping The IHH *Schull Backpackers' Lodge* (☎ 028-28681) is on

Colla Rd, a little before the Planetarium. Beds are IR£6.50, doubles from IR£17 and camping is possible.

B&Bs Two good B&Bs are at opposite ends of the village. Coming in from Ballydehob a sign on the left points the way to *White Castle Cottage* (☎ 028-28528), overlooking Roaring Water Bay and the ruins of a castle. Singles/doubles are from IR£16 to IR£26. More expensive is *Corthna Lodge Country House* (☎ 028-28517), a short distance out of the village and signposted at the Goleen end; its rooms are IR£22/36.

Hotels In Schull the *East End Hotel* (☎ 028-28101) in Main St has singles/doubles ranging from IR£22 to IR£35. *Colla House* (☎ 028-28105), at Colla, is similarly priced.

Places to Eat
The *Courtyard* in Main St is a bar down an alley beside a wholefood shop of the same name with a coffee bar at the back. The coffee bar serves light meals that includes a vegetarian choice, the bar has tasty seafood and is open till 10 pm. To sample some of the locally baked bread with coffee there is nowhere better than *Adele's*, in Main St. At night, except for Tuesday, Adele's also has a good restaurant (☎ 028-28459) with main dishes around IR£8. The largest bar menu is to be found at the *Bunratty Inn* at the Goleen end of the village. The mussels are excellent.

There are two cheese-making farms near Schull; their produce features on village menus, and you can also visit them and buy cheese wholesale. Contact either *Gubbeen House* (☎ 028-28231) or *West Cork Natural Cheeses* (☎ 028-28593) to check they are open and to get directions.

Getting There & Away
Twice a day a bus leaves Clonakilty, at 10.25 am and 7.05 pm, for Schull via Skibbereen and Ballydehob. The bus leaves Schull at 8.05 am and 5.30 pm from near the AIB bank at the Goleen end of the village.

During the summer a boat for Clear Island leaves from the pier. See the Baltimore Getting There & Away section for details of the Schull-Baltimore boat service.

Getting Around
Bicycles can be hired from Cotter's Yard (☎ 028-28165) in Main St, for IR£8 per 24 hours, or from the hostel or the Black Sheep Inn (☎ 028-28203).

WEST OF SCHULL TO MIZEN HEAD
The road west from Schull leads to the small village of Goleen. The surrounding area is, in the words of the local TD (member of parliament), in danger of declining into a land of 'briars, bullocks and bachelors'. From Goleen one road runs out to Mizen Head and the other to Crookhaven.

Crookhaven
The village is built on the far side of a spur of land that runs eastwards enclosing a harbour. The road from Goleen comes down to the north side of the harbour, passing the remains of a once-thriving stone quarry. Crookhaven was once very important as the most westerly harbour along the coast. Mail from America was collected here and the place was a busy port for sailing and fishing ships from all over the world.

Today the village still attracts sailing people and there are a couple of B&Bs, pubs and seafood restaurants.

Barleycove
This is West Cork's most splendid beach, and because a smaller beach nearer the camp site attracts holidaymakers, Barleycove itself is never crowded. It's a great place for children, with long stretches of sand and a safe sandy area where a stream flows down to the sea.

Mizen Head
The Mizen Head Signal Station was completed in 1910, complementing the Fastnet Lighthouse and giving extra protection to Atlantic-bound ships. It is on a small island connected to the mainland by a superb little suspension bridge that gives exciting views of the nearby rock formations. Following complete automation in 1993 it is now open

to the public for IR£2.50/1.50, daily from 11 am to 5 pm in the summer.

For an interesting walk follow the main path beyond the car-park area and pass beneath the concrete arch on the right. Just a little farther on, a path goes up to the right by rough steps, which lead to the top of the cliff and more spectacular views. Head for the old signal house, but keep to the left of it and avoid the cliff edge. A path makes its way around a huge cleft and eventually comes to a sheep fence. The fence can be climbed and the open heath crossed to Three Castle Head. The whole journey to Three Castle Head would take at least an hour and should only be undertaken on a fine dry day when visibility is clear.

Three Castle Head

A prime reason for making the journey to Three Castle Head is to visit the 13th-century castle at the end of the headland. Once a stronghold of the O'Mahoneys, it is mentioned in the 'Annals of Innisfallen' as having been built in 1217. Today it stands a lonely ruin by the side of a supposedly haunted lake, with a sheer drop to the sea behind it.

Leaving the car park of the Barley Cove Beach Hotel, do not turn left for Mizen Head but go right and then left at the first T-junction. This quickly leads to another junction with a sign pointing left to the Ocean View B&B. Go right instead, follow the road to its end, and go through the farm gate on the right. Take the path up to the house, follow the sign to the left and walk north for ten minutes.

Places to Stay

Camping There is a popular camping and caravan site (☎ 028-35302) at Barleycove, open from May to September. Family tents are IR£7.

B&Bs Crookhaven has *Marconi House* (☎ 028-35168), on the right when entering the village, where Guglielmo Marconi (1874-1937), the Italian physicist who developed radiotelegraphy, erected a radio

mast in 1902. Singles/doubles are IR£18/34-38. The closest accommodation to Mizen Head is at the *Barley Cove Beach Hotel* (☎ 028-35234). B&B during the summer is from IR£50/84. Along the road from the hotel to Three Castle Head there are a couple of small farms offering B&B in summer.

Places to Eat

In Goleen the *Heron's Cove Restaurant* (☎ 028-35225) is open from mid-morning to last dinner orders at 9.45 pm. Crookhaven has a couple of pubs serving food, such as the *Welcome Inn* and the *Crookhaven Inn* with a bar menu until 8 pm, mostly featuring seafood open sandwiches. *Marconi House* also has a restaurant open for breakfast at IR£4, lunch starting at IR£7 and dinner around IR£14. On the left just before entering the village, *Journey's End* restaurant offers seafood lunches and dinner from around IR£12. At the *Barley Cove Beach Hotel* there is a restaurant, bar food and afternoon tea. Lunch in the restaurant is around IR£10 while dinner is IR£18.50.

On the left on the road between Schull and Goleen, and just before the right turn-off to Durrus, is the *Altar Restaurant* (☎ 028-35254). The menu looks good and includes local seafood and vegetarian dishes, with main courses starting at around IR£10.

Getting There & Away

The Clonakilty to Goleen bus leaves Clonakilty at 7.05 pm and stops in Rosscarbery, Leap, Skibbereen, Ballydehob and Schull. It can be flagged down anywhere along the road. There is no bus to Crookhaven or west of Goleen.

Getting Around

Bicycles can be hired from the Barleycove Caravan and Camping Park.

BANTRY

Bantry (*Beanntrai*) narrowly missed fame in the late 18th century, thanks to the storms that prevented a massive French landing. A local Englishman, Richard White, was rewarded with a peerage for his efforts in trying to alert the military in Cork. His grand home is open to the public and this, along with an exhibition devoted to the events of 1796, is now the main attraction of the town.

Before Irish independence, Bantry Bay was a major anchorage for the British navy, and after WW II Spanish trawlers were regular visitors to the town. The deep waters of the bay were also exploited by Gulf Oil who built an oil terminal on Whiddy Island and brought an unexpected prosperity to the town. The island is close to Bantry Harbour and can be seen from the Cork road when entering the town. In 1979 a fire broke out at the terminal and 51 lives were lost. The terminal is said to be reopening in some modified form; the island's storage tanks remain intact and are visible from the Bantry-Glengarriff road.

Orientation & Information

The two main roads into Bantry both lead to the large Wolfe Tone Square, now mostly given over to a free car park, but once the location of an important cattle market on the first Friday of each month. A fair of sorts is still held on that day, and some of the region's

many expatriates, known as 'hippies' or 'blow-ins' to the locals, are to be found selling their wares.

From the end of May to the end of September the tourist office (☎ 027-50229) is open on the south side of the square. The square also houses a laundrette and there's a decent bookshop close by.

Museum

There is a small museum just behind the fire station (open May to September, Tuesday and Thursday, from 10.30 am to 1 pm, Wednesday and Friday 3 to 5.30 pm). It houses a modest local history collection.

Bantry House

Bantry House is superbly situated overlooking the bay. Parts of the house date back to the mid-18th century, but the fine north front overlooking the sea was added in 1840. The gardens are well-kept and the house is noted for its French and Flemish tapestries and the eclectic collection assembled by the 2nd earl of Bantry during his overseas peregrinations between 1820 and 1850. Entry is IR£3/1.75, and is open from 9 am to 6 pm daily, to 8 pm

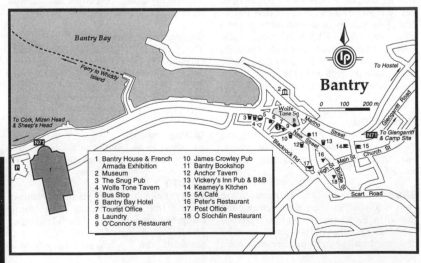

Bantry

0   100   200 m

1 Bantry House & French Armada Exhibition
2 Museum
3 The Snug Pub
4 Wolfe Tone Tavern
5 Bus Stop
6 Bantry Bay Hotel
7 Tourist Office
8 Laundry
9 O'Connor's Restaurant
10 James Crowley Pub
11 Bantry Bookshop
12 Anchor Tavern
13 Vickery's Inn Pub & B&B
14 Kearney's Kitchen
15 5A Café
16 Peter's Restaurant
17 Post Office
18 Ó Síocháin Restaurant

during the summer. The old kitchen, with range intact, is now a tearoom and craft shop. The grounds can be viewed free of charge.

French Armada Exhibition Centre

Considering how Lord Bantry received his title it's rather ironic that in the grounds of the house there is now a French Armada exhibition celebrating the sorry saga of the attempted French landing of 1796. The exhibit centres around the scuttled French frigate *La Surveillante*, which it was hoped might be raised from Bantry Bay in time for the 1996 centenary but this is not to be. Entry is IR£3/1 but a combined ticket with Bantry House saves IR£2.

On the main Bantry to Cork road, about three km outside town and almost opposite Barry's garage, there is an **anchor** from one of the French ships, found by a trawler in 1964.

Kilnaruane Pillar Stone

This is worth seeking out because of its rare representation of the kind of boat that St Brendan may have used to reach America. Coming out of Bantry towards Cork it is signposted on the left immediately after the Westlodge Hotel. The stone is in a field 500 metres along on the right but cannot be seen from the road. Look for a faded pink corrugated tin roof and a gateway through to a field.

Cruises

Whiddy Island can be reached by a boat (☎ 027-50310) which leaves from the pier during the summer for IR£5 return. On the island the *Bank House* pub and restaurant (☎ 027-51739) serves bar food and meals, mostly seafood. A four-course dinner costs around IR£20.

Festival

In the second week of May, Bantry holds a Mussel fair with various musical events and free mussels distributed around the pubs.

Places to Stay

Camping The nearest camp site is *Eagle Point* (☎ 027-50630), six km from town on the road to Glengarriff.

Hostel The IHH *Bantry Independent Hostel* (☎ 027-51050) is off the Glengarriff Rd at Bishop Lucy Place; take the fork by the Key Properties office and continue uphill almost to the top. The nightly cost is IR£5.50 and a double room is IR£15.

B&Bs There are plenty of B&Bs strung out along the Glengarriff Rd. *Shangri-La* (☎ 027-50244), from IR£20/28, is one of these that has a good reputation but it tends to fill up quickly. In town *Vickery's Inn* (☎ 027-50006), a venerable old place that was once the town's coaching inn, has singles/doubles from IR£14/28.

Hotels The *Bantry Bay Hotel* (☎ 027-50062) is near Wolfe Tone Square and has singles/doubles for IR£30/50. Bantry's other hotel is the *Westlodge* (☎ 027-50360), a charmless building a couple of km outside of town on the road to Cork. Singles/doubles are IR£55/90 but, notwithstanding its swimming pool, similar rates are charged at the far superior *Sea View Hotel* (☎ 027-50073) at Ballylickey. To get there take the road for Glengarriff and it's on the right after a few km, before reaching a sharp bend where the road to Macroom is signposted.

Places to Eat

A number of pubs serve bar lunches including the *Wolfe Tone Tavern* and *The Snug*. The only vegetarian place in town is *5A* in Barrack St but it closes at 5.30 pm. *Kearney's Kitchen*, on the other side of the road, has the best array of sandwiches and snacks in Bantry.

O'Connor's (☎ 027-50221) is a highly acclaimed seafood restaurant right next to the tourist office. Lunch costs around IR£5-9 and dinner dishes are around IR£12. *Ó Síocháin* on Bridge St has a standard café-style menu with main courses around IR£6. *Vickery's Inn*, opposite the supermarket, does a three-course lunch for around IR£6, specials cost less, and dinner is IR£12; the food is unadventurous but filling. *Peter's* on New St is a steak house with meals from IR£7.

CORK

Larchwood House Restaurant (☎ 027-66181) is outside town but worth the journey for the five course dinner costing over IR£20. To get there turn right at the sign about three km out on the road to Glengarriff. Further along the road at Ballylickey the IR£19 dinner at the *Sea View* is also excellent.

Entertainment

The *Wolfe Tone Tavern* near the square has musical evenings and *James Crowley* nearby is another reliable venue throughout the summer. The *Bantry Bay Hotel* is also worth a look and the *Anchor Tavern*, even without music, is an interesting old pub.

Getting There & Away

During summer only there is an express bus service between Cork and Killarney that stops in Bantry. It leaves for Glengarriff, Kenmare and Killarney at noon and departs for Skibbereen, Clonakilty and Cork at 6.10 pm. Throughout the year there are three buses a day between Cork and Bantry.

The private Berehaven bus travels between Castletownbere and Bantry via Glengarriff. The first bus leaves Bantry at 11.25 on Monday, and 3.45 pm on Tuesday, Friday and Saturday. The bus stop is next to the Wolfe Tone Tavern.

Getting Around

Bicycles can be hired from Carrowell (☎ 027-50278), on the right side of the Glengarriff road. From the top of Barrack St it is less than a km away. The daily rate is IR£5 to IR£6 and longer rentals can be negotiated. The hostel also has bikes.

GOUGANE BARRA FOREST PARK

There is a green island in lone Gougane Barra
Where Allua of song rushes forth as an arrow,
In deep vallied Desmond – a thousand wild fountains
Come down to that lake from their home in the
      mountains.

J J Callanan, 18th-century Cork poet

This is the most picturesque part of inland Cork. The source of the River Lee is a mountain lake, fed by numerous streams. St

Finbar, the founder of Cork, came here in the 6th century and established a monastery. He had a hermitage on the island in the lake, which is now approached by a short causeway. There is a small modern chapel on the island.

A road runs through the park in a loop and a number of meandering paths lead off it. There is a signboard map in the park, and it is worth heading for Bealick's summit for the fine views. Take the road to Glengarriff from Bantry and after five km turn right at the bridge, signposted for Macroom. There is a signposted turning to the left for Gougane Barra about 28 km before Macroom.

Places to Stay & Eat

Near the main park entrance is the *Gougane Barra Hotel* (☎ 026-47069), with singles/doubles for IR£42/70. Bar food is available and there is a café next door as well as a gift shop.

Carrying on along the road to Macroom, you come to Ballingeary and the IHH *Tig Barra Hostel* (☎ 026-47016). It is about three km from the turn-off to Gougane Barra to the left of the main road. Beds are IR£5, there's one double for IR£14 and camping is available.

B&B is available from *Kelleher* (☎ 026-47172) at Cois na Coille, Gurteenakila. As the name might suggest, people around Ballingeary speak Irish.

Sheep's Head Peninsula

This is the least visited of Cork's three peninsulas although it has a charm all of its own. There are no substantial antiquities, but a loop road runs close to the sea for most of the way. There are wonderful seascapes to appreciate and country walks where other visitors will be few and far between.

The second turning on the right after leaving Bantry for Cork is the beginning of the **Goat's Path Scenic Route**, which approaches the peninsula from the northern side. The southern part of the loop road begins farther along the main road, just past the Esso garage.

WALKING TOURS
The start of a walk to the top of **Seefin** (334 metres) is at the top of the Goat's Path, about two km north of the village of Kilcrohane. Across the road from here rests a forlorn imitation of Michelangelo's *Pietà*, erected by an American with local family roots. While there is no obvious path it is not difficult to aim for the summit and reach it in less than 45 minutes. There are fine views from the top, and not many people go there.

A good three-hour walk could also be begun from the top of the Goat's Path. Standing near the *Pietà* statue and facing Bantry Bay locate an old road about 100 metres to the right; recognisable by a low wall of slate on the sea-facing side. Follow this utterly remote track until it joins a surfaced road that heads out farther west along the peninsula and eventually crosses over to the southern side from where the main road leads back to Kilcrohane. A left turn at the village church would return you to the start of the walk at the top of the Goat's Path.

PLACES TO STAY
Just west of Ahakista a sign points the way to *Hillcrest* B&B (☎ 027-67045) with singles/doubles from IR£19.50/29. There are other B&Bs dotted along the road and the rates are almost identical so it's just a matter of picking one that takes your fancy.

In the village of Kilcrohane, the *Dunmahon* (☎ 027-67092) has singles/doubles from IR£14/28.

The *Dunbeacon Campsite* (☎ 027-61246) is about five km from Durrus on the road to Goleen. The charges are IR£2.50 per person; showers are 50p though there is also one free shower with a donation box!

PLACES TO EAT
Durrus
Cronin's is a pub with bar food and *Jim's Place* on the other side of the road serves bar food and evening meals. Opposite the post office, where the road to Kilcrohane begins, there is a small café. Just outside Durrus, on the road to Goleen, *Blair's Cove* (☎ 027-61127) is reputed to serve wonderful seafood and meat dishes. Dinner is around IR£30.

Ahakista & Kilcrohane
Calling Ahakista a village is stretching the meaning of the word village: there are two unprepossessing pubs (one of which doesn't bother with a name and may be closed), no shops but one outrageously expensive Japanese restaurant. The unnamed pub with the tin roof serves soup and sandwiches, and has a surprisingly delightful garden at the back. *Shiro Japanese Dinner House* (☎ 027-67030) is opposite the pub and has only two tables.

Of the two pubs in Kilcrohane, *Fitzpatrick's*, just north of the church, is very friendly and serves light refreshments. Dinner at the *Dunmahon* is IR£8.

GETTING THERE & AWAY
There is no public transport apart from one Saturday bus between Bantry and Kilcrohane. Hitching is easier along the road that runs along the southern side of the peninsula, via Durrus.

Beara Peninsula

The appeal of the Beara Peninsula lies in its startling natural beauty, best experienced by climbing the hills and cycling the roads. It's a lot bigger and much wilder than its neighbouring peninsula to the south. While the Mizen Head and Sheep's Head peninsulas are lush and green, reminiscent of the Ireland imagined by long-departed emigrants, the Beara is desolate, a harsh and rocky landscape which had to be fought for survival. A quick visit could easily extend itself into a longer stay.

It's wonderful walking country, and the Beara Way is a new long-distance walk, 197 km long, linking Glengarriff with Kenmare via Castletownbere, Bere Island, Dursey Island and the north side of the peninsula.

CORK

Much of the route is along green roads and is well signposted. For more details see the Activities chapter.

ORIENTATION & INFORMATION
There are small tourist offices in Castletownbere and Glengarriff but both open only during the summer and close for lunch. Kenmare and a small part of the peninsula to the west of the town are in Kerry and therefore covered in that chapter.

A trip round the coastal roads is 137 km. You could drive it in one day, but little would be achieved except a lot of gear changes. The spectacular Healy Pass joins Adrigole with Lauragh in Kerry. Castletownbere is well placed as a base for exploring the peninsula.

GETTING THERE & AWAY
A local bus leaves Bantry at 3.45 pm on Tuesday, Friday and Saturday, stopping in Glengarriff and then Castletownbere. On Monday its departure times are 11.25 am and 8.20 pm. On Thursday the service originates in Cork, from where it departs at 6 pm, reaching Bantry at 7.45 and Glengarriff at 8.25 pm. These local buses depart from Castletownbere at 10.30 am on Tuesday, Friday and Saturday, 7 am and 4.30 pm on Monday, and 7.30 am on Thursday (bound for Bantry and Cork).

GLENGARRIFF
This village's fame is due to its proximity to Garnish Island and its location on the main West Cork to Killarney road. The village itself is strung out along the main road with the Eccles Hotel at one end. At the other end, the roads to Kenmare and the Beara Peninsula divide. Its sheltered position at the head of Bantry Bay, together with the influence of the Gulf Stream, give it a particularly mild climate, and the local flora is lush and sometimes exotic.

During the second half of the 19th century Glengarriff (*An Gleann Garbh*) became a popular retreat for prosperous Victorians. They would sail from England to Ireland then take the train to Bantry from where a paddle steamer chugged over to Glengarriff.

By 1850 the road to Kenmare had been blasted through the mountains and the link with Killarney was established.

A major attraction is the Italianate garden on Garnish island.

Information
During July and August tourist information (☎ 027-63084) is available from the small portacabin in the car park outside the Eccles Hotel. It opens from 9.30 am to 5 pm (closed between 1 and 2 pm).

Scuba Diving
Both Bantry and Dunmanus Bay have exciting sites for scuba diving and a new diving centre *Bantry Bay Divers* (☎ 027-63072/51310), based in Main St, is recommended for both dedicated and occasional divers. Package trips are arranged and other water activities can be organised. Contact Tim Doyle for details.

Garnish Island
This small island (15 hectares) was turned into an Italianate garden in the early years of the 20th century. It was designed by Harold Peto, who brought in exotic plants never before seen in Ireland, and they continue to flourish, providing a blaze of colour in a landscape usually dominated by greens and browns. There is a walkway on the island to a Martello Tower.

Boats leave from the seafront in the village (☎ 027-63333) and from the Blue Pool just a little way west on the Castletownbere road (☎ 027-63170); IR£5/2.50. The OPW gardens on the island (☎ 027-63040) have a separate entrance charge of IR£2.50.

Glengarriff Woods
The woods were part of the estate of the White family of Bantry House in the 18th century. Oak and pine were planted, and after the government took over in the 1950s the range of trees was expanded. The thick cover of trees maintains humid conditions that allow a profusion of ferns and mosses to flourish. At the beginning of the walk look out especially for very small white flowers

on red stems rising from rosettes of leaves: kidney saxifrage, rare elsewhere.

The woodlands and bogs also provide a home for the Kerry slug *(Geomalacus maculosus)*, only found here and in parts of Kerry and the Iberian Peninsula. Coffee-coloured with cream spots, it has been described as the aristocrat of slugs.

Leave Glengarriff in the direction of Kenmare; the entrance to the woods is about one km along on the left.

Places to Stay

Camping *Dowling's Caravan & Camping Park* (☎ 027-63154) is two km west of Glengarriff on the road to Castletownbere. It has its own licensed bar and music in the summer. Close by is *O'Shea's Caravan & Camping Park* (☎ 027-63140). Their tent rates are IR£6.50 and IR£6 respectively, but Dowling's also charges IR£1 extra per adult.

Hostels At the Bantry end of the village *O'Mahony* (☎ 027-63033) has beds for IR£5 and two double rooms for IR£12. Just over a km from the village, signposted on the road to Kenmare, *Glengarriff Independent Hostel* (☎ 027-63211) charges the same rates. The bunk beds are not robust but there's a good-sized kitchen.

B&Bs On the seafront, *Mrs Guerin* (☎ 027-63079) has three beds for IR£14 each and *Island View House* (☎ 027-63081) has singles/doubles from IR£18/27.

Hotels *Eccles Hotel* (☎ 027-63003) is the grand old hotel of Glengarriff, boasting literary guests that have included Thackeray, Yeats and Shaw. Facing the sea on the main road at the Bantry end of the village, it offers singles/doubles from IR£35/50. When there's live music downstairs it can get noisy. The other hotel in the village is *Caseys* (☎ 027-63010) and the rates are identical.

Places to Eat

The *Blue Loo* pub, opposite the post office where the road splits for Kenmare and Castletownbere, does bar food. Open fish

sandwiches for about IR£5 are served at *Barry's* pub, on the other side of the road, which also boasts a seafood restaurant with main dishes around IR£12. *Caseys* hotel has pub food all day and dinner is IR£15. *Eccles* has a good bar menu and afternoon tea is pleasant amid the faded elegance of the foyer, if the giant television is switched off.

Getting There & Away

The bus stop is opposite Barry's Restaurant. The Cork to Killarney (two hours) bus leaves for Kenmare and Killarney at 12.25 pm and for Bantry, Clonakilty and Cork at 5.30 pm. This is a summer-only service, from 8 June to 26 September. All year there is an express service between Cork and Glengarriff (2½ hours) that travels inland via Dunmanway.

The private Berehaven bus departs for Bantry at 7.45 am and 5.20 pm on Monday, 11.20 am Tuesday, Friday and Saturday, and 8.15 am on Thursday (travelling on to Cork on Thursday). It leaves for Castletownbere at 11.55 am and 8.50 pm on Monday, 4.15 pm on Tuesday, Friday and Saturday, and 8.25 pm on Thursday.

Getting Around

Jem Creations Craft Workshop (☎ 027-631130), next to the Blue Loo pub, has bikes for hire.

CASTLETOWNBERE

Castletownbere is the largest whitefish port in Ireland and when its full name – Castletownberehaven – is used it shares with Newtownmountkennedy in County Wicklow the proud claim of having the longest place name in Ireland. The town developed out of the mining industry at Allihies, and it is the main town on the peninsula.

Tourist information (☎ 027-70344) is available during the summer from a garden shed squeezed in next to the fire station in the town square. It's open from 11 am to 5 pm, Monday to Saturday, closing between 1 and 2 pm.

There is a good supermarket, a post office with a limited bureau de change, a laundrette and a string of pubs, some with music at night.

A sign to the west of the town points to a **stone circle** which is 1.5 km along the road on the right-hand side.

Places to Stay

Camping The *Adrigole Hostel* on the Castletownbere side of Adrigole village also has camping space. Before Castletownbere the *Wheel Inn Holiday Centre* (☎ 027-70090) is pleasantly situated with views of Bere Island. The *Beara Hostel*, on the other side of town, has camping for IR£3.50 per person.

Hostels The *Adrigole Hostel* (☎ 027-60132), is just west of the village. About three km west of Castletownbere, just past the sign for Dunboy, the *Beara Hostel* (☎ 027-70184) is also on the main road. The *Garranes Hostel* (☎ 027-73147) is between Castletownbere and Allihies, superbly located on the Bantry Bay side a couple of km off the road (hard work if you're pushing a loaded bike). Next door is a Buddhist retreat centre.

B&Bs There are half a dozen B&Bs, including *Mrs S Murphy* (☎ 027-70099) along West End, and *Mrs Harrington* (☎ 027-70252) on the road to Glengarriff. *Craigie's Cametringane House* (☎ 027-70379) has singles/doubles for IR£29/50.

Places to Eat

The *Old Cottage Restaurant*, just before entering town from the Glengarriff side, and *Jack Patrick's* in town both do lunch and dinner. There is also the *Old Bank Seafood Restaurant* and on the way out to Dursey the *Hole in the Wall* pub has sandwiches and snacks. The *Berehaven Inn* has a set lunch for around IR£5.

Stephanie's is a pleasant restaurant on the main street at the west end of town, serving local seafood. Dinner is around IR£25 per person. *Niki's*, on the right when you enter the town from the east, has its home inside an old pharmacy and has seafood dinners for

around IR£12. It also does reasonable lunches and breakfasts.

Getting Around

Bikes can be hired from the SuperValu supermarket (☎ 027-70020) in the centre of town.

BERE ISLAND

The island is about the same size as Manhattan but has a different kind of appeal. The very deep anchorage helped make it the base for the British navy and the whole Allied fleet spent some time here before the Battle of Jutland. At the outbreak of WW II, Winston Churchill wanted to continue using it, and a deal for the return of the six northern counties was in the air. However, it was not to be. In 1994 a ferry carrying people across to the island sank and four people died.

The enjoyment of the Beara Way's 21-km walk is the best reason for visiting the island. There are a couple of pubs and small shops but tourist accommodation is limited to one B&B, *Mrs O'Sullivan* (☎ 027-75011) at Harbour View. It would make sense to ring in advance.

A ferry service (☎ 027-75009) for **Bere Island** runs from Castletownbere quay; IR£15 return for a car including driver, IR£3/1.50 for other passengers. During July and August there are seven boats a day, from 10.30 am to 6 pm.

DUNBOY CASTLE & PUXLEY MANSION

Little now remains of Dunboy Castle, the fortress of the O'Sullivans, who ruled supreme for three centuries before succumbing to the English with cannon and 4000 men in 1602. It's signposted after Castletownbere.

Don't make the mistake of following the sign for Dunboy Castle and thinking the grand ruins you see are the magnificent remains of a Gaelic stronghold. This is Puxley Mansion, bearing testimony to the vast wealth generated by the copper mined on the estate of the Puxley family. It was built in the 19th century, and although it was burnt down by the IRA in 1921, enough of it remains to show the extravagance of its style. Check out the Italian marble of the columns still standing in what was designed to be the grand hallway.

It is possible to camp in the scenic grounds of *Puxley Castle*. Enquiries should be made at the house on the right after passing the main gate.

ALLIHIES & THE COPPER MINES

Copper was discovered in 1810 and mining started two years later. It brought wealth to the Puxley family who owned the land but low wages and dangerous, unhealthy work conditions for the workforce, which at one time numbered 1300 men, women and children. Experienced miners from Cornwall were brought into the area, and the ruins of their stone cottages remain. As late as the 1930s, over 30,000 tonnes of pure copper were being exported but by 1962 the last mine was closed. Daphne du Maurier's novel *Hungry Hill* (Penguin) is based on the Puxley family.

Walking Tour

The mines are just north of the village of Allihies, 19 km west of Castletownbere, and signs point the way to the remains of an untidy quarry. An old road leads up to the ruins of a chimney stack, from where the road can be followed further up, passing an old reservoir on the right. Mine shafts are scattered around the place but they are fenced off and the main chimney stack can be approached in relative safety. The track eventually leads to Eyeries and can be followed for as long as you wish. Half an hour's walk leads to a point with a view of Coulagh Bay and Kenmare Bay beyond. You can climb the hills by cutting over the moor to the right, but it is best to consult one of the local walking guides like *West Cork Walks* by Kevin Corcoran (O'Brien Press, Dublin).

Places to Stay & Eat

At Allihies there is the An Óige *Allihies Hostel* (☎ 027-73014). There is also the IHH *The Village Hostel (Bonnie Braes)* (☎ 027-73107) in the village with beds for IR£6,

three double rooms for IR£15. Camping is also possible and bikes can be hired.

There are also a couple of B&B places: *Sea View Cluin Village* (☎ 027-73004) from IR£15/26, and *Mrs O'Sullivan* (☎ 027-73019) at Glenera for IR£14/24.

In the village meals are available at the homely *Atlantic Seafood Restaurant*, and *O'Neil's* pub does bar food.

DURSEY ISLAND

At the end of the peninsula the island of Dursey is only 250 metres away, and a cable car connects the 20 or so inhabitants and their cattle with the mainland. Three hundred people sought refuge here in 1602, when Dunboy Castle was under siege by the English; they were slaughtered and thrown into the sea.

The best time to go across is between 9 and 11 am; confirm your return time with the cable-car operator. Note that cattle get precedence over humans in the queue for the ride! Normally the service resumes between 2.30 and 5 pm.

While there is no tourist accommodation available on the island it is easy to find somewhere to camp. The Beara Way's 11-km walk loops the island, and the signal tower is an obvious destination for a slightly shorter walk. Bikes are not allowed on the cable car.

Just by the cable car point for Dursey Island, the coffee shop, *Windy Point House* (☎ 027-73017), does B&B.

SUGARLOAF MOUNTAIN

After leaving Glengarriff for Castletownbere there is a turning on the right after eight km. It is half a km after a disused school on the right of the road, opposite a blue sign in the middle of nowhere announcing that this is a Community Alert Area. After turning right, follow the road for 1.5 km, leaving your bicycle or car near the single two-storey house with pine trees behind it or near the bungalow just past it.

Sugarloaf Mountain (581 metres) is best approached by walking up behind the houses and crossing an old road. A steady approach up the side of the mountain would reach the triangulation point at the summit in about an hour. From the top there are excellent views: the Caha Mountains to the north, Hungry Hill to the west, Garnish Island to the east and Bantry Bay spread out to the south. On the way up, around the old road, it is not difficult to spot the great butterwort, an insectivorous plant, in May and June.

HUNGRY HILL

Hungry Hill is the highest point on the peninsula at 686 metres. A sign points to one route to the top, seven km west of Adrigole. A longer but more comfortable ascent begins by ignoring this sign, carrying along the road, and turning right just past a church on the right side of the road. This road goes north until blocked by a wire sheep gate. A vehicle could be left just before this or taken past for another km or more. The overgrown road eventually stops near some lakes and from here, keeping the lakes to the left, you head up the east ridge and climb the summit from the north side. A quicker descent can be made by following the stream down the south-west side to some farmhouses and a road that connects with the one where you began. The whole journey will take at least five hours but the rockscapes are fabulous and the views of West Cork from the stone circle at the top are tremendous. Less arduous would be a walk to the end of the road and a picnic by the lakes.

North Cork

The chief reason for visiting north Cork is for the fishing and the golf. There is a small but distinguished number of country houses open to the public for evening meals and short stays, often with fine gardens. North Cork is not the budget traveller's territory: permission for a day's fishing on the Blackwater could cost IR£30, and a night for two in a country house with dinner could easily approach IR£200. There are no hostels or official camp sites, but B&B places are never far away and the towns all have affordable places for meals.

FERMOY

This small town has around 5000 people and a pub for roughly every 200 of them, if anything a little below par for Ireland. Fishing is *the* attraction, and the town hosts a Fishing Festival in the week that straddles May and June, in an attempt to lure visitors from England during their Bank Holiday weekend and then Irish anglers the week after for their Bank Holiday weekend.

Information

The tourist office (☎ 025-31811) is in the same shop as a travel agent in the main square. It is open all year from 9 am to 6 pm.

Fishing

In Fermoy fishing enquiries should be made to Jack O'Sullivan (☎ 025-31110) at 4 Patrick St, just two doors down from the tourist office, in a men's clothes store of the same name.

MALLOW

Twice the size of Fermoy, Mallow (*Mala*) is a prosperous town in the Blackwater Valley that caters for fishing, golfing and horse racing. It's well provided with restaurants and pubs. In the 19th century visitors to the town's spa christened it the 'Bath of Ireland'. The tourist office (☎ 022-42222) is on Bridge St near the castle. It is open 9.30 am to 5.30 pm, from May to September.

AROUND MALLOW

About 13 km north-east of Mallow, **Doneraile Forest Park** is a large 18th-century park with herds of deer, open without charge from 11 am to 7 pm or sundown in winter. The nearby town of the same name was once owned by the English poet Edmund Spenser, and the slight remains of **Kilcolman Castle**, where he wrote part of the *Faerie Queene*, are five km to the north. The first recorded steeplechase in 1752 ended in Doneraile after heading off from the steeple of a church in nearby Buttervant. Half way between

Mallow and Fermoy on the N72 near the town of Castletownroche **Annes Grove Gardens** (☎ 022-26145) is a small, formal 18th-century garden.

From Mallow to Killarney, a distance of 49 km, the landscape is nondescript; the only worthwhile detour would be to the 17th-century **Kanturk Castle**. It is said that the mortar was mixed with the blood of the builders who were forced to work on it. The English, however, objected to such a massive mansion being built by an Irish chief, and did not allow the roof to be installed. The roofless remains are very well preserved.

Kanturk Town has fishing possibilities (☎ 029-50257) and the superior *Assolas Country House* (☎ 029-50015).

Camping (☎ 029-50257) is possible in the town park, and near the Bank of Ireland the café serves meals till 2 or 3 am.

Inland Cork

The most popular route from Cork is to Kinsale and then the coastal road through Clonakilty and Skibbereen. From Skibbereen the Mizen Head Peninsula is close by and the main road heads north to Bantry.

An alternative route from Cork to Bantry is inland via Macroom, and the road from Macroom to Bantry has its own scenic attractions, most notably at Gougane Barra. The quickest route between Killarney and Cork is also via Macroom.

There is one other inland route to Bantry which takes the main road to Bandon and Dunmanway. This is actually the quickest way to reach Bantry and the Beara Peninsula from Cork but it is the least interesting. The road is a good one for driving but has few attractions along the way except the IHH *Shiplake Mountain Hostel* (☎ 023-45750) where bikes can be hired and local cycling trips suggested.

MICHAEL COLLINS AMBUSH SITE

Michael Collins, commander-in-chief of the army of the new Provisional Government that had just won independence from Britain, left Macroom on the morning of 22 August 1922, on a quick tour of West Cork. He was recognised by anti-Treaty forces, who were holding a secret meeting in the area. In the evening they ambushed his car and Collins was shot dead. It seems that Collins ignored his companions' advice to drive on after the first shots were fired, choosing instead to make a fight of it.

The site of the ambush is marked by a stone memorial with an inscription in Irish. Each year, on the anniversary of the killing, a commemorative service is held by the roadside.

About 200 metres past the memorial there is another stone inscribed with the words: 'On this road too died 17 terrorist officers of the British forces on 28/11/20.'

The site is about 10 km from Macroom on the road to Dunmanway.

County Kerry

While the town of Killarney bursts at the seams during the summer months and the Ring of Kerry has queues of tour coaches, the rest of the county is easily big enough for visitors to find some solitude. The tourist hype does little to detract from the wild splendour of the landscape. There are countless opportunities for long and short walks, easy and stiff climbs and bike rides galore where your only companions will be the birds soaring above, the odd cow or sheep and a few like-minded travellers. Especially beautiful is the Dingle Peninsula, and the Iveragh Peninsula to the south has even more opportunities for open-air activities. There is, of course, the usual full quota of pubs with lively music at night and there are a number of small towns with historical places of interest. And there's Killarney.

Killarney & Around

KILLARNEY
By the time you reach Killarney (*Cill Airne*) you will have seen plenty of heavily touristed Irish towns but this is the Numero Uno. There is more registered accommodation here than anywhere else outside the capital. On the other hand there are lots of easy escapes if you want to explore the delights of Kerry and avoid the excesses. However, on the whole, Killarney is still more a tourist town than a tourist trap.

Information
Killarney's busy but efficient tourist office (☎ 064-31633) is in the town hall right in the centre of town and is open from 9.15 am to 5.30 pm Monday to Saturday. There is a laundrette lurking behind the Spar supermarket at the Plunkett St end of College St. The Killarney Bookshop is at 32 Main St.

Money can be changed at the tourist office and the American Express Travel Service,

Highlights
- The 9th-century Gallarus Oratory on the Dingle Peninsula
- Climbing Mt Brandon on the Dingle Peninsula
- Walking the second half of the Dingle Way from Dunquin to Tralee
- Great Blasket Island off the tip of the Dingle Peninsula
- Day-long cycling trips from Killarney
- Rowing out to Inishfallen Island from Killarney for a picnic
- Walking all or part of the Kerry Way and escaping the brouhaha of Killarney
- Avoiding the ritualised Ring of Kerry and cycling or driving through the Ballaghbeama Pass
- The boat trip to Skellig Michael and the astonishing 7th-century monastery perched at the top of this lump of rock in the Atlantic Ocean
- Cycling or driving through the Healy Pass from Lauragh south to County Cork

around the corner on East Avenue Rd, is open till 9 pm weekdays and 7 pm on Saturday and Sunday.

A huge Dunnes supermarket has its entrance on New St.

St Mary's Cathedral
Built in 1842-55, this church was designed by the architect Augustus Pugin. During the

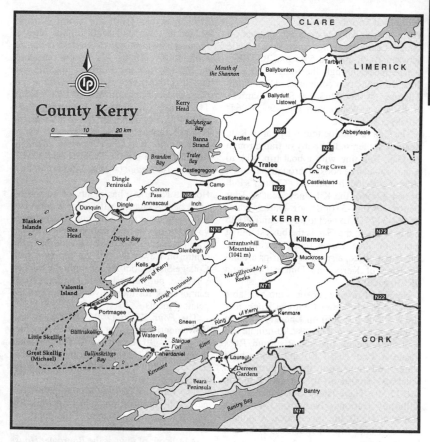

County Kerry

famine years the building was used to house the destitute. It's cruciform with a square tower and a spire that reaches 87 metres. It's in Cathedral Place at the far end of New St.

National Museum of Irish Transport
This interesting collection of old cars, bicycles and assorted odds and ends includes an 1844 Meteor Starley Tricycle found in a shop's 'unsold stock' in 1961! It also has a 1910 Wolseley that belonged to the Gore-Booth family and was used by Countess Markievicz and W B Yeats.

The museum is in East Avenue Rd. It's open April to October, from 10 am to 8 pm daily, and until 6 pm during the rest of the year. Entry is IR£2.50/1.50.

Fishing
Fishing for trout and salmon is possible in the Rivers Flesk and Laune as well as in the lakes themselves. There are also many small lakes with brown and rainbow trout around the southern side of Killarney towards Kenmare, but there is no coarse fishing in the region. Permits, licences, equipment and information are available from O'Neill's (☎ 064-31970) at 6 Plunkett St.

Organised Tours

There are 11 daily watercoach cruises on Lough Leane, leaving from Ross Castle between 10.30 am and 5.45 pm. Bookings can be made through the tourist office or direct from the two companies: Destination Killarney (☎ 064-32638) at Scotts Gardens or Killarney Watercoach Cruises (☎ 064-31068) at 3 High St.

The Gap of Dunloe tour – by car to Kate Kearney's, then saddle pony or trap through the Gap, finishing with a boat trip back to Killarney – can be booked through the tourist office, Castlelough Tours at O'Connor's Pub (☎ 064-32496), the Killarney Boat & Tour Centre (☎ 064-31068), or Deros Tours (☎ 064-31251). Expect to pay around IR£25 and be warned: the Gap is the busiest tourist spot in the area. Deros Tours, just opposite the tourist office, also do coach trips around the Ring of Kerry and Dingle Peninsula (IR£10 each).

Natural history water tours are available from the Field Studies Centre at Knockreer House (☎ 064-35960) on Knockreer Estate to the west of town. There's a 90-minute trip on Lough Leane that departs from Ross Castle at 8 am (IR£7.50) and a three-hour water and land tour that departs from Muckross House at 10 am and 1.30 pm (IR£12.50). There is also a day trip around Killarney National Park from Muckross House at 10.30 am, involving a woodland walk and boat trip on Muckross Lake and Lough Leane.

For organised horse-riding trips enquire at Kilarney Riding Stables (☎ 064-31686) or Rockland Stables (☎ 064-32592).

Kerry Country Rambles (☎ 064-35277) at 53 High St can be contacted to enquire about walking trips in the region.

Places to Stay

Camping The *Fossa Caravan & Camping Park* (☎ 064-31497) is 5.6 km west of town on the road to Killorglin. A tent is IR£3.50 per night for a cyclist or hiker, IR£8 for a car and two people. Almost next door, with similar rates but fewer facilities, is the *Beech Grove Caravan & Camping Park* (☎ 064-31727), across from the Hotel Europe. Nearer to town and with similar rates is *Fleming's Whitebridge Caravan & Camping Park* (☎ 064-31590). It's 1.6 km out along the N22 road to Cork. Further along this road and less expensive is *White Villa Farm Caravan and Camping Park* (☎ 064-32456). The *Flesk Caravan & Camping Park* (☎ 064-31704) is one km out of town on the N71 to Kenmare.

The only Killarney hostels offering camping space are the *Park* (☎ 064-32119) and *Donash Lodge* (☎ 066-64554).

Hostels Killarney has plenty of hostels all more or less charging IR£6 for a dorm bed and many have transport waiting to engage you at the bus or train station. The small but friendly *Súgán* (☎ 064-33104) is right in the centre on Lewis Rd, by the junction with College St, no doubles. At night the kitchen serves a public restaurant, and residents cannot cook for themselves but can get discounted meals.

The *Four Winds* (☎ 064-33094) is also conveniently central at 43 New St; doubles are IR£19. Off the same street, a lane leads to *Neptune's Killarney Town Hostel* (☎ 064-35255), a big place with some en suite doubles.

The *Railway Hostel* (☎ 064-35299) is a new well-equipped place just off Park Rd, within staggering distance of the pubs, and close to the bus and rail stations.

A little out of town is the *Bunrower House Hostel* (☎ 064-33914), under the same ownership as the Súgán. Heading for Kenmare, take a right turn at the Esso garage on the road signposted for Ross Castle. It's a 20-minute walk and there's regular free transport between the two hostels.

The large An Óige *Killarney International Hostel* (☎ 064-31240) is two km west of the centre at Aghadoe House; it costs IR£6.50 per night. A hostel bus meets trains from Dublin and Cork. The IHH *Fossa Holiday Hostel* (☎ 064-31497) is slightly farther out and has some hostel accommodation near its camp site.

The comfortable and well-equipped *Atlas*

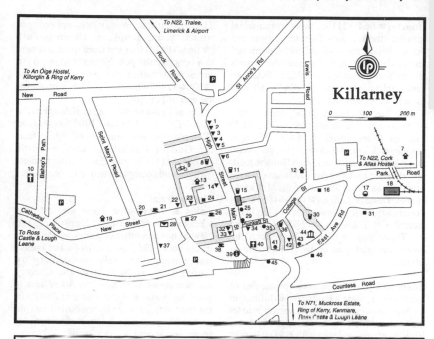

Killarney

PLACES TO STAY

- 7 Railway Hostel
- 12 Súgán Hostel & Restaurant
- 13 Neptune's Hostel
- 16 Arbutus Hotel
- 19 Four Winds Hostel
- 24 Belvedere Hotel
- 27 Eviston House Hotel
- 31 Great Southern Hotel
- 46 Killarney Park Hotel

PLACES TO EAT

- 1 Bricín Restaurant
- 2 Gaby's Restaurant
- 3 Foley's Restaurant
- 4 Swiss Barn Restaurant
- 5 Robertino's Restaurant
- 6 Allegro Restaurant
- 14 Sheila's Restaurant
- 20 Dunnes Supermarket
- 21 Grunt's Café
- 22 Country Kitchen
- 23 Big Ali's Diner
- 26 Caragh Café
- 32 Stella's Restaurant
- 33 Flesk Restaurant
- 34 Strawberry Tree Restaurant
- 37 An Taelann Restaurant
- 38 Cyrano's Café
- 42 Kiwi's Retreat

PUBS

- 8 Courtney's Pub
- 11 O'Connor's Pub
- 15 Laurels Pub
- 30 Scott's Gardens
- 36 Kiely's Bar

OTHER

- 9 O'Sullivan's Bike Hire
- 10 St Mary's Cathedral
- 17 Bus Station
- 18 Railway Station
- 25 Killarney Bookshop
- 28 Post Office
- 29 O'Neill's Fishing Tackle & Bike Hire
- 35 Laundrette
- 39 Tourist Office & Town Hall
- 40 St Mary's Church
- 41 American Express
- 43 Destination Killarney, Lake Tours
- 44 National Museum of Irish Transport
- 45 Jaunting Cars Pick-up Point

Hostel (☎ 064-32119), more commercial than the others, is a km from the railway and bus station off the road to Cork. A dorm bed tends to be a IR£1 more than the other hostels and there are doubles for IR£22 (IR£25 en suite) and a triple en suite is IR£33. All beds include a continental breakfast.

Two hostels near Killarney have a free pick-up service from town. The IHH *Peacock Farm Hostel* (☎ 064-33557) is in Gortdromakerry, Muckross. To get there, take a left turn on to the Lough Guitane road, just after the *jaunting car* (traditional horse-drawn transport) entrance at Muckross House. *Donash Lodge* (☎ 066-64554) is at Longfields, Firies North, about 15 km in the direction of Tralee on the N22. If you take the Tralee bus or train to Farranfore, the hostel will pick you up by arrangement in advance.

B&Bs Killarney has an awesome number of B&Bs, but finding a room can be difficult in the high season. As usual the answer is to let the tourist office do the looking. Muckross Rd is particularly dense with B&Bs. Expect to pay up to IR£50 a double in some of the smart guesthouses, like *Kathleen's Country House* (☎ 064-32810) three km out of town on the road to Tralee. The average price of a regular B&B for a single/double is IR£18.50/30.

Hotels Places costing between IR£50 and IR£80 for a double include *Eviston House* (☎ 064-31640) and the *Belvedere* (☎ 064-31133), both in New St. Also central is the *Arbutus* (☎ 064-31307) on College St, with a friendly atmosphere. Strung out along Muckross there's *Whitegates* (☎ 064-31164) and the *Lake* (☎ 064-31035).

Moving up into the IR£100-plus range there's the *Killarney Ryan* (☎ 064-31555) on the Cork road or the *Great Southern* (☎ 064-31262), built in the 19th century opposite the railway station, for the convenience of Victorian travellers. A modern hotel which is just as posh and plush is the *Killarney Park* (☎ 064-35555) in Kenmare Place. Along Muckross Rd there's the *Gleneagle* (☎ 064-

31870), with a holiday atmosphere that attracts younger folk, or *Muckross Park* (☎ 064-31938) four km from town and next to a very popular pub. Nearer to town on the same road there's the sedate *Cahernune* (☎ 064-31895), built in 1877 as a home for the earl of Pembroke.

Out at Fossa on the road to Killorglin, the *Hotel Europe* (☎ 064-31900) boasts an Olympic-size swimming pool, while near the Gap of Dunloe the *Dunloe Castle* (☎ 064-44111) is a modern building in its own grounds complete with a ruined castle.

Places to Eat

Cafés & Takeaways There are fast-food takeaways in Main St and Plunkett St, and New St has a number of places where quick meals under IR£5 are available. For breakfast or lunch-time sandwiches or salad try *Grunts Café* on New St or the *Country Kitchen* almost next door. *Big Ali's Diner* is good for pizza, soup, snacks and desert. In the Innnishfallen Arcade, just down from the tourist office, *Cyrano's* has a wide menu of meals and is popular with locals.

Mid-Range Restaurants At the following places a lunch will cost about IR£5 and dinner around IR£10. In High St the *Allegro* is more of a café with chicken, pizza and pasta dishes. Near the tourist office on Main St, *Stella's* is a straightforward place of the '& chips' variety with an IR£8 set dinner and main courses around IR£6-10. Just round the corner on New St, the *Caragh Café* is similar. Farther down High St from the tourist office, *Sceilig* has a more upmarket menu with pizza, pasta and specials at around IR£6. A few doors down is the similarly priced *Sheila's*.

The *Súgán* hostel opens its restaurant during the evenings and vegetarian meals make up 90% of the reliable menu. It's closed on Monday. The vegetarian *An Taelann* (☎ 064-33083) is tucked away down Bridewell Lane, off New St just past the post office. The *Bricín*, above a small bookshop in High St, has vegetarian meals but their cheaper food is only available at lunch time. The *Swiss Barn* in High St serves Swiss specialities from IR£12-21 but the tourist menu has meals around IR£10 and the deserts are difficult to turn down.

Among the hotel restaurants, the *Colleen Bawn* in the Eviston House Hotel has a decent tourist dinner, sometimes invaded by coach parties. (Go downstairs to the Danny Mann lounge, to see a wall display on the origin of the restaurant's name.) At the main junction of New, High and Main Sts, the *Laurels* pub and restaurant is a very popular place.

Kiwi's Restaurant is in the lane that joins East Avenue Rd with College St, and you can bring your own wine to accompany the tourist meals of IR£11 and IR£16.

Expensive Restaurants In this category an evening meal for two will cost from IR£15 and up and many of the restaurants are in High St. At the top end of the street is *Foley's* (☎ 064-31217), offering mainly seafood. Nearby, *Gaby's* (☎ 064-32519) is another seafood place where dinner is IR£25. *Robertino's* (☎ 064-34966), close by, is an Italian place with a IR£15 dinner. The *Flesk* restaurant, down the road in Main St, is not so expensive with a set tourist dinner for IR£8. The *Strawberry Tree* in Plunkett St is an old pub with promising organic and wholefood dishes, with a seafood emphasis, around IR£15.

Entertainment
Killarney has lots of pubs and many have music although it's often highly tourist-oriented. Top of the list in that department would have to be the *Laurels* on Main St; their music pub is back behind the main pub, reached by the side alley. It's extremely touristy, with a nightly show in summer from 9.30 to 11 pm and an entry charge of IR£3. Entertainment is along the 'And this is for all the Canadians in the audience' (or Germans, Scots, Australians, you name it) lines, but it's good-humoured and well done.

More expensive musical entertainment can be had at the *Great Southern Hotel* (☎ 064-35392). The *Killarney Manor*

Banquet (☎ 064-31551) hosts a dinner and musical entertainment experience for around IR£30, open from April to October; a reservation is best made, as coach parties often fill the place. *Scott's Gardens*, between College St and East Ave Rd, also has music most nights.

O'Connor's on High St is popular with young people who spill out into the side alley on summer nights. *Courtney's*, across the road on High St, has authentic Irish music. Other pubs to try include *Charlie Foley's* on New St and *Kiely's Bar*, the *Jug O'Punch*, the *Dunloe Lodge* and the *Tatler Jack Bar*, all on College St.

The *Danny Mann Lounge* in the Eviston House Hotel usually has a band and sometimes a display of Irish dancing. The hotel also has a disco.

Getting There & Away
Air Kerry Airport (☎ 066-64644) is at Farranfore, about 15 km north of Killarney off the N22. There are direct Aer Lingus flights to Dublin, and Manx Airlines flights to Luton and Manchester.

Bus Bus Éireann (☎ 064-34777) operates from next to the railway station, with regular links to Tralee, Cork, Galway, Limerick, Shannon, Westport, Waterford and Rosslare. The Ring of Kerry has its own service in the summer, departing Killarney at 8.45 am and 1.25 pm (no early bus on Sunday) for Killorglin, Cahirciveen, Waterville, Caherdaniel, Sneem and back to Killarney.

In July and August there is a private bus service (☎ 066-72249) between Killarney and Cahirciveen which can be booked at the tourist office. Single/return fare is IR£5/8.

Train Travelling by train to Cork involves changing at Mallow, but there is a direct route to Dublin via Limerick. Phone ☎ 064-31067 for details.

Getting Around
Bicycles are the ideal way to explore the Killarney area as the sights are scattered, many of them only accessible by bike or on

foot, and in summer the traffic jams can be horrendous. A number of places hire bikes at around IR£5 a day. There's O'Sullivan's (☎ 064-31282) in Pawn Office Lane off High St, and the Laurels pub has its own bike hire (☎ 064-32578) in Old Market Lane that runs alongside the pub. The hire includes a map, panniers and repair kit, and there are good deals for group or weekly hire. O'Neill's (☎ 064-31970) on Plunkett St has children's bikes and will deliver free to your accommodation. Some of the hostels have their own bike-hire service.

If you're not on two wheels, Killarney's traditional transport is the jaunting car, complete with a driver known as a *jarvey*. The pick-up point is on East Avenue Rd just past the tourist office but they also congregate in the N71 car park opposite Muckross House and at the Gap of Dunloe.

AROUND KILLARNEY
Knockreer Estate
You can walk to the Knockreer Estate, just beyond the cathedral to the west of town. There's fine scenery around Lough Leane (the Lower Lake), the restored Ross Castle and Inisfallen Island on the lake with its ancient monastery ruins. Knockreer House is open during the summer, and has exhibitions on the wildlife and history of the area.

Ross Castle
Ross Castle dates back to the 14th century when it was a residence of the O'Donoghues, and it was the last place in Munster to succumb to Cromwell's forces under the command of Ludlow. According to a prophecy, the castle would only be captured from the water. In 1652 Ludlow had floating batteries brought up river from Castlemaine, then transported overland before launching them on to the lake. Seeing the prophecy about to be fulfilled, the defenders reportedly surrendered promptly.

The castle has been restored – perhaps a little too clinically – by the OPW and entrance is IR£2.50/1. From Killarney, turn right opposite the Esso garage at the beginning of the Kenmare road, just past the roundabout. The castle is at the bottom of the road near the car park.

Muckross House & Gardens
Once you escape the suburbs to the south, you can dive into the extensive grounds of the Muckross Estate. Muckross Abbey was founded in 1448 and put to the torch by Cromwell's troops in 1652. The tombs of the abbey's founder, various Kerry chieftains, and several noted Irish poets are to be found in the choir.

Muckross House has museum exhibits as well as period furnished rooms. It's open daily from 9 am to 7 pm in summer, and till 5.30 pm in winter. Entry is IR£3/1.25. Next to the house there is an exhibition dealing with life in Kerry in the 1930s and while the entrance charge is the same a joint ticket to the house and farm saves IR£2. Both places are run by the OPW.

Continuing east from Muckross House you come to the Meeting of the Waters, Torc Waterfall and finally the road climbs up to Ladies' View which takes its name from Queen Victoria's ladies-in-waiting, who liked it.

The house is six km from town and vehicle access is about one km beyond the Muckross Park Hotel on the N71 Kenmare road. There is a car park about a mile before this on the N71, and directly opposite is an entrance for pedestrians and cyclists. During the summer there is a tourist bus leaving from outside O'Connor's pub (10 am & 2.30 pm) to the house (IR£4 return).

Inisfallen Island
The first monastery on the island is said to have been founded by St Finian the Leper in the 7th century. The island's fame dates from the early 13th century when the *Annals of Inisfallen* were written here. The Annals, now resident at Oxford University, remain a vital source of information for early Irish history. Nothing is now left of the original monastery, but there is a 12th-century oratory with a carved Romanesque doorway and a ruined priory nearby.

From Ross Castle, boats can be hired for

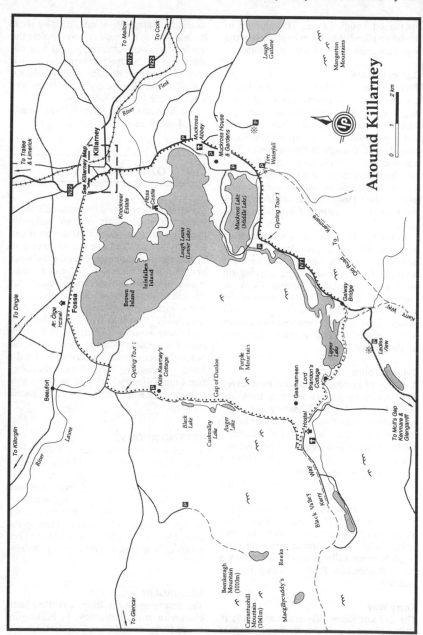

Around Killarney

To Mallow

To Cork

N72

N22

Lough Guitane

Mangerton Mountains

Flesk

River

To Tralee & Limerick

Killarney

See Killarney Map

Muckross Abbey

Muckross House & Gardens

Torc Waterfall

N22

Knockreer Estate

Ross Castle

Muckross Lake (Middle Lake)

Cycling Tour 1

0   1   2 km

To Kenmare (Old Road)

To Dingle

Ar. Óige Hostel

Fossa

Brown Island

Innisfallen Island

Lough Leane (Lower Lake)

N71

Galway Bridge

Kerry Way

Upper Lake

Beaufort

Cycling Tour 1

Kate Kearney's Cottage

Gap of Dunloe

Purple Mountain

Gearhameen

Lord Brandon's Cottage

Ladies' View

To Killorglin

Laune

River

Black Lake

Cushvalley Lake

Auger Lake

Hostel

To Moll's Gap Kenmare & Glengarriff

Black Valley

Kerry Way

Beenkeragh Mountain (1010m)

Carrantuohill Mountain (1041m)

Macgillycuddy's Reeks

To Glencar

rowing on Lough Leane. The journey to Inisfallen Island, which can be seen from the departure point, takes at least 20 minutes.

Gap of Dunloe

This is Killarney tourism at its worst. Every day throughout the summer, cars and buses disgorge countless visitors at Kate Kearney's cottage who then proceed to take a pony-and-trap ride through the Gap of Dunloe (no cars allowed through in the summer). The one-hour trip costs IR£25 in a trap for four. Two-hour trips can be negotiated. You could also walk through the narrow gorge to the Black Valley Hostel at the other end, but don't do this in summer if you want to be alone.

At the turn of this century some 20 men were garrisoned in a Royal Irish Constabulary barracks on the Gap to safeguard the passage of tourists who were arriving on tours established by Thomas Cook & Company in London. Only the ruins of the barracks remain, for the burgeoning crowds of tourists are now welcomed into the county with open arms by a local population grateful for the income.

Cycling Tours

A variety of cycle tours suggest themselves from Killarney and two return trips are marked on the Around Killarney map. One is an adventurous 30-km ride via the Gap of Dunloe and Black Valley Hostel, although the last third of this journey is best undertaken on a dry day. A longer trip is an 80-km journey via Lake Acoose and Moll's Gap and its route is marked out on the ring of Kerry map.

See the Activites chapter for more details of both these trips. The Ring of Kerry seems the obvious choice for a long cycle but it can be busy with traffic. Cutting across the peninsula between Killorglin and Waterville via the Ballaghbeama Pass is highly recommended.

Kerry Way

The 215-km Kerry Way starts and ends in Killarney and is undoubtedly the best way of

seeing the Iveragh Peninsula, rock by rock. It could take up to nine days to complete the whole route, without rushing, and a viable alternative is to do the first three days to the town of Glenbeigh (hostel accommodation is available for all three nights) and then take a bus or hitch back to Killarney.

See the Activities chapter for more details and advice on maps and supplies.

Ring of Kerry

The Ring of Kerry, the 179-km circuit of the Iveragh Peninsula, is one of Ireland's premier tourist attractions. Although it can be 'done' in a day by car or bus, or three days by bicycle, the more time you take the more you'll enjoy it. Getting off the beaten tourist track is also worthwhile. The Ballaghbeama Pass cuts across the peninsula's central highlands with some spectacular views and remarkably little traffic. Anticlockwise is the 'right' way to tackle the ring but in the high season it's probably worth doing it in the 'wrong' direction in order to avoid the tourist buses – all shuffling round in the same direction from Killarney – as well as being able to keep on the side of the road with the scenic views.

GETTING AROUND

The Ring of Kerry bus leaves Killarney in summer at 8.45 am and 1.25 pm (no early bus on Sunday), and stops at Killorglin, Cahirciveen, Waterville, Caherdaniel and Sneem before returning to Killarney. If you're planning a leisurely trip around the Iveragh Peninsula it's worth picking up the timetable from Killarney Bus Station. For details of other buses in the area ring ☎ 064-34777.

KILLORGLIN

The first town on the Ring, travelling anticlockwise from Killarney, is Killorglin, famed for its annual Puck Fair Festival.

Apartheid Without the Name

As you travel round Ireland, you can hardly help noticing the little huddles of caravans clustered in lay-bys on the outskirts of towns. These are home to many of the country's estimated 30,000 tinkers (or travellers, as many prefer to be called these days), a group so unpopular with society at large that they might as well be lepers.

There are many theories to explain the tinkers' origins. Some suggest that they are descendants of children left orphaned by the famine of the mid-19th century, others that they are descendants of families driven westwards by Oliver Cromwell in the 17th century. However, study of their language suggests that the tinkers have been around for much longer than this and that they may actually be descendants of Bronze Age tinsmiths and related to Europe's other gypsy and nomadic groups.

Until recently, tinkers had a distinct place in society. Before the days of Tupperware, their tin receptacles had a real value, as did their donkeys and mules before the advent of tractors. And until radio and television came along, villagers saw their arrival in the district as a way of keeping in touch with what was happening in the world outside. Now, however, all these roles have vanished and the tinkers are left to make ends meet as best they can.

Despite the apparent poverty of the families you see in the lay-bys and the beggars on the streets, some tinkers actually make a good living from the scrap business or from dealing in secondhand cars. Others sell copper or the lead from old car batteries. A few have even grown wealthy trading in antiques. But even when they own fine houses, most still keep their caravans and spend part of every year on the road.

The tinkers have a dismal reputation for drinking and fighting (although they would argue that this is a fine case of the pot and the kettle), and inevitably there are complaints that they leave sites dirty and strewn with litter. Community ties remain very strong, families of 12 children are still common, and single parents are almost unheard of...perhaps not surprisingly since many girls are married as soon as they turn 16.

But the tinkers face an uphill struggle to lead worthy lives. Pubs often refuse to serve them and hotels will turn away bookings for wedding receptions if it's suspected that the happy couple are actually travellers. When their children are admitted to mainstream schools, most other parents forbid their offspring to mix with them, thus depriving them of the social benefits of education. As a result, special schools are sometimes set up for travelling children, guaranteeing that integration doesn't take place. ∎

The Puck Fair Festival

This is a rumbustious three-day celebration that takes place annually during the second weekend in August. The name of the festival derives from the custom of installing a billy goat (a puck), horns festooned in ribbons, on a pedestal in the town centre and leaving it there while everyone takes advantage of the special licensing hours. Pubs stay open till 3 am, although it often seems that they simply serve for three days nonstop. Accommodation is hard to come by if you haven't booked in advance.

Places to Stay

Camping Just under two km from the bridge in Killorglin, on the road to Killarney, is the small unregistered *West Camping Site*

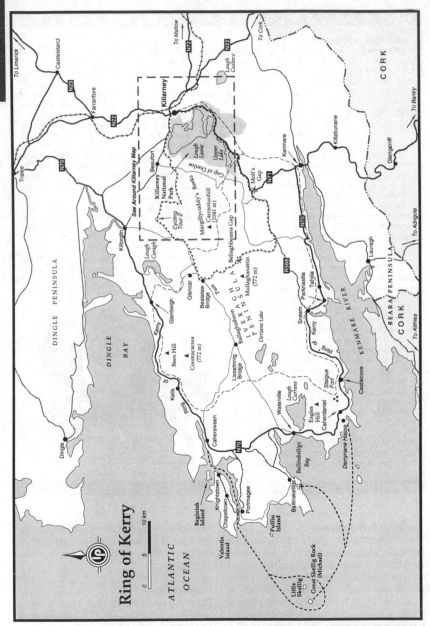

Ring of Kerry

(☎ 066-61240). The Laune Valley Farm Hostel also has camping space.

Hostel About two km from the bridge, on the road to Tralee, the IHH *Laune Valley Farm Hostel* (☎ 066-61488) comes complete with satellite TV. A bed in a dorm is IR£6, doubles IR£16.

B&Bs There is the usual string of B&Bs on the roads in and out of town.

Places to Eat
Lunch for IR£6 is available from *Bunkers*, a combined pub/restaurant/takeaway. Less expensive is the *Starlite Diner* café in the town centre. *Nick's Restaurant* (☎ 066-61219) in Main St does seafood and steaks in the IR£12 to IR£20 bracket. A more interesting menu is at *Bianconi* (☎ 066-61146), a cosy pub and restaurant next door, with seafood and meat dinners from IR£13 and bar food available until 9.30 pm. There is also a pizza bar that closes with the pub.

For something more sedate try a relaxing dinner, country house style and surrounded by antiques, at *Caragh Lodge* (☎ 066-69115) for around IR£25. A stroll by the lake and a drink in the lounge precede dinner; afterwards there are drinks by the fireside.

Entertainment
Two pubs have regular music at night. *Bianconi* has a piano player while the *Old Forge* has traditional ballad sessions.

Getting Around
Bicycles can be hired from O'Shea's Cycle Centre (☎ 066-61919/61180) in Lower Bridge St. Bikes are IR£6 a day, weekly IR£35, and helmets and panniers can also be rented.

GLENBEIGH
Between Killorglin and Glenbeigh, on the main road next to the Red Fox pub, the **Kerry Bog Village Museum** recreates an early 19th-century Kerry home. Admission is IR£2.50/1, open from 8.30 am to 7 pm.

Glenbeigh, 10 km west of Killorglin, is nestled at the floor of Seefin Mountain and this small town has the attraction of a superb Blue Flag beach (unpolluted and safe for swimming with lifeguards on duty during the day), as well as being on the Kerry Way.

Rossbeigh Strand
The five km of sand look across to the Dingle Peninsula and even with a camp site in the vicinity it is easy to find a quiet spot. Swimming is safe and the mud flats at the eastern spit of land is good birdwatching territory. To get there, bear right for three km at the Y-junction at the Cahirciveen end of town.

Places to Stay
Camping The *Glenross Caravan & Camping Park* (☎ 066-31590/68451) is in town next to the Glenbeigh Hotel; two people with a tent and car will be charged IR£8.50, two people without a car and with or without a bike IR£7. The other camp site, *Falvey's* (☎ 066-68238), is on the road out to Kells; the corresponding rates here are IR£10 and IR£7.

Hostel At the Killorglin end of town the *Hillside House Hostel* (☎ 066-68228) is the only available budget accommodation, charging IR£5 per night.

B&Bs *Village House* (☎ 066-68128) has rooms from IR£25/32 in town, while *Ocean Wave* (☎ 066-68249), a few doors away, charges IR£19/28, as does *Ocean Star* (☎ 066-68123).

Hotels The *Towers Hotel* (☎ 066-68212), in the centre of town, is a cosy, relaxed place well used to families. Singles/doubles are from IR£40/60. The other two hotels are at opposite ends of town: the *Falcon Inn* (☎ 066-68215) is at the Cahirciveen end with rooms from IR£20/35, while the *Glenbeigh* (☎ 066-68333) is by the side of the road to Killarney with rooms from IR£20/36.

Places to Eat
Nowhere has really inexpensive food. The pubs are best for lunch, including the *Red*

Fox Inn out of town towards Killorglin. On the beach the *Ross Inn* has pub food.

The three hotels all have restaurants for dinner. The fresh seafood at the *Glenbeigh* is excellent, the atmosphere a little quieter than the others and a set dinner costs IR£16.50. Set dinners are IR£18 at the *Towers* and IR£12.50 at the *Falcon Inn*.

Entertainment

The *Towers* and *Glenbeigh* hotels have music in their bars and the *Red Fox Inn* usually has something happening at weekends. The *Ross Inn* has bands, and local shops display posters for events there.

KELLS

Between Glenbeigh and Cahirciveen, near Kells, the route of the old Great Southern & Western Railway (a branch line which ran from Killorglin to Valentia Harbour Station, just west of Cahirciveen, and closed in 1960) can be clearly seen on the hillside, with its tunnels and retaining walls. The small beach near Kells is three km off the road, but it doesn't look very clean. On the main road there is the Caitin Beatear's pub/heritage centre.

Places to Stay

The *Kells Bay Caravan & Camping Park* (☎ 066-77647) is 1.5 km off the road and signposted. *Mrs Golden* (☎ 066-77601) at the post office does B&B or there is *Seaview* (☎ 066-77610) down by the beach.

Places to Eat

Caitin Beatear's is a pub and restaurant and the thatched roof is a magnet for coach parties. Irish stew and seafood feature on the menu and musical sessions are held regularly throughout the summer. It doubles as a small heritage centre with wall displays, farm machinery, and a Neolithic standing stone not far away. Snacks and tourist information are available at *Pat's* craft shop at the Cahirciveen end of Kells.

CAHIRCIVEEN

As late as 1815, there were only five houses in Cahirciveen. Daniel O'Connell, whose name is indissolubly linked with the early 19th-century campaign for the Catholics' right to become MPs, came from near here. The ruins of his home can still be seen on the left of the new bridge entering town from the Kells end. There are also some prehistoric sites in the area.

Information

The tourist office (☎ 066-72777) is in The Barracks. Coming from the Kells end of town turn right at the junction of Bridge and Church Sts.

Continue across the bridge for White Strand, about five km away and safe for swimming.

The Skellig Experience boat tour (see the Valentia section below) departs from Cahirciveen every day except Monday and Friday at 12.15 pm, returning at 5.15 pm. Cost is IR£18/9.

The Barracks

Another heritage centre, but this one is superbly situated in what was once an intimidating Royal Irish Constabulary (RIC) barracks. The building was burned down in 1922 by Anti-Treaty forces but has now been reconstructed to its remarkable state. The story goes that the plans for this building got mixed up with ones intended for India; when you see the place you might believe in this particular piece of blarney.

Exhibits inside have information on Daniel O'Connell and other subjects of local interest. There is a coffee shop serving meals and Skellig trips can be booked here. Admission is set at IR£3/2 but may be reduced a little in future.

Places to Stay

Camping *Mannix Point Caravan & Camping Park* (☎ 066-72806), a 15-minute walk from the town, is well run and charges a flat rate of IR£3 per person, including showers. As with the hostel, boat operators for the Skelligs will pick up passengers from the camp site.

Camping is also possible at the hostel.

RICHARD STEWART

SEAN SHEEHAN

SEAN SHEEHAN

RICHARD STEWART

RICHARD STEWART

SEAN SHEEHAN

County Kerry

A: St Mary's Cathedral, Killarney
B: Dingle Peninsula
C: The Bog Village Museum, near
   Glenbeigh

D: Tombstone, Muckross Abbey,
   Killarney
E: Tunnel near Killarney
F: Ring of Kerry, near Kells

TONY WHEELER

TONY WHEELER

TONY WHEELER

TOM SMALLMAN

A	
C	B
D	

Counties Limerick & Tipperary

A: Street sign in Limerick City
B: King John's Castle, Limerick City
C: Cottage in Adare, County Limerick
D: Rock of Cashel, Tipperary

Hostel The IHH *Sive Hostel* (☎ 066-72717) is at the east end of the long main street. Beds are IR£6 and there's one double for IR£15. Trips to the Skelligs can be arranged from here.

B&Bs In Newmarket St *O'Driscoll's Town House* (☎ 066-72531) has rooms, as well as being a pub and restaurant. *Mount Rivers* (☎ 066-72509) costs from IR£15/28 and is an attractive old house on the road east to Killarney.

Hotel The only hotel here is the charmless *Ringside Rest* (☎ 066-72543) on Valentia Rd, which offers singles/doubles for IR£22/38.

Places to Eat

Meals at *Grudles* and *Ben's Bistro* (which is open till 10 pm) are the best value at around IR£5. Food can be taken away from the *Red Rose Restaurant* in Church St opposite the O'Connell Memorial Church.

The *Old School House* (☎ 066-72426) has a reputation for first-class seafood, at around IR£20 a head. *The Point Bar* pub has a restaurant with excellent seafood and salads plus lovely views of Valentia.

Entertainment

The *Sceilig Rock Bar* has traditional music. There is also the *Harp* which sometimes has discos. The *Shebeen* is more touristy. The *Anchor Bar* doesn't have music but there's a good atmosphere and *Mike Murt's* pub is equally good in this respect.

If you don't like any of these, then there are almost 50 more to visit!

Getting There & Away

Apart from the regular Ring of Kerry bus service there is a private bus service (☎ 066-72249) between Cahirciveen and Killarney. It departs from the pier at 5.15 pm and the single/return fare is IR£5/8.

Getting Around

Bicycles can be hired from Casey's (☎ 066-72474) on the main street.

VALENTIA ISLAND

Valentia is 11 km long and three wide but even so, it doesn't really feel like an island, especially if you come by road. In the summer it's a popular resort and scuba-diving centre.

The main town is Knightstown, three km from the Ring of Kerry road and accessible by ferry. It is named after the Knight of Kerry who once owned it. Most visitors reach the island by the long bridge from Portmagee, turning right at the other end of the bridge for the road to Chapeltown and then Knightstown.

See the following Skellig Island section for information about the Skellig Experience Centre on Valentia Island.

Heritage Centre

The main item of interest here is the history of the Valentia-US cable. The island was chosen as the site for the first transatlantic telegraph cable, and when the connection was made in 1858, the town of Cahirciveen was in direct contact with New York, but not with Dublin! It worked for 27 days before it failed, but went back into action some years later. The telegraph station was in operation until 1966.

The centre is open from May to September, from 11 am to 6 pm, and is in an old school on the road from Knightstown to the quarry.

The Quarry

In the 19th century the quarrying of slate was an important activity, with boats from the nearby harbour carrying away the roofing slates and flagstones. If you ever wondered what Charing Cross railway station in London and San Salvador station in El Salvador have in common, the answer is that they were both roofed with slate from Valentia.

Today the site features a disused quarry tunnel that has been converted into a tasteless religious grotto, but despite this the place retains a sense of history.

KERRY

Beginish & Church Islands

These two small islands are both in the harbour. The beach on Beginish is excellent and swimming is safe here. Church Island, to the east, has the remains of an 8th-century oratory and some beehive huts. Enquire at the Royal & Pier Hostel about boat trips to the islands.

Angling & Diving

For sea angling trips contact Dan McCrohan (☎ 066-76142) at Knightstown. For diving there are three reliable centres: Des Lavelle (☎ 066-76124),the Valentia Hyperbaric Diving Centre (☎ 066-76225) and Valentia Island Sea Sports (☎ 066-76204).

Places to Stay

Hostels There are three hostels on Valentia Island. The *Ring Lyne Hostel* (☎ 066-76103) is at Chapeltown, half way between the bridge and Knightstown. Beds here are IR£5, 50p for a shower and doubles are IR£10. The *Royal & Pier Hostel* (☎ 066-76144), down by the harbour, has beds for IR£5 and IR£6.50. You can book here for trips to the Skelligs.

The An Óige *Valentia Island Hostel* (☎ 066-76141) at Knightstown occupies three of the former coastguard station cottages.

B&Bs Before Knightstown, *Glenreen Heights* (☎ 066-76241) has singles/doubles from IR£18.50/29. In Knightstown by the harbour, the Victorian building that is now home to the *Royal & Pier Hostel* also does B&B for IR£16 a head. Also on the waterfront, *Lavelle's* (☎ 066-76124), once part of the original transatlantic telegraph station, is now a diving centre, with rooms for IR£16/29.

Places to Eat

At the western end of Knightstown the *Islander Café* is OK but the *Gallery Kitchen* is more inviting, being a restaurant, wine bar and sculpture gallery. Meals are available to non-residents at the *Ring Lyne*, which has a bar and restaurant; three-course meals at

IR£6-9 are served till 10 pm. The *Royal Pier Hostel* also has a restaurant and an evening meal is IR£9. At Chapeltown, *Curran's petrol station* has a coffee shop doing light meals and snacks.

For pub food, *Boston's* serves very good home-cooked dishes. Two of the pubs at Portmagee, the *Bridge Bar* and the *Fisherman's Bar*, are also worth trying.

Entertainment

In Chapeltown the *Ring Lyne* has musical sessions after 9.30 pm, most evenings of the week. In Knightstown, *Boston's Bar* comes alive on Friday and Sunday. In Portmagee the *Bridge Bar* is worth checking out and sometimes has free set-dancing lessons.

Getting There & Away

The Maurice O'Neill bridge at Portmagee leads to Valentia Island. For pedestrians and cyclists there is a ferry from Reenard to Knightstown that takes 15 minutes.

A ferry service operates between Valentia and Dingle, departing from Knightstown at 9.30 am and 4.45 pm, single fare is IR£10/5, return IR£12/6.

Getting Around

There are no buses on the island but bikes can be hired from Curran's (☎ 066-76297) at Chapeltown.

SKELLIG ISLANDS

I tell you the thing does not belong to any world that you and I have lived and worked in: it is part of our dream world.
George Bernard Shaw, 1910.

A boat trip to the Skellig Islands (*Oileáin na Scealaga*) is one of the highlights of Ireland, and Shaw's comment still holds good. The 217-metre jagged rock of Skellig Michael, the larger of the two, looks like the last place on earth that anyone would try to land, let alone establish a community. Yet early Christian monks survived here from the 7th until the 12th or 13th century. They were influenced by the Egyptian Coptic Church founded by St Anthony in the deserts of

Egypt and Libya, and their desire for solitude led them to this remote, most westerly corner of Europe.

After the introduction of the Gregorian calendar in 1582, Skellig became a popular spot for weddings. Marriages were forbidden during Lent, but since Skellig operated by a different calendar, a quick trip over to the islands allowed those unable to wait for Easter to tie the knot. In time these annual pilgrimages became an excuse for other jollifications, and crates of alcohol were hauled over to facilitate the merrymaking. There is even a record of the police being called to the island.

The Monastery

The monastic buildings are perched on a saddle in the rock, some 150 metres above sea level. The oratories and beehive cells vary in size, the largest cell having a floor space of 4.5 by 3.6 metres and they're all astounding. The projecting stones on the outside have more than one possible explanation: steps to reach the top and release chimney stones, or maybe holding places for turf that covered the exterior. There are interior rows of stones in some of the cells, and the guides who live on the rock during the summer will provide a possible explanation for these as well.

Very little is known about the life of the monastery, but there are records of a Viking raid in 812 and again in 823. Monks were killed or taken away but the community recovered and carried on.

Bird Life

From the boat, look out for the diminutive storm petrel, a black bird that darts around over the water like a swallow, and the large fulmar with a wingspan of 107 cm. Kittiwakes – seagulls with black-tipped wings – are easy to see and hear around the covered walkway just after stepping off the boat. They spend the winter at sea but thousands come to Skellig Michael to breed between March and August.

On the rock itself the delightful puffins with their multicoloured beaks and waddling

steps are all around. The puffin lays one egg in May at the end of a burrow and the parent bird will be seen guarding its nest, with as much dignity as it can manage.

The boat trip should take you past the Small Skellig where some 20,000 pairs of gannets breed. Check beforehand if the boat will pause to look for basking seals. The visitors' centre at the Skellig Experience has a good display on the birdlife and is worth visiting in advance.

The Skellig Experience Centre

This visitor centre – a Bord Fáilte venture – is well worth a visit and has interesting exhibitions on the life and times of the monks, the history of the lighthouses on Skellig Michael, and the wildlife. A 15-minute audiovisual show deals with the monastery.

The boat trip does not actually land on Skellig Michael. It does get close, however, and there are good opportunities for photography; the onboard commentary is good too. The centre and boat have access for the disabled.

Admission to the centre only is IR£3/1.50 while the cruise, (departing daily at 2.30 pm) and centre is IR£15/13.50. The Skellig Experience visitors' centre is on the left just before the bridge from Portmagee to Valentia.

Getting There & Away

Joe Roddy (☎ 066-74268) operates a 40-minute boat journey from Ballinskelligs which, given the name, may well be the monks' original departure point. He is also very knowledgeable on the history and ornithology of the rocks and will gladly dispense information. His boats usually go around 10-11 am but ring to confirm.

Other boats from Ballinskelligs are Sean Feehan (☎ 066-79182) and J B Walsh (☎ 066-79147).

Brendan O'Keefe (☎ 066-77103) operates from Portmagee and can be contacted at the Fisherman's Bar pub in Portmagee. Also departing from Portmagee are Murphy's (☎ 066-77156) and Casey's (☎ 066-77125). The latter's main booking office is in Cahirciveen (☎ 066-72437/72069).

On Valentia, Lavelle's (☎ 066-76124) or the Royal & Pier Hostel (☎ 066-76144) do trips. Near Caherdaniel, Sean O'Shea (☎ 066-75129) also runs a trip.

The standard fare for most of the operators is IR£20 but you may be able to negotiate reductions for students or children.

WATERVILLE

This popular resort is on a narrow bit of land between Ballinskelligs Bay and Lough Currane. Charlie Chaplin was probably the town's most famous visitor, and photographs of him here can be seen in the Butler Arms pub.

The *Waterville Leisure Hostel* (☎ 066-74644) is at the Cahirciveen end of town. Beds are IR£6.50/14, meals are available and bikes can be hired. *Waterville Camping & Caravan Park* (☎ 066-74191) is 1 km north of town off the main road to Cahirciveen.

Fishing

There are lots of angling possibilities around Waterville. Lough Currane is a free fishing lake for sea trout while the Inny River is a breeding ground for wild salmon and trout. Sea angling takes in mackerel, pollack and shark. For information ask at O'Sullivan's, a tackle shop between the hostel and Silver Sands on the main street, or enquire at the Lobster Bar (☎ 066-74183).

SKELLIG RING

The Skellig Ring is a scenic route that leaves the main road to Cahirciveen after Waterville. It begins with a turn to the left, clearly signposted, and goes down to an unmarked junction: the short road to the left goes to Ballinskelligs Bay, the road straight on goes to the departure point for the Skelligs, and a right turn eventually leads to Portmagee. It makes an interesting cycling route, but there are lots of small unmarked roads and it's easy to take a wrong turning.

Ballinskelligs Monastery

The exact relationship between this monastery and the one on Skellig Michael is not clear. It was probably founded after the

monks left Skellig in the 12th or 13th century. The sea is gradually wearing away at the ruins and it's the sort of place that children like to explore. Take the road down to Ballinskelligs Bay and walk to the remains from there.

Ballinskelligs Bay

At the western end of this Blue Flag beach are the last remnants of a castle, a 16th-century stronghold of the McCarthys.

Places to Stay

The An Óige *Ballingskelligs Hostel* (☎ 066-79229) is reached by turning right at the small junction after passing the Sigerson Arms on the Skellig Ring. The *Sigerson Arms* (☎ 066-79104) has half a dozen beds from IR£16/30 and overlooks the bay near the hostel.

Places to Eat

After leaving Waterville, but before reaching the beach, the *Sigerson Arms* is passed on the left. This pub is about the only place where food can be found.

CAHERDANIEL
Derrynane National Historic Park

The coastal area around Caherdaniel was once the centre of large-scale smuggling with France and Spain, a source of wealth for the O'Connells. They owned Derrynane House and the surrounding parkland, evading official restrictions on the purchase of land by Catholics with the help of a co-operative Protestant.

The house is open to the public and is largely furnished with items relating to Daniel O'Connell, the campaigner for Catholic emancipation. The dining room is full of early 19th-century furniture and silver given to O'Connell by grateful Catholics. The drawing room is renowned for its table, which was carved over a period of four years by two men. The adjoining parkland includes a sandy beach and Abbey Island, which can usually be reached on foot across the sand. A little way to the east of the house is an Ogham stone.

The house is open from May to September, Monday to Saturday, from 9 am to 6 pm, Sunday 11 am to 7 pm. It's closed November to March and during the remaining time it's open afternoons only and closed Monday. Admission is IR£2/1.

Activities

Caherdaniel competes with Valentia as the base for diving off the Iveragh Peninsula. There are two companies offering courses and equipment hire. One of them, the Derrynane Diving School (☎ 066-75110) includes a half-day discovery course for those without certificates. Celtic Adventures (☎ 066-75277) organise a variety of outdoor courses including diving trips off the Skellig Islands, abseiling, rock climbing and hill walking. Derrynane Sea Sports (☎ 066-75266) is the place to contact for canoeing, wind-surfing and water-skiing.

Places to Stay

There are two camp sites: the *Wave Crest* (☎ 066-75188) which has lots of facilities but only 10 tent pitches, and *Ocean Billow* (☎ 066-75188). There are two hostels: the *Carrigbeg* (☎ 066-75229) with singles/doubles for IR£5.50/14 and the IHH *Village Hostel* (☎ 066-75227) which costs IR$6 plus a 50p shower; no doubles here. B&Bs include *Mrs O'Sullivan* (☎ 066-75124) from IR£18.50/27 and *The Old Forge* (☎ 066-75140) from IR£18/28.

STAIGUE FORT

This 2000-year-old fort is one of the finest dry-stone buildings in Ireland. The five-metre circular wall is up to four metres thick and surrounded by a large bank and ditch. It is similar in style to the Grianan of Aileach in County Donegal but has not been restored to the same degree.

The exact age of the fort is not known but it probably dates from the 3rd or 4th century AD. It cannot be seen from the sea, although it has sweeping views down to the coast. It may have been a communal place of refuge, or a royal residence as the sophisticated staircases incorporated into the walls suggest. The answer is

lost in time, but the fort remains an astonishing testimony to the skill of its builders.

It's about three km off the main road, reached by a country lane which narrows as it climbs to the site. In summer the road and carpark are the scene of absurd traffic jams! There's an honesty box by the gate asking for 50p, children free.

SNEEM

Visitors have differing reactions to the oddly named town of Sneem (pronounced 'shneem', derived from the Irish *snaidhm*, meaning 'knot' or 'twist', from the snaky river.) It's quaint to some, while to others, who never see the place in winter, it seems to have sold out completely to tourism.

Museum

The small museum, housed in the old courthouse, looks like a cluttered antique shop inside. The curator, Tim Reilly, may talk about the exhibits. A newspaper cutting shows that Charles de Gaulle stayed in Sneem in 1969 – perhaps recovering from the ferment of 1968.

The museum is open seven days a week during the summer, from 10 am to 5.30 pm (closed 1 to 2 pm), and admission is 50p.

Places to Stay

Camping There is a small camp site (☎ 064-45181) in town. Turn down past the bridge, near the church. Campers can fish in the river nearby. Camping should also be possible at the hostel.

Hostel The *Harbour View* (☎ 064-45276) is about to open, located off the main road at the Kenmare end. Beds are IR£6-7.50 and en suite doubles IR£18.

B&Bs *Woodvale House* (☎ 064-45181) is next to the camp site in town and is owned by the same family. Singles/doubles are IR£20/30. *Derry East Farmhouse* (☎ 064-45193) is out of town on the road to Waterville and has singles/doubles from IR£18.50/27, and an evening meal for IR£12.

Hotel The *Great Southern* (☎ 064-45122) is a few km along the Kenmare road, and costs IR£146 for a double. The guest list includes Charles de Gaulle, Princess Grace of Monaco and Bernard Shaw (who wrote most of *St Joan* here).

Places to Eat

There are a few places offering snacks and meals. Either side of the pretty bridge *The Green House* and *Riverside* (with a wider menu) do sandwiches. *Stone House*, at the Caherdaniel end, does lunch for IR£5 and dinner around IR£8-12. Also at this end of the village the *Sacre Coeur Restaurant* does seafood for around IR£10, a little less for meat dishes.

The *Pygmalion Restaurant* at the Great Southern is the most prestigious place on the Ring of Kerry. Dinner is around IR£30.

Getting There & Away

Apart from the regular Ring of Kerry bus service there is a bus between Kenmare and Sneem operating in July and August.

Getting Around

Burns Bike Hire (☎ 064-45140) in town is open all week. Bikes are IR£5 a day and IR£30 a week.

KENMARE

This pastel-painted little town is a good alternative to Killarney as a base in the Ring of Kerry area. It's very touristy, crowded with restaurants, but not as big as Killarney. Henry, Main and Shelbourne Sts make a neat triangle defining the town centre. Henry St is dedicated to tourism, with almost every place a pub, a restaurant or a B&B.

Information

The tourist office (☎ 064-41233), near the town square, is open from 9.30 am to 7 pm in the summer, Monday to Saturday and also Sunday in July and August. Pick up the free Heritage Trail leaflet that maps out the town's places of historical interest.

The Kenmare Bookshop is on Shelbourne St near the Main St corner.

Things to See & Do

An ancient **stone circle** is signposted from the park end of Main St, beyond the Henry St junction. The **Kenmare Heritage Centre** is entered through the tourist office. It focuses on the history of the area and admission is IR£2/1. **River Cruises** (☎ 064-83171) on Kenmare Bay depart from the pier near the suspension bridge and last for just under two hours. The cost is IR£7.50/4.50.

Places to Stay

Camping The *Ring of Kerry Caravan & Camping Park* (☎ 064-41366) is four km west of town on the Sneem road. Large/small tents are IR£6.50/2 plus IR£1.50 per adult.

Hostels The IHH *Fáilte Hostel* (☎ 064-41083) is at the junction of Henry and Shelbourne Sts. Beds are singles/doubles IR£6/16. *Kenmare Private Hostel* (☎ 064-41260) is on Main St but it wasn't open earlier in the year so ring first to check. Seven km beyond Kenmare on the road to Killarney, behind a Catholic church, the *Bonane Hostel* (☎ 064-41098) has beds at IR£6, and camping is possible but without the use of the kitchen.

B&Bs There are plenty of B&Bs and one of the best is *Sallyport House* (☎ 064-42066), at the Bantry end of town just before the bridge. Doubles are from IR£40 and there are delightful river views.

Hotels Two of Ireland's most expensive hotels compete for business in Kenmare: the *Park* (☎ 064-41200) and the *Sheen Falls Lodge* (☎ 064-41600). The Park is the oldest and has a superb interior full of antiques. The Sheen Falls is next to the old Kenmare cemetery, with the remains of a 7th-century church and a walk down to the sea. A double at either will set you back over IR£200.

The *Wander Inn* in Henry St charges from IR£18/25.

Places to Eat

Cafés Try the simple *Clifford Café* on Main

St with its outdoor patio, or the fancier *Mickey Ned's*.

Foley's on Henry St does a pub lunch and dinner. *Le Brasserie* opposite does lunch for around IR£5.

Restaurants Places in town include the *Purple Heather Bistro* on Henry St and *An Leath Pingin* on Main St. Near the Fáilte hostel, *Virginia's* serves meat dishes under IR£10 and Guinness fruit cake. The *Old Bank House Restaurant* (☎ 064-41589) at the top of Main St has main dishes around IR£12, while *Giuliano's* next door is a pizzeria open daily for lunch and dinner with main dishes around IR£5-10.

Especially good restaurants are the *Waterfront* (☎ 064-41299) at the Riversdale House hotel, where a seafood dinner is IR£20, and *The Lime Tree* (☎ 064-41225), a cosy and attractive place in Shelbourne St with main dishes around IR£12.

Things to Buy
Quills Woollen Market has a large store in the centre of town.

Getting There & Away
Apart from the main Ring of Kerry bus service there is a July and August service between Sneem and Kenmare. The bus stop is outside Brennan's pub on Main St.

Getting Around
Finnigan's (☎ 064-41083) at the Fáilte Hostel has bikes for hire.

Beara Peninsula

Most of this peninsula is in County Cork, but a small part in the north-east is in Kerry.

CYCLING & WALKING TOURS
About one km west of Lauragh on the R572 there is a road off to the left marked for Glanmore Lake. Take the first turning to the right along this road and follow it until it comes to an end by a couple of farms, the

first of which has a stone circle in its back yard. Although the road ends, a pathway continues across the stream and into the valley until it ends by the remains of some stone dwellings. This is a pleasant and undemanding walk which takes less than an hour from the stone circle.

A more exhilarating walk is to head up behind the house with the stone circle, crossing a sheep fence and keeping to the right of the stream. A stiff climb leads to a hanging valley with mountains on both sides. Avoid the one on the left and head right to climb the shorter summit of Cummeennahillan (361 metres). From here you can walk along the ridge of the mountain and down through holly woods and invasive rhododendrons through another farm to the Glanmore Lake road. The longer trek takes at least a couple of hours, but a wander around the top of Cummeennahillan offers tremendous views from the top and a fine descent along the hanging valley.

LAURAGH
The 11-km Healy Pass offers the most scenic views when commenced at Lauragh, which is also home to **Derreen Gardens**. The gardens are now over a century old and were planted by the fifth Lord Lansdowne. An abundance of interesting plants thrive here, including spectacular New Zealand tree ferns and red cedars that are normally found in rainforests. The gardens are open April to September from 11 am to 6 pm and admission is IR£2.50. They are just west of Lauragh, which can be reached from Kenmare or from Adrigole in the south, via the Healy Pass.

The *Creveen Lodge Caravan & Camping Park* (☎ 064-83131) is 1.5 km south-east of Lauragh on the Healy Pass road and is open from Easter to the end of September. The An Óige *Glanmore Lake Hostel* (☎ 064-83181), five km from Lauragh, is open from April to September. *Mountain View* (☎ 064-83143), distinctively located on the Healy Pass, does B&B for IR£18/26 and dinner for IR£11.

Tralee & North Kerry

The north Kerry landscape is mediocre at best and many travellers rush through the area on the way to Clare via the ferry at Tarbert. However, there are some places of historical interest and the coastal strip is popular with Irish holidaymakers.

TRALEE

Tralee (*Trá Lí*) has some tourist attractions but may not detain you for long. The Dingle Peninsula is the major reason for coming here and the town makes a useful stopover, being well-provided with hostels, places to eat and lively music pubs. The Rose of Tralee festival, in the last week of August, is based around a renowned beauty contest and most of the B&B places increase their prices by IR£3 or IR£4 for its duration, helping to create a seedy commercialism that lingers on after the crowds have departed.

The town has a long history of rebellion. In the 16th century the last ruling earl of the Desmonds was captured south of the town and executed. His head was sent to Elizabeth I, who had it exposed on London Bridge. The Desmond property was given to Sir Edward Denny. The Desmond castle once stood at the junction of Denny St and the Mall .

Tralee has a strong Republican tradition, and until quite recently there was a Sinn Fein office in the town.

Information

The tourist office (☎ 066-21288) is open all year and seven days a week in July and August from 9 am to 7 pm (closed Sunday in May and June). It is at the side of the Ashe Memorial Hall. The building is named after Thomas Ashe, a Kerryman who in 1916 led the largest Easter Rising action outside of Dublin. He died the following year from medical neglect after being forcibly fed while on hunger strike in prison.

Kerry the Kingdom

Upstairs in the Ashe Memorial Hall is a museum that gives a compact history of Ireland, with a Kerry bias of course. Downstairs an exhibition recreates the 15th-century walled town of Tralee and visitors are shunted around in little buggies with a voice-over commentary. Children enjoy it and a commentary in French and other languages is available here and in the museum.

The exhibition is open from 9.30 am to 6 pm during July and August, and from 3 to 5 pm the rest of the year including Sunday. Admission is IR£3.95/2.50.

Steam Railway

Between 1891 and 1953 a narrow-gauge railway connected Tralee with Dingle. The first short leg of the journey, from Tralee to Blennerville, has been reopened. The train leaves Ballyard (☎ 066-28888) on the hour, from 11 am to 5 pm, and the fare is IR£2.50/1.50.

Blennerville Windmill

This is the largest working mill in Ireland or Britain. It was built around 1800 by the local landlord, and fell into disuse by 1880 before being restored to its present grandeur. A short video tells the story of its history and there are guided tours.

There is also an exhibition about the thousands of emigrants who boarded the coffin ships for a new life in the USA. There are craft shops and a cafeteria.

The windmill is open from 10 am to 6 pm from Monday to Saturday (8 pm in August), 1 to 6 pm on Sunday, from March to early November. Admission is IR£2.50/1.50. To get there, take the main road west to Dingle for just over one km. It is difficult to miss.

Siamsa Tire

This is the National Folk Theatre of Ireland (pronounced 'shee-am-sah-tee-reh') whose performances, in song, dance and mime, recreate aspects of Gaelic culture. The shows are folksy at best. Events take place at the company theatre (☎ 066-23055), close to the tourist office, at 8.30 pm throughout the summer. Admission is IR£8/7.

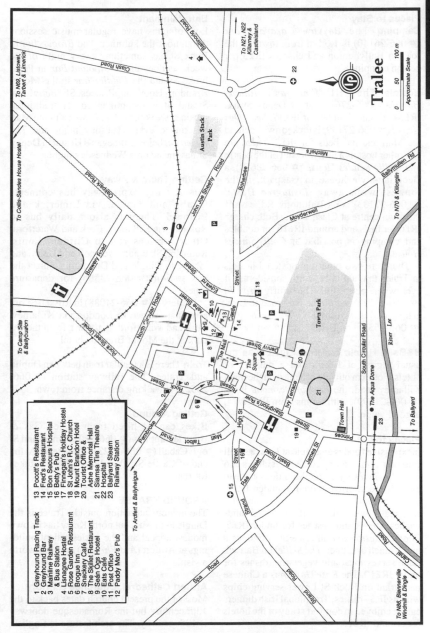

Tralee

0   50   100 m
Approximate Scale

1   Greyhound Racing Track
2   Greyhound Bar
3   Mainline Railway
    & Bus Station
4   Lisnagree Hostel
5   Rose Garden Restaurant
6   Brogue Inn
7   Snackery Café
8   The Skillet Restaurant
9   Seán Ogs Hostel
10 Eats Café
11 Post Office
12 Paddy Mac's Pub
13 Pocott's Restaurant
14 Fred's Restaurant
15 Bon Secours Hospital
16 Betty's Pub
17 Finnegan's Holiday Hostel
18 St John's R.C. Church
19 Mount Brandon Hotel
20 Tourist Office &
    Ashe Memorial Hall
21 Siamsa Tíre Theatre
22 Hospital
23 Ballyard Steam
    Railway Station

Places to Stay

Camping The *Bayview Caravan Park* (☎ 066-26140) is 1.6 km from town on the road to Ballybunion and charges IR£3 per person camping.

Hostels The IHH *Finnegan's Holiday Hostel* (☎ 066-27610), at 17 Denny St has IR£6 beds and doubles for IR£17. *Seán Ógs Hostel* (☎ 066-27199) is tucked away behind the Mall and has beds for IR£5. There are two other hostels a little way out of the centre and *Collis-Sandes House* (☎ 066-28658), a Georgian-style house in Oakpark, is the longest walk away. *Lisnagree Hostel* (☎ 066-27133) is on Ballinorig Rd, east of the town centre at Clash Cross. Both charge IR£6 for beds and around IR£16 for doubles and camping is possible at *Collis-Sandes House*.

There are two other unregistered hostels in Tralee that are only worth considering if everywhere else is full. The scruffy *Drive In* (☎ 066-21272) out on the N69 road to Limerick, and the noisy *White House* pub (☎ 066-25311) on Boherbee in town.

B&Bs & Hotels Tralee has more than the usual legion of B&Bs and a number of hotels. Four km outside of Tralee on the main Killarney road, the *Earl of Desmond* hotel (☎ 066-21299), with rooms from IR£28/44, is good value.

Places to Eat

Inexpensive food is available at *Eats*, a small café on a corner along Ashe St. It closes at 6 pm. The *Snackery* on the Mall does a cheap breakfast and fried food for under IR£5. *Fred's Restaurant* on Castle St is more of a café really but with a wide menu of sandwiches, steaks and pastries for under IR£5. *Pocott's Restaurant* on Ashe St is fine for a quick lunch or dinner. *The Skillet* on Barrack Lane serves meat and vegetarian dishes for under IR£10. The *Rose Garden* is a Chinese restaurant on Rock St Lower serving chips with its IR$7 dishes. Traditional Irish dinners can be enjoyed in comfort at any of the hotels for around IR£12.

Entertainment

Lots of pubs have regular music sessions throughout the summer. The *Brogue Inn* in Rock St has something every night of the week, as does the *Greyhound Bar* in Pembroke St and the *Fiddler Bar* in the Mount Brandon Hotel on Princes St. *Betty's* on Strand St is recommended for traditional music at weekends. *Paddy Mac's* in the Mall has music every Tuesday night and *The Basement* below Finnegan's Hostel in Denny St has music on a Wednesday night.

Getting There & Away

Bus A daily expressway bus connects Dublin and Tralee, via Limerick and Listowel. There is also a daily bus to Rosslare via Killarney, Cork and Waterford. Other services run to Clifden, Ennis, Kenmare, Shannon, Westport and Derry, and locally to Dingle and Dunquin. Contact the bus station (☎ 066-23566) for departure times.

Slattery's (☎ 066-24088) in Russell St run a regular service to London via Killarney, Cork and Waterford, departing from the car park at the Mount Brandon hotel.

Train There is a regular train between Dublin and Tralee. The railway station (☎ 066-23522) is walking distance from town.

Getting Around

Bikes can be hired from Tralee Gas & Bicycle Supplies (☎ 066-22018) in Strand St or E Caball (☎ 066-22231) in Ashe St. At the end of Castle St, O'Halloran also has bikes for rent.

AROUND TRALEE

The obvious attraction outside Tralee is the Dingle Peninsula but north Kerry has its own modest appeal and the ecclesiastical buildings at Ardfert (*Ard Fhearta*) are well worth a visit.

Ardfert Cathedral, Churches & Priory

Most of the present church dates back to the 13th century but the Romanesque doorway is 12th century. The architecture is English, but St Brendan the Navigator was educated in Ardfert and founded a monastery here. Set into one of the interior walls is an effigy popularly said to be of the saint. The cathedral is on the road to Ballyheigue from Tralee, which passes through Ardfert. It's run by the OPW, opens daily from 9.30 am to 6.30 pm and admission is IR£1.50/60p.

Turning right in front of the cathedral and going down the road for less than one km brings you to the remains of a **Franciscan friary**, dating from the 13th century but with 15th-century cloisters.

Banna Strand

This eight-km stretch of sandy beach will always be better known for its history than for its recreational qualities. Sir Roger Casement (1864–1916) landed here on 21 April 1916 from a German submarine. He was planning to bring in rifles for the Easter Rising but was arrested as soon as he landed. He was tried for treason and executed in London but many years later his body was returned to Ireland. Approaching the beach there is a sign pointing left to the Casement memorial. It is one km down to the left, past the caravan park.

The beach itself is safe for swimming, as is the smaller but equally sandy beach at Ballyheigue to the north.

Crag Caves

One of Ireland's more recent tourist attractions, the caves were discovered in 1983 when problems with water pollution led to a search for the source of the local river. The entrance to the caves had been known for years but they had never been explored.

The caves are open March to November, from 10 am to 6 pm (closing at 7 pm in July and August), with guided tours for IR£3/2. Coffee and snacks are available.

From Tralee or Killarney look for the sign on the right of the N21 after Castleisland. Coming from Limerick on the N21 the turning is on the left at the top of the hill approaching Castleisland.

Places to Stay & Eat

You can camp for free on the sand dunes at Banna, and there are public toilets, but no showers, at the main entrance to the beach. There are a couple of caravan parks stretched along the beach that attract Irish holidaymakers. A little farther north at Ballyheigue there is another safe beach, and camping is possible at *Casey's Caravan & Camping Park* (☎ 066-33195). Camping is also possible at the IHH *Breakers Hostel* (☎ 066-33242) which is on Cliff Rd at Ballyheigue. Beds are IR£5.50, doubles IR£13. The *Banna Beach Hotel* (☎ 066-34103) has rooms from IR£20/40.

In Ardfert, *O'Sullivan's* pub does bar food. After Ardfert but before Banna the *Bayside Bistro* is open till 8 pm and does the usual meat and fish dishes, including takeaway service. Dinner at the *Banna Beach Hotel* is around IR£12 and bar food is available throughout the day.

Getting There & Away

There is a bus between Tralee and Ballybunion that stops near Banna and in Ardfert.

RATTOO ROUND TOWER & MUSEUM

The only complete round tower in Kerry has six floors and is in fine condition. The top windows face the four points of the compass which indicates that this was an important monastic site in the 9th and 10th centuries. Nothing else remains from that era. To the east are the ruins of a 15th-century church.

The tower is visible from the main road before entering the small town of Ballyduff and the turning is signposted.

Just outside Ballyduff, there is a small museum at Knappogue (☎ 066-31000), dedicated to the history of North Kerry.

BALLYBUNION

In June 1834 a longstanding feud between two Ballybunion (*Baile an Bhuinneánaigh*) families culminated in a massive brawl on the beach, involving over 3000 combatants. During the summer the beach is still crowded, but only with Irish holidaymakers who have made Ballybunion a popular

KERRY

seaside resort. Apart from the usual seaside attractions there is little to see except the ruins of Ballybunion Castle that overlook the beach. Tourist information is available from a small cubicle, on the left as you enter the Ambassador Golf Hotel.

LISTOWEL
Listowel's only real attraction is the annual Writers' Week, although there are some places of interest in the vicinity. Tourist information is available from the Arts Centre (☎ 068-22590) in the middle of the market square, from June to September. McGuire's in Church St is the only bookshop in town.

Writers' Week
John B Keane is probably the most famous writer associated with Listowel, especially since the filming of *The Field*. He owns a pub in the town and usually features in Writers' Week. Brian McMahon, a short story writer, is another literary talent from the town.

The literary festival, which is the main reason for visiting Listowel, takes place each May – details from Writers' Week, PO Box 147, Listowel, County Kerry. Many of the events take place in the St John's Arts Centre (☎ 068-22566) in the square.

Getting There & Away
Situated on the Shannon estuary, the town is just south of the car ferry that crosses to County Clare. The ferry leaves either every hour or every half-hour according to demand.

AROUND LISTOWEL
Carrigafoyle Castle
The location of this castle is very attractive, perched above the Shannon estuary. It was probably built at the end of the 15th century by the O'Connors, who ruled most of northern Kerry. It was besieged by the English in 1580, later retaken by O'Connor but fell again to the English under George Carew in 1600, during the suppression of O'Neill's rebellion, and was finally destroyed by Cromwell's forces in 1649. Climb the spiral

staircase to the 29-metre top for a good view of the estuary.

The castle is 1.5 km west of the village of Ballylongford, which can be reached from Listowel, Ballybunion or Tarbert.

Lislaughtin Abbey
This Franciscan friary was also founded by the O'Connors in the late 15th century. When the castle was attacked in 1580, this friary was also raided and three elderly friars were murdered in front of the altar. In the National Museum in Dublin there is a processional cross from this abbey, known as the Ballylongford Cross.

Take the small road to Saleen from the village of Ballylongford and the ruins of the abbey come into view.

Dingle Peninsula

Less touristy and just as beautiful as the Ring of Kerry, the Dingle Peninsula is the Ireland of *Ryan's Daughter* and *Far and Away*, with an extraordinary number of ring forts, high crosses and other ancient monuments. Dingle is the main town. Ferries run from Dunquin to the bleak Blasket Islands, off the tip of the peninsula.

TRALEE TO DINGLE VIA CONNOR PASS
There are two routes from Tralee to Dingle, though they both follow the same road out of Tralee past the windmill. Near the village of Camp a right fork heads off to the Connor Pass, while the main road via Annascaul brings you to Dingle more quickly. The Connor Pass route is more beautiful, and goes past the Castlegregory Peninsula, which divides Brandon and Tralee bays. The broad and empty beaches around Castlegregory are perfect for surfing and those close to the Sandy Bay Caravan Park have been particularly recommended. Bring your own gear.

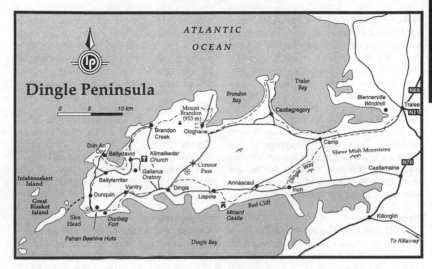

Connor Pass

This pass, sometimes spelt with a single 'n', is the highest in Ireland at 456 metres and has impressive views of Dingle harbour and Mt Brandon to the north.

Places to Stay

Camping There are three camp sites near Castlegregory. The *Anchor Camping & Caravan Park* (☎ 066-39157) is close to the beach: 19 km from Tralee, three km before Castlegregory, and signposted on the main road. Large/small tents are IR£8/7 a night. *Seaside Caravan & Camping Park* (☎ 066-30161) is also on the beach, but the coin-operated hot showers put people off. The *Green Acres Caravan & Camping Park* (☎ 066-39158) is close to Crutch's Country House Hotel. Large/small tents here cost IR£8/6 plus IR£1 per adult.

Hostels The *Connor Pass Hostel* (☎ 066-39179) is by the road at Stradbally, close to Castlegregory, and the proprietor runs the pub opposite. Beds are IR£6, no doubles.

In Castlegregory itself the *Euro-Hostel* (☎ 066-39133) is part of Fitzgerald's bar in the village. Beds are IR£5, showers 50p and family rooms are available. *Lynch's Hostel* (☎ 066-39128) charges similar rates.

B&Bs *Griffin's* (☎ 066-39147) at the Tip Top Farmhouse, on the main road about one km from Castlegregory, does B&B from IR£13.50/27. *Mrs Ferriter* (☎ 066-39263) at Beenoskee, Cappateigue, charges from IR$18.50/27 and is on the Connor Pass road.

Hotel Tucked away between Tralee and Dingle on the Connor Pass road, *Crutch's Country House Hotel* (☎ 066-38118) has singles/doubles from IR£40/60.

Places to Eat

In Castlegregory, *Barry's* is a pizza and burger place. The *Fermoyle Restaurant* at Crutch's Country House Hotel serves dinner for IR£18 and bar food is also available here.

Getting Around

In Castlegregory there are two shops that hire bikes during the summer: Lynch's and Finn's. They are both in the small village and both charge IR£5.

TRALEE TO DINGLE VIA ANNASCAUL

For drivers this route has little to recommend it other than being faster than the Connor Pass route. By bicycle it is less demanding. On foot the journey constitutes the first three days of the Dingle Way.

Dingle Way

This is a 178-km circular route from Tralee that continues past Dingle to Dunquin and returns to Tralee via Castlegregory. The whole walk takes eight days but the last four days, from Dunquin back to Tralee, are easily the best in terms of scenery. See the Activities chapter for further details.

Places to Stay

The IHH *Bog View Hostel* (☎ 066-58125) is a converted school halfway between Tralee and Dingle. It is a friendly place, and the rates are IR£6 for a bed, IR£6 for a bed in a two-bed room and IR£16 for a private room with a double bed. Meals are also available, bikes can be hired and there's a free pickup service.

A few km past the Bog View on the road to Dingle is the well-equipped IHH *Fuschia Lodge Hostel* (☎ 066-57150). Beds here are from IR£ 6 and doubles are from IR£15 and there is camping space. The hostel near Lispole is the *Seacrest* (☎ 066-51390) and beds are IR£5 but there is only one double at IR£15. The Seacrest is just over one km from the village and has a free pick-up service.

Places to Eat

Inexpensive vegetarian meals are available at the *Bog View Hostel*, though you'd better check if you're not actually staying there.

In Annascaul the *Anchor Restaurant* has dishes at IR£10. *Brackluin House* in the village also does evening meals. The *South Pole* bar commemorates Tom Crean, a villager, who went to the South Pole with Scott.

CASTLEMAINE TO DINGLE

Travelling from Killarney to Dingle the quickest route is by way of Killorglin and Castlemaine. At Castlemaine a road heads west to Dingle, soon meeting the coast and passing Inch on the way to joining the main Tralee road to Dingle. Apart from the odd pub or two there is little provision for food so bring your own. Also bring your own gear for surfing at Inch where the waves average one to three metres.

Minard Castle

This 15th-century castle has been in a dangerous condition since its destruction by Cromwellian forces in the 17th century. Children should not be left unsupervised.

The castle is signposted on the left after leaving Inch on the way to Dingle; it is three km from the main road.

Places to Stay

Camping & Hostel About 16 km from Castlemaine, just before Inch, the *Inch Hostel* (☎ 066-58181) is a friendly place with beds for IR£5.50 and private rooms for IR£12. Camping is also possible at IR£3 per person and including the use of hostel facilities.

B&Bs At the Castlemaine end of Inch, *Waterside* (☎ 066-58129) has ocean views from some rooms. Rooms are IR£18.50/28.

On the other side of Inch *Red Cliff* (☎ 066-57136) was once owned by Dr Eamonn Casey, Bishop of Galway, who used it for a liaison. The mother of his son went public in 1992, and journalists turned up in force. See the section on Bishop Casey in the Galway chapter.

Entertainment

Foley's pub in Inch has music in summer. The main attraction locally is the six-km sand spit that runs into Dingle Bay – a location for the film of *The Playboy of the Western World*. The sand dunes were once home to Iron Age settlements. Cars are allowed on the beach but be careful because – and this is supported by personal experience – vehicles regularly get stuck in the wet sand.

DINGLE

The attractive little port of Dingle (*An Daingean*) makes a good base for exploration of the Dingle Peninsula, and has a famous resident dolphin. And while, like Kinsale in County Cork, it has a disproportionate number of quality restaurants there is also a healthy number of affordable eating places.

Information

The tourist office (☎ 066-51188) is in the centre of town and opens from April to October. One-hour guided walks of historical Dingle (☎ 066-51937) depart from outside the tourist office at 11.30 am and 2.30 pm for IR£2.50.

There is a bureau de change at the Craft Village on the Wood. There is a laundrette at the end of Green Lane, the lane opposite the church in Green St.

Activities

Look in at the Mountain Man shop (☎ 066-51868) on Strand St for details of their walks programme. They are mostly half-day trips, costing IR£12, in the beautiful countryside west of Dingle. There is also a whole-day hike up Mt Brandon for IR£18.

For scuba diving there are a number of places worth contacting for their details. One is in Ventry (☎ 066-59876), another out at Ballyferriter (☎ 066-56105).

Enquire at the tourist office for details of sea fishing trips or contact the boatman himself (☎ 066-51163). The Skellig Experience cruise (see the earlier Skellig Islands section) departs daily from Dingle at 11.15 am except on Monday and Friday.

Fungie the Dolphin

Dolphins are not usually a common sight in Dingle Bay, but in the winter of 1983 the crews of fishing boats began to notice a solitary bottlenosed dolphin that followed their vessels, jumped about in the water and on more than one occasion leapt over their boats. He came to be known as Fungie, the nickname of a local fisherman, and is now an international celebrity.

During the summer, boats leave the pier regularly for a one-hour trip that takes you out to the dolphin. The cost is IR£5/3.50 and while there's no charge if the dolphin isn't

around, he usually turns up. A boat also leaves each morning at 8 am for those who want to swim with Fungie; the trip lasts two hours and the cost is IR£10/5.

It's just as easy to watch Fungie from the shore. From Dingle take the road to Tralee and turn right down a lane about 1.5 km from the Shell garage. The turning is easy to miss so look for a set of whitish gateposts beside the lane. Coming from Tralee look for the Ballytaggart Hostel on the right and further on a blue sign for Pax House nursing home on the left. About 100 metres further on are the whitish gateposts and the lane going down to the left. At the bottom of the lane is a tiny parking space and if you walk along the sea wall towards the old tower you will come to the mouth of the harbour. If you're in a car, remember when parking that this land is owned by someone who needs access to his fields.

Wetsuits can be hired from Flannery's (☎ 066-51337) in a two-storey house near the pier, or from Seventh Wave (☎ 066-51548), just across the bridge on the road out west. Seventh Wave have children's suits as well and a small display relating to Fungie. The cost is around IR£12 for the whole day. The Ballintaggart Hostel also has wetsuits for hire, mainly for residents.

Places to Stay

Camping Three of the hostels provide for campers: the *Seacrest*, furthest out of town near Lispole, the *Ballintaggart* a little way outside of Dingle and the *Westlodge/ Westgate* in town.

Hostels The *Grapevine Hostel* (☎ 066-51434) is a new place on Dykegate St with IR£6 dorm beds and IR£6.50 in the four-bedroom rooms. In town, *Lovett's* (☎ 066-51903) is a small family house with beds for IR£6. It's down the road that is opposite the garage, less than 100 metres from the town roundabout, on the way to Tralee.

The *Marina Hostel* (☎ 066-51065) is near the pier and has 20 beds for IR£6 and private rooms for IR£15. Close to town is the

KERRY

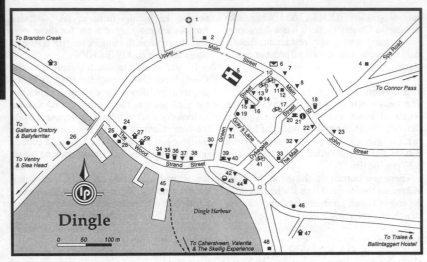

Dingle

0   50   100 m

Dingle Harbour

To Brandon Creek

To Connor Pass

To Gallarus Oratory & Ballyferriter

To Ventry & Slea Head

To Cahersiveen, Valentia & The Skellig Experience

To Tralee & Ballintaggert Hostel

Upper   Main   Street

Spa Road

Green   Street

Grey's Lane

Dykegate   Street

John   Street

The Mall

Strand   Street

The   Wood

PLACES TO STAY

2   Boland's B&B
3   Rainbow Hostel
4   Hillgrove Hotel
12 Benner's Hotel
27 Westlodge/Westgate Hostel
28 Ocean View B&B
29 Marina Hostel
33 Captain's House B&B
34 Marina Inn
38 Murphy's Pub/B&B
46 Alpine House
47 Lovett's Hostel
48 Skellig Hotel

PLACES TO EAT

7   Adams Restaurant & Bar
8   Whelan's Restaurant
11 Lord Baker's Restaurant
13 El Toro Restaurant
16 Café Ceol
20 An Café Liteártha
22 Old Smokehouse
23 Doyle's Seafood Restaurant
30 Fenton's Restaurant
31 Beginish Restaurant
32 Shamrock Restaurant & B&B
37 Armada Restaurant

39 Oven Door Café
40 Forge Restaurant
42 Greany's Restaurant

PUBS

15 Dick Mack's
18 Small Bridge Bar
35 Máire de Barra Pub
36 Star Bar
44 O'Flaherty's

OTHER

1   Hospital
5   St Mary's Church
6   Post Office
9   Bike Hire
10 Moriarty Bike Hire
14 Laundrette
17 Bike Hire
19 Lisbeth Mulcahy Shop
21 Tourist Office
24 Craft Village
25 Brian De Staic Jewellery
26 Seventh Wave
41 Bike Hire
43 Bus Stop
45 Pier & Dolphin Boats'
    Departure Point

Rainbow Hostel (no phone), similarly priced and with a free pick-up from the bus stop. Unlike some hostels, the kitchen here is big enough to handle a crowd. Near the Craft Village on the Wood, *Westlodge/Westgate Hostel* (☎ 066-51476) has views of the sea but there's an army camp look about the place notwithstanding a stove that encourages camaraderie at night.

Along the road to Tralee is the IHH *Ballintaggart Hostel* (☎ 066-51454). It has a free shuttle service to and from town, bike hire, a bureau de change, pony trekking and a resident ghost, and charges IR£6 a night.

B&Bs A couple of pubs down by the pier have gone into B&B; the *Marina Inn* (☎ 066-51660) offers B&B for IR£12 or just a bed for IR£8. *Murphy's* (☎ 066-51450) has rooms with separate bathroom for IR£13 per person, plus tea and coffee making facilities. A quieter place is *Ocean View* (☎ 066-51659) at 133 The Wood, a small town house on the water's edge with singles/doubles for IR£13/30. On the Mall, *Captain's House* (☎ 066-51531), from IR£22/32, is very pleasantly situated. The *Shamrock Restaurant* on the Mall has budget accommodation at IR£6 and IR£9 including breakfast.

Alpine House (☎ 066-51250) is a guesthouse on the road to Tralee, just east of the roundabout with singles/doubles from IR£16.50/30. The rooms are bigger than most, and the sea views are terrific. In town *Boland's* (☎ 066-51426) has beds from IR£18/28. The comfortable *Doyle's Townhouse* (☎ 066-51174) at the bottom of John St costs IR£39/62.

Hotels *Benner's* (☎ 066-51638) on Main St is attractively and comfortably furnished, with singles/doubles from IR£38/76. With higher prices and about four times the number of rooms is the *Skellig Hotel* (☎ 066-51144). A 10-minute walk from town south-east of the roundabout brings this idiosyncratic, some would say charmless, building into view. The strange-looking foyer area is supposed to represent clocháns, the beehive huts found in the area. There are

doubles only at just under IR£100. The normal-looking *Hillgrove* (☎ 066-51131) is on Spa Rd, within walking distance of town, and rooms are from IR£30/40.

Places to Eat
Dingle has some good restaurants, and while many are expensive there are also a number of places offering cheap meals. Cheap here means paying around IR£6, while expensive means a bill in the IR£50-plus region for two.

Cafés & Pubs *An Café Liteártha*, on Dykegate St, is a bookshop with a good, small inexpensive café at the back serving drinks and sandwiches.

At *Café Ceol*, at the end of the lane opposite the church in Green St, dinner is served upstairs while the café is below. Pleasant surroundings match congenial prices, around IR£7, and vegetarians are well catered for. Another unpretentious place is the *Old Smokehouse* at the corner of the Mall and Main St. Pizza, lasagne and the like are all around IR£5. The *Oven Door* is a pleasant little café at the corner of Green St and Strand St, open until 10.30 pm with pizzas around IR£5.

The pub strip is along by the pier and most of the pubs serve bar food all day. *Murphy's* serves a traditional bacon and cabbage meal for IR£4 until 9 pm. The *Star Bar* has food until 9.30 pm, mostly steaks and seafood for between IR£5-10. The *Máire de Barra* pub is the least attractive of the pubs but serves inexpensive food. *Benner's Hotel* has a very comfortable bar serving pub lunches.

Restaurants Along the Mall, the *Shamrock Restaurant* is squarely aimed at budget-minded travellers and families. Lunch specials are IR£5. Farther down again, near the roundabout, *Greany's Restaurant* does fish & chips for IR£4, other fish dishes for IR£6 and a set dinner for IR£9.45. The *Forge Restaurant* nearby has standard meals in the IR£5 to IR£10 range.

Opposite St Mary's Church in Green St, *El Toro* does lunch for about IR£7 and from 5.30 pm there are IR£6 pizzas and seafood between IR£8-17. On Main St, *Adams* is a new establishment with a bar on one side and a small restaurant area on the other side serving vegetarian and fish dishes for between IR£4-8. You can have a quiet drink away from the fishing folk of the pier pubs while perusing the menu and wine list.

The *Armada*, above the Star Bar opposite the pier, has seafood and grills for between IR£9-15. *Lord Baker's* (☎ 066-51277) in Main St is a seafood restaurant with a set dinner from 6 pm for IR£13.50. Nearby, *Whelan's Restaurant* is another evening seafood place with a set dinner for IR£16. *Fenton's Restaurant* in Green St has a set dinner for IR£16. *Doyle's Seafood Bar* (☎ 066-51174) at the bottom of John St is a good reputation. They do dinner only, and most main courses are in the IR£12 to IR£15 range.

Excellent value for money though is the *Beginish Restaurant* (☎ 066-51588) in Green St. It can always be relied on for a good seafood or vegetarian meal and the place has a genteel air.

Entertainment

Many of the pubs have live music, and three in particular are worth checking out: *O'Flaherty's* near the roundabout, *Murphy's* down by the pier and the *Small Bridge Bar*, at the end of Main St by the bridge. In Green St, *Dick Mack's* is an old-style pub with the shop counter on one side and the drinking counter opposite.

Things to Buy

At the Craft Village on the Wood there are a number of workshops specialising in leatherware and garments. If you want your name inscribed in Ogham script on a piece of jewellery go to Brian de Staic. They also have an outlet in Green St.

Green St is worth strolling down for its craft shops and Lisbeth Mulcahy is recommended for its pottery and woven garments like scarves – expensive but nice. Her husband has his own workshop west of Dingle near Ballyferriter (see that section).

Getting There & Away

Buses stop outside the car park at the back of the Super Valu store. Buses leave Tralee at 1.45 pm Monday to Friday, at 4.15 pm Monday to Saturday, with an extra evening bus at 8.10 pm in the summer. Two buses daily depart Killarney for Dingle in the summer at 10.30 am and 1.30 pm.

From Dingle (☎ 066-23566) the earliest of three daily buses to Tralee leaves at 7.25 am (two daily on Sunday at 2 pm and 4.40 pm). The other two, at 2.45 and 5 pm, go on from Tralee to Killarney.

A ferry to Valentia departs daily at 11.15 am and 6.30 pm. Bikes are carried free on the one-hour journey.

Getting Around

There are several bike-rental places and the daily rate is IR£5. Moriarty (☎ 066-51316) on Main St does the Raleigh Rent-a-Bike scheme. Around the corner in Green St there is another bike-rental place, and in Dykegate St two more, one at each end.

WEST OF DINGLE

The area west of Dingle has the greatest concentration of ancient sites in Kerry if not the whole of Ireland, and to do them justice you should use one of the local specialist guides, on sale in the An Café Liteártha or the tourist office. The sites listed here are among the most interesting and easiest to find.

The land west of Dingle has other attractions. It is a genuine Irish-speaking area. The landscape is dramatic, except when it's hidden in mist, and there are striking views of the Blasket Islands from Slea Head. The sandy beach nearby, Coumenole, is lovely to walk along but like most of those in the area it is treacherous for swimming.

Tourism came late to Dingle but the area is handling it well, avoiding the tackiness of Killarney. In 1971, David Lean made the film *Ryan's Daughter* here. Much of it was shot near Dunquin, and the ruins of the film's schoolhouse can still be found. Film buffs should enquire at Kruger's pub in Dunquin.

Orientation

If you cross the bridge west of Dingle and turn north just after Seventh Wave, you come to a Y-junction after five km. To the right are Kilmalkedar Church (two km) and Brandon Creek; from here you could return to Dingle on a circular route. If you turn left at the Y-junction, you come to Gallarus Oratory and the Riasc site, from which you can reach Ballyferriter and Dunquin, for boats to the Blasket Islands. The road continues down the coast and back to Dingle, via Ventry.

Kilmalkedar Church

This 12th-century Romanesque church was once part of a complex of religious buildings. The characteristic Romanesque doorway has a tympanum with a head on one side and a mythical beast on the other. The church has an Ogham stone and an alphabet stone. About 50 metres away is a two-storey building known as St Brendan's House, believed to have been the residence of the medieval clergy. The road connecting these two ruins is the beginning of the Saint's Rd, the traditional approach to Mt Brandon.

Brandon Creek

St Brendan set off from this inlet in the 5th century and sailed to America, according to the information board. As Tim Severin proved, this voyage could have been done hundreds of years before Columbus. The fishing boats add to the creek's atmosphere, and on a warm day the water is inviting.

Carry on along the road that you turned off to reach the church. After a few km turn right at the junction that points to An Dooneen B&B and carry on for nearly two km until reaching the tiny village of Bothar Bui where the IHO hostel is. Carry straight on to the next junction and turn left for Brandon Creek which is about one km along this road. A right turn at this junction returns to Dingle.

Gallarus Oratory

Simple but stunning, this superb dry-stone oratory is reason enough for visiting the Dingle Peninsula. It is in perfect condition, apart from a slight sagging in the roof, and

Gallarus Oratory was used for private prayer

has withstood the assault of the elements for some 1200 years. The interior and exterior walls may have been plastered, as some sign of mortar remains. Shaped like an upturned boat, it has a doorway on the west side and a small round-headed window on the east side. Inside the doorway are two projecting stones with holes which once supported the door.

Bear left at the Y-junction (see the Orientation section earlier), and after two km turn left at the sign. The oratory is half a km down the road on the left.

Riasc Monastic Settlement

The remains of this 5th or 6th-century monastic settlement are impressive. Excavations have revealed, among other finds, the foundations of an oratory first built with wood and later stone, a kiln for drying corn and a cemetery. Most interesting is a pillar with beautiful Celtic designs.

A sign points the way from the Y-junction (see Orientation). Follow the road for four km and just before a T-junction there is a rotting sign to the site which is pointing back the way you came. Follow instead the sign for the Reask View B&B and the site is half a km up this road.

Ballyferriter

This small village is named after Piaras Ferriter, a poet and soldier who emerged as a local leader in the 1641 rebellion and was the last Kerry commander to submit to Cromwell's army. Near the village are the

Three Sisters hills, Smerwick Harbour and the remains of **Dún An Óir Fort**. During the 1580 rebellion in Munster, the fort was held by an international brigade of Italians, Spaniards and Basques. On 17 November, English troops under Lord Grey attacked the fort and the people inside surrendered. 'Then putt I in certeyn bandes who streight fell to execution. There were 600 slayne', said the poet Edmund Spenser, who was secretary to Lord Grey.

To reach Ballyferriter go north on the R559 road towards the Gallarus Oratory. At the Y-junction four km from Dingle take the left fork. After another three km take a left turn at a T-junction just after an iron bridge. After about 300 metres turn right at a brown sign for the An Oíge hostel and the Golf Links Hotel. Ballyferriter is one km further along that road.

To get to Dún An Óir, head out of Ballyferriter in a westerly direction. After one km turn right at a brown sign to Smerwick Harbour. After a further 1.5 km, the right fork at a Y-junction. After 2.6 km, turn right at the T-junction and after roughly 300 metres you'll see a signpost to the fort, indicating a poorly surfaced road.

Social, cultural and historical aspects of life on the Dingle Peninsula and the Blasket Islands are the concern of the **Ballyferriter heritage centre** (☎ 066-56100). It is open over Easter and from June to the end of September, seven days a week, from 10 am to 6 pm. Admission is IR£1/50p.

Louis Mulcahy Pottery

This is not the only pottery shop on the peninsula but it is certainly one of the most interesting. Visitors can see the potters at work and the two floors of the shop display a variety of pieces, costing from IR£5 to IR£500. Tea sets, bowls, lamps, vases, platters – if it can be fashioned from clay you are likely to see it here. Purchases can be mailed overseas from the shop (☎ 066-56229). The workshop is on the road just after Ballyferriter and before Dunquin.

Dunbeg Fort & Beehive Huts

This promontory fort has a sheer drop to the Atlantic and four outer walls of stone. Inside are the remains of a house and a beehive hut as well as an underground passage. The fort is eight km from Dunquin.

From Dunbeg Fort to Slea Head there are many beehive huts, forts and church sites. The **Fahan** huts are accessible from more than one place and you will see signs pointing the way from the road. There is usually a 50p admission charge.

The Blasket Centre

This heritage centre at Dunquin is devoted to what was the distinctive lifestyle of the Blasket Islanders and there is a restaurant and small bookshop. The audiovisual show can be seen in French and German. Admission to this OPW centre is IR£2.50/1 and opening hours are from 10 am to 7 pm daily.

Mt Brandon

At 953 metres Mt Brandon is the second-highest mountain in Ireland. There are two main routes up: a gradual one from the west and a more exciting one from the east. You should give yourself at least five hours for the climb. Gill & Macmillan's *New Irish Walk Guides: Southwest* by Sean O'Suilleabhain has details of both routes. The book is available in Dingle.

If you want to climb the mountain, with or without a guidebook do make sure there is no danger of a mist descending, as the top is frequently shrouded in cloud. If you do get caught, you may need a compass to make your way down. Travelling along the road from Dingle to Brandon Creek you will see two signs pointing the way. The traditional way up the mountain is by way of the Saint's Rd that starts at Kilmakedar Church. The eastern, more demanding, approach starts just beyond the village of Cloghane which is signposted on the left after leaving Dingle and descending the Connor Pass.

The ruins of St Brendan's Oratory mark the summit. The legend is that the navigator saint climbed the mountain with his seafaring monks before they set out in their curraghs for the journey to Greenland and America.

There is a shower available at the An Bothar pub for 50p (see B&Bs in the following section).

Places to Stay

Camping The most westerly camp site in Europe is *Campaill Teach An Aragail* (Oratory House Camp) (☎ 066-55143) near Gallarus Oratory. A family tent costs IR£7 a night, two cyclists IR£5. Free camping is possible near Ferriter's Cove (see Ballyferriter) but there are no facilities.

Hostels The IHH *Tigh An Phoist Hostel* (☎ 066-55109) is at Bothar Bui village, attached to a shop, with beds for IR£6.50 and doubles for IR£15. On Tuesday and Friday the Dingle to Ballydavid bus goes close but ask to be dropped off at the Caragh church. By road follow the directions for Brandon Creek above.

An Cat Dubh (☎ 066-56286), (Black Cat Hostel), is at Ballyferriter, just past the Granville Hotel on the road to Dunquin.

The An Oíge *Dunquin Hostel* (☎ 066-56145) at Dunquin is perfect for visiting Great Blasket Island, being close to the ferry departure point.

B&Bs Dunquin has *Kruger's* (☎ 066-56127) and is as close as possible to the Blasket Islands. From the pub it is a short walk to the ferry. The place is still in the Kruger family, and the story of a male member of the family is recounted on one of the pub's walls, along with photographs relating to two films made in the locality, *Ryan's Daughter* with Robert Mitchum and Sarah Miles and *Far & Away* with Tom Cruise and Nicole Kidman. A bed is IR£13.50.

Ballyferriter has a few B&Bs dotted around the vicinity. *Mrs Ferris* (☎ 066-56282) is 3 km away and charges IR£18.50/27.

An Bothar (☎ 066-55342) is a friendly pub doing B&B for IR£13.50 per person and is ideally located if you want to climb Mt Brandon. To get there, go to the Tigh an Phoist Hostel and carry on until a junction. The road to the left goes to Brandon Creek.

Turn right instead; the B&B is half a km along the road to Dingle. From Dingle a more direct route would be to turn right before the bridge over the river. If you take this route you will meet two other B&Bs before An Bothar.

Hotels The two hotels west of Dingle are both in Ballyferriter. *Ostan Dun An Oir* (☎ 066-56133) is reached by taking the first right turn after the An Cat Dubh Hostel on the road from Ballyferriter to Dunquin. Singles/doubles are IR£40/60 and there's an outdoor heated swimming pool.

The *Granville* (☎ 066-56116) is just before the An Cat Dubh Hostel. Singles/doubles here are from IR£18/36.

Self-Catering If you want to spend a week exploring the Dingle Peninsula, there are two groups of self-catering cottages. *Dingle Wine Strand Cottages* (☎ 061-53582) have 22 cottages near Ballyferriter. Summer rates start at over IRT£300 a week but they do sleep eight. The postal address is Geraldville, North Circular Rd, Limerick.

Ventry Holiday Cottages (☎ 066-51588) sleep six and are a little less expensive. The postal address is Mr Moore, Green St, Dingle.

Places to Eat

Ballyferriter is the best place for a meal. The *Gallery Restaurant* is part of the *Teach Pheig* pub and the three-course meal for around IR£6 is available day or night. Vegetarian meals are prepared on request. The nearby *Ostan Dun An Oir Hotel* also does food.

On the road from Dunquin to Slea Head the *Pottery Café* does meals and snacks and *An Bracan Feasa*, over 13 km from Dunquin, is a self-service restaurant by the side of the road.

In the Mt Brandon area, bar food is available at the *An Bothar* pub, and near the Riasc monastic site the *Tig Ohric* pub does sandwiches.

Getting There & Away

There is a daily bus service from Dingle to Dunquin, via Ventry, Slea Head and Ballyferriter. During the summer there is also a bus service between Killarney and Dunquin, via Inch and Dingle. The bus leaves Killarney weekdays only at 10.20 am and reaches Dunquin at 1.05 pm. It leaves from the hostel at Dunquin at 2.55 pm for the return journey.

BLASKET ISLANDS

There are four big islands and three smaller ones. Great Blasket is the largest and the most visited. It is six km by 1.2 km, and is mountainous enough for strenuous walks including a good one detailed in Kevin Corcoran's *Kerry Walks*. There are the remains of an old church and the views are wonderful.

The last islanders left for the mainland in 1953 but lyrical stories of their lives survive. Three books in particular are currently in print and easily available in Dingle. The best is the English translation of Thomas O Crohan's *The Islandman*; the other two are Maurice O'Sullivan's *Twenty Years A-Growing* and translation of Peig Sayers' *Peig*.

For some time the government has been trying to buy up the empty property lots on the Great Blasket, and compulsory purchase

orders have now been processed for the most part. There are plans to renovate some of the dilapidated homes on the island and to build a pier which will allow larger boats to ferry visitors across.

Places to Stay & Eat

There is no accommodation on the island but camping is free. There is a café serving snacks and campers could arrange for meals to be cooked.

The An Oíge *Dunquin Hostel* on the mainland is within walking distance of the ferry point.

Getting There & Away

Boats (☎ 066-56455) operate throughout the summer, weather permitting, costing IR£10 return.

On Monday and Thursday the first bus for Dunquin leaves Dingle at 8.50 am and this will still give you half an hour before the first boat leaves around 10 am. In the summer there is a daily bus leaving Dingle at 12.30 and 3.10 pm, 10.30 am on Sunday. The last boat from Great Blasket leaves around 3 pm.

Counties Limerick & Tipperary

Both these counties tend to be passed through while going to or leaving somewhere more interesting. This is fair enough in the sense that neither county can compete with the attractions of neighbouring Cork, Kerry, Clare or Galway. But it is also true that both County Limerick and Tipperary have worthwhile places of interest that invite the traveller to slow down and stop rather than just tear through to reach somewhere else. The city of Limerick makes an obvious base for seeing the neighbouring attractions and County Tipperary has the major site of the Rock of Cashel as well as a surprising number of other locations worth your time.

County Limerick

In the past the siege of Limerick played centre stage in the struggle between Ireland and England, and the imposing remains of the city's castle bear testimony to this decisive event in Ireland's history. Apart from the historical interest and amenities of Limerick City itself, there are fascinating historic and prehistoric sites to the south of the city that make ideal excursions by bicycle. The nearby town of Adare is one of the prettiest in Ireland, in dramatic contrast with the proletarian Limerick City.

LIMERICK CITY

Limerick (*Luimneach*) is an instantly recognisable name and one of the larger cities in Ireland. For a long time it was regarded by tourists as one of the dullest cities in the country, but this is no longer the case. There are a number of places in and around the city worth visiting and Limerick is now a place of interest in its own right, rather than just a convenient crossroads. There is a variety of eating establishments and a very lively music scene that exists quite independently from the tourist trade.

Highlights
- Lough Gur, a remarkable Stone Age archaeological site south of Limerick City
- King John's Castle and the collection of Irish art and antiquities in the Hunt Museum, both in Limerick City
- The spectacular Rock of Cashel in County Tipperary, best visited early in the morning before the tour buses arrive

History
History has weighed heavily on the city of Limerick since the Vikings first arrived in the 10th century. The Vikings and the native Irish fought over the town until Brian Ború's forces defeated the Norsemen at the Battle of Clontarf in 1014.

After the arrival of the Normans in Ireland, King John paid a visit in 1210 to celebrate the completion of his castle, work on which had started 10 years earlier.

In 1690, Limerick acquired heroic status in the ongoing saga of the English occupation of Ireland. After the Battle of the Boyne, the defeated Jacobite forces withdrew west behind the famously strong walls of Limerick. Surrender seemed only a matter of time, but the Irish Jacobite leader Patrick Sarsfield slipped out with 600 men and launched a

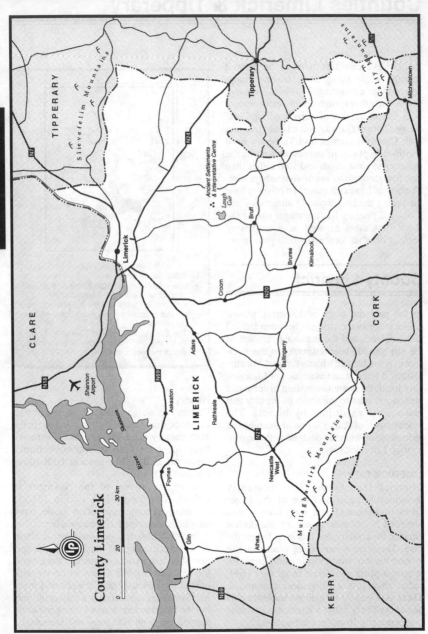

surprise attack on the English supply train. Cannons, mortars and 200 wagons of ammunition were destroyed. Sarsfield and his followers returned undetected to Limerick.

Months of bombardment followed and eventually Sarsfield sued for peace with dignity. The terms of the Treaty of Limerick were agreed and Sarsfield and about 12,000 soldiers, many with their wives and children, were allowed to leave the city and set sail for France. The treaty also guaranteed religious freedom for Irish Catholics, but the English later reneged on it, and enforced fierce anti-Catholic legislation. Decades of unrest followed, and this act of betrayal came to symbolise the injustice of British rule.

In 1919 a general strike took place in the city to protest against British military rule. A Strike Committee took charge of running essential services, and for one week the city of Limerick operated outside all legal structures. The Strike Committee even issued its own banknotes. It became known as the Limerick Soviet.

Orientation & Information

The tourist office (☎ 061-317522), with a bureau de change, is at Arthur's Quay near the river. It is open Monday to Friday from 9 am to 6.30 pm in July and August (9.30 am to 5.30 pm on Saturday and Sunday). The rest of the year it is open from 9.30 am to 5.30 pm, Monday to Friday (half day on Saturday). The post office is on Lower Cecil St and the railway and bus station is to the south-east of the town, near Parnell St.

The main street through town changes names from Patrick St to O'Connell St, The Crescent and then Quinlan St as it runs south.

Laundrettes can be found in Cecil St and Ellen St. One of the city's better second-hand bookshops, O'Brien's Bookshop, is next to the Savoy Centre in Bedford Row. There's a branch of the Eason bookshop chain on O'Connell St.

St Mary's Cathedral

This is the oldest building in the city, founded in 1172 by Donal Mor O'Brien, King of Munster. The Romanesque west doorway survives from this period, with the chancel and chapels added in the 15th century. There are grand tombs, memorial stones, and splendid black oak misericords – support ledges for choristers, carved with pictures of animals and other figures dating from around 1489. The graveyard outside has many 18th-century tombstones.

Between June and September at 9.15 pm there is a *son et lumière* show on the history of the city and church; admission is IR£2.50/1.50.

King John's Castle

The castle was built at the beginning of the 13th century on the site of an earlier fortification to administer and guard the rich Shannon region. The new cannon technology necessitated stronger walls and defences than ever before, and the castle became the most formidable bastion of English power in the west of Ireland.

Two floors of the interpretative centre set forth the tragic and heroic story of Limerick. In the courtyard there are replicas of three classic machines of early castle warfare: two catapults – a mangonel and a trebuchet, the latter capable of hurling a 200-kg missile – and a battering ram.

Underneath the castle there are some fascinating archaeological excavations showing the development of the castle and attempts by the besiegers to tunnel beneath the walls.

The castle is open between April and October seven days a week from 9.30 am to 5.30 pm (last admission is 4.30 pm). Admission is IR£3.50/1.90.

Across the river from the castle the **Treaty Stone** marks the spot on the riverbank where the Treaty of Limerick was signed. The subsequent English sellout rankles in Limerick to this day.

City Museum

The museum occupies two three-storey houses, dating back to 1751, in the corner of John's Square, near St John's Cathedral. There's an extensive collection on the history of the city over the last two centuries,

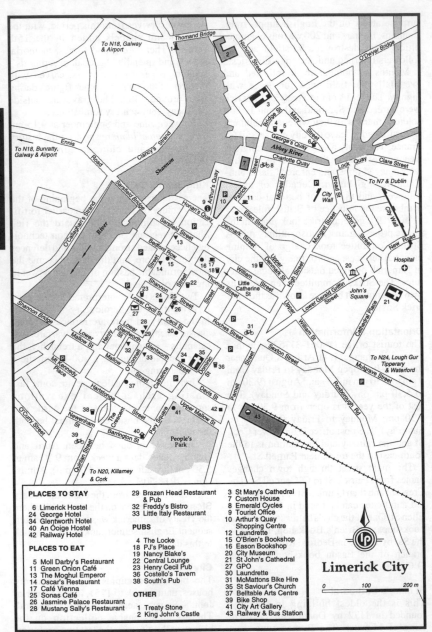

Limerick City

PLACES TO STAY
6 Limerick Hostel
24 George Hotel
34 Glentworth Hotel
40 An Ooige Hostel
42 Railway Hotel

PLACES TO EAT
5 Moll Darby's Restaurant
11 Green Onion Café
13 The Moghul Emperor
14 Oscar's Restaurant
17 Café Vienna
25 Sonas Café
26 Jasmine Palace Restaurant
28 Mustang Sally's Restaurant

29 Brazen Head Restaurant & Pub
32 Freddy's Bistro
33 Little Italy Restaurant

PUBS
4 The Locke
18 PJ's Place
19 Nancy Blake's
22 Central Lounge
23 Henry Cecil Pub
36 Costello's Tavern
38 South's Pub

OTHER
1 Treaty Stone
2 King John's Castle

3 St Mary's Cathedral
7 Custom House
8 Emerald Cycles
9 Tourist Office
10 Arthur's Quay Shopping Centre
12 Laundrette
15 O'Brien's Bookshop
16 Eason Bookshop
20 City Museum
21 St John's Cathedral
27 GPO
30 Laundrette
31 McMattons Bike Hire
35 St Saviour's Church
37 Belltable Arts Centre
39 Bike Shop
41 City Art Gallery
43 Railway & Bus Station

but surprisingly little on the Limerick Soviet, except for banknotes issued by the strikers.

It's open from Tuesday to Saturday, 10 am to 1 pm and 2 to 5 pm, entrance free.

Hunt Museum

Situated at the time of writing in Limerick University, this museum should soon be in Custom House, in the city centre. It contains probably the finest collection of Bronze Age, Celtic and medieval treasures outside Dublin. It is not a big museum and there's an explanatory leaflet that lists and describes all the contents. One of the major attractions is a superb Bronze Age shield. The only other of its kind in Ireland is in the National Museum in Dublin.

It should be open from May to September, seven days a week, and the present admission is IR£2/1.

City Art Gallery

The permanent collection includes work by artists such as Jack B Yeats and Sean Keating. It is open all year from 10 am to 1 pm and from 2 to 6 pm Monday to Friday, and from 10 am to 1 pm only on Saturday. There is no charge for admission. The gallery is in a corner of People's Park, not far from the An Oíge hostel.

St Saviour's Dominican Church

This 19th-century church contains a statue of Our Lady that was given to the Dominicans of the city in 1640 by a rich Limerick citizen. He wanted to do something to atone for the fact that his uncle had sentenced a man to death for allowing a priest to say mass in his house. The church is open from 7.30 am to 8.15 pm Monday to Saturday, 7.30 am to 2.45 pm on Sunday. It's in Dominic St, off Glentworth St.

Places to Stay

Camping The *Shannon Cottage Caravan & Camping Park* (☎ 061-377118) is about 12 km from Limerick, reached by turning left at Birdhill – the signpost is easily missed – on the N7 road to Dublin. After Birdhill follow the signs to O'Brien's Bridge and turn sharp

right after crossing the bridge. Small/family tents costs IR£8/11 plus IR£1 per adult and IR£3 for a hiker or cyclist.

Hostels The An Oíge *Limerick Hostel* (☎ 061-314672) is at 1 Pery Square, a short walk across People's Park from the bus and railway station, and a bed is IR£6.50. The large independent *Limerick Hostel* (☎ 061-415222) is at Barrington's House on George's Quay and costs IR£6 in rooms for two to four. Single rooms are excellent value at IR£7. Both hostels tend to be a little strict but the spacious and recently redecorated independent one is preferable.

B&Bs *Alexandra* (☎ 061-318472) at 6 Alexandra Terrace, O'Connell Ave, the Cork road, is handily close to the centre and has singles/doubles from IR£17.50/28. Otherwise the Ennis Rd (N18) running out of Limerick to Ennis and Galway is lined with B&Bs for several km, including *Clifton* (☎ 061-451166) just one km out with singles/doubles for IR£22/32. One km further on, *Parkview* (☎ 061-451505) has rooms for IR£18/28. Further out again, just next to the Ryan hotel, *Mrs Gavin* (☎ 061-453690) has three doubles from IR£27, sharing washroom facilities.

Hotels There are lots of big hotels strung out along the Ennis Rd (N18) and they are nearly all unnecessarily expensive for the average traveller. The least expensive is the *Railway Hotel* (☎ 061-413653) on Parnell St across from the station, with rooms from IR£16/40. The *George Hotel* (☎ 061-414566) is centrally located on O'Connell St. It's a comfortable hostelry – though sometimes noisy at night – with singles/doubles from IR£34/48, excluding breakfast, and an overnight garage. The *Glentworth Hotel* (☎ 061-413822), in the street of the same name, has rooms for IR£35/52, excluding breakfast. Just one km from town on Ennis Rd, *Woodfield House* (☎ 061-453022) has singles/doubles from IR£ 35/56.

If you want to splash out, the *Limerick Inn*

(☎ 061-326666) has rooms from IR£86/104, excluding breakfast.

Places to Eat

Cafés & Takeaways For cheap eats try the modern *Sails Restaurant* in the equally modern Arthur's Quay shopping centre across from the tourist office. *Café Vienna* on William St is OK for sandwiches, pizzas and salads and *WoKing*, opposite the George Hotel, is a fast-food Chinese place with a sit-in counter and a take-away service. Just next door *La Romana* does mostly pasta dishes for around IR£6 and, next door again, *Sonas* makes its own delicious chocolate and ice cream and good coffee. *McDonald's* have an outlet on O'Connell St.

Restaurants Decent meals are available from 5.30 pm at *Freddy's Bistro* (☎ 061-418749), tucked away down Theatre Lane which runs between Lower Mallow and Lower Glentworth Sts; it's open every day except Monday and dishes range from vegetarian chilli for IR£7 to seafood for IR£10. *Oscar's Restaurant*, part of the Savoy Centre cinema complex accessible from Henry St or Bedford Row, has a wide menu of affordable dishes. *The Moghul Emperor* is an inexpensive Indian restaurant at the corner of Henry St and Sarsfield St.

The *Green Onion Café* in Ellen St does pasta and pitta dishes from IR£6-10 from 6 pm. The *Brazen Head* restaurant and pub, on the corner of Lower Glentworth and O'Connell Sts, has an interesting menu of fish, curries, pizza and tacos. Next door, the new *Mustang Sally's* is a bright tex-mex joint open from 5 pm and costing about IR£10.

On George's Quay, just up from the independent Limerick Hostel, there is *Moll Darby's* pizzeria (☎ 061-417270) with meals from IR£8 to IR£15 and outdoor tables. The alfresco mood can be maintained at the *The Locke* bar next door. Another Italian place is the *Little Italy Restaurant* at the bottom end of O'Connell St with dishes around the same price.

The *Jasmine Palace* (☎ 061-42484) is the best Chinese place in town, and conveniently located on O'Connell St. A Cantonese-style meal for two would be about IR£30.

The *George Hotel* has a set dinner for IR£15.50 and a less expensive à la carte menu. Between 3 and 5.30 pm there is a budget menu with dishes for around IR£5.

Entertainment

The music scene shifts by the night but there's often something on at the popular *Nancy Blake's* on Upper Denmark St. Other possibilities include the busy *Central Lounge* on O'Connell St; *Costello's Tavern* on Dominic St and *South's Pub* on The Crescent. At the Henry St end of Lower Cecil St the *Henry Cecil* is worth checking out, as is the *The Locke* on George's Quay. *P.J.'s Place* on Little Catherine St has a nominal thatched roof and traditional music at night.

The *Belltable Arts Centre* (☎ 061-319866) on O'Connell St is a regular venue for the travelling theatre companies that tour Ireland in the summer.

Getting There & Away

Air Shannon Airport (☎ 061-471444), just over the border in County Clare, handles both domestic and international flights. The airport is 24 km from Limerick and takes over half an hour by car.

Bus Bus Éireann services operate from the bus and railway station (☎ 061-313333), a short walk south of the centre. There are regular connections to Dublin, Cork, Galway, Killarney, Rosslare, Donegal, Sligo, Derry and most other centres. There is a Bus Éireann desk in the tourist office.

Train There are services to all the main towns served by rail: eight trains daily to Dublin; two daily to Rosslare Harbour, Cahir and Tipperary. Other routes involve changing at Limerick Junction, a station 20 km southeast of Limerick. Enquire for details at the tourist office or the station itself (☎ 061-315555).

Getting Around

Regular buses connect Shannon Airport with

the Limerick bus and railway station. There are bus services from Shannon to Dublin.

As Limerick is quite a small city with a lot of one-way streets, there are only bus services out to the suburbs and not around the city centre itself. A walk across town, from St Mary's Cathedral to the railway station, takes about 15 minutes.

If you're driving, you can obtain parking discs from the tourist office. Otherwise, use the large car park attached to the adjacent Arthur's Quay shopping centre where you pay by the hour but discs are not required. The tourist office also houses a Bus Éireann desk and Limerick City Tours (☎ 061-301587) who conduct a two-hour walking tour that begins at 11 am and 2.30 pm, Monday to Friday, from June to August. It costs IR£3.50/1. For IR£1.50 the tourist office sells a map with two walking trails by the River Shannon.

Bicycles can be hired at Emerald Cycles (☎ 061-416983), 1 Patrick St and returned in Dublin, Cork or Galway. The rate is IR£7 a day, IR£30 a week and IR£6 extra if returning outside of Limerick. Bikes can also be hired at the Bike Shop (☎ 061-315900) on Quinlan St, from the An Óige Hostel and from McMattons (☎ 061-415202) at 25 Roches St.

AROUND LIMERICK CITY

There are a few places south of Limerick that could be taken in on a day's tour by car. It could also be done by bike over a few days. The road that leads to Lough Gur, the R512, continues on through the village of Bruff to the historic town of Kilmallock. From there, it is a short journey to the village of Bruree, former home of Eamon de Valera. From Bruree a country road leads across to Bruff and the R512 back to Limerick. Apart from pubs in Bruree and more pubs and an ice-cream parlour in Kilmallock, there is little to recommend in the way of food. Picnic spots, however, are not difficult to find.

Accommodation can be found in Bruff, Kilmallock and Bruree, but the best B&B is in Kilmallock (see the following Kilmallock section).

Lough Gur

Gathered around a small horseshoe-shaped lake south of Limerick are a number of Stone Age remains. Coming from the city, the first is a 4000-year-old **stone circle** by the side of the road. With its 113 stones it's one of the largest in Ireland. One km farther along the road a left turn goes up towards Lough Gur; 100 metres past a church there is a **wedge tomb** on the other side of the road.

Another two km along is the **interpretive centre** which runs a half-hour slide and video presentation on the prehistoric remains. There is also a small **museum** with Neolithic artefacts and a replica of the Lough Gur shield that is now in the National Museum in Dublin. The 700 BC shield is 72 cm in diameter with six raised bosses designed to weaken the impact of an enemy's sword. The charge for the museum and presentation is IR£1.90/1. The centre's open from 10 am to 6 pm from early May to the end of September.

The area around the lake can be explored on foot; there are burial mounds, standing stones, ancient enclosures and other remains dotted around. A festival is held here around the summer solstice (21 June); check with the tourist office or the interpretive centre for details.

To get there, start by taking the N24 road to Waterford south from Limerick. There is a sign to Lough Gur indicating a right turn at the roundabout outside town. After 18 km there is parking space on the left for the stone circle.

Kilmallock

Kilmallock was once the third largest town in Ireland, after Dublin and Kilkenny. It developed around an abbey founded in the 7th century by St Mocheallóg, hence its Irish name *Cill of Mocheallóg* which means 'church of Mocheallóg'. From the 14th to the 17th centuries it was the seat of the earls of Desmond.

On the way into town from the Limerick road, the first place to see is the four-storeyed **King's Castle**, a 15th-century tower house with the street pavement running through it.

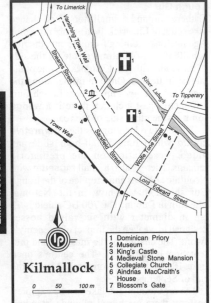

Kilmallock

0   50   100 m

1 Dominican Priory
2 Museum
3 King's Castle
4 Medieval Stone Mansion
5 Collegiate Church
6 Aindrias MacCraith's
  House
7 Blossom's Gate

On the other side of the road a lane leads down to a tiny **museum** that houses a small local collection and a model of the town in 1597. The museum is open from 1.30 to 5.30 pm on Monday to Friday and from 2 to 5 pm on Saturday and Sunday; it's hardly worth the IR£1/50p entry charge.

Beyond the museum and across the River Lubagh is the 13th-century **Dominican Priory**, with an attractive 13th-century east window and a tower and south window added in the 15th century. Kilmallock surrendered to Cromwell's forces in the 1640s and the priory was sacked and partly destroyed.

Back on to King's Castle and a little farther on to the right is a **medieval stone mansion** – just one of the 30 or so that once housed the prosperous merchants and landowners of the town. Returning to the main street and continuing up Sarsfield St there's a turning on the left that goes down to the **Collegiate Church**. This has a round tower,

which may have belonged to an earlier monastery on the site. The fine door in the south wall of the north transept is original 13th-century, while the impressively carved door on the south side of the nave dates from the 15th century.

Not far from the junction of Sarsfield St and Lord Edward St is **Blossom's Gate**, the only surviving gate of the original medieval town wall, traces of which can be seen in the vicinity. Along Wolfe Tone St, you'll find a 15th-century house, where the Irish poet Aindrias MacCraith died in 1795.

If you want to spend a night here, *Deebert House* (☎ 063-98106) is a good B&B, with singles/doubles from IR£18.50/28.

Bruree

Eamon de Valera was born in New York in 1882, to an Irish mother and Spanish father. His father died when he was two years old, and his mother sent the young Eamon to Ireland in 1885 with his uncle. As a child he lived in a small cottage in Bruree and attended a Christian Brothers school in the nearby town of Charleville. The cottage where he spent his formative years is open to the public, but there's precious little in it. At the Kilmallock end of the village there is a sign pointing to the cottage and it is just over one km from this sign. Look for a parking space on the left next to a small slate-roofed cottage. The key to the house is available from the next house 200 metres farther up the road on the right-hand side.

The museum at the other end of Bruree also contains a variety of items associated with de Valera, as well as a local collection of folk objects. It is open Tuesday to Friday from 10 am to 5 pm, and between 2 and 5 pm on Saturday and Sunday; admission is IR£2/1. The village can be reached off the N20 road connecting Limerick and Cork; it is 32 km from Limerick, twice as far from Cork. If coming from Kilmallock there is a small direct road to Bruree.

LOUGH DERG WAY

This walking trail begins in Limerick City and ends at the village of Dromineer in

Eamon de Valera

As a young teacher of mathematics, de Valera attended a meeting in 1911, which was organised to protest at the visit to Ireland of the British monarchy. He found himself listening to the idea of an independent Irish republic and was quick to join the new Irish Volunteers. During the 1916 Easter Rising he commanded an outpost on a main road, and ambushed British reinforcements travelling into Dublin, securing the greatest military success of the rebellion.

Like the other leaders, he was sentenced to death for his role in the uprising but his US citizenship helped secure him a life sentence instead. In June 1917, he was included in an amnesty and was elected Sinn Féin MP for East Clare. He was president of Sinn Féin from 1917 to 1926. In 1918 he was imprisoned in Lincoln Prison in England but escaped in 1919 with the aid of a duplicate key.

When the IRA split in 1921 over the Anglo-Irish Treaty, de Valera led the anti-Treaty forces in a bitter civil war. After the war he continued to be elected, this time for the Irish parliament, but refused to swear the contentious oath of allegiance to the British king. Eventually he managed to enter parliament, skirting the oath by claiming his motive in entering parliament was to ensure its abolition. He formed a new party, Fianna Fáil, and established a government in 1932. Its new constitution abolished the oath and included a claim of sovereignty over the six counties of the North. That claim is still part of the constitution and has contributed to the difficulties in reaching a settlement to the Troubles.

De Valera's idyllic vision of self-sufficient rural communities has since been ridiculed. He is probably held in less regard now than at any time in the 20th century. ■

County Tipperary. See the Activities chapter for details.

FOYNES

If you're heading west from Limerick, pause at Foynes to visit the interesting little **Flying Boat Museum**, a reminder of Foynes's brief role as the eastern terminus of the first trans-atlantic airline service. There's a sister museum to Foynes at La Guardia Airport in New York, the US terminus of the pioneering pre-WW II flying-boat operations.

Entry is IR£2.50/1, and it's open from 10 am to 6 pm seven days a week from March to the end of October.

ADARE & AROUND

This attractive village south-west of Limerick is tourist Ireland at its most sanitised and manicured. Charming thatched cottages and antique shops abound. The comely layout of the village was created by the third earl of Dunraven in the first half of the 19th century. Coach tours make an obligatory stop in Adare (*Áth Dara*) and its cultivated pretti-ness means high prices for food and accommodation.

Information

The tourist office (☎ 061-396255) is on the main street and open mid-March to the end of October from 9 am to 6 pm (7 pm in July and August), closing at 1 pm on Sunday.

Adare Friary

The ruins of a Franciscan friary, founded by the earl of Kildare in the 15th century, and restored in 1875, stand in the middle of the Adare Manor golf course beside the river Maigue. Permission to enter should be obtained from the club house. The church has a well-preserved sedilia (set of seats for priests in the south wall of the chancel) and windows.

Desmond Castle

Dating back to the early 13th century, the castle was partly rebuilt in the following century and besieged by English forces in 1580. When Cromwell's army took possession in the 17th century, this castle had already lost its strategic importance. Restoration work by the OPW is currently in progress and the castle is best viewed from the bridge on the main road at the north end of the village.

Adare Manor

The earl of Dunraven enlisted the architectural help of James Pain and A W Pugin when creating his mansion in 1832. The enormous entry hall is divided by Gothic stone arches and there's a rococo panelled staircase worth seeing. The house is now an expensive hotel, open for viewing by non-residents who cough up IR£2. There should be no charge if you are going to have a drink in the hotel bar – you might change your mind on the way to the bar and go for a pleasant stroll through the grounds by the river instead.

Churches

In the village itself there are two churches of interest. The tower and south wall of the **Church of the Most Holy Trinity**, the village's Catholic church, are part of a 13th-century monastery which came to an end when the monks were murdered in 1539, during the dissolution of the monasteries.

The Church of Ireland parish church is the **Augustinian Friary**, founded in the 13th century. The tower was added in the 15th century, but the original stonework is well preserved.

Matrix Castle

This fine 15th-century Norman tower has been carefully preserved and is full of artefacts and objets d'art. Tours start at 10.30 am and continue at regular intervals until 6.30 pm, seven days a week. Entrance is IR£3/2. The castle is 13 km west of Adare on the N21, near the village of Rathkeale.

Places to Stay

B&Bs abound and accommodation in these is best arranged through the tourist office. On Main St, *Village House* (☎ 061-396554) charges from IR£16/30 and *Elm House* (☎ 061-396306), at around IR£30 for a double, has been recommended. The top-notch place is *Adare Manor* (☎ 061-396566) charging as much as a ridiculous IR£285 for a single.

Places to Eat

There is nowhere inexpensive to eat. The village pubs are the best bet for lunch. Dinner at *Adare Manor* starts at IR£32. On the main street the *Mustard Seed*, not quite as pricey, has a reputation as one of Ireland's best restaurants.

Getting There & Away

Adare is 16 km south-west of Limerick and the five daily Tralee (County Kerry) to Dublin buses stop at Adare before going on to Limerick. For details contact either the Bus Éireann desk at Limerick tourist office (☎ 061-301587) or the Limerick bus station (☎ 061-313333).

County Tipperary

County Tipperary occupies a fair chunk of the south midlands of Ireland and is the sort of land farmers dream about owning. Limey, superbly fertile soil puts Tipperary at the heart of Irish farming; particularly around the southern area known as the Golden Vale, which has some of the country's richest pastures. Most Tipperary farmers earn a good living and that wealth is reflected in the shops, streets and towns of the region.

Tipperary is mostly flat in the centre, with hills intruding over the borders from other counties. The River Suir cuts through the heart of the county and every major town lies on the banks of the Suir or one of its tributaries. Some of the towns have very active animal fairs or marts, especially Tipperary Town – which is, incidentally, not the major settlement: prosperous Clonmel, Cahir and Nenagh are far larger.

No WW I movie would be complete without some British private singing:

> It's a long way to Tipperary,
> It's a long way to go...

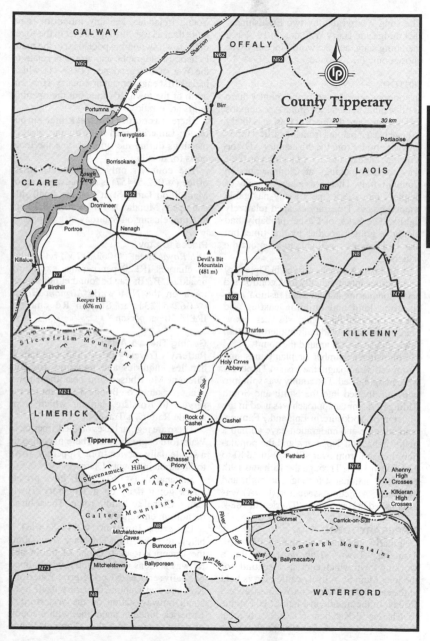

The song was written by two Englishmen, Jack Judge and Harry Williams, in 1912 as a marching song, and the word Tipperary was chosen only for its sound.

HISTORY

In common with the rest of the country there is substantial evidence of Stone Age humans in Tipperary, and the Rock of Cashel is likely to have been inhabited from the earliest times in that period. From the 9th century AD, the Vikings sailed up the River Shannon on their way to rich pickings at Clonmacnois in County Offaly. There was a local scarcity of helpless monasteries near easily navigable waterways, so Tipperary escaped relatively lightly. The Rock of Cashel probably had plenty of golden goodies by that time, but also had defences well able to keep out the raiders.

In 1185 the Normans arrived in Tipperary with serious intent, quickly took control and set to conquering in their usual fashion, confiscating land and building castles and abbeys. Some of the region was later recovered by the Irish, who built numerous small tower-house castles around the county.

Following a number of plantations and Cromwell's campaign, the Irish in Tipperary were marginalised. The county was split into two and divided into the North and South Ridings. (A similar approach was used in the division of Yorkshire in England.) Famine, land struggle and emigration have all had a major impact on Tipperary, and the population dropped from over 430,000 in 1840 to 135,000 in 1981. Through the 18th and 19th centuries, nationalist feelings ran high, and the Gaelic Athletic Association (GAA) was established in Hayes Hotel, Thurles, in 1884.

TIPPERARY TOWN

Originally an Anglo-Norman settlement, Tipperary Town (*TiobraidÁrann*) is a working town which consists essentially of the long Main St. A lively cattle mart is held at the east end of Main St on Wednesday and Friday. In the middle of Main St is a statue to Charles T Kickham (1822-82), a local novelist (author of *Knocknagow*) and a

Young Irelander. The tiny **museum** is no more than a large display cabinet in the foyer of the town swimming pool, next to the mart. Letters, photographs and artefacts relate to the War of Independence (1919-21) which had its first engagement in a quarry a few km north of the town. It's free, but the opening hours are erratic.

There is a **country racetrack** three km out on the Limerick road with regular weekly meetings during the summer. See the local press for details.

The county's only year-round tourist office (☎ 062-51457) is off the west end of Main St on James St. It's on the small side and opens Monday to Friday from 9.30 am to 6 pm, closing on Saturday at 1.30 pm.

Places to Stay

The *Royal* Hotel (☎ 062-51204) on Bridge St charges IR£20 per person, excluding breakfast. B&Bs can be found either side of town on the N24 while *Airmont House* (☎ 062-51231) in Station Rd charges IR£14.50 per person.

Getting There & Away

Rafferty's Travel (☎ 062-51555) on Main St handles enquiries and bookings for Bus Éireann. Most buses stop near the Brown Trout restaurant on Bridge St, except for the service to Rosslare Harbour which stops outside Rafferty's Travel.

There are regular buses on the Limerick to Waterford express route. There may also be a single daily service from Tipperary Town to Shannon in County Clare

Kavanagh's (☎ 062-51563) have private buses going daily on a Tipperary Town, Cahir, Cashel to Dublin route. These buses do not run on Sunday.

Limerick Junction (☎ 062-51406) is barely three km from Tipperary Town along the Limerick road. It is one of the busiest railway stations in the country, with numerous daily services to Cork, Kerry, Waterford, Rosslare and Dublin. Tipperary itself has a small railway station on the Waterford to Limerick Junction main line, with a couple of daily services to Cahir, Clonmel, Waterford and Rosslare Harbour and multiple connections from Limerick Junction.

Getting Around

Farther up the hill from the tourist office on James St is *O'Carroll's* (☎ 062-51229) which rents out bikes in the summer months at reasonable rates.

GLEN OF AHERLOW & GALTEE MOUNTAINS

South of Tipperary Town are the Slievenamuck Hills and then the Galtee Mountains, separated by the gently beautiful Glen of Aherlow. Between Tipperary and Cahir is **Bansha** at the eastern end of the glen, which marks the start of a 20-km through trip to Galbally, an easy bike ride. It is a nice area for low-key hiking, and there is plenty of country accommodation. Cahir is a good base from which to explore the Galtees.

Places to Stay

Ballinacourty House Caravan & Camping (☎ 062-56230) has excellent caravan and camping facilities, as well as a fine garden, restaurant, wine bar and tennis court. This oasis is 10 km west-south-west of Bansha on the road to Galbally and is open from mid-April to September. A tent with a car is IR£6.25 plus IR£1 per adult and IR£4 without a car.

The An Óige *Ballydavid Wood House* (☎ 062-54148) is an old hunting lodge in the south-east corner of the glen three km off the Tipperary to Cahir road on the north slopes of the Galtees, 10 km from Cahir, and a bed is IR£6. There are more hostels in and near Cahir.

The Georgian *Bansha House* (☎ 062-54194) is only 200 metres from Bansha village and does B&B from IR£17/30.

Close by Bansha House is *Bansha Castle* (☎ 062-54187), a lovely castellated 19th-century house and former residence of some of the Butlers of Ormond. B&B is from IR£21/32 and dinner from IR£15.

Getting There & Away

The express Tipperary Town to Waterford bus stops at Bansha and there are five or six buses daily in both directions. For details, contact Rafferty's Travel (☎ 062-51555) in Tipperary Town.

ROCK OF CASHEL

The Rock of Cashel (☎ 062-61437) is one of the most spectacular archaeological sites in the country. For 20 or 30 km in every direction there is a grassy plain, but on the outskirts of Cashel is a huge lump of limestone, bristling with ancient fortifications. Mighty stone walls encircle a complete round tower, a roofless abbey, the finest 12th-century Romanesque chapel in Ireland, and numerous smaller buildings and high crosses. For over a thousand years, the Rock of Cashel was a symbol of power, the base of kings and churchmen who ruled over the region and large swathes of the country as a whole.

The word Cashel is an anglicised version of the Irish *Caiseal* meaning 'fortress', and it's easy to imagine that the site developed in territory hostile to the Church. From the Dublin road, the Rock is concealed by smaller hills, until the last minute. The site is busy, especially in summer, so try and go first thing in the morning or in the late afternoon.

In the 4th century, the Rock of Cashel was chosen as a base by the Eóghanachta clan from Wales, who went on to conquer much of Munster and become kings of the region. For some 400 years it rivalled Tara as a centre of power in Ireland.

The clan's links with the church started early; St Patrick converted their leader in the 5th century in a ceremony in which the saint accidentally stabbed the king in the foot with his crozier. The king, thinking this was a painful initiation rite, bore the pain with fortitude. Possibly he was afraid to react, considering the actions taken by St Patrick on previous occasions against unbelievers.

The clan lost possession of the Rock in the 10th century to the O'Brien, or Dál gCais, tribe under the leadership of Brian Ború. In the first year of the 12th century, King

Muircheartach O'Brien presented the Rock to the Church, a move designed to curry favour with the powerful bishops and also to stop the Eóghanachta ever regaining the Rock, as they could never ask the Church to return such a present. So the Eóghanachta, by now the MacCarthys, moved to Cork; as a sign of goodwill Cormac MacCarthy built Cormac's Chapel in 1127 before leaving.

This chapel proved to be too small. A new cathedral was built in 1169 but was replaced in the 13th century.

In 1647, the Rock fell to a Cromwellian army under Lord Inchiquin which sacked and burned its way to the top. Early in the 18th century the Protestant church took it over for 20 years, and this was the last time the rock was officially used as a place of worship. The roof of the abbey only collapsed in the late 18th or early 19th century.

The Rock of Cashel is open all year round: from mid-September to mid-March, it's open daily from 9.30 am to 4.30 pm; between March and early June it's open daily from 9.30 am to 5.30 pm; while from June to mid-September it's open daily from 9 am to 7.30 pm. Admission is IR£2.50/1, and final admission is 40 minutes before closing time.

Hall of the Vicars Choral The entrance to the Rock is through this 15th-century house, which now contains the ticket office, a small exhibition centre and the audiovisual presentation room. The presentation runs every half hour for 20 minutes, detailing the Rock's history and attractions as one of the strongholds of the Christian faith. The exhibits downstairs include some rare silverware and **St Patrick's Cross**, a 12th-century crutched cross with a crucifixion scene on the west face and interlacing and animals on the opposite side; it's in poor condition, though. Tradition held that the kings of Cashel and Munster – including Brian Ború – were inaugurated at the base of the cross.

The Cathedral This 13th-century Gothic structure overshadows the other ruins. Entry is through a small porch across from the Hall of the Vicars Choral, leading into a tiny nave.

The west end of the cathedral is formed by the Archbishop's Residence, a 15th-century, four-storey castle which had its great hall built over the nave. Soaring above the centre of the cathedral is a huge, square tower with a turret on the south-west corner.

Scattered throughout are monuments, panels from 16th-century altar-tombs and coats of arms of the Butlers. On the north side of the choir is the recess tomb of Archbishop Hamilton. Opposite this is the tomb of Miler Mac Grath, who died in 1621. Miler was Catholic Bishop of Down and Connor until 1569, when he switched to the Protestant faith and ordained himself to the status of Protestant Archbishop of Cashel with the blessing of Elizabeth I. Her forces were busy at the time torturing and executing his rival, the Catholic Archbishop Dermot O'Hurley.

Round Tower On the north-east corner of the cathedral is the sandstone 11th or 12th-century round tower, the earliest building on the Rock. It is 28 metres tall and the doorway is 3.5 metres above the ground – perhaps for structural rather than defensive reasons.

Cormac's Chapel This is the Rock of Cashel's pièce de résistance, standing completely intact on the south side of the cathedral. Built from 1127, Cormac's Chapel is a small, solid, stone-roofed chapel of cruciform shape, with two tall, square towers on either side. Compared with other churches of the same era, the chapel is sophisticated in design, and displays influences from Britain and continental Europe – including the unusual square towers on either side of the nave.

Outside are impressive Romanesque arches, richly carved. Above the north door (opposite the entrance) in the minute courtyard adjoining the cathedral is a carving of a Norman helmeted figure firing an arrow at a huge lion which has just killed two animals.

The interior of the chapel is dark, its windows either blocked up – perhaps to shield the murals from light – or in the constant shadow of the cathedral.

The barrel-vaulted nave is only 12 metres

long, with a fine archway into the east chancel, boasting many finely carved heads and capitals. The south tower leads to a stone-roofed vault or croft above the nave. Inside the main door to the chapel on the left is the sarcophagus said to house King Cormac, dating from between 1125 and 1150. The deeply cut, interlacing design is highly developed, with motifs found more commonly on metalwork from earlier centuries.

Hore Abbey

The 13th-century Hore Abbey is set in farmland less than one km north of the base of the Rock. It was the last daughter house – a religious house which was affiliated to the main monastery – of Mellifont's Cistercians and was a gift from a 13th-century archbishop who expelled the Benedictine monks after dreaming that they had plans to murder him. The ruins are fairly extensive and it's a pleasant walk (signposted) from the base of the Rock.

CASHEL

Cashel (*Caiseal Mumhan*) is prosperous and thoroughly touristy, with plenty of restaurants, bars, B&Bs and hotels. It's also home to a small folk museum, folk village, Irish music centre and a library with some rare manuscripts.

The town hall stands in the middle of the main street, and contains Cashel's seasonal tourist office (☎ 062-61333), which is open from April to September. A small museum is also open here during the same period, Monday to Saturday, 10 am to 6 pm.

Things to See

Around town there are a number of ruins which, due to the overpowering presence of the Rock, are sometimes overlooked. The first right-hand turn after leaving the Rock leads onto Dominic St with its small **Dominican Friary** ruin from 1243 which, unlike Hore Abbey, has been engulfed by the town. On this road is the **Folk Village**. The far end of Dominic St leads to the centre of town.

Up a lane directly opposite the Cashel Palace Hotel is the **GPA Bolton Library**

Carving of a Norman figure above the north door of Cormac's Chapel, Cashel

(GPA stands for Guinness Peat Aviation). This small building, which was once a chapter house in the grounds of the Protestant cathedral, is now home to valuable manuscripts and first editions. It's open all year round from 9.30 am to 5.30 pm daily, and from 2.30 pm on Sunday. Admission is IR£2/1.

The **Cashel Palace Hotel** is a lovely Queen Anne residence built by Edward Lovett Pearce (architect of the Bank of Ireland in College Green, Dublin) for Archbishop Bolton in 1730.

One km along the Clonmel Rd is the museum of **Bothán Scóir**, a careful if slightly romanticised reconstruction of a peasant cottage. It is opened only on request; ring ☎ 062-61360.

Places to Stay

Camping & Hostels The IHH *O'Brien's Farm Hostel* (☎ 062-61003), a converted coach house, is a friendly and well-equipped place. It is in Dundrum Rd, just across from Hore Abbey and literally in the shadow of the Rock of Cashel, as a reader put it when recommending the hostel. Beds are from IR£6, doubles from IR£18, and camping is also possible. The IHH *Cashel Holiday Hostel* (☎ 062-62330) is at 6 John St, a turning off Main St, and beds here are IR£6 and there are two double rooms at IR£17 each.

B&B On Main St, *Bailey's* (☎ 062-61937) is a Georgian townhouse with B&B from IR£12.50/25. Across from the Dominican friary on Dominic St is *Abbey House* (☎ 062-61104), a stone's throw from the Rock and Main St, with rooms from IR£14/28. *Ros-Guill House* (☎ 062-61507) is one km away on the Kilkenny to Dualla road and has views of the Rock and exceptionally good breakfasts; singles/doubles are from IR£20/28 and it's open April to October. *Maryville* (☎ 062-61098) is at Bank Place in Cashel and has identical rates.

Hotels *Kearney's Castle Hotel*, (☎ 062-61044), in Main St, is a 15th-century square tower once known as Quirke's Castle, with rooms from as little as IR£25/40. In Dundrum, 10 km to the north-west, are *Dundrum House* (☎ 062-71116) and *Rectory House* (☎ 062-71266). Both are excellent: the former is an 18th-century Palladian villa offering B&B for IR£51.50/86.50, while the latter charges IR£42/68 for B&B.

The *Cashel Palace Hotel* (☎ 062-61411) on Cashel's Main St is exquisite, with an unbeatable view of the Rock. A private footpath joins the two. The bad news is that B&B erodes the budget by between IR£85 for a single and IR£104 for a double, excluding breakfast.

Places to Eat
Two excellent coffee shop cum restaurants are the *Bakehouse* (☎ 062-61680) on Main St near the traffic lights, and the *Coffee Stop* also on Main St on the corner near the GPA Bolton Library.

There are a few takeaways in Cashel, though none of the fast-food chains have made it out this far. The *Friar St Fryry* on Friar St serves good burgers & chips. The *Spearman's Restaurant* behind the town hall on Main St has middle-of-the-road fare, and next door is *O'Neill's* coffee shop. Beside the Rock of Cashel car park, *Granny's Kitchen* has cheap snacks including desserts flavoured with Guinness. All these places are around IR£and under for most items on their menus.

The Cashel Palace Hotel has two restaurants: the *Four Seasons* and the *Buttery*. The first has a good à la carte menu at over IR£30 for dinner. The second is cheaper and more informal. A full dinner at *Dundrum House* costs IR£26; IR£18 at *Rectory House*.

The best restaurant in the region is *Chez Hans* (☎ 062-61177) just off Main St at the Dublin end of town. It's inside a converted church and the food is terrific. Dinner costs from IR£20 a head.

Entertainment
Down the hill past the Rock's car park is *Brú Ború* (☎ 062-61122), a centre for traditional Irish music which serves it up seven nights a week during the summer season. Starting at 9 pm there is music, song, dance, storytelling and crack galore. Admission is IR£5 for the night, and there is an optional pre-show banquet. They also have a genealogy centre and a coffee shop and restaurant.

For a more authentic Irish music scene, head for the *Golden Vale* pub on Monday nights; it's in the village of Dundrum, 10 km north-west of Cashel on the R505. For a quiet drink, try *Davern's Pub* or *Dowling's*, both on Main St.

Getting There & Away
Bus Éireann runs one bus daily each way on the Dublin to Clonmel and Limerick route. There are four daily each way on the Dublin to Cork Expressway service, with three on Sundays. Rafferty's Travel (☎ 062-62121) on Main St handles tickets and enquiries for Bus Éireann.

Kavanagh's (☎ 062-51563) have private buses going daily on a Tipperary Town, Cahir, Cashel, Dublin route leaving Cashel for Dublin at 8.30 am. Coming back, they leave Dublin (George's Quay near Tara St Station) at 6 pm and arrive in Cashel at 8.30 pm. They also do a daily run between Cashel and Clonmel, departing from Cashel at noon, and another to Thurles, departing at 3.45 pm. These buses do not run on Sunday.

Getting Around
Both the hostels hire out bicycles, and places within cycling range include Cahir Castle.

ATHASSEL PRIORY

Twenty km west of Cashel, the N74 brings you to Tipperary Town. A third of the way along is the village of Golden, from which you can detour south for two km to Athassel Priory. This extensive and long-abandoned Norman monastery sits peacefully on the west bank of the River Suir. It was built around 1200 by William de Burgh, who wanted it to be one of the richest and most important in the country. The native Irish, in the guise of the earl of Desmond and the O'Briens, burned the priory and its accompanying town in 1319 and again in 1329. What's left today are the remains of a gatehouse, gateway, surrounding walls and the cloisters or arched passageways where monks would walk in prayer, as well as some foundations of various other monastic buildings, including the chapter house.

CAHIR

Cahir (pronounced 'Care') is 15 km due south of Cashel, lying at the eastern tip of the Galtees and on the banks of the River Suir. Cahir (*An Cathair*) is a prosperous place on the main Dublin to Cork road, which ensures constant heavy traffic. There is a tourist information point in the reception area of Cahir Castle.

Cahir Castle

Cahir's most noteworthy feature is the great 15th-century Butler castle near the town centre. The Butlers were granted lands in the area in 1192, but didn't get round to building their first castle until the 13th century. The castle is remarkably intact and one of the largest in Ireland. Its occupants surrendered to Cromwell in 1650 without a struggle – memories were fresh of the battering the place had suffered in 1599 at the hands of the earl of Essex and his meagre two cannons – and it has been extensively restored. Some of John Boorman's *Excalibur* was filmed in Cahir Castle.

The castle sits on a rocky island in the River Suir, and comprises three wards or yards, surrounded by a thick fortifying curtain wall, with the main structural towers

and halls around the innermost ward. Entry to the castle is along the sloping barbican running parallel to the inner-ward wall, and then through to the reception area. This opens out into the small middle ward, overshadowed by the large gatehouse and keep to the right. Go through this gatehouse, under the reconstructed and fully functioning portcullis, and you come to the inner ward. Its buildings are sparsely furnished – it's a pity to have such fine rooms so empty.

Beside the north-east tower is the small **well tower** which offers the best vantage point over the river. The tower spirals down to the river and therefore once provided a vital water supply during any extended siege.

The large, garden-like outer ward has a 19th-century cottage at the far end, housing an audiovisual show on other sites in the region.

Cahir Castle, run by the OPW, is open daily all year round: between April and mid-June and mid-September to mid-October it's open from 10 am to 6 pm. From mid-June to mid-September, it's open from 9 am to 7.30 pm. The rest of the year it's open from 10 am to 4.30 pm, but closed from 1 to 2 pm. Admission is IR£2/1.

Swiss Cottage

A little over two km south of town in Cahir Park is the Swiss Cottage, also run by the OPW, a thatched hunting lodge with mature gardens and parkland, and an elevated view of the River Suir. Access to the cottage is only by guided tour. It was designed by John Nash and is slowly recovering from a period of decay; many fine little features remain.

The cottage is open from mid-March to November, daily from 10 am to 6 pm between May and September. Call ☎ 051-640787 for the varying hours at other times of the year. Admission is IR£2/1.

Places to Stay

Cahir has two independent hostels nearby. The run-of-the-mill IHH *Lisakyle Hostel* (☎ 052-41963) is two km south of town on a back road to Ardfinnan past the Swiss

Cottage, and also has camping facilities for IR£3.50 per person. Beds in the hostel are IR£6 and there's one double at IR£15. In town, Maurice Condon's shop opposite the post office on the Dublin road acts as their office for any enquiries.

The excellent IHH *Kilcoran Farm Hostel* (☎ 052-41906) is slightly harder to find. It's six km west of Cahir, signposted 1.6 km off the N8 Mitchelstown road at a petrol station. It's on an organic farm, and has free showers, kitchen facilities and donkey rides for kids. There are no dorm beds and it's a flat IR£7 per person.

The An Óige *Ballydavid Wood House* hostel (☎ 062-54148) is in the Glen of Aherlow 10 km north-west of Cahir and a bed is IR£6.

One km along the Cashel to Dublin road is *Ashling* (☎ 052-41601) with B&B from IR£19/29. Also along this road, three km from Cahir, is *Springhill* (☎ 052-41754), with B&B for IR£18.50/29.

If you come to Cahir to view a castle, you could well stay the night in one. The 16th-century *Carrigeen Castle* (☎ 052-41370) on the Cork road is often mistaken for Cahir Castle. It's actually a B&B, with four grand double rooms at IR£28 and IR£34 or IR£20 single.

Right in the centre of town, the *Castle Court Hotel* (☎ 052-41210) on Church St is a pleasant little family-run hotel costing IR£35/60. The *Kilcoran Lodge* hotel (☎ 052-41288) is six km along the Cork road. Facilities include a pool and health club. B&B goes from IR£47.50/90.

Places to Eat

There are a couple of takeaways and cheap places to eat. Opposite Cahir Castle car park and above a craft shop is the *Crock of Gold*, a tiny restaurant which serves up light lunches and dinner throughout the day. The *Earl of Glengall* in the square has solid IR£5 pub lunches though the day. There are two Italian-style restaurants, the *Italian Connection*, with dishes around IR£7, and *Roma* which is a little less expensive and enjoys a better atmosphere.

Getting There & Away

For buses, Cahir is on the main Dublin to Cork express route, the Limerick to Waterford express route, and the Kilkenny to Cork and Cork to Athlone express routes. A less frequent service runs from and to Tralee with connections on the northbound bus to Galway, Sligo, Derry, Drogheda, Dundalk and Belfast. The bus stop is outside the Crock of Gold craft shop and restaurant, across the road from Cahir Castle. For information on bus times, ring ☎ 062-51555.

Kavanagh's (☎ 062-51563) have private buses going daily on a Tipperary Town, Cahir, Cashel to Dublin route. These buses do not run on Sunday.

Two trains a day on the Cork to Rosslare Harbour line stop at Cahir. For train information, contact Thurles Railway Station (☎ 0504-21733). Cahir is on the main Waterford to Limerick Junction railway line.

MITCHELSTOWN CAVES

The Galtee Mountains are sandstone, but on the southern side is a narrow band of limestone, which is home to the Mitchelstown Caves. They're found near Burncourt, 15 km south-west of Cahir, signposted off the road to Mitchelstown. They are also signposted from the centre of Ballyporeen. These caves are among the most extensive in the country, far superior to the Dunmore Caves of Kilkenny and much less developed for the tourist.

In 1833, Michael Condon was quarrying limestone when he lost his crowbar down a crack in the rock. His efforts to retrieve it opened up the system they called New Caves. There was an earlier known cave system nearby – now called the Old Caves – which were used in prehistoric times and include the largest chamber of the system. However, it is the New Caves that form the basis of the tour. It is through Condon's original opening that exploration begins. Internal temperatures are pretty constant at around 13°C. Underground, there are nearly two km of passages and spectacular chambers full of text-book formations, inventively labelled from classical and biblical sources.

The caves (☎ 052-67246) are open all year round from 10 am to 6 pm. Call at the English's farmhouse opposite the car park for tickets and a tour guide. Admission is IR£2.50/2.

Places to Stay

Five km due north of the caves on the slopes of the Galtees is the An Óige *Mountain Lodge Hostel* (☎ 052-67277), north off the main Mitchelstown to Cahir road. It's open from March to September and is a handy base to explore either the Galtees or the Mitchelstown Caves.

Getting There & Away

Buses from Dublin to Cork and back on the express route pass through Mitchelstown. Ring ☎ 062-51555 for details.

CLONMEL

Clonmel (*Cluain Meala*) is the largest, liveliest and most cosmopolitan town in Tipperary. It's also the largest inland town in the county. The approach to Clonmel is attractive, particularly from the Kilkenny side, along a good road with well-tended houses and hedges, while the river and mountains give the town a fine backdrop. The town's long prosperity has left it with many fine features.

History

After the Norman invasion, Clonmel came under the influence of the de Burgos and the earls of Desmond, which created tension with the Butlers until 1583, when the Butlers were finally victorious. In 1650, Cromwell laid siege to the town for three weeks. The garrison under the command of Hugh Dubh O'Neill exhausted their arsenal in the struggle, and on 17 May they sneaked undetected out of town. The remaining townspeople held out for a fair and honourable surrender. Cromwell had lost 2000 men in this single siege, more than in the whole remainder of his Irish campaign; he fell for the ruse and agreed to the town's request.

Over the centuries the town's wealth has attracted many businesspeople. One of them is now synonymous with Clonmel. Charles Bianconi (1786-1875) arrived in Ireland from northern Italy at the age of 16, sent by his father in an attempt to break a liaison he had formed with a spoken-for young lady. In 1815, Bianconi set up a coach service between Clonmel and Cahir, and the company quickly grew, becoming a nationwide passenger and mail carrier. For putting Clonmel on the map, Bianconi was twice elected mayor. The company's former headquarters is now Hearn's Hotel on Parnell St – Hearn was an assistant to Bianconi.

Orientation

The heart of Clonmel lies on the north bank of the River Suir. Set back off the quays and running parallel to the river, the main street from east to west starts off as Parnell St, becoming Mitchel St, O'Connell St, under West Gate and on to Irishtown and Abbey Rd. Running north off this long thoroughfare are Dillon, Gladstone, O'Neill and Cantwell St. Many of the town's narrow streets are one way.

Information

The tourist office (☎ 052-22960) in the Chamber of Commerce buildings opposite Hearn's Hotel is open from June to early September, 9 am to 5 pm. The post office is in a courtyard of the one-time county gaol at the north end of Emmet St, which runs north off Mitchel St. The Post House is a good bookshop on Gladstone St.

Walking Tour

A good starting point for a quick tour of the town is **Hearn's Hotel**, which still has material relating to its former incarnation as Bianconi's headquarters.

South off Parnell St is Nelson St with the **County Courthouse** designed by Richard Morrison in 1802. It was here that the Young Irelanders of 1848 including Thomas Francis Meagher were tried and sentenced to the penal colonies of Australia. Back on Parnell St is the **County Museum**, which exhibits the shirt worn by Michael Hogan, who was captain of the Tipperary Gaelic Football team in Croke Park when they played Dublin on 21 November 1920. In retaliation for the deaths of 14 British Army intelligence officers, the British police auxiliaries known as the Black & Tans opened fire on the crowd and players, killing Hogan and 13 others. This was the first of the Bloody Sundays.

West along Mitchel St, past the town hall and south down Abbey St, is the **Franciscan Friary**. Although dating from 1269, much of what is visible is from the late 19th century. The tower is 15th century. Inside, near the door, is a 1533 Butler tomb depicting a knight and his lady. Back up on Mitchel St at the corner of Sarsfield St is the **Main Guard**. It was a Butler courthouse from 1674, based on a design by Christopher Wren, and still bears their coat-of-arms even though it was converted into shops in 1810.

Spanning the far end of O'Connell St is the **West Gate**, an 1831 reconstruction of an old town gate which once arched over the street here. On the east side is a plaque commemorating Laurence Sterne (1713-68), a native of the town and author of *A Sentimental Journey* and *Tristram Shandy*. Just before the arch is Wolfe Tone St which heads north past the old **Wesleyan Chapel** to **Old St Mary's Church**, built in 1204 by William de Burgh. The north and west sides of the site include some of the original medieval town wall.

Through West Gate is Irishtown, named after those native Irish who worked inside the town but were forbidden by law from living within its walls. On the south side of this street is the decorative **St Mary's Church**.

Places to Stay

The *Powers the Pot Hostel* (☎ 052-23085) has a Clonmel address even though it lies nine km south-east of town on the northern slopes of the Comeragh Mountains, well inside County Waterford. To get there, cross south over the river in Clonmel and follow the road to Rathgormack. It has a good little restaurant and camping is also possible. Beds are IR£6.

Many B&Bs can be found on Marlfield

Rd, due west of Irishtown and Abbey Rd. *Benuala* (☎ 052-22158) charges from IR£13/24 while *Hillcourt* (☎ 052-21029) is from IR£18.50/27. *Amberville* (☎ 052-21470) on Glenconnor Rd, north off Western Rd beside St Luke's Hospital, is well within walking distance of the town centre. B&B is from IR£18.50/27.

Three km from Clonmel, in Marlfield, is *New Abbey* (☎ 052-22626) with B&B doubles only, at IR£27 and IR£31.

Hearn's Hotel (☎ 052-21611) in the town centre does B&B for IR£32 per person. The *Hotel Minella* (☎ 052-22388) is a four-star hotel with gardens; it's south of the River Suir and is almost two km east of town on the Coleville road (follow the south quays east). B&B costs from IR£40/70.

The fine *Clonmel Arms Hotel* (☎ 052-211233) is down from the main street towards the river on Sarsfield St and costs from IR£42/80, excluding breakfast.

Places to Eat

There are plenty of cheap cafés, coffee shops and delis. *Niamh's* is a cosy coffee shop and deli on Mitchel St, while *Nuala's/Hickey's Bakery* right by the Westgate has fresh homemade snacks and good coffee. Both are open all day until 6 pm.

In the Marystone Centre, *Coyle's Coffee House* is similar, open until 5.30 pm. At 14 Abbey St is the Rainbow Warehouse, with an organic market on Friday and Saturday and the *Abbey Restaurant* (☎ 052-21457), which serves excellent cheap vegetarian dishes. It's open all day until 5.30 pm.

Bar food is available in *Tierney's Pub* on O'Connell St, *Kinsella's Bar* in Irishtown, the *Market Tavern* on Market St or *Mulcahy's* (☎ 052-22825) pub and restaurant on Gladstone St which is open from 10 am to 10 pm and serves dinner for about IR£11. The pub also has the more expensive *Mellary Restaurant*. The *Clonmel Arms Hotel* on Sarsfield St is one of the best places in town for a bar lunch and is reasonably priced.

The *Emerald Garden* (☎ 052-24270) is a good Chinese restaurant on O'Connell St.

The reasonably priced and pleasant *La Scala* (☎ 052-24147) is on Market St off Gladstone St.

Entertainment

Pubs Clonmel is lively at night. *Lonergan's* and *Chawke's Bar* on Gladstone St are fine for a pint. Many other bars, such as the *Coachman* on Parnell St and *Mulcahy's*, have local bands and Irish music nights in the summer. There are Irish music and dance sessions in the *Mellery Room* on Gladstone St.

Nightclubs Most of the hotels have nightclubs. *Club Nineties* in the Clonmel Arms Hotel is open Thursday to Sunday, while the Hotel Minella is home to *Streamers* on Saturday night.

Spectator Sports Clonmel is at the heartland of Irish greyhound racing and coursing. At the east end of Parnell St on Davis St is the greyhound track (☎ 052-21118), which has dog racing on Monday and Thursday at 8 pm. Powerstown Park Racecourse (☎ 052-22852) is north of the town and has a year round fixture list – though events may be a few weeks apart. Consult the local press for details.

Getting There & Away

Bus Bus Éireann (☎ 051-79000) has two buses daily each way to Dublin and Cork, with a more complicated timetable to Waterford, Limerick and Kilkenny. Contact the Waterford Bus Travel Information Centre, or ask at the Clonmel Railway Station for details. Rafferty's Travel (☎ 052-22622) act as Bus Éireann's ticket agent and the bus stop is at the railway station. Kavanagh's (☎ 062-51563) have private buses going daily between Cashel and Clonmel, leaving Cashel at noon and Clonmel at 3 pm. These buses do not run on Sunday.

Princess Coaches (☎ 052-21389) have a single daily service (Thursday to Monday) each way between Clonmel and Dublin.

Train The railway station (☎ 052-21982) is north of Gladstone St on Prior Park Rd, within walking distance from the town centre. Clonmel is on the Cork to Limerick to Rosslare Harbour line, with two trains each way daily, one on Sunday. There is no direct rail link to Dublin, but there are connections from Waterford or Limerick Junction.

AROUND CLONMEL

Directly south of Clonmel are the Comeragh Mountains in County Waterford, and there is a fine scenic route south to Ballymacarbry and the Nire Valley. Instead of coming back the same way you can do a circle, heading down to Ballymacarbry from the east and heading back up to Clonmel from the west side. For more details about this area see under the Nire Valley section in County Waterford.

The **Munster Way** long distance walk (see the Activities chapter) passes through Clonmel following the old towpath along the River Suir. At Sir Thomas Bridge the trail cuts south away from the river and into the Comeraghs to Harney's Cross Rds before rejoining the River Suir again at Kilsheelan Bridge from where it follows the river towpath all the way to Carrick-on-Suir. From Clonmel, you can walk parts of the trail along the towpath as a shorter outing. The main road between Clonmel and Carrick-on-Suir also follows the river through some lovely countryside.

CARRICK-ON-SUIR

This market town is 20 km east of Clonmel. With brewing and wool industries, Carrick-on-Suir grew to considerable importance during the Middle Ages. For a long time, the seven-arched 15th-century bridge was the only crossing point of the river for 40 km from the Suir's mouth at Waterford Harbour. In the 18th century, the population was 11,000, almost twice what it is today. Old warehouses still crowd the waterfront. Compared to Clonmel, Carrick-on-Suir is quiet and unsophisticated. It's surrounded by rich green farmland and the Comeragh Mountains can be seen in the distance.

Most places only make a fuss of their famous inhabitants long after their demise, but Carrick-on-Suir was quick to honour Sean Kelly, who was one of the world's greatest cyclists during the late 1980s. The town square now bears his name.

The Munster Way has one terminus at Carrick-on-Suir, winding its way west to Clonmel before heading south into Waterford. For more details see the Activities chapter.

Ormond Castle

Carrick-on-Suir was once the property of the Butlers, the earls of Ormond, who built the 14th-century castle at the east end of Castle St. Anne Boleyn, one of Henry VIII's six wives, is rumoured to have been born here, though many other castles claim this distinction. She was the great-granddaughter of the 7th earl of Ormond. The Elizabethan mansion next to the castle was built by the 10th earl of Ormond, Black Tom Butler, in anticipation of a visit by his cousin, Queen Elizabeth I, who unfortunately never got round to seeing the result of his efforts.

Some of the rooms have fine 16th-century stuccowork, especially the Long Gallery, with its depictions of Elizabeth and the Butler coat of arms. Considering the turmoil of the period, it is interesting to note the house's almost complete lack of defences. The castle, run by the OPW, is open mid-June to September, every day from 9.30 am to 6.30 pm, and admission is IR£2/1.

Tipperary Crystal

Only 22 km away from Waterford City and its world-famous glass industry, Carrick-on-Suir is home to one of the many regional crystal enterprises which have sprung up, attempting to rival their neighbour. The factory (☎ 051-41188) is along Clonmel Rd and is open to the public. There is a crystal outlet and coffee shop.

Places to Stay

Centrally located on Sean Kelly Square is *Orchard House* (☎ 051-41390), with B&B from IR£15/28. The *Grand Inn* (☎ 051-47035) is a 17th-century stone coaching inn, once a stopover on the Bianconi coach line. It's now an unusual B&B costing from

IR£16.50/27. It's nine km north on the main N76 Clonmel to Kilkenny road at Nine-Mile House, not far from the Ahenny crosses.

The *Carraig Hotel* (☎ 051-41455) on Main St has rooms from IR£25/40 for B&B.

Places to Eat

The *Carraig Hotel* is probably the best place to eat in town; dinner is IR£15. Otherwise, the choice of eateries is limited. The *Park Inn Pub* is good for pub food.

Entertainment

Cooney's attracts the younger crowd for drinks, while *Kehoe's* has an older mixture and the occasional music night.

Getting There & Away

Bus There are extensive bus services to and from the town. For details ring ☎ 051-79000. On the Limerick to Waterford express route there are up to five buses on weekdays and three on Sunday, serving Tipperary Town, Cahir, Clonmel, and Carrick-on-Suir. Other regular buses serve Clonmel, Dublin, Galway, Rosslare Harbour, Tralee, Cork and Kilkenny.

Train There are two trains daily on the Cork to Rosslare Harbour line. For information contact Thurles Railway Station (☎ 0504-21733). Carrick-on-Suir is on the main Waterford to Limerick Junction line with daily services and connections to Dublin, Limerick, Cork, Tralee, Mallow, Cahir, Clonmel, Waterford and Rosslare Harbour.

AHENNY & KILKIERAN HIGH CROSSES

Roughly five km and eight km north of Carrick-on-Suir and signposted off the road to Windgap are the two groups of high crosses at Ahenny and Kilkieran. The more easily found are the more distant crosses in the village of Ahenny.

The two Ahenny crosses are impressive, both four metres tall and dating from the 8th century. They are somewhat unusual in that they're almost exclusively covered in an interlacing design in high relief. Only on the base are there any panels depicting the more typical religious scenes. They are said to represent the transition from the older abstract designs of high crosses to the pictorial scenes found on many later crosses. Another odd feature are the removable cap stones, sometimes known as mitres (bishop's hats). Legend has it that these caps can cure migraine headaches if placed on the sufferer's head. The victim would have more than migraine to worry about – the stones are on the large side.

On the base of the north cross is a panel depicting seven religious men. The story goes that these were seven bishops who had returned from Rome, each carrying a bag of sand as a memento of their visit. Robbers ambushed them and mistook their bags for purses. The robbers murdered them, convinced that the bishops had turned their gold into sand to save it from being stolen.

There is the base of a third cross still here. This cross was supposedly the most beautiful of those at Ahenny and rumour has it that it was stolen about 200 years ago. The story goes that the ship which was carrying the cross out of Waterford was lost at sea off Passage East, and that the cross lies somewhere on the sea floor.

About two km nearer Carrick-on-Suir and east off this road are the three Kilkieran crosses in a small graveyard. The west cross is similar to those in Ahenny: four metres tall, richly decorated and with mitre intact. The other is extremely plain. The most interesting is the needle-like Long Shaft Cross, a shape unique in Ireland.

At the far end of the cemetery is a holy well whose waters are said to cure headaches. There must have been a plague of headaches at the time, given the number of cures to be found in the area.

THURLES

This large market town 22 km north of Cashel was founded by the Butlers in the 13th century, but little of note has been built in Thurles (*Durlas*) since then.

Information

There is a tourist information desk (☎ 0504-

23579) in the Centrefield building on the Slievenamon road, which is north off Liberty Square. It's open May to August from 9.30 am to 5.30 pm, Monday to Saturday. There is a regional museum housed in the same building.

Things to See

There are two poor, square tower-house ruins left: the 15th-century **Barry's Castle** by the bridge and the other **Black Castle** at the opposite end of Liberty Square, behind shops. There's an incongruous **bird sanctuary** on an island in the middle of the River Suir. A few hundred metres farther on is the **Catholic cathedral**, built in the 1860s in the Italian Romanesque style.

Back in the square is **Hayes Hotel** where, as every Irish schoolchild learns, the Gaelic Athletic Association or GAA was founded in 1884. It was set up to foster the pursuit of Irish sports and pastimes, particularly Gaelic football and hurling, which it continues to oversee. Over the years, the GAA has been the most successful of the Gaelic revivalist groups.

The town square has unfortunately become one big ugly car park.

Getting There & Away

Bus Éireann (☎ 051-79000) buses stop at Thurles once daily on the Dublin (2¼ hours) to Cahir (35 minutes) route.

Thurles is on the busy Dublin to Limerick and Dublin to Cork rail lines. For details contact Thurles Railway station (☎ 0504-21733).

HOLY CROSS ABBEY

Six km south-west of Thurles is the picturesque Holy Cross Abbey right beside the River Suir. The abbey was in ruins until the early 1970s, but a massive restoration project turned the Cistercian cloisters and chapels into a living church.

Holy Cross was home to a relic of the True Cross, a splinter of wood said to be from Jesus' cross, which attracted pilgrims to the abbey from its foundation in the 1160s. The splinter of wood was said to have been presented by Pope Pascal II to the King of Munster, Murtagh O'Brien, in the early years of the 12th century. It was the only cross relic in the country and was passed on to the nuns of the Ursuline Convent in Cork in the 19th century.

The buildings and cloisters you see today are from the 15th century, when the abbey was largely remodelled. The ground plan is typically Cistercian; a fine cruciform church with a square tower and cloisters to the east. The interior has been recently restored and whitewashed, and contains a modern altar. Look out for the small fleurs de lis and other symbols carved on the old stone pillars, the individual trademarks of the stonemasons. There is also a fine medieval fresco showing a hunting scene on one side of the church.

Built into the side of the abbey complex is a nice old pub, which does good food.

TEMPLEMORE & THE DEVIL'S BIT

Templemore, 12 km north of Thurles, is the chief training centre for the Gardaí, the Irish police force and is probably the one place where everyone sticks rigorously to speed limits. The railway station is on the Dublin to Limerick and Dublin to Cork lines.

Six km north-west is the Devil's Bit Mountain, a deep cut in the western end of the Slieve Bloom Hills.

The devil is supposed to have taken a bite out of the mountain and flown off. One version says that the devil didn't like the flavour, so he spat it out 34 km away where it became the Rock of Cashel. Another version claims that he was flying over Cashel when he spotted St Patrick preaching and such was the devil's anger that he dropped the rock. Unfortunately, unbelievers have hard evidence against both versions, as the Devil's Bit Mountain is sandstone while the Rock of Cashel is limestone!

The journey here is along lonely country roads and is fine for walkers heading for the Slieve Blooms, but is not really worth a detour.

NENAGH & AROUND

Nenagh (*An tAonach*) is a busy country town serving a large section of northern Tipperary.

It's on the main Dublin to Limerick road, and suffers from heavy traffic.

There is a tourist office (☎ 067-31610) on Connolly St, open May to September.

Things to See

Nenagh Castle was the seat of the first Butler of Ireland, Theobald Walter, in the early 13th century and remained in the family's possession for 400 years. The Walters changed their name to Butler and in the late 14th century moved their principal seat of power to Kilkenny Castle (see Kilkenny City and Castle for more details). All that remains of the family castle at Nenagh now is a circular **donjon** or tower dating from 1217. It is over 30 metres tall; the final eight metres were added by the Bishop of Killaloe in 1860.

Across the road is a Doric courthouse and beside it a convent, originally a prison. Some of the buildings are now home to the **Nenagh heritage centre** (☎ 067-32633). The centre is in two parts. The first is the Gatehouse and gaol, where criminals were hanged in the last century. The exhibits are related to those events. Up the driveway is the Governor's House, with a display of art and photographs of an old country schoolroom, a kitchen, a forge, a dairy, and an exhibit on Lough Derg.

The centre is open 16 May to 28 September, Monday to Friday between 10 am and 5 pm. It's closed on Saturday and opens from 2.30 to 5 pm on Sunday. Admission is IR£1.50.

Getting There & Away

Bus The bus stop in Nenagh is on Banba Square in the middle of town although some services stop at Nenagh Railway Station. There are frequent buses on the Dublin to Limerick express route. A less frequent service runs to Tralee with connections on the northbound bus to Galway, Sligo, Derry, Drogheda, Dundalk and Belfast. There are a couple of buses daily to Roscrea, Killaloe and Limerick (only one on Sundays) and some of these stop at Nenagh railway station only. From late June to early September the Galway to Rosslare Harbour bus stops at Nenagh.

Tuohy's Coaches (☎ 067-312900), a private company, has a daily bus to Dublin, leaving from O'Meara's Hotel at 8.25 am; an extra one on Mondays leaves at 6 am. It also has services to Scarriff in County Clare and Galway City.

Train Two Dublin to Limerick trains stop at Nenagh every day. For details ring Thurles Railway Station (☎ 0504-21733).

Getting Around

J Moynan (☎ 067-31293) on Pearse St is the main bike dealer. In Dromineer, Shannon Sailing Ltd (☎ 067-24295) can provide canoes (IR£3 an hour), yachts or motor boats to explore the lake. Their two-hour cruise on the *Ku-Ee-Tu* is also available from May to September, costing IR£5 for adults, children IR£3. It departs daily at 3 pm.

ROSCREA

On the eastern edge of the county is the medium-sized town of Roscrea (*Ros Cré*), which like Mountrath in Laois can be used as a base for exploring the Slieve Bloom Hills to the north-east. Roscrea would be quite a pleasant country settlement but for the main Limerick to Dublin road which cuts through the town.

Roscrea owes its origin to a 5th-century monk, St Crónán, who set up a way station for the travelling poor. Today, most of the town's historical structures are on or near the main street.

Things to See

As you hit town from the Dublin side, you are faced with a truncated **round tower** built into the wall of a builder's yard, while across the road are the remains of St Crónán's second monastery: the gable end of **St Crónán's Church** with its finely worked

stone Romanesque doorway, and a **high cross**, both of which date from the 12th century. The rest of the church was torn down in the early 19th century. The site of St Crónán's first monastery is almost two km east of town and south of the main Dublin road.

A 7th-century illuminated manuscript, 'The Book of Dímma', originated from here and can now be seen in Trinity College, Dublin.

In the centre of town is the OPW-restored, 1280 **Norman Castle**, with substantial remains of a gatehouse, walls and towers. Inside the courtyard of the castle is **Damer House**, the Queen Anne residence of the Damer family, which houses **Roscrea heritage centre** with some fine period furniture and a wonderful staircase. The centre also mounts various exhibitions of local interest throughout the year. It is open from June to September, daily from 9.30 am to 6 pm, and admission is IR£2.50/1. From October to May it is open Sunday only from 10 am to 5 pm.

Getting There & Away

Bus Frequent Dublin to Limerick express buses stop at Roscrea. There are a couple of buses daily to Nenagh, Killaloe and Limerick, but only one on Sunday. A less frequent service runs from and to Tralee with connections on the northbound bus to Galway, Sligo, Derry, Drogheda, Dundalk and Belfast. Roscrea is also on a daily Cork to Athlone express route which serves Fermoy, Cahir, Cashel, Thurles and Templemore and Birr. For bus details phone Rafferty's Travel (☎ 062-51555) in Tipperary Town.

Train Two Cork to Limerick trains stop at Roscrea every day. For details ring Thurles Railway Station (☎ 0504-21733).

County Kilkenny

A verdant farming county, Kilkenny is peppered with solid stone walls, medieval ruins and stands of old trees. The Normans liked this part of Ireland and settled here in numbers, leaving their stamp on Kilkenny City which is a league above most midland towns. The county's most attractive areas are along the rivers Nore and Barrow with charming villages like Inistioge and Graiguenamanagh, while nearby Jerpoint Abbey and Kells Priory are two of the finest medieval monastic settlements in the country.

Since medieval times, Kilkenny's history has been inextricably linked with the fortunes of one Anglo-Norman family, the Butlers, earls of Ormond. After arriving in 1171, they made the region their own, promoting first the Norman cause and then that of the English royal household. They were based in Kilkenny City.

In Irish minds, Kilkenny is most closely associated with the ancient game of hurling. Many local shops plaster their windows with accessories of the game and photos of the great teams of the past. For the visitor, walking the stretch of the South Leinster Way that crosses the southern portion of the county offers an opportunity to see some of rural Ireland at its prettiest.

Highlights
- Jerpoint Abbey and Kells Priory, two of the finest medieval monastic settlements in Ireland
- The rivers Nore and Barrow with charming villages such as Inistioge which has a 10-arched stone bridge
- Kilkenny City, perhaps the most attractive large town in the country

GETTING THERE & AWAY
Bus
The Bus Éireann (☎ 01-836 6111, 051-79000) express Waterford to Dublin service takes in Mullinavat, Thomastown and Gowran en route, and has five buses daily in each direction. Thomastown is also on a summer only (mid-June to early September) express bus route between Galway, Thurles, Kilkenny City and Rosslare Harbour. There is one bus daily in each direction.

Another express route runs between Waterford and Longford stopping at Thomastown, Bennettsbridge (a request stop) and Kilkenny City en route, with one bus daily in each direction.

Rapid Express Coaches (☎ 01-679 1549) stops at Gowran, Thomastown and Mullinavat on its Dublin to Waterford and Tramore run; Monday to Saturday there are seven buses a day, five on Sunday.

See also Getting There & Away under Kilkenny City and Castlecomer.

On Thursday only, a single bus runs from New Ross to Kilkenny City (1¼ hours) via Inistioge, Thomastown and Bennettsbridge. Northbound, it leaves New Ross at 10 am; southbound, it leaves Kilkenny Railway Station at 1.15 pm.

Train
The Iarnród Éireann (☎ 01-850 836 6222)

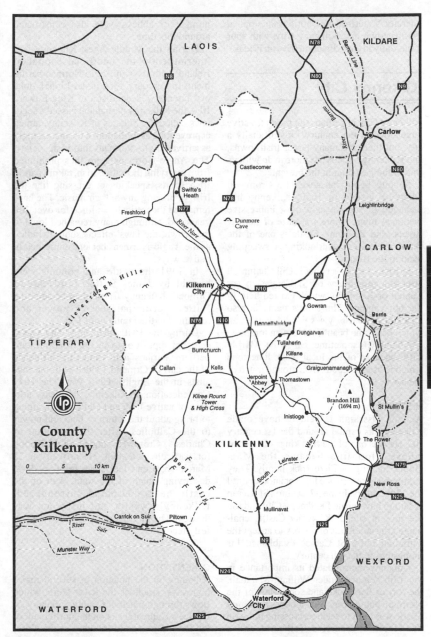

County
Kilkenny

intercity Waterford to Dublin train stops at Thomastown and Kilkenny City, with four trains daily in each direction (five on Friday).

Kilkenny City

Kilkenny City is perhaps the most attractive large town in the country. It's officially a city, but there are many larger Irish towns, and Kilkenny's status has more to do with its role in the past than in the present.

Despite being ransacked by Cromwell when he visited in 1650, Kilkenny has managed to survive as a most impressive medieval town. There's a maze of narrow streets, and Kilkenny Castle is one of the finest in Ireland, overlooking a sweeping bend in the river.

In Irish, the city's name is Cill Chainnigh after the monastery of St Cainneach (or Canice or Kenneth), which existed here in the 6th century. The saint's name is also attached to the city's splendid cathedral, which has some beautiful Norman tombs.

Kilkenny is sometimes called the 'Marble City' because of the local black limestone which is used to good effect around much of the town.

HISTORY

Aengus Ossraigh is said to have made Kilkenny his capital around the 1st century BC. He was one of the first kings of Ossory, whose bloodline became the MacGiollaPhadruig or Fitzpatrick family. They continued to rule in one form or another until the 12th century. In the 5th century, St Kieran is said to have visited Kilkenny City and, on the present site of Kilkenny Castle, challenged the chieftains of Ossory to accept the Christian faith. St Canice established his monastery in the 6th century.

Kilkenny consolidated its importance in the 13th century, under William Marshall, the earl of Pembroke and son-in-law of the Norman conqueror, Strongbow. Kilkenny Castle was built to secure a crossing point on the Nore. St Canice's Cathedral and a number of abbeys were also constructed around this time.

During the Middle Ages, Kilkenny was intermittently the unofficial capital of Ireland, with its own Anglo-Norman parliament. In February 1366 under Lionel, duke of Clarence – second son of King Edward III – the Kilkenny parliament passed a set of laws called the Statutes of Kilkenny, aimed at preventing assimilation of the increasingly assertive Anglo-Normans into Irish society. The Anglo-Normans were thus prohibited from marrying the native Irish, taking part in Irish sports, speaking or dressing like the Irish or playing any of their music. The laws remained theoretically in force for over 200 years and, although many remained loyal to the crown, the laws' effects soon dwindled as the Anglo-Normans became enmeshed in native ways.

In 1391 the castle and grounds were bought by James Butler, third earl of Ormond. Kilkenny Castle then became the Butlers' principal seat of power and remained in the family until 1967.

During the 1640s, Kilkenny City was a centre of opposition to the English Protestant parliamentarians, and – under the influence of the earl of Ormond – sided with the royalists in the English Civil War. The 1641 Confederation of Kilkenny, an uneasy alliance of native Irish and Old English, aimed to bring about the return of land and power to the Catholics. After the execution of Charles I, Cromwell singled out Kilkenny for particular attention. He arrived on 22 March 1650 and laid siege for five days, destroying much of the south wall of the castle before Ormond surrendered. Kilkenny's wealth and influence was destroyed by this defeat, from which it never fully recovered.

ORIENTATION

Kilkenny, at the junction of several major highways, straddles the River Nore, which flows through much of County Kilkenny. St Canice's Cathedral sits on the north bank of the River Bregagh (a tributary of the Nore)

KILKENNY

The Butler Family

Kilkenny City and castle are intimately associated with the Butler family, the earls of Ormond. This Anglo-Norman clan were originally known as the Walters, but changed their name after Theobald Walter was given the title of Chief Butler of Ireland by Henry II in 1185. The title was nice but what went with it was even better: the butlerage or duty charged on all wine imported into Ireland and England. When a descendant, Walter Butler, was strapped for cash in 1811, he sold the right for nearly £216,000, an extraordinary sum in those days. The three wine glasses on the family shield commemorate this important source of the family wealth.

The Butlers owned vast tracts of land in Tipperary and Kilkenny. During Henry VIII's reign, the family's power extended across much of southern Ireland. The Butlers lost out under Cromwell when the earl was exiled but his wife, Lady Ormond, managed to hang on to the estates. Because her treasonous husband was not in control, Cromwell didn't take away the family's positions or titles.

The Butlers bounced back with the restoration of Charles II in 1660 and picked the victorious side at the Battle of the Boyne in 1690 (although a Catholic cousin controlled the castle for the opposition), only to go down in flames when they backed a planned Spanish invasion of England in 1714. They later managed to reclaim some of their influence but never again reached their earlier heights. Both Tipperary and Kilkenny have numerous castles built by the family, including Carrick-on-Suir Castle (in Tipperary), the finest Elizabethan mansion in the country. ∎

at the north of the city centre outside the city walls.

From the cathedral, Kilkenny's main thoroughfare runs south-east, past St Canice's Place to Irishtown (where the common folk were once concentrated, outside the city walls, but now only the name remains) then over the bridge, eventually becoming Parliament St, which then splits in two. The eastern fork, St Kieran's St, meets Rose Inn St which leads north-east to John's Bridge over the River Nore. The western fork, High St, carries on south to Patrick St. Most places of interest can be found on or close to High St/Parliament St, parallel to the river, or John St on the other side of the river across John's Bridge. South from Rose Inn St, the Parade leads up to Kilkenny Castle, a long-time centre of Anglo-Norman power, which dominates the southern side of the city.

INFORMATION

The tourist office (☎ 056-51500) is in the Shee Alms House of 1581, a lovely stone townhouse on Rose Inn St. It's open April to September from 9 am to 6 pm Monday to Saturday, on Sunday from 11 am to 1 pm and 2 to 5 pm; October from 9 am to 1 pm and 2 to 5.30 pm Monday to Saturday; and November to March from 9 am to 1 pm and 2 to 5.15 pm Tuesday to Saturday. It has excellent maps and guides to the city and county.

The CityScope Exhibition takes place upstairs every half hour, and comprises a half-hour commentary explaining the sights, which are pinpointed on a model of medieval Kilkenny. Admission is IR£1.

The main post office (☎ 056-21879), open from 9 am to 5.30 pm Monday to Saturday (from 9.30 am on Wednesday), is on High St. Brett's Launderette (☎ 056-63200), on Michael St, west off John St, is open from 8.30 am to 8 pm Monday to Saturday. The Book Centre, 10 High St, has a range of books and maps on Ireland, while farther north, at No 67, the Ossory Bookshop has second-hand books as well as new ones.

KILKENNY CASTLE

The first structure on this strategic site overlooking the River Nore was a wooden tower built in 1172 by the Anglo-Norman conqueror of Ireland, Richard de Clare, better known as Strongbow. Twenty years later, his son-in-law William Marshall erected a stone

PLACES TO STAY

1 Newpark Hotel
2 The Brog Maker
4 Kilkenny B&B
5 Bregagh House B&B
14 Kilkenny Tourist Hostel
19 Ormonde Tourist Hotel
21 Dunromin B&B
23 St Mary's B&B
24 Mrs Dempsey's B&B
40 Lacken House
50 Club House Hotel

PLACES TO EAT

10 Parliament House Restaurant
15 Italian Connection
25 Emerald Garden
31 The Pantry
42 Uncle Sam's
44 Lautrec's Bistro & Wine Bar

46 Castle Diner
48 Moghul Restaurant
51 The Teashop
52 Restaurant Rinucinni

PUBS

9 Pump House & John Cleere
18 Peig's Bar
27 Daniel Bollard's
28 Kyteler's Inn
30 Jim Holland's
38 Edward Langton's
49 Caisleán Uí Cùain

OTHER

3 St Canice's Cathedral
6 Watergate Theatre
7 St Francis Abbey
8 Smithwick Brewery

11 Black Abbey
12 Black Freren Gate
13 Rothe House
16 Grace's Castle/Old Jail & Courthouse
17 Brett's Launderette
20 McDonagh Railway & Bus Station
22 St Mary's Cathedral
26 Confederation Hall Monument & Plaque
29 Market Cross Shopping Centre
32 Ossory Bookshop
33 Post Office
34 Butter Slip
35 Bateman's Quay
36 St John's Priory
37 Kilkenny College
39 JJ Wall Bike Hire
41 Regent Cinema
43 Tholsel (City Hall)
45 Tourist Office/Shee Alms House
47 Book Centre
53 Kilkenny Castle
54 Kilkenny Design Centre

KILKENNY

To Sundown House

To Castlecomer, N77, Athy & Dublin

Bishops Hill

Vicar Street

Greens Bridge

Greensbridge

New Road

Castlecomer Road

Wolfe Tone Street

Michael Street

John's Quay

John Street

Maudlin Street

Dublin Road

To N10, Carlow & Dublin

Butts Green

Dean St

St Canice's Place

Hightown

Bregagh

River

Abbey St

Parliament Street

Blackmill Street

Dominic Street

James Street

Kickham Street

Parnell Street

Kieran's Street

High St

Stephen Street

Friary Street

Gaol Road

Rose Inn St

The Parade

Pudding Lane

Patrick Street

Ormonde Road

New Street

Walkin Street

College Road

John's Bridge

River Nore

Kilkenny City

0   150   300 m

To Hotel Kilkenny, N76, Callan & Cork

To N10, Knocktopher & Waterford

To Thomastown & Nore Valley

castle with four towers, three of which survive in the present structure.

The castle was bought by the powerful Butler family in 1391, and their descendants continued to live there until 1935. Maintaining such a structure became an enormous financial strain and most of the furnishings were finally sold at auction. The castle was handed over to the city in 1967 for the princely sum of IR£50 and is now administered by the OPW.

The castle's 20 hectares of gardens extend to the north-east, with a formal rose garden, a fountain to the north end and a well-kept park with a children's playground to the south. Entry to the grounds is free.

Inside the castle, many of the rooms have only recently been opened to the public. The **Long Gallery** (the wing of the castle nearest the river), with its vividly painted ceiling and extensive portrait collection of Butler family members over the centuries, is quite remarkable and the focus of the 40-minute guided tour. It was the most significant part of the work carried out in 1826. The castle also has contemporary art exhibitions in the **Butler Gallery**, and in the basement, the castle kitchen now houses a popular summertime restaurant (see Places to Eat).

For IR£4 you can see and hear traditional Irish music performances in the castle on Tuesday at 8.30 pm during July and August.

Kilkenny Castle (☎ 056-21450) is open from 10 am to 7 pm daily between June and September. From October to March, it opens from 10.30 am to 12.45 pm and 2 to 5 pm Tuesday to Saturday, while on Sunday it's open 11 am to 12.45 pm and 2 to 5 pm. In April and May it opens from 10 am to 5 pm daily. Entry is IR£3/1.25.

ST CANICE'S CATHEDRAL

St Canice's Cathedral dominates Irishtown at the northern end of Parliament St. The approach on foot from Parliament St leads you over Irishtown bridge and up St Canice's Steps. The steps date from 1614, and the walls contain fragments of medieval carvings. Around the cathedral are a graveyard, an almost intact round tower and an 18th-century bishop's palace. Although the cathedral in its present form dates from 1251, it has a much longer history and contains some remarkable tombs and monuments. The *Guide for Visitors* is an excellent investment.

This site may well have had pre-Christian significance. Legends relate that the first monastery was built here by St Cainneach, Canice or Kenneth, Kilkenny's patron saint, who moved here from Aghaboe, County Laois, in the 6th century. There are records of a wooden church on the site, which was burnt down in 1087. The 30-metre-high **round tower** beside the church is the oldest structure within the cathedral grounds and was built somewhere between 700 and 1000 AD on the site of an earlier Christian cemetery. Apart from missing its crown, the round tower is in excellent condition, and you can admire the fine view from the top for 50/30p. It's a tight squeeze and both hands are needed to climb the steep ladders.

St Canice's was built in early English Gothic style and suffered a history of catastrophe and resurrection. Its first disaster, when the bell tower collapsed in 1332, is connected with the story of Kilkenny's legendary witch, Dame Alice Kyteler. In 1650, Cromwell's forces defaced and damaged the church, even using it to stable their horses. Repairs began in 1661, but there was still a great deal to be done a century later. The various additions over the centuries have not been faithful to the church's original design.

Throughout the church, both on the walls and in the floor, are ancient **graveslabs**. On the north wall opposite the entrance is a slab inscribed in Norman French to Jose de Keteller, who died in 1280; despite the difference in spelling he was probably the father of Kilkenny's witch, Alice Kyteler. On the same wall, read the verse to Mary Stoughton who died in 1631. The stone chair of St Kieran embedded in the wall dates from the 13th century.

In 1354, some magnificent **stained glass** was made for the church's east window, depicting the Life, Passion, Resurrection and Ascension of Jesus. A papal visitor in 1645 was so impressed he offered to buy it for

KILKENNY

£700, a huge sum in those days. The offer was rejected, and only five years later Cromwell's troops comprehensively destroyed the 300-year-old masterpiece. The replacement dates from 1875.

In the south transept is a beautiful **white tomb** with effigies of Piers Butler, who died in 1539, and his wife Margaret Fitzgerald. Tombs and monuments to a number of other notable members of the Butler family crowd this area of the church.

There's no entry fee to the church but donations are accepted.

BLACK ABBEY

The Dominican Black Abbey on Abbey St, off Parliament St, was founded in 1225 by William Marshall and takes its name from the monks' black habits. After Henry VIII's dissolution of the monasteries in 1543, it was turned into a courthouse. After Cromwell's visit in 1650, it remained a roofless ruin until restoration in 1866. Much of what survives dates from the 18th and 19th centuries.

Nearby to the south-west, off James St, is the small and less-interesting Catholic **St Mary's Cathedral of the Assumption** (☎ 056-21253). One of the side altars was the work of stonemason James Pearse (father of Patrick, a 1916 Easter Rising leader), and this altar was added to the cathedral during renovations around 1890. The cathedral was founded in 1843, and was named 'the famine church', as its construction provided employment for many local people during lean periods.

ROTHE HOUSE

Rothe House (☎ 056-22893), on Parliament St, is a fine old Tudor house dating from 1594. The house, which formerly belonged to a merchant, was built around a series of courtyards, and now has a museum with a sparse collection of local items from various periods displayed in its old timber-vaulted rooms.

In the 1640s, the wealthy Rothe family played a part in the Confederation of Kilkenny, and Peter Rothe, son of the original builder, had all his property con-

fiscated. His sister was able to reclaim it, but just before the Battle of the Boyne (1690), the family supported James II and this time lost the house permanently. In 1850, a banner from the confederation was discovered in the house and is now in the National Museum, Dublin.

Rothe House is open April to October from 10.30 am to 5 pm Monday to Saturday, 3 to 5 pm on Sunday. The rest of the year it only opens from 3 to 5 pm on Saturday and Sunday. Entry is IR£1.50/60p (students IR£1).

SMITHWICK BREWERY

The Smithwick Brewery, on Parliament St, has an audiovisual display and tastings during July and August at 3 pm Monday to Friday. The brewery was founded in 1710 and as well as Smithwick's own brands, Budweiser is brewed here under licence. The Franciscan monks of the restored St Francis Abbey on the brewery site were reputed to be expert brewers. This national monument was founded by William Marshall in 1232, but was desecrated by Cromwell in 1650.

OTHER BUILDINGS & SITES

Various remnants of the old Norman city walls can still be traced, but **Black Freren Gate**, just north-east of the Black Abbey on Abbey St, is the only gate still standing.

Shee Alms House, on Rose Inn St, was built in 1582 by local benefactor Sir Richard Shee and his wife to provide help to the poor. The house continued in this role as a 12-bed hospital until 1740. It's now home to the tourist office. The **Tholsel** or city hall on High St was built in 1761 on the site where Dame Alice Kyteler's maid, Petronella, was burnt at the stake in 1324. Just north of the Tholsel is the **Butter Slip**, a narrow alleyway, built in 1616 to connect High St with Low Lane (now St Kieran's St), once lined with the stalls of butter sellers.

St Kieran's St commemorates a church said to have been built here by the saint around 430 AD. The history of Kyteler's Inn built in 1324 is better documented as this was

The Witch of Kilkenny

Dame Alice Kyteler ran through four husbands in suspicious circumstances. She acquired some powerful enemies along the way and was charged with witchcraft in 1324. Witnesses claimed to have seen her sweeping dust to the door of her son, William Outlawe, while chanting, 'to the house of William, my son, lie all the wealth of Kilkenny town'. Worse still, she had supposedly been seen sacrificing cocks and consorting with the devil. She was duly convicted, along with her sister, her son and her maid. Dame Alice managed to escape to England but the unfortunate maid, Petronella, was left behind and burnt at the stake outside Kilkenny's Tholsel. No-one knows the fate of the sister.

Alice's son escaped from his sentence by offering to re-roof part of the cathedral with lead tiles. He carried out his side of the bargain, but the new roof proved too heavy and collapsed in 1332, bringing the church tower down with it.

Kytoler's Inn, 27 St Kieran's St, Dame Alice's former home, is now a restaurant and bar. ■

the site of wealthy Dame Alice Kyteler's home.

On the corner of Parliament St and the road leading down to Bateman's Quay, a **monument and plaque** beside the Bank of Ireland marks the site of the Confederation Hall, where the national parliament met from 1642 to 1649. Next door is **Grace's Castle** originally built in 1210 but lost to the family and converted into a prison in 1568 and later into a courthouse (1794), which it remains today. Rebels from the 1798 Rising were executed here.

On the eastern side of the river stand the ruins of **St John's Priory**, which was founded in 1200 and was noted for its many beautiful windows until Cromwell's visit. Nearby, St John's **Kilkenny College**, on the east end of Lower John St, dates from 1666. Its students included Jonathan Swift and the philosopher George Berkeley. It now houses Kilkenny's county hall.

ORGANISED TOURS

Tynan Tours (☎ 056-65929), 10 Maple Drive, conducts hour-long walking tours of the city six times daily (four on Sunday) starting from the tourist office. They cost IR£2.50/60p (students IR£2).

FESTIVALS

The highlight of the city's year is the Kilkenny Arts Week Festival which takes place in late August, with exhibitions, music, drama and theatrical events all over the city. It's very busy so if you aim to be in town, book ahead. The Confederation of Kilkenny Festival, which commemorates the time when Kilkenny was Ireland's capital, takes place in June bringing the streets to life, with parades, sideshows and historic pageantry.

PLACES TO STAY
Camping

The nearest officially approved camp site with proper facilities is eight km south near Bennettsbridge; see that section later for details.

Hostels

The IHH *Kilkenny Tourist Hostel* (☎ 056-63541), 35 Parliament St, is neat, clean and central, has a kitchen and laundry and is open year round. It has 25 beds at IR£5.50 a night in dorms or IR£8 in private rooms. *Ormonde Tourist Hostel* (☎ 056-52733), John's Green, is close to the railway and bus station and has dorm beds for IR£7, doubles for IR£10 per person. It has good facilities including kitchen, laundry, TV room and security lockers; there's no curfew and it's open all year round.

An Óige has a hostel in *Foulksrath Castle* (☎ 056-67674), a 16th-century Norman castle 13 km north of Kilkenny in Jenkinstown near Ballyragget. It's in a beautiful

KILKENNY

setting and costs IR£4 to IR£5 a night in dorms. During the summer, they serve reasonably priced meals. Buggy's Buses (☎ 056-41264) operates a bus service between Kilkenny and the hostel. It leaves from the Parade in Kilkenny at 11.30 am and 5.30 pm from Monday to Saturday; from the hostel it leaves at 8.25 am and 3 pm. The fare is IR£1.50 and the journey takes about 20 minutes.

B&Bs

There are plenty of B&Bs, especially south of the city out along Patrick St and on Castlecomer Rd north of the city. Close to the centre, *Mrs Dempsey's* (☎ 056-21954) and *St Mary's* (☎ 056-22091) are two small town houses side by side on quiet James St. Each has six rooms. Mrs Dempsey charges IR£14/16 per person without/with bathroom. St Mary's charges IR£16/18 and has big breakfasts.

Also central is *Bregagh House* (☎ 056-22315), on Dean St near St Canice's Cathedral, costing IR£20/34 a single/double with bathroom. A few doors down is *Kilkenny* (☎ 056-64040), where rooms are IR£20/30 a single/double or IR£25/35 with attached bathroom.

Dunromin (☎ 056-61387), Dublin Rd near the railway station, has top-notch breakfasts, and costs IR£18/30 with bathroom. *The Bróg Maker* (☎ 056-52900), on Castlecomer Rd near the Newpark Hotel, is a pub and guesthouse offering B&B for IR£25 per person.

Sundown House (☎ 056-21816), one km out on the Freshford road, has rooms for IR£13.50/15 per person without/with bathroom. To get there, go north along Parliament St, turn right at the traffic lights in Irishtown and head north for one km. Watch for the sign.

Hotels

The attractive old *Club House Hotel* (☎ 056-21994) on Patrick St has B&B from IR£38.50, good food and a private car park. A new extension is being built onto the back of the hotel.

The modern *Newpark Hotel* (☎ 056-22122), north of the railway station along Castlecomer Rd, has swimming pools, saunas, a gym and 20 hectares of parkland. All its rooms have bathrooms. The cost per person is from IR£37/60 to IR£60/115 a single/double depending on the season. *Hotel Kilkenny* (☎ 056-62000), about 10 minutes' walk from the city centre on College Rd, has excellent facilities and costs IR£45/92 to IR£60/115 a single/double depending on the season.

Country Houses

Blanchville House (☎ 056-27197), Maddoxtown, is a lovely 19th-century Georgian house on its own farm about eight km east of the city. B&B is IR£25 to IR£30 per person, and dinner is IR£17.50. It's open from March to the end of October. To get there, go along the main Carlow road (N10) and take the first right after the Pike pub, then it's three km to a crossroads and Connolly's pub. Turn left here and it's almost two km down the road on the left.

Lacken House (☎ 056-61085), just out of town on Dublin Rd, is more expensive at IR£36/60 a single/double. This is a highly rated country house with an excellent restaurant.

PLACES TO EAT
Cafés & Takeaways

In summer, the restaurant in the *Kilkenny Castle Kitchen* is a good place for lunch or for delicious home-made scones and you don't have to pay the castle admission charge to eat there. Across the road from the castle, the restaurant upstairs in the *Kilkenny Design Centre* (open from 9 am to 5 pm daily) is excellent for snacks or lunch. It attracts coach parties. Always packed and popular is the *Pantry*, a small self-service coffee shop on St Kieran's St that does a set lunch for IR£3.95; they also have their own bakery nearby next to the Butter Slip.

The *Teashop*, on Patrick St, is an unpretentious place with sandwiches for IR£1.20. There's also a branch of *Bewley's* downstairs in the Market Cross Shopping Centre.

Castle Diner, on Rose Inn St, is a US-style fried chicken and burger place, and *Uncle Sam's*, on High St with a small courtyard in front, does burgers and cheap pizzas.

Pub Food

Kilkenny has plenty of pubs serving reasonable food. On St Kieran's St, the Kyteler's Inn has a rustic little restaurant downstairs, *Alice's* (☎ 056-21604), and a bar upstairs. While the food isn't brilliant, the place is popular. A mixed grill costs IR£6.75 and chicken kiev IR£7.50.

North-east of the river, *Edward Langton's* (☎ 056-21728), 69 John St, is a wonderful pub and restaurant that has won many awards. Lunch-time meals like roast beef will cost a reasonable IR£5, sandwiches from IR£3.50 including chips. Set dinners, served until 11 pm, cost from IR£14 to IR£17.

Caisleán Uí C'uain (the Castle Inn) (☎ 056-65406), 2 High St, is another popular pub which turns out good food including a popular buffet in summer, at lunch times only. Pasta or Irish stew cost around IR£6.

Restaurants

There are several Italian-Irish restaurants around the city. The *Italian Connection* (☎ 056-64225), 38 Parliament St, is good value with pizzas at IR£4 to IR£6 and pasta from IR£5. A more up-market Italian place is *Ristorante Rinuccini* (☎ 056-61575), a cellar restaurant on the Parade opposite the castle with delicious pastas, all freshly prepared. Main dishes cost from IR£6 and there are choices for vegetarians.

Near Kyteler's Inn on St Kieran's St is the late-night *Lautrec's Bistro & Wine Bar* (☎ 056-62720), open until 1 am, which serves an eclectic range of dishes including Italian, Mexican and Indian from IR£4.45 upwards.

Parliament House Restaurant, on Parliament St opposite Kilkenny Tourist Hostel, serves traditional food such as Irish stew (IR£6.25) and homemade soup (IR£1.90).

Kilkenny has some excellent ethnic restaurants. On High St, the Chinese *Emerald Garden* (☎ 056-61812) does main courses from IR£7. The Indian *Moghul Restaurant* (☎ 056-21239), on Pudding Lane (down the alley between Manning Travel and the Book Centre at the south end of High St), is very good, with main meat courses from IR£8, and vegetarian ones from IR£4.

Widely regarded as the best local restaurant is *Lacken House* (☎ 056-61085), just out of town on Dublin Rd. Dinner will cost you IR£22 or more.

ENTERTAINMENT
Pubs

There's no shortage of pubs in Kilkenny and music is often being played in several of them on any given night. At the castle end of High St, the popular, trendy and stylishly old-fashioned *Caisleán Uí C'uain* lays claim to being the town's music pub. The music includes Irish, blues and jazz. Further north on High St, *Jim Holland's*, a bare stone and pine place, has a cellar where rock/pop bands perform at weekends and Irish music is heard on Wednesday nights.

A string of pubs line the northern end of Parliament St. The *Pump House*, 26 Parliament St, is another place offering rock/pop as well as traditional music. *John Cleere* (☎ 056-62573), at No 28, has regular, year-round productions of plays, revues, poetry readings and anything else that's going. Monday night is Traditional Irish Music & Folk night. Spontaneous sessions can happen any time.

Daniel Bollard's is a nice, traditional bar on St Kieran's St. Over the river, *Edward Langton's*, on John St, has discos on Tuesday and Saturday nights; admission is IR£4. Also on John St, *Peig's Bar*, a traditional pub, often has Irish music.

Theatre

The *Watergate Theatre* (☎ 056-61674), on Parliament St, has drama, comedy and musical performances by both professional and amateur groups. See also the *John Cleere* pub in the previous section.

Cinema

The *Regent* is a single-screen cinema at the end of William St, a cul-de-sac whose entrance is opposite the Tholsel.

THINGS TO BUY

On the other side of The Parade from Kilkenny Castle are the former Castle Stables (1760) which have been tastefully converted into the famous Kilkenny Design Centre, with an outstanding collection of Irish goods and crafts for sale. Behind the shop through the arched gateway is the Castle Yard and the studios of various local craftspeople, with gift shops.

GETTING THERE & AWAY

Bus

Bus Éireann (☎ 056-64933) also operates out of the railway station and on its Dublin to Cork route provides services to and from Dublin up to eight times a day Monday to Saturday, five on Sunday. There are three buses daily to/from Cork City.

On the Galway to Rosslare Harbour and Waterford to Longford routes, one bus a day passes through in each direction.

J J Kavanagh & Sons (☎ 056-31106) run private coaches, largely for college students, on Friday and Sunday to/from Carlow, Limerick and Cork. The bus stop is outside St John's Church.

Train

McDonagh Railway Station (☎ 056-22024) is on Dublin Rd, north-east of the town centre via John St. There are four trains daily each way (five on Friday, three on Sunday) on the Dublin (Heuston Station) to Waterford line. The journey to and from Dublin takes just under two hours. For the full timetable check with the station or phone ☎ 01-850 836 6222 for Dublin and Waterford departure times.

GETTING AROUND

Buggy's Buses (☎ 056-41264) has a daily service Monday to Saturday from The Parade to Foulksrath Castle (which houses the An Oige hostel), Ballyragget, Dunmore Cave and Castlecomer.

J J Wall (☎ 056-21236), 88 Maudlin St, rents bikes at IR£5 a day, plus a deposit of IR£40. The countryside around Kilkenny is fine cycling territory and there's a lovely day excursion to Kells, Inistioge, Jerpoint Abbey and Kilfane.

You can rent a car from Barry Pender Motors (☎ 056-65777) on Dublin Rd. There are quite a few cab companies in town; try Kilkenny Cabs (☎ 056-52000) or Michael Howe (☎ 056-65874).

Central Kilkenny

A tour of the county south of Kilkenny City takes in much of the Nore Valley and sections of the Barrow Valley. The most scenic parts are from Graiguenamanagh in the east, down to The Rower and then north on the road to Inistioge, Thomastown, Kells and finally to Callan near the border with Tipperary. There is still a fair chunk of the county below this arc, with pleasant rolling countryside and quiet backroads.

BENNETTSBRIDGE

Bennettsbridge, a village south of Kilkenny City on the River Nore, has two of Ireland's most renowned potteries. In a big old mill by the river, **Nicholas Mosse Pottery** (☎ 056-27126/05) turns out hand-made spongewear: creamy brown pottery with sponged patterns. The factory shop, on the right on the way down to the mill, is open Monday to Saturday from 10 am to 6 pm (and in July and August on Sunday from 2 to 6 pm).

Stoneware Jackson Pottery (☎ 056-27175), which is almost two km north of Bennettsbridge on the minor road to Kilkenny City, produces pale-blue pottery with dark blue swirls and pink dots. It's open Monday to Friday from 9 am to 1 pm and 2 to 5.30 pm, Saturday from 9.30 am to 1 pm and 2 to 6 pm.

Places to Stay & Eat

The only official camp site for a long way in any direction is the *Nore Valley Camping & Caravan Park* (☎ 056-27229), on a farm. If you're coming into Bennettsbridge from Kilkenny City (along the R700 Thomastown road), turn right just before the bridge and the park is signposted. They charge IR£5 per tent or IR£3 if you are hiking or cycling. It's open March to the end of October. There are also a couple of B&Bs just out of the village on the Thomastown road.

The *Nore Tavern* (☎ 056-27275), a pleasant bar and restaurant about 50 metres from the bridge, has snacks during the day and more formal meals in the evening.

KELLS

Only 13 km south of Kilkenny City, Kells is not to be confused with its namesake in County Meath. This is a treat of a hamlet, nestling beside a fine stone bridge on the King's River – a tributary of the Nore. In Kells Priory, the village has one of Ireland's most impressive monastic sites.

Kells Priory

The earliest remains of the magnificent Kells Priory date from the late 12th century with the bulk of the present ruins from the 15th century. In a sea of rich farmland, a protective wall, largely intact, connects seven dwelling towers. Inside the walls are the remains of an Augustinian abbey and the foundations of some chapels and houses. It's unusually well fortified for a monastery, and the heavy curtain walls hint at a troubled history. Indeed, within a single century from 1250, the abbey was twice fought over and burnt down by squabbling warlords.

Kilree Round Tower & High Cross

Three km south at Kilree (signposted from the abbey car park) there's a 29-metre round tower and a simple early high cross, said to mark the grave of a 9th-century Irish high king, Niall Caille. He is supposed to have drowned in the King's River at Callan some time in the 840s while attempting to save a servant. His body was found near Kells. His final resting place and cross are outside the church grounds, as he was not a Christian.

Burnchurch Castle

Five km due north of Kells, after turning west at the first crossroad, is Burnchurch Castle, a 15th or 16th-century Fitzgerald castle and adjoining round gate tower. It's possible to climb the square tower.

THOMASTOWN

Thomastown is a little market town, nicely situated by the River Nore. It's also on the main Dublin to Waterford road (N9) and would be more attractive but for the constant rumble of heavy traffic. However, locals and visitors usually ignore this aspect of the town and concentrate on its drinking establishments, of which it has 11. Some have music and others have reasonable food. There are also some good craft shops; at the edge of town on the Waterford road, the Grennan Mill Craft School (☎ 056-24557) has a craft shop open Monday to Saturday from 9 am to 7pm.

Named after a Welsh mercenary in 1169, Thomastown has some fragments of a medieval wall, and **Mullin's Castle** down by the bridge is the sole survivor of 14 castles. There is also the 13th-century **Church of St Mary**, now under restoration. The main point of interest around here is the magnificent nearby Cistercian abbey at Jerpoint (see Around Thomastown later).

From Inistioge to Thomastown is a gentle eight km journey along the River Nore valley, with a couple of crossings on old stone bridges, passing people fishing amongst the reeds.

Getting There & Away

Bus Bus Éireann (☎ 056-64933) has up to five connections Monday to Saturday between Dublin and Waterford with a stop at Mullinavat and Gowran. See also the introductory Getting There & Away section at the start of this chapter. The bus stop in Thomastown is outside O'Keeffe's Supermarket (the store with the petrol bowser in front of it) on Main St.

Train The town is on the main railway line between Dublin and Waterford with the same service as Kilkenny City. The train takes about 15 minutes to Kilkenny City, 25 minutes to Waterford and two hours to Dublin. The station is one km west of town past Kavanagh's Supermarket.

AROUND THOMASTOWN
Jerpoint Abbey

Just south-west of Thomastown on the Waterford road, Jerpoint Abbey (☎ 056-24623), one of Ireland's finest Cistercian ruins, was established by a king of Ossory in the 12th century. It has been partially restored. The fine tower and cloister are late 14th or early 15th century. Fragments of the monastery's cloister are particularly interesting with a series of often amusing figures carved on the cloister pillars. There are also stone carvings on the church walls and in the tombs of members of the Butler and Walshe families. Faint traces of a 15th or 16th-century painting remain on the north wall of the church. This chancel area also contains a tomb thought to be that of Felix O'Dullany, Jerpoint's first abbot and bishop of Ossory, who died in 1202.

According to local legend, St Nicholas (or Santa Claus) is buried near the abbey. The Knights of Jerpoint, while retreating in the Crusades, removed his body from Myra in modern-day Turkey and laid him to rest in the Church of St Nicholas to the west of the abbey. The grave is marked by a broken slab and decorated with a carving of a monk.

Entry to Jerpoint Abbey is IR£2/1. The abbey is open daily from mid-June to September from 9.30 am to 6.30 pm; and between the end of September to mid-October daily from 10 am to 1pm and 2 to 5 pm; and from April to mid-June from 10 am to 1 pm and 2 to 5 pm Tuesday to Saturday, and afternoons only on Sunday. Guided tours are available on request.

There is no public transport here, but it's only 1.5 km from Thomastown.

Kilfane

Just three km north of Thomastown on the Dublin road is the village of Kilfane, with a small ruined 13th-century church and Norman tower, well-hidden 50 metres off the road but signposted. The church has a remarkable stone carving of Thomas de Cantwell; the carving, called the Cantwell Fada or 'long Cantwell', depicts a tall, thin knight in detailed chainmail armour, brandishing a shield decorated with the coat of arms of the Cantwells. Some of the graves are of Irishmen who perished in WW I.

Tullaherin

Another three km north off the main road at Tullaherin, where St Ciaran is buried, is a ruined church with a damaged, leaning, 22-metre round tower dating from the 9th century, and a small museum.

INISTIOGE

Inistioge (pronounced 'Inishteeg') is a delightful little village, with a 10-arched stone bridge spanning the River Nore and a picturesque tree-lined square. The Protestant church to the north of the newer Catholic church sits in part of a medieval priory with some old graveslabs. The village is 10 km south-east of Graiguenamanagh on the opposite side of Brandon Hill, and there's a pleasant journey across through a gap in the mountains. At the bottom of the hill that leads to Woodstock House Demesne is a pottery which produces lovely simple work in light pastel colours.

One km south on Mt Alto is the **Woodstock House Demesne**, and the hike up to it is well worth the effort for the panorama of the valley below and the demesne itself. The 18th-century house was one of the finest in the county, but was destroyed during the Civil War in 1922. The ruin is closed but the elevated garden and forest are now a state park with picnic areas and trails and are open to the public. For another fine walk, follow the river bank and climb any of the surrounding hills. Inistioge is on the South Leinster Way.

The *School House Café*, by the river, is a good place to stop for tea, sandwiches and cakes.

Getting There & Away

On Thursday only, a single bus runs between New Ross and Kilkenny City, calling at Inistioge en route. Northbound, it leaves Inistioge at 10.40 am; southbound, it leaves at 1.50 pm.

GRAIGUENAMANAGH

Graiguenamanagh (pronounced 'Greg-na-mana') is a small market town on a very attractive stretch of the River Barrow. It lies 23 km south-east of Kilkenny City at the northern foot of Brandon Hill (516 metres).

If you're driving, to get to Graiguenamanagh from Kilkenny City head east on the Carlow road (N10) then turn off south for Gowran following the R702 which loops through County Carlow, then turn right (south-west) onto the R705 which leads into County Kilkenny and to Graiguenamanagh. From Thomastown, head north along the N9 and turn right (east) at Kilfane.

Duiske Abbey

This 13th-century abbey is Graiguenamanagh's prime attraction. The name comes from the Irish *Dubh Uisce* or 'Black Water', a tributary of the River Barrow. Duiske Abbey has been completely restored, and its pleasantly simple interior is in everyday use.

Inside the abbey to the right of the main entrance is the Knight of Duiske, a 14th-century carving in high relief of a knight in chain mail reaching for his sword. On the floor nearby is a glass panel which reveals some of the original 13th-century floor tiles some way below the present floor level. In the grounds are two early high crosses, brought here in the last century from the surrounding countryside for protection. The larger, heavier Ballyogan Cross has panels on the east side depicting the Crucifixion, Adam & Eve, Abraham's sacrifice of Isaac, and David playing the harp. The west side shows the Massacre of the Innocents.

Other Attractions

As well as Duiske Abbey, there are more monastic remains eight km south along the River Barrow towpath at **St Mullins** in

County Carlow. **Brandon Hill** has a megalithic cairn and stone circle on the summit, with fine views of the Barrow Valley and Blackstair Mountains to the east.

The area is good for unstrenuous **walking** up the mountain, along the road to Inistioge or south along the river towards New Ross. Graiguenamanagh is also on the South Leinster Way.

GOWRAN

The village of Gowran, 12 km east of Kilkenny City, is famous for its **racecourse** and 13th-century **St Mary's Church** which has some fine carvings and several tombs of the Butler family. There is a nice guesthouse here – *Whitethorns* (☎ 056-26102), 300 metres off the main Dublin to Kilkenny road. B&B is IR£18.50/27 a single/double or IR£20/30 with bathroom.

For bus services to/from Gowran, see the Getting There & Away section at the start of this chapter. The bus stop is outside Comerford's shop.

Southern Kilkenny

Much of southern Kilkenny is sparsely populated. Gentle hills separate the river valleys of the Nore, Barrow and the Suir. Carrick-on Suir in Tipperary and Waterford City are within easy reach, with a wide choice of accommodation and restaurants. Southern Kilkenny is crossed by the **South Leinster Way**, which runs from Carrick-on-Suir, through Piltown, Mullinavat, Inistioge, Graiguenamanagh and on to Borris in County Carlow. See the Activities chapter for more details.

If you want to stay in the area or have a stopover as you walk the South Leinster Way, then **Mullinavat**, 12 km north of Waterford on the Kilkenny road (N9), is an agreeable spot to spend a relaxing day or two. Signposted two km south of Mullinavat, *Tory View* (☎ 051-85513) has B&B in smallish rooms for IR£13/15 per person without/with bathroom, and evening meals are available.

Alternatively, there is the 1644 *Rising Sun* (☎ 051-98173), a beautiful old stone building on Mullinavat's Main St. All rooms have bathroom, phone and TV but at IR£26/40 a single/double for B&B it's a bit pricey. The upstairs restaurant is good, bar food is available in the lounge and you can have high tea in the afternoon.

Express buses between Dublin and Waterford call at Mullinavat; see the Getting There & Away section at the start of this chapter. The bus stop is outside Mulhearn's on Main St.

Northern Kilkenny

CASTLECOMER & AROUND

An attractive town, 18 km north of Kilkenny, Castlecomer is on the River Dinin which flows across the Castlecomer Plateau.

The town became a major mining centre for anthracite after it was discovered nearby in 1636, and the mines only closed for good in the mid-1960s. The anthracite was widely regarded as being the best in Europe with very little sulphur and producing almost no smoke. Castlecomer saw action in the 1798 Rising when the Fenian rebels, led by Father John Murphy, took the place while en route from Wexford to the midlands. There is little to do here, but the tree-lined square and neat townhouses are pleasant.

Things to See

Eight km west-south-west of Castlecomer is **Ballyragget**, with an almost intact square tower in the 16th-century Butler Castle. Five km south of Castlecomer on the road to Kilkenny is the 16th-century square-towered **Foulksrath Castle** in a similar style.

Almost two km south of Ballyragget is **Swifte's Heath**, home to Jonathan Swift during his school years in Kilkenny, and now offering B&B accommodation. Eight km south-west of here is **Freshford** which has a finely worked Romanesque doorway set into the 18th-century Protestant church.

Freshford was the site of a monastery founded in the 6th century by St Lachtain.

Places to Stay

Foulksrath Castle is now a busy An Óige hostel (☎ 056-67674) and the setting is superb. For more details see Places to Stay under Kilkenny City.

In Castlecomer, the *Avalon* pub and guesthouse (☎ 056-41302), on the square near the bridge, are housed in the old mine offices. B&B is good value at IR£15/28 a single/double. Alternatively, the 1824 *Wandesforde House* (☎ 056-42441) has six rooms, all with a bathroom; B&B is IR£20/36 and dinner is IR£15.

Getting There & Away

Castlecomer, on Bus Éireann's (☎ 056-64933) route between Cork, Kilkenny and Dublin, is serviced by four buses daily Monday to Saturday, three on Sunday. The bus stop is outside Houlihan's. New Princess Coach Services (☎ 056-31555) runs buses twice daily between Clonmel, Kilkenny, Castlecomer, Athy and Dublin; from Castlecomer it takes 75 minutes to Dublin. The bus stop is outside Dillon's pub. Buggy's Buses (☎ 056-41264) runs a local service Monday to Saturday between Castlecomer and Kilkenny City.

DUNMORE CAVE

Dunmore Cave (☎ 056-67726), about 10 km north of Kilkenny on the Castlecomer road (N78), is a large cave divided into three parts with many limestone formations.

According to some texts, marauding Vikings killed 1000 people at two ring forts near Dunmore Cave in 928 AD. A number of survivors fled and hid in the caverns from where the Vikings tried to smoke them out by lighting fires at the entrance. It is thought that the Vikings found the people who were hiding, dragged off the men for slaves and left the women and children to suffocate.

Excavations in 1973 uncovered the remains of at least 44 people, mostly women and children. They also found a number of coins dating from the 920s but none from any later date. One theory suggests that the coins were dropped by the Vikings (who often carried them in their armpits, secured with wax) while enthusiastically engaged in the slaughter. However, there are few marks of violence on the skeletons, which lends weight to the theory that the people suffocated.

The limestone cave is well lit and spacious. After a steep descent through the large entrance, there are two detours to the left with stalactites, stalagmites and columns, including the six-metre Market Cross stalag-

mite. It's damp and cold, so a sweater or coat is advised. The guided tour is optional but worthwhile.

The cave is open mid-March to mid-June from 10 am to 5 pm Tuesday to Saturday and 2 to 5 pm Sunday; mid-June to September from 10 am to 7 pm daily; and October to mid-March from 10 am to 5 pm Saturday and Sunday. Entry to the cave is IR£2/1.

Buggy's Buses (☎ 056-41264) runs a local bus daily Monday to Saturday to Castlecomer, which stops along the main road about one km from the cave.

Central South

The four counties of Carlow, Kildare, Laois and Offaly make up a large portion of the Irish midlands. Sites of archaeological interest include the High Cross at Moone in Kildare, Kildare Town's cathedral, the Browne's Hill Dolmen just outside Carlow Town, the Rosse Estate and observatory in Birr and, most impressive of all, Clonmacnois on the banks of the River Shannon, which is probably the most important monastic site in the country.

County Kildare

Kildare (*Cill Dara*), to the west and southwest of Dublin, is mostly rich green farmland in the south, while the fringe of the extensive Bog of Allen peatland lies to the north-west of the county. Underlying the pasture and bog is a limestone plain.

The main towns are dominated by traffic, but this should be much less of a problem when the local councils finish building bypasses to the worst affected towns. The county is crossed by nearly all the main road and rail arteries to the rest of the country, and by the 18th-century Grand and Royal canals, now enjoying a new lease of life. The River Barrow marks the county's eastern border, while the Curragh plains form a great sweep of unfenced countryside to the south.

HISTORY
Early archaeological sites of any significance are few and far between, with little remaining of the Bronze Age hill forts on Knockaulin, the Hill of Allen and Lyons Hill in the north-east of the county. Away from Dublin, South Kildare has some fine monastic remains, chiefly at Moone near Castledermot.

From the 12th to the 16th centuries, Kildare and indeed much of Ireland was controlled by the Norman Fitzgerald family,

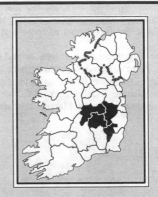

Highlights
- High Cross at Moone in Kildare which was erected in the 8th or 9th century and is six metres tall
- St Brigid's Cathedral in Kildare Town
- Browne's Hill dolmen, outside Carlow Town, which is 5000 years old
- Birr Castle & Demesne, which are among the finest in Ireland, and Birr Observatory & Telescope, which at one time was the largest in the world
- Clonmacnois, overlooking the River Shannon, is Ireland's most important monastic site

whose principal base was Maynooth Castle. Through skilful diplomacy, they managed for a long time to coexist with the crown and sustain their power and influence.

A serious setback to this power and influence occurred in 1536 when the English defeated a rebellion led by Silken Thomas Fitzgerald, the 10th earl of Kildare. He had renounced his allegiance to the king two years earlier after it was rumoured his father had been killed in London by Henry VIII. But the family became Protestant and through some clever diplomacy regained much of its land and titles over the next few decades. From then on the Fitzgeralds were part of the Protestant ascendancy and their

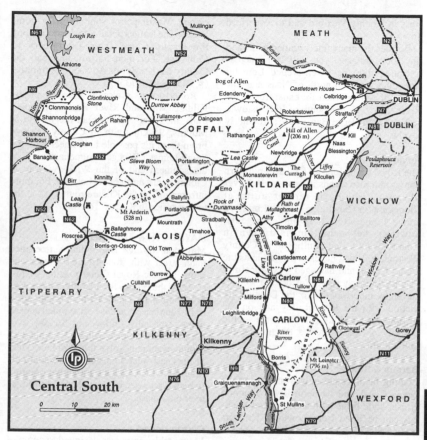

Central South

0   10   20 km

power waxed and waned over the ensuing centuries.

Close to Dublin, Kildare was well within the English-controlled Pale, and 18th-century landowners felt secure enough to build some of the grandest mansions in the country. Castletown House near Celbridge is an outstanding example.

GRAND & ROYAL CANALS

The Grand and Royal canals were built in the 18th century to revolutionise goods and passenger transport, but the railways superseded them during the 19th century and the canals

slowly fell into disuse. Today, they are owned by the OPW and are a pleasant way of drifting across the country.

Grand Canal

The Grand Canal, opened in 1779, carried passengers until 1852 and goods until 1960. The canal threads its way from Dublin through County Kildare, dividing near Robertstown. From there one branch heads west through Tullamore to join the River Shannon at Shannon Harbour in County Offaly, the other turns south to join the River Barrow at Athy, providing passage to New

Ross in County Wexford and to Waterford Town.

Besides the many finely crafted locks and tiny lock cottages, you will come across treasures like the seven-arched Leinster Aqueduct, five km north of Naas near the village of Sallins, where the canal crosses the River Liffey. Farther south of Robertstown, sections of the River Barrow are particularly lovely.

Royal Canal

The Royal Canal follows Kildare's northern border and also wends its way to the River Shannon, joining it farther north at Cloondara (or Clondra) in County Longford above Lough Ree. It is only navigable, however, between Blanchardstown in County Dublin and Mullingar in County Westmeath. It was never as profitable as the Grand Canal, and has aged less gracefully than its southerly sister. Restoration work is currently underway to link the Dublin City section with the River Liffey and on the section west of Mullingar. The canal should be fully navigable around the turn of the millennium.

Barges & Boats

Boating facilities are only available on the Grand Canal, and six-berth River Shannon cruiser-style boats with showers and kitchens can be hired from Lowtown Cruisers (☎ 045-60427), 13 km west of Naas, one km west along the north bank of the canal over the bridge from Robertstown. The cost per week is IR£900 in the high season, IR£580 in the low, and no experience is necessary. During the summer there are also day trips from Robertstown. There are 45-minute trips on a refurbished canal barge, the *Eustace*, from Robertstown on Sunday afternoons between 2 and 6 pm for IR£2/1; for details phone ☎ 045-60808.

Walking Along the Canals

The canal towpaths are ideal for walkers, and Robertstown is a good starting-point for many canal walks. Three *Canal Bank Walks* leaflets can be picked up at tourist offices,

certain Maxol petrol stations or at some B&Bs. The leaflets detail a 45-km trail along the Grand Canal from Edenderry to Celbridge. For more information call the County Kildare Sports Advisory Committee (☎ 045-79502/97358)

Robertstown is also at the hub of the Kildare Way and River Barrow towpath trails, the latter stretching all the way to St Mullins, 95 km south in County Carlow. From there it's possible to connect with the South Leinster Way at Graiguenamanagh or the southern end of the Wicklow Way at Clonegal, just north of Mt Leinster. For more information on the Kildare routes ask at the tourist office in Kildare Town.

MAYNOOTH & AROUND

Maynooth (*Maigh Nuad*) has a tree-lined main street with stone-fronted houses and shops and the Royal Canal passing by just south of the centre. As it's only 24 km west of Dublin on the N4, Maynooth is a dreadful traffic bottleneck, and is best avoided at peak times, especially Friday and Sunday evenings. The new bypass, when it is completed, should eventually solve this problem. Main St runs east-west. Leinster St runs south off Main St to the canal and the railway station (which is accessed by a couple of footbridges over the canal).

Carton House

Maynooth's centre was designed to complement the entrance to Carton House, on the Dublin (east) end of the main street. This splendid Georgian mansion was built by the Fitzgeralds, the earls of Kildare, in the mid-18th century and later belonged to the duke and duchess of Leinster. Unfortunately you cannot see the luxurious interior, but you are free to wander around the gardens.

Carton House was designed by Richard Castle, architect of the Fitzgeralds' town house, now Leinster House (the Irish Parliament), in Dublin and Russborough House in Wicklow. Castle is buried in St Mary's Church beside the gate of St Patrick's College.

St Patrick's College
St Patrick's College & Seminary (☎ 01-628 5222), also called Maynooth College, at the west end of town has been turning out Catholic priests since 1795 and became a college of the National University in 1910. Ironically, the seminary was founded by the English, who were growing alarmed at the prospect of Irish priests studying in France, where they might pick up disturbing ideas about revolution and republicanism.

Maynooth Castle
The castle, parts of which date from the 13th century, is by the entrance to St Patrick's College. The gatehouse, keep and its great hall survive, and the key can be picked up from the house opposite at 9 Parson St.

The castle was home to the Fitzgeralds. After the rebellion of 1536, led by Silken Thomas Fitzgerald, the English laid siege to the castle. The castle's garrison surrendered after being assured of leniency. In what became known as the 'Pardon of Maynooth', Thomas and his men were summarily executed. The castle was badly damaged in Cromwellian times and ceased to be lived in when the Fitzgeralds moved to Kilkea Castle in the mid-17th century.

Canoeing
The town of **Leixlip** on the River Liffey between Maynooth and Dublin is an important canoeing centre. It's the starting point of the Irish Sprint Canoe Championships and annual 28-km International Liffey Descent Race, when the Electricity Supply Board (ESB) releases 30 million tonnes of water from the Poulaphouca Reservoir in County Wicklow into the river to bring it up to flood level. Canoes can be hired here from the Kilcullen Canoe & Outdoor Pursuits Club (☎ 045-81240) which is based in Kilcullen, 10 km south-west of Naas.

Places to Stay
B&Bs *Park Lodge* (☎ 01-628 6002), 201 Railpark, one km south of Maynooth near the bridge, charges IR£20/30 a single/double for B&B. *Windgate Lodge* (☎ 01-273415),

about two km farther south of Maynooth in Barberstown, costs IR£18/30.

Hotels The attractive old *Leinster Arms* pub (☎ 01-628 6323), in the centre of Maynooth on Main St, has rooms with bathroom for IR£20 per person. Breakfast is an extra IR£5. If your trunkload of cash is weighing you down, the lovely Georgian *Moyglare Manor* (☎ 01-628 6351) is a couple of km north of Maynooth. It's one of the best country houses in Ireland and costs IR£90/130 a single/double including breakfast, plus at least another IR£25 for dinner. The dining room is full of works of art, and lunch here is a special treat.

Places to Eat
The *Elite Coffee Shop & Bakery*, in the middle of Main St, is a self-service place that has freshly baked bread and cakes and serves snacks. For a more substantial meal the *Country Restaurant*, downstairs under the craft shop just off Main St near the castle, serves solid helpings of standard food from IR£3 to IR£5.

The *Leinster Arms* has pub food, a carvery and the more formal *Plough Restaurant*. It serves food from 12.30 to 9.30 pm and prices are reasonable at IR£4 to IR£6 for a main course. Out of town, *Moyglare Manor* (☎ 01-628 6351) is good although expensive (see Places to Stay).

Entertainment
Brady's and *Caulfield's* are two pubs on Main St where you can share a drink with the locals, while the *Leinster Arms* has bands and is popular with students. *Cassidy's Roost* bar at the west end of Main St has a facade dominated by Greek statuary.

Getting There & Away
Bus From Middle Abbey St in Dublin, suburban bus Nos 66 and 67 go to Maynooth, plus there are numerous long-distance buses passing through en route to Galway and Sligo. For information consult the timetable or ring ☎ 01-873 4222. The Maynooth bus stop is outside Brady's pub on Main St.

Train Maynooth is linked to Dublin by the Western Suburban line and is on the main Dublin to Sligo line with three to four trains daily in each direction. Call ☎ 01-850 836 6222 for details.

CELBRIDGE

Celbridge, a plain village on the River Liffey, 6.5 km south-east of Maynooth, is the home of the magnificent Palladian Castletown House.

Castletown House

This huge Irish mansion, with its tree-lined avenue from the village (continue straight ahead after entering the gate), is said to be the largest private house in Ireland. It was built between 1722 and 1732 for William Conolly, who started life as the son of a pub owner and rose to become the speaker of the Irish House of Commons. Castletown House was no small undertaking and Conolly financed it from the fortune he made as a land agent in the chaotic aftermath to the Battle of the Boyne.

Castletown was designed by Alessandro Galilei, and continued by Edward Lovett Pearce (creator of the Bank of Ireland building on College Green, Dublin), who oversaw the building of the two sweeping columned wings. The house remained in the Conolly family until its 1965 takeover by the Irish Georgian Society; in 1979 it was given to the voluntary Castletown Foundation who maintained the house until it came under the management of the OPW in 1994.

Many of Castletown's magnificent rooms were decorated well after the building had been finished. Lady Louisa, great-grand-daughter of Charles II and wife of William Conolly's grandnephew Tom, took a particular interest in the finer details. The Francini brothers from Italy did the plasterwork in the hall adjacent to the main hall, and their magnificent work continues up the main staircase.

Scattered throughout are paintings from Joshua Reynolds and Nathaniel Hone. Off the upstairs landing is a glass case containing stuffed hedgehogs and stoats which are dis-played in an absurd classroom scenario, holding books at their desks.

Castletown has two associated follies, commissioned by William Conolly's wife, Katherine, to provide employment for the poor. The **Obelisk** was designed by Richard Castle and can be seen from the Long Gallery at the back of the house. Completed in 1740, it consists of a series of arches, piled one upon another and topped by an obelisk reaching 40 metres in height. The Conolly family used it for picnics.

The other folly, the even more curious **Wonderful Barn**, is off to the north-east on private property just outside Leixlip and dates from 1743. It is made up of four domes mounted one on top of another and scaled by a spiral staircase.

Castletown House (☎ 01-628 8252) is open April to September from 10 am to 6 pm Monday to Friday, from 11 am to 6 pm Saturday, and from 2 to 6 pm Sunday; October from 10 am to 5 pm Monday to Friday, and from 2 to 5 pm Sunday; and November to March from 2 to 5 pm Sunday; admission is IR£2.50/1. At weekends there is a coffee shop in the basement. You can picnic on the lawn or take a stroll down to the River Liffey from the car park. The OPW has begun spending IR£3 million to restore the house and transform it into a national showpiece.

Coming from Dublin on the N4, turn left just before the Spa Hotel in Lucan. Dublin bus Nos 67 or 67A to Celbridge will drop you off at the gate.

Celbridge Abbey

At the other end of Main St, beside the River Liffey, is Celbridge Abbey (☎ 01-628 8350), built in the 1690s by Bartholomew van Homrigh, a Dutch merchant who became Lord Mayor of Dublin. His daughter, Vanessa, was a close friend of Jonathan Swift, whose visits to her at the abbey she marked by preparing a bower and planting laurel trees. Henry Grattan, the 18th-century parliamentarian, used to visit his uncle here.

The abbey, now owned by the St John of God Brothers, is a private residence but the picturesque grounds are open to the public March to September from noon to 6 pm Tuesday to Sunday; admission is IR£1.50/1. Facilities include a model railway, river walks, picnic areas and a café.

Places to Stay
One km out of Celbridge on the Dublin road, *Green Acres* (☎ 01-627 1163), a B&B with singles/doubles at IR£18.50/30 including bathroom, is open year round. *Mt Carmel* (☎ 01-627 3461), a little farther out, has similar facilities and rooms for IR£18/30 and is open March to October. More expensive is *Setanta House* (☎ 01-627 1111) in Celbridge, an elegant old family-run hotel; the cost is IR£42.50 to IR£45 per person.

Places to Eat
Connolly's Restaurant near the abbey is a pleasant place serving light meals. For good pub food try the *Castletown Inn* with main courses for IR£4 or *Celbridge House*, one km out of town on the Maynooth road, which also has Irish music nights on Wednesday and Friday.
Michelangelo (☎ 01-624 2086), near the gates to Castletown House, is about as upmarket as Italian restaurants go. Dinner will cost from IR£20. It's closed Sunday and Monday.

Getting There & Away
Bus Nos 67 and 67A go from Middle Abbey St in Dublin to Celbridge, departing every 40 minutes.

STRAFFAN
South-west of Celbridge on the road to Clane, in the village of Straffan, is the **Straffan Steam Museum** (☎ 01-627 3155), housed in the former church of St Jude in Lodge Park. The museum contains models of steam locomotives, plus several working steam engines and displays on the history of steam power. It's open Easter to September from 11 am to 6 pm Tuesday to Sunday; and October to Easter from 2 pm to dusk Sunday and public holidays; admission is IR£3/1.50.
At the **Straffan Butterfly Farm** (☎ 01-627 1109), Ovidstown, you can see butterflies flying freely around in a tropical greenhouse, while in glass cases there are stick insects, bird-eating spiders and reptiles. The farm is open 1 May to late August from noon to 5.30 pm daily.

BODENSTOWN
In the Bodenstown churchyard is the last resting place of Theobald Wolfe Tone (1763-98), founder member of the Society of United Irishmen and a leader in the 1798 Rising. He committed suicide in prison in Dublin, after he was captured during an attempt to invade Ireland with the aid of the French fleet. To get to Bodenstown take the Naas road south out of Clane and turn left (east) after three km.

OUGHTERARD
One km north of the village of Kill on the N7 is Oughterard, with the remains of a 10th-century round tower and church. Even those who have no interest in ecclesiastical monuments might like to know that here lies Arthur Guinness, a man who needs no introduction.

BOG OF ALLEN
The Bog of Allen is Ireland's best known raised bog, a huge expanse of peat that once covered a large part of the midlands. The bog stretches like a large brown desert through three counties – Offaly, Laois and Kildare – but like other raised bogs it's rapidly being turned into potting compost and fuel.

RATHANGAN
The sleepy Victorian village of Rathangan, surrounded by the Bog of Allen, is on the Grand Canal 20 km west of Naas but well off the beaten track. There is good coarse fishing; for information and boat hire contact John Conway (☎ 045-24331) at the camping ground.

Peatland World
If you are interested in the finer aspects of bogs, on the R414 nine km north-east of Rathangan in a converted farm in Lullymore

is Peatland World (☎ 045-60133), an interpretive centre dealing with every aspect of Ireland's bogs. It has displays covering flora, fauna, fuel, conservation and archaeological finds, as well as a video presentation and trails through parts of the bog. It's open from 9.30 am to 5 pm weekdays and from 2 to 6 pm weekends; admission is IR£2/1 (students IR£1.50).

Places to Stay
Carasli Caravan & Camping Park (☎ 045-24331) on the outskirts of Rathangan charges IR£5 per tent, 50p per occupant and IR£1 for power. The entrance is beside the Jet service station. It rents caravans for IR£100 a week and has free fishing for tench, roach and bream behind the park on the River Barrow. John can also help with local tourist information and may even give you a tip for a horse at the Punchestown races.

Milorka (☎ 045-24544) is one km along the Portarlington road in Kilnantogue. The excellent rooms cost IR£15 per person for B&B, and evening meals are available.

Places to Eat
Tommies, on the main street, does reliable burgers, fish & chips etc for IR£2 to IR£3, and *Dillon's Bar* and the *Village Pump* are worth trying for pub food.

Getting There & Away
On Tuesday and Thursday only there is a single Bus Éireann (☎ 01-8366111) service between Rathangan and the Busáras in Dublin, via Robertstown, Clane, Sallins and Naas. The bus leaves Rathangan at 9.30 am and leaves Dublin on the return journey at 4.25 pm.

HILL OF ALLEN
The Hill of Allen rises above the flatlands of Kildare, which as you travel north or west change from green to the desolate brown of the Bog of Allen. Nine km north-west of Newbridge and marked today by a folly, the hill has been a strategic spot through the centuries with its commanding views in all directions. The Iron Age fortifications are said to mark the home of Fionn McCumhaill, the leader of the *Fianna*, a mythical band of warriors who feature in many tales of ancient Ireland.

ROBERTSTOWN
The tiny hamlet of Robertstown might have had all passing traffic diverted for the past 100 years. It's 12 km north-west of Naas, and its old buildings overlook the Grand Canal, which is spanned by a stone bridge. The village has grown and declined in parallel with the canal. On summer Sundays, the refurbished barge, *Eustace*, sitting out the front of the cheerily orange-red canal hotel offers short cruises (☎ 045-60808). (See the Grand & Royal Canals section earlier.)

The countryside around Robertstown, with its rich farmland, narrow lanes and small stone bridges, is delightful in summer.

Getting There & Away
On Tuesday and Thursday a single Dublin to Rathangan bus passes through Robertstown. Contact Bus Éireann (☎ 01-8366111) for details.

NAAS
Kildare's county town of Naas (pronounced 'Nace') is about 27 km south-west of Dublin. The N7 highway to Cork, Kerry and Limerick bypasses it to the north. There is a scenic route from Naas (*An Nás*) to Wicklow Town, via Blessington, through the Sally Gap and over the Wicklow Mountains.

Tourist information is available from the Maxol service station on the Dublin road just north of the town centre or from the Apollo Travel Agency (☎ 045-76934), 19 North Main St.

Jigginstown House
Naas' only ruin of note is Jigginstown House, one km south on the N7 to Kildare Town. It was begun by Thomas Wentworth, earl of Strafford, and Lord Deputy of Ireland from 1632 to 1641, with the intention of entertaining Charles I. It would have been one of the largest brick buildings in Ireland

if he hadn't lost his head – literally. It was never finished.

Motor Racing
Mondello Park (☎ 045-60200), Ireland's premier racing and rally circuit, is seven km to the north-west of Naas, signposted off the M7 motorway. For around IR£80 you can have a lesson in a single-seater Formula Vee racing car with the Racing & Rally School.

Horse Racing
Punchestown Racecourse (☎ 045-97704) is a famous and beautifully situated steeple-chase track, three km south-east of Naas. The season runs from October to April and the highlight is the National Hunt festival in late April. During the summer there are meetings at Naas Racecourse (☎ 045-97391). More a local affair than the Curragh or Punches-town, it's just as enjoyable.

Getting There & Away
Naas is well served by buses. There are hourly double-deckers to Dublin, as well as intercity services to Limerick, Kilkenny, Waterford, Clonmel, Portlaoise, Kildare, Carlow and Newbridge. The bus stop is on Main St opposite the post office; for intercity bus times ring ☎ 01-836 6111 and for local Dublin buses call ☎ 01-873 4222. Rapid Express Coaches (☎ 01-679 1549) has seven buses a day stopping in Naas on its Dublin to Waterford and Tramore run.

CURRAGH
The town of Newbridge (*Droichead Nua*) is the gateway to the Curragh, at around 20 sq km one of the largest pieces of unfenced fertile land in the country and home to the Curragh Racecourse (☎ 045-41205) and a large military training barracks (☎ 045-41301). The Curragh has been home to horse racing for centuries and today its wide open spaces are used extensively by horse trainers to exercise their thoroughbred charges.

The N7 highway runs through the Curragh between Newbridge and Kildare Town.

Horses & Horse Racing
Kildare has more horseflesh per sq km than any other Irish county, and the racecourses are home to some of the biggest meetings of the year. The calcium-rich grass breeds strong-boned horses, while excellent stud facilities and generous tax concessions attract many foreign horse owners.

Travelling through Kildare you will see plenty of studs, most of which are private and not too keen on visitors. You can, however, visit the state-owned National Stud just outside Kildare Town. You could also check out a thoroughbred auction in Goff's Sales(☎ 045-77211/83), Kildare Paddocks, a huge complex beside the main Dublin road (N7) near Kill, north-east of Naas. There, you will see spindly thoroughbred foals and yearlings change hands for unbelievable sums.

Almost everyone in Ireland goes to the races. At race meetings you can see all of Irish society at play: the glitterati in their private boxes swilling champagne, and the ordinary punters oblivious to everything except their bets – and, between races, their drink.

Kildare has three of Ireland's most famous tracks, and there is racing all year round. The best known is the Curragh Racecourse (☎ 045-41205), over two km south-west of Newbridge on the road to Kildare Town. The racecourse takes its name from the expanse of open countryside surrounding it, which also holds one of the country's biggest army camps. The Curragh Race-course season runs from March to November and has some of the biggest meetings of the country's racing calendar, including the 1000 and 2000 Guineas in May, the Irish Derby in June, the Irish Oaks in July and the St Leger in September.

Five km south of Naas is Punchestown (☎ 045-97704), a top-notch steeplechase course where every April they hold the Irish National Hunt Festival. And finally, just to the north, Naas has its own local racetrack (☎ 045-97391), which holds well-attended meetings every two weeks or so during the summer and less frequently in winter. ■

KILDARE TOWN

Kildare is a cathedral and market town 24 km south-west of Naas, and its busy little triangular square with a pub on each side is a pleasant change from the county's other nondescript urban centres.

Information

The county's main tourist office (☎ 045-226596), in Market House in the centre of the square, is open Easter to October from 10 am to 6 pm Monday to Saturday and is closed for lunch from 1 to 2 pm.

St Brigid's Cathedral

St Brigid, one of the country's best loved saints, is remembered by St Brigid's Cross, a simply constructed four-pointed cross woven from reeds and found today in many homes and gift shops. In the 5th century she founded a religious centre, unusual in that it was shared by nuns and monks, who were separated only by screens in church. A fire was kept burning perpetually in a fire temple, looked after by nuns and out of bounds to males, tended only by virgins over the age of 30. It lasted until the 16th-century dissolution of the monasteries. The restored fire pit can be seen in the grounds of the 13th-century Protestant St Brigid's Cathedral, whose solid presence looms over the square. The cathedral is open from 10 am to 5 pm Monday to Friday.

Round Tower In the cathedral grounds is a 10th-century round tower, Ireland's second highest at 31.5 metres. Its original conical top has been replaced with an unusual Norman battlement which allows access to the outside roof but has ruined the tower's profile. You can climb to the top for IR£1/50p from 10 am to 1 pm Monday to Saturday or between 2 and 5 pm any day.

Irish National Stud

More than any other county, Kildare is synonymous with the multi-million-pound bloodstock industry, and Kildare Town is twinned with another famous horse-breeding centre, Lexington-Fayette in Kentucky,

USA. The Irish National Stud (☎ 045-21251), just one km south of the centre in Tully, was set up in 1900 by Colonel Hall Walker, then given to the crown in 1915, in return for which he became Lord Wavertree. He must have wanted the title badly. He had been remarkably successful with his horses, although his breeding and training techniques fell somewhere outside the everyday. On the birth of each foal, he devised a horoscope based on the position of the stars and planets and from this decided whether to keep it or not.

The stud remained in the hands of the British until 1943 when they in turn passed it on to the Irish government. Today its purpose is to breed high-quality stallions who will mate with approved mares from Ireland's private studs. The intention is to improve the overall quality of Irish bloodstocks.

For a IR£4/2 (students IR£3) entry fee to both the stud and the Japanese Gardens (see below), visitors are free to wander around the impossibly tidy compound, walk through the various stables, paddocks and meadows, or pop into the foaling unit where they can watch a video of the birth of a foal. The small but interesting Irish Horse Museum examines the role horses have played in Irish life over the years and includes the skeleton of Arkle, who won the prestigious Cheltenham Gold Cup race in Britain three years running in the 1960s. If there was a saint among Irish horses, Arkle was it. He was the object of national adoration and after his death in 1968 the country went into mourning.

Adjacent to the stud, the **Japanese Gardens** (☎ 045-21617) were created for Lord Wavertree between 1906 and 1910. He went to Japan to bring back two superb gardeners, Tasa Eida and his son Minoru, as overseers and they employed 40 local men for the four years it took to complete the work. The gardens were planted to symbolise the stages of the Life of Man, but you need a tour guide or leaflet to follow the cycle. The trees, paths and ponds are all symbolic. There is a large visitors' centre with a coffee shop, a children's play area and a selection of expensive bonsai trees for sale.

The stud and gardens are open Easter Sunday to the end of October from 10.30 am to 5 pm Monday to Friday, from 10.30 am to 6 pm Saturday and public holidays and from 2 to 6 pm Sunday.

Places to Stay
In Maddenstown, near the Irish National Stud, *St Mary's* (☎ 045-21243), run by Agnes Winters, charges IR£14 per person for B&B. *Catherine Singleton's* (☎ 045-21964), 1 Dara Park, has three rooms at IR£20/30 for singles/doubles with bathroom.

Nearer town, *Fremont* (☎ 045-21604), just south of the town square on the Tully road, charges IR£19/28 singles/doubles. The *Lord Edward Guesthouse* (☎ 045-22389), part of the Silken Thomas pub on the square, has singles/doubles for IR£18/30 with bathroom and breakfast. *Rossa House* (☎ 045-21210), a good guesthouse just on the Dublin edge of town, charges IR£18/28 without bathroom or IR£19/32 with; breakfast is included.

Nearby, the *Curragh Lodge Hotel* (☎ 045-22144) has 10 rooms with bathroom for IR£25 per person.

Places to Eat
Silken Thomas (☎ 045-22232), a vast old-world bar, takes up one corner of the square and has a restaurant offering good lunches for around IR£6 and dinner from IR£9.50 to IR£12, as well as sandwiches and pub food. *Boland's Pub* (☎ 045-21263) on the opposite side of the square has good light snacks. *Gallops Restaurant*, in the Curragh Lodge Hotel, serves breakfast specials for IR£3.50 and four-course dinners in the evening for IR£9.

Getting There & Away
Kildare Town is 30 minutes by train from Dublin on the Waterford, Tralee, Galway, Limerick and Cork lines; there are more than 10 trains daily. For details ring ☎ 01-850 836 6222. The main N7 highway from Dublin to the west of Ireland passes through Kildare and Bus Éireann has numerous express

coaches from the Busáras (☎ 01-836 6111) which take about one hour.

MONASTEREVIN
Monasterevin (*Mainistir Eimhín*) is 11 km west of Kildare Town on the N7 and the River Barrow. The 18th-century **Moore Abbey** is built on the site of an ancient Cistercian monastery founded by St Evin and was home in the 1930s to the famous Irish tenor John McCormack. In a remarkable piece of 18th-century engineering, an **aqueduct** carries the Grand Canal across the River Barrow here.

Bus Éireann services to Monasterevin are the same as those to Kildare Town.

NAAS TO CARLOW TOWN
The 48-km stretch of the N9 highway between Naas and Carlow Town offers a number of interesting side trips.

Getting There & Away
The Naas to Carlow Town road is well served by long-distance buses on the Dublin to Carlow, Clonmel and Kilkenny routes. Some of these buses will drop you off at Kilcullen, Ballitore, Moone, Castledermot and Athy, though you should check beforehand because some buses go straight through to Athy or Carlow. On the way to Kilkenny they pass through Leighlinbridge and Castlecomer. Bus Éireann (☎ 01-836 6111) has two or three buses daily from Dublin and J J Kavanagh & Sons' private bus company (☎ 0503-43081) offers a similar service.

Kilcullen
The tiny village of Kilcullen is on the River Liffey, 12 km east of Kildare Town. Nearby at **Old Kilcullen**, the scant remains of a high cross and round tower are all that is left of an early Christian settlement.

On the edge of the Curragh, four km northwest of Kilcullen on the west side of the L19, **Donnelly's Hollow** was the scene of numerous victories of Dan Donnelly (1788-1820), Ireland's greatest bare-knuckle fighter of the last century. It's said he had a reach so long that he could touch his knees without having to stoop, and that a fight here attracted about 20,000 spectators. An obelisk at the centre of the deep hollow details his glorious career. His 'footprints' lead up the slope from the centre of the hollow.

Back in Kilcullen his mummified arm can be seen in **The Hideout** (☎ 045-81232), a famous and wildly eccentric pub. The arm arrived here after Donnelly's grave was robbed.

Beginners are welcome at **Golden Falls Waterski Centre** (☎ 045-64270) in Ballymore Eustace on the Wicklow border not far from Kilcullen, which is open June to September.

Ballitore & Timolin

At Ballitore on the River Greese the **Crookstown Mill & Heritage Centre** (☎ 0507-23222) has a functioning water mill and a display covering milling and baking through the centuries. It also has a coffee shop and is open April to September from 10 am to 4 pm daily; admission is IR£2. Ballitore was originally settled in the 18th century by Quakers, and their influence can be seen throughout the area in the finely built stone courtyards, buildings and graveyards. One of the settlers was an ancestor of Ernest Shackleton, the Antarctic explorer, who was born nearby in Kilkea House. The **Quaker Museum** (☎ 0507-23133) is in the old schoolhouse where Edmund Burke, the political philosopher, studied as a pupil. It's open from 11 am to 6 pm Tuesday to Friday, from 11 am to 5 pm Saturday and from 3 to 5 pm Sunday.

Two km west is the **Rath of Mullaghmast**, an Iron Age hill fort where Daniel O'Connell, champion of Catholic emancipation, held one of his 'monster meetings' in 1843.

Three km south of Ballitore and just north of Moone, the village of Timolin is home to the **Irish Pewter Mill & Craft Centre** (☎ 0507-24164). *Woodcourte House* (☎ 0507-24167) in Timolin has a tennis court, runs arts & crafts weekends and offers B&B for IR£15 with bathroom. Take the turn beside the Sportsman Inn in Timolin and the

house is about 200 metres on the right past the Irish Pewter Mill.

Moone

The barely noticeable village of Moone is just south of Timolin and 29 km south-west of Naas. One km west in an early Christian monastic churchyard is the magnificent **Moone High Cross**. This 8th or 9th-century masterpiece is slender and, at six metres, remarkably tall. The numerous crisply carved panels display biblical scenes including the Loaves & Fishes, the Flight into Egypt and a wonderful representation of the Twelve Apostles. Unfortunately, an ugly wire fence has been erected around the cross to protect it.

The 18th-century *Moone High Cross Inn* (☎ 045-24112) is a delightful bar about 100 metres west of the N9, one km south of Moone village. It does plain but hefty pub food including a great Irish stew.

Kilkea Castle

This 12th-century castle (☎ 0503-45156), completely restored in the 19th century, is five km north-west of Castledermot on the Athy road and was once the second home of the Maynooth Fitzgeralds. The castle grounds are supposed to be haunted by the son of Silken Thomas, Gerald the Wizard Earl, who rises every seven years from the Rath of Mullaghmast to free Ireland from its enemies. This is a neat trick as the Wizard Earl was buried in London. A great deal of reconstruction and restoration was carried out on the castle in the 19th century.

Although the castle is now a very exclusive hotel you can still have a drink in the bar and pick up a booklet on the building's history. Among its oddities is an **Evil Eye Stone** set high up on the exterior wall at the back of the castle. Thought to date from the 13th or 14th century, this is a depiction of various half-human, animal and birdlike figures engaging in some rather unseemly erotic behaviour. The castle has formal gardens and a forest park.

Accommodation costs IR£85/150 a single/double with bathroom and breakfast.

Castledermot

Castledermot's ruined Franciscan friary is right by the road at the south end of town on Abbey St. The friary dates from the mid-13th century and the key is available from the adjacent cottage.

A little farther north on Main St and back from the road is a churchyard, the site of a monastery founded originally by St Diarmuid in 812 AD. There are two fine 9th or 10th-century granite high crosses beside the remains of a round tower 20 metres high and a 12th-century Romanesque church doorway. The round tower has a medieval battlement added on top.

Places to Stay & Eat The old stone *Kilkea Lodge* (☎ 0503-45112) has big open fires and is more expensive than most B&Bs at IR£25 a night. The small and intimate *Doyle's Schoolhouse Inn* (☎ 0503-44282) has an unusual menu and is consistently rated as one of the best restaurants in the county. Dinner will cost around IR£22 and reservations are essential. It also offers B&B at IR£22.50 per person.

ATHY

Founded in the 12th century, Athy (pronounced 'A-thigh') sits at the junction of the River Barrow and the Grand Canal near the County Laois border. Athy (*Áth Í*) has the feel of a genuine country town, with a pleasant but somewhat dilapidated old square. The 15th-century tower of White Castle, built by the earls of Kildare who once owned the town, is now a private house overlooking the River Barrow.

The tourist office, in the town hall building on Emily Square, is open year round from 10 am to 1 pm and 2 to 4.30 pm Monday to Friday. The town hall also houses a local museum and library.

There is coarse, salmon and trout fishing on the Grand Canal and the River Barrow. For information check with Kane's pub (☎ 0507-31434). The Athy Golf Club (☎ 0507-31729) has a nine-hole course. Six km north-east on the road to Naas is the 18-metre **Ardscull Motte**, one of the largest

of these defensive structures to be built by the Normans.

Places to Stay & Eat
There are a number of B&Bs in and around Athy. *Forest Farm* (☎ 0507-31231), a small country farmhouse five km out of Athy on the Dublin road, and *Ballindrum Farm* (☎ 0507-26294), a few km farther out in Ballindrum, both have rooms for IR£13.50/14.50 per person without/with bathroom.

The *Blackboard* (☎ 0507-38748), in Stanhope St just off Emily Square, is a straightforward restaurant/snack bar with main courses from IR£5.25. For cheap and cheerful pub food, try the *Castle Inn* on Leinster St, or the *Leinster Arms* on the corner of Emily Square. The *Duck Press Restaurant* (☎ 0507-38952), on Leinster St over the river, is good for lunch or dinner.

Tonlegee House (☎ 0507-31473), in a beautiful setting beside the remains of an old church south out of town on the Kilkenny road, is an excellent restaurant but expensive at about IR£20. There are guest rooms upstairs at IR£40/60 a single/double.

Getting There & Away
Buses on the Naas to Carlow Town road, of which there are a number, stop at Athy, following the Dublin to Carlow, Clonmel and Kilkenny routes. Contact Bus Éireann (☎ 01-836 6111) or New Princess Coach Services (01-679 1549) for details.

County Carlow

Carlow (*Ceatharlach*), the second smallest Irish county, has the scenic Blackstairs Mountains to the east, the Killeshin Hills to the west, and sections of the rivers Barrow and Slaney, with quietly picturesque villages such as Rathvilly, Leighlinbridge and Borris. The Dublin to Carlow Town route via southwest Wicklow runs through some wild and lightly populated country.

The rest of Carlow is mainly undulating

farmland, where you will often see sugar beet piled by the roadside awaiting collection. Browne's Hill Dolmen is the county's most interesting archaeological feature and is just outside Carlow Town.

HISTORY

Despite its proximity to the Pale, for a long time Carlow remained a hotbed of Irish patriotism, thanks mainly to the fearless MacMurrough Kavanaghs, ancient kings of Leinster. They dominated the region from the 13th century up to Cromwellian times.

One chief in particular, Art Óg, based in Borris, posed such a threat to the Pale that in 1394 King Richard II came over from England to subdue him with a force of 10,000 men. After fierce fighting, Art Óg capitulated, but no sooner had a treaty been agreed and Richard hightailed it back to London, than Art Óg along with the Ulster O'Neills turned on the occupying English army and savaged them. At the pivotal Battle of Kellistown in 1398, Richard's cousin Roger Mortimer, heir to the throne, was killed. In 1399, Richard returned, bent on revenge.

This time Art Óg was ready and gave Richard a miserable time, defeating him again and again. Meanwhile back in London, trouble was brewing for Richard and he was overthrown and killed on his return. The spirit of resistance stayed alive in County Carlow and more than 600 rebels died in Carlow in the 1798 Rising. The local rebel leader was Father John Murphy, immortalised in the song *Boulavogue*, who was captured and executed in Tullow.

CARLOW TOWN

Carlow was a frontier town for many centuries due to its strategic location on the River Barrow, on the border with the Pale. Today, it's a busy market and industrial centre serving a large rural area. The town itself is unremarkable except for Browne's Hill Dolmen on the outskirts. Carlow was the first town outside Dublin to have electric street lighting, from power generated downstream at Milford. Railway pioneer William

Dargan, who founded the National Gallery in Dublin, was born here.

History

After the Normans arrived in Ireland, a motte-and-bailey fort was erected here in 1180, and shortly afterwards succeeded by Carlow Castle, built by William Marshall, Strongbow's successor in the region. A wall was built to protect Carlow Town in 1361.

During Cromwell's tour of the country, the town surrendered to his son-in-law Ireton in 1650.

In 1798 on Tullow St, over 600 Irish rebels were killed in the bloodiest fighting of the rising. A Celtic high cross marks the Croppie Grave, in Graiguecullen gravel pits just over the river, where most were buried in quick-lime.

Orientation & Information

Dublin St is the city's principal north-south axis, Tullow St is the main shopping street and College St runs between the two. The northern end of Dublin St divides into Dublin and Athy Rds. The tourist office (☎ 0503-31554), in Traynor House on the corner of Tullow and College Sts near the cathedral, is open from 9.30 am to 5.30 pm Monday to Friday and from 10 am to 6 pm Saturday, but is closed at lunch times. The post office is just south of the town centre on the corner of Kennedy Ave and Dublin St.

Carlow Castle

Officials at Carlow Castle, on Castle St, once had to be paid danger money to live here among the native Irish. The castle survived Cromwell's attentions and would be largely intact if a Dr Middleton had not decided to turn it into an asylum and blew it up in 1814; the mighty four-walled castle was reduced to a single wall flanked by two towers. Enquire at the Corcoran's Mineral Waters factory on Castle Hill about access to what's left.

Courthouse

It's said that the plans for Carlow and Cork courthouses got mixed up, so this little town ended up with William Morrison's splendid

1830 building, based on the Parthenon in Athens, while Cork had to make do with a less-impressive design. The cannon beside the steps was taken from the Russians during the Crimean War. The courthouse is at the northern end of Dublin St.

Cathedral of the Assumption
Down College St from the courthouse, this 1833 cathedral has an elaborately carved pulpit and some fine stained-glass windows. John Hogan's statue of Bishop Doyle, better known as JKL (James of Kildare & Leighin) for his work as a supporter of Catholic Emancipation, includes a woman who represents Ireland, rising up against her oppressors.

County Museum
This small museum on local history is in the town hall, on Centaur St off the Haymarket, and is open May to September from 11 am to 5.30 pm Monday to Saturday and from 2.30 to 5.30 pm Sunday; admission is IR£1/50p. A **market** dealing in mostly second-hand goods takes place in the car park next to the museum during the week.

Places to Stay
The independent *Carna Hostel* (☎ 0503-31700), on Pembroke St, is open May to September and charges IR£5.50 for a dorm bed. *Red Setter House* (☎ 0503-41848), 14 Dublin St, is a very good central B&B that has singles/doubles with bath for IR£16.50/31 and its own car park.

Getting There & Away
Bus Bus Éireann (☎ 01-836 6111) has regular services to Dublin (six daily, 1½ hours), Kilkenny (one daily, 45 minutes) and Waterford (five daily, 1¼ hours). Rapid Express Coaches (☎ 0503-43081) has seven buses daily to Dublin and Waterford. Bus Éireann and Rapid Express buses leave from near the latter's office on Barrack St south of the post office.

Train The railway station (☎ 0503-31633) is on Railway St in the north-east of town. Carlow is on the Dublin to Waterford and Kilkenny line with at least four trains daily in each direction and three on Sunday.

Getting Around
A E Coleman (☎ 0503-31273), 19 Dublin St, is a Raleigh dealer with bikes for IR£7 a day or IR£30 a week. Contact Carlow Cab Service (☎ 0503-32404) for taxis.

AROUND CARLOW TOWN
There is no public transport to the following sights, but the first two at least are within easy cycling distance.

Browne's Hill Dolmen
This 5000-year-old granite monster is believed to have the largest capstone in Europe, weighing in at over 100 tonnes. The structure when completed would have been covered with a mound of earth. The dolmen is three km east of town on the R726 Hacketstown road; a path leads around the field to the dolmen.

Killeshin Church
Killeshin Church is five km west of Carlow Town on the Abbeyleix road just inside County Laois. See that section later for more details.

Milford
One of the nicer drives to the south is via Milford on the minor road that follows the River Barrow valley. The village lies about half way between Carlow Town and Leighlinbridge. The old mill at Milford was the site of the turbine which first powered Carlow Town's electric street lighting in the 1890s. John Alexander, the present owner, still runs a turbine here and supplies electricity to the Electricity Supply Board (ESB). There's good salmon and trout fishing here.
The Locks (☎ 0503-46261), in a picturesque spot by the River Barrow near the old mill, is a guesthouse that has singles/doubles for IR£14/26 with bathroom and breakfast.

TULLOW
Tullow is a well-known angling town on the River Slaney in the north of the county.

Father John Murphy, a local leader of the 1798 Rising, was captured and executed in the market square on 2 July 1798. A memorial to him stands in the town centre. Tullow Museum, beside the town bridge, is open on Sunday and Wednesday afternoons.

Five km due east of Tullow on Shillelagh Rd is the Iron Age ring fort of **Rathgall**, dating from the 8th century BC. The fort is protected by three outer ring walls, which are overgrown. The final wall is still in good condition, though somewhat lower nowadays. It is said that Rathgall is the burial site of the kings of Leinster.

Places to Stay

For somewhere to stay, try the early Georgian *Sherwood Park House* (☎ 0503-59117) south of Tullow in Kilbride just off the N80, about half way between Ballon and Kildavin. B&B costs IR£25/40 a single/double with bathroom.

Getting There & Away

Tullow is on Bus Éireann's (☎ 01-836 6111) Dublin to Waterford route, which stops at Tullow, Enniscorthy and New Ross. There are two buses daily in each direction.

LEIGHLINBRIDGE

Leighlinbridge, just off the main Kilkenny road, 13 km south-west of Carlow Town, has one of Ireland's first Norman castles. The rather uninspiring **Black Castle** dates from 1181 and overlooks the first bridge to be built over the River Barrow. This pleasant little village also produced Captain Myles Kehoe, the last of General Custer's men left alive at the 1876 Battle of Little Big Horn in Montana, USA.

Three km west is **Old Leighlin**, the site of a 6th-century monastic settlement founded by St Laserian. There is a small cathedral with some finely carved stonework and a Romanesque doorway; it is nowhere near as good as the one in Killeshin, however.

Places to Stay & Eat

Nevin's (☎ 0503-21202), next to the Lord Bagenal Inn, has simple rooms for IR£12 per person. The owner, Martin Nevin, is a teacher with a great interest in local history.

The choice of restaurants outside Carlow Town is limited. The popular *Lord Bagenal Inn* (☎ 0503-21668), on Leighlinbridge's main street, has a restaurant and a bar serving food. It's an inviting place with a big open fire, excellent steaks (IR£10), fish and pasta (IR£5.50) and good vegetarian food. The restaurant is open from 6 to 10.30 pm Tuesday to Saturday and until 9 pm Sunday. The inn was once visited by Brian Mulroney when he was prime minister of Canada.

Getting There & Away

There are plenty of buses passing through daily, on the Dublin to Carlow and Kilkenny route. See the introductory Getting There & Away section under Naas to Carlow Town earlier for details.

BORRIS

The Georgian village of Borris is 16 km south of Leighlinbridge and is overlooked by a disused railway viaduct with 16 arches. **Borris House** is the residence of the MacMurrough Kavanaghs, descendants of the ancient kings of Leinster, and is still in the family's possession, Andrew MacMurrough Kavanagh being the present occupant.

A most remarkable MacMurrough Kavanagh was Arthur (1831-89), who was born with only rudimentary limbs yet learned to ride and shoot and later became an MP. The castle is only open for viewing by appointment. The entrance is at the north end of town near the White House pub.

Borris is a starting point for the Mt Leinster Scenic Drive (which can also be walked) and is also on the South Leinster Way. Alternatively, there is a lovely 10-km walk along a towpath beside the River Barrow to Graiguenamanagh, a picturesque little village just inside County Kilkenny.

Places to Stay & Eat

Breen's (☎ 0503-73231), a B&B on Church St, has rooms at IR£17/27 a single/double. Half way between Borris and Bagenalstown, the *Lorum Old Rectory* (☎ 0503-75282) is overlooked by the Blackstairs Mountains and charges IR£25/40, with excellent dinners at IR£16.

The *Green Drake Inn* (☎ 0503-73116) has fairly good pub food and a restaurant where dinner will cost around IR£12.

Entertainment
The *White House* pub, at the north end of Main St, usually has music on weekends, while the *Green Drake* pub has traditional Irish and contemporary music Thursday to Sunday. *O'Shea's*, a bar cum grocery and hardware store also on Main St, is good for a quiet drink.

Getting There & Away
J J Kavanagh & Sons' private bus company (☎ 0503-43081) includes Borris in its single daily Carlow Town to Limerick service. Foley's (☎ 0503-24641) private buses stop at Borris on their twice daily route between Graiguenamanagh and Kilkenny. Neither of these services operates on Sunday.

MT LEINSTER
Mt Leinster at 796 metres has some of the finest hang-gliding in the country. It's also worth the hike up for the panoramic views over counties Carlow, Wexford and Wicklow. To get there from Borris, follow the Mt Leinster Scenic Drive signposts 13 km towards Bunclody in County Wexford. See the Counties Wexford & Waterford chapter for more details. It takes a good two hours on foot or 20 minutes by car.

ST MULLINS
A quiet village on the River Barrow 12 km south of Borris, St Mullins has numerous ecclesiastical ruins. The scant remains of a round tower, various abbeys and chapels were all part of St Moling's original 7th-century monastery. St Moling's Well is by the stream, and a number of people who died during the 1798 Rising were buried in the graveyard, including some who were executed for manufacturing pikes, the rebels' favourite (but unfortunately for them, rather

ineffective) weapon. Across the road from the graveyard the grass-covered mound is a good example of a small Anglo-Norman motte.

There is no public transport to St Mullins.

THE SOUTH LEINSTER WAY
Just south-west of Clonegal, on the north slopes of Mt Leinster, is the tiny village of **Kildavin**, the starting point of the South Leinster Way. Carlow Town and St Mullins are also on the Kildare Trails. See the Activities chapter for details.

County Laois

Laois, pronounced 'Leash', is a 1½-hour drive south-west of Dublin and is as far inland as counties get in Ireland. It's the only inland county surrounded on all sides by neighbours none of which touch the coast. For most visitors Laois is simply somewhere you pass through en route to Limerick or Cork. It's a fairly uninteresting landscape of raised bogs and poor farms, but there are some pleasant country towns and the unspoiled Slieve Bloom Mountains.

HISTORY
Most of Laois is underlain by carboniferous limestone deposited some 330 million years ago. The grey rock breaks through the soil and forms low hills in the east of the county. Some of these, such as Lugacurran and Dunamase, have fortifications dating back to the Iron Age, although the first significant human traces are from the Bronze Age. While no site is of special significance, various burial places and artefacts have been uncovered over the years.

Considering the county's relative proximity to Dublin's Pale, Irish families such as the O'Mores, O'Dunnes, O'Dowlings and O'Dempseys controlled the county for a remarkable length of time. There were interruptions from the Normans in the 12th and 13th centuries, but their influence was only really weakened by the arrival of plantation settlers from England and Scotland in the mid-16th century.

Much of present-day Laois owes its shape to these plantations, the first in Ireland. It was called Queen's County after Queen Mary I, and Portlaoise was given the name Maryborough, while neighbouring Offaly was known as King's County. Many of the towns were developed by Quaker settlers. Laois only really became safe for the settlers when the O'More and Fitzpatrick clans were shifted to Kerry in the 17th century, shortly before Cromwell came along to finish the job. Today Laois has one of the highest Protestant to Catholic ratios in the South.

PORTLAOISE

Although founded by the O'Mores just before the plantation, Portlaoise (*Port Laoise*) is mostly modern, and only the courthouse by Richard Morrison on the corner of Main and Church Sts is of note. The old centre has little charm and has been bypassed by a loop to the south where most of the town's commercial development is happening. However, plans are in the pipeline to revitalise the centre and pedestrianise Main St.

To the west are the Slieve Bloom Mountains, while to the east is the only historic site of interest worth a special detour, the Rock of Dunamase on the Stradbally road.

Bristling with wire fencing at the east end of town is the 1830 Republic of Ireland's maximum-security prison.

Information

The tourist office (☎ 0502-21178), in the shopping-centre car park beside the bypass on James Fintan Lawlor Ave, has lots of information on the region. To get there from Main St, go through the lane beside Dowling's café. The office is open May to September from 10 am to 1 pm and 2 to 6 pm Monday to Saturday; the rest of the year it is open from 2 to 6 pm Monday to Friday. The post office is nearby.

Places to Stay & Eat

There are a couple of B&Bs, *Donaghue's* and

No 8, on James Finlan Lawlor Ave opposite the county hall, or you could try the *Regency Hotel* (☎ 0502-21305), on Main St, which has rooms with bathroom from IR£22. The rate includes breakfast and there's a bar and restaurant downstairs.

Dowling's, also on Main St, serves good hot food (around IR£4) and sandwiches during the day.

Getting There & Away

Bus Portlaoise is on one of the busiest main roads in the country at the junction of the N8 and N7, with a large number of daily Bus Éireann (☎ 01-836 6111) buses passing between Dublin and Cashel, Cork, Limerick and Kerry. It is also on a Waterford, Kilkenny, Carlow, Athlone and Longford route. J J Kavanagh & Sons' private bus company (☎ 056-31106) has two buses a day to Carlow.

The bus stop in Portlaoise is at Egan's Hostelry on Lower Square at the bottom of Main St.

Train Portlaoise is one hour from Dublin on the main railway line to Tipperary, Cork, Limerick and Kerry and is serviced by numerous daily trains. The train station (☎ 0502-21303), on Railway St, is about a five-minute walk north of the town centre.

ROCK OF DUNAMASE

Six km east of Portlaoise along the Stradbally road, this fractured limestone hill is covered with the remains of fortifications. It's only 65 metres high, but the surrounding countryside is so flat that the summit gives a fine view in all directions. You can see the round tower at Timahoe to the south and the cooling tower of Portarlington power station to the north.

The remains include an Iron Age ring fort and a 12th or 13th-century keep. The slopes of Dunamase can be treacherous, particularly on the north side, and these natural barriers would have complicated any assault on its defenders. First sacked by the Vikings in the 840s, Dunamase was later given away by Dermot MacMurrough, king of Leinster, as part of his daughter Aoife's dowry when she married Strongbow, the Norman invader of Ireland. Dunamase was then reinforced by William Marshall, Strongbow's successor, who built three baileys on the spot.

The local clan, the O'Mores, captured the rock from the English near the end of the 15th century and held it until it was retaken 150 years later in 1641, by Charles Coote. He was a leading Parliamentarian and one of Cromwell's most able leaders in Ireland. Recaptured five years later by Catholic forces, it was finally taken and wrecked by Cromwell's henchmen Reynolds and Hewson in 1650.

Hewson gave his name to the hill to the south-west, which has the ruined 9th-century church of Dysert, and the earth embankments 500 metres to the east are known as Cromwell's lines, although they are in fact the remains of a much older two-ringed fort.

The main ruins consist of a badly shattered 13th-century castle on the highest point (best seen from the north side) surrounded by an outer wall of which little remains. You enter the complex through the twin towered gate structure, which leads to the outer bailey and fortified courtyard to the south-east.

J J Kavanagh & Sons' private bus service (☎ 056-31106) has two daily buses from Portlaoise to Carlow which pass by the rock. It's a good hour's walk from the town centre.

EMO COURT & DEMESNE

Emo Court was the county seat of the 1st earl of Portarlington and is 13 km north-east of Portlaoise, signposted off the main road to Dublin. The rather unusual house with its prominent green dome was designed by James Gandon (architect of Dublin's Customs House) and served as a Jesuit novitiate for many years. The estate has long walks winding through forests and by Emo Lake, and is littered with Greek statues. From the Emo village gate it is a two-km walk to the house.

The house is now owned by the OPW and at the time of writing was closed for restoration. Contact the OPW or the tourist office in Portlaoise for details of opening times and admission fee.

South of Emo village off the main Portlaoise road is **St John's Church**, in Coolbanagher, also designed by Gandon. This church was built in 1786 by Lord Carlow, the 1st earl of Portarlington, to replace a thatched church which was destroyed in 1779. It's simple Georgian architecture at its best and inside is a Gothic 14th or 15th-century carved baptismal font.

Emo is just off the main Portlaoise to Dublin road, and there are daily buses in both directions.

STRADBALLY

The village of Stradbally (or Strathbally), 10 km south-east of Portlaoise, was once a seat of the mighty O'More clan. Most of the present buildings date from the 17th century.

The O'Mores were the force behind the Franciscan friary which was established here in 1447. The family were the holders of 'The Book of Leinster', a manuscript compiled between 1151 and 1224 to record all the knowledge of Aéd Crúamthainn, a scribe to the high kings of Ireland. This book contained, among other things, vivid descriptions of the banqueting hall at Tara, the seat of the high kings, and is now to be found in the library at Trinity College, Dublin.

Stradbally Steam Museum

The museum (☎ 0502-252136) has a collection of fire engines, steam tractors and steam rollers, lovingly restored by the Irish Steam Preservation Society. Housed in a tightly packed warehouse, the prize exhibits include a Merryweather horse-drawn fire engine from 1880.

The 1895 Guinness Brewery steam locomotive in the village is used six times annually for a day trip to Dublin. During the three-day Steam Rally in early August the 40 hectares of Cosby Hall are taken over by all types of steam-operated machines and vintage cars. The museum is open from 2 to 6 pm Sunday.

Getting There & Away

J J Kavanagh & Sons' private bus service (☎ 056-31106) has two daily buses from Portlaoise to Carlow via Stradbally. Stradbally is also on a Waterford to Longford Bus Éireann (☎ 01-836 6111) twice daily service which passes through Kilkenny, Carlow, Stradbally, Portlaoise and Athlone.

PORTARLINGTON

There are still traces of Portarlington's (*Cúil an tSúdaire*) former prosperity in many of its buildings. It grew under the influence of French Huguenot and German settlers introduced by Lord Arlington, who was granted tracts of land here after the 17th-century Cromwellian wars. Many of the finer 18th-century buildings are a result of the efforts of Henry Dawson, earl of Portarlington, to improve the town. His family encouraged bankers and upmarket tradespeople like silversmiths to settle here. Unfortunately, many of their houses are now suffering from neglect.

The 1851 **St Paul's Church**, on the site of the original 17th-century French church, was built for the Huguenots, and some of their tombstones stand in one corner of the churchyard. The River Barrow kinks around the town on its journey east; stretches along the borders with counties Kildare and Carlow are lovely.

The large cooling tower of the peat-fuelled **power station** is a local landmark. Built in 1936, the power station was the first in Ireland to use peat to generate electricity.

Getting There & Away

Portarlington is on the main railway lines between Dublin and Galway, Limerick, Kerry and Cork, with numerous daily trains in both directions. For details contact Portlaoise railway station (☎ 0502-21303). There are no buses to Portarlington.

LEA CASTLE

On the banks of the River Barrow four km east of Portarlington on the Monasterevin road (R420), this 13th-century ruin was the stronghold of Maurice Fitzgerald, 2nd baron

of Offaly. It consists of a fairly intact towered keep with two outer walls running down to the Barrow and a twin-towered gatehouse. It was burned in 1315 by Edward Bruce, the brother of King Robert Bruce of Scotland. Edward came to Ireland at the invitation of Irish chieftains in 1315 to create trouble for the Anglo-Normans/English. He hoped this would distract the English and lessen their pressure on his brother in Scotland.

Crowned high king of Ireland, Edward Bruce created a lot of trouble for the forces and colonisers loyal to England, until he was killed in 1318 at the Battle of Faughart near Dundalk. His remains are said to be buried in a churchyard at Faughart four km from Castleroche.

In the 16th century Silken Thomas sought refuge after his failed rebellion against Henry VIII. In 1650 the castle was blown up by Cromwell's forces, fresh from their success at Dunamase. The castle stairways were filled with explosives to maximise the damage.

Much of the remains are now covered in ivy, and at the right time of the day, such as early morning or evening, the place is tranquil and evocative. Access to the castle is through a dilapidated farmyard half a km to the north off the main Monasterevin road.

MOUNTMELLICK

Mountmellick is an attractive if rather faded little market town with many Georgian houses, 10 km north of Portlaoise on the River Owenass. Its fortunes rose with Quaker settlers who produced linen which was exported by barge on a branch of the Grand Canal which runs away to the east. It became something of a boom town in the late 18th and early 19th centuries with many different industries and was home to the first sugar-beet factory in Ireland built in 1851. The small visitors' centre (☎ 0502-24525) with a display on Quaker life and Mountmellick embroidery is open from 10 am to 5 pm Monday to Friday (plus summer weekends from 2 to 6 pm).

Getting There & Away

Mountmellick is on the twice-daily Waterford to Longford Bus Éireann (☎ 01-836 6111) route which passes through Kilkenny, Carlow, Stradbally, Portlaoise and Athlone. There is also a daily service to and from Dublin via Naas, Newbridge, Kildare and Portlaoise.

MOUNTRATH & AROUND

Like so many other Irish settlements, Mountrath has associations with St Patrick and St Brigid, who are supposed to have established religious houses here, although there are no traces left today. Much of the town and surrounding land belonged to Sir Charles Coote, an ardent parliamentarian and supporter of Cromwell during and after the Cromwellian wars in the 1640s. Mountrath's halcyon days were in the 17th and 18th centuries, when the linen industry generated a fair amount of local wealth.

The town is 13 km south-west of Portlaoise and lies on the Mountrath River, a tributary of the Nore. The Slieve Bloom Mountains are only eight km to the north-west.

St Fintan's Tree

Three km east on the Portlaoise road, there is little left of Clonenagh, the site of the 6th-century monastery of St Fintan. St Fintan's Tree is a large sycamore with a water-filled groove in one of its lower branches which is said to never dry out. The tree has long been a place of pilgrimage and the many coins embedded in the trunk are offerings by pilgrims who attribute healing powers to the water. The ruined church on the opposite side of the road is unrelated.

Ballyfin House

Eight km north of Mountrath off the Mountmellick road is Ballyfin House, built by Sir Charles Henry Coote in 1850 to the designs of Richard Morrison (better known for his courthouses). It has been described as the finest 19th-century house in Ireland, and is pleasantly sited overlooking a small lake in quiet, rolling countryside. Inside, it is well preserved, and some of the ornamentation is completely over the top. The dining room is

also known as the 'gold room', and someone ran amok with plasterwork and gold paint. It would look at home in Versailles. Sir Charles reckoned all good houses should have a lake, and the one in front is artificial.

Another and more intriguing piece of aristocratic eccentricity at this time was megalithomania, a passion for building imitation Stone Age monuments. Ballyfin has an excellent example on the right of the avenue about 200 metres short of the house. It's a rough stone shelter hidden among the trees on the far side of the fence. These sorts of extravagances were being built just a couple of years after the famine when half the population was starving or leaving the country. The mansion now has a school housed in a rather unattractive modern wing and you can drive up and have a look.

Places to Stay & Eat

The Lodge (☎ 0502-32756), on Coote Terrace, is run by Mrs Wallis, who has four rooms with separate bathroom for IR£17/30 a single/double with breakfast. If you are hungry, the choice is fast food or pub food. *Phelan's Restaurant*, on Main St by the square, has reasonable burgers and chips.

Entertainment

On the pub front most of the action is in *Kavanagh's*, on the main square, which has live bands at the weekends. For music or a quiet drink in a traditional country pub, head out to the *Village Inn* in Coolrain just northwest of Mountrath. It has Irish music at weekends.

Getting There & Away

Mountrath is on the main Bus Éireann (☎ 01-836 6111) Dublin to Limerick route, with up to four buses a day going in each direction. The bus stop is in front of Darcy's.

SLIEVE BLOOM MOUNTAINS

One of the best reasons for visiting Laois is to explore the Slieve Bloom Mountains (Slieve is pronounced 'shleeve'). Their name means Mountains of Bladhma, after a Celtic warrior who used the mountains as a refuge.

CENTRAL SOUTH

Though they cannot compare for spectacle with their cousins in Wicklow and the west, the absence of visitors adds to their appeal. They are well signposted by the county council and you can't miss the brown signs on almost every road that leads to the hills.

The highest point is Mt Arderin (528 metres) south of the Glendine Gap on the border with Offaly. On a clear day it's possible to see the highest points of all four of the ancient provinces of Ireland. East is Lugnaquilla in Leinster, west is Nephin in Connacht, north is Slieve Donard in Ulster and south-west is Carrauntuohill in Munster.

Mountrath to the south and the lovely village of **Kinnitty** to the north of the hills are both good bases to work from. **Glenbarrow**, south-west of Rosenallis, has a gentle walk up by the River Barrow which has its source just a few km farther up in the hills. There are some waterfalls, a large moraine on the north side of the river and some unusual plants in the area, including orchids, butterwort and blue fleabane. Other spots worth checking out are **Glendine Park** near the Glendine Gap, and the **Cut** mountain pass. The road skirting north of the mountains from Mountmellick to Birr via Clonaslee and Kinnitty is particularly scenic.

Slieve Bloom Way

The Slieve Bloom Way is a 70-km signposted trail which does a complete circuit of the mountains taking in almost all the major points of interest. See the Activities chapter.

WEST LAOIS

South of the Slieve Bloom Mountains, **Borris-on-Ossory** on the N7 was once known as the Gate of Munster and was a major coaching stop in the 18th century before the railways developed. Borris-on-Ossory is on a Bus Éireann express Dublin to Limerick route, with up to six buses daily in each direction.

About three km farther west on the same road, **Ballaghmore Castle** (☎ 0505-21453) controlled the edges of the Fitzpatrick family lands. Ballaghmore means 'great way or

road'. It is one of several small castles which have opened their doors to the public. The square tower fortress dates from 1480 and has faithfully been restored. If you have good eyesight you may spot the *Sheila-na-gig* in the south wall. These fertility symbols, usually rough carvings of women displaying their genitals, are found all over the country but are usually quite hard to spot. Ballaghmore Castle is open daily; admission is IR£2.50/1.50.

ABBEYLEIX

Abbeyleix, 14 km south of Portlaoise, is as well tended a country town as you will find. The town grew around a 12th-century Cistercian monastery in nearby Old Town, though no traces of it remain. The town centre was moved to its present location in the 18th century by the local landowner, Lord de Vesci, and he supervised the layout of tree-lined streets, neat town houses and a fountain in the square.

Abbeyleix House, his mansion, was erected in 1773 from a design by James Wyatt and is two km south-west of town on the Rathdowney road, but it is not open to the public. In the local Catholic church, you can see carpets on display that were manufactured in Abbeyleix for the *Titanic*.

Getting There & Away

Abbeyleix is on an express Bus Éireann (☎ 01-836 6111) route between Dublin and Cork, with up to four buses daily. J J Kavanagh & Sons' private bus service (☎ 056-31106) has a daily Portlaoise, Abbeyleix, Durrow, Cullahill, Urlingford bus and another Friday-only service on the Carlow to Limerick run.

TIMAHOE

The tiny village of Timahoe is just a handful of houses around a grassy square, 10 km north-east of Abbeyleix on a minor road (R426). Seven roads converge just south of the village at a fine **round tower**. The 30-metre tower, with a large circumference of 17 metres, has a slight tilt and is all that remains of a 12th-century monastery. It now stands in the grounds of a converted Church of Ireland church. The tower has a beautifully worked Romanesque entrance some five metres above the ground which has carved human faces with beards. The ruins behind are of an associated church which was converted into a castle before falling into decay.

The church's 6th-century founder was St Mochúa, who, legend relates, had a wondrous pet fly which would parade on a book, keeping pace with the saint's reading and marking the lines so he would not lose track.

DURROW & CULLAHILL

In **Durrow**, about 10 km south of Abbeyleix at the junction of the N77 and N8, neat rows of houses surround a manicured green, which on the west side has an imposing gateway to Castle Durrow (1716). It's a large Palladian villa which is now in the hands of private owners and which you can see from the entrance avenue. Entry to the castle is by appointment only.

The attractive *Castle Arms Hotel* (☎ 0502 36117), on the square, charges IR£25 per person for B&B. There is a restaurant, and entertainment most weekends.

Cullahill is a tiny, well-kept hamlet on the main N77 road eight km south of Durrow. The *Sportsman Inn* (☎ 0502-37119) is an excellent place to pause and has the best bar food in the region, served from 10.30 am to 7 pm Monday to Saturday.

Getting There & Away

Durrow and Cullahill are on the main Dublin to Cork bus route and Durrow is served by up to four Bus Éireann (☎ 01-8366111) express coaches daily. There is no official stop at Cullahill, so you will need to check with the bus driver beforehand if he will drop you off there.

J J Kavanagh & Sons' private bus company (☎ 056-31106) has a daily service to Portlaoise, Abbeyleix, Durrow, Cullahill and Urlingford.

KILLESHIN CHURCH

Killeshin Church is a mere five km from Carlow Town. Killeshin used to be one of the biggest settlements in Laois and had one of the finest round towers in the country. It's said the tower was destroyed in the 18th century by a local farmer who was afraid it might collapse and kill his livestock.

The shattered 11th-century church is all that's left of Killeshin's ancient town and monastery. The church has a steeply arched Romanesque doorway bearing fine, intricate carvings of patterns and human heads.

County Offaly

Offaly is home to Clonmacnois, one of the most extensive and attractive monastic sites in the country. The county has the typical flat and boggy landscape of central Ireland, including the extensive Bog of Allen and Boora Bog between Ferbane and Kilcormac. The mighty River Shannon forms part of Offaly's border with Galway, while the Grand Canal also threads its way through the county. Offaly shares the Slieve Bloom Mountains with County Laois.

HISTORY

County Offaly produced a major archaeological surprise in 1977, when deep in Boora Bog slivers of flint called microliths were discovered. These had been used in the knives and weapons of the middle Stone Age, some 8000 to 9000 years ago. The find showed that nomads were living in the centre of Ireland around this time. After these hunter-gatherers came Ireland's first farmers. Offaly's extensive bogs would not have been attractive to them, the acid bog being unsuitable for agriculture, and few traces of them have been found.

Later on, the glacial ridges or *eskers*, standing well drained and dry above the surrounding peatlands, were used for ancient highways and settlements such as Clonmacnois. The early Christians liked the isolation and the protection afforded by the peatlands, but were virtually defenceless against the Vikings, who sailed up the River Shannon and attacked any settlement within reach.

During the Middle Ages, Offaly was a stronghold of the O'Connor, O'Carroll and O'Dempsey families, who used the landscape to their advantage, retreating into the bogs in time of trouble.

The modern shape of the county arose out of the plantations of 1556, when Offaly (King's County) and Laois (Queen's County) were shired or divided among subjects loyal to the crown. Originally, Daingean was the official county capital, named Philipstown after King Philip of Spain, Mary I's husband. But the town never really got going, unlike Tullamore and Birr, which became the two main settlements in Offaly.

BIRR

On the River Camcor, a small tributary of the River Shannon in the south-west of the county, Birr is Offaly's most attractive town. With formal, tree-lined avenues and Georgian terraces, Birr retains much of its 18th and 19th-century character. Many traditional shopfronts survive along Connaught and Main Sts, and all the main roads converge on Emmet Square, where a statue of the duke of Cumberland (victor of the Battle of Culloden) stood on the central column until 1925. In one corner is Dooly's Hotel dating from 1747, formerly a coaching inn on the busy route west. The buildings around Emmet Square are attractive and the central area of the square surrounding the column has been repaved. The square, however, would still benefit from some trees.

History

After starting life as a 6th-century monastic site founded by St Brendan of Birr, the town acquired an Anglo-Norman castle in 1208. The Gaelic O'Carroll family gained control of the castle and kept it until the 17th century. In the plantations of 1620, the O'Carroll family castle and the 580-hectare estate were handed over to Sir Laurence Parsons, and Birr became known as Parsonstown. Parsons

laid out streets, established a glass factory and issued decrees to the scruffy townspeople that anyone who 'cast dunge rubbidge filth or sweepings in the forestreet' was to be fined four pennies. Any woman who was caught working as a barmaid was to 'be set in the stocks by the constable for three whole market days'.

Later, the Parsons became earls of Rosse. The present earl and his wife still live on the estate, which has remained in the family for 14 generations.

Information

The tourist office (☎ 0509-20110), on Rosse Rowe, is housed in the building almost directly opposite the castle gates, and is open May to September from 10 am to 5.30 pm daily. Out of season the person in the castle ticket office just inside the gates has brochures and leaflets and may be able to help you with any queries. The post office is in the north-west corner of Emmet Square.

Birr Castle & Demesne

Most visitors to Birr come to see the castle and grounds, which are among the finest in Ireland. Most of the present structure dates from around 1620 when Sir Laurence Parsons was granted the estate. A later Laurence presided over alterations to the castle in the early 19th century, which left it almost exactly as you see it today. In 1820 the castle was fortified again after a local Protestant woman, Mrs Legge, convinced her brethren that the Catholics were going to rise up and kill them in their beds.

The demesne, which runs north from the castle, consists of 50 hectares of magnificent gardens set around a large artificial lake. The gardens hold over 1000 species of shrubs and trees from all over the world. Of particular interest is the collection from the Himalayas and China, brought back from the 6th earl's 1935 honeymoon in Peking. You will also find the tallest box hedges in the world, which were planted in the 1780s and now stand some 12 metres high. A catalogue of the plant collection is available at the entrance.

Birr Observatory & Telescope

The castle grounds hold one of the most impressive and extraordinary structures in Ireland. The third earl of Rosse, William Parsons (1800-67), wanted to build the biggest telescope in the world. The resulting 'leviathan of Parsonstown', a 72-inch (183-cm) reflector telescope completed in 1845, remained the largest in existence for 75 years, attracting astronomers and scientists from all over the world. The instrument was used to map the surface of the moon, and made a multitude of discoveries including the spiral galaxies. Amazingly, the telescope was built in Birr using local engineering and materials.

The Science Museum in London now has the telescope's huge 72-inch reflector, but the massive walls, 22 metres long and 16 metres high, remain. The telescope's 18-metre wooden tube is 2.5 metres in diameter and was controlled by an impressive mechanism of pulleys and cables, none of which remain in place. A detailed model is on hand, though. Also within the enclosure is a small exhibition on the history and achievements of the telescope, with a five-minute recorded talk by the British astronomer Patrick Moore.

This remarkable family (all of whom were educated at home) were not just stargazers. The next earl of Rosse, Lawrence Parsons, was just as bright as his father, and built a device to measure the heat given off by the moon. Charles Algernon Parsons, Lawrence's brother, invented the steam turbine for the earliest British iron battleships, while their mother, Mary Rosse, the third earl's wife, was a pioneer in 19th-century photography. ∎

Today the castle is the private home of Lord and Lady Rosse and is not open to casual visitors, although group visits may be possible if arranged well in advance. Enquiries should be directed to: Estate Office (☎ 0509-20056), Rosse Row, Birr, County Offaly. The gardens are open May to September from 9 am and 6 pm daily, and for the rest of the year from 9 am to 1 pm and 2 to 5 pm daily; admission is IR£3.20/1.60.

Other Attractions

There's a comprehensive Tourist Trail leaflet available at the tourist office and **Birr Heritage Centre**, which is on St John's Mall east of Emmet Square and is open April to September from 2.30 to 5.30 pm Monday to Saturday and from 3 to 5 pm Sunday. **St John's Mall** has John Henry Foley's 1876 statue to the 3rd earl of Rosse and a Russian cannon from the Crimean War. Nearby is the **Seffin Stone**, a megalithic stone found in an early Christian monastery and said to have marked the centre of Ireland. Some fine Victorian houses built between 1870 and 1878 are on the side of the square opposite the Birr Heritage Centre.

Emmet St, to the north of Emmet Square, meets **Oxmantown Mall** at St Brendan's

Church of Ireland. This mall is the town's prettiest, with a regiment of trees and the castle gates at the western end. The massive stone walls of the Birr Estate form the western limits of the town. South-west of the square are the remains of **Old St Brendan's Church**, reputed to be the site of the first settlement of St Brendan in the 6th century.

There is a fine **riverside walk** along the River Camcor from Oxmantown Bridge near the Catholic church, running east out to Elmgrove Bridge.

The **Birr Outdoor Education Centre** (☎ 0509-20029), Roscrea Rd, offers courses in walking, sailing, canoeing and rock climbing in the nearby Slieve Blooms. The centre also has an exhibition on the ecology of the mountains. The Birr Golf Club (☎ 0509-21184) has an 18-hole course.

Places to Stay

Hostel The nearest hostel is the *Crank House Hostel* in Banagher, 13 km to the north. (See that section later.)

B&Bs *Ard na Gréine* (☎ 0509-20256), in Hillside one km from Birr along the Roscrea road, and *Ard Abhainn* (☎ 0509-21257), a

CENTRAL SOUTH

good place in Riverstown two km along the Borrisokane road, charge IR£18.50/27 for singles/doubles, although Ard Abhainn is only open June to the end of November. B&Bs in town are not too cheap. The Georgian *Ormond House* (☎ 0509-20291), in Emmet Square, and *Stables* (☎ 0509-20263), in Oxmantown Mall, both charge from IR£20 for a room with bath.

Hotels The friendly *County Arms Hotel* (☎ 0509-20791) is walking distance from the centre on Railway Rd, which becomes the road to Roscrea. The 1810 house has various less-pleasing modern extensions but there is plenty of space, the rooms are well equipped and B&B costs IR£42/78 a single/double.

Originally a 1747 hunting lodge, *Dooly's* (☎ 0509-20032), on Emmet Square, is another good hotel. It has 18 comfortable rooms and B&B is IR£29/50.

Country Houses The 18th-century *Tullanisk House* (☎ 0509-20572) has delightful rooms on part of the Birr Estate. It's almost two km from Birr on the Banagher road up a long avenue on the right. B&B costs from IR£32 to IR£42.

Places to Eat
The *Castle Kitchen* is a lovely little place in the same building as the tourist office that does vegetarian dishes as well as the regular food. *Dooly's Hotel* (☎ 0509-20032) in Emmet Square has an excellent cafeteria-style coffee shop (open 10 am to 10 pm), and lunch is available at the bar from 12.30 to 2.30 pm, while the restaurant in the front of the hotel serves dinner.

North of the square and near the castle walls is the *Stables Restaurant* (☎ 0509-20263), in a converted mews on Oxmantown Mall. It serves a four-course dinner Tuesday to Saturday for IR£16 and lunch on Sunday; the food is straightforward but consistently good. The *County Arms Hotel* (☎ 0509-20791) does a good lunch in the bar and a more than acceptable dinner in the evenings for around IR£18.

Tullanisk House (☎ 0509-20572) blends old English and Far Eastern influences in a IR£22 set dinner (see Places to Stay).

Entertainment
Foster's Bar, on Connaught St at the back of Dooly's, is an old-style pub which gets a good crowd at weekends and usually has music. The *Palace Bar* on O'Connell St often has live bands at weekends. *Kelly's* is a locals' haunt, just off the square towards the castle. *Mary Walshe's Bar* has Irish music on Friday and Saturday nights. In Dooly's Hotel you'll find *Melba's Nite Club* open Saturday and Sunday nights.

Getting There & Away
The Bus Éireann stop is in Emmet Square. Call the tourist office or Athlone (☎ 0902-72651) for times. There is a single bus passing through on the Dublin to Portumna route and one daily each way between Cork and Athlone.

Kearn's Coaches (☎ 0509-20124/776) has services from Dublin and Tullamore through Birr to Portumna. There are three buses passing through Birr on Sunday, Monday and Friday, two on Saturday and one Tuesday to Thursday between Tullamore and Portumna. Up to two buses a day go from Portumna to Birr and Dublin. The bus stop is near the post office in Emmet Square.

Getting Around
P L Dolan & Sons (☎ 0509-20006), on the corner of Main St and Wilmer Rd, has good bikes for IR£8 a day. Kearn's Coaches (☎ 0509-20124/776) also has a taxi service.

LEAP CASTLE
South-east of Birr between Kinnitty and Roscrea (in Tipperary) are the remains of Leap Castle. It lies in one of the few areas of Offaly rich in pre-Christian ring forts and burial mounds, and the site has some good views of the Slieve Bloom Mountains.

The castle was originally an O'Carroll family residence, watching over a crucial route between Munster and Leinster, and was renowned for a 'smelly ghost'. It was said by locals to be one of the most haunted castles in Europe. The castle was destroyed in 1922 during the Civil War. The ruins consist of a blocky central tower sitting between two later lower wings.

There is no bus servicing this site.

SLIEVE BLOOM MOUNTAINS
It's a bit of an exaggeration to call them mountains, but the Slieve Blooms in the south-east of the county are little visited, and have moorlands, pine forests and hidden river valleys. It's a lovely journey from Birr to the hamlet of Kinnitty, the jumping-off point for the mountains. There's a good trip over the hills to Mountrath (County Laois), and a pleasant drive around the northern flanks of the hills between Kinnitty and Mountmellick (also in County Laois).

For more details see the County Laois section earlier.

RIVER SHANNON & THE BOGS
The River Shannon forms the border between Offaly and Galway until it veers off west to Lough Derg south of Banagher, and it dominates the region geographically and commercially. Towns like Banagher grew up beside the river when it was a busier highway than it is today.

The Grand Canal also threads its way through the county, entering to the east near Edenderry and passing through Tullamore before joining the River Shannon at Shannon Harbour, just north of Banagher.

Offaly has two extensive peatlands: the Bog of Allen in the east and Boora Bog in the west. The Bog of Allen is an enormous brown expanse that stretches over into Kildare and which – along with many of Offaly's other bogs – is being mined by the huge machines of the Bord na Móna (Irish Turf Board) for potting compost and briquettes for fuel. Some of Offaly's bogs, however – most particularly Clara Bog – are remarkably untouched, and these are internationally recognised for their plant and animal life.

BANAGHER & AROUND
The riverside town of Banagher, 12 km north of Birr, is one of the few crossing points of the River Shannon in this area. Going north, the next crossing point is at Athlone. Banagher has some pleasant pubs and restaurants and a busy marina, but is otherwise quiet.

Anthony Trollope was a post office clerk here in 1841, and wrote his first novels here. Charlotte Brontë spent her honeymoon here, and her husband, the Reverend Arthur Bell Nicholls, spent the rest of his life here after she died in England. Cuba Ave is named in honour of a local boy, George Frazer, who became governor of that island.

There is a tourist information desk (☎ 0509-51458) in Crank House on Main St. The post office is farther up Main St near the Brosna Lodge Hotel; the Bank of Ireland is beside the hotel.

Eskers
The flat bog lands in west Offaly have in many areas been prevented from draining off into the River Shannon by *eskers*. These are long, winding, glacial ridges made up of fossilised coarse sand and gravel deposits from meltwater rivers that ran underneath glaciers. Over time the vegetation built up layers of peat, as deep as 10 metres in places. The best known of these eskers is the Esker Riada, which translates as the Kings' Road; this great esker ran across much of the country and was used as the principal highway between Leinster and Connaught. You can still see parts of it today, near the main road to Dublin. Clonmacnois sits on part of this esker in the north-west corner of Offaly.

Esker is one of the few Irish words to enter the English language. ■

Things to See

About three km south of Banagher and 10 km north-west of Birr in Lusmagh near the confluence of the rivers Little Brosna and Shannon is **Cloghan Castle**. The well-preserved keep has an adjoining 19th-century house and protective walls. The owners have a fine flock of Jacob's sheep.

Cloghan Castle has been in use for nearly 800 years, starting life as a McCoghlan stronghold, and seeing over the ensuing centuries more than its fair share of bloodshed. The present owner, Brian Thompson, has brought together an interesting and varied assortment of antiques. Pride of place in the main hall goes to the enormous antlers of an Irish elk. At the end of the 45-minute tour, in the rustic dining room, the visitor can examine some Cromwellian armaments and marvel at just how heavy their breastplates were.

The castle is open May to September from 2 to 6 pm Wednesday to Saturday; admission is IR£3. There is no bus service here, but the owners will collect people from the Banagher tourist desk at the Crank House by prior arrangement.

Crank House, on Main St, is a locally run cooperative and, as well as the hostel, contains a tourist information desk, an exhibition room for local artists and a coffee shop. Also on the premises is the office of Crann (☎ 0509-51718), a non-governmental organisation set up to restore some of the deciduous trees that once covered much of Ireland. Visitors are invited to sponsor their own tree.

Seven km north-east of Banagher is **Cloghan**, where all six roads out of town lead into wide tracts of peat. Five km from Cloghan, on the road north-west to Shannonbridge, the 16th-century **Clonony Castle's** four-storey square tower is enclosed by an overgrown castellated wall. Local tales relate that Anne Boleyn, the second wife of Henry VIII, was born here, but that's unlikely. Her cousins Elizabeth and Mary Boleyn are buried beside the ruined tower.

On the County Galway side of the River Shannon is an early 19th-century **Martello Tower**. Eight km south of Banagher on the County Galway side is the delightful **Meelick Church**, one of the oldest in use in Ireland.

You can hire canoes from Shannon Adventure Canoeing Holidays (☎ 0509-51411), 21 Cuba Ave, for trips on the River Shannon or Grand Canal.

Places to Stay

The only hostel in the region is the excellent Crank House Hostel (☎ 0509-51458), Main

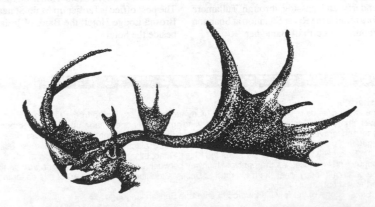

Antlers of the extinct giant Irish elk in the main hall of Cloghan Castle

St, which charges IR£7 a night in two and four-bed rooms and is open all year. There are several B&Bs in Banagher, the cheapest of which is *Ashling* (☎ 0509-51228), Cuba Ave, which has rooms with bath for IR£15/27 a single/double.

Getting There & Away
Kearn's Coaches (☎ 0509-20124/776) includes Banagher on its daily Portumna to Dublin service. Bus Éireann has a bus to Galway on Tuesday in July and August.

Getting Around
Kieran Doneghan (☎ 0509-51178) has a cycle shop on Main St near Crank House and rents bikes.

SHANNONBRIDGE
A narrow bridge crosses the river at this point into County Roscommon. Shannonbridge is an unremarkable little village except for a 19th-century **fort** on the west bank just up from the bridge, where heavy artillery was placed to bombard Napoleon, if he was cheeky enough to try to invade via the river. Part of the road north towards Clonmacnois runs along the top of the esker on which Clonmacnois is also built.

Just south of Shannonbridge, a 45-minute train tour on the **Clonmacnois & West Offaly Railway** (☎ 0905-74114) takes you through the Blackwater section of the Bog of Allen on the narrow-gauge line which used to transport the peat. During the nine-km trip, the bog landscape is explained in detail, with an emphasis on its special flora. The journey begins near the Bord na Móna Blackwater peat-fired power station which is visible for miles. Trips go on the hour from 10 am to 5 pm daily April to October, and cost IR£3/2.20. Tickets are available from the coffee shop.

CLONMACNOIS
Ireland's most important monastic site is superbly placed, overlooking the River Shannon from a ridge. It consists of a walled field containing numerous early churches, high crosses, round towers and graves. Many of the remains are in remarkably good condition and give a real sense of what these monasteries were like in their heyday. The site is surrounded by low marshy ground and fields known as the Shannon Callows. These are home to many wild plants and are one of the last refuges of a seriously endangered bird, the corncrake.

History
Clonmacnois (or Clonmacnoise) is roughly translated as 'Meadow of the sons of Nós', and its Irish name is *Cluain Mhic Nóis*. The glacial ridge called the Esker Riada on which it stands was once one of the principal cross-country routes between Leinster and Connaught. St Ciarán, the son of a chariotmaker, is said to have founded the site in 545 AD and died only seven months later after building the first church with the personal assistance of Diarmuid, the high king of Tara.

The monastery's beginning was humble, as only eight followers of Ciarán had set out with him, but it became an unrivalled bastion of Irish religion, literature and art. Between the 7th and the 12th centuries monks from all over Europe came to study and pray here. Clonmacnois was one of the reasons Ireland became known as the 'island of saints and scholars' while much of Europe languished in the Dark Ages. Such was Clonmacnois' importance that the high kings of Connaught and Tara were brought here for burial, and many lie in the cathedral, also known as the Church of Kings. The last high king of Tara, Rory O'Connor, who died in 1198, is among them.

Most of the remains date from the 10th to 12th centuries, as the earlier buildings of wood, clay and wattle have long since disappeared. The monks would have lived in small huts scattered in and around the monastery, which would probably have been surrounded by a ditch or rampart of earth. It was recorded that there were 106 houses and 13 churches here in 1179 when the site was ravaged by fire. These scattered Irish sites contrast with the strict layout and planning of many monasteries in continental Europe. The river became a deadly conduit when

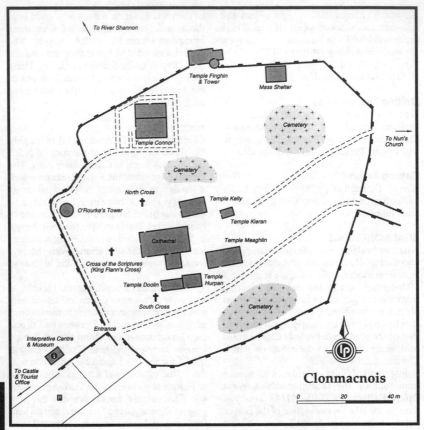

Viking raiders used it to penetrate right into the heart of Ireland. Clonmacnois was pillaged repeatedly between 830 and 1165 (records suggest on at least eight occasions). It must be said that the Vikings were by no means the only ones guilty of attacking the place; it was burned down at least 12 times between 720 and 1205 and attacked over 25 times by native Irish forces between 830 and 1165. After the 12th century, it went into decline and by the 15th century it was the home of a bishop of only minor importance. Its final destruction came at the hands of the English in 1552 when it was plundered by

the regiment based in Athlone: 'Not a bell, large or small, or an image, or an altar, or a book, or a gem, or even glass in a window, was left which was not carried away'.

Among the treasures which survived this continuous onslaught are the crozier of the abbots of Clonmacnois in the National Museum and the *Leabhar na hUidhre* ('The Book of the Dun Cow'), now in the Royal Irish Academy in Dublin.

Information

The OPW has a number of facilities including a museum, an interpretive centre

(☎ 0905-74195) and a coffee shop. There is also a tourist office (☎ 0905-74134) in the car park open April to October from 10 am to 1 pm and 2 to 6 pm.

Clonmacnois is open June to mid-September from 9 am to 7 pm daily; mid-September to October and mid-March to May from 10 am to 6 pm; and November to mid-March from 10 am to 5 pm. Visiting early or late will help you avoid the crowds. Admission is IR£2.50/1. An audiovisual show provides a good introduction to the site.

There are river cruises to Clonmacnois from Athlone in County Westmeath; see the Central North chapter for details.

High Crosses

In the compound are seven church buildings and three replicas of 9th-century high crosses (the originals are in the museum). The sandstone **Cross of the Scriptures** is the most richly decorated and has unique upward-tilted arms. Its west face depicts the Crucifixion, soldiers guarding Jesus' tomb and the arrest of Jesus. On the east face are scenes of St Ciarán and King Diarmuid placing the corner stone of the cathedral. It's also known as King Flann's Cross because a rough inscription on the base is said to attribute it to him. He died in 916 AD.

Nearer the river the **North Cross** dates from around 800 AD, but only the shaft remains, with lions, rich spirals and a single figure, thought to be the Celtic god Cerrunnos or Carnunas, who sits in a Buddha-like position. The two-headed snake is associated with him. The richly decorated **South Cross** has more carvings, including the Crucifixion on the west face.

Cathedral

The biggest building at Clonmacnois, the cathedral, or MacDermot's Church, was built in the 12th century, but incorporates part of a 10th-century church. Its most interesting feature is the intricate 15th-century Gothic doorway with carvings of St Francis, St Patrick and St Dominic and a badly worn Latin inscription which, roughly translated,

Cross of the Scriptures, Clonmacnoise

says: 'This doorway was erected for the eternal glory of God'.

The door is also known as the Whispering Door because a whisper carries from one side of it to the other. It is said that lepers would come here to confess; because of the door's unusual acoustic properties the priest was able to hear the confession from a safe distance.

Around the altar are said to be buried the last high kings of Tara: Turlough Mór O'Connor (died 1156) and his son Ruairí or Rory (died 1198).

Temples

The small churches are called temples, but the word is in fact a derivation of the Irish word *teampall*, meaning 'church'. Past the scant foundations of the **Temple Kelly** (1167) is the tiny **Temple Kieran**, less than four metres long and 2.5 metres wide. Also known as St Ciarán's Church, it is traditionally thought to be the burial place of St Ciarán, the site's founder; his hand was kept here as a relic until the 16th-century, but is now lost. The remarkable Crozier of the Abbots and a chalice are supposed to have been discovered in here in the 19th century.

The floor level in Temple Kieran is lower than outside because local farmers have for centuries been taking clay from the church to place in the four corners of their fields, where it is said to protect crops against an eelworm parasite and cattle against red-water disease. The floor was covered in slabs to stop further digging but the tradition continues in the early spring when handfuls of clay are taken from outside the church.

Near the south-west corner of the temple is a bullaun, or ancient grinding stone, which is reputed to have been used for making medicines for the monastery's hospital. Today the rainwater which collects in it is said to cure warts.

Continuing round the compound there is the 12th-century **Temple Meaghlin**, with its attractive windows, and the twin structures of **Temple Hurpan** and **Temple Doolin**. Doolin is named after Edmund Dowling, who repaired this church in 1689 and made it the family crypt. At the same time he may have restored Temple Hurpan, which is also known as Claffey's Church.

Round Towers

Overlooking the River Shannon is the truncated O'Rourke's Tower, a 20-metre tower named after the high king of Connaught, Fergal O'Rourke (died 964 AD). The top of the tower is said to have been blown apart by lightning in 1135, but the tower was used up to 1552. The top few levels of masonry are decidedly inferior to the rest.

Temple Finghin and its round tower are on the northern boundary of the site, also overlooking the Shannon. The quaint building, also known as MacCarthy's Church &

Tower, appears in most photographs of Clonmacnois and dates from around 1160 to 1170. It has some fine Romanesque carvings and the unusual miniature tower's cone roof has stones set in a herring-bone pattern. This is the only Irish round tower roof that has never been altered. Most round towers were used by monks for protection when their monasteries were attacked, but this one was probably used as a bell tower as the doorway is at ground level.

Other Remains

The **Temple Connor** is a little, roofed church still used by Church of Ireland parishioners on the last Sunday of the summer months. Beyond the boundary wall, a half km east through the modern graveyard, is the secluded **Nun's Church** with its fine Romanesque doorways. Above the west doorway is a Sheila-na-gig. West of the church is a cairn said to be the burial place of a servant of St Ciarán who, legend has it, was not allowed to be buried in the monastery graveyard after losing St Ciarán's dun cow.

West of the settlement on the ridge near the car park is a motte with a 13th-century **castle**, now in ruins. It is said to have been built by John de Grey, Bishop of Norwich, to watch over the Shannon.

Museum

The museum near the entrance consists of three beehive-like structures echoing the design of the early monastic dwellings. It contains the originals of the three principal high crosses described and various artefacts uncovered during excavation, including silver pins, beaded glass and an Ogham stone.

The museum and entrance buildings also contain many of Clonmacnois' 8th to 12th-century graveslabs. This is the largest collection of early Christian graveslabs in Europe. Many are in remarkable condition with inscriptions clearly visible, often starting with *oroit do* or *ar* meaning 'a prayer for'.

Places to Eat
The Clonmacnois interpretive centre has a tearoom serving good coffee, sandwiches and snacks.

Getting There & Away
Clonmacnois is seven km north of Shannonbridge and about 24 km south of Athlone. There is no public transport service directly to Clonmacnois.

CLONFINLOUGH STONE
Three km east of Clonmacnois, near Clonfinlough Catholic Church, is a curious limestone boulder half buried in the ground. Its surface is engraved with crosses and markings resembling human forms. They are thought to date from the Stone Age and the patterns resemble similar ones found in Spain and France. Some suggest the carvings depict a prehistoric battle. To get there find Clonfinlough Church; a rough path behind leads over fields to the stone.

TULLAMORE
Tullamore (*Tulach Mór*), Offaly's county town 80 km due east of Dublin on a nice stretch of the Grand Canal, is pleasant enough. Charleville Castle is the main attraction – there isn't much to the Irish Mist liqueur factory which is nominally another attraction. The market square and some of the old houses are attractive.

Founded in 1750 by the Bury family of Limerick, Tullamore soon superseded Philipstown (now Daingean) as the county capital. In 1785 a hot-air balloon crashed and started a fire that consumed hundreds of homes!

Information
The tourist office (☎ 0506-52617), open June to August from 10 am to 5 pm Monday to Friday, is on Bury Quay between the Irish Mist factory and the canal. In the same building as the tourist office is the Offaly Historical Archaeological Society (open from 9.30 am to 4 pm Monday to Friday), which may be able to help you when the tourist office is closed. The post office is on O'Connor Square, the main square in the town.

Continental Cleaners are 50 metres beyond the car park at the back of High St Mall.

Charleville Forest Castle
The great Gothic structure of Charleville Forest Castle (☎ 0506-21279) sits in a large estate a km to the west of the town centre on the Birr road. What some call a 'Gothic fantasy castle' with its spires and turrets was the family seat of the Burys, who in 1798 commissioned the design from Francis Johnston, one of Ireland's most famous architects.

From the entrance on Charleville Rd, south of town on the road to Limerick, there is a 1.5 km lane (take the right fork after you enter the gate) to the castle itself which is popular with joggers. (Tullamore Harriers is one of Ireland's premier running clubs.) The castle's interior has deteriorated although some of the rooms have been maintained and furnished. The Hutton-Burys are the present owners and intend to restore the property and turn it into a classy hotel.

Tours operate haphazardly between 11 am and 5 pm Wednesday to Sunday from June to September and weekends only in April and May – it's worth checking this with the tourist office first. The 30-minute tour costs IR£2.50/1.50 (students IR£2) and the castle grounds are also worth exploring.

Irish Mist Factory
The Irish Mist factory is beside the tourist office on Bury Quay. This internationally famous liqueur is a secret combination of herbs and spirits, only blended here. The Irish Mist Visitor's Centre has closed down, so you won't even get a sample tasting these days! There is, however, a movement afoot to have it reopened.

Cruises
Celtic Canal Cruisers (☎ 0506-21861) has boats available by the week from IR£256 for two people in the low season up to IR£1095 for nine people in the high season. You can

cruise west to the River Shannon joining it at Shannon Harbour or east to Edenderry, Laytown and down into the Grand Canal and River Barrow systems.

Getting There & Away

The Bus Éireann (☎ 0506-21431) stop is at the railway station, south of town on Western Relief Rd off Charleville Rd. From Tullamore there is one bus daily each way on the Dublin (1¾ hours) to Portumna (one hour) route, and one daily on the Waterford to Longford route. Kearn's Coaches (☎ 0509-20776) has three buses Monday, Friday and Sunday, two on Saturday and one Tuesday to Wednesday through from Tullamore on its Dublin to Portumna route.

There are seven trains daily to Dublin (one hour) and Galway (2¼ hours) on weekdays, and five at weekends.

Getting Around

You can hire bicycles from Buckley Cycles (☎ 0902-81606), on Brewery Lane, for IR£7/30 a day/week.

RAHAN

Eight km west of Tullamore at Rahan are the ruins of two old **chapels** with fine Romanesque carvings around the doorways. The Protestant church nearby is still used. Rahan is thought to be one of the earliest Christian sites in Ireland, founded by St Camelacus or St Cartage in the 7th century.

There is a lovely eight-km **walk** from Rahan along the Grand Canal to Tullamore. About three km from Rahan you will see the ruined remains of Ballycowan Castle and an aqueduct where the Brosna River flows under the canal.

DURROW ABBEY

St Colmcille (also known as St Columba) founded a monastery at Durrow Abbey in the 6th century, and the monastery's scriptorium later produced the 'Book of Kells', a Latin gospel now in Trinity College, Dublin. The book was kept here for over 800 years until the 16th-century dissolution of the monasteries, when it fell into the hands of a local

farmer. The book's bright illustrations survived being immersed in the farmer's cattle's drinking water to ward off evil spirits. In 1661 the local bishop handed it over to Trinity College.

The 'Book of Kells' fared better than the rest of the monastery. It was damaged in 1186 by Hugh de Lacy, who literally lost his head in the process, a local man taking exception to de Lacy using the monastery stones for a castle. The castle was being built on the fortified mound nearby.

Today, the site's only prominent structures are a Georgian mansion and a derelict 19th-century Protestant church; on a gloomy day, the bedraggled ivy-clad walls and gravestones do have a certain atmosphere. Some high kings of Tara are said to have been buried here including Donal (who died in 758) and a grandson of Brian Ború, Murcadh, who died in 1068. The ancient remains include St Colmcille's Well to the north-east of the church and a 10th-century high cross. On the east face of the cross are panels of King David, Abraham's sacrifice of Isaac and the Last Judgement, while the west face includes soldiers guarding Jesus' tomb, and the Crucifixion.

Durrow Abbey is seven km north of Tullamore down a long lane west off the N52 Kilbeggan road.

DAINGEAN

Daingean, once known as Philipstown, is on the Grand Canal 14 km east of Tullamore, and was the administrative centre for the plantation of Offaly (King's County) until Tullamore took over in 1834. Five km due north of Daingean near the hamlet of Croghan is **Croghan Hill**, an extinct volcano, which offers fine views of the surrounding bog, with some burial cairns and Bronze Age earthworks.

EDENDERRY

On the River Boyne bordering County Kildare and the Bog of Allen, Edenderry is 16 km north-east of Daingean. Edenderry sprang to life with the arrival of the Grand Canal in 1802, but its origins go back to the

TOM SMALLMAN

TOM SMALLMAN

TOM SMALLMAN

County Kilkenny

Top: The Marble City Bar, Kilkenny City
Middle: Kilkenny Castle & grounds, Kilkenny City
Bottom: House in Bennettsbridge

TOM SMALLMAN

TOM SMALLMAN

TOM SMALLMAN

TOM SMALLMAN

A	
B	C
D	

Central South
A: Emily Square, Athy, County Kildare
B: Market house & town square, Kildare Town
C: Ballaghmore Castle, County Laois
D: Clonmacnois monastic site, County Offaly

14th century and the de Berminghams, whose ruined **Carrickoris Castle** is seven km north of town on Carrick Hill. Three km north-west on the Rhode road is the scanty monastic site of **Monasteroris**. It was built for the Franciscans by John de Bermingham in 1325 to quell his conscience over his father's massacre of 32 local chieftains 20 years before in Carrickoris Castle. The name Edenderry came from the oakwoods that once blanketed the hills around the town. The local O'Connor family used to harry the English and retreat into the bogs that cover the region. There is a pleasant walk from the town hall along the canal towpath out to the Downshire Bridge.

Places to Stay & Eat
Bella Vista (☎ 0405-31179), on St Mary's Rd, has B&B with four rooms (shared bathroom) for IR£12 per person. There isn't a lot of choice for dining but *Eden Inn* and *An Cuán Cistin*, both on Main St, serve plain, dependable food all day for IR£3 to IR£4.

Entertainment
Popular pubs include *Patrick Larkin* on Main St which gets a good young crowd. *M Regan's* usually has bands at weekends while the *Huntsman* has American line dancing on Tuesday night.

Getting There & Away
Bus Éireann (☎ 01-836 6111) has up to four buses a day to Dublin (two on Sunday). A single daily bus goes to and from Tullamore.

County Clare

County Clare is almost a peninsula, with the Shannon Estuary cutting deep into its southern border and Galway Bay on the northern side. Wedged between Kerry and Galway, Clare's land is mostly poor, with a large sweep of limestone rock in the north of the county forming the famous Burren region.

Clare is in some ways unfortunate. It doesn't get the good press of either Kerry or Galway, although it has special charms of its own. There is some spectacular scenery, particularly around the Cliffs of Moher, and the attraction of the Burren grows with every visit. This limestone landscape has countless monuments, castles and rare flowers, and there are some wonderful walks.

Many of Clare's towns and villages have resisted plastic-sign disease as well as the prettification that you see in many more heavily touristed places. Ennis, Clare's county town, retains its charming narrow streets, while villages like Ennistymon have many of their old shops and pubs – the latter often hosting traditional music sessions on long summer evenings. The county has some 250 castles in various stages of preservation: Knappogue near Quin and the famous tower house at Bunratty, which holds 'medieval banquets', are fine examples. There's scuba diving at Kilkee, Doolin and Fanore, excellent rock climbing at Ballyreen near Fanore, and caving all over the Burren.

A couple of villages have become havens for particular types of visitor. Doolin attracts music lovers and backpackers, while genteel Ballyvaughan has become a weekend retreat for a wealthier bunch.

The shortest route to Clare if you're travelling up the coast is via the car ferry between Killimer and Tarbert. See the Killimer section for details. Shannon Airport in Clare is Ireland's second-largest airport (see the Shannon Airport section).

Highlights
- The spectacular Cliffs of Moher
- The pub music scene in the village of Doolin
- Walking all or part of the 45-km Burren Way and/or the 3-hour walk to Hag's Head
- Walking and cycling in the Burren and viewing the Poulnabrone Dolmen, especially at sunset or early in the morning
- Bunratty Castle – despite the kitsch

Ennis & Around

ENNIS
Ennis (*Inis*), Clare's principal town, is a busy market centre with a population of 16,000. It lies on the banks of the River Fergus which runs south into the Shannon Estuary. The town's medieval origins can be seen in the narrow streets, and there are many old shops and pubs. The friary, founded in the 13th century, is its most important historic site. Ennis is the cathedral town for the Catholic diocese of Killaloe.

History
The O'Briens, kings of Thomond, built a castle here in the 13th century and were also

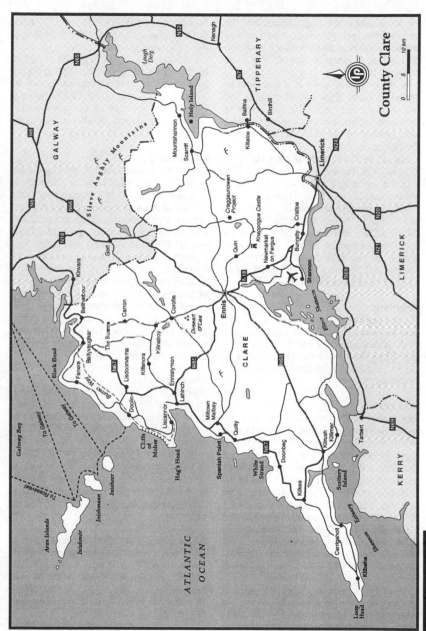

County Clare

the force behind the impressive friary, the town's principal attraction. Much of the wooden town was destroyed by a great fire in 1249 and again by one of the local O'Briens in 1306.

In the centre of town is a memorial to Daniel O'Connell, whose election to the British Parliament by a huge majority in 1828, forced Britain to lift its bar on Catholic MPs and led to the 1829 Act of Catholic Emancipation.

Eamon de Valera was MP for Clare from 1917 to 1959. There is a bronze statue to him near the courthouse and a small De Valera Museum on Harmony Row (no admission fee), which also houses extraneous material like the shovel used by Parnell to turn the first sod of the West Clare Railway in 1885 and a ship's door from the Spanish Armada. The museum is open all year from 11 am to 5.30 pm on Monday and Thursday, and 11 am to 8 pm on Tuesday, Wednesday and Friday.

Orientation
The old town centres on O'Connell Square, and the principal streets – O'Connell St, High St (becoming Parnell St), Bank Place and Abbey St – fan out from here. The large but not particularly attractive cathedral is on O'Connell St.

Information
The tourist office (☎ 065-28366) is a 20-minute walk outside Ennis, on the N18 road to Limerick and Shannon. There is no bus. If leaving town it is on the left side of the road just before the West County hotel. Money can be changed here. From mid-May to the end of September it's open daily from 9 am to 6 pm. The rest of the year the hours are 9.30 am to 5.15 pm, Monday to Saturday and closed from 1 to 2 pm. The location suits those with vehicles. In town local tourist information is available from Upstairs Downstairs (☎ 065-41670) at O'Connell Square.

The GPO is on Bank Place, north-west of O'Connell Square. Ennis Bookshop on Abbey St is excellent. Apart from the banks you can also change money at McMahon's

Insurances (☎ 065-28307) on O'Connell Square. Ennis Hospital (☎ 065-24464) is along the Galway road.

On Saturdays, there is a market at the Old Market Place. For general shopping, use the huge Dunnes supermarket which can be entered half way down O'Connell St. Perhaps the success of the supermarket accounts for all the derelict shops along Parnell St.

Ennis Friary
Ennis Friary was founded by Donnchadh O'Brien, king of Thomond, sometime between 1240 and 1249, though a lot of the present structure was completed in the 14th century. Partly restored, it has an impressive five-section east window and a McMahon tomb (1460) with alabaster panels depicting scenes from the Passion, including the Entombment of Christ. At the height of its fame in the 15th century, the friary was one of Ireland's great centres of learning, with over 300 monks in residence. Being an OPW site there are often the usual informative guided tours. It's open late May to late September daily from 9.30 to 6.30 pm. The entrance fee is IR£1/40p.

Places to Stay
Hostels The IHH *Abbey Tourist Hostel* (☎ 065-22620) on Harmony Row is a stone's throw from the O'Connell monument. It's an excellent place with 90 beds from IR£5.50 a night.

The *Walnut House Hostel* (☎ 065-28956) is older, run-down and nowhere near as spruce as its rival in town. A single bed with no breakfast is IR£8, B&B is IR£22 in double rooms. It's on O'Connell St, past the cathedral.

B&Bs Ennis is not short of guesthouses. In Ennis town, near the Quinnsworth shopping centre just off Francis St, is *Avonlea* (☎ 065-21632) on Clon Rd. Good rooms all with bathrooms are IR£19/28. *Ardlea House* (☎ 065-20256) on Clare Rd has rooms from IR£18/28.

Clare Manor House (☎ 065-20701) is

Ennis

0   75   150 m

To N68, Kilrush,
& Killimar
Car Ferry

To N18, West County Hotel,
Limerick, Shannon Airport,
Bunratty Castle & Tourist Office

To Quin, Knappogue
Castle & Craggaunowen

PLACES TO STAY

2 Avonlea B&B
4 Abbey Tourist Hostel
8 Queen's Hotel
27 Old Ground Hotel
28 Walnut House Hostel
32 Ardlea B&B

PLACES TO EAT

5 Cloister Pub & Restaurant
7 Cruise's Pub & Restaurant
11 Considine's Bar
15 La Fontana Restaurant
16 Bewley's Coffee Shop
21 Coffee Brook Café
22 Silver House Restaurant

PUBS

14 Ciaran's Bar

20 Woody's Bar
23 Brogan's Bar
24 PJ Kelly's Bar
25 Usual Place
29 Brandon's Bar

OTHER

1 Ennis Courthouse
3 De Valera Museum
6 Ennis Friary
9 St Columba's Church
10 Post Office
12 Tierney's Bike Hire
13 Ennis Bookshop
17 Upstairs Downstairs
18 O'Connell Monument
19 Franciscan Friary
26 Dunnes Shopping Centre
30 Ennis Cathedral
31 Cinema
33 Railway & Bus Station

about 1.5 km along the Limerick road. The six rooms, all with bathrooms, are IR£20/32 for singles/doubles. *Laurel Lodge* (☎ 065-21560) is on the right-hand side along Clare Rd and has doubles for IR£32.

Two km from Ennis on Tulla Rd is *Newpark House* (☎ 065-21233), a 300-year-old country house with excellent breakfasts, and good value with rooms from IR£20/35. To get there go along the Scarriff road and turn right at the Amber Inn.

Hotels The *Old Ground Hotel* (☎ 065-28127) is on Station Rd near the centre of

town where rooms are IR£80/100. On Abbey St the comfortable *Queen's Hotel* (☎ 065-28963) is a notch below the Old Ground with rooms from IR£40/60.

The other two hotels are out of town. The *West County Inn* (☎ 065-28421), just south of Ennis on the road to Limerick, has B&B from IR£72 excluding breakfast, and the *Auburn Lodge* (☎ 065-21247), which is just north of Ennis on the road to Galway, has B&B from IR£40/60.

If you fancy a luxurious manor house in the country, *Carnelly House* (☎ 065-28442) is five km north of Ennis in Clarecastle. B&B

CLARE

is a mere IR£73 a night per person and dinner is IR£28 or more per person.

Places to Eat

Cafés & Takeaways *Bewley's* has a branch on Bank Place near High St and the coffee and light meals are usually excellent. Another good lunch time place is the *Coffee Brook* in Market St. Both are closed in the evenings. *Enzo's* is a good burger place at 32 Abbey St. *Considine's Bar* at 26 Abbey St has a reasonable coffee shop with food all day.

Pubs & Restaurants Have a look at *Cruise's Pub & Restaurant* (☎ 065-41800) near the friary, full of old-world charm and superb for a drink and a meal. Bar food is served until late at night and the restaurant opens for lunch and dinner.

Brogan's pub at 24 O'Connell St has good bar food; a three-course lunch will cost you IR£5. Near Brogan's, *Brandon's Bar* has similar fare, in the IR£5 to IR£9 range. The *Old Ground Hotel* is a huge old place with lunches at tables in the bar. Rock solid Irish fare – cabbage and piles of spuds – costs around IR£5 in a comfortable setting. Further up O'Connell St, *Silver House* is a Chinese restaurant with dishes around IR£6.

Howley's pub-cum-restaurant (☎ 065-29923) on Parnell St serves very good food; dinner will cost you IR£20 or more. *La Fontana* Italian restaurant (☎ 065-41458), is also on scruffy Parnell St; an unlikely setting for a smart upmarket establishment serving dinner around IR£18 from 6 pm seven days a week and lunch on Sunday.

Cloister's Pub & Restaurant (☎ 065-29521) on Abbey St near the friary is one of Ennis's best restaurants. It's also the most expensive, charging from IR£25 per person for dinner. They also do excellent meals in the bar from noon to 10 pm from IR£5.

Entertainment

As capital of a renowned music county, Ennis is not short of good music pubs. *Brogan's* pub is one of the best known and has sessions on Tuesday.

Ciaran's Bar is a small but very cosy place near the Queen's Hotel on Francis St. It's popular with the local football crowd, and has Irish music on Thursday, Friday and Saturday. *Woody's* pub up Parnell St is a little out from the town centre, and has rock music and a trendy crowd. The *Usual Place* pub in the market is an old-style local.

Brandon's Bar has live music some nights as does *P J Kelly's Bar* at 5 Carmody St. *Considine's* on Parnell St has occasional Irish sessions and don't be put off the schizophrenic decor. The exterior looks suitably traditional but leads into a gross plastic area – fortunately, there's an authentic Irish bar at the other end!

One km along the Gort road north of town is a low wooden music hall, *Cois Na hAbhna* (☎ 065-20996), where *ceilidhs* (sessions of traditional music and dancing) are held every Wednesday night, June to September from 8.30 to 11.30 pm. It also sells tapes, books and records.

Getting There & Away

Train For regular trains, Limerick (☎ 061-418666) is the nearest station. There are, however, various special shopping trains that leave Ennis Railway Station (☎ 065-40444) for Dublin via Limerick. Check with the station as times vary.

Bus The Bus Éireann depot (☎ 065-24177) is at the railway station. Buses run from Limerick to Ennis (35 minutes) six times a day. There is a direct service to and from Dublin (4½ hours) on weekdays, six buses to and from Galway (two hours), four a day to and from Cork (three hours) and 15 a day to Shannon Airport (30 minutes).

Getting Around

Michael Tierney (☎ 065-29433) at 17 Abbey St is part of the Raleigh Rent-a-Bike scheme and has well-maintained mountain bikes for IR£7 a day or IR£30 a week plus deposit. TMT Rentals (☎ 065-24211) at 71 O'Connell St can fix you up with anything from a car to a motor home.

AROUND ENNIS

To the north of Ennis is the early Christian site of Dyseart O'Dea. To the south-east are castles, theme parks and other attractions. East of Ennis, the countryside rolls gently to the River Shannon and Lough Derg while west the farms get smaller and the land poorer as you approach the Atlantic. Shannon International Airport is 22 km to the south-east.

Getting Around

There are local and express buses covering most areas around Ennis but the frequency of service is hugely variable. Many buses run only in summer and on certain days, so you would be best to confirm times and destinations with Ennis bus station (☎ 065-24177).

The express service running between Limerick and Galway can sometimes be picked up in Ennis to get to Clarecastle, Newmarket-on-Fergus and Bunratty. A bus service also operates to Limerick via Clarecastle and Newmarket-on-Fergus.

A summertime weekday service travels north-west to Ennistymon and then south along the coast to Kilkee.

Dyseart O'Dea

Nine km north of Ennis on the road to Corofin is Dyseart O'Dea, where St Tola founded a monastery in the 8th century. The church and High Cross – known as the White Cross of Tola – date from the 12th or 13th century. The cross depicts Daniel in the Lions' Den on one side and a crucified Christ above a bishop carved in relief. Look for the carvings of animal and human heads on the south doorway of the Romanesque church. There are also the remains of a round tower.

In 1318, the O'Briens and the de Clares of Bunratty fought a pitched battle nearby, which the O'Briens won, thus postponing the Anglo-Norman conquest of Clare. O'Dea Castle nearby has a museum and interpretive centre and is open May to September from 10 am to 6 pm; admission is IR£1.80.

Getting There & Away In July and August, there is a daily bus from Monday to Friday

coming from Limerick, which leaves Ennis for Corofin and Ennistymon at 2.15 pm, passing by Dyseart O'Dea en route. During the rest of the year, a bus heads out of Ennis on the same route on weekdays only. Phone the Bus Éireann depot at Ennis for specific details.

Quin

Quin, a tiny village 11 km east of Ennis, was the site of Ireland's greatest find of prehistoric gold, the Great Clare Find of 1854. While working on the Limerick to Ennis railway, labourers uncovered a huge hoard of Celtic gold. Sadly, very few of the several hundred torcs, gorgets and other pieces made it to the National Museum in Dublin; most were sold and melted down. The source of this and much of ancient Ireland's gold may have been the Wicklow Mountains.

Quin Abbey Surrounded by fresh green countryside, Quin's Franciscan friary was founded in 1433 using part of the walls of an older de Clare castle built in 1280. An elegant belfry rises above the main body of the abbey and you can climb the narrow spiral staircase and look down on the very fine cloister and surrounding countryside.

Despite many periods of persecution, Franciscan monks lived here until the 19th century. The last friar, Father Hogan, who died in 1820 is buried in one corner. Another occupant is the impressively named Fireballs McNamara, a notorious duellist and member of the region's ruling family. McNamara castles dot the surrounding countryside. Just beside the friary is a 13th-century Gothic church, St Finghin's.

Knappogue Castle

Knappogue Castle, three km south of Quin, was built in 1467 by the McNamaras. They held sway over a large part of Clare from the 5th to mid-15th centuries and built 42 castles in the region. Knappogue's huge walls are intact, and it has a fine collection of period furniture and fireplaces.

When Oliver Cromwell came over from England in 1649 to subdue the Irish, he used

Knappogue as a base while he was in the area; one of the reasons it was spared destruction. The McNamara family regained the castle after the Restoration in 1660, when many old Irish families had their estates returned to them.

Knappogue Castle is open from mid-April to October, between 9.30 am and 5.30 pm. Admission is IR£2.50/1.30. It has a small souvenir shop in the courtyard.

It also hosts **medieval banquets** (☎ 061-360788), from May to October – usually twice-nightly, but depending on demand. The times are 5.30 and 8.45 pm and the cost is IR£29.90. See the Bunratty section for more details. Knappogue, unlike Bunratty, lays on knives and forks.

Craggaunowen Project

Six km east of Quin, the Craggaunowen Project includes recreated ancient dwelling places such as a crannóg and ring fort; real artefacts like a 2000-year-old oak road, and related items such as Tim Severin's leather boat the *Brendan*, which crossed the Atlantic in 1976-77.

Craggaunowen Castle itself is a small and well-preserved McNamara fortified house. The Craggaunowen Project is open mid-March to November from 10 am to 6 pm, latest admission 5 pm. The entry fee is IR£3.50/2.75. They have a nice little restaurant for light snacks or lunch. Cullaun Lake nearby is a popular boating and picnic spot with forest trails.

Dromoland Castle

Just north of Newmarket-on-Fergus is Dromoland Castle (☎ 061-368144), a magnificent building and one of Ireland's best hotels. It sits in 220 hectares of vast and beautiful gardens by the River Fergus. Inside, oak panels and silken fabrics adorn every wall. B&B at IR£254/268 is beyond most travellers' budgets, but venture in for a drink in the bar.

Mooghaun Ring Fort In Dromoland Demesne are the remains of one of Europe's largest Iron Age hill forts: three circular

earthen banks enclosing some 13 hectares. The fort's occupants may have been the owners of the huge gold hoard uncovered nearby in Quin in 1854. Access to the fort is through Dromoland Forest which is signposted off the Newmarket to Dromoland road.

East & South-East Clare

Clare's eastern boundary is formed by the River Shannon and Lough Derg, the Republic's largest lake, which stretches some 48 km from Portumna in Galway, to just south of Killaloe. Farther south the road between the two towns swings past the lake through some gentle countryside and picturesque hamlets like Mountshannon. From high ground, there are panoramic views across the lake to the Silvermine Mountains in Tipperary.

East Clare is fishing and shooting country, and the villages on the eastern shores of Lough Derg are favoured by hunting types.

South East Clare is visually unremarkable compared with the county's Atlantic coastline or the lakeside scenery north of Killaloe. Most people pass through quickly, taking in diversions like **Bunratty Castle**, **Quin Abbey** or Cratloe's ancient oakwoods. Twenty-four km west of Limerick City is Shannon Airport, until recently the arrival and departure point for transatlantic flights to Ireland.

SHANNON AIRPORT

Shannon, Ireland's second airport, sits in the apparent wilderness of South-East Clare. Like Gander Airport in Newfoundland, Shannon Airport used to be a vital link in the transatlantic air route, as piston-engined planes barely had enough range to make it across the ocean. If you come through Shannon, the extensive runways and numerous departure gates are reminders of a prosperous past. It is said that Irish coffee (a healthy slug of whiskey in a strong coffee) was invented at Shannon Airport for early transatlantic passengers.

Duty-Free
The world's first duty-free when it opened in 1947, Shannon has a huge stock of Irish and international goods. It's worth a browse and is a good place to rid yourself of any leftover cash. However, prices for international goods – jewellery, perfumes etc – are the same as in any duty-free, while Irish tweeds, pottery, clothes and crystal cost the same (if not less) in any high street shop.

Information
There is a tourist office (☎ 061-471664, 471665) in the arrivals hall, open 6 am until 6 pm daily. For flight information, phone ☎ 061-471444. The Bank of Ireland counter is open from the first flight until 5.30 pm.

Places to Stay
B&Bs The nearest hostels are in Limerick and Ennis. There are plenty of B&Bs five km from the airport in Shannon and 11 km away in Bunratty. Only 400 metres from Shannon town centre is *Moloney's B&B* (☎ 061-364185) at 21 Coill Mhara St, down a quiet cul-de-sac, with two doubles for IR£27 and IR£30. Less than three km from the airport, on a hill overlooking the estuary is the stylish, modern *Lohan's B&B* (☎ 061-364268) at 35 Tullyglass Crescent, Shannon, charging IR£20/30.

Hotels The comfortable *Great Southern Hotel* (☎ 061-471122), directly in front of the airport terminal, costs IR£44 per person, excluding breakfast.

On the road into Shannon town is the *Oak Wood Arms Hotel* (☎ 061-361500), with B&B from IR£50/80. For more accommodation, see the sections on Bunratty, Ennis and Newmarket-on-Fergus.

Places to Eat
The airport has the café-style *Courtyard* and the more upmarket *Lindbergh Room*, but it's worth going to Shannon Town, where *Mr Pickwick's* (☎ 061-364290) is a cheap and

cheerful place offering a full Irish breakfast for IR£2.25, a set lunch for IR£3.75 and dinner for IR£11.95, as well as a three-course tourist dinner for IR£7.95. In the town centre, the *Terrace Bar* in the Shannon Knights Inn does reasonable bar food.

Getting There & Away
Air Aer Lingus (☎ 061-471666), Ryanair (☎ 061-471444), Delta (☎ 061-471837) and Aeroflot (☎ 061-472299) operate from Shannon.

Bus There are 13 Bus Éireann buses a day to Ennis; nine on Sundays. The ticket office (☎ 061-474311) in the airport opens at 7 am, the first bus leaves at 8 am and the fare is IR£5. There are also services to Limerick (six daily, 40 minutes, IR£3.50), Galway (three daily, one hour 50 minutes, IR£10) and Dublin (one daily, leaving at 8.05 am, IR£10).

Taxi A taxi locally will cost you about IR£1 a mile plus a pickup charge. A taxi to Limerick costs about IR£17, with possible extra charges for luggage or unsocial hours.

BUNRATTY
Bunratty (*Bun Raite*) overlooks the Shannon Estuary. The castle is in excellent condition and well worth a look, but it's a prime tourist attraction and is besieged by coach tours in summer. With an attendant Folk Park and Durty Nelly's pub nearby, the area is starting to resemble a medieval theme park. The historical reality is in danger of being mistaken for a Disney-world creation. Go early in the day.

Bunratty Castle
The Vikings built a fortified settlement at this spot, a former island surrounded by a moat. Then came the Normans: Thomas de Clare built the first stone structure on the site in the 1270s. The present castle is the fourth or fifth structure to occupy the location beside the romantically named River Ratty.

The castle was built in the early 1400s by the ubiquitous McNamara family, but fell shortly afterwards to the O'Briens, kings of Thomond, in whose possession it remained until the 17th century. Admiral Penn, father of William Penn, founder of Pennsylvania, resided here for a short time.

In modern times, a complete restoration was carried out, and today the castle's magnificent Great Hall holds a very fine collection of 14th to 18th-century furniture, paintings and wall hangings. Combined admission to the castle (☎ 061-361511) and Folk Park is IR£4.50/2, open daily 9.30 am to 5.30 pm in the winter and 7 pm in the summer.

Bunratty Medieval Banquets
Today, Bunratty Castle's Great Hall hosts 'medieval banquets' (☎ 061-360788, or Freephone 1-800-269811), replete with comely maidens playing the harp, court jesters cracking corny jokes, food à la Middle Ages (a pale imitation) all washed down with mead, a kind of honey wine much favoured by the Irish in times gone by. You eat with your fingers. A seat at the banquet table will set you back IR£29.90 and they are heavily booked with coach parties. The whole thing is stage Irish but taken in spirit can be quite fun.

The banquets at Knappogue and Dunguaire castles are generally smaller, quieter and often more pleasant. All run two banquets each night during the summer at 5.30 pm and 8.45 pm.

Bunratty Folk Park
Bunratty Folk Park is a reconstructed traditional Irish village, with cottages, a forge and working blacksmith, weavers weaving and buttermakers making butter. There is a complete village street with post office, pub and small café, some of them transplanted from the the site of Shannon Airport. Agricultural machinery buffs will find a good collection here in Bunratty House overlooking the Folk Park.

Every evening between May and September, **Shannon Ceilidhs** are held in the Folk Park, serving up music, dancing, Irish stew, apple pie and soda bread. It's meant to demonstrate how the peasants passed their time while the gentry gorged themselves in the safety of their castles. The cost is IR£25.90 per person and there are ceilidhs every evening at 5.30 pm and 8.45 pm. For bookings ring the same numbers as for the medieval banquets.

Places to Eat
If you are hungry and looking for quantity at reasonable prices, hotels like the *Bunratty Castle* do a huge lunch for around IR£8, which will keep you going for the day. *Durty Nelly's* (☎ 065-364861), the gaily coloured pub beside the castle, has fairly good bar food and also houses two restaurants. The *Oyster* downstairs is open from noon to 10 pm and the *Loft* upstairs from 6 to 10 pm. Both are fine, with main courses from IR£12 to IR£15.

In the Folk Park, *Mac's* pub does light meals. *Avoca Cottage Café*, in Avoca Handweavers just down the road from the castle, does excellent lunches. Meals in both are around IR£5. *Truffles Restaurant* (☎ 061-36117) in the Fitzpatrick Bunratty Shamrock Hotel is a good hotel restaurant, with dinner costing around IR£20.

MacCloskey's (☎ 065-364082) in Bunratty House Mews is the best and most expensive restaurant in the area. Dinner costs IR£25 or more a head, but the food, with mostly Irish ingredients, is top class.

Entertainment
Durty Nelly's was built in the early 1600s, and the atmosphere is laid on by the shovel load. A peat fire burns in front of rough wooden chairs and benches. It can be good fun and does attract a local crowd as well as visitors. There is music most evenings.

Mac's pub in the Folk Park has Irish music on Wednesday and Friday evenings and is accessible even after the Folk Park is closed.

Things to Buy
Avoca Handweavers beyond the Fitzpatrick Bunratty Shamrock Hotel do a good selection of tweeds, crafts and woollen suits. Opposite the same hotel is Sweaters Galore with every conceivable Irish jumper

(sweater). Mike McGlynn Antiques is worth a look, as is Bunratty Cottage Antiques near the castle. Along the Limerick to Shannon road is Ballycasey Craft Workshops, home to weavers, silversmiths, leatherworkers and potters.

Getting There & Away
The bus stop for Bunratty is outside the Fitzpatrick Bunratty Shamrock Hotel. Bunratty is on the main Limerick to Galway road so there are plenty of express services in both directions. From Limerick bus & railway station (☎ 061-313333), express buses leave on weekdays between 9 am and 5 pm (afternoons only on Sunday).

Buses travelling south through Bunratty leave Ennis Railway Station (☎ 065-24177) daily from noon onwards. Bunratty is also served by the numerous daily buses on the Shannon Airport to Limerick route.

Getting Around
Bikes can be hired at Hanrahan's (☎ 061-361696), 12 Firgrove, Hurlers Cross, almost four km north of Bunratty on the main road to Ennis.

CRATLOE
Three km from Bunratty just north of the main road to Limerick is Cratloe, a picturesque village overlooking the Shannon estuary. Nearby are hills covered in oak forest – a rare sight in Ireland today, although it once blanketed the countryside. The oak roof beams of Westminster Hall in London are supposedly from Cratloe. To reach the woods, go along the Kilmurry road from Cratloe, under a railway bridge and turn right. There are some fine walks in the area and views over the estuary from Woodcock Hill.

Places to Stay
Cratloe has a fair selection of guesthouses. *Cratloe Heights* (☎ 061-357253), Ballymorris, charges from IR£18/28. The *Grange* (☎ 061-357389), similarly priced, is on the Grange Wood road two km off the main Limerick road; turn north at the Limerick Inn Hotel.

Getting There & Away
While there is no bus service directly to Cratloe, there are plenty of buses passing through Bunratty nearby. Visitors can hire a bike in Bunratty (see the Getting Around section for Bunratty earlier) or walk out to Cratloe.

KILLALOE & AROUND
Killaloe (*Cill Dalue*) is one of the principal crossings on the River Shannon, and a fine old 13-arched bridge spans the river. On the Tipperary side of the bridge, Killaloe's other half is called Ballina and some of the best pubs and restaurants are on that side. From Killaloe, the Shannon is navigable all the way up to Lough Key in County Sligo, and in summer the town buzzes with weekend sailors.

The town itself has a fine setting, with the Slieve Bearnagh hills rising abruptly to the west, the Arra Mountains to the east and Lough Derg right on its doorstep.

Orientation & Information
The narrow street running from the river on the Killaloe side is Bridge St, which turns right becoming Main St. The tourist office (☎ 0619-376866) is right beside Shannon Bridge.

Killaloe Cathedral
This cathedral, which is also known as St Flannan's Cathedral, dates from the 12th century and was built by the O'Brien family on top of an earlier 6th-century church. Take a look at the carvings around the Romanesque doorway, which dates from an older chapel; these carvings are among the finest in the country.

Near the doorway, the early Christian Thorgrim Stone is unusual in that it bears both the old Scandinavian runic script and Irish Ogham script. It could be the gravestone of a converted Viking. In the cathedral grounds is St Flannan's Oratory, of 12th-century Romanesque design.

Mountshannon
North of Killaloe, on the south-western shores of Lough Derg, Mountshannon is an

CLARE

idyllic 18th-century village. Its stone houses overlook the lake, while anglers pass the evenings in pubs, discussing the day's catch. With luck, you will find Irish music in summer.

The small stone harbour is usually busy with fishing boats and is the port for trips to Holy Island, one of Clare's finest early Christian settlements.

Holy Island

From Mountshannon, there are boats to Iniscealtra or Holy Island, the site of a monastic settlement thought to have been founded by St Cáimín in the 7th century. Here you'll see a round tower which is over 27 metres tall, despite being minus its top storey. You'll also find four old chapels, a hermit's cell and some early Christian gravestones dating from the 7th to the 13th century. One of the chapels has an elegant Romanesque arch; inside the chapel there's an inscription in Irish, which translated reads 'Pray for Tornog who made this cross'.

The Vikings gave this monastery a rough time, but under the subsequent protection of Brian Ború and others it flourished. The Holy Well was once the focus for a lively festival, which was banned in the 1830s because a lot of nonreligious behaviour was creeping in.

Other Sights

The journey north on either side of Lough Derg to Mountshannon or Portroe is very scenic. About 1.5 km north of Killaloe, **Beal Ború** is an earthen mound or fort said to have been Kincora, the palace of the famous Irish king, Brian Ború, who defeated the Vikings at the Battle of Clontarf in 1014. Traces of Bronze Age settlement have been found. With its commanding view over Lough Derg, this was obviously a site of strategic importance.

Three km north again is Cragliath Hill which has another fort, **Griananlaghna**, named after Brian Ború's great-grandfather King Lachtna.

Activities

Shannonside Activity Centre (☎ 061-376622) is an approved sailing centre, offering sailing at IR£10 to IR£20 an hour, windsurfing at IR£8 an hour, canoeing at IR£3 to IR£5 an hour, pony trekking at IR£8.50 an hour, hillwalking, and biking. Road bikes can be hired by the hour (IR£2), day (IR£7.50) or week (IR£35), and mountain bikes cost IR£12 a day. It's three km out of town on the Scarriff road.

Places to Stay & Eat

Killaloe *Lough Derg Holiday Park* (☎ 061-376329) is a camp site 5 km from Killaloe along Scariff road on the lake shore charging IR£7 a night.

On the Tipperary side of the bridge in Ballina, *Gooser's Pub & Restaurant* has some of the best food in town. The restaurant at the back is fine, but expensive at about IR£20 for dinner. *Simply Delicious*, a coffee shop just down from Gooser's, has snacks and lunches for under IR£5.

The *Lantern House* eight km out along the Scariff road, does simple but wholesome food, including a substantial and reasonable high tea from 6 to 7 pm.

Mountshannon The *Lakeside Caravan & Campsite* (☎ 061-927225) charges IR£5 plus 50p per adult for a tent; hostel accommodation is available in mobile homes or chalets and costs IR£6 per night. There are boats and equipment for hire for windsurfing, rowing and sailing. To get there, go along the Portumna road from Mountshannon and take the first turn right.

Derg Lodge (☎ 061-927180) in the village offers B&B from IR£13/26. *Oak House* (☎ 061-927185), a country house overlooking the lake six km from the village, costs IR£18.50/27. In the village, the delightful *Mountshannon Hotel* (☎ 061-927272) charges IR£53/61.50. Dinner is IR£10.

Entertainment

Good pubs in the village are *Irish Molly's*, *Gooser's* and *Crotty's* and most have traditional music at weekends.

CLARE

Getting There & Away

There are regular buses (☎ 061-42433 for details) from Killaloe to Limerick, Nenagh, Roscrea and Scarriff.

On Saturday only there is a single bus which leaves Limerick railway station in the afternoon and travels to Whitegate via Scarriff and Mountshannon. The journey time to Mountshannon is one hour and 25 minutes. A bus leaves Mountshannon for Limerick each Saturday at 8.50 am.

Getting Around

The Mountshannon Hotel has boats for hire at IR£15 a day. Shannonside Activity Centre (☎ 061-376622), three km along the Scarriff road, has bikes for hire (see the Activities section). Guerin's Ivy Stores in the village also has bikes for hire at IR£7 a day.

NORTH TO GALWAY

North of Mountshannon, the road swerves away from the lake and the views are nondescript. Inland is an area known as the **Clare Lakelands**, based around Feakle. There are numerous lakes with good coarse fishing.

South-West & West Clare

Loop Head at the county's south-western tip is a mighty wedge splitting the Atlantic rollers. North of Kilkee, a popular seaside resort, the road moves inland but there are some worthwhile detours along lonely coast roads and beaches where Spanish Armada ships were wrecked over 400 years ago. The coast between Kilkee and Loop Head has some outstanding cliff scenery. White Strand, Kilkee, Spanish Point and Lahinch have good beaches.

To the north and north-west of Ennis are a number of small villages, such as Corofin and Ennistymon. These are both at the very southern limits of the remarkable Burren region which includes the Hag's Head (a superb walk with excellent views) and the Cliffs of Moher, one of Ireland's most spectacular natural features. From there the road dips downhill towards Doolin, a famous backpacker's rest stop and Irish music centre.

GETTING THERE & AWAY

This region has infrequent local bus services to the coastal towns and villages; some buses run from Limerick and others from Galway, and services are more frequent in summer. Phone Ennis bus station (☎ 065-24177) for exact times and fares.

One express service has its terminus in Ennis or Ennistymon and runs through Lahinch, Lisdoonvarna, Doolin and Kilkee. Another bus goes to Galway, Kinvara, Ballyvaughan, Lisdoonvarna, Ennistymon, Lahinch, Miltown Malbay, Doonbeg, Kilkee and Kilrush. There is also a service to Limerick, Ennis, Ennistymon, Lahinch, Liscannor, the Cliffs of Moher and Doolin, as well as one covering the route between Kilkee, Kilrush, Doonbeg, Quilty, Miltown Malbay, Lahinch, Ennistymon, Ennis and Limerick.

A small bus known as a 'nipper' runs three times daily during the summertime between Lahinch and Lisdoonvarna, passing through Liscannor, the Cliffs of Moher and Doolin en route.

KILLIMER

Killimer is a nondescript village, close to the Shannon estuary and Moneypoint, Ireland's largest power station. At 900 megawatts, Moneypoint is capable of supplying 40% of the country's needs and burns two million tonnes of coal a year. It has a visitors' centre and a guided tour.

The Colleen Bawn, or 'white girl', was a woman called Ellen Hanly who was murdered in 1819 and thrown into the River Shannon by her husband, John Scanlon. Her body washed ashore and was buried in Killimer graveyard. Scanlon was hung. The story has inspired novels, plays and operas; unfortunately her tombstone has been dismantled by souvenir hunters.

Getting There & Away

A car ferry runs from Killimer to Tarbert across the Shannon estuary all year. From April to September, the schedule is a daily one from 7 am (9 am on Sunday) to 9 pm. Ferries depart every half hour. The cost is IR£2 for bikes and/or foot passenger, IR£6 for cars (IR£8.50 return), and it can be very busy at peak times.

KILRUSH

This small town overlooks the Shannon Estuary and the hills of Kerry to the south and is not a particularly attractive place. Kilrush has the west coast's newest and biggest marina. If you happen to be interested in stained glass, the Catholic church has some nice examples by well-known craftsman Harry Clarke. East of town is Kilrush Wood, which has some fine old trees and a picnic area. The nearby harbour at Cappa is where you catch the boat to Scattery Island, out in the estuary.

Kilrush has banks, a post office, and a tourist office (☎ 065-51577) on the square which is open through the summer, closed at lunch times. There is also a Kilrush in Landlord Times exhibition, IR£1/50p, housed in the old town hall in Market Square.

Bikes can be hired at Gleeson Wholesale (☎ 065-51127) on Henry St for IR£7 per day, or IR£35 per week plus a deposit of IR£40.

SCATTERY ISLAND

This island is about two km south-west of Cappa pier and is the site of a Christian settlement founded by St Senan in the 6th century. The island is windswept and treeless, and has one of the tallest and best preserved round towers in Ireland. It's over 32 metres high and the entrance is at ground level instead of the usual position high above ground level. There are the remains of five medieval churches.

In order to build his monastery, St Senan had to rid the island of a monster. The Irish name for the island is *Inis Cathaigh*, Cathach being the legendary sea serpent whose lair was on the island. St Senan banished the monster with the help of the angel Raphael.

A local virgin named Cannera wanted to join him, provoking much speculation in rhyme about how he withstood the temptation.

> Legend hints that had the maid,
> Until morning's light delayed,
> And given the saint one rosy smile,
> She'd ne'er have left his lonely isle.

Scattery was a beautiful but unfortunate site for a monastery, as it was all too easy for the Vikings to sail up the estuary and raid the place, which they did repeatedly in the 9th and 10th centuries. They occupied the island for 100 years until 970 when they were dislodged by Brian Ború.

An exhibition on the history and wildlife of Scattery is housed in an information centre on Merchants Quay in Kilrush. Here there is no admission charge. It's open May to September, daily from 9.30 am to 6.30 pm.

During the summer, boats (☎ 065-52031) run from Cappa pier to the island for IR£3 return. There is no scheduled timetable as the trips are subject to demand.

KILKEE

During the summer, Kilkee's wide bay is thronged with day trippers and holidaymakers from all over Clare and Limerick. Kilkee first became popular in Victorian times when rich Limerick families built seaside retreats here. Today, the town is a little too thick with guesthouses, amusement arcades and takeaways.

Visitors come for the fine sheltered beach and the Pollock Holes, natural swimming pools in the Duggerna Rocks to the south of the beach. St George's Head to the north has good cliff walks and scenery, while south of the bay the Duggerna Rocks form an unusual natural amphitheatre. Farther south is a huge sea cave. These sights can be reached by driving to Kilkee's west end and following the coastal path. The west end is also where you will find most of the best B&Bs.

Information

The seasonal tourist office (☎ 065-56112) is on O'Connell St just off the seafront and the staff are very helpful. It's open June to August, 10 am to 6 pm, closed from 1 to 2 pm and on Sunday.

Activities
Kilkee is a well-known diving centre. There are shore dives from the Duggerna Rocks fringing the west side of the bay, or boat dives on the Black Rocks farther out. Right at the tip of the Duggerna Rocks is the small inlet of Myles Creek, and there is excellent underwater scenery out from it. A diving centre by the harbour has air available and equipment for hire.

Places to Stay
Camping There are plenty of caravan and camp sites. *Cunningham's* (☎ 065-56430) is open May to September and charges IR£7 per night plus IR£ per adult. To get there find the Victoria Hotel on the seafront and turn inland. *Green Acres* (☎ 065-57011), with a flat IR£6 charge, is six km south of Kilkee on the R478.

Hostels The IHH *Kilkee Hostel* (☎ 065-56209) is clean, well-run and open all year round. It's 50 metres from the seafront on O'Curry St, and costs IR£6 a night in a dorm. There are no double rooms. They have a well-equipped kitchen, a laundry room, and a small coffee shop.

B&Bs There are countless guesthouses, usually a little more expensive than other areas. There are some good ones at the west end of Kilkee.
Dunearn (☎ 065-56545) and *Harbour Lodge* (☎ 065-56090) are at the west end near the Victoria Hotel. Doubles are around IR£30. At busy times, you may have to take whatever the tourist office can get you.

Hotels There are plenty of hotels in Kilkee, but for the extra money you don't get much extra luxury. *Halpin's Hotel* (☎ 065-56032) is a pleasant family-run hotel on Erin St. B&B is from IR£24/48.

Places to Eat
There are plenty of fast-food joints. For good home cooking at reasonable prices try the *Pantry* (☎ 065-56576), halfway up O'Curry St from the seafront on the right. The *Hideout* pub on Erin St has bar food. The *Strand* pub on the seafront is also worth trying. Meals at all these places are around IR£5.
Krazy Kraut's (☎ 065-56240) on the Strand does good seafood snacks and lunches during the day and full dinner in the evenings. Almost two km north of Kilkee is the popular *Manuel's Seafood Restaurant* (☎ 065-56211), only open for dinner, which costs IR£20 or more.

Entertainment
Kilkee has plenty of resort diversions. Across from the hostel on O'Curry St is the *Myles Creek* pub, Kilkee's trendiest spot. The pub is on the band circuit and attracts many of Ireland's best young rock groups. *O'Mara's* on the same street and the popular *Strand* on the seafront have sessions during the week.
There is horse racing on the beach in late August.

Getting Around
Bicycles can be hired at Williams (☎ 065-56041), on Circular Rd near the Catholic church, for IR£7.50 a day or IR£30 a week.

SOUTH OF KILKEE TO LOOP HEAD
The land from Kilkee south to Loop Head is poor and flat but the cliff scenery is spectacular: the coast is peppered with sea stacks, arches and wave-sculpted rocks. It's a glorious day's bike ride down to the Head and back. Better still, if you have the energy, is the 24-km cliff walk between Loop Head and Kilkee. The cliffs compare with the more famous Cliffs of Moher to the north and are much less visited.

Intrinsic Bay
Just south of Kilkee is Intrinsic Bay, named after the *Intrinsic*, a ship wrecked here in

CLARE

1856 en route to America. When the *Edmund* sank nearby in 1850, 100 people drowned.

The summit shadowing the bay is Lookout Hill. To the north are Diamond Rock and **Bishop's Island**, the latter a remarkable pillar of rock with a medieval oratory perched on the summit. The oratory is attributed to the 6th-century St Senan who also built the settlement on Scattery Island in the Shannon estuary. Later, a selfish bishop is supposed to have lived here while his people starved in a famine; when the gap to the mainland widened in a storm the bishop himself starved to death.

Kilbaha

On the minor coast road, seven km from Loop Head, Kilbaha's tiny church contains an unusual relic of more repressive times. The 'little ark' is a small wooden altar used by Catholics in the 1850s. To hold mass, the altar was wheeled below the high-tide mark where it was outside the jurisdiction of the local Protestant landlord. A stained-glass window above the church door depicts the ark in use. Father Michael Meehan, the courageous local priest who had the ark built, is buried in the church.

There is a 'submerged forest', a collection of 5000-year-old tree stumps (probably pine) on the shore east of Rinvella Bay, near Kilbaha. They were originally preserved in peat bog, which was washed away as the sea level rose, leaving the stumps visible.

Carrigaholt

On 15 September 1588, seven tattered ships of the Spanish Armada took shelter off Carrigaholt, a tiny village inside the mouth of the Shannon estuary. One, probably the *Annunciada*, was torched and abandoned, sinking somewhere out in the estuary. Today, Carrigaholt has a safe beach and the substantial remains of a McMahon castle overlooking the water.

The *Long Dock* (☎ 065-58106) on West St is a cosy pub-cum-restaurant, with bar food, seafood dinners and Irish music on Friday night. Also worth trying is *Fennell's* pub which has music some nights.

Loop Head

On a clear day, Loop Head, Clare's southern-most point, has magnificent views south to the Dingle Peninsula crowned by Mt Brandon, and north to the Aran Islands and Galway Bay. There are bracing walks in the area and a long hike running along the cliffs to Kilkee.

Cúchulainn's Leap

Loop is a corruption of 'leap', and legend has it that the Celtic warrior Cúchulainn was being chased all over Ireland by a hag called Mal. Cornered on this headland, he leapt onto a seastack and when she tried to follow him, Mal fell to her death. The sea turned crimson and her body washed ashore at various points along the coast, giving Hag's Head and Malbay their names. West of the lighthouse, you will find the seastack in question; the gap is known as Cúchulainn's Leap. ■

NORTH OF KILKEE

North of Kilkee, the real west of Ireland quickly reasserts itself. The road runs inland for some 32 km until it reaches Quilty. Take the occasional lane to the west and search out little-visited places like Ballard Bay and White Strand, north of Dunbeg or Doonbeg. Ballard Bay is eight km north of Doonbeg, where an old telegraph tower looks over some fine cliffs. Doonegal Point has the remains of a promontory fort.

There is good fishing for bass, pollock and mackerel all along the coast, and safe beaches at Seafield, Lough Donnell and Quilty.

Doonbeg

Doonbeg is a tiny fishing village halfway between Kilkee and Miltown Malbay. Near the mouth of the River Doonbeg, another Armada ship, the *San Esteban*, was wrecked on 20 September 1588. The survivors were later executed at Spanish Point.

White Strand is a quiet beach, two km long and backed by dunes. For campers the side roads around Doonbeg are good places to pitch a tent and watch the sun go down. There are two ruined castles nearby, Doonbeg and Doonmore.

Places to Stay & Eat The Igoe Inn in Doonbeg has the *Olde Kitchen Restaurant* (☎ 065-55039), which docs steak and seafood (dinners only) for IR£12 to IR£18. *An Tintean* (☎ 065-55036) is a seafood restaurant and guesthouse, with turf fires and good rooms with bathrooms. B&B from IR£18/30. The *San Esteban* (☎ 065-55105) is one km from Doonbeg in (try and pronounce this) Rhynnagonnaught. B&B is from IR£15/25.

Entertainment *Morrissey's* pub in Doonbeg often has music as does *Tubridy's* pub on Thursday. The *Ocean View Bar* has Irish music on Tuesday, Saturday and Sunday during the summer.

Quilty

The small village of Quilty lies on a particularly bleak stretch of coast. Quilty is a centre for seaweed production; kelp and other weeds are collected, dried on the stone walls and sent for processing. The resulting alginates are used in toothpaste, beer and agar. Quilty has a good beach and boats are available for deep-sea angling.

One of the most powerful ships of the Spanish Armada, the *San Marcos,* was wrecked off nearby Mutton Island in September 1588. It had taken a terrible battering in the English Channel and only four of the 1000 sailors on board survived the wreck.

Local **guesthouses** include *Clonmore Lodge* (☎ 065-87020), just over one km from the village. B&B from IR£12/20.

Miltown Malbay

Like Kilkee, Miltown Malbay was a resort favoured by wealthy Victorians. Having said that, the town isn't actually on the sea: the beach is three km away at Spanish Point. Every year Miltown Malbay hosts a Willie

Clancy Irish Music Festival as a tribute to one of Ireland's greatest pipers. The festival usually runs in the first week in July, when the town is overrun with wandering minstrels, and drink is consumed by the bucketload. You can also find music in the surrounding villages.

Spanish Point

There is an excellent beach at Spanish Point, and when the waves are running there's good surfing.

The beach gets its name from the execution of 60 Armada survivors on Cnoc Na Crocaire (the 'Hill of the Gallows') nearby. They had swum ashore, only to be executed by the local head honcho, Boetius Clancy, Sheriff of Clare, and Turlough O'Brien, the local chief who was loyal to the English crown.

Lahinch

Lahinch is the archetypal seaside resort, full of fast-food joints, amusement arcades and places to stay. The town sits on a protected bay with a fine beach, and the surfing can be good. In 1943, an off-course US bomber landed on the beach and the 12 airmen were repatriated through Northern Ireland. Lahinch is very busy in the summer; you may prefer to move on to Ennistymon, Liscannor or Doolin.

There is a seasonal (June to August, 10 am to 6 pm) tourist office (☎ 06581730) near the post office at the south end of Main St, which is open between 10 am and 7 pm. Surfboards can be rented on the seafront from the Surf Shop. There is pony trekking (☎ 065-71385) en route to Liscannor.

The IHH *Lahinch Hostel* (☎ 065-81040), along Church St, has beds for IR£6, doubles for IR£16, and there's a laundry.

The bus which runs between Limerick and Lisdoonvarna (more frequently in summer) stops at Lahinch. Contact Ennis bus station (☎ 065-24177) for exact times and fares.

ENNISTYMON

Ennistymon, a lovely little town just three km inland from Lahinch, is on the banks of the River Inagh. The town started out as a settlement around a castle built by Turlough O'Brien in 1588, the year of the Spanish Armada. The town's appearance has scarcely changed in the last 20 or 30 years and its charm derives primarily from the many well-maintained old pubs and shops.

The bridge over the River Inagh is just above the well-known 200-metre rapids known as the **Cascades**, which are impressive if the river is in flood. There is trout and salmon fishing, and some good Irish music pubs.

Orientation & Information

Kam Knitwear (☎ 065-71387) has some tourist information and is on the Ennis Rd about five minutes' walk south of the town square. Markets are held in the town centre on Tuesday. Ennistymon is essentially one long main street called Church St.

Things to See

The **River Inagh** runs directly behind and parallel to Church St. The rapids known as the Cascades are just down the lane beside the Archway Bar to the south of the Square. It's a pleasant stroll around here in the evening. When the Inagh is in flood, though, the waters can rise almost to the houses. Down river, the Falls Hotel is a former residence of the McNamaras and has its own hydropower generator.

Places to Stay

Hostels The *White House Hostel* (☎ 065-26793) is a very basic hostel on a corner in Main St and costs IR£4 per person.

B&Bs & Hotel In the town centre is *San Antone* (☎ 065-71078), part of McMahon's pub, IR£17/27. *Station House* (☎ 065-71149) is about half a km south of the square on the Ennis road, IR£18.50/27.

The *Falls Hotel* (☎ 065-71004) is a comfortable old country house in 20 hectares of wooded gardens with rooms from IR£30/54.

Places to Eat

Franco's Pizza & Takeaway on Church St is one of the very few decent low-priced eateries in Ennistymon. *Sugan Chair* is a modest restaurant on Main St. *Cooley's House* pub on Church St has reasonable bar food and music most evenings during the summer. The *Archway Bar*, just south of the square, serves run-of-the-mill food until 9 pm. For something more substantial or upmarket try the *Falls Hotel* where dinner is IR£19.50, or make the journey out to Lahinch.

Entertainment

Daly's pub on Church St (also known as the *Matchmaker's Shack*) is a cosy, traditional place and gets a good crowd. It's one of the best places in town for Irish music with sessions most nights in summer. *Phil's Place* across from the Archway Bar has music on Saturday and Sunday nights, while *Nagle's Bar* has music on Wednesday and weekends. *Cooley's House* pub has music at weekends and *Carrigg's* is worth a look.

Getting There & Away

The bus which runs between Limerick and Lisdoonvarna (more frequently in summer) stops at Ennistymon. Contact Ennis bus station (☎ 065-24177) for exact times and fares.

LISCANNOR & AROUND

This small fishing village offers a fine view over Liscannor Bay and Lahinch, as the road winds past on its way to the Cliffs of Moher and Doolin. Liscannor has given its name to a characteristic flagstone with wormlike ripples on the surface. The stone is widely used locally for floors, walls and even roofs.

John P Holland, the inventor of the submarine, was born here. He emigrated to the USA, and he hoped his invention would be used to sink British warships.

Things to See

On the way to the Cliffs of Moher and close to Murphy's and Considine's pubs is the **Holy Well of St Brigid** where people with all sorts of problems come to pray and drink the healing waters. There is usually a collection of discarded crutches and sticks near the well, so it obviously works!

The well's significance probably predates Christian times, as its Irish name suggests a connection with a pre-Christian god, Crom Dubh. People from all over Clare and the Aran Islands make the pilgrimage to the well in July, particularly on the last weekend of the month, and there can be from 100 to 400 people there on the Sunday.

Clahane Beach to the west of Liscannor is good and safe. A 'lost city' and church known as Kilstephen are supposed to sit on an underwater reef in Liscannor Bay. On **Slieve Callan** to the south is buried the Celtic hero Conan, who is said to lie with the key to the lost church.

Places to Stay & Eat

The IHH *Liscannor Village Hostel* (☎ 065-81385) in the centre of the village is a big, well-run place with beds for IR£5.50 and doubles for IR£14.

Coming from Lahinch, just before the village on the right, is *Sea Haven B&B* (☎ 065-81385), IR£19/28, with good, hard beds. Five km out of Liscannor, you'll find the closest B&B to the Cliffs of Moher – the friendly *Moher Lodge* (☎ 065-81269), IR£18/29.

For cheap meals, try the *Village Hostel*, the pubs or the small coffee rooms at the Cliffs of Moher. There is good fresh seafood at the *Captain's Deck Restaurant* (☎ 065-81666) in the middle of the village. It's open 6 to 10 pm with main courses from IR£9 to IR£15. They have a simpler set dinner from 6 to 7.30 pm for IR£12. There is a small seafood restaurant tucked away in a tiny cottage near the Holy Well of St Brigid a few km to the west.

Entertainment

There are a string of pubs in Liscannor, most with music. *Joseph McHugh's* is the best known and is as genuine an old Irish pub as you will find anywhere, down to the groceries and other oddments piled on the shelves (ask to see the bull's penis). For music, try McHugh's on Tuesday or the equally good

Egan's next door. *Vaughan's Bar* has music almost every night during the summer. Alternatively, travel on to Doolin.

Getting There & Away

The bus which runs between Limerick and Lisdoonvarna (more frequently in summer) stops at Liscannor. Contact Ennis bus station (☎ 065-24177) for exact times and fares.

The O'Briens

The eccentric O'Briens were one of Clare's most important ruling families. The ruined square castle on the point outside Liscannor was built by the O'Connors, taken later by the O'Briens and at the time of the Spanish Armada was occupied by Turlough O'Brien, who was loyal to the English crown and co-executioner of the Spanish survivors washed up at Spanish Point. Cornelius O'Brien, a rather idiosyncratic descendant, lived in the now ruined manor house north of Liscannor. That O'Brien was MP for Clare in the mid-19th century. To the west is a monument to Cornelius, erected in 1853 by his tenants with some persuasion from the man himself. He also erected the viewing tower at the Cliffs of Moher. ∎

HAG'S HEAD

Hag's Head forms the southern end of the touristy but magnificent Cliffs of Moher. There is a superb walk to Hag's Head (see below) where a signal tower was erected in case Napoleon tried to make a surprise attack on the west coast. The tower is built on the site of an ancient promontory fort called Mothair which has given its name to the famous cliffs to the north.

Hag's Head is named after the formidable Mal, who chased the legendary Celtic hero Cúchulainn all over Ireland. She fell to her death off Loop Head to the south, and her body was reputedly washed ashore here (and in various other places). Some say the headland looks like a seated woman looking out over the Atlantic.

CLARE

Hag's Head Walk

Hag's Head is an excellent place to view the Cliffs of Moher and the walk out is more than worth the effort. To get there, go just over five km out of Liscannor towards the Cliffs of Moher until, just past Moher Lodge B&B, you'll spot a rough track turning to the left. You can only drive a short distance and then have to walk along the path out towards the point and tower. There is a huge sea arch at the tip and another visible to the north. The hike there and back takes about three hours.

CLIFFS OF MOHER

One of Ireland's most spectacular sights, the Cliffs of Moher, rise from Hag's Head to the south and reach their highest point (230 metres) just north of O'Brien's Tower before slowly declining farther north again. On a clear day, the views are tremendous: the Aran Islands stand etched on the waters of Galway Bay and beyond lie the hills and valleys of Connemara in western Galway.

From the cliff edge, you can just hear the booming far below as the waves eat into the soft shale and sandstone. Often, sections of the cliff give way, and they are generally so unstable that few birds or plants live on them. Sunset is by far the best time to visit and there is a bracing eight-km walk along the cliff edge down to Hag's Head. Part of the walk was walled off with Liscannor stone by the eccentric local landlord Cornelius O'Brien, who built the lookout tower to impress lady visitors.

The seastack – covered with seabirds and their guano – just below the tower is called Breanan Mor and is itself over 70 metres high.

Information

The visitors' centre (☎ 065-81171) for the Cliffs is open from March to October and has tourist information, a shop, a reasonable café and a bureau de change. It must be said that the cliffs are one of the most visited attractions in the country: coaches roll up ceaselessly during the day and stage Irish characters hang about playing tin whistles and looking for money.

The car park costs IR£1.

A Risky Route

The cliffs just north of Moher are known as *Aill Na Searrach* or the 'Cliff of the Colts' because some fairy horses are supposed to have leapt into the sea at this point. There is a precipitous and dangerous path to the base of these cliffs, only to be attempted by the fittest walkers, and only in dry weather – be warned. The beginning of the path is about two km north of the official Cliffs of Moher entrance.

Where the road comes off the mountain, there is a small bridge and a rough track leading to a galvanised gate. Cross the field to the dip on the left, where the path begins. At the bottom, massive boulders have been worn smooth and piled high by the Atlantic rollers.

You can also reach this path by following the clifftop path north from O'Brien's Tower, as if you were walking to Doolin. You can clearly see the path which zigzags down to the rocky beach.

Getting There & Away

The bus which runs between Limerick and Lisdoonvarna (more frequently in summer) stops at the Cliffs of Moher as well as the nearby small towns of Ennistymon, Lahinch and Liscannor. Contact Ennis bus station (☎ 065-24177) for exact times and fares. The small bus known locally as the 'nipper' calls at the Cliffs of Moher as well as Liscannor and Doolin en route between Lahinch and Lisdoonvarna, and runs three times daily June to September and not at all during the rest of the year.

The Burren Area

Between Kinvara and Corofin in northern Clare is the Burren region, an extraordinary and unique place. *Boireann* is the Irish for 'rocky place', and when you see the miles of polished limestone stretching in every direction you'll know why one of Cromwell's generals was moved to exclaim that there is 'neither water enough to drown a man, nor a tree to hang him, nor soil enough to bury him' – which shows what was on their minds.

Along the coast are a few settlements including Doolin, a very popular Irish music centre, and Ballyvaughan, an attractive little village on the south coast of Galway Bay.

East of Ballyvaughan the Burren peters out, near Kinvara. This area has a lot of historical sites, notably Corcomroe Abbey and the churches of Oughtmama. The deeply indented coastline has plenty of wildlife and fine walks.

INFORMATION

The nearest tourist information point to the Burren is at the Cliffs of Moher. A must if you intend spending any time here is Tim Robinson's *Burren Map & Guide*. It's available in many shops and shows just about every object and place of interest on the Burren.

GEOLOGY

The Burren is the most extensive limestone region in Britain or Ireland. The craggy limestone landscape is known as 'karst' after a similar area in Slovenia. The Burren is all limestone except for a cap of mud and shale which sits on the higher regions from Lisdoonvarna north to Slieve Elva.

During the Carboniferous period 350 million years ago, this whole area was the bottom of a warm shallow sea. The remains of coral and shells fell to the seabed, and coastal rivers dumped sand and silt on top of these limey deposits. Time and pressure turned the layers to stone: limestone underneath, shale and sandstone above.

Massive rumblings in the earth's crust some 270 million years ago buckled the edges of Europe and forced the seabed above sea level, at the same time bending and fracturing the stone sheets to form long, deep cracks. Wind, rain and ice have since removed most of the overlying shale, leaving mountains of limestone.

The difference between the areas of

The Burren & the Interpretive Centre

The Office of Public Works (OPW) decided to build an interpretive centre near Mullaghmore Mountain and Lake, half way between Corofin and Gort. This is a particularly beautiful spot and the prospect of a tourist centre, complete with coaches, car parks and toilets, in such a delicate place caused uproar. Construction work began in early 1993 and just about every biologist, conservationist and man, woman or child who had a feeling for the Burren objected. Until that time, the OPW had not had to go through normal planning procedures and could build almost anything it liked anywhere it liked, with little scope for objectors' views to be expressed or heeded.

The row split the community. No prospect of providing jobs is rejected lightly, so feelings on both sides were very strong. Many local politicians backed the centre which was being built with the aid of grants from the EU. The opponents of the centre wanted it to be built somewhere else, such as in a local village, where it would have caused minimum disruption.

In May 1993, the battle was won – for the time being – by the opponents to the centre, who took the OPW to court. The verdict was that the OPW had to go through normal planning procedures for any of its developments and thus the interpretive centres were now illegal. The car park and foundations had already been laid at Mullaghmore, but work was immediately abandoned. Even those beginnings have provided an unsightly blot on the landscape. It still remains to be seen if the OPW applies for planning permission and attempts to complete the buildings.

Overall, the OPW does a reasonable job in protecting Ireland's national heritage. But it recently it appears to have been rushing to package every region or site of interest with interpretive centres, which detract from the very beauty and isolation that people come to these places to appreciate. By far the best way to explore the Burren is to get a map and head off on your own. ∎

CLARE

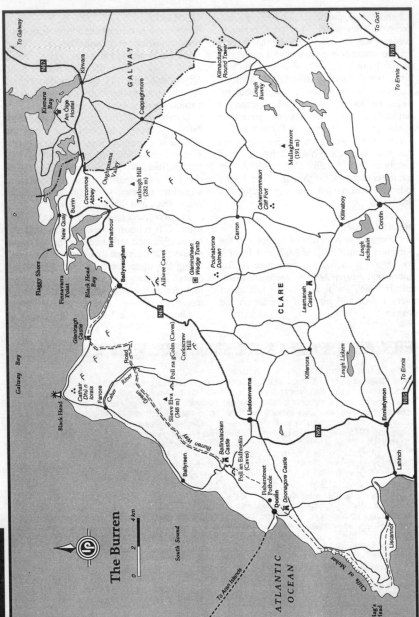

The Burren

0 2 4 km

CLARE

porous limestone and nonporous shale is acute. Shale country is a depressing dull green, covered in acid bogs, marshes and reeds. On limestone the soil is sparse, water disappears and grey rock predominates.

Being slightly acidic, rainwater dissolves the limestone, widening the vertical cracks, which are known as grikes. The horizontal slabs are called clints. The water follows weak points in the rock, carving out underground rivers and caverns. Springs and rivers appear and disappear. Near the surface, the roofs of caves collapse, forming dark swallowholes and squared-off valleys. Rainwater is caught on top of the shale and eventually drains off at the edges into the limestone, which it erodes. A ring of caves appears along the shale/limestone boundary.

The southern boundary of the Burren is roughly where the limestone dips under the shale between Doolin and Lough Inchiquin. Underneath the limestone of the Burren is a huge mass of granite, which surfaces to the north-west in Connemara, County Galway.

During numerous Ice Ages, glaciers have scoured the hills, rounding their edges and sometimes polishing the rock to a mirror finish. They also dumped a skin of rock and soil over the region. Huge boulders were carried by the ice, incongruous aliens on a sea of flat rock. Seen all over the Burren, these 'glacial erratics' are often a visibly different type of rock.

The only surface river in the Burren is the River Caher, which flows down the Khyber Pass before meeting the sea at Fanore. The valley is lined with glacial sediments which stop the water from leaking away.

FLORA & FAUNA

Soil may be scarce here, but the small amount that gathers in the cracks is limey, well-drained and rich in nutrients. This and the soft Atlantic climate support an extraordinary mix of Mediterranean, Arctic and Alpine plants.

The Burren is a stronghold of Ireland's most elusive mammal, the pine marten. They are rarely seen, although there are certainly some living near Gleninagh Castle and up

the Caher Valley. Badgers, foxes and even stoats are common throughout the region. Otters and seals live along the shores around Belharbour, New Quay and Finnavarra Point. The estuaries along this northern coast of the Burren are rich in birdlife and frequently have brent geese during the winter. More than 28 of Ireland's 33 species of butterfly are found here, including one endemic species, the Burren green.

Unfortunately, modern farming and EU land-improvement grants have had their effect on the Burren. Weedkillers and fertilisers encourage grass and little else. Many ring forts and stone walls have been bulldozed into extinction.

ARCHAEOLOGY

The Burren's bare limestone hills were once lightly wooded and covered in soil. Towards the end of the Stone Age, about 6000 years ago, the first farmers arrived in the area. They began to clear the woodlands and use the upland regions for grazing. Over the centuries, the soil was eroded and the huge mass of limestone we see today began to emerge.

Despite its desolation, the Burren supported quite large numbers of people in ancient times, and has over 2500 historic sites. Chief among them is the 5000-year-old Poulnabrone Dolmen, one of Ireland's finest ancient monuments.

There are at least 65 megalithic tombs erected by the Burren's first settlers. Many of these tombs are wedge-shaped graves, stone boxes tapering both in height and width and about the size of a large double bed. The dead were placed inside and the whole structure was covered in earth and stones. Gleninsheen, south of Aillwee Caves, is a good example.

Ring forts dot the Burren in prodigious numbers. There are almost 500 in all, including Iron Age stone forts like Ballykinvarga and Cahercommaun near Carron.

In later times, many castles in the area were built by the region's ruling families, and these include Leamenah Castle near Kilfenora, Ballinalacken Castle near Doolin

CLARE

and Gleninagh Castle on the Black Head road.

Green roads are the old highways of the Burren, crossing hills and valleys to some of the remotest corners of the region. Unpaved and possibly dating back thousands of years, they are now used mostly by hikers and the occasional farmer. Many are signposted.

CAVING

Serious caving is not for the fainthearted. If you fancy trying it, take a course or at least find an experienced guide.

Tim Robinson's Burren map has many of the cave entrances marked on it and some equipment can be hired at the Bridge Hostel in Fanore. Kilfenora Caving & Outdoor Centre (☎ 065-71422) offers caving, walking, pony trekking and climbing. Serious cavers should consult *The Caves of Northwest Clare* by Tratman.

GETTING THERE & AWAY

For precise times and other details of the buses to the Burren area, ring either Ennis, Limerick or Galway bus stations. Various buses pass through the Burren: a local service runs between Ennis, Ennistymon, Lisdoonvarna, Doolin, Kilrush and Kilkee; another service connects Galway City with Ballyvaughan, Lisdoonvarna, Ennistymon, Lahinch, Kilkee and Tralee, on summer weekdays only; and another runs from Galway City to Kinvara, Ballyvaughan, Lisdoonvarna and Doolin – this service has one bus a day between Monday and Saturday in winter and up to three buses a day in the summer months, from mid-June to the end of September.

From Limerick, a bus to Doolin passes through Ennis, Lahinch, the Cliffs of Moher, Ennistymon, and Lisdoonvarna, and this service consists of one bus a day between Monday and Saturday in winter and two every day between mid-June and the end of September.

Buses from Galway City follow the Burren coast via Kinvara, Ballyvaughan, Blackhead, Fanore and Lisdoonvarna to Doolin. There is usually one bus daily in winter, except Sunday, and two every day in summer, from mid-June to the end of September.

GETTING AROUND
Walking
Walking is by far the best way of seeing the Burren. Particularly good walks are the green road (old highway) from Ballinalackan Castle to Fanore and back through a hidden valley which forms part of the Burren Way; and the climb up Black Head to Cathair Dhun Iorais Iron Age fort. The 45-km Burren Way (see the Activities chapter) runs down through the Burren from Ballyvaughan to Doolin and then south to the Cliffs of Moher and Liscannor. The southern portions of this walk are described in more detail under the section on Fanore and under Doolin.

Guided hill walks are available through Burren Hill Walks Ltd (☎ 065-77168) based at Corkscrew Hill, Ballyvaughan.

Bicycle
Cycling is the second best way to see the Burren, and good mountain bikes are available from the Doolin Hostel (☎ 065-74006) or Burkes Garage (☎ 065-74022) on the square in Lisdoonvarna, for IR£6. You can easily ride a bike along the green roads.

DOOLIN
Doolin straggles unattractively for miles along the road, but despite appearances it has some of the best music pubs in the west, two of the best restaurants for kilometres, and plenty of good cafés, hostels and guesthouses. It's also an excellent base for the Burren, which lies just to the north. There is a ferry to the smallest Aran island of Inisheer, and the Cliffs of Moher are only a few km to the south.

Doolin's popularity among backpackers and music lovers has rocketed over the past few years, and at night the pubs are packed with a cosmopolitan crowd. In high season it can be difficult to get a bed, so book ahead.

Orientation & Information
Doolin – or Fisherstreet on some maps – is made up of three parts. Coming from Lisdoonvarna you first hit the Catholic church, then after less than one km the upper village or Roadford area with shops, restaurants and hostels, and the post office. Then there's a slightly bigger gap before reaching Fisherstreet or the lower village, which has the Doolin Hostel, more shops and O'Connor's pub. It's one more km to the harbour and the ferry to the Aran Islands.

There are no banks, but you can change money and travellers' cheques in the Auld Doolin Hostel as well as in O'Connor's pub just over the bridge.

Walking Tours
A number of people operate excellent walking tours of the Burren. They come and go, so check hostel and shop windows for details.

Places to Stay
Camping Down by the harbour is the excellent *Doolin Camping & Caravan Park* (☎ 065-74127), with a good kitchen, showers and laundrette. Nearby *Riverside Camping* (☎ 065-74314) has been recommended. *Nagles* camp site (☎ 065-74458) is beside the quay. The average price at these camp sites is IR£5 a night.

Hostels Budget travellers are well catered for in Doolin. The IHH *Aauld Doolin Hostel* (☎ 065-74006) is in the lower village. A bed costs from IR£7.50, doubles IR£18; they are very busy so book ahead. *Paddy Moloney's Doolin Hostel* (☎ 065-74006), under the same ownership and across the road, is an older place and beds are from IR£6.75, doubles IR£18.

In the upper village, Roadford, the *Rainbow Hostel* (☎ 065-74415) is near McGann's pub. It is smaller and older than the Doolin Hostel, and its front room has an open turf fire. They have 16 beds for IR£6.50 and one doubles for IR£14. They are open all year.

Off the road on the way down to O'Connor's pub from the upper village is the *Aille River Hostel* (☎ 065-74260), a converted farmhouse with turf fires. The cost is IR£6 a night, doubles IR£14.

B&Bs *Killilagh House* (☎ 065-74392) in the upper village is on the right going south past the post office. Excellent rooms with bathrooms are from IR£25/30. Continuing on past McGann's pub and around the bend on the left is the equally good *Doolin House* (☎ 065-74259) at IR£28/36. *Moloney's* (☎ 065-74006) is near the Doolin Hostel, same family, and charges IR£28 for doubles only.

Other good B&Bs include *Island View House* (☎ 065-74346), from IR£18.50/27, three km from Doolin on the Lisdoonvarna road via Garrahy's Cross or, near the harbour *Atlantic View* (☎ 065-74189) with doubles only for IR£24.

Hotel *Aran View* (☎ 065-74061) is a very comfortable and friendly country house hotel one km north of town past the Catholic church. Rooms from IR£30/50.

Places to Eat
Both *O'Connor's* in the lower village and *McGann's* in the upper village serve really good bar food. McGann's have Irish stew for around IR£6. The *Apple Tree* restaurant is opposite Moloney's hostel and is open from 8 am to 9.30 pm.

Doolin Craft Gallery one km along the Lisdoonvarna road, does delicious light meals. The *Doolin Café*,opposite the post office, and *Ilsa's Kitchen*, by the bridge just up from O'Connor's, do good snacks. The *Aran View* hotel does an excellent dinner for IR£18.

If you feel like splashing out, there are two really nice restaurants, the *Lazy Lobster* (☎ 065-74390) and, next door to McGann's, *Bruach na h'Aille* (☎ 065-74120), both in the upper village. Count on about IR£20 per person including wine.

Entertainment
Doolin is renowned for Irish music, and you can hear it almost every night during the

CLARE

summer and occasionally during the winter. *O'Connor's* pub is the best known (note the international collection of police department badges behind the bar) but *McGann's* staff can be friendlier. On a good night, the atmosphere in either pub is hard to beat. *McDermott's*, in Roadford near the post office, is more favoured by locals and is quieter. Watch out for sessions in nearby Lisdoonvarna or Kilfenora. Even if you're not staying in the *Aran View* hotel, its bar provides a pleasant way to escape the tumult in the village.

Things to Buy
The Doolin Craft Gallery is past the church on the way to Lisdoonvarna and is excellent, with a huge range of woollen sweaters (jumpers), batik and crafts.

Getting There & Away
Ferry Doolin Harbour is the jumping-off point for the ferry to Inisheer – also spelt Inis Thiar or Inis Oírr – the smallest of the three Aran Islands. In May, June, July and August, there is also a single daily sailing to the biggest Aran island, Inishmór. Otherwise you can get onward connections from Inisheer.

There are two rival companies. Doolin Ferries (☎ 065-74189/77086 or at the pier 065-74455) have the bigger boats, the *Happy Hooker* and the *Tranquility* while Inis Thiar Ferries (☎ 065-74500) operate two smaller boats, the *Dorothy D* and *Saoirse*. There is keen competition for clients, and ugly advertisements are springing up along the road to the harbour.

It takes around 30 minutes to cross the eight km to Inisheer and the return fare is IR£12. Ferries run from April to September, and in June, July and August each company operates around seven sailings a day beginning at 9.30 am and the last returning from Inisheer at around 7 pm. If you intend only to spend the day on Inisheer you should get an early ferry out and book a place on the last one home.

From May through to August, Doolin Ferries operate the single daily sailing to

Inishmór, leaving at 10 am and departing Inishmór to come back to Doolin at 4 pm. The trip takes 50 minutes and the fare is IR£10 one way.

Bus The Bus Éireann stop is outside Paddy Moloney's Doolin Hostel (☎ 065-74006) near O'Connor's pub. For fares and times check with the hostel or ring ☎ 065-24177 or ☎ 061-418855. There are Bus Éireann buses between Doolin and Ennis, Galway Bus Station (☎ 091-63555) and Limerick Bus Station (☎ 061-313333). There are connections on to Dublin. For more details, see the Getting There & Away section under the Burren Area.

Getting Around
All the hostels have bikes for around IR£7 a day or IR£35 a week plus deposit. There's another place (☎ 065-74429) just opposite the post office renting bikes, including ones for children.

AROUND DOOLIN
Caves
Doolin is very popular with cavers. The British seem particularly fond of this pastime and use Doolin as a base, spending their days crawling through dirty holes and their nights drinking pints of Guinness. The Fisherstreet potholes are nearby, and Poll Na gColm, five km north-east of Lisdoonvarna, is Ireland's longest with over 12 km of mapped passageways.

A few hundred metres south of Ballinalacken Castle, you will see some low cliffs on the east or inland side across a field. These hide the entrance to Poll an Eidhnain or Ionáin, a cave which, after a difficult and mucky passage, widens to a chamber containing a six-metre stalactite claimed to be the tallest in Western Europe. The cavern is difficult to get to and the farmer is not keen on trespassers, so ask first.

The rocks to the north of Doolin Harbour are honeycombed with an unusual system of undersea caves called the Green Holes of Doolin. They are the longest known undersea caves in temperate waters – one of them has been followed inland underwater for a km. Nondivers can look into 'Hell', a large gash in the rocks, north of the harbour and about 50 metres from the sea. The gash is about six metres and the heaving water at the bottom leads to a maze of submarine passages.

Doonagore Castle
If you follow the coast road for about three km south of Doolin you will come to Doonagore Castle, a restored 15th-century tower with its surrounding walled enclosure or *bawn*. There is a lovely view from here over Doolin and the Aran Islands, a perfect sunset spot for photographers.

Ballinalacken Castle
Five km north of Doolin en route to Fanore is Ballinalacken Castle. Sitting astride a small cliff, this 15th-century O'Brien tower house is in excellent order. The stairway is intact and there are good views of the Burren from the top. Look out for an original fireplace perched halfway up the interior with the date 1679 carved on it.

Just beside the gateway to Ballinalacken Castle and guesthouse, a minor road leads inland up into the Burren. After about a km, it meets one of the Burren's ancient green roads, and in good weather this route up to Fanore is a lovely walk. It also forms part of the Burren Way. There is a more detailed description of the return part of this route in the section on Fanore.

LISDOONVARNA
Lisdoon, as the town is generally called (its Irish name is *Lios Dúin Bhearna*), is well known for its mineral springs where people have been coming for centuries to drink and bathe. It also used to be home to some serious matchmakers, who for an appropriate fee would fix you up with a soulmate. Most aspiring suitors would hit town in September after the hay was in.

Today, genuine matchmaking is a little thin on the ground, but the Matchmaking Festival, which runs over a couple of weekends in September, is still a great excuse for drinking, merriment and music in the pubs. And with all those singles events, some romances must begin.

Orientation & Information
Lisdoonvarna is essentially a one-street town with a square in the middle where you turn west for Doolin and the coast. The town has plenty of shops, pubs and smart hotels with fine restaurants.

The Spa Wells Centre
The centre (☎ 065-74023) is the only working spa in the country. It has the main sulphur spring, a pump house, massage room, sauna and mineral baths, in nice wooded surroundings. The iron, sulphur, magnesium and iodine in the waters are supposed to be good for rheumatic and glandular complaints. So if you have a spot of hyperthyroidism or ankylotic spondylitis, this is the place for you. You can drink the water, but it tastes hideous and the aftertaste can last for ages.

Places to Stay & Eat
The IHH *Burren Holiday Hostel* (☎ 065-74300) is just outside of town on the road to Ennistymon. Beds are IR£6.50, doubles IR£16. Meals are available at the attached Kincora pub, where there is often music at night, and bikes can be hired during the day. There are 11 hotels in the town, all charging about IR£37/50 for singles/doubles, and *Whites Imperial* (☎ 065-74042) is one of the best.

In town, the *Irish Arms* is a popular pub serving food and music at night. *The Half Door* is a pleasant café with delicious home baked snacks. The *Orchard Restaurant* at the Spa View hotel (☎ 065-74026) in town has been praised by food critics and a dinner ranges from around IR£10 for a vegetarian choice to IR£15 for lobster.

Getting There & Away
For information regarding bus services to Lisdoonvarna, see the Getting There & Away section under the Burren Area.

CLARE

Getting Around

Burke's Garage (☎ 065-74022) near the Spa Hotel has bikes for hire.

BALLYREEN

Ballyreen or Ballyryan is no more than a deserted stretch of coast about five km south of Fanore, but it's a lovely spot and a good place to camp. There's a cliff called Ailladie, which has some of Ireland's finest rock climbing. For divers, a barely visible track leads to a small inlet which has some excellent underwater scenery on the left, dropping quickly to a depth of about 20 metres, with vertical walls and gullies covered in jewel anemones.

Offshore after heavy rain you may see currents of brown water coming through the clear surface water. These are resurgences: fresh water flooding from an undersea cave. On land, glaciers have polished the limestone to a mirror-like finish. The incongruous stones and boulders are glacial erratics.

Getting There & Away

There is no direct bus to Ballyreen. The coastal bus service which covers the Burren area starts from Galway and goes to Kinvara, Ballyvaughan, Blackhead, Fanore, Lisdoonvarna and Doolin, returning by the same route. There is usually one bus daily from Monday to Saturday in winter and two or three buses a day between June and August.

FANORE

Fanore, five km south of Black-Head, could hardly be called a village. It's more like a stretch of coast, with a shop, a pub, and a few houses every now and then along the road. It has a fine sandy beach with an extensive backdrop of dunes: the only safe beach between Lahinch and Ballyvaughan. Behind the dunes is an accompanying caravan and camp site.

The remains of a Stone Age settlement were discovered near the small river that runs down through the dunes. Along the road south of the beach are a scattering of 10th and 11th-century church ruins.

Information

Four km south of the beach is a small shop and post office with a public phone. O'Donoghue's pub is just down the road and is a friendly place with music on Saturday nights. There are no other shops or bars along the coast. John McNamara at the Admiral's Rest Restaurant organises Wildlife Weekends (see the Places to Stay & Eat section).

Things to See & Do

Just behind Fanore Beach, a road goes inland and up the Khyber Pass, or Caher River Valley. This is the only surface river in the Burren. The first few km are very pleasant and there is a village up on the left, deserted since the Famine. There are foxes, badgers and pine martens in the area, though you are unlikely to see any.

There are a couple of lovely walks. On the coast road about 400 metres south of the beach, a small road goes inland. After about a km, it meets an old green road which can be followed south to Ballinalackan Castle, part of the Burren Way.

Alternatively, you can park at the Admiral's Rest Restaurant and go straight up through the fields to the green road. On top of this hill are two caves. Poll Dubh is, according to the restaurant's proprietor, an easy cave for amateurs, with delicate stalactites on view. The other, Poll Mor, is home to badgers, foxes, hares and rabbits.

There is a very well-preserved ring fort and souterrain on top of a hill at the south end of Fanore. Heading for Doolin, past the last house, the fort is on top of the hill about one km inland.

There is another good walk south of here. Travelling south, just past the Fanore town sign, the dip before the last hill on the left turns out to be a wonderful hidden valley, which also comes out eventually on the green road to Ballinalackan Castle.

Places to Stay & Eat

At the north end of Fanore, a few hundred metres inland from where the river crosses the road, is the *Bridge Hostel* (☎ 065-76134). It's a converted police station, with

22 beds at IR£5.50 per night in dorms or IR£7 per person in the two doubles, and they are open March to October.

At the south end of Fanore is the *Admiral's Rest B&B & Seafood Restaurant* (☎ 065-76105) run by John McNamara. Clean, tidy rooms cost IR£18/27 for B&B and dinner is IR£13. John organises a Burren Wildlife Weekend twice a year, in May and October.

Getting There & Away
On Tuesday and Thursday only, one bus a day makes the run between Galway and Lisdoonvarna, stopping at Ballyvaughan, Blackhead, Fanore and Ballinalacken Castle en route.

BLACK HEAD & THE FORT OF IRGHUS
Black Head, Clare's north-westernmost point, is a bleak but imposing mountain of limestone dropping swiftly into the sea. The head has an unstaffed lighthouse and good shore angling for bass and cod. If you are lucky, you may see dolphins.

There is a great hike up the head to a large Iron Age stone fort: *Cathair Dhun Iorais*, the 'Fort of Irghus', a legendary builder. The views across Galway Bay and the Aran Islands are exceptional, especially with the steep walls of the fort as a backdrop.

Inland, the hills rise to 318 metres and farther back is Slieve Elva (345 metres) capped with shale. Some of the intervening summits are marked with Bronze Age cairns. On your way up to the fort you cross an old green road.

BALLYVAUGHAN & AROUND
Ballyvaughan is a small pretty fishing village on a quiet corner of Galway Bay. In the past few years, it has been attracting upmarket visitors, and its nice pubs, restaurants and places to stay make it a good base for visiting the northern part of the Burren.

Just west of the village, past the holiday cottages and the Tea Gardens restaurant, is the quay and Monk's Bar. The harbour was built in 1829 when boats traded with the Aran Islands and Galway, often bringing in turf which was scarce in this area.

Ballyvaughan is a T-junction. Going south and inland brings you to the centre of the Burren, Aillwee Caves, Poulnabrone Dolmen and Lisdoonvarna. Turning west brings you out on the magnificent coast road to Black Head and down towards Doolin. North-east you reach Kinvara and County Galway.

Information
At some point, there will be a tourist information centre in the village; they are currently looking for premises.

The post office is on Main St. There are no banks but you can change money in Manus Walsh's Craft Shop on Main St or the Whitethorn Craft & Visitor Centre, east of Ballyvaughan on the way to Kinvara. Alternatively try Hyland's Hotel or Monk's Bar.

Corkscrew Hill
Five km south of Ballyvaughan on the Lisdoonvarna road is a series of very severe bends up Corkscrew Hill. The road was built as part of a famine-relief scheme in the 1840s. From the top there are spectacular views of the north Burren and Galway Bay with Aillwee Mountain and Caves on the right and Cappanawalla Hill on the left with the ruins of Newtown Castle at its base. From here, the route to Lisdoonvarna is through boggy and fairly boring countryside.

Gleninagh Castle
Down a narrow leafy lane and just off the coast road, about six km west of Ballyvaughan, is Gleninagh (Ivy Glen), a 16th-century O'Lochlain castle. The O'Lochlains were chieftains in this region and people lived here as late as 1840. If the gate is locked, you can squeeze or climb through with a bit of effort; there is a stair to the top. In front of the castle is a still-used holy well, and the ruins of a medieval church. To the east you may find a small horseshoe-shaped mound of earth: a *fulachta fiadh* or Bronze Age cooking place.

Places to Stay
You can camp in many of the fields around Ballyvaughan or along the coast just beyond

the harbour. There are no hostels in Ballyvaughan. The nearest are north on the way to Kinvara at Doorus, or west on the coast in Fanore.

For B&B, *Meadowfield* (☎ 065-77083) is 200 metres along the road to Kinvara and costs from IR£15/29. Almost opposite is *Oceanville* (☎ 065-77051), with doubles around IR£28. *Stonepark House* (☎ 065-77056) in Bishops Quarter, a km and a bit along the Kinvara road, costs IR£16/26. There are many more out around Doorus and New Quay and they all get busy, so book ahead.

A particularly good B&B is *Rusheen House* (☎ 065-77092), a little over one km out on the inland road to Lisdoonvarna. It's not cheap at IR£30/40, but the rooms and breakfast are top class. *Hyland's Hotel* (☎ 065-77037) in the middle of Ballyvaughan is a small, family-run hotel with a cosy atmosphere, costing around IR£31/53. They serve bar food and the restaurant is good as hotels go.

Places to Eat
You are spoiled for choice. The *Tea Garden* in an old cottage down towards the harbour, has top-notch soups, salads and home-cooked desserts. They are open till 6 pm. *Monk's Bar*, a popular place on the harbour, has melt-in-your-mouth mussels, seafood and brown bread.

The *T-Junction Café* in the village centre does a good breakfast and serves reasonable snacks all day. Most bars in town serve pub food. The restaurant at the *Aillwee Caves* is great for soups, salads and desserts. The *Whitethorn Craft & Visitor Centre*, north of town en route to Kinvara, has a good coffee-shop-cum-restaurant, open until 9.30 pm between Thursday and Saturday. The tourist menu is IR£13.

Claire's Restaurant (☎ 065-77029) in the village is the best around and the food is top class. Dinner will cost you IR£20 or more a head.

Entertainment
Monk's Bar has music almost every night in summer. *Hyland's Hotel* has music at weekends while *O'Brien's* has music from Thursday to Sunday night. *O'Lochlainn's*, on the left as you head down to the harbour, is a lovely old country pub, much less touristy than Monk's.

Getting There & Away
See the Burren Area's section on Getting There & Away for details of public transport to and from Ballyvaughan.

Getting Around
Monk's Bar (☎ 065-77059) by the harbour has bikes for hire at IR£6 a day, plus deposit.

CENTRAL BURREN
The road through the heart of the Burren runs between Ballyvaughan and Corofin via Leamenah Castle. Travelling south from Ballyvaughan, turn left before Corkscrew Hill at the sign for the Aillwee Caves. The road goes past Gleninsheen Wedge Tomb, Poulnabrone Dolmen and into some really desolate scenery.

To the south of the Burren, it's worth taking a diversion to Kilfenora to take in the Burren Centre and Kilfenora's cathedral and high crosses.

Aillwee Caves
The Aillwee Caves (☎ 065-77036) are a good place to pass a rainy afternoon. The main passage penetrates for 600 metres into the mountain, widening into larger caverns, one with its own waterfall. The caves were carved out by water some two million years ago. Near the entrance are the remains of a brown bear, extinct in Ireland for over 10,000 years.

Aillwee was discovered in 1944 by Jack McCann, a local farmer, and today has a discreetly designed outer building with an excellent café. Behind the cave entrance there is a relatively easy scramble up 300-metre Aillwee Mountain. There are fine views from the summit.

You can only go into the cave as part of a guided group and tours are IR£3.85/2.20. Aillwee is open April to September 10 am to

6 pm. Try and visit early in the day before the crowds arrive.

Gleninsheen Wedge Tomb

This tomb is known in folklore as the 'Druid's Altar' though the druids lived a long time after this was built. The tomb is just beside the road, a little over a km north-west of Poulnabrone Dolmen. It's thought to be from 4000 to 5000 years old and like most of the other tombs in the Burren is up here on high ground.

A magnificent gold collar was found nearby in 1930 by a boy hunting rabbits. The collar was in a crack in the limestone and at first the boy thought it was part of a coffin. It is reckoned to be one of the finest pieces of prehistoric Irish craftwork. Dating from around 700 BC, it's now on display at the National Museum in Dublin.

Poulnabrone Dolmen

Poulnabrone Dolmen is one of Ireland's most photographed ancient monuments, the one you see on all the postcards with the sun setting behind it. The dolmen is a three-legged tomb, sitting in a sea of limestone without a house in sight. At quiet times of day, this is a truly lovely place. It is eight km inland from Aillwee and signposted from the road.

Poulnabrone was built over 5000 years ago. It was excavated in 1989 and the remains of more than 25 people were found among pieces of pottery and jewellery. Radiocarbon dating suggests they were buried between 3800 and 3200 BC. When the dead were originally buried here, the whole structure was covered in a mound of earth which has since eroded away. Poulnabrone means 'the hole of the quern' and the capstone weighs five tons. Try and visit early in the morning or at sunset for good photographs. Better still, try a moonlit night.

Try to ignore the intrusive iron shed which has been built in the neighbouring field by a local farmer.

Cahercommaun Cliff Fort

Perched on the edge of an inland cliff, three km south of the tiny village of Carron, is the great stone fort of Cahercommaun. It was inhabited during the 8th and 9th centuries by a group of people who hunted deer and grew a small amount of grain. There are the remains of a souterrain or underground passage leading from the fort to the outer face of the cliff.

To get there, go south from Carron and take a left turn for Kilinaboy. After 1.5 km a path on the left leads up to the fort.

East of Carron

If you turn east at Carron, you have two options. The first is to turn north after about two km, which takes you on a magnificent drive through a valley to Cappaghmore in County Galway. If instead you continue directly east you come close to the lovely Mullaghmore Mountain. Later, just over the Galway border on the main road to Gort, is Kilmacduagh, a monastic site with a splendid round tower.

KILFENORA

The tiny, windswept village of Kilfenora lies on the southern fringes of the Burren, eight km from Lisdoonvarna. Most visitors come to see the monastic remains, five High Crosses and a tiny 12th-century cathedral. The village itself is a touch forlorn, but has some attractive shopfronts and pubs.

Burren Display Centre

The Burren Display Centre (☎ 065-88030) was built by the local community and has a fair amount of information on the Burren and guidebooks for sale. There is a display, a video presentation and plenty of literature for sale. Entry is IR£2.50/1.25 but if you know some of the basic geography of the Burren the cost might be better spent on the very decent café attached to the centre.

Kilfenora Cathedral

The pope has the honour of being bishop of Kilfenora and in the past the ruined 12th-century cathedral was an important place of pilgrimage. St Facthna founded the monastery here in the 6th century and it later became capital of Kilfenora diocese, the smallest in the country.

The cathedral is the smallest one you are ever likely to see. Only the ruined structure and nave of the more recent Protestant church are actually part of the cathedral. The chancel has two primitive carved figures on top of two tombs. They are thought to be bishops and it must be said that neither were very handsome gentlemen. The theory goes that after the Black Death in the 14th century there was a general decline in craft skills across the continent, and these poor carvings may be examples of this.

High Crosses

Kilfenora is best known for its high crosses, three in the churchyard and a large 12th-century example in the field about 100 metres to the west.

The most interesting one is the 800-year-old Doorty Cross, standing prominently near the front door of the church. It differs significantly from the standard Irish high cross so beloved of photographers and the Irish Tourist Board, in that it is without the usual pierced disc or wheel on top. It was lying broken in two until the 1950s when it was re-erected. The Doortys are a Tipperary family whose ancestors were bishops here, and you can see the name on many recent headstones.

The east face of the cross is the better preserved. One interpretation of the carvings has Christ on top ordering two figures in the middle to destroy the devil/bird at the bottom, which is misbehaving. The west face is much less clear. Christ still appears to be on top, this time surrounded by birds. Directly underneath are delicate designs and a man on horseback holding the ends of the patterns. Some say it is Christ's entry into Jerusalem. One theory suggests the cross may commemorate Kilfenora being made headquarters of the diocese in the 12th century.

Places to Stay

A km along the Lisdoonvarna road is the welcoming *Mrs Howley's* (☎ 065-88075), at IR£18.50/27.

The *Burren Farmhouse* (☎ 065-71363), two km along the Ennistymon road, is equally pleasant and has three doubles for IR£27.

Places to Eat

The *Burren Display Centre* has a reasonable tearoom, open 9.30 am to 6 pm. *Vaughan's* pub (☎ 065-88004) on the green has bar food.

Entertainment

Vaughan's pub has regular Irish music sessions during weeknights and Saturday. *Nagle's Bar* has music at weekends only.

COROFIN

Corofin is a small village on the southern fringes of the Burren. Commonly found in the area are *turloughs*, small lakes which often disappear in dry summers. O'Brien castles abound in this boggy countryside, two of them on the shores of nearby Lake Inchiquin.

Corofin is home to the **Clare Heritage Centre** which has a genealogy facility for people with Clare ancestors and a display covering the period around the famine. Over a quarter of a million people lived in Clare before the famine in 1845; a century later there were less than 75,000. Opening hours are 10 am to 6 pm and admission is IR£2/1.

About four km north-east of Corofin, on the road to Leamaneh Castle and Kilenora, look for the small town of Kilinaboy. The ruined church here is worth seeking out here for its sheila na gig over the doorway.

Places to Stay

Camping & Hostel The IHH *Corofin Village Hostel* (☎ 065-37683) is a fine hostel and camp site with good facilities on Main St in Corofin. A bed in a dorm is IR£6, doubles IR£15. Camping for two people is IR£6 and cyclists pay IR£3.

B&Bs There are plenty of B&Bs in the area, many of them in Kilinaboy, one to two km

SEAN SHEEHAN

TONY WHEELER

JOHN MURRAY

County Clare
Top: Thatched cottage
Middle: Ennis Abbey, Ennis
Bottom: Turlough (Temporary Lake), The Burren

SEAN SHEEHAN

JOHN MURRAY

JOHN MURRAY

County Galway & Aran Islands

Top: Westport, County Mayo
Middle: Salmon fishing, Connemara, County Galway
Bottom: Inisheer, Aran Islands, County Galway

along the road north to Lisdoonvarna. Good ones include *Cottage View* (☎ 065-27662), one km from Corofin, at IR£15/27. *Clifden View* (☎ 065-37779) has three rooms at IR£18.20/27 for singles/doubles.

Places to Eat

Near the heritage centre is a reasonable coffee shop serving light meals all day. For pub food try the *Angler's Rest. Bofey Quinn's* on Main St is a very popular pub and seafood restaurant serving simple but delicious snacks and meals, open until 10.30 pm for meals between Easter and September.

Getting There & Away

There is an infrequent bus service from Kilkee or Doonbeg to Ennis and Limerick via Corofin. Check with Ennis bus depot (☎ 065-24177), or the Corofin Village Hostel for times.

LEAMENAH CASTLE

Leamenah is a well-preserved castle-cum-fortified-house, five km east of Kilfenora and eight km north of Corofin. The road north to Ballyvaughan brings you through some of the wildest parts of the Burren and past a number of its highlights such as Poulnabrone Dolmen.

The castle's name is pronounced 'Lay-im-on-ay' and is Irish for 'deer's leap' or 'horse's leap'. If you look carefully, you will see that there are two parts joined together. The five-storey tower house on the right was built around 1480 by the O'Briens and is much more solid and better defended than the main house which Conor O'Brien added in 1640. This has four storeys and its most appealing features are the largely intact stone window frames.

The whole building was originally surrounded by a high wall. Just above the tower house entrance is a vertical shaft or murder hole. If this was the 15th century and you were an uninvited guest, all manner of unspeakable things could be dropped on top of you including boiling oil, tar, arrows and anything else handy. There is a fine view from the top of the tower.

Conor O'Brien, builder of the house, was killed in 1651 fighting for the royalists against Cromwell. His wife, the infamous Maire Rua McMahon, reportedly refused to take his body back into Leamenah Castle. After his death, she offered to marry one of Cromwell's soldiers to ensure her son Donough didn't lose his inheritance. Marry one she did, but they still lost the estate. Despite this setback she and her new husband, John Cooper, stayed together. They regained their property in 1675 but later records suggest she was suspected of murdering Cooper; she was tried for the crime but acquitted. She died in 1686.

NORTH-EAST CLARE

Low farmland stretches south from County Galway until it meets the bluff limestone hills of the Burren. The Burren begins just west of Kinvara and Doorus where the road forks, going inland to Carron or along the coast to Ballyvaughan.

From Oranmore in County Galway all the way down to Ballyvaughan, the coastline wriggles along small inlets and peninsulas; some like Finnavarra and New Quay are worth a detour. Just inland near Bellharbour is the largely intact Corcomroe Abbey, and the ancient churches of Oughtmama lie up a quiet side valley.

Galway Bay forms the backdrop to some outstanding scenery: bare stone hills shining in the sun, with small hamlets and rich patches of green wherever there is soil.

Getting There & Away

There is a bus service between Galway City and Cork which passes through Kinvara and Ballyvaughan on summer weekdays only. Another service running between Galway and Doolin also stops in those two places, and offers one bus daily in winter and two or three in summer. Infrequent buses on the Burren coastal route from Galway can drop you in Kinvara or Ballyvaughan; there is usually one bus daily in winter, from Monday to Saturday, and two each day in summer. Details of these bus services are available from Galway bus station (☎ 091-562000) or Ennis bus station (☎ 065-24177).

New Quay & the Flaggy Shore

New Quay, on the Finnavarra Peninsula, is about two km off the main Kinvara to Ballyvaughan road. There are a couple of thatched cottages on the peninsula and the ruins of a 17th-century mansion.

Linnane's pub in New Quay serves excellent seafood and is right next door to Ireland's biggest oyster farm.

The Flaggy Shore, west of New Quay, is a particularly nice stretch of coastline. Layers of limestone march boldly into the sea, and behind the coastal path swans parade gently on Lough Muirí. There are otters in the area. On the way out to Finnavarra Point is Mt Vernon Lodge, the summer home of Augusta Lady Gregory, playwright and friend of W B Yeats. She was prominent in the Anglo-Irish literary revival.

On Finnavarra Point is one of the west coast's few **Martello towers**, built in the early 1800s to warn Galway in case Napoleon came sailing by and sneaked into Ireland by the back door. The road loops back and joins the main road beside a small lake which is very rich in birdlife including ducks, moorhens and herons.

Bellharbour

Bellharbour is no more than a crossroads with some thatched holiday cottages, about eight km east of Ballyvaughan. There is an excellent walk along an old green road which begins behind the modern St Patrick's Catholic Church, one km north of Bellharbour, and threads north along Abbey Hill.

Just inland from here is Corcomroe Abbey, the valley and churches of Oughtmama, and the interior road that takes you right through the heart of the Burren.

Wildlife

You can almost be guaranteed seals along the coast west of Bellharbour. Go about one km along the Ballyvaughan road until you spot a large dark green farm shed in on the right. Follow the path down to the shore and you may see seals. This inlet is also thick with birds, and winter visitors include brent geese from Arctic Canada.

Corcomroe Abbey

Corcomroe is a Cistercian abbey one km inland from Bellharbour. It lies in its own small valley surrounded by low hills and is a very peaceful place. Another name for it is 'St Mary's of the fertile rock'. It was founded around 1180 by Munsterman Donal Mor O'Brien. His grandson, King Conor O'Brien

---

Legend of Corcomroe

In 1317, the Battle of Corcomroe was fought very near the abbey. Two O'Brien clans were fighting for control over Clare. Legend has it that one of the chieftains, Donough, was passing by Lough Rask on his way to battle, when he saw a witch washing a pile of bleeding limbs in the lake. The witch told Donough that her name was Bronach Boirne and that the corpses were of his army, if he insisted on going into battle; and that, to make matters worse, Donough's own head was in the pile.

Donough's men tried to capture her, but she flew up in the air and rained curses on them. To reassure his men, Donough told them Bronach was the lover of his arch rival Dermot and her warnings merely a ploy to frighten them off. Unfortunately for Donough, by that night he and most of his army were lying dead in the abbey.

Incidentally, on nearby Moneen Mountain is a pass called Mam Catha, the 'pass of the battle', which could refer to the route taken by Donough and his army. Dermot, the victor, later defeated de Clare of Bunratty, halting the spread of Norman influence in Clare for some time. ■

who died in 1267, occupies the tomb in the north-east wall, and there is a crude carving of him below another effigy of a staring bishop armed with a crozier. Some fine Romanesque carvings are scattered throughout the abbey.

Oughtmama Valley

Oughtmama is a lonely and deserted valley hiding some small and very old churches. To get there turn inland at Bellharbour, left at the Y-junction, and up to a clump of trees and a house on the right. A rough track here will bring you east up a blind valley to the churches. St MacDuach, who also built churches on the Aran Islands, founded the monastery here in the 6th century. The three churches were built in the 12th century by monks looking for peace and solitude.

It's a hardy walk up Turlough Hill behind the chapels but the views are tremendous. Near the summit are the remains of an Iron Age hill fort.

County Galway

County Galway is likely to be one of the highlights of any visit to Ireland. Stretching from Ballinasloe in the midlands through the wilds of Connemara to the craggy Atlantic coastline beyond Clifden, Galway (*Gaillimh*) has a huge amount of interest packed into its 5940 sq km. It is the second largest county in Ireland after Cork – and Galway City is the west coast's liveliest and most populous settlement.

Galway's neighbour to the south is County Clare, and the Burren limestone region peters out near Kinvara, a picturesque little coastal town just inside the Galway border. However, the limestone surfaces out to sea in a long, grey reef; this forms Galway's three Aran Islands, which are famous for their folklore, woollen sweaters, bleak scenery and Irish-speaking population.

Galway's landscape is extremely varied. Lough Corrib cuts off the rugged coastal region from the largely flat interior which makes up the bulk of the county.

Highlights
- Walking in the Connemara National Park
- The scenic journey through the Lough Inagh Valley in Connemara
- Inishmór (Aran Islands) and especially Dún Aengus perched on the edge of its southern cliffs
- Walking or cycling on Inishmaan & Inisheer (Aran Islands)
- Cycling or walking the Sky Road west of Clifden in Connemara
- The pubs and cultural life of Galway City
- Inishbofin and Inisturk islands

Galway City

Galway City is a delight, with its narrow streets, old stone and wooden shopfronts, good restaurants and bustling pubs. It is also the administrative capital of the county, and home to the local government, University College Galway, and a regional college to the east of town. There is a ferry to the Aran Islands from the docks, although you are better off travelling farther west and taking a boat from near Spiddal or Rossaveal.

In marked contrast to most of the depopulated west coast, Galway is one of Europe's fastest growing cities. Large factories and a bustling sense of energy underlie its relative economic security.

Galway City is a gateway for Connemara and the west, as it sits at the southern tip of Lough Corrib which forms a natural border

to the region. The city is also a handy base for exploring the Burren, which begins some 30 km to the south in Clare.

Galway City has always attracted a bohemian crowd of musicians, artists, intellectuals and young people. This is partly due to the presence of the university, but the main attractions are the nightlife and pubs where talk and drink flow by the bucketful. The city is a major Gaelic centre and Irish is widely spoken. The Druid Theatre is one of the best in the country, and the city hosts an annual and hugely popular arts festival every summer. The place goes wild during Galway Race Week in the last week in July. If you

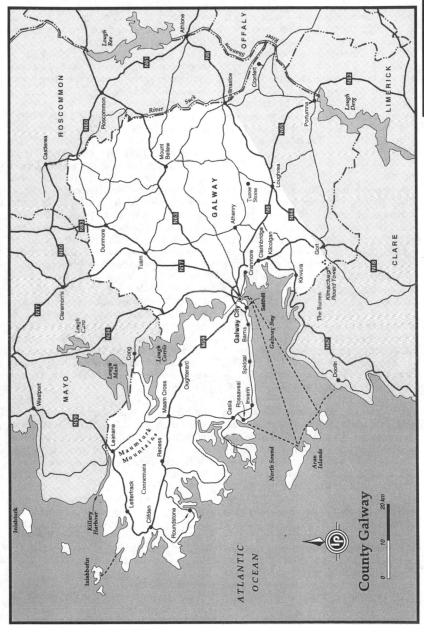

County Galway

haven't booked, accommodation is going to be very difficult to find at these times.

While the city centre deserves its accolades, the approaches and suburbs don't. Coming from the east, you pass by huge modern hotels, barren housing developments and the ugly regional college. The coast road west through the beach resort of Salthill and on to Spiddal is one of the worst examples of ribbon development in the country. Only after Spiddal do the bungalows thin out.

HISTORY

Galway grew from a fishing village in the Claddagh area at the mouth of the river to become an important walled town when the Anglo-Normans under Richard de Burgo captured territory from the local O'Flahertys in 1234. The Irish for outsider or foreigner is 'gall', which may be the origin of the city's Irish name, Gaillimh. The town walls were built by the Anglo-Normans from around 1270.

Galway City became something of an outpost in the wild west. In 1396, Richard II granted a charter to the city which effectively transferred power from the de Burgos to 14 merchant families or 'tribes'. This led to the name 'City of the Tribes' by which Galway is commonly known. These powerful families were mostly English or Norman in origin. But, of course, there were tribes outside the walls as well as inside. Clashes with the leading Irish families of Connemara were frequent, and at one time the city's west gate bore the prayer and warning: 'From the fury of the O'Flahertys, good Lord deliver us.' To ensure fury was kept at bay, the city fathers warned that no uninvited 'O' nor Mac' should show his face on Galway's fair streets.

English power throughout the region waxed and waned, but the city maintained its independent status, under ruling merchant families who were mostly loyal to the English crown. Galway's relative isolation encouraged a huge trade in wine, spices, fish and salt with Portugal and Spain. At one point, it rivalled Bristol and London in the volume of trade passing through the docks. Many of the ruling families educated their sons in mainland Europe.

For a long while Galway prospered. A huge fire in 1473 destroyed much of the town and created space for a new street layout with many solid stone buildings being erected in the 16th and 17th centuries.

Galway's faithful support of the English crown led to its downfall when Cromwell turned up. The city was besieged in 1651 and fell in April 1652, after nine months' resistance. Cromwell's forces under Charles Coote wreaked their customary havoc and Galway's long period of decline was under way. In 1691 the city again took the wrong side and King William's forces added to the destruction. The important trade with Spain was almost at an end, and with Dublin and Waterford taking most of the sea traffic, Galway stagnated until its recent revival.

ORIENTATION

Galway's tightly packed town centre lies on both sides of the River Corrib, which connects Lough Corrib with the sea. Eyre Square and most of the main shopping areas are east of the river. There are three main bridges; the northernmost, Salmon Weir Bridge, looks over a weir and is overshadowed by Galway Cathedral.

Just west of the river mouth is the historic, but now totally redeveloped, Claddagh area, while slightly farther west is the beach resort of Salthill, a popular area for accommodation and restaurants. Eyre Square is just west of the combined bus and railway station, near the tourist office and is a good central meeting point.

From Eyre Square, the meandering main shopping street starts as Williamsgate St and becomes William St and then Shop St before splitting into Guard St and High St. High St then becomes Quay St and crosses the River Corrib on Wolfe Tone Bridge.

INFORMATION

The tourist office (☎ 091-563081) is just east of Eyre Square and opens seven days a week from 8.30 am to 8 pm during July and

August. In June it's 9 am to 7 pm. At the height of the season it is busy and there can be a delay of an hour or more in making accommodation bookings. There's another branch at the junction of Seapoint Promenade and Upper Salthill Rd at Salthill.

A USIT travel office is located at the Kinlay House hostel.

English language classes are taught at the Cultural Institute (☎ 091-568300) in Lowstrand House in Flood St and there is also a Language Centre on the first floor of the Bridge Mills Shopping Centre. The Alliance Française de Galway is also located here.

Banks
All Irish banks have branches in the city centre. The building societies also have bureaus de change and are open Monday to Friday from 9.30 am to 5 pm. The main tourist office also changes money. The bureau de change in the Eyre Square Shopping Centre is open seven days a week until late evening.

Post
The GPO is on Eglington St, north of William St. It's open Monday to Saturday from 9 am to 6 pm.

Laundry
There's a laundrette on Sea Rd, near Upper Dominick St on the west side of the river. Others can be found in the Old Malte Arcade off High St in the centre and at Salthill, near the Stella Maris Hostel.

Books & Bookshops
Hawkins House is a good bookshop at 14 Churchyard St, right by the Collegiate Church of St Nicholas. Kenny's Bookshop is on High St above the gallery of the same name. There's also a branch of Eason's on Shop St and Byrne's second-hand bookshop across from Bewley's Café on Middle St.

A copy of *Medieval Galway – A Rambler's Guide & Map* (Tir Edas) is available in most bookshops.

EYRE SQUARE
This is the focal point for the eastern and most extensive part of Galway City. In spite of Galway's civic pride, the square shows no great imagination in its layout. The bus and railway station is at the western corner, the tourist office just off the southern corner. This side of the square taken up almost entirely by the Great Southern Hotel, a great grey limestone building. To the west of the square is Browne's Doorway of 1627, a fragment from the home of one of the city's merchant rulers.

In the centre is the John F Kennedy Memorial Park. Kennedy visited the city in 1963 and a stone tablet in the square commemorates the event. Ronald Reagan also dropped by in 1984, when the town was celebrating its 500th anniversary – and the university gave him a doctorate! To the north of the square is a controversial statue to the Galway-born writer Pádraic O'Conaire (1882-1928), a noted hell-raiser. It's one of the better examples of modern sculpture in the country. Finally there's a curious object behind Browne's Doorway, which is supposed to evoke the sails of a traditional Galway hooker. It was designed by Eamon O'Doherty and erected during the city's quincentennial in 1984.

COLLEGIATE CHURCH OF ST NICHOLAS OF MYRA
This church on Shop St with its curious pyramidal spire dates from 1320 and is not only Galway's most important monument, but is also the biggest medieval parish church in Ireland. Although it has been rebuilt and enlarged over the centuries, much of the original form has been retained. After Cromwell's victory, the church suffered the standard indignity of being used as a stable. Much damage was done but at least it survived; 14 other Galway churches were razed to the ground. Look for the damaged stonework. The church has numerous finely worked stone tombs and memorials. The two bells date from 1590 and 1630.

Parts of the floor are paved with gravestones from the 16th to the 18th centuries and

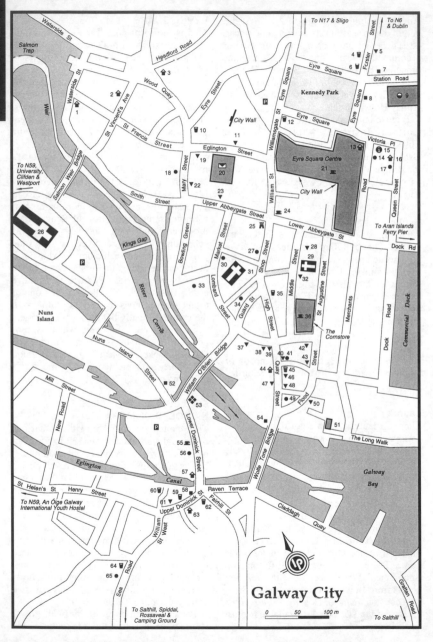

Galway City

To N17 & Sligo
To N6 & Dublin
Salmon Trap
Waterside St
Headford Road
Eyre Square
Kennedy Park
Station Road
Wood Quay
City Wall
Eyre Square
Victoria Pl
Eglinton Street
Eyre Square Centre
City Wall
Upper Abbeygate Street
Lower Abbeygate St
To Aran Islands Ferry Pier
Dock Rd
Bowling Green
The Cornstore
Commercial Dock
Nuns Island
River Corrib
Dock Road
Nuns Island Street
William O'Brien Bridge
Wolfe Tone Bridge
The Long Walk
Mill Street
New Road
Eglinton
Lower Dominick Street
Galway Bay
St Helen's St
Henry Street
Canal
Raven Terrace
To N59, An Óige Galway International Youth Hostel
Upper Dominick Street
Fairhill St
Claddagh Quay
William St West
Sea Road
Grattan Road
To Salthill, Spiddal, Rossaveal & Camping Ground
0   50   100 m
To Salthill

0   50   100 m

PLACES TO STAY

1 Corrib Villa Hostel
2 Salmon Weir Hostel
3 Woodquay Hostel
7 Great Western House Hostel
8 Great Southern Hotel
12 Skeffington Arms Hotel & Pub
13 Kinlay House Hostel
16 Celtic Tourist Hostel
44 Quay Street Hostel
52 St Martin's B&B
54 Jury's Galway Inn
57 Galway City Hostel
58 Arch View Hostel
63 West End Hostel

PLACES TO EAT

5 Eyre House Restaurants
6 Dragon Court Restaurant
11 Conlon's Restaurant
19 Salsa Mexican Restaurant
21 Sails Café
22 Kashmir Restaurant
23 Brannagan's Restaurant
24 Food for Thought Café
28 Aideen's Wine Bar & Restaurant
32 Brasserie Restaurant
36 Bewley's Café
37 Country Basket
38 Hungry Grass
39 Neachtain's Bar & Restaurant
40 Quay West Restaurant
42 Pasta Mista
43 Sev'nth Heaven
46 Fat Freddy's Pizzeria
47 McDonagh's Restaurant
48 La Mezza Luna

50 Shama Indian Restaurant
55 Left Bank Café
61 Kebab House

PUBS

4 Rabbitt's Bar & Restaurant
6 An Púcán Bar
10 MacSwiggan's Pub
35 King's Head Pub
45 Quay's Bar
59 Taylor's Bar
60 Blue Note
62 Monroe's Tavern
64 Crane's Bar

OTHER

9 Bus & Railway Station
14 Galway Cycle Hire
15 Tourist Office & Aran Islands Ferry Offices
17 Celtic Cycles
18 Laundrette
20 Post Office
25 Lynch's Castle
26 St Nicholas' Cathedral
27 Eason's Bookshop
29 Augustinian Church
30 Lynch's Memorial Window
31 St Nicholas Collegiate Church
33 Nora Barnacle's House
34 Hawkins House Bookshop
41 Druid Theatre
49 Punchbag Theatre
51 Spanish Arch & Museum
53 Bridge Mill Shopping Centre
56 Arts Centre
65 Laundrette

the Lynch Aisle holds the tombs of the powerful Lynch family. A large block tomb in one corner is said to be the grave of James Lynch, a former mayor of Galway, who condemned his son to death for killing a young Spanish visitor. None of the townsfolk would act as hangman, and the mayor was so dedicated to upholding justice that he personally acted as hangman, after which he went into seclusion – or so the story goes. The Lynch Memorial Window, on Market St outside the church, tells the tale and claims to be the spot where he carried out the execution.

At the end of the aisle is the 'empty frame' which is said to have once held a picture of the Virgin Mary, which later turned up in Gyor in Hungary.

It's claimed that Christopher Columbus paused in Galway to hear mass and pray at the church. The supposed Galway detour took place either because one of his crew was a Galway man or because Columbus wished to investigate tales of St Brendan's earlier voyage to the Americas.

BOWLING GREEN

Across the road from the Lynch Memorial is Bowling Green. No 8 Bowling Green was once the home of Nora Barnacle, who married James Joyce. There is now a small museum dedicated to the couple, open Monday to Saturday, IR£1. Joyce only visited the house on two occasions, in 1909 and 1912. When James Joyce's father heard of his son's partner he remarked how 'she'll stick to him' which indeed she did. Her biography *Nora* by Brenda Maddox (London, 1988) is an excellent read.

LYNCH'S CASTLE

On the corner of Shop and Abbeygate Sts, parts of the gargoyled old stone townhouse called Lynch's Castle date back to the 14th century. Most of the present building, however, dates from around 1600. Reputed to be the finest town castle in Ireland, it now houses a branch of the AIB Bank. The Lynch family were the most powerful of the 14 ruling tribes, and members of the family held the position of mayor no less than 80 times between 1480 and 1650 – including the notorious James Lynch, whose tomb is in St Nicholas' Church.

Lynch's Castle has numerous fine stone features on its facade including the coats of arms of Henry VII and the earl of Kildare, as well as the gargoyles, unusual in Ireland.

THE SPANISH ARCH

A 1651 pictorial view of Galway clearly shows its extensive city walls – but since the visits of Cromwell in 1652 and King William in 1691, and the subsequent centuries of neglect, the walls have almost completely disappeared. Located near the river, the Spanish Arch seems to have been an extension of the walls, through which ships unloaded their goods – often wine and brandy from Spain. This area used to be the fish market.

The unremarkable Galway City Museum is by the arch. It's open Monday to Saturday from 10 am to 1 pm and 2.15 to 5.15 pm.

It Could Happen to a Bishop

Or so goes the Irish saying, and in 1992 it certainly happened to Dr Eamonn Casey, the Bishop of Galway. I happened to be in Galway on the morning the 'shock' announcement was made that the Bishop had zipped off to Rome to tender his resignation. Why? Well no-one was saying, certainly no-one from the church, but there was talk of a woman in the USA whom he once knew. And it was said she had a son. Before you could whisper 'celibacy?' the bishop was on his way to New York, flying 1st class, and then, before you could whisper 'disgraced bishop' he was following that well-trodden route to South America popularised by escaping Nazis and British train robbers.

The bishop wasn't saying and the church certainly wasn't, but his ex-girlfriend and their 18-year-old son soon were, and the damage-control efforts provided high drama for the next few weeks. Pages of analysis followed in the papers. My journeys on Irish roads were enlivened by a fascinating series of radio call-in programmes. Some callers tore into the woman, accusing her of leading the poor man astray. One caller even developed (at length, Irish call-ins tend to be at length) a fascinating theory that it was a KGB plot and she was a highly trained operative, skilled in the seduction of randy bishops. At the end of 20 minutes of this fellow, I was uncertain whether or not this was some kind of skit. The caller who summed it up for me announced that despite all the pontificating, he and his friends found the whole thing hilarious.

Some more serious analysis questioned the whole point of priestly celibacy. The good bishop certainly hadn't. At the same time that he was concealing the existence of his son, he was a conservative on abortion, contraception, celibacy and other sex-related issues. Well, he was a good Catholic, said one of the commentators, since he certainly didn't practise birth control.

The question of Irish double standards also got a wide airing; how much sympathy would have been expressed for a nun who got herself 'in trouble'? What didn't get much questioning was the small matter of IR£70,000 which the good bishop had 'borrowed' from church funds in order to keep things quiet. As the shit hit the fan it was quickly repaid by 'friends of Dr Casey' and the church announced that the financial issue was closed as far as they were concerned. Well – would you trust a bishop who had received speeding tickets in his BMW?

Tony Wheeler

ST NICHOLAS' CATHEDRAL

From the Spanish Arch, a pleasant riverside path runs all the way up river and across the Salmon Weir Bridge to the second site in the town dedicated to St Nicholas. Galway Cathedral is a huge and imposing structure, opened in 1965. Tasteful it is not, and critics vie for the most acidic descriptions of this monument to inelegance.

Inside things are a little less grandiose, but it's a mishmash of styles and intentions. Even the cathedral's name is a mouthful; correctly, it's the Catholic Cathedral of Our Lady Assumed into Heaven and St Nicholas.

Until 1992, the cathedral was the base of Bishop Eamonn Casey, one of Ireland's most flamboyant and well-liked clergymen. But in 1992 it emerged that he was the father of a teenage son, and Casey fled Ireland. The story made headlines all over the world.

SALMON WEIR

The Upper or Salmon Weir Bridge crosses the River Corrib in front of the cathedral. Just upstream is the great weir where the waters of the Corrib cascade down one of their final descents before the sea, one km to the south. The weir controls the water levels above it, and when the salmon are running you can often see them waiting in the clear waters before making the rush upstream to spawn. You may see them jumping up the weir; a fish pass allows them easier passage.

The earliest records of Galway include references to the de Burgo family owning the fisheries on the town's weirs. Today they are owned by the Central Fisheries Board. The salmon and sea trout season is usually from February to September. Most fish pass through the weir during May and June. Fishing licences are obtainable from the Fishery Office (☎ 091-62388), Nuns Island, Galway.

CLADDAGH

Galway's main fishing area used to centre around the Claddagh district. Up to 3000 people and 300 boats were based here at one stage. Many of the boats were traditional Galway vessels with sturdy black hulls and rough rust-coloured sails, known as *púcáns* and *gleótógs*, today collectively called Galway hookers.

Claddagh used to have its own characteristic costume and dialect, and a king. Although the traditional Claddagh is gone, you can still wear a Claddagh ring with a crowned heart nestling between two hands. If the heart points towards the hand then the wearer is taken or married, towards the fingertip means he or she is looking for a mate. The Claddagh ring was the wedding ring used throughout much of Connaught from the mid-18th century.

SALTHILL

Beyond Claddagh, but still within walking distance of the city, is Salthill, a traditional large seaside resort. The beaches are often packed in hot weather but are not particularly good.

ORGANISED TOURS

During the summer months Bus Éireann runs a variety of tours from Galway and Salthill, including day trips to Connemara or the Burren and shorter trips to Cong or the Knock Shrine. Contact the railway station or the tourist office for details. The *Corrib Princess* does afternoon cruises on the Corrib River from Woodquay, just up river from the Salmon Weir. Bookings can be made at the tourist office.

FESTIVALS

A Jazz Festival in February is now well established. Around Easter there is the Cúirt Festival of Literature which is growing in importance every year. The city parties with a vengeance at the Galway Arts Festival in late July. The whole town turns out for this two-week extravaganza of theatre, music and art. There's even a parade.

The last week of July is Galway Race Week which is as much an event off the course as on it. The racecourse, six km from the city centre at Ballybrit, hosts a traditional Irish fair.

The Galway International Oyster Festival takes place towards the end of September.

PLACES TO STAY

Galway has a huge variety of accommodation, but you may still have difficulty finding a bed in summer. There is more accommodation in Salthill a couple of km to the south-west.

Camping

The *Silver Strand Caravan & Camping Park* (☎ 091-592452) is on the coast, just beyond Salthill. Large/small tents are IR£6.50/6 plus 50p per adult. The *Spiddal Caravan & Camping Park* (or Pairc Saoire an Spidéil in Irish) (☎ 091-83372) is 18 km west of Galway on the coast road. Large/small tents are IR£4/3.

Hostels

There are legions of hostels. A newish one is *Great Western House* (☎ 091-561150) in Frenchville Lane adjacent to the bus and train station, with beds for IR£6.50 plus double rooms and a sauna. The modern 150-room *Kinlay House* (☎ 091-65244), opposite the tourist office, is well equipped, has a variety of rooms from IR£7 and includes a light breakfast. Around the corner on Queen St the not-so-attractive *Celtic Tourist Hostel* (☎ 091-566606) has beds for IR£6.50 and IR£17 doubles.

The *Quay St Hostel* (☎ 091-568644) at 10 Quay St has 97 beds and charges IR£6.60, doubles IR£23. *Corrib Villa* (☎ 091-562892) is at 4 Waterside St, near the Salmon Weir Bridge. It costs IR£5.90 and there are no doubles. The *Woodquay Hostel* (☎ 091-562618) costs IR£6.90 and has a decent kitchen but cramped washrooms and rickety bunks. It's just north of the city centre, in St Anne's House at 23-24 Woodquay. Around the corner in St Vincent's Ave is the *Salmon Weir Hostel* (☎ 091-561133). Beds are IR£6.50.

The *Arch View Hostel* (☎ 091-586661), with 60 beds at IR£6.50, is hidden away at the junction of Upper and Lower Dominick Sts, just west of Wolfe Tone Bridge. Close by, on the other side of the canal, is the *Galway City Hostel* (☎ 091-566367) at IR£6.60; again, no doubles. Back on Upper Dominick St is the *West End Hostel* (☎ 091-583636) with 58 beds for IR£7 and four doubles at IR£20. Continue north-west from Upper Dominick St through the name changes Henry St, St Helen's St to St Mary's Rd, then turn left to find the huge An Óige *Galway International Youth Hostel* (☎ 091-527411). This is a summer hostel in St Mary's College, open only for July and August. It's between central Galway and Salthill. You can take bus No 1 from Eyre Square. It costs IR£8, including a light breakfast, and also has family rooms.

In Salthill, the *Grand Holiday Hostel* (☎ 091-521150) is right on the promenade and has rooms with two or four beds as well as family rooms, from IR£6.50 a night. The similarly priced *Stella Maris Holiday Hostel* (☎ 091-521950) is at 151 Upper Salthill. The *Mary Ryan Hostel* (☎ 091-23303) is at 4 Beechmount Ave, Highfield Park, beyond Salthill to the south of the centre. It's about a 20-minute walk from the centre; or you could take bus No 2 from Eyre Square to Taylor Hill Convent. It costs IR£6.50 and has one en suite double for IR£16; ring before heading out there to make sure there are rooms available. The *Galway Tourist Hostel* (☎ 091-25176) is also just beyond Salthill, at Gentian Hill, Knocknacarra. It's just past the golf course and camp site, pleasantly situated near the water and with a camping area.

B&Bs

In summer you may have to travel to the suburbs. There are not many B&Bs around the city centre, but it's worth trying Mrs Sexton's *St Martin's* (☎ 091-568286) at 2 Nuns Island Rd, which is delightfully situated backing right on to the river. Costs are from IR£15 per person.

There are plenty of places less than 10 minutes' walk away on the Newcastle Rd which is west of the river and runs in a north-south direction, becoming the N59 to Clifden. At 113 Upper Newcastle *Burke's House* (☎ 091-524394) charges from IR£18.50/27 while *Newcastle Lodge* (☎ 091-527888) has doubles only from

IR£28. At 4 Greenfields Rd is *Edelweiss* (☎ 091-524501), with singles/doubles for IR£18.50/29.

Salthill and adjacent Renmore are good hunting grounds for B&Bs which typically cost IR£15 per person. Upper and Lower Salthill Rds are packed with places. Particularly good places include *Norman Villa* (☎ 091-521131), at 86 Lower Salthill, for IR£16/26. *Devondell* (☎ 091-523617) is down a cul-de-sac at 47 Devon Park, Lower Salthill.

In Upper Salthill try *Mandalay* (☎ 091-524177), at 10 Gentian Hill, which costs from IR£15/26. Also in Gentian Hill is *Bay View House* (☎ 091-526140) in a cul-de-sac, which costs IR£15/29.

Hotels

On Eyre Square, the *Skeffington Arms* (☎ 091-563173) is an attractive, though sometimes noisy, place charging from IR£27/50. *Jury's Galway Inn* (☎ 091-566444) on Quay St has a flat room rate of IR£53, which is good for families. The price rises to IR£75 between 24 and 30 July.

The sumptuous *Great Southern Hotel* (☎ 091-564041) takes up one complete side of Eyre Square and a room is IR£107 for the privilege.

PLACES TO EAT
Cafés & Takeaways

There are lots of restaurants, cafés and pubs around the river end of Quay St. *Hungry Grass* on Upper Cross St has good snacks for around IR£4. *Neachtain's* on Quay St is a pub serving some of the best bar food to be found anywhere, and has a reasonable restaurant upstairs.

Conlon's Restaurant on Eglington St is reasonably priced and the fish is good. There's a *Bewley's Café* in the Cornstore on Middle St, while *Sails*, another popular tea-and-coffee specialist, is in the Eyre Square Centre.

The choice isn't so good on the other side of the river. The *Left Bank Café* on Lower Dominick St is a good sandwich place.

Restaurants & Pubs

The Quay St area is crowded with restaurants, but finding a quiet one can be difficult. *Sev'nth Heaven* (☎ 091-563838) is right beside the Druid Theatre on the corner of Courthouse Lane and Flood St and does excellent pasta and pizza for around IR£6-10. *Fat Freddy's* on Quay St is similar. *La Mezza Luna* nearby is a good Italian place with main courses in the IR£6 to IR£10 range. *McDonagh's*, directly opposite, is a good fish & chip restaurant and a takeaway bar is attached. The *Quay West* (☎ 091-563015), opposite the hostel on Quay St, is relatively new and has a IR£14 set dinner.

Two Indian restaurants are *Shama* (☎ 091-566696) on Flood St near Spanish Arch and, more vegetarian-friendly, *Kashmir* (☎ 091-566674) on Mary St. The popular *Dragon Court* (☎ 091-565388) Chinese restaurant which is above a pub on Forster St has a set dinner for two for IR£30; try the IR£5 lunch first. *Rabbitt's*, another pub on Forster St, is good for steaks and seafood at around IR£15. Opposite, *Eyre House Restaurants* has a substantial high-tea menu between 5.30-7.30 pm for IR£6-10 and an early bird dinner during the same hours for IR£13-17.

Despite the French name, the reasonably priced *Brasserie* (☎ 091-561610) on Middle St has a lot of US/Mexican food – tacos, steaks and good ice cream. *Brannagan's*, on Abbeygate Upper, is another interesting place, with a mixture of Mexican and European dishes; it's open every day from 5 pm and is in the IR£10 range. A new place on Eglington St is *Salsa Mexican Restaurant* which serves dishes around IR£7 and IR£3.50 cocktails. Well worth seeking out for the lovely pizza is *Aideen's Wine Bar & Restaurant* tucked away in Buttermilk Walk off Middle St. The location helps keep it less crowded than many others.

One of the best restaurants in the country is *Drimcong House* (☎ 091-85115) 14 km along the Clifden road past Moycullen. It cannot be recommended highly enough and has a very reasonable (for its bracket) set menu under IR£20.

ENTERTAINMENT
Pubs

There's lots going on in Galway's pubs. On Quay St is the cosy *Neachtain's*, which has a great atmosphere. Back from the river on High St, the *King's Head* has music most nights in summer. *MacSwiggan's* on Daly's Place is big and busy. The upstairs of *Quay's Bar* on Quay St draws a great crowd in summer.

There are some glossier but less atmospheric pubs around Eyre Square, including the popular *Skeffington Arms* ('the Skeff') on the square, *An Púcán Bar* just off the square at 11 Forster St (music most nights) and *Rabbitt's Bar* at 23 Forster St.

On the west side of the river there's the busy *Monroe's Tavern* on the corner of Upper Dominick St and Fairhill. *Taylor's Bar* on Upper Dominick St and *Crane's Bar*, round the corner on Sea Rd, both have music, as does *O'Connor's* at Salthill, another popular place.

The Blue Note, at 3 William St West, has live jazz a few nights each week, and is recommended.

Theatre

Galway has three good theatres. The *Druid Theatre* (☎ 091-568617) on Chapel Lane and the newer *Punchbag Theatre* (☎ 091-565422) have packed summer programmes. *An Taibhdhearc* (☎ 091-562024) on Middle St regularly puts on plays in Irish. The Arts Centre at 47 Dominick St is also worth checking out.

THINGS TO BUY

The Eyre Square Centre is a big shopping centre right off Eyre Square by the tourist office. They've cunningly incorporated a reconstructed stretch of the old city wall in this modern centre. Other shopping centres are Bridge Mills, in an old mill building right by the river, and the Cornstore on Middle St. Outside of town, the Royal Tara China factory at Mervue is worth a look. Take the N6 Dublin Rd and take the first left after Ryan's Hotel. Some 15 km south of Galway on the N18 there's the Clarenbridge Crystal Shop selling all things Irish.

GETTING THERE & AWAY
Air

Galway Airport (☎ 091-755569) is in Carnmore, 10 km east of the city. Take the main Dublin road to Oranmore and turn north, then watch out for the signs to the airport. A taxi to or from the airport costs around IR£10. There is one bus a day to and from the airport and Galway bus station. There are two Aer Lingus flights each day to and from Dublin.

Bus

The bus station is behind the big grey Great Southern Hotel off Eyre Square in the centre of town, next to the railway station. For current travel information ring ☎ 091-562000/563555. There are regular services from Galway to all major cities and points in between.

Feda O'Donnell's private buses (☎ 091-761656) run daily between Donegal and Galway via Sligo, departing from the cathedral except on Sunday evening when it leaves from Eyre Square.

Train

Ceannt Railway Station is beside the bus terminus (☎ 091-564222 ext 156). There are four or more trains to and from Dublin (2¾ hours), Monday to Saturday, fewer on Sunday. Connections with other train routes can be made at Athlone and Mullingar.

GETTING AROUND

You can walk to most points of interest and out to Salthill from the centre, but there are regular buses from Eyre Square. Local Bus Éireann bus No 1 runs from Eyre Square to Salthill and Blackrock; bus No 2 goes from Knocknacarra through Eyre Square to Renmore; bus No 3 runs between Eyre Square and Castlepark and bus No 4 runs to Newcastle.

Drivers will need parking discs for parking on the street; these are available from newsagents. The car park near the

Bridge Mills Centre is next to a police station, so it should be safe.

Taxi
Galway Taxi (☎ 091-561111) is on Mainguard St, Corrib Cabs (☎ 091-567888) are on Eyre St north off Eyre Square, and there are also a couple of taxi ranks on Eyre Square.

Bicycle Rental
The Kinlay House, Stella Maris and Galway City hostels all rent bikes.

Galway Cycle Hire (☎ 091-61600) is next to the tourist office. Celtic Cycles (☎ 091-66606), on Queen St, is the local Raleigh dealer and rents bikes for IR£7/30 a day/week. Rent-a-Bike (☎ 091-568223) is on Dominick St and Europa Cycles (☎ 091-563355) is near Galway Cathedral.

South of Galway City

Many visitors will pass through the small area of County Galway south of the city, on their way to or from the spectacular limestone Burren in County Clare. Worth visiting in the area are the tranquil monastic settlement and round tower at Kilmacduagh.

CLARINBRIDGE & KILCOLGAN
Sixteen km south of Galway, Clarinbridge and Kilcolgan are the focus for Galway's famous Clarinbridge Oyster Festival held during the second weekend in September. *Paddy Burke's Bar & Restaurant* (☎ 091-96107) in Clarinbridge, is an old-fashioned place famous for its association with the festival. A little farther south, signposted off the road in Kilcolgan, is *Moran's on the Weir* (☎ 091-96113), a wonderful thatched pub and restaurant overlooking the bay, where the famous Galway oysters are reared. During the festival, the world oyster-opening championships are held at Moran's. This place is highly recommended and a good stopover on the way to or from Clare.

Getting There & Away
Clarinbridge is on the main Galway to Gort, Ennis and Limerick road and is served by numerous Bus Éireann buses from Galway bus station. Kilcolgan is also on the main road, and Moran's pub is about 1½ km to the west.

KINVARA
Kinvara is a delightful village tucked away on the south-east corner of Galway Bay. A small stone harbour is home to a number of the Galway 'hookers'. For all its quaintness, Kinvara is a relatively quiet spot and doesn't attract anything like the numbers of people that Ballyvaughan 24 km to the west does. A few km west of Kinvara, you come to County Clare and the Burren limestone region.

Dunguaire Castle
Dunguaire Castle is north of Kinvara on the shore and was erected around 1520 by the O'Hynes. It later passed through the hands of Oliver St John Gogarty (1878-1957), a noted writer and wit. The castle is supposedly built on the site of the 6th-century Royal Palace of Guaire, king of Connaught.

Today, it's in superb condition, and each floor of the castle is set up to reflect a particular period in its history, right down to the last mildly eccentric owner who lived here through the 1960s. It has a gift shop, guided tours, and medieval banquets à la Bunratty held during the summer (☎ 061-360788) – however, they're on a more intimate scale than Bunratty's. Just south of Dunguaire is a bare stone arch, the only remains of an older castle.

There is an entrance charge to the castle of IR£2.10/1.15.

Festival
Every August the village hosts 'Cruinniú na mbád' – the 'gathering of the boats' festival – in celebration of these traditional craft.

Places to Stay & Eat
The IHH *Johnston's Hostel* (☎ 091-37164) is on Main St, open from June to September. Beds are IR£6 and there's a camp site.

Six km south and well-signposted off the main road to Ballyvaughan is the An Óige *Doorus House* (☎ 091-37512). The hostel building was once owned by a count called Floribund de Basterot, who entertained such notables as W B Yeats, Lady Augusta Gregory, Douglas Hyde and Guy de Maupassant here. Yeats and Lady Gregory are said to have first mooted the idea of the Abbey Theatre while they were here. It's a good base for exploring the Burren.

Many local B&Bs are south of town around the Doorus Peninsula. *Burren View Farm* (☎ 091-37142) charges IR£13.50/27.

There is an excellent little coffee shop, *Café*, overlooking the harbour with snacks and light meals available all day. *Partners* on Main St serves meals and snacks and is pleasant enough.

Getting There & Away
One Bus Éireann route serves Galway, Kinvara, Ballyvaughan, Lisdoonvarna, Ennistymon, Lahinch, Miltown Malbay, Doonbeg, Kilkee and Kilrush.

Another route serves the Burren coast, running to and from Galway City via Kinvara, Ballyvaughan, Blackhead, Fanore, Lisdoonvarna and Doolin. There are usually two or three buses each day in summer. Contact Galway City bus station (☎ 091-62000) for details of bus times on all these routes.

KILMACDUAGH & COOLE PARK
Five km south-west of Gort is the extensive monastic site of Kilmacduagh. Beside a small lake is a well-preserved round tower, the remains of a small cathedral (Teampall Mór MacDuagh), a church of St John the Baptist and various other little chapels. The original monastery is thought to have been founded by St Colman MacDuagh at the beginning of the 7th century, and such was its importance that it became the focus for a new diocese in the 12th century. St MacDuagh founded the monastery under the patronage of King Guaire of Connaught who gave his name to Dunguaire Castle in Kinvara. The round tower is 33 metres tall

Teampall Mór MacDuagh at Kilmacduagh

and leans some 60 cm from the perpendicular. The doorway is seven metres above ground level. There are fine views over the Burren.

About five km to the north-east of Gort is Coole Park. It was the home of Lady Augusta Gregory, co-founder of the Abbey Theatre, and the exhibition depicts the literary and natural history of the site. It's an OPW site and opens daily from 9.30 am to 6.30 pm from mid-June to the end of August (otherwise closed Monday and shorter hours). Admission is IR£2/1.

Connemara

Connemara (*Conamara*) is the wild and barren region north-west of Galway City. It's a stunning patchwork of bogs, lonely valleys, pale grey mountains and small brown lakes. Its devotees – Irish, French, Americans – buy up remote cottages as holiday homes or spend a small fortune on a week in a castle hideaway during the salmon fishing season.

Connemara is not a distinct geographical region like the Burren. At its heart are the Maumturk mountains and the grey quartzite peaks of the Twelve Bens, which offer tremendous hill walking. They look south over a plain dotted with lakes, melting southwards into the sea around Carna and Roundstone in a maze of rocky islands, tortuous inlets and sparkling white beaches. The coast road west of Spiddal eventually enters this maze, and it is well worth losing yourself for a day, in search of Carraroe, Roundstone, Lettermullen Island and Ballyconneely Bay. Pink Galway granite is the predominant rock in this lower country, while the mountains and northern part of the region are made of a mixture of quartzite, gneiss, schist and marble. However, the best scenery is in the middle of the region. The journey from Maam Cross over to Leenane and especially the trip up the Lough Inagh Valley and around by Kylemore Lake would be difficult to surpass anywhere in the country.

One of the most important Gaeltachts in the country begins just west of Galway City around Barna and stretches west through Spiddal and Inverin, and along much of the coast as far as Carna. Ireland's national Irish-language radio station, Radio Na Gaeltachta, is based out here and does much to sustain the language.

Heading west from Galway City you have two options: the coast road through Salthill, Barna and Spiddal, or the inland route through Oughterard which leads directly to the heart of wild and beautiful Connemara.

The Folding Landscapes map company have produced a superb map of Connemara which is a must if you intend any detailed exploration. Their *Connemara, A Hill Walker's Guide* by Tim Robinson and Joss Lynam is also invaluable.

GETTING THERE & AWAY

There are numerous Bus Éireann services serving most parts of Connemara, many of which originate from Galway City bus station (☎ 091-562000), so check there for times and fares. Services can be very sporadic and many only operate in the summertime.

A service runs between Galway, Oughterard, Maam Cross, Recess, Roundstone, Ballyconneely and on to Clifden; usually one of the summer weekday buses on this service diverts at Maam Cross and travels to Clifden via Leenane. Another less frequent service runs between Westport, Leenane, Kylemore, Letterfrack and Clifden with one bus a day during the summer only.

Galway, Cong, Leenane and Clifden are connected by an infrequent service on weekdays only. Another runs between Galway, Spiddal, Inverin, Rossaveal, Carraroe, Lettermore and Lettermullen Islands. On weekdays only a bus runs between Galway, Oughterard, Maam Cross, Ros Muc, Recess, Glinsk, Carna and Moyrus.

SPIDDAL

Just 17 km from Galway City, Spiddal *(An Spidéal)* is a lively little roadside settlement with some good pubs. East of the village is an Irish college which gives summer courses in the Irish language. On the Galway side of Spiddal is Standún's, a massive craft shop which also operates a bureau de change. Nearby, just in front of an extensive craft village, is a good beach which can get crowded during summer. If you are looking for open landscapes and wild coastlines, leave Spiddal behind and head west towards Roundstone.

SPIDDAL TO ROUNDSTONE

West of Spiddal, the scenery gradually improves and at Casla you can turn west off the main road for Carraroe *(An Cheathrú Rua)* and into a maze of inlets and islands. Before Casla, you will notice the signs for Rossaveal *(Ros an Mhil)*, the main departure point for ferries to the Aran Islands. It is well worth heading out to Carraroe and back across a series of rugged islands, all connected to the mainland. **Carraroe** is famous for its fine beaches, including the Coral Strand which is composed entirely of shell and fragments of coralline seaweed. **Lettermore, Gorumna** and **Lettermullen** islands are low and bleak, with a handful of farmers eking out an existence from tiny, rocky fields. Fish farming has become big

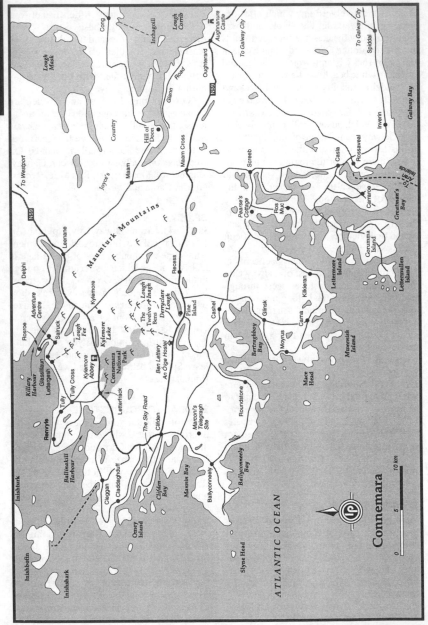

Connemara

business out here and there are salmon cages floating in some of the bays.

From Screeb you can head up to Maam Cross or continue along the coast down to **Carna**, a small fishing village with a marine biology research station nearby. Carna has cheap accommodation and food at *Mac's Bar & Hostel* (☎ 095-32240). From Carna there are some good walks out to **Mweenish Island** or north to **Moyrus** and out to **Mace Head**. Back on the coast road, it's a lovely journey back up to Cashel and south again to Roundstone. There's a pleasant walk from Roundstone to the top of Errisbeg, just follow the small road past *O'Dowd's* pub.

Places to Stay & Eat

There is the An Óige Inverin Hostel (%y091-593154) west of Spiddal in Inverin, by the main road, and there are bikes for hire. A bed is IR£6.50. There is also the Connemara Tourist Hostel (%y091-593104) in Inverin, with similar rates.

The *Carraroe's Caravan & Camping Park* (☎ 091-95266) is one km and signposted from the village of Carraroe. It costs IR£5 to pitch a tent.

There are plenty of B&Bs along the road – one that has been recommended as a relaxing place is *Col Mar* (☎ 091-83247) a couple of km west of Spiddal; it costs from IR£18/27.

There are some exclusive hotels tucked away out here, which are good places to stop for a sandwich, drink or meal if you can rise to their prices. The lovely *Ballynahinch Castle Hotel* (☎ 095-31006), south of Recess, was formerly the home of Humanity Dick (1754-1834), a local landlord, MP and one of the chief forces behind the Royal Society for the Prevention of Cruelty to Animals (RSPCA). Ballynahinch Castle is well worth a visit even if it's just a for a drink in the bar and a quick scout around the delightful grounds. B&B is from IR£75/114.

Near Cashel, the *Zetland House Hotel* (☎ 095-31111) has B&B for IR£80/130, while the *Cashel House Hotel* (☎ 095-31001) charges IR£65/130.

ROUNDSTONE

The small fishing village of Roundstone *(Cloch na Rón)* is 16 km south-west of Recess on a western extension of Bertraghboy Bay. Looming behind the neat stone harbour is Errisbeg at 300 metres, the only significant hill along this section of coastline. From the summit there are wonderful views across the bay to the distant humps of the Twelve Bens.

The village itself consists essentially of one main street of tall houses, pubs and shops overlooking the water. The small harbour is home to lobster boats and *currachs*, a featherlight rowing boat of black tar on canvas laid over a wicker frame. At the head of the pier is the home of Tim Robinson, the man behind Folding Landscape Maps – the interesting and detailed maps of the Burren, the Aran Islands and Connemara that you will see for sale everywhere. His house is open to visitors during the summer.

Just south of the village is an IDA (Industrial Development Agency) craft complex with various small factory shops selling everything from teapots to *bodhráns*, the goatskin drums beloved of traditional Irish musicians. Farther south off the road to Ballyconneely are the magnificent white beaches of Gorteen and Dogs Bay.

Places to Stay & Eat

Gurteen Beach Caravan & Camping Park (☎ 095-35882) is two km west of town near the beach and charges IR£6 a night for two people. For B&B, *St Joseph's* (☎ 095-35865) on Main St overlooking the harbour, costs IR£18/27. *Roundstone House Hotel* (☎ 095-35864) is also on Main St, with good views over the bay to Connemara, charging IR£33/50.

O'Dowd's Pub (☎ 095-35809) in the village has good food in the bar and a restaurant with excellent oysters. There is a nice coffee shop in the IDA Craft Park just outside the village, open all day. *Beola Restaurant* (☎ 095-35871) on Main St serves seafood in the IR£12 range. They are open for lunch and dinner, but O'Dowd's is a better bet.

ROUNDSTONE TO CLIFDEN

Twelve km west of Roundstone is **Ballyconneely**. If you detour south off the Clifden road towards the Connemara Golf Club, you pass the ruins of **Bunowen Castle** before reaching the shore at **Trá Mhóir**, or 'great beach', a superb expanse of pure white sand.

Back on the road north to Clifden you pass another fine beach and coral strand in **Mannin Bay**.

OUGHTERARD

The small town of Oughterard, 27 km along the main road from Galway City to Clifden, calls itself 'the Gateway to Connemara'. And sure enough, just west of town, the countryside opens to sweeping panoramas of lakes, mountain and bog that get more spectacular the farther west you travel.

Oughterard itself is a pleasant little town and one of Ireland's principal angling centres. It has a number of good cafés, pubs, and restaurants as well as some fairly exclusive country house establishments hidden in the surrounding countryside.

The focus of the anglers' attention is Lough Corrib, just out of sight to the north of town. Nearby attractions include Aughanure Castle to the east and the lovely drive along the Glann Rd by Lough Corrib to a vantage point overlooking the Hill of Doon.

Information

There is a tourist information point at the Galway end of town (☎ 091-82808).

There are banks on Main St, and more bureaus de change in Fuschia Crafts on Main St, Keogh & Sons on the square and even the Spar supermarket. Keogh's Laundrette is on Main St.

Aughanure Castle

Three km east of Oughterard and off the main Galway road is the 16th-century O'Flaherty fortress, Aughanure Castle, built on the site of earlier structures. The O'Flahertys controlled the region for hundreds of years after they fought off the Normans, and these 'fighting O'Flahertys'

were constantly at odds with the forces of Galway City. The six-storey tower house stands on a rocky outcrop overlooking Lough Corrib and has been extensively restored. Surrounding the castle are the remains of an unusual double bawn or perimeter fortification. Underneath the castle, the lake washes through a number of natural caverns and caves.

The castle, run by the OPW, is open daily from 9.30 am to 6.30 pm in the summer and the entrance fee is IR£2/1.

Places to Stay

Hostels *Canrawer House Hostel* (☎ 091-82388) is a spanking new hostel at the Clifden end of town, just over one km down a signposted turning. The bunk beds are IR£7.50, five regular beds with their own bathroom are IR£8.50 and the one double room en suite is IR£18. It looks good: the kitchen is big, boats can be hired and camping is IR£5.

The IHH *Lough Corrib Hostel* (☎ 091-82866) is on Camp St. From the centre of town, turn north for the Hill of Doon drive, and it's about 200 metres along on the left. They have two-person Canadian-style canoes for hire, IR£10 for half a day, as well as bikes. There are tent sites and boat trips to Inchagoill Island in Lough Corrib. Beds are IR£5.50.

B&Bs There are legions of B&Bs around Oughterard, but they can be expensive. *Woodlawn House* (☎ 091-80198) in Doon, Rosscahill – on the Galway City side of Oughterard – does B&B from IR£18.50/27. Further east of Oughterard and travelling towards Portacarron and the lake, you'll see plenty of signposts.

If you turn north at the main crossroads in Oughterard and travel five km along Glann Rd towards the Hill of Doon, you come to the excellent *Glann House* (☎ 091-82127), charging IR£18/27.

Hotels The *Corrib Hotel* (☎ 091-82204) on Bridge St is a comfortable old hotel from IR£35/50. *Currarevagh House* (☎ 091-

82312) is a 19th-century mansion just outside Oughterard on the shore of Lough Corrib, renowned for its massive meals and quality accommodation, charging from IR£42/84.

Places to Eat
On Main St, the *Corrib County* is an excellent low to medium-priced restaurant with good coffee, lunches and dinners. There is another cosy coffee-shop-cum-snack-restaurant, *O'Fatharta's*, farther east on Main St. For good pub food and meals try the *Boat Inn* on the Square. *Keogh's Bar* on the Square also does reasonable pub food.

On Bridge St, the western extension of Main St, is the upmarket *Water Lily* (☎ 091-82737), right on the river. Also on Bridge St, the *Corrib Hotel* does a good four-course dinner for around IR£15.

Entertainment
Power's Bar on Main St often has music in summer. So do *Faherty's* and the *Boat Inn* on the Square.

Getting Around
Bikes can be hired from Lough Corrib Hostel and the tourist office.

LOUGH CORRIB
The Republic's biggest lake, Lough Corrib is over 48 km long and covers some 200 sq km. It virtually cuts off western Galway from the rest of the country and has over 360 islands. The largest one, Inchagoill, has a monastic settlement and can be visited from Oughterard or Cong.

Lough Corrib is world-famous for its salmon, sea trout and brown trout and the area attracts legions of anglers from all over the world. The highlight of the fishing year is the mayfly season when countless billions of these small lacy insects hatch over a few days (usually in May) and drive the fish and fishermen into a frenzy. The hooks are baited with live flies which join their brothers and sisters dancing on the surface of the lake. The main run of salmon does not begin until June.

The owner of Canrawer House Hostel is a good contact for information and boat hire.

Inchagoill Island
The largest island on Lough Corrib, some seven km north-west of Oughterard, Inchagoill is a lonely place hiding many ancient remains. Most fascinating is an obelisk, a burial marker to 'Lia Luguaedon Macc Menueh', the 'stone of luguaedon son of Menueh'. It stands some 75 cm tall near the 'Saints' Church', and some people claim the Latin writing on the stone is the oldest Christian inscription in Europe apart from those in the catacombs in Rome. It's certainly the oldest Latin inscription in Ireland.

Teampall Padraig or St Patrick's Church is a small oratory of a very early design with some later additions. The prettiest church is the 'Saints Church'; it's of early Romanesque design and was probably built in the 9th or 10th centuries. There are carvings around the arched doorway. The name Inchagoill means 'Island of the Foreigner'. The island can be reached by boat from Cong in County Mayo or Oughterard. Look out for details in shop windows or check with the hostels.

MAAM CROSS TO LEENANE
West of Oughterard, Maam Cross *(Crois Mám)* is the first settlement along the Clifden Rd. *Peacockes* is the huge and touristy bar/shop/restaurant/petrol station, with a tacky model donkey and 'traditional' Irish cottage, by the turn-off for Leenane. The trip to Leenane is lovely but if you have only one run through the region it's better to stay on the Clifden road and turn up the Lough Inagh Valley instead. It's also a nice journey south towards Screeb and the coast. *Tullaboy House* (☎ 091-82305) is an excellent farmhouse B&B five km from Maam Cross towards Oughterard on the N59. It costs IR£18.50/27.

LEENANE & DELPHI
The Irish name, *An Lionan*, means 'Shallow Sea-Bed', referring to the way the sea edges its way in to Killary harbour. Leenane itself

makes a convenient stopover on the way north and the road north-west to Louisburgh is startlingly beautiful. Like nearby Cong the town can boast a film connection, having been the location for *The Field* which was shot in 1989 and based on a John B Keane story about an argument over the ownership of a field. The dance and pub scenes were filmed in the village and the church scene in Ashleagh church near the village.

Leenane Cultural Centre
The centre focuses on the woollen industry and gives demonstrations of carding, spinning and weaving, with a 15-minute video that sets the historical and social scene. Locally made woollen garments are on sale. Admission is IR£2.50 and there's a coffee shop that serves dinner in the evening.

Delphi
The Brownes of Westport were originally a Catholic family, but they converted to Protestantism in order to avoid the constraints of the penal laws. This paved the way for one of the family to be ennobled as marquess of Sligo at the time of the Act of Union in 1801, and the 2nd marquess gave the unlikely name of Delphi to his fishing lodge in Galway. A friend of Byron, he had travelled in Greece and returned home with the thought that his fishing territory bore an uncanny resemblance to the area around Delphi.

At Delphi Lodge (☎ 095-42213) permits are available for fishing in the local waters, and an adventure centre (☎ 095-42208) has organised sports throughout the summer.

The *Delphi Hostel* (☎ 095-42208) has beds from IR£5.50, camping space and bikes for hire.

RECESS & AROUND
Recess is nothing more than a few houses on the main road between Clifden and Maam Cross. Turning north here brings you on a minor road through the wonderful Lough Inagh Valley. If, instead, you continue along the main road from Recess towards Clifden, there are some marvellous views over Lough

Derryclare and Pine Island, familiar from many postcards. The grassy layby overlooking the island is an excellent place to camp. About one km west of here off the Clifden road is a dead-end road heading north into a great valley enclosed by a ring of six of the Twelve Bens. It's a beautiful drive up this road and there's a challenging circuit hike of the six peaks.

Back on the main Clifden Rd and another one km west is the An Óige *Ben Lettery Youth Hostel* (☎ 095-511366). It's an excellent and popular base to explore the Twelve Bens and makes a good starting or finishing point for the walk mentioned previously. The hostel is eight km from Recess, 13 km from Clifden.

Lough Inagh Valley
The journey north up the Lough Inagh Valley is one of the most scenic in the country. There are two fine approaches up valleys from the south, starting on either side of Recess, and the long sweep of Loughs Derryclare and Inagh accompanies you for most of the way. On the west side are the brooding Bens, while just out of the valley on the north side is the picturesque drive along Kylemore Lake.

Half way up the Inagh Valley is the *Inagh Valley Lodge*, an upmarket country house hotel. It's a worthwhile place to stop for a snack, particularly in good weather. The location is magnificent.

Towards the northern end of the valley, a track leads off the road west up a blind valley, which is also well worth exploring.

Kylemore Abbey & Lake
Just outside the northern end of the beautiful Inagh Valley is the almost equally scenic Kylemore Lake with its accompanying abbey. The road skirts the northern shore of the lake, winding through overhanging trees with magnificent views across the silent lake. South of the lake are the Twelve Bens and Connemara National Park, while the mountains behind the abbey are Dúchruach (530 metres) and Binn Fhraoigh (545 metres).

The lake passes under the road and extends to the north, where you will see the castellated towers of the 19th-century Gothic Kylemore Abbey among the trees (and rhododendron bushes, which are slowly choking the oak wood). The abbey was built for a wealthy English businessman, Mitchell Henry, after he had spent his honeymoon in Connemara and fallen in love with the region. During WW I, a group of Benedictine nuns left Ypres in Belgium and eventually set up in Kylemore, turning the place into an abbey.

Today, the nuns run an exclusive convent boarding school with some sections open to the public and a small craft shop and tea room. You can walk up behind the abbey to a statue overlooking Kylemore Lake. The abbey is 17 km from Clifden.

Pearse's Cottage

Padraic Pearse (1879-1916) – who has so many streets named after him – was one of the leaders of the Gaelic revival and in 1908 he founded a bilingual school, St Edna's, in Dublin. He was the least political of the 1916 rebels, being heavily imbued with a religious need for a blood sacrifice, but nevertheless was the commander-in-chief of the insurgents and was proclaimed president of the provisional government. After the revolt he was executed by the British. He wrote some of his short stories and plays in this cottage.

Admission to the OPW cottage is IR£1/40p, open mid-June to mid-September from 9.30 am to 6.30 every day (closed from 1.30-2.30 pm). It is easily reached from either Screeb or Cashel.

CLIFDEN

Clifden, the capital of Connemara, is some 80 km west of Galway City at the head of Clifden Bay. Astride the Owenglen River, the tightly packed houses and the two needle-sharp spires of the town's churches are shadowed by the steep backdrop of the Twelve Bens to the east. A landlord, John D'Arcy, was the main force behind the establishment of the town around 1812, but the

famine ruined the family and their estate along the Sky Rd is now deserted.

Opinions differ about Clifden. Some travellers feel it's not as relaxing a place as they hoped it would be. Judge for yourself.

Information

The seasonal tourist office (☎ 095-21163) is on Lower Market St and opens from June to September. Other times enquire at Island House on Lower Market St.

Activities

There are superb cycling possibilities and if Map 31 in the Ordnance Survey Discovery Series is available, this is all you need to plan your tours. Connemara Contours (☎ 095-21379), near the tourist office at The Island House, run guided walking trips to local geographical and natural interest sites. A half-day walk is about IR£10, while an enjoyable six-day walking holiday including accommodation and all meals is IR£440.

See the Around Clifden section below for good local walks and cycles.

The Clifden Trekking Centre (☎ 095-21350), at the Galway end of Main St, organise short treks on horses and ponies.

Places to Stay

Camping & Hostels The *Clifden Town Hostel* (☎ 095-21076) is on Market St and costs IR£6. The IHH *Leo's Hostel* (☎ 095-21429) is nearby, right by the square; it costs IR£6.50 for a dorm bed in high season, and also has camping space. *Brookside Hostel* (☎ 095-21812), on Hulk St, is down by the river in a quiet location. These three are open year round. There is another hostel in Cleggan to the north-west.

B&Bs & Hotels In town, *Kingston House* (☎ 095-21470) on Bridge St costs from IR£18.50/27. Many B&Bs are to the south in the direction of Ballyconneely. One km from Clifden and signposted off the road is *Mallmore House* (☎ 095-21460), with B&B for IR£15. *Actons* (☎ 095-44339), at Claddaghduff at the end of Sky Rd, has been

GALWAY

warmly recommended. Rates are from IR£20/32.

Clifden House (☎ 095-21187), a hotel in town is from IR£12/40. *Barry's* (☎ 095-21287) on Main St charges from IR£30/50 while the *Alcock & Brown* hotel (☎ 095-21006) in the town centre does B&B for IR£35/50.

Places to Eat
My Tea Shop on Main St next to Barry's hotel has a dubious 'greenie' but it's friendly and serves meals around IR£5.

For pub food, try *Mitchell's Bar* on the Square. *E J Kings* on the Square serves pub food all year round with a more formal restaurant during the summer. The food is good and reasonably priced. On Main St, the *D'Arcy Inn* is opposite Barry's hotel, and does similar fare with the accent on seafood. It has menus in French and German, and meals are under IR£10. *An Tulan*, opposite the church, has a conventional menu with lunch around IR£5 and a set dinner for IR£10.

O'Grady's Seafood Restaurant (☎ 095-21450) is one of the best restaurants in west Galway, open for lunch and dinner. *Doris's* (☎ 095-21427) on Market St is also worth trying.

Out at Claddaghduff, the cliff-top *Acton's Restaurant* (☎ 095-44339) does good food, and exhilarating views of the Atlantic are thrown in for free.

Getting There & Away
The Bus Éireann stop is outside Cullen's on Market St. For information phone ☎ 091-62000. Buses go between Galway and Clifden via Oughterard and Maam Cross or via Cong and Leenane. For more details, see the Getting There & Away section under Connemara. Michael Nee (☎ 095-51082) runs a private bus to and from Clifden daily.

In summer there is a daily express bus from Galway to Clifden at 11.15 am, and 12.15 and 6 pm. Express buses from Clifden to Galway leave at 8 am, and 12.30 and 1.30 pm. In summer a bus leaves from the Island

House on Market St at 11.30 am for Cleggan, gateway to Inishbboffin Island.

Getting Around
Mannions (☎ 095-21160), Railway View, Clifden, hire out bicycles and so do most of the hostels.

AROUND CLIFDEN
The road south of Clifden takes you out past the fine beach at **Mannin Bay** to **Ballyconneely**. Heading directly west from Clifden, the Sky Rd takes you on a loop out to a townland known as Kingston and back to Clifden through some rugged coastal scenery. The round trip is about 12 km and can easily be walked or cycled. The deeply indented coastline farther north brings you to the tiny village of **Claddaghduff**. Turning west here down by the Catholic church you come out on Omey Strand, and at low tide you can drive or walk across the sand to **Omey Island**, a small low island of rock, grass and sand with a few inhabited houses. During the summer there are horse races held on Omey Strand.

Back on the mainland to the north is **Cleggan**, the boarding point for ferries to Inishbboffin island.

Alcock & Brown Memorial
In a bog, almost six km south-west of Clifden en route to Ballyconneely, is a memorial to John Alcock and Arthur Brown, the two pilots of the first nonstop transatlantic flight. The flight began in Newfoundland and ended when their Vicker Vimy biplane crash-landed in Derrygimlagh Bog on 15 June 1919. They were not injured, and the memorial was erected in 1959.

Appropriately, the building nearby (now ruined) was a wireless station built three years earlier in 1906 by Marconi for his first transatlantic wireless communications.

LETTERFRACK
Letterfrack, founded by the Quakers in the mid-19th century, is barely more than a few pubs and a crossroads some 15 km north-east of Clifden. It lies at the head of Ballinakill

Harbour, but the sea is only visible from west of the crossroads and from the entrance to the national park.

The small *Old Monastery* hostel (☎ 095-41132) has been recommended as a great deal because of its free breakfast, friendliness, and IR£5 evening meal option which includes a vegetarian choice. There are also bikes for hire and camping is possible, so it is worth considering as a base for visiting Connemara National Park.

North from the crossroads you come to Tully Cross, which has a line of neat, thatched rent-a-cottages and some nice little pubs. West of here is Tully where *An Teach Ceoil* (☎ 095-43446) has regular music and Irish dancing sessions.

There is a tourist information point (☎ 095-43950) in the Credit Union office in Tully Cross.

Diamond's (☎ 095-43431) in Tully and King's (☎ 095-43414) in Lettergesh rent bikes.

CONNEMARA NATIONAL PARK

Connemara National Park – managed by the OPW – covers an area of 2000 hectares of bog, mountain and heath in the countryside east of Letterfrack. The headquarters and visitors' centre (☎ 095-41054) are housed in pleasant old buildings just south of the crossroads in Letterfrack.

The park encloses a number of the Twelve Bens, including Bencullagh, Benbrack and Benbaun. The heart of the park is Gleann Mór, the 'big glen', through which flows the River Polladirk. There is fine walking up the glen and over the surrounding mountains.

The visitors' centre will give you an insight into the park's flora, fauna and geology, as well as showing maps and various trails. Bog biology is interesting, so a wander round is not a waste of time. It has an indoor eating area and rudimentary kitchen facilities for hillwalkers.

There are guided nature walks on Monday, Wednesday and Friday during the summer, leaving the centre at 10.30 am and taking two to three hours. Bring good boots ('knee-high' recommends a reader) and rain-

wear. There are also short, self-guided walks. If the Bens look too strenuous, you can hike up Diamond Hill nearby.

The entry fee is IR£2/1.

NORTH OF LETTERFRACK

There is some fine coastal scenery along the coast north of Letterfrack, especially from Tully Cross east to Lettergesh and Salruck, home to the Little Killary Adventure Centre.

Just short of Salruck is Glassillaun Beach, a breathtaking expanse of pure white sand. There are other fine beaches at Gurteen and at Lettergesh, where the beach horseracing sequences for John Wayne's film *The Quiet Man* were shot. There are fine walks all along the coast and around Renvyle Point to Derryinver Bay. There's an excellent hillwalk, which takes four to five hours each way, from Lettergesh post office up Binn Chuanna and Maolchnoc and then down to Lough Fee.

Getting There & Away

There's a bus between Galway and Clifden which calls at Cong, Leenane, Salruck, Lettergesh Post Office, Tully Church, Kylemore, Letterfrack, Cleggan and Claddaghduff en route. One bus a day in either direction travels that route on summer weekdays only.

Activities

Little Killary Adventure Centre (☎ 095-43411) is a well-run place offering accommodation, plus courses in canoeing, sailing, rock climbing, and just about every other adventure sport you can think of. The owners, Jamie and Mary Young, are an adventurous pair; Jamie has canoed around Cape Horn. On Glassillaun Beach is *Scubadive West* (☎ 095-43922), offering courses and diving on the surrounding coast and islands.

For sea trips or deep-sea angling contact John or Phil Mongan (☎ 095-43473) at Derryinver and for horse trekking contact Joe O'Neill (☎ 095-42269).

Places to Stay & Eat
Camping *Renvyle Beach Caravan & Camping* (☎ 095-43462) is west of Tully and they charge IR£5.50 a night for tents or IR£2.50 per hiker or cyclist. East of Tully Cross near Lettergesh Beach is the *Connemara Caravan & Camping Park* (☎ 095-43406), a little more expensive.

Hostels The An Óige *Killary Harbour Hostel* (☎ 095-43417) is 13 km north-east of Tully Cross on Rosroe Pier, eight km off the N59, and charges IR£6 a night. The philosopher Wittgenstien stayed here for seven months in 1948. Some food and supplies are available at the hostel, but the nearest shop is five km away in Lettergesh, so stock up in advance. There is a fine hike from the hostel along an old green road by the fjord to Leenane.

Hotels *Renvyle House Hotel* (☎ 095-43511) is a converted country house in Renvyle and was once owned by Oliver St John Gogarty. It's the best place in the area to have a drink or snack or relax after a walk and B&B runs from IR£60/90.

KILLARY HARBOUR & AROUND
Mussel rafts dot long, dark Killary Harbour, which looks like a fjord but may not actually have been glaciated. It's 16 km long, over 45 metres deep in the centre and has a superb anchorage. Mweelrea Mountain (815 metres) towers over its northern shores. From Leenane at the head of the harbour, the road runs west for a couple of km along the southern shore before veering inland. However, you can continue walking along the shore to Rosroe on an old green road.

County Mayo begins just north of Leenane and there is magnificent scenery around the north side of Killary and up into Delphi and Doolough, one of the most scenic valleys in the country.

CLEGGAN
Cleggan is a small fishing village 16 km from Clifden and many visitors pass through en route to Inishbofin Island.

There are a couple of B&Bs around Cleggan as well as the IHH *Masters House Hostel* (☎ 095-44746) which also offers camping. Beds are IR£6 and doubles IR£16.

There is a bus to Cleggan from Clifden every day at 8 am during the summer, and Cleggan is on an infrequent Galway City, Cong, Leenane, Clifden route. For details contact Bus Éireann (☎ 091-62000).

INISHBOFIN ISLAND
Inishbofin Island is a haven of peace and tranquillity, nine km out in the Atlantic from Cleggan. The island is compact; six km long by three km wide. Its highest point is a mere 95 metres above sea level. Good sheltered beaches, open grasslands, grassy lanes and a strong sense of offshore isolation are what make Inishbofin special.

The island is made of some of the oldest rocks in Ireland. The birdlife includes corncrakes, choughs, corn bunting and a variety of seabirds.

Just off the north beach is Lough Bó Finne from which the island gets its name. Bó Finne neans 'fair or white cow'.

According to legend, the island was once a mysterious and forgotten place, permanently enveloped in a thick blanket of fog. Some fishermen came upon the island, lit a fire near the lake and immediately the mist began to clear. Coming out of the mist was a woman with a long stick driving a white cow or 'bó finne' in front of her. She hit the white cow with the stick, turning it to stone. Irritated at such behaviour, the fishermen grabbed the stick and struck her, upon which she also turned to stone.

Until the late 19th century, there were two white stones by the lake: the remains of the cow and its owner.

History
Inishbofin's main historical figure of note was a St Colman who at one stage was a bishop in England. He fell out with the English church in 664 over their adoption of a new calendar system, and exiled himself to Inishbofin where he set up a monastery. North-east of the harbour is a small 13th-century church and hollowed stone, or bullaun, which are said to occupy the site of Colman's original monastery.

Grace O'Malley, the famous pirate queen who was based on Clare Island, also used Inishbofin as a base in the 16th century.

Cromwell's forces captured Inishbofin in 1652 and used it as a prison camp for priests and clerics. Many died or were killed, and one bishop was reputedly chained to Bishop's Rock near the harbour and drowned as the tide came in.

Information

Inishbofin has a small post office and a grocery shop, but no banks. The bars and the hotels will usually change travellers' cheques and US dollar or pounds sterling cash.

Places to Stay & Eat

Hostel & Camping The IHH *Inishbofin Island Hostel* (☎ 095-45855) is a fine hostel 500 metres up from the harbour. It costs IR£5.50 for a bed and doubles are IR£14. Camping is also possible here but you can camp on most unfenced ground and by the beaches.

Hotels The modern and comfortable *Day's Hotel* (☎ 095-45803) has turf fires and a dining room looking out over the sea. Rooms are from IR£15.50/31. The food is creative, with excellent fresh fish. A four-course dinner is IR£14. *Day's Bar* next door has a good atmosphere. There are bikes for hire.

The *Doonmore Hotel* (☎ 095-45804) has B&B from IR£17/34. Seafood is their speciality and dinner is IR£14. They also have bikes for hire.

Getting There & Away

Boats leave regularly from Cleggan, usually starting at 11.30 am and two more at 2 and 6.45 pm in July and August. They depart from Inishbofin at 9.30 am and 1 and 5 pm. The fare is around IR£10 return and bikes are free. Ring for details of the *Dun Aengus* and the *Queen* (☎ 095-44642/45806).

Aran Islands

The same stretch of limestone that created Clare's Burren region surfaces in the middle of Galway Bay to form the three Aran Islands (*Oileáin Árainn*): Inishmór, Inishmaan and Inisheer. The islands are like one long, undulating reef, with no significant hills or mountains – although on the western side of Inishmór and Inishmaan, the land rises enough to allow for some dramatic cliffs dropping into the Atlantic. As in the Burren, the limestone creates a spectacular moonscape: sheets of grey rock with flowers and grass bursting from the cracks.

The islands have some of the most ancient Christian and pre-Christian remains in Ireland. Farming was once much easier to pursue here than on the densely forested mainland. The most ancient significant remains on the islands are massive Iron Age stone forts, such as Dún Aengus on Inishmór and Dún Conchuir on Inishmaan. Almost nothing is known about the people who built these structures, partly because their iron implements quickly rusted away. In folklore, the forts are said to have been built by the Fir Bolg, a Celtic tribe who invaded Ireland from Europe in prehistoric times.

Christianity reached the islands remarkably quickly and some of the earliest monastic settlements were founded by St Enda or Éanna, in the late 4th and early 5th centuries. Any remains you see today are later, from the 8th century on. Enda appears to have been an Irish chief who converted to Christianity and spent some time studying in Rome before seeking out a suitably bleak spot for his monastery. Many great monks studied under him on Aran, including Colmcille or Columba who went on to found the monastery on Iona in Scotland.

From the 14th century on, control of the islands was disputed by two Gaelic families, the O'Briens and the O'Flahertys. During the reign of Elizabeth I, the English took control and in Cromwell's times a garrison was stationed here.

As Galway City's importance waned so too did that of the islands. They became a quiet and windy backwater.

The islands' isolation allowed Irish culture to survive when it had all but disappeared elsewhere. Irish is still the native tongue, and until recently people wore traditional Aran dress: bright red skirts and black shawls for women and baggy woollen trousers and waistcoats with a colourful belt or *crios* around the waist for men. The classic white Aran sweater knitted in complex patterns was born here. You may still see old people wearing some elements of the traditional dress, particularly on Inishmaan. The other Aran trademark is the currach.

Even the smallest patches of rocky land are bordered by stone walls. Over the centuries, tonnes of seaweed were brought up from the beaches, mixed with sand and laid out on the bare rock to start walls. The walls may be hundreds or even thousands of years old. So have respect for them, and replace any stones you dislodge. On Inishmaan and Inisheer many of the walls are up to eye level, and it's a joy to walk for hours along the sandy lanes between them.

The elemental nature of life on the islands has always attracted writers and artists. John Millington Synge (1871-1909) spent a lot of time on the islands and his play *Riders to the Sea* is set on Inishmaan. His book *The Aran Islands* is the classic account of life out here and is readily available in paperback. The American Robert Flaherty came to the islands in 1934 to shoot *Man of Aran*, a dramatic account of daily life. It became a classic and there are regular screenings of it in Kilronan on Inishmór. The islands have produced their own talent, particularly the writer Liam O'Flaherty (1897-1984) from Inishmór. His outstanding novel *Famine* makes an appropriate introduction to an interesting writer who wandered around North and South America before returning to Ireland in 1921 and fighting on the Republican side in the Civil War.

The mapmaker Tim Robinson has written a wonderful account of his explorations on Aran, *Stones of Aran* (Penguin), and his *The Aran Islands – a map & guide* is superb. A recent publication in paperback is *The Book of Aran*, published locally by Tír Eolas, consisting of articles by 17 specialists covering diverse aspects of the islands' culture.

Today, the islands have become major attractions with quick and convenient travel connections to the mainland, a plethora of B&B and hostel accommodation and a veritable armada of mountain bikes waiting to be hired out. Inishmór – the largest – is exceedingly busy during the summer with armies of day trippers and shuttle buses all over the island.

If you have the time try to get to the smaller islands, particularly Inishmaan – the least visited – and allow yourself a few days for exploration. Inisheer is the smallest and closest to land, just eight km out from Doolin in Clare.

GETTING THERE & AWAY
Air
If speed is important or seasickness a mortal fear, you can fly to the islands with Aer Arann (☎ 091-593034) for IR£35 return, or IR£33 if you are travelling in a group of four or more people. For IR£18 you can fly one way and take the ferry the other. Nine-seater planes can be hired privately for IR£350 an hour and they also do regular 20-minute pleasure flights which cost IR£20 per person (minimum of six required).

Flights operate to all three islands, and take less than 10 minutes. The mainland departure point is at Minna, near Inverin, 38 km west of Galway. A connecting bus from outside the Galway City tourist office costs IR£4 return.

Ferry
There are several companies and several routes to the islands. The services from Rossaveal, 37 km west of Galway, are popular because the crossing is quick and the services are frequent. The ferry companies compete fiercely with offers of inclusive accommodation and family fares or with claims of impossible speed. Aran Ferries (☎ 091-568903) have a desk in the tourist

office in Galway City, as do O'Brien Shipping (☎ 091-567676). Island Ferries (☎ 091-561767) have two offices near the tourist office. Doolin ferries (☎ 065-74500) handle the route from Doolon in Clare. Bicycles usually travel free.

To/From Galway City There are direct services from Galway between June and September on Aran Ferries' *Galway Bay*. This is a journey of about 46 km to Inishmór. It takes 90 minutes, costs IR£18 return and operates twice daily in July and August, once a day in June and September.

O'Brien Shipping also operate a single daily boat service to all three Aran Islands from June to September, which usually departs from the Galway docks at 10 am.

To/From Rossaveal Also operated by Aran Ferries, the *Aran Flyer* takes less than half an hour to Inishmór. From April to October, there are three sailings a day in each direction. Island Ferries' (☎ 091-61767) slightly slower *Aran Seabird* also operates from Rossaveal. During the summer, there are at least five sailings a day from Rossaveal. The regular adult return fare from Rossaveal is IR£15 and both companies charge IR£3 for the return Galway to Rossaveal bus trip. Car parking at Rossaveal costs IR£2 a day, IR£3 overnight. O'Brien Shipping go from Rossaveal to Inishmaan and Inisheer.

In summer the Island Ferries' service from Rossaveal to Inishmór continues on to the smaller islands of Inishmaan and Inisheer.

To/From Doolin Two ferry companies operate from Doolin in County Clare to Inisheer and Inishmór. It's only eight km to Inisheer, taking about 30 minutes and costing about IR£7 one way or IR£10 return. For more details, see the Doolin section in County Clare.

Inter-Island Ferries Inter-island services are irregular but there's usually something connecting with the mainland arrivals. Typical inter-island fares are IR£10 return.

GETTING AROUND
Inisheer and Inishmaan are small enough to explore on foot but on larger Inishmór bikes are the way to go.

INISHMÓR
The island, which has the Irish name *Árainn Mór*, slopes up from its comparatively sheltered northern shores to the southern edge, then plummets straight into the turmoil of the Atlantic. Once you have climbed the hill west of Kilronan, all you can see is rock, stone walls and boulders, with the odd patch of deep green grass and potato plants. There is a fine beach at Kilmurvey west of Kilronan, and it's nice to stay out here away from the bustle of the island capital. Inishmór has a population of around 900.

Orientation
Inishmór is 13 km long and three km wide, running along a north-west to south-east axis. All ferries and boats arrive and depart from Kilronan (*Cill Ronáin*) on Cill Éinne bay on the south-eastern side of the island. The airstrip is two km farther south-east, on the other side of the bay facing Kilronan. One principal road runs the length of the island with many smaller lanes and paths leading off.

Information
There is a small seasonal tourist office (☎ 099-61263), open from June to September, on the waterfront in Kilronan. There is also a small post office and branch of the Bank of Ireland which opens on Tuesday and Wednesday in July and August. Many of the shops and craft shops will change money.

Things to See
Inishmór has three impressive stone forts, probably about 2000 years old. Halfway down the island, **Dún Aengus**, perched on the edge of the sheer southern cliff, is one of the most amazing archaeological sites in the country. It has a remarkable 'chevaux de frise'; a defensive forest of sharp stone spikes around the exterior of the fort to stop any would-be attackers.

GALWAY

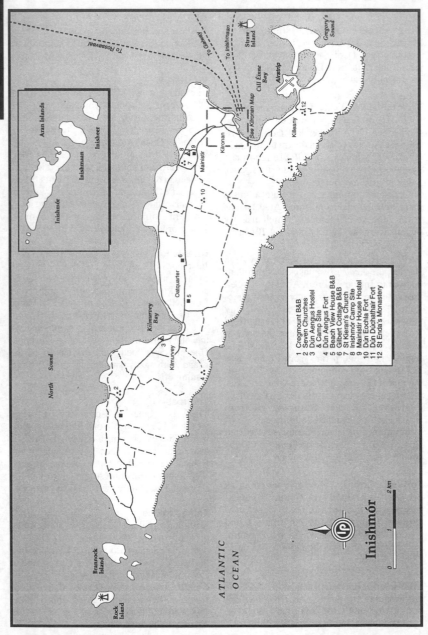

Inishmór

Aran Islands
Inishmór
Inishmaan
Inisheer

North Sound

Kilmurvey Bay

ATLANTIC OCEAN

Brannock Island

Rock Island

Kilmurvey

Oatquarter

Mainistir

Kilronan

Killeany

Cill Éinne Bay

Airstrip

Straw Island

Gregory's Sound

See Kilronan Map

To Galway
To Inishmaan
To Inisheer
To Rossaveal

1 Cregmount B&B
2 Seven Churches
3 Dún Aengus Hostel & Camp Site
4 Dún Aengus Fort
5 Beach View House B&B
6 Gilbert Cottage B&B
7 St Kieran's Church
8 Inishmór Camp Site
9 Mainistir House Hostel
10 Dún Eochla Fort
11 Dún Dúchathair Fort
12 St Enda's Monastery

0   1   2 km

Folklore suggests that Aengus was a king of the Fir Bolgs, a legendary Celtic tribe from Europe who are said to have retreated to Aran and built these forts after falling out with the mainland chiefs. Other sources say that he was a 5th-century Irish chief and pupil of St Enda, the islands' most important saint.

Dún Aengus is a magical place and should not be missed. Try and go at a quiet time such as late evening when there are few visitors about.

Half way between Kilronan and Dún Aengus is the smaller **Dún Eochla** fort, a perfect circular ring fort. Directly south of Kilronan and dramatically perched on a promontory is **Dún Dúchathair**. It's surrounded on three sides by cliffs and is less visited than Dún Aengus.

The ruins of numerous stone churches trace the island's monastic history. The small **St Kieran's** (*Teampall Chiaráin*), with a high cross in the churchyard, is near Kilronan. Past Kilmurvey are the ruins of various small early Christain remains known rather inaccurately as the **Seven Churches** (*Na Seacht Teampall*), consisting of a couple of ruined chapels, monastic houses and some fragments of a high cross. Near the airstrip are the sunken remains of a church said to be the site of **St Enda's monastery** in the 5th century.

Inishmór now has the ubiquitous **Heritage Centre** offering an introduction to the landscape and culture of the three islands. It is easily found in Kilronan and is open seven days a week from 10 am to 7 pm between April and October; admission is IR£2.

Places to Stay

Camping *Inishmór Camp Site* (☎ 099-61185) has a fine setting near the beach in Mainistir, almost two km north-west of Kilronan and about a 30-minute walk from the pier. Facilities are basic and they charge IR£2 per person. There is also free camping beside Dún Aengus Hostel and you can use the hostel's facilities for a nominal charge.

Hostels In Kilronan the *Aran Islands Hostel* (☎ 099-61255) is only a short walk from the pier and has dorm beds for IR£6. It's on top

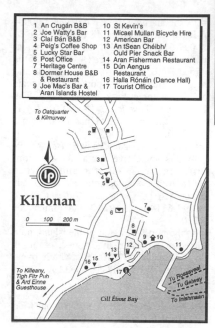

1 An Crugán B&B
2 Joe Watty's Bar
3 Claí Bán B&B
4 Peig's Coffee Shop
5 Lucky Star Bar
6 Post Office
7 Heritage Centre
8 Dormer House B&B & Restaurant
9 Joe Mac's Bar & Aran Islands Hostel
10 St Kevin's
11 Micael Mullan Bicycle Hire
12 American Bar
13 An tSean Chéibh/ Ould Pier Snack Bar
14 Aran Fisherman Restaurant
15 Dún Aengus Restaurant
16 Halla Rónáin (Dance Hall)
17 Tourist Office

Kilronan

of the Joe Mac pub – convenient for a Guinness, not so good for light sleepers. *St Kevin's* hostel is next door and accommodation should be available here also in the summer. *Dún Aengus Hostel* (☎ 099-61318) is near the beach on the west side of Kilmurvey Bay some seven km from Kilronan. This is a nice country house with 42 beds, two, three or four to a room. They charge IR£6 a night and there are free rides in and out of Kilronan.

The *Mainistir House Hostel* (☎ 099-61199), which has a bus meeting the ferries, has beds for IR£7 and doubles for IR20; both include a breakfast of porridge and scones. Some travellers have reported a frosty regime.

Aran Ferries offers special discounts with Aran Islands Hostel, Island Ferries with Mainistir House. For example, you can get one night's B&B, and return fares by bus and ferry from Galway for around IR£25.

B&Bs In Kilronan village about 800 metres

from the harbour is *An Crugán* (☎ 099-61150) which costs IR£13. *Claí Bán* (☎ 099-61111) is IR£12, or IR£14 with own bathroom. *Dormer House* (☎ 099-61125) is a good B&B not far from the harbour and their restaurant is very popular with locals and dinner there costs around IR£14. The *Ard Einne Guesthouse* (☎ 099-61126) is west of the village and has rooms from IR£22/26.

Farther away, *Beach View House* (☎ 099-61141) is some five km north-west from Kilronan in Oatquarter and charges IR£18/26 for singles/doubles, IR£11 for dinner. Also here is the cosy *Gilbert Cottage* (☎ 099-61146) at IR£12 and dinner for IR£10.

At the north-west end of the island, nine km from Kilronan in Creggakeerain, is *Cregmount* (☎ 099-61139), which overlooks Galway Bay and costs IR£13.

Places to Eat

In Kilronan, about the best place for pub food is *Joe Watty's Bar* (☎ 099-61155) on the way north-west out of Kilronan. There's also the *Ould Pier* snack bar and, a little farther from the centre, *Peig's Coffee Shop* near the Lucky Star bar with good snacks all day. *Dún Aengus* (☎ 099-61104) overlooking Cill Éinne Bay Bay in Kilronan has a set dinner for IR£12 and serves good grills, steaks, chips and lovely scones and fruitcake. It's open from breakfast to late evening. The *Aran Fisherman* is under the same management and has a wide range of meat, seafood and vegetarian dishes from around IR£6.

Mainistir House Hostel has a reputation for good food: breakfasts with home-made bread and good coffee, and dinner costing IR£6 for residents and IR£7 for non-residents. They offer plenty of choice on their menu of seafood and vegetarian dishes, and the buffet dinner at 8 pm often includes some excellent vegetarian options. Also try *Gilbert Cottage* (☎ 099-61146) which does good evening meals, most costing around IR£10. Outside of Kilronan, at the end of the road leading to Dún Aengus fort, there is the *An Sunda Cáoch* café.

Entertainment

There's music in most Kilronan pubs at night. For Irish music, try *Joe Watty's Bar* or *Joe Mac's*, or *Tigh Fitz* west of the village. The *American Bar* has rock music and draws a young crowd.

Robert O'Flaherty's classic *Man of Aran* is shown regularly at the Dance Hall (*Halla Rónáin*) in Kilronan and shows how much life has changed here in the last 60 years. Admission is IR£3.

Getting Around

Daily rates for bike hire are around IR£5 but the islands are tough on bikes, so check any bike over carefully before agreeing to rent it.

Micael Mullan (☎ 099-61132), just up from the pier, seems to have pretty good machines. Costelloes (☎ 099-61241) is the other bike hire company, offering similar bikes for similar prices; it's near the American Bar. The rocky back roads are definitely mountain bike territory. You can bring your own bike out on the ferries.

There are plenty of small tour buses which offer speedy trips to some of the island's principal sights for around IR£5. Michael Hernon (☎ 099-61303) is one such operator and can be used for evening transfers to Kilronan. However, walking and cycling will give you more of a sense of the place. Pony traps with a driver are also available for an island trip from Kilronan to the west of the island from around IR£20.

INISHMAAN

Inishmaan (*Inis Meáin*) is the least visited of the three Aran Islands and well worth the effort of getting there.

Inishmaan is lozenge-shaped and about five km long by three km wide. The fields are bordered by high stone walls, and it's a delight to wander along these boreens and take in some of the tranquillity that attracted the playwright J M Synge and the evangelical nationalist Patrick Pearse. **Synge's Chair** is a sheltered spot where the writer is said to have spent many an hour. It is at the west of the island near the end of a path that leads to a sheer cliff.

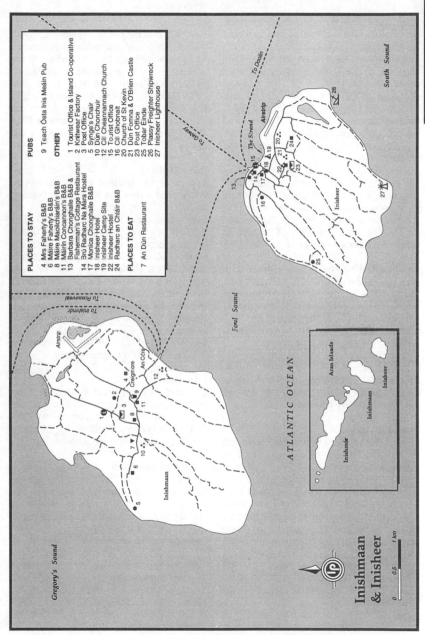

PLACES TO STAY

4 Mrs Faherty's B&B
6 Máire Faherty's B&B
8 Máire Maoilchiaráin's B&B
11 Máirín Concannon's B&B
13 Barbara Chonghaile B&B &
   Fisherman's Cottage Restaurant
14 Brú Radharc Na Mara Hostel
17 Monica Chonghaile B&B
18 Inisheer Hotel
19 Inisheer Camp Site
22 Inisheer Hostel
24 Radharc an Chláir B&B

PLACES TO EAT

7 An Dún Restaurant

PUBS

9 Teach Ósta Inis Meáin Pub

OTHER

1 Tourist Office & Island Co-operative
2 Knitwear Factory
3 Post Office
5 Synge's Chair
10 Dún Chonchuir
12 Cill Cheannannach Church
15 Tourist Office
16 Cill Ghobnait
20 Church of St Kevin
21 Dún Fonna & O'Brien Castle
23 Post Office
25 Tobar Éinde
26 Plassy Freighter Shipwreck
27 Inisheer Lighthouse

Inishmaan
& Inisheer

0   0.5   1 km

Most of the houses on Inishmaan are in the centre of the island, while the principal boat landing stage is at An Córa on the east side. There is a reasonable beach just north of the slip. The airstrip is on the north-east corner of the island.

Inishmaan does not seem to be hell bent on attracting tourists. It is the home of a knitwear factory which exports fine woollen garments to some of the world's most exclusive shops. There is a factory shop on the island.

The main archaeological site is **Dún Chonchúir**, a massive stone ring fort, built on a high point and offering good views of the island on a fine day. It's similar to Dún Aengus on Inishmór, but it's built inland overlooking a limestone valley. Chonchúir is said to have been a brother of Aengus. Dún Chonchúir's age is a bit of a mystery; it's thought to have been built somewhere between the 1st and the 6th centuries AD. The thatched cottage on the road before you head up to the fort is where J M Synge spent his summers between 1898 and 1902.

Cill Cheannannach is a rough 7th or 8th-century church south of the pier.

Information
The Island Co-operative (☎ 099-73010) is north of the post office, and the manager and his family are very helpful.

Places to Stay & Eat
There is free camping by the beach just north of An Córa landing slip. One of the best B&Bs on the island is *Mrs Faherty's* (☎ 099-73012) in Creigmore about 500 metres north-west of the pier, which costs IR£13/22. *Mrs Máire Maoilchiaráin's* (☎ 099-73016) is a good B&B on a corner south of the post office, similarly priced. Another good one in the village is *Máirín Concannon's* B&B (☎ 099-73019), across the road from the island's only pub. *Máire Faherty's* B&B (☎ 099-73027), charging from IR£10.50/21 is west of the village past the entrance to the Dún Chonchúir.

Most B&Bs serve evening meals for around IR£10. The island has just one pub,

Teach Ósta Inis Meáin (☎ 099-73003) in Baile an Mhothair, serving snacks, sandwiches, soups and seafood platters between 11.30 am and 6 pm. This is a terrific little bar and hums with life on summer evenings.

The island's only restaurant is *An Dún* (☎ 099-73068), just opposite the entrance to Dún Chonchúir. It offers reasonably priced omelettes, pasta for lunch for around IR£6 and dinner for around IR£10 per main course.

INISHEER
Inisheer is the smallest of the three Aran Islands and only eight km off the coast of Doolin in County Clare. The view from the ferry is of a sheltered white beach backed by modern bungalows – few traditional thatched cottages and buildings survive – overlooked by a squat stone 15th-century castle. To the south there's a maze of fields without a building in sight. The island has a timelessness about it, and a summer stroll through its sandy lanes is hard to beat. Despite a regular ferry service, the absence of archaeological sites and tourist amenities keeps the number of visitors down and this helps make Inisheer rather special.

Information
During the summer there is a tourist information desk at the harbour. You can also contact the Island Co-operative (☎ 099-75008). Bikes are available for hire at a couple of houses near the pier.

Things to See & Do
The 16th-century O'Brien **castle** overlooks the beach and harbour. It is built within the remains of a ring fort from around the 1st century AD. Nearby is an 18th century signal tower. On the beach is the 10th-century **Teampall Chaoimhain** or Church of St Kevin, with some gravestones and shells from an ancient midden or dumping ground. The **Heritage House** is a typical stone built thatched cottage with some interesting old photographs. It has a craft shop and a café.

Cill Ghobnait (church of Saint Gobnait) is west of the main pier and this small 10th-

GALWAY

century church is named after Gobnait, who fled here from Clare trying to escape an enemy who was pursuing her. A two-km walk south-west of the church leads to **Tobar Éinde** (Well of St Enda).

The best parts of Inisheer are uninhabited and the signposted Inis Oírr Way walk is recommended. The eastern road to the lighthouse is more popular but the coast around the west side is wilder. On the eastern shore is the rusting hulk of the *Plassy*, a freighter wrecked in 1960 and thrown high up onto the rocks. The uninhabited lighthouse on the island's southern tip with its neat enclosure is off limits.

Places to Stay & Eat
Camping *Inisheer Camp Site* (☎ 099-75008) by the strand is open from May to September. They charge IR£2 per tent and have basic facilities.

Hostels The *Brú Radharc Na Mara Hostel* (☎ 099-75087) near the pier costs IR£6 a night and has three double rooms for IR£16. It also does B&B for IR£12 and is open all year round and has bikes for hire. The smaller *Inisheer Hostel* (☎ 099-75077) is near the post office.

B&Bs *Radharc an Chláir* (☎ 099-75019) is near the castle, charges from IR£15/25, does a IR£10 dinner, and is tourist-board approved. Other B&Bs have similar rates. Try *An Cladach* (☎ 099-75033) in West Village or there's *Mrs Barbara Chonghaile* (☎ 099-75025) or *Monica Chonghaile* (☎ 099-75034), also in West Village not far from the pier.

Hotel The modern Inisheer Hotel or *Óstán Inis Oirr* (☎ 099-75020) is just up from the strand. It offers B&B from IR£19/35. The restaurant serves reasonable seafood and dinner is IR£14. The bar is a little vacuous but you should check out the old *National Geographic* pictures of the island on its walls which show the islanders in their traditional dress.

Pub The *Fisherman's Cottage* (☎ 099-75073) is a pub with very good seafood, not far from the pier in the western part of the village. Lunch is around IR£6, most main courses for dinner are around IR£12 and vegetarian meals are also available.

Eastern Galway

Eastern Galway is markedly different from the wild and bleak landscape of Connemara and west Galway. The two regions are separated naturally by Lough Corrib. Eastern Galway is relatively flat, and its underlying limestone has given it a well-drained, fertile soil. This is the largest section of the county but it lacks any areas of significant interest. Big towns like Ballinasloe, Loughrea and Tuam (*Tuaim*) serve prosperous farming regions.

In the south-east corner of the county, the lakeside town of Portumna is an attractive place and a popular base for boating and fishing on Lough Derg.

CLONFERT CATHEDRAL
Around 15 km south of Ballinasloe is the tiny 12th-century cathedral at Clonfert. The monastery is said to have been founded in the middle of the 6th century by St Brendan the Navigator and was ravaged several times by Vikings between 840 and 1180. The remarkable Romanesque doorway, with its human and animal heads dates from the 1160s.

BALLINASLOE
The biggest town in eastern Galway, Ballinasloe (*Béal Átha na Sluaighe*) was a strategic crossing point over the River Suck. In the early 1100s, Turlough O'Connor, king of Connaught, built a castle to guard the river crossing and this became the nucleus of the town's development. Around eight km west of town, Aughrim was the site of a crucial victory by William of Orange over the Catholic forces of James II in 1691. There is a small museum here and *Hyne's Hostel*

(☎ 0905-73734) nearby, part of the family home, charges IR£5.50 a night.

Today, Ballinasloe is on the main Dublin to Galway road with most traffic diverted south around the town centre. The town is pleasant enough, but there is no real reason to stay here except possibly over the eight days in October when the Ballinasloe Horse Fair attracts legions of horse buyers, horse sellers and drinkers.

LOUGHREA

Loughrea (*Baile Locha Riach*) is a large and busy market town 26 km east of Galway City. It gets its name from the lake at the west end of town. Loughrea has improved a lot in recent years with many plastic signs and garish shopfronts replaced by much more appealing and traditional frontages. **St Brendan's Catholic Cathedral** is renowned for its stained glass.

Seven km from Loughrea near Bullaun is the remarkable **Turoe Stone**, a phallic standing stone covered in delicate La-Tène-style carvings in relief. It dates from between 300 BC and 100 AD. There are similarly carved stones in Brittany, associated with the La Téne Celts. The stone was not found here

The Turoe Stone with its La-Tène-style carving

originally but at an Iron Age fort a few km away.

PORTUMNA

The main attraction here is the recently opened **Portumna Castle & Gardens**, built in the early 17th century by Richard Burke and boasting a formal garden of some pretension. It's an OPW site, open daily from mid-June to mid-September from 9.30 am to 6.30 pm. Entrance is IR£2/1.

Counties Mayo & Sligo

Despite a shared history of rural poverty and a common geography of remote and underpopulated places, the smaller county of Sligo – thanks largely to the poet W B Yeats – is better known to many travellers. But the qualities of landscape and sense of place that inspired the poet belong equally to both counties. And, apart from a small number of towns like Sligo, Westport and Cong, both counties are ideal for anyone wishing to escape the tourist trail. Mayo in particular is just waiting to be discovered by intrepid travellers who want to escape from other tourists.

County Mayo

Mayo (*Maigh Eo*) has an identity that distinguishes itself on many different levels: an introspective landscape, a Connaught accent with its own inflection and a people who seem far removed from cosmopolitan Dublin or touristy Killarney. The relative poverty of the land meant that the invaders left it to last, but what delayed the English is what attracts today's visitors: lakes, mountains, boglands, and a population density among the lowest in Europe.

The recent history of Mayo is one of massive and ongoing emigration and apart from the small industries that sustain Castlebar's relative prosperity, there is a chronic lack of employment opportunities for young people.

CONG

Drive straight through and this small town would be just another dot on the map, but there's a great deal hidden behind that ordinary main street. In 1951 director John Ford along with John Wayne & Co came here to film *The Quiet Man* and there are still many reminders of that momentous event.

Highlights
- Cycling or driving from Louisburg to Leenane through the Doolough Valley
- Achill Island off the coast of West Mayo
- The lonely expanses of bogland in the Belmullet Peninsula
- North Mayo – its historical and prehistoric sights
- The museum and art gallery in Sligo Town
- Carrowmore Megalithic Cemetery outside Sligo Town
- Discovering WB Yeats' County Sligo
- Inishmurray Island

Information

Tourist information (☎ 092-46542) is available from May to September, daily from 10 am to 6 pm, from the old courthouse building opposite the abbey in Abbey St. Get a copy of the Heritage Trail brochure to explore the town and discover the fascinating history of the 1123 Cong Cross, now in the National Museum in Dublin. The local booklets *The Glory of Cong* and *Cong – Walks, Sights, Stories* have more information.

Guided tours focusing on *The Quiet Man* locations depart from the tourist office at 8.45 am each morning and last about 90 minutes.

The post office is on Main St.

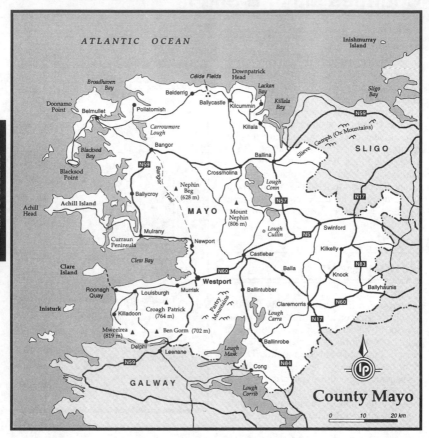

Cong Abbey

This 12th-century Augustinian abbey, founded by the high king Turlough O'Connor, occupies the site of a 6th-century abbey. It has a carved doorway on the north side and fine windows and decorated stonework in the Chapter House. Just west of the abbey on a small island in the nearby river stands the monks' fishing house, where a bell was rung every time a fish was caught. The modern Catholic church, in a corner of the abbey site, is a remarkable piece of festering ugliness plonked down with utter disregard for its surroundings. The market cross, at the junction of Main St and Abbey St, is the reconstructed remains of a 14th-century high cross.

Ashford Castle

This Victorian castle, once the home of the Guinness family and now a private hotel, stands on the site of an early Anglo-Norman castle built by the de Burgos family after their defeat of the native O'Connors of Connaught. The interior is strictly for residents and it costs IR£2/1 just to enter the grounds and view the fairytale exterior. However, the jetty for cruises on Lough Corrib (IR£7,

IR£6 for students) is beside the castle, and it's also possible to enter the grounds by way of the exit road that comes out in Abbey St, or by crossing the river from the abbey and walking along the other bank.

Places to Stay

Camping You can camp at the *Cong Caravan & Camping Park* (☎ 092-46089), on Lisloughrey Quay Rd, for IR£3.50 per person, or at the *Cong Hostel* or *Courtyard Hostel*.

Hostels The IHH *Quiet Man Hostel* (☎ 092-46089) on Abbey St is right in the centre of town; beds are IR£6 and doubles IR£14. Two km out of town in Lisloughrey, off the road to Galway, the popular IHH *Cong Hostel* (☎ 092-46089) has better facilities and charges IR£6.50 for a bed and IR£16 for a double room. There's also the *Courtyard Hostel* (☎ 092-46203), five km out in Cross,

with beds for IR£5.50 and two doubles for IR£13.

B&Bs In and around the town there's a typical collection of B&Bs. Central places include *Lydon's* (☎ 092-46228) charging from IR£12/24 and the *White House* (☎ 092-46358), across from the abbey and charging from IR£17/28.

There are a few B&Bs down the street by the side of Connolly's food store, the *River Lodge* (☎ 092-46057) being typical. Singles/doubles here are IR£18/30.

Hotels *Ryan's Hotel* (☎ 092-46243) has rooms at similar prices to the B&Bs. *Danagher's* (☎ 092-46028) is a hotel at the town's main junction with singles/doubles for IR£25/50, which sounds like a giveaway compared to the IR£254/268 charged at *Ashford Castle* (☎ 092-46003). Some of the

MAYO & SLIGO

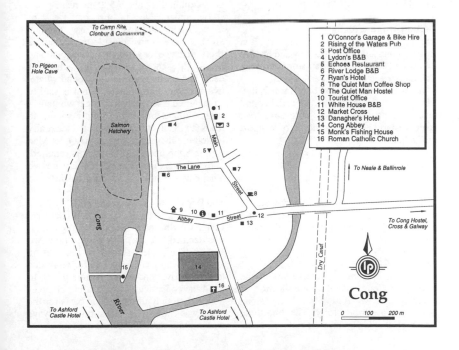

1 O'Connor's Garage & Bike Hire
2 Rising of the Waters Pub
3 Post Office
4 Lydon's B&B
5 Echoes Restaurant
6 River Lodge B&B
7 Ryan's Hotel
8 The Quiet Man Coffee Shop
9 The Quiet Man Hostel
10 Tourist Office
11 White House B&B
12 Market Cross
13 Danagher's Hotel
14 Cong Abbey
15 Monk's Fishing House
16 Roman Catholic Church

To Camp Site, Clonbur & Cornamona
To Pigeon Hole Cave
Salmon Hatchery
The Lane
Main Street
Street
Abbey Street
Cong
River
Dry Canal
To Neale & Ballinrole
To Cong Hostel, Cross & Galway
To Ashford Castle Hotel
To Ashford Castle Hotel

Cong

0   100   200 m

boxy rooms at the castle can actually prove disappointing but they do provide *The Quiet Man* on the in-house video ready for viewing any time of the day or night.

Places to Eat

The *Rising of the Waters* pub in Main St has light meals, while at the other end of the street is *The Quiet Man Coffee Shop*. Nearby, *Danagher's Hotel* has a fine old bar, a straightforward eating area and a fancier restaurant. Vegetarian food is hard to come by though Danagher's will do an omelette for IR£4. Bar food in the IR£7 to IR£10 range is available at *Ryan's Hotel* and dinner between 5 and 7 pm is IR£16.50. *Lydon's* is a restaurant as well as doing B&B and their tourist menu has been recommended.

If your credit card didn't stretch to the Ashford Castle, consider unleashing it on *Echoes* on Main St, a restaurant which proves great food can exist in Ireland – but count on more than IR£50 for two, including a bottle of wine.

Getting There & Away

From Monday to Friday, there's a Bus Éireann connection with Galway and bus No 243 from Galway to Clifden stops at Cong. The bus stop is outside Ryan's Hotel.

If travelling by car or bike farther into Mayo, avoid the main N84 to Castlebar and take the longer, but much more attractive, route west to Leenane and north to Westport via Delphi.

Getting Around

There are enough interesting sites close to Cong to make a bike worth having. They can be hired from O'Connor's on Main St; it's the combined garage, supermarket, bar and craft shop. All three of the hostels also have bikes for hire.

AROUND CONG

There's a surprising amount to see in the vicinity of Cong, including a collection of caves, a canal which never worked, a stone circle and a curious folly. The limestone strata of the Cong area account for the numerous caves, for the failure of the canal and for the local phenomenon known as 'the rising of the waters', where water from Lough Mask percolates through the limestone and emerges from the ground at Cong before flowing down to Lough Corrib.

Caves

The Cong area is riddled with caves, many of them only a short walk from the village. The Pigeon Hole is about 1.5 km west of Cong and can be reached by road or by the walking track from across the river. Stone steps lead down into the cave, which at times can be rather wet. There's a local legend about two fairy trout who dwell in the cave.

From the Pigeon Hole, take the L101 road towards Clonbur, passing the Giant's Grave turn-off and continuing to a lane turning south about five km from Cong. A stream flows into the extensive Ballymaglancy Cave, which is off the road to the right. The cave has stalactites and stalagmites and has been explored for about 500 metres.

Two other caves are just to the east of Cong, beside the road to Cross. Captain Webb's Cave is just outside the village, a short distance beyond the dry canal and behind the school grounds. It's actually a deep, water-filled hole in the ground where, two centuries ago, a local villain is said to have hurled a succession of local women. A further 200 metres from Cong, a wide path leads to Kelly's Cave, which is usually locked up; the key is kept at the Quiet Man Coffee Shop and a IR£ deposit is required. Lady's Buttery and Horse Discovery are two other caves beside a road to the castle.

The Dry Canal

Lough Mask is about 10 metres higher than Lough Corrib, and in the mid-18th century it was decided to cut a canal between the two loughs. The project started in 1848, using labourers who were desperate for work due to the deprivations of the famine years. In 1854 the construction was nearing completion, but already the economic basis for the canal was coming into question as railways were rapidly spreading across the country. At

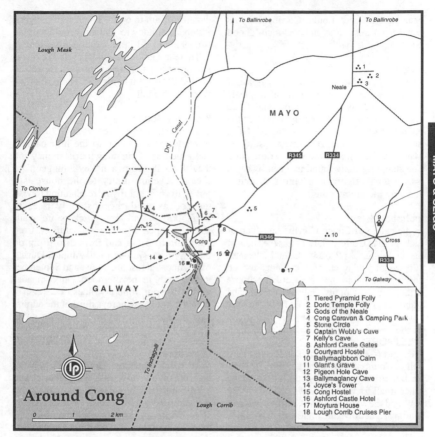

Around Cong

0   1   2 km

1 Tiered Pyramid Folly
2 Doric Temple Folly
3 Gods of the Neale
4 Cong Caravan & Camping Park
5 Stone Circle
6 Captain Webb's Cave
7 Kelly's Cave
8 Ashford Castle Gates
9 Courtyard Hostel
10 Ballymagibbon Cairn
11 Giant's Grave
12 Pigeon Hole Cave
13 Ballymaglancy Cave
14 Joyce's Tower
15 Cong Hostel
16 Ashford Castle Hotel
17 Moytura House
18 Lough Corrib Cruises Pier

this point a much greater problem was discovered – the canal was not watertight. The porous limestone simply soaked up any water that flowed into the canal. Although various schemes for sealing the canal bed were considered, the whole expensive project was abandoned in 1858. The dry canal, complete with locks for raising and lowering the water level, runs just to the east of Cong.

Circles & Graves

The stone slabs of the megalithic burial chamber known as the Giant's Grave can be conveniently visited between the Pigeon Hole and the Ballymaglancy Cave. A path leads into the forest to the south of the R345 road to Clonbur, about three km from Cong. About 100 metres from the road take the turn-off to the left; the grave is off that path to the right.

There are several stone circles in the area, including an excellent one just to the east side of the road from Cong to Neale at Nymphsfield, about 1.5 km out of Cong. Just north of the road from Cong to Cross is Ballymagibbon Cairn, supposedly the site of a legendary Celtic battle. Moytura House, near the shores of Lough Corrib, takes its name from this battle and was a childhood home of Oscar Wilde.

Neale

The village of Neale, five km north-east of Cong, has several interesting sites. Neale Park is on the east side of the road and if you take the turn-off at the northern end of the village, the curious stone known as the 'Gods of the Neale' is about 200 metres east of the main road, just inside the walls of the park. The slab, originally found in a nearby cave, is carved with figures of a human, an animal and a reptile in low relief.

Inchagoill Island

In the centre of Lough Corrib, the island of Inchagoill in County Galway has the ruins of the 5th-century St Patrick's Church, the later 12th-century Church of the Saint, and an ancient obelisk in the graveyard. For more details see the County Galway chapter. The island can be reached by boat from the jetty next to Ashford Castle.

WESTPORT

Westport (*Cathair na Mart*), in the southern half of County Mayo, didn't acquire its post-card prettiness gradually, unlike so many other small Irish towns. It was designed that way, and the Mall, with the Carrowbeg River running right down the middle of it, is as nice a main street as you could find. The present Westport House was built on the site of an O'Malley castle, which was surrounded by about 60 hovels, the original settlement of Westport. These were moved when the house was planned, and the Brownes, who came here from Sussex in the time of Elizabeth I, even had the course of the river altered to allow the Mall to act as a grand approach to the gates of the house. This wasn't entirely successful, as even today the Mall is subject to occasional flooding.

Information

The tourist office (☎ 098-25711) on the Mall is open all year round. Between April and September, it opens from Monday to Satur-day from 9 am to 6 pm. The rest of the year, it's open Monday to Thursday and Saturday from 9 am to 5.15 pm and closes for lunch.

There is a laundrette in High St. For information about fishing enquire at Hewetson (☎ 098-26018) on Bridge St. The post office is on North Mall.

Westport House

The present house dates from 1730. Commercialisation is taken to the hilt: name a tacky method of pursuing tourist money and they'll do it, from a hokey 'dungeon' to cheap souvenirs. Entry to the house is a pricey IR£6/3, but if you're planning to visit the zoo as well the cost only rises to IR£6.50/3.25, and family tickets are available. It's open Monday to Saturday from 10.30 am to 6 pm and from 2 to 6 pm on Sunday from 27 June to 20 August. During May, June, the rest of August and September it opens only in the afternoon. Only consider a visit if your itinerary doesn't take in a stately home elsewhere; a third of the admission price buys an informative town guide and map from the tourist office, which provides greater insight into the social history of Westport.

To reach Westport House in a vehicle, head out of town towards Croagh Patrick and Louisburgh and the entry road is on the right. An alternative approach is on foot via the Hotel Westport. Enter through the iron gates to the right of the hotel's entrance and follow the path until you reach the sign for the zoo on the right. Go down to the left here, cross the small red bridge and follow the river to the right. It takes about 10 minutes to walk there from the hotel.

Heritage Centre

The centre has an interesting selection of local artefacts and documents, including the spinning wheel presented by the people of Ballina to Maud Gonne, the dynamic political rebel who was married briefly to Major John MacBride and was the object of Yeats' adoration. Also housed in this centre are the records of the trial of Patrick Egan, who commandeered Westport House during the

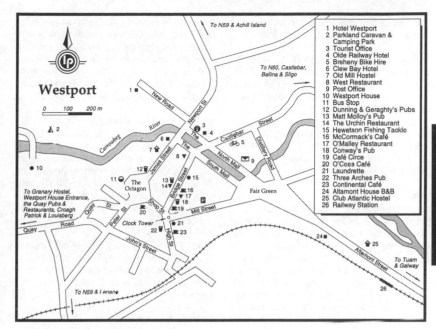

Westport

0   100   200 m

To N59 & Achill Island

To N60, Castlebar,
Ballina & Sligo

To Granary Hostel,
Westport House Entrance,
the Quay Pubs &
Restaurants, Croagh
Patrick & Louisburg

Clock Tower

Fair Green

To Tuam
& Galway

To N59 & Lenane

1 Hotel Westport
2 Parkland Caravan &
   Camping Park
3 Tourist Office
4 Olde Railway Hotel
5 Breheny Bike Hire
6 Clew Bay Hotel
7 Old Mill Hostel
8 West Restaurant
9 Post Office
10 Westport House
11 Bus Stop
12 Dunning & Geraghty's Pubs
13 Matt Molloy's Pub
14 The Urchin Restaurant
15 Hewetson Fishing Tackle
16 McCormack's Café
17 O'Malley Restaurant
18 Conway's Pub
19 Café Circe
20 O'Coes Café
21 Laundrette
22 Three Arches Pub
23 Continental Café
24 Altamont House B&B
25 Club Atlantic Hostel
26 Railway Station

MAYO & SLIGO

1798 Rising. The centre is open all year from 10 am to 5 pm on weekdays (2 pm in winter), 3 to 6 pm at the weekend. Admission is IR£1 and it's just outside town on the road to Louisburgh.

The Octagon Monument

This was erected in 1845 to the memory of an eminently forgettable local banker and a statue of the man stood upon an octagonal podium at the top of the column. During the Civil War, Free State troops decapitated the statue and it was later removed. In 1990 a more politically correct statue of St Patrick replaced the unfortunate capitalist.

Places to Stay

Camping Camping is recommended at the *Club Atlantic Hostel*. The alternative, the *Parkland Caravan & Camping Park* (☎ 098-25141) on the Westport House estate and accessible by the same road that leads to the house, charges an outrageous IR£16 for

one night's pitch. If the hostel sites are full, consider the camp site 16 km away near Louisburgh. See the Louisburgh section for details.

Hostels The well-equipped IHH *Old Mill Hostel* (☎ 098-27045) is right in the centre on James St and costs IR£6 a night. There is one double room for IR£11. The IHH *Club Atlantic Hostel* (☎ 098-26644), on Altamont St near the railway station, has even more facilities; beds are IR£6.50 and double rooms are IR£17. If you are heading down to Cong, take the opportunity to view *The Quiet Man* free of charge on the hostel's video.

Westport hostels also include the *Granary* (☎ 098-25903) on Quay Rd, just before the Westport House entrance. Beds are IR£5.

B&Bs The tourist office will book rooms in the town's plentiful supply of B&Bs, but if you should arrive late, try *Altamont House*

(☎ 098-25226) which is within walking distance of the railway on Altamont St.

Hotels *Clew Bay* hotel (☎ 098-25438) on James St has rooms from IR£30/50. The *Olde Railway Hotel* (☎ 098-25166) is next to the tourist office. Thackeray chose to stay here on his tour around Ireland in the 19th century and the Victorian connection is carefully maintained. It costs from IR£35/50. *Hotel Westport* (☎ 098-25122), on New Rd, is functional by comparison but charges about the same.

Places to Eat

Bridge St has a fair selection of cafés. Try *McCormack's* in the middle of Bridge St where lunch is around IR£5 or *Café Circe* further down. The *West* is a pub and restaurant and offers a tourist menu around IR£7.

The *O'Malley Restaurant* has a vast and varied menu of pizza, steak and seafood. Expect to pay around IR£10 for dinner. Almost opposite is *The Urchin* restaurant; the interior is plain, but the menu is more promising and dinner is under IR£10.

Round the corner on High St is the excellent *Continental Café* with good vegetarian food. On the Octagon, *O'Cee's* is a popular soup-and-sandwich place.

On the Quay, just outside of town on the road to Louisburgh, there are a number of pubs and restaurants mostly specialising in seafood. Near the entrance to Westport House, *Quay Cottage* (☎ 098-26412) has a nautical theme and evening meals are IR£8-15. On the Quay the *Moorings* restaurant (☎ 098-25874) is in the house where Major John MacBride, briefly married to Maud Gonne and executed after 1916, was born. Both these places only open for dinner. Nearby, the *Asgard Tavern*, the *Towers Bar* and *Ardmore House* all serve pub food, lunch and dinner.

Entertainment

There are a number of pubs, including those on Quay Rd, with music throughout the summer. *Matt Molloy's* on Bridge St is owned by Matt Molloy of the Chieftains. The

Three Arches near the clocktower has regular sessions while *Conway's* on Bridge St is a quieter, old-style place. Two pubs rubbing shoulders and facing the Octagon, *Dunning* and *Geraghty's*, have tables out on the pavement and on a fine day a Mediterranean mood can be conjured up here.

Getting There & Away

Bus There are bus connections to Achill, Ballina, Belfast, Cork, Galway, Limerick, Shannon, Sligo and Waterford. Buses depart from the Octagon at present. A private bus (☎ 095-41043) leaves Clifden at 10 am, arriving in Westport just before midday and leaving for the return journey at 5 pm from the Octagon.

Train The railway station (☎ 098-25253) is up Altamont St from the Club Atlantic Hostel and within walking distance. There are three daily connections with Dublin (3½ hours) via Athlone.

Getting Around

Bicycles can be hired from the Club Atlantic Hostel or from Breheny Bike Hire on Castlebar St just north of the Mall.

AROUND WESTPORT
Croagh Patrick

Croagh Patrick towers to the west of Westport. It was from the top of this mountain that St Patrick performed his snake expulsion act – Ireland has been snake-free ever since. Climbing the 765-metre peak is a holy feat for thousands of pilgrims on the last Sunday of July. The really enthusiastic make the rocky ascent barefoot. If the weather's clear the two-hour climb (one if you're in a real hurry) gives fine views at any time of year.

Unfortunately, the extensive instructions at the bottom of the peak about making a properly pious ascent neglect to add a suggestion that 'thou shalt not litter'. As a result, the upper reaches of this holy mountain are richly carpeted with empty soft-drink cans.

The trail begins at Campbell's pub in the

village of Murrisk, west of Westport. There is a sign between the pub and the car park pointing the way and there's no mistaking the route.

Louisburgh

The town gets its name from the fact that it was laid out by the 1st Marquess of Sligo, who had a relation who fought against the French at the Battle of Louisburgh in Canada. The town is home to the **Granuaile Visitor Centre**, dedicated to the life and times of Grace O'Malley (1530-1603), the pirate queen and the most famous of the O'Malley clan. The centre also includes a Famine Exhibition. Admission is IR£2.25/1.25 and, during the summer, it's open from 10 am to 7.30 pm, closed Sunday.

There are some excellent **beaches** in the vicinity, Old Head Beach and the Silver Strand are particularly sandy and safe and are suitable for surfing and other adventure sports. About 4 km from Louisburgh and just off the main road to Westport is the *Old Head Forest Caravan & Camping Park* (☎ 098-66021). Large/small tents cost IR£6.50/5.50 plus 50p per person. The beach is only 300 metres away.

Doolough Valley

There are two roads connecting Westport and Leenane but the one nearest the coast, via Delphi (see the Galway chapter), travels through the Doolough Valley and crosses the border between Mayo and Galway. It is wildly beautiful, not least because of the lonely expanse of Doo Lough (the dark lake) with the Mweelrea Mountains behind. At the southern end of the lake Ben Gorm rises to 702 metres. The landscape changes from snooker table green and sparkling wet stone to a forbidding grey, as shadows envelop everything when cloudbanks spread in from the Atlantic.

During the famine, the valley was the scene of tragedy when some 600 men, women and children walked from Louisburgh to Delphi Lodge in the hope that the landlord would offer them some food. Help was flatly refused, and on the return journey around 400 perished through hunger and exposure. On the road there is a memorial.

Large deposits of gold, worth in excess of IR£400 million, are believed to be in the area. A High Court decision has decided that a mining company can move in and disregard Mayo council's veto on any threat to the natural beauty of the area.

MAYO & SLIGO

Granuaile – Grace O'Malley – the Pirate Queen

Granuaile (1530-1603) was the daughter of a Connaught chief who established her own fleet and commanded her own army. From her Clare Island base she attacked the ships of those who had submitted to the English. In 1566 she married Richard Burke (her first husband had died years earlier), a neighbouring clan chief, and her power grew to such an extent that the merchants of Galway pleaded with the English governor to do something about her.

In 1574 her castle was besieged, but she turned the siege into a rout and sent the English packing. In 1577 she was held in prison but, mysteriously, managed to get herself released on a promise of good behaviour. Over the next few years she craftily entered a number of alliances, both with and against the English!

In 1593 she travelled to London and was granted a pardon after meeting with Queen Elizabeth I, who offered to make her a countess. Grace declined, for she already considered herself Queen of Connaught.

Back in Ireland she appeared to be working for the English, but the final recorded reference to her in the English State Papers of 1681 makes it seem likely that she was still fiercely independent. An English captain tells of meeting one of her pirate ships, captained by one of her sons, on its way to plunder a merchant ship. She was over 50 by then. ∎

Killadoon

Killadoon is a small village on the coast reached by turning off the main Louisburgh to Leenane road via the Doolough Valley. The main attractions here are the panoramic ocean views and the sandy beaches. An inexpensive hotel in the area is *Killadoon Beach Hotel* (☎ 098-68605) with singles/doubles from IR£14/28.

Getting There & Away

There is a daily bus service between Westport and Killadoon via Murrisk for Croagh Patrick and Louisburgh, but there is no bus to Delphi.

CLARE ISLAND

Clare Island (population 200) has the ruins of an abbey and a castle, both associated with Grace O'Malley, the pirate queen. The tower castle was her stronghold, although it was altered considerably when the coastguard service took it over in 1831. Grace is supposed to be buried in the small abbey, which contains a stone with her family motto: 'Invincible on land and sea'.

The island is also one of the dwindling number of places where you can find choughs (which look like blackbirds but with red beaks).

The island has safe, sandy beaches and is perfect for walking and climbing on a clear day. The highest point of Knockmore Mountain is at 462 metres and it dominates the landscape. The island's only hotel, the Bay View, has tourist information and attracts sea anglers, scuba divers and sailing folk.

Places to Stay & Eat

Free camping should not be a problem. The *Bay View Hotel* (☎ 098-26307) beside the harbour is the main accommodation centre and singles/doubles are IR£19/22. There are a number of B&Bs, the least expensive being IR£12 per person at *Ballytoughey Lodge* (☎ 098-25412) which also offers organised treks and residential study tours. *Mary O'Malley* (☎ 098-26216), five km from the harbour, for IR£15/24 or – more unique – *Clare Island Lighthouse* (☎ 098-45120)

which dates back to 1806 but has all the comforts one would expect for a IR£45 double room.

If you're going for just one day, it's best to take your own lunch – although food is available at the Bay View and the B&Bs all do evening meals for residents and non-residents.

Getting There & Away

A scheduled ferry service (☎ 098-26307) runs from Roonagh Quay, a few km west of Louisburgh, to the island. There are usually two sailings a day.

INISTURK ISLAND

Signs of pre-Christian life have been found on this island but it is believed that the ancestors of many of the inhabitants there today were probably expelled or driven there in Cromwellian times.

This island does not receive many tourists notwithstanding two sandy beaches on its east side, wonderful flora and fauna and a rugged landscape ideal for random walking. Contact the island's tourist association (☎ 098-45510/45641) for details of transport from Roonagh Pier and Cleggan Pier in County Galway. There is no regular ferry.

This small island has one bar in the community centre. There used to be a shebeen near the pier but the police came over from Louisburgh and closed it down. Bed and breakfast is available from a few of the farm houses and they will provide home-grown food for dinner.

The company (☎ 095-44642) that runs a boat to Inishbofin also now runs a service to Inisturk.

NEWPORT

This small town on the banks of the River Newport is often just passed through on the way to Achill, but it deserves a closer look.

Towards the end of the 19th century the Great Western Railway ran a line from Westport to Achill Sound, which continued to operate until 1937. In 1987 the route was pedestrianised and now offers an interesting walk, with views of the river and Newport House.

On the road out to Achill, there is a mural on the gable end of a house depicting the arrest of Father Manus Sweeney who led the Achill contribution to the 1798 Rising and was later executed.

Near this mural, opposite the Angler's Bar, a tourist information office is due to open for the summer (☎ 098-41822). Newport is also the beginning, or end, of the Bangor Trail. See the Bangor section.

Places to Stay & Eat

Walsh's Bridge Inn on Main St serves light food for around IR£5, and the café farther down the street is about the same price. Entering Newport from the Westport road the *Black Oak Inn*, which has a small restaurant, is on the right. Dinner at Newport House is a stiff IR£28, but the snug little bar is worth a visit any time.

Getting There & Away

In the summer, from 25 May to 26 September, bus No 124 from Achill to Belfast stops at Newport and goes on through Ballina, Sligo and Enniskillen. Throughout the year, bus No 255 links Achill and Ballina via Newport. The bus stop is outside Chambers' pub.

AROUND NEWPORT

Borrishoole Abbey

The abbey was founded in 1486 by the Dominicans. What remains is a solid tower and the east window of the cloisters. It is beside the river that drains Lough Furnace into the sea. About 2.5 km beyond Newport on the Newport-Achill road, a sign points the way down to the left.

Rockfleet Castle

Formerly known as Carrigahowley, this castle has a strong association with Grace O'Malley.

The story goes that after the death of her first husband she married a second time, on condition that at the end of the first year either party could summarily dissolve

the marriage. This duly occurred; she shut herself up in Rockfleet and announced the divorce when her husband tried to enter!

Whether the story's true or not, the castle does look impregnable. Grace O'Malley is supposed to have lived out the rest of her years here, and successfully repulsed an English force which besieged the castle. To get there, turn left at the sign about five km beyond Newport on the road to Achill.

Mulrany

This small town stands on the isthmus between island-studded Clew Bay and Bellacagher Bay and boasts a lovely, big beach. To reach the sand, either take the footpath opposite the now-closed Mulrany Bay Hotel or continue a little way past the hotel and bear left following the Atlantic Drive sign and then left again where the sign points to Mallaranny Strand, another Blue Flag beach.

At some time in the future the Mulrany Bay Hotel may reopen under new management. Hopefully they will retain the Lennon Suite, named after John Lennon when he came here for a visit and ended up purchasing one of the small islands in Clew Bay.

Places to Stay & Eat

The An Óige *Traenlaur Lodge* hostel (☎ 098-41358), charging IR£6, is eight km from Newport, signposted on the road to Achill. Achill seems the obvious destination if you're travelling from Newport, but the Curraun Peninsula, joined to Achill Island by bridge, has a couple of B&Bs where you can get away from it all. *Curraun House* (☎ 098-45228) is attached to the George Pub and serves food for lunch and dinner and B&B is IR£12.50. To get there, follow the Atlantic Drive road from Mulrany; the place is on the south-west corner of the peninsula, just before a sign points right up to Achill Sound. Farther up this road, just before the Sound, *Mrs Cannon* (☎ 098-45134) has a bungalow and charges the standard IR£13.

The beach at Mulrany has a field marked out for camping and there are public toilets

MAYO & SLIGO

nearby. A local farmer turns up periodically to collect his dues.

ACHILL ISLAND

Joined to the mainland by a bridge, remote Achill Island combines views, moorland and mountains in one handy package. For most of the 20th century it has remained forgotten by tourists and, many of the islanders would assert, the Dublin government as well. The deserted village of Slievemore is the most dramatic example of a process of decay that continues to this day. The amount of arable land is limited and there are few employment opportunities to keep young people around. As people move away, the small houses are bought up as holiday homes. In recent years, the island has also become a favourite destination for jaded Dubliners in search of solitude and sand.

Information

Tourist information (☎ 098-45384) is available from an office near the souvenir shop on the right side just after crossing onto the island. A few km farther along on the road to Keel, an Esso garage (☎ 098-47242) also dispenses tourist information.

O'Malley's at Keel is a post office and will change money.

Slievemore Deserted Village

Different explanations have been given for the abandonment of Slievemore some time in the middle of the 19th century. The 'booley houses' were summer residences for the owners of grazing cattle. The inhabitants, it seems, moved permanently down to the coast at Dooagh, and the famine years may have forced them to seek a living nearer the sea. Another factor may have been a proselytising Potestant group which came here in 1834. There has been talk of renovating a couple of the ruins and establishing an interpretive centre; local people will provide varying explanations as to why this venture has not taken off.

Beaches

Achill has some beautiful beaches which never seem crowded and are often deserted even in good weather. Two of them, at Keel and Keem, are Blue Flag beaches and the ones at Dooega, Dooagh, Dugort and Dooniver are equally sandy.

Activities

The island is perfect for walking and even the highest point of Slievemore at 671 metres presents no problems. It can be climbed from behind the deserted village and from the top there are terrific views of Blacksod Bay. A longer climb would take in Croaghaun (668 metres), Achill Head and a clifftop walk along what are claimed to be the highest cliffs in Europe. The walk is covered in the *New Irish Walk Guides: West & North* (Gill & Macmillan) by Whilde & Simms.

Sea angling gear is sold by O'Malley's at Keel, who also know about boat hire.

Other activities include windsurfing, hang-gliding from the top of Minaun and rock climbing. If you're interested in any of these, it's worth calling in at the Activity Centre on the road to Keel. McDowell's Hotel hires out canoes and surfboards.

Places to Stay

Camping The first camp site is at *Alice's Harbour Inn*, just before the bridge to Achill Sound. In the north, close by the Valley House, is *Lavelle's* (☎ 098-47232/47277), charging IR£5, and *Seal Caves Caravan Park* (☎ 098-43262), charging IR£4.50/2.50 for large/small tents and 50p per person. Finally, at Keel there is *Keel Sandybanks Camping Park* (☎ 098-32054) charging IR£5.50.

Hostels The *Railway Hostel* (☎ 098-45187) is on the east side of the bridge over Achill Sound, opposite the police station. Beds are IR£5 and doubles IR£12. The excellent *Wild Haven Hostel* (☎ 098-45392) is just across the bridge on the left near the church. The basic rate is IR£5 and two-bed rooms cost IR£1 extra. Breakfast and evening meals can be ordered in advance at this very homely hostel.

The *Valley House Hostel* (☎ 098-47204), with a licensed bar and IR£5 beds, is in the

MAYO & SLIGO

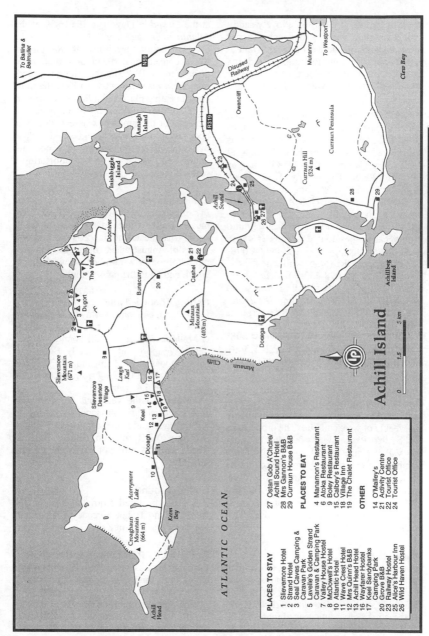

Achill Island

ATLANTIC OCEAN

Clew Bay

PLACES TO STAY
1 Slievemore Hotel
2 Strand Hotel
3 Seal Caves Camping & Caravan Park
5 Lavelle's Golden Strand Caravan & Camping Park
7 Valley House Hostel
8 McDowell's Hotel
10 Atlantic Hotel
11 Wave Crest Hotel
12 Mrs Quinn's B&B
13 Achill Head Hotel
16 Wayfarer Hostel
17 Keel Sandybanks Camping Park
20 Grove B&B
23 Railway Hostel
25 Alice's Harbour Inn
26 Wild Haven Hostel

27 Ostan Gob A'Choire/ Achill Sound Hotel
28 Mrs Gannon's B&B
29 Curraun House B&B

PLACES TO EAT
4 Manamon's Restaurant
6 Atoka Restaurant
9 Boley Restaurant
15 Calbey's Restaurant
18 Village Inn
19 The Chalet Restaurant

OTHER
14 O'Malley's
21 Activity Centre
22 Tourist Office
24 Tourist Office

0   1.5   5 km

north of the island, with some lovely sandy beaches within walking distance. To get there, take the road to Keel and turn right at the Bunacurry junction signposted for Dugort. The other hostel is the *Wayfarer* (☎ 098-43266) in the village of Keel.

B&Bs & Hotels At the Bunacurry junction, where the road to Keel has a turning right for Dugort, the *Grove* (☎ 098-47108) has rooms with shared bathrooms for IR£15/28. In Keel itself, *Mrs Quinn* (☎ 098-43385) charges from IR£20/29. The nearby *Achill Head Hotel* (☎ 098-43108) has rooms from IR£14/28. The *Ostan Gob A'Choire*, also known as the Achill Sound Hotel (☎ 098-45245), on the west side of the Achill Sound bridge, has singles/doubles for IR£24/44.

At Dugort, the *Slievemore Hotel* (☎ 098-43224) charges IR£15/36, while the nearby *Strand Hotel* (☎ 098-43241), delightfully located facing the sea and close to a small beach, is IR£18/36. *McDowell's Hotel* (☎ 098-43148) on Slievemore Rd has rooms from IR£15/36.

Out at Dooagh, the *Wave Crest* (☎ 098-43115) has singles/doubles from IR£13/26. The other hotel here, the *Atlantic Hotel* (☎ 098-43239) charges from IR£19/38.

Rental Accommodation There are a number of bungalows and cottages available for weekly or weekend hire. The proprietors of the Atoka Restaurant (☎ 098-47229), near the Valley House hostel, are agents for a number of properties and enquiries could be made there. Or contact the Bord Fáilte reservation service for the west of Ireland (☎ 091-63081). During July and August expect to pay from IR£160 to IR£280 a week.

Places to Eat
If you are camping or hostelling, stock up at Sweeney's supermarket which is just across the causeway when travelling to Achill. O'Malley's at Keel has a minimarket. Nearly all the hotels serve lunch or dinner to non-residents, with dinner costing from IR£13.50

at the *Strand* in Dugort to IR£16.50 at the *Atlantic* in Dooagh.

At Dugort the cosy little *Atoka Restaurant* has a conventional menu of grilled meat dishes around IR£6. Farther along the road, *Manamon's* is worth a try. At Keel the most popular eating place is the *Boley Restaurant* (☎ 098-43147); if this is full try farther down the road at the junction where *Calbey's* is open all day and serves breakfast. Also close by is the *Village Inn* serving pub food and dinner and *The Chalet* restaurant offering a seafood menu.

Entertainment
In summer a number of pubs and hotels have music. The best time of the year for traditional Irish music and dance is the first two weeks of August when Irish culture is promoted through a number of workshops, which end up in the pubs at night.

Getting There & Away
In the summer, from 25 May to 26 September, bus No 124 runs from Dooagh, outside O'Malley's, to Keel, Achill Sound and then on to Westport and eventually Belfast. It leaves Dooagh at 7.30 am and Achill Sound 20 minutes later. Coming from Westport the bus leaves at 5.45 pm.

Throughout the year, bus No 255 runs across the island from Dooagh, taking in Keel, Dugort and Dooega before crossing to Mulrany, Westport and finally Ballina. Check with the tourist office for the current schedule.

Getting Around
Bikes can be hired from the hostels, the Achill Sound Hotel, Sweeney's supermarket, or O'Malley's in Keel.

BELMULLET PENINSULA & BANGOR
Probably the least visited corner of the whole of Ireland, this strange and remote land, known as the Mullet or the western Barony of Erris, has a population density of only 10 people per sq km. The peninsula is 30 km in length rarely rising to more than 30 metres

above sea level and it is obvious that the boggy land offers a poor livelihood.

Information

The Erris Tourist Information Centre (☎ 097-81500) is on the main road as you enter Belmullet from the east. The travel agent, McIntyre's Travel (☎ 097-82199), in the main street of Belmullet also has local information. Bikes can be hired from the Cycle Centre (☎ 097-81424) in American St.

Belmullet

This forlorn-looking place will never win the Tidy Towns competition. Belmullet was founded in 1825 by the local landlord, William Carter, and built on an unimaginative plan, with one main street and side roads at right angles. Carter also designed a canal joining Broadhaven Bay with Blacksod Bay to the south, and a new bridge now crosses the narrow channel.

Blacksod Point

The road south from Belmullet curves around the tip of the peninsula before rejoining itself at Aghleam. Near the point are the remains of an old church, and the view across the bay takes in the spot where *La Rata Santa Maria Encoronada*, part of the 1588 Spanish Armada, came in and was later burned by the captain, who then left to join two other Spanish ships that had found refuge farther north in Elly Bay.

The road south to Blacksod Point goes past sandy Mullaghroe Beach, which is inviting on a warm day. In the early years of this century a whaling station operated at Ardelly Point, just north of the beach. There is also a decent beach at Elly Bay.

Doonamo Point

This typical promontory fort is the main point of interest north of Belmullet and is built on a spit of land and defended by water on three sides. There are other forts farther north near Erris Head but this one is the most accessible.

Bangor

The main reason for being here is to begin or end the long-distance Bangor Trail that connects Bangor and Newport. This is an extraordinary walk that takes you through the bleakest and most remote landscape to be found anywhere in Ireland. If it rains you may curse the place but on a dry day it offers a unique experience. There is a small tourist information office in Bangor which sells the useful *County Mayo – The Bangor Trail* by McDermott and Chapman and this is also available in Keohane's bookshop in Ballina. Unfortunately, more than one of the 1:50,000 Ordnance Survey maps is needed to cover this trail.

Places to Stay & Eat

There is the usual run of bungalowed B&Bs on the main road approaching Belmullet, but there are singles/doubles for IR£13/22 at the *Western Strands Hotel* (☎ 097-81096) on Main St. If the 10 rooms here are full, *Mrs Gaughan* (☎ 097-81181) has rooms at Mill House in nearby American St for the same rates.

The *Owenmore River Lodge* (☎ 097-83497) is a hostel just outside of Bangor and camping is also possible here. Some 16 km east of Belmullet at Pollatomish, signposted on the road to Ballycastle, the An Óige *Poll an tSomais* hostel (IR£5.50) is located. There's a sandy beach nearby and headland walks. There is also the *Kilcommon Lodge* hostel (☎ 097-84621) at Pollatomish with beds for IR£5 and double rooms for IR£12.

As for food, the best advice is to bring your own! In Belmullet the hotel serves snacks and a dinner for IR£10 and there's a café at the top end of Main St that does soup and sandwiches. There is also the *Anchor Bar* and, a couple of km along the road to Bangor, the *Glenside Tavern* does pub food and meals in its restaurant.

Getting There & Away

One bus runs on weekdays from Ballina to Belmullet and then south to Blacksod Point. Contact the bus station in Ballina or the tourist office in Belmullet for the schedule.

MAYO & SLIGO

BALLINA & AROUND

The largest town in the county is renowned for its fishing, and is a good base for exploring north Mayo. The tourist office has free maps of interesting walks near the town. Ballina (*Béal an Átha*) itself is a typical Connaught town, with a shabbiness and conservatism rooted in long deprivation and isolation. There is little to see in the town except the authentic hungry face of County Mayo. It was an unlikely environment for the childhood of its most famous inhabitant – Mary Robinson, the liberal, pro-feminist president of Ireland.

Information

The tourist office (☎ 096-70848) is on Cathedral Rd overlooking the River Moy and is open from 10 am to 5.45 pm (closed 1 to 2 pm) Monday to Saturday from May to September. There is a laundrette on Tone St and Keohane's bookshop on the other side of the road acts as a bureau de change.

Rosserk Abbey

Situated close to the River Rosserk, a tributary of the Moy, the Franciscan abbey dates back to the middle of the 15th century. It is remarkably well preserved and there is an interesting carved piscina (a perforated stone basin for carrying away the water used in rinsing the chalices) in the chancel. Like Rathfran Abbey near Killala, Rosserk was burned down by the English governor of Connaught in the 16th century.

To get there, leave Ballina on the R314 for Killala and after 6.5 km turn right at the sign and take the first left at the next crossroads. Beware of the loose sign at this junction which may point in any direction. Continue for another km and turn right at the next sign for the abbey.

Moyne Abbey

This abbey was established around the same time as Rosserk, also by the Franciscans. It, too, was burned down by Bingham, the Connaught governor, in the 16th century and perhaps he did a better job on this one, as it is in worse condition than its neighbour.

After leaving Rosserk Abbey go back to the main road and continue north for another three km until the abbey is seen on the right across a field. After returning across the field continue north-west for 1.5 km until the main R314 is reached. Turn right for Killala or left for Ballina.

Fishing

The River Moy is one of the most prolific salmon rivers in Europe and a leaflet listing the fisheries and contacts for permits is available from the tourist office.

Nearby, Lough Conn is also an important brown trout fishery and, while a boat is required, there is no shortage of places renting boats and gillies around the lake. Pontoon is a good base for trout fishing in both Lough Conn and Lough Cullen, and again there are plenty of places hiring boats and dispensing advice. The daily rate for hiring a boat is around IR£25.

Places to Stay & Eat

The *Salmon Weir* (☎ 096-71903) is a new hostel in Barrett St, down by the river with IR£6 beds and IR£18 for an en suite double. The well-equipped *Belleek Camping Park* (☎ 096-71533) is 2.5 km north of town off the road to Killala. The best hotel, complete with swimming pool, is the *Downhill* (☎ 096-21033) with singles/doubles for IR£65/110.

Cafolla's is a café and takeaway on Bridge St and *Padraic's*, next to Keohane's bookshop, has a wide selection of quick meals. There are lot of pubs on Pearse St serving bar food.

Getting There & Away

Bus Ballina has good connections. Bus Éireann buses (☎ 096-71800) go west to Achill, east to Sligo and the North, and south to Limerick, Shannon and Cork.

There are also a couple of private bus companies that run scheduled trips at cheaper rates. Treacy's (☎ 096-70968) run a daily return service from outside Dunne's store at the bottom of Pearse St and the Quay St car park in Sligo. Also, Barton Transport

(☎ 01-6286026) run a daily return service between Ballina and Dublin.

Train The Westport to Dublin train stops at Ballina, up to four times daily. Connections to other routes can be made at Athlone.

Getting Around
Bicycles can be hired from Gerry's Cycle centre on the Crossmolina Rd (☎ 096-70455) or from the hostel.

CROSSMOLINA
The town itself is undistinguished, but it serves as a quiet retreat for anyone wishing to fish in Lough Conn or explore the lakes and scenery around Mt Nephin. The mountain (806 metres) takes under two hours to climb and is described, along with other walks in Mayo, in the *New Irish Walk Guides: West & North* (Gill & Macmillan) by Whilde and Simms.

Research & Heritage Centre
If you have a family connection with North Mayo this is the place to contact (☎ 096-31809). An initial assessment will cost about IR£15 and if this looks promising, your full family record would be researched for between IR£50 and IR£100.

The heritage centre houses a collection of old farm machinery and domestic implements. It is open Monday to Friday 9 am to 4 pm and Saturday morning between June and October.

Errew Abbey
The abbey is the remains of a house of Augustinian canons built around 1250 on the site of an earlier 7th-century church. In common with other abbeys in Mayo, the monks wisely chose to live close to where they could fish, and the location of Errew Abbey is particularly picturesque.

To get there, take the road from Crossmolina that leads to the heritage centre, and one km after the centre turn left at the sign and keep going for another five km.

Places to Stay & Eat
The best food in Crossmolina is to be found in *Hiney's* pub in the town centre, though the *Dolphin* hotel is also worth checking out. *Enniscoe House* (☎ 096-31112) serves an evening meal for IR£20 and this friendly 18th-century home does B&B from IR£48/76.

Getting There & Away
There are regular bus connections to Ballina and Castlebar. The bus stop is outside Hiney's pub.

KILLALA & AROUND
It is claimed that St Patrick founded Killala and the 25-metre round tower is evidence of the town's early ecclesiastical history. The tower was struck by lightning in 1800 and the cap is a later reconstruction. The Anglican cathedral in the town is supposed to have been built on the site of the first Christian church where St Patrick installed Muiredach as the town's first bishop.

It's the French connection that really puts this small town on the map. On 22 August 1798, over 1000 troops under the command of General Humbert landed in Killala Bay, the plan being that Irish peasants would rise in rebellion and help Napoleon in his war against the English. At first there were dramatic successes, with Killala, Ballina and Castlebar falling to the joint enemies of England. On 8 September, however, Humbert was defeated in Longford. The best account of Humbert's arrival in Killala was written by the Protestant Bishop Stock. He was put under house arrest by the French, and his *Narrative* is available in bookshops in Ballina and Castlebar.

Information
Tourist information (☎ 096-32166) is available during the summer from a council building on the left if you're entering Killala on the Ballina road.

Rathfran Abbey
The Dominicans came here in 1274 and built a friary; only the ruins now remain. In 1590

MAYO & SLIGO

the friary was closed down and burned by the English but the monks remained in the community until the 18th century.

Take the R314 road that heads north out of Killala and after five km turn right after crossing the river. After another couple of km turn right at the crossroads.

Breastagh Ogham Stone
The stone is 2.5 metres high but the Ogham writing is not easy to read. It's in a field by the left side of the R314 just past the crossroads which has the turning for Rathfran Abbey (not the earlier crossroads which has a sign for both the Stone and Abbey). Cross the ditch just where the sign points to the Stone.

Kilcummin
This is the spot where General Humbert and his 1067 men landed in 1798. A right turn off the main R314 is signposted for Kilcummin. It is remarkably undramatic.

The imagination is more easily kindled by the sculpture of the French revolutionary soldier helping a prostrate Irish peasant. It's on the main road just after the turning to Lacken Bay and it records that at this particular place the first French soldier died on Irish soil.

Lackan Bay & Downpatrick Head
Lackan Bay is wonderfully sandy and ideal for young children. Downpatrick Head has a fenced off blowhole which occasionally shoots up plumes of water. The rock stack just off shore is Dun Briste.

Places to Stay & Eat
The well-run An Óige *Killala Hostel* (☎ 096-32172), IR£6, is easily the best place for accommodation. The B&Bs are mostly outside of town, like *Rathoma House* (☎ 096-32035) which charges IR£17/29, or *Beach View* (☎ 096-32023), reached by turning right at the sign to the beach.

The hostel serves breakfast, a packed lunch for IR£3.50 and dinner for IR£6. There are a couple of pubs in town serving food and the *Golden Acres* has been recommended.

Getting There & Away
The Ballina to Ballycastle bus stops outside the hostel.

BALLYCASTLE
Ballycastle boasts some of the oldest and most extensive Stone Age archaeological excavations in Europe.

Information
A tourist information point (☎ 096-43256) is open from 10 am to 5 pm (closed 1 to 2 pm) during the summer. If you're entering the town from Killala it is on the right side of the main street at the bottom of town. A video on Céide Fields can be viewed here.

Céide Fields
Over 5000 years ago there was a wheat and barley farming community with domesticated cattle and sheep, just a few km west of Ballycastle. The growth of the bog led to the decline and eventual end of the community and their stone walls and farm buildings disappeared into the bog. Perhaps the farmers, gradually diminishing the soil's fertility, contributed to the growth of the bog or maybe the wet climate made it inevitable. Whatever the cause, the farms lay buried for thousands of years but have now been excavated and opened to the public as the oldest enclosed landscape in Europe and the most extensive Stone Age monument in the world.

The OPW Interpretive Centre incorporates an exhibition court and audiovisual room detailing aspects of the site's architecture, botany and geology (a script of the exhibition is available in French and German). There is also a panoramic viewing platform and tearooms. Admission is IR£2.50/1

Céide Fields is eight km west of Ballycastle on the main R314 road.

Places to Stay & Eat
B&B is available from *Hilltop House* (☎ 096-43089), on the road to Downpatrick Head, but the *Céide House* pub (☎ 096-43105) in town also has rooms. Another possibility (enquire at the tourist point), is

May's, where apparently Maud Gonne once stayed.

Beyond Céide Fields at Belderrig, where there is another prehistoric farm site, the *First Fence* (☎ 096-43114) does B&B.

The *Céide House* and the *Castle Lounge* pubs in town serve food for around IR£5. The other possibility is *Doonferry House*, a little more expensive, which is a few km west of town on the road to Céide Fields and has a restaurant and bar.

Getting There & Away
A bus runs between Ballina and Ballycastle, stopping outside the Castle Lounge pub.

CASTLEBAR & AROUND
Although this is Mayo's county town it has little appeal compared to Westport or even Ballina. The old shops have been replaced by modern stores and there is little to evoke the history of the place. But Castlebar (*Caislean an Bharraigh*) does have a place in history, for it was here in 1798 that General Humbert and his army of French revolutionary soldiers and dispossessed Irish peasants encountered the numerically stronger English forces under the command of General Lake. The defeat of the English and their ignominious cavalry retreat became known as the Races of Castlebar.

There is a monument in the Mall to the 1798 Rising. The Mall was once the cricket ground of the Lucan family who own a significant amount of property in the area. There is still a Lucan St close by the tourist office, and some tenants in Castlebar are still paying rent to the Lucan estate, or at least they were until the notorious Lord Lucan disappeared after the murder of his children's nanny in London in 1974. The tenants are refusing to pay the rent until he returns and the family want him declared officially dead so that a new Lord Lucan can inherit the estate – including the rents!

Information
The tourist office (☎ 094-21207) is on Linenhall St near the main shopping centre

and is open from Easter to September from 9.30 am to 5.30 pm (closed 1 to 2 pm).

Turlough Round Tower
The 9th-century tower stands next to a ruined 18th-century church and a graveyard that is still in use.

The tower is a few km out of Castlebar on the main road to Ballina, which branches off to the right at the north end of town just after the Sacred Heart Home. The road to the left goes to Pontoon and Crossmolina.

Michael Davitt Memorial Museum
The museum in Strade is attached to the church and houses a small collection of material relating to the life and times of Michael Davitt (1846-1906), who is buried in the churchyard.

Take the N5 Dublin Rd and turn off onto the N58 to Strade (also spelt Straid). It is 16 km from Castlebar.

Ballintubber Abbey
The only church in Ireland that was founded by an Irish king and is still in daily use, Ballintubber Abbey was over 200 years old when Columbus went to America. It was founded in 1216 next to the site of an earlier church founded by St Patrick after he came down from his vigil on Croagh Patrick. It is one of the most impressive church buildings in Ireland and well worth a visit.

Features of the church include the 15th-century west doorway and 13th-century windows on the right side of the nave. The nave roof was erected in 1965 and is an Irish oak reproduction of the timber one burned down by Cromwell's soldiers in 1653. Inside the church a IR£1 guide leaflet describes the church in detail.

Take the N84 south to Galway and after about 13 km a signposted road on the left leads to the abbey.

Places to Stay & Eat
The IHH *Hughes House Hostel* (☎ 094-23877), on Thomas St around the corner from the tourist office, is open June to September and has dorm beds for IR£5.90.

The *Davitt Restaurant* on Rush St is also around the corner from the tourist office and has fish meals for around IR£5. Along Main St the *Mandalay* is OK for burgers and the like. For more comfort, try the *Imperial Hotel* where the bar food is OK and dinner is IR£16.

Getting There & Away

An express bus connecting Westport and Dublin stops outside Flannelly's pub in Main St three times daily in each direction. There is also a direct bus south to Shannon and Cork and east to Sligo and Belfast. The Westport to Dublin train stops at Castlebar; the station is out of town on the road to Galway.

Getting Around

Raleigh bikes can be hired from Robinson's (☎ 094-21355) on Spenser St.

KNOCK

This once undistinguished village has been famous for over a century as the site of visions and miracles.

There is a tourist office (☎ 094-88193) near the church that opens from May to September, seven days a week from 10 am to 6 pm.

Knock Church

On a wet evening in 1879, two women of Knock were apparently struck by the sight of Mary, Joseph and St John standing in light against the south gable end of their church. Others were called to witness the apparition and a church investigation quickly confirmed the miracle. Other miracles followed as the sick and disabled claimed amazing recoveries after visiting the church, and another church commission upheld Knock's status in 1936. Today, the Knock industry continues unabated and crowds of dutiful worshippers are always to be found praying in and outside the basilica of Our Lady, Queen of Ireland, which can accommodate 12,000 people.

Knock Folk Museum

This is one of the better folk museums and also serves as an ideal introduction to the Knock phenomenon. There is plenty of material on the apparition and subsequent church commissions of enquiry, including bizarre photographs of the display of crutches left behind by grateful pilgrims. The museum also houses an extensive collection of craft tools, costumes and various artefacts relating to rural life in the west of Ireland. It is all attractively presented.

The museum is in a separate building near the church and is open from 10 am to 5 pm from May to October. Entry is IR£2/1.

Getting There & Away

Knock Airport (☎ 094-67222) is 15 km north by the N17 and there is a daily flight from Dublin. There are bus connections from Westport, Sligo, Galway, Shannon, Dublin, Cork and the North.

County Sligo

William Butler Yeats (1865-1939) was educated in Dublin and London, but his poetry is inextricably linked with the county of his mother's family. He returned to Sligo (*Sligeach*) many times, becoming a close friend of the Gore-Booth family who lived at Lissadell. There are plentiful reminders of his presence in the county town and in the rolling green hills around it.

SLIGO TOWN

One of the more interesting portrayals of Yeats is a sculpture outside the Ulster Bank in Sligo Town which has his poetry tattooed over every inch of his body. Hard to find are two of his most famous lines, from his poem *Easter 1916*:

> All changed, changed utterly:
> A terrible beauty is born...

The poem pays homage to the executed rebels of the Easter Rising, including John MacBride who was married to Maud Gonne. Yeats' unrequited love for Maud Gonne underlies many of his greatest love poems.

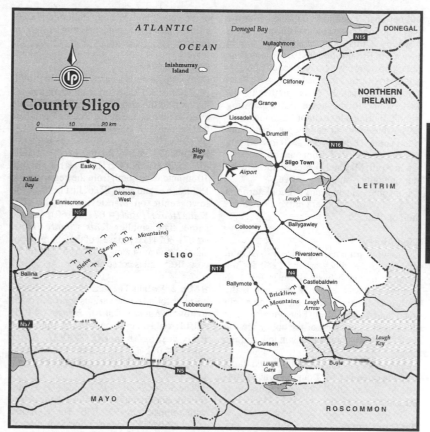

MAYO & SLIGO

Politics divided them, for while she remained a rebel and a socialist all her life, Yeats ended up alarmingly close to fascism.

Yeats apart, the town's main attractions are a few km outside at Carrowmore and Knocnarea.

Information

The tourist office (☎ 071-61201) is on Temple St, just south of the centre. It opens seven days a week in July and August, closing at 2 or 6 pm on Sunday. During the rest of the year it opens from 9 am to 5 pm, Monday to Friday. There is also a tourist

information desk in the Quinsworth shopping arcade which has an entrance on O'Connell St opposite the Ritz. The post office is on Wine Street, opposite Michael Quirke's butcher's shop. Pam's Laundrette is in Johnston Court, off O'Connell St and the Washeteria is nearby on Harmony Hill. Keohane's Bookshop on Castle St is the place to go for books by and about Yeats.

Museum & Art Gallery

Although there is other material here, the main appeal is the Yeats room, chock-a-block with manuscripts, photographs, letters and newspaper cuttings connected with the poet. The room also contains an apron dress worn by Constance Markievicz while interned in Britain after the 1916 Rising. The gallery upstairs has a good selection of paintings by Irish artists like George Russell, Sean Keating and Jack B Yeats, brother of the poet, who said he never did a painting without putting a thought of Sligo into it.

The museum and gallery are open from 10.30 am to 12.30 pm and 2.30 to 4.30 pm, Tuesday to Saturday from June to September. In April, May and October it opens in the morning only. Admission is free.

For some contemporary art, look through the window of Michael Quirke's butcher's shop on Wine St.

Sligo Abbey

The town's founder, Maurice FitzGerald, established the abbey around 1250 for the Dominicans but it burnt down in the 15th century and was rebuilt. It was put to the torch once more – and for the last time – in 1641, and ruins are all that remains. The oldest remaining parts of the abbey are the choir, the 15th-century east window and the altar.

If the abbey is locked, a key is available from the caretaker, Mr Loughklin, at 6 Charlotte St. It's an OPW site and admission is IR£1.50/60p.

The Courthouse

The Victorian architecture of the courthouse is very unusual for Ireland and it stands out as a reminder of the other power that once ruled the land. The exterior is extravagantly Gothic and modelled on the London Law Courts. Inside, the building still functions as a working courthouse, and on a busy day the foyer takes the overspill from the small public gallery.

Yeats Memorial Building

Near the corner of O'Connell St at the Douglas Hyde Bridge is the Yeats Building (☎ 071-42693), the centre for the Yeats International Summer School, an annual international gathering of scholars. The rest

of the year it houses an art gallery and travelling exhibitions, with paintings often up for sale.

Places to Stay

Camping There is a camp site at Strandhill (☎ 071-68120) eight km from town and off the road to the airport. The other camp site close to Sligo is the one at Rosses Point (see that section).

Hostels On Pearse Rd the excellent IHH *Eden Hill Hostel* (☎ 071-43204) is about a 10-minute walk south from the centre on the Dublin road and costs IR£6. Just north of the town centre on Markievicz Rd the IHH *White House Hostel* (☎ 071-45160) costs the same. The smaller *Yeats County Hostel* (☎ 071-60241) is just west of the centre, opposite the railway station at 12 Lord Edward St, costs IR£5 and is not so attractive.

B&Bs & Hotels The less expensive B&Bs are to be found on the various approach roads to town. *Renate Central House* (☎ 071-62014) on Upper John St is a traditional B&B costing from IR£18.50/27. *Bonne Chere* (☎ 071-42014) is a small hotel, centrally located on High St, and charges from IR£24/44.

The *Silver Swan* (☎ 071-43231) is a comfortable and friendly hotel close to the centre with rooms from IR£45/70. The *Clarence Hotel* (☎ 071-42211) on Wine St is a small place costing IR£33/52. The stately *Southern Hotel* (☎ 071-62101) charges from IR£43/62.

Places to Eat

The *Ritz Restaurant* on O'Connell St is a big place, likely to be crowded but good for lunch or snacks. Also on O'Connell St is *Beezies*, a big old-fashioned place with a very standard Irish menu of almost anything with chips. *Bistro Bianconi*, another O'Connell St eating house, serves very good Italian dishes for around IR£10, including vegetarian choices. Round the corner on Grattan St, the popular *Gulliver's* has a similar menu. The tourist-oriented *Bonne*

MAYO & SLIGO

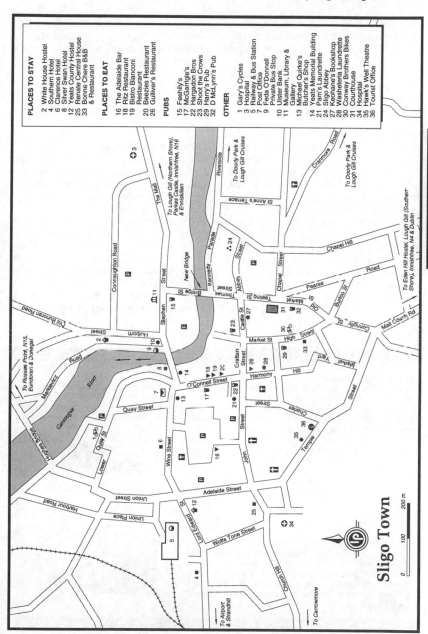

Sligo Town

PLACES TO STAY
2 White House Hostel
4 Southern Hotel
6 Clarence Hotel
8 Silver Swan Hotel
12 Yeats County Hostel
25 Renate Central House
33 Bonne Chere B&B
   & Restaurant

PLACES TO EAT
16 The Adelaide Bar
18 Ritz Restaurant
19 Bistro Bianconi
   Restaurant
20 Beezies Restaurant
26 Gulliver's Restaurant

PUBS
15 Feehily's
17 McGarrigle's
22 Hargadon Bros
23 Shoot the Crows
29 Harry's Pub
32 D McLynn's Pub

OTHER
1 Gary's Cycles
3 Hospital
5 Railway & Bus Station
7 Post Office
9 Feda O'Donnell
   Private Bus Stop
10 Ulster Bank
11 Museum, Library &
   Gallery
13 Michael Quirke's
   Butcher's Shop
14 Yeats Memorial Building
21 Pam's Laundrette
24 Sligo Abbey
27 Keohane's Bookshop
28 Washeltería Laundrette
30 Conway Brothers Bikes
31 Courthouse
34 Hospital
35 Hawk's Well Theatre
36 Tourist Office

Chere Restaurant on High St has lunch and dinner specials. In the Quinsworth car park area, *The Adelaide Bar* is popular with town people.

The bar food at the comfortable *Southern Hotel* near the railway station is reasonable. The restaurant downstairs serves dinner for IR£19 and lunch specials are served in the bar.

Entertainment

Pubs Sligo has the usual phenomenal number of pubs, many with music at night. The deservedly popular *D McLynn's* is on Old Market St just south of the Courthouse. *TD's* on Hughes Bridge St (the Donegal road) has bands most nights of the week.

Shoot the Crows on Castle St at Market Square and *Feehily's* on the corner of Bridge and Stephen Sts are other very popular small pubs. Jazz on a Wednesday is to be found at *McGarrigle's* on O'Connell St.

Hargadon Bros on O'Connell St doesn't have music but this ancient-looking place is almost a living museum, and you can become part of the display. Serious drinking is best conducted at *Harry's* pub on High St, where there are lots of special offers and it is likely to be busy at 11 in the morning.

Theatre The *Hawk's Well Theatre* (☎ 071-61526) is next to the tourist office in Temple St and it is always worth checking to see what is on.

Getting There & Away

Air From Sligo Airport (☎ 071-68280) there are two daily nonstop Aer Lingus flights to Dublin. Flights to other parts of Ireland and Europe are all routed through Dublin.

Bus Bus Éireann (☎ 071-60066) has three services a day to and from Dublin (four hours). There's also a Galway-Sligo-Derry service and other connections. Buses operate from the railway station which is just to the west of the centre.

Feda O'Donnell Coaches (☎ 075-48114) run a daily service between county Donegal

---

William Butler Yeats

The most famous of Irish poets was born in 1865 in a Dublin suburb. His mother was from Sligo and Yeats spent a lot of time there as a child. At the age of nine he moved with his family to London, but six years later they were all back in Ireland. His early interest in the occult led to him being one of the founder members of the Dublin Hermetic Society, and the budding poet became more and more interested in Irish mythology.

As his poetry became better known, he became friends with William Morris, George Bernard Shaw and Oscar Wilde. His most important encounter, though, was with Maud Gonne whose nationalism and socialism provided a healthy balance to his predilection for mysticism and an ill-defined romanticism. The story of their relationship has attracted a lot of speculation – especially the sexual side (did they/didn't they?) – with Maud Gonne finally refusing to marry him. She took the title role in his 1902 play *Cathleen ni Houlihan* which has been credited as the catalyst for the 1916 Easter Rising.

Yeats became a senator of the new Irish state in 1922 and the following year he received the Nobel Prize for Literature. In 1928 he moved to Italy where, in the years to follow, his flirtation with fascism sat uneasily alongside his enormous stature as a poet of world renown. He died in 1939. ■

and Galway which arrives in Sligo at 10.45 am and departs 15 minutes later. The bus from Galway arrives at 6 pm.

Train The railway station (☎ 071-69888) is close to town for the Dublin service via Mullingar. From Mullingar train connections to Galway and Mayo can be made.

Getting Around
There's a bus service from the airport into town or a taxi costs about IR£6. Bike hire is available from Conway Bros (☎ 071-61370), opposite the Bonne Chere Restaurant on High St, or Gary's Cycles (☎ 071-61370) on Lower Quay St. The Eden Hill Hostel and the White House Hostel also have bikes for hire.

AROUND SLIGO TOWN
Rosses Point
The scene of a battle between two Irish warlords in 1257, Rosses Point is now a picturesque seaside resort easily reached on a town bus, with a lovely Blue Flag beach. Easy to spot is the Metal Man, a brightly coloured buoy that marks the way for boats coming into Sligo.

Carrowmore Megalithic Cemetery
Carrowmore's megalithic cemetery has over 60 stone circles and passage tombs, making it one of the largest Stone Age cemeteries in Europe. Over the years, many of the stones have been removed – a survey in 1839 noted 23 more sites than now exist – and a complicating factor is that some of the best stones are on private land. For various reasons, some of the landowners are not encouraging visitors and one farmer has dumped two old cars on either side of stones in his field.

The dolmens were the actual tombs and were probably covered with stones and earth, so it requires an act of imagination to picture what this area, 2.5 km wide, might once have looked like when it was dotted with round mounds.

The OPW site centre is open daily 9.30 am to 6.30 pm from May to September and entry is IR£1.50/60p.

To get there, leave town by Church Hill and carry on for five km; the site is clearly signposted.

Knocknarea
A couple of km north-west of Carrowmore is the hilltop cairn grave of Knocknarea. About 1000 years younger than Carrowmore, which still makes it quite a venerable age, the huge cairn is popularly supposed to be the grave of the legendary Queen Maeve (Queen Mab in English). The 40,000 tons of stone have never been excavated despite speculation that a tomb on the scale of the one at Newgrange in County Meath may lie buried underneath.

Leave town as for Carrowmore and a sign shows the way to Knocknarea. If leaving the Carrowmore Centre, continue down the road and turn right at the junction with a church. At the next crossroads turn left, signposted Mescan Meadhbha Chambered Cairn, and leave your vehicle at the car park. From here it is only half an hour to the summit and panoramic views.

Magheraghanrush Court Cairn
This impressive court tomb stands on a wooded limestone hill with fine views of Lough Gill. The court area is not outside the front entrance, but in the centre of the tomb with two burial chambers opening off at one end and another one at the other end. The site has been dated to around 3000 BC.

Take the N16 out of Sligo and turn off on the R286 for Parke's Castle. Almost immediately after joining this road turn left at the Y-junction on a minor road signposted for Manorhamilton, ignoring the road to the right that is signposted for Parke Castle and Dromahair. Continue along the minor road for about three km, park in the Forestry car park and follow the trail through the trees. The tomb is made difficult to find because of the forestry work.

Places to Stay
Rosses Point *Greenlands Caravan & Camping Park* (☎ 071-77113) is next to the golf course near the beach. The two hotels at

MAYO & SLIGO

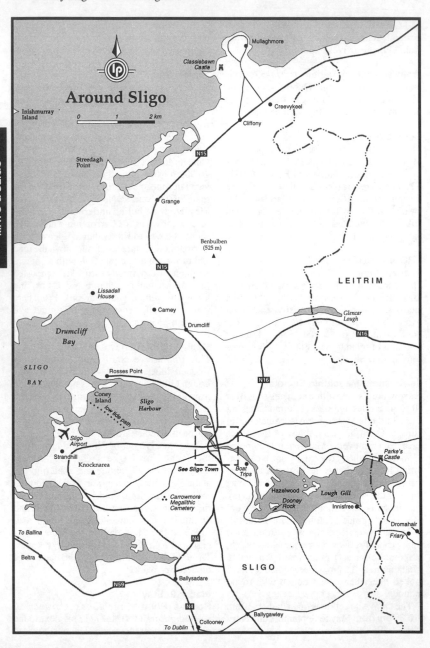

Around Sligo

0   1   2 km

Inishmurray Island

Mullaghmore

Classiebawn Castle

Creevykeel

Cliffony

N15

Streedagh Point

Grange

N15

Benbulben (525 m)

LEITRIM

Lissadell House

Carney

Drumcliff

Glencar Lough

Drumcliff Bay

N16

SLIGO BAY

Rosses Point

Coney Island

low tide path

Sligo Harbour

N16

Sligo Airport

Strandhill

Knocknarea

See Sligo Town

Boat Trips

Hazelwood

Dooney Rock

Lough Gill

Parke's Castle

Innisfree

Dromahair

Friary

Carrowmore Megalithic Cemetery

To Ballina

Beltra

N4

SLIGO

N59

Ballysadare

N4

Colooney

To Dublin

Ballygawley

Rosses Point are quite different in character: *Yeats Country* (☎ 071-77211) attracts families, while *Ballincar House Hotel* (☎ 071-45361) is relaxed and peaceful, away from the beach. Rates at Yeats Country are from IR£39/58, at the Ballincar House Hotel from IR£60/100.

B&Bs are not difficult to find although they can fill up quickly. Try *Mrs Gill* (☎ 071-77202) at Kilvarnet House or, one of the closest to the sea, *Mrs Brady* (☎ 071-77245) at Coral Reef. Both have doubles for IR£30.

Carrowmore The place to stay for a quiet retreat is *Mrs McKiernan* (☎ 071-61449) at Glenwood. It is close to the Carrowmore Centre and has its own stone circle in a nearby field. Closer to Knocknarea and with similar prices is *Mrs Carter* (☎ 071-62005) at Primrose Grange House, just along the road that leads to the Knocknarea car park.

Places to Eat
A day out to Carrowmore and Knocknarea requires a packed lunch, but there is no shortage of eating places at Rosses Point. The *Bunker* pub on the main road leading to the beach always has pub food, and the *Reveries Restaurant* (☎ 071-77371), close to the Yeats Country Hotel, is open for dinner in the evening. Close by is the *Moorings Restaurant*, which serves mostly seafood.

Best of all, if your budget stretches to IR£25 a head, is the restaurant at the *Ballincar House Hotel* (☎ 071-45361). A French chef has left a legacy of imaginative cooking which quite sets this place apart.

Getting There & Away
Apart from the town buses (☎ 071-60066) which run out to Rosses Point, there is no public transport to the other places of interest in the area. A bicycle hired in Sligo would be the best way of getting around. While it is possible to walk to both Carrowmore and Knocknarea from town, it is a long day's trek on foot there and back.

LOUGH GILL
A round trip of 48 km would take in most of the lough as well as Parke's Castle which, though inside the Leitrim border, is more likely to be visited on a day trip from Sligo. There are legends associated with Lough Gill; one that can be put to the test is the story that a silver bell from the Dominican Abbey in Sligo was thrown into the lough and only those who are free from sin can still hear its pealing.

Dooney Rock
There are good views of the lough and its islands from the top of Dooney Rock. In *The Fiddler of Dooney*, Yeats immortalises the Rock, although his poem about Innisfree has become more famous.

Leave Sligo on the N4 going south and after half a km turn left at the sign to Lough Gill. Another left at the T-junction brings you onto the R287/L117 road and the viewpoint of Dooney Rock.

Innisfree
If Yeats hadn't written *The Lake Isle of Innisfree*, this tiny island near the south-east shore would not attract so many visitors and it would probably have kept the air of tranquillity that the poet was moved by:

I will arise and go now, and go to Innisfree,
And a small cabin build there, of clay and wattles made;
Nine bean rows will I have there, a hive for the honey bee,
And live alone in the bee-loud glade.

From the Dooney Rock car park turn left at the crossroads and after three km turn left again for another three km. A small road leads down to the lake.

Creevelea Abbey
This was the last Franciscan friary to be founded in Ireland before they were suppressed in the Reformation. The pillars in the cloister have some interesting carvings of St Francis, one displaying his stigmata and another one showing him in a pulpit with birds perched on a tree. It was burnt in 1590 by Bingham but repaired by the monks

before they were again ejected by Cromwellian forces. They returned yet again and thatched the church roof, remaining until the end of the 17th century.

From Innisfree (*Inis Fraoigh*), return to the R287/L117 and continue east until the sign for the abbey is seen in the village of Dromahair.

Parke's Castle
The placid setting of the castle, with swans drifting by on the lake, belies the fact that the early plantation architecture was created out of insecurity and fear by an unwelcome English landlord. The three-storeyed castle, which has been carefully restored, forms part of one of the five sides of the bawn, which also has two rounded turrets at the corners. This is an OPW site so try to join one of the knowledgeable guided tours after viewing the 20-minute video which gives a general introduction to the antiquities of the area and is likely to whet your appetite for other excursions.

The castle (☎ 071-64149) is open from 9.30 am to 6.30 pm every day between June and September, with shorter hours in October, April and May. Admission is IR£2/1.

From Creevelea Abbey, continue east along the R287/L117. To return to Sligo from Parke's Castle turn west onto the R286/Ll16.

Places to Stay & Eat
There are not many eating places on a tour of Lough Gill and a picnic lunch might be best. *Parke's Castle* has a small but friendly café. In Dromahair's Main St the *Stanfords Village Inn* (☎ 071-64140) does a IR£15 dinner. And dinner costs IR£12 at the *Breffni Centre* (☎ 071-64199).

Getting There & Away
Bicycle/Car Leave for the northern shore via the Mall, past the hospital, and turn right off the N16 onto the R286. Following the signs to the right for Hazelwood leads to a parking area where a 4 km sculture trail is situated. Ignoring the Hazlewood turn off and staying on the R286 leads to the northern shore of

Lough Gill and around to Innisfree. The southern route is less interesting until reaching Dooney Rock.

Cruises *The Wild Rose Water-Bus* (☎ 071-64266) cruises Lough Gill on a daily basis from Doorly Park (half an hour's walk east of town) and Parke's Castle for IR£4.50/1.50. There is also a IR£3.50/1.50 tour around Innisfree, and one-way trips between Parke's Castle and Sligo. There is a shuttle bus service from The Adelaide Bar at 2 pm but you need to inform the bar staff beforehand.

NORTH OF SLIGO TOWN
Drumcliff & Benbulben
W B Yeats died in 1939 in Roquebrune, France but his wishes were that 'if I die here, bury me up there on the mountain (the mountain cemetery in Roquebrune), and then after a year or so, dig me up and bring me privately to Sligo.' True to his wishes, his body was interred in the churchyard at Drumcliff in 1948, where his great-grandfather had been rector – although it was hardly a private affair, as the photographs in the Sligo museum make clear. The grave is on the left near the church and alongside Yeats is buried Georgie Hyde-Lees whom he married in 1917, when she was 15 and he was 52. The famous epitaph was his own composition:

> Cast a cold eye
> On life, on death.
> Horseman, pass by!

Nearly 1300 years earlier, St Colmcille chose the same location for the foundation of a monastery (see next page) and the remains of the round tower, damaged by lightning in 1936, can still be seen. A 10th-century high cross is nearby, depicting Adam and Eve, Cain's murder of Abel, Daniel in the Lions' Den and Christ in Glory. On the west side of the cross, the Presentation in the Temple and the Crucifixion can be made out.

Look for the round tower on the N15 road from Sligo. Going by bus you need to take the 8.45 am bus from Sligo because the next

The Battle of the Book

After Drumcliff, the first left turn goes to the village of Carney and just north of the village, in Cooldrumman, is where the Battle of the Book took place in the year 561. At the time, St Colmcille borrowed a rare psalter from St Finian and made a pirate edition for his own use. When St Finian found out and demanded the copy, the resulting argument found its way to the high king of Ireland who was asked to arbitrate. The delivered judgement was 'To every cow its calf and to every book its copy'. St Colmcille refused to accept the judgement and in the battle that followed over 4000 people were slain. Struck with remorse and shame, St Colmcille built a monastery at Drumcliff before departing forever into voluntary exile on Iona in Scotland. ■

one is at 4.15 pm which means you'll miss the two daily return buses that pass through Drumcliff at 12.30 and 4.53 pm.

Glencar Lough

Fishing apart, the attraction of the lake is the scenic waterfall which is signposted from the car park. Yeats refers to this picturesque spot in *The Stolen Child* and the surrounding countryside can be appreciated by walking east along the road and taking the steep trail that heads north to the Swiss valley.

From Drumcliff it's less than 5 km to the lake and there is also a bus service from Sligo.

Lissadell House

This is the ancestral home of the Gore-Booth family, the most famous member of whom was Constance Markievicz (1868-1927), a friend of Yeats and a participant in the 1916 Rising. The death penalty she received for this was later withdrawn and she lived to become the first woman elected to the House of Commons. Like many Irish rebels since, she refused to take her seat – although later, while still in prison, she became a member of the first Republican Dáil in 1918, and in 1919 she became Europe's first woman minister.

Constance's sister Eva was a poet, and Yeats's poem *In Memory of Eva Gore-Booth and Con Markievicz* is inscribed on a sign at the entrance to the house.

> The light of evening, Lissadell,
> Great windows, open to the south,
> Two girls in silk kimonos....

Yeats was a frequent visitor to Lissadell and in 1894 he wrote of the interior: 'Great sitting room as high as a church and all things in good taste.'

The house is open June to September, Monday to Saturday, from 10.30 am to 12.15 pm and 2 to 4.15 pm. The entrance charge is IR£2/50p (likely to increase soon) and the guided tour, which is very informative and interesting, takes about 45 minutes to complete.

To get there, take the N15 road out of Sligo and turn left in Drumcliff.

Mullaghmore

If you turn left at Cliffony, off the N15, the main road to Mullaghmore first passes **Streedagh Beach**, a grand stretch of sea and sand that was the final resting place for many of the 1300 sailors who perished when three ships from the Spanish Armada were wrecked nearby.

The beach at Mullaghmore is also delightfully wide and safe. It was in this bay, however, that the IRA assassinated Lord Mountbatten and members of his family in 1979 by blowing up his yacht. On the way to the Mullaghmore headland you pass **Classiebawn Castle** that was built for Lord Palmerston in 1856 and became the home of Lord Mountbatten. The castle is not open to the public.

Inishmurray Island

If access was easier to arrange, a visit to uninhabited Inishmurray would be a must. It contains the remains of three churches, beehive cells and open-air altars. The old monastery is surrounded by a stone wall with five separate entrances to the central area that contains the churches and altars. The monastery was founded in the early 6th century by St Molaise, and a wooden statue of the saint that once stood in the main church is now in the National Museum in Dublin.

The early monks on Inishmurray assembled some fascinating pagan relics. There is a collection of cursing stones; those who wanted to lay a curse did the Stations of the Cross in reverse, turning over the stones as they went. There were also separate burial grounds for men and women and a strong belief that if a body was placed in the wrong ground it would move itself during the night.

Only six km separate Inishmurray from the mainland but there is no regular boat service and the lack of harbour makes any landing subject to the weather. Trips can be arranged through either Lomax Boats (☎ 071-66124) or Brendan Merrifield (☎ 072-41874) from Mullaghmore, or from Streedagh Point through Joe McGowan (☎ 071-66267), or from Rosses Point through Tomas McCallion (☎ 071-42391). If you're lucky, a fishing group might be going out and an arrangement could be made; otherwise you need a group of at least six to make it economical.

Creevykeel Court Cairn
Just past Cliffony is a court tomb with a wide high front which tapers away to a narrow end. The unroofed court stands outside the front entrance and at some later stage, chambers were added to the west side of the cairn. It was constructed around 2500 BC.

Places to Stay
Celtic Farm Hostel (☎ 071-63337), located at Grange, is a useful base for the north of Sligo. Connemara ponies can be hired for riding on the beaches and B&B is currently available here – but as the place is up for sale, be sure to ring first. *Mrs Waters* (☎ 071-63350) at Shaddan Lodge near Streedagh Beach does B&B from IR£18/27.

At Drumcliff there are a number of B&Bs including *Mrs Hennigan's* (☎ 071-63211) at Benbulben Farm, Barnaribbon where singles/doubles are from IR£17/27.

At Mullaghmore the *Beach Hotel* (☎ 071-6610) has an indoor swimming pool. Singles/double are IR£39/58 and fishing trips can be arranged.

Places to Eat
Vegetarian food is available at the *Celtic Farm Hostel*. If you're visiting Drumcliff the *Yeats Tavern* is open seven days a week until 10 pm. Lunch specials are good value. The place is about 100 metres past Yeats' grave on the left of the main road.

Getting There & Away
There are regular bus connections between Sligo, Drumcliff, Grange and Cliffony as nearly all the buses to Donegal and Derry will take the N15. In Drumcliff the buses stop outside the creamery, in Grange it's outside Rooney's shop and in Cliffony it's Ena's pub. The first bus stopping at all these places leaves Sligo at 8.45 am.

SOUTH & WEST OF SLIGO TOWN
Collooney
The **Teeling Monument** can be found at the northern end of this village. It commemorates the daring of Bartholomew Teeling who was marching with Humbert's French-Irish army when it encountered stiff resistance from an English gunner. Teeling charged up to the gunner and killed him, thus allowing the army to march on to an eventual defeat at the battle of Ballinamuck in Longford. Although the French were treated as prisoners of war, Teeling and 500 other Irishmen were executed.

The other attraction near Collooney is **Markree Castle** (☎ 071-67800) which is signposted off the main road on the left after leaving the village. The castle has remained in the same family since Cromwell's time. When Charles Kingsley stayed here in the 19th century he wrote that he cried over the misery inflicted on the local peasantry, while at the same time exalting in the excitement of fishing for salmon in the estate's river. And it is said that Mrs Alexander wrote the hymn *All Things Bright & Beautiful* after her stay there. The castle now functions as a hotel; singles/doubles start at IR£58/96.

B&B at IR£15 is available from *Tess & Des Lang* (☎ 071-67136) at Union Farm just one km outside the village.

Ballymote

This small town, definitely off the tourist trail, has two points of interest. **Ballymote Castle**, on the road from town to Tubbercurry, looks like a designer ruin but this is the real thing; an early 14th-century castle fought over between Irish chiefs before succumbing to the English in 1577 and now crumbling away in obscurity. It was from here that O'Donnell marched to disaster at the Battle of Kinsale in 1601.

The **Protestant church** is also worth a glance, if only to read the plaque saying that the clock was paid for by the tenants of Ballymote estate as a mark of respect to Sir Robert Gore-Booth of Lissadell. Unlike many of these tributes this one was genuine; Robert Gore-Booth mortgaged Lissadell House during the Famine to raise money for food for the starving. Constance Markievicz, his daughter, received a minute-long ovation from the local peasantry here after her release from an English jail in June 1917.

There are a few B&Bs here: *Mrs Mullin* (☎ 071-83449) at Millhouse and *Mrs McGettrick* (☎ 071-83398) at Hillcrest both charge around IR£14 per person and are signposted from the village. More upmarket is *Temple House* (☎ 071-83329), an old Anglo-Irish home, which gets its name from the Knights Templar. Singles/doubles from IR£42/76.

There are plenty of unpretentious pubs to choose from and *Donald H Tighe* serves reasonable bar food. The *Corran Restaurant* is good for lunch or dinner and serves a variety of conventional dishes from IR£5 to IR£12.50.

Tubbercurry

Sometimes spelt Tobercurry, this is another off-the-beaten-track town. It comes alive around the middle of July when a music summer school takes the place over. On the second Wednesday in August, the town's big Fair Day is celebrated. Nearly all the pubs have musical links, and the first place to call in at is *Killoran's* on the long main street, which is multi-purpose functioning as a combined pub/restaurant/takeaway/travel agent/off-licence/ tourist office.

Carrowkeel Passage-Tomb Cemetery

Situated on a hilltop in the Bricklieve Mountains overlooking Lough Arrow, this place is uplifting, with panoramic views on a clear day, and also a little spooky given the 14 cairns, various dolmens and scattered remnants of other graves. The place has been dated to the late Stone Age (3000-2000 BC).

The site, off the main N4 road, is closer to Boyle than Sligo. In the village of Castlebaldwin turn right, if coming from Sligo, at the sign, and then left at the fork as indicated. The site is a couple of km uphill from the gateway. You can take bus No 275 from Sligo and ask to be put off at Castlebaldwin.

Coopershill House (☎ 071-65108) is close to the Carrowkeel Passage-Tomb Cemetery, halfway between Sligo and Boyle, and is a handsome retreat for anyone wanting to relax in a Georgian family mansion. Bed & breakfast here is from IR£52/84 for singles/doubles and you would want to stay two nights to enjoy the boating and fishing that is available.

For a down-to-earth Irish meal with good wine and open log fires, splash out IR£21 for a dinner at *Coopershill House* (☎ 071-65108).

Lough Arrow

Lough Arrow has its own tourist office (☎ 079-66232) open during July and August from 9.30 am to 5.30 pm, seven days a week. It is situated on the main N4 road just north of Boyle, within spitting distance of County Roscommon. The centre is geared towards motoring tourists.

Lough Arrow is of interest to anglers. Mayfly Holidays (☎ 071-65065) of Ballindoon, Riverstown, do B&B plus

MAYO & SLIGO

packed lunches and boat hire at IR£12 a day. Inside information on fishing spots is free.

Getting There & Away
Bus The Bus Éireann Dublin to Sligo express stops outside Quigley's in Collooney as does the Galway-Derry express which goes on to Tubbercurry. Bus No 248 runs through Collooney, Ballymote and Tubbercurry on the way to Athlone and a local bus runs from Sligo to Collooney.

Train The Dublin train also stops at Collooney and Ballymote three times daily.

West of Sligo Town
The interesting places west of town are Carrowmore and Knocknarea, mentioned earlier,

and Strandhill is the only other place close to town that might be worth a visit. There is a pub and the beaches are sandy, though not always safe for swimming, and at low tide there you can walk across to Coney Island. The story goes that New York's own Coney Island was named by a man from Rosses Point.

The main route west to Mayo is pleasant enough, but there is little to detain the visitor. The town of Easky has the ruins of a 15-century castle and the surfing possibilities are highly regarded. The sandy beach at Enniscrone, further west, is a popular holiday spot for Irish families and the *Atlantic Beech* camp site (☎ 096-36132) is only 12 km from Ballina. An attraction here are the putative health-restoring qualities of a seaweed and hot sea-water bath.

The Central North

Someone once described Ireland as a dull picture with a wonderful frame – and indeed most visitors do just travel around the coast which forms the frame and rarely venture inland to explore the picture. But while the six counties of the central north – Cavan, Monaghan, Roscommon, Leitrim, Longford and Westmeath – may never attract the tourist hordes, they do have a number of places of great interest.

Cavan, Monaghan and Donegal, together with the six counties of Northern Ireland, make up the province of Ulster.

Since the ceasefire and the start of the peace process all border crossing points between the Republic and the North have been opened.

County Cavan

The low, undulating county of Cavan (*An Cabhán*), with its population of just over 3300, is barely a two-hour drive from Dublin and lies just south of the border with Northern Ireland. Cavan is dominated by lakes, bogs and drumlins; small round hills deposited and shaped by retreating glaciers during the last Ice Age, which ended some 10,000 to 12,000 years ago. In the far north-west of the county, the wild and barren Cuilcagh Mountains are the source of the River Shannon, at over 300 km long the mightiest river in Ireland or Great Britain.

Cavan is also famous for its potholed roads, which are often twisty and badly signposted to boot. The roads seem to go over the drumlins, whereas in neighbouring Monaghan they go round them.

Cavan was the birthplace of Percy French, the late 19th-century songwriter responsible for *The Mountains of Mourne*.

HISTORY

Archaeological evidence suggests that Cavan was inhabited as far back as Neolithic

Highlights
- Excellent fishing
- Monaghan County Museum in Monaghan Town, one of the best regional museums in Ireland and home to the Cross of Clogher
- Boyle Abbey, just east of Boyle, one of the finer Cistercian abbeys in Ireland
- The superb Drumanone Dolmen, just outside of Boyle, one of the largest in Ireland
- The 24-km Shannon-Erne Waterway, with its 34 stone bridges and 16 locks, stretching from the village of Leitrim, four km north of Carrick-on-Shannon, to the southern shore of Upper Lough Erne

CENTRAL NORTH

times. Magh Sleacht, a plain in the north-west of the county near the border village of Ballyconnell, was one of the most important druidic centres in the country around the 5th century, when St Patrick was converting the Irish to Christianity. The principal Celtic deity was Crom Cruaich, whose significance swiftly diminished as the Christian teachings of Patrick spread. In the 12th century, the Anglo-Normans made a concerted effort to get a foothold in Cavan, but the landscape proved difficult to penetrate and the region remained under the control of the Gaelic O'Reilly clan for many years.

Their grip on power began to slip in the

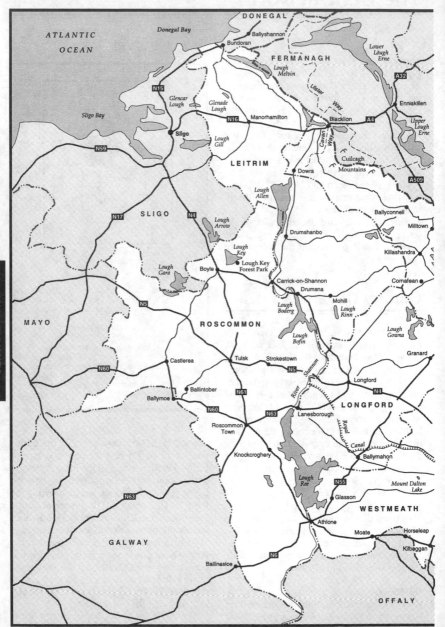

CENTRAL NORTH

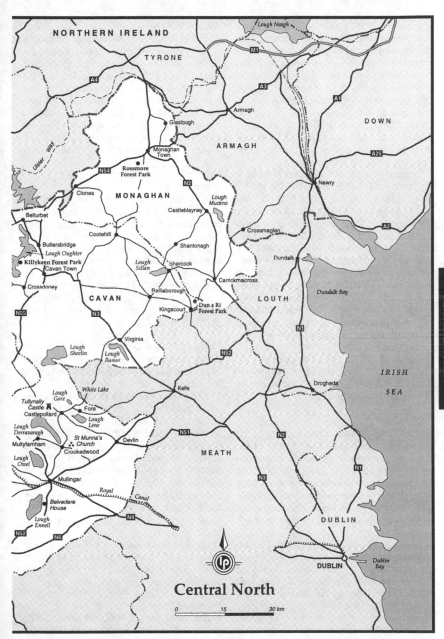

Central North

0   15   30 km

16th century. The English 'shired' the county into baronies, dividing these amongst clan members loyal to the English crown. The end came when the O'Reillys joined with the other Ulster lords – the O'Donnells and the O'Neills – in the Nine Years War (1594-1603) against the English and were defeated.

As part of the plantation of Ulster after 1609, Cavan was divided up amongst English and Scottish settlers, and the new town of Virginia was created, named after Elizabeth I, the Virgin Queen.

In the 1640s, with Charles II in trouble in England, the Confederate Rebellion led by Owen Roe O'Neill took place in opposition to the plantation. O'Neill, a returned exile, had one major victory over the English at the Battle of Benburb in County Tyrone in 1646. Only with the conclusion of the English Civil War and the arrival of Cromwell in 1649 were the English again able to take control. Owen Roe O'Neill died in suspicious circumstances in 1649 in Cloughoughter Castle near Cavan Town; poisoning was suspected.

The Irish population generally remained in poverty and the famine of the 1840s led to massive emigration. After the War of Independence in 1922, the Ulster counties of Cavan, Monaghan and Donegal were included with the South. With the border so close, Republicanism is strong.

FISHING

Anglers from all over Europe converge on Cavan to fish the many lakes along the southern and western border of the county. Cavan has more than its fair share of lakes, some 365 in total according to the locals; one for every day of the year! The fishing is excellent; primarily coarse fishing for pike, bream, perch and roach but also some game angling for trout in Lough Sheelin.

Some of the lakes like Lough Sheelin are recovering after years of serious pollution from the numerous pig farms in the area, and as the fish return so do the anglers. Most lakes are well signposted, with the types of fish available also marked. Some of the villages and guesthouses depend heavily on anglers, many of whom return year after year.

CAVAN TOWN

The most important settlement in the county is the rather ordinary Cavan Town. Its slightly peculiar layout centres around the two parallel Farnham and Main Sts. Main St has the feel of an Irish country town with typical shops and pubs on each side, while in contrast, Farnham St more closely resembles a city avenue with some elegant Georgian houses, a large courthouse and garda station, a couple of churches and a Catholic cathedral.

Information

The tourist office (☎ 049-31942), on the corner of Farnham and Thomas Ashe Sts, is open June to September from 9 am to 5 pm Monday to Friday, from 9 am to 1 pm the rest of the year. The post office is on the corner of Main St and Market Square. You can leave your laundry at the Supaklene laundrette on Farnham St about 100 metres from the bus station. There's also a small, local genealogical office, signposted up the hill off Farnham St, in Cana House.

Things to See & Do

Cavan developed around a 13th-century Franciscan friary of which there are no traces left today. On the site in Abbey St is an 18th-century **Protestant church tower** which marks the grave of Owen Roe O'Neill, though it must be said that it's not very impressive. One km from the town centre on the Dublin road is Ireland's second-oldest crystal factory, **Cavan Crystal** (☎ 049-31800). It's open Monday to Friday from 9.30 am to 5.30 pm, Saturday 10 am to 5 pm, and Sunday 2 to 5 pm. There are free factory tours by arrangement where you can see the handmade crystal being blown and cut. They also have a gift shop.

Courses in **canoeing** are given by local Irish Canoe Union instructors on the River Erne. See the noticeboard in Louis Blessing's pub.

Places to Stay

B&Bs *Roses Brough House* (☎ 049-30311), on the Dublin road, has rooms for IR£16/26 with separate bathroom. *Bridge Restaurant* (☎ 049-31538), 5 Coleman Rd, is by the bridge, close to the Bus Éireann station. It offers B&B in spacious rooms for IR£18 per person, plus a IR£3 key deposit. *Oakdene* (☎ 049-31698), 29 Cathedral Rd at the north end of town, has four reasonable rooms for IR£18.50/30 a single/double. *Halcyon* (☎ 049-31809), 600 metres along the Cootehill road and then right by McDonald's shop, has five rooms at the same rates.

There are some real gems out of town, if you are prepared to push on a little. *Lisnamandra House* (☎ 049-37196) is about eight km along the Crossdoney road and well signposted on the left-hand side. B&B is IR£18.50/30 with a shower, dinner is IR£14 and you should book ahead. Breakfast is wonderful.

Hotels In the centre of town, on Main St, you could try the very popular *Farnham Arms Hotel* (☎ 049-32577) with B&B for IR£28/54 a single/double. *Hotel Kilmore* (☎ 049-32288), on the Dublin road near the Crystal Factory, has B&B for IR£38/72.

Places to Eat
The town has fast-food places like *Uncle Sam's* on College St, or *Una's Takeaway* on Main St. *Galligan's Restaurant* (☎ 049-61323), just off Main St on Bridge St, is good for inexpensive lunches and early dinners; fish is IR£6.25. Serving a good cup of coffee, *Melbourne Bakery* is a small restaurant-cum-coffee-shop halfway up Main St. The *Farnham Arms Hotel* has a comfortable lounge with reasonable food. *Bridge Restaurant* is a good, reasonably priced place to eat with chicken dishes from IR£2.50 and fish from IR£3. It's open from 9 am to 9 pm.

The best place in town is the *Olde Priory Restaurant* (☎ 049-61898), on Main St in an old convent basement opposite the Melbourne Bakery. It serves pizzas from IR£4.20 and also does seafood, kebabs and vegetarian dishes. It has a bar and is closed Monday.

Entertainment
McGinty's Corner Bar, on College St, has won a regional 'pub of the year' title and sometimes has music at weekends. There are heaps of pubs on Main St. The *Black Horse Inn* is popular with locals and has pool tables. You will occasionally find jazz in *Louis Blessing's* rustic bar. *Linus McDonnell's*, on Thomas Ashe St, is another attractive place.

The town's small *cinema* is on Towne Hall St, which runs between Farnham and Main Sts.

Getting There & Away
The Bus Éireann (☎ 049-31353) station is at the south end of Farnham St near the bridge. The ticket office is open Monday to Saturday from 7.30 am to 8.30 pm.

Cavan is on the Dublin to Donegal, Galway to Belfast and Athlone to Belfast routes. On weekdays there are five daily buses to Dublin (1¾ hours), three buses to Belfast (three hours) and two to Galway (3¾ hours). Bus Éireann also has services running from Cavan Town through the county to Bawboy, Ballyconnell, Belturbet, Virginia, Kells, Dunboyne, Dunshaughlin and many other small towns.

Wharton's Bus (☎ 049-37114) has private daily buses between the Lakeland Hotel and Parnell Square, Dublin. Buses leave Cavan at 8 am Monday to Saturday, at 7 pm on Sunday.

Getting Around
'On Yer Bike Tours' (☎ 049-31932), in the Abbeyset Printers building on Farnham St, rent bikes for IR£7/30 a day/week plus deposit. They also offer day or week-long leisurely group cycling tours of the area with many excursions, including Corleggy Cheese Farm, well known for its goats' cheese.

AROUND CAVAN TOWN
Kilmore Cathedral
This modest Protestant cathedral, built in 1860, is about five km west on the R198 Crossdoney road to Killykeen Forest Park. On the west side of this relatively modern

building is a fine 12th-century Romanesque doorway brought here from an Augustinian monastery on one of Lough Oughter's many islands. If you look closely, you'll notice that some of the stones have not been replaced in the right order. In the churchyard is the grave of Bishop Bedell (1571-1642) who commissioned the first translation of the Old Testament into Irish; there's a copy of it on display in the chancel.

Killykeen Forest Park

This forest park is 12 km north-west of Cavan Town on the shores of Lough Oughter. Lough Oughter winds a tortuous path around the undulating landscape and the park has some fine walks, nature trails, fishing spots and good chalets for rent amongst its 243 hectares of trees and inlets. Many of the low wooded islands in the lake are likely to have been crannógs – fortified, artificial islands.

To the north, within the park, is the inaccessible **Lough Oughter Castle**, built in the 13th century by the O'Reillys on an island in the lake and the place where the rebel leader Owen Roe O'Neill died, reputedly from poisoning. The best way to get near it is from the south-east, along a narrow road running north from the village of Garthrattan. On **Inch Island**, also within the park, there is a ring fort.

Admission to the park is IR£1 for a car, IR£3 for a family. There are self-catering chalets (☎ 049-32541) on the shores of Lough Oughter which sleep six and can be rented for IR£360 a week or IR£200 on weekends (three nights).

Canadian-style canoes can be rented (☎ 049-32842) for a paddle on Lough Oughter or the Erne waterways and there's fishing and horse-riding within the park.

Pighouse Folk Museum

From Crossdoney you'll see signposts for the Pighouse Folk Museum (☎ 049-37248) in Corr House, Cornafean. Its hodgepodge of artefacts dating from the 1700s are preserved in the original pighouse and barns. If you like rummaging through other people's attics,

then you'll love this place. It's almost worth the trip anyway, for the view it affords of the drumlins and valleys. The museum is open by appointment, so phone ahead to see if Mrs Faris is going to be there. Admission is free.

Drumlane Monastic Site

One km south of Milltown, north of Killeshandra on the road to Belturbet, is Drumlane, a 6th-century monastic site; though the small plain church and peculiar round tower just over 11 metres high, were built later. The monastery was founded by St Mogue and the site's location between two small lakes – Drumlane and Derrybrick – and the surrounding hills is its most attractive feature.

Butlersbridge

Six km north of Cavan Town is the pretty hamlet of Butlersbridge on the River Annalee. **Ballyhaise House** nearby was designed by Richard Castle (responsible for Dublin's Leinster House) and is worth a quick look for its fine brickwork. It is now an agricultural college.

Just near the river in Butlersbridge, *Ford House* (☎ 049-31427) has six rooms for IR£13 to IR£15 per person B&B. The *Derragarra Inn*, a pub by the river, which often seems to be the busiest place in the county, has good bar food, a reasonably priced tourist menu and peat fires.

Belturbet

A small town on the River Erne 16 km north-west of Cavan Town on the N3, Belturbet is an angling centre with cruises available up Lough Erne during the summer. Turbet Tours (☎ 049-22360) has sailings on the Shannon-Erne Waterway from June to September aboard the *Erne Dawn* between Belturbet and Ballyconnell. The 2½-hour tour costs IR£5/3.

At *Fortview House*, (☎ 049-38185) B&B is IR£16/27 for singles/doubles. *Hilltop Farm* (☎ 049-22114) has 10 rooms with B&B at IR£18.50/27 to IR£20.50/31 for singles/doubles. Both places have facilities for anglers.

Bus Éireann (☎ 049-31353) stops here five times daily in each direction on its route between Cavan Town and Donegal (2¼ hours). The bus stop is outside O'Reilly's Garage.

Lough Sheelin

Lough Sheelin, 24 km south of Cavan Town, is noted for its game angling for brown trout. The two main accommodation centres are the villages of Finnea (just over the border in County Westmeath) and Mountnugent at opposite ends of the lough. In Mountnugent there are several places where you can stay and hire boats for fishing: Sheelin Shamrock Hotel (☎ 049-40387), Crover House Hotel (☎ 049-40206) and Ross House (☎ 049-40218).

WEST CAVAN

West Cavan, sometimes known as the Panhandle because of its distinctive shape, is dominated by the starkly beautiful, but little visited Cuilcagh Mountains. To the southwest, Magh Sleacht, the area around Kilnavert and Killycluggin, is supposed to have been a druidic centre dedicated to the deity Crom Cruaich. In the far north-west corner of the county, the road travels parallel to the border before forking. The left fork heads west to Dowra and Blacklion; this is a desolate area with some interesting ancient sites. The right fork heads north to Swanlibar and the border.

Getting There & Away

There are few buses servicing this remote part of the county. The express Donegal to Dublin buses pass through Ballyconnell, Bawnboy and Swanlinbar four times daily. Swanlinbar is also on the Athlone to Derry run. The Galway to Belfast bus stops in Blacklion only once a week, on a Monday; but on the Westport to Belfast route the bus stops once a day. Contact the Bus Éireann (☎ 049-31353) station in Cavan Town for information.

Ballyconnell

Ballyconnell, 29 km north-west of Cavan Town and seven km west of Belturbet, is the gateway to the region. There's not a lot in the village itself but it's a good base from which to explore. There are tours available on the Shannon-Erne Waterway; see Belturbet earlier for details.

Places to Stay The county's only hostel, *Sandville House Hostel* (☎ 049-26297), is three km south of Ballyconnell, signposted off the Belturbet road, in a peaceful rural two-hectare setting. A dorm bed is IR£5 and there is an area to pitch a tent. The Dublin to Donegal bus stops at the Slieve Russell Hotel on request, and if you ring the hostel beforehand they can arrange to pick you up.

Ballyconnell has lots of B&Bs. *Snugborough House* (☎ 049-26346) has four rooms at IR£14/32 with bath. *Angler's Rest* (☎ 049-26391) is a pub-cum-guesthouse which has rooms for IR£14/26 B&B with shared bathroom. You can get snacks and light meals in the pub.

The huge *Slieve Russell Hotel* (☎ 049-26444), two km south-east of Ballyconnell, is something of a legend. Built by a local millionaire, it features marble, fountains, restaurants, bars, nightclubs, a swimming pool and a golf course. It even has its own private helicopter and hangar. B&B is normally IR£80/140 a single/double, but there are frequent weekend and midweek specials.

Dowra & the Black Pig's Dyke

Dowra is on the upper reaches of the River Shannon and between the river and Slievenakilla to the east is a five-km section of the mysterious Black Pig's Race or Dyke, a worm-like earthworks which wriggles across much of the region. It may have been an ancient fortification and frontier of Ulster, perhaps an earlier version of Hadrian's Wall in Scotland.

Blacklion

Five km south of Blacklion are the remains of a **cashel** or ring fort with three large circular embankments. Inside is a sweathouse, a stone beehive hut which served as a type of Turkish bath and was used mostly in the 19th century. Between Dowra and

Blacklion there are the remains of quite a number of these curiosities.

Lough MacNean House (☎ 072-53022), on Main St, is one of the few B&Bs around Blacklion, and costs IR£20/36 a single/double. It also provides dinner in the evening.

The Cavan & Ulster Ways

Blacklion and Dowra are the ends of the Cavan Way, and Blacklion is also on the Ulster Way. See the Activities chapter.

EAST CAVAN

Heading east, from Cavan Town you move into the heart of drumlin country. The history of foreign settlement has left its mark on the fabric and layout of the main towns.

Getting There & Away

Four express Bus Éireann (☎ 049-31353) buses on the Donegal to Dublin route pass through Virginia, and there are also three daily passing through between Cavan Town and Dublin. Cootehill is on a Dundalk to Cavan Town route with a single bus on Friday only; and there are two daily buses on weekdays from Cootehill to Monaghan Town, with just one on Saturday.

On Tuesday a Dundalk to Cavan Town bus travels through Kingscourt. There is also a Cootehill-Kingscourt-Dublin service which has three buses on Monday and Saturday and two on each of the other weekdays.

Virginia

On the shores of Lough Ramor in the southeast corner of the county, Virginia's origins go back to the Plantation of Ulster in the early 17th century. It was named after Elizabeth I, the Virgin Queen. Six km to the north-west is **Cuilcagh House**, home of the Sheridan family, where Jonathan Swift is said to have come up with the idea for *Gulliver's Travels* while visiting in 1726. There is a nine-hole golf course just out of town, on the Dublin side, in the grounds of the Park Hotel.

Places to Stay & Eat Five km south of Virginia on the southern tip of Lough Ramor is the somewhat run-down *Lough Ramor Camping & Caravan Park* (☎ 049-47447). It has tent sites, of which there are only seven, for IR£5 per person; motorcyclists pay IR£4, hikers and cyclists IR£3.50.

On the lakeshore one km from Virginia on the Dublin road, *St Kyran's* (☎ 049-47087) is open April to September and costs between IR£15/26 for a single/double without bathroom. Across the road is *Hillside House* (☎ 049-47125) with three rooms at IR£13 per person. Two km west along the Oldcastle road is the *White House* (☎ 049-47515), with three rooms for IR£13.50 to IR£15 per person.

Just outside Virginia, the *Park Hotel* (☎ 049-47235) is an 18th-century building overlooking a small lake, with rooms at IR£50 per person. They also have a little nine-hole golf course and good but pricey food.

Sharkey's Hotel, on Main St, does teas, coffees and snacks all day and lunches in the bar.

Cootehill

Farther to the north, the small, neat market town of Cootehill is named after the Cootes, a planter family who, after acquiring confiscated land from the O'Reillys, were instrumental in founding the town in the 17th century. This colourful clan had many interesting members, including Sir Charles Coote, one of Cromwell's most ruthless and effective leaders, and Richard Coote (1636-1701) who became governor of New York State, and then New Hampshire and Massachusetts.

The Coote mansion, **Bellamont House** (1729), was designed by Edward Lovett Pearce (architect of the Bank of Ireland in College Green, Dublin, and supervisor of Castletown House in Kildare) and is described as one of the best Palladian villas in Ireland. It's open in the afternoons (no admission fee) and for exclusive overnight stays.

Places to Stay & Eat *Knockvilla* (☎ 049-52203), on Station Rd, a small cul-de-sac off the Shercock road, costs IR£13 to IR£14 per person. Also worth trying is the *Beeches* (☎ 049-52307), Station Rd, which has single/doubles for IR£18.50/30 with bathroom. One km on the Cavan side of Cootehill is *Riverside House* (☎ 049-52150), an excellent B&B for IR£13.50 to IR£15.50 and open all year.

The *Coffee Pot*, on Market St, has good coffee, cakes, sandwiches (IR£1.20) and lunches during the day. The *White Horse Hotel*, at the end of the same street, has a good carvery lunch and other dishes for around IR£5.

Shercock

Shercock is a pretty little village on the shores of Lough Sillan, 13 km south-east of Cootehill. The lake is noted for its pike fishing. *Lakelands Caravan & Camping Park* (☎ 042-69488), about one km west of the village in a tranquil setting beside the lake, charges IR£4 per tent plus 50p per person, and is open at Easter and from June to mid-September.

Kingscourt

In the far east of the county, Kingscourt is a fairly drab village. **St Mary's Catholic Church** has some superb 1940s stained-glass windows by the artist Evie Hone. The church has views of the surrounding region, and just to the north-west is **Dun a Rí Forest Park**, with wooded walks and picnic spots.

Places to Stay & Eat *Mackin's Hotel* (☎ 042-67208), on Church St, is an ordinary country hotel with 20 rooms from IR£15 per person. *Cabra Castle* (☎ 042-67030), three km out of Kingscourt on the Carrickmacross road, is an imposing structure with its own nine-hole golf course, but it isn't cheap. B&B is IR£65/80 a single/double. It's worth trying for a snack or meal at lunch or dinner time.

County Monaghan

Few visitors pass through Monaghan's (*Muineachán*) landscape of neat round hills,

crisscrossed by unkempt hedgerows and countless scattered farms. The hills are drumlins, dumped by the glaciers of the last Ice Age in a belt stretching from Clew Bay in County Galway across the country to County Down. It's pleasant but never spectacular scenery; walkers and cyclists may enjoy the many peaceful country lanes if the weather is cooperative. Monaghan has fewer lakes than neighbouring Cavan, though the fishing is still good.

Patrick Kavanagh (1906-67), one of Ireland's most respected poets, was born in this county, in Inniskeen. *The Great Hunger* which he wrote in 1942, and *Tarry Flynn* written in 1948 evoke the atmosphere and often grim reality of life for the poor farming community.

The barren terrain has restricted the development of large-scale mechanised farming, but despite this, Monaghan's farming cooperatives are amongst the most active and forward-looking in the country. Monaghan is noted for its lace and the eyestraining tradition of making this extraordinarily fine material continues in Clones and Carrickmacross, the centre of the industry since the early 19th century.

HISTORY

The earliest traces of humans in this region go back to before the Bronze Age. None of these sites measure up to the magnificent monuments of County Meath, though the Tullyrain Ring Fort close to Shantonagh in the south of the county is worth a look, as are Mannor Castle near Carrickmacross and the crannóg in Convent Lake in Monaghan Town. Like Cavan, Monaghan is lacking in religious remains despite its proximity to Armagh, the principal seat of St Patrick. The round tower and high cross in Clones in the west of the county are among the scant remains from this period of Irish history.

The Anglo-Normans were also less influential here than elsewhere. The county was controlled through the early Middle Ages by many Gaelic clans including the O'Carrolls, McKennas and MacMahons. Enemies for a long time of the O'Neills of Armagh, these families united with them on the losing side of the Nine Years War (1594-1603) against the English.

Unlike Cavan and much of Ulster, Monaghan was largely left alone during the plantation of Ulster. The transfer of Monaghan land to English hands came later, after the Cromwellian wars, and much of it was granted to soldiers and adventurers or bought by them from the local chieftains (under pressure and often for a fraction of its worth). These new settlers levelled the forests and built numerous planned towns and villages, each with their own Protestant church. The planning and architecture exemplified their tidy, austere and no-frills approach to life. Disapproving of Irish pastoral farming methods, they introduced arable farming, and the linen industry later became seriously profitable.

Monaghan's historical ties with Ulster were severed by the partition of Ireland in 1922, and although Republicanism is quite strong, it is not as visible as you might expect. A number of towns have Sinn Féin advice centres.

MONAGHAN TOWN

The county town of Monaghan is 141 km north-west of Dublin and just eight km south of the border with the North. It's the only town of any size in the county. Its design and buildings reflect the influence of the British newcomers of the 17th and 18th centuries and of the money generated by the linen industry in the 18th and 19th centuries. Compared to many midland towns, Monaghan is a pleasant surprise; many of the town's important buildings are elegant limestone edifices built to last more than one lifetime. The locals have developed an excellent regional museum.

History

Nothing remains of the ruling MacMahons' 1462 friary or their earlier forts, but in Convent Lake, just behind St Louis's Convent, there is a small crannóg now overgrown which served as the headquarters for the family around the 14th century.

After the turbulent wars of the 16th and 17th centuries, the town was settled by Scottish Calvinists who built a castle using the rubble of the old friary, some fragments of which can be seen near the Diamond. The 19th-century profits from the linen industry transformed the town and brought many sturdy new buildings.

Orientation & Information

Monaghan's principal streets form a roughly continuous arc, broken up by the town's three main squares or 'diamonds' – Church Square, the Diamond and Old Cross Square. Most of the sights and important buildings can be found on these thoroughfares. To the west of this arc at the top of Park St is Market Square. Here, the tourist office (☎ 047-81122), in Market House, which dates from 1792, is open Monday to Friday from 9 am to 1 pm but these hours may be extended. The post office is on Mill St which runs between Hill St and North Rd.

You can get your laundry done at the Supreme Laundrette on Park St just down from the tourist office.

There are two small lakes, Peter's Lake to the north of the courthouse and Convent Lake with its crannóg at the south-west corner of town. A one-way traffic system operates through the centre of town,

Monaghan County Museum

Monaghan County Museum (☎ 047-82928) is behind the tourist office at the junction with Hill St and is one of the best regional museums in Ireland. Taking up two Victorian houses, it includes exhibits from Stone Age to modern times, and has displays on the local lace and linen industries, the abandoned Ulster Canal (which runs just to the south of the town and is being renovated) and, of course, the border with the North.

The museum's prized possession is the **Cross of Clogher**, a bronze 13th or 14th-century altar cross. Usually, local treasures such as this are whisked away to the National Museum in Dublin. Local and national artists have exhibits in the Art Gallery wing. The museum is open Tuesday to Saturday from

11 am to 5 pm, closed from 1 to 2 pm, and admission is free.

From June to September, the museum runs heritage walks of the town.

Other Sights

At the top of Market St is **Church Square**, the first of the three diamonds, with an 1857 **obelisk** for a Colonel Dawson who was killed in the Crimean War. Overlooking the square is a fine Doric-style 1830 **Courthouse**, the former Hibernian Bank (1875) and the Gothic St Patrick's Church.

In the centre of town, the **Diamond** is the town's original market place, with a Victorian sandstone fountain presented to the town in 1875 in honour of the Baron of Rossmore, a member of the area's former leading family. This spot was once occupied by the **Market Cross**, with its fancy sundial, which was moved to Old Cross Square at the east end of Dublin St to accommodate the Baron's memorial.

The birthplace of **Charles Gavan Duffy**, one of the leaders of the Young Ireland Movement and a founder of the *Nation* newspaper, is at 10 Dublin St. In the 1840s, the *Nation* set out to teach the native Irish about themselves, their history and literature, as well as presenting a non-sectarian view of Irish news. Later, Duffy moved to Australia, where he became Premier of Victoria. Nearby, the **Sinn Féin Advice Centre** has a display of Republican literature.

South of the Ulster Canal on the Dublin road, **St Macartan's Catholic Cathedral** with its slender spire was designed by J J McCarthy (responsible for the College Chapel in Maynooth, County Kildare), and is said to be his finest building, though some feel it has been marred by the later addition of incongruous Carrara marble statues. It has good views of the surrounding area. **Convent Lake** with its crannóg is at the bottom of Park St, over the canal.

Places to Stay

B&Bs The central, clean and efficient *Ashleigh House* (☎ 047-81227), 37 Dublin St, has 10 rooms with singles/doubles at

IR£18/30 with bath, IR£14/26 without. On the Clones road south of the centre, *The Cedars* (☎ 047-82783) has three rooms at IR£18.50/31.

Hotels The fine, red-brick *Westenra Hotel* (☎ 047-81517), at the Diamond in the centre of town, has 17 rooms with bathroom at IR£25 per person for B&B. The Georgian-style *Lakeside Hotel* (☎ 047-83519), on North Rd beside Peter's Lake, is reasonably priced with rooms from IR£20. The modern *Four Seasons Hotel* (☎ 047-81888), about two km north on the Derry road in Coolshannagh, is more expensive at IR£40/72 for singles/doubles.

Places to Eat

Pizza D'Or (☎ 047-84777), in Market Square behind the tourist office, turns out good, takeaway pizzas from IR£4.50 and is open from 5 pm until late. The *Genoa Restaurant & Ice Cream Parlour*, on Dublin St, is a popular fast-food place serving pizzas, steaks and good ice cream. Just down from the Genoa is *Mediterraneo* which has mainly Italian food for around IR£5 but also does a vegetable curry. The *Coffee Shop Restaurant & Deli*, on Church Square, has standard food like burgers and chips and is busy at lunch times. *Andy's Lounge & Restaurant*, in Market Square across from the tourist office, is one of the better places in town for food or a quiet drink.

Entertainment

Some of the best pubs are on Dublin St, including *McGinn's* and *McKenna's*, both small but popular with the locals; McKenna's has the occasional music night. On the Old Cross Square is *McConnon's Olde Cross Inn*. One of the most popular pubs in town is *Terry's* on Park St, near the museum. *Jimmy's*, on Mill St across from the post office, is a quieter locals place.

The *Garage Theatre* (☎ 047-81021) hosts professional theatre companies as well as local, amateur drama groups. The *Diamond Screen* is a three-screen cinema beside the car park in the Diamond Centre shopping area.

Getting There & Away

From the Bus Éireann bus station (☎ 047-82377), on North Rd beside the former railway station, there are numerous daily intercity services within the Republic and to the North. These include five to Dublin (two hours), four to Derry (two hours) and three to Belfast (two hours) and Armagh (40 minutes). There are also many daily local services to the nearby towns of Ballybay, Castleblayney and Carrickmacross.

McConnon's (☎ 047-82020) private bus company has two daily buses from Church Square to Dublin's Parnell Square serving Carrickmacross and Castleblayney en route, and one daily bus to Clones.

Getting Around

Clerkin's Cycles (☎ 047-81434), on Market Square behind the tourist office, sometimes rents out bikes.

ROSSMORE FOREST PARK

The park, three km south-west of Monaghan on the Newbliss road, was originally the home of the Rossmores, but only the buttresses to their castle walls and the entrance stairway remain. Besides forest walks and picnic areas, the park has Californian sequoias, some of the tallest trees in Ireland. Other items include the Rossmores' pet cemetery as well as Iron Age wedge and court tombs. A gold collar or 'lunula' from 1800 BC was found here in the 1930s and removed to the National Museum in Dublin. Fishing in the lakes here is popular. Admission to the park is free for pedestrians and IR£1.50 if you bring a car.

GLASLOUGH

Glaslough, nine km north-east of Monaghan Town, is a neat little village of cut-stone cottages set beside its namesake, Glaslough (Green Lake), so called because of its curious green colour. To get there from Monaghan Town, take the N2 Omagh road north, turn right (east) onto the N12 for about two km then turn left (north) onto the R185.

Beside the village is the 500-hectare demesne of **Castle Leslie** (☎ 047-88109), a magnificent 19th-century Italianate mansion overlooking the lake. The castle's attractions include a toilet used by Mick Jagger. Greystones Equestrian Centre (☎ 047-88100) has some fine hacks in the demesne, where there are 40 km of trails.

The castle and gardens are open from May to the end of August, from 2 to 6 pm Sunday to Thursday, and admission is IR£3/1.50 which includes a tour and coffee or tea. On Sunday afternoons only, teas of hot scones with cream and plenty of calorific desserts are served in the conservatory.

CLONES & AROUND

The border town of Clones, 19 km south-west of Monaghan, was the site of an important 6th-century monastery which later became an Augustinian abbey. The bus stop and small tourist office are in the central Diamond or square. Clones is the birthplace of the former world-champion boxer, Barry McGuigan.

Things to See & Do

As well as the scant remains of the **abbey** founded by St Tiernach on Abbey St ,there is a truncated **round tower** in the old cemetery south of town; what is left of the round tower is just 22 metres high and the layout suggests it may be an early example from the 9th century. There's also a fine **high cross** in the town centre and the Protestant **St Tiernach's Church** looking out over the Diamond.

The Ulster Way in Northern Ireland runs through **Newtownbutler** in Fermanagh, eight km to the north-west of Clones. North of Newtownbutler, there is a **scenic drive** from Derrnawilt to Lisnaskea. South-east of Clones, the road from Newbliss to Cootehill is quite pretty and takes you to the edge of **Bellamont Forest** which straddles the border with Cavan.

Places to Stay & Eat

The *Lennard Arms Hotel* (☎ 047-51075), on the Diamond, has 10 rooms with B&B for IR£15 or IR£17.50 with own bathroom. The *Lennard Arms* pub (☎ 047-51075), just off the Diamond, has B&B from IR£15 and is replete with Barry McGuigan memorabilia.

Creighton Hotel (☎ 047-51284), on Fermanagh St, is popular with anglers. It has 16 simple but comfortable rooms with bathroom at a reasonable IR£18.50 B&B per person. This is also a nice place for a snack or lunch.

For a real treat, *Hilton Park* (☎ 047-56007, fax 047-56033) is an ideal place to forget the 20th century and blow any spare cash that is weighing you down. Five km south along the L46 then L44 to Scotshouse, this country house has its own estate and serves top-class food in regal surroundings. Many of the ingredients are grown on the estate's organic farm (☎ 047-51023). B&B in splendid rooms is IR£38 to IR£55.50 per person and dinner for residents only is IR£22.50 or more.

Getting There & Away
Bus Éireann (☎ 047-82377) has buses from Clones through Monaghan Town and on to Dublin. Ulsterbus (☎ 01365-322633 in Enniskillen) has a number of daily buses on a route which takes in Monaghan Town, Clones, Enniskillen and Belfast. McConnon's (☎ 047-82020) has a daily bus between Clones, Monaghan, Carrickmacross and Dublin.

CARRICKMACROSS & AROUND
At one time a stronghold of the MacMahon clan, Carrickmacross owes its origins to the third earl of Essex, who was a favourite of Queen Elizabeth I and built a castle here in the 1630s. The site of the castle is now occupied by the St Louis Convent. An extensive hand-made lace industry helped the early English and Scottish planters to develop this pleasant little town, which consists of one wide street boasting some good Georgian houses and an old Protestant church.

Things to See & Do
There's **fishing** in many of the lakes around Carrickmacross including Loughs Capragh, Spring and Monalty, and in Lough Fea. Contact Jimmy MacMahon at the Carrick Sports Centre (☎ 042-61714) for information on where to fish. Lough Fea also has an adjacent mansion and demesne with oak parkland. Five km south-west along the R179 Kingscourt road is **Dun a Rí Forest Park** with trails and picnic spots.

Mannan Castle is an enormous and heavily overgrown motte-and-bailey, five km north-west of Carrickmacross in Donaghmoyne. This fortified Norman mound has fragments of a stone castle dating from the 12th century. Both structures were built by the Pipard family, who were given an estate here in 1186 by England's King John.

Places to Stay
Carrickmacross has lots of B&B accommodation to choose from. The *Shirley Arms* pub (☎ 042-63299), on Main St, has reasonable singles/doubles for IR£20/38 with bathroom. A farmhouse on the Kingscourt road south of town, *Arradale House* (☎ 042-61941) has six rooms all with bathroom for IR£17/30.

Things to Buy
The nuns of St Louis revived the lace-making craft at the end of the 19th century and today the local lace cooperative (☎ 042-62085/62506) runs the remaining small-scale lace industry. They have a display with some of their handiwork for sale in the Lace Gallery at the bottom of Main St.

When Di married Charles, her wedding gown was trimmed with Carrickmacross lace.

Getting There & Away
Seven Bus Éireann (☎ 047-82377) buses a day to Dublin (1¼ hours) pass through Carrickmacross, at least three on a Letterkenny to Dublin route, two on a Coleraine to Dublin route and one going between Clones and Dublin. Collins (☎ 042-61631) private bus company has four buses a day to Dublin, three on Sundays. McConnon's (☎ 047-82020) private bus service includes Carrickmacross on its Dublin to Monaghan and Clones route, which also passes through

Castleblayney, and has two daily buses Monday to Saturday.

The bus stop is outside O'Hanlon's shop on Main St.

INNISKEEN

The village of Inniskeen, birthplace of the poet Patrick Kavanagh (1905-67), is 10 km north-east of Carrickmacross. Patrick Kavanagh is buried in the local graveyard where his cross reads 'And pray for him who walked apart on the hills loving life's miracles'.

The **Patrick Kavanagh Literary Resource Centre** (☎ 042-78560), housed in the village's plain chapel, is open all year from 11 am to 5 pm Monday to Friday, from 2 to 7 pm on Saturday and Sunday. Nearby, the forlorn skeletal ruin of a **round tower** is all that is left of the 6th-century monastery of St Daig.

CASTLEBLAYNEY

Castleblayney, about half way between Carrickmacross and Monaghan Town on the N2, is nicely situated near Lough Muckno, County Monaghan's most expansive and most scenic lake. This small town takes its name from Sir Edward Blayney and his family who built their castle by the lake in 1622 and were responsible for the construction of the plain Georgian courthouse, Church of Ireland church and the former Catholic church - an uncommon gesture by a landowner at the time.

Blayney's Castle was sold in the last century to the Hope family and became Hope Castle. In the demesne is the **Lough Muckno Leisure Park** (☎ 042-46356), which has lakeshore and woodland trails as well as golf, cycling, canoeing, sailing and waterskiing. Accommodation is available in a 50-bed IHH *hostel* for IR£10; it's open April to October.

Getting There & Away

Castleblayney is on the main Monaghan Town to Dublin route, with seven buses daily in each direction. McConnon's (☎ 047-82020) private bus service also has a number

of daily buses from Clones and Monaghan through Castleblayney and on to Dublin. The bus stop is outside Hanratty's.

County Roscommon

County Roscommon (*Ros Comáin*) is more a transit route than a destination in itself, but apart from the lacklustre county town there are places well worth visiting. Strokestown has one of the more interestingly presented mansions in the country as well as a unique Famine Museum. Just south of the Sligo boundary, the town of Boyle is also worth a stop.

Much of its western border follows the River Suck, while its eastern border is formed by a number of loughs and the River Shannon which flows between them. Fishing is a major attraction.

STROKESTOWN

Strokestown, on the N5 between Longford Town and Tulsk, is about 18 km north-west of Roscommon Town.

An unnecessarily wide avenue leads to the arched entrance to **Strokestown Park House** (☎ 078-33013), built in the 1730s for Thomas Mahon, whose ancestors were granted a 12,000-hectare estate by Charles II after the Restoration. The architect was Richard Castle, who introduced the Palladian style into Ireland, gratifying the desire of the Anglo-Irish gentry for impressive family homes. By 1979, when the family sold up, the estate had dwindled to 120 hectares. *Woodbrook* (see the Books section in the Facts for the Visitor chapter) is the perfect book to read after a visit and is available here.

Even children will enjoy the tour, which takes in a schoolroom and a child's bedroom, complete with 19th-century toys and funny mirrors. The 45-minute tour provides a fascinating glimpse into the whole Anglo-Irish ascendancy and costs IR£3/1 (students £2). The house is open June to mid-September, from noon to 5 pm Tuesday to Sunday.

The fascinating material on the Great Irish

Famine is housed in the **Famine Museum** (☎ 078-33013) in the old stable yards.

When the potato crop failed in the 1840s, Major Denis Mahon (landlord of Strokestown at the time) and his land agent simply evicted the hundreds of starving peasants who could no longer contribute to the estate's coffers and chartered ships to transport them away from Ireland. These overcrowded 'coffin ships', which carried immigrants to the USA and elsewhere, resulted in more suffering and deaths. In 1847 Major Mahon was shot dead just outside the town and one of the documents on display is a newspaper account of how Patrick Hasty and Owen Beirne committed the deed. Their signed confession looks as dubious as the ones which convicted the Birmingham Six of terrorist outrages in Britain in the 1970s.

As well as depicting the famine and its causes, the material draws parallels with world hunger and poverty today. The Famine Museum is open mid-May to October, from 11 am to 5 pm Tuesday to Sunday. Admission is IR£2.50/1 (students £2).

Places to Stay
Church View House (☎ 078-33047) is a D&B four km east of town with singles/doubles for IR£16/32.

Getting There & Away
The Bus Éireann (☎ 071-60066) express bus from Sligo to Athlone (via Roscommon Town and Boyle) stops in Strokestown. If you're travelling by car from Roscommon Town or Sligo, turn east off the N61 at the village of Tulsk to get to Strokestown. The bus stop is outside Corcoran's.

BOYLE
Boyle (*Mainistir na Búille*) is in the north-west of the county at the foot of the Curlew Mountains, on the River Boyle between Lough Key and Lough Gara, and close to the Sligo border. The town's main attractions are the fine Boyle Abbey, the impressive Drumanone Dolmen just outside town and Lough Key Forest Park.

Information
The tourist office (☎ 079-62145), in King House on the corner where Military Rd meets Main St, is open 1 May to late September from 10 am to 5 pm Monday to Friday. The friendly tourist officer may be contacted (☎ 079-62249) outside office hours if necessary. The post office is on Carrick Rd, south of the river.

Boyle Abbey
Beside the N4, just to the east of Boyle, is one of the finer Cistercian abbeys in Ireland, with remains dating back to its 12th-century foundation by the austere monks from Mellifont in County Louth. In 1659 military forces occupied the abbey and turned it into a fort. Originally, the western side of the abbey was set aside for the monks' sleeping quarters; later, the military forces had a dog kennel built into the left side of the gatehouse entrance.

The interesting 13th-century nave, in the northern part of the abbey, has Gothic arches on one side which are narrower than the Romanesque arches on the other. The capitals are also distinctively different. On the southern side of the abbey, once the refectory area, there is a fine 16th-century stone chimney built after the monks left and the abbey became a fortified home. Edward King, whose death by drowning in 1637 inspired the English poet John Milton to compose *Lycidas*, is buried here.

The abbey is open daily from 9.30 am to 6.30 pm June to mid-September. Entry is IR£1/40p (family IR£3). It is possible to view the abbey at other times by asking for the keys from the neighbouring Abbey House guesthouse.

Drumanone Dolmen
The superb Drumanone Dolmen measures 4.5 by 3.3 metres and is one of the largest in Ireland. To get there, take Patrick St west out of town for two km, bear left at the junction sign for Lough Gara for another km, passing under a railway arch. A brown sign indicates the path across the railway line.

Lough Key Forest Park
This 350-hectare park (☎ 079-62363), on the N4 three km east of Boyle, was part of the

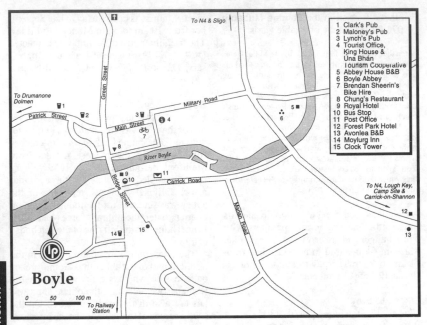

1 Clark's Pub
2 Maloney's Pub
3 Lynch's Pub
4 Tourist Office,
  King House &
  Una Bhán
  Tourism Cooperative
5 Abbey House B&B
6 Boyle Abbey
7 Brendan Sheerin's
  Bike Hire
8 Chung's Restaurant
9 Royal Hotel
10 Bus Stop
11 Post Office
12 Forest Park Hotel
13 Avonlea B&B
14 Moylurg Inn
15 Clock Tower

Boyle

CENTRAL NORTH

Rockingham estate until it was sold to the Land Commission in 1957. Rockingham House was destroyed by a fire in the same year; all that remains are some stables and other outbuildings. The inexpensive café is open 12.30 to 6 pm and in summer there is a restaurant for lunch and dinner. Lough Key is at the northern limit for cruising on the Shannon. Rowing boats are available for a pricey IR£6 an hour. The park is open daily year round and entry costs IR£1.

Organised Tours
The Úna Bhán Tourism Cooperative (☎ 079-63033), whose office is in the grounds of King House, organises week-long cycling, horse-riding and fishing tours that include accommodation on a working farm. Contact Ruth Moran for details.

Places to Stay
Camping The *Lough Key Forest Caravan Park* (☎ 079-62363) is in the Forest Park, so

indicate your intention to camp to avoid the IR£1 entrance charge. Camping costs IR£7.25 for a family tent, or IR£2.50 per hiker, cyclist or motorcyclist; electricity is an extra IR£1.50.

B&Bs *Lynch's* pub, right in town on Main St, has plain but adequate rooms at IR£15 without bath. The better located – beside the abbey and river – but slightly more expensive *Abbey House* (☎ 079-62385) charges IR£18.50 per person for rooms with bath. At *Avonlea* (☎ 079-62538), on the N4 just outside the town and opposite the Forest Park Hotel, rates are IR£19.50 with bath. Three km further south on the N4, Mrs Kelly in *Forest Park House* (☎ 079-62227) offers B&B for IR£18.

Hotels The 18th-century *Royal Hotel* (☎ 079-62016) in town, has rooms with bath for IR£33.50 per person, while the *Forest*

Park Hotel (☎ 079-62229), just outside town on the N4, charges IR£50.

Places to Eat

The *Royal* and *Forest Park* hotels do lunch and dinner, while *Lynch's* pub on Main St does coffee and snacks. Farther along in Patrick St, reasonable pub food is available at *Maloney's*. Overlooking the river, *Chung's* Chinese restaurant is open Friday to Wednesday from 5.30 pm.

Entertainment

The *Railway Bar* near the station, *Clark's* in Patrick St, and the *Moylurg Inn* near the clock tower have music and a decent drop of Guinness.

Getting There & Away

From outside the Royal Hotel on Bridge St the Bus Éireann (☎ 071-60066) express bus leaves once daily to Sligo (40 minutes) and Dublin (3¼ hours). From Boyle, a train goes three times daily (four on Friday) between Sligo (40 minutes) and Dublin (2¼ hours) via Mullingar.

Getting Around

You can hire bikes from Brendan Sheerin's cycle shop (☎ 079-62010) in Main St for IR£7/35 daily/weekly.

ROSCOMMON TOWN

The small county town of Roscommon, sitting at the crossroads of several major highways, has a few sights of interest that make it worth a stopover. It gets its name from 'Ros', meaning wooded height, and St Coman who was the see's first bishop.

Things to See

The Norman **Roscommon Castle** built in 1269 was almost immediately destroyed by Irish forces, and rebuilt in 1280. The mullioned windows were added in the 16th century and the massive walls and round bastions give it an impressive look, standing alone in a field at the north end of town.

At the other end of town are the remains of a 13th-century **Dominican priory**, the most notable feature of which is an effigy of the founder, carved around 1300; it's set in the north wall near where the altar stood.

The town square's Bank of Ireland used to be the **courthouse**. Close by is the **old gaol**, where executions were carried out by 'Lady Betty'. She had herself been condemned to death after confessing to the murder of a lodger in her house, who turned out to be her own son. She escaped death by offering to take over from the incapacitated executioner.

French Park, about 1½ km outside Roscommon, is home to the **Douglas Hyde Interpretive Centre**. Hyde was one of the founding members of the Gaelic League and was later elected the first president of the Republic in 1938. He is buried nearby.

Places to Stay

The *Gailey Bay Caravan & Camping Park* (☎ 0903-61058) is in Knockcroghery beside Lough Rea about 10 km south of Roscommon Town on the N61 to Athlone; a sign points east just near the railway station and it's a couple of km up the road. A tent is IR£4 plus IR£1 per person; IR£3 for a hiker or cyclist.

In Roscommon Town, the *Royal Hotel* (☎ 0903-26317), in Castle St, has rooms with shower and toilet for IR£35 per person and is also the best place for a meal. On the Galway road there are B&Bs such as Mrs Campbell's *Westway* (☎ 0903-26927) with singles/doubles for IR£12/22 with separate bathroom, and Mrs O'Grady's *The Villa* (☎ 0903-26048) from IR£15/24.

Getting There & Away

Bus Éireann (☎ 071-60066) express buses stop in the town three times daily (once on Sunday) between Westport (2¼ hours) and Dublin (2¾ hours). Roscommon Town is also served by trains three times daily (four on Friday) on the Dublin (two hours) to Westport (1½ hours) line.

WEST ROSCOMMON

The village of Ballintober (*Bail an Tobair*), about 15 km north-west of Roscommon Town off the N60, is dominated by the

14th-century **Ballintober Castle**, once the home of the fierce O'Conors of Connaught. Cromwellian forces took the castle in 1652 but it was later restored, only to be lost again after the defeat of the Catholics at the Battle of the Boyne in 1690. The large central courtyard has polygonal towers at each corner and the whole edifice is a good example of an early Irish castle.

Further west past Castlerea on the N60, the 1878 **Clonalis House** (☎ 0907-20014) is open to the public May to September from 11 am to 5.30 pm Monday to Saturday (2 to 6 pm Sunday) for IR£2. The house is rather cold and lacks atmosphere, but it does have the harp of Turlough O'Carolan (1630-1738), the great blind harpist and composer, and a copy of the last Brehon Law (Irish common law dating back to pre-Christian times) judgement handed down in 1580.

County Leitrim

Leitrim stretches 80 km from the border with Longford to Donegal Bay in the north-west, with a short coastline of about five km around Tulloghan. Lough Allen splits the county in two; the attractions in the northern part with its mountains and glens are more accessible from Sligo and are covered in the Sligo chapter. The southern part of Leitrim's main interest is its lush scenery of lakes and drumlins, but while a walking or cycling tour of the area would be enjoyable most visitors just speed through on their way north.

CARRICK-ON-SHANNON

Carrick-on-Shannon (also known simply as Carrick, or in Irish as *Cora Droma Rúisc*), on the border with Roscommon and the main town in the county, marks the upper limit of navigation on the River Shannon. Apart from boating and fishing trips, there is little to keep the visitor here.

Information

The tourist office (☎ 078-20170), on West Quay beside Carrick Bridge, is open May to September from 9 am to 1 pm Monday to Thursday and from 9.30 to 1 pm on Friday. During the rest of the year, tourist information (☎ 078-20857) is available from an office in the old town hall. A signposted walking tour takes in all the buildings and places of local interest.

Costello Chapel

At the top of Bridge St, next to Flynn's bar, is the spooky little Costello Chapel. It measures only five by 3.6 metres and was built in 1877 by the distraught Edward Costello after the death of his wife. She is buried on the left side under a heavy slab of glass and her husband was interred on the other side in 1891. Further intimations of mortality come from the fact that the chapel was built on the site of the old courthouse where 19 men were hung in the 19th century.

Boating

Michael Lynch (☎ 078-20034), based near the tourist office, has rowing boats for hire at IR£6 an hour, or between IR£20 and IR£30 a day with a motor. Barges for hire are available through Shannon Barge Lines (☎ 078-20520) while Tara Cruisers (☎ 078-20736), based at the Rosebank Marina on the Dublin road, have more upmarket launches.

Places to Stay

Camping is free on the river bank near the tourist office. Tokens for the showers at the nearby marina can be purchased from the marina office. The IHH *Town Clock Hostel* (☎ 078-20068), in the town centre at the junction of Main and Bridge Sts, has dorm beds for IR£5 and is open May to the end of August.

Carrick has lots of B&Bs. On Station Rd, near the railway station on the Roscommon side of the river, *Villa Flora* (☎ 078-20338) and *Ariadna* (☎ 078-20205) both cost IR£18 per person for rooms with separate bathroom. The *Bush Hotel* (☎ 078-20114), in the centre of town, has B&B with own bathroom from IR£26 per person.

Places to Eat

On the corner near the bridge and tourist office, *Coffey's* is a busy, inexpensive self-service place. Next door *Cryan's* pub does a IR£2.95 lunch. On Bridge St *Mariner's Reach* has lunch specials for IR£2.50 to IR£3.50, but even better is the four-course bar special until 10 pm for IR£5. Just past Geraghty's bike shop on Main St the *Coffee Shop* in the Bush Hotel is another reasonably priced place for coffee and light meals.

Getting There & Away

The bus stop is outside Coffey's self-service restaurant on the corner near the bridge and tourist office. Bus Éireann's (☎ 071-60066) main Dublin (three hours) to Sligo (one hour) express bus stops there three times daily in each direction. There are also buses to Limerick, Cork, Waterford, Galway, Belfast and Derry.

The railway station (☎ 078-20036) is a 15-minute walk from the bridge on the Roscommon side of the river. Turn right over the bridge, then left at the service station. Carrick has three trains daily to Dublin (2¼ hours) and Sligo (one hour), four on Friday.

Getting Around

You can hire bikes from Geraghty's (☎ 078-21316), on Main St, for IR£6/25 per day/week; they also rent out rods and tackle on a daily or weekly basis. The visitor's guidebook from the tourist office includes details of suggested cycling tours.

AROUND CARRICK-ON-SHANNON

The countryside around Carrick with its quiet lanes and gently undulating landscape makes cycling a good way of getting around.

Turlough O'Carolan

There are two places to visit in Leitrim connected with the famous blind poet, composer and harpist, Turlough O'Carolan (1670-1738). He is buried in **Kilronan church**, which preserves a 12th-century doorway. To reach the church, take the R280 north from Carrick-on-Shannon and at the village of Leitrim turn left (west) on the R284 to Keadue (also spelt Keadew). In Keadue turn left (west) on the R284 to Sligo.

O'Carolan spent most of his time in **Mohill** where his patron, Mrs MacDermot Roe, was based and a sculpture on the main street of the town commemorates the association. To reach Mohill from Carrick-on-Shannon, follow the N4 to Dublin then turn left (east) shortly after Drumsna onto the R201.

Lough Rynn Estate

Lough Rynn, south of Mohill, was the home of the Clements family, the earls of Leitrim; and the various 19th-century buildings put up during the time of the third earl are open to the public. Within the wooded estate (☎ 078-31427) there's a picnic site, restaurant and guided tours of the principal buildings. It's open daily May to the end of August from 10 am to 7 pm. Admission to the grounds is IR£3.50 per car, IR£1.50 per person and the tour is another IR£1/50p.

Drumshanbo

Drumshanbo, about nine km north of Carrick-on-Shannon on the southern shores of Lough Allen, is mainly a centre for coarse fishing. The Sliath an Larainn Visitor Centre (☎ 078-41522) has an interesting audiovisual display (IR£1/50p) on the history and culture of the locality, and a non-functioning replica of an ancient Irish sweathouse (similar to a sauna). The centre is open April

The Sweathouse

Sweathouses, used to help cure aches and pains, were built of stone with a small opening or doorway. A turf fire would be lit inside for several hours and when the sweathouse was sufficiently hot the fire was removed. The patient would then go inside and sit or lie on a pile of rushes or straw until they felt they had sweated enough. They would then emerge and take a dip in a nearby cold running stream. ∎

CENTRAL NORTH

to October from 10 am to 6 pm Monday to Saturday, 2 to 6 pm on Sunday.

Mrs Mooney (☎ 078-41013), 2 Carrick Rd, on the left if you're entering town from Carrick-on-Shannon, does B&B for IR£11 per person, and provides tourist information.

SHANNON-ERNE WATERWAY

The Shannon-Erne Waterway stretches from the River Shannon beside the village of Leitrim four km north of Carrick-on-Shannon, through north-west County Cavan to the southern shore of Upper Lough Erne, just over the border in County Fermanagh. The 240-km waterway is a series of rivers and lakes linked by canal. The original canal, named the Ballinamore-Ballyconnell Canal, was completed in 1860, but soon fell into disuse with the coming of the railway. Today, the waterway with its 34 stone bridges and 16 locks is busy with boats and pleasure cruisers. Emerald Star (☎ 01-679 8166), 47 Dawson St, Dublin 2, rents cruisers on the waterway.

The waterway is jointly operated by the OPW in the South and the Department of Agriculture in Northern Ireland.

LEITRIM WAY

The Leitrim Way begins in Drumshanbo and finishes in Manorhamilton, a distance of 48 km. See the Activities chapter for details.

County Longford

County Longford's (*An Longfort*) history dates back to prehistoric times; St Patrick visited here and for centuries it was the centre of power of the O'Farrell family who arrived in the 11th century. During the 1798 Rising, the British army under Lord Cornwallis defeated a combined Irish and French army at Ballinamuck, 16 km north of Longford Town. The famine of the 1840s saw large-scale emigration and many Longford migrants went to Argentina, where one of their descendants, Edel Miro O'Farrell, became president of that country in 1914.

Longford Town is solidly agrarian and very prosperous, to judge by the number of restaurants and hotels, but of little interest to the tourist; many people pass through travelling between Dublin and Mayo or Sligo. Carriglass Manor (☎ 043-45165), five km north-east, has been the home of the Huguenot Lefroy family since 1810, and is open to the public in summer.

The Royal Canal from Dublin passes through the county to meet the River Shannon near Cloondara west of Longford Town. The canal's towpath provides an interesting walking route through the county.

The main attraction for most visitors to County Longford, however, is the fishing around Lough Ree and Lanesborough.

LANESBOROUGH

Also spelt Lanesboro, this small town is the site of one of Ireland's first turf-fired generating stations, which dominates the skyline. It's close to the banks of the River Shannon and provides a flow of warm water into a channel. When the mayfly appear in May, then later in August and September, this stretch of water becomes prime angling territory. Bream and tench are caught early in the morning and at night, while roach are available throughout the day. The water is only just over a metre deep. This is not the only place to fish and enquiries should be made at the Pricewyse tackle shop in the middle of Lanesborough. You can hire boats from Mark Shields at MJS Motorcycles (☎ 043-21510) on Main St.

The river divides County Longford from County Roscommon and the town is linked by bridge to Ballyleague on the Roscommon side.

Places to Stay

B&B is available at *Dunamase House* (☎ 043-21201), on Rathcline Rd south-east of the centre of Lanesborough, for IR£18.50/27 a single/double. In Ballyleague, *Noreen Dunne* (☎ 043-21150) runs a friendly place and has rooms with separate bathroom for IR£12 per person; there's a TV room downstairs.

The *Flagship Restaurant* (see Places to Eat) has a room in a house beside the river at IR£17.50 per person. The only hotel is the somewhat run-down *Sliabh Bán* (☎ 043-21790), also known as the Anchor, with rooms at IR£15 per person including B&B. Self-catering accommodation is available through the *Lough Ree Arms* pub (☎ 043-21145).

Places to Eat
The *Flagship Restaurant*, on a converted barge on the river is a good friendly place, open from 8 am to 10 pm; fish with salad and chips is IR£7 and it does snacks as well. *Samantha's* café, good for coffee and sandwiches, and the *Upper Deck Restaurant* are both on Main St. The *Lough Ree Arms* does reasonable pub food.

Getting There & Away
Lanesborough is on the N63, halfway between the towns of Longford and Roscommon. The nearest bus and railway stations are at these two towns. Coming from Athlone follow the N55 into County Longford then turn left (north-west) at Ballymahon.

County Westmeath

Characterised by lakes and rich pasture land, the county of Westmeath is more noteworthy for its beef than its scenic splendour or historic sites. An exception to the lacklustre landscape is an area north of Athlone, known as Goldsmith Country, while the places of genuine interest in Westmeath – and there are some – are mostly in the vicinity of Mullingar.

MULLINGAR
Mullingar (*An Muileann gCearr*) is a prosperous marketing town, with a commuter train service each morning to Dublin, and much of the surrounding area is rather like the rich countryside of England. There are some fine fishing loughs in the vicinity and a preserved bog that delights naturalists. The town itself is one of the few places outside the capital that James Joyce visited. There are also three private museums, each with their own low-key appeal, and Mullingar makes a good base for some interesting local excursions.

The Royal Canal, linking Dublin with the River Shannon via Mullingar, was constructed in the 1790s as a rival to the Grand Canal. It never managed to compete successfully with its rival, and, by the 1880s, passenger business had ceased. There was a slight revival during WW II with a turf trade to Dublin, but it finally closed in 1955. Plans to build a motorway to Dublin over the canal course were shelved and restoration work west of Mullingar is in progress.

Information
The main tourist office (☎ 044-48761), on the Dublin road on the outskirts of town, is open Easter to the end of September from 9 am to 1 pm and 2 to 5.30 pm Monday to Friday. Another tourist office (☎ 044-44044), operated by the local chamber of commerce, is in town next to the Market House Museum. It's open year round Monday to Friday from 9.30 am to 5.30 pm, Saturday and Sunday from 10 am to 1 pm and 1.30 to 4 pm. The post office (☎ 044-48563) is on Dominick St.

Cathedral & Ecclesiastical Museum
The Cathedral of Christ the King was built just before WW II and has large mosaics of St Anne and St Patrick by the Russian artist Boris Arrep. There is a small museum over the sacristy, entered from the side of the church, which has vestments worn by St Oliver Plunkett (see Drogheda in the Meath & Louth chapter for the whereabouts of his head).

Guided tours (IR£1/50p) operate between 3 and 6 pm on Thursday, Saturday and Sunday. Otherwise call at the church house to the right of the cathedral inside the gates or phone ☎ 044-48338.

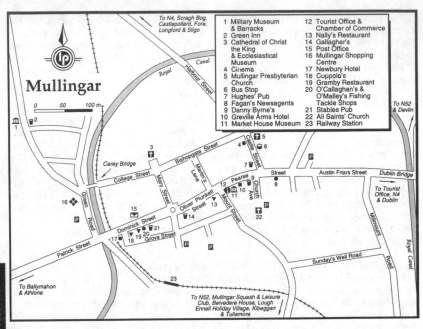

Mullingar

To N4, Scragh Bog, Castlepollard, Fore, Longford & Sligo

1 Military Museum & Barracks
2 Green Inn
3 Cathedral of Christ the King & Ecclesiastical Museum
4 Cinema
5 Mullingar Presbyterian Church
6 Bus Stop
7 Hughes' Pub
8 Fagan's Newsagents
9 Danny Byrne's
10 Greville Arms Hotel
11 Market House Museum
12 Tourist Office & Chamber of Commerce
13 Nally's Restaurant
14 Gallagher's
15 Post Office
16 Mullingar Shopping Centre
17 Newbury Hotel
18 Coppola's
19 Gramby Restaurant
20 O'Callaghan's & O'Malley's Fishing Tackle Shops
21 Stables Pub
22 All Saints' Church
23 Railway Station

To N52 & Devlin

To Tourist Office, N4 & Dublin

To Ballymahon & Athlone

To N52, Mullingar Squash & Leisure Club, Belvedere House, Lough Ennell Holiday Village, Kibeggan & Tullamore

Military Museum & Barracks

The Columb Barracks (☎ 044-48391) were built by the British in 1813 and the museum is just inside the main entrance on the right, in what were once the punishment cells. The museum is home to a delightful miscellany of artefacts, including army chamber pots and a weighing chair for recruits. Entry is free but you need to call ahead first.

The barracks and museum can be reached by taking College St past the cathedral, crossing the canal by the small Carey Bridge and walking across the road toward the church spire; or alternatively by turning right into Green Rd off the main street and following the road round to the left past Mullingar Shopping Centre. The entrance is opposite the Green Inn.

Market House Museum

Market House Museum (☎ 041-48152), on Pearse St, has an even odder collection, including axe-heads, fossils, a German army

helmet, a rubber bullet from the North, a shillelagh, a stone hot water bottle and a grand butter churn. It's open mid-May to mid-September from 2 to 5.30 pm Tuesday to Saturday. Entry is 50p/20p, but call first to make an appointment.

Activities

A visitors' fee of IR£3 opens the doors of the Mullingar Squash & Leisure Club (☎ 044-40949), Lynn Industrial Estate, which offers squash, sauna, snooker and indoor bowls. Or you can go swimming at the local swimming pool (☎ 044-40488), off Austin Friars St, for IR£1.70.

Festivals

The Mullingar Festival (☎ 044-44044) is usually held in the second week of July. It is a low-key affair, the highlight of which is the election of the Queen and the Bachelor of the Festival. Later in the month there is a two-day Agricultural Show.

The Joyce Connection

James Joyce came to Mullingar in his late teens in 1900 and 1901 to visit his father, John Joyce, who had been sent to the town to compile a new electoral register. John Joyce worked in the Courthouse, which is still standing in Mount St, and the Joyces stayed at Levington Park House near Lough Owel.

Parts of *Stephen Hero*, an early novel that would later become *A Portrait of the Artist as a Young Man*, are set in Mullingar. The Greville Arms Hotel is mentioned, as are the *Westmeath Examiner* office, the Royal Canal and the Military Barracks (where the military museum is situated). In the lobby of the Greville Arms there is a wax model of Joyce.

In *Ulysses*, Leopold Bloom's daughter, Millie, is working in Mullingar, employed in a photographer's shop. This is now Fagan's newsagents and sub-post-office on Pearse St near the junction with Castle St, but at the time of Joyce's visits it was owned by a photographer, Phil Shaw. Mullingar also makes brief appearances in *Finnegans Wake*. ■

Places to Stay

Camping at *Lough Ennell Holiday Village* (☎ 044-48101), eight km south of town on the N52 road to Tullamore, costs IR£4 per person and it can get busy on sunny weekends. Most of the B&Bs are on the approach roads from Dublin and Sligo. *Woodside* (☎ 044-41636) has singles/doubles from IR£15/28 and *Moorlands* (☎ 044-40905) charges IR£18/30 for rooms with bath. Both are on the Dublin road. The *Newbury Hotel* (☎ 044-42888) on Dominick St costs IR£20/36, or there's the more expensive *Greville Arms Hotel* (☎ 044-48563), on Pearse St, which has singles/doubles from IR£35/60.

Places to Eat

Coppola's, next to the Newbury Hotel, offers takeaways. At *Nally's Restaurant*, 9 Oliver Plunkett St, main meals are around IR£4 to IR£5 during the day, but the evening à la carte menu is a little more expensive; there is a good vegetarian selection. The *Gramby Restaurant*, on Dominick St, is a little more upmarket and is open daily from 8 am to 10 pm. The bar food in the *Greville Arms*, on Pearse St, is good and they have a *James Joyce Restaurant* with dinner for around IR£16. *Gallagher's* pub, on Oliver Plunkett St, has a lunch time house special of soup with a brown scone for IR£1.30.

Entertainment

Hughes' pub, on the corner of Castle and Pearse Sts, has traditional music on Wednesday night and jazz on Thursday, while the *Stables* in Dominick St attracts blues bands. *Danny Byrne's* has music on Thursday and Sunday nights and a wide selection of beers. The *Greville Arms Hotel* has dancing on Sunday night, and for country & western fans American line dancing with lessons on Monday night.

Getting There & Away

Bus Éireann (☎ 01-836 6111) runs two daily buses from Galway (three hours) to Dundalk (2¼ hours), five from Dublin (1½ hours) to Ballina (2¾ hours), and three from Dublin to Sligo (2½ hours) – all stopping at Mullingar. They depart and arrive from opposite the cinema in Castle St.

Trains stop at Mullingar (☎ 044-48274) four times daily in each direction on the Dublin (one hour) to Sligo (two hours) line.

AROUND MULLINGAR
Belvedere House & Gardens

Belvedere was the scene of a tale which finds its way into Joyce's *Ulysses*.

The house was built around 1740 for the recently remarried Lord Belfield, first earl of Belvedere. He soon accused his young wife of adultery with his younger brother Arthur, and imprisoned her here. She remained under house arrest for 31 years. When the earl of Belvedere's death finally released her she was still dressed in the fashion of 30 years earlier. She died still protesting her innocence. Belvedere also sued his brother and had him jailed in London for the rest of his life.

Not far from the house, the **Jealous Wall** was deliberately built by Lord Belfield as a ready-made 'ruin' to block a view of the neighbouring house of a second brother, George, with whom he also fell out. Belvedere House & Gardens (☎ 044-40861) are 5.5 km south of town on the N52 road to Tullamore, just before Lough Ennell Holiday Village. The house itself is closed; entrance to the gardens is IR£1. Opening hours are April to October from 9 am to 6 pm Monday to Saturday, from 10 am to 6 pm Sunday; November to March from 10 am to 4.30 pm Monday to Saturday, from 2 to 6 pm Sunday.

Locke's Distillery

Sixteen km south-west of Mullingar on the N52 road to Tullamore past Belvedere House & Gardens, Locke's Distillery (☎ 0506-32134) in the small town of Kilbeggan still has a working mill wheel. Open from 9 am (10 am on Sunday) to 6 pm daily the IR£2/1 tour concludes with the customary glass of malt whiskey. Lunch and snacks are served at the adjoining coffee shop.

Crookedwood & Around

Crookedwood, about five km north-east of Mullingar off the R394, is a small village on the shores of Lough Derravaragh. The lough is associated with the tragic legend of the Children of Lir who were transformed into swans by a jealous stepmother.

Two ecclesiastical sights near Crookedwood are worth a visit. Three km west is the **Multyfarnham Franciscan Friary**. In the present church, parts of a 15th-century church remain and there are outdoor Stations of the Cross set beside a stream.

East of Crookedwood, a small road leads up two km to **St Munna's Church**. It dates from the 15th century, replacing an earlier 7th-century church founded by St Munna. This fortified church has a lovely location and there is a grotesque figure over the north window. Keys to the church are available from the nearby bungalow.

Scragh Bog

Scragh Bog is a nature reserve and home to the rare wintergreen, *Pyrola rotundifolia*, which flowers around willow and beech trees in midsummer. Other, less rare plants are members of the sedge family, orchids and sphagnum species, and there is a profusion of insects. This small bog is seven km north-west of Mullingar near Lough Owel on the

Adolphus Cooke the Eccentric

Mullingar was home not only to the paranoiac Lord Belvedere, but also to the bizarre Adolphus Cooke. This character served under Wellington and survived a shipwreck and a desert island before becoming convinced that his grandfather had been reborn as a turkey. Later, he sentenced his dog to death for its loose morals, but when the executioner was attacked by the turkey he realised that the dog was probably also related to him and granted it a reprieve. He wanted his library and favourite chair to be buried with him, and his extraordinary grave is tucked away in a fading Protestant churchyard outside Mullingar. He thought he might be reborn as a bee.

To get there, take the N52 road to Devlin for 12 km until, after passing a small number of houses, you come to a junction with a sign pointing straight on to Kells. Follow this road for another half km and turn into the fancy arched entrance on the left to the Bee Hive Nite Club. Pass the first sheepgate immediately on the right, but cross over the second black gate just after it. Follow the side of the field under the trees and the old church is about 200 metres along. The unmistakeable beehive grave is easily found. ■

N4 road to Longford. The Wildlife Service does not recommend unaccompanied visits and waterproof boots are a necessity.

Tullynally Castle & Gardens

This family seat of the Pakenham family and the earldom of Longford is another pretend castle. The original fortress was converted into a house in the first half of the 18th century and various additions were made over the next 150 years. The most notable feature is the extensive Gothic facade which is visually impressive despite the crooked TV aerial and satellite dish. The laundry is wonderfully preserved and there are many workaday items worth examining.

The house is open daily mid-June to mid-August from 2 to 6 pm with the first tour beginning at 2.30 pm. The charge is IR£3.50/2 and this includes admission to the 12 hectares of gardens and parkland which are open separately May to September from 10 am to 6 pm for IR£2/50p. It might be worth telephoning (☎ 044-61159) at other times about the possibility of going round with a coach tour.

Take the N4 north-west out of Mullingar then follow the R394 road right (north) to Castlepollard. From there the castle and gardens are signposted two km north-west.

Fishing

Trout fishing is popular in loughs around Mullingar, including Lough Owel, Lough Derravaragh, Lough Glore, White Lake, Lough Lene, Lough Sheelin, Mt Dalton Lake, Pallas Lake and Lough Ennell – where in 1894 an 11.7-kg trout was landed, still the largest trout ever caught in Ireland. The fishing season is March or May (depending on the lake) to mid-October, and all the lakes except Lough Lene are controlled by the Shannon Regional Fisheries Board; you can get details from Limerick City (☎ 061-55171) or Mullingar (☎ 044-48769). For further information contact the tourist offices in Mullingar, O'Callaghan's or O'Malley's on Dominick St or Sam's Tackle Shop on Castle St. Sam's can provide boats on Lough Owel or Lough Ennell, *ghillies* (a

guide) and permits. For Lough Derravaragh contact Mr Newman (☎ 044-71111), for Lough Owel contact Mrs Doolan (☎ 044-42085), and for Lough Ennell contact Mrs Hope (☎ 044-40807).

Swimming

Swimming is possible in Loughs Lene, Ennel and Owel, but Derravaragh is very deep and has no shallows.

FORE VALLEY

Just outside the small village of Fore, in the north-east of the county near the shores of Lough Lene, lies a group of early Christian sites that date back to 630 AD when St Fetchin founded a monastery. There are no visible remains of this early settlement, but there are three later buildings still standing in the valley plain, and they are closely associated with a legend that Seven Wonders occurred here.

The Fore Valley is a great area to explore by bicycle or on foot.

The Seven Wonders

The oldest of the three buildings is **St Fetchin's Church**, which may well mark the original monastery. The chancel and baptismal font inside are early 13th century, and over the unusually large entrance there is a huge lintel stone carved with a Greek cross. It was supposed to have been placed through the divine power of St Fetchin's prayers and as such it makes up one of the Seven Wonders of Fore.

A path runs up from the church to the attractive little **Anchorite's Cell**, which dates back to the 15th century and is another of the Seven Wonders. The Seven Wonders pub in the village keeps the key to the cell.

Down on the plain, on the other side of the road, there are extensive remains of a 13th-century **Benedictine priory**, built on what was once bog (another Wonder). In the next century it was turned into a fortification; hence the castle-like square towers, each of which formed a separate residence, and loophole windows. The west tower is in a dangerous state – keep clear. Two other

Wonders are a mill without a stream and water that flows uphill. The mill site is marked and legend has it that St Fetchin caused water to flow uphill, towards the mill, by throwing his crozier against a rock near Lough Lene, about 1.5 km away.

The final two Wonders, incidentally, are water that will not boil and a tree which will not burn. Both are associated with St Fetchin's well which is passed on the way to the friary from the road.

To get to the Fore Valley from Mullingar take the take the N4 north-west out of Mullingar then follow the R394 road right (north) to Castlepollard. From there the road to Fore is signposted.

ATHLONE

Despite its historic importance, due mainly to its strategic position midway on the River Shannon, the county town of Athlone (*Baile Átha Luain*) is a fairly ordinary place; there's more life and interest in Mullingar. It does, however, have a number of attractions, mostly out of town. A visit to the castle is worth considering and there are fishing and boat trips along the river to Lough Ree or to Clonmacnois.

Orientation & Information

Athlone is in the far south-west of Westmeath on the border with Roscommon. It's on the main Dublin to Galway road (the N6) and the River Shannon flows north through town into Lough Ree. The obvious landmarks in town are Athlone Castle and St Peter & Paul Cathedral, prominently located on the west bank of the river by the bridge and overlooking Market Square. The castle contains the tourist office and museum. Cars can be parked behind the castle down by the river without the usual parking discs.

The tourist office (☎ 0902-94630) is open April to October from 9.30 am to 5.30 pm Monday to Saturday and is just inside the castle grounds. The office has a Tourist Trail booklet that offers the reader a choice of a three-hour walk, or two 1½-hour walks. The local chamber of commerce has an information office (☎ 0902-73173) open year round

at the Jolly Mariner Marina by the river on the east bank.

The post office is on Barrack St beside the cathedral.

Athlone Castle & Museum

The Normans probably had a camp by the ford over the river before they built a castle here in 1210. In 1690 the castle held out for James II, but the following year the bridge came under determined Protestant attack, and this time the Jacobite city fell to the troops under William of Orange's Dutch commander, Ginkel. The Jacobites retreated to Aughrim and were decisively defeated there by Ginkel. Major alterations took place between the 17th and 19th centuries and the ramp that forms the present entrance is one of these relatively recent additions. The oldest surviving part is the central keep where the museum now is.

Athlone Museum has two floors, the upstairs being designated a folk museum, containing a fascinating miscellany of objects. Downstairs has artefacts from prehistoric times. There's also an old gramophone which belonged to John McCormack (1884-1945), a native of Athlone and arguably the world's greatest tenor. The gramophone is in working order and there are records of his songs which you can ask to be played.

The museum is open daily April to October from 10.30 to 4.30 pm and entry is IR£2.50/80p (students IR£1.50, family IR£6). The price includes a visit to the **interpretive centre** which is an audiovisual presentation of the town's history and flora & fauna.

Fishing

Just below the Church St end of the bridge on the east bank opposite the castle, the Strand Tackle Shop is the place to go for information, boats and rods. A day's hire of boat and guide for mostly pike fishing would cost around IR£80. You can fish for free along the Strand.

River Cruises

Several companies offer cruises from Athlone. Between July and September, Rosanna Cruises (☎ 0909-92513) has a Wednesday cruise on its Viking ship south to Clonmacnois, the ancient monastic site in County Offaly. It costs IR£6/4, and departs at 10 am. Every day of the week there are cruises north to Lough Ree for IR£4/2.50. The first boat leaves the Strand at 11 am and a timetable is available from the tourist office.

Getting There & Away

The Bus Éireann depot (☎ 0902-73322) is beside the railway station and express buses stop there on many routes from the east to the west coast. There are eight buses daily to Dublin (two hours) and Galway (1½ hours), three to Westport (2¾ hours) and two to Mullingar (one hour).

From Athlone Railway Station (☎ 0902-72651) there are three daily trains to Westport (two hours) in County Mayo, seven to Galway (70 minutes) and up to 11 to Dublin (1½ hours). The railway station is on the east bank. To get there, take Northgate St north off Costume Place then, near St Vincent's Hospital, turn right into Southern Station Rd.

Getting Around

Bicycles can be hired for IR£9/30 per day/week from Hardiman's (☎ 0902-78669), opposite the Athlone Shopping Centre on the road out of town to Dublin.

AROUND ATHLONE
Lough Ree

Just north of Athlone, Lough Ree, one of the three main lakes formed by the River Shannon, is noted for the historical monastic remains on its many islands and for the excellent trout fishing.

It is also home to many migratory birds who come here to nest; particularly swans, plovers, mallard ducks and curlews to name a few of the more common ones.

Sailing is popular and the Lough Ree Yacht Club (☎ 0902-75976), established in 1770, is one of the world's oldest.

Goldsmith Country

From Athlone the N55 north-west to County Longford runs close to the eastern side of Lough Ree and through Goldsmith Country, so called because of the area's associations with the 18th-century poet, playwright and novelist, Oliver Goldsmith. The gentle aspect of the landscape makes it ideal for cycling.

Cycling Tour

The following tour pretty much follows the signposted Lough Ree Trail, a booklet for which is available from the tourist office in Athlone.

Five km north-west of Athlone, the road comes to the village of Ballykeeran to the west of which is the Lough Ree Caravan Park. About three km further is the village of Glasson (or Glassan), which Swift called Auburn in his poem *The Deserted Village*. Just north of the village a left turning goes to the Killinure spur on the shore of Lough Ree. The turning is marked by No 8 on the Lough Ree Trail roadsign and it is 2.5 km to a junction, marked as No 11 on the tourist trail road sign. From there, another left goes down to the marina at Killinure where you can rent boats.

Back at the No 11 junction the road continues north for another 2.5 km to a junction, No 14 on the tourist trail signs. Turning left leads to Manto's pub (by the shore opposite Inchmore Island) where you can hire boats. Turning right at No 14 leads after three km to the village of Tubberclaire (or Tuberclare), which takes its name from a holy well, back on the N55.

Continuing north the road leads into Goldsmith Country proper, with the reminders and remains of:

The never-failing brook, the busy mill,
The decent church that topt the neighbouring hill.

Only the site remains of the schoolhouse where the young Goldsmith and his fellow pupils wondered at the wisdom of their teacher:

And still they gazed, and still the wonder grew
That one small head could carry all he knew.

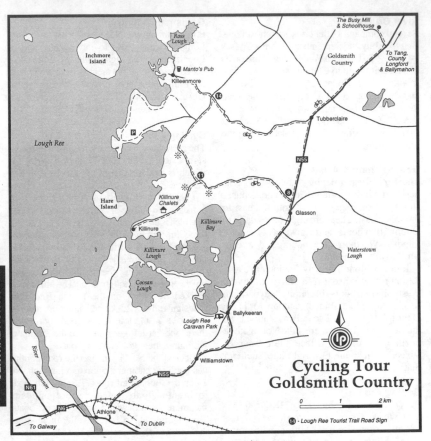

**Cycling Tour
Goldsmith Country**

0   1   2 km

⑭ - Lough Ree Tourist Trail Road Sign

From Tubberclaire northward Goldsmith Country extends into County Longford. From the site of the schoolhouse it's about 15 km back south to Athlone on the N55. The whole tour takes a couple of hours.

Places to Stay Camping is possible at *Lough Ree Caravan Park* (☎ 0902-78561) where tent sites are IR£2.50 per person or at *Manto's* (☎ 0902-85204), which also does B&B for IR£20 per person. Self-catering chalets are available at Killinure, Glasson, Tubberclaire and at Manto's and enquiries should be made at the tourist office in Athlone.

Moate

The village of Moate, halfway between Athlone and Kilbeggan on the N6, about 40 km south-west of Mullingar, gets its name from a nearby motte. **Moate Museum** is a small folk museum with displays of 19th-century farm tools, kitchenware and the like. It is open June to August from 11 am to 1 pm and 2 to 6 pm Monday to Friday and entry is IR£1/25p.

County Donegal

County Donegal matches anywhere else in Ireland for bleakness, dramatic cliffs and hectares of peat bogs; it can be great if the weather isn't equally bleak and dramatic. Despite being in the South, County Donegal extends farther north than anywhere in the official North. It is virtually separated from the rest of the Republic by the westward projection of County Fermanagh in Northern Ireland, and is sufficiently far from Dublin to deter the worst of the crowds.

Roughly one third of Donegal falls into the Gaeltacht, where Irish is more widely spoken than English. You'll see signs pointing to offices of Údarás na Gaeltachta, a government agency which tries to promote the social, economic and cultural strengths of the Gaeltacht area. Round Gweedore in particular, they have been instrumental in creating an industrial zone where more than 800 people are employed in production of yarn, plastic, radiators and so on.

Tourism in Donegal is extremely seasonal, and many attractions and almost all the tourist offices close except between June (interpreted pretty narrowly) and September.

Unless you're entering Donegal from the North you will be travelling there from Sligo on the N15, passing Bundoran and Ballyshannon on the way to Donegal Town.

Although you could get round Donegal by bus, it would be a slow experience, especially in winter; for example, the bus takes more than five hours to get from Bunbeg to Derry, a distance of just 89 km. This is very much walking and cycling country. When driving, be prepared for switchback roads, suicidal sheep, signs only in Irish, signs hidden behind vegetation or no signs at all.

Donegal Town

The town gets its name from the Vikings, who had a fort here in the 9th century, Dhún na nGall being 'the fort of the foreigner'. The

Highlights
- Getting drenched in Glenveagh National Park
- Staying up till all hours over pub music sessions in Donegal Town
- Gazing down on Slieve League cliffs
- The view from Grianán of Aileach
- Walking the Bloody Foreland and Horn Head
- Glebe House and Gallery
- Relaxing in Ramelton village

town's importance later developed due to its being the main seat of the O'Donnells, the family that controlled this part of Ireland before the 17th century.

Donegal Town is principally the jumping-off point for the rest of the county, but it's a pleasant and very popular little place. The triangular Diamond is the centre of Donegal, often choked with traffic in summer; there are some good shops selling quality souvenirs and garments.

INFORMATION

The tourist office (☎ 073-21148) is by the river on Ballyshannon Rd and close to the Diamond but is only open Monday to Friday from 9 am to 4 pm. Ask for *A Signposted Walking Tour of Donegal Town* if you want to take in all the sights. The post office is in Tirchonaill St.

DONEGAL

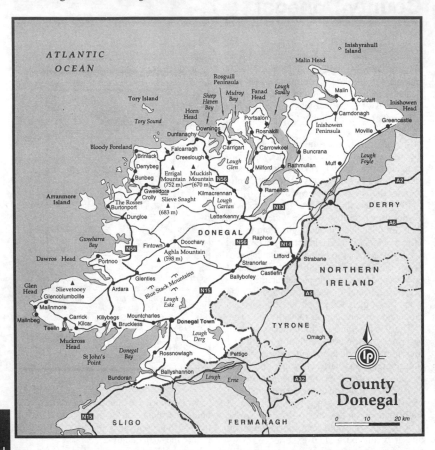

ATLANTIC OCEAN

County Donegal

0   10   20 km

Permits are required for fishing in most of the local rivers and these are available, along with licences for salmon and sea trout, from Doherty's (☎ 073-21119) on Main St. The shop will dispense information freely and provide a map of the local fishing spots.

DONEGAL CASTLE
Built on a rocky outcrop over the River Eske, what remains of this castle is still impressive. Originally, it was home to Hugh Roe O'Donnell, who may well have burnt it down rather than see it fall into the hands of the English at the end of the 16th century. Sir

Basil Brooke, the Englishman into whose hands it did fall, rebuilt it in Jacobean style. Notice the floral decoration on the corner turret and the decorated fireplace on the 1st floor. Brooke also built the three-storey manor house adjoining the castle.

In 1995, the castle was undergoing extensive restoration. It used to open from June to September but you should expect the admission fee of 80p to go up when it reopens.

THE DIAMOND OBELISK
In 1474, Hugh O'Donnell and his wife Nuala O'Brien founded a Franciscan monastery by

the shore in the south of town. It was accidentally blown up in 1601 and very little of it now remains. What makes it famous is that four of its friars, driven by the realisation that the arrival of the English meant the end of Celtic culture, chronicled the whole of known Celtic history and mythology from 40 years before the Flood to AD 1618 in 'The Annals of the Four Masters'.

The obelisk in the Diamond commemorates the prescient Four Masters. The National Library in Dublin displays facsimile pages of their work, which remains an important source for early Irish history.

FESTIVAL
Donegal Town has its own festival for three days at the end of June, featuring song, dance and story-telling, with arts and crafts thrown in. The tourist office should have the details.

New Music from Old Roots
The true origins of traditional Irish music are, of course, lost in the proverbial mists of time. However, clues to its humble origins lie in the very instruments themselves. Take the bodhrán, for example, the simple drum that resembles nothing as much as a giant cymbal. Originally it was probably shaken to separate the corn from the chaff, while the small knuckle-ended 'beater' was banged against it to frighten wrens away from the fields.

Like much that is Celtic, Irish traditional music may have found its way overland from Asia and India some 2000 years ago. The Irish harp may even have been developed in Egypt.

Until around 1700, this harp was the most important instrument in Irish music, although it was a smaller version than that used today; wooden-framed and with wire strings that were sounded with the fingernails rather than the fingertips. Just as the great painters of the Renaissance depended on the patronage of wealthy Italian merchants, so the harpists found support and patronage among Ireland's Gaelic chieftains. Consequently, music suffered a serious setback in 1607 when the episode known as the Flight of the Earls saw the chieftains flee to the continent, leaving the harpists to turn itinerant music teachers to support themselves. The most famous of these itinerant musicians was Turlough O'Carolan, some of whose tunes are still played today.

Traditionally, music was performed as a background to dancing, so the 17th-century Penal Laws did nothing to help by banning all expressions of traditional culture including dancing. Music was forced underground, which goes some way towards explaining the homely feel of much Irish music today. Until the late 18th century, Irish music was also primarily an oral tradition. In 1762, a book of 49 airs was published in Dublin. Then in 1792 Edward Bunting attended a Belfast harp festival and recorded the tunes he heard. His manuscripts are still housed in the library of Queen's University, Belfast.

In 1847 the Great Famine dealt traditional music – at least in Ireland – another blow as musicians either died or emigrated in search of a better life. However, within the Irish diaspora the traditions lived on, indeed were clung to as part of the immigrant's usual yearning for identity. To the standard repertoire of songs new themes were added, as musicians sang nostalgically of the homeland and celebrated their new lives. Piano backing was added to some tunes while others were speeded up.

Eventually the tide turned. Recordings of the music being made in America in the 1920s travelled back across the Atlantic and sparked renewed interest in what had been lost. Copying the Irish Americans, musicians at home also began to experiment by adding new instruments to the traditional line-up of fiddle, whistle, pipes and drum.

In the 1960s, Sean O'Riada of Cork set up Ceoltoiri Chualann, a band featuring a fiddle, flute, accordion, bodhrán and uilleann pipes, and began to perform music to listen to rather than dance to. When his band performed at the Gaiety Theatre in Dublin they gave a whole new credibility to traditional music. Members of the band went on to form the Chieftains, who played an important role in introducing Irish music to an international audience. Others who followed on and helped develop 'traditional' music into its current forms included Planxty, the Bothy Band (who introduced the bazooki), Moving Hearts and the Horslips who added a very 1970s rock twist. ∎

DONEGAL

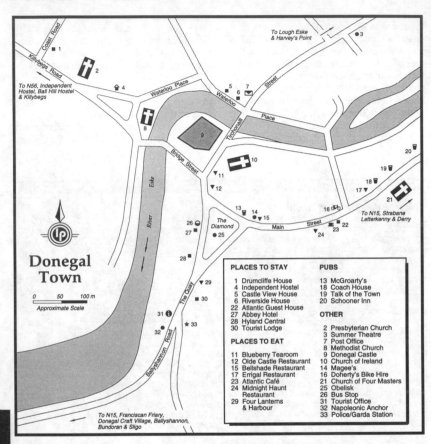

Donegal Town

0 50 100 m
Approximate Scale

PLACES TO STAY

1 Drumcliffe House
4 Independent Hostel
5 Castle View House
6 Riverside House
22 Atlantic Guest House
27 Abbey Hotel
28 Hyland Central
30 Tourist Lodge

PLACES TO EAT

11 Blueberry Tearoom
12 Olde Castle Restaurant
15 Bellshade Restaurant
17 Errigal Restaurant
23 Atlantic Café
24 Midnight Haunt
  Restaurant
29 Four Lanterns
  & Harbour

PUBS

13 McGroarty's
18 Coach House
19 Talk of the Town
20 Schooner Inn

OTHER

2 Presbyterian Church
3 Summer Theatre
7 Post Office
8 Methodist Church
9 Donegal Castle
10 Church of Ireland
14 Magee's
16 Doherty's Bike Hire
21 Church of Four Masters
25 Obelisk
26 Bus Stop
31 Tourist Office
32 Napoleonic Anchor
33 Police/Garda Station

DONEGAL

PLACES TO STAY
Hostels

The IHH *Donegal Town Independent Hostel*
(☎ 073-22805) is two kilometres out of town
on the Killybegs Rd, with a summer overflow house (☎ 073-22030) available just
across the river from the town centre. The
cost is IR£5.75 in both hostels, or IR£6.75 in
the two private rooms. You can also camp in
the grounds for IR£3.75 per person. In 1995,
the hostel was for sale, so it might be wise to
phone ahead to check.

The An Óige *Ball Hill Hostel* (☎ 073-
21174) in Ball Hill has an absolutely

stunning setting at the end of a quiet road,
right on the shores of Donegal Bay. To get
there, keep going along the Killybegs road
and look out for the signs on the left-hand
side of the road about five km out. Beds cost
IR£5 to members and IR£6.25 to non-
members. It's pretty remote, so stock up on
food before arriving.

B&Bs

There are plenty of B&Bs within walking
distance of the centre. *Drumcliffe House*
(☎ 073-21200) on Coast Rd off the
Killybegs Rd is a pleasant old place with

beds for IR£13.50. Waterloo Place, past the castle and down a few steps beside the river, has a couple close by each other: *Riverside House* (☎ 073-21083) and *Castle View House* (☎ 073-22100) both of which have doubles for IR£27. On Main St the *Atlantic Guest House* (☎ 073-21187) has decent singles/doubles from IR£17.50/25. The *Tourist Lodge* (☎ 073-23060) opposite the tourist office at the Quay has triple rooms which are good value at £30. If these are all full, there are plenty of others about town, including several fairly basic B&Bs opposite the tourist office; ask for rooms at the back to escape noise from the road.

Hotels
The *Abbey Hotel* (☎ 073-21014) and the *Hyland Central* (☎ 073-21027) are both in the Diamond; singles/doubles at the former are from IR£36/62, at the latter from IR£50/80.

For something rural and relaxing try the *Arches Country House* (☎ 073-22029) on the Lough Eske ring road. It has beds for IR£15. More expensive at IR£30 per person is the nearby *Ardnamona* (☎ 073-22650), a late 18th-century house with a splendid garden. Beautifully sited on the shores of Lough Eske and signposted from the Killybegs road is *Harvey's Point Country Hotel* (☎ 073-22208) with singles/doubles from IR£48/55.

PLACES TO EAT
Quite apart from supermarkets and fast fooderies, there are half a dozen places to eat very close to the busy Diamond. The *Atlantic Café*, the *Abbey Hotel* and the slightly fancier *Olde Castle Restaurant* all feature absolutely standard menus. *Stella's Salad Bar* in *McGroarty's* pub offers lunches with a healthy twist. The *Errigal Restaurant* in Main St does good fish & chips with mushy peas for around IR£3. The Chinese *Midnight Haunt*, also in Main St, has surprisingly good Chinese food with main courses at around IR£6 to IR£8. The recommended *Bellshade Restaurant* on the 1st floor of Magee's store does breakfast for IR£3.95 and lunches with

vegetarian possibilities. Round the corner by the *Olde Castle*, the *Blueberry Tearoom* over a lampshop does quiches, chicken curries and sandwiches.

Opposite the tourist office in the Quay there's *Four Lanterns* for fast food, with the snazzier *Harbour* grill doing seafood, pizzas and steak right next door.

For a real treat, try the Swiss-owned restaurant at *Harvey's Point Country Hotel* (☎ 073-22208), six km out of town on the small road to Lough Eske and the Blue Stack Mountains. Midweek, a five-course dinner costs IR£22.50, but on Saturday nights there are candlelit four-course gourmet dinners with entertainment laid on for IR£20. Reservations and formal attire are the rule.

ENTERTAINMENT
Numerous pubs can also be found within a stone's throw of the Diamond. Worth checking out for the music are the *Coach House* on Main St and the new *Talk of the Town* further down, which has live music on Wednesday. The *Schooner Inn* beyond Main St on the road out to Derry is also worth frequenting for its food and its music.

The *Summer Theatre* is run by a local theatre group and presents Irish plays in O'Cleary Hall by the junction up past the castle. Posters will be in the shops and tourist office.

THINGS TO BUY
Well worth a browse is Magee's in the Diamond. It has its own garment factory, and sells its tweed rolls at IR£16 per yard. A mailing service is available. Tweed jackets cost around IR£150, skirts IR£60 and there are lots of Aran sweaters around IR£80. Prices and quality can be compared with the Four Masters store almost next door, which has two floors of garments and gifts.

Also worth visiting is the Donegal Craft Village, a complex of small art and craft workshops, by the side of the N15 on the way to Bundoran about 1.5 km from town. Pottery, crystal, batik, garments and jewellery are all made on the premises. Its coffee shop is open seven days a week.

GETTING THERE & AWAY

There are Bus Éireann connections with Derry, Enniskillen and Belfast in the North, Sligo and Galway to the west and Limerick and Cork in the south. The bus stop is outside the Abbey Hotel and information is available by phoning ☎ 073-21101.

Feda O'Donnell (☎ 075-48114, 091-61656) runs a private coach to and from Galway every day, via Bundoran and Sligo. It leaves from the Garda station in Donegal at 9.45 am every day and reaches Galway at 1.15 pm. There are also departures at 4.20 pm on Sunday and at 1.15 and 5.20 pm on Friday. The bus leaves the cathedral in Galway at 4 pm daily – ring for details.

It is also worth checking out McGeehan's Coaches (☎ 075-46150) which does a Donegal to Dublin return trip for IR£15 and also departs from outside the Garda station.

GETTING AROUND

Doherty's (☎ 073-21119) on a corner along Main St hires out bikes for £6 a day.

Around Donegal Town

LOUGH DERG

From 1 June to 15 August, Lough Derg is alive with pilgrims who spend three days on a small island in the middle of the lake where St Patrick is believed to have stayed and fasted. Anyone over the age of 14 is welcome, and some 30,000 turn up every year – but be warned: the penitential aspect is taken seriously. The pilgrimage starts with a 24-hour vigil; only one meal a day is allowed; and everyone is expected to complete the Stations of the Cross in bare feet on the first day, having fasted from the preceding midnight. The pilgrims reach the island by boat from Pettigo, but outside the pilgrim season, there is no regular boat service to the island.

A new **Visitor's Centre** (☎ 072-61546) in Main St, Pettigo, details Lough Derg's Celtic past and recounts the story of St Patrick. It's open daily April to September from 10 am to 5 pm Monday to Saturday and from noon to 5 pm on Sunday. Admission is IR£2/1, twice that if you want a boat trip of the lough thrown in.

Places to Stay & Eat

There is no need to book accommodation on the island; just turn up at Pettigo and pay on the spot for accommodation and the boat fare. In Pettigo, *Avondale* (☎ 072-61520) on the Lough Derg Rd and *Hill Top View* (☎ 072-61535) at Billary just before Pettigo on the road from Donegal offer B&B from around IR£14 a person.

Getting There & Away

Pettigo and Lough Derg are extremely remote, at the end of a road across the moors. During the pilgrim season, a special bus (☎ 01-836 6111) leaves Dublin each day and there are bus connections from Sligo and Belfast. The local bus from Sligo stops at Bundoran and Ballyshannon, but not Donegal. The first boat leaves at 11 am, the last at 3 pm. Further information is available from the Prior (☎ 072-61518/61550), St Patrick's Purgatory, Lough Derg, Pettigo, County Donegal.

LOUGH ESKE

This is a place for fishing or for cycling or walking over the Blue Stack Mountains. If walking, consider using the *New Irish Walk Guides: West & North* (Gill & Macmillan), available from the bookstores in Donegal's Diamond. There's also an interesting walk around the hills of Lough Derg.

Getting There & Away

Leave Donegal on the N56 to Killybegs and turn right just past the bridge following the signs to *Harvey's Point*. The ring road eventually joins the N15 to the north-east of Donegal so it makes a convenient cycling trip. If you hire a bike from O'Doherty's in Donegal, they'll give you a photocopied map.

ROSSNOWLAGH

If you want a beach holiday without the amusement arcades, then Rossnowlagh is

DONEGAL

the place to visit. The sandy beach is stunning, extends for nearly five km and mostly attracts surfers.

Places to Stay & Eat
Camping is available at the *Manor House Caravan & Camping Park* (☎ 072-51477). It costs IR£6.50 per night to camp (IR£3.50 for cyclists), and there's a shop, take-away food outlet and restaurant at the camp site, which is open July and August.

Sand House (☎ 072-51777) is the beach hotel, charging from IR£40 per person. The front rooms have magnificent sea views.

BALLYSHANNON
This is a busy, hilly little town set above the River Erne with a small adjunct of shops and houses south of the river and connected by a bridge. It could be more appealing than Bundoran as a base for exploring the coastline before Donegal. It's also very convenient for trips into the North, with regular buses to Belleek and Enniskillen.

Allingham's Grave
The poet William Allingham (1824-89) was born in Ballyshannon and is buried in the graveyard. It's signposted first left up Main St after Dorrians Imperial Hotel. The tombstone is on the left side of the churchyard.

Donegal Parian China Visitor Centre
Parian china is lighter and more translucent than bone china. All the pieces available are on display in the Centre, which is by the side of the N15 on the way to Bundoran. Prices range from around IR£10 for small pieces to IR£250 for a full tea set. Free guided tours, a tea room, a bureau de change and mail order service are all laid on here. The Centre is open daily from 9 am to 6 pm June to September, and from 9 am to 5.30 pm Monday to Saturday the rest of the year.

Places to Stay
The IHH *Duffy's Hostel* (☎ 072-51535) is less than one km out of town on the road to Donegal, has 18 beds for IR£5 each and is open from March to October. You can camp in the garden for £3.50 a head. There's a secondhand bookshop in the garage behind the hostel.

Macardle House (☎ 072-51846), is at 55 Assaroe Heights and is signposted on the corner opposite the Seán Og pub. Singles/doubles are IR£18.50/27. The best hotel is the grand *Dorrians Imperial* in Main St (☎ 072-51147), with singles/doubles for IR£44/77.

Places to Eat
Cúchulainn's, on the corner opposite the Seán Og pub, is a pub and takeaway with a restaurant upstairs. Across the road, *Embers* in Paddy Donogher's pub does seafood, pasta and a few vegetarian options. The *Kitchen Bake*, where the two main streets meet, serves cakes and coffee. The bar at *Dorrians Imperial Hotel* serves pub food at lunch time and dinner is around IR£15, depending on what's on.

A coffee and craft shop has recently opened in the restored mills of a 12th-century Cistercian abbey founded by monks from Boyle. To get there go past the Thatch Pub on the road to Rossnowlagh and turn left into Abbey Lane, or the next left if you need parking space.

Entertainment
Pubs have live music throughout the summer, but the perfect time to be entertained in Ballyshannon is during the August bank holiday weekend music festival, the first weekend in August. The pubs to check out are *Seán Og's* in Market St, the *Thatch* at the top of Main St as you turn towards Rossnowlaugh, and the *Cellar* which is in the southern part of town across the roundabout on the other side of the river heading towards Sligo. The *Abbey Centre* (☎ 072-51375) in the north of town has one cinema screen and does occasional plays (and bingo!) too.

Getting There & Away
The bus station (with some truly disgusting public toilets) is close to the roundabout and near the very distinctive clock tower of

DONEGAL

Gallogery's Jewellers. There are daily Bus Éireann buses (☎ 074-21309) to Bundoran, Derry, Donegal, Glencolumbcille, Sligo and Dublin.

The Feda O'Donnell bus (☎ 075-48114) departs from outside Maggie's Bar for Donegal, Letterkenny, Dunfanaghy and Crolly at 6.35 pm Monday to Saturday (also 12.30 pm on Saturday), 8.30 pm on Friday and 11 pm on Sunday. The single fare for anywhere in Donegal is IR£4. It leaves for Sligo (IR£4) and Galway (IR£8) at 10 am Monday to Saturday; also at 1.30 and 5.30 pm on Friday, and 4.30 and 8.30 pm on Sunday.

Getting Around
Duffy's Hostel has a few bikes for hire.

BUNDORAN
A mildly depressing place, Bundoran is one of the most popular seaside resorts in the whole of Ireland. It comes alive during the summer but is mostly just driven through for the rest of the year and it's not hard to see why. The main street, made up of East End and West End, is a series of games arcades, including some real antique shove ha'penny games, restaurants of the fish & chips variety, and souvenir shops. Bundoran is used mainly by Catholic Northerners and at nights the traditional music in the pubs favours the rebel song over the folk song.

Information
The tourist office (☎ 072-41350) is a kiosk opposite the Holyrood Hotel, on the left as you come into town from Sligo. It's open from the end of May to the middle of September from 10 am to 1 pm and 2 to 6 pm daily. Outside peak season, you'd be lucky to find it open even at the times posted on the door.

Activities
Children enjoy Waterworld where a slide pool, wave pool and restaurant pack them in by the hundred. The noise level in here probably breaks several EU standards. Tickets cost IR£2.50 for the under-sixes, IR£3.50 for the under-16s and IR£4 for oldies.

An activity that might appeal to children and their parents is horse riding; the Stracomer Riding School (☎ 072-41787) organises hourly sessions as well as residential courses.

Just north of the town centre, Tullan Strand is a handsome sandy beach with waves big enough to deter swimmers. The strange cliffside rock formations have whimsical names like the Fairy Bridges and the Puffing Hole.

Places to Stay
Should you decide to give Bundoran a whirl, there's the IHH *Homefield Hostel* (☎ 072-41288) in Bayview Ave, with 30 dorm beds for £8 a head and a few private rooms for £10. Going for B&B you're spoilt for choice, though nothing stands out. Waterworld keeps a handy list for when the tourist office is closed. Going upmarket, the *Holyrood Hotel* (☎ 072-41232), at the southern end of the main street, is big and new, with rooms for IR£42/60 in high season.

Places to Eat
There's no shortage of cafés and fast-food places along the main street but they're all much of a muchness. During the summer months the *Kitchen Bake*, midway along the street in a converted 19th-century church, does at least offer light lunches in more imaginative surroundings.

Getting There & Away
Bus Éireann buses (☎ 074-21309) stop in the centre of town opposite Pebbles Boutique, and there is a direct daily service to Dublin, Derry, Sligo and Galway. Ulster Buses stop on the patch of wasteland known as Railway Yard; turn down beside the Railway Tavern to find it. Ulster Bus has direct services to Belfast and Enniskillen. The Feda O'Donnell bus (☎ 075-48114) from Crolly to Galway stops in Bundoran outside the Holyrood Hotel at 10.05 am every day. If it's open, the tourist office can help with other bus times.

Getting Around
There is a bike hire place (☎ 072-41526) at the south end of town, with bikes for IR£4.50 a day or IR£20 a week. You'll need to leave a IR£20 deposit.

MOUNTCHARLES TO BRUCKLESS
The first town on the coastal road west of Donegal, Mountcharles, has a safe and sandy beach, angling possibilities, and an interesting story-telling festival. Four of the eight pubs have live music at weekends. The road west to Bruckless passes through the village of Inver, which has its own small beach. A little farther west at Dunkineely, a minor road runs down the promontory to St John's Point, but there is no sand here.

Fishing
Michael O'Boyle (☎ 073-35257) has a boat available for deep-sea angling at IR£10 a day and rod and tackle can be hired for another IR£5 a day. He leaves from the Mountcharles pier; take the first turning on the left as you come into the village from the Bundoran side.

Storytelling Festival
Seamus MacManus was a villager who told stories around the village pump in the 1940s and 1950s. In the past, the festival organised by the Seamus MacManus Society consisted of lectures, walks and sessions with modern storytellers. It didn't take place in 1995, but there are hopes of reinstating it for 1996. The Donegal Town tourist office (☎ 073-21148) should be able to help you, or try Bosco House Hostel.

Places to Stay
Mountcharles *Bosco House Hostel* (☎ 073-35382) is difficult to miss on the main street. It is open all year and a bed is IR£5. Nearby is the *Coast Road Guest House* (☎ 073-35018) with beds for IR£13, and near the church *Clybawn House* (☎ 073-35076) has singles/doubles for IR£17.50/27.

Bruckless The inviting *Gallagher's Farm Hostel* (☎ 073-37057), with 18 beds in con-

verted farm outhouses, is halfway between Dunkineely and Bruckless on the main N56 road. Beds cost IR£6 with another IR£3 for breakfast. Camping is also possible here at IR£3 a head and there are separate kitchen facilities. Guests get given a list of walks in the area. *Bruckless House* (☎ 073-37071), just past the hostel, is a cut above the usual B&B and a night in this 18th-century home costs from IR£20.

Places to Eat
Apart from the pubs and the hostels there is little choice, so stock up before leaving Donegal or Killybegs.

Getting There & Away
Bus No 299 leaves Donegal at 9.10 am, and 4.15 and 6.15 pm stopping outside Mulhern's in Mountcharles, the Inver post office and McGinley's shop in Dunkineely.

South-Western Donegal

KILLYBEGS
Depending on your viewpoint, Killybegs could be said to have an important and successful fishing industry, or to have been blighted by the large fishmeal processing plant on the eastern outskirts, which casts an offputting stench across much of the town. The wild-looking and secluded Intra Beach, a couple of km beyond town, is more fun to explore than swim from.

Information
The tourist information point (a board with maps) is in the car park by the harbour.

MacSweeney's Tomb
A right turn in town up the steep hill brings you to St Catherine's Church, which contains the tomb slab of Niall Mor MacSweeney, with its Celtic-style carved gallowglasses. Gallowglasses were Scottish mercenaries who first came to the north and west of Ireland in the late 13th century. At first they were only hired by the big chiefs

DONEGAL

but, by the late 15th century, their descendants were being employed around the country as personal bodyguards and police officers.

Fishing

In summer the *Arctic Cloud* departs Blackrock Pier daily at 10 am, returning at 6 pm, with the opportunity to fish for pollock, cod, whiting etc. For details phone Anthony Doherty on ☎ 073-31079. Inclusive B&B and angling deals can be arranged for groups of eight people.

Places to Stay

If you decide to stay in Killybegs, it's important to pick a guesthouse on the western outskirts (Intra Rd) to avoid the worst of the fishy pong. Clean and friendly is the recommended *Oilean Roe* (☎ 073-31192), one km west on Intra Rd, with singles from IR£16.50 and doubles from IR£25. Alternatively there's *Glenlee House* (☎ 073-31026) just across the road, charging IR£18/28. The *Bay View Hotel* (☎ 073-31950) in the town centre has a leisure centre and pool, and charges £48/80 in high season. It can't entirely escape the smells, though.

Places to Eat

Cope House guesthouse on Main St houses the Hai Kong Chinese restaurant, while *Barnacles* in the Lone Star, down a side street opposite, is a seafood restaurant where a meal can be enjoyed for under IR£10. The *Harbour Bar* nearby has a claustrophobic little boxroom upstairs serving meals and snacks. The big Bayview Hotel has a downstairs brasserie and an upstairs restaurant specialising, not surprisingly, in seafood. You can also pick up fish & chips opposite the car park.

Getting There & Away

Bus No 299 runs between Strabane and Killybegs via Donegal Town and the bus stop is outside Hegarty's shop. There is also a service to Portnoo via Ardara and Glenties. Bus No 296 heads out west to Kilcar, Glencolumbcille and Malinmore.

McGeehan's bus (☎ 075-46101) to Dublin stops at the Pier bar at 8.10 am (also 3.45 pm on Sunday).

KILCAR

Either Kilcar or neighbouring Carrick will serve as a base for exploring the local indented coastline and the Slieve League cliffs. Outside of Kilcar, just a five-minute walk from the hostel, is a small, sandy beach.

Information

Tourist information is available from the Craft Shop (☎ 073-38002), open seven days a week in the summer. They can provide details of two local walks, which take in many of the prehistoric sites.

Donegal Tweed

Opposite the Craft Shop is a small tweed factory employing 25 workers. Free guided tours operate from Monday to Friday. In the Craft Shop, the tweed can be bought by the metre (IR£8.50). You're unlikely to get better prices than this elsewhere in Donegal.

Slieve League

Carrick, five km from Kilcar, is where you turn off for Teelin and the Bunglas viewing point for Slieve League, a cliff face which drops over 300 metres straight into the sea. To drive to the cliff edge, take the turn-off signposted Bunglas from the Donegal-Killybegs-Glencolumbcille road at Carrick, and continue beyond the narrow track signposted Slieve League to the one signposted Bunglas.

Another way to view the changing colours of the rock face is by boat from Teelin Pier (☎ 073-39079/39117). Between June and September, provided the weather's good, the boat leaves at 11.30 am and 2.30 pm and costs IR£6/3. It only operates with a minimum of six people.

Starting from Teelin, experienced walkers can spend a day walking via Bunglas and the somewhat terrifying One Man's Path to Malinbeg, near Glencolumbcille.

Places to Stay

There are two hostels in Kilcar, both on the Glencolumbcille side of the village. *Dún Ulún House* (☎ 073-38137) charges IR£7.50 per person for hostel beds and IR£12.50 for B&B. The IHH *Derrylahan Hostel* (☎ 073-38079), over one km from the village, charges IR£5 in 7-bed dorms. A phone call from Kilcar village or Carrick will get you a lift to the hostel. Derrylahan hostel allows camping for IR£3 and private rooms for two cost IR£14. There's a small shop and plentiful cooking facilities; all the waste is dutifully separated out for recycling. For B&B *Kilcar Lodge* (☎ 073-38156) in Main St has singles/doubles from IR£20/29.

The Slieve League pub in Carrick also has a *hostel* (☎ 073-39041), with rooms for IR£5.

Places to Eat

The thatched *Piper's Rest* pub serves light food while the *Village Restaurant* in Main St is open during July and August with meals around IR£10. On the road between Kilcar and Killybegs the panoramically-situated *Blue Haven* (☎ 073-38090) serves lunch and dinner, with a more imaginative menu than you might expect; a full meal might cost about IR£15 but there are main courses for around IR£5.

Getting There & Away

Buses connect Kilcar and Carrick with Donegal Town and Glencolumbcille. Enquire at the Craft Shop for full details of the times, which change at weekends and from summer to winter. There is usually a 10 am and 6.15 pm bus leaving Donegal Town and taking about an hour to reach Kilcar. McGeehan's bus (☎ 075-46101) leaves Kilcar, outside John Joe's, at 7.50 am (also 3.30 pm on Sunday).

GLENCOLUMBCILLE

The village name, the Glen of St Colmcille (also spelt Columbkille or Columcille, all meaning Columba's church in Irish), derives from the fact that St Colmcille lived in the valley, and the remains of his church can still be seen. Every 9 June, his feast day, the locality becomes the focus for a penitential three-hour tour.

Information

The Lace House Centre (☎ 073-30116) dispenses information and sells a useful archaeological guide to the area, *A Guide to 5000 Years of History in Stone*.

Beaches

The beach opposite the Folk Village can be dangerous due to the undercurrents and it's worth making the short journey west of Glencolumbcille to Doonalt where there are two sandy beaches. Another beach can be found at the end of the road to Malinbeg, where steps descend to a sheltered cove.

Folk Village

This heritage centre is the most tangible evidence of the work of a priest who played a remarkable role in Glencolumbcille's development. Father James McDyer came here from Tory Island in 1952 and was galvanised into action by a community with a 75% emigration rate. He organised cooperatives and diversified farming practices as well as promoting tourism. By 1964 emigration had dropped to 20% and the village became a symbol of a 'Save the West' consciousness.

The heritage centre was established long before they became trendy – even before there were EU grants to help pay for the expense of setting one up. There are three replicas of buildings as lived in by people from the 18th and 19th centuries, with genuine period fittings. The shebeen house sells local wine for IR£3.50 alongside marmalade and fudge. The old National School is also open to visitors, and there's a short nature trail up the hill behind.

The museum is open in summer from 10 am to 6 pm Monday to Saturday, noon to 6 pm on Sunday. There's a IR£1.50/1 charge for the hourly tour of the site's buildings and entry to the museum. The café sells excellent Guinness cake.

DONEGAL

Malinmore Adventure Centre

Overlooking Malin Bay, this new outdoor pursuits centre (☎ 073-30123) offers scuba diving, canoeing, snorkelling, fishing, orienteering, boat trips and other activities.

Irish Language Courses

Every summer, the village hosts a number of adult courses in aspects of Irish language and culture, and non-Irish speakers are welcome. Fees range from IR£40 for a weekend language course to IR£55-70 for a week's course in the design and practice of weaving, hill walking, set dancing, painting or archaeology.

Rental accommodation sharing with other course participants can also be arranged at IR£50 per person. Details are available from Oideas Gael (☎ 073-30248), Gleann Cholm Cille, County Dhún na nGall.

Places to Stay

The *Dooey Hostel* (☎ 073-30130) is about 1.5 km beyond the village and offers everything from camping space (IR£3.50 per person) to dorms (IR£5.50) to private rooms (IR£6.50). Rather surprisingly for somewhere as remote as this, it also offers wheelchair access. Driving, take the turn beside the Glenhead Tavern. Walking or cycling, there's a short cut up a track beside the Folk Village. At Malinmore, about two km past the Folk Village, *Ros Mór* (☎ 073-30083) is a B&B charging IR£15 a person, and nearby is the *Glencolumbcille Hotel* (☎ 073-30003), with doubles for IR£59.

Places to Eat

The *Bialanni Restaurant* is near the Folk Village and seafood dishes are available for around IR£5. There is also a restaurant and afternoon teahouse above *Lace House*, open daily until 9.30 pm and offering unexpected curries alongside soup and sandwiches.

Things to Buy

Between Glencolumbcille village and the Folk Village are the Donegal Woollen Centre shops, with a large selection of Donegal tweed jackets, caps and ties alongside lambswool scarves and shawls. Also available are Aran sweaters and handwoven rugs. Most of the shops are open seven days a week.

Inside the Lace House, Rossan sells knitted garments, jackets and rugs. Visitors can tour the factory to view the production of sweaters.

Getting There & Away

The Bus Éireann bus (☎ 074-21309) leaves for Donegal daily at 8.25 am, with an extra bus on Saturday at 11.30 am. McGeehan's private bus (☎ 075-46101) leaves daily for Donegal and Dublin. From Dublin the bus leaves the Royal Dublin Hotel at 6 pm (extra buses on Friday at 4.30 pm and on Monday at 10 am), arriving at Glencolumbcille at 11 pm. Departure from Glencolumbcille is at 7.30 am (extra buses on Sunday at 3 pm) from outside Biddy's. McGeehan's run to Letterkenny, also leaving at 7.30 am.

Getting Around

Bicycles can be hired from the Glencolumbcille Hotel for IR£6 a day.

ARDARA

The road from Glencolumbcille to Ardara is by way of the scenically stunning Glengesh Pass, a glaciated valley which suddenly opens up before you, with long winding bends carrying the road down to the river. Before entering Ardara, a small road to the left runs down to the tiny village of Maghera and its attractive beach with caves that can be explored. Be careful as some of them flood when the tide comes in. The small peninsula that extends from Ardara and divides Loughros More Bay from Loughros Beg Bay is also well worth walking or cycling.

Ardara Heritage Centre

A brand-new heritage centre tells the story of Donegal's role in the tweed-weaving industry and gives you the chance to watch a handloom weaver in action and ask questions. A video upstairs describes the surrounding area. There's also a handy tea shop. It's open daily from Easter to October 10 am to 6 pm, Sunday 2 to 6 pm. Admission costs IR£2 and children usually get in free.

Ardara Weavers Fair

The Ardara Weavers Fair had its origins in the 18th century but went into decline early this century. Recently it has been revived and now takes place in early June. Phone ☎ 075-41262 for details.

Places to Stay

Laburnum House (☎ 075-41146) on the corner of the Portnoo Rd right in the centre does B&B for IR£11.50. The big, old *Nesbitt Arms* (☎ 075-41103) has singles/doubles from IR£20/36 in high season.

Places to Eat

The best place for snacks or a meal is *Nancy's* in the *Chas McHugh* pub. This small dark bar has lots of atmosphere and serves burgers, various seafood dishes including garlic oysters (IR£4.50), and a ploughman's lunch for IR£3.20. *Charlie's West End Café* at the Killybegs end of Main St can do you breakfast, as well as soups, sandwiches and steak.

Entertainment

The *Central Bar* has live music nightly and invites all musicians to join in.

Things to Buy

There are a few shops specialising in locally made knitware and prices are competitive. Aran cardigans and sweaters are between IR£35 and IR£75, scarves around IR£12, and tweed jackets from IR£90 to IR£150. Compare prices and styles at Kennedy's and Bonner & Son, almost side by side on Front St, and John Molloy on the Killybegs road.

Getting There & Away

The Killybegs bus departs at 10 am and 5.05 pm, reaching O'Donnell's in Ardara in about half an hour. At noon and 7 pm buses leave for Killybegs. The Bus Éireann express (☎ 074-21309) from Dublin to Donegal is

extended to Ardara on Friday, and a Sunday bus leaves for Dublin at 4.30 pm.

McGeehan's bus (☎ 075-46150/46101) also runs to Dublin each morning from the post office at 8.30 (extra Sunday bus at 3.45 pm). The Glencolumbcille-Letterkenny bus, via Glenties, also stops in Ardara.

DAWROS HEAD

The two camping and caravan sites are packed out every summer with holidaymakers from the North and consequently the area is busier than you might expect. The beach at Narin is a big crowd-puller and at low tide you can walk out to Iniskeel Island to the remains of a monastery founded by St Connell, a cousin of St Colmcille.

Doon Fort

Signposts off the road from Narin to Rosbeg lead to a lake in the centre of which sits 2000-year-old Doon Fort, a fortified oval settlement. To reach it, you need to hire a rowing boat. The signs lead you to the site; alternatively, phone ☎ 075-45317. It'll cost you IR£3 for an hour.

Armada Site

In 1588 the *Duquesa Santa Ana* ran aground off Tramore Beach. The survivors temporarily occupied O'Boyle's Island in Kiltoorish lake, but then marched south through Ardara to Killybegs where they set sail again in the *Girona*.

Places to Stay

Dunmore Caravans (☎ 075-45121) is on the Strand Rd at Portnoo and accepts tents for IR£5 – ring first to check there's a space available. The other camp site, the *Tramore Beach Caravan & Camping Park* (☎ 075-51491) at Rosbeg, charges IR£7 a tent for two people. Take the road from Ardara to Narin and turn off to the left following the signposts.

There are a few B&Bs at Narin and Portnoo that open for the summer season. *Carnaween House* (☎ 075-45122) charges

DONEGAL

IR£13 and *Thalassa Country Home* (☎ 075-45151) IR£14.

Getting There & Away
In the summer a Bus Éreann bus leaves Killybegs at 10 am and 5.05 pm for Portnoo. The buses leave Portnoo for the return journey at 12.15 and 6.15 pm.

GLENTIES
In this small town there are a number of pubs offering music at night and the place is busy with Northerners. The town was home to Patrick MacGill (1896-1937), the Navvy Poet, and a small festival in his honour takes place during the last week in August. There's a board with tourist information beside the gardaí station in the main street.

St Connell's Museum & Heritage Centre
The local history museum beside the old courthouse has a small collection of local artefacts, including an impressive set of early 20th-century bathroom furniture in the basement and reminders of the old railway line. It's open mid-May to mid-September from 10 am to 12.30 pm and from 2 to 4.30 pm, Monday to Friday and from 10.30 am to noon on Saturday. Admission is IR£1/50p.

The museum is opposite the beautiful slope-roofed St Conal's Church, designed by the Derry architect Liam McCormack and built between 1972 and 1974.

Places to Stay
Clean, spacious IHH *Campbell's Hostel* (☎ 075-51491) is on the left beside the museum as you enter from Glencolumbcille. A bed in a dorm with en-suite facilities is IR£5 and there are several twin rooms for IR£13. There's also a big kitchen-cum-common room, with welcoming fire. Two B&Bs are along Glen Rd about one km out of town: *Claradon* (☎ 075-51113) and *Avalon* (☎ 075-51292), which both have singles/doubles for IR£16/27. *Highlands Hotel* (☎ 075-51111) on the main street has singles/doubles from IR£18/34.

Places to Eat
The *Highlands Hotel* serves substantial meals even on a Sunday evening. Otherwise, there are several fast food places and a chip shop in the main street.

Getting There & Away
On weekdays a Bus Éireann bus (☎ 074-21309) connects Portnoo and Killybegs, stopping outside the post office in Glenties at 10.45 am and 5.50 pm on the way to Portnoo and at 12.40 and 6.40 pm on the way to Killybegs.

On Friday an express bus leaving Dublin for Donegal at 5.15 pm extends its service to Glenties, arriving at 10.30 pm. On Sunday the bus leaves Glenties at 4.15 pm and reaches Dublin at 9.45 pm.

McGeehan's bus (☎ 075-46101) from Glencolumbcille to Dublin stops outside the Highlands Hotel, at 8.15 am from Glencolumbcille (extra bus on Sunday at 3.30 pm), and 10.25 pm from Dublin. There is also a bus to Fintown and Letterkenny.

INLAND TO THE FINN VALLEY
This is the only part of Donegal that isn't well travelled by visitors – a blessing if you want to get away on your own for some fishing, hill walking or cycling. The River Finn is a good salmon river, especially if there has been heavy rain before the middle of June. Sea trout are also available and fishing gear is available from Mcelhinys in Ballybofey.

There's good **hill walking** on the Blue Stack Mountains and along the Ulster Way, but you need to be prepared with maps and provisions. The Finn Farm Hostel dispenses maps and advice and will even arrange a pick-up at the beginning or end of the trip. A long one-day trek could start from the hostel and end at the Lodge Hostel in Doochary village, Campbell's Hostel in Glenties or the new hostel in Fintown.

Horse riding is best arranged through the Finn Farm Hostel which organises lessons at IR£7 an hour. Experienced riders can take a horse for the whole day for IR£30. Six-day trips across the border can also be arranged.

The main town is **Ballybofey**, linked to Stranorlar by an arched bridge, and a dreadful traffic bottleneck. In Ballybofey's Protestant church, the grave of Isaac Butt, founder of the Irish Home Rule movement, can be found.

Despite its name, **Fintown** is a much smaller settlement, just a cluster of houses, hostel, shop, post office, garage and pubs. Nevertheless a narrow-gauge railway has just been renovated and will be running short excursions alongside the lough; phone ☎ 075-46280 for details.

Places to Stay

The IHH *Finn Farm Hostel* (☎ 074-32261) is two km from Ballybofey and the left turn off the road is signposted on the road to Glenties. When you think you're lost and there can't possibly be a hostel along the green road you're on, you'll see it. A bed is IR£5.50, while camping costs IR£3 (IR£2 if you can manage without the hostel's indoor facilities). The new *Fintown Hostel* (☎ 075-46244) charges IR£5 for a bed and is beautifully sited above Lough Finn, with the Finnian's Rainbow pub at the end of the drive.

There are B&B possibilities in both Ballybofey and Stranorlar. *Finn View House* (☎ 074-31351), Lifford Rd in Ballybofey, has beds for IR£13.50, while *Mrs Fahey* (☎ 074-31312) on the Letterkenny Rd in Stranorlar charges from IR£16/25 for single/doubles. *Kee's Hotel* (☎ 074-31018) in Stranorlar, where the mail horses were changed on the Derry-Sligo run in the 19th century, has singles/doubles for IR£38.50/65 which includes free use of the leisure club's swimming pool and sauna. *Jackson's Hotel* (☎ 074-31021) is a little cheaper with high season doubles from IR£52.

Places to Eat

The big hotels will be able to do you a meal. Otherwise, there's the small *Red Rose Café* in Ballybofey, or the equally small *Caifa na Locha* run by a women's co-operative in Fintown; both do tea and light meals. Caifa na Locha is open seven days a week in summer.

Entertainment

There's a small theatre in Ballybofey but really you'd be better off getting to grips with the area's traditional music outlets. The Finn Farm Hostel is a centre for a community work scheme aimed at reviving dying musical traditions, so if you stay during the week you'll be able to hear the musicians practising; at weekends you'll have to make do with a tape of their best efforts. Also nearby is *Glen Tavern*, midway between Glenties and Fintown and renowned for its traditional music evenings.

Getting There & Away

The Bus Éireann (☎ 074-21309) Galway-Derry express stops outside the shopping centre in Ballybofey, connecting the area with Sligo, Donegal and Letterkenny. Local buses connect Ballybofey with Killybegs and Letterkenny.

McGeehan (☎ 075-46101) runs a Glencolumbcille-Letterkenny bus that stops in Fintown, at 9 am for Letterkenny and 5.35 pm for Glenties, Ardara, Killybegs and Glencolumbcille (except Sunday). There is also a McGeehan bus from Fintown to Ballyfoley at 12.10 pm on Thursday, Friday and Saturday.

Getting Around

Bicycles can be rented from Kee's Hotel in Stranorlar for IR£6 a day.

North-Western Donegal

The various epithets earned by Donegal's scenery – wild, spectacular, dramatic and so on – are nowhere more justified than in the north-west of the county. Despite the absence of large towns you are rarely far from a village or pub, and the area around Gweedore claims to be one of the most densely populated rural regions in Western Europe.

DONEGAL

The stretch of land between Dungloe in the south and Crolly in the north is a bleak and rocky Gaeltacht area known as the Rosses. The main attraction here is the island of Arranmore, reached by ferry from the village of Burtonport.

The other accessible island, the visually distinctive Tory Island further to the north, is even more appealing. The coast around here, between Bunbeg and Dunfanaghy, is absolutely superb and there are wonderful cycling tours to be enjoyed around Bloody Foreland and Horn Head.

DUNGLOE
Information
In theory, the tourist office (☎ 075-21297) in Dungloe (*Dúngleo*) is open from 10 am to 6 pm (closed 1 to 2 pm) Monday to Saturday from June to September. To reach it, turn left immediately in front of the Bridge Inn when coming from the south. If it's closed the adjacent festival office (see next section) may be able to help; bear in mind that they do this out of the kindness of their heart. The nearest good beach is just north of Maghery.

Festival
In the last week of July, Dungloe plays host to the Mary of Dungloe festival, named after a popular song. Thousands of people crowd into town for a series of events culminating in a contest to pick the year's 'Mary'. Supposedly, she's selected on the basis of personality but the fact that only women aged 18 to 25 are eligible to enter rather gives the lie to this. This is a big, boozy affair, and although it's sometimes graced by big names like folk singer Christy Moore, some people might well want to avoid Dungloe while it's in progress. If you do want to attend, book a bed well ahead. For more details phone ☎ 075-2154.

Places to Stay
The IHH *Greene's Hostel* (☎ 075-21021) in Cranmore Rd charges IR£7 a bed in six and eight-bed dorms. There's also space for tents: IR£5 if you're hitching or cycling. You can also hire a bike here. *Sweeney's Hotel*

(☎ 075-21033) in the high street charges IR£20 per person plus a 10% service charge. If singer Daniel O'Donnell's your man, you might want to press on to his home village of Kincasslaugh in the Rosses peninsula to stay at the *Viking House Hotel* (☎ 075-43295), owned by Daniel and run by his family. Beds cost IR£25.95/IR£41.80.

Places to Eat
The *Bridge Inn* pub near the tourist office does light snacks, or there's the nearby *Courthouse Restaurant* (☎ 075-22000) for more substantial seafood meals. For a quiet spot, seek out *Scrumptious* in the otherwise uninspiring Dungloe Centre shopping arcade. Other possibilities for dinner include *Sweeney's Hotel* in the high street, or the *Riverside Bistro* as you leave town on the north side.

Annagry is a small village four km west of Crolly and 10 km north of Dungloe, where you will find the snazzy *Danny Minnies Restaurant* (☎ 075-48201) which does good seafood (about IR£15 for an evening meal) or lunch for around IR£6.

Getting There & Away
There is a private bus (☎ 075-21105) that runs to Larne, the Northern Ireland ferry port, each day in July and August with a 20-minute stopover in Letterkenny. The bus leaves from outside Doherty's at 9 am. McGeehan's bus (☎ 075-46101) leaves from outside Sweeney's Hotel at 7.45 am for Dublin.

There is a small airport at Carrickfinn (☎ 075-48284) near Dungloe, with scheduled services to Glasgow with British Airways and to Birmingham and Edinburgh with Macair.

ARRANMORE
This small island (*Árainn Mhór*), 14 km by five km, has some spectacular cliff scenery and sandy beaches, as well as pubs and a small festival held each August. The island has been inhabited for thousands of years, and a prehistoric fort can be discerned on the south side. The western and northern parts

are wild and rugged with hardly any houses to disturb the sense of isolation. For fishing trips in the area phone ☎ 075-42077.

Places to Stay

The An Óige *Arranmore Island Hostel* (☎ 075-21574) is open from May to the end of October but is pretty basic and keen on the rulebook. There is also the *Glen Hotel* (☎ 075-20505) with 10 beds for IR£15 each. You can also arrange B&B for IR£14 with *Mrs Annie Bonner* (☎ 075-20532) through her husband Cornelius, the boatman.

Places to Eat

There are a number of pubs on the island doing food and meals are usually available at *Bonners Restaurant* at the pier, but if staying over, bring your own food to be on the safe side. There is a small shop not far from the hostel.

Getting There & Away

Throughout the year, the ferry (☎ 075-20532) plies the 1.5 km from Burtonport to Kilranaan; the trip takes 20 minutes and costs IR£5 return. In summer there are eight daily ferry crossings, usually starting from 8.30 am.

BURTONPORT

The otherwise uninteresting port village of Burtonport village does have one small claim to fame. Back in 1974 the Atlantis commune was established here by Jenny James, who practised a form of primal therapy which soon led to her followers being dubbed 'the Screamers'.

Eventually the commune relocated to the Columbian jungle and another group arrived to take its place. 'The Silver Sisters' chose to live a Victorian lifestyle, complete with Victorian dress, and soon even more peculiar stories were circulating about them. Now they, too, have moved on, leaving Burtonport to sink back into anonymity. Jenny James tells her own story, complete with tales of IRA threats, in *They Call Us the Screamers* (Caliban Books, 1983).

GWEEDORE, DERRYBEG & BUNBEG
Information

Derrybeg (*Doirí Beaga*) and Bunbeg (*An Bun Beag*) virtually run into each other and share an information centre (☎ 075-31510) on the main road which is open (in summer only) from 10 am to 6 pm. It has a bureau de change, as does the post office further down the road which is more likely to be open. The Gweedore (*Gaoth Dobhar*) tourist office (☎ 074-65070) is equally elusive. Failing either office being open, there's a tourist information point in the car park of the Allied Irish Bank on the main Bunbeg-Derrybeg road.

Places to Stay

The wonderfully remote and friendly *Screag An Iolair Hill* ('Eagle's Nest') hostel (☎ 075-48593) is signposted up in the hills above Crolly to the south of Gweedore. It charges IR£5 and offers a free pick-up service if you don't fancy the 5 km walk from the main road. Eamonn, who runs it, is a mine of information on traditional music.

Bunbeg has plenty of B&Bs, with *Atlantic View* (☎ 075-31550) on Strand Rd offering singles/doubles from IR£18/29, and *An Teach* (☎ 075-31569) beside the Allied Irish Bank charging IR£15/26. It's run by an Irish-Honduran couple.

There are a couple of prettier places beside Bunbeg Harbour: *The Haven* (☎ 075-31014) in a 250-year-old soldier's retreat with beds from IR£12.50 and *Bunbeg House* (☎ 075-31305) with beds from IR£14. In summer traffic to the harbour might detract a bit from their charm though. *Fernfield* (☎ 075-31258), further away at Middletown, charges IR£16/26.

The *Óstán Gweedore* (☎ 075-31177) hotel which is right by Bunbeg beach has the best facilities, including a leisure complex. It probably has the best views too, but they've been bought at the price of inflicting an eyesore on everyone outside. B&B for two is IR£70 (IR£90 with an evening meal). The *Seaview Hotel* (☎ 075-31076), also in Bunbeg, charges from IR£35/55.

DONEGAL

Places to Eat

Moonies Restaurant is opposite the Seaview Hotel, but only opens during summer evenings. The *Seaview* itself does grills and steak-style meals, with main courses for about IR£4.50. *Bunbeg House* by Bunbeg harbour has dinner for IR£15 and also serves afternoon teas.

Entertainment

For traditional pub music it would be hard to beat the Monday night sessions at *Teach Hiúdaí Beag* (☎ 075-31016) in Bunbeg high street.

Getting There & Away

Feda O'Donnell Coaches (☎ 075-48114) has buses leaving Gweedore for Letterkenny, Donegal, Sligo and Galway. They depart at 7.10 am Monday to Saturday with extra buses on Friday, from the Bunbeg crossroads, the Seaview Hotel and Molloy's supermarket. In Galway the bus leaves the Cathedral at 4 pm daily, at 5.30 pm on Friday, and at 8 pm from Eyre Square on Sunday.

Getting Around

You can hire a bike for IR£5 a day from Gweedore Tool Hire in Bunbeg high street (☎ 075-31066).

THE DUNLEWY CENTRE

Right beside Lough Dunlewy, Dunlewy *(Dún Lúiche)* is a small village at the foot of Errigal Mountain (740 metres), Donegal's highest peak. Here the Dunlewy Centre *Ionad Cois Locha* reconstructs the home of Manus Ferry, the last of the local weavers who died in 1975. Visitors can watch all the stages of weaving in operation and then go outside to see assorted farm animals, walk along the lake shore or take a boat ride on the lake with a storyteller on board to fill them in on local history, geology and folklore. There may well be music here as well (call ☎ 075-31699 to find out). There's an excellent café with a turf fire for cold days and a big shop selling everything from sweaters to tapes of local music.

A ticket for the house and grounds costs IR£2.20; for a boat trip it's IR£2.50; combined it's IR£4. A combined family ticket is particularly good value at IR£10. The Centre is open from Easter until the end of October from 10.30 am to 6 pm Monday to Saturday and 11 am to 7 pm Sunday.

ERRIGAL MOUNTAIN & THE POISONED GLEN

You don't need to be an experienced mountaineer to climb Errigal Mountain, but it can be a tough walk and you should always be wary of damp, misty days when visibility can be snuffed out with little warning. There are two paths up to the summit: the easier tourist route which covers five km and takes roughly two hours to complete; and the tougher 3.25-km walk along the north-west ridge which involves scrambling over scree for perhaps 2½ hours. Details of both routes are available at the Dunlewy Centre.

There are all sorts of stories about how the Poisoned Glen got its name. The more prosaic suggest it's because poisonous Irish spurge used to grow here, or because the original name *An Gleann Neamha* (Heavenly Glen) became corrupted to *An Gleann Nimhe* (Poisoned Glen). Another story has it that the British were once camped here and the Irish poisoned the water to kill their horses. Most imaginative of all is the version that says the ancient giant Balar was killed here by his exiled grandson Lughaidh, whereupon the poison from his eye split the rock and poisoned the glen.

Whichever story you choose, it's possible to walk through the glen, although some of the ground is rough and boggy, so it's as well to take advice on the precise route before starting out. From the Dunlewy Centre a return walk along the glen would be about 12 km and take up to two hours.

Places to Stay

There's a simple An Óige *hostel* (☎ 075-31180) at Errigal, which is three km west of the village of Dunlewy and eight km west of Gweedore. Beds cost IR£6 in high season. To get to it from Bunbeg keep going past the junction of the road leading to the Dunlewy

Centre and it's on the left after the Texaco garage. Another independent hostel is due to open nearby, at the junction with the road to the Dunlewy Centre. Eventually there will probably be accommodation at the Centre itself.

GLENVEAGH NATIONAL PARK

The Dunlewy Centre is right beside the 10,000-hectare Glenveagh National Park (*Pairc Naísúnta Ghleann Bheatha*), in a lake-filled valley overlooked by the Derryveagh Mountains. Much of the land making up the park was once farmed by tenants, 244 of whom were evicted by land-owner John George Adair in the winter of 1861. A plaque on a gable end at Ardaturr farm commemorates their fate. Adair was responsible for the building of Glenveagh Castle in 1870. After the mysterious disappearance of the second owner, the land was bought in 1937 by American Henry McIlhenny who eventually sold it to the state and later donated the castle and gardens.

John George Adair's wife Cornelia was responsible for the introduction of two things that define the appearance of the modern national park: the herd of red deer, and the rhododendrons which, despite their beauty, are seen as a pest, preventing broad-leaved trees from seeding themselves and running riot in the landscape. Enjoy them while you can since their days are numbered.

Features of the park include a nature trail through woods of Scots pine and oak to a stretch of blanket bog, and a viewing point, just a short walk behind the castle.

The excellent visitor centre hosts a useful audiovisual show on the ecology of the park and the infamous landlord. There's also an extremely imaginative toy theatre representation of the story. The restaurant serves hot food and snacks, and the reception sells midge-repellent, as vital in summer as walking boots and waterproofs are in winter. In July and August guided walks of the park leave every Wednesday at 11 am.

The park is open all year, and the visitor centre is open Easter to October from 10 am to 6.30 pm, seven days a week. June to September it's open until 7.30 pm on Sunday, while in October it closes on Friday. The charge is IR£2/1, family IR£5. Camping is not allowed in the park.

If you'd like to get more involved with the park, *Groundwork* in Dublin organises summer workcamps to help clear the rhododendrons. For a cost of IR£10, a week's food and accommodation comes with the labour. Groundwork is at 39 Upper Fitzwilliam St, Dublin 2 (☎ 01-836 6821).

Glenveagh Castle

The castle built by John George Adair was modelled on Balmoral in miniature, but Henry McIlhenny restored it as a comfortable gentleman's home with lots of reminders of the deer hunting so crucial to society life. A guided tour takes in a series of rooms which look as if McIlhenny has just left them. Some of the nicest, including the tartan-draped music room and the guest room for female visitors, are in the round tower. The drawing room also has a splendid 300-year-old Adams-style fireplace bought from the Ards estate by McIlhenny.

On a dry day the gardens are spectacular. They were nurtured for decades and include a variety of features: a terrace, an Italian garden, a walled kitchen garden and the Belgian Walk laid by Belgian soldiers who stayed here during WW I. In July and August there are guided tours of the gardens on Tuesday and Thursday at 2 pm.

The castle is open the same hours as the visitor centre, although the last guided tours leave about 45 minutes before closing time. Admission costs IR£2. Free minibuses run from the visitor centre to the castle roughly every 15 minutes. The pleasant tearoom does sandwiches and cold snacks.

BLOODY FORELAND

The headland (*Cnoc Fola*) gets its name from the colour of the rocks, and the road to it is wonderfully remote and ideal for cycling. The tiny village of Brinlack, about one km past the viewing point, has a thatched cottage doing tea and cakes (mid-June to August only).

DONEGAL

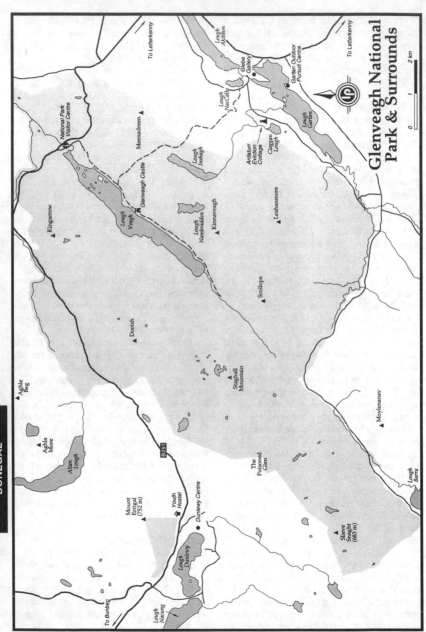

Glenveagh National Park & Surrounds

0   1   2 km

To Letterkenny

To Letterkenny

Lough Akibbon

Glebe Gallery

Gartan Outdoor Pursuit Centre

Lough NacCally

Lough Gartan

National Park Visitor Centre

Meenadreen

Lough Inshagh

Ardaturr Eviction Cottage

Claggan Lough

Glenveagh Castle

Kingarrow

Lough Veagh

Lough Nambraddan

Kinnaveagh

Leahanmore

Doish

Scollops

Aghle Beg

Staghall Mountain

Moylenanav

Aghla More

Altan Lough

R251

Mount Errigal (752 m)

Youth Hostel

Dunlewy Centre

The Poisoned Glen

Lough Barra

Slieve Snaght (683 m)

To Bunbeg

Lough Dunlewy

Lough Nacung

Places to Stay

There is a small hotel, the *Foreland Heights* (☎ 075-31785), near the viewing point. Singles/doubles are IR£30/45.

TORY ISLAND

Not so long ago a visit to Tory Island (*Oileán Tóraigh*) was a precarious venture; visitors could be stranded for days in bad weather. With modern boats, this is no longer a problem and the island is trying to attract as many visitors as possible.

Tory Island has its own indigenous school of painters whose work has been exhibited around Europe. The most accomplished of them, James Dixon, didn't start painting until he was in his 60s, when he was inspired by the English landscape artist Derek Hill, who began visiting Tory in 1956. Dixon saw him at work, claimed he could do better and was duly presented with paints and paper. He died in 1970. Patsy Dan Rogers is now the senior artist working on Tory. There is a permanent exhibition in the island's community hall.

Things to See

St Colmcille is said to have founded a monastery on the island in the 6th century. The only remains of this monastic era are near West Town: the **Tau Cross**, a small undecorated T-shaped cross on the pier, and the **Round Tower**, with a circumference of nearly 16 metres, built of rounded beach-stones and rough granite with a round-headed doorway some way above the ground.

The north-eastern side of the island has cliffs with colonies of puffins. The south-west is quite different, very flat but with dangerous offshore rocks. It was here that the British gunboat *Wasp* was wrecked in 1884 while on a mission to collect taxes from the inhabitants. There are no sandy beaches and just one pebbly one, but the cliff walks and a visit to the island's one pub at night make a stay here well worthwhile.

Places to Stay

The accommodation situation has improved dramatically over the last few years. The

Tory Island Hostel (☎ 074-65145) has beds for IR£6 and there are a few unregistered B&Bs in the two villages. *Óstán Tóraigh* (☎ 074-35920) has beds from IR£30/40.

Places to Eat

There's a small café on the island. Otherwise you can get pub food or full à la carte meals at the *Óstán Tóraigh*.

Getting There & Away

Turasmara Teo is a new boat service operating from Bunbeg (☎ 075-31991) and Magheraroarty (☎ 074-35061). Bunbeg is just west of Gweedore while Magheraroarty is reached by turning off the N56 at the western end of Gortahork near Falcarragh. The road is signposted Coastal Route/Bloody Foreland. Twice a week there is also a service from Port-na-Blagh and Downings near Dunfanaghy.

Between June and September the boat leaves Bunbeg at 9 am and returns from Tory at 7 or 9 pm. The boat from Magheraroarty leaves at 11.30 am and returns from Tory at 4.30 pm. On Wednesday from June to September, the boat leaves Port-na-Blagh at 2 pm and returns at 6.30 pm. Each Saturday there is also a 2 pm departure from Downings, returning at 6.30 pm. There are several extra services in July and August. No matter where you leave from, the fare is IR£12 return.

Bicycles are carried free on all the boats. For further information phone ☎ 075-31320/31340.

FALCARRAGH

This rather uninspiring village (*An Fal Carrach*), along with neighbouring Gortahork, has a significant Irish-speaking community. During the summer the pubs come alive at night, many with traditional music.

Beach

You can reach the beach by following signs marked *Trá* from either end of the main street. At the eastern end turn left beside the An Saibleann supermarket opposite the

Bank of Ireland. At the T-junction turn right until another sign marked *Trá* points down to the left and you're there. The beach is superb for walking but not for swimming. From the supermarket it's four km to the beach.

Places to Stay

The *Shamrock Lodge Hostel* (☎ 074-35859) has 18 beds in the village pub of the same name and charges IR£6 a bed. It's perfect for people who want a lively nightlife close to hand, but not for anyone wanting to get to sleep before 1 am.

Sea View (☎ 074-35552) is one km off the road going to Dunfanaghy and charges IR£13/25 for B&B. Nearer to Falcarragh itself *Chestnut Lodge* (☎ 074-35243) only does B&B in July and August. Doubles cost from IR£25.

Places to Eat

The *Gweedore* pub has a restaurant upstairs, and there's a coffee shop virtually next door.

Getting There & Away

The Feda O'Donnell bus (☎ 075-48114) from Crolly to Galway stops outside the phone box on Main St in Falcarragh at 7.50 am, reaching Letterkenny an hour later and Galway at 1 pm. There are extra buses on Friday, and on Sunday it leaves at 2.20 pm.

The Lough Swilly bus (☎ 074-22863) leaves for Derry at noon and 6.40 pm, Monday to Friday. This bus stops on Main St near the hostel.

DUNFANAGHY

Dunfanaghy (*Dún Fionnachaidh*) is a popular holiday resort in its own small and discreet way; the vast sandy stretches of the beach, when the tide is out, are a big draw, and there are a couple of smart hotels as well as a hostel, which is expanding to meet the demand. Compared to beaches in the south-west of Ireland, those around Dunfanaghy are idyllically empty, and it makes a good base for trips south to Letterkenny or west to Tory Island.

Information

There is no tourist office but the post office has a bureau de change facility, open until 5.30 pm on weekdays. Only punts can be issued so you will be disappointed if you wanted pounds for a visit to the North.

Dunfanaghy Workhouse & The Gallery

After the passing of the Poor Law in 1838, workhouses were set up around Ireland to house the destitute in circumstances that were deliberately intended to be unattractive. Men, women, children and the sick were separated from each other, and their lives were rigorously governed, with hard work the general rule. Dunfanaghy's workhouse opened in 1845, just before the onset of the famine which caused the number of residents to swell; by 1847 it had to be expanded to accommodate 600 people, double the number originally planned.

The workhouse has now been opened as a small heritage centre, with information about local history in general as well as its own. It's open from Easter to September (and maybe longer...phone ☎ 074-36540 to check), from 10 am to 5 pm on weekdays and from noon to 5 pm at weekends. Admission is IR£2/1, too much for what is actually offered.

The Gallery next door started life as a fever hospital. Nowadays it houses art and crafts.

Horn Head

Horn Head (*Corrán Binne*) has some of Donegal's most spectacular coastal scenery, with a pleasing absence of ugly residential development. The towering headland, with quartzite cliffs over 180 metres in height, could be reached by continuing on from the end of the walk (described in the following section) but the route is perilous at times. Consult the *New Irish Walks Guide: West & North* for details.

An alternative is to take the scenic route by bike or car from the Falcarragh end of Dunfanaghy. The road circles the headland with tremendous views on a fine day: the islands of Inishbofin, Inishdooey and

Inishbeg to the west, as well as Tory island, Sheep Haven Bay to the east, Malin Head to the north-east, and even, on a good day, the coast of Scotland. You could easily spend a day walking this area, with breaks for a swim and a bite to eat.

Walking

For an exhilarating walk, take the road west to Falcarragh for about four km and turn right at the first track past the Corcreggan Mill Cottage Hostel. Follow the track down to the sea dunes by first passing a farm and then crossing a field on a clearly indicated pathway. The vast and lovely Tramore Beach opens up below the sand dunes, and you may well be the only person here. Turn to the right and follow the beach to the end where you can find a way up onto a path that leads north to Pollaguill Bay. From the bay you can continue to the cairn at the end of the bay and follow the coastline for a stupendous view of the 20-metre Marble Arch, carved out by the sea.

Organised walks are also offered by Donegal Walking Holidays (☎ 074-36376), Sessiagh Cottage, Woodhill, Dunfanaghy.

Other Activities

Horse riding can be arranged through Arnold's Hotel, which also offers a programme of birdwatching, painting and photography holidays; phone ☎ 074-36208 for more details.

Places to Stay

Overlooking a glorious, deserted beach, *Corcreggan Mill Cottage Hostel* (☎ 074-36409) is a pleasantly cosy and well-organised place, four km from the Esso garage in Dunfanaghy on the road to Falcarragh. Beds in dorms cost IR£6 (IR£7

The Corncrake Crisis

Not so long ago, Irish rural nights were regularly riven by the distinctive *crek-crck* cry of the lovelorn male corncrake. But in 1988 an all-Ireland survey found only 903 birds still calling, and by 1994 this had fallen to just 130. Nowadays, corncrakes survive only in North Donegal and in the Shannon Callows, Mayo and small areas of the west coast.

The corncrake is a dowdy, secretive bird which winters in south-east Africa before arriving in Ireland to breed in April each year. But, like so many endangered species, it has habits that render it peculiarly vulnerable to modern life. Having laid their eggs in long grass, the females will stay with their chicks even as a mowing tractor's blades descend on them. Even if they realise the danger, long centuries of programming make them reluctant to rush for the safety of open ground.

With the hands at two minutes to midnight for the corncrake, the Irish Wildbird Conservancy (IWC) now offers grants to farmers who will delay mowing until August when the nesting season is over, or cut the grass in 'corncrake-friendly' fashion. A 24-hour Corncrake Hotline (☎ 074-65126) has been set up and you'll see notices in shop windows inviting people to ring it if they hear one. An IWC officer will then visit the site and decide if a nest is in need of protection.

In 1994 just 45 corncrakes were heard calling in County Donegal. The good news is that by mid-1995, the number had risen slightly to 60. ■

DONEGAL

in semi-private areas), and camping is also possible at IR£3 per person. It's a no smoking set-up with no TV or radio, and guests can earn themselves a free vegetarian meal by helping out with the organic garden.

The biggest hotel is *Arnold's* (☎ 074-36208) with singles/doubles from IR£40/60 in high season. The *Carrig Rua* (☎ 074-36133) charges about the same. Both hotels welcome children. *Rosman House* (☎ 074-36273) does B&B from IR£5 per person. At the *Corncrake's Rest* (☎ 074-36501) you might get lucky and hear a rare corncrake; to see one would be even luckier. B&B costs from IR£14 per person.

Arnold's Hotel has a chalet for rent at IR£230 a week during July and August.

Places to Eat

For coffee and cake, try the café attached to Dunfanaghy Workhouse on the N56. The restaurant in *Arnold's Hotel* has good views over the sea and serves hearty dinners from IR£14; the menu at the *Carrig Rua Hotel* is very much the same. The *Danny Collins Restaurant* (☎ 074-36205) is also worth a visit and *Danann's* (☎ 074-36150) is popular, with main courses for around IR£8. It's open from 6 pm, and reservations will often be necessary. Dunfanaghy also has a couple of fast-food places on the main street. Nearby at Port-na-Blagh, *The Cove* (☎ 074-36300) comes highly recommended and reservations are likely to be necessary. Reckon on between IR£15 and IR£20 a head.

Things to Buy

McAulliffe's craft shop, on the main street, has a selection of Irish tweeds and crystal.

Getting There & Away

The McGinley bus (☎ 075-48167) for Letterkenny and Dublin leaves Annagry at 6.45 am and reaches Dunfanaghy around 7.30 am. On Friday there are buses leaving for Dublin at 7.30 and 11.30 am, and 3.30 pm. From Dublin the buses leave at 5.45 pm daily and at 4.15 pm on Friday and 8.30 pm on Sunday.

The Feda O'Donnell bus (☎ 075-48114) to Galway stops in the Square at 8 am and 2.30 pm on Sunday, with extra buses on Friday.

The Lough Swilly bus (☎ 074-22863) leaves at 7.30 am and 12.20 and 5.15 pm for Derry, Monday to Friday only, and leaves Derry for Dunfanaghy at 8.50 am and 5 pm.

AROUND DUNFANAGHY

Ards Forest Park

The park has way-marked nature trails, varying in length from a couple of km to 13 km, and is also a wildfowl sanctuary. It covers the north shore of the Ards Peninsula which was once an estate of over 800 hectares. In 1930 the southern part was taken over by Capuchin monks; the grounds of their friary buildings are open to the public. The park is open free until 9 pm in summer; a guidebook costs IR£1.

The park is five km north of Creeslough off the N56.

Creeslough

This small village (*An Craoslach*) is on the N56 near an inlet of Sheep Haven Bay, and has an interesting modern church, best viewed against the outline of distant Muckish Mountain.

The mountain (659 metres) is a distinctive landmark, visible after leaving Letterkenny on the N56 and dominating the coast between Dunfanaghy and the Bloody Foreland. The hardest climb is from the Creeslough side; a road turns off to the left two km north-west of Creeslough, by a small derelict shop, on the N56. After six km along here a rough track begins the ascent. The easier route to the top is by way of Muckish Gap, off the inland road from Falcarragh. Consult *New Irish Walks: West & North* for details of both routes.

Doe Castle

The castle (*Cais Léan Na dTuath*) was once the stronghold of the Scottish MacSweeney family, once employed by the O'Donnells. It was built in the early 16th century and was constantly fought over by the MacSweeney brothers. Early in the 17th century it passed into English hands and was repaired and lived in until well into the 19th century. The curious tomb slab that rests against the tower near the entrance is thought to belong one of the MacSweeneys. It is picturesquely located on a very low promontory with water on three sides and a moat hewn out of the rock on the land side. The best view is from the Carrigart to Cresslough road.

The castle is five km from Creeslough on the Carrigart road and is clearly signposted. Admission is free, and if the gate is locked a key is available from the nearby house.

Places to Stay

At Port-na-blagh, the nearest town to Dunfanaghy, the *Hotel Port-na-blagh* (☎ 074-36129) has singles/doubles from IR£34.50/69 and that's about it apart from self-catering. *Creeslough Holiday Cottages* (☎ 074-38101) have a number of modern detached cottages that sleep seven adults and cost around IR£320 per week in July and August.

Places to Eat

You'll do better looking for somewhere to eat in Dunfanaghy or Letterkenny rather than along the N56 that joins them, although there is the inexpensive *Red Roof Restaurant* near Creeslough. Creeslough also has a couple of cafés.

If you are hostelling or camping, there are supermarkets at Creeslough, Dunfanaghy and Falcarragh. During the day Lurgyvale Thatched Cottage is open as a teashop (see that section for details).

Letterkenny & Around

Letterkenny is Donegal's largest town and could be used as a base for exploring the surrounding areas as an alternative to staying in smaller Dunfanaghy in the north or Dungloe in the west.

LETTERKENNY

Letterkenny (*Leitir Ceanainn*) is the county town and has grown considerably since

Derry was effectively cut off from its hinterland by the partition of Ireland. There's not a great deal to detain a tourist here, although it makes a pleasant enough place to spend the night en route to or from Derry.

Information

Main St, said to be the longest main street in Ireland, runs from Dunnes Stores at one end to the Court House at the other end and divides into Main St Upper and Lower. At the top of Main St Upper there is a junction with High Rd leading off to the left and Port Rd going right and down to the bus station and the road out to Derry.

The tourist office (☎ 074-21160), on the main Derry road outside town, is geared towards the motorist; you could walk there from the roundabout where the buses stop but it wouldn't be a very enjoyable experience. In the town itself, there's a Chamber of Commerce visitor centre (☎ 074-24866) at 40 Port Rd but it's not the county's most helpful. Both offices dispense an inexpensive signposted walking tour of the town which will help you focus on the highlights.

County Museum

This small modern museum has a collection of local archaeological finds including some interesting Iron Age stone heads and early Christian material upstairs. Downstairs there are temporary displays, often on the local tweed-making and weaving industries, and some very telling photos about the realities of life in 19th-century rural Ireland to counterbalance the rather rosy model on display upstairs. The museum is on High Rd, past the Manse Hostel, and is open from 10 am to 12.30 pm and 1 to 4.30 pm, Monday to Friday, afternoons only on Saturday. Entrance is free.

Fishing

There are a number of salmon and trout rivers in the area surrounding Letterkenny as well as various loughs. The Letterkenny and District Anglers' Association is open to visitors and there are shops in town where membership and permits are available. At 50

DONEGAL

Port Rd there is McGrath's newsagent and there is a tackle shop, Mr O'Neill's, in Main St Upper.

Other Activities

The Letterkenny leisure centre (☎ 074-25251) opposite the Manse Hostel (see Places to Stay) has swimming for IR£2/1, family IR£6, including use of the sauna before 3 pm.

Festival

A four-day international festival of music and dance (☎ 074-27856) is held at the end of August. It features a variety of music from Celtic rock to folk and jazz and includes a crafts day, street music and competitions.

Places to Stay

The *Manse Hostel* (☎ 074-25238) is on High Rd at the top of Main St with beds for IR£5, private rooms for IR£6.50 and family rooms also available. It's friendly, with lots of info on what to see and do locally and Diane, the proprietor, is from Melbourne, Australia. In theory there's a second hostel at 24 Port Rd (☎ 074-25315) but its business hours seem pretty arbitrary.

For B&B you could try *Covehill House* (☎ 074-21038) set back from the Port Rd and therefore likely to be fairly quiet. Beds cost £18/30. Near the Manse Hostel, *Carmel's* (☎ 074-21332) above a newsagent's is better than it looks from the outside and has beds for IR£16. In the centre of town *Gallagher's Hotel* (☎ 074-22066) at 100 Main St is currently overpriced at £27/48 but a refit is supposedly in the pipeline. If you arrive late and everything's full the modern *Hotel Clanree* (☎ 074-24369) is on the outskirts as you approach from Derry and charges IR£45/80 in high season.

Places to Eat

Best place for a pizza or home-made pasta is *Pat's Pizza* in Market Square. *Pat's Too* midway along Main St sells part-cooked pizzas to take away as well as kebabs and pitta bread sandwiches. Close to Pat's Too is the *Central Bar* which does pub food. In

Church St *Bakersville* is pleasant enough for coffee and snacks, or there's the *Quiet Moment* tearoom in Upper Main St for baps and salads. The *Tasty Bite*, also on Main St, opens for breakfast (IR£3.50) at 7.30 am. Inside the new Courtyard Shopping Centre in Main St, opposite Market Square, there's a good coffee shop one floor down, and *Galtee's Restaurant* in the basement with a few tables outside looking onto a mural so you can appreciate the Donegal scenery even when it's raining outside.

For dinner, *Gallagher's Hotel* (☎ 074-22066) in Main St Upper has a set menu for IR£12.95. The *Mount Errigal* hotel (☎ 074-22700) also does good dinners but it's on the outskirts of town. The *Taj Mahal* (☎ 074-27554) in Main St does standard Indian and Pakistani food. There's also the more distinctive *Arboretum Restaurant* (☎ 074-24333), tucked away in Villa Court off Port Rd, where a set dinner costs IR£9.95.

Entertainment

There's a four-screen cinema in Port Rd. Inside the Courtyard Shopping Centre you'll find a giant chessboard, snakes and ladders board and skittles to keep children amused.

Getting There & Away

The main bus station (☎ 074-22863) is by the big roundabout on the edge of town where the road to Derry begins. Bus Éireann, Lough Swilly and the other private companies all use this area and the adjacent supermarket car park.

Bus Éireann (☎ 074-21309) runs an express service from Dublin to Letterkenny via Omagh, and the Derry-Cork express stops at Letterkenny, Sligo, Galway and Limerick. The Derry-Galway bus also stops at Letterkenny before travelling on to Donegal, Bundoran, Sligo and Galway.

Lough Swilly (☎ 074-22400) runs a regular service from Derry to Dungloe, via Letterkenny and Dunfanaghy, as well as a more direct route between Letterkenny and Derry. The single fare to Derry is IR£4.20.

McGinley's (☎ 074-35201) run a bus from Annagry to Dublin through Letterkenny.

DONEGAL

There's a Feda O'Donnell bus (☎ 075-48114) from Crolly to Galway through Letterkenny. It goes on to Donegal, Bundoran, Sligo and Galway.

McGeehan (☎ 075-46101) runs a Letterkenny-Glencolumbcille service from Monday to Saturday. The fare is IR£6 single.

Doherty's Travel (☎ 075-21105) has a coach to Glasgow that leaves from outside Dunnes store at 5 pm; it's a daily service in July and August.

Getting Around

In summer, bikes can usually be hired from Church Street Cycles (☎ 074-25041) at 11 Church St. The street name is not indicated but it's about halfway along the main street and signs point to Conwal Parish Church and St Eunan's College.

COLMCILLE HERITAGE CENTRE

Colmcille (St Columba in English) was born in Gartan and the exhibition is devoted to his life and times, with a lavish display on the production of illuminated manuscripts.

Look for the Gartan clay that is associated with the birth of Colmcille. The clay is only found on a townland belonging to the O'Friel family, whose oldest son is the only one allowed to dig it up. The story is that Colmcille's mother, on the run from pagans, haemorrhaged during childbirth and her blood changed the soil's colour from brown to pure white. Ever since, the clay has been regarded as a charm. Ask nicely and the staff may produce some from below the counter.

In 1995 the centre (☎ 074-37306) was undergoing restoration. It's usually open over Easter and from mid-May to the end of September. Hours should be 10.30 am to 6.30 pm, Sunday 1 to 6.30 pm, and the charge was IR£1/50p, students 70p.

On the way to the heritage centre you'll also see signs to the ruins of Colmcille's Abbey and to the site of the saint's birthplace, marked by a cross erected by Cornelia Adair in 1911.

Getting There & Away

Leave Letterkenny on the R250 road to Glenties and Ardara and a few km out of town turn right on the R251 to the village of Churchill. Alternatively, from Kilmacrennan on the N56 turn west and follow the signs.

GLEBE HOUSE & GALLERY

The early 19th-century Glebe House was formerly a rectory and then a hotel. It was bought by the artist Derek Hill in 1953 for IR£1000. A fascinating guided tour of the house takes about 40 minutes.

Derek Hill was born in England in 1916 and worked in Germany before travelling to Russia and the east. He visited Armenia with Freya Stark and became interested in Islamic art and things oriental. The kitchen has a wonderfully folksy style and is full of paintings by the Tory Islands artists, including a bird's-eye view of West End village by James Dixon (see the Tory Island section). There is some original William Morris wallpaper in several rooms. Don't miss the weird bathroom with forward-flushing loo.

Glebe House would be worth visiting for the works of art alone. Landseer, Pasmore, Hokusai, Picasso, Augustus John, Jack B Yeats and Kokoschka are all represented. The gardens are also wonderful.

The house is open from mid-May to September and over the Easter period from 11 am to 6.30 pm daily except Friday. The charge is IR£2/1, family IR£5. It's on the shore of Lough Gartan close to the Colmcille Heritage Centre.

DOON WELL & ROCK

During penal times it was believed that wells like this had remarkable curative properties, and some people still believe this to be the case to judge by the bits of cloth left hanging in the nearby bush. There are good views from the top of the rock, which is where the O'Donnell kings were inaugurated.

Getting There & Away

There are a number ways of reaching the well. The most straightforward route is by taking the signposted turn-off from the N56 just north of Kilmacrennan.

GARTAN OUTDOOR EDUCATION CENTRE

The centre is set in its own 35-hectare estate and conducts a variety of courses throughout the summer: rock climbing, sea canoeing, windsurfing and hill climbing. Courses are run for both adults and children and full details are available from the Gartan Outdoor Education Centre (☎ 074-37032), Churchill, Letterkenny, County Donegal. Including hostel accommodation, a weekend multi-skill course for adults costs about IR£60, a five-day course about IR£155.

NEWMILLS VISITOR CENTRE

In the village of Newmills, just off the N56 between Creeslough and Kilmacrennan, an old flax and corn mill have been restored and opened to the public with a visitor centre explaining the role of these products and how they were produced. The mills had only just reopened in 1995 and, as the project expands there will also be a riverside walk to a two-room 19th-century scutcher's cottage and a village forge. The waterwheels attached to the mill should also start turning again. The mills are open daily May to October from 10 am to 6.30 pm (last tour 5.45 pm). Admission is IR£2/1.

LURGYVALE THATCHED COTTAGE

In a flagstone-floored cottage (☎ 074-39216) filled with rural artefacts, Susan and Sheila dispense tea and scones with home-made jam to famished motorists for IR£1.50. On Thursday evenings traditional music sessions are held with dancing and a singsong. Also during the summer there are demonstrations of traditional crafts on the first Sunday of the month. On cold, wet days the big log fire is particularly inviting.

Getting There & Away

The cottage is next to the road bridge on the N56 in the village of Kilmacrennan, easily spotted because of the large numbers of old farming implements scattered about.

LIFFORD

About 22 km south of Letterkenny, along the N14, is the small town of Lifford. It was once the judicial capital of the county, a position now held by Letterkenny.

Lifford Old Courthouse Visitors' Centre

Recently the fine 17th-century courthouse has been given a new lease of life as a heritage centre (☎ 074-41228), looking at both the historic role of Donegal's Gaelic chieftains and at some of the cases tried in the court and their verdicts.

For those who can't tell their O'Neills from their O'Donnells, some of the information provided in the Clans Room can be pretty heavy going. Descend into the courtroom, though, and the stories of Napper Tandy, Half-hanged McNaughten and other 'criminals' are riveting, and it's amazing how often they culminated with the villain sentenced to transportation to Australia!

Downstairs again and you fetch up in the icy cells where there are models of some of the prisoners whose cases you've already heard. Now you hear their side of the story. Down here there's also a small café serving soup, sandwiches and teas. The Courthouse is open Easter to October, Monday to Friday from 10 am to 6 pm, and Saturday and Sunday 2 to 6 pm. Admission costs IR£2.50/1.

Cavanacor House

At Rossgier, three km north of Lifford off the N14, Cavanacor House (☎ 074-41143) is an attractive 18th-century building, once inhabited by Magdalen Tasker, who was the great-great-great-grandmother of James Knox Polk, president of the USA from 1845 to 1849. James II is said to have dined beneath a sycamore in the front garden during the Siege of Derry in 1689. Three rooms in the house are now open to visitors, although the gallery at the back housing the paintings and sculptures created by its current owners is probably more interesting.

Cavanacor is open from Easter to September Tuesday to Saturday noon to 6 pm, and Sunday 2 to 6 pm. Admission is IR£2/1. There's an inviting tearoom too.

Places to Stay

Gateway Hotel (☎ 074-41700) is in Church St right in the centre of Lifford. It has beds from IR£20 per person. Cheaper beds are also available at *Rossborough House* (☎ 074-41132) and *Haw Lodge* (☎ 074-41397), both in Sligo Rd and both from about IR£14 a head.

North-Eastern Donegal

ROSGUILL PENINSULA

From Carrigart it is a 15-km journey around this small peninsula on the road marked Atlantic Drive. Carrigart itself has a lovely beach which is relatively deserted because the camp sites at Downings (also called Downies) draw the crowds to the other end of the long strand. The best beach for swimming is Trá na Rossan and the nearby hostel is an added attraction. On no account go swimming in Boveeghter Bay or Mulroy Bay as both have had drownings.

There are no tourist attractions to detract from the scenery, but there is plenty of social life at night in the Downings pubs, packed with holidaymakers from the North staying at the camp site.

Places to Stay

Casey's Caravan Park (☎ 074-55376) has limited camping space so it's best to ring first and check. A family tent is IR£8 a night, and a small tent IR£7.

The An Óige *hostel* (☎ 074-55374) at Trá na Rosann is open all year. It is six km from Downings and hitching is the best bet if you're without wheels.

Singles/doubles at the oddly designed *U Hol-Tel Carrigart* (☎ 074-55114) range from IR£32.50 per head to IR£40 and there's an indoor pool. Nearby at Hill House (☎ 074-55221) in Dunmore, B&B is from IR£13/26.

There is a little more choice in Downings: *Bay Mount* (☎ 074-55395) and *An Crossóg* (☎ 074-55498) both do B&B for IR£14 a

head. There's a hotel, *Beach* (☎ 074-55303), with 21 beds costing from IR£16/28.

Places to Eat

Carrigart itself is the best bet for food. The *North Star* pub has bar food and *Weavers Restaurant & Wine Bar* has meals for around IR£5.

Getting There & Away

There is a local bus between Carrigart and Downings, but that's of limited use for visitors from elsewhere. You really need your own transport for this area.

FANAD HEAD PENINSULA
Western Side

On the western side of the Fanad Peninsula, Carrowkeel (also called Kerrykeel) has an attractive location overlooking Mulroy Bay and nearby is the 19th-century **Knockalla Fort**, built to warn of any approaching French ships. There is also **Kildooney More portal tomb** to visit, but that's about it. The small villages of Milford and Rosnakill have little to attract visitors and there are no particularly good beaches.

Getting There & Away The Swilly bus leaves Letterkenny at 10.10 am and 6.10 pm and reaches Milford an hour later. From Milford it takes a further 10 minutes to Carrowkeel and 35 minutes to Portsalon, handy for the camp site.

Eastern Side

The eastern side of the Fanad Peninsula is far more interesting and either Ramelton or Rathmullan would make a good base for a quiet break. Accommodation is relatively limited so it would be wise to book ahead.

Ramelton

The first town you come to is pretty Ramelton, founded in the early 17th century by William Stewart and with some fine Georgian houses and stone warehouses. When the railway was routed to Letterkenny instead of Ramelton, a hush descended on the town. Not altogether surprisingly, it was picked as

DONEGAL

the location for filming the 1995 TV series set during the Irish Famine, *The Hanging Gale*.

In Back Lane the old **Meeting House** dating from around 1680 now houses a genealogy centre (☎ 074-51266). The ruined **Tullyaughnish Church** is also worth a visit because of the Romanesque carvings in the east wall which were taken from a far older church on nearby Aughnish Island. Shops in the main square sell the useful *Ramelton...an illustrated guide to the town* for IR£2.

Places to Stay There are several good B&Bs here. At the quiet northern end of town is *Crammond House* (☎ 074-51055) where beds from IR£13.50 come with a warm welcome. Near the town centre *Clooney House* (☎ 074-51125) charges IR£15/28.

Places to Eat A couple of km out of Letterkenny, before reaching Ramelton, *Carolina House Restaurant* (☎ 074-22480) is a smart establishment that specialises in fish. It only opens during the evenings, Tuesday to Saturday, and dinner is in the IR£20 bracket.

In Ramelton itself *Fish House* is attractively placed in an old stone building by the river and serves tea and light meals from 10 am to 7 pm, with last orders for food at 6.20 pm. For something more substantial *Mirabeau Steak House* (☎ 074-51138) cooks gigantic steaks with home-made sauces. The fish dishes are good but vegetarians would need to put in a special order.

Getting There & Away The Swilly bus (☎ 074-22863) weaves its way across the peninsula, leaving Letterkenny at 10.10 am, and 4.20 and 6.10 pm and taking 20 minutes to reach Ramelton.

Rathmullan

Like Ramelton, Rathmullan feels as if it has been bypassed by time, although in the 16th century it was the scene of momentous happenings. In 1587, 15-year-old Hugh O'Donnell, heir to the powerful O'Donnell clan, was tricked into boarding a ship at Rathmullan and taken to Dublin as a prisoner. He escaped four years later on Christmas Eve and, after unsuccessful attempts at revenge, died in Spain, aged only 30.

In 1607, despairing of beating the English, Hugh O'Neill, the earl of Tyrone, and Rory O'Donnell, the earl of Tyrconnel, boarded a ship in Rathmullan harbour and left Ireland for good. This decisive act, known as the Flight of the Earls, marked the effective end of Gaelic Ireland. In the aftermath of the earls' flight, large-scale confiscation of their estates took place, preparing for the plantation of Ulster with settlers from Scotland and England.

Heritage Centre This small, rather wordy centre (☎ 074-58229) focuses on the Flight of the Earls, and will mainly appeal to the historically minded. It's housed in an early 19th-century fort built by the British fearing Napoleon's intentions, and is open from 10 am to 6 pm (noon to 6.30 pm on Sunday) from Easter to September. Admission costs IR£1/50p, family IR£3. In lieu of a tourist office, the heritage centre can help with enquiries about local accommodation etc.

The sandy area near the pier outside the centre is the only clean part of the town's beach but there's a strong smell of fish from the quayside warehouse.

Rathmullan Priory This Carmelite friary was founded around 1508 by the MacSweeneys, and was still in use in 1595 when an English commander named George Bingham raided the place and took off with the church plate and vestments. The fact that it looks so well preserved is due to Bishop Knox's renovation in 1618; he wanted to use it as his own residence. It was from immediately outside the priory that the earls departed in 1607.

Places to Stay The newly refurbished *Water's Edge Inn* (☎ 074-58182) does B&B for IR£25 per person. it's just south of town and most of the rooms have fine views of Lough Swilly. There's also the small

Martello (☎ 074-58207) immediately opposite the heritage centre offering B&B from IR£11. The nearest hostel is further north at Bunnaton.

Rathmullan has three hotels, each quite different in style. The *Pier Hotel* (☎ 074-58178), originally a 19th century coaching inn, has 10 beds from IR£20 each and is very much a family establishment. *Rathmullan House* (☎ 074-58188) is a swanky country house with its own indoor heated swimming pool and sauna. Singles/doubles start at IR£25 per person in low season. *Fort Royal* (☎ 074-58100) has its own private beach and organises sporting activities; singles/doubles are from IR£30/70.

Places to Eat The *An Bonnan Bui* is a pleasant place for meals, with Guinness casseroles taking their places alongside crêpes and tacos on the menu. It's down the road near the pier that has the White Harte pub on the corner and opens on Friday and Saturday from 7 to 10 pm and on Sunday from 3 to 9 pm. The *Water's Edge Inn*, just south of town, does bar food as well as full à la carte meals with lovely lake views. The *Pier Hotel* and *Fort Royal* also do bar food as well as restaurant meals.

Getting There & Away The Swilly bus arrives in Rathmullan at 10.45 am and 6.45 pm from Letterkenny and departs straightaway for Portsalon (morning only) via Milford and Carrowkeel.

Portsalon & Fanad Head

Portsalon, once a popular holiday resort with Northerners, has little to offer except a long stretch of golden sand which is safe for swimming. It's another eight km to Fanad Head, which also has little to detain the traveller, other than the scenic drive to get there.

INISHOWEN PENINSULA

The Inishowen Peninsula, with Lough Foyle to the east and Lough Swilly to the west, reaches out into the Atlantic and ends with the most northerly point in the whole of

Ireland, Malin Head. The landscape is typical of Donegal: rugged, desolate and mountainous. Sites of antique interest abound, but there are also some wonderful beaches and plenty of places where travellers can go off alone. Tourist offices in Donegal, Letterkenny or Derry have free leaflets about walks for the Inishowen (*Inis Eoghain*) area, complete with maps. Proximity to Derry meant that the peninsula attracted few outsiders during the Troubles. Provided the peace holds, that should all change now.

The route below follows the road out of Derry up the coast of Lough Foyle to Moville and then north-west to Malin Head before following the western side down to Buncrana. If coming from Donegal the peninsula could be approached from the Lough Swilly side by turning off for Buncrana on the N13 road from Letterkenny to Derry. Leaving from Derry, though, the first village in the Republic is Muff. A scenic drive (*Inis Eoghain 100*) is clearly signposted round the peninsula.

Muff to Moville

The tiny village of Muff is only eight km from Derry. At night the pubs have their fair share of Northerners, and past Muff along the coast there are larger pubs catering to the same market.

Places to Stay The *Muff Hostel* (☎ 077-84188; from Derry 0003-84188), charging IR£5 a night, is in the village at the northern end just before the Renault garage; turn left if you're coming from Derry. The hostel is up this narrow road on the left. Camping is possible and bikes can be hired, but it's best to phone ahead to avoid a gruff reception. *Mrs Reddin* (☎ 077-84031), next to the post office on Main St, does the only village B&B. Rooms are pretty basic but it's only IR£12 a head.

Beyond Muff and just before Moville there is a hotel and a bunch of B&Bs at Redcastle. Next to the village post office, *Fernbank* (☎ 077-83032) does B&B from IR£13. The *Redcastle Country Hotel*

DONEGAL

(☎ 077-82073) has all the facilities of a big hotel and singles/doubles from IR£35/60.

Places to Eat There are a few pubs serving sandwiches and a village café doing takeaways, but no restaurants. More substantial meals are available at the *Redcastle Country Hotel* further up the coast before Moville; their tourist menu has three-course meals from IR£6.50 to IR£12, served from 11 am to 6.30 pm. After 7 pm, dinners starts at IR£14.50. There are a couple of cafés at Quigley Point, a few km out of Muff and also on the coast road.

Getting There & Away Lough Swilly buses (☎ 01504-262017 in Derry) run eight buses a day from Derry on the Cardonagh service that stops at Muff, as well as five buses a day to Stroove that also go through Muff. There is no Sunday service on either route. Worth considering is their eight-day unlimited travel ticket for IR£15.

Moville

Now a sleepy seaside town, Moville was once a busy port where emigrants set sail for a new life in America. The coastal walkway from Moville to Greencastle takes in the

TOM SMALLMAN

TOM SMALLMAN

TOM SMALLMAN

Central North
Top Left: Lough Key, County Roscommon
Top Right: Saints Peter & Paul Cathedral and Market Square, Athlone, County Westmeath
Bottom: Main Street, Mullingar, County Westmeath

PAT YALE

PAT YALE

PAT YALE

County Donegal

Top Left: Tree festooned with offerings beside Doon Well
Top Right: Bilingual Guinness ad
Bottom: Garden gnomes

stretch of coast where the steamers used to moor.

Cooley Cross & Skull House

By the gate of the Cooley gravehouse is a three-metre, slender high cross, unusual due to the ringhole in its head through which the hands of negotiating parties were clasped to seal an agreement. In the graveyard itself there is a small building known as the Skull House, still containing some old bones. It may be associated with St Finian, the monk who accused Colmcille of plagiarising a manuscript of his in the 6th century. He lived in a monastery here that was founded by St Patrick and which survived into the 12th century.

Approaching Moville from the south, look out for a turning on the left (if you pass a church, you've gone too far) which has a sign on the corner for Clarke's furniture store. The graveyard is just over one km up this road on the right.

Places to Stay The IHH *Moville Holiday Hostel* (☎ 077-82378) is in Malin Rd and charges IR£6 a head. There are also a few B&Bs around Moville. *Barron's Café* (☎ 077-82472) in town has beds for IR£12, while on the road out of town *Iona House* (☎ 077 82173) is a small homely place charging IR£14. There are two hotels: *Foyle* (☎ 077-82025), charging from IR£17/34 or the more expensive *McNamara's* (☎ 077-82010), from IR£26 per person.

Places to Eat In Moville itself, *Barron's Café* and the two hotels are the best bets: dinner at *McNamara's* costs IR£17, while *Foyle* has a Saturday night set dinner for IR£11. *Rosatos* also serves food until 9 pm.

Greencastle is so close that, if you have your own transport, the places there are worth looking at. *The Old Fort Inn* (☎ 077-81044) is inside a Napoleonic fort and you can dine either in the officers mess bar or the soldiers canteen bar.

Greencastle

In 1305 Greencastle Castle was built by Richard de Burgo, known as the Red Earl

because of his florid complexion. The castle functioned as a supply base for English armies in Scotland and for this reason was attacked by the Scots under Robert Bruce in the 1320s. In 1555 the castle was demolished, and little now survives.

Four Lough Swilly buses travel daily between Derry and Stroove, passing through Greencastle, but there is no Sunday service.

Inishowen Head

A right turn outside Greencastle leads to Stroove whence a sign indicates Inishowen Head is one km to the left. It's possible to drive or cycle part of the way but it's also an easy walk to the headland from where views take in the Antrim coast as far as the Giant's Causeway. A more demanding walk continues to the sandy beach of Kinnagoe Bay. At Stroove, where the road left goes to the headland, a right turn goes to Dunagree Point and back to Greencastle but this loop has little to recommend it.

Carndonagh

Information Inishowen Tourism (☎ 077-74933) at the top of Bridge St could show Bord Fáilte a few things when it comes to supplying visitors with out-of-season information. It's open Monday to Friday from 9.30 am to 5.30 pm, and daily from mid-June to September, provided enough staff can be found.

Things to See In Bridge St there's a small **history museum** which opens in summer, provided staff are available.

At the Buncrana end of Carndonagh, the 8th-century **Carndonagh High Cross** has been re-erected against the wall of an Anglican church. Next to the cross are two small pillars, one said to show a man with a sword and shield, possibly Goliath, next to David and his harp. In the graveyard there is a pillar with a carved marigold on a stem. On the other side of the stone there's a Crucifixion scene.

On the road to Ballyliffin, in a small church by the post office, a collection of local folk items are on display in the **Folk**

DONEGAL

Museum. It only opens in July and August, Monday to Saturday from 2 to 4 pm.

Places to Stay Near the High Cross a sign points the way to *Teirnaleague* (☎ 077-74471) where B&B costs from IR£12.

Places to Eat In the main square there's *Trawbreaga Bay* for main meals, but for something lighter, head down Malin St to *The Corncrake Restaurant and Coffee Shop* (☎ 077-74534) which is open from 10 am to 5 pm on weekdays (later in summer) and until 9 pm at weekends. Here you can tuck into dishes like mussels in garlic for IR£3.50 or sea trout for IR£7.50.

If you're off to Malin Head for the day or going on to the camp site at Clonmany, stock up with eatables at the Contra supermarket in Malin Rd.

Getting There & Away A Lough Swilly bus leaves Buncrana for Carndonagh at 8.40 am, 1 and 6.15 pm, returning from Carndonagh at 7.30 and 10 am. They also run a bus between Derry and Carndonagh but neither service runs on Sunday.

North West Busways (☎ 077-82619) operate a service between Letterkenny and Moville via Carndonagh and Buncrana. They also run buses to Malin Head, although the timing is such that you'd need to stay the night before coming back again.

Around Carndonagh
There are several neighbouring antiquities that can be visited from the main Moville-Carndonagh road.

Clonca Church & Cross The carved lintel over the door of this 17th-century building is thought to come from an earlier church. In the north-east corner the interesting tombstone was erected by one Magnus MacOrristin and has a sword and hurling stick carved on it. The remains of the cross show the Miracle of the Loaves and Fishes on the east face and geometric designs on the sides.

Look for the turn-off to Culdaff, on the right if coming from Moville, on the left after about 6 km if coming from Carndonagh. The Clonca Church and Cross are 1.5 km on the right.

Bocan Stone Circle There are better stone circles in Ireland. This one has only a few of probably over 30 original stones left but the surrounding views help to conjure up the kind of significance the place must have held some 3000 years ago.

From Clonca Church, continue along the road until a T-junction is reached. Turn right here and after about half a km turn left. The stone circle is inside the first field on the left.

Carrowmore High Crosses Like the Bocan Stone Circle, these high crosses may prove a little disappointing. One is basically a decorated slab showing Christ and a ministering angel, while on the other side of the road there is a taller cross with stumpy arms.

From Bocan Stone Circle and Clonca Church, retrace the route back to the main Carndonagh-Moville road and turn left and then almost immediately right. Don't be surprised to find the sign to the crosses pointing in the wrong direction.

Malin Head
At the top of the Inishowen Peninsula is Malin Head, the most northerly point of Ireland, and a familiar name to listeners to radio weather forecasts. The tower on the cliffs was built in 1805 by the British Ambassador and used later as a Lloyds signal station. The huts were used by the Irish army in WW II as lookout posts.

Above nearby Ballyhillion Beach the *Cottage* serves tea and food all week from June to September, Sunday only between March and May and in October.

The pretty plantation village of Malin is centred round a triangular green. One of the Inishowen walk leaflets (see the Inishowen section) outlines an interesting circular route from the village green that takes in a local hill with terrific views as well as Lagg Presbyterian Church, which is claimed to be the oldest in Ireland. Children will love the massive Lagg sand dunes by the church.

Places to Stay There is one small hotel, the *Malin* (☎ 077-70606), in the village. Singles/doubles are from IR£22/42. B&B is also available from *Mrs Gallagher* (☎ 077-70649) for IR£11. At Malin Head there are a few more B&Bs, the most northerly in Ireland offered by *Mrs Hickox* (☎ 077-70249), who charges from IR£13.

Getting There & Away The best way to approach Malin Head is by the R238/242 from Carndonagh, rather than up the eastern side from Culdaff.

Ballyliffin & Clonmany
This small resort area attracts more Irish than overseas visitors. There's plenty of accommodation in the area.

About one km from Ballyliffin is the lovely expanse of Pollan Bay Beach, which is unfortunately not safe for swimming. A walk to the north brings you to the ruins of Carrickbrackey Castle (also spelt Carrickabraghy), dating back to the 16th century. To reach the beach, turn down the road in Ballyliffin by the thatched cottage and the Atlantic ballroom. There is one sign on the road but it's only visible from the Clonmany side.

The other beach is at Tullagh Bay, immediately behind the camp site at Clonmany. It's great for an exhilarating walk but the current can be strong and swimming is not recommended when the tide is going out. Someone drowned here in 1992.

Places to Eat The *Strand Hotel* does lunch for IR£8 as well as bar food, while in the evening, dinner costs from IR£10 a head. Both the *Strand* and the *Ballyliffin* do pub food, as does a nameless pub at the junction in Clonmany.

Entertainment Most of the pubs and hotels have music sessions throughout the summer. In Clonmany, *McFeeley's* is a very popular

pub and *Mackey's Tavern*, near the camp site, has lively music sessions at the weekend.

Getting There & Away A Lough Swilly bus runs between Buncrana and Carndonagh three times daily, Monday to Saturday. It leaves Buncrana at 8.40 am, 1 and 6.15 pm and departs from Carndonagh at 7.30 and 10 am and 4.15 pm; 20 minutes later from Clonmany.

Ballyliffin to Buncrana
There are two routes from Ballyliffin to Buncrana: the scenic coastal road via the Gap of Mamore and Dunree, or the speedier, inland road. The Gap of Mamore descends dramatically between Mamore Hill and the Urris Hills into a valley where the road follows the River Owenerk most of the way to Dunree.

The main reason to pause in Dunree would be to visit the **Guns of Dunree** military exhibition in Dunree Fort. Back in 1798, Wolfe Tone, with the help of the French, planned to arrive in Lough Swilly and march on Derry. The British constructed six forts to guard the lough and the museum tells the whole story. It's open June to September Monday to Saturday from 10.30 am to 6 pm, opening at 12.30 pm on Sunday. The charge is IR£1.50/70p and there's a small café at the site. Fulmars nest on the rocks below the fort, so close you can see them easily.

Buncrana
After Bundoran this must be the most popular resort in Donegal for holidaymakers from Derry and the North, but unlike Bundoran it contrives to suggest there is life beyond tourism. It has a long sandy beach which is safe for swimming, all the pubs you could hope for, and several places of interest to while away your spare hours.

Information Despite the huge signs trumpeting the tourist information office in Swilly Terrace opposite the leisure centre as you come in from Letterkenny, you'll be lucky to find it open except in July and August. Don't be fooled by the sign outside the Roadside Café either. The council simply erected it one

DONEGAL

day and it's been there ever since, pointing nowhere at all! A taxi service (☎ 077-61366) is available from here though.

Tullyarvan Mill This community-run exhibition, craft shop and café is well worth a visit. The exhibition is devoted to the restoration of the mill, local history, flora & fauna, and is attractively presented. Downstairs the small craft shop has pottery at prices that are not as outrageous as usual. The place is also worth checking out for its lively traditional music evenings that take place regularly throughout the summer.

The centre should be open in summer from 10 am to 6 pm Monday to Friday, afternoons only at weekends, but because it's staffed by volunteers it sometimes closes unexpectedly, so phone ☎ 077-61613 to check before making a special journey. To visit the exhibition costs IR£1.50/75p.

To find the place, take the road out to Dunree and the mill is signposted on the right after the bridge.

Vintage Car & Carriage Museum The vehicles being exhibited are likely to change from time to time as the owner buys and sells, but would anyone part with a '29 Rolls or a '57 Chevy? These and many others fill up the large garage incongruously located behind a bungalow on the seafront. During the summer it is open from 10 am to 8 pm and costs IR£1.50/50p; other times by appointment (☎ 077-61130).

O'Docherty's Keep At the north end of the seafront an early 18th-century six-arched bridge leads to a tower house built by the O'Dochertys, the local chiefs, in the early 15th century. It was burnt by the English and then repaired for their own use. The big house nearby was built in 1718 by John Vaughan who also built the bridge.

Places to Stay There is no shortage of B&Bs around town but they can fill up during August. *Golan View* (☎ 077-62644) is close to the town centre and charges IR£15 a head. *Kincora* (☎ 077-61174) in Cahir

O'Doherty Ave charges from IR£18 single, IR£26 double.

The *White Strand* (☎ 077-61144) hotel has beds from IR£18 and the *Lake of Shadows Hotel* (☎ 077-61005) has a heated indoor pool and singles/doubles from IR£22/40.

Places to Eat At the Clomany end of town, the *Roadside Café* lives up to its name, and a takeaway service is also available. The café at the Tullyarvan Mill serves cakes and drinks at sensible prices, but the best place in terms of choice is probably the *Ubiquitous* (☎ 077-62530) at 47 Upper Main St despite the fact that its name makes little sense now that it's dropped the word 'chip'!

Across the road *Wing Tai House* is a Chinese restaurant that does serve chips with everything. The *Four Lanterns* next door dishes up fast food, while *McDaids* bakery opposite does snacks. Despite its old-fashioned name, *Dorothy's Kitchen* in Church St, off Main St, stays open dishing out burgers and kebabs until 1 am. On the Derry road heading out of town, the *Drift Inn* is a strange, Gothic-looking pub converted from a railway station. It also serves food.

Entertainment The main form of entertainment is found, unsurprisingly, in the town's many pubs strung out along the main street. The *Atlantic Bar* can be relied on for live music at weekends, as can *O'Flaitbeartaiz*. For somewhere quiet and relaxing, try *Roddens*. There's a one-screen cinema at the end of Main St.

Getting There & Away From Buncrana, Lough Swilly buses (☎ 077-61340) run a daily service to Derry (IR£2.40 single). There is also a service to Carndonagh.

South of Buncrana
Fahan Cross Slab A monastery was founded in Fahan by St Colmcille in the 6th century and the stone slab in the graveyard beside the Anglican church has been dated to the century after. Each face is decorated with a cross, and the Greek inscription, which is

not easily made out, is the only one known from this early Christian period.

Grianán of Aileach This impressive hilltop stone fort offers panoramic views of the surrounding countryside: Loughs Swilly and Foyle, Inch Island and distant Derry. The walls are four metres thick and enclose an area 23 metres in diameter. The fort may be at least 2000 years old, but the site has pagan associations that go back much further. Between the 5th and 12th century it was the seat of the O'Neills before being demolished by Murtogh O'Brien, king of Munster. You might be wondering how a fort that was demolished 800 years ago could possibly look so complete. The answer is that between 1874 and 1878 an amateur archaeologist from Derry set about reconstructing the fort and this is mostly what you see today.

The design of the attractive circular **church** at the foot of the hill was obviously modelled on that of the fort. It's by Derry architect Liam McCormack and was built in 1965-67.

Grianán of Aileach Visitor's Centre The late 19th-century church of Christchurch at Burt, at the bottom of the hill with the fort, has been converted to house a small display on its history up among the roof rafters. There's a life-size model of Muirchertach na gCochall Craicinn, a 10th-century ancestor of the O'Neills and king of Aileach from 938 to 943. In 942 he went on an extended tour of Ireland recorded in verse by Cormacan

Eigean, but here he looks remarkably like a New Age Traveller! There are also models of members of Christchurch's Victorian congregation and information about the local flora & fauna. The centre is open daily from 10 am to 6 pm (until 10 pm in high summer) and admission is IR£2/1 child. Because space is limited, things could get pretty cramped in peak season.

Places to Stay Inch Island (connected to the mainland by a causeway) is not much visited by tourists but does have one interesting B&B. *O'Doherty's* (no phone) is on the right of the pier, just past the sign to the strand, and there is usually a US flag flying outside next to an Irish one. If you carry on along the road, you will come across the *Meitheal* holistic centre (☎ 077-60323) where a bed and meals are available for around IR£10. People pay to meditate here.

Places to Eat Set fair to become *the* place to eat around here is the *Grianán of Aileach Visitor's Centre*. Most of Christchurch has in fact been turned into a restaurant with character (the bar counter created out of a Boer war memorial slab, the reservations book resting in the pulpit). It's open for lunch from noon to 2.30 pm and for dinner from 6 to 10 pm, and there's plenty of choice, including several vegetarian options. Phone ☎ 077-68512 for reservations. If you don't fancy such formality, there are a few tables on the ground floor for coffee, open sandwiches and other snacks.

DONEGAL

Counties Meath & Louth

Heading north from Dublin along the coast takes you through the counties of Meath and Louth before you cross the border into County Down in Northern Ireland. This low, coastal landscape is the opposite of the mountainous country to the south of Dublin, rising only slightly inland to the plain known in folklore as Murtheimne, the stage for many events in the Iron Age saga of the Cattle Raid of Cooley. The climax of the saga took place on Louth's beautiful Cooley Peninsula, and many places there owe their names to the legendary heroes and battles of that time.

The scenery in Meath and Louth is reminiscent of old England: verdant, settled farmland with fine old farmhouses throughout. Here lie some of the most remarkable legacies of the earliest Irish people: the tombs of Newgrange and Loughcrew and also the fine monasteries at Monasterboice, Mellifont and Kells, built later by Irish Christians.

Highlights
- Prehistoric remains at Newgrange and Knowth
- Eating oysters in Carlingford
- Tracking the remains of medieval Trim
- The Hill of Tara
- Mellifont Abbey and Monasterboice

County Meath

Meath, Dublin's immediate neighbour to the north-west, has long been one of Ireland's premier farming counties, a plain of impossibly rich soil stretching north to the lakelands of Cavan and Monaghan and west before running into the bleak Bog of Allen. Hidden among the huge fields and old stands of trees, you will glimpse the solid houses of Meath's former settlers and today's wealthy farmers – many of them grown even wealthier since EU farming policies started offering subsidies for letting land lie fallow!

For a large county, Meath has surprisingly few major settlements. Navan, Trim and Kells are simply medium-sized towns, while places like Ashbourne, Dunshaughlin and Dunboyne on the southern fringe are becoming commuter suburbs of Dublin. The county's principal attractions are its ancient sites, and the isolated hills such as Tara and Slane have immense historical significance.

HISTORY
Meath's rich soil, laid down during the last Ice Age, attracted settlers as early as 8000 BC, who worked their way up the banks of the River Boyne and began to transform the landscape from forest to farmland. Brugh na Bóinne is an extensive prehistoric necropolis, dating from around 3000 BC, which lies on a meandering section of the Boyne between Drogheda and Slane. There's a group of smaller passage graves at Loughcrew on the Slieve na Caillighe Slieve na Calliaghe hills.

The Hill of Tara in Meath was the foremost spiritual and political centre of Ireland;

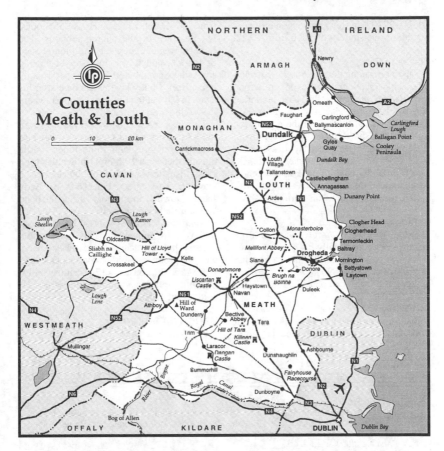

Counties Meath & Louth

for 1000 years it was the seat of power for Irish high kings until the arrival of St Patrick in the 5th century. Later, Kells became one of the most important and creative monastic settlements in Ireland and lent its name to the famed 'Book of Kells', now displayed in Trinity College, Dublin.

THE COAST

Meath's paltry 10 km of coastline includes a number of small resorts with sand dunes and safe beaches. The Elizabethan **Maiden Watch Tower** in Mornington at the mouth of the Boyne provides a fine view of Drogheda, five

km to the west, and the Boyne estuary. **Laytown** is a busy little place with golf, tennis and good windsurfing. It hosts annual horse races on the beach in mid-August. Barely one km away to the south, **Bettystown's** claim to fame is that the magnificent Tara Brooch was found here. It is now on display in the National Museum, Dublin.

Places to Stay

Ardilaun (☎ 041-27033) at 41 Beach Park, Laytown, is near the beach, and a single costs IR£13 or IR£15 with bathroom. It's open from May to September. The *Neptune*

(☎ 041-27107) in Bettystown is an ordinary, medium-priced hotel with B&B from IR£22.

Places to Eat

In Laytown, facing the sea, *Paddy Traynor's* offers chicken & chips and so on. In Bettystown, *Gary Lynch's* near the beach is similar. Nearby, the *Coastguard Restaurant* (☎ 041-28251) is one of the best in the region. It's right on the shore, and dinner costs from IR£18.95. It's open Tuesday to Saturday from 6.30 pm and on Sunday for lunch. You'll probably have to book at weekends. Almost next door is *Tea & Talent*, with coffee, teas and light meals during the day.

Entertainment

In Laytown, the *Cottage Inn* is a nice thatched pub and usually has a good crowd at weekends. The *Lyons Pub* is also popular. In Bettystown, *McDonagh's* is another popular, old-fashioned place.

DULEEK

Duleek claims to have had Ireland's first stone church, and the town's name comes from 'An Damh Liag' or House of Stones, but no trace of the church remains. The founder was the energetic and omnipresent St Patrick, and it was built by St Cianán somewhere around 450. En route to Armagh, Brian Ború's body lay in state here after his death in 1014 at the Battle of Clontarf, where the Vikings were defeated.

Duleek's abbey and tower ruins date from the 12th century and contain a number of excellent effigies and tombstones, while outside there is a 10th or 11th-century high cross. The town square of Duleek has a wayside cross, erected in 1601 by Lady Jennet Dowdall in memory of her husband William Bathe and herself.

Annesbrook House (☎ 041-23293) is open mid-May to September. This comfortable country house is surrounded by extensive wooded grounds but it's rather expensive at IR£30/50. The house is a 17th-century building with Georgian additions, and George IV paid a visit in 1821.

BRUGH NA BÓINNE

There was extensive settlement along the

Battle of the Boyne

On 1 July 1690, the forces of the Catholic James II were defeated by those of the Protestant William of Orange at the Battle of the Boyne. The victory is still celebrated by Protestants in Northern Ireland as the Glorious Twelfth – the date having been adjusted in 1752 when the Gregorian calendar was adopted.

There is little to see of the battle site except green fields. Nevertheless, a visit may give some understanding of the forces that shaped Ireland then and now, which are examined in the History section of the Facts about the Country chapter.

The battle site is near Oldbridge, four km west of Drogheda, and is clearly marked with a huge orange billboard. A trail leads to a slight rise overlooking the battlefield. Before the battle, William's army camped just west of Oldbridge in what is now Townley Hall demesne and Forest Park. The Jacobite camp was stretched out along the slopes of Donore Hill, four km south of Oldbridge. James's command post was near the ruined church on the summit.

On 1 July, William's men crossed the river near Slane and Oldbridge, and despite the death of the able Marshal Schomberg (an obelisk at the base of the bridge marks the spot), they outflanked James's forces and in the face of brave resistance routed them. The losers retreated to Donore, then to Duleek, where they spent the night, and then to the Shannon and Dublin.

James himself fled south to Dublin and then to Waterford, whence he crossed back to France and ignominious exile. Remnants of the Catholic forces regrouped and fought on for another year, but symbolically and politically the struggle was over. ■

Boyne Valley in prehistoric times, and the necropolis known as Brugh Na Bóinne (Brugh is pronounced 'broo') was built in the area. This consists of many different sites, the three principal ones being Newgrange, Knowth and Dowth. They were the largest artificial structures in Ireland until the construction of the Anglo-Norman castles.

Over the centuries these tombs decayed, became covered by grass and trees and were plundered by everybody from Vikings to Victorian treasure hunters, whose carved initials can be seen on the great stones of Newgrange. The countryside around them is littered with countless other ancient mounds and standing stones.

Newgrange

Newgrange is a huge, flattened, grass-covered mound about 80 metres in diameter and 13 metres high. The mound covers the finest Stone Age passage tomb in Ireland; one of the most remarkable prehistoric sites in Europe. It dates from around 3200 BC, earlier than either Stonehenge or the Pyramids. The purpose for which it was constructed remains uncertain. It may have been a burial place for kings or a centre for ritual – although the alignment with the sun at the time of the winter solstice might also suggest it was designed to act as a calendar.

Over the centuries Newgrange, like Dowth and Knowth, deteriorated and was even quarried at one stage. There was a standing stone on the summit until the 17th century. The site was extensively restored in 1962 and again in 1975.

A superbly carved kerbstone with double and triple spirals stands guarding the tomb's main entrance. The front facade has been reconstructed so that tourists don't have to clamber in over it. Above the entrance is a slit or roof box, which lets light in. Another beautifully decorated kerbstone stands at the exact opposite side of the mound. Some experts say that a ring of standing stones encircled the mound, forming a Great Circle about 100 metres in diameter, but only 12 of these stones remain – with traces of some others below ground level.

Holding the whole structure together are the 97 boulders of the kerb ring, designed to stop the mound from collapsing outwards. Eleven of these are decorated with motifs similar to the one on the main entrance stone, although only three have extensive carvings.

The white quartzite was originally brought from Wicklow, 80 km to the south, and there is also some granite from the Mourne Mountains in Northern Ireland. Over 200,000 tonnes of earth and stone also went into the mound.

You can walk down the narrow 19-metre passage, lined with 43 stone uprights, some of them engraved, which leads into the tomb chamber, about a third of the way into the colossal mound. The chamber has three recesses, and in these are large basin stones which held cremated human bones. Along with the remains would have been funeral

Detail of the Threshold Stone at Newgrange, Ireland's finest Stone Age passage tomb

offerings of beads and pendants, but these must have been stolen long before the archaeologists arrived.

Above, massive stones, many with intricate engravings, support a six-metre-high corbel-vaulted roof. A complex drainage system means that not a drop of water has penetrated the interior in 40 centuries.

At dawn on the winter solstice – the shortest day of the year – the rising sun's rays shine directly through the slit above the entrance, creep slowly down the long passage and illuminate the tomb chamber for 17 minutes. Places to experience this annual event, and for the days immediately on either side when the sun enters most of the way, are booked up until 2009 and the waiting list is now closed.

However, for the legions of daily visitors, there is a simulated winter sunrise for every group taken into the mound. Make sure you are near the centre of the chamber floor, otherwise somebody is bound to be in your line of sight.

A couple of things puzzled the archaeologists. The light comes all the way down the passageway a few minutes after sunrise, not at the precise moment, and surprisingly it stops short of illuminating the centre of the back wall. Recent studies by cosmic physicists have found that the earth's position has shifted; when the mound was built, the sunlight would have illuminated the whole chamber precisely at sunrise.

According to Celtic legend, the god Aengus lived at Newgrange, and the hero Cúchulainn was conceived here.

Guided tours take place (☎ 041-24488) daily 9.30 am to 7 pm from June to September (to 6 pm in May). In March and April, and October, hours are 10 am to 5 pm. From November to February the site closes half an hour earlier at 4.30 pm. The last tours leave about half an hour before closing time. Entry is IR£3/1.25.

In summer, particularly on weekends, Newgrange is crowded (it's the busiest single tourist site in the country), and it's best to come during the week and/or first thing in the morning. Large groups must be booked

in advance and because of this and the limited space inside the tomb, individual visitors may find themselves with a long wait at peak times.

Across the road, a seasonal tourist office (☎ 041-24274) is open April to October. Work has started on a controversial interpretive centre for the Brugh Na Bóinne. Once it's completed, visitors will be ferried to the tomb in shuttle buses from the car park. Eventually, the tomb may even be closed altogether to protect the fragile carvings. If that happens, visitors will have to make do with a reproduction.

A few hundred metres down the hill from the tomb is Newgrange Farm (☎ 041-24119), a 133-hectare working farm with a wide range of animals on view, a picnic area and a coffee shop. It's a good place to wait for the Newgrange tour to begin. It's open for farm tours from 10 am to 5.30 pm Monday to Friday and 2 to 5.30 pm on Sunday from April to September; in July and August, it's also open on Saturday afternoons. Admission is IR£2 for adults or children.

Dowth
The circular mound at Dowth is similar in size to Newgrange – about 63 metres in diameter – but at 14 metres high is slightly higher. It has suffered badly at the hands of everyone from roadbuilders to treasure hunters to antiquarians, who scooped out the centre of the tumulus in the last century. For a time, Dowth even had a teahouse perched on the summit, erected by a local lord. Relatively untouched by modern archaeologists, Dowth shows what Newgrange and Knowth looked like for most of their history.

There are two entrance passages leading to separate chambers (both barred), and a 24-metre early Christian souterrain with beehive structures at either end which connect up with the west passage. The nine-metre-long west passage leads into a small cruciform chamber, in which a recess acts as an entrance to an additional series of small compartments, a feature unique to Dowth.

To the south-west is the entrance to a shorter passage and smaller chamber.

Unfortunately, as a result of a dispute between the landowners and the Office of Public Works (OPW), the site at Dowth is closed to visitors for the foreseeable future.

North of the tumulus and visible from the summit are the ruins of **Dowth Castle** and **Dowth House**.

A native of the area was one John Boyle O'Reilly (1844-90). For his part in the Irish Republican Brotherhood, O'Reilly was deported to a penal colony in Australia from where he later escaped to the USA. As editor of the *Boston Pilot* newspaper he made an influential contribution to liberal opinion. The people of Boston erected a memorial to him in their city centre while the locals did the same here in the churchyard beside the castle.

Knowth

Knowth (*Cnóbha*), the third principal burial mound of the necropolis, was built around the same time as Newgrange, and seems set to surpass its better-known neighbour, both in the extent and importance of the discoveries made here. It has the greatest collection of passage grave art ever uncovered in western Europe.

Modern excavations started at Knowth in 1962 and soon cleared a 34-metre passage to the central chamber, much longer than the one at Newgrange. In 1968 a second 40-metre passage was unearthed on the opposite side of the mound. Although the chambers are separate, they are close enough for archaeologists to hear each other at work. Also in the mound are the remains of six Christian beehive souterrains similar to the one at Dowth. Three hundred carved slabs and 17 'satellite graves' surround the main mound.

Human activity at Knowth continued for thousands of years after its construction and accounts for the site's complexity. The Beaker people, so called because they buried their dead with a characteristic beaker, occupied the site in the Bronze Age (circa 1800 BC), as did the Celts in the Iron Age (circa 500 BC). Remnants of bronze and iron work-

ings from these periods have been discovered. Around 800 to 900 AD it was turned into a rath or ring fort, a stronghold of the powerful UiNeill (O'Neill) family. In 965, it was the seat of Corgalach McMaelmithic, later a high king of Ireland. The Normans built a motte-and-bailey here. In about 1400 the site was finally abandoned. Excavations are likely to continue for the next decade.

Partly because of the excavations and partly because the later buildings on the site weakened the internal structures, making it difficult for anyone to walk along the passage, only parts of the site are open for guided tours. It's open from 10 am to 5 pm May to October, from 9.30 am to 6.30 pm, with the last tour at 5.45 pm, from mid-June to mid-September. Admission costs IR£2/1.50.

Getting There & Away

Newgrange, Knowth and Dowth are all well signposted. Newgrange is 13 km west of Drogheda, just north of the River Boyne. Dowth is between Newgrange and Drogheda, while Knowth is about one km north-west of Newgrange or almost four km by road.

There are no buses to any of the sites, but a couple of buses between Slane and Drogheda on Monday, Wednesday and Friday will drop you on the main road about three km from Newgrange. For IR£10, Bus Éireann also runs a bus and bike scheme which allows you to catch the 10 am Dublin to Drogheda bus on any weekday, picking up a bike to explore the area at Drogheda station and returning to Dublin on the 5.20 pm bus. There's a IR£20 deposit, and hire of a bike helmet adds another IR£1 to the cost.

Alternatively, Mary Gibbons Tours (☎ 283 9973) take in both Newgrange and Knowth on Monday, Wednesday and Friday afternoon tours, leaving Dublin Tourism on O'Connell St at 1.20 pm. The IR£14 cost includes admission to both sites.

SLANE

Slane is perched on a hillside overlooking the River Boyne, at the junction of the N2 and N51, 15 km west of Drogheda. Built as a manorial village for Slane Castle, it is a charming little place with stone houses, cottages and mature trees. Just to the south of the centre is the massive grey gate to Slane Castle.

A curious quartet of identical houses face each other at the junction of the main roads. A local tale relates that they were built for four sisters who had taken an intense dislike to each other and kept watch on each other from their residences! At the bottom of the hill, the River Boyne glides by under the narrow bridge.

The Hill of Slane

Above the village, one km north, is the Hill of Slane. Tradition holds that St Patrick lit a paschal (Easter) fire here in 433. Such a fire was in direct contravention of a decree issued by Laoghaire, the high king of Ireland, that no flame should be lit in sight of Tara. Patrick's act thus symbolised Christianity's triumph over paganism. According to legend, Laoghaire was furious, but was restrained by his druids who warned that 'the man who had kindled it would surpass kings and princes'. Instead, the king set out to meet Patrick and question him. The king's attendants were ordered to ignore the saint and all but one (named Earc) greeted him scornfully.

During the encounter, St Patrick killed one of the cursing men and then summoned an earthquake to subdue the king's guards. Finally, he plucked a shamrock and used its three leaves to explain the paradox of the Trinity. The king made peace and although he refused to be converted, he allowed Patrick to continue his work. Earc was converted and became Bishop of Slane. On the eve of Easter Sunday the local parish priest still lights a fire on the hill.

The site originally had a church associated with St Earc and, later, a round tower and castle, but nothing remains of either. Later a motte-and-bailey were constructed and are still visible on the west side of the hill. A ruined church, tower and other buildings come from an early 16th-century Franciscan friary. On a clear day it's said that you can see seven Irish counties as well as the Boyne Valley from the top of the tower.

St Earc is said to have become a hermit in old age, and a small tumbledown 16th-century church marks the spot where he is thought to have spent his last days around 512 to 514. It's on the north river bank, behind the Protestant church on the Navan road. Its reputation as a hermitage came from two hermits named O'Brien who lived here in the 16th century. The ruins are on the private Conyngham estate and are only open to the public on 15 August.

Modern Ireland still has three hermits officially recognised by the church.

Ledwidge Museum

About one km out of the village on the Drogheda road is the Ledwidge Museum (☎ 041-24285). This labourer's cottage was the birthplace of Francis Ledwidge, a poet who died on the battlefields of Belgium in 1917 at the age of 29. Admission is IR£1, and it is open 9 am to 1 pm and 2 to 7 pm, April to September only.

Slane Castle

Slane Castle, the private residence of the earl of Mountcharles, is two km along the Navan road and is best known in Ireland as the setting for major outdoor rock concerts. Bruce Springsteen, the Rolling Stones and Guns 'n' Roses have appeared here, but events have dwindled of late due to local antipathy to hordes of young rock fans.

Built in 1785 in Gothic Revival style by James Wyatt, the building was altered later by Francis Johnson for the visit of George IV to Lady Conyngham. She was allegedly his mistress, and it's said the Dublin to Slane road was built unusually straight and smooth to speed up the randy king's journeys.

Unfortunately much of the castle, including some notable furniture, was destroyed by fire in 1991, whereupon it was discovered that the earl, a Name at Lloyd's, was underinsured. Money is now being raised for restoration. The castle and grounds are closed to the public.

MEATH & LOUTH

Places to Stay

Hostel The nearest hostel is in Kells. See that section for details.

B&Bs Near the village centre, *Castle Hill House* (☎ 041-24696) at 2 Castle Hill, Slane, costs IR£13.50 per person. *Boyne View* (☎ 041-24121), up the hill towards Slane from the bridge, is a little more expensive at IR£18.50/27 a single/double.

Hotels The lovely old *Conyngham Arms* (☎ 041-24155) is near the crossroads in Slane village, and has 15 rooms at IR£22.50 to IR£34.50 per person. They have a reasonable restaurant and you can get good snacks in the bar from 10.30 am to 7 pm.

Places to Eat

The *Roadhouse Rest* is attached to a petrol station three km south of Slane on the Dublin road, and does generous servings of straightforward food.

The *Craft Shop*, in Slane on the Drogheda road, has a very nice tearoom in summer where you can also get lunches. For a serious meal try the *Conyngham Arms* near the crossroads or *Bartle's Steakhouse* (☎ 041-24664) on the crossroads.

Getting There & Away

Bus From Dublin, Slane is on the Letterkenny and Armagh Bus Éireann routes as well as the less busy routes to Portrush and Derry. There's a service between Slane and Drogheda about three times a day. The stop is at Conlon's shop near the crossroads. For information ring ☎ 01-836 6111.

Train Only the coast is serviced by the Dublin (Connolly Station) to Belfast line, with the occasional stop at Mosney, a holiday camp two km south of Laytown, and Laytown itself, before Drogheda.

SLANE TO NAVAN

The 14-km journey between Slane and Navan follows the Boyne Valley past a number of great houses, ruined castles, round towers and churches; they're only of mild interest compared to the fine sites elsewhere in County Meath.

Dunmoe Castle lies down a horrendously bumpy cul-de-sac four km from Navan. This D'Arcy castle is a 16th-century ruin with good views of the countryside and of an impressive red-brick manor, Ardmulchan House, on the far side of the River Boyne. Cromwell is supposed to have fired at the castle from the opposite bank in 1649. Local legend holds that a tunnel used to run from the castle vaults under the river. Near Dunmoe Castle is a small overgrown chapel and graveyard, with a crypt containing members of the D'Arcy family. Ardmulchan House, though somewhat dilapidated, is still used as a private residence.

You can't miss the fine 30-metre round tower and 13th-century church of **Donaghmore**, a km nearer Navan. The site has a profusion of modern gravestones, but the tower with its Crucifixion scene above the door is interesting and there are carved faces near the windows.

NAVAN

The county town of Navan (*An Uaimh*) at the confluence of the Rivers Boyne and Blackwater is disfigured by a busy road which cuts off the river from the town. Navan was the birthplace of Sir Francis Beaufort of the British Navy, who in 1805 devised the internationally accepted scale for wind strengths. The town has a carpet factory and some big furniture stores. Tara mine, Europe's largest lead and zinc mine, is three km along the Kells road.

Orientation & Information

Market Square is the town hub, with Ludlow, Watergate and Trimgate Sts leading off from it in the direction of the former town gates. In the absence of a tourist office you'll have to make do with a map in the town hall car park at the end of Watergate St.

The post office is on tatty Kennedy Rd off Trimgate St, as are the banks and the Garda station. The Bizzy Laundry is beside the Lyric Cinema on Brew's Hill.

Places to Stay
Hostels The nearest hostel is in Kells. See that section for details.

B&Bs *Riverside Lodge* (☎ 046-28762) at 19 Watergate St has beds for £14 above a restaurant. *Tower View* (☎ 046-23358) is three km along the Slane road and costs IR£12 per person. *Lios Na Greine* (☎ 046-28092), almost two km south of Navan on the R153 Duleek/Ashbourne road, has three rooms at IR£18.50/27.

Balreask House (☎ 046-21155) is three km from Navan and has rooms at IR£17/28; go two km along the N3 Dublin road until the Old Bridge Inn, turn right and it's one km along. *Swynnerton Lodge* (☎ 046-21371), one km from Navan on the main road to Slane, is a 19th-century fishing lodge overlooking the Boyne. They cater for fishing and shooting and charge IR£23 to IR£36 per person. Dinner is IR£14.

Hotels The *St Laurence Hotel* (☎ 046-28833) in Market Square offers B&B for IR£25/39 a single/double.

The *Ardboyne Hotel* (☎ 046-23119) is a first-class hotel on the Dublin road, charging IR£44.50 to IR£70 per person B&B. The *Beechmount Hotel* (☎ 046-21553), just outside Navan on the Trim road, costs IR£22 to IR£28.

In Kilmessan, 10 km south of Navan, the delightful little *Station House Hotel* (☎ 046-25239) costs IR£25 to IR£30. Light meals are available at lunch times and they have a good restaurant open Monday to Saturday 6 to 9.30 pm, with an early bird menu before 8 pm.

Places to Eat
Snacks *Susie's Cookhouse* in Watergate St does good light lunches, as do the *Pepper Pot*, the *Coffee Dock* and *Tasty Bites*, all in Trimgate St. The *Times Square Coffee House* in the St Laurence Hotel in Market Square is another lunch possibility.

Pub Food Try the comfortable *O'Flaherty's*, on the corner of Trimgate St and Brew's Hill,

Bernard Reilly's on Trimgate St or the *Round O* on Flower Hill at the edge of town on the Slane road. The *Flat House Pub* near the roundabout just out on the road to Trim also serves good, solid food.

Restaurants On Brew's Hill, the popular *China Gardens* (☎ 046-23938) does excellent Chinese and limited European food. On Ludlow St across from Bermingham's Pub is *Mimmo Valdi's Ristorante*, offering a predictable menu of Italian dishes.

Entertainment
O'Flaherty's and *Bernard Reilly's* are popular, modern and comfortably furnished pubs on Trimgate St. *Robbie O'Malley's* on Watergate St is similar.

The tiny *Bermingham's Pub* on Ludlow St has an old wooden frontage and faded posters inside. They have music on Thursday and Sunday morning. The *Lantern Lounge* at the bottom of Watergate St has an Irish music night on Wednesday. There are nightclubs in the Ardboyne and Beechmount hotels.

The *Palace Cinema* in Ludlow St still rakes up enough audience for two screens but the *Lyric* in Brew's Hill is now a small theatre; call ☎ 046-23969 for programme details.

Getting There & Away
Bus Éireann buses stop at McDonagh's Electrical Shop in Kennedy Rd and in Market Square. Times are posted on the wall, or call ☎ 01-836 6111 for info. There are regular buses to and from Dublin's Busáras and less frequent ones to Kells for IR£2.25 single.

Sillan Tours (☎ 042-69130), based in Shercock in County Cavan, have two coaches for Dublin leaving the Square every morning at 7.20 and 7.30 am.

Getting Around
Clarke's Sports (☎ 046-21130), on Trimgate St, is the local Raleigh dealer, with bikes for IR£7 a day or IR£20 a week; plus a deposit of IR£50.

AROUND NAVAN

There are some nice walks in the area, particularly following the towpath that runs beside the River Boyne towards Slane. On the south bank, you can go out about seven km as far as Hayestown and the Bridge o' the Boyne with ease, passing Dunmoe Castle on the opposite bank and Ardmulchan House on the same side as the path. See under Slane to Navan earlier. Going from the bridge towards Slane is trickier as the path is rough and in some places switches to the opposite side of the bank, with no bridge for you to follow suit.

Just west of town is **Navan Motte**, a scrub-covered mound which tradition holds to be the burial site of Odhbha, the wife of a Celtic prince who had abandoned her for Tea (pronounced Tay-ah), the lady who gave her name to Tara. Odhbha pursued her husband to Navan and died from a broken heart. The mound is thought in reality to have formed naturally; it was then adapted by the Normans as a motte-and-bailey.

Two km south-east of town are the impressive remains of **Athlumney House**, built by the Dowdall family in the 15th century with 17th-century additions. This relatively intact castle was said to have been set alight in 1690 by its then owner Launcelot Dowdall, after James's defeat at the Battle of the Boyne. Dowdall vowed that the conquering William would never shelter or confiscate his home. He watched the blaze from the opposite bank of the river before leaving for France and Italy. The grounds are now occupied by a convent.

Close to the Kells road, five km northwest of Navan, is the large ruin of another castle which once belonged to the Talbot family. **Liscartan Castle** is made up of two 15th-century towers joined by a hall-like room.

TARA

The Hill of Tara has occupied a special place in Irish legend for up to 5000 years, although we don't know exactly when people first settled on this gently sloping hill with its commanding views over the plains of Meath.

One of the many mounds on the hill was found to be a Stone Age passage grave from about 2500 BC, and during the Bronze Age important people were certainly being buried here.

Much of Tara's (*Teamhair*) pagan significance seems to have derived from its associations with the goddess Maeve (Medbh) and the mythical powers of the druids or priest-kings who ruled over part of the country from here. By the 2nd and 3rd centuries AD, Tara was the seat of the most powerful rulers in Ireland, a place where the high king and his royal court had their ceremonial residence, feasted and watched over the realm. Whilst Tara's kings may have been more powerful than the others, they would by no means have held sway over the whole country, as there were countless other petty kings and chieftains controlling many smaller areas.

Tara's remains are not visually impressive. Only mounds and depressions in grassy meadows mark where Iron Age hill forts and surrounding ring forts once stood. But on a mellow summer evening, when the shadows lengthen and the sun highlights the hill's earthworks, you can sit back, appreciate the view and get some sense of the commanding power of the place.

As the focus of Irish political influence and a centre of pagan worship, Tara was targeted by the early Christians. A great pagan *feis* or festival is thought to have been held around what is now Hallowe'en. On Tara – if not on the Hill of Slane – St Patrick supposedly used the three-leaved shamrock to illustrate the idea of the Holy Trinity (the Father, the Son and the Holy Ghost acting as one unified force) hence the adoption of the shamrock as a national symbol.

After the 6th century, once Christianity had a widespread hold and Tara's pagan significance waned, Tara's high kings began to desert her. Diarmait McCerrbeoil was the last to stage the great *feis* here. However, the kings of Leinster continued to be based here.

In August 1843, Tara saw one of the greatest crowds ever to gather in Ireland. Daniel O'Connell, the 'Liberator' and leader of the opposition to union with Great Britain, held one of his 'monster meetings' at Tara, and 750,000 people came to hear him speak. During a recent excavation, traces of O'Connell's wooden platform were uncovered on the Mound of the Hostages.

The Hill of Tara is an open site, open at all hours without charge.

Visitor Centre

The former Protestant church (with a window by the well-known artist Evie Hone) now houses the Tara Visitor Centre where a 20-minute audiovisual presentation on the site is shown. During the summer the tour from here is a must, as the anecdotes really bring the remains to life. Admission to the Visitor Centre (☎ 046-25903) and a tour costs IR£1/40p. It's open, and tours are available from June to September, 9.30 am to 6.30 pm, and in May and October from 10 am to 5 pm.

Rath of the Synods

The names applied to Tara's various humps and bumps were adopted from ancient texts, and mythology and religion intertwine with the historical facts. The Protestant church grounds and graveyard spill onto the remains of the rath of the Synods, a triple-ringed fort supposed to be the location of some of St Patrick's early meetings or synods. Excavations on the rath suggest it was used between 200 and 400 AD for burials, rituals and living quarters. Originally the ring fort would have contained wooden houses surrounded by timber palisades.

During a digging session in the graveyard in 1810, a boy found a pair of gold torcs (necklaces of twisted gold strips), now in the National Museum in Dublin. Later excavations brought a surprise when Roman glass, shards of pottery and seals were discovered, showing links with the Roman Empire, even though it never extended its power to Ireland.

The poor state of the rath is due in part to a group of British 'Israelites' who in the 1890s dug the place up looking for the Sacred Ark of the Covenant, much to the consternation of the locals. The Israelites' leader claimed to see a mysterious pillar on the rath, but unfortunately it was invisible to everyone else. After they failed to uncover anything, the invisible pillar moved to the other side of the road, but before the adventurers had time to start work, worried locals chased them away.

The Royal Enclosure

To the south of the church, the Royal Enclosure (*Ráth Na Ríogh*) is a large, oval Iron Age hill fort, 315 metres in diameter, surrounded by a bank and ditch cut through solid rock under the soil. Inside the Royal Enclosure are smaller sites.

Mound of the Hostages This noticeable bump in the north corner of the rath (*Dumha Na nGiall in Irish*) is the most ancient known part of Tara and the most visible of the remains. Supposedly a prison cell for hostages of King Cormac, son of Art, in the 3rd century AD, it is in fact a small Stone Age passage grave dating from around 2500 BC and later reused by Bronze Age people. The passage contains some carved stonework but is closed to the public.

The mound produced a treasure trove of artefacts including some Mediterranean beads of amber and faïence from the 16th century BC. Over 35 Bronze Age burials were found here, as well as a mass of cremated remains from the Stone Age.

Cormac's House & Royal Seat Two other earthworks inside the enclosure are Cormac's House (*Teach Cormaic*) and the Royal Seat (*Forradh*). Although they look similar, the Royal Seat is a ring fort with a house site in the centre, while Cormac's House is a barrow, or burial mound, in the side of the circular bank. Cormac's House commands the best views of the surrounding lowlands of the Boyne and Blackwater valleys.

Inside Cormac's House is the phallic **Stone of Destiny** or Lia Fáil, originally located near the Mound of the Hostages and representing the joining of the gods of the earth and the heavens. It is said to be the inauguration stone of the kings of Tara. The would-be king stood on top of it, and if the stone let out three roars, he was crowned.

Other legends claim the stone is the pillow on which Jacob rested his head and dreamt of an angel descending on a ladder from heaven, with whom he fought. The stone was supposedly later brought to Ireland by Jewish refugees. Others say that it ended up as the Stone of Scone in Westminster Abbey, used during coronations. The mass grave of 37 men who died in a skirmish on Tara during the 1798 Rising is near the stone.

Enclosure of King Laoghaire

South of the Royal Enclosure is the Enclosure of King Laoghaire, a large but worn ring fort where the king is supposedly buried standing upright in his armour to look out for his enemies.

The Banquet Hall

North of the churchyard is Tara's most unusual feature, the Banquet Hall or Teach Miodhchuarta which translates as the 'House of Mead-Circling' (mead, which was a popular tipple, is fermented from honey). This rectangular earthwork measures 230 metres by 27 metres along a north-south axis. Tradition holds that it was built to cater for thousands of guests during feasts like the feis. Much of this information about the hall comes from the 12th-century 'Book of Leinster' and 'The Yellow Book of Lecan', which even include drawings of it.

Opinion varies as to the site's real purpose. Its orientation suggests that it was a sunken entrance to Tara, leading directly to the Royal Enclosure. More recent research has uncovered graves within the compound and it is possible that the banks are in fact the burial sites of some of the kings of Tara.

Gráinne's Fort

Gráinne's Fort (*Ráth Gráinne*) and the north and south Sloping Trenches (*Claoin Fhearta*) off to the north-west are burial mounds. Gráinne's Fort was named after the goddess daughter of King Cormac who was betrothed to Fionn McCumhaill. She eloped with Diarmuid, one of the king's warriors, on her wedding night and started the epic saga of Diarmuid and Gráinne. When the king of Leinster laid siege to Tara around 220 AD, Tara's inhabitants are said to have been slaughtered in the Sloping Trenches.

Getting There & Away

Tara is nine km from Navan and 40 km from Dublin, signposted off the Dublin to Navan (N3) road.

Buses linking Dublin and Navan pass within one km of the site; ask to be dropped off at Tara Cross and follow the signs.

From April to October, Bus Éieerann often include the Hill of Tara in their Newgrange and Boyne Valley tours, costing £15 for the day. To check that it will be included on a particular day call ☎ 01-836 6111.

AROUND TARA

Five km south of Tara on the Kilmessan road is **Dunsany Castle** (☎ 946-25198), the residence of the lords of Dunsany, former owners of the lands around Trim Castle. The Dunsanys are related to the Plunkett family, the most famous Plunkett being St Oliver, who was executed, and whose head is kept in a church in Drogheda.

The present Lord Dunsany opens his house to visitors from mid-June through to September; it's best to ring ahead and check. Admission is IR£3, and they prefer people to come as part of group tours organised by the Drogheda tourist office and the Irish Georgian Society. There's an impressive private art collection (although paintings by Van Dyck and Jack B Yeats have been stolen) and many other treasures related to important figures in Irish history like Oliver Plunkett and Patrick Sarsfield.

About 1.5 km north-east of Dunsany is the ruined **Killeen Castle**, the seat of another line of the Plunkett family. The 1801 mansion was built around an 1180 Hugh de Lacy original and comprises a neo-Gothic structure between two 12th-century towers.

According to local lore, the surrounding lands were divided at one point amongst the two branches of the family by a race. Starting at the castles, the wives had to run towards each other and a fence was placed where they met. Luckily for the Killeen side, their castle is on higher ground and they made considerable gains, as their woman was running downhill against the uphill struggle faced by Dunsany's representative.

Another five km south-east on the Dublin road is the town of **Dunshaughlin** with **Fairyhouse Racecourse** seven km beyond. The Easter holiday races of 1916 attracted a large contingent of British soldiers out of Dublin while the Rising was beginning.

TRIM

Trim is a pleasant, rather sleepy little town on the River Boyne, with several interesting ruins. The name comes from *Baile Átha Troim*, meaning 'ford of the elder bushes'. The medieval town was a jumble of streets and once had five gates. At one stage, there were also seven monasteries in the immediate area. Sadly, few visitors pause to inspect the impressive ruins of Ireland's largest Anglo-Norman structure, Trim Castle, a sprawling construction surmounted by a huge keep.

According to locals, Queen Elizabeth I considered Trim as a possible site for Trinity College, which eventually ended up in Dublin. The Duke of Wellington went to school for a time in St Mary's Abbey/Talbot Castle, which served as a Protestant school in the 18th century. There's an unlikely local tradition that he was born in a stable south of the town, which probably arose from the duke's observation that being born in a stable didn't make one a horse, and thus his birth in Ireland didn't make him Irish! A Wellington monument stands at the junction of Patrick and Emmet Sts. After defeating Napoleon at the Battle of Waterloo, the Iron Duke went on to become prime minister of Great Britain and in 1829 passed the Catholic Emancipation Act which repealed the last of the repressive penal laws.

Trim was once home to the county jail, giving rise to the ditty:

> Kells for brogues
> Navan for rogues
> And Trim for hanging people.

Orientation & Information

Once a notorious traffic bottleneck, Trim now has a by-pass to the east of the centre which has eased things considerably. The helpful tourist office (☎ 046-37111) in Mill St is open from 9.30 am to 5 pm daily, closing between 1 and 1.30 pm at weekends. It sells a handy little *Trim Tourist Trail* walking tour booklet for 60p. The post office is at the junction of Emmet St and Market St.

In the same building as the tourist office on Mill St is the Meath heritage centre (☎ 046-36633) with an extensive genealogical database for people trying to trace Meath ancestors. Noel French at the heritage centre also runs group tours of Trim and other sites of interest in Meath.

The Power & the Glory

Immediately next door to the tourist office in Mill St is the Trim Visitor Centre, the Power and the Glory, which outlines the medieval history of Trim in audio-visuals. It makes a good starting point for your visit and is open daily from 11 am to 6 pm from April to September. Admission is IR£2/1.

Trim Castle

Hugh de Lacy founded Trim Castle in 1173 but Rory O'Connor, said to have been the last high king of Ireland, destroyed this motte-and-bailey within a year. De Lacy did not live to see the castle's replacement, and the building you see today was begun around 1200.

Although King John visited Trim in 1210 to bring the de Lacy family into line, giving the castle its alternative name of King John's Castle, he never actually slept in the castle – on the eve of his arrival, Walter de Lacy locked it up and left town, forcing the king to camp in the nearby meadow.

De Lacy's grandson-in-law, Geoffrey de Geneville, was responsible for the second stage of the keep's construction in the mid to late 13th century. De Geneville was a crusader who later became a monk at the Dominican abbey which he founded in 1263, just outside the northern wall of the town near the Athboy Gate.

Henry of Lancaster, later Henry IV, was

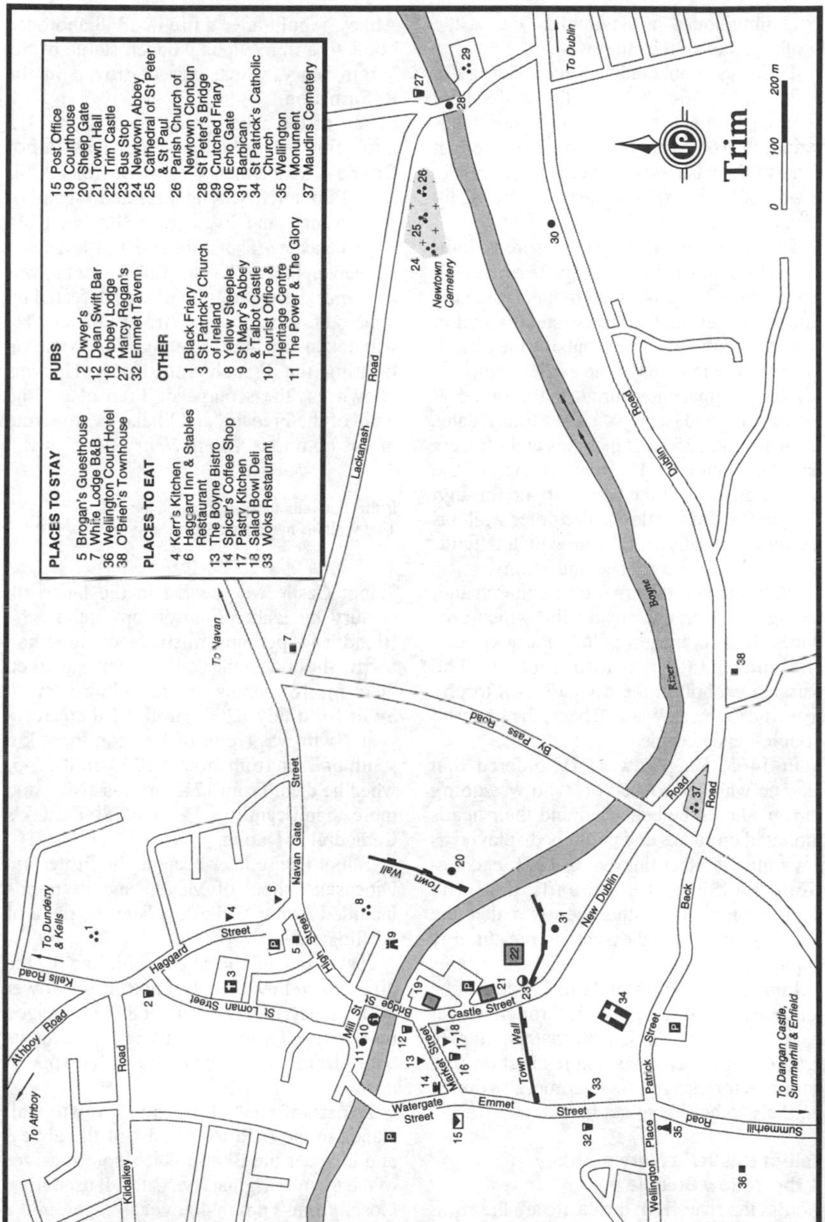

PLACES TO STAY

5 Brogan's Guesthouse
7 White Lodge B&B
36 Wellington Court Hotel
38 O'Brien's Townhouse

PLACES TO EAT

4 Ker's Kitchen
6 Haggard Inn & Stables Restaurant
13 The Boyne Bistro
14 Spicer's Coffee Shop
17 Pastry Kitchen
18 Salad Bowl Deli
33 Woks Restaurant

PUBS

2 Dwyer's
12 Dean Swift Bar
16 Abbey Lodge
27 Marcy Regan's
32 Emmet Tavern

OTHER

1 Black Friary
3 St Patrick's Church of Ireland
8 Yellow Steeple
9 St Mary's Abbey & Talbot Castle
10 Tourist Office & Heritage Centre
11 The Power & The Glory
15 Post Office
19 Courthouse
20 Sheep Gate
21 Town Hall
22 Trim Castle
23 Bus Stop
24 Newtown Abbey
25 Cathedral of St Peter & St Paul
26 Parish Church of Newtown Clonbun
28 St Peter's Bridge
29 Crutched Friary
30 Echo Gate
31 Barbican
34 St Patrick's Catholic Church
35 Wellington Monument
37 Maudlins Cemetery

Trim

0   100   200 m

MEATH & LOUTH

once imprisoned in the Dublin Gate at the southern part of the outer wall.

Trim was conquered by Silken Thomas in 1536, and in 1647 by Catholic Confederate forces, opponents of the English parliamentarians. In 1649 it was taken by Cromwellian forces under Charles Coote, and the castle, town walls and Yellow Steeple were badly damaged.

The grassy two-hectare enclosure is dominated by a massive stone keep, 25 metres tall and mounted on a Norman motte. Inside are three lofty levels, the lowest one divided in two by a central wall. Just outside the central keep are the remains of the earlier wall.

The principal outer curtain wall, some 500 metres long and largely standing today, dates from around 1250 and includes eight towers and the gatehouse. The finest stretch of the outer wall is from the River Boyne through Dublin Gate to Castle St. The outer wall has a number of sally gates from which defenders could sally out to meet the enemy.

Within the north corner was a church and, facing the river, the Royal Mint which produced Irish coinage (called 'Patricks' and 'Irelands') into the 15th century. The Russian cannon in the car park is a trophy from the Crimean War and bears the imperial double-headed eagle.

In 1465, King Edward IV ordered that anyone who had robbed or 'who was going to rob' should be beheaded and their heads mounted on spikes and publicly displayed as a warning to other thieves. In 1971, excavations in the castle grounds near the depression south of the keep revealed the remains of 10 headless men, presumably hapless criminals.

In theory, the ruins of Trim Castle can be reached by a riverside path or through the car park on Castle St. Unfortunately, a programme of excavations and restoration will continue for many years to come, so you are unlikely to be able to get inside.

Talbot Castle/St Mary's Abbey & the Yellow Steeple

Across the river from the castle are the ruins of the 12th-century Augustinian St Mary's Abbey, rebuilt after a fire in 1368 and once home to a miraculous wooden statue of the Virgin Mary, which was destroyed in the Reformation.

Part of the abbey was converted in 1415 into a fine manor house – known as **Talbot Castle** – by the then Viceroy of Ireland, Sir John Talbot. (He was later created 1st earl of Shrewsbury, and lived for a time in King John's Castle.) The Talbot coat of arms can be seen on the north wall. Talbot went to war in France, where in 1429 he was defeated by none other than Joan of Arc at Orleans. He was taken prisoner, released and went on fighting the French until 1453. He was known as 'the scourge of France' or 'the whip of the French', and Shakespeare wrote of this notorious man in *Henry VI*:

Is this the Talbot so much feared abroad
That with his name the mothers still their babes?

Talbot Castle was owned in the late 17th century by Esther Johnson or 'Stella', the friend and perhaps mistress of Jonathan Swift. She bought the castle for £65 and lived there for 18 months before selling it on to Swift for a tidy £200. He lived there for a year. Swift was rector of Laracor, three km south of Trim from around 1700 until 1745, when he died. From 1713 he was also – and more significantly – Dean of St Patrick's Cathedral in Dublin.

Talbot House later became the Protestant Diocesan School of Meath, and its pupils included Arthur Wellesley, later the duke of Wellington.

Just north of the abbey building is the 40-metre Yellow Steeple, once the bell tower of the abbey, dating from 1368 but damaged by Cromwell's soldiers in 1649. It takes its name from the colour of the stonework at dusk.

A part of the 14th-century town wall stands in the field to the east of the abbey, and includes the **Sheep Gate**, sole survivor of the town's original five gates. It used to be closed from 9 pm to 4 am each night, and a toll was charged for sheep entering to be sold at market. Unfortunately, you can only gaze on these two monuments from across a field.

Newtown Trim
East of town on the Lackanash road, Newtown Cemetery contains an interesting group of ruins.

What was the parish church of Newtown Clonbun contains the 16th-century tomb of Sir Luke Dillon, Chief Baron of the Exchequer during the reign of Elizabeth I, and his wife Lady Jane Bathe. The effigies are known locally as 'the jealous man and woman', perhaps because of the sword which lies between them.

Rainwater which collects between the figures is claimed to cure warts. Place a pin in the puddle and then jab your wart. When the pin becomes covered in rust your warts will vanish. Some say you should leave a pin on the statue as payment for the cure.

The other buildings here are Newtown's **Cathedral of St Peter & St Paul** and the 18th-century **Newtown Abbey**, or the Abbey of the Canons Regular of St Victor of Paris, to give it its full name. The cathedral was founded in 1206 and burnt down two centuries later. Parts of the cathedral wall were flattened by the Big Wind in January 1839, which also damaged sections of the Trim Castle wall. The abbey wall throws a superb echo back to **Echo Gate** across the river.

East again from these ruins, and just over the river, is the **Crutched Friary**. There are ruins of a keep and traces of a watchtower and other buildings from a hospital set up after the crusades by the Knights of St John of Jerusalem. **St Peter's Bridge** beside the friary is said to be the second oldest in Ireland. *Marcy Regan's*, the small green and gold pub beside the bridge, claims to be Ireland's second oldest pub, and is now open every evening except Wednesday.

Other Attractions
The site of the Dominican **Black Friary** lies north of the town, near the junction of the Athboy and Kells roads. Only a few mounds remain.

At the other end of town, **Maudlin's Cemetery** has the bronze statue of Our Lady of Trim, linked sentimentally although not in reality with a wooden statue put in St Mary's Abbey after its 1368 restoration. The statue was reputed to have miraculous powers. It survived the abbey's suppression in 1540 and later came into the possession of a powerful local family. After the sack of Drogheda in 1649, Cromwell's commander lodged in the house and the statue was burnt as firewood.

On the western outskirts, signposted from the town centre, are the award-winning **Butterstream Gardens**, open April to September from 11 am to 6 pm (except on Mondays). Admission costs IR£3.

Places to Stay
B&Bs *Brogan's Guesthouse* (☎ 046-31237) in the centre of Trim in the High St has an old-world flavour and charges IR£14. They have an adjoining bar and do lunches. *White Lodge* (☎ 046-36549) is 500 metres out of town at the north end of the Trim by-pass on the road to Navan, overlooking the castle and near the modern Lady of Trim statue. B&B is IR£13.50 or IR£15.50 with bathroom. *O'Briens Townhouse* (☎ 046-31745) on the Dublin road costs IR£14.50.

Crannmór (☎ 046-31635) is a converted farmhouse about one km along the road to Dunderry which costs IR£14.50 with bathroom.

Hotels The fairly ordinary-looking *Wellington Court* (☎ 046-31516) is the town's only hotel, with well-equipped singles/doubles at IR£35/50.

Places to Eat
Emmet St has takeaways and also a Chinese restaurant, *Woks* (☎ 046-36368). *Spicer's* bakery and coffee shop in Market St is good for a snack. For a more substantial lunch, try the *Salad Bowl Deli* or the *Pastry Kitchen* next door. Across the street *The Boyne Bistro* also does soups, sandwiches as well as more

substantial lunches. The *Dean Swift Bar* in Bridge St and the *Emmet Tavern* in Emmet St are fine for bar food and lunches, as is the *Abbey Lodge* on Market St.

The *Stables Restaurant* (☎ 046-31110) in the Haggard Inn on Haggard St is one of the best places to eat in town and has a three-course tourist menu for around IR£10. Nearby is *Kerr's Kitchen* (☎ 046-37144) where the service is a bit iffy, but the cakes look excellent.

Getting There & Away
The Bus Éireann stop is right by Trim Castle. Bus Éireann services between Dublin's Busáras and Athboy/Granard pass through Trim four times daily (twice on Sunday) in each direction. A single ticket costs £5, as does a midweek day return.

There are daily buses to/from Warrens-town, Kiltale and Batterstown.

AROUND TRIM
Jonathan Swift (1667-1745), author of *Gulliver's Travels*, was the rector of **Laracor** for 15 years before becoming Dean of St Patrick's Cathedral in Dublin in 1713. Laracor is three km from Trim on the road south to Summerhill, but nothing remains of the rectory which stood by the bridge.

Three km farther south, **Dangan Castle**, built by the Wellesley family, was the home of the Duke of Wellington as a boy. The castle is also supposed to have been the birthplace of Don Ambrosio O'Higgins (died 1801), the Spanish viceroy of Peru and Chile at the end of the 18th century. His son Bernardo O'Higgins went on to become the Liberator of Chile, and Santiago's main thoroughfare is named after him. The mansion's current state is the result of the efforts of Roger O'Conor, its last owner, who set it alight on a number of occasions in 1808-09 for the insurance.

On the road you might spot the huge slender mast of **Atlantic 252**, a long-wave radio station which broadcasts to Britain from Ireland.

Summerhill, nine km from Trim, is a pleasant, sleepy little village with a large and tidy green, but there's nothing much to do here except have lunch at *Shaw's* restaurant. Swift's connection with the area includes a curious folly in **Castlerichard**, a hamlet 10 km west of Summerhill. By the church over the old bridge is a large pyramid of stone inscribed with the word 'Swifte'.

Near the small town of Athboy is **Rathcarn**, 12 km north-west of Trim, one of the few Irish-speaking or Gaeltacht outposts outside the remote western seaboard. Rathcarn's population is descended from a group of Connemara people, who were settled on an estate here in the 1930s.

BECTIVE ABBEY
Bective Abbey lies halfway between Trim and Navan, south off the R161 on the Kilmessan road and the west bank of the Boyne.

Founded in 1147, Bective Abbey was the first Cistercian offshoot spawned by Mellifont Abbey in Louth. The remains seen today are 13th and 15th-century additions and consist of the chapter house, church and alleys with fine cloisters. After the dissolution of the monasteries in 1543, it was used as a fortified house, and the tower was built.

In 1186, Hugh de Lacy, lord of Meath, desecrated the abbey in Durrow, County Offaly, to build a castle, which offended a local man variously known as O'Miadaigh and O'Kearney, who lopped off de Lacy's head and fled. Although de Lacy's body was interred in Bective Abbey, his head went to St Thomas's Abbey, Dublin. A dispute broke out over who should possess all the remains, and it required the intervention of the Pope to decide matters, with St Thomas's Abbey winning out. Their interest was not so much in reuniting the head and torso out of respect for the dead, as in the prestige that went with possessing the complete body of such an important and powerful man.

KELLS
Almost every visitor to Ireland pays homage to the 'Book of Kells' in Dublin's Trinity College but fewer pause to see where it came from. Little remains of the ancient monastic

site in the town of Kells (*Ceanannas Mór*), but there are some fine high crosses in various states of preservation; a 1000-year-old round tower; the even older St Colmcille's House; and an interesting display in the gallery of the local church. Otherwise, present-day Kells is a fairly uninspiring place and doesn't reflect its past glory.

St Colmcille established the monastic settlement here in the 6th century and, in 807, monks arrived from a sister monastery on the remote Scottish island of Iona, retreating from a Viking onslaught in which 68 of their brothers were killed. It is thought that they brought the bones of their revered saint and the 'Book of Kells' with them. The book was stolen in 1007, but the thief was only after its gold case and it was later found buried in a bog. Kells proved to be little safer than Scotland, for Viking raids soon spread to Ireland and Kells was plundered on five occasions between 807 and 1019.

Orientation & Information
The main road to Donegal and Northern Ireland almost bypasses the town. Turning off the main road at the Market High Cross brings you down to Farrell St, where you'll find most of the shops and pubs including Maguire's Foodstore, a useful newsagency and grocery which sells disposable mousetraps amongst other remarkable objects.

Detail of an illustration from the 'Book of Kells'

There is no tourist office, but the hostel is helpful with queries if you're staying there.

Round Towers & High Crosses
The comparatively modern and uninteresting Protestant church west of the town centre stands on the grounds of the old monastic settlement. If the church is open (only likely in the height of summer) the gallery has an exhibit on the settlement and its famous illuminated book, with a facsimile on show.

The churchyard has a 30-metre-high, 10th-century round tower on the south side. It's minus its original roof, but is known to date back to at least 1076, when Muircheartach Maelsechnaill, king of Tara, was murdered in its confined apartments.

Inside the churchyard are four 9th-century high crosses in various states of repair. The West Cross at the far end of the compound from the entrance is a stump of a decorated shaft with scenes of the Baptism of Jesus, the Fall of Adam and Eve, and the Judgement of Solomon on the east face, and Noah's Ark on the west face. All that is left of the North Cross is the bowl-like base stone.

Near the tower is the best preserved of the crosses, the Cross of Patrick & Colmcille, with its semi-legible inscription 'Patrici et Columbae Crux' on the east side of the base. Above it are scenes of Daniel in the Lions' Den, the Fiery Furnace, the Fall of Adam and Eve and a hunting scene. On the opposite face are the Last Judgement, the Crucifixion, and riders with a chariot and a dog on the base. The council plans to move this cross into a hall to protect it from the elements.

The other surviving cross is the unfinished East Cross. On the east side is a carving of the Crucifixion and a group of four figures on the right arm. The three blank, raised panels below these were prepared for carving but the sculptor never got around to them.

Finally, a square church tower dating from the 15th century stands beside the modern church. Above the door is an inscription detailing the addition of the spire in 1783 by the earl of Bective from a design by Thomas

Cooley, architect of Dublin's City Hall. Below this are a number of tombstones and stone heads set into its walls.

St Colmcille's House

From the churchyard exit, St Colmcille's House is left up the hill, amongst the row of houses on the right side of the road. From June to September it may be open. Otherwise, pick up the keys from Mrs Carpenter at No 1 Lower Church View, the first brown house on the right at the bottom of the hill, before walking up.

This squat, solid survivor from the old monastic settlement resembles St Flannan's, Killaloe, and St Kevin's Church in Glendalough, County Wicklow, in its construction. The original entrance door to the 1000-year-old building was over two metres above ground level and, inside, a very long ladder leads to a low attic room under the roofline.

Market High Cross

The Market Cross stands in Cross St in the town centre, marking the furthest extent of the 10th-century monastery. It is said that it was moved here by Jonathan Swift, and in 1798 the British garrison executed rebels by hanging them from the crosspiece, one on each arm so the cross wouldn't fall over. It has suffered some damage over the years: the shaft has had chunks taken out of it and the pinnacle is missing. On the east side are Abraham's sacrifice of Isaac; Cain and Abel; the Fall of Adam and Eve; guards at the tomb of Jesus; and a procession of horsemen. On the west face, the Crucifixion is the only discernible image. Finally, on the north face is a panel of Jacob wrestling with the angel. The council also plans to move this cross indoors out of the way of traffic pollution.

Places to Stay

Kells Independent Youth Hostel (☎ 046-40100) is next door to Monaghan's pub on the Cavan road, 200 metres uphill from the bus stop. A bed in a dorm costs IR£6 and in a private room IR£7. There's a full kitchen and other facilities. Camping costs IR£3 per person. You may have to check in at the pub rather than at the hostel itself.

Alternatively, the *Headfort Arms Hotel* (☎ 046-40063) in John St does B&B for £27.50 a head. It has a nightclub and restaurant attached.

The wonderful 200-year-old *Lennoxbrook House* (☎ 046-45902) is five km north of Kells on the road to Cavan. The double rooms cost IR£15 per person B&B. It's open February to November and serves dinner for IR£12.

Outside Kells in Crossakeel, *Deerpark Farm* (☎ 046-43609) costs from IR£30 for doubles, with delicious home-made bread for breakfast.

Places to Eat

In the centre of Kells, *Penny's Place* (☎ 046-41630) in Market St is an excellent café with home-made food and drinks; the brown bread alone would take some beating. It's open until 6 pm, Monday to Saturday. *O'Shaughnessy's* pub nearby does reasonable sandwiches and lunches. Next to the post office in Farrell St, the *Round Tower* (☎ 046-40144) has a good restaurant and does substantial pub lunches too. *McGee's* on the corner opposite Maguire's does afternoon teas. *Monaghan's* pub, on the main street, does lunch for around IR£3 and dinner with main courses from IR£4.

Entertainment

In the centre, *O'Shaughnessy's* features lots of rustic timber, while the *Blackwater Pub* has regular Irish music sessions. *Monaghan's* is next door to the hostel so it gets a good young crowd and often has music at weekends.

Getting There & Away

The Bus Éireann stop in Kells is outside the Video Box video rental shop close to the Market Cross. Times are posted at the stop or phone ☎ 01-836 6111. Buses run from Dublin to Kells and Cavan and back almost hourly between 7.30 am and 10.30 pm. Two of the buses are express coaches on their way to and from Donegal. There are also regular services to Navan and Dunshaughlin.

AROUND KELLS
Hill of Lloyd Tower
The 30-metre Hill of Lloyd tower is visible from behind the hostel and it's easy to see why it became known as the 'inland lighthouse'. Built in 1791 by the earl of Bective in memory of his father, it has been renovated and if it's open you can climb to the top for IR£1, or picnic in the surrounding park. The tower is two km west of Kells, off the Crossakeel road.

Crosses of Castlekeeran
A little farther down the Crossakeel road, signposted to the right, are the Crosses of Castlekeeran. Access is through a farmyard, from where the farmer's friendly dog may accompany you through the field. Four plainly carved early 9th-century crosses, one in the river, are surrounded by an overgrown cemetery, while at the ruined church in the centre are some early grave slabs and an Ogham stone.

CAIRNS OF LOUGHCREW
The Loughcrew Hills beyond Oldcastle are also known as Slieve na Calliaghe and give marvellous views east and south to the plains of Meath and north into the lake country of Cavan. On the summit of three of the hills are the remains of 30 Stone Age passage graves built around 3000 BC, but reused up to the Iron Age. In some cases, a large mound is surrounded by numerous, smaller satellite graves. Like Newgrange, larger stones in some of the graves are decorated with spiral and motif patterns. Archaeologists have unearthed bone fragments and burnt bones, stone balls and beads. Some of the graves look like a large pile of stones, while others are less obvious, the cairn having been removed.

To get there from Kells, head for Oldcastle. About five km from Oldcastle you will see a sign for the Slieve na Calliaghe hills. Turn right, and at the first house on the right collect the keys to the cairn entrances from Basil Balfe (please phone ☎ 049-41256 first).

If anybody's there to collect it, a deposit of IR£5 (hikers can leave their backpacks as collateral!) is required and a leaflet about the sites is available. A torch (flashlight) is useful on dull days. Coming from the east, the first hill is of little interest; the most interesting and intact remains are on the next two, Carnbane East and Carnbane West.

Carnbane East
Carnbane East has a cluster of sites; Cairn T is the biggest at about 35 metres in diameter, and has numerous carved stones. One of its outlying kerbstones is called the 'Hag's Chair' and is covered in gouged holes, circles and other marks. You need the gate key to enter the passageway and a torch to see anything in detail. It takes about half an hour to climb Carnbane East from the car park. From the summit on a reasonably clear day, you should be able to see the Hill of Tara to the south-east while the view north is into Cavan with Lough Ramor to the north-east and Lough Sheelin and Oldcastle to the north-west.

Carnbane West
From the same car park, it takes about an hour to the summit of Carnbane West where Cairn D and L are both some 60 metres in diameter. Cairn D has been seriously disturbed in an unsuccessful search for a central chamber. Cairn L, north-east of D, is also in poor condition, although you can enter the passage and chamber, where there are numerous carved stones, and the curved basin stone where human ashes were placed.

County Louth

Although the smallest county in Ireland, Louth is home to the two principal towns of Ireland's north-eastern region. Drogheda makes a good base for exploring the Boyne Valley, with its prehistoric sites to the west and the monastic relics to the north. Dundalk is a border town to the north and a gateway to the scenic Cooley Peninsula.

Just west of Dundalk, the lonely moorlands of the Cooley Peninsula are the setting for a large part of Ireland's most famous fable, the Táin Bó Cúailnge or the Cattle Raid of Cooley. The low mountains are really a part of Northern Ireland's Mourne Mountains, but are cut off from them physically by the flooded valley of Carlingford Lough and politically by the border which runs up the centre of the lough.

HISTORY

Humans have lived in this region since about 7000 BC, but Louth's Stone Age relics like the Proleek dolmen and passage grave near Dundalk pale in comparison with the Brugh na Bóinne relics in County Meath. Only with the coming of the Iron Age does Louth rival its neighbour.

The north of the county and the Cooley Peninsula are the setting for legends of Cúchulainn, one of the most famous heroes of ancient Ireland, who was born and raised around Faughart, just north of Dundalk. Cúchulainn was the lead player in the story of the Táin Bó Cúailnge (The Cattle Raid of Cooley), one of the great Celtic myths. *The Táin* by Thomas Kinsella (Dolmen Press) is a modern version of this compelling and bloody tale.

St Patrick introduced Christianity in the 5th century, and numerous religious communities sprang up in the region. The monastery at Monasterboice and the later Cistercian abbey at Mellifont, both near Drogheda, are the county's most interesting archaeological sites.

Irish society underwent a huge upheaval, with the arrival of the Anglo-Normans in the 12th century. Hugh de Lacy's reward for his Irish conquests was the fertile land of Meath and Louth. Mottes, such as the one at Millmount in Drogheda, were first built around this time to defend the Anglo-Normans against the hostile Irish.

The Normans' stone castles came later, and smaller satellite castles such as Termonfeckin, north-east of Drogheda, dot the countryside. The Norman invaders were responsible for the development of Dundalk, and for the two towns on opposite banks of the Boyne, which united in 1412 to become what is now Drogheda.

These new settlers would become some of the staunchest defenders of Ireland in later centuries, particularly against the English parliamentarians. In 1649, Cromwell's forces massacred the native Irish and old English Catholic defenders of Drogheda for refusing to surrender.

Ireland succumbed to English control in 1690, after the Battle of the Boyne where the Protestant William of Orange defeated his father-in-law, the English Catholic king, James II. James had enlisted the help of the Irish in return for greater religious and political freedom, and his defeat resulted in a new influx of Protestant settlers.

DROGHEDA

The historic town of Drogheda hugs a bend on the River Boyne, five km from the sea. It's a compact settlement, with a small village-like adjunct to the south of the river around Millmount. Unfortunately, the city centre is congested and distinctly run-down in places.

Once fortified, Drogheda still has one town gate in fine condition, together with some interesting old buildings and the curious hump of Millmount south of the river. The embalmed head of the Catholic martyr St Oliver Plunkett (1629-81) is housed in St Peter's Roman Catholic Church.

The town's name comes from *Droichead Átha*, the Bridge of the Ford, after the bridge built over the river by the Normans to link the two earlier Viking settlements. Drogheda featured in novelist Colleen McCullough's blockbuster *The Thornbirds*.

History

There was probably a rough settlement here before the 10th century, but Drogheda really began to take shape around 910, when the Danes built defences to guard a strategic crossing point on the River Boyne. In the 12th century, the Normans built a bridge and expanded the two settlements forming on either side of the river. They also built a large defensive motte-and-bailey castle on the south side at Millmount.

MEATH & LOUTH

A Moving Head

In the north transept of Drogheda's St Peter's Church, a ghastly relic lurks inside a soaring reliquary of solid brass and unbreakable glass. Closer inspection reveals the leathery head of St Oliver Plunkett, hanged by the English in 1681 for his supposed part in the 'Popish Plot'.

Plunkett was born at Loughcrew, near Oldcastle, in 1629, a descendant of king Brian Ború who had defeated the Danes at Clontarf in 1014. In 1645 he was sent to Rome to complete his education and stayed in Italy for 25 years. Ordained in 1654, he became Archbishop of Armagh and Primate of all Ireland in 1670. Following his consecration, he returned to Ireland in 1670. In the first three years of his mission he confirmed 48,655 people, ordained many priests and set up what may been the first integrated Roman Catholic and Protestant school in Drogheda.

Oliver Plunkett

But Plunkett lived during a time when the English were particularly paranoid about the supposed threat from Roman Catholicism, and in 1679 he was seized and imprisoned in Dublin, accused of involvement in the 'Popish Plot'. This was an entirely fabricated conspiracy dreamt up by Titus Oates, a ne'er-do-well with a long history of dubious dealings, who claimed in 1678 that he had uncovered a plot to kill Charles II and turn the country over to the Jesuits. Despite Oates's past, he was believed and about 35 men were put to death for supposed involvement. Plunkett was accused of planning the invasion of Ireland by foreign powers and in 1680 he was moved to London's Newgate Prison. Tried and convicted of treason, he was hanged at Tyburn on 1 July 1681. The very next day the plot was revealed as a sham. Oates himself was flogged, pilloried and imprisoned for perjury, only to be pardoned and granted a pension after the revolution of 1688.

At the time of Plunkett's execution, the custom was to quarter the body and then burn the parts. Plunkett's friends obtained permission to remove the body, but only just managed to snatch the head from the fire, scorch marks are still visible on the left cheek and nose. The head and forearms were placed in tin boxes, and the rest of the body buried in St Giles Cemetery. Later it was exhumed and sent first to a Benedictine monastery in Germany and then to Downside in England. The head, meanwhile, was taken to Rome and then to Drogheda where the Sisters of Sienna looked after it for the next 200 years.

In 1920 Plunkett was beatified and the head was given to the new parish church of St Peter's, 'the Oliver Plunkett Memorial Church'. Following a miraculous cure in a Naples hospital which was attributed to Plunkett's intervention, the pope canonised him in October 1975.

In 1990 the priest of St Peter's decided to have the head examined since it was showing signs of decay. At the same time a living descendant of the saint provided a blood sample so that Turin Shroud-style DNA tests could be carried out to verify its authenticity. The tests having proved satisfactory, the saint's head was replaced in its reliquary inside an inner capsule containing silica gel which would make it easier to maintain the correct humidity level. The reliquary was then enclosed in a pedestal shrine over one metre high and with a soaring nine-metre stone spire. Beside it is displayed the original certificate of authenticity, dated 1682. ∎

By the 15th century, Drogheda was one of Ireland's four major walled towns. Many Irish parliament sessions were held here, and Poyning's Law, passed in 1494, is the most famous piece of legislation from Irish medieval times. It diminished prospects of home rule or independence for Ireland by granting the English crown the right to veto any measures the Irish proposed to enact.

In 1465, the Irish parliament had conferred on Drogheda the right to a university, but the plan foundered in 1468, when the earl of Desmond was executed for treason. During the period of the Pale, when only a

Drogheda

small portion of the country around Dublin was fully controlled by the English, Drogheda was a frontier town. Farther north were the fractious Ulster folk, definitely beyond the Pale.

In 1649, the town was the scene of Cromwell's most notorious Irish slaughter. Marching north from Dublin he met with stiff resistance at Drogheda and when his forces overran the town on the third assault, the defenders were shown no mercy. The order went out to kill every man who had borne arms, and it's estimated that nearly 3000 were massacred, including civilians and children.

The defenders were a combination of native Irish and old English Catholic Royalists led by Sir Arthur Aston, who was beaten to death with his own wooden leg. Some of the survivors were shipped to Barbados. When 100 people hid in the steeple of St Peter's Church of Ireland, Cromwell's men simply burnt the church down. 'A righteous judgement of God upon these barbarous wretches,' was Cromwell's summation of the butchery. Drogheda also plumped for the wrong side at the Battle of the Boyne in 1690, but surrendered the day after James II was defeated.

PLACES TO STAY

13	Harpur House Hostel
27	Westcourt Hotel
41	St Gobnait's B&B
42	Orley House B&B

PLACES TO EAT

6	Golden House
14	La Pizzeria
15	Burke's Restaurant
17	Rumble's Restaurant
19	Moorland Café
20	Swan House
28	Snackmaster Restaurant
33	A Little Mouthful
38	Butter Gate Restaurant

PUBS

8	Branagan's Pub
11	C Ní Cairbre
21	Weavers Pub
25	Gwent Arms
30	Goodfellow's Bar

OTHER

1	Our Lady of Lourdes Hospital
2	Church of Our Lady of Lourdes
3	Cottage Hospital
4	Magdalene Tower
5	PJ Carolan Bike Hire
7	Courthouse
9	St Peter's Church of Ireland
10	Presbyterian Church
12	St Laurence's Gate
16	Old Gate Bakery
18	St Peter's Catholic Church
22	Police/Garda Station
23	Tourist Office
24	Cinema
26	Post Office
29	Drogheda Arts Centre
31	Tholsel
32	Wise Owl Bookshop & Coffee Shop
34	Bus Station
35	St Mary's Catholic Church
36	Butter Gate
37	Millmount & Museum
39	St Mary's Church of Ireland
40	Railway Station

It took many years for the town to recover from these events, but in the last century a number of Catholic churches were built. The massive railway viaduct and the string of quayside buildings hint at the town's brief Victorian industrial boom, when it was a centre for cotton and linen manufacture and for brewing.

Orientation & Information
Drogheda sits astride the River Boyne with the principal shopping area on the north bank along the main street, called West St and Laurence St. The area south of the river is residential, dull and dominated by the mysterious Millmount mound. The main road to Belfast skirts around the town to the west.

The scruffy tourist office (☎ 041-37070) is at the west end of West St but only opens in July and August from 10 am to 6 pm Monday to Saturday. The main post office is on the middle of West St, next door to the Westcourt Hotel. Most of the main banks are also on West St.

There's a terrible traffic problem and disc parking is in operation throughout the town. Discs can be bought in newsagents.

St Peter's Church
On West St, the Gothic-style St Peter's Catholic Church dates from 1791 and dominates the centre of town. In a glittering brass and glass case in the north transept you can see the head of St Oliver Plunkett (1629-81), executed by the perfidious English and now surrounded by flowers, candles and the attentions of the devout.

St Laurence's Gate
Astride Laurence St, the eastward extension of the main street through town, is St Laurence's Gate, the finest surviving portion of the city walls and one of only two surviving gates from the original 11.

The 13th-century gate was named after St Laurence's Priory which once stood outside the gate; no traces of it now remain. It consists of two lofty towers, a connecting curtain wall and the entrance to the portcullis. This imposing pile of stone is not in fact a gate but a barbican, a fortified structure used to defend the gate, which was farther behind it. When the walls were completed in the 13th century, they ran for three km around the town, enclosing 52 hectares.

MEATH & LOUTH

Millmount & Museum

Across the river from the town centre, in a village-like enclave amid a sea of dull suburbia, is Millmount, an artificial hill overlooking the town. Although it may have been a prehistoric burial mound along the lines of nearby Newgrange, it has never been excavated. There's a tale that it was the burial place of a warrior-poet who arrived in Ireland from Spain around 1500 BC. Throughout Irish history, poets have held a special place in society and have been both venerated and feared.

The Normans constructed a motte-and-bailey on top of this convenient command post overlooking the bridge. It was followed by a castle, which in turn was replaced by a Martello tower in 1808. It was at Millmount that the defenders of Drogheda made their last stand before surrendering to Cromwell. Later, an 18th-century English barracks was built around the base, and today this has been converted to house craft shops, museums and a restaurant, though the courtyard retains the flavour of its former life.

The tower played a dramatic role in the 1922 Civil War and the Millmount Museum has a colourful (and somewhat romanticised) painting of its bombardment. The top of the tower offers a fine view over the centre of Drogheda, on the opposite side of the river.

Millmount Museum A section of the army barracks has been converted into a museum (☎ 041-33097) with interesting displays about the town and its history. They include three wonderful late-18th-century guild banners, perhaps the last in the country. There's an excellent example of a coracle, a tiny boat used to get around by water from earliest times. The pretty, cobbled basement is full of gadgets and kitchen utensils from bygone times, including a cast-iron pressure cooker and an early model of a sofa bed. Across the courtyard, the **Governor's House** contains a chronological account of Drogheda's history, along with a slide show and temporary exhibitions.

The museum is open 10 am to 6 pm, Tuesday to Sunday April to October and entry is IR£1/50p. During the winter, it's open afternoons only. The Governor's House is open Tuesday to Sunday afternoons only to 5 pm, and admission costs another IR£1. You can drive up to the hilltop or climb Pitcher Hill via the steps from St Mary's Bridge.

Butter Gate The 13th-century Butter Gate, just north-west of the Millmount, is the only genuine town gate to survive. This tower with its arched passageway predates the remains of St Laurence's Gate by about a century. St Mary's Churchyard to the south-east contains some of the original town wall and is reputedly where Cromwell breached the walls in 1649.

Other Buildings

On the corner of West and Shop Sts is the **Tholsel**, an 18th-century limestone town hall, now occupied by the Bank of Ireland. Off Hardmans Gardens is the more recent and charming **Church of Our Lady of Lourdes**.

North of the centre on William St is **St Peter's Church of Ireland**. This contains the tombstone of Oliver Goldsmith's uncle Isaac, as well as another on the wall depicting two skeletal figures in shrouds, dubiously linked to the Black Death. This is the church whose spire was burnt by Cromwell's men with the death of 100 people seeking sanctuary inside. Today's church (1748) is the second replacement of the original destroyed by Cromwell. It stands in an attractive close approached through lovely wrought-iron gates. Note the old 'Blue School' of 1844 on one side.

On Fair St the modest 19th-century **Courthouse** is home to the sword and mace presented to the town council by William of Orange after the Battle of the Boyne.

Topping the hill behind the main part of town is the **Magdalene Tower**, dating from the 14th century, the belltower of a Dominican friary which was founded in 1224. Here, England's King Richard II accepted the submission of the Gaelic chiefs with suitable ceremony in 1395 after arriving with a great army, but peace lasted only a few months and his return to Ireland led to his overthrow in 1399. The earl of Desmond was beheaded here in 1468 because of his treasonous connections with the Gaelic Irish. The tower is reputed to be haunted by a nun.

Organised Tours

The Drogheda Historical Society occasionally runs summer tours of the town; phone ☎ 041-33097 (the Millmount Museum) to check if anything is scheduled.

Places to Stay

Hostel *Harpur House* (☎ 041-32736) on William St is near the centre of town. A bed costs IR£6 in the dorms or IR£9 in the double rooms. They also do standard B&B for IR£12.

B&Bs It's advisable to book ahead during the summer months. Near town, south of the river, *Orley House* (☎ 041-36019), 100 metres off the main Dublin road in a housing estate, costs from IR£15 per person. Nearby, on the main Dublin road, is *St Gobnaits* (☎ 041-37844), costing IR£15 per person. An old priests' house near Harpur House was due to open as a B&B; ask at the tourist office ... if it's open!

Harbour Villa (☎ 041-37441) is two km along the river towards the sea on the Mornington road. It overlooks the estuary and has small but pleasant rooms at IR£19/30 for singles/ doubles. At the mouth of the estuary near the beach in Baltray is *Aisling House* (☎ 041-22376) with rooms at IR£13.50 to IR£18.50 per person.

Hotels The smart, new *Westcourt Hotel* (☎ 041-30965) in West St is right in the town centre, with beds from IR£33/55 a single/double; it's worth asking about special weekend bargain breaks. The *Rossnaree Hotel* (☎ 041-37673) is good and costs IR£20 to IR£35. The excellent restaurant has a set dinner from IR£13. The *Boyne Valley Hotel* (☎ 041-37737) is a 19th-century mansion with rooms at IR£33 to

IR£46 per person including breakfast. Both hotels are just along the main Dublin road.

Places to Eat

Cafés & Fast Food *A Little Mouthful* (☎ 041-42887) at the river end of Shop St and the corner of North Quay does excellent sandwiches and soup in pine-filled surroundings. Right next door, *The Wise Owl* bookshop also has a pleasant coffee shop. The *Snackmaster Restaurant* (☎ 041-34760) on Dominick St is run by an Egyptian who serves good, reasonably priced meals. The *Moorland Café* on West St does good coffee, snacks and light meals.

The busy, Italian-owned *La Pizzeria* (☎ 041-34208) on Peter's St features pizzas from IR£5, from 6 to 11 pm. Down an alley opposite, *Burke's Restaurant* does soups for IR£1.10 and main courses from IR£2.50. Other possible lunch stops in Peter's St might be the *Olde Gate Bakery*, with soups for just 50p, or *Rumble's Restaurant*.

The popular Chinese *Swan House* (☎ 041-35838) is in West St next door to Weavers and the *Golden House* on Trinity St also has Chinese food.

Pub Food The popular *Weavers* pub on West St does pub food, as well as three-course meals for IR£3.95 provided you eat between 5 and 8 pm. *Branagan's* (☎ 041-35607) on Magdalene St is also popular, with straightforward lunch and evening meals and main courses in the IR£4 to IR£9 range. About a km along the Dublin road, the *Black Bull Inn* (☎ 041-37139) was once a winner of the 'regional pub of the year' title, and gets the local vote. Dinner costs from around IR£10.

Restaurants The cosy *Buttergate Restaurant* (☎ 041-34759) beside the Millmount Museum has excellent food, with meals before 7 pm at IR£7 and others at IR£15 to IR£20. It's open Tuesday to Saturday for dinner and on Sunday for lunch and dinner. The *Forge Gallery Restaurant* (☎ 041-26272) 10 km northwest of town in Collon is one of the best restaurants in the region.

MEATH & LOUTH

Entertainment

Weavers (☎ 041-32816) on West St always has a youngish crowd and often has music at weekends. *Bridie Macs* attached to the *Westcourt Hotel* also offers a wide range of musical possibilities. The *Gwent Arms* on West St is also lively, with music from jazz to rock & roll on offer, especially at weekends. The *Black Bull Inn*, about one km along the Dublin road, has country music on Thursday, and rock and pop on Friday.

C Ní Cairbre (Carberry's) pub, on North Strand near Laurence St, has Irish music sessions on Tuesday. In theory it's open from 7.30 am; in reality, opening hours vary depending on who's expected!

The *Earth* nightclub in the *Westcourt Hotel* is popular. The *Rossnaree* and the *Boyne Valley* hotels on the Dublin Rd also have nightclubs, respectively the *Place* and *Luciano's*. Entry is usually IR£5.

There is a modern two-screen cinema (☎ 041-30188) at the back of the Abbey shopping centre off West St. In Stockwell St the *Drogheda Arts Centre* (☎ 041-33946) stages theatrical and musical events.

Getting There & Away

Bus Drogheda is only 48 km north of Dublin, on the main N1 route to Belfast. The Bus Éireann station (☎ 041-35023) is on the corner of John St and Donore Rd, just south of the river, and there are hourly connections with Dublin and Dundalk as well as numerous links to Belfast and other centres. There is a handy expressway service from Drogheda to Galway once every morning. You can get off at Athlone for connections to Limerick, Sligo and Donegal.

Capital Coaches (☎ 042-40025) have a daily Dundalk to Dublin service through Drogheda.

Train Drogheda Railway Station (☎ 041-38749) is just south of the river and east of the town centre, off the Dublin road. Drogheda is on the main Belfast to Dublin line and there are five or six express trains (and many more slower ones) daily each way, with four on Sunday.

The train crosses the river just downstream from Drogheda on Sir John McNeill's mid-19th-century Boyne Viaduct, a fine piece of engineering which dominates the seaward view.

Getting Around

Drogheda itself is infinitely walkable, and many of the surrounding region's interesting sites are within easy cycling distance. P J Carolan (☎ 041-38242), 77 Trinity St, is part of the Raleigh Rent-a-Bike scheme and has good bikes for IR£6 a day.

There are taxi ranks on Laurence St and on Duke St, just off West St, or call 24 Hour Cabs (☎ 041-37663).

AROUND DROGHEDA

Drogheda makes an excellent base for exploring the Boyne Valley sites to the west – see the County Meath section of this chapter for more details. In Louth itself, Mellifont and Monasterboice are two famous and picturesque monastic sites a few km north of Drogheda. Travelling to or from Northern Ireland there's a coast route, the faster and duller N1 main road route and a more circuitous inland route via Collon and Ardee which can include Mellifont and Monasterboice.

Beaulieu House

Five km east of Drogheda on the Baltray road is Beaulieu House, built between 1660 and 1666. The land had belonged to the Plunkett family since Anglo-Norman times, and was confiscated under Cromwell. This lovely red-brick mansion is thought to have been designed by Sir Christopher Wren (architect of St Paul's Cathedral in London), and its steep roof and tall chimneys are distinctive.

In 800 years the estate has been in the possession of only two families, first the Plunketts and then the ancestors of Lord Tichbourne. There's an impressive art collection. Although it's a private residence, there are occasional tours by the Drogheda Historical Society, operating out of the Millmount Museum; phone ☎ 041-33097 to see if anything is planned.

Counties Meath & Louth

A: Village pub/store, Carlingford, Louth
B: Harbour & castle, Carlingford, Louth
C: Church ruins, Slane, County Meath

D: West Cross, Monasterboice, County Louth
E: Drogheda, County Louth

A	B
C	D
E	F

Belfast

A: Robinson & Cleaver Building
B: Rebuilt city centre pub
C: Marching bands, Sandy Row
D: Commemorating the city's women
E: Symbol of renewal
F: Grand Opera House

Mellifont Abbey

Mellifont Abbey (☎ 041-26459), eight km north-west of Drogheda beside the River Mattock, was Ireland's first Cistercian monastery. The name comes from the Latin 'melli-fons' or 'honey fountain'. In its prime, Mellifont was the Cistercians' most magnificent and important centre in the country but, while the remains are well worth seeing, they don't really match the site's former significance.

In 1142 St Malachy, bishop of Down, brought in a new troop of monks from Clairvaux in France to combat the corruption and lax behaviour of the Irish monastic orders. These strait-laced new monks were deliberately established at this remote location, far from any distracting influences. The French and Irish monks failed to get on, and the visitors soon returned to the continent, but within 10 years nine more Cistercian monasteries followed, and Mellifont was eventually the mother house for 21 lesser monasteries. At one point, as many as 400 monks lived here.

Mellifont not only brought fresh ideas to the Irish religious scene, it also heralded a new style of architecture. For the first time in Ireland, monasteries were built with the formal layout and structure that was being used on the continent. Only fragments of the original settlement remain, but the plan of the extensive monastery can easily be traced. Like many other Cistercian monasteries, the buildings clustered around an open cloister or courtyard.

To the north side are the remains of a principally 13th-century cross-shaped church. To the south, the chapter house, probably used as a meeting hall by the monks, has been partially floored with medieval glazed tiles, originally found in the church. Here also would have been the refectory or dining area, the kitchen and the warming room, the only place where the austere monks could enjoy the warmth of a fire. The east range would once have held the monks' sleeping quarters.

Mellifont's most recognisable building, and one of the finest pieces of Cistercian architecture in Ireland, is the *lavabo*, an octagonal washing house for the monks. It was built in the 13th century and used lead pipe to bring water from the river. A number of other buildings would have surrounded this main part of the abbey.

After the dissolution of the monasteries, a fortified Tudor manor house was built on the site in 1556 by Edward Moore, using materials scavenged from the demolition of many of the buildings. In 1603, this house was the scene of a poignant and crucial turning point in Irish history. After the disastrous Battle of Kinsale, the vanquished Hugh O'Neill, the last of the great Irish chieftains, was given shelter here by Sir Garret Moore until he surrendered to the English Lord Deputy Mountjoy. After his surrender, O'Neill was pardoned, but despairing of his position fled to the continent in 1607 with other old Irish leaders in the Flight of the Earls. In 1727 the site was abandoned altogether.

A new visitor's centre next to the site describes monastic life in greater detail. Entry is IR£1.50/60p and the grounds are open 9.30 am to 6.30 pm from mid-June to mid-September, from 10 am to 5 pm from May to mid-June and from mid-September to the end of October. At other times of year, entrance is free. A back road connects Mellifont with Monasterboice.

Monasterboice

Just off the N1 road to Belfast, about 10 km north of Drogheda, is Monasterboice (*Mainistir Bhuithe*), an intriguing monastic site containing a cemetery, two ancient church ruins, one of the finest and tallest round towers in Ireland and two of the best high crosses.

Down a leafy country lane and set in sweeping farmland, Monasterboice has a special atmosphere, particularly at quiet times. The site can be reached directly from Mellifont via a winding route along narrow country lanes.

The original monastic settlement at Monasterboice is said to have been founded by St Buithe in the 4th or 5th century, although the site probably had pre-Christian significance. The saint was a follower of St Patrick, whose name somehow got converted to Boyne, and the river is named after him. It's said that he made a direct ascent to heaven via a ladder lowered from above. An invading Viking force took over the settlement in 968, only to be comprehensively expelled by Donal, the Irish high king of Tara, who killed at least 300 of the Vikings in the process.

Entrance to Monasterboice is free and there is a small gift shop outside the compound. To avoid the crowds, come early or late in the day.

High Crosses Monasterboice's high crosses are superb examples of Celtic art with an important didactic use, bringing the gospels alive for the uneducated – cartoons of the scriptures, if you like. Like Greek statues, they were probably brightly painted, but all traces of colour have long disappeared.

Muiredach's Cross, the one nearest to the entrance, dates from the early 10th century. The inscription at the foot reads 'Or do Muiredach Lasndernad i Chros' – 'A prayer for Muiredach for whom the cross was made'. Muiredach was abbot here until 922.

The subjects of the carvings have not been positively identified. On the east face from the bottom up are thought to be: on the first panel, the Fall of Adam and Eve and the murder of Abel; on the second, David and Goliath; on the third, Moses bringing forth water from the rock to the waiting Israelites; and on the fourth, the Three Wise Men bearing gifts to Mary and Jesus. The Last Judgement is at the centre of the cross with the risen dead waiting for their verdict, and farther up is St Paul in the desert.

The west face relates more to the New Testament and from the bottom up depicts the arrest of Christ, Doubting Thomas, Christ giving a key to St Peter, the Crucifixion in the centre, and Moses praying with Aaron and Hur. The cross is capped by a representation of a gabled-roof church.

The West Cross is near the round tower and stands 6.5 metres high, making it one of the tallest high crosses in Ireland. It is much

more weathered, especially at the base, and only a dozen or so of its 50 panels are still legible.

The more distinguishable ones on the east face include David killing a lion and bear, the sacrifice of Isaac, David with Goliath's head and David kneeling before Samuel. The west face has the Resurrection, the crowning with thorns, the Crucifixion, the baptism of Christ, Peter cutting off the servant's ear in the garden of Gethsemane and the kiss of Judas.

A third, simpler cross in the north-east corner of the compound is believed to have been smashed by Cromwell's forces and has only a few straightforward carvings. Photographers should note that this cross makes a great evening silhouette picture, with the round tower in the background.

The round tower, minus its cap, stands in a corner of the complex. It's still over 30 metres tall but is closed to the public. In 1097, records suggest, the tower interior went up in flames destroying many valuable manuscripts and other treasures. The church ruins are later and of less interest.

COLLON

Collon, a small village 10 km north-west of Drogheda, was planned along English lines in the 18th century. It is now home to the newer Mellifont Cistercian monastery, founded in 1958, which is housed in the former landlord's residence north of the village.

On Main St, the *Roundhouse Restaurant* is a medium-priced family restaurant with average food but is closed on Monday. Also closed on Monday (and Sunday) is the expensive and highly recommended *Forge Gallery Restaurant* (☎ 041-26272), which features meat, fish, game and some vegetarian dishes; a set dinner costs £22. It's in an old forge building and exhibits paintings by local artists.

ARDEE

This sleepy market town (its Irish name is *Baile Átha Fhirdhia*) on the narrow River Dee is 10 km north of Collon on the N2. Its long tidy main street is dominated by Ardee Castle to the south and Hatch's Castle to the north.

History

For such a small town, Ardee has a colourful history. It takes its name from Áth Fhír Diadh, or Fear Diadh's ford, inspired by the well-known tale of the combat between Cúchulainn and Fear Diadh or Ferdia, as recorded by the ancient tale of the Cattle Raid of Cooley.

The duel was a result of the desire of Maeve, the Queen of Connaught, to get her hands on the Brown Bull of Cooley, which belonged to Ulster. All of Ulster's soldiers had fallen mysteriously sick, but at this ford the young Cúchulainn defeated her army one by one as they tried to get across. Maeve finally persuaded a childhood friend and foster brother of Cúchulainn called Ferdia to take him on. Cúchulainn won, and the defeated Ferdia had the ford named after him as was the Celtic custom. A broken tumulus grave to the west of the river is called Ferdia's Grave.

In the 12th century, the area was turned into a barony and the town remained in English hands before being taken by the O'Neills in the 17th century. James II had his headquarters here for two months in 1689 prior to the Battle of the Boyne.

Things to See

Ardee Castle, a square tower dating from the 13th century, was an important outpost on the edge of the English Pale. It later became a courthouse and is now under restoration to house a museum and gift and coffee shop. Hatch's Castle also dates from this time, and it remained in the hands of the Hatch family from Cromwellian times until 1940. It is still a private residence.

The river bank can be explored around the ford, where there is a well-tended riverside walk.

Places to Stay

The *Railway Bar* (☎ 041-53279) in Market St does B&B for £14 a head. *Carrig Mor*

(☎ 041-53513), two km south of Ardee on the main Dublin to Donegal road, has rooms at IR£18.50 single or IR£27 to IR£29 double. There's also accommodation at *Gable's Restaurant* (☎ 041-53789) in Dundalk Rd for IR£17 to IR£23 per person.

For a real treat, try the lovely Georgian *Red House* (☎ 041-53523), which stands in its own demesne. Take the Dundalk road past Gable's Restaurant and it's about 500 metres along among trees on the left. The elegant rooms cost IR£36 to IR£42 per person including breakfast, and dinner is another IR£20.

Places to Eat

Caffrey's bakery and coffee shop in the centre does light meals, as does *Auberge* further along. *Brian Muldoon & Sons* on Main St does a good steak.

Gable's Restaurant (☎ 041-53789) costs IR£19 for the set dinner and their desserts are particularly memorable. They're open Tuesday to Saturday and bookings are advisable. Chinese takeaways are available from *Chinese Palace* (☎ 041-53998) near the river.

Popular pubs in town include the *Lemon & Clove* and the *Irish Harp* across the road.

AROUND ARDEE

The Jumping Church of Kildemock

Three km south-east of town is the area's oddest landmark, the remains of the Jumping Church of Kildemock. On a thunderous night in February 1715, a storm caused a section of St Catherine's Church to shift from its foundations.

Rather than settle for this rather straightforward explanation, the locals decided the church had miraculously jumped to exclude the remains of an excommunicated member of the flock who had been buried within its walls. Thus was born the 'jumping church'.

In the churchyard is a gravestone to Sara and William Orson, decorated with an unusual skull and crossbones.

Tallanstown

North of Ardee, the main road forks to Monaghan and Dundalk. The slightly more interesting route to Dundalk is via Tallanstown, with nearby Louth Hall which belonged to the Plunkett family, the barons of Louth. Oliver Plunkett took shelter here among his relations in the 1670s. It is not open to the public.

Louth Village

North of Tallanstown, the county's namesake is an insignificant little place with some mildly interesting remains. St Mochta's is a small 11th or 12th-century church with enclosure and stone roof. St Mochta was British and a follower of St Patrick; he founded a monastery here in the early 6th century. Nearby is the church of a 15th-century Dominican friary, sometimes called Louth Abbey.

Ardpatrick

To the east of Louth is Ardpatrick and Ardpatrick House, the home of Oliver Plunkett. There is a mound here where he is supposed to have illegally ordained priests. It was a good vantage point to spot any advancing English soldiers.

THE COAST ROAD

While the most visually rewarding route to travel between Drogheda and Dundalk is the minor inland route via Mellifont and Collon, the coastal route is also scenic. The latter heads off north under the railway viaduct, passes Baltray with its championship golf course and continues on quiet country roads to Termonfeckin.

Termonfeckin

A 6th-century monastery was founded in Termonfeckin by St Féichín of Cong, County Mayo. All that remains are some gravestones and a 10th-century high cross. Nearby is a well-preserved 15th-century castle or tower house (you get the key from across the road, 10 am to 6 pm) which has two small corbel-vaulted alcoves and an anticlockwise spiral staircase (most go clockwise).

Clogherhead

A couple of km farther north is the busy seaside and fishing centre of Clogherhead, with a good, shallow Blue Flag beach. The area around town is pleasant for strolling with enjoyable walks along the coast (partially marred by vistas of caravan parks) or out to **Port Oriel**, an attractive little harbour with views of the Cooley Peninsula and the Mourne Mountains farther north. During the summer, Port Oriel is home to a fleet of trawlers and smaller fishing boats.

On the south side of the headland is the **Red Man's Cave**. At low tide a reddish fungus becomes visible, covering the cave walls. Local stories describe the fate of some people fleeing from Cromwell, whose hiding place was revealed by a barking dog. They were discovered and slaughtered, and their blood splashed on the walls, where it remains to this day. The cave is hard to find so it's sensible to ask a local for directions, but even if you don't find it the walk is satisfying enough.

Annagassan

A minor road with picture-book views continues 12 km north to Annagassan, on the north side of Dunany Point, at the junction of the Dee and Glyde rivers. It's claimed locally that Annagassan is the site of the Vikings' first settlement in Ireland. Records suggest they sacked a monastery here in 842 and may be responsible for the promontory fort, which is now a low mound overlooking the village.

Castlebellingham

North of Annagassan, the coast road joins the busy main N1 at Castlebellingham, only 12 km from Dundalk. The village grew up around its 18th-century mansion, which is something of a disappointment after the imposing castellated entrance. The mansion is on the site of an earlier castle burnt down by James II's troops; the owner, Thomas Bellingham, worked as a guide to William of Orange during his visit to Ireland in 1689-90. The building is now a hotel and restaurant (☎ 042-72176).

The human grandfather of all Irish frogs is buried in the local graveyard. Dr Thomas Guither, a 17th-century physician, is supposed to have reintroduced frogs to Ireland by releasing imported frog spawn in a pond in Trinity College, Dublin. Frogs, along with snakes and toads, had supposedly received their marching orders from St Patrick 1000 years earlier.

Places to Stay

The coast road doesn't have too many places to stay but *Cross Garden* (☎ 041-22675), one km south of Clogherhead on the Termonfeckin road, overlooks the sea and has very comfortable rooms for IR£18/28 single/double.

Places to Eat

The excellent *Triple House Restaurant* (☎ 041-22616) at the top of the hill in Termonfeckin serves a lot of fish and some meat. There's a three-course menu prior to 7 pm for IR£10; after that expect to pay IR£15 or more. It's closed Monday. For cheaper food, try the nearby *Harbour Bar* which does soup and sandwiches.

Clogherhead's pubs are pretty ordinary but the *Waterside Inn* is a comfortable bar in Termonfeckin.

DUNDALK

Halfway between Dublin and Belfast, Louth's charmless county town is only 13 km from the border and is widely regarded as a Republican stronghold.

History

Dundalk's name is derived from Dún Dealgan, a prehistoric fort which was reputedly the home of the hero Cúchulainn. The town grew under the protection of a local estate controlled by the de Verdon family who were granted lands here by King John in 1185. In the Middle Ages, Dundalk was at the northern limits of the English-controlled Pale, strategically located on one of the main highways to the North.

Orientation & Information

Northbound traffic sweeps round to the east of the town centre. The tourist office (☎ 042-35484) is in Market Square near the Maid of Éireann statue. It's open 9.30 am to 5.30 pm Monday to Friday with a lunchbreak from 1 to 2 pm; in July and August it opens at weekends too. At other times there are boards and maps with tourist info dotted around town. The main post office is on Clanbrassil St.

Things to See

The **Courthouse** on the corner of Crowe and Clanbrassil Sts is a fine neo-Gothic building with large Doric pillars, designed by Richard Morrison who also designed the courthouse in Carlow. In the front square is the stone **Maid of Éireann**, commemorating the Fenian Rising of 1798.

At the top of Church St, **St Nicholas' Church** or the Green Church is the burial site of Agnes Burns, elder sister of Robert, the Scottish poet. She married the local rector, and the monument was erected by the townspeople to honour them both. The 15th-century tower to the right of the church is the oldest structure on the site.

The richly decorated **St Patrick's Cathedral** was modelled on King's College Chapel in Cambridge and in front of it on Jocelyn St is the **Kelly Monument** to a local captain drowned at sea in 1858. Also in Jocelyn St is the newly opened **Dundalk Museum** (☎ 042-27056), open Tuesday to Saturday from 10.30 am to 5.30 pm, and Sunday 2 to 6 pm. Admission costs IR£2/60p.

At the east end of Jocelyn St is the Seatown area of Dundalk with its **castle** (really a Franciscan friary tower) and a derelict sail-less **windmill**, the tallest in Ireland. If you arrive in Dundalk by train you pass the 1820 **Garda station** on St Dominick's Place on the way into town. Its first prisoner is believed to have been its architect, who misappropriated funds and was arrested for non-payment of bills.

Places to Stay

Camping There is camping at *Gyles Quay*

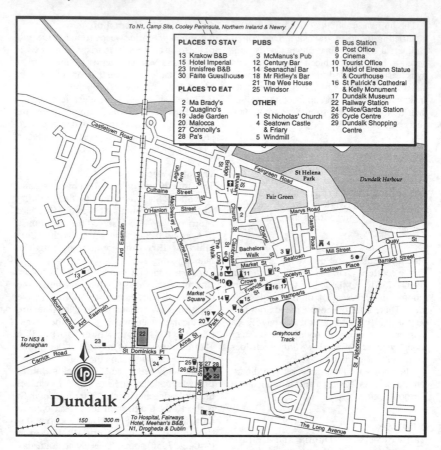

PLACES TO STAY

13 Krakow B&B
15 Hotel Imperial
23 Innisfree B&B
30 Fáilte Guesthouse

PLACES TO EAT

2 Ma Brady's
7 Quaglino's
19 Jade Garden
20 Malocca
27 Connolly's
28 Pa's

PUBS

3 McManus's Pub
12 Century Bar
14 Seanachaí Bar
18 Mr Ridley's Bar
21 The Wee House
25 Windsor

OTHER

1 St Nicholas' Church
4 Seatown Castle & Friary
5 Windmill
6 Bus Station
8 Post Office
9 Cinema
10 Tourist Office
11 Maid of Eireann Statue & Courthouse
16 St Patrick's Cathedral & Kelly Monument
17 Dundalk Museum
22 Railway Station
24 Police/Garda Station
26 Cycle Centre
29 Dundalk Shopping Centre

Dundalk

Caravan Park (☎ 042-76262) 16 km west, off the road to Greenore. Open April to September, it has excellent facilities and charges IR£7 per tent.

Hostels The nearest hostels are on the Cooley Peninsula in Omeath, 16 km away and Carlingford, 24 km away.

B&Bs An excellent B&B is the *Fáilte Guesthouse* (☎ 042-35152) on the corner of Hill St and The Long Ave, which charges IR£16/28 for singles/doubles. Another which is just as good is *Mrs Meehan's Rosemount* (☎ 042-35878)

near the Carroll's cigarette factory about three km south of town on the main Dublin road. B&B there is IR£18 single and IR£28 double in high season.

Innisfree (☎ 042-34912) in Carrick Rd close to the railway station is a pleasant old house with rooms at IR£13 or IR£16 per person. *Krakow* (☎ 042-37535) on Ard Easmuin St, north from the railway station, has rooms for IR£13 to IR£15 per person and dinner is available for IR£11.

Hotels The *Hotel Imperial* (☎ 042-32241) on Park St has a better interior than the outside would suggest. Singles/doubles are IR£45/56 including breakfast. The *Fairways Hotel* (☎ 042-21500) on the Dublin road is modern, plush and costs IR£39/69.

The *Ballymascanlon Hotel* (☎ 042-71124) is a manor-house hotel with a swimming pool, squash courts, nine-hole golf course and other sporting facilities. It is six km north of Dundalk on the way to Carlingford and costs IR£50 to IR£75 B&B.

Places to Eat
Dundalk has plenty of cheap eateries. Try *Connolly's*, a small restaurant upstairs in the shopping centre on The Ramparts south of the town centre and east of Dublin St. The *Malocca Restaurant* (☎ 042-34175) on Park St will have something for the pickiest eater: curries, burgers, pizzas and sandwiches. *Ma Brady's* is a homely place at 7 Church St where a substantial dinner will cost IR£5 to IR£10. The *Windsor* pub on Dublin St, does light meals all day.

Better places in town would include *Quaglino's* (☎ 042-38567), an Italian restaurant near the post office where dinner will cost from IR£17. The *Jade Garden* (☎ 042-30378) is an excellent Chinese restaurant on Park St near Dundalk shopping centre, with dinners from IR£8. *Cluskey's Restaurant* (☎ 042-74223), 12 km along the Carrick road is small, comfortable and will cost from IR£15 for dinner.

Entertainment
Several good pubs can be found around Park St. *Mr Ridley's* has pop/rock most nights while *Seanachaí Bar* has Irish music on Tuesday night, jazz on Wednesday and whatever is going at weekends. The *Century Bar* at Roden Place, the *Wee House* in Anne St and *McManus's* in Seatown are alternatives.

The three-screen *Adelphi Cinema* is across from the tourist office.

Getting There & Away
Bus Bus Éireann run an almost hourly service to Dublin and a less-frequent one to Belfast. The bus station (☎ 042-34075) is behind Clanbrassil St, up from the tourist office. There are plenty of local buses and daily connections to centres nationwide. Capital Coaches (☎ 042-40025) operate a daily Dundalk-Drogheda-Dublin service.

Train The railway station (☎ 042-35521/35522) is a few hundred metres west of Park St on Carrickmacross St. Six trains daily (three on Sunday) operate on the Dublin to Belfast line.

Getting Around
The Cycle Centre (☎ 042-37159), opposite the huge shopping centre at 44 Dublin St south of the town centre, rents bikes for IR£ a day or IR£ a week. The taxi rank is beside the tourist office, or call A-1 Cabs (☎ 042-26666) or Dixon's (☎ 042-30000).

INTO NORTHERN IRELAND
If you are heading for Derry, take the N53 to the west of town, while for Belfast continue north on the main N1 route. If you are hiking or cycling and want to go directly to the Mourne Mountains you can, during the summer, get a ferry from Omeagh to Warrenpoint.

Driving north from Dundalk, you will be across the border long before you realise it. Northern Ireland begins about 13 km north of Dundalk, somewhere after the closed Irish customs post and before the first petrol station advertising cheap petrol (by southern standards). Watch the road: the surface improves and there's a concrete kerb once you're in the North.

The British army checkpoints are no longer obviously staffed, although the structures are still in place just in case the ceasefire breaks down.

CASTLEROCHE
Five km north-west of Dundalk on the Castleblayney road, Baron de Verdon's 1230 Castleroche Castle is impressively sited on a pinnacle of rock. The triangular remnants of the building include a twin-towered entrance house and protective wall. One of the windows on the west side is 'Fuinneóg an Mhurdair', meaning the Murder Window, as

the baroness was said to have had the architect thrown from it to prevent any similar castles ever being built.

FAUGHART

Faughart, four km from Castleroche, has fine views and is reputed to be the birthplace of St Brigid, Ireland's most revered saint after St Patrick. She was the daughter of a local chieftain and settled in Kildare in the 6th century. The grotto and church here mark the spot of a monastery associated with her, and devotions are still carried out on 1 February, her feast day.

In the west corner of the graveyard is the grave of Edward Bruce, a king of Ireland who died in 1318. As part of the Gaelic revival he was invited to Ireland from Scotland and crowned by the Ulster lords, who hoped he would create trouble for the English in Ireland. He accepted the job, hoping this would relieve English pressure at home on his brother, Robert Bruce of Scotland. The hero Cúchulainn is said to have been born near here.

THE COOLEY PENINSULA

Just west of Dundalk, the lonely moorlands of the Cooley Peninsula are the setting for a large part of Ireland's most famous fable, the Táin Bó Cúailnge or the Cattle Raid of Cooley. The low mountains are really a part of Northern Ireland's Mourne Mountains, but are cut off from them physically by the flooded valley of Carlingford Lough and politically by the border which runs up the centre of the lough. The peninsula is a world of its own and has strong Republican traditions.

The best way to explore the peninsula is by first circumnavigating it on the ring road, perhaps detouring closer to the sea at **Gyles Quay** which has a camp site and safe beach, before arriving in Carlingford and Omeath. Carlingford is probably the best base from which to venture inland over the peninsula's

---

The Táin Bó Cúailnge – The Cattle Raid of Cooley

This remarkable tale of greed and war is one of the oldest stories in any European language and the closest thing Ireland has produced to the Greek epics. Queen Maeve, the powerful ruler of Connaught, was jealous because she could not match the white bull owned by her husband Ailill. She heard tales of the finest bull in Ireland, the brown bull of Cooley, and became determined to rectify the situation.

Maeve gathered her armies and headed for Ulster, where she conspired with her druids to place the Ulster armies under a spell. A deep sleep descended on them, leaving the province undefended. The only obstacle remaining was the boy warrior Cúchulainn, who tackled Maeve's soldiers as they tried to ford the river at Ardee in County Louth. Cúchulainn killed many of them and halted their advance. Maeve eventually persuaded Cúchulainn's half-brother and close friend, Ferdia, to take him on, but he was defeated after a momentous battle and died in Cúchulainn's arms.

The struggle continued across Louth and on to the Cooley peninsula, where many place names echo the ensuing action. Sex rears its head regularly in the Táin, for Maeve was more interested in her chief warrior Fergus than in her husband Ailill. At various spots in the saga, they sneak off to make love and in one instance Ailill steals the sword of the distracted Fergus, to shame him and show how careless he was.

While Maeve's soldiers were being despatched in all sorts of ways by Cúchulainn, Maeve had managed to capture the brown bull and spirit him away to Connaught. The wounded Cúchulainn defeated her armies but the bull was gone. In the end, the brown bull killed Ailill's white bull and thundered around Ireland leaving bits of his victim all over the place. Finally, spent with rage, he died near Ulster at a place called Druim Tarb, the ridge of the bull. Cúchulainn and Ulster then made peace with Maeve and thus the saga ended. ∎

hilltops, soaked in the legends of the Cattle Raid of Cooley, through Windy Gap to the **Long Woman's Grave** and beyond to the picturesque country roads and forests that make the place a haven for walkers.

PROLEEK DOLMEN & GALLERY GRAVE

Heading north from Dundalk, turn right after three km towards the Ballymascanlon Hotel, the start of the peninsula ring route. In the grounds of the hotel, up by the 5th green of the golf course (there is a signposted trail for non-golfers) is the fine Giant's Load Proleek Dolmen and Gallery Grave.

Local legends say it is the grave of Para Buí Mór MhacSeóidín, a Scottish giant who came here to challenge Fionn MacCumhaill, leader of the fabled Fianna warriors. It dates from 3000 BC, and the 47-tonne capstone sits precariously on three uprights. The pebbles on top are recent additions and come from the belief that if you can land a stone on top, any wish will be granted. Single women who achieve this are guaranteed marriage within a year.

CARLINGFORD

Near Carlingford (*Cairlinn*), the peninsula's mountains and views display themselves to dramatic effect. This pretty village, with its cluster of narrow streets and whitewashed houses, nestles on Carlingford Lough, beneath 587-metre Slieve Foye. After visiting in 1914, the Reverend Laurence Murray wrote of its 'medieval suggestiveness', and that suggestiveness survives today in the street plan and the crumbling walls and towers dotted around the village. Hard though it is to believe it, not much of this was appreciated until the late 1980s, when the villagers got together to show what can be done to revive a dying community. The story of their efforts is vividly told in the heritage centre (see below).

Plans for a proper tourist information centre exist, but in the meantime you can get quite a lot of information from Carlingford Heritage Centre, where a good town trail leaflet is available.

The Mourne Mountains are just a few km north across the lough. Carlingford is the starting point for the 50-km Táin Way.

Carlingford Heritage Centre

Holy Trinity Church (☎ 042-73454) in Churchyard Rd in the centre of the village had been redundant for several years before funds became available to turn it into a heritage centre. The work has been carried out in such a way that the information boards are encased within closeable doors so that the church can double as a concert hall outside visiting hours. Above the door, a fine mural shows what the village would have looked like in its medieval heyday when the Mint and Taafe's Castle would have been right on the waterfront. A short video describes the village history and explains what has been done to give it new life over the last few years.

The Centre is open on weekdays from 9.30 am to 4.30 pm, and on weekends and bank holidays from noon to 6 pm. Admission costs IR£1/50p.

King John's Castle

Carlingford was first settled by the Vikings, and in the Middle Ages became an English stronghold under the protection of the castle. It was built on a pinnacle in the 11th to 12th centuries to control the entrance to the lough. On the west side, the entrance gateway was constructed to allow only one horse and rider to pass through at a time. King John's name stuck to a remarkable number of places in Ireland, given that he spent little time in or near any of them! In 1210 he spent a couple of days here en route to a nine-day battle with Hugh de Lacy at Carrickfergus Castle in Antrim. It is suggested that the first few pages of the Magna Carta, the world's first constitutional bill of rights, were drafted while he was here.

Other Sites

Near the disused railway station is **Taafe's Castle**, a 16th-century tower house which stood on the waterfront until the land in front was reclaimed to build the shortlived railway line. The **Mint**, in front of the hostel near the square, is of a similar age, but although Edward IV is thought to have granted a charter to a mint in 1467 no coins were produced here. The building has some interesting Celtic carvings around the windows. Near it is the **Tholsel**, the only surviving gate to the original town, although much altered in the 19th century when its defensive edge was softened in the interests of letting traffic through.

To the west of the village centre are the remains of a **Dominican Friary**, built around 1305 and used as a storehouse by oyster fishermen after 1539. A ruinous, aisleless church and traces of the southern dormitory range survive.

Carlingford is the birthplace of Thomas D'Arcy McGee (1825-68), one of Canada's founding fathers. A bust commemorating him stands opposite Taafe's Castle.

Cruises

Carlingford Pleasure Cruises (☎ 042-73239) run one-hour and all-day cruises between May and September. The one-hour cruises cost IR£2 per person and departure times depend on the tides. Byrne's fishing boat (☎ 042-71349) does boat trips during the summer; if you're not part of a group, Sunday is your likeliest day.

Festivals

In mid-August, the pubs are packed morning to midnight when the village is overrun by 20,000 visitors to the Oyster Festival, with funfairs, live bands and buskers alongside the official oyster-opening competitions and tastings. Carlingford goes event-crazy with summer schools, medieval festivals, leprechaun hunts and homecoming festivals almost every weekend between June and September.

Places to Stay

Hostels The IHH *Carlingford Adventure Centre & Hostel* (☎ 042-73100) is on Tholsel St just off the main street. Dorm beds cost IR£8 in rooms for two to eight people, and bedding costs IR£1 extra. The adventure centre exists to teach rock climbing, orienteering, hill walking and windsurfing to

groups, so you would be wise to check whether any large and potentially noisy gaggles of school kids will be staying at the same time as you.

B&Bs Carlingford is a far nicer place to stay than Dundalk and its B&Bs are of a high standard. There aren't many of them though, so in summer and at weekends it's wise to book ahead. In the middle of the village, *Carlingford House* (☎ 042-73118) charges IR£15 per person and has a big drawing room with an open turf fire – but come alone and they slap on a single supplement even in low season. *Viewpoint* (☎ 042-73149) overlooks the harbour in the village on the Omeath road. The motel-style rooms cost IR£16.50 per person, including an excellent breakfast.

Mourneview farmhouse (☎ 042-73551), a km out of Carlingford in Belmont, costs IR£15 per person. *Shalom* (☎ 042-73151) is a half km along the Greenore road overlooking the village, and has rooms with bathrooms at IR£18/28.

Hotels *McKevitt's Village Hotel* (☎ 042-73116) on Market Square has singles at IR£38, doubles at IR£56, and boasts a good bar and restaurant. *Jordan's* also has some very comfortable, spacious rooms for IR£60 a head.

Places to Eat

The *Carlingford Arms* pub does hefty helpings of pub food; two people could manage perfectly well with one serving of fish & chips. *PJ's* does half a dozen oysters with brown bread for £3. *Magee's Bistro* in Dundalk St has a very varied menu featuring dishes like fajitas and moussaka. Unfortunately, it's only open Thursday to Saturday from 7 to 10 pm and on Sunday from 1 to 6 pm. There's a minimum charge of IR£4.95.

Jordan's Restaurant (☎ 042-73223) in Newry St is a cosy place overlooking the water, with surprisingly sophisticated food. The menu ranges from oysters to unusual Irish dishes like *crubeens* – pig's trotters. There's a set dinner for IR£21; for à la carte count on around IR£30 per person with drinks.

It's a good idea to make reservations in summer. The bistro at the front is slightly cheaper.

When everything else is closed, *McKevitt's* may still be serving food. You can also get breakfast here for IR£3 even if you're not staying.

Entertainment
Popular pubs include the *Carlingford Arms*, the *Central Bar*, which often has Irish music. *PJ's* pub, off the Square on Tholsel St, is a traditional Irish bar with a grocery shop upfront and a leprechaun's suit of clothes, hammer and anvil on a window ledge.

Northern Ireland

ERECTED
IN MEMORY OF
CHARLES WILLIAM VANE
3RD MARQUIS OF LONDONDERRY
K G
BY HIS TENANTRY AND FRIEND

1857

Northern Ireland

Until recently, a quarter of a century of bad publicity had rendered much of Northern Ireland a tourism no-go area. However, despite the fear engendered by the bombings and shootings, drunken and erratic Irish drivers were – and probably still are – a much greater danger to tourists in Ireland, North or South. The accent is distinctly different in the North, there's another currency and they measure distances in miles, but otherwise the changes across the border are insignificant. The Northern Irish are certainly no less friendly to foreign visitors than are their compatriots in the South.

The rewards of a foray to the North are certainly well worthwhile – the Antrim Coast Road is a truly stunning stretch of coastline, there are some fascinating early Christian remains around Lough Erne, and Derry has one of the best preserved old city walls in Europe. But even with the coming of peace and the ending of the military roadblocks, the signs of the Troubles can't be ignored: the wall murals in Belfast and Derry, fortified police stations and circling helicopters are still as much a part of Northern Ireland as green fields and noisy pubs.

HISTORY

With the industrial revolution, Belfast and the surrounding counties became the major industrial centre on the island, but the wealth of Belfast's industrial expansion went primarily to the Protestant community. In the late 19th and early 20th centuries, when Home Rule for Ireland became a possibility, the Protestant citizens of Belfast joined the Ulster Volunteer Force in large numbers to resist any such move. The Catholic minority felt increasingly alienated, and while violence was nothing like as frequent as today there was the odd sectarian attack.

Northern Ireland's relationship with the Republic of Ireland was tenuous from the moment of partition. In the Government of Ireland Act of 1920 Lloyd George split

Ireland into two and allowed for parliaments both north and south. The division of the island was a rough and ready one. The Ulster Unionist leaders demanded only the six of Ulster's nine counties where they were supported by half or more of the population. While the South was overwhelmingly Catholic with a very small Protestant minority (5%), the balance was very different in the North, with a substantial Catholic minority (over 30%) and many areas, especially in South Armagh, where Catholics were actually in the majority.

The Anglo-Irish Treaty of 1921 which partitioned the country and granted Ireland its independence was less than completely clear on the future of the North. A Boundary Commission was supposed to reconsider the borders and make adjustments as necessary, something it never did.

On 22 June 1921 the Northern Ireland parliament came into being, with James Craig as the first prime minister. In 1923 the Civil War in the South ground to an exhausted halt with reluctant acceptance of Ireland's division. In the North, Catholic nationalists elected to the new Northern Ireland parliament took up their seats with equal reluctance, but only in 1925, after the Boundary Commission had collapsed. The politics of the North became increasingly divided on religious grounds, with one prime minister declaring that the government of Northern Ireland was 'a Protestant parliament and a Protestant state' and another proudly proclaiming that he did not employ a single Catholic.

The Northern Ireland parliament sat from 1920 until 1972 and the Protestant majority made sure their rule was absolute by systematically excluding Catholics from power. There was widespread discrimination against Catholics in housing, employment and social welfare. The Protestant reluctance to share the country with Catholics was exacerbated by the shortage of things to share out anyway. The effects of the 1930's depression were even more severe in Northern Ireland than elsewhere in the UK, with unemployment averaging 25%. Per capita income was only about 60% of the level in Britain, and indicators in every area from housing to public health were considerably worse than elsewhere in Britain.

The government at every level from local councils to the Stormont parliament was Protestant-dominated and consistently followed a 'jobs for the (Protestant) boys' mentality. In the early 1970s when Belfast's population was 25% Catholic, only 2.5% of Belfast Corporation jobs were held by Catholics. In 1922, the bitter struggle going on in the South spilled over the border and serious rioting broke out in Belfast. In 1935 11 people died in further riots in Belfast. But in spite of all this, Northern Ireland remained relatively peaceful for many years after partition.

In WW II, Belfast was heavily bombed, with many deaths and large areas of the city flattened. The first US Army forces to land in Europe passed through Belfast on 26 January 1942. The strong support given to Britain's war effort further entrenched British backing for Northern Ireland's continued existence and independence. In 1949 the creation of the Republic of Ireland cut the South's final links, via the British Commonwealth, with the North, but even though the new republic's constitution enshrined its eventual goal of regaining the North, this caused little stir. It was not until the 1960s that Northern Ireland's basic instability began to show itself.

The government, under Prime Minister Terence O'Neill, took the first tentative steps towards dealing with the problems of the North's Catholics. A meeting with the South's prime minister and a visit to a Catholic girls' school were hardly earthshattering moves, but the reaction to these symbolic initiatives propelled the Reverend Ian Paisley to the front of the stage as the ranting personification of Protestant extremism.

The next innocent addition to what was soon to become a very messy stew was the creation of the Northern Ireland Civil Rights Association in 1967, to campaign for fairer representation for the North's Catholics. It was in Derry (Londonderry) that Protestant political domination was at its most outrageous, and in Derry that 50 years of Catholic anger at the rigging of council elections finally boiled over in the late 1960s. Derry's population was split approximately 60% Catholic to 40% Protestant, yet the city's council was consistently elected with exactly the reverse ratio. This was accomplished not only by a long-running gerrymander of the electoral boundaries, but also by handing out more votes to the Protestants via residency and home-ownership requirements. In October 1968 a civil rights march in Derry was violently broken up by the Royal Ulster Constabulary and the Troubles were under way.

In January 1969 People's Democracy, another civil rights movement, organised a Belfast to Derry march to demand a fairer division of jobs and housing and an end to unfair voting practices. Just outside Derry a Protestant mob attacked the marchers. The police stood to one side and then compounded the problem with a sweep through the predominantly Catholic Bogside area of Derry. Further marches and protests followed, but increasingly exasperation on one side was met with violence from the other, and far from keeping the two sides apart the police were becoming part of the problem.

Finally in August 1969 British troops were sent into Derry and, two days later, Belfast, to maintain law and order. Though the British army was initially welcomed by the Catholics, it soon came to be seen as a tool of the Protestant majority. The peaceful civil rights movement lost ground, and the hibernating IRA found itself with new and willing recruits for an armed struggle for independence from among the beleaguered Catholic minority. Socialists like Bernadette Devlin provided a brief flash of leadership, but it was 'the men with the guns' who soon called the tune.

For 25 years the story of the Troubles, as they were euphemistically known in Northern Ireland, was one of lost opportunities, intransigence on both sides and fleeting moments of hope. Suspected IRA sympathisers were interned without trial, and on 'Bloody Sunday' (30 January 1972) in Derry 13 civilians were killed by troops. Northern Ireland's increasingly ineffective parliament was abolished in 1972, although substantial progress had been made towards meeting the original civil rights demands. A new power-sharing arrangement was worked out in the 1973 Sunningdale agreement, but it was first rejected by the Protestants and then killed stone dead by the massive and overwhelmingly Protestant Ulster Workers' Strike of 1974. Northern Ireland has been ruled from London ever since.

Whilst continuing to target people in Northern Ireland, the IRA also moved their campaign of violence and terror to mainland Britain, bombing pubs and shops and killing many civilians. Their activities were increasingly criticised by citizens on all sides of the political spectrum, and by all mainstream political parties in Britain and the Republic. Meanwhile Loyalist paramilitaries were running a sectarian murder campaign against Catholics. The Troubles rolled back and forth throughout the 1970s, and although they slowed down during the 1980s an answer to the Irish problem seemed nowhere nearer. Passions reached fever pitch in 1981 when Republican prisoners in the North went on a hunger strike, demanding the right to be recognised as political prisoners. Ten of them fasted to death, the best known being an elected MP, Bobby Sands.

The waters were further muddied by an incredible variety of parties, groups, splinter groups and even splinters of splinter groups, each with its own agenda. The Royal Ulster Constabulary (RUC) was reorganised and retrained, while the IRA split into 'official' and 'provisional' wings from whom sprang even more extreme republican organisations like the Irish National Liberation Army (INLA). Protestant loyalist paramilitary organisations sprang up in opposition to the IRA, and violence was frequently met with violence, indiscriminate outrage with indiscriminate outrage.

In 1985 the Anglo-Irish Agreement gave the Dublin government an official consultative role in Northern Ireland affairs for the first time. The idea was to make Northern nationalists feel that someone was looking out for their interests. However, the Unionist politicians were outraged by what they saw as meddling by the Republic and protested against and boycotted anything to do with the agreement. From 1985 onwards there was a steady increase in the level and professionalism of violence from the loyalist side of the divide.

It's easy to line up the 'if onlys' when it comes to the problems of Ireland. If only the Home Rule movement had not encountered such violent opposition to Irish independence in the early part of this century, Ireland might be one country today and the problem would be simply not exist. Northern fears might have been reduced if only the Republic had not pandered to them by allowing the Catholic church's prejudices (on sex, marriage, censorship and the position of the church) to insinuate themselves into so many corners of the country.

Northern Catholics' antipathy to Northern Protestants might have been much less if only they had been treated with a modicum of fairness between the 1920s and 1970s. Northern fears of Southern impoverishment might have been lower if only the Republic's government had not pursued its vision of a rural arcadia for longer than was sensible. The British army's unpopularity might have been far less if only it hadn't over-reacted to IRA provocation. And the North's unwillingness to countenance any agreement with the South might have been less if only the IRA had not been so callously indiscriminate in their violence or, equally frequently, so callously inept.

Back in 1970 the British home secretary, the hapless Reginald Maudling, was castigated for observing that the best hope for Northern Ireland was to achieve 'an acceptable level of violence'. Twenty years later that was precisely what had been achieved.

However, by 1995 external circumstances started to alter the picture. Membership of the

European Union had reduced the differences between North and South, while economic progress in Ireland had shrunk the disparity between Northern and Southern standards of living. The importance of the Catholic church in the South had also diminished.

In 1991, the various factions had met for talks under Peter Brooke, the British government's representative in Northern Ireland. Further talks were held in 1992. On the surface nothing much seemed to come of all this, but behind the scenes individuals, and particularly the Social Democratic & Labour Party (SDLP) leader John Hume, continued to beaver away, trying to persuade the mouthpieces of the main groups that something had to give.

Then, 25 years after the Troubles began, seemingly out of the blue, on 31 August 1994 the Sinn Féin leader Gerry Adams announced a 'permanent cessation of violence' on behalf of the IRA. For some months afterwards the British government quibbled over the precise meaning of those words, but in October 1994 the Combined Loyalist Military Command also announced a ceasefire. Most British troops were then withdrawn to barracks and roadblocks were removed. Since then an edgy peace has held sway while all the parties restate their conflicting agendas.

In 1995 the British and Irish governments published two Framework documents intended to act as a basis for discussion on the way forward. The first, *A Framework for Accountable Government in Northern Ireland*, set out the British government's proposals for restoring democracy through a new 90-member Assembly to be elected by proportional representation and with 'substantial legislative and administrative powers'. In the second, *A New Framework for Agreement*, the British and Irish governments put forward their joint proposals for relationships within the island and between the two different governments.

Although it was stressed that these were discussion documents and that nothing would be imposed on anyone without a referendum being held first, both sides – but more conspicuously the Unionists – dug their heels in, once again reeling off their objections as if the preceding 25 years had never taken place.

This description of the years of conflict has been written in the past tense in the hope that the violence really is at an end. However, this is by no means a certainty. Although there have been no major incidents since the ceasefires, caches of arms and bomb-making materials have occasionally been uncovered, and paramilitary punishment attacks (particularly the kneecapping of supposedly anti-social individuals) have been stepped up.

More alarmingly, as the months slipped by and the first anniversary of the IRA ceasefire passed, Sinn Féin leaders grew restive about having so little to show in return for their gesture. There were even mutterings about a return to violence if talks did not begin soon. In May 1995 Gerry Adams had met Sir Patrick Mayhew, the Northern Ireland secretary, in the USA, but after that the peace process stalled again. The main sticking point was that John Major's government, beleaguered at Westminster and with so small a majority in the House of Commons that it depended on the support of Unionist MPs, refused to allow overt all-party talks to start unless the IRA first 'decommissioned' their weapons.

To the IRA this would be tantamount to surrender, and they continued to argue that no arms could be given up until the British troops withdrew and all political prisoners were freed. To the British government – and the tabloid press – there are no political prisoners, only convicted terrorists. A by-election in the strongly Unionist seat of North Down resulted in victory for an independent Unionist, who was even more opposed to the peace talks than the official Unionists. And so the dialogue of the deaf continued.

GOVERNMENT

Northern Ireland is part of the United Kingdom of Great Britain and Northern Ireland, and is governed from London. The main Protestant parties in the North are the

The Public Faces of Conflict
Gerry Adams

The *Daily Telegraph* once claimed that the bearded, bespectacled Sinn Féin President Gerry Adams could be mistaken for a Liberal Democrat candidate canvassing in Oxford. Elsewhere he's been described as resembling a sociology lecturer at one of the old polytechnics. A glance at his CV quickly dispels any such illusions.

Gerry Adams

Adams was born in Belfast in 1948 into a staunchly Republican family and by the age of 16 had already joined Fianna, the IRA's youth wing. A year later, allegedly, he joined the IRA itself, rising rapidly through its ranks until, it is thought, he became chief of staff. Throughout the '70s he was in and out of jail on a variety of charges and non-charges, but on his release he was elected to the Northern Ireland Assembly. In December 1982 he was excluded from Britain following a bomb outrage. Elected to the House of Commons as MP for West Belfast in 1983, he refused to take up his seat in a 'foreign Parliament'. He lost his seat at the 1987 general election.

It was Gerry Adams who articulated the belief that Irish freedom could only be bought by someone with a bullet in one hand and a ballot paper in the other, and throughout the Troubles, it was Adams who regularly featured in news broadcasts, organising and participating in paramilitary funerals. However, by 1988, when he met SDLP leader John Hume for talks, the tone of his public utterances had begun to soften.

In 1994 it was again Adams, as Sinn Féin President, who announced the IRA ceasefire. This led to a lifting of the absurd British broadcasting ban which had meant his words could only be read on television by an actor. Since then Adams has walked the world stage, meeting Presidents Clinton and Mandela, and tirelessly expounding the Republican cause. He is the author of several books, including *Free Ireland: Towards a Lasting Peace* in which he sets out his vision for the future.

Ian Paisley

If Gerry Adams is the man to set the hackles rising on one side, the Reverend Ian Paisley, leader of the Democratic Unionist Party, has much the same effect on the other side. Paisley, however, with his white hair, burly build and habit of throwing off microphones and stomping out of TV interviews, could never be mistaken for anything other than what he is, namely the extremist face of Protestant Unionism.

Born in Ballymena in 1926, Paisley took longer than Adams to get into his political stride. Motivated by desire to exclude Catholics from power, he established the Protestant Unionist Party in 1970, later replacing it with the Democratic Unionist Party. Although some of Paisley's views are unexpected (he opposed internment without trial, for example), he has been astonishingly persistent in opposing virtually every attempt at a settlement, resigning his parliamentary seat in protest at the 1985 Anglo-Irish Agreement, only to win it back again with an increased majority in the ensuing by-election.

It's easy to parody Paisley (the man who wanted *The Sound of Music* banned because it featured a novice nun, the man who called Mrs Thatcher a liar from the House of Commons gallery and showered the Northern Ireland Minister Nicholas Scott with bits of torn-up order paper in one of his more mature protests) but that would be to understate his importance. In *The Independent* David McKittrick wrote that 'it seemed impossible to conceive of an arrangement which included him since he was more interested in protest than power – but it also seemed impossible to establish a workable arrangement without him, since he had the capacity to bring it down'. Even the normally open-minded travel writer Dervla Murphy was moved to write that she had recognised an 'evil influence' after listening to Paisley preach a sermon of pure hatred at his Matryrs' Memorial Free Presbyterian Church in Belfast at the height of the Troubles. ■

Ulster Unionist Party, currently led by David Trimble, and the Democratic Unionist Party, led by the controversial Reverend Ian Paisley. Trying to occupy the middle-of-the-road Catholic and nationalist ground is the Social Democratic & Labour Party (SDLP), led by John Hume, while Sinn Féin ('Ourselves Alone') is the political wing of the IRA and attracts the hard-line nationalist voters. Their current leader is Gerry Adams, with Martin McGuinness as his deputy.

ECONOMY

Northern Ireland's shipbuilding and other industries have declined dramatically, but new industries have developed and, of course, the region is heavily subsidised by Britain and, increasingly, by the European Union. Traditionally the North has been regarded as an economic black hole for Britain and much of the spending has been on defence and security. Northern Ireland suffers from male unemployment of around 14%, which, while very significant, is not as high as in the Republic. It's higher than the British average, largely as a result of the region's de-industrialisation; arguably it would be much worse without the attention and money which has poured into Northern Ireland in the last 20 years or so.

Half of the working population in the North are employed in one way or another by the government and there are many departments doing work for mainland Britain. Agriculture employs around 8% of the labour force and manufacturing and construction around 24%. Unemployment in Northern Ireland used to be far greater amongst the Catholic community (and still is), but the imbalance has started to narrow.

The coming of peace brought an almost instant dividend in the shape of a 20% boom in tourism, especially from Britain and the Republic. And in the first half of 1995 the tourist office counted 156,000 vacationers – a 56% gain from the same period in 1994. If this continues it's estimated that it could result in the creation of some 20,000 new jobs. On the other hand, jobs will be lost amongst security guards, glaziers and others who managed to do well financially out of the conflict.

In the 1980s Northern Ireland was dubbed the 'independent Keynesian republic', as it seemed to be the one area of Thatcher's Britain exempt from public spending cuts. Huge expenditure on public housing turned the region's appalling housing conditions around. Northern Ireland also boasts better hospital standards than the British average. Its educational test results also continue to outpace the rest of the UK, perhaps because the old 11-plus and grammar school system have been retained.

Belfast

Had the Troubles never happened, the capital of Northern Ireland would simply have been a big, rather ugly industrial city, nicely situated and with some imposing and impressive Victorian architecture but well past its prime. As it is, the strife which tore Belfast apart for a quarter of a century has given it quite another edge. If your only view of the city has been through the media's lens, you may be surprised to find it's actually busy and bustling, even prosperous in parts, with more glossy shopping centres and shiny new cars than Dublin.

However, a 'black taxi' ride through the strictly divided working-class areas of the Falls and Shankill Rds in West Belfast will show you the flip side of the coin. Since the outbreak of peace in 1994, obvious reminders of sectarian hatred have retreated to the suburbs, but much of the city centre is pedestrianised for security reasons, and reminders of the Troubles linger on in the armoured Land-Rovers ('tangis') straight out of *Mad Max*, the heavily fortified police stations and the helicopters buzzing overhead,

You may be reassured to know that no tourists have been killed or injured since the Troubles got going in the early 1970s. In fact statistically Belfast is a much safer city for a visitor than even the most touristically inclined US metropolis.

Another feature of Belfast is its size; the centre is compact, the traffic relatively light and most points of interest are within easy walking distance of each other. The rocks and green slopes of Cave Hill, with the outline of 'Napoleon's Nose', loom over the city to the north, while the sweep of Belfast Lough cuts right into the city centre from the north-east.

HISTORY

Compared with many other cities, Belfast is relatively new, with few reminders of its pre-19th-century existence. The city's name

Highlights
- Soaking up the nightlife along the 'Golden Mile'
- Learning about the Troubles on the Living History tour
- Animal watching in Belfast Zoo
- Rubbing shoulders with the crowds in the Crown Liquor Saloon
- Taking a (free) City Hall tour

comes from Beál Feirste, or 'mouth of the sandy ford', a reference to the River Farset which used to flow through the town centre but is now contained inside an underground pipe. In 1177, the Norman John de Courcy built a castle by the River Lagan, and a small settlement grew up around it.

Both were destroyed 20 years later, and the region was controlled for a long time afterwards by the Irish O'Neill family. In 1613 King James I gave Belfast a charter as a city for the first time but even during the late 17th century it was hardly more than a village; the population was a mere 550 in 1657. The first significant wave of foreign settlers were Huguenots: French Protestants, fleeing from persecution in France, who laid the foundations for a thriving linen industry. More Scottish and English settlers arrived, and other industries such as rope-making, tobacco, engineering and shipbuilding were also developed.

A strong antagonism between Protestants and Catholics only really developed during the 19th century. Prior to this, Belfast had produced many Protestant supporters of an independent Ireland and a fairer society. The United Irishmen, who pushed for increasing independence from England, were actually founded in Belfast in 1791, and the struggle for fairer trading terms enjoyed Protestant and Catholic support. The 1798 Rising, for example, was not purely religious. In Belfast a number of Protestant ministers who supported the revolt were hanged.

During the 18th and 19th centuries Belfast was the one city in Ireland which really experienced the industrial revolution. Sturdy rows of brick terraced houses were built for the factory and shipyard workers. A population of around 20,000 people in 1800 grew steadily to around 400,000 at the start of WWI, by which time Belfast had nearly overtaken Dublin in size. Some suspected that the frequent adjustments to the Dublin city boundaries were made partly in order to ensure the city's population remained a step ahead of the northern upstart.

Queen Victoria visited Belfast in 1849 and her brief foray through the city has been immortalised by a large number of streets and monuments named after her. Belfast was granted city status by Victoria in 1888.

The division of Ireland after WW I and independence in the South gave Belfast a new role as the capital of Northern Ireland. It also marked the end of the city's industrial growth although the decline did not really set in until after WW II. For nearly 50 years from 1922 until the late 1960s, Northern Ireland was a comparatively quiet place and as a result it was studiously ignored by the British government. The Protestant-dominated Unionist government was left to run things as it saw fit, and since Catholic complaints were relatively subdued, and were generally suppressed when they did get too loud, the underlying instability of the region was not noticed.

Since the initial outbreak of rioting in 1969, Belfast has seen more than its fair share of violence and bloodshed, and shocking pictures of extremist bombings and killings, often matched by security force brutality, have made the city a household name around the world. The mayhem reached its peak in the 1970s, and through the 1980s and into the 1990s Belfast appeared to have simmered down to an 'acceptable' level of violence. Then in 1994, seemingly out of the blue, the declaration of peace by both main parties to the conflict raised hope that things might at last improve.

Greater Belfast's population of around 500,000 is about one-third of that of Northern Ireland. While unemployment is relatively high, there is a burgeoning middle class which benefits from the reasonable tax rates and the relative cheapness of housing costs in particular. Belfast has plenty of new cars and neat suburban houses, the city restaurants always seem to be full, and huge expenditure on public housing has smartened up even the bleak areas of West Belfast. The city is much livelier and more cheerful than its grim reputation leads visitors to expect.

ORIENTATION

The city centre is a compact area with the imposing City Hall in Donegall Square as a convenient central landmark. North of the square is Donegall Place/Royal Ave which leads to Donegall St and Belfast Cathedral. This is Belfast's principal shopping district. Reminders of the Victorian era can be found in the stately buildings surrounding City Hall, in the narrow alleys known as the Entries off Ann and High Sts and in the museum-like Crown Liquor Saloon on Great Victoria St.

If you are looking for restaurants or accommodation head south from the square down Great Victoria St or Dublin Rd to University Rd, where you will find Queen's University, the Botanic Gardens and the Ulster Museum. This stretch is called the Golden Mile, and at night it's the most energetic and cheerful area of a generally hard-working city.

The main Europa Bus Station is behind the rebuilt Europa Hotel, in Glencall St. A new city centre train station is being built right beside it.

To the east of Donegall Square is Chichester St which runs down to the Royal Courts of Justice, the Oxford St bus station and the River Lagan, an area which is being extensively developed and will eventually boast a large conference and concert centre, the Belfast Waterfront Hall. East of the river are Samson and Goliath, the giant cranes dominating the Harland & Wolff shipyards. The Short's aircraft factory is beside the Belfast City Airport.

West of the centre the Westlink Motorway divides the city from West Belfast and does nothing to improve the appearance of the place. The (Protestant) Shankill Rd and the (Catholic) Falls Rd run west into West Belfast. The 'Peace Line' built between the two was intended as a safety measure to discourage extremists of either ilk from creating mayhem then scuttling quickly back to their side of the tracks. Since peace broke out in 1994 it's possible to cross from one side to the other without problem, although, ironically, new stretches of wall were being erected even as the terms of the ceasefire were being debated. Beyond the Falls Rd lie even more run-down, deprived areas like Andersonstown and the Ardoyne.

It's worth remembering that Belfast grew out of the industrial revolution and, like cities in England's depressed north, has fallen on hard times, particularly in areas like West Belfast. Nevertheless, a great deal of renovation and reconstruction, much of it part-funded by the European Regional Development Fund (ERDF) or the International Fund for Ireland (IFI), is, belatedly, going on. A brand-new cross-harbour rail link, the Dargan Bridge, opened alongside the new Lagan road bridge in 1995.

INFORMATION
Tourist Information
The Northern Ireland Tourist Board office (☎ 01232-246609) is at St Anne's Court, 59 North St. In July and August, the peak of the summer season, it's open from 9 am to 7.30 pm Monday to Friday, 9 am to 5.15 pm on Saturday and noon to 4 pm on Sunday. For the rest of the year it's open Monday to Saturday from 9 am to 5.15 pm. Outside these hours, a computerised database outside gives details of accommodation, etc. You can pick up information about the whole of Northern Ireland here, and book accommodation both within Northern Ireland and in Britain. There's also a bureau de change and souvenir shop. The tourist information office also stocks four Civic Festival Trails to guide you round the best of the city centre's buildings.

There are also tourist information offices in the City and International airports; the City airport branch is open daily from 5.30 am to 10 pm, while the International airport branch is open more or less round the clock except from November to February when it closes between 11 pm and 7 am.

The Irish Tourist Board, or Bord Fáilte (☎ 01232-327888), at 53 Castle St is open Monday to Friday 9 am to 5 pm and Saturday 9 am to 12.30 pm from March to the end of September only. The Youth Hostel Association of Northern Ireland (YHANI) (☎ 01232-315435) is at 22-32 Donegall Rd, off Shaftesbury Square. The AA (☎ 0345-500600) is at 108 Great Victoria St; for breakdowns phone ☎ 0800-887766. The RAC (☎ 01232-232640) is at 14 Wellington Place; for breakdowns phone ☎ 0800 828282.

The women's centre at 30 Donegall St (☎ 01232-243363) can help with enquiries about specific women's issues. Travellers with disabilities can call Disability Action at 2 Annadale Ave on ☎ 01232-491011 for advice; the tourist office also produces a useful free brochure, *Accessible Accommodation in Northern Ireland*. The Northern Ireland Gay Rights Association (☎ 01232-664111) in Cathedral Buildings, Lower Donegall St should be able to advise on gay and lesbian matters.

The Central Library in Royal Ave (☎ 01232-243233) is open on Monday and

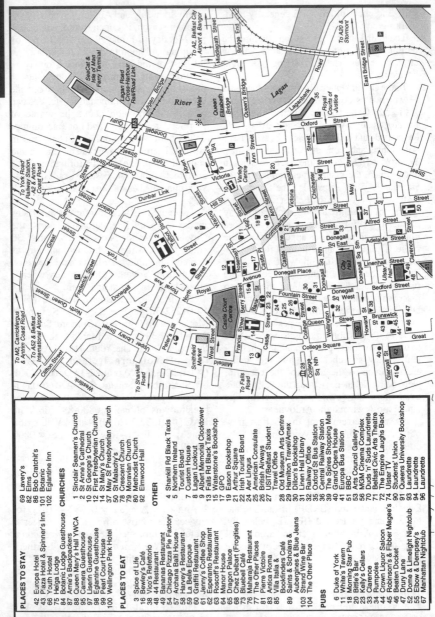

PLACES TO STAY

42 Europa Hotel
43 Plaza Hotel & Spinner's Inn
66 Youth Hostel
75 Helga Lodge
84 Botanic Lodge Guesthouse
87 Arnie's Backpackers
88 Queen Mary's Hall YWCA
95 Camera Guesthouse
97 Liserin Guesthouse
98 Eglantine Guesthouse
99 Pearl Court House
100 Wellington Park Hotel

PLACES TO EAT

3 Spice of Life
16 Bewley's Café
38 Vico's Refettorio
48 Restaurant
49 Banana Restaurant
54 Chicago Pizza Pie Factory
57 Archana Balti House
58 Harvey's Restaurant
59 La Belle Epoque
60 Graffiti Restaurant
61 Jenny's Coffee Shop
62 Esperanto Restaurant
63 Roscoff's Restaurant
64 Manor House
65 Dragon Palace
68 Chez Delbart (Frogities)
73 Bluebell Café
76 Maharaja Restaurant
77 The Other Places
81 Pierre Victoire
83 Antica Roma
85 Villa Italia &
   Bookfinders Café
89 Saints & Scholars &
   Auberges & Blue Jeans
103 Strand Wine Bar
104 The Other Place

PUBS

6 Duke of York
11 White's Tavern
18 Morning Star Pub
20 Bittle's Bar
23 Kelly's Cellars
33 Clarence
34 Rumpoles
44 Crown Liquor Saloon
45 Robinson's & Fibber Magee's
46 Beaten Docket
47 Drury Lane
52 Dome & Limelight Nightclub
55 Elbow & Dempsey's
67 Manhattan Nightclub

69 Lavery's
82 Elms
86 Bob Cratchit's
101 Pizza Hotel
102 Eglantine Inn

CHURCHES

1 Sinclair Seamen's Church
2 St Anne's Cathedral
10 St George's Church
12 First Presbyterian Church
14 St Mary's Church
37 May St Presbyterian Church
50 St Malachy's
78 Crescent Church
79 Moravian Church
80 Methodist Church
92 Elmwood Hall

OTHER

4 Shankill Rd Black Taxis
5 Northern Ireland
   Tourist Board
7 Custom House
8 Lagan Lookout
9 Albert Memorial Clocktower
13 Falls Rd Black Taxis
15 Waterstone's Bookshop
17 GPO
19 Eason Bookshop
21 Arthur Square
22 Irish Tourist Board
24 Aer Lingus
25 American Consulate
26 British Airways
27 USIT/Belfast Student
   Travel
28 Old Museum Arts Centre
29 Hamilton Travel/Amex
30 Dillon's Bookshop
31 Linen Hall Library
32 Railway Office
35 Oxford St Bus Station
36 Central Railway Station
39 The Spires Shopping Mall
40 Grand Opera House
41 Europa Bus Station
51 BBC
53 Arts Council Gallery
56 MGM Cinema Complex
70 Duds 'n 'Suds Laundrette
71 Belfast Civic Arts Theatre
72 The Empire Laughs Back
74 Ulster TV
90 Students' Union
91 Queens University Bookshop
93 Laundrette
94 Laundrette
96 Laundrette

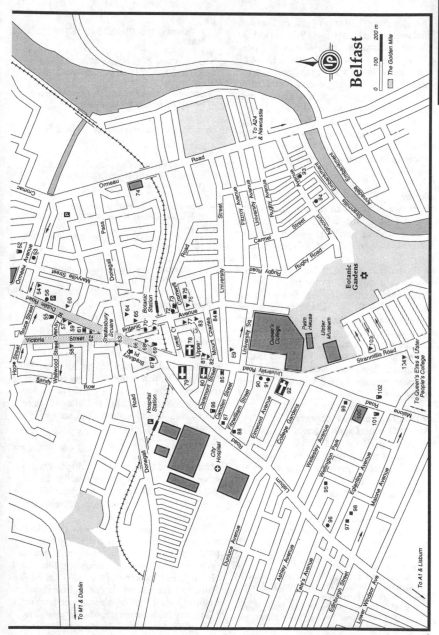

Belfast

0   100   200 m

The Golden Mile

Thursday from 9.30 am to 8 pm, on Tuesday, Wednesday and Friday from 9.30 am to 5.30 pm and on Saturday from 9.30 am to 1 pm.

The Buzz is Belfast and Northern Ireland's commercial 'what's on' magazine, but the fact that it's bi-monthly renders it useless for rapidly changing events and cinema programmes. What's more, it's appallingly written and costs £1.75. The newly established *That's Entertainment* is a much better bet for listings, not least because it's free. Pick it up in Belfast's tourist offices or at the youth hostel.

Money
There are branches of the major Northern Irish banks in the centre of Belfast and numerous cash machines which dispense money to Visa and MasterCard (Access) customers.

The tourist office in St Anne's Court has a bureau de change, as do the post offices in Castle Place and Shaftesbury Square. Hamilton Travel (☎ 01232-322455) at 10 College St, opposite British Airways, is an American Express agent with foreign exchange facilities but doesn't handle client mail. There is a branch of Thomas Cook with exchange facilities in Donegall Place, and another at the International Airport which stays open until 8 pm.

Post & Telecommunications
The GPO is on Castle Place at the junction of Donegall Place and Royal Ave. Other convenient post offices are in Shaftesbury Square and at the junction of University Rd with Malone Rd.

Belfast's phone code is 01232.

Embassies & Consulates
Some countries with consular representation in Belfast are:

Denmark, Sweden
c/o G Heyn & Sons Ltd, Head Line Buildings, 10 Victoria St, Belfast BT1 3GP (☎ 01232-230581)
Greece, Norway, Portugal
c/o M F Ewings (Shipping) Ltd, Hurst House, 15-19 Corporation Square, Belfast BT1 3AJ (☎ 01232-242242)

Italy
7 Richmond Park, Belfast BT9 5EP (☎ 01232-668854)
Spain
c/o McClure & Company, 171-75 Victoria St, Belfast BT1 3GP (☎ 01232-320148)
USA
Consulate General, Queen's House, 14 Queen St, Belfast BT1 6EQ (☎ 01232-328239)

Other consulates in Northern Ireland are:

Belgium
c/o John Preston & Company, Flax House, 29-31 Lisburn St, Hillsborough, County Down (☎ 01846-682671)
France
Drumdarragh, 72 Ballymoney Rd, Craigavad, Holywood, County Down (☎ 01231-72248)
Germany
c/o AVX Ltd, 1 Ballyhampton Rd, Larne BT42 2ST (☎ 01574-260777)
Netherlands
25 Randalstown Rd, County Antrim BT41 (☎ 0184 94 63535)

Travel Agencies
The USIT/Belfast Student Travel office (☎ 324073) is at 13B Fountain Centre, College St. The Queens University Travel Centre (☎ 241830), in the Student Union Building in University Rd, is also run by USIT and is open to non-students of Queens too. Travellers Tales Ltd (☎ 239412) inside the Spires Shopping Mall in College Square is a more conventional travel agency with a positive attitude.

Bookshops
Mainstream bookshops include Waterstone's at 8 Royal Ave, Eason at 16 Ann St and Dillon's at 42 Fountain St. Queen's University also has a bookshop opposite the main university building.

For a wide selection of books on Ireland and good advice on what to read, try Familia (☎ 235392) at 64 Wellington Place. If you're prepared to penetrate the double grilles, the Green Cross bookshop (☎ 243371) at 51-3 Falls Rd has a range of books on Irish issues, mainly giving the Republican perspective. It's run by the wives of Republican prisoners.

Bookfinders at 47 University Rd is a

second-hand bookshop with a popular café at the back. Bookrite (☎ 244137) at 25 Lower North St, near the tourist office, has a good range of second-hand books at fair prices. Roma Ryan's at 73 Dublin Rd stocks prints and rare books.

See the Books & Bookshops section in the Facts for the Visitor chapter for books on Northern Ireland's turbulent history, visitors' accounts and fiction by Northern Irish writers. *Belfast – The Making of the City* (Appletree Press paperback, Belfast, 1983, £7.99) covers Belfast during its prime years from 1800 to 1914.

Laundry
In the university area there are laundrettes at 46 and 120 Agincourt Ave and at 160 Lisburn Rd. More fun is Duds 'n' Suds at 37 Botanic Ave, which incorporates a snack bar. It's open Monday to Friday from 8 am to 9 pm, Saturday from 8 am to 6 pm and Sunday from noon to 6 pm.

Shops
Shops are open until 9 pm on Thursday.

Medical Services
The Royal Victoria Hospital (☎ 240503) is on the Falls Rd west of the city centre; bus Nos 12, 13, 14 and 15 pass by. Belfast City Hospital (☎ 329241) is on the Lisburn Rd; bus No 58 passes by. If you need an ambulance or an emergency service phone ☎ 999.

Dangers & Annoyances
Even at the height of the Troubles Belfast was not a particularly dangerous city for tourists to visit. The callous violence between the IRA (and its various offspring) and the equivalent Protestant paramilitaries was usually aimed at specific people. Nevertheless security precautions used to affect tourists as much as anyone else. Since the ceasefire things have lightened up considerably and you're now no more likely to be stopped and asked for your ID on a Belfast street than on a London one.

It continues to make sense to be careful where you park your car though. Cars illeg-

ally (or suspiciously) parked can expect rough treatment. In practice this is not quite as fearsome as it sounds; even in the bad times you were unlikely to come back to find the bomb squad in action just because you'd overstayed a parking meter for 10 minutes! For the time being parking is still not allowed at all in the prominently marked Control Zones. Indeed it's still wise to use proper car parks wherever possible, whatever the cost, if only because Belfast has a notorious problem with 'joy-riding'; the police view is that guarded multi-storeys are the best bet. The tourist office has a leaflet showing all the car parks, or for information you can phone ☎ 253026.

Unfortunately as the political troubles have died down, so the normal crime rate has started to creep up. As anywhere, you should always lock your car when you leave it and take anything valuable with you. If you leave it in the car, make sure it's out of sight and bear in mind that many insurance policies exclude items stolen from cars.

From the visitor's point of view one of the irritating legacies of the Troubles is an absence of luggage storage facilities at bus or train stations. You may need to open your bag for inspection before going into some public buildings, but this type of security measure is now more commonplace in Dublin than Belfast! Some letterbox slits are also partially closed to prevent anything bulkier than a letter being posted through them. To outsiders police stations can also look offputtingly fortified. Take heart though. If you need to report a 'normal' crime like a lost camera, just march up to the door and press the buzzer. Someone will emerge to help you out.

Given that no one knows what may happen in the future it's still a good idea to carry some form of identification on you; a passport is particularly good as it proves you're a real visitor. If you want to take photos of fortified police stations and other quasi-military paraphernalia, ask first to be on the safe side.

You're unlikely to get into furious political or religious arguments in Belfast pubs because both topics are studiously avoided with outsiders. In staunchly single-minded pubs of either persuasion, outsiders are just as studiously avoided!

AROUND THE CENTRE

Donegall Place runs north from Donegall Square then changes its name to Royal Ave. The city's busy and mainly pedestrianised shopping centre spreads out on either side of this important avenue. The pedestrianisation of the centre is in part a by-product of the Troubles. At their height in the 1970s, terrorist activities turned the whole centre into a heavily militarised zone, but the security presence is very low-key now, and modern city planning would probably have got around to excluding cars in any case. The **Cornmarket**, just east of Donegall Place, takes its name from an older agricultural Belfast but is still a popular, if scruffy, meeting place. Two modern shopping centres, the Castle Court in Royal Ave and the Variety Centre in High St, are symbols of the vibrant Belfast that has grown up in spite of the Troubles.

Belfast City Hall

The industrial revolution transformed Belfast, and that rapid rise to muck-and-brass prosperity shows to this day. The Portland-stone City Hall in Donegall Square was completed in 1906. Built in the Classical Renaissance style, much to the disdain of architectural purists, it has some fine Italian marble inside and a great deal of pomp and splendour outside. The first meeting of the Northern Ireland Parliament was held here in 1921, but it subsequently met at the Union Theological College until Stormont was completed in 1932.

The most noticeable feature of the exterior used to be the huge 'Belfast Says No' banner displayed along the top of the building. It was placed there by the Unionist city fathers to show their objections to the Anglo-Irish Agreement, which was signed in 1985 and formed the basis of ongoing consultations between Britain and the Republic over the North. Most Unionist city councillors also refused to take part in council affairs while the agreement was in force. In 1988 the City Hall was bombed and the stained glass windows in the Great Hall were destroyed. When the building was uncovered after cleaning in 1994, the banner had disappeared, a small symbol of a greater willingness to negotiate

The hall is fronted by a statue of a rather dour Queen Victoria. Statues of city mayors also guard the building on the Donegall Square North side. At the north-east corner of the City Hall grounds is a statue of Sir Edward Harland, the Yorkshire-born marine engineer who founded the Harland & Wolff shipyards. In its prime the shipyard was one of Belfast's biggest businesses and it still survives, if in much quieter form. The yard's most famous construction was the ill-fated *Titanic* which sank in 1912, after colliding with an iceberg on its maiden voyage to America. A memorial to the disaster and its victims stands on the east side of City Hall.

The Marquess of Dufferin (1826-1902), whose career included postings as ambassador to Constantinople in Ottoman Turkey, St Petersburg in Tsarist Russia, Paris and Rome, and as governor-general to Canada and viceroy to India, has an extremely ornate temple-like memorial on the west side of the City Hall. He was responsible for adding Burma to the British Empire in 1886. Look out, too, for monuments to the United States of America Expeditionary Force which arrived in Belfast in January 1942, and to the Boer War.

Free tours of the City Hall lasting approximately one hour are available every Wednesday morning at 10.30 am; in July, August and September there are twice daily tours at 10.30 am and 2.30 pm (weekdays only). Amongst other things, you get to see the Council Chamber with red and blue flashing lights to tell councillors when they've overtalked their allotted 10 minutes, a painting of the proclamation of Edward VII outside City Hall (slashed by a visitor in 1991 and now behind glass) and some highly fanciful images in the grey and white marble of the hall. For more information call ☎ 320202 ext 2227.

Linen Hall Library

At 17 Donegall Square North, looking across the square to the City Hall, the Linen Hall Library was established in 1788 (although not in this building), and has a major Irish collection, most of which survived an IRA incendiary device planted inside. It includes the most complete collection of early Belfast and Ulster printing and key research collections in Irish and local studies; look out for *An Essay on the Antiquity of the Irish Language, being a Collation of the Irish and Punic Languages with a Preface Proving Ireland to be the Thule of the Ancients.*

Thomas Russell, the first librarian, was a founder member of the United Irishmen and a close friend of Wolfe Tone – a reminder that this movement for independence from Britain had its origins in Belfast. Russell was hanged in 1803 after Robert Emmet's abortive rebellion. For over a century the library was in the White Linen Hall, which was built from 1784 but demolished to make way for the City Hall. The entrance doorway to the present library is draped with stone linen and topped by the red hand of Ulster.

The library is open to its members from 9.30 am Monday to Saturday, to 4 pm on Saturday, 8.30 pm on Thursday and 5.30 pm on the other days. A limited number of non-members are admitted to the library to browse each day. It may be possible to arrange a tour by phoning ☎ 321707, although you'd probably need to be part of a group.

Other Donegall Square Buildings

Donegall Square, with the City Hall squarely in the middle, is undoubtedly the centre of Belfast. If you come into town by local bus you're likely to be dropped here as most local bus services arrive and depart from around the square.

It has a number of interesting buildings, but easily the most magnificent is the wonderfully ornate **Scottish Provident Building** built from 1899 to 1902, and overlooking the City Hall from Donegall Square West. It's decorated with a veritable riot of statuary, including several allusions to the industries that assured Victorian Belfast's

The Red Hand of Ulster

The symbol of the province of Ulster is a striking red hand which you'll see displayed on coats of arms, in stained-glass windows and, vividly, above the entrance to the Linen Hall Library in Donegal Square North. The story goes that way back in the Middle Ages when Viking raids were a regular occurrence, a group of Vikings had already settled the land and looked on in horror as another raiding vessel approached. The chief announced that the land would belong to whoever put their hand on it first, whereupon he sliced off his own hand and threw it forward, thus beating the raiders to it. Impressed by this, the O'Neill clan later adopted the red hand as their emblem, and it went on to become the symbol of Ulster. ■

prosperity, as well as sphinxes, dolphins and a variety of lions' heads. Nowadays it houses a gift shop.

The building was the work of the architectural partnership of Young & MacKenzie who counterbalanced it in the same year with the **Pearl Assurance Building** on the Donegall Square East corner. Between these two examples of turn-of-the-century extravagance is the equally fine **Robinson & Cleaver Building**, once the Royal Irish Linen Warehouse and then Belfast's finest department store.

The Entries

The area immediately north of High St was the oldest part of Belfast but it suffered considerable damage during WW II bombing. The narrow alleyways known as the **Entries** run off High St and Ann St in the pedestrianised shopping centre. At one time they were bustling commercial and residential centres: Pottinger's Entry had 34 houses in 1822. Today pubs are just about all that survives down these reclusive hideaways. The **Morning Star** on Pottinger's Entry is one of the most attractive of these wonderful old Belfast bars.

Joy's Entry commemorates the Joy family. In 1737 Francis Joy founded the *Belfast News Letter*, the first daily newspaper in Britain. It's still in business today. One of his grandsons, Henry Joy McCracken, was executed for supporting the 1798 United Irishmen's revolt.

The United Irishmen were founded in 1791 by Wolfe Tone in Peggy Barclay's tavern in **Crown Entry**. They used to meet in **Kelly's Cellars** on Bank St off Royal Ave. **White's Tavern** on Wine Cellar Entry is the oldest pub in the city and is still a popular lunch-time meeting spot.

Albert Memorial Clocktower

W J Barre's 1867 Albert Memorial Clocktower in Queen's Square at the junction of High St and Victoria St is not so dramatically out of kilter as the famous tower in Pisa, but it is, nevertheless, a leaning tower.

Around the Clocktower

Looking across the River Lagan from the clocktower, west Belfast is dominated by the huge cranes of the Harland & Wolff shipyards. Many of the buildings around the clocktower are the work of Sir Charles Lanyon, the pre-eminent architect of Belfast in its prime. The modern Queen Elizabeth Bridge crosses the Lagan just to the south, but immediately south again is **Queen's Bridge** with its ornate lamps. Completed in 1843, this was Lanyon's first important Belfast construction. Immediately north of the clocktower is a disused white stone building originally completed in 1852 by Lanyon as a head office for the Northern Bank.

Further north stands **Clifton House**, built in 1774 as a poorhouse and the finest surviving 18th-century building in Belfast. East towards the river is the **Custom House**, built by Lanyon in Italianate style in 1854-57. On the waterfront side the pediment carries sculptured portrayals of Britannia, Neptune and Mercury. In 1995 the Custom House was undergoing complete renovation; it's possible that parts of it will be opened to the public once the work is completed.

Follow the waterfront round to the SeaCat and Isle of Man ferry terminal beside the **Harbour Office**. The office has exhibits relating to the city's maritime history but is only rarely open to the public. The Belfast Churches section describes the intriguing Sinclair Seamen's Church which is right next door.

Lagan Lookout Visitor Centre

A weir has recently been built across the River Lagan to make it possible to control the flow of water and keep ugly mudflats covered up. As part of the general development of this area, which is overlooked by the new Lagan Bridge (M3 motorway), the Lagan Lookout Visitor Centre offers a state-of-the-art explanation of how the weir works and why it was needed, with interactive computers to bring things to life. Through the windows of the circular building you can view not just the weir but also the distant Harland & Wolff shipyard and the site of the new conference centre.

From March to September it's open Monday to Friday 11 am to 5 pm, opening at noon on Saturday and 2 am on Sunday. In winter it closes at 3 pm Monday to Friday and opens 1 to 4 pm Saturday and 2 to 4 pm Sunday. Admission is £1.50/75p.

Crown Liquor Saloon

Across from the Europa Hotel on Great Victoria St, the Crown Liquor Saloon was built by Patrick Flanagan in 1885 and displays Victorian architectural flamboyance at its most extravagant. Owned by the National Trust, who have removed some newer embellishments, and operated by Bass Ireland, this pub is on every visitor's itinerary; you need to get there early to have any hope of standing space, let alone a seat. The exterior is decorated with a myriad different coloured and shaped tiles, while the interior has a mass of stained and cut glass, marble, mosaics and mahogany furniture. Gas mantles provide atmospheric lighting.

A very lengthy and highly decorated bar

dominates one side of the pub while on the other is a row of ornate wooden snugs topped by stirring mottoes. The snugs come equipped with brass plates for striking matches and with bells which were once connected to the bell board behind the bar, enabling drinkers to demand top-ups without ever leaving their seats. The bells have since been disconnected and you'll have to take your chance in the crush around the bar; men appear to take precedence over women when it comes to getting served.

In 1993 the Crown was lucky to survive the bomb which devastated the Opera House and destroyed Robinson's immediately next door. Above the Crown is the **Britannic Bar** which displays all sorts of memorabilia from the *Titanic*; the entrance is around the corner in Amelia St.

Grand Opera House

One of Belfast's great landmarks is the Grand Opera House (☎ 01232-241919), just north of the Europa Hotel and across the road from the Crown Liquor Saloon on Great Victoria St. Opened in 1895, the Opera House was closed for a considerable part of the 1970s before a restoration project completely refurbished both the interior and the red-brick exterior.

It has suffered grievously at the hands of the IRA in recent years. A 450-kg truck bomb was their 1991 Christmas gift to Belfast culture, and a multi-million-pound reconstruction had barely been completed before they parked another well-loaded truck outside on 20 May 1993. Since then the interior has been restored to over-the-top Victoriana, with purple satin in abundance and swirling wood and plasterwork. It's constantly busy with music shows, operas and plays.

SOUTH OF THE CENTRE
Sandy Row

Just a block west of Great Victoria St, the road which leads from the city centre to the university, is the curving Sandy Row. This used to be the main road south out of the city, and it's still a working-class Protestant enclave, wedged in beside the wealthier Golden Mile area. Here you'll find red, white and blue kerbstones and Unionist murals, just like on the Shankill Rd in West Belfast. Van Morrison fans may remember that he wandered 'up and down the Sandy Row' in his 1968 album *Astral Weeks*. The Crescent Bar at the Lisburn Rd end of Sandy Row looks grim but is popular with young people from both sides of the politico-religious divide.

Ulster Museum

The Ulster Museum (☎ 381251) is beside the Botanic Gardens near the university. As well as a quick rundown on Irish history, there are good displays on Irish art, wildlife, dinosaurs, steam and industrial machines, minerals and fossils; allow several hours to see everything properly. Items from the 1588 Spanish Armada wreck of the *Girona* (see Dunluce Castle in County Antrim) are a highlight, especially the gold jewellery which includes a ruby-encrusted salamander and an inscribed gold ring. Many of the Armada ships were wrecked along the west coast of Ireland, but the *Girona* came to grief on the north-east coast, off the Giant's Causeway. The wreck was investigated by the Belgian marine archaeologist Robert Stenuit in 1968, 380 years later.

The museum was designed in 1911 but not completed until late in the 1920s. An extension was added in 1971, and the complex includes a shop and the Collections Café overlooking the Botanic Gardens. Entry to the museum is free and it's open 10 am to 5 pm Monday to Friday, from 1 pm Saturday and from 2 pm Sunday. Bus No 69 or 71 will get you there from the centre.

Botanic Gardens

The somewhat tatty Botanic Gardens are a restful oasis away from the busy main road and worth a wander about. The gardens date from 1827 and their centrepiece is the fine Palm House with its cast-iron and curvilinear glass construction, built between 1839 and 1852 and housing palms and other hot-house flora. Even though Belfast's pre-eminent

Van Morrison

James Joyce claimed that Dublin could be recreated using his books as the plan. Belfast, on the other hand, could probably be sketched out from Van Morrison's songs. The Belfast Cowboy fronted the Northern Ireland band Them to fleeting success in the swinging '60s with songs like *Here Comes the Night* and the classic *Gloria*, but in 1966 Them fell apart, and their short, intense and utterly uncharismatic lead singer moved to the USA where he managed one top-10 hit and a quickly forgotten solo LP. Morrison might have become just another '60's rock & roll victim, when he drifted back to Ireland. But in 1968 he was back in the USA and in just two days recorded *Astral Weeks*, an LP which to this day critics hail as one of the seminal records of the era. Over 20 records later, every one of them a solid success, 'Van the Man's' unique blend of folk, jazz, blues, gospel and a healthy slug of Celtic mysticism has given him one of the most loyal followings in rock music.

Even in *Astral Weeks* those Belfast clues started to appear. One track is named *Cyprus Avenue*, after a street in east Belfast, while *Madame George*, the record's most enigmatic and intriguing song, wanders 'up and down the Sandy Row', a staunchly Protestant street just south of the city centre. More recently the 1991 *Hymns to the Silence* conjures up Belfast in the late 1950s and early 1960s in the track titled *On Hyndford St*. The 1990 record *Enlightenment* also journeys back to a forgotten Belfast of the 1950s *In the Days Before Rock 'n' Roll*.

The 1989 *Avalon Sunset* has a track titled *Orangefield*, after the unmemorable Belfast suburb of that name, but *Coney Island* on the same record is a positive delight. It's a real wander around Northern Ireland, taking you from Downpatrick to St John's Point for a spot of birdwatching and good crack! Then it's on to Strangford Lough, Shrigly, Killyleagh, the Lecale District, Ardglass and finally Coney Island, all with a flavour so golden you wish you could be there too.

Views of Belfast also appear on his record sleeves, most notably on the 1984 *Live at the Grand Opera House Belfast*, while two different views of Hyndford St pop up on the sleeve and sleeve notes for *Hymns to the Silence*. It's a reminder that for all his mellow music Van Morrison is a notably prickly character, visibly uncomfortable on stage and famously difficult with journalists. When the Belfast Blues Society tried to put a commemorative plaque on his former home on Hyndford St in the east Belfast suburb of Bloomfield, he set the lawyers on them. They must have failed: the plaque's there at No 125. ■

architect Charles Lanyon played a part in its creation, the Palm House was essentially the work of Richard Turner of Dublin who also built glasshouses in the Dublin Botanic Gardens and at Kew Gardens in London and worked on the 1851 Crystal Palace in London. Just inside the gardens at the Stranmillis Rd gate is a statue to Belfast-born Lord Kelvin who invented the Kelvin Scale which measures temperatures from absolute zero (-273°C or 0°K). The gardens are open daily from 8 am to sunset.

From April to September the Palm House is open Monday to Friday from 10 am to noon and 1 to 5 pm, Saturday and Sunday from 2 to 5 pm. In winter it's open on weekdays from 1 to 4 pm and at weekends from 2 to 4 pm. The unique Tropical Ravine tucked in beside the Ulster Museum was designed by Charles McKimm of Donaghadee in 1887 as an enclosed sunken glen with balconies for visitors to look down on the plants. Ferns, cycads, bananas and lilies all grow here. It keeps the same opening hours as the Palm House.

Belfast has a number of other parks and gardens, and the Parks Department produces a booklet titled *On Foot in Belfast* detailing good walks in and around the city.

Queen's University

One km south of Donegall Square and City Hall is the muted red and yellow brick Queen's College building of Queen's University, Northern Ireland's most prestigious university. It caters for around 8000 students and has a particularly strong reputation in medicine, engineering and law. Although the plan of the college building is based on Magdalen College in Oxford, it was, once again, Charles Lanyon who was responsible for the design. Queen Victoria was present for the laying of the foundation stone in 1845, and the building was completed in 1849. The lofty entrance hall leads into the quadrangle. On the south side a chimney has brickwork spelling out VR 1848 (Victoria Regina). Beyond the college building is Old Library, designed by Lanyon's assistant W H Lynn and built in 1864, then extended in 1913.

Surrounding the university are quiet tree-lined streets with small cafés full of students. University Square, on the north side of the campus, dates from 1848-53 and is one of the finest terraced streets in Ireland. It was once known as the Harley St of Belfast, and is now owned by the university. Behind the Queen's College building, across Botanic Ave, is the colonnaded Union Theological College, originally the Presbyterian College. It opened in 1853 and it too was a Lanyon design. From the partition of Ireland it served as the Northern Ireland parliament, until 1932 when the Stormont building took over for the next 40 years.

CHURCHES

Although Belfast has numerous churches, none are of great interest. Most of the Protestant churches are only open for very limited hours, in many cases only on Sunday and even then only around service times. The tourist office has a leaflet listing service times in all the churches.

St Anne's Anglican Cathedral was built in pseudo-Romanesque style between 1899 and 1904 and stands on boggy ground just north of the city centre. Unusually, only one person is actually buried inside it and that is Edward Carson, whose opposition to Home Rule was a principal cause of the separation of Ireland and Northern Ireland.

A slab simply announcing 'Carson', can be found about half way along the right wall of the nave, together with a wall memorial. In the north aisle look out for a Book of Common Prayer written in a Japanese prisoner-of-war camp in Korea using

home-made ink on cigarette paper. The cover was created out of pillowcase material provided as the end of World War II drew near to create a less distressing impression of the living conditions the prisoners had had to endure.

In the pedestrianised central shopping area, the **First Presbyterian Church** on Rosemary St dates from 1783 and has an interesting oval-shaped interior with enclosed pews, each entered by a door. It's open on Sunday, and also on Wednesday from 10.30 am to 12.30 pm.

On High St at the corner with Victoria St, right across from the Albert Memorial Clocktower, stands the 1816 Anglican **St George's**. The church's most noticeable feature may be its superb classical portico, but that didn't start life here. Instead it was originally the front of Ballyscullion House in Bellaghy, between Belfast and Derry. The colourful earl of Bristol (who also happened to be the bishop of Derry) abandoned the house before it was completed and the facade was dismantled and rebuilt here. See the section on the Mussenden Temple near Derry for more on this unusual character.

Further north of the centre, on Corporation Square beside the Harbour Office and the Isle of Man and SeaCat ferry terminal, the 1857 **Sinclair Seamen's Church** is one of Belfast's most interesting churches. It was designed by that busiest of Belfast architects, Charles Lanyon, and features a pulpit designed to look like a ship's bow and enough nautical memorabilia to qualify as a marine museum!

The Catholic **St Malachy's** on Alfred St, just south of the centre, was built in 1844 and has interesting pink-trimmed turrets, an ornate fan-vaulted ceiling and a pulpit frosted like a wedding cake. In the south transept look out for relics of St Benedict Joseph Labre, an 18th-century Trappist monk whose exemplary life story is detailed in the booklet (30p) on sale at the back of the church. Nearby is the 1829 **May St Presbyterian Church**, a classical-style building also known as the Cooke Memorial Church after the pedantic Dr Henry Cooke who actually dedicated his religious life to arcane arguments about Biblical interpretations; his memorial notes 'his eminent and successful labour for the truth against the prevailing errors of the time.' He also laboured in the Protestant cause and served as a prototype for the modern 'Orangeman'.

The northern end of University Rd, the Golden Mile area south of the centre, harbours a cluster of Victorian churches. The 1887 **Crescent Church** was built of Scrabo stone in a style modelled on 13th-century French church designs. The pierced tower, looking like an open framework, is an instantly recognisable landmark. Across the road the **Moravian Church** also dates from 1887 and was also built of Scrabo stone. Completing this University Rd trio is the 1865 **Methodist Church**, just a few steps further along the road. There are elements of Italian design in this church which was the work of W J Barre, best known for the leaning Albert Memorial Clocktower in the docks area.

Built in 1862 in an exotic interpretation of Italian architectural styles, **Elmwood Hall** also started life as a church but is now used as a university concert hall. It's further along University Rd, opposite the Queen's College building. The **Knockbreda Parish Church**, Belfast's oldest church, dates from 1737 and is on the A24 south of the centre and just before the ring road. Perched on a hill, it was designed by Richard Castle, who was also responsible for many buildings in Dublin including Leinster House.

ART GALLERIES

The Ulster Museum has a collection of Irish art on the top floor, but Belfast's principal modern art gallery is the **Arts Council Gallery** (☎ 321402) in the old Ormeau Baths, near the BBC building on Ormeau Ave. The **Old Museum Arts Centre** at 7 College Square North, a fine building dating back to 1831, houses temporary exhibitions of modern art. It's open from Monday to Friday from 10 am to 5.30 pm; ring the doorbell for admission. **Malone House** (☎ 681246) has exhibitions on Belfast parks

and an art gallery. It's well to the south of the centre in Barnett's Demesne on Upper Malone Rd and is open Tuesday to Saturday from 10 am to 4.30 pm; bus Nos 70 and 71 pass by.

Private galleries in Belfast include the Crescent Arts Centre (☎ 242338) at 2 University Rd, the Bell Gallery (☎ 662998) at 13 Adelaide Park, the Fenderesky Gallery (☎ 235245) at 5 Upper Crescent and the Eakin Gallery (☎ 668522) at 237 Lisburn Rd.

WALK 1 – PRINCE ALBERT TO QUEEN VICTORIA

This walking tour takes you from a memorial to Prince Albert, Queen Victoria's husband, to another to Queen Victoria herself, exploring the city's Victorian heartland on the way. Sadly, many of the grand 19th-century buildings stand empty and boarded-up. The leaning (1) **Albert Memorial Clocktower** on Queen's Square makes an easily located start for the walk. Immediately north of the clocktower is (2), the 1852 building Sir Charles Lanyon designed for the **Northern Bank**, now owned by the First Trust Bank but disused.

This walk passes by several other Lanyon buildings including the grand 1857 (3) **Custom House**; restoration work should have given this a new lease of life by the time you read this. From the waterfront side you can see the sculptured pediment at the front of the building. Across the road is the now disused Calder Fountain, erected in memory of a naval commander who installed cattle troughs in Belfast in the 1840s and founded the local Society for the Prevention of Cruelty to Animals.

Turn down Albert Square and cross Victoria St to Waring St where the grandiose 1860 (4) **Ulster Bank** survived wartime bombing that obliterated much of this area. The imposing building has iron railings decorated with the red hand of Ulster, cast-iron lamp standards, soaring columns and sculptured figures of Britannia, Justice and Commerce. The rooftop figures were by Thomas Fitzpatrick who was also responsi-

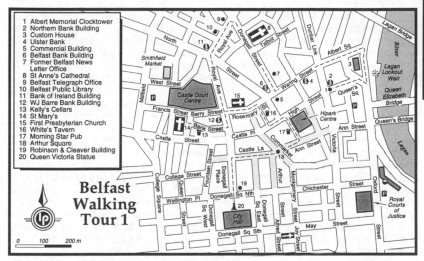

1 Albert Memorial Clocktower
2 Northern Bank Building
3 Custom House
4 Ulster Bank
5 Commercial Building
6 Belfast Bank Building
7 Former Belfast News
  Letter Office
8 St Anne's Cathedral
9 Belfast Telegraph Office
10 Belfast Public Library
11 Bank of Ireland Building
12 WJ Barre Bank Building
13 Kelly's Cellars
14 St Mary's
15 First Presbyterian Church
16 White's Tavern
17 Morning Star Pub
18 Arthur Square
19 Robinson & Cleaver Building
20 Queen Victoria Statue

**Belfast
Walking
Tour 1**

0   100   200 m

ble for the carvings on the nearby Custom House. Inside it's even more impressive, with cute blue cherubs playing instruments to customers queuing to access their accounts.

At the junction of Waring St with Donegall St is the deserted 1822 (5) **Commercial Building**, easily identified by the prominent name of the Northern Whig Printing Company. Opposite is the (6) **Belfast Bank Building**, now occupied by the Northern Bank and the oldest public building in the city (although bearing little relationship to its original design). The building started life as a single-storey market house in 1769, became the Assembly Rooms, with the addition of an upper storey, in 1777 and in 1845 was remodelled by Charles Lanyon to become the bank buildings.

Turn up Donegall St, looking for Commercial Court, a narrow laneway hiding the Duke of York pub. The former home of the (7) *Belfast News Letter* at No 59 is an 1873 building decorated with bas-relief portraits of literary figures – we'll meet a similar decorative style on Walk 2. The imposing (8) **St Anne's Cathedral** was built from 1899 but has little of interest inside apart from the

grave of Edward Carson. At Royal Ave turn left, noting the modern offices of the (9) *Belfast Telegraph* and then the red sandstone (10) **Belfast Public Library**. Continue along Royal Ave as it bends to the left, but look back to the (11) **Bank of Ireland Building**, a fine example of 1920s Art Deco and elegantly placed at the junction of North St and Royal Ave.

Past the Castle Court Centre and the Virgin Megastore is the 1868 (12) **W J Barre Building** designed by the man who was also responsible for the Albert Memorial Clocktower at the start of this walk. The building is now owned by the First Trust Bank. Turn right by the bank into Bank Place and (13) **Kelly's Cellars**, a whitewashed 18th-century pub where the United Irishmen once met. Just beyond the pub is the elaborate grotto of (14) **St Mary's**, the first Catholic church in Belfast, which opened in 1784. Return to Royal Ave and backtrack to the Virgin Megastore then turn right into Rosemary St, past the 1783 (15) **First Presbyterian Church** with its curious elliptical interior.

A few steps further, a right turn leads into Winecellar Entry where Belfast's oldest pub,

(16) **White's Tavern**, lurks. It's been here since 1630 although it was rebuilt in 1790. Turn right, then left down High St with its narrow 'entries'. On the right is Pottinger's Entry sheltering the (17) **Morning Star Pub**. Pottinger's Entry emerges on to pedestrianised Ann St: note the arm holding up an umbrella which emerges from the building opposite the entry.

Turn right down Ann St to (18) **Arthur Square**, where five pedestrianised streets meet with a bandstand, newsstands, buskers, preachers, hawkers and all sorts of other activities. This was once the central traffic junction in the city but the traffic has long been diverted. It was also the site of the Abercorn, a popular café before the Troubles, until one crowded Saturday lunch time in 1972 a terrorist bomb destroyed it; redevelopment has removed all trace of the place. Continue along Castle Lane and turn left down Donegall Place with the City Hall towering in front of you. At the corner of Donegall Place and Donegall Square North is the ornate carved stone facade of the (19) **Robinson & Cleaver Building**. Resolutely guarding the front of the City Hall the (20) **statue of Queen Victoria** in time-honoured 'not amused' pose marks the end of this walk.

WALK 2 – QUEEN VICTORIA TO LORD KELVIN

The (1) **statue of Queen Victoria** in front of the City Hall concluded Walk 1 and marks the beginning of this walk south of the city centre to the university area, botanic gardens and the restaurant-studded Golden Mile. See the City Hall section for information about this symbol of Belfast at the height of the industrial revolution. Standing in front of the Victoria statue and looking, like her, down Donegall Place, you can see the (2) **Robinson & Cleaver Building** on the corner of the square and Donegall Place. To the right on the corner of the square is the magnificent redbrick (3) **Pearl Assurance Building**. To the left is the even more magnificent (4) **Scottish Provident Building**, now housing a gift shop.

Bid Victoria farewell and turn left along Donegall Square North noting the (5) **Linen Hall Library** whose history, though not all at this site, dates back to 1788. Continue down Wellington Place towards the (6) **statue of Dr Henry Cooke** (1788-1868). It's typical that this prickly character should stand not beside the road but right in the middle of it. We'll be meeting him again shortly. Behind his statue is the (7) **Technical Institute** of 1907 and the (8) **Royal Belfast Academical Institution** or 'Inst' of 1814. The Inst is a story of frustrated plans – it stands on College Square which is actually only half a square because the west and south sides were never built. The building itself was not completed to its original plans due to shortage of funds and the Technical Institute was plonked in front of it due to another college cash shortage.

Turn left down College Square past the bulk of the ornate (9) **Presbyterian Church House** which dates from 1905 and is decorated with angels, eagles and dragons and now houses the Spires Shopping Mall and a café. Turn left on to Howard St, which shortly becomes Donegall Square South and takes you along the back of the City Hall. The White Linen Hall once occupied the City Hall site and as a result the surrounding area was crowded with linen warehouses, most of them long gone.

On the corner with Linenhall St is (10) **Yorkshire House**, with 16 sculptured heads of various personages, real and imaginary. Donegall Square South changes names to become May St and passes the (11) **May St Presbyterian Church**, built in 1829 and also known as the Cooke Memorial Church. Yes, it's named after the same Dr Henry Cooke who stands resolutely in the middle of the street on College Square. Continue along May St to Joy St. Across the road is an empty car parking lot, of zero interest except for the (12) **Dunlop plaque** on the east wall which explains that this was the former site of John Boyd Dunlop's workshop, where he developed the first pneumatic tyre in the 1880s.

Turn down Joy St and then right on to Russell St and left past (13) **St Malachy's Church**. Another right takes you on to Clarence St and past the (14) **Robinson Patter-son architectural office**, an intriguing redevelopment of a 19th-century warehouse which sliced the end off the building and glassed it over to produce a building which won a 'Building of the Year' architectural award. Turn right into Bedford St, past the (15) **Ulster Hall**, dating from 1862; on the opposite side of the road murals painted to look as if they were done on damask linen illustrate scenes of linen manufacture.

Turn left into Franklin St to Brunswick St, passing Surf Mountain, a reminder to surfing enthusiasts that Northern Ireland has some good waves, then backtrack past the Drury Lane pub and down Amelia St to the wonderful (16) **Crown Liquor Saloon**. Across the road are the (17) **Europa Hotel** and the (18) **Grand Opera House**, which could also qualify for a 'much bombed' accolade. Turn south down Great Victoria St, noting the memorial statue to working women just south of the Europa Hotel; the occasional interesting building can't make up for the fact that this road is in dire need of redevelopment.

Shaftesbury Square, Belfast's answer to Piccadilly Circus, marks the start of the university area. Glance back at the junction to the (19) statuary tacked on the front of the Ulster Bank Building; the figures are known locally as Draft and Overdraft. Continue across Shaftesbury Square, more a road junction than a square in the conventional sense, noting Donegall Pass which runs off the junction to the left (east). This is the only remaining 'pass' into Belfast, a reminder that the city was once bounded on this side by private land belonging to Lord Donegall, and the passes through Cromac Woods were the only access to the city. Today Donegall Pass is guarded at the Shaftesbury Square end by a typically forbidding (20) **RUC guardpost**.

Bradbury Place runs south from the junction; a narrow alley (Albion Lane) disappearing down the back of the buildings was once used as a discreet back entry to (21) **Lavery's Gin Palace**. Today it's just a popular student pub, but Lavery's has a long bohemian and literary tradition in Belfast. Bradbury Place becomes University Rd and

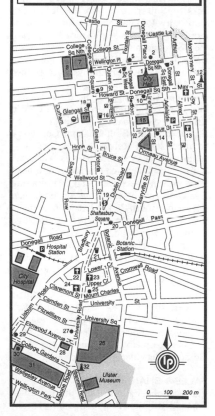

Belfast Walking Tour 2

1 Queen Victoria Statue	15 Ulster Hall
2 Robinson & Cleaver Building	16 Crown Liquor Saloon
3 Pearl Assurance Building	17 Europa Hotel
	18 Grand Opera House
4 Scottish Provident Building	19 Ulster Bank Statues
5 Linen Hall Library	20 RUC Guardpost
6 Dr Henry Cooke Statue	21 Lavery's Gin Palace
7 Technical Institute	22 Moravian Church
8 Royal Belfast Academical Institution	23 Crescent Church
	24 Methodist Church
9 Presbyterian Church House	25 Mount Charles Villas
10 Yorkshire House	26 Queen's College
11 May St Presbyterian Church	27 Student's Union
12 Dunlop Plaque	28 Elmwood Hall
13 St Malachy's Church	29 Gate Lodge
14 Robinson Patterson Office	30 McArthur's Hall
	31 Methodist College
	32 Lord Kelvin Statue

on the right side of the road is the 1887 (22) **Moravian Church**. A left turn takes you into Lower Crescent, beside the 1887 (23) **Crescent Church**, with its instantly recognisable skeleton-like bell tower.

The green behind the church is enclosed by Lower Crescent, Crescent Gardens and Upper Crescent. Walking round the green takes you past mid-19th-century, neoclassical-style terraces, built by Robert Corry, a local entrepreneur, and possibly designed by Charles Lanyon. Across University Rd, W J Barre's (24) **Methodist Church** of 1865 completes the trio of University Rd churches. Continuing along University Rd the next street left is Mt Charles with a group of (25) stylish **villas** dating from 1842. University Square, also to the left from University Rd, has another fine group of terraced houses. Queen Victoria herself laid the foundation stone for (26) **Queen's College** in 1845. It's the principal building of Queen's University and was yet another Charles Lanyon design.

Across University Rd from the college building is the modern (27) **Student's Union**, a stark contrast to the exotic (28) **Elmwood Hall**. Built by John Corry, the architect son of Robert Corry whose crescents were seen earlier on this walk, the Italian-inspired church building is now used as a university concert hall. Walk along Elmwood Ave beside Elmwood Hall, then left on to Lisburn Rd and left again, beside a toy-like (29) **gate lodge** into College Gardens. The road takes you past (30) **McArthur's Hall** and the grandiose (31) **Methodist College**, built in High Victorian style in 1865-68. Cross University Rd to enter the Stranmillis Rd gate of the Botanic Gardens. Just inside the gate is a (32) **statue of Lord Kelvin** (1824-1907) who invented the Kelvin Scale and patented inventions for underwater submarine cables. By now you'll probably be ready to collapse in one of the Golden Mile's many cafés.

FALLS & SHANKILL RDS

The Catholic Falls Rd and the Protestant Shankill Rd have been battlefronts for the Troubles, and apart from the occasional bright flash of a wall mural they're grey and rather dismal. For visitors they're quite safe, and more modern (and enlightened) public housing is not only replacing the old Victorian slums but also the 1960s tower blocks. These areas are worth venturing into, if only to see the large murals expressing local political and religious passions. King Billy riding to victory in 1690 on his white steed and hooded IRA gunmen are two of the more memorable images. Less noticeable to first-time visitors are the red, white and blue-painted pavement kerbs which adorn staunch Protestant loyalist areas, and the green, white and orange kerbs in the Catholic areas.

West Belfast grew up around the linen mills which propelled the city into its industrial revolution prosperity. It was an area of low-cost working-class housing, and even in the Victorian era was divided along religious lines. The advent of the Troubles in 1968 solidified the sectarian division, and the construction of the Westlink Motorway neatly divided the area, and its problems, from central Belfast. Since the start of the Troubles, working-class religious segregation has grown steadily and West Belfast is now almost wholly Catholic. Although the Shankill Rd is the Protestant flip side of the Catholic Falls Rd, it's actually in retreat, and were it not for its strong symbolic importance, the shrinking proportion of Protestants in West Belfast would undoubtedly be even smaller.

There are other Protestant working-class enclaves around the city, such as along the Newtownards Rd to the east of the centre, where you'll also see the brightly painted sectarian murals. If you don't fancy a tour (see Organised Tours), the ideologically sound way to visit the sectarian zones of the Falls and Shankill Rds is by black taxi. These recycled London cabs run a bus-like service up and down their respective roads from terminuses in the city. Shankill Rd taxis go from North St, Falls Rd taxis from Castle St, both sites close to the modern Castle Court Centre. The Falls Rd taxis occupy the first line at the Castle St taxi park, with signs up in Gaelic. They're used to doing tourist circuits of the Falls and typically charge £10 for a one-hour visit which takes in the main points of interest from republican murals to British army bases.

If you simply want to share a black taxi down the Falls Rd the fare is 55p to 75p depending on the distance, and your fellow passengers are likely to be women and children returning from a city shopping trip or men coming back from the pubs. Fares are similar on the Shankill Rd taxis. Alternatively bus Nos 12, 13, 14 or 15 will take you down the Falls Rd; bus Nos 39, 55, 63 or 73 go down the Shankill.

Falls Rd

The Falls Rd taxis start from the taxi park beside the Smithfield Market, a pale reflection of the bustling market which used to operate here. Separated from the city centre by the Westlink Motorway, but actually a very short distance west of the centre, the ugly and infamous Divis Flats take their name from Divis Mountain, the highest summit in the hills which surround Belfast. They were constructed in the late 1960s during the world-wide mania for high-rise public housing, and as elsewhere in the world they quickly became 'vertical slums'. During their planning and construction they were actually welcomed by local residents as both an alternative to substandard housing and as a way of retaining the local community. Extremely fearful of losing their congregations, the Catholic churches in the vicinity were particularly enthusiastic backers.

Predictably the Divis Flats were as disastrous in Belfast as elsewhere, and the Troubles quickly turned them into the scene of many confrontations between residents and the army. Today most of the flats have been replaced with modern housing. Divis Tower, a single block of high-rise flats, still overlooks the other buildings and the motorway. At the start of the Troubles the Irish Republican Socialist Party colonised its roof, winning it the nickname 'The Planet of

the IRPS'. When the British army took their place, this was changed, predictably, to 'The Planet of the Apes'. The top storeys are still occupied by the British army who come and go by helicopter. Taking pictures without permission might not be a particularly bright idea, but provided the peace holds you're unlikely to get into serious trouble.

Across the road a huge mural of the Madonna and Child decorates what was once the Brickfields Barracks, the first purpose-built police barracks in Belfast, now a refuge for homeless men.

From Divis Tower Divis St runs west, becoming the Falls Rd which runs in a south-westerly direction through the area known as the Lower Falls. On the right are a swimming pool and the heavily protected Sinn Féin offices; the massive boulders are to deter car bombers. If you turn right (north) off the Falls Rd into the side streets you'll quickly come up against the 'Peace Line', a rough corrugated iron wall separating Catholics from their Protestant neighbours. In places you could almost lean out of a back window and touch the wall.

On the other side of the Falls Rd in the Lower Falls, the old slums which stood here before the Troubles have been replaced with neat rows of houses, a reminder of the huge sums spent to improve public housing in the 1970s and 1980s; even at the height of the Thatcher era, Northern Ireland remained relatively immune to public spending cutbacks. The Falls Rd passes the Royal Victoria Hospital, which developed a well-earned reputation for dealing with medical emergencies at the height of the Troubles in the 1970s.

The area's famous murals are found along the Falls and in adjacent streets. It's a constantly changing art show, with new murals appearing over old, and demolition and reconstruction removing and replacing the canvases. Along the Falls Rd itself you're unlikely to have problems taking pictures but be warned that there have been stories of gangs of small boys extorting cash for photos in quieter side streets. Beyond the Lower Falls the road is less interesting until it reaches the Milltown Cemetery, the main site for republican burials housing the graves of numerous noted republicans who have died in shoot-outs, hunger strikes and other events of the Troubles.

The junction of Glen Rd and Andersonstown Rd marks the end of the Falls Rd with a strongly fortified army base looking down the Falls from its position in the fork. It's one of four 'forts' in West Belfast. Andersonstown (Andytown) is about three km from the centre and beyond here is Twinbrook, another staunchly republican suburb and the former home of Bobby Sands, the first 1981 hunger striker to die. In the surprisingly neat, tidy and modern development where he lived, one end of a block has been turned into a memorial. More murals, slogans and graffiti can be found in the Ballymurphy area by taking Whiterock Rd or Springfield Rd, north of the Falls, but these are thoroughly impoverished areas where a stranger will be very noticeable.

Shankill Rd

The Shankill Rd begins not far west of Belfast Cathedral and runs north-west towards the Crumlin Rd. Although the Shankill has been given less media and tourist attention than the Falls it's also of interest. The street's name comes from *sean chill*, the old church, and once again the brightly painted murals, including some of the Derry apprentice boys slamming the city gates in 1689, are the central attraction. Here the villains and heroes have switched roles, and the hooded and menacing paramilitaries are members of the UDA and other Protestant groups, instead of the IRA or INLA.

Hoardings round a break in the terraced shops are a reminder of one of the nastier and more recent events of the Troubles, the IRA bombing of Frizzell's fish shop in October 1993 which claimed nine lives. At the far end of Shankill Rd, look out for St Matthew's, a church built in shamrock shape in 1872.

NORTH & EAST OF THE CENTRE
Around Belfast
Harland & Wolff Shipyards
Although you can't easily visit the Harland

& Wolff shipyards, they certainly dominate East Belfast, separated from the city centre by the River Lagan. The giant cranes known as Samson and Goliath, one of them over 100 metres high and 140 metres long, straddle a 550-metre-long shipbuilding dock. The shipyard was founded in 1833 but it was under the Yorkshire engineer Edward Harland, who recruited the German marine draughtsman Gustav Wolff in 1858, that it assumed its leading role in Victorian shipbuilding. There's a statue of Sir Edward Harland by the City Hall. The good ship *Titanic* was built here and more recent constructions have included oil tankers and passenger vessels, including the *Canberra* in 1960.

The Harland & Wolff dry dock is one of the biggest in the world, capable of handling ships of up to 200,000 tons. With substantial British government support the shipyard managed to continue in existence through the 1970s and 1980s, when most European shipbuilding crumbled before Asian competition. Current employment is at a fraction of its former levels. In its heyday 60,000 people worked here; by the 1970s it had fallen below 10,000; by the mid-1980s it was down to 5000; and by the early 1990s below 2000. Work at the yards today is primarily maintenance rather than new construction.

Stormont
The former home of the Northern Ireland parliament is eight km east of the centre, off the A20. The regal 1932 building in Neoclassical style stands at the end of an imposing avenue, fronted by a defiant statue of Lord Carson, the Dublin-born architect of the fierce Ulster opposition to union with Ireland. This is where the Northern Ireland parliament met until 1972 when power was transferred to London. Now it's home to the Northern Ireland Secretary. You can walk in the extensive grounds, but visits to the parliament buildings must be arranged in advance (☎ 520600). Visits were suspended in 1995 when extensive restoration work was required after Stormont was damaged by a fire. Local bus Nos 22 and 23 run directly to

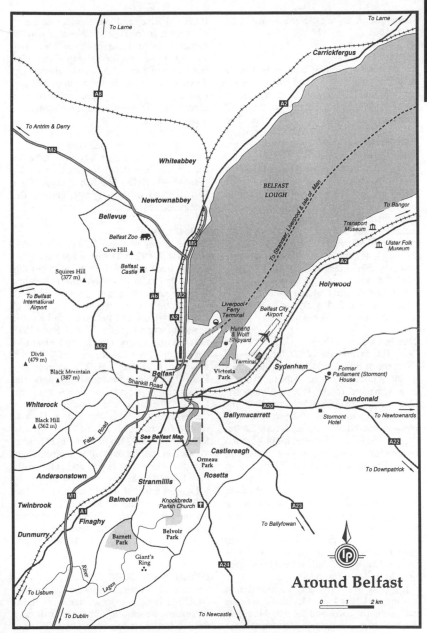

Around Belfast

0   1   2 km

Stormont from Donegall Square West in the city centre.

Belfast Zoo

Belfast Zoo (☎ 776277) is an exceptionally good one and has pursued an aggressive policy of building new and large enclosures for its exhibits, most recently for the small primates and chimps and gorillas. The sealion and penguin pool with its underwater viewing is particularly good. Some of the more unusual animals include tamarins, spectacled bears and red pandas, but children flock to the meerkats and to the ring-tailed lemur colony. The zoo enjoys a splendid location on the slopes below Cave Hill with views out over Belfast Lough, and the animal enclosures are laid out down the hillside, making for some strenuous walking. Opening hours are 10 am to 6 pm in summer, with last admissions at 5 pm, and entry is £4.20 for adults and £2.10 for children. Senior citizens and children under four get in free. Bus Nos 2, 3, 4, 5, 6 or 45 will take you to the zoo from Donegall Square West.

Cave Hill Country Park

Cave Hill Country Park (☎ 776925) covers 750 acres of northern Belfast on the shores of Belfast Lough. Walks through the grounds are waymarked (make sure you've noted which colour arrows you need to follow for any specific route), and it's a pleasant stroll from the zoo back as far as Belfast Castle. Cave Hill itself is 355 metres high; from the top there are panoramic views over Belfast, Belfast Lough and even parts of Scotland on a clear day.

The park contains evidence of prehistoric occupation in the form of several raths and a *crannóg*. On top of Cave Hill one such ringfort is known as McArt's Fort, a prominent spot from which members of the United Irishmen including Wolfe Tone looked down over the city in 1795 and pledged to struggle for independence for Ireland.

The peak was originally named after a 9th-century Ulster king, Matudhain, a name that gradually corrupted to Ben Madigan. One look at its profile, which dominates the

Belfast skyline, and you'll understand why it's known as 'Napoleon's Nose' in popular parlance. In previous centuries Cave Hill was a popular site for lighting Hallowe'en bonfires and for rolling hand-painted eggs downhill at Easter. To the north of McArt's Fort are five man-made caves, some of them accessible. To the south side there's a disused limestone quarry.

The Country Park encompasses two nature reserves, at Ballyaghagan and Hazelwood. There are five park entrances: beside Belfast Castle and the zoo; at Carr's Glen Linear Park, Ballysillan Rd; at Upper Cave Hill Rd; and in the Upper Hightown Rd. Admission is free.

Belfast Castle

On the slopes of Cave Hill stands Belfast Castle (☎ 776925). There has been a 'Belfast Castle' since the late 12th century, but this particular model was only built, in the then fashionable Scottish Baronial style, in 1870. The Castle was presented to the City of Belfast in 1934 and became a fashionable venue for weddings after WW II. From 1978 to 1988 the Council undertook extensive renovation of the Castle, parts of which are now open again as a posh restaurant (see Places to Eat) and for social functions. The cellars also house a bistro, tavern and shop. Upstairs, there's a small Cave Hill Heritage Centre with details of the history, flora & fauna of the area. It's open daily April to September from 9 am to 9 pm, and October to March (and Sundays all year) from 9 am to 6 pm. Admission is free and you usually have to ask for the key at reception.

Legend has it that the Castle's residents will only experience good fortune as long as a white cat lives there, a tale commemorated in the formal gardens with nine portrayals of cats in mosaic, painting, sculpture and garden furniture.

ORGANISED TOURS

There is a 3½-hour, £6.50/4.50 Citybus tour (☎ 458484) taking in all the city sights including Stormont, the shipyards and Belfast Castle. It begins at Castle Place at

1.30 pm every Wednesday during the summer months.

This is now supplemented with a very popular 'Living History' tour, taking in the sites and areas associated with the Troubles; if you feel nervous about walking up and down the Falls or Shankill Rds or venturing into the Ardoyne or Andersonstown alone, this tour would fit the bill nicely, although some might have qualms about ghoulish voyeurism. During the summer, tours leave Castle Place at 9.30 am and 4 pm on Tuesday, Thursday and Saturday; at other times of the year there may be only one tour a week. For more information phone ☎ 458484. Tickets cost £6.50 each and the tour lasts for two and a half hours with a short break for tea. The souvenir booklet alone almost justifies the tour price.

Ulsterbus also runs evening tours of Belfast during July and August. They leave Castle Place at 7 pm and tickets must be reserved in advance (☎ 458484). Other summer tours take in the Lagan Valley and Carnfunnock Country Park. Information on all tours can be picked up at the tourist office, at the Europa bus station or at the kiosk in Donegall Square West.

On summer Saturday afternoons pub tours leave the tourist office in North St at 2 pm. Itineraries are fairly flexible, but are likely to include the Duke of York, White's Tavern, Kelly's Cellars, Robinsons and the Crown Liquor Saloon, after which the day is yours. Tickets cost £5, no drinks included. For bookings and information phone Maggie Shannon on ☎ 658337.

CUTURAL EVENTS
Every May Belfast hosts a Civic Festival when all sorts of events take place all over town. As part of it there's a Taste Fest during the last weekend in May. Different restaurants from around town set up stalls in the Botanic Gardens and tempt those prepared to pay £1.50 to come in and then fork out another £5 for a book of sampling vouchers. It's worth noting that some buildings around town which may otherwise be closed become accessible during the Civic Festival.

The tourist office will be able to supply a programme for this. There's also the Belfast Folk Festival which takes place in mid-June.

PLACES TO STAY
Accommodation in Belfast is both scarce and expensive, particularly in the better guesthouses and hotels. Fortunately a brand-new youth hostel is ideally situated in Donegall Road, just off Shaftesbury Square, within walking distance of the city centre. Most of the B&Bs are clustered together in the Golden Mile area near the university. At the other end of the scale expensive hotels are either right in the centre or well out of it.

Camping
Camping possibilities close to Belfast are very restricted. The Northern Ireland Tourist Board produce a *Camping & Caravanning* brochure but the two sites close to Belfast are very small and intended only for caravans or campervans. Tent sites can be found along the coast beyond Bangor towards Portaferry. *Belvoir Forest* (☎ 491540) is just five km south of Belfast off the A504. This is a small and comparatively basic site, charging £4 per night for caravans. *Jordanstown Lough Shore Park* (☎ 863133/868751) is 10 km north of central Belfast on Shore Rd in Newtownabbey. Although this is a better equipped site, costing £6 per night and mainly intended for caravans, it's still very small and there is a maximum stay of two consecutive nights.

Hostels
The cheapest place to stay in Belfast is *Arnie's Backpackers* at 63 Fitzwilliam St (☎ 242867) where beds cost £7 a head. Arnie's has laundry and cooking facilities but, with only 19 beds, demand for space far exceeds supply. It makes sense to book ahead. Bus Nos 70 and 71 pass the end of Fitzwilliam St.

The YHANI *Belfast International Youth Hostel* (☎ 315435) is at 22-32 Donegall Road, between Shaftesbury Square and Sandy Row. Beds cost £9 a head or £10.50

in a double room, with another £1 for single occupancy. There's a laundry and a Backpackers Café, but no cooking facilities. Such is the demand for beds that YHANI has already requisitioned the vacant plot next door for expansion. Until that happens (not before 1997 sadly), it's also trying to hire extra rooms in town to accommodate the overflow. You can get there by train to Botanic Station or by bus from Donegall Square; bus Nos 69, 70 and 71 pass nearby, while Nos 89 and 90 stop outside.

From June to the end of September *Queen's Elms* (☎ 381608) run by the university at 78 Malone Rd offers excellent accommodation. The rooms are mainly singles and cost £7.40 for students, £11.85 for non-students. There are cooking and laundry facilities too. Rooms may also be available for short periods over Christmas and Easter. *Queen Mary's Hall* (☎ 240439) is the YWCA at 70 Fitzwilliam St. In theory it has single and double rooms at £13.50 per person including breakfast, but in practice it's usually full of long-term resident students. At 30 Adelaide Park, further south off Malone Rd, is the *Ulster People's College* (☎ 665161) which does bed and continental breakfast for £12, bed and cooked breakfast for £14.

B&Bs

The tourist office will make B&B reservations, sometimes in return for a minimal booking fee; credit card bookings can be made on freefone number 0800-317153. Many of the B&Bs are in the university area with prices around £15-20. This area is close to the centre, safe and well stocked with restaurants and pubs. Botanic Ave, Malone Rd, Wellington Park and Eglantine Ave are good hunting grounds. Botanic Ave near Queen's University is a pleasant residential street. The comfortable *Helga Lodge* (☎ 324820) at 7 Cromwell Rd, just off Botanic Ave, costs £17/32 for singles/doubles. Note the colourful orange frontage and the flowers. All rooms have their own bathrooms with TV and phones.

Nearby is the handsome *Botanic Lodge Guesthouse* (☎ 327682) at 87 Botanic Ave,

where the rooms all have TV and cost £18/40. Bus Nos 83, 85 or 86 will get you to these two. Also in this popular university area, the *Queen's University Common Room* (☎ 665938) offers B&B for £26.50/33.50 at 1 College Gardens.

Eglantine Ave, just 1.5 km south of the city centre, is quiet and packed with guesthouses and B&Bs. To reach them catch a bus along the Lisburn Rd from Donegall Square. The *George* (☎ 683212) at No 9 is £16.50/33.

At No 17 is *Liserin Guesthouse* (☎ 660769), costing £17/34. The *Eglantine Guesthouse* (☎ 667585) at No 21 has B&B for £18/34. At No 30 is *Marine House* (☎ 662828) at £17/34. *East Sheen House* (☎ 667149) at No 81 charges £14/28. At 11 Malone Rd *Pearl Court House* (☎ 666145) has B&B for £17.50 per person; at the time of writing it was for sale but likely to continue as a B&B under new ownership. Further up the road at No 67 Pearl Blakely also runs the smaller *Pearl Court Lodge* (☎ 662985) where beds cost £18 a person. More expensive places include the Edwardian *Camera House* (☎ 660026) at 44 Wellington Park where B&B for singles/doubles cost £40/56.

Along the Antrim Rd, good cheapies include *Drumragh House* (☎ 773063) at No 647. It's three km north from the city centre, close to the zoo and costs £18/32. Also out here is *Aisling House* (☎ 771529) at 7 Taunton Ave off the Antrim Rd, in a quiet residential area with B&B at £16/30; the breakfasts come highly recommended.

Hotels

There's no longer a shortage of hotel beds in Belfast, but prices are still comparatively high, except at weekends when business travellers go home and prices drop accordingly. The much-bombed *Europa Hotel* (☎ 327000) is a Belfast landmark – many city directions begin with 'Do you know the Europa?' Now part of the Hastings Group, it's one of the city's best hotels and costs from £130 for a double. The modern *Plaza Hotel* (☎ 333555), another victim of bombing, is at 15 Brunswick St, behind the Crown Liquor Saloon and only a short stroll from the Europa. Rooms cost £75/85 including breakfast, with prices plummeting to £45/55 at weekends.

The *Wellington Park Hotel* (☎ 381111) is another smaller hotel at 21 Malone Rd, close to the Ulster Museum and Queen's University. Doubles here cost £90 including breakfast, but the setting is nothing special. The *Malone Lodge* (☎ 382409) at 60 Eglantine Ave has rooms including breakfast at £59/76 dropping to £35/48 at weekends. In University Rd, at No 75 *Renshaws Hotel* (☎ 333666) has singles for £49.50 and doubles for £69.50, while *Dukes* (☎ 01232-236666) at No 65 is pricier at £81.50 single and £98 double.

Belfast's glossiest hotel (there's even an external glass lift) is the modern *Stormont Hotel* (☎ 658621), directly across from the Stormont parliament building on Upper Newtownards Rd. It's some distance out from the centre and costs £120 for a double room, but you even get a rubber duck to float in the bathtub.

Immediately opposite the terminal at Belfast International Airport at Aldergrove, the *Aldergrove Airport Hotel* (☎ 01849-422033) has excellent rooms and facilities at £64.50 per room (weekday rate) or £55 per room (weekend rate).

Country Houses

The lovingly restored *Cottage* (☎ 01247-878189) at 377 Comber Rd, Dundonald, about 16 km south-east of the city has two bedrooms with B&B for £17/32. The Georgian *Holestone House* (☎ 01960-352306) is in wooded grounds at 23 Deer Park, Doagh, Ballyclare, 21 km north-west of the city, and B&B starts from £25/35. Off the main road to Carrickfergus is the pleasant *Glenavna House Hotel* (☎ 01232-864461) at 588 Shore Rd, Newtownabbey, standing in quiet parkland, with rooms at £65/80.

PLACES TO EAT

Belfast has a surprising number and variety of restaurants including one of the very best restaurants in all of Ireland. More than one journalist has noted that the Troubles seemed to have given the citizens of Belfast a positive passion for eating out! Although there are plenty of pubs, cafés and fast-food places around the centre, Belfast's best eating is found south of the city centre along the Golden Mile towards the university, where there are eating houses to suit all purses from the professorial to the penny-pinching.

Cafés & Fast Food

The Donegall Road youth hostel's decent

Europa Hotel

A mid-1993 article on war zone hotels in *The Guardian* gave the Europa the blue riband as 'the world's most bombed hotel', ahead of such strong contenders as the Holiday Inn, Sarajevo, and the Commodore, Beirut. When the Europa opened in the late 1960s it was several stars better than anything Belfast had previously seen, but with the start of the Troubles it quickly took on a new role as the nerve centre for a nervous city as well as the most visible target for bomb-happy terrorists.

During the 1970s the Europa was bombed no less than 29 times, but every single time the broken glass was swept up, new drinks appeared on the bar and life continued. The Europa was where journalists from around the world gathered to interview paramilitary spokespeople from both religious extremes, who often left by the back door just as military personnel entered by the front to conduct yet another press briefing.

However, two big blasts – the latter in May 1993 – almost brought the Europa to its knees. The British government once again picked up the repair bill, new owners have taken over, and the Europa reopened for business in 1994. ∎

Backpackers Café is open to non-residents too. Food is reasonably priced and you can fill up on the Ulster Fries, but service can be slow and the café closes at about 8.30 pm. After that the *Kebab House* across the road from the hostel does a mix and match assortment of tasty kebabs, Indian dishes and fish and chips.

The streets around the hostel are prime hunting ground for cheap meals, the cafés in Botanic Ave in particular usually crammed with students from Queens. Immediately round the corner, Bradbury Place can seem like one solid fast food shop, with everything from filled potatoes for £1.75 at *Spuds* to excellent fish and chips at *Bishops*. There's also a small vegetarian café in the back of a shop in Shaftesbury Square which opens for cheap light lunches from noon to 4.30 pm.

At 81 Dublin Rd *Jenny's Coffee Shop* is a pleasant little café cum sandwich bar, next door to *La Boulangerie* where you can get an after-lunch pastry. Monro's at No 33 is perfect for coffee and cake before or after a film in the MGM Centre across the road; it closes at 10 pm.

At 50 Botanic Ave near the Botanic Rail Station, the friendly *Bluebell's* serves soup and sandwiches, with good ice cream and excellent cappuccinos to follow. It's also open for breakfast from about 11 am on Sunday morning. Across the road in *Queen's Espresso* at No 17 you can get a cheap breakfast or lunch in more sedate surroundings. Further up the road at No 79 there's a branch of the extremely popular *The Other Place* where burgers and fries come to an accompaniment of Beatles' tracks and lots of student jollity.

The Other Place has a second, equally popular branch in Stranmillis Rd, down past *Bonnie's Museum Café* which is perfect for a quick bite after inspecting the Ulster Museum.

Heading up University Rd towards Queens, *Bookfinder's Café* at the back of the bookshop at No 47 is an excellent place for a quick lunch. The *Student Union Cafeteria* on the ground and 1st floors of the Student Union building directly opposite Queen's College is also good for rock-bottom meals if in uninviting surroundings. At 3 Fitzwilliam St *The Mortarboard* serves coffee until late provided you don't mind the religious overtones. For late coffee with burgers instead, *Steady Eddie's* diner at 44 Bradbury Place, south of Shaftesbury Square, is often open until 1 am.

The city centre has its representatives of the international fast-food chains including *McDonald's, Pizza Hut, Burger King* and *Kentucky Fried Chicken*. There's also a food hall offering fish and chips, Chinese, pizzas and more in the Variety Centre in the High St. More atmospherically there's also a branch of the popular *Bewley's Café* chain in Donegall Arcade off Rosemary St. If that looks too pricey, *Delaney's* or the *Chalet d'Or* nearby in Rosemary St are rougher and readier lunch spots. For rock-bottom, cholesterol-rich breakfasts until 11.45 am head straight for *Spires* in the Spires Mall on College Square; for 99p you can fill up on five fried items or go for a doughnut and cappuccino. For £1.99 you get nine items, with tea or coffee thrown in. *Bambrick's* at 58 Wellington Place also does breakfasts (five items for £1) and light lunches, but doesn't open until 9.30 am.

Out towards Donegall Quay *Le Café* at 38-42 Hill St is an enterprise worth supporting. It's a training centre for people studying for National Vocational Qualifications and does light lunches.

Should everything else fail, Belfast is famous for its excellent bread (don't miss the soda farls) and you'll find innumerable bakeries around the city centre and along Botanic Ave near the university.

Pub Food

At the *Crown Liquor Saloon* (☎ 249476) on Great Victoria St in the centre you can get oysters and Irish stews, and at the same time take in the magnificent décor. They serve food from 11 am to 3 pm, but you'll need to get there early to get a seat. Even more central is the *Clarence* (☎ 238862) in a basement on Donegall Square East beside the City Hall. It offers good although somewhat more expensive bar lunches as well as more sophisticated main courses from around £7.

Keeping a low profile at 81 Chichester St, on the corner of Victoria St near the Royal Courts of Justice, *Rumpole's* (☎ 232840) is good for steak-type lunches. A block further north at 103 Victoria St, *Bittle's Bar* (☎ 311088) is in an interesting triangular building which can also be entered from 70 Upper Church Lane. It specialises in local dishes like *champ*, an Ulster speciality consisting of mashed potatoes and spring onions. *White's Tavern* (☎ 243080) at Winecellar Entry between Rosemary and High Sts is one of Belfast's most historic taverns and a popular lunch time meeting spot.

The *Duke of York* (☎ 241062) is another oldie, popular with journalists from the nearby local papers and stuffed with printing memorabilia. It serves excellent solid pub lunches for less than £5 along with overpriced fruit juices. It's hidden away down Commercial Court, an alleyway leading off Donegall St just south of St Anne's Cathedral. The *Kitchen Bar* (☎ 324901) in Victoria Square is another popular lunch time rendezvous where you'll be lucky to get a seat. If you do, you can tuck into *champ* or pizzas on a soda bread base.

Restaurants
Bottom End The *Spice of Life* (☎ 332744) at 62 Lower Donegall St, opposite St Anne's Cathedral is a relaxed wholefood and vegetarian café, open Monday to Wednesday from 9.30 am to 5 pm, and until midnight on Thursday, Friday and Saturday. Deep pan pizzas and other American food can be found at the *Chicago Pizza Pie Factory* (☎ 233555) at the back of the MGM cinema complex on Dublin Rd; a Saturday brunch including beer costs just £3.50.

There are numerous cheaper restaurants south of the centre in the Golden Mile area and around the university. *Harvey's* (☎ 233433) at 95 Great Victoria St does good pizzas and some diet-crushing desserts.

Italian restaurants are particularly popular. *Graffiti* (☎ 249269) at 50 Dublin Rd

serves excellent, filling pasta dishes, while there are often queues to get into *Villa Italia* (☎ 328356), a vibrant Italian restaurant and pizzeria at 37-41 University Rd; they'll give you a doggy bag for any leftovers. In Shaftesbury Square *Speranza* (☎ 230213) does good pizzas and even better sundaes. *Vico's Refettorio* (☎ 321447) at 10 Brunswick St also turns out excellent pizzas and other Italian dishes. *Esperanto* (☎ 248708) at 89 Dublin Rd also turns out reasonably priced pizzas and pricier à la carte dishes.

Chez Delbart (also known as *Frogities*) (☎ 238020) is a fairly cheap and cheerful French restaurant at 10 Bradbury Place where you can get good *crêpes*. There's also a branch of *Pierre Victoire* at 30 University Rd (☎ 315151) which serves *crêpes* from Monday to Thursday from 6 to 11 pm. Midweek it also does a good-value set lunch for £4.90, but on Friday and Saturday nights it's à la carte only.

If you can stand the frenetic atmosphere *Aubergines and Blue Jeans* (☎ 233700), next door to *Saints and Scholars* (see Restaurants – Top End) at 1 University St, serves all sorts of interesting goodies in a crazy décor with blue jeans much in evidence. Get there before 7 pm and two people can tuck into a 'Pauper's Platter' for £15.50; the 'Beggar's Banquet' for four is £28. The Irish stir-fry consists of wok-fried potatoes, mushrooms, sausages and onions for £3.95, or there's a big breakfast including soda bread and hash browns for £3.25. Don't dream of dropping by between 7 and 9.30 pm at weekends unless you've reserved a table in advance.

There are also plenty of Indian and Chinese restaurants in the university area. The *Archana Balti House*, upstairs at 53 Dublin Rd (☎ 323713), offers a curry named after the metal *balti* in which it's cooked and served, a style which started in Birmingham and swept the British Midlands. It says everything for Belfast's recent troubled history that this is the Archana's third incarnation; the previous two were both lost to bomb blasts.

The *Maharaja* (☎ 234200), upstairs at 62 Botanic Ave, is a more traditional Indian restaurant in the heart of the university area. In the same area, the *Dragon Palace* (☎ 323869) at 16 Botanic Ave offers Chinese food, or you can turn the corner past the forbidding checkpost to *Manor House* (☎ 238755) at 47 Donegall Pass which has excellent Cantonese food. There are many other Indian and Chinese restaurants around Belfast, many of them further from the centre along Lisburn Rd and Ormeau Rd.

Finally, the *Greek Shop* (☎ 333135) at 43 University Rd, next door to Bookfinders, does pleasing if not especially cheap Greek meals.

Top End Close to the centre the tropical ambience at *Bananas* (☎ 339999) at 4 Clarence St may feel a trifle odd, but the adventurous international mix of dishes (kebabs, moules, tiger prawns, chicken tikka) is well done and reasonably priced. It's open Monday to Friday for lunch, Monday to Saturday for dinner and shares a kitchen with the more formal *44 Restaurant* (☎ 244844), which is next door but in Bedford St at No 44. You'll need to book to get into either on a Saturday night.

The *Strand Wine Bar & Restaurant* (☎ 682266) at 12 Stranmillis Rd, right behind the Ulster Museum, offers traditional dishes and a popular Sunday brunch, although at £5.99 you might feel you could forego the buck's fizz. Surprisingly for a newly refurbished fairly upmarket restaurant it doesn't have a non-smoking area. Pricier French cuisine can be sampled in *La Belle Epoque* (☎ 323244) at 61 Dublin Rd, Belfast's most authentic French restaurant. It's closed on Sunday.

The stylish *Antica Roma* (☎ 311121) is at 67 Botanic Ave near the university. Also near the university at 3 University St is *Saints and Scholars* (☎ 325137) where advance booking is essential. This is where John Major and Peter Brooke dined while negotiating over the 1994 ceasefire arrangements. *Bocoose* (☎ 238787) at 85 Dublin Rd offers modern British cookery which tends to mean small portions beautifully cooked. If you'd like to try it without busting your budget, get

there between 5 and 7.30 pm when there are 'early bird' specials from £6.95.

Behind an anonymous frosted glass facade *Roscoff* (☎ 331532) at 7 Lesley House, Shaftesbury Square, serves superb food in very modern surroundings. Paul Rankin has a tremendous reputation (and his own TV programme) and this is one of only three restaurants in Ireland with a Michelin star; the other two are in Dublin. A complete dinner could set you back £40 per person but lunch is cheaper (set 'business lunches' cost £14.50) and on some nights there's a set dinner for £21.50.

You can also eat in the *Belfast Castle Restaurant* (☎ 776925) provided you remember to book ahead and allow at least £15 a head. Cream tea in the basement café might be nearly as satisfying.

ENTERTAINMENT

To find out what's on where and when, pick up a free copy of *That's Entertainment* at the youth hostel or tourist office.

Pubs

At lunch times many of the city centre pubs are crammed to overflowing. In the evenings, the same is equally so, but many pubs here and along the Golden Mile have bouncers on the door and operate an ad hoc dress code: look too scruffy and you'll be turned away. Large groups of men without accompanying women are not looked on favourably; conversely, lone women will sometimes find service slow and frosty.

Belfast has some pubs which are as much museums as drinking places, particularly the wonderful old *Crown Liquor Saloon* opposite the Opera House, which even teetotallers should have a look at. The *Britannic Bar* upstairs opens at 5 pm and, with its plush seating and soft lighting, has been described as the pub to which local men bring their mistresses!

The narrow alleys known as the Entries shelter a plethora of older pubs. Good ones to sample include the rough-edged *Morning Star* on Pottinger's Entry, the historic *White's Tavern* on Winecellar Entry and the *Globe*

Tavern on Joy's Entry. Other older pubs in the centre include *Kelly's Tavern* (1720) on Bank St, the *Clarence* on Donegall Square East beside the City Hall or the *Duke of York*, hidden away down Commercial Court near St Anne's Cathedral. Also very popular are the linked up *Kitchen* and *Parlour* bars at the junction of William St and Victoria Square.

Belfast also has its share of modern pubs, many of them themed, like the popular *Drury Lane* at 2 Amelia St, overlooking the modern Blackstaff Square behind the Crown Liquor Saloon, where the sculpture of a butterfly emerging from a chrysalis symbolises its rebirth after yet another bombing incident. At the opposite side of the same square is the *Spinner's Inn* below the Plaza Hotel, named after a spinner of yarns who stands in effigy in one of the many alcoves.

Also off the same square, and completely rebuilt after it was destroyed by a bomb, is *Fibber Magee's*, heavily disguised as a grocer's shop. Inside, it's a bit like plunging into a heritage centre, with salamis and hot-water bottles supposedly for sale hanging from the beams, a draper's counter at the back and a model man asleep in front of the range. Don't be fooled by any of this – it really is a pub. Push through the doors at the back and you'll emerge in *Robinson's*, with a mock-up library amongst other distractions. Upstairs is the *Shoe Shine*, a themed Manhattan speakeasy bar. Upstairs again and you'll emerge in *Spot Robinson's* where bands play (☎ 01232-247447 for details). Down in the basement is the *Rock Bottom* where Belfast's beautiful bikers and their molls hang out. On Great Victoria St, just a few steps south from the Crown Liquor Saloon, the *Beaten Docket* is equally popular with younger Belfastians.

In the university area *Bob Cratchit's* on Lisburn Rd is a trendy, modern pick-up joint. Somewhat less trendy *Lavery's* on Bradbury Place is popular with an extraordinary range of clients, from students to bikers to hardened drinkers, and has a long and colourful history as Lavery's Gin Palace. On the corner of Dublin Rd and Ventry St, the *Elbow* caters for 18 to 21-year-olds, while *Dempsey's* next door focuses on an older clientele, with themed alcoves done up to represent rooms from a range of European countries. The *Elms* is another popular student pub at 36 University Rd. Farther south the *Eglantine Inn* and the *Botanic* are institutions, packed at weekends with crowds of students. Known as the Egg and Bott, they face each other across Malone Rd.

Cinema

Belfast's biggest cinema complex, the 10-screen *MGM Centre* (☎ 245700; recorded programme details 243200), is at the north end of Dublin Rd, just south of the city centre and five minutes' walk from the youth hostel; admission is £3.80 except on Sundays when it's £2.30 all day. The *Yorkgate* (☎ 755000), with five screens, is north of the centre near the York Rd Railway Station. The *Queen's Film Theatre* (☎ 244857) near the university is the closest Belfast has to an art house cinema; tickets are £3.30, or £2 for students. *That's Entertainment* lists what's on where but without the times.

Theatre & Music

The Belfast *Grand Opera House* (☎ 241919) on Great Victoria St is host to a mixture of good theatre, opera and music shows. The booking office at 17 Wellington Place is open Monday to Saturday from 9.45 am to 5.30 pm (☎ 241919) or you can get recorded details of the current programme on ☎ 249129. On Botanic Ave in the university area the *Belfast Civic Arts Theatre* (☎ 324936) chiefly puts on popular plays or comedies. Further out from the centre on Ridgeway St, the *Lyric Theatre* (☎ 381081) has a more serious bent and includes Irish plays in its repertory. Performances also take place at *Whitla Hall* in Queen's University.

Northern Ireland's excellent Ulster Orchestra often plays in the *Ulster Hall* (☎ 323900) on Bedford St , and this is also the venue for larger rock music events (and for lunch time organ recitals and even boxing bouts). The *Group Theatre* (☎ 329685) next door stages plays by local playwrights.

King's Hall (☎ 665225) at Balmoral is

another centre for big rock events; get there by bus down Lisburn Rd or by train to Balmoral Station. Performances also take place at *Elmwood Hall*, the church building now used as a concert hall on University Rd directly opposite Queen's College. The *Crescent Arts Centre* (☎ 242338), at 2 University Rd, is another smaller music venue. *St Anne's Cathedral* also hosts occasional lunch time organ recitals. Both the *Factory* at 52 Hill St and *The Old Museum Arts Centre* (☎ 235053) in College Square North host 'arty' live events.

Discos & Nightclubs

Music, either disco or live, features in many of Belfast's pubs including the *Eglantine Inn* (☎ 381994), the *Botanic* (☎ 660460), the *Elbow* (☎ 233003), *Spot Robinson's* (☎ 247447), the *Duke of York* (☎ 241062), the *Kitchen Bar* (☎ 324901) and *Bob Cratchit's* (☎ 332526). The *Elms* (☎ 322106) and the *Chicago Pizza Pie Factory* (☎ 233555) also have live music. Further out from the centre the *Rosetta Bar* (☎ 649297) at 75 Rosetta Rd is a rock venue.

The *Errigle Inn* (☎ 641410) at 320 Ormeau Rd, south of the centre, is also popular. Nightclub-style discos can be found at the *Limelight* (☎ 325968) at 17 Ormeau Ave, at *Vico's* (☎ 321447) in Brunswick St, and at the *Manhattan* (☎ 233131) at Bradbury Place close to the university. The *Crow's Nest* in Skipper St and the *Parliament Bar* in Dunbar St are popular gay hangouts. Monday night is also gay night at the *Limelight*. When there's music on most of these places levy entry charges, typically between £1 and £5 depending on the night and the venue.

Comedy

The *Empire Laughs Back* (☎ 228110), inside a redundant church at 42 Botanic Ave, is the in place for stand-up comedy, with shows every Tuesday night starting at 9 pm. Be there by 7.30 pm if you want to get a seat. Acts consist of a local warm-up followed by a more established comedian. Tickets cost £3.50 and you get your laughs in what is

otherwise a barn-like pub with more *Titanic* memorabilia lining its walls.

THINGS TO BUY

The Craftworks Gallery (☎ 236334) at 15-19 Linenhall St specialises in Northern Irish crafts with work from craftspeople all over Ulster, but you're unlikely to find many bargains. For Irish linen and all things tackily Irish (shamrocks, leprechauns et al), try Smyth's Irish Linen at 65 Royal Ave (☎ 242232) which runs a VAT-free scheme for foreign visitors.

For camping gas cylinders, other camping equipment or for surfing gear, Surf Mountain (☎ 248877) at 12 Brunswick St in the centre is excellent. There's also the Scout Shop Ski and Camp Centre at 12-14 College Square East (☎ 320580) which retains mildly off-putting security arrangements on the door.

For music, try the Vintage Record Shop at 54 Howard St (☎ 314888). For more general shopping, Donegall Arcade, off Rosemary St, is popular with Belfast trendies. St George's Market (near the Central Station) takes place on Tuesday and Friday from 7 am to 3 pm. At the moment it's a depressing undercover jumble-sale of a place, but plans exist to revamp it as part of the Laganside development.

GETTING THERE & AWAY

See the introductory Getting There & Away chapter for international flights and ferries to Belfast.

Air

There are flights from some regional airports in Britain to the convenient Belfast City Airport (☎ 457745), but everything else goes to Belfast International Airport (☎ 01849-422888), 30 km north of the city by the M2.

There are tourist offices at both airports and a branch of Thomas Cook at the international airport which is open until 8 pm daily and where you can change up to £50 of Northern Irish banknotes into more familiar mainland sterling notes.

For more details see the introductory Getting There & Away chapter.

Ferry

Ferries to and from Northern Ireland come into one of three terminals. Closest to the centre is the SeaCat and Isle of Man terminal on Donegall Quay, a little further out is the Liverpool terminal, while the Larne terminal is 30 km north along the coast. There are trains from Larne to Belfast's Central Station. Ulsterbus services to and from Belfast's Europa Bus Station also connect with the Larne ferries.

Norse Irish Ferries (☎ 779090) have a service between Belfast and Heysham, to the south of Liverpool, and operate from the Liverpool terminal. Isle of Man Steam Packet (☎ 351009) operates between the Isle of Man and Belfast from the SeaCat terminal on Donegall Quay; it is linked to Donegall Square and the bus and train stations by a 90p bus run.

SeaCat (☎ 312002) operate huge Australian catamaran car ferries that make a 1½-hour crossing between Belfast City and Stranraer. The conventional ferries to and from Scotland dock at Larne, 30 km north of Belfast, where both Stena Sealink and P&O have their offices. Stena Sealink (☎ 01574-273616) operates between Stranraer and Larne; the trip takes two to three hours. P&O (☎ 01574-274321) operates between Cairnryan and Larne.

Bus

Belfast has two separate bus stations. The smaller of the two is in Oxford St beside the river, with bus connections to Counties Antrim, Down and Derry (the eastern side). By 1996 this bus station should have been moved across the road and modernised as part of the Laganside development.

Buses to everywhere else in Northern Ireland, the Republic, the International Airport and the Larne ferries leave from the bigger, more modern Europa Bus Station in Glengall St, right behind the Europa Hotel, where there's a café, shop, phones and toilets. Note that buses to Larne Town, as opposed to the harbour, leave from the Oxford St bus station.

Pick up bus timetables free at the Europa Bus

Station or phone ☎ 01232-320011 for Ulsterbus information or ☎ 01232-333000 for timetable information. Ulsterbus produce an excellent free *Exploring Ulster* booklet with information on bus services and fares to major attractions accessible by bus from Belfast.

There are four Belfast-Dublin services daily (three on Sunday) taking about three hours and costing £9.50 one-way. For connections to Derry and Donegal contact the Lough Swilly Bus Company (☎ 01504-262017) in Derry. Because of security concerns there are no left-luggage facilities at Belfast train and bus stations although the situation might eventually change if the peace holds.

Students are eligible for 15% reductions on Ulsterbus fares of more than £1 on production of their ISIC card.

Train

For tickets and information, Northern Ireland Railways Travel (☎ 230671) is at 17 Wellington Place close to the City Hall. Information about local trains is also available from Belfast Central station (☎ 899411).

A new station is being built behind Great Victoria St, next to the Europa Bus Station. When the new station is completed Belfast will have that rare thing, a truly integrated transport system, with buses and trains linking both airports to the central railway station and bus station.

Until it is completed the closest station to the city centre is the Central Railway Station (☎ 899400) on East Bridge St east of the city centre. Trains to all destinations including Larne, Derry, Dublin, Newry, Portadown and Bangor arrive and depart from here. A free bus to Donegall Square in the city centre leaves from outside every 10 minutes. Dublin-Belfast trains run up to six times a day (three on Sunday) and take about two hours at a cost of £14.00 one-way. All of them stop at Portadown or Dundalk, and some stop at Lisburn and Newry as well.

On Sundays you can buy a £2 go-as-you-please-ticket, allowing you to travel all over the Northern Irish rail network.

The nearest station to the university/youth

BELFAST

hostel area is Botanic which can be reached direct from the City Airport.

Car

The principal motorways out of Belfast are the M1 heading south-east towards Fermanagh, the M2 past Aldergrove Airport and on to Derry, and the M5 north-east towards Carrickfergus. If you're heading for Dublin take the M1 and then branch off on the A1, which becomes the N1 south of the border.

GETTING AROUND
To/From the Airports

Belfast International Airport (☎ 01849-422888) is 30 km from the city. Buses connect it with the Europa Bus Station behind the Europa Hotel for £3.70 or £6.40 return. There are two services an hour, 19 daily even on Sunday. A taxi would cost £18 (fares are listed inside the terminal building).

The more convenient Belfast City Airport (☎ 457745) is only six km from the centre, and you can cross the road from the terminal to the Sydenham Halt train station whence a train to Botanic would cost 65p. Suburban trains and Bus No 21 service the City Airport for less than £1; a taxi fare to the city centre is about £5. Services run roughly every half-hour on weekdays, less frequently at weekends. A bus into town would cost 70p. A taxi fare to the city centre is about £5.

Bus

Very short trips in the centre are just 42p, but in general around the city the standard bus fare is 73p. The fare increases by zones as you travel farther, but 73p will get you all the way to Cave Hill or the Zoo. A multitrip ticket costs £2.30 and gives you four rides at slightly lower cost and much greater convenience. A Day Ticket gives you unlimited travel within the City Zone from 9.30 am on weekdays or all day on weekends for £2. A seven-day bus pass costs £10.

Most local bus services depart from Donegall Square, near the City Hall. Timetables are available from the kiosks on Donegall Square West, or you can phone

☎ 246485 for information. Single tickets should be bought from the driver, but multiple tickets need to be purchased in advance from kiosks in Castle Place or Donegall Square West.

Belfast has a good system of night buses to enable people to join in the nightlife. Most of them leave from Shaftesbury Square at around midnight and 1 and 2 am. You buy tickets in advance from a mobile ticket booth between 9 pm and 1.50 am; they're £2 a shot. There are even buses to outlying towns like Antrim, Carrickfergus, Lisburn, Bangor and Newtownards so, if you wished, you stay in any of these places and still take advantage of the Belfast nightlife. These buses leave between 11.30 pm and 1.30 am and tickets cost £3 single.

Taxi

Black taxis operate bus-like services down the Shankill Rd from North St and down the Falls Rd from Castle St. Fares are 55p to 75p. Regular taxis are pricey with a £2 flagfall. For security reasons, hailing taxis on the street is not normal in Belfast. Possibilities to call include Fonacab on Great Victoria St (☎ 233333) or Jet Taxis (☎ 323278) beside the youth hostel.

Car

If you're driving be fastidious about where you park. Although things have eased considerably since the ceasefire you still shouldn't park within the well-marked Control Zones. Tales of foolish tourists coming back to find their car about to be blown up by a bomb demolition squad are, however, essentially urban myths. Terrorism aside, Belfast has a bad reputation for joy-riding.

There are plenty of car parks in Belfast, and it's wise to use them, even though they're often rather expensive. Multi-storey car parks are probably the safest places to leave your vehicle.

Rental Avis (☎ 240404) has desks at both the Belfast airports; its city office is at 69 Great Victoria St. Hertz is at the City Airport (☎ 732451) and the International Airport

(☎ 01849-422533). McCausland Car Hire is at the International Airport (☎ 01849-422022) and the City Airport (☎ 454141). Europcar (☎ 757401) is at 58 Antrim Rd, the City Airport (450904) and the International Airport (01849-423444). CC Economy Car Hire (☎ 840366) is at 2 Ballyduff Rd.

Bicycle

McConvey Cycles (☎ 491163) at 467 Ormeau Rd rents bicycles for £8 a day or £40 a week. A deposit of £30 is required. The tourist office can supply a leaflet outlining four possible cycle routes in Northern Ireland.

Counties Down & Armagh

County Down

County Down is Northern Ireland's sunny south-east, being relatively dry. Neighbouring Belfast delivers hordes of day trippers to the many seaside resorts on the coast from Bangor to Newcastle and beyond. The shoreline runs from the flat finger-like Ards Peninsula, encompassing the drowned drumlins and nature reserves of Strangford Lough, to the Mourne Mountains which coax the traveller farther south. In the famous lyrics by Percy French, the Mournes 'sweep down to the sea'; they are the highlight of Down. Besides tourists, more permanent visitors reside in the numerous retirement homes in the seaside towns – look out for elderly pedestrians! The interior of the county is well past its Industrial Revolution heyday but Hillsborough retains much of its Georgian splendour. The main Belfast to Dublin road crosses into the Republic just south of Newry at an imposing, seemingly unstaffed security checkpoint.

Highlights
- Walking in the Mourne Mountains and the Silent Valley
- Vintage train-spotting at the Ulster Folk & Transport Museum
- Mount Stewart House & Gardens
- Discovering Armagh Town
- Shopping, especially for antiques, in Hillsborough
- Visiting Down Cathedral

HISTORY

The history of Down goes back 7000 years. The county has its fair share of early monuments; the Giant's Ring near Belfast and the Legananny Dolmen near Ballynahinch are two of the best examples. St Patrick landed in Strangford Lough in 432, and died in the area in 461. The whereabouts of his remains is disputed, though Downpatrick Cathedral is the favoured site. By the time of his death the crusade he had started in Ulster had made Ireland Christian and turned him into one of the few genuinely national heroes. After his death, Irish monasteries flourished and multiplied, surviving repeated Viking attacks.

They were finally to lose out to the Normans, who ousted the Irish monks and built Grey Abbey on the Ards Peninsula and Inch Abbey near Downpatrick. Castles were

their main priority, however, and many along the coast survive today. The Scottish and English settlers who arrived with the plantation of Ulster in the 17th century were given large tracts of land previously occupied by the native Irish. They built towns and roads, and were responsible for the development of the linen industry in the 17th and 18th centuries.

BELFAST TO BANGOR

Belfast creeps east along the south shores of Belfast Lough towards the Irish Sea. The A2 road out of Belfast follows the railway line and is a pleasant route to the Ards Peninsula.

Ulster Folk & Transport Museum

This is one of the finest museums in Ireland, 11 km north-east of Belfast, near Holywood.

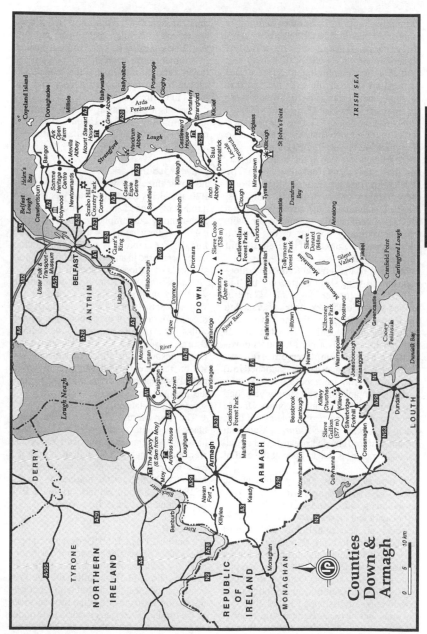

Counties
Down &
Armagh

0   5   10 km

Farmhouses, forges, churches and mills (almost 30 buildings in all) have been carefully reconstructed on the wooded 60-hectare site, with plenty of human and animal extras combining to give strong impressions of Irish life over the last few hundred years. From industrial times, there are complete terraces of 19th-century Belfast and Dromore houses. During the summer, activities such as thatching and horse ploughing are displayed for visitors.

On the opposite side of the road the transport museum is a sort of automotive zoo. The Dalchoolin Transport Galleries display horse carts, donkey *creels* (baskets), carriages, bicycles and one of the prototypes for a VTOL – a vertical take-off and landing aircraft. Particularly popular is the section which records the sinking of the Belfast-built *Titanic* in 1912.

Included in the large automobile collection is a gull-wing stainless steel car, built in Belfast after former American General Motors whiz kid John de Lorean persuaded the British government that to invest £80 million in manufacturing a flash new car would help reduce Northern Ireland's horrifyingly high unemployment figures. Unfortunately the new car was launched into a market suffering from recession and much of the development money simply vanished into numbered Swiss bank accounts. One de Lorean car put in a starring role as the time machine in *Back to the Future*. (A warrant remains out for John de Lorean.) A new road transport gallery is due to open at the end of 1995.

A separate railway gallery looks at the history of Irish railways, with lots of preserved locos, videos and sound effects.

The park and museum (☎ 01232-428428) are open all year round: July and August from 10.30 am to 6 pm (Sunday noon to 6 pm); April to June and during September 9.30 am to 5 pm (Saturday 10.30 am to 6 pm, Sunday noon to 6 pm); October to March 9.30 am to 4 pm (Saturday and Sunday noon to 4.30 pm). Admission is £3.50/2.20.

Trains and buses to Bangor stop nearby; get off the train at Cultra Station. Bear in mind, though, that the site has been designed for drivers; it's hilly and spread out and you'll need a good half day to do it justice. In summer there's a café in the reconstructed 'town' centre; for the rest of the year snacks can be had in the railway gallery and full meals in Cultra Manor.

There is a fine coastal walk of some six km from Holywood to Helen's Bay, with more pleasant seashore trails continuing north-east to Grey Point.

Crawfordsburn Park

Just over three km west of Bangor off the B20 at Helen's Bay, this country park has a number of wooded and coastal walks, and a 20th-century gun emplacement. The large-calibre artillery have been trained on Belfast Lough since before WW I, though a shot has never been fired in anger. The command post and lookout station also remain.

The park is open from 9 am to 8 pm all year and admission is free; phone the visitors' centre (which has a café) on 01247-853621 for details of occasional free guided walks. The park is accessible on Belfast-Bangor bus No 2 or by train to Crawfordsburn (unstaffed) or Helen's Bay station, the latter a wonderful little Victorian railway station dating from 1865 and built by the marquess of Dufferin, who owned the surrounding estate.

The 17th-century *Old Inn* in the pretty black and white village of Crawfordsburn has bags of character but isn't cheap; at weekends a single is £40, a double £60; it's even more during the week. For a slap-up meal, try *Deane's on the Square* (☎ 01247-852841) at Station Square, Helen's Bay where dinner costs £19 for two courses.

BANGOR

It's barely 21 km from Belfast to Bangor (*Beannchar*), a seaside resort and dormitory town for Belfast commuters. The Belfast to Bangor railway line was built in the late 19th century to connect the capital with what was then a flourishing resort. What little survives of the original Victorian charm is now under siege from amusement arcades and cheap restaurants, and Main St contrives to look like any British high street, its identity swamped beneath the chain stores. At the bottom of Main St, however, a newly developed marina, with fountains, landscaped parking, promenades and a staggeringly outsize public toilet block, has given it back a touch of glamour. The Pickie Fun Park, with mute-swan pedaloes, continues the more kitsch tradition of British seaside resorts.

History
The town goes back to the 6th century, when the Abbey of St Comgall made Bangor one of the great centres of the early church. St Comgall was a teacher and friend of St Columbanus and St Columcille, two of Ireland's most famous saints. Because Bangor was close to the sea and so often the first landfall after their journey from Scandinavia, the Vikings repeatedly attacked Bangor Abbey, which was abandoned by the 10th century; only one wall remains today. The one priceless surviving relic – 'The Antiphonary of Bangor', a small 7th-century prayer-book, the oldest surviving Irish manuscript – is now housed in Milan's Ambrosian Library.

Orientation & Information
The bus and train stations are side by side in Abbey St at the top of Main St, near the post office. At the bottom of Main St is the marina, with B&Bs clustered to east and west. For information on Bangor and the North Down region call in to the helpful Tower House tourist office housed in a tower originally built as a fortified customs post in 1637 in Quay St (☎ 01247-270069). It's open Monday to Saturday from Easter to June and seven days a week in July and August; closed winter weekends.

North Down Heritage Centre
Surrounded by Castle Park, this small museum (☎ 01247-271200) is housed in the converted laundry, stables and stores of Bangor Castle in Castle Park Ave. It contains an early 9th-century handbell, some ancient swords, a milepost with distances in Irish

miles, and a facsimile of 'The Antiphonary of Bangor', as well as details of the North Down Coastal Path. It's open Tuesday to Saturday, 11 am to 4.30 pm (5.30 pm in July and August), and Sunday from 2 to 4.30 pm; closed on Monday. Admission is free.

Places to Stay
B&Bs A cluster of virtually identical guesthouses lining Seacliff Road offer B&B from £11 to £15 a head; amongst the cheapest are *Bayview* at No 140 (☎ 01247-464545), *Pierview* at No 28 (☎ 01247-463381) and *Snug Harbour* at No 144 (☎ 01247-454238). More guesthouses are grouped in Queen's Parade overlooking the marina; try *Mardee Guesthouse* (☎ 01247-457733) at £13/26 for singles/doubles, the *Battersea Guesthouse* (☎ 01247-461643) at £13/26 or the friendly *Ashley House* (☎ 01247-473918) at £15/28. *Emmaus* (☎ 01247-456887) on Holborn Ave has rooms for as little as £11/21.

Hotels The *Tedworth Hotel* (☎ 01247-463928), spectacularly sited in Lorelei off Princetown Rd with views of the marina, does B&B at around £45/55 for singles/doubles. The brand-new *Marine Court Hotel* at 18-20 Quay St (☎ 01247-451100) offers B&B for £65/80, while on Seacliff Rd the *Sands Hotel* (☎ 01247-270696) does B&B for £49.50/68, or less at weekends.

Country House Almost five km west of Bangor and south-west of Groomsport is the modern *Sandeel Lodge* (☎ 01247-883139), at 18 Sandeel Lane off the Groomsport to Donaghadee road. It has a heated swimming pool, sea views and well-furnished bedrooms, at £45-plus for B&B. It's near the National Trust reserve of Ballymacormick Point and Orlock.

Places to Eat
Main St is thick with takeaways and cheap restaurants. In the High St *Wolsey's* (☎ 01247-460495) is a bar-eating house worth trying for lasagne and pizza, while *Jenny Watt's* (☎ 01247-270401) offers chow

mein, *champ* and chilli to musical accompaniment on Tuesday and Sunday. At 94 Main St, the *Heatherlea Tea Rooms* (☎ 01247-453157) serve terrific light meals all day. On Crosby St the *Honey Tree* (☎ 01247-457817) does reasonably priced Cantonese food, and *Simas* (☎ 01247-271722) good Indian food, costing £13.50 for a set dinner. The popular *Sorrento's Pizzeria* on the 1st floor of 8 Quay St (☎ 01247-274804) offers marina views alongside cheap pizzas. For lunch in attractive surroundings, head for the *Castle Garden Restaurant* attached to the North Down Heritage Centre.

The best places for more expensive meals are the *Sands Hotel* (☎ 01247-270696) on Queen's Parade, and *O'Hara's Royal Hotel* (☎ 01247-271866) on Quay St, where the unprepossessing exterior belies the good dinners for £14.50 to be had inside. But by far the most stylish eating place in Bangor is *Café Brazilia* in Bridge St overlooking the marina (☎ 01247-272763), which serves filled baguettes and cakes to kill for from 9 am to 5 pm daily except Sunday; from Wednesday through to Sunday it also opens for dinner (filled potato skins to steaks) from 6.30 to 9 pm.

Just outside Groomsport on the Donaghadee road is the excellent *Abelboden Lodge* (☎ 01247-464288). Dinner costs £16 or more, and there are always good vegetarian dishes. It is open from 5 pm to 11.30 pm and closed Monday and Sunday. It also does high teas.

Getting There & Away

Bus Ulsterbus Nos 1 and 2 from Belfast depart from Oxford St Bus Station (☎ 01232-320011) for Bangor's Abbey St Bus Station. There's a bus each way every 20 minutes or so on weekdays (and every half hour or hour at the weekends) and the one-way fare is around £1.80. From Bangor bus No 6 heads for Newtownards, while Nos 3 and 7 travel across the north of the Ards Peninsula to Donaghadee and Millisle. All these services run roughly hourly. For timetable details ring ☎ 01247-271143.

Train There is a regular half-hourly service to Bangor (and the Folk & Transport Museum) from Belfast's Central railway station (☎ 01232-899400). Bangor Station (☎ 0247-474143) is in Abbey St.

Road The A21 runs south from Bangor to Newtownards, while the A2 links it to Belfast to the west and to Donaghadee to the east.

Getting Around

A1 Car Hire (☎ 01247-464447) at 14 Dufferin Ave has a small fleet on offer, as does *Low Cost Car & Van Hire* (☎ 01247-271535) at 12 Church St.

SOMME HERITAGE CENTRE

Just before Newtownards on the A21 is the Somme Heritage Centre, which relates the circumstances leading up to the WWI Somme campaign of 1916 from the perspective of men of the 10th (Irish), 16th (Irish) and 36th (Ulster) divisions. It's a high-tech show, with short films, a talking model of a wandering preacher and costumed interpreters to explain everything on a 25-minute guided tour. You even walk through a mock-up trench, although inevitably health and safety requirements make this a pretty sanitised experience. There's nothing at all celebratory about the displays, intended as a memorial to the men who died.

It's open July and August Monday to Saturday 11 am to 6 pm, Sunday noon to 6 pm, and the rest of the year from Tuesday to Sunday noon to 5 pm. Admission costs £3.50/2.50, and there's a café and shop. Bus No 6 passes the entrance but you have to dash across a busy dual carriageway. There's ample parking space outside.

ARK OPEN FARM

Immediately opposite the Somme Heritage Centre, on the other side of the dual carriageway, is the Ark, an open farm with displays of rare breeds of sheep, cattle and poultry, alongside a few llamas and a solitary donkey. It's open from 1 March to 31 October,

Monday to Saturday from 10 am to 6 pm, Sunday 2 to 6 pm (☎ 01247-812672).

NEWTOWNARDS

Newtownards, like Bangor, was founded as a 6th-century ecclesiastical centre. There's a ruined 13th-century **Dominican friary** on Court St (open July and August from 1 to 5 pm, admission 50p), and the scant remains of **Movilla Abbey** and its 13th-century church 1.5 km to the east. There is some fine 18th-and 19th-century architecture in town, especially along Church St. Most striking is the 18th-century **Market House** on High St which once housed the town's prison; nowadays a bustling **market** takes place in the square in front of it every Saturday. The **Market Cross** in High St dates back to the 17th century.

Information

The Leisure Services Department inside the Ards Borough Council building at 2 Church St (☎ 01247-812215) can provide limited information on Newtownards and the Ards Peninsula but is closed at weekends. During summer a mobile information booth in Regent St is open all week.

Scrabo Hill Country Park

The park was once the site of extensive prehistoric earthworks, but these were largely removed during the construction of the 1857 Memorial Tower in honour of the marquess of Dufferin. The summit (after 122 steps) of the 41-metre tower offers some expansive views of Strangford Lough. The park (☎ 01247-811491) is two km south-west of town. It is open all year round, while the tower is open from 11 am to 6.30 pm every day except Friday. Admission to both is free.

Places to Stay

B&Bs There's no budget accommodation in central Newtownards, which can easily be visited on a day trip from Belfast or Bangor. The attractive modern *Cuan Chalet* (☎ 01247-812302) is on Milecross Rd west of town. B&B is £14 single or sharing, and it's open all year round. *Greenacres*

(☎ 01247-816193), in lovely gardens overlooked by the Memorial Tower, is at No 5 Manse Rd near the Ards Shopping Centre; B&B costs £20/32 a night with bathroom.

Hotel The neat, three-star *Strangford Arms Hotel* (☎ 01247-814141) at the far end of Church St does B&B from £35 to £65 a night.

Places to Eat

Cheap meals are as hard to come by as cheap B&Bs. *Smyth's Café* is a typical greasy spoon in West St behind the bus station. Otherwise, one of the best bets is *Knott's Coffee Shop* at 45 High St where the café at the rear is much bigger and more attractive than the facade might suggest; it's open all day (except Sunday) until 5 pm. The *Regency Restaurant & Coffeeshop* at 5 Regency Rd (☎ 01247-814347) also does good lunches (and dinners on Friday and Saturday).

On Court St the *Ming Court* (☎ 01247-815073) and the nearby Indian *Ganges* (☎ 01247-811426) are both good but neither is particularly cheap; there are Chinese and Indian takeaways a short walk away in Castle St. For Italian food try *Roma's* (☎ 01247-812841) at 4 Regent St or *Giuseppe's Ristorante* (☎ 01247-812244) at 33 Francis St.

The *Gaslamp* (☎ 01247-811225), also on Court St in the heart of Newtownards, is famous for opening on Christmas Day if the demand is there. The food is good, expensive (£18-20) and French, from an older age when helpings were bigger and sauces heavier. The *Strangford Arms Hotel* (see Places to Stay) has a good restaurant, which does a set dinner, including wine, for £12.50.

Getting There & Away

Bus The new Ulsterbus station is on Church St. There are buses roughly every half hour to Bangor and Belfast, and less frequent services along the east and west sides of the Ards peninsula.

DOWN & ARMAGH

DOWN & ARMAGH

Getting Around

The Strangford Arms Hotel (see Places to Stay) rents bikes for £7.50 a day.

STRANGFORD LOUGH

Cut off from the sea by the Ards Peninsula (see below), except for a one-km wide strait at Portaferry ('The Narrows'), Strangford Lough is almost a lake. It is 25 km long, about six km wide on average and up to 45 metres deep. Large colonies of grey seals live in and around the lough, particularly at the southern tip of the peninsula where the exit channel widens out into the sea. Birds abound on the shores and mudflats, including brent geese wintering from Arctic Canada, eider ducks and many species of wader. Underwater the muddy lough has a very diverse marine biology, which can be studied at closer quarters at Exploris in Portaferry (see below). Killer whales have occasionally come into the lough and spent a few days there, causing a sensation. The lough is a great leisure resource, with boats and yachts plying their way up and down its sheltered waters.

At Portaferry, however, 400,000 tonnes of tidal water surge through the strait four times a day; you can get some idea of the current's remarkable strength by watching the Portaferry/Strangford ferry being whipped sideways by the riptide.

There are boat trips around the lough; see under Strangford in the Lecale Peninsula section farther on for details.

The western side of Strangford Lough is nothing like as scenic or interesting as the east, although it's the route followed by the Ulster Way walking trail. The main roads between Belfast and Downpatrick (A7) and Comber and Killyleagh (A22) are remarkably straight, considering the number of drumlins locally.

ARDS PENINSULA

The beckoning-finger-shaped Ards Peninsula slots in between the eastern side of Strangford Lough and the Irish Sea, with Newtownards and Donaghadee acting as gateways. From Newtownards the A20 heads south, following the lough shore, passing Mt Stewart and Grey Abbey, before arriving at Portaferry, linked by ferry across 'The Narrows' to Strangford on the western shore of the lough. The A2 heads back north along the peninsula's seaward side, passing through the fishing port of Portavogie (fallen on hard times in the 1990s as EU fishing quotas bite) to Millisle and Donaghadee. Due to the shortage of accommodation in Newtownards, Portaferry and Donaghadee, it may be best to explore the Ards using Bangor as a base for day trips. Relatively flat, the peninsula is about six km wide and 35 km long, with some good beaches. Dotted the length of the peninsula are the remains of tower-houses, built after Henry VI offered a £10 subsidy to anyone constructing a tower to protect the border in 1429; most date from the 16th century.

Nowadays the Ards is an agricultural region where farmers are diversifying into ostrich-rearing and daffodil-bulb cultivation. It's a world away from the tension and industrial grittiness of Belfast, but you'll still spot red, white and blue kerbstones testifying to strong sectarian feeling. Watch out for dried *dulse*, Ards edible seaweed, on sale in greengrocers'; it tastes much as you'd expect – strong, salty, very much an acquired taste.

Mount Stewart House & Gardens

Eight km south of Newtownards on the A20 is Mount Stewart. The magnificent 18th-century house and gardens were the home of the marquess of Londonderry, though much of the landscaping was carried out early this century by Lady Edith, wife of the 7th marquess, for the benefit of her children. The 35 hectares form one of the finest gardens in Ireland or Britain and are now in the charge of the National Trust.

The gardens are a cosmopolitan affair, with gardens, woodlands and lakes, elegantly populated by a vast collection of plants and statues. Unusual creatures from history (dinosaurs and dodos) and myth (griffins and mermaids) join forces with curious giant frogs and duck-billed platypuses, a world of adventure for children. The

18th-century owners constructed the **Temple of the Winds**, a folly in the classical Greek style built on a high point above the lough.

The classical house still has lavish plasterwork, marble nudes and valuable paintings (including works by George Stubbs, the painter of animals). Kings have stayed here in bedrooms dedicated to the great European cities. Viscount Castlereagh was born here; he went on to become British foreign secretary and was responsible for the passing of the Act of Union in 1801, dissolving the Dublin Parliament and making Ireland legally a part of Britain. Another member of the family was a general under the Duke of Wellington.

The opening hours are unusually complicated. The gardens are open daily April to September from 10.30 am to 6 pm and at the weekends during October. The house (☎ 012477-88387) is open daily (except Tuesday) May to September and at weekends during April and October from 1 to 6 pm. The temple is open the same days as the house but only from 2 to 5 pm. Access to the gardens, house and temple costs £3.30, or for 70p you can bypass the house. There is a shop and tearoom in the grounds. Bus Nos 9, 9A and 10 pass the gate except on Sunday.

Places to Stay Along the A20 Mount Stewart road from Newtownards is *Ballycastle House* (☎ 012477-88357) an 18th-century farmhouse near the Mount Stewart gardens. B&B is £16 with top-class breakfasts.

Grey Abbey

In the antique-shop-choked village of Grey Abbey three km south-east of Mount Stewart are the fine ruins of a Cistercian abbey founded in 1193 by Affreca, wife of the Norman John de Courcy. The abbey was a daughter house of Holm Cultram Abbey in Cumbria and was used for worship as late as the 18th century. What remains is a characteristic 12th-century Cistercian ground plan, consisting of a large cruciform church, two chapels and parts of a refectory, chapter house and rest rooms.

Parts of the church, including the west doorway, were built in early Gothic style even though Romanesque still reigned supreme elsewhere in Ireland. At the far end of the church is a carved tomb possibly depicting Affreca; her husband may be represented by the effigy in the north transept. The grounds, overlooked by 18th-century Rosemount House, are awash with trees and flowers on spreading lawns, making this an ideal picnic spot. A sweet-smelling physic (herb) garden has been replanted, and there is a small visitors' centre.

During April to September the grounds are open from 10 am to 7 pm, Tuesday to Saturday, and Sunday 2 to 7 pm. They are closed on Monday except bank holidays. Admission is £1/50p.

Places to Stay *Mervue* (☎ 012477-88619) at 28 Portaferry Rd has B&B at £15/30 in the low season and £17.50/35 in summer; all rooms have their own bathroom. At 93 Newtownards Rd *Gordonall* (☎ 012477-88325) offers farm B&B for £14.

Portaferry

Portaferry is the most substantial settlement on the Ards Peninsula. A neat huddle of streets, it was originally called Ballyphilip; its new, duller name relates to its position as the terminus for the short ferry ride across the lough to Strangford. The renowned marine biology station on the waterfront uses the lough as an outdoor laboratory. The town itself is a sleepy place that feels like the end of the road, which of course it is. In good weather, you can sit outside the pubs on the waterfront and watch the lough and the ferry go by. There is a small 16th-century tower-house on Castle Lane with the state-of-the-art **Exploris**, Northern Ireland's only aquarium (☎ 012477-28062), next door, concentrating on marine life from Strangford Lough and the Irish Sea.

The latter is open all year round, daily from April to August, 10 am to 6 pm, opening at 1 pm on Sunday. The rest of the year it's open from 10.30 am to 5 pm daily, Sunday 1 to 5 pm. Admission is £3.25, children £2.15 and it's hellishly overcrowded during school holidays. There's a tearoom inside and picnic tables outside.

Places to Stay There's a *youth hostel* at 11 The Strand (☎ 012477-29598) opposite the ferry slipway; beds here cost £7.75 in winter, £8.95 in summer. On the Square in the centre of the village the modest signless and nameless guesthouse at No 22 (☎ 012477-28412) offers B&B at £13/25. At 15 High St, *White's* (☎ 012477-28580) charges £14/28 for singles/doubles. *Lough Cowey Lodge* (☎ 012477-28263) is a few minutes out of Portaferry at 9 Lough Cowey Rd. B&B is £14 a head. Moving upmarket, the seafront *Portaferry Hotel* (☎ 012477-28231) does B&B for £47.50/80.

Places to Eat In and around the Square are a few fast-food cafés. More inviting are *Café Kim* and *Harlequin*, both across the road from Exploris and offering good, cheap lunches. The *Portaferry Hotel* serves delicious seafood in its restaurant; in the bar the emphasis is also on seafood, with snacks available from 12.30 to 2.30 pm. High teas are served from 5.30 to 7 pm.

Getting There & Away
Bus Ulsterbus Nos 9 & 10 go to Portaferry and Grey Abbey from Belfast or Newtownards every hour or so. You can also pick up buses round the peninsula in Newtownards.

Ferry The ferry (☎ 01396-86637) sails every half hour from Portaferry to Strangford and back between 7.45 am and 10.45 pm Monday to Friday, 8.15 am to 11.15 pm on Saturday, and 9.45 am to 10.45 pm on Sunday. The journey time is only around five minutes. The fare is £2.50 for a car and driver, £1.50 for motorcyclists and their bikes, and 60p for car passengers and those on foot.

Ballyhalbert
Bayview (☎ 012477-58908) at 187 Harbour Rd has three rooms from £13 a head for B&B. It also serves high tea for £5 and dinner for £9; you need to order early though.

Ballywalter
In Ballywalter, *Windmill Hollow* (☎ 012477-58755) at 166 Whitechurch Rd does B&B for £20 a head. *Greenlea Farm* (☎ 012477-58218) is a modernised farmhouse, charging £13.50/27 which also offers pre-bookable evening meals. The *Pink Geranium* at 1 Harbour Rd does straightforward grills, snacks and teas.

Millisle
Behind Millisle's dreary high street lies a pretty shoreline, with a stone wall running out to sea, handy for watching the eider ducks and brent geese bobbing offshore. About 1.5 km north-west along Moss Rd is **Ballycopeland Windmill** (☎ 01247-861413), an 18th-century tower mill which was in commercial use until 1915. It's been restored to working order, and has an adjacent visitors' centre. From June to September it's open from 10 am to 7 pm Tuesday to Saturday, and 2 to 7 pm on Sunday. From April to June it opens weekends only: Saturday 10 am to 7 pm, Sunday 2 to 7 pm. Admission is £1/50p. Bus No 7 from Donaghadee passes the entrance.

Places to Stay
B&Bs In Millisle, *Crossdoney* (☎ 01247-861526) at 216 Abbey Rd does B&B for £13.50/27, while *Mount Erin House* (☎ 01247-861979) at 46 Ballywater Rd charges £15/28.

Donaghadee
Donaghadee is an extremely pretty small port, encircled by harbour walls designed by John Rennie in 1819 and completed by his son, Sir John Rennie, who designed several of London's bridges. In summer it's possible to get a boat out to the **Copeland Islands**, which were abandoned to the birds at the turn of the century; enquire at the Harbour Office

at the southern end of the harbour. Back in the village, Grace Neill's Bar dates from 1611. Among its 17th-century guests were Peter the Great, tsar and later emperor of Russia, who popped by for lunch in 1697 on his grand tour of Europe, and in the 19th century John Keats who found the place 'charming and clean' but who was 'treated to ridicule, scorn and violent abuse by the local people ... (who) objected to my mode of dress and thought I was some strange foreigner'.

Places to Stay

Camping *Donaghadee Caravan Park* (☎ 01247-882369) on the Millisle Rd has tent sites for £5 a night. *Ballywhiskin Caravan and Camping Park* (☎ 01247-862304) in Millisle has pitches for only £4.

B&Bs Two of the cheapest B&Bs around Donaghadee are *Woodside* (☎ 01247-883653) at 7 Newtownards Rd, and *Bridge House* (☎ 01247-883348) on 93 Windmill Rd, three km from Donaghadee; both do B&B for £14/28. The *Deans* (☎ 01247-882204) at 52 Northfield Rd, Donaghadee, has beds for £17/28 for singles/doubles.

Places to Eat

Along the seafront *Harlequin* at 5 Shore St does coffees and light lunches, while *Dunallen Hotel* at No 27 offers lunches with a view. *The Captain's Table* at 6 The Parade does fish & chips, while *Moorings Restaurant* (☎ 012477-882239) does simple meals until 9 pm except on Sunday. At No 35 *The Olde Seafarers Tavern* does lunches from noon to 2.30 pm, with bistro meals from 5.30 to 9 pm on Thursday to Saturday; a meal for two inclusive of wine is £21. In the Market House on New St *Coffee Plus* offers light meals and coffee breaks in daytime (closed Sunday). Finally, for a pint and a bite in historic surroundings, the *Grace Neill's* pub at 33 High St fits the bill perfectly.

Western Shore of Strangford Lough

Castle Espie Centre Two km south-east of Comber is a haven for fledgling ornitholo-

gists, and for a large gathering of geese, ducks and swans, in the hands of the Wildfowl & Wetlands Trust. The centre (☎ 01247-874146) is open 10.30 am to 5 pm daily, Sunday 11.30 to 6 pm (5 pm October to March). There's a small restaurant.

Admission is £2.60/1.30, family £6.50. Best time to visit is May/June when the grounds are overrun with goslings, ducklings and cygnets.

Trench Farm (☎ 01247-872558) is almost four km from Comber on the Ringcreevy Rd, with B&B at £15 a head. Comber's *Old Schoolhouse* (☎ 01238-541182) just south of town is the area's best known restaurant, though it is expensive. It concentrates on seafood and has a set dinner for £14. On Sunday it only opens for lunch. Six km south of Comber on the A22 in the hamlet of Lisbane is *Lisbarnet House* for good, inexpensive and familiar food like garlic steaks.

Nendrum Abbey The abbey is on Mahee Island, connected to the lough's western shore by a causeway; the remains of 15th-century Mahee Castle guard the causeway. Nendrum is earlier than Grey Abbey on the opposite shore; it was built in the 5th century under the guidance of St Mochaoi (St Mahee). The scant remains provide a surprisingly clear outline of its early plan. Foundations exist from a number of churches, a round tower, beehive cells and other buildings, as well as three concentric stone ramparts and a monks' cemetery, all in a wonderful country setting. A particularly interesting relic is the vertical stone sundial, which has been reconstructed with some of the original pieces. The ruins were only uncovered in 1844, even though the island has long been inhabited.

Access to the site is free although there's a small visitors' centre which charges 75/40p. An excellent video compares Nendrum to Grey Abbey, and there's some interesting material about the concept of time and how we measure it, presented in child-friendly fashion. The centre opens April to September Tuesday to Saturday 10 am to 7 pm, Sunday 2 to 7 pm. In winter it only opens on Saturday from 10 am until 4 pm and from 2 to 4 pm on Sunday.

Tides Reach (☎ 01238-541347) in Whiterock Bay, Killinchy, is south-west of Mahee Island on the lough shore. There is a boat at guests' disposal. B&B is £18.50/35 for singles/doubles in rooms with TV and bathroom. *Barnageeha* (☎ 01238-541011) at 90 Ardmillan Rd, Killinchy, does B&B from £20 per person.

Killyleagh The A22 continues south to Killyleagh, an old fishing village dominated by the impressive hilltop **castle** of the Hamilton family. Built originally by the Norman John de Courcy in the 12th century, this partly 14th and 17th-century structure sits on the original motte-and-bailey and was heavily restored in 1850 to create the romantic version we see today. It's in private hands but the gates are left open so you can peer through. Outside the gatehouse a plaque commemorates Sir Hans Sloane, the naturalist born in Killyleagh in 1660 whose collection was the basis for the founding of the British Museum. He also gave his name to Sloane Square in London. The parish church has the tombs of members of the Dufferin family, some of whom lost their lives in the battles of Trafalgar and Waterloo.

The *Dufferin Arms* in the High St near the castle is good value for meat and fish dishes.

LECALE PENINSULA
The knob of land protruding east from Downpatrick underneath Strangford Lough is known as the Lecale Peninsula. If you follow the coastline from the south, you'll probably end up in Strangford, with the option of taking the ferry across to Portaferry and the Ards Peninsula. St John's Point, the southern tip of the Lecale Peninsula, is surmounted by an automatic lighthouse. It's a wonder that St John managed to get a mention around this part of the world, because the Lecale Peninsula is unequivocally St Patrick's territory.

St Patrick (as you'll probably know by now) was originally kidnapped from Britain by Irish pirates and spent six years tending sheep on Slemish Mountain in County Antrim before escaping back to Britain. After religious training, he returned to Ireland to preach the faith in 432 and is said to have landed near the mouth of the Slaney Burn river. Patrick's first church was in a sheep shelter near Saul, to the north-east of Downpatrick. Using Saul as his base, he made forays out into the country, returning to Saul after some 30 years of evangelising. He's buried nearby, or so the locals believe.

Strangford This is a small and very quaint fishing village 16 km north-east of Downpatrick. The Vikings sailed into the lough and noted the strong tidal currents through the strait – hence 'strong fjord'. Most of the village is in a conservation area dominated by **Strangford Castle**, another 16th-century tower-house; the keys are available from 39 Castle St, 10 am to 7 pm daily. Steps up at the end of Castle St (opposite the castle) lead to a network of paths and a fine view of the lough. There's a large and noisy colony of nesting terns on Swan Island, just off the slipway.

Ninety-minute tours around the lough on the *Islander Marine* (☎ 01396-881303) leave from the slip, operating from April to October on Wednesday, Saturday and Sunday at 3.30 pm. The fare is £6. For details of the car ferry to Portaferry, see Getting There and Away in the Portaferry section above.

The excellent *Lobster Pot Bar* (☎ 01396-881288) on the Square does seafood and is open for lunch and dinner. The *Cuan Bar & Restaurant* (☎ 01396-881222) also on the Square does hot and cold buffet lunches. The *Cottage Grill* next door is cheaper. Officially, Strangford has no B&Bs, but ask around and something may turn up.

Castleward This huge estate stretches away from the inlet to the west with the house two km along the Downpatrick road. It was built in the 1760s by Lord and Lady Bangor – Bernard Ward and his wife Anne who were quite a pair. Their tastes were poles apart, and diverging all the time. The result was Castleward House (and a subsequent divorce). Bernard favoured the neoclassical

PAT YALE

PAT YALE

TONY WHEELER

PAT YALE

TONY WHEELER

PAT YALE

A	B
C	D
E	F

Counties Down & Armagh

A: Commemorative statue, Crossmaglen County Armagh
B: Pleasure boating, Bangor, County Down
C: Bangor, County Down

D: Roadside hoarding, County Armagh
E: Abbey ruins in Grey Abbey, County Down
F: Donaghadee harbour, County Down

PAT YALE

VITA · VERITAS · VICTORIA

PAT YALE

PAT YALE

County Derry

Top Left: Mural, Derry youth hostel
Top Right: Derry Coat of Arms
Bottom: Symbol of hope, Derry

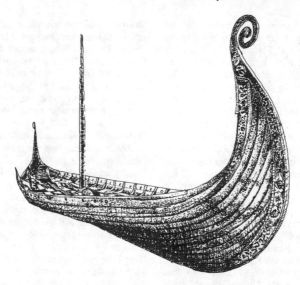

The Osebery, a Viking long ship similar to those that first sailed into Strangford Lough

Palladian approach, and was victorious in the design of the front facade and the classical staircase. Anne had leanings towards the Strawberry Hill Gothic style, which she implemented on the back facade and in her Gothic boudoir with its incredible fan vaulting. The rest of this great house is a mixture of their different aesthetic views.

Around the grounds are some decent walks with vistas of the lough, a Greek folly, a fine 16th-century Plantation tower-house, Castle Audley by the lough, a Victorian laundry museum, and tearooms (open the same hours as the house) which also do light lunches. The garden lakes have plenty of birds. Castleward Estate (☎ 0139-6881204) is in the hands of the National Trust.

The house is open daily (except Thursday) from 1 to 6 pm May to August and at the same time at weekends during April, September and October. Admission to the house is £2.60. The grounds are open all year round until dusk and admission is £3.50 for a car in summer, £1.75 in winter or after the house has closed for the day. Castleward Estate has

a park (☎ 0139-6881680) for caravans and tents at £6 a night. Otherwise, accommodation in the area is scarce and you're better off heading for Portaferry or even Newcastle.

Strangford to Dundrum
A string of castles stretches from Strangford to Dundrum along the A2 road, the majority of them large and in good condition.

Kilclief Castle Only four km south of Strangford, Kilclief Castle guards the seaward mouth of the strait. This is the oldest tower-house castle in the county, built in the 15th century by the adulterous bishop of Down. It has some elaborate details and is viewed as the prototype for other castles in the region. It's open in July and August Tuesday to Saturday from 10 am to 7 pm and Sunday 2 to 7 pm. Admission is 75/40p.

Ardglass Thirteen km south of Strangford is Ardglass, a fishing village with no less than seven castles or fortified houses from the 14th and 16th centuries. Ardglass (*Ard*

Ghlais) Castle (now the clubhouse for the local golf club) and Gowd Castle adjoining it, have Horn and Margaret Castle towers nearby, while King's and Queen's Castles reside on a hilltop above the village. The only one open to the public is **Jordan's Castle** on Low Rd, a four-storey tower near the harbour. Like the others this was built by wealthy merchants at the dawn of economic development in Ulster. The castle now houses a local museum and a collection of antiques gathered together by its last owner.

It's open June to September from 10 am to 7 pm Tuesday to Saturday, and from 2 to 7 pm on Sunday, closed Monday and lunch times 1 to 1.30 pm. Admission is 75p. On the hill north of the village is a 19th-century folly built by Aubrey de Vere Beauclerc as a gazebo for his disabled daughter.

In Ardglass on the Killough Rd is *Coney Island Park* (☎ 01396-841210) with tent spaces at £8 a night. On the B1 road from Ardglass to Downpatrick is *Strand Farm* (☎ 01396-841446), a small B&B with two rooms at £12.50. *Aldo's* (01396-841315) on Castle Place in Ardglass serves seafood or à la carte dinners for over £10, Tuesday to Saturday from 5 to 10 pm.

Killough Four km west of Ardglass is a seaside village planned by Castleward's Lord Bangor, who constructed the road which runs dead straight from here to their estate 12 km to the north. The harbour has long silted up but the village still has a picturesque, vaguely continental feel, the tree-lined streets and buildings around Palatine St and Palatine Square exemplifying this. The Palatines were 17th-century German refugees escaping the Thirty Years War (1618-48).

A worthwhile walk is south to the 10th-century church ruins and nearby lighthouse of St John's Point, a round trip of about four km. From here the beaches return to the coastline, especially west of here at Minerstown and Tyrella Strand, a seven-km stretch of firm sand but privately owned so that you must pay to use it.

Clough This small town lies at the northern end of a long and narrow inlet which is almost landlocked by a spit formed by Tyrella Strand. It's at the crossroads of east and south Down and is home to yet another castle. Clough Castle at the junction of the A24 and A25 is a good example of a Norman motte-and-bailey with a small stone keep.

Dundrum The final castle on this trip is four km south of Clough on the shore of the bay. Dundrum Castle was built in 1177 by de Courcy on the site of an earlier Irish fortification. The extensive ruins dominate the village, a rugged fortress on a rocky outcrop amidst the trees. De Courcy's castle was made of wood, and his successor, de Lacy, was probably responsible for most of the walls in the first years of the 13th century. King John confiscated the castle in 1210 and added the donjon at the highest point, its thick walls still containing the accessible stairway to the top. After a few changes in ownership it was captured from the Magennises by Cromwell, who blew it up in 1652.

You can walk up to the castle from the village centre or there's a car park beside it. From April to September opening hours are from 10 am to 7 pm, Tuesday to Saturday, and 2 to 7 pm on Sunday. It closes at 4 pm during the rest of the year and on Monday and lunch times 1 to 1.30 pm all year. Admission is 75p.

The down-at-heel *Bay Inn* (☎ 01396-755 1209) on Main St has rooms for only £10. There's pub food available in places like the *Murlough Tavern* or the *Marina Bar*. The *Bucks Head Restaurant* (☎ 01396-755 1868) does good seafood lunches and dinners.

DOWNPATRICK & AROUND

Downpatrick's name (which in Irish is *Dún Pádraig*) comes from Ireland's patron saint who is associated with numerous places in this corner of Down. From Saul and Downpatrick Cathedral, he developed the island into what was to become the 'land of saints and scholars'. St Patrick had tried to land in Wicklow but was blown ashore at Strangford Lough near Saul. Downpatrick is the county's administrative centre and capital, 32 km south of Belfast. It was settled long before the saint's arrival, his first church here being constructed inside the dún or fort of Rath Celtchair, an earthwork still visible to the south-west of the cathedral. The place later became known as Dún Padraic, anglicised to Downpatrick in the 17th century.

In the 11th century St Malachy moved the diocesan seat to Bangor, but the transfer was short-lived. In 1176 the Norman John de Courcy claimed to have brought the relics of St Columcille and St Brigid to Downpatrick to rest with the remains of St Patrick. This may have been a ploy to protect the churches of the town from the native Irish, who were disgruntled because the Irish clergy had been removed and replaced with Benedictines and Cistercians. Later the town declined along with the cathedral until the 17th and 18th centuries, when the Southwell family developed it into more like what we see today. Much of the Georgian work is centred around English, Irish and Scotch Sts, which radiate from the town centre, although the best of it is in the Mall leading up to the cathedral. The street names derive from the ethnic ghettoisation of Downpatrick in the 17th century.

Information

The tourist office (☎ 01396-612233) is in Market St opposite the bus station. It's open Monday 10 am to 5 pm, Tuesday to Saturday 9.30 am to 5 pm, and Sunday 11 am to 5 pm. On Saturday it closes for lunch from 1 to 2 pm.

Down Cathedral

Sixteen hundred years have created a cathedral that is a conglomerate of reconstructions. Repeated Viking attacks wiped away all trace of the earliest churches and monasteries here, while the Irish Augustinians produced little before being evicted by the Norman Benedictines. Their cathedral and settlements were destroyed by Edward Bruce in 1315. The rubble of those times was used in the 15th-century construction, which was finished in 1512 and lasted until 1538; after the dissolution of the monasteries it fell into ruins. Today's structure is a 17th and 18th-century reconstruction with a few additions.

In the grounds are a 9th-century high cross in poor condition and, to the south, a turn-of-the-century monolith with the inscription 'Patric'. It has been believed since de Courcy's time that the saint is buried somewhere nearby. The legend goes that Patrick died in Saul, where his followers were told by angels to place his body on an ox-cart and that the angels would guide the cart to the spot where the saint was to be buried. They supposedly halted at the church on the hill of Down, now the site of the cathedral. The interior (open daily from 9 am to 5 pm) reveals a bygone era of churchgoing. The private pews are the last of their kind still in use in Ireland. Note the pillar capitals, the east window representing the Apostles, and the fine 18th-century church organ.

There is a memorial to an Oliver Cromwell, though not 'the' Cromwell. All the treasured relics of St Patrick wouldn't save a church in Ireland from destruction if it housed that man's body!

Inch Abbey

Visible across the river from the cathedral is this abbey, built by de Courcy for the Cistercians in 1180 over an earlier Irish monastic site. The Cistercians arrived from Lancashire in England with a strict policy of non-admittance to Irishmen and managed this for nearly 400 years before closing in 1541. Much of the remains consists of foundations and low walls only; the groomed setting in the marshes of the River Quoile is its most memorable feature.

The grounds are open all year round. From April to September the abbey's open daily (except Monday, and lunch times 1 to 1.30 pm) 10 am to 7 pm, Sunday 2 to 7 pm. The rest of the year it closes at 4 pm. Admission is 75/40p. To get here head out of town for one km on the Belfast road and turn left just before the Abbey Lodge Hotel.

Down County Museum/ St Patrick Heritage Centre

Down the Mall from the cathedral is the county museum (☎ 01396-615218), housed in an extensive 18th-century gaol complex. The gatehouse contains exhibits on the life of St Patrick, while the main buildings deal with the history of the county. In the cell block at the back are models of some of the prisoners incarcerated here. Perhaps the biggest exhibit of all is outside, for a short signposted trail from here leads to the **Mound of Down**, a good example of a Norman motte-and-bailey.

The museum is open on Tuesday to Friday from 11 am to 5 pm, and on Saturday from 2 to 5 pm. July to September it's also open on Monday from 11 am to 5 pm and Sunday from 2 to 5 pm. Admission is free.

The Mall itself is the mòst picturesque street in Downpatrick, with some marvellous 18th-century architecture, including Soundwell School built in 1733 and a courthouse with a finely decorated pediment.

Quoile Countryside Centre

Signposted off the Strangford Rd is the small Quoile Countryside Centre, an educational centre with lots of info on the local flora & fauna. It's right beside the ruins of **Quoile Castle**, a 17th-century tower-house which stood on the shores of the River Quoile when it was first built. Access to the lower floors is via the Countryside Centre which is open free from 11 am to 5 pm throughout the year.

Places to Stay

B&Bs Accommodation in Downpatrick is very thin on the ground. *Hillcrest* (☎ 01396-612583) on Strangford Rd charges £14. Farther afield is the 200-year-old *Havine Farm* (☎ 01396-851242), about seven km south-west of Downpatrick and three km north of Tyrella in Ballykilbeg. It has four bedrooms and B&B is £13 in a truly rural environment.

Hotels The not very inviting two-star *Abbey Lodge Hotel* (☎ 01396-614511) has rooms at £39.50/54 for singles/doubles.

Places to Eat

By far the best place to eat is in the *Arts Café* (☎ 01396-615283) in the Down Arts Centre, a fine red-brick Victorian building, hard to miss at the centre of town. It opens Monday to Saturday from 9 am to 5 pm (to 9 pm on Thursday) but closes on Sunday. The *Golden Dragon* on Scotch St combines Chinese and European menus. Arriving by bus it would be difficult to miss *Harry Afrika's Diner & Restaurant* (☎ 01396-617161) immediately opposite. It's open for breakfast and Sunday lunch, and from 5.30 to 7.30 pm every day you can get a 4-course dinner for £5.95. For pub grub *Denvir's Pub* in Mall St would be a good choice. The *Abbey Lodge Hotel* has a good seafood-orientated restaurant with a set dinner for £12.50.

Getting There & Away

Ulsterbus No 15 departs from Belfast's Victoria St Bus Station (☎ 01232-333000) for Downpatrick Station (☎ 01396-612384) on Market St every half hour or so.

Saul

Saul is three km outside Downpatrick off the Strangford road to the north-east. Upon landing near here in 432, St Patrick made his first convert, Díchú, the local chieftain, who gave St Patrick a sheep barn ('sabhal' meaning barn in Irish) from which to preach. This was the saint's favourite spot; he returned here regularly and came here to die. Just west of the village is the supposed site of the barn, marked now by a mock 10th-century church and round tower built in 1932 to mark the 1500th anniversary of his arrival. There is a surviving wall of a medieval abbey beside this church. At the same time a massive 10-metre statue was erected on nearby Slieve Patrick, with Stations of the Cross along its ascent to occupy any climbing pilgrims.

Streull Wells

Two km east of Downpatrick, on a back road behind the hospital, is the final pilgrimage site associated with the saint. Since the Middle Ages the waters from these wells have been popular cures for all ills, with one well specially set aside for eye ailments. The site's popularity was at its peak in the 17th century, and the men's and women's bath houses date from this time.

CENTRAL COUNTY DOWN

South of Belfast is pastoral countryside, with towns like Craigavon, Lurgan, Saintfield, Ballynahinch, Hillsborough and Banbridge servicing the region. Hillsborough is a particularly attractive little town, but Moira too has a quiet charm. Craigavon is an ugly sprawl, best avoided except that many bus services connect there. Only Slieve Croob south-west of Ballynahinch breaks the flatness of the terrain. Down's greatest megalithic monuments are in this region, including the Giant's Ring and the Legananny Dolmen.

Giant's Ring

This earthwork is within easy reach of Belfast, only eight km south of the city centre, west of the A24 in Ballynahatty. The ring is a huge prehistoric enclosure nearly 200 metres in diameter, enclosing nearly three hectares. In the centre is the **Druid's Altar**, a dolmen from around 4000 BC. Prehistoric rings were commonly believed to be the home of fairies, and consequently treated with respect, but this one was commandeered in the last century as a racetrack. The four-metre embankment was a natural grandstand and course barrier.

Legananny Dolmen

This is perhaps Ulster's most famous Stone Age monument, and features extensively in tourist literature. Situated on the south-eastern slopes of Slieve Croob (528 metres), the tripod dolmen is less bulky than most, and its elevated position has the great backdrop of the Mournes to the south. On Slieve Croob is the source of Belfast's River Lagan,

and the mountain is crowned with the remains of a court cairn. Farther up, the summit also presents a much wider panorama of the county. To reach the mountain, head west from Ballynahinch to Dromara; from here are roads leading south-east across the slopes.

Ballynahinch

Ballynahinch, 20 km south of Belfast, was once a spa town and is now a plain market and agricultural centre. It does have a tourist office of sorts (☎ 01238-561950) in the Ballynahinch Centre at 55 Windmill St. The nearby **Seaforde Tropical Butterfly House** (☎ 01396-811225) has hundreds of free-flying tropical butterflies and much more safely caged tropical insects and reptiles. Just over 12 km south of Ballynahinch on the A24, it might make a good place to break a journey south to Newcastle and is open April to September Monday to Saturday from 10 am to 5 pm and on Sunday from 2 to 6 pm. Admission costs £2/1.20.

Moira

Moira, near the County Antrim border, owes much of its attractive appearance to the Rawdon family from Yorkshire who settled here in the 17th century and built a huge mansion in a demesne which is now a public park. The broad main street was laid out in the 18th century and retains many elegant buildings like the town hall and St John's Parish Church. If you want to get away from the main tourist route through Northern Ireland, *Albany House* (☎ 01846-611351) at 35 Main St does B&B for £25/40, or you can camp in the Moira Demesne Transit Caravan Park (☎ 01846-619974) for just £1.50 a night.

Hillsborough

The gracious town of Hillsborough is 15 km south-west out of Belfast. It was founded in the 1640s by a Colonel Hill who built a fort here to quell Irish insurgents. Fine Georgian architecture rings the Square and runs down Main St where there are several antique shops.

At the top of Main St, the most notable building is **Hillsborough House**, built in the

1780s; as the official royal residence in Northern Ireland, and the official residence of the Secretary of State for Northern Ireland, the British government's main person, it still hosts official receptions and is not open to the public. The most notable exterior feature is the elaborate wrought-iron gates dating from 1745 which were designed for Richhill Castle near Armagh and brought here when the House was restored after a fire.

Nearby are the Georgian **Market House** and **Court House**, while at the bottom of Main St stands **St Malachy's Parish Church**, one of Northern Ireland's most splendid churches, with twin towers at the ends of its transepts and a graceful spire at the west end. Originally dedicated in 1663, St Malachy's was restored and improved in 1774 by the first marquis of Downshire, who was also responsible for its fine Snetzler organ. Inside, the nave and transepts are filled with box pews and there are some impressive 18th and 19th-century wall tablets as well as a 17th-century copy of the Bible in Irish.

Beside the church, only the ramparts of **Hillsborough Fort** date from Colonel Hill's day; the structures dotted around them mostly date from the 19th century. The fort (☎ 01846-683285) is open daily except Monday from April to September from 10 am to 7 pm (closed for lunch from 1 to 1.30 pm) and on Sunday from 2 to 7 pm. Admission is free.

There are fine views over Hillsborough forest and lake from the ramparts.

Places to Stay *Growell House* (☎ 01238-532271) at 207 Dromore Rd has two rooms at £16 a head. Mrs Silcock at 16 Lisburn St also lets out rooms for £18 a head (☎ 01846-683334).

Places to Eat The *Plough Inn* at the top of Main St boasts that it's been offering 'beer and banter' since 1758; upstairs is *Clouseau's* wine bar, with excellent food available. On Sunday, food is only served between 7 and 9 pm in both sections. The *Hillside Bar* (☎ 01846-682765) on Main St is also handy, serving good bar food until

7.30 pm (8 pm on Friday) and nouvelle cuisine and seafood in its more formal restaurant until 9 pm. Dinner is expensive, from around £20. *Ritchies* on the corner of Ballynahinch St does the usual bar meals: steaks, lasagne and burgers. In the Square there's also *La Glacerie*, should the weather be good enough to brave ice cream.

At 23 Dromore Rd the *White Gables Hotel* (☎ 01846-682755) has a nice little restaurant which relies on the best of local produce for its à la carte menu. Dinner costs between £12 and £15. It also serves food in the bar and has tea rooms for the less hungry.

Getting There & Away Bus Nos 38 and 238 run regularly from Belfast's Europa Bus Station. Busy buses also run back and forth between Hillsborough and Lisburn.

Banbridge
Fifteen km south-west of Hillsborough is Banbridge, another Industrial Revolution town. The tourist office (☎ 018206-23322) is at 200 Newry Rd.

Things to See Near the centre is the **statue to Captain Francis Crozier**, complete with polar bears which look like no other polar bears you're likely to encounter. A native of Banbridge, he was commander of HMS *Terror* in the 1840s, and explored the uncharted Antarctic continent. Later he went with Sir John Franklin in search of the elusive North-West Passage. Franklin died on that voyage in 1847, and Crozier and his crew starved to death a year later, their bodies remaining lost in the Arctic for 10 years. Crozier lived in the fine blue and grey Georgian house, now colonised by solicitors, across the road from the statue.

Bridge St features an unusual Victorian central **underpass** which enabled horse coaches to manage the steep hill but makes the street seem unattractively cluttered nowadays.

Banbridge is the start of a **Brontë Homeland Drive** which travels the River Bann valley to Rathfriland 12 km to the south. Patrick Brontë, father of the famous literary sisters, was born here and taught in a local school. The locals like to think that her father's tales of the Mournes inspired the bleak setting for Emily's *Wuthering Heights*. Milking this tenuous connection for all it's worth, there's the **Brontë Homeland Interpretive Centre** in what was Drumballyroney church, 13 km south from Banbridge (☎ 018206-31152); it's open March to October Tuesday to Friday 11 am to 5 pm, and Saturday and Sunday 2 to 6 pm; admission is £1, children 50p.

Organised Tours The tourist office is the 'gateway' for the so-called Linen Homelands (Banbridge, Craigavon and Lisburn). It's here that you can join tours of the linen towns on Wednesday and Saturday from May to the end of September. Tours kick off at 9.30 am and take in the Linen Centre in Lisburn, a local flax farmer in Dromore and one of the linen factories which are still in production, returning to Banbridge around 4 pm. The charge is £12 a head, and advance booking is essential; phone ☎ 018206 23122.

Places to Stay *Lisdrum* (☎ 018206-22663) is on the main road to Newry, in well over 10 hectares of nicely tended gardens. Its flatlets, each with a small lounge, cost £15 for B&B. It's open all year round.

Places to Eat Banbridge is something of a culinary wasteland. *Rosamar's Restaurant* at 14 Bridge St does sandwiches and soups, and there's fast food available at *Friar Tuck's*, also on Bridge St. On a Sunday, head for *Shalamar Tandoori* at 42 Bridge St which stays open until 11 pm. The *Lucky Star* immediately opposite sells Chinese.

Getting There & Away Bus Nos 38 and 238 run regularly from Belfast's Europa Bus Station, through Dromore, Hillsborough and Lisburn.

SOUTH DOWN & MOURNE MOUNTAINS

The relatively compact yet impressive Mourne Mountains have long resisted human settlement. Today they are surrounded on all sides by towns and villages, but are crossed only by the B27 road between Kilkeel and Hilltown. The reservoirs of the Silent Valley and Spelga are among the few intrusions on nature. The steep and craggy granite peaks have suffered less than other similar ranges from glaciation. There are no low polished hills to be found here. The highest peak, and indeed the most accessible, is **Slieve Donard** (848 metres). In its shadow, the town of Newcastle is the best base for exploring this or other peaks, as the Mourne Countryside Centre here provides detailed information. The less adventurous can visit the numerous forest parks around Newcastle. For walkers, J S Doran's *Hill Walks in the Mournes* is worth getting. Alternatively, Newry and Downpatrick tourist offices stock *St Patrick's Vale: The Land of Legend* which describes 31 possible walks for £1. The **Silent Valley Park** plunges into the range's heart, surrounded by most of the peaks. **Ben Crom**, **Slieve Muck** and **Slievelamagan** are good for strenuous hiking. Westwards is the B27 road which passes **Spelga Reservoir**, a picturesque drive in the evening, when the sun goes down behind **Eagle Mountain** and **Pigeon Rock Mountain**. There's good rock climbing in this area. As in Connemara, the farmers here have produced the characteristic patchwork of small fields with dry-stone walls out of the boulder-strewn landscape. The biggest of the walls, the **Mourne Wall**, is a different kettle of fish; it was built early this century to provide employment and to enclose the catchment area of the Silent Valley reservoir; it stretches for 35 km over numerous peaks.

Newcastle

All along the coast from the north of the county the Mournes beckon. If you stick to the coastline you'll eventually end up in Newcastle, 46 km away from Belfast. Despite its marvellous setting with the huge Slieve Donard stretching up behind the town as a backdrop, Newcastle itself is a dreary place, the Bangor of south Down, awash with fast-food joints, amusement arcades and general seaside tackiness. To be fair, it also boasts five km of beaches. Now that peace has descended Newcastle is well positioned to catch the Southern holiday market; be warned that everywhere can book out when it's a public holiday in the Republic.

Information There is a tourist office (☎ 013967-22222) in the Newcastle Centre & Tropicana Complex on Central Promenade. It's open seven days a week, all year round, from 10 am to 5 pm Monday to Friday and noon to 5 pm on Saturday (longer hours in summer). For more details on the Mournes, drop into the Mourne Countryside Centre (☎ 013967-24059) just south of the Newcastle Centre. During the summer months (from 9 am to 7 pm weekdays, noon to 6 pm weekends) it provides more information on history and scenery in the form of exhibitions, brochures and maps of suggested walks. On Monday and Saturday at 10 am free guided walks of varying distances (four to 14 km) into the mountains leave from the centre. In winter it's open 11 am to 5 pm Monday to Friday, noon to 6 pm at weekends.

Places to Stay The YHANI *Newcastle Youth Hostel* (☎ 013967-22133)) is near Slieve Donard Hotel on the promenade at 30 Downs Rd. It charges £6.30 a night including bed linen, and is open from March to December.

For value for money there are few B&Bs better than *Glenside Farmhouse* (☎ 013967-22628) one km from Tollymore Forest Park on Tullybrannigan Rd with simple rooms available for only £10. The *Briers* (☎ 013967-24347) is a delightful old farmhouse almost one km from Newcastle at 39 Middle Tollymore Rd; B&B is £25/35 a single/double. The modern 14-bed *Golf Links House* (☎ 013967-22054) is at 109 Dundrum Rd, next to the Royal County Down Golf Club, hence the name. B&B is good value at £14 and four-course evening meals cost another £8.

If all you want to do on reaching Newcastle is get out again *Old Town Farm* (☎ 013967-22740) at 25 Corrigs Rd could fit the bill nicely. Turn right immediately after the Burrendale Hotel (see below) and take the first right down a country lane to the far end. Bcds cost from £15. At £30, the *Donard Hotel* (☎ 013967-22203) on Main St is the cheapest hotel. It's not to be confused with the dominating *Slieve Donard Hotel* (☎ 013967-23681) on Downs Rd, which offers rooms for a minimum of £68 but has all the extras.

Bryansford Rd has some good-value hotels like the *Brook Cottage Hotel* (☎ 013967-22204), with pleasant rooms at £20 a night for a single. Finally there's the *Burrendale Hotel & Country Club* (☎ 013967-22599), a three-star establishment with spacious rooms for £51/80 for singles/doubles and the best restaurant in Newcastle.

Places to Eat Main St abounds with every kind of fast food. On the seafront the *Strand Palace Restaurant* is marginally more upmarket but with main courses for around £5. Next door is the *Mariner Restaurant* (☎ 013967-23473) where dinners come with musical accompaniment. The popular *Mario's* on Central Promenade tends towards Italian as well as à la carte dishes in comfortable surroundings. The *Pavilion* on Downs Rd opposite the entrance to the Slieve Donard Hotel is more seafood-orientated, and has an à la carte selection; a set dinner costs £10.

If you're prepared to venture farther afield the *Tea House* in Tollymore Forest Park (see below) is designed to resemble a treehouse and has fine views of the park. It's open 10.30 am to 5 pm in the week and till 6.30 pm at weekends (closed November/December). You could get a decent light lunch for under £5 here. The *Burrendale Hotel* (☎ 01367-22599) has a high-quality restaurant with a set dinner at £16. Snacks are also available in the *Cottage Bar*, but both eating places take last orders at 9 pm on Sunday.

The *Slieve Donard Hotel* restaurant (☎ 013967-23681) isn't bad either and booking is essential for a table. Life is less formal (and cheaper) at the *Percy French Pub Restaurant* by the gates.

Getting There & Away The bus station (☎ 013967-22296) is in Railway St and there is an hourly service from Belfast on Ulsterbus Nos 18 and 20 through Ballynahinch. Alternatively go from Belfast to Downpatrick and connect with Ulsterbus No 17 between Newcastle and Downpatrick.

Getting Around During July and August Ulsterbus No 34A tours from Newcastle (☎ 013967-22296) to the Silent Valley and the Spelga Dam, with three buses on weekdays, two on Saturday. Wiki Wiki Wheels at 10B Donard St near the main roundabout rents bikes for £6.50 a day, £30 a week. In nearby Castlewellan on Clarkhill Rd is Ross Cycles (☎ 013967-78029), the region's main Raleigh dealer. Bikes are £7.50 a day or £30 a week.

Around Newcastle
Newcastle is an ideal base from which to explore the Mournes, and there are three forest parks close by, for walks, hikes and pony treks. **Donard Park** at the south edge of town is the best place from which to ascend Slieve Donard. On a good day the three-hour effort is well rewarded, with Down's patchwork of fields, Scotland, Wales and the Isle of Man all on show at varying splendid perspectives. Two cairns can be found near the summit and were long believed to have been cells of St Donard, who retreated here to pray in early Christian times.

Tollymore Forest Park is three km northeast of town. Its 500 hectares offer lengthy walks along the Shimna River and the north slopes of the Mournes. The park (☎ 013967-22428) is open every day, 10 am to sunset and admission is £2.50 for a car. The visitor centre is housed in a 19th-century barn designed to look like a church and displays the single plaster plaque that survives from Tollymore House as well as info on the flora, fauna and history of the park. Normally it opens at weekends from noon to 5 pm.

Guided walks leave from outside at 2.30 pm on summer weekends. Tollymore Outdoor Centre (☎ 013967-22158) runs courses on hill walking, rock climbing and canoeing. Bus No 34 runs from Newcastle to Tollymore but there's no Sunday service except in July and August.

Farther north-east is the finest but slightly smaller park, **Castlewellan Forest Park** (☎ 013967-78664), and its lovely lake. Trout fishing is allowed (daily permit £7) and there is also boat hire. The Arboretum here is well established, dating from 1760, and is internationally known, with a wide variety of fine shrubs and trees. Opening hours and admission are identical to those of Tollymore. Just outside the park is the **Mount Pleasant Horse Trekking Centre** (☎ 013967-78651), which caters both to the experienced rider and to the beginner, with various treks into the park for £7 an hour inclusive of guide.

Places to Stay There are plenty of camp sites on offer though they can fill up at the height of summer. Both *Castlewellan* (☎ 013967-78664) and *Tollymore* (☎ 013967-22428) have spaces for tents from £5 to £8.50 depending on the season. Nearer the town is *Lazy BJ Park* (☎ 013967-23533) on the Dundrum road, which is similarly priced.

Mournes Coast Road
The coastal drive along the A2 south and around the sweeping Mourne slopes is the most memorable journey in Down. Annalong, Kilkeel, Rostrevor and Warrenpoint offer convenient stopping points, from which you can detour into the mountains. If you take the Head Rd, following the sign for the Silent Valley one km north of Annalong, you go through the beautiful stone-wall countryside, past the Silent Valley, and back to Kilkeel.

Annalong This busy little tourist spot with its shingle beach is 12 km south of Newcastle. Overlooking the harbour is the **Annalong Corn Mill** (☎ 013967-68736) an 1830 watermill, nicely preserved, which still mills flour. The café and antique shop are open sporadically, while the mill is open more or less year round in the afternoons from 2 to 6 pm; admission is £1.30, children 65p. For B&B in the £14 to £16.50 range there are *Dairy Farm* (☎ 013967-68433) and the neighbouring *Sycamores* (☎ 013967-68279), both on Major Hill. Annalong's *Glassdrumman Lodge* (☎ 013967-68451) is a very expensive guesthouse (£65/85 for singles/doubles) which also serves up French cuisine from £20 a go. It has the *Kitchen Garden* for more moderately priced meals. Back down to earth is the *Harbour Inn* (☎ 013967-68678) down by Annalong's waterfront, serving up fish, steaks and pub food daily.

Kilkeel Kilkeel, nine km farther south, is larger than Annalong, with a quayside fish market. From here the B27 ventures north into the mountains. *Chestnut Park* camp site (☎ 016937-62653) is good, with pitches at £8 a night. B&Bs within the £15 range are *Mourne Abbey Guesthouse* (☎ 016937-62426) just south of town at 16 Greencastle Rd, and *Ashcroft Farmhouse* (☎ 013967-62736) five km north-west on the A2 in Ballymartin. Both only open from April to September. Out of season, *Hill View* (☎ 016937-64269), six km north of Kilkeel, just off the B27 is open all year round and does B&B at £17.50/30 a single/double. The homely *Kilmorey Arms Hotel* (☎ 016937-62220) is at 41 Greencastle St and costs £27/44. It does a medium-priced menu of familiar à la carte dishes.

Silent Valley Just east of Kilkeel is the Head Rd, which leads to the beautiful Silent Valley six km north of here. In the valley the Kilkeel River has been dammed to provide water for Belfast. The dry-stone **Mourne Wall** surrounds the valley and climbs over the summits of 15 of the nearby peaks. Two metres high and over 35 km long, it was built in 1910-22 and outlines the watershed of the springs which feed the two lakes.

At the south end of the valley is the Silent Valley information centre (☎ 01232-

746581). From the car park (admission £2) there's a bus up the valley to the top of Ben Crom. This operates daily during July and August and costs £1 return; in May, June and September buses run at weekends only. Otherwise it's a fine walk. The centre and coffee shop are open from 10 am to 6 pm from April to September and until 5 pm during the rest of the year.

Greencastle Six km south-west of Kilkeel on the tip of a promontory across Carlingford Lough is Greencastle. The first castle was built in 1261 as a companion to Carlingford Castle on the opposite side of the lough in County Louth. However, the square, turreted remains date from the 14th century. Once the property of the earls of Kildare, it was seized by the crown and given to the Bagenal family of Newry in the 1550s. They maintained it as a royal garrison until it was destroyed by Cromwell's forces in 1652. The rooftop provides a good vantage point west up the lough. The interior is open every day except Monday from April to September, 10 am to 7 pm, Sunday 2 to 7 pm. During winter it's open weekends, Saturday 10 am to 4 pm, Sunday 2 to 4 pm. It's closed lunch times 1 to 1.30 pm. Admission is 50p.

Cranfield Point to the south-east is the most southerly tip of Northern Ireland.

Rostrevor From Kilkeel the journey is westward along Carlingford Lough. Thirteen km to the west, Rostrevor is a pretty Victorian seaside resort of a couple of streets at the base of Slievemartin. Just before entering the town from the north, the road passes a large **obelisk** to Major General Ross, a British commander in the American War of 1812. His achievement was the capturing of Washington DC and the burning of the White House. Up until this point the presidential residence was stone grey, but it had to be painted white to cover the smoke and scorch marks left behind by Ross's men.

From **Kilbroney Forest Park** to the north-east of the town, there's a forest drive and then a footpath to the top of Slievemartin, or a strenuous trek up the steepest side of the mountain. The Kilbroney Forest Park *camp site* (☎ 016937-38134) on Shore Rd costs only £4.80 a tent.

Near Rostrevor, two km inland by the Fairy Glen riverside walk, is the attractive early 18th-century *Forestbrook House* (☎ 016937-38105) on Forestbrook Rd. It charges £14 for B&B. A larger hotel is planned for Rostrevor and may have opened by the time you read this; the tourist office in Warrenpoint (see below) should be able to tell you.

For something to eat in Rostrevor try the *Cloughmor Inn* on Bridge St for toasted sandwiches, or the *Corner House* opposite for something more substantial even on Sunday (6 to 9 pm). Failing that, there's the *Wok Way* Chinese and the *Chicken Range* takeaway, both in Bridge St. The *Glen Bar* in Bridge St should make a pleasant watering hole once renovations are complete.

Warrenpoint At the head of the lough, on the way to Newry, is Warrenpoint, another spacious and picturesque resort. It's one of the livelier towns around, with an active nightlife in the pubs and halls, although for many people it will always be associated with an incident in 1979 when the IRA detonated a bomb hidden in a haycart, killing fifteen soldiers and seriously injuring eight others.

For somewhere to stay you could try *Fern Hill House* (016937-72677) at 90 Clonallon Rd where B&B is £15, or the slightly cheaper *Glen Rosa* (☎ 016937-72589) at 40 Great Georges St South. For pub food, try *Bennett's* on Church St, or the *Duke of Mourne* on Duke St, with the *Tai-Pan* above it for good Chinese food. Alternatively *Diamonds* (☎ 016937-52053) in the Square has an extensive menu with something to suit most tastes.

The *Red Star Ferry* (☎ 016937-72682) operates from Warrenpoint to Omeath in County Louth from June to September. It's more like a tour as it only takes passengers, not cars. It operates every 20 minutes between 1 and 6 pm from the beach or Marine Parade and costs £1.50 return. A 90-minute cruise around the lough on the *Maiden of Mourne* (☎ 016937-72950) costs £3. For sailing timetables and tickets you could also call into the tourist information office in the Church St town hall (☎ 01637-52256) which is open from 9 am to 5 pm on weekdays all year round and at weekends during the summer.

Just over three km west of Warrenpoint is the small **Burren Heritage Centre** which has information about the court tombs and crannógs of the area, along with a collection of embroidery, tools and bits and pieces rescued from local churches. It has a craft shop and teashop attached. Opening hours are from 11 am to 6 pm Tuesday to Saturday, and 2 to 6 pm Sunday from April to September, and 10 am to 5 pm on weekdays in winter. Admission is £1.

On the main road from Warrenpoint to Newry you'll see **Narrow Water Castle**, a medieval tower-house, standing on the shores of the lough and the round tower of **Clonallan** monastic settlement on the opposite shore.

Newry

Newry (*An tIúr*) has long been a frontier town, guardian of the Gap of the North which lies between the Mournes to the east and Slieve Gullion to the south-west. Its name derives from a yew tree which was planted here by St Patrick in an early monastery, of which nothing remains. A stone castle was first built in the town in 1180 by de Courcy, but it was repeatedly attacked. Cistercian monks came to shelter near the castle, until their abbey was taken over by Nicholas Bagenal in the 1570s. As Grand Marshal of all English forces in Ireland, the powerful Bagenal attracted the attention of some of the local rulers. One, Sean 'the Proud' O'Neill, had completely destroyed the castle and house in 1566. In 1575 Bagenal used the rubble to construct the first Protestant church built in Ireland since the Reformation. He is buried in the grounds of St Patrick's Church of Ireland on Stream St which may eventually become a museum.

The Newry canal, built in 1740, was a

forerunner of the English network which led England into the Industrial Revolution. It brought trade, and later its decline led to the decline of the town.

After a long period in the doldrums, Newry is starting to find its feet again. Its position on the main Dublin to Belfast road makes it a magnet for shoppers, in particular for Southerners who come for the cheaper merchandise, especially around Christmas. The coming of peace also promises to benefit a town which was always too close to the borders to be popular with tourists. A Regeneration Project is already up and running, and one of its earliest achievements was producing a town trail (see later section).

Information There's a small but very helpful tourist office (☎ 01693-68877) inside the town hall. June to September it's open from 9 am to 5 pm Monday to Friday and 10 am to 4 pm Saturday, while in winter it closes at weekends and from 1 to 2 pm on weekdays. The Arts Centre & Museum beside the town hall also has a few shelves in the lobby stacked with brochures and free booklets. The Newry Bookshop (☎ 01693-64999), just off Monaghan St beside Dunnes Stores, has a fairly good selection on offer.

Newry Museum The small Newry Museum (☎ 01693-66232) in the Arts Centre on Bank Parade presents a detailed historical account of the town, and has some intriguing exhibits, including Admiral Nelson's cabin table from the HMS *Victory*. This piece sits near the base of the entrance stairs, its glass case bearing only a small plaque naming the benefactor. The museum is open from 11 am to 4.30 pm weekdays except Monday, 10 am to 1 pm on Saturday, closed Sunday. Admission is free.

Town Hall The red-brick town hall was built in 1893 on the border of Counties Down and Armagh. So fierce was the rivalry between the two counties that it was erected right on the border, which meant building it on a three-arched bridge over the Clanrye river. The cannon outside was captured during the Crimean War and given to the town in memory of the men who volunteered to fight in the war.

Newry Canal You can hardly miss Newry Canal in the centre of town where it shadows the river, separated from it by a narrow strip of land. It runs for 29 km out to Lough Neagh. Victoria Lock, south of the town, has been restored for visitors; the town authorities are now looking for £25 million to restore the whole canal and reopen it for leisure traffic.

Town Trail While it's certainly not a pretty town, Newry repays a bit of foot-slogging, especially if you've picked up a copy of the new town trail, either from the tourist office or from the Newry Regeneration Project offices at 10-20 The Mall (☎ 01693-250303). Depending on how much time you've got there are two versions, a long and a short trail, both starting from the town hall.

Places to Stay *Ashton House* (☎ 01693-62120) is on Fathom Line on the Omeath Rd, close to town. It does B&B for £14, and all rooms have their own bathroom. The modern *Hillside* (☎ 01693-65484) is eight km north off the Belfast road and charges £14 for B&B in a single room. Finally for somewhere central, *Castle View*(☎ 01693-68786) on Chapel St charges £15 for B&B in a single room. The large modern *Mourne Country Hotel* (☎ 01693-67922) was bombed in 1993 but should have reopened by the time you read this.

Places to Eat There are numerous places to stop for a bite. The *Friar Tuck* fast-food outlets on Monaghan St and Sugar Island are good of their kind. *Snaubs* in Monaghan St has a range of healthier possibilities including vegetarian options and good bread. The *Ambassador* on Hill St is good for familiar set fare at reasonable prices: cottage pie for £3, roast beef for £4. It accepts punts for pounds on a one for one basis. For good steaks the *Brass Monkey* on Trevor Hill is the usual grill and is relatively cheap. Chinese dishes are best in the *Rose Garden Restaurant & Take-away* on Sugar Island, with dinner at around £10. Pub food can be had in the *Quayside Inn* on Canal St.

Entertainment The two-screen Savoy Cinema is in Merchants Quay (☎ 01693-67549).

Getting There & Away From Belfast's Europa Bus Station (☎ 01232-320011) on Glengall St buses run regularly to Newry Station (☎ 01693-63531) on Edward St. From the Mall in Newry, Ulsterbus No 39 leaves once or twice an hour for Kilkeel, passing through Rostrevor and Warrenpoint.

Getting Around A Taxis (☎ 01693-69988) are one of the many companies in the town.

County Armagh

County Armagh could be – should be – a major tourist attraction. Quite apart from the venerable town of Armagh, there are some wonderful prehistoric sites, and sights, in the surrounding countryside and a week or more could easily be spent here. Unfortunately, modern history came close to rendering the county a no-go area. Apart from small Protestant outposts like Bessbrook, County Armagh is strongly Catholic and its nationalist identity is keenly felt. The resolve of its people to refuse incorporation into the UK is steadfastly maintained; nowhere else is there so strong a sense of Ireland being occupied by a foreign force. Even with the peace, the evidence of barely suppressed conflict is everywhere apparent, but Armagh is also very beautiful and deserves more visitors.

ARMAGH TOWN

Armagh (*Ard Mhacha*), one of the towns most worth visiting in the North, has suffered badly from the social and political unrest; witness the boarded-up remains of the courthouse, destroyed by a huge bomb in 1993. Here, as elsewhere, the ceasefire offers hope for a rapid tourist peace dividend, and both the St Patrick's Trian and Navan Fort developments are indicative of an effort to turn things round quickly.

History

This compact little city lays claim to being one of Ireland's oldest settlements. Legend has it that the hill now home to the Church of Ireland cathedral was once the power base of Queen Macha, wife of Nevry, some time during the first millennium BC. She gave her name to the city, whose Irish form, Ard Macha, means 'Macha's height'. St Patrick set up the first Christian church in Ireland here, on a site at the base of the hill. Later the local chieftain, a convert to the new religion, gave Patrick the hilltop, and a church of some kind has stood on that spot for over 15 centuries, predating Canterbury as a Christian religious site. By the 8th century Armagh was one of Europe's best known centres of religion, learning and craftwork. Its fame was its undoing, as the Vikings raided the city 10 times between 831 and 1013, taking slaves and valuables, and leaving many dead in their wake. Brian Boru, who died in 1014 near Dublin during the last great battle to defeat the Vikings, was buried on the north side of the cathedral. With the Vikings gone, the Irish clans fought each other for the city, and the Norman settlement in the 12th and 13th centuries saw more attacks. But the religious life continued, with the conversion from Celtic Christianity to Catholic customs in the 12th century and the establishment of a Franciscan friary in 1263. What the Vikings and Normans hadn't managed, the Reformation did. The monasteries and educational establishments were destroyed by either English or Irish forces fighting yet again for control of the city. By the 17th century little was left of a once flourishing city.

During the plantation, Irish landowners were thrown off their lands, and settlers from England and Scotland took their place. Today's Armagh City is a largely Georgian construct and owes its distinctive architecture to Richard Robinson, a Church of

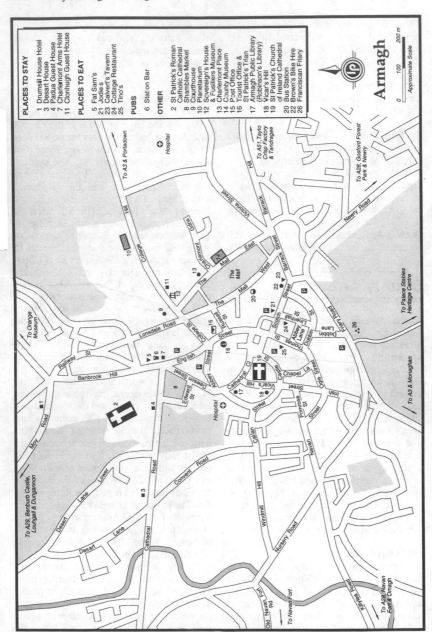

PLACES TO STAY

1 Drumsill House Hotel
3 Desart House
4 Padua Guest House
7 Charlemont Arms Hotel
11 Clonhugh Guest House

PLACES TO EAT

5 Fat Sam's
21 Jodie's
23 Calvert's Tavern
24 Cottage Restaurant
25 Tino's

PUBS

6 Station Bar

OTHER

2 St Patrick's Roman
  Catholic Cathedral
8 Shambles Market
9 Courthouse
10 Planetarium
12 Sovereign's House
  & Fusiliers Museum
13 Charlemont Place
14 County Museum
15 Post Office
16 Tourist Office &
  St Patrick's Trian
17 Armagh Public Library
  (Robinson's Library)
18 St Patrick's Church
  of Ireland Cathedral
19 Vicar's Hill
20 Bus Station
22 Brown's Bike Hire
26 Franciscan Friary

Armagh

0   100   200 m

Approximate Scale

Ireland primate. By the time of his arrival in 1765 the town had recovered, economically at least, from the many invasions and had a flourishing linen industry. In 1995 its old city status was restored again.

Information

The helpful tourist office (☎ 01861-527808) is in English St inside the building housing St Patrick's Trian (see below). It's open from 9 am to 5.30 pm, Monday to Saturday, and Sunday 2 to 5 pm all year round and can provide information on the limited places to stay, restaurants and music bars. The car park next door charges 25p for two hours and 75p for four. If you are intending to spend just one day here don't do it on Sunday when, like the rest of Northern Ireland, Armagh more or less closes down.

St Patrick's Church of Ireland Cathedral

The core of the building dates back to medieval times while the rather dull sandstone-clad exterior is the result of a 19th-century restoration by Primate Beresford. Around the exterior are a series of carved heads, and inside, along with the chilly wooden pews of established religion, are some interesting plaques and an 11th-century Celtic cross. The chapter house has assorted paraphernalia from the ancient city. Every time anyone has knocked down a house or rebuilt a wall and found some ancient object, it has been deposited here, unexamined and unexplained. There is usually someone around who can tell you what's known about the collection.

On the west wall of the north transept a plaque commemorates the burial of Brian Ború. Near the cathedral, **Vicar's Hill** is one of the oldest terraces in Ireland, built in the 18th century by Richard Castle in the Palladian style. The ghost of a green lady is said to haunt the area. Beside St Patrick's Cathedral on the corner of Abbey St is the **Public Library**(☎ 01861-523142), also known as Robinson's Library, which has several ancient manuscripts, a set of 1838 Ordnance Survey maps and a first edition of *Gulliver's Travels*, annotated by Swift himself. The library is open from 10 am to 1 pm and 2 to 4 pm, Monday to Friday; other times by appointment.

St Patrick's Roman Catholic Cathedral

From the Church of Ireland cathedral you can walk down Dawson St and Edward St to the other St Patrick's Cathedral, built between 1838 and 1873, with the famine interrupting building work for a while. It is built in the Gothic Revival style, with huge twin towers dominating the approach up flight after flight of steps. Inside it seems almost Byzantine, with every piece of wall and ceiling covered in brilliantly coloured mosaics. The sanctuary was modernised in 1981 by Liam McCormick and has a distinctive tabernacle holder and crucifix which – seem out of place among the mosaics and statues of the rest of the church.

The Mall

Back along English St (stopping to admire the Shambles at the corner of English St and Cathedral Rd) and Russell St, you come to the Mall: not a collection of supermarkets and dress shops, but a pleasantly laid out park which once held horse races, cock fighting and bull baiting sessions, until Richard Robinson decided it was a bit low-class for a city of learning. Now several war memorials stand sentinel over the flowerbeds.

At the top of the Mall behind wire mesh fences, barbed wire and video cameras used to stand the **courthouse**, built in 1809 by Armagh man Francis Johnston, who later became one of Ireland's most famous architects. It was destroyed by a huge bomb in 1993 and the site is still under restoration. On the opposite corner the **Sovereign's House**, built for the Armagh equivalent of the mayor, was also damaged by the explosion.

Farther along the Mall East, away from the courthouse, is a series of Georgian terraces. Charlemont Place is a creation of Francis Johnston, and so is the County Museum's portico, fronting a more workaday building originally put up as a school.

County Museum

In the Mall East, Armagh has one of Ireland's nicer small museums (☎ 01861-523070), its showcases pleasantly filled with prehistoric axeheads, items found in bogs, old clothes, corn dollies and strawboy outfits, plus some very dead stuffed wildlife, and military costumes and equipment. It's open from 10 am to 5 pm, Monday to Saturday (with a one-hour lunch break on Saturday), but sometimes closes on bank holidays. Admission is free.

Royal Irish Fusiliers Museum

The Fusiliers Museum was in the old Sovereign's House, near the courthouse and consisted of much paraphernalia of war: polished silver and brass, medals and the little personal items that survived from the many battles the Fusiliers fought. Unfortunately in the 1993 attack on the courthouse, this museum was also damaged and had to close. It may open again in the future; phone ☎ 01861-522911 or check with the tourist office.

Planetarium

A healthy walk up College Hill from the Mall brings you to the Observatory & Planetarium. The Observatory is not open to the public but the Planetarium (☎ 01861-523689) is. Both buildings are set in gardens which are open to the public during office hours. The Observatory is over 200 years old but still contributes to astronomical research. The Planetarium now has a new Eartharium Gallery designed to give visitors 'a global view of our home'. Both galleries stand in an Astro Park, laid out to show the relationships of the different planets to each other.

The Planetarium is open January to March and September to December Monday to Friday 10 am to 5 pm (with daily shows at 3 pm) and Saturday 1.30 to 5 pm (shows at 2 and 3 pm). From April to June it also opens on Sunday from 1.30 to 5 pm (with shows at 2 and 3 pm). In July and August there are hourly shows on weekdays. Admission to everything costs £3.50/2.50. The exhibition

downstairs is free and quite interesting, with lots of hands-on stuff, a shop and a café.

Palace Stables Heritage Centre

The heritage centre is 10 minutes walk out of town off Friary Rd and stands in the grounds of the Palace Demesne, built by Archbishop Robinson when he was appointed primate of Ireland in 1769. Just as you turn into the demesne, you'll see the ruins of the Franciscan friary dating back to the 13th century. Much of its stonework was taken to build the demesne walls.

The Palace Stables now house a set of tableaux meant to illustrate how a guest would have been entertained in the days of Richard Robinson, but as there are no real artefacts except in the coachman's kitchen downstairs, it's of fairly limited interest. There's a nice coffee shop and craft shop and a children's play room. The Palace Stables are open Monday to Saturday 10 am to 7 pm and Sunday 1 to 7 pm. You have to go round with a guide. The palace itself now houses council offices but the ground floor lobby still retains some of the grandeur of earlier days, with fine portraits of George III and his wife, and it's hoped that tours will eventually include some of the rooms.

Next door to the palace the Primate's Chapel, designed by Thomas Cooley with a little help from Francis Johnston, is now deconsecrated. Inside are fine oak carvings, an elaborate coffered ceiling and stained-glass windows. Beside it steps lead down to a tunnel. Archbishop Robinson didn't like the smell of cooking, so the kitchen was in an outside building connected to the palace by a tunnel. There's also an interesting ice house which would once have been filled to the brim with ice, which didn't melt as long as it wasn't exposed to outside air.

St Patrick's Trian

The old second Presbyterian church behind the tourist office has been turned into a heritage centre (☎ 01861-527808), focusing on the theme of 'faith' in a city so associated with St Patrick. For children there's also a Land of Lilliput exhibition with a rather wonderful model of Gulliver tied down on the ground while the Lilliputians climb all over him. The story of his adventures there is then retold by a gigantic, seemingly real model of Jonathan Swift's famous creation. Inside the centre there's also a restaurant and shop. It's open April to September Monday to Saturday from 10 am to 7 pm, Sunday 1 to 7 pm, and October to March Monday to Saturday 10 am to 5 pm, Sunday 2 to 5 pm. Admission costs £3/1.50, family £8.

Places to Stay

Camping There are no hostels but if you have a tent you can camp at *Gosford Forest Park* (☎ 01861-551277) south of town on the A28 near Markethill. It has a good camp site with lots of facilities and you don't need to get an advance permit. Camping is £5 to £8 a night.

B&Bs Beyond the cathedral in Cathedral Rd are *Padua Guest House* (☎ 01861-522039) at No 63, with rooms at £18 single, and the slightly cheaper *Desart House* (☎ 01861-522387) at No 99 with beds at £15. On College Hill a few doors up from the Fusiliers Museum is pleasant *Clonhugh Guest House* (☎ 01861-522693), also charging £15 per person.

Hotels The *Charlemont Arms Hotel* (☎ 01861-522028) in English St charges £25 single and £42 double with bathroom. On Moy Rd is *Drumsill House Hotel* (☎ 01861-522009). It's small, offers B&B at £40/55 for singles/doubles and has a nightclub at weekends.

Places to Eat

In town there are lots of places to get lunch but evening meals are more of a problem. In St Patrick's Trian the *Pilgrim's Restaurant* does pleasant lunches, including vegeburgers, and has a few outdoor tables for decent days. *Tino's* on Thomas St does fairly inexpensive food in heated trays, so early is best. Despite its rather offputting name, *Fat Sam's* in Lower English St is a bright, stylish place doing tasty jacket potatoes with assorted fillings for around £1.95.

In Gazette Arcade off Scotch St is the *Cottage Restaurant*, with muzak and single flowers in vases on the table. It has a good selection of lunches at around £3. For evening meals at reasonable prices there is *Jodie's* in Scotch St, which also does lunch specials for £3 or less and afternoon coffee. Other than that, the two hotels offer evening meals at around £10 to £15. The Charlemont does children's meals while both do inexpensive lunches. *Calvert's Tavern* at the corner of Scotch and Barrack Sts is open until 9.30 pm even on Saturday.

Entertainment

Rafferty's bar, beside Wellworth's in town, has traditional music on Saturday nights, while the *Station* bar in Lower English St has live music of some kind on Tuesday and Thursday. Out of town, *McAleavey's*, 7.5 km south in Keady, has traditional music, set dancing and singing on Wednesday.

Getting There & Away

The bus terminal (☎ 01861-522266) is in the Mall West. There are connections with Belfast (roughly hourly) and Enniskillen, and a service to Dublin that involves a change of bus at Monaghan. The Belfast-Galway bus also stops in Armagh. A return fare to Belfast is £7.

Getting Around

Bikes can be hired from Brown's Bikes (☎ 01861-522782) at 21A Scotch St for £4 per day.

AROUND ARMAGH TOWN
Navan Fort

A little over three km west of Armagh is Navan Fort or Emain Macha, an Irish Camelot and the principal archaeological site in Ulster. The Egyptian geographer Ptolemy marked this site on his map of the known world in the 2nd century AD, naming it Isamnion.

Legend has it that a pregnant woman called Macha was forced to race against the king's horses here; at the end of the race she died giving birth to twins, and the name Emain Macha means 'twins of Macha'. Another legend says that it was the great Queen Macha who began this place, marking out the area with her brooch.

Whatever its origins, the hill was the site for homes and a huge temple during both the Iron and Bronze Ages. At one stage an enormous timber structure was filled with lime and deliberately burnt, suggesting that it was sent on its way to heaven rather than sacked by its enemies. Close by is a Bronze Age pond now called the King's Stables where remains of bronze castings have been found.

An impressive new visitor centre designed in the shape of a Bronze Age building details the excavation of the site and retells the legends associated with it. Afterwards it's just a ten-minute walk behind the centre to the site itself which can seem uninspiring on a dull day, but offers magnificent views on a good one. The centre is open Monday to Friday all year from 10 am to 5 pm, Saturday from 11 am and Sunday from noon. In April,

May, June and September it stays open till 6 pm on weekdays, and in July and August until 7 pm (also opening an hour earlier at 11 am on Sunday). Admission costs £3.75/2.10. There's a small tearoom and shop. You can get there on bus No 73 from Armagh or it's just about walkable.

Orange Museum

This Orange Order museum is 10 km north from Armagh at Loughgall and was created in 1961 on the premises of what was then a pub. It is open during office hours; enquire in the building next door. It contains sashes and banners, and weapons from the Battle of the Diamond in 1795 between Protestant 'Peep o' Day Boys' and Catholic 'Defenders'. This took place at Diamond Hill five km north-east of the village and led to the founding of the Orange Order.

Ardress House

The 17th-century Ardress House (☎ 01762-

The Orange Order

Wherever there's a sizeable Protestant population in Northern Ireland, you will come across buildings, ranging from sheds like scout huts to imposing mansions, designated as 'Orange Lodges'. The Orange Order is a secretive Irish Protestant political society named after King William III of Orange, the 'hero' of the Battle of the Boyne. It owes its origins to a quarrel between Protestants and Catholics in County Armagh in 1795 which blew up into the 'Battle of the Diamond' as the Protestant 'Peep o' Day Boys' and the Catholic 'Defenders' slogged it out for supremacy.

The battle over, the Protestants determined to set up what was originally called the Orange Society to defend Protestantism and the Protestant succession to the English throne from what they saw as a creeping tide of green Catholicism. Lodges quickly spread through Ireland, into Britain and thence to the colonies. Secret societies always make governments twitchy (viz the Freemasons) and this one was no exception. In 1835 the House of Commons petitioned the king to abolish all secret societies and those excluding people on grounds of their religion. The target was clearly the Orange Order, but the petition was not successful.

Since then the Orange Order has flourished, bearing much responsibility for strengthening the resistance to the granting of Home Rule in 1912 and objecting to almost any proposals for sorting out the mess in the North which wouldn't leave the Protestants riding high. There have been sporadic efforts to stop their provocative 'marching season' which extends from Easter through to the 12 July when they round things off with a giant celebration of 'their' victory in 1690, complete with pipes, drums and outsize bonfires. To an outsider, these marches can look colourful and harmless, quirky variations on carnival floats and Salvation Army bands, but it's worth remembering that many of these middle-aged 'apprentice boys' in their sashes and bowler hats represent the intractable 'No Surrender' face of Irish politics which has made it so difficult to make any headway over the years. ∎

851236) started life as a farmhouse and was upgraded to a manor house in 1760. Much of the original interior remains and the farmyard still functions, with a piggery and smithy. There are pleasant walks around the wooded grounds. From April to June and in September it opens at weekends and on bank holidays from 2 to 6 pm. In July and August it opens daily except Tuesday. In May to June and September the farm part is open noon to 4 pm. Admission is £2/1, family £5. Ardress House is reached by taking the road to Loughgall, which is on the right shortly after the beginning of the A29 to Dungannon. It's 14 km from Armagh.

The Argory

A fine country house in 315 acres of woodland, The Argory (☎ 018687-84753) retains most of its 1824 fittings; some rooms are lit by acetylene gas from the house's private plant. It's open the same hours as Ardress House and admission costs £2.20 (£1.10 child) or £1 if you just want to see the grounds. It's on the Derrycaw Rd, 3½ km from Moy.

Tayto Crisp Factory

The crisps (potato chips) factory at Tandragee on the A51 can be inspected. The factory is inside a castle which was destroyed and rebuilt on many occasions, the last rebuilding, by Lord Mandeville, taking place in 1836. Every stage of the potatoes' mutation from living vegetable to addictive snack can be seen, and you get to sample the freshly made delicacies. Phone ☎ 01762-840249 well in advance to arrange a tour or see if there is one you can tack on to. Tours usually operate at 10.30 am and 1.30 pm Tuesday and on Friday mornings only.

Benburb Castle & Museum

The castle was founded by Shane O'Neill, who had a stronghold here long before the English arrived; not a trace of this now remains. In 1611 Sir Richard Wingfield added a barn which does still stand. In the 19th century floors were raised and a private house was incorporated into the building.

During WW II American troops used the place as a hospital and the towers were altered to allow access to the roofs. Benburb Castle is now entering its fifth life as a tourist attraction restored along 17th-century lines. At the moment the key to the building can be collected from the Benburb Valley Heritage Centre at the Servite Priory nearby, but when the restoration is complete it will open at regular hours.

Half a mile's walk from the castle is the new **Benburb Valley Heritage Centre** in a restored linen mill. Although work here is not yet complete, the mill is open from 10 am to 5 pm Tuesday to Sunday. Admission is £2/1.

The village of Benburb in County Tyrone is 11 km north-west of Armagh; take the A29 and then turn left onto the B128. The centre is on the left and clearly marked, and the castle is a short distance farther along the road.

Gosford Forest Park

At this relaxing picnic spot children will enjoy the weird and wonderful poultry on display. Nature trails work their way around the park and through the trees and in the middle of it all is a vast mock-Norman castle that is not open to the public. Admission to the park (☎ 01861-551277) is £2.50 if you're in a car, £1 if you're on foot. A child is charged 50p. The park is by the side of the A28, south-east of town near Markethill. Town buses to Markethill stop outside.

SOUTH ARMAGH

During 'the Troubles' the notoriety of south Armagh earned it the forbidding epithet of Bandit Country, which was hardly likely to attract visitors. The intensity of the armed conflict between the IRA and the British army was nowhere more evident or dramatic. Many small towns were effectively sealed off by the British military, and army helicopters buzzed overhead. Even now wreaths by the roadside bear silent homage to the many victims of the fighting, and it would be hard to venture into the remoter areas without being made aware of the demands of the

Catholic side for any peace settlement: the disbanding of the RUC, the freeing of all political prisoners, demilitarisation (by which they mean the total withdrawal of the British army) and a united Ireland.

The area is strongly Catholic with small Protestant communities living a beleaguered existence amid more Irish tricolours than ever graced the Republic. Now that the army has retreated there's nothing to stop you visiting what is a lovely part of Ireland with some interesting archaeological and ecclesiastical places to see. It's unlikely that anyone will ask any questions even though helicopters still buzz overhead, and the hilltops still sprout listening posts and watchtowers.

To our knowledge, no tourist has ever been attacked in south Armagh even at the height of the Troubles, but you should still exercise caution. If you have a British accent, don't assume a warm welcome awaits in local pubs even now.

Most places worth seeing could be taken in on a half-day trip by car. On a bicycle give yourself the whole day. The following itinerary starts from Armagh or Newry.

Bessbrook
This small town was founded in the mid-19th century by a Quaker industrialist, and the layout of the houses and shops later gave the Cadbury family the idea of building Bournville near Birmingham in England. Most of the buildings are made from local granite and arranged around two squares. Originally everyone here worked in the manufacturing of linen, and because of the Quaker influence no pubs were built. Even now there's not even a café in town. From Newry take the A25 west and turn right onto the B133 to Bessbrook. From Armagh take the B31 south to Newtownhamilton and turn left onto the A25 and then, before Newry, left again onto the B133.

Camlough
Camlough is only a short distance from Bessbrook but quite different in character and political allegiance, as the flying tricolours make plain. There is a fish and chip

shop here and a couple of pubs serving bar food. To get to Camlough, do not return to the B133, but leave Bessbrook from the other end that you came in and turn left immediately after the army control box. Continue down to the main road and turn right back onto the A25. Camlough is a short distance along this road.

Killevy Churches
Surrounded by beech trees, these ruined Siamese-twin churches were built on the site of a 5th-century nunnery founded by St Monenna and plundered by the Vikings in 923. During the Middle Ages a convent of Augustinian nuns was founded, but it was dissolved in 1542; the last abbess was Alicia O'Hanlon. The eastern church is 15th-century, while the western one is 12th-century and the massive lintel on the western door with the granite jambs may be 200 years older still. Originally, the two churches were nearly a metre apart but became joined at an unknown date.

To the north, the traditional site of St Monenna's grave is marked by a granite slab, and a signed walkway leads to a holy well. Heading west out of Camlough, turn left at the crossroads, keeping the lough on the right. A junction on the road points right to the churches and left to Bernish Rock Viewpoint. The churches are five km from Camlough and can be visited at any time.

Clonlum South Cairn
From the Killevy churches, travel south, passing after one km a sign on the left side of the road to the tomb. Mainly of specialist interest, this tomb is on the way to the Slieve Gullion Forest Park. The stones enclose a single chamber with the big stone slabs bearing a now broken capstone.

Slieve Gullion Forest Park
From the Clonlum South Cairn continue along the road for about 1½ km and turn right into the B113 for the Forest Park. The coniferous forest covers the lower slopes of Slieve Gullion and a gorgeous 13-km drive takes in a walk to a lake. The drive emerges

from the trees to picturesque views of the Ring of Gullion, a circle of small hills around Slieve Gullion. Slieve Gullion can be climbed from the south or north. The south approach has a forest road for the first part of the journey, while the north approach is made a little easier because of a rough path all the way. On the summit there are two early Bronze Age cairns.

The park's interpretive centre was being extensively rebuilt at the time of writing. In the past it was only open on Sunday from 1 to 7 pm, but with luck the hours should lengthen when the work is finished. To check phone ☎ 01693-848084. The park itself is open from Easter to September from 10 am. Admission is £2 per car.

Ballymacdermot Cairn
From the Slieve Gullion Forest Park turn right at the exit, down to a crossroads and left for the road back to the churches. Turn right at the junction where the churches are, in order to return to the crossroads where the sign for Bernish Viewpoint was seen earlier. Go straight across and carry on for a couple of km. At a junction a sign points left for the cairn. The cairn is in an attractive position on the slopes of Ballymacdermot Mountain overlooking a plain. There are two burial chambers with sections of the roofs still intact. When the site was excavated some 30 years ago, Neolithic artefacts were found. From the cairn the road continues three km into Newry.

Kilnasaggart Stone & Moyry Castle
From Ballymacdermot Cairn, retrace the three km back to the crossroads, and this time turn left for Jonesborough. At the next junction, by a post office and corner shop, turn right (signposted for Forkhill) for 1.5 km and then left for Jonesborough at the sign. After one km turn left at the T-junction signposted for Crossmaglen and Jonesborough, and after a couple of hundred metres turn right as indicated by the sign. From here it is a short distance to another T-junction where you should leave your bicycle or car. Follow the

footpath across two fields and stiles to the stone.

The 8th-century granite pillar marks the site of an early Christian cemetery on the great Slighe Miodhluachra road from Drogheda to Dunseverick on the Causeway Coast in County Antrim. The Irish inscription records a dedication by Ternohc, son of Ceran Bic. On the other side are a number of carefully inscribed crosses inside circles. From the T-junction it is a short walk to the right and Moyry Castle, built in 1601 by Lord Mountjoy to secure the Moyry Pass (the Gap of the North). All that remains is a tower with gunloops.

Crossmaglen
From the T-junction nearest to the Kilnasaggart Stone, retrace the 1.5 km to the crossroads and turn left. After a couple of hundred metres turn right, signposted for Newry. The B113 is straight ahead; take a left for Forkhill. Turn left in the village of Forkhill and carry on for about two km until an unmarked T-junction is reached. Turn right for Crossmaglen (*Crois Mhic Lionnáin*). This small town has a fierce reputation, with more than 20 soldiers having been killed in the square alone. Peace or no, it's still dominated by a sprawling, ugly army-cum-police post built right against the houses. Notwithstanding this, people go about their daily business as if oblivious to the helicopters and the listening devices.

There are no specific sights to see in what would otherwise be a sleepy little backwater but the army post makes a visit here educational, not to mention sobering if you're British. About seven km from Crossmaglen on the road to Newry there is a small **folk museum** containing a miscellany of mostly local items. It keeps very irregular opening hours.

Places to Stay
In Crossmaglen *Murtagh's Bar & Lounge* (☎ 01693-861378) at 13 North St offers B&B from £13.50 a head. On the B30 back to Newry, just after the junction with the A29, *Lima* (☎ 01693-861944) at 16 Drumalt

Rd, Silverbridge, charges £12.50 a head with another £8.50 for dinner. *Likane Farmhouse* (☎ 01693-868348) at 10 Corliss Rd does rock-bottom B&B from £10 a head.

Places to Eat

In Forkhill the *Welcome Inn* on the main street, near a small antique shop, does soup and sandwiches most of the time. In Crossmaglen the *Glen* in the square is a pleasant café doing light meals like burgers and curried chips. There are also a few pubs in the square offering bar food. *Chums* is close to the Glen while *McConville's Place* is across the other side.

Getting There & Away

Ulsterbus No 42 runs four services a day between Newry and Crossmaglen, except on Sunday.

Counties Derry & Antrim

Ireland is not short of fine stretches of coast, but the Causeway Coast from Portstewart in County Derry to Ballycastle in County Antrim, and the Antrim Coast from Ballycastle to Belfast, are as magnificent as you could ask for. Most spectacular of all is the surreal landscape of the Giant's Causeway, familiar from many a postcard and calendar, and looking like some weird image from a Magritte painting.

GETTING AROUND

In winter it's difficult to explore the Causeway and Antrim Coasts using public transport, but in summer there are two regular bus services. The Antrim Coaster – No 252 – operates between Belfast and Coleraine twice daily, Monday to Saturday from late May to late September. It leaves Belfast at 9.10 am and 2 pm, and Coleraine at 9.50 am and 4.10 pm. The trip takes about four hours. The Bushmills Open Topper – No 177 – is an open-top double-decker bus that runs (weather permitting) from the Giant's Causeway to Coleraine four times daily in July and August. It leaves the Giant's Causeway at 10.15 am and 12.30, 3.05 and 4.55 pm; from Coleraine it goes at 9.20 and 11.30 am and 2.10 and 4 pm. The trip takes about an hour.

DERRY & ANTRIM

Highlights
- Seeing the Giant's Causeway 'in the flesh'
- Walking round Murlough Bay
- Tottering across Carrick-a-rede Rope Bridge
- Camping in Glenariff Forest Park
- Discovering the origins of the Troubles in Derry's Tower Museum
- Learning more than you ever dreamt of knowing about linen at Lisburn's Linen Heritage Centre
- Exploring the Walled Town of Derry
- Visiting ruinous Dunluce Castle
- Visiting much less ruinous Carrickfergus Castle
- Having lunch in Cushendun

County Derry

The chief attraction of the county is the town of Derry (*Doire*) itself, nestled poetically by the wide sweep of the River Foyle. There is a terribly sad contrast between the cosy feel of the town itself and its recent past, scarred by injustice and bitterness. Inland from Derry the towns are dour and staunchly Protestant, evoking and living out the history of apartheid they represent. After the defeat of Hugh O'Neill in 1603, this part of the county was systematically planted with English and Scottish settlers and there is little here to attract the tourist. Back on the coast, though, the atmosphere perks up in Portstewart.

DERRY CITY

Although Derry is now more peaceful than at any time since the 1960s, there can still be a sharp edge to its atmosphere; in May 1995 rioting broke out inside the walls when British Prime Minister John Major arrived to visit the Tower Museum. Derry is as safe to visit as anywhere else in Northern Ireland, although it might not be wise to hang around some of the nationalist pubs in the Bogside

DERRY & ANTRIM

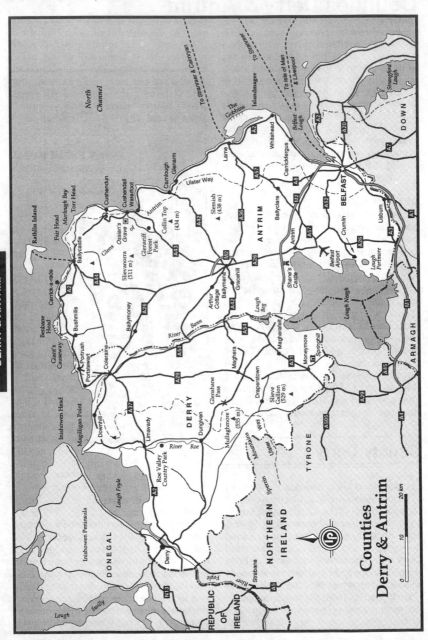

North
Channel

To Stranraer & Cairnryan
To Stranraer
To Isle of Man
& Liverpool

The
Gobbins

Islandmagee

Belfast
Lough

Strangford
Lough

DOWN

A2

A20

A7

Whitehead

Carrickfergus

Larne

Glenarm

A2

A8

Camlough

Ulster Way

Glenarm

Antrim

A57

BELFAST

Cushendun

A43

Slemish
(438 m)
▲

Ballyclare

Belfast
Airport

Lisburn

A52

A1

Cushendall
Waterfoot

Collin Top
(434 m)
▲

A42

A36

Antrim

Crumlin

A3

Ossian's
Grave

A26

A57

Lough
Portmore

A26

Ballycastle
▲

Glens

Glenariff
Forest
Park

M2

Shane's
Castle ■

M1

Slievanorra
(511 m)
▲

Ballymena

Gracehill

ARMAGH

Fair Head
Murlough Bay
Torr Head

Arthur
Cottage

A42

Lough
Beg

Rathlin Island

A44

Lough Neagh

A45

Benbane
Head
Carrick-a-rede

A2

Ballymoney

A26

River Bann

A54

Magherafelt

A31

Moneymore
Springhill

A29

Giant's
Causeway

Bushmills

Portrush
Portstewart

Coleraine

A54

Maghera

Draperstown

Slieve
Gallion
(529 m)
▲

A505

A5

Magilligan Point

Downhill

A37

A29

Glenshane
Pass

Mullaghmore
(555 m)
▲

TYRONE

Inishowen Head

Limavady

DERRY

Dungiven

Sperrin Mountains
Ulster Way

Lough Foyle

A2

Roe Valley
Country Park

River Roe

NORTHERN
IRELAND

Counties
Derry & Antrim

DONEGAL

Inishowen Peninsula

Derry

River Foyle

Strabane

A5

A5

Swilly

Lough

REPUBLIC
OF
IRELAND

M3

0   10   20 km

or Creggan late at night if you have an English accent. For the time being, the walled city area retains a slight air of schizophrenia, the Shipquay St side being lively and relaxed while the Bishop Gate end is blighted by the forbidding RUC and army post. Provided the peace lasts, expect all this to change and not at snail's pace either. Already McDonald's and Marks & Spencer have earmarked plots and three new hotels are planned.

History

Although you sometimes get the feeling that Derry's history started in 1688, in fact there has been a settlement on the site since the 6th century AD when St Columba (otherwise known as St Columb, Columcille or Colmcille) founded a monastic community on the hillside, probably where the Church of Ireland chapel of St Augustine stands today. In the Middle Ages Derry seems to have escaped the worst of the Viking raids and had a burst of independent prosperity in the 12th and 13th centuries under the Mac Lochlainn dynasty.

In the late 16th century Queen Elizabeth I became determined to conquer troublesome Ulster, and an English garrison arrived in Derry in 1566. In 1600 a second, more lastingly successful attempt to secure the town was made during the Nine Years War (1594-1603) against the O'Neills and O'Donnells. In 1603 an English trading colony was established and given city status. Sir Cahir O'Doherty attacked this settlement in 1608 and virtually wiped it out, but in 1609 James I determined to settle matters for good by granting land to English and Scottish settlers. The wealthy London trade guilds were put in charge of 'planting' Derry and were responsible for the present layout of the walled city and for the walls themselves.

In 1688 the gates of Derry were slammed shut by 13 apprentice boys before the Catholic forces of King James II, and some months later the great Siege of Derry commenced. For 105 days the Protestant citizens of Derry withstood bombardment, disease and starvation. Rejecting proffered peace terms, they declared that they would eat the Catholics first and then each other before surrendering. By the time a relief ship burst through the boom on the River Foyle and broke the siege, an estimated quarter of the

The Derry Skeleton

Round about town you'll soon spot the Derry skeleton, a mournful figure with his skull leant to one side, adorning the city's coat of arms. There are several stories to explain how he came to be there. One suggests that he is associated with the 1689 Siege of Derry; another that he represents Sir Cahir O'Doherty who had sacked Derry in 1608 to avenge an insult. Neither of these explanations is likely to be right though, because the skeleton was already gracing the arms in 1600 when the first plantation of Derry took place.

The most convincing suggestion is that the skeleton represents one Walter de Burgo, an Anglo-Norman knight and the nephew of the Red Earl, Richard de Burgo. He is said to have fallen out with his cousin William de Burgo, the earl of Ulster, who had him imprisoned in a dungeon in Greencastle in County Donegal. There he eventually starved to death in 1332. If this story is true, the castle also shown on the coat of arms would probably be Greencastle. In 1311 Edward II granted the Inishowen Peninsula and the island of Derry to Richard de Burgo, thus explaining how his nephew ended up immortalised on the city's coat of arms. ∎

city's 30,000 inhabitants had died. It was not the final victory for the Protestant forces, but the long distraction gave King William time to increase his army's strength, and it thus played an important role in his victory at the Battle of the Boyne on 12 July 1690.

In the 19th century Derry was one of the main ports from which the Irish emigrated to the USA, a fact commemorated by the statue of a departing family standing in Waterloo Place. It also played a vital role in the transatlantic trade in shirts and collars; supposedly, local factories provided uniforms for both sides in the American Civil War. To this day Derry still supplies the American president with twelve free shirts every year.

More recently Derry has been a flashpoint for the Troubles. Resentment at the long-running domination and gerrymandering of the council by Protestants boiled over in the civil rights marches of 1968. Simultaneously, attacks on the Catholic Bogside district began, but by the time of the 12 July celebrations in 1969 the people there were prepared. Confrontation between Catholics and Protestants led to a veritable siege of the Bogside, and for over two days the community withdrew behind barricades. It was as if the Bogside had seceded from the UK, and even the government in the South began to talk of Ireland's duty to protect its own. Open warfare and disintegration could only be prevented by military intervention, and on 14 August 1968 British troops entered Derry.

In 1972 the city's 'Bloody Sunday' saw the deaths of 13 unarmed Catholic demonstrators at the hands of the army. Today the old Bogside estate has been rebuilt, giving a curiously modern and neat feel to what was once a violent ghetto.

Orientation

The old centre of Derry is the small walled city on the west bank of the River Foyle. At its heart is the square called the Diamond, with Shipquay St, Ferryquay St, Butcher St and Bishop St converging on it. Arriving by train you'll fetch up on the east side of the River Foyle, while buses stop on the west bank, just round the corner from the walled city. The Craigavon road bridge has linked the two banks of the river since 1933; farther downstream is the Foyle Bridge, built to

---

What's in a Name?

Derry's original name was *Daire Calgaigh*, meaning 'oak grove of Calgach'. In the 10th century it was renamed *Doire Colmcille*, or 'the oak grove of St Columba', in remembrance of the 6th-century saint who had established the first monastic settlement on the site. However, in 1609 when the English government decided to 'plant' Derry properly, it signed an agreement with the Corporation of London to provide the necessary settlers. To commemorate this fact the new city's name was lengthened to Londonderry.

Until the Troubles, people readily abbreviated the town's name to 'Derry'. At that point, however, what anyone called it suddenly became a touchstone for their political views, with Protestant Unionists dogmatically asserting the full Londonderry and Catholic Republicans equally firmly shortening it to Derry. Although the city is still officially called Londonderry, in 1984 the city council was renamed Derry City Council.

The naming controversy has persisted until today, turning the normally straightforward business of buying a bus ticket into a political minefield; you can easily judge someone's position on the conflict by noting whether they react to your Derry with an emphatic *London*derry or vice versa. All over the country, but especially in the border areas, you'll see the word 'London-' scratched off offending signposts.

Luckily, not everyone takes the Derry/Londonderry controversy so seriously. In Belfast, for example, wags have dropped both possibilities, opting instead for the simple 'Stroke City'! ∎

provide a second crossing point in 1984. The
Catholic Bogside area is below the walls to
the west while to the south is a Protestant
estate known as the Fountain. There are car
parks on Butcher St and beside the station.

Information

The tourist office in Pittsburgh House at 8
Bishop St in the walled city houses both the
Northern Ireland Tourist Board (☎ 01504-
267284) and Bord Fáilte (☎ 01504-369501).
The still to be completed Heritage Centre at
4-22 Butcher St (☎ 01504-373177) houses
the genealogy centre; it's open from Monday
to Friday from 9 am to 5 pm for anyone
wishing to trace their ancestors.

All the banks will change punts into
pounds and vice versa. Outside banking
hours there's a bureau de change (☎ 01504-
260636) on the top floor of the Richmond
Centre, which is open until 5.30 pm from
Monday to Wednesday and Saturday, and
until 9.30 pm on Thursday and Friday.

The USIT travel office at 33 Ferryquay St
(☎ 01504-371888) is open Monday to
Friday from 9.30 am to 5.30 pm and on
Saturday from 10 am to 1 pm.

Bookshops The Bookworm at 16-18 Bishop
St (☎ 01504-261616) is excellent for material
on the Troubles, and sells the useful little *Political
Guide to Derry* with a street map of places
associated with the city's political life, past and
present (£2). Alternatively there's the Shipquay
Bookshop on Shipquay St.

Laundry There's a laundrette in Oakgrove
Manor youth hostel. Alternatively, visit
Duds 'n' Suds at 141 Strand Rd, positively
the most glamorous laundrette you'll meet
anywhere in Europe – it has a pool table,
electronic games and a snack bar! It's open
8 am to 9 pm Monday to Friday and until 8
pm on Saturday. A wash and dry costs £3.

City Walls

Until recently, the presence of the army and
of protective iron bars made Derry's magnificent city walls hard to appreciate and
impossible to walk round. Provided the

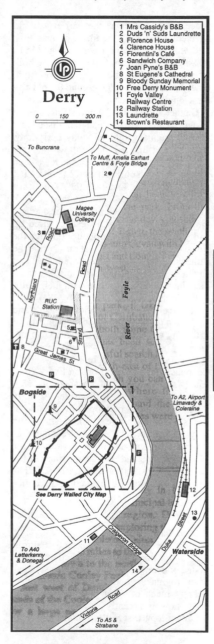

peace holds, however, the barriers should have come down by the time you read this. The walls were built between 1613 and 1618 making Derry the last walled city to be built in Ireland. They're about eight metres high, nine metres thick, and go around the old city for a length of 1.5 km.

Gunner's Bastion, Coward's Bastion and Water Bastion have all been demolished and the four original gates (Shipquay, Ferryquay, Bishop's and Butcher's) rebuilt, while three new gates (New, Ferry and Castle) have been added. Derry's sobriquet, the Maiden City, derives from the fact that the walls have never been breached. The south-west end, overlooking the cathedral on the inside and the Bogside to the north-west, is wired up and provides an army lookout point for the Bogside. Behind the wall that runs beside the cathedral is the Fountain estate, a fenced and battered area that suggests the Protestants there have a lot in common with their Catholic neighbours.

An excellent overview of the Bogside and its defiant murals can be had by going up on to the city walls between Butcher's Gate and the army post. There you will also see behind you in Society St the Apprentice Boys' Hall. Cannons, given by the London livery companies and reminders of the siege of 1689, still point out over the Bogside. An ugly pillar, that used to be topped by a statue of the Reverend George Walker, stands on Royal Bastion. The 2.7-metre statue of Walker, who was one of the leaders of the 1698 resistance and who kept a diary of the siege, was blown off by the IRA in 1973. The restored statue stands beside the Apprentice Boys Hall.

Walled City

After a 1981 survey discovered that almost 30% of the inner city was bombed out, abandoned or derelict, the Inner City Trust began work to make good the damage. Consequently much of what you see inside the walls now is recently restored and has a toy-town look that will no doubt fade with the years.

Tower Museum

Just inside Coward's Bastion, the modern O'Doherty's Tower houses the excellent Tower Museum which tells the story of Derry right through from the days of St Columcille to the present through traditional exhibits and audiovisuals; allow a good two hours to do it justice. It's open Tuesday to Saturday 10 am to 5 pm all year round, and Monday to Saturday from 10 am to 5 pm and Sunday 2 to 5 pm in July and August. Admission costs £2.75/1.

St Columb's Cathedral

Standing within the walls of the old city, St Columb's Cathedral dates from 1628 and shares the austerity of many other Church of Ireland cathedrals, with dark, carved wooden pews, an open timbered roof resting on the carved heads of past bishops and deans, and a gruesome skull-and-crossbones wall tablet in the north aisle. Beside the pulpit is a cross of nails donated by Coventry Cathedral. Unusually, the bishop's throne is placed in the nave; the 18th-century mahogany chair inside the canopy is a beautifully carved example of what is known as Chinese Chippendale.

In the porch is a mortar shell lobbed into the city during the siege by the Jacobites, which carried the terms of surrender. The Chapter House, now designated a museum, contains some bits of flag, old photos and the huge padlocks used to close the city gates in the 17th century. Built in a style known as Planter's Gothic with an embattled exterior, the cathedral now sits rather forlornly surrounded by the barbed wire and surveillance cameras of a more recent siege. Walk around the building to admire the architecture and watch the video cameras watching you. It's open Monday to Friday 9 am to 5 pm, and visitors are asked to donate £1 towards its upkeep.

Derry's Other Churches

The Catholic cathedral of St Eugene in Great James St was dedicated to St Eugene in 1873 by Bishop Keely, and the handsome east window is a memorial to the bishop.

The Long Tower Church, Derry's first post-Reformation Catholic church, stands on the site of the older Tempull Mor church, the cathedral church of the Derry diocese during the Middle Ages. The Long Tower Church was erected in 1784 in neo-Renaissance style and stands just outside the city walls in the Bogside.

Guildhall

Just outside the city walls, the red-brick Guildhall (☎ 01504-365151) was originally built in 1890 and rebuilt after a fire in 1908. As the seat of the old Londonderry Corporation, which institutionalised the policy of discriminating against Catholics over housing and jobs, it incurred the wrath of nationalists and was bombed twice by the IRA in 1972. One of the convicted bombers was elected to the new council in 1985! The Guildhall is noted for its fine stained-glass windows, including one of George V's coronation upstairs; others on the stairs commemorate the various London livery companies that played so divisive a role in the city's development. It is open from 9 am to 5.30 pm, Monday to Friday.

Bogside & the Free Derry Monument

As you step out of Butcher's Gate, the Bogside comes into view, and down on the left is the famous 'You Are Now Entering Free Derry' monument. This was once the end wall of a row of old houses; the area has been rebuilt with modern low-level flats, and is now traversed by a dual carriageway. During the early 1970s, until the army's Operation Motorman smashed the barricades in July 1972, this was a no-go area as far as the military authorities were concerned. It took 5000 soldiers with Chieftain tanks to bring down the barriers. The monument, with its much repainted slogan, remains as a defiant response to the army watchtowers that continue to look down on the Bogside.

Bloody Sunday Memorial

On Sunday, 30 January 1972, some 20,000 civilians marched through Derry in protest at the policy of internment without trial. It now seems clear that the 1st Battalion of the Parachute Regiment opened fire on the unarmed marchers. By the end of the day 13 unarmed people were dead, some shot through the back, and a 14th subsequently died of his injuries. None of those who fired the 108 bullets, or those who gave the order to fire, were ever brought to trial or even disciplined. The subsequent enquiry was a whitewash. To reach the monument leave the walled city by Butcher's Gate; it's a little to the right down near the roadside. The actual incident happened in the enclosed square across the road.

Craigavon Bridge

The double-decker bridge spanning the River Foyle was erected in 1933 and used to carry trains on the lower deck and cars on the upper. Since Northern Ireland's railways were pruned back in 1965, it has carried cars on both decks.

Foyle Valley Railway Centre

Just outside the walled city by the bridge, the centre stands on what was once the junction of four railway lines. Exhibits inside tell the story of the railways, and you can take a 20-minute, four-km excursion on a train with diesel engine. The museum is open April to September, Tuesday to Saturday from 10 am to 4.30 pm, Sunday 2 to 5.30 pm. Admission is free but the excursion costs £2/1.

Harbour Museum

A small, old-fashioned maritime museum, with models of ships and the figurehead of the *Minnehaha*, takes up two rooms of the old Londonderry Port Building on Guildhall St. It's open Monday to Friday from 9 am to 5 pm, and is free.

Amelia Earhart Centre

In 1932 when Amelia Earhart became the first woman to fly solo across the Atlantic she mistook Derry for Paris and landed in a field in what is now the suburb of Ballyarnett (five km north-west of Derry) where a small cottage contains pictures and memorabilia.

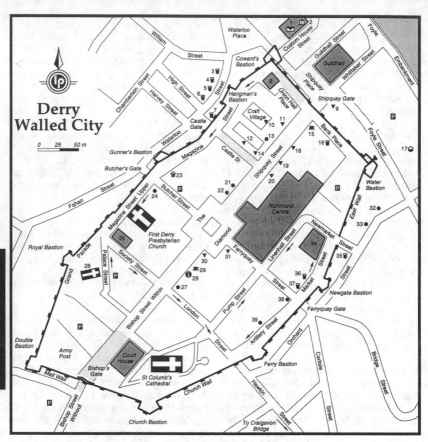

The Centre is open Monday to Thursday 9 am to 4.30 pm, Friday 9 am to 1 pm, admission free. Access is temporarily disrupted, so if you want to see the centre, it's best to phone ☎ 01504-265234 for advice before setting out.

The Fifth Dimension
By the time you read this, a new heritage centre telling the story of the Celts should have opened in Butcher St, just down the road from Oakgrove Manor hostel. The heritage centre is planned to open daily from 10 am to 8 pm.

Organised Tours
Between May and September walking tours depart from the tourist office at 10.30 am and 2.30 pm, Monday to Friday. They cost £1.50 (children and students free) and last about 1½ hours. Every Tuesday and Thursday during July and August a bus tour of the city departs from the bus station at 2 pm; it lasts over two hours and costs £3 (children £2).

Places to Stay
Provided the peace holds, Derry is likely to find the number of would-be visitors outstripping the stock of available beds, at least

PLACES TO STAY			7	Castle Bar
			16	Metro Bar
23	Oakgrove Manor Youth Hostel		35	Badger's Place
			36	Linen Hall
PLACES TO EAT			37	Anchor Inn

		OTHER	
9	Open Oven	1	General Post Office
10	Thra'n Maggie's	2	Harbour Museum
11	Wheeler's	8	O'Doherty's Tower & Tower Museum
12	Boston Tea Party	13	Bridie's Cottage
14	Galley Restaurant	17	Bus Station
15	Bewley's Café	21	Shipquay Bookshop
18	The Townsman	22	Donegal Shop
19	Marlene's Diner	24	Fifth Dimension/Genealogy Centre
20	Beehive Restaurant	25	Apprentice Boys' Hall
29	Malibu Café	26	St Augustine's Church
30	The Sandwich Company	27	Bookworm Bookshop
31	Austin's Department Store	28	Tourist Office
		32	Orchard Gallery
PUBS		33	St Columb's Hall
		34	Rialto Entertaiment Centre
3	Gweedore	38	USIT Travel Office
4	Peadar O'Donnell's	39	The Playhouse
5	Dungloe		
6	Bound for Boston		

DERRY & ANTRIM

until some of the planned new hotels come on line. Booking ahead is advisable, especially in July when an annual gathering of O'Dohertys from around the world puts even greater strain on the accommodation supply.

Hostels The YHANI hostel is in the newly-restored *Oakgrove Manor* at 4-6 Magazine St, inside the city walls near Butcher's Gate (☎ 01504-372273), just 150 metres from the bus station. The cheapest dorm beds without breakfast cost £7, but there's a variety of rooms ranging up to singles at £17.50 for B&B. Cooking and currency exchange facilities are available. If it's full, the *Muff Hostel* (☎ 077-84188) costs IR£5 a night and is eight km from Derry, across the border in Muff, County Donegal. Lough Swilly buses run there regularly for £1.10 but it would be wise to ring ahead as Muff has only one other B&B. In summer you may be able to stay at *Magee University* (☎ 01504-371371) on Northland Rd, at £11.50 a head without breakfast (£6.50 student rate).

B&Bs *Ms Joan Pyne* (☎ 01504-269691) offers B&B for £15 a head in a lovely 19th-century house with stripped pine fittings at 36 Great James St, within walking distance of the bus station. Farther north, at 15 Northland St, there is the slightly officious (but very well run) *Clarence House* (☎ 01504-265342), charging between £15 and £25 a head. Farther along at No 16, *Florence House* (☎ 01504-268093) is slightly cheaper at £14 per person. Farther north again at 86 Duncreggan Rd, *Mrs Cassidy* (☎ 01504-374551) charges £13. You can get to these places on Bus No D6 or by shared black taxi from Foyle St.

Farmhouse accommodation costs about the same as B&B and there are quite a few places out at Eglinton on the A2 to Limavady. For example *Longfield Farm* (☎ 01504-810210) and *Greenan Farm* (☎ 01504-810422) are both £28 for a double. The tourist office has a complete list and will make bookings.

Hotels Two top hotels, at around £80 a double, can be found south of the city and on the east side of the river. The *Beech Hill House Hotel* (☎ 01504-49279) is at 32 Ardmore Rd, Ardmore, while the *Everglades*

Hotel (☎ 01504-46722) is closer in on Prehen Rd, just off the A5 (Victoria Rd). Three other hotels are also on the east side of the river but north of the city. The *Broomhill* (☎ 01504-47995) is £60 a double and is easy to find on the Limavady Rd. A little farther out the *White Horse Hotel* (☎ 01504-860606) is at 68 Clooney Rd and costs £42.50 a room. Nearby and beside the Caw Roundabout at 14 Cloney Rd, the circular *Waterfoot Hotel* (☎ 01504-45500) has doubles including breakfast for £57.

Places to Eat

Cafés & Fast Food Inside the walled city there is plenty of choice along Shipquay St. The *Beehive Restaurant* in the Richmond shopping centre is open until 9 pm on Wednesday, and serves inexpensive meals throughout the day for around £4. Across the road the *Galley Restaurant* boasts home cooking at reasonable prices.

A little farther down Shipquay St, *Wheeler's* dishes up fast food, as does *Marlene's Diner* opposite, which is open until the early hours on Friday night and opens Sunday evening too. At the bottom the latest branch of *Bewley's Café* occupies a fine newly-restored, ex-bank building. *The Sandwich Company* on the corner of the Diamond and *Malibu*, beside the tourist office, are also handy lunch stops. More upmarket is the *Boston Tea Party* in the Craft Village off Shipquay St, which offers sandwiches, quiche, lasagne and good cakes but is only open until 5.30 pm.

Austin's department store on the Diamond has a coffee shop with cakes and sandwiches and fine views over the city centre. Across from the Guildhall, *Open Oven* does good sandwiches, as does *Cappuccino's* opposite the bus station which opens at 7 am. Heading along Strand St, inexpensive places include *Fiorentini's* and another branch of *The Sandwich Company* which opens on Thursday, Friday and Saturday nights for excellent Mexican food.

Pub Food & Restaurants On Shipquay St, the *Townsman* (☎ 01504-260820) is particu-

larly popular at lunch time. Pub food is also available at the *Anchor Inn* and the *Linen Hall* by Ferryquay Gate. The *Dungloe* on Waterloo St is pleasantly untarted up, with photographs of the old Bogside on the walls. *Thra'n Maggies* (☎ 01504-264267) in the Craft Village off Shipquay St is one of the few places to dine in the walled city; it's open till 9.15 pm on weekdays, till 10 pm on Sunday, and a meal won't bust the budget.

On Victoria Rd, just across the bridge from the centre, *Brown's* (☎ 01504-45180) is pleasantly trendy with interesting food at only moderately expensive prices; it's open until 11 pm Tuesday to Saturday, for lunch only on Sunday and closed altogether on Monday. More expensive meals can be enjoyed at the *Seminole* restaurant (☎ 01504-46722) at the Everglades Hotel (dinner for between £10 and £15) or at the *Beech Hill House Hotel* (☎ 01504-49279) (dinner from £15).

Entertainment

Derry does a fine line in themed pubs, many of them masquerading as shops. The liveliest are those along Waterloo St, like the *Gweedore*, which hosts regular music and quiz functions, the *Bound for Boston*, the *Dungloe* and the *Castle Bar*. *Peadar O'Donnell's* is also good for traditional music. The *Metro Bar* on Bank St, just inside the walls, is very popular. Others include the *Anchor Inn* and the *Linen Hall* by Ferryquay Gate, *Badger's Place* on the corner of Newmarket and Orchard Sts just outside the walls, and the *Forum* right beside the bus station and looking like a tea merchant's. You can pick up the *Good Pub Guide to Derry* free in the *The Townsman* in Shipquay St for more suggestions.

Bridie's Cottage in the Craft Village holds music and dance sessions on Wednesday evenings in summer. Classical music shows are often scheduled during the summer months for performance at *Magee University* or the *Guildhall*. The tourist office will have the details. The *Orchard Gallery* (☎ 01504-269675) in Orchard St has regular exhibitions, concerts and drama. Theatrical

TONY WHEELER

PAT YALE

PAT YALE

PAT YALE

TONY WHEELER

TONY WHEELER

A	B
C	D
E	F

County Antrim

A: Carrickfergus Castle
B: Orange Hall, Lisburn
C: Clough Williams-Ellis houses, Cushendun
D: Ireland's smallest church, Portbradden

E: Dunluce Castle
F: Hexagonal basalt columns, Giant's Causeway

TONY WHEELER

TOM SMALLMAN

Counties Tyrone & Fermanagh
Top: Beaghmore Stone Circles, County Tyrone
Bottom: Rural scene near Enniskillen, County Fermanagh

events take place regularly in summer at the *Playhouse* in Artillery St (☎ 01504-264481), the *Rialto Entertainment Centre* nearby in Linenhall St (☎ 01504-260516) and *St Columb's Hall* in Orchard St (☎ 01504-262880).

Things to Buy

Derry Craft Village is tucked away in one of the corner blocks of the walled city. It contains a number of craft shops selling Derry crystal (with a mail service), handwoven cloth and other items crafted by local people. If you're interested in traditional music Soundsaround (☎ 01504-374511) has an excellent selection. Most of the shops are open Monday to Saturday from 9.30 am to 5.30 pm and some open on Sunday during the summer.

Close to the Diamond in Shipquay St, the Donegal Shop sells garments, tweeds and souvenirs. Austin's on the corner in the Diamond is also worth a look as Ireland's oldest department store. In James St Art Glass sells modern glass in a 19th-century porticoed glassworks.

Getting There & Away

Air About 13 km east of Derry, Eglington Airport (☎ 01504-810784) has direct British Airways flights to Glasgow (£100 return) and Manchester (£106 return). Jersey European offers direct flights to Belfast, Dublin and Paris, with connections via Belfast to Birmingham, Blackpool, Bristol, Exeter, Guernsey, the Isle of Man, Jersey, Leeds and London; for more information call ☎ 01232-457200. Macair offers direct flights to Edinburgh; details from 01920-486323. Bus No 143 to Limavady stops near the airport; otherwise a taxi will cost about £7.

Bus Ulsterbus services between Belfast and Derry operate with similar frequency. Bus No 212, the Maiden City Flyer, is the fastest (1 hour 40 mins), followed by bus No 272 that goes via Omagh; a single ticket costs £5.50. A bus to Portstewart and Portrush leaves at 2.15 pm on Thursday and Sunday for most of June, and on Thursday, Friday

and Saturday in most of July and August. Each day at 8.20 am a bus leaves Derry for Cork, arriving at 7.15 pm. The bus from Cork leaves at 9.15 am and arrives in Derry at 8.30 pm.

Bus Éireann operates a Derry-Galway service three times daily, via Donegal and Sligo. It's £14 single to Galway, although midweek you can get a return for the same price. Lough Swilly buses (☎ 01504-262017) connect with County Donegal, across the border.

During the summer a bus leaves for Buncrana at 7.05 and 8 pm, and for Malin Head at 11 am and 4.15 pm Monday to Friday. On Sunday the Derry-Buncrana bus leaves at 1 and 6.15 pm. There is also a very useful Derry to Dungloe service, via Letterkenny and Dunfanaghy.

Feda O'Donnell's private buses (☎ 075-48114, 0141-631 3696) include a service from Letterkenny to Glasgow via Derry. It leaves from the bus station at 11 am, reaching Larne at 1 pm and Glasgow around 8 pm. The coach from Glasgow leaves at 8 am from the Citizens Theatre in Gorbles St (☎ 0141-631 3696) and reaches Derry around 4 pm. Services may not run if not enough passengers have booked. The bus station (☎ 01504-262261) is just outside the city walls, on Foyle St near the Guildhall.

Train Northern Ireland Railways have a half dozen daily Belfast-Derry services (only two on Sunday) taking about three hours. The earliest train for Portrush departs at 6.20 am (11.05 on Sunday), the last one at 7 pm. The railway station (☎ 01504-42228) is on the east side of the River Foyle. There's a free bus link into the town centre from outside the station.

Getting Around

Auto Cabs (☎ 01504-45100) and Central Taxis (☎ 01504-261911) operate from the city centre, and will go to all areas. Local buses leave from Foyle St in front of the bus station, where there are also shareable black cabs to outlying suburbs like Shantallow.

COLERAINE

Despite standing on the banks of the River Bann, Coleraine is not particularly attractive, and the pedestrianised town centre could be any English shopping area. But Coleraine is an important transport hub for County Derry and you could well find yourself waiting here for a bus or train connection. There are plenty of shops catering to the largely Protestant population, who first arrived in 1613 when the land was given by James I to loyal Londoners. The University of Ulster was established just north of town in 1968, much to the chagrin of Derry which had lobbied hard to win it. Efforts are being made to brighten things up and repair recent bomb damage, with the town hall, St Patrick's church and the birthplace of the obscure 19th-century illustrator Hugh Thomas in Church St all undergoing renovation.

Information

The tourist office (☎ 01265-44723) is near the railway station on Railway Rd and next to the leisure centre. It's open from 9 am to 5 pm Monday to Saturday, closing at 6 pm on Friday and Saturday in summer.

Mountsandel Mount

The age and purpose of this large oval mound south of Coleraine is something of a mystery. It may have been an early Christian stronghold or a later Anglo-Norman fortification. Just to the north-east of the mound, a Mesolithic site dating back to the 7th millennium BC has been excavated; post-holes, hearths and pits bear testimony to the early inhabitants of the area. The site is signposted from the Lodge Rd roundabout. At the T-junction after the roundabout turn right. There's parking at the heavily fortified courthouse on the right; from there cross over the road where a sign points the way. From here it is a 15-minute walk through the forest. Bicycles are not allowed.

Places to Stay

In the *Lodge Hotel* (☎ 01265-44848) on Lodge Rd, which joins Railway Rd, doubles are £70. In summer, you can get a bed for £11.70 at the *University* (☎ 01265-44141) but it's often full and cannot be relied on. The *Town House* (☎ 01265-44869) at 45 Millburn Rd charges from £14 for B&B, while *Coolbeg* (☎ 01265-44961) at 2E Grange Rd on the outskirts of town charges from £17 per person.

All the other B&Bs are out of town; the tourist office has a complete list. *Camus House* (☎ 01265-42982) is off the A54, five km south of town; the house is 17th-century and is worth £20/35 a single/double. *Tullan's Farm* (☎ 01265-42309), 46 Newmills Rd, is a working farm just one mile from Coleraine; rooms cost from £25. Grandest of all is *Blackheath House* (☎ 01265-868433), built as the home of an eccentric 18th-century bishop of Derry, who would surely have approved of the indoor swimming pool. The house is 13 km south of Coleraine at 112 Killeague Rd, Blackhill, and costs £60 for two.

Places to Eat

There are plenty of eating places around the pedestrianised precinct. *Twenty Two*, opposite Woolworths, does breakfast for £1.50 and hearty lunches for around £3. *Brook's Wine Bar*, round the corner near the car park, serves burgers and steaks until 9 pm. *Kitty's Pattisserie* in Church Lane does good cheap coffee and cakes. *MacDuffs* at Blackheath House (☎ 01265-868433) is open to non-residents for dinner, which costs from £15. It's closed on Sunday and Monday. If you're just passing through, you could do worse than patronise the *Whistlestop Café* in the train station, which is right next door to the bus station; soda bread filled with bacon and egg costs £1.45, as do a variety of tasty pies. It's closed Sunday though.

Getting There & Away

The Belfast-Derry trains stop at Coleraine and there is a branch line to Portrush. The Ulsterbus Atlantic Express bus No 218 travels between Portrush, Portstewart and Belfast via Coleraine and Antrim. In summer, the Antrim Coaster travels between Coleraine and Belfast. Bus No 234 takes an hour to reach Derry for £3.80.

LIMAVADY

You're unlikely to want to linger in Limavady, a pitstop of a town with a handful of attractive 19th-century houses. Its only claim to fame is that one Jane Ross (1810-79) heard a travelling fiddler playing the *Londonderry Air* – aka *Danny Boy*, probably the most famous Irish song of all – and noted it down; a blue plaque on the wall of 51 Main St where she lived commemorates the fact.

Information

The tourist office (☎ 015047-22226) is at 7 Connell St and open from 9 am to 12.30 pm and 1.30 to 5 pm Monday to Saturday. Outside those hours there's a computerised database in the wall.

Roe Valley Country Park

The park (☎ 015047-22074) stretches for five km either side of the River Roe, just south of Limavady. The area is associated with the O'Cahans, who ruled the valley until the Plantations. The 17th-century settlers saw the flax-growing potential of the damp river valley and the area became an important linen manufacturing centre. In the visitors' centre there are some excellent old photographs of the flax

---

DERRY & ANTRIM

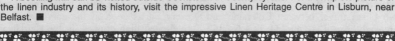

Linen

The manufacture of linen, probably the earliest textile made from plants, was once of vital significance to the Ulster economy. Linen was made in ancient Egypt and introduced into Britain by the Romans. The real boost to linen-making in Ulster, though, came with the arrival of Huguenot weavers seeking sanctuary in the late 17th century.

The flax plant was sown in the north of Ireland from March to May and harvested in mid-August. The first stage in the harvesting was the pulling of the flax plants and bundling them into stacks for open-air drying. The seeds were removed and crushed for linseed oil or kept for the following year's planting. The second stage was a messy and smelly one, entailing the soaking of the bundles of flax in freshwater ponds, or 'lint holes', for up to two weeks. This process of 'retting' softened the outer stem and the 'scutching' could begin.

Scutching separated the dried flax stem; with the introduction of water wheels in the 18th century, large wooden blades pounded and loosened the flax. The fibres were then ready for spinning on a wheel before being woven into lengths of cloth. Some of this unbleached linen was sold as 'brown linen', hence the number of Brown Linen Halls that used to exist.

The next stage was the bleaching, carried out in the open air after the cloth had been soaked in water for hours. Huge lengths of the cloth were stretched out across fields and left in the sunlight. The moisture in the material reacted with the sunlight to produce hydrogen peroxide which bleached the cloth. The final stage involved the hammering of the cloth by wooden hammers, or beetles, which smoothed out the material and made it ready for selling to the public. Bleached linen was sold through the many White Linen Halls.

At its height the linen industry was so important that Belfast was sometimes referred to as 'Linenopolis'. Flax growing died out in the North towards the end of the 19th century but was reborn during WW I with the demand for parachute material. There was a similar resurgence during WW II, but most of the linen now purchased is made in Scandinavia with the aid of chemicals. In recent years there has been an attempt to reintroduce flax growing in Ulster, and the occasional field of blue flax flowers may be spotted.

A beetling mill can be visited outside Cookstown in County Tyrone. For a complete picture of the linen industry and its history, visit the impressive Linen Heritage Centre in Lisburn, near Belfast. ■

industry and around the park are relics of that time. The weaving shed now houses a small museum near the main entrance. The scutch mill, where the flax was pounded, is a 45-minute walk away, along the river, past two watch towers that were built to guard the linen when it was spread out in the fields for bleaching. The park also contains Ulster's first domestic hydro-electric power station, opened in 1896. The plant is open to visitors free of charge on request at the visitor's centre next door.

The park itself is always accessible and the visitors' centre is open from 9 am to 5 pm all year. The café keeps the same hours but from Easter to September only. The park is clearly marked off the B68 road between Limavady and Dungiven. Bus No 146 from Limavady to Dungiven will drop you on the main road, but there is no weekend service.

Places to Stay

Camping is at the *Roe Valley Country Park* (☎ 015047-22074), just off the B68 to Dungiven; you'll be charged £5 for a tent. The *Gorteen House Hotel* (☎ 015047-22333) at 187 Roe Mill Rd charges £42 a double. If you're coming in from Derry on the A2 turn right just after crossing the bridge and follow Roe Mill Rd down until it turns to the left past a cemetery; the hotel is off to the right. Otherwise, the pistachio-coloured 19th-century *Alexander Arms* (☎ 015047-63443) at 34 Main St offers B&B for £16 or £18 a head depending on the floor.

Places to Eat

The *Alexander Arms* on Main St is OK for bar food; lunch would cost about £5. It's open until 10 pm on weekdays but only does lunch on Sunday. *Gentry's* (☎ 015047-22017), on the same street, offers a choice between Indian food and pizzas, and is open seven days a week. At 54 Main St *McNulty's* has been wrapping up fish & chips for half a century.

Getting There & Away

Two buses travel between Coleraine and Limavady, Nos 134 and 234. Bus No 143 runs to Derry almost hourly. There is no direct bus to Belfast but connections can be made at Coleraine or Dungiven.

DUNGIVEN

Despite the defiant Irish flags flying on the bridge, Dungiven exudes an air of desolation, with most of the shops in the high street boarded up and abandoned. Its only attractions are nearby ecclesiastical sites and one of the North's few independent hostels, which could make it a better base than Limavady if you're travelling between Belfast and Derry or if you want to explore the Sperrin Hills.

Dungiven Priory

The remains of this Augustinian priory date back to the 12th century, when they replaced a pre-Norman monastery.

The church contains the ornate tomb of Cooey-na-Gal, a chieftain of the O'Cahans who died in 1385. On the front of the tomb are figures of six kilted gallowglasses, mercenaries from Scotland hired by Cooey O'Cahan as minders and earning him the nickname na-Gal ('of the foreigners'). In the 17th century another foreigner, Sir Edward Doddington, who built the walls of Derry, remodelled the priory and an adjacent small castle built by the O'Cahans. He constructed a private dwelling of which only the foundations remain.

Nearby is a bullaun, a hollowed stone originally used by the monks for grinding grain but now collecting rainwater and used by people seeking cures for illnesses.

The priory is signposted off the A6 road to Antrim.

Maghera Old Church

The church site goes back to a 6th-century monastery that was plundered by the Vikings in 832. The present ruined nave is 10th-century while the Romanesque door on the west side is two centuries younger. There are interesting motifs on the door jambs, and the lintel carries a fine Crucifixion scene that is every bit as good as the carvings on the celebrated high crosses. In the churchyard there is an unmistakable pillar stone, carved with a ringed cross, which is said to mark the grave of the 6th-century founder, St Lurach.

The town of Maghera is on the A6 Derry to Belfast road, and the best approach is from Dungiven via the Glenshane Pass. Rising to 555 metres the road through the Sperrin Mountains offers dramatic views. In town turn right at the north end of the main street into Bank Square and then left to the car park. Bus Nos 116/278 offer an infrequent service between Coleraine and Maghera.

Places to Stay
The *Flax Mill Hostel* (☎ 015047-42655), Mill Lane, Derrylane, Dungiven, has no electricity and costs £4.50 a night or £2 to camp. The hostel is five km from Dungiven: take the A6 to Derry and after crossing the river take the first road on the right, signposted for Limavady and the Roe Valley Country Park. Then take the third road on the left, Altmover Rd, and the hostel is (unsigned) down the first lane on the right. The German-run hostel is sometimes full with groups from Germany but every effort is made to accommodate other travellers. *Mrs McMacken* (☎ 015047-41346), 132 Main St, does B&B for £12 per person per night, with 50% discount for children under twelve.

Places to Eat
When it comes to food, Dungiven hits rock bottom. The *Carraig Rua* at 40 Main St may be serving evening meals but in less than inviting surroundings. If you're travelling to Maghera on the A6, *Ponderosa* at the top of the Glenshane Pass does steaks and seafood.

Getting There & Away
Express bus No 212 between Derry and Belfast operates 10 times daily (five times on Sunday) and stops on Main St in Dungiven. Ulsterbus No 146 travels between Limavady and Dungiven.

PLANTATION TOWNS
The rest of inland Derry, to the south of Dungiven, is strong Protestant territory made up of towns planned and created by London companies with gracious thanks to King William of Orange for the grants of land. In Draperstown, Magherafelt and Moneymore the kerbstones are often painted red, white and blue, and for weeks after 12 July, when the victory of King Billy over the Catholics is celebrated, flags and banners proclaim the diehard patriotism of the locals.

Springhill
An interesting example of early Plantation architecture is to be found at Springhill, 1.5 km south of Moneymore on the B18. The original house was built about 1695 by the Conynghams who came here from Scotland after acquiring the 120-hectare Springhill estate. It was built at the same time as Hezlett House near Portstewart, but has little in common with that more humble abode. The central block has a high pitched roof, enlarged by the addition of the wings in the 18th century which give a more solid air of Baroque assurance to the house. The barn is also late 17th-century and was built to accommodate a warning bell. The Williamite war was over but then, as now, a certain siege mentality remained. Inside the house is some old oak furniture, a library, a collection of weapons and many costumes.

The house (☎ 016487-48210) is open 2 to 6 pm at weekends from April to September and daily during July and August. Admission is £2.20, children £1.10.

PORTSTEWART
When the English novelist Thackeray visited Portstewart in 1842, he noted the 'air of comfort and neatness'; 150 years later this still rings true and the place has an air of superiority that distinguishes it from the more proletarian Portrush, only six km farther down the coast in County Antrim. A day could easily be passed visiting the excellent beaches in the vicinity, and the town makes a convenient base for the Giant's Causeway and other coastal attractions.

Orientation & Information
Portstewart consists of one long promenade. To the east it heads along the coast to

DERRY & ANTRIM

Ballycastle, and to the west to a fine beach. If you're coming from Derry the place is wonderfully relaxed; there is no Control Zone and cars can be left unattended anywhere. The attractions that lie farther west can only be reached in a roundabout manner by going inland to Coleraine and then north again up the other side of a narrow inlet.

The tourist office (☎ 01265-832286) is in the red-brick town hall at the western end of town and is open 10 am to 4 pm, Monday to Saturday in July and August.

In summer you can hire speedboats and try parascending; phone ☎ 01265-824099 for details.

Portstewart Strand
The beach is 20 minutes' walk or a short bus ride west of town along Strand Road. Despite the fact that the Strand is a National Trust site, vehicles are allowed to use the firm sand which can accommodate over 1000 cars. If someone is on duty (unlikely out of season) there's a £2 charge to take cars on the beach.

Festival
In May the North-West 200 motorcycle race is run on a road circuit between Portrush, Portstewart and Coleraine. This classic race is one of the last to be run on closed public roads anywhere in Europe; most such events are now considered too dangerous. It attracts up to 70,000 spectators.

Places to Stay
Camping Camp sites are plentiful along the coast road. *Carrick Dhu Caravan Park* (☎ 01265-823712) is on Ballyreagh Rd, while the *Golf Links Hotel Caravan Park* (☎ 01265-823539) and *Margoth Caravan Park* (☎ 01265-822531) are both on Dunluce Rd. Pitching a tent for one night at any of them costs between £6 and £9. There is also the *Portrush Caravan Park* (☎ 01265-823537) on the Portrush to Coleraine road, opposite the Magherabuoy Hotel; a tent for up to four people will cost £8. The *Benone Tourist Complex* (☎ 015047-50555) and the larger *Golden Sands Caravan Park* (☎ 015047-50324) are

both at Benone Beach and charge from £4.50 for a tent for two.

Hostel The *Causeway Coast Hostel* (☎ 01265-833789), at the eastern end of town at 4 Victoria Terrace, Atlantic Circle, charges £5.50 per person in four, six or eight-bedded dorms, £6.50 in private rooms. It has its own kitchen and laundry, and welcoming fires in winter. Real baths also make a nice change from just showers.

B&Bs B&Bs are easy to find around Atlantic Circle at the eastern end of town, although some of them have a distinctly aged clientele. Typically, *Salem* at No 5 (☎ 01265-834584) charges £13 for B&B, with another £5 for dinner. At 23 The Promenade, the centrally placed *Craigmore* (☎ 01265-832120) costs £28 for a double plus £6 each for dinner. *Mount Oriel* at No 74 (☎ 01265-832516) and *Akaroa* next door at No 75 (☎ 01265-832067) charge £15 each.

Hotels The *Portmor Bay* (☎ 01265-832688) in Kinora Terrace, at the end of Atlantic Circle, costs £35 for a basic double and £40 for a room with bathroom while the pretty lemon *Windsor* (☎ 01265-832523) on the Promenade charges £50 a double. The *Edgewater* (☎ 01265-833314), farther out at 88 Strand Rd, is also pleasant, with doubles from £55.

Self-Catering Describing themselves as 'exclusively adult', the cottages at *Rock Castle* (☎ 01265-832271) overlook Portstewart Strand and vary from £130 a week for a one-bedroom unit in the low season to £400 for a two-bedroom unit in the high season.

Places to Eat
For reasonably priced hot or cold lunches, try *Squires* at 18 The Promenade, which also does early evening meals. The *Heathron Diner* at No 31 is similar. You can hardly miss *Morelli's*, midway along the Promenade, which dispenses mouth-watering ice cream sundaes. Next door, but part of the

DERRY & ANTRIM

same complex, is *Nino's* which does hot meals as well as ice cream and usually has a vegetarian special for less than £4. Up some stairs and round the back, the *Outback*, yet another part of the same complex, serves steaks in the evenings.

The *Montagu Arms* at 68-9 The Promenade (☎ 01265-834146) has a carvery but does toasted sandwiches as well, as does *Shenanigans* nearby. Dinner costs around £10 in the *Windsor Hotel* restaurant on the Promenade or at the *Edgewater Hotel* where the bar and restaurant have great views of the broad beach. The *Ashiana* at 12 The Diamond (behind the town hall) has a mixed menu of Indian and European dishes and kebabs, while the *York Bar* in Station Rd also has a good reputation. Heading out of town *Some Plaice Else* (☎ 01265-824945) is a large seafood restaurant at 21 Ballyreagh Rd on the sea side of the coast road between Portstewart and Portrush.

Getting There & Away
Bus See Getting Around at the start of this chapter for information on the summertime Antrim Coaster and Open Topper bus services along the coast. Departures are from the Promenade bus stop in Portstewart. Ulsterbus No 218 leaves Portstewart for Belfast eight times daily on weekdays, four times on Saturday and twice on Sunday, stopping at Coleraine, Ballymoney and Antrim. Bus No 243 leaves for Derry at 8.25 am, arriving at 9.25 am Thursday and Sunday for most of June. For most of July and August it runs on Friday and Saturday as well. It leaves Derry at 2.15 pm. Bus No 140 plies back and forth between Coleraine and Portstewart, with services roughly every half hour (fewer on Sunday) and a single fare of 95p.

Train The nearest station is at Portrush, with connections to the Derry-Belfast train at Coleraine. See the Portrush section for details.

AROUND PORTSTEWART
To reach the attractions west of Portstewart take the A2 from Coleraine and head west.

Hezlett House, Castlerock
The house was built in the late 17th century, a single-storey thatched cottage noted for its cruck truss roof gables of stone and turf strengthened with wooden crucks or crutches. The interior decoration is Victorian. The house is owned by the National Trust and open daily (except Tuesday) at Easter and during July and August, from 1 to 6 pm. From April to June and September it's open the same hours Saturday and Sunday only. Admission is £1.50/75p and there is a car park across the road. The house is eight km west of Coleraine at Liffock on the A2.

Mussenden Temple & Downhill
An eccentric and very rich bishop of Derry was also the earl of Bristol, and his fine home at Downhill was built in 1774. It was burnt down in 1851, rebuilt in 1870 and abandoned after WW II. The roof was taken down for its scrap value and the remains of the small castellated building now stand forlornly in a field. The major attraction, a short walk from the house, is the curious little Mussenden Temple, perched right on the cliff edge and built by the energetic bishop to house either his library or his mistress – opinions differ! He conducted an affair with the mistress of Frederick William II of Prussia well into his old age.

It is a pleasant walk to the temple and the reward is fine views of the sand at Portstewart and Magilligan, the railway line below disappearing into a tunnel, and the hills of Donegal across the water. The beach immediately below is where the bishop set his own clergy to race on horseback, rewarding the winners by appointing them to the more lucrative parishes. In the distance shadowy outlines of the Scottish mountains are usually visible. The bishop inscribed a quotation from Lucretius on a frieze:

It is pleasant to see from the safe shore
The pitching of ships and hear the storm's roar.

The inscription is thoroughly appropriate on a windy day. The site is about 20 km west of Portstewart by road, much closer as the crow

DERRY & ANTRIM

flies. It is now owned by the National Trust but there is no admission charge. The temple is open April, May, June and September on Saturday and Sunday from noon to 6 pm. July, August and Easter it is open daily the same hours. Bar food is available at the nearby *Downhill Inn* which opens its restaurant at 6 pm. Immediately past the Downhill Inn, Bishop's Rd forks up to the left, leading over the mountains to Limavady, with terrific views from Gortmore picnic area.

Benone/Magilligan Beach

Some 10 km in length and hundreds of metres wide at low tide, this Blue Flag beach – called both Benone and Magilligan – is worth a visit. It sweeps out to Magilligan Point where a Martello tower stands and from where sailplanes and hang-gliders can be seen riding the wind. Look for the sign to the Benone Tourist Complex on the A2.

County Antrim

Just east of Ballycastle the distinctive cliffs of Fair Head mark the point where the coast turns southwards and the Antrim coast makes its way down to Larne before turning inland for Carrickfergus and Belfast Lough. This coastal strip is known as the Glens of Antrim after the series of nine valleys which cut across the range of hills between Ballycastle and Larne. The A2 road runs along the coast for most of the way and it's an exciting route for cyclists. The short run between Waterfoot and Carnlough is particularly fine.

Inland, Antrim (*Aontroim*) is perhaps the least interesting part of Northern Ireland, and Antrim Town has little to recommend it. To the south of nearby Lisburn the infamous Long Kesh prison was the scene of the hunger strikes in 1981 which led to the deaths of 10 men who were campaigning for the right to be recognised as political prisoners. The Thatcher government refused to negotiate and allowed them to die one by one.

Most visitors pass along Antrim's coast and there is little here to remind one of the Troubles. The scenery is delightful all the way and everyone is drawn towards a coastline that bears the distinguished name of the Giant's Causeway.

PORTRUSH

This is a busy little resort, bursting at the seams with holidaymakers from all round the North in summer. Not surprisingly, many of its attractions are unashamedly focused on families.

Information

The tourist office (☎ 01265-823333) in the Dunluce Centre opens daily from 9 am to 8 pm from June to September (shorter hours at other times) and closes altogether from mid-November to the end of February.

Things to See & Do

Boat trips (☎ 01265-823369 or contact the tourist office) depart regularly in the summer for cruising or fishing. For pony trekking contact the Ballywillan Riding Centre (☎ 01265-823372), half a mile from the town centre on Ballywillan Rd, or Maddybenny Farm (☎ 01265-823394 or 01265-823603 after 6 pm). Portrush is also carving out a name for itself as a surfer's paradise. The friendly Troggs surf shop at 8 Bath St (☎ 01265-823923) does board and wetsuit hire, surf reports and general advice. Ask here, too, about the possibility of renting a bike.

Waterworld (☎ 01265-822001) by the harbour has pools, flumes and spa baths for children to play in, while the **Dunluce Centre** has a 'turbo tour', a hands-on nature trail with lots of buttons to press, and animated shows on local myths and legends. In summer it's open daily 10 am to 9 pm, but usually closes at 5 pm in winter; an inclusive ticket costs £4.50 from April to September, 50p less at other times.

Places to Stay

Bus No 177 runs to the *Margoth Caravan Park* (☎ 01265-822531) at 126 Dunluce Rd and *Skerryview Camping* (☎ 01265-823537) at 60 Loguestown Rd; both charge from £7 for a tent. *Macools* is an unusually clean 20-bed independent hostel with sea views at 5 Causeway View Terrace (☎ 01265-824845). Beds in single sex dorms cost £5 a head (£7.50 in the one private room), and there are laundry and cooking facilities. Double rooms at *Magherabuoy House* (☎ 01265-823507) are £70, while at the *Eglinton Hotel* (☎ 01265-822371) they are £65. The *Langholm Hotel* (☎ 01265-822293) charges £40.

B&Bs can easily fill up during the summer months and it's advisable to book in advance through the tourist office. Guesthouses with sea views on Landsdowne Crescent include *Clarmont* (☎ 01265-822397) at No 10, *Alexandra* (☎ 01265-822284) at No 11 and *Belvedere* (☎ 01265-822771) at No 15, all charging around £35 a double in the high season. The *Clarence* (☎ 01265-823575) at 7 Bath Terrace also overlooks the sea and is less expensive.

With more character, there's the *Old Manse* dating from 1850 at 3 Main St (☎ 01265-824118) which charges from £30 a double. If you arrive late, there are also a few B&Bs immediately opposite the station in Eglinton Rd, including *Atlantic View*, *Glenshane* and *An Uladh*.

Places to Eat

Cafés and fast-food places jostle with amusement arcades all the way along Main St and you need to head for the harbour end to find better. *Ramore* (☎ 01265-823444), overlooking the harbour, is Portrush's premier eating place, and can be unbelievably busy at lunch times. The wine bar is open for lunch from 12.30 to 2.15 pm (there are very good value lunch specials for £3.95), and then again from 5 pm, while the pricier restaurant upstairs does not open its doors until 7 pm.

Rowland's at 92 Main St, near the harbour, does main courses for about £7.50. Around the corner from here *Skerries Pantry* in Bath St is fine for snacks. *Dionysus* on Eglinton St is open daily and serves Greek and European dishes from £5. It's next to the *China*

House which does marginally pricier Chinese standards. Some of the hotels are also reliable eating places. At *Magherabuoy House* generous helpings make the Sunday lunch particularly good value at £8.50.

Entertainment

What was once the Londonderry Hotel on Main St now houses the linked *Atlantic* and *McNally* bars which stay open until 1 am. The *Harbour Bar*, unsurprisingly by the harbour, is immensely popular at night. The flashiest local disco is *Kelly's*, just over a mile out of town; a taxi will charge £3 to get you there.

Getting There & Away

Bus See Getting Around at the start of this chapter for information on the summertime Antrim Coaster and Open Topper bus services along the coast. Ulsterbus No 218 leaves daily from Portrush for Belfast, travelling inland via Portstewart, Coleraine, Ballymoney, Ballymena and Antrim; there are only three or four services on Saturday and two on Sunday. The bus terminal is on Dunluce Ave near the railway station.

Train Portrush is served by train from Coleraine roughly every hour for the 12-minute journey. The earliest train leaves Coleraine at 7.05 am, the latest at 10.25 pm; from Portrush the times are 6.35 am and 10.41 am respectively. At Coleraine connections can be made for Belfast or Derry. Travelling to Dublin from here, changing at Coleraine and Belfast, would take nearly five hours. Contact Portrush Station (☎ 01265-822395) for more details.

Getting Around

For taxis call Andy Brown's on ☎ 0500-822223 or North West Taxis on ☎ 01265-824446. They're both near the red-brick town hall. A taxi to the Giant's Causeway would cost about £5.

PORTBALLINTRAE

Portballintrae ('the port of the town of strand') is little more than a small harbour ringed with houses and a couple of seaside-style hotels. During WWI it was the only place in the UK to be shelled by a German submarine. Luckily, the result was no worse than a crater on the outskirts of town and the downing of the electric tram lines.

Dunluce Castle

The site was used for defensive purposes long before a stone castle was constructed, as shown by the existence of a 1000-year-old souterrain. Parts of the castle date from the 14th century. In the 16th century it came into the hands of the Scottish Sorley Boy Mac-Donnell family, who extended the buildings and tried to strengthen its walls after a serious artillery attack by the English. In the 17th century a manor house with medieval floorplan and Renaissance embellishments was built inside the walls.

The south wall, facing the mainland, has two openings cut into it which were made to hold cannons salvaged from the wreck of the *Gerona*, a Spanish Armada vessel that foundered nearby. Perched 30 metres above the sea, the castle was of obvious military value, and there are extensive remains inside the walls, giving a good idea of life here. The palatial hall needed two fireplaces, while the kitchen area has ovens, storage space and a drainage system all built into the stone. The lower yard retains the original cobbling and was surrounded by service rooms, some of which collapsed into the sea in 1639; servants and a night's dinner were lost. An audiovisual display tells the castle's history.

The castle is open from April to the end of September from 10 am to 7 pm Monday to Saturday and 2 to 7 pm on Sunday. The rest of the year it's 10 am to 4 pm Monday to Saturday and 2 to 4 pm on Sunday. Entry is £1.50/75p. The castle is beside the A2 coast road, just west of Portballintrae.

Places to Stay

The *Portballintrae Caravan Park* (☎ 012657 -31478) is in Ballaghmore Rd and has space for 11 tents at £5 a night. The very accommodating *Keeve-Na* (☎ 012657-32184), right beside the camp site in Ballghmore Rd, does

B&B for £14 a head. The sea-facing *Bayhead Guest House* (☎ 012657-31441) at 8 Bayhead Rd charges from £39 for a double. The *Bayview Hotel* (☎ 012657-31453) has an indoor heated swimming pool and costs £70 for a double while the better *Beach House Hotel* (☎ 012657-31214) charges £64 a double.

Places to Eat

Sweeney's Public House & Wine Bar (☎ 012657-32404) on Seaport Ave serves steak, fish and a few vegetarian dishes casually in front of a log fire or more formally in an upstairs restaurant with harbour views. The *Beach Hotel* also dishes up decent dinners.

BUSHMILLS

On the River Bush, Bushmills is a small town off the A2 between Portrush and Ballycastle. At its centre is the Diamond, with a grim grey circular clocktower and war memorial whence Main St makes its way to the famous Bushmills Distillery.

Bushmills Distillery

This is the only place in the world where Bushmills whiskey is distilled. Whiskey was first officially distilled here in 1608, but records indicate that the activity was going on for hundreds of years before that. After the noisy and rather technical tour of the industrial process, you are rewarded with a tot of the hard stuff in the Potstill Bar, where an exhibition area has been created in what were once malt kilns.

The distillery is open all year, Monday to Thursday, 9 am to noon and 1.30 to 3.30 pm, and from 9 to 11.45 am on Friday. During July, August and September it opens from 9 am to 4 pm Monday to Friday and from 10 am to 4 pm on Saturday as well. Opening hours are sometimes extended over public holidays; call ☎ 012657-31521 to check. Admission costs £2, children free. The distillery is signposted from the town of Bushmills on the A2 coast road. Buses drop you in the Diamond whence it's about a one-km walk west along Main St.

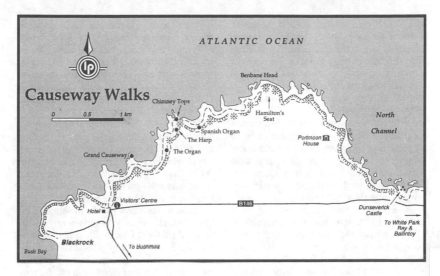

ATLANTIC OCEAN

Causeway Walks

Chimney Tops

0   0.5   1 km

Benbane Head

Hamilton's Seat

Spanish Organ
The Harp
The Organ

Grand Causeway

Portmoon
House

Visitors' Centre
Hotel ■

Blackrock

To Bushmills

Bush Bay

B146

North

Channel

Dunseverick
Castle
To White Park
Bay &
Ballintoy

Places to Stay

Ardeevin (☎ 012657-31661) at 145 Main St, on the way to the distillery, does B&B for £13 a head. *The Sycamores* (☎ 012657-31145), at 56 Priestland Rd just off the A2, charges the same and will accept payment in Irish punts. The pleasantly quiet *Bushmills Inn* (☎ 012657-32339), on Main St, charges £48 single and £78 a double midweek, but weekend breaks at £82 including dinner are good value. *Pineview* (☎ 012657-41527) is a farmhouse five km from Bushmills on the B66 and charges £27 a double.

The spectacularly-sited YHANI hostel at White Park Bay is six km east of Bushmills on the A2 coast road overlooking a lovely bay (see the Along the Coast section later in this chapter).

Places to Eat

A *coffee shop* in the Diamond serves snacks and sandwiches, but you'll do better at *Valerie's Pantry* where cream tea costs £1. It's on Main St as you walk to the distillery and is open every day from May to August. You can pay in punts if you want to. The *Bushmills Inn* has a very attractive restaurant serving everything from toasted sandwiches

to full à la carte dinners. Strangely in a place synonymous with Irish whiskey, the *Scotch House* pub on Main St boasts a wide range of Scotch whiskies.

GIANT'S CAUSEWAY

The chances are you've seen pictures of the North's number one tourist attraction long before getting here. A bishop of Derry, who became interested in geology after seeing Vesuvius erupt, commissioned the paintings of the site that led to its fame. Today, school geography books still regard its inclusion as mandatory. The hexagonal basalt columns are impressive, and do look as if a giant might have playfully tipped out all 37,000 of them, if you count the ones under the water. According to legend the giant in question, Finn McCool, fancied some stepping stones to the Scottish island of Staffa where, indeed, similar rock formations are to be found.

The modern story is that red-hot lava erupted from an underground fissure and crystallised some 60 million years ago into the shapes that we see today. The phenomenon is clearly explained in the visitors' centre, alongside the surprising fact that the Causeway only came to general notice as late as 1740. The audiovisual section, however, is more of an animated tourist brochure, debatably worth the charge of £1 (children 50p). It costs nothing to make the pleasant 1.5 km pilgrimage to the actual site. From mid-March to the end of October minibuses with wheelchair access ply the route every 15 minutes (80p/40p).

Different areas of the rock formations have their own names, most of them invented by the many Victorian guides who made a summer living by escorting the tourists who arrived on the electric tram from Coleraine. Past the main spill of columns, the pathway brings into view a formation that does deserve its own name. Chimney Tops was identified by ships of the Spanish Armada in 1588 as part of Dunluce Castle, and consequently fired upon.

Two well-established footpaths at different levels start from just outside the visitors' centre, but a landslip means that it is not possible to join them up as a circular walk for the time being. From the clifftop at Hamilton's Seat, there is one of the best views of the Causeway and headlands to the west, including Malin Head and Inishowen.

If you want to go farther, the path continues around Benbane Head, and the sandy beach of White Park Bay comes into view. On the right is Portmoon House. The headlands become lower and lower until the path reaches the main road near Dunseverick Castle. The walk from the visitors' centre to the castle and back is around 15 km.

From below the remains of the castle a path winds up and round to the east, ending at Ballintoy. It crosses a number of small wooden bridges before reaching the beach of White Park. There is a YHANI hostel here, so the whole 16-km journey from the Giant's Causeway could be done in one day.

These walks follow the North Antrim Cliff Path, which actually begins west of the visitors' centre at Blackrock, a short walk of about 2.5 km. A useful 45p map from the visitors' centre details the walks, including the various rock formations that can be seen along the way.

The Giant's Causeway (*Clochán an Aifir*) can be visited free of charge any time but the car park costs £2. In winter the visitors' centre (☎ 012657-31855) is open from 10 am to 4.30 pm Monday to Friday and 10 am

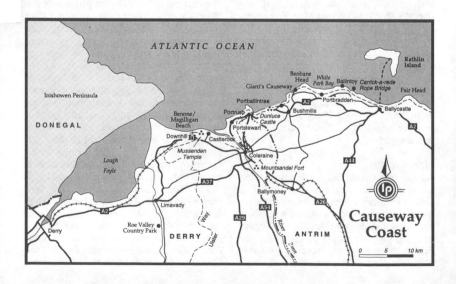

to 5 pm Saturday and Sunday. In spring it stays open half an hour later every day. Then in summer it opens from 10 am to 7 pm Monday to Friday and from 10 am to 7.30 pm Saturday and Sunday. It only closes completely on Christmas Day and Boxing Day. There's a National Trust shop and a café in the same building but they close earlier; you can buy sandwiches, etc in two small shops outside.

Next to the visitors' centre, and mainly of interest to children, the Causeway School Museum opens July and August from 10 am to 4.30 pm; 75/50p, or £2 for a family.

Places to Stay

If you want to stay as close to the Causeway as possible, the *Causeway Hotel* (☎ 01267-31226) is within spitting distance at £50 for a double. The nearest hostel is in White Park Bay (see below). Otherwise, you could stay in Bushmills or Portballintrae, or even in Portrush or Ballycastle, and still visit the Causeway perfectly easily. *Lochuber* (☎ 012657-31385), on the coast road at 107 Causeway Rd, just 1.5 km from the Causeway, charges £26 for two, while at 23 Causeway Rd *Carnside* (☎ 012657-3133/) charges £30.

Places to Eat

The Causeway visitors' centre *café* is OK but you'll get a more substantial meal at the *Causeway Hotel* outside. The restaurant here is extremely popular, so it's wise to book in advance (☎ 01267-31226).

Getting There & Away

The B146 Causeway to Dunseverick road runs parallel to the A2 but closer to the coast and can be joined just east of Bushmills or near White Park Bay. Infrequent buses between Portrush and Ballycastle also pass the site. See the introduction to this chapter for information on the summertime Antrim Coaster and Open Topper bus services along the coast. It's only five minutes by bus from the Giant's Causeway to the Diamond in Bushmills and another five minutes to Portballintrae. If you're unlucky with the buses, a taxi would cost £5 from Portrush or £8 from Ballycastle.

Getting Around

The YHANI hostel at White Park Bay (see below) is the only place around with bikes for hire.

Dunseverick Castle

This is an older castle than Dunluce, but unfortunately very little remains. It was once the home of Conal Cearnac, a famous wrestler and swordsman said to have been present at the Crucifixion; he reputedly moved the stone at Christ's sepulchre. St Patrick is also said to have visited the castle, and a road was laid from here to Tara, the headquarters of the pagan high kings of Ireland. The castle remains are spectacularly sited by the side of the B146 which is reached off the A2 coast road.

Along the Coast

Signposted off the A2 is **Portbradden**, a hamlet of half a dozen pretty harbourside houses. Tiny blue and white St Gobban's church is said to be the smallest in Ireland, and it's easy to believe it. Visible from Portbradden and accessible via the next road junction off the A2 is the spectacular **White Park Bay** with its sweeping sandy beach. The YHANI *hostel* (☎ 012657-31745) has a common room positioned to soak up the view. Beds cost £6.30 or £5.30 for a child, and bikes can be hired for £8 a day (£6 for hostellers). A few km farther along, **Ballintoy** is another picture-postcard village set around a harbour. Look out for the idiosyncratic home-made house on the right on the way down. Right by the harbour *Roark's Kitchen* serves teas, coffees and light lunches in summer. Bearing in mind the minuscule size of the place, though, it's best to avoid visiting at the peak of the season.

Carrick-a-rede Rope Bridge

It's a scary traipse across the Carrick-a-rede ('rock in the road') rope bridge to a small island with a salmon fishery and hundreds of nesting fulmars. The 20-metre bridge sways some 25 metres above the rock-strewn water. It's especially frightening if it's windy, but there are secure handrails to help steady your nerves and your balance; stout footwear is advised and no more than two people should cross simultaneously. The bridge is put up every spring by fishermen who work the fishery. Once on the island there are good views of Rathlin Island and Fair Head to the east. You can cross the bridge free, but the National Trust car park costs £1.50; it's a 1.25-km walk from there to the bridge.

There's a small information centre and café open at weekends from Easter to June and daily from 11 am to 6 pm from July to mid-September. If you want to stay nearby *Glenmore House* on the A2 is convenient. It serves teas and coffees too.

BALLYCASTLE

Ballycastle, where the Atlantic Ocean meets the Irish Sea, also marks the end of the Causeway Coast. It's a pretty, small town, with plenty of 18th and 19th-century architecture, and its location makes it a natural base for exploring the coasts to the west or south. The beach itself may be nothing special but there's a seaside feel to the harbour area; great change can be expected if plans for a new ferry route to Campbelltown in Scotland come to fruition. The Giant's Causeway, Bushmills distillery and the rope bridge are all less than 16 km away and the Glens of Antrim are due south.

Information

The tourist office (☎ 012657-62024) is in the Moyle District Council Office on Mary St; in winter it's only open Monday to Friday from 9 am to 5 pm, but from June to September it stays open seven days a week until 7 pm. You can pick up a free copy of the Ballycastle Heritage Trail leaflet here. To charter a boat for fishing trips contact Mr McCaughan (☎ 012657-62074).

Museum

The tiny museum in the town's 18th-century courthouse on Castle St is open from 2 to 6 pm in July and August, free of charge.

Bonamargy Friary

The remains of this Franciscan friary are one km east of town on the A2 to Cushendun, on the Ballycastle golf course. The friary was founded around 1500 and was used for two centuries. To the south of the friary a vault contains the bodies of the MacDonnells, the earls of Antrim, including Sorley Boy Mac-Donnell from Dunluce Castle. There is no admission charge.

Festival

There is a three-day music and dance festival in June and a bigger Ould Lammas Fair held on the last Monday and Tuesday of August. This is one of the oldest established fairs in Ireland, dating back to 1606, and is associated with the sale of two traditional foods. *Yellowman* is a soft toffee while *dulse* is a dried seaweed that is sold salted and ready to eat, although some people toast it. Always available during the Ould Lammas Fair, dulse is on sale generally from June to September while yellowman is available throughout the year. The Fruit Shop at the Diamond often stocks both delicacies.

Places to Stay

Camping *Silver Cliffs Holiday Village* (☎ 012657-62550) is a big, noisy caravan and camp site, north-west of town and within walking distance. It is also expensive at £8 per tent. Comfortable four-berth caravans can be hired for £20 a night. On the A2 to Cushendun, 10 km from Ballycastle, *Watertop Open Farm* (☎ 012657-62576) has space for a few tents (£5 each) and is a good place for children, with pony trekking and farm tours on offer. *Fair Head Caravan Park* (☎ 012657-62077) on Whitepark Rd also has limited camping space at £7 a tent.

Hostel The independent *Castle Hostel* (☎ 012657-62337) is at 62 Quay Rd, just past the Marine Hotel and charges £5 a night. It's clean, welcoming and unusually spacious. The next nearest one is the YHANI hostel at White Park Bay.

B&Bs If you want to be close to the sea, the *Fairhead View* (☎ 012657-62822) is on North St, above the harbour; a double costs £24. At 42 Quay Rd, an architecturally

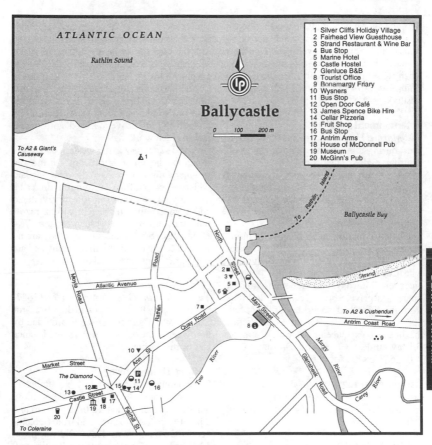

1 Silver Cliffs Holiday Village
2 Fairhead View Guesthouse
3 Strand Restaurant & Wine Bar
4 Bus Stop
5 Marine Hotel
6 Castle Hostel
7 Glenluce B&B
8 Tourist Office
9 Bonamargy Friary
10 Wysners
11 Bus Stop
12 Open Door Café
13 James Spence Bike Hire
14 Cellar Pizzeria
15 Fruit Shop
16 Bus Stop
17 Antrim Arms
18 House of McDonnell Pub
19 Museum
20 McGinn's Pub

DERRY & ANTRIM

attractive road despite the noise from the A2, *Glenluce* (☎ 012657-62914) charges £30. Other possibilities along Quay Rd include *Fragens* at No 34 (☎ 012657-62168), *Ammiroy* at No 26 (☎ 012657-62621) and *Silver Springs House* at No 20 (☎ 012657-62080) charging between £13 and £15 a person.

Hotels The *Marine Hotel* (☎ 012657-62222) is right on the seafront and costs £60 a double. The smaller *Antrim Arms Hotel* (☎ 012657-62284) inland on Castle St charges £35 a double.

Places to Eat
On the seafront the *Strand Restaurant and Wine Bar* does all-day breakfasts for £3.30 and is open for evening meals until 10.30 pm. Nearby the *Marine Hotel* also serves dinner until 10.30; a four-course Sunday lunch would set you back £8.95. In the streets leading off the Diamond there are the usual small cafés, including the *Open Door* in Castle St which is pleasant enough but closes at 5.30 pm. Right on the Diamond the *Cellar Pizzeria* (☎ 012657-63037) serves up standard Italian fare in cosy little booths, while *Wysners* (☎ 012657-62372) at 16 Ann

St is good for lunch or afternoon tea; there's also a restaurant upstairs which opens on Friday and Saturday evenings. *Donelly's Coffeeshop*, at 28 Ann St, is another good lunch stop. For fish & chips, try the *Golden Chip*, *Macs Takeaway* or *Checkers*, all on Castle St.

Entertainment
The *Marine Hotel* has live music at weekends during the summer and a disco on Saturday nights. There's more live music at *McGinn's* pub and at the popular *House of McDonnell*, which has traditional music sessions on Friday nights. Both are on Castle St.

Getting There & Away
See the introduction to this chapter for information on the summertime Antrim Coaster bus services. Bus No 171 links Ballycastle with Coleraine, but there are just two services on Saturday and none on Sunday. There is a private bus, McGinns, that runs from the Diamond on Friday at 4 pm and Sunday at 7.30 pm to Belfast. From Belfast the bus leaves Queen's Gate at 6 pm on Friday and 9.30 pm on Sunday. Call ☎ 012657-63451 for details.

Getting Around
James Spence at 66 Castle St rents bicycles for £5 a day. For a taxi, try *Del's Taxis* on ☎ 012657-62822.

RATHLIN ISLAND
Only 22 km from Scotland's Mull of Kintyre, Rathlin Island (*Reachlainn*) is itself only six km long and nowhere more than 1.5 km across. It has a pub, a restaurant, two shops, a camp site and a guesthouse, along with approximately 100 inhabitants and thousands of seabirds. The island, which Pliny mentions as Ricnia, was raided by Vikings in AD 795 and suffered again in 1595 when Sorley Boy MacDonnell sent his family here for safety only to have them massacred by the English along with all the inhabitants. Its most illustrious visitor was Robert the Bruce who spent some time in 1306 in a small cave on the north-east point learning a lesson

about fortitude. Watching a spider's resoluteness in repeatedly trying to spin a web gave him the courage to have another go at the English, whom he subsequently defeated at Bannockburn.

Another claim to fame is the fact that Rathlin was the first place to have a wireless. Marconi's assistant contacted Rathlin by radio in 1898 to prove to Lloyd's of London that the idea worked.

A bird sanctuary at the western end of the island is the chief attraction. During the summer a minibus waits at the quayside and will take you out for £2 return (children £1). The service does not run to a timetable so check your return time. Kittiwakes, razorbills and puffins can be seen around West Lighthouse, but by late summer they are no longer nesting or rearing their young and are difficult to spot from the land.

Places to Stay
The *Rathlin Guesthouse* (☎ 012657-63916/7) is by the harbour and does B&B for £26 for two. Camping space is provided by the owner of the one pub, just a short distance east of the harbour.

Getting There & Away
From January to March and November to December boats leave Ballycastle at 10.30 am and 4 pm and leave Rathlin at 9 am and 3 pm. From April to June and from September to October boats leave Ballycastle at 10.30 am and 5 pm, and leave Rathlin at 9 am and 4 pm. In July and August they leave Ballycastle at 10.30 am and 12.15, 5 and 6.45 pm, and leave Rathlin at 9 and 11.15 am and 4 and 6 pm. A single fare is £3.40/1.65, and a day return £5.60. It's wise to show up well in advance of the scheduled sailing time, and be warned that boats may not sail when the weather's bad.

MURLOUGH BAY
The coast between Ballycastle and Cushendun is best covered not by the main A2 but by a more scenic coastal road that takes in Murlough Bay. This is the most stupendous part of the Antrim coastline.

Leave your transport at the first car park-there are three altogether – where a map display sets out the walking possibilities.

Walk No 1 is from the first car park to Coolanlough, and is a 3½ km return trip. The views from Fair Head are magnificent. From a vantage point 186 metres above the sea, Rathlin Island is to the left, while out to sea the peaks of the Isle of Arran can be seen on a clear day behind the Mull of Kintyre. The walk also takes in Lough na Cranagh with an ancient crannóg in the middle.

The second walk begins from the second car park farther down the road; follow the clear pathway to the west. It leads to some abandoned coal mines, indicated only by arches in the rock, which are probably not safe to explore. By following the main road down past the second car park you come to a third parking area on the right. From here the road down becomes a green track and ends in a cul-de-sac by a small house.

Between the first and second car parks, the remains of a cross can be seen, a memorial to Roger Casement whose family came from this area. Casement, who was hanged in London in 1916 for enlisting the aid of Germany in the nationalist struggle, made a last request to his cousin: 'Take my body back with you and let it lie in the old churchyard in Murlough Bay.' It was 50 years before the British consented to release the body.

Getting There & Away

From Ballycastle take the sign pointing to Torr Head and Cushendun Scenic Route, as opposed to the A2 that goes to Cushendun. From Cushendun take the Scenic Route to Torr Head. The A2 goes inland between Cushendun and Ballycastle and cannot compete with the grandeur of the coastal route. The only reason for travelling on this part of the A2, apart from speed, is to visit the Watertop Open Farm or Ballypatrick Forest, an over-organised forest park.

CUSHENDUN

The distinctive black and white houses at the southern end are National Trust property, the work of Clough Williams-Ellis, designer of Portmeirion in North Wales, who came here to work for Lord Cushendun.

Information

The National Trust tourist office (☎ 012667-61506) is open daily 12.30 to 6 pm in July and August. From Easter to June and in September it opens the same hours on Saturday and Sunday only. It can provide general tourist information as well as details of NT properties. Permits for fishing on the River Dun that runs into Cushendun Bay are available from McFetridge's shop, 116 Tromara Rd, Castle Green.

Walking

The village is on the Ulster Way (see the Activities chapter) and part of the walk could be undertaken from here. North from Cushendun the walk goes inland before heading down to Murlough Bay and then along the coast to Ballycastle. Going south the walk goes inland nearly all of the way to Cushendall.

Places to Stay

There is only one hotel, the *Bay Hotel* (☎ 012667-61267), with rooms at £28 for a double. A few doors away, the largish *Cushendun* (☎ 012667-61266) calls itself a guesthouse, perhaps because it's only open during July and August. A double here is £30. The *Villa* (☎ 012667-61252) at 185 Torr Rd does B&B for £35 double. Camping is possible at *Cushendun Caravan Park* (☎ 012667-61254), 14 Glendun Rd, run by the local council. Self-catering houses and flats around Cushendun go for around £125 to £250 a week. Try *Ash Cottage* (☎ 01238-510877) or else try *Mullarts Apartments* (☎ 012667-61221) inside a converted church.

Places to Eat

The *tearoom* round the corner from the National Trust office serves hot snacks and salads. Bar food is available at the *Bay Hotel* and the *Cushendun*, and both places serve evening meals. If you phone beforehand, the

Villa does home-made meals until 7.30 pm for around £8.

Entertainment

On the opposite side of the harbour to the National Trust office a drink can be enjoyed, if you can squeeze in, at *McBride's* pub. *Pubs of the North* by J J Tohill reckons that McBride's is the smallest pub in Ireland at 1.5 by 2.8 metres. No children are allowed in, but maybe that's because they take up valuable space.

Getting There & Away

Ulsterbus No 150 links Cushendun with Ballymena, from where a connection to Belfast can be made. Bus No 162 travels to Larne five times daily and six times on Saturday, and it's a short hop from Larne to Belfast. See the introduction to this chapter for information on the summertime Antrim Coaster bus services along the coast.

CUSHENDALL

The red sandstone tower at the crossroads of this picturesque little village was built in the early 19th century by Francis Turnly. From the village the B14 road runs inland to the Glenariff Forest Park, in the loveliest of Antrim's nine glens, whence the A43 rejoins the A2 south of Cushendall at Glenariff, also known as Waterfoot.

Information

The tourist office is now in Mill St, opposite the library (☎ 012667-71180). It's open all year Monday to Friday 10 am to 1 pm and 3 to 5 pm, mornings only on Saturday. Boats and tackle can be hired for sea fishing from Red Bay Boats (☎ 012667-71331/71373) on the main road.

Layde Old Church

This ruined church and churchyard stand beside a fast-flowing stream that heads straight down to the sea. The church was founded by Franciscans but was used as a parish church from the early 14th century until 1790. The tombstones in the graveyard include MacDonnell memorials, and there's

a very pagan-looking one with a hole cut through it immediately on the left after entering the grounds. The church is over one km up a steep coast road (not the A2) which goes north to Cushendun and passes the YHANI hostel. There is a car park outside.

Ossian's Grave

Romantically, but inaccurately, named after the legendary warrior-poet of the 3rd century AD, this Neolithic court tomb consists of a two-chambered burial ground once enclosed by an oval cairn. The site is signposted off the A2 outside Cushendall on the Cushendun side. Park at the farm and walk up.

Glenariff Forest Park

Over 800 hectares of woodland make up the park, and the main attraction is a waterfall, about half an hour's walk from the visitors' centre. Views of the valley led Thackeray to exclaim that it was a 'Switzerland in miniature'. There are various walks, not all of them clearly marked; the longest is a three-hour circular mountain trail. There is a £2.50 charge for cars (£1.50 for motorcycles) or there's parking at the Manor Lodge Restaurant, on the road to the park. Even pedestrians have to pay £1 (children 50p).

Places to Stay

Camping & Hostel Camping is possible at the *Glenariff Forest Park* (☎ 012667-58232), while the *Glenville Caravan Park* (☎ 012667-71520) on the Layde road has a small camping area, charging £5 for a tent for two. *Cushendall Caravan Park* (☎ 012667-71699) on the coast road is bigger and pricier at £7.25 a tent. The *YHANI Hostel* (☎ 012667-71344) costs £6.30 and is on the Layde road that leads from Cushendall village up to Layde Old Church.

Hotels & B&Bs The *Thornlea Hotel* (☎ 012667-71223) has doubles for £45. Next door *Trosben Villa* (☎ 012667-71130) does B&B for from £20 a head. Farther up the road, at 1 Kilnadore Rd, *Mountain View* (☎ 012667-71246) is cheaper, with beds from £13. Right in the centre is *Riverside*

Guest House (☎ 012667-71655) at 14 Mill St with singles/doubles for £16/28. Near Glenariff, *Glen Vista* (☎ 012667-71439) at 245 Garron Rd does B&B at £24 for a double.

Places to Eat

Gillans Coffee Shop in Mill St does light lunches. Midweek, the *Thornlea Hotel* has a set dinner menu for £8.50; at weekends it's à la carte only. The hotel also serves afternoon tea and a high tea for £5. More expensive still is a country house dinner at *McAuley's* (☎ 012667-71733) at 63 Ballyeamon Rd. Glenariff Forest Park has its own *Waterfall Restaurant* with meals from £5 to £8; it's open daily March to October. On the road to the park the *Manor Lodge* does steaks and, in Waterfoot, pub food is available from the *Mariners' Bar* or the *Glenariff Inn*.

Getting There & Away

The buses serving Cushendall are the same as the ones for Cushendun: No 150 to Ballymena, No 162 to Larne, No 252 to Portrush and Nos 120/150 to Belfast.

Getting Around

The YHANI hostel hires out bikes for the standard £6 a day.

CARNLOUGH

The good beach attracts holidaymakers, and there are many buildings made of the fine local limestone, dating from when the building work was commissioned by the marquess of Londonderry in 1854. The limestone quarries were in use until the early 1960s, with the white stone bridge across the village carrying trains that brought the stone down to the harbour for export.

The tourist office is in the post office, just by the Londonderry Arms Hotel.

Places to Stay

Camping Both *Bay View Caravan Park* (☎ 01574-885685) and *Whitehill Caravan Park* (☎ 01574-885233) have limited camping space.

Hotel The prosperous and solid *Londonderry Arms Hotel* (☎ 01574-885255) was built as a coaching inn by the Marchioness of Londonderry in 1848. It was eventually inherited by a distant relation of hers, William Churchill, who sold it to the present owners. A standard double is £65, but there are various specials worth enquiring about if staying more than one night: for example, two nights' B&B at the weekend with one 5-course dinner thrown in costs £60 per person.

Places to Eat

The *Londonderry Arms Hotel* serves up locally caught fish, and a wild salmon steak for £8 is difficult to resist. The *Arkle Bar* in the hotel, named by loyal followers of the Irish horse that won 27 of its 35 races before being put down in 1970, is decorated with photographs of the famous horse. The *Glencloy Inn* (☎ 01574-885226) at the junction of Harbour Rd and Bridge St does food: a Sunday dinner for two inclusive of a bottle of wine is £20. The *Harbour House Tea Rooms* (☎ 01574-885056) upstairs overlooking the harbour serves teas and light meals until 9 pm.

Getting There & Away

Bus No 128 travels to and from Ballymena five times a day on Monday to Saturday, with connections to Belfast. Bus No 162 between Cushendun and Larne stops at Carnlough. See the introduction to this chapter for information on the summertime Antrim Coaster bus services.

GLENARM

Five km from Carnlough, this is the oldest village in the glens and the first one you come to if travelling up from Belfast or Larne. The pavements are made from attractive black and white pebbling and many of the buildings are coated white from the limestone dust of the local quarries. In the glen stands **Glenarm Castle** which dates back to the early 17th century; it was remodelled in the 19th century and is privately owned.

Places to Stay & Eat

Drumnagreagh Hotel (☎ 01574-841651) has doubles for £57, and *Dunluce* (☎ 01574-841279), 5 The Cloney, charges £12.50 per person for B&B. The hotel is the best place for a meal, though the *Heather Dew Tavern* is OK for grills and salad and there is often live music here at weekends. If you're coming from Carnlough, turn right at the crossroads for *Margaret's Guest House* (☎ 01574-847307), which has a café and does B&B for £14 a head.

Getting There & Away

The buses that serve Carnlough stop at Glenarm as well.

LARNE

Arriving from Scotland, Larne (*Lutharna*) offers a poor introduction to the spectacular Antrim coast and the rest of Northern Ireland. Conversely, if you've travelled down the coast, you might almost have forgotten the North's troubles until the sectarian graffiti around Larne brings it all rudely back again. There's not much to linger in for in Larne.

Despite the quite impressive 'ancient monument' signposting, **Olderfleet Castle** is an uninspiring example of a ruined 16th-century tower-house, crumbling away at the end of a row of terraced housing; to get there from the ferry terminal, take Olderfleet Rd along the seafront and turn right following the signpost at the roundabout. More imposing is the 19th-century round **Chaine Memorial Tower**, north of the ferry terminal in Chaine Memorial Rd. It was built to commemorate James Chaine, an MP in the 'imperial parliament of Great Britain and Ireland' from 1855 to 1874, and was paid for by 'contributions of every class in this mixed community irrespective of creed or party'. Chaine played an important role in getting Larne Harbour expanded to handle traffic with North America.

Heading along Curran Rd into town you'll pass two other reminders of Larne's American links. A statue of a family group commemorates the 52 people who emigrated

to Boston from Larne on the *Friend's Goodwill* in 1717, while a plaque commemorates the arrival of the first Americans into Larne during WWII in 1942.

Orientation & Information

It's about 15 minutes' walk from the ferry terminal to the town centre; take Fleet St on the right as you leave the terminal and then turn right again along Curran Rd. Inside the ferry terminal there's a small tourist information with a helpful list of B&B phone numbers right beside the phone booths to ring up and book. The main tourist office (☎ 01574-260088) is in Narrow Gauge Rd and is open Monday to Saturday 10 am to 6 pm; outside those hours it has a computer database and list of hotels displayed outside. Leaving Larne Town station, it's in the car park on the far side of the roundabout outside.

Places to Stay

Camping The most convenient camp site, if you're just off a ferry or you want to stay near the terminal, is *Curran Caravan Park* (☎ 01574-273797), five minutes from the harbour, on the left of Curran Road, and reached by following the sign to the town centre. It costs £5 a night. One of Ireland's better little camp sites is at *Carnfunnock Country Park* (☎ 01574-270541), nearly five km north of town off the A2. It's a modest place but well run and very pleasantly situated. A tent costs £5 a night. There's also *Browns Bay Caravan Park* (☎ 01574-260088) on Islandmagee, at £5.

B&Bs Closest to the harbour are a couple of B&Bs in Olderfleet Rd: the *Manor Guesthouse* at No 23 (☎ 01574-273305) with rooms from £13.50 per person, and the *Bellevue* at No 35 with beds from £12. Along Curran Rd, also within walking distance of the harbour, are *Moneydara* (☎ 01574-272912) at 149 Curran Rd and the comfortable *Seaview Guest House* (☎ 0574-272438), across the road at No 156, both charging from £13 a head. Even cheaper is

Killyneedan at 52 Bay Rd (☎ 01574-274943) with beds from £11.

Hotels The *Curran Court Hotel* (☎ 01574-275505), at 84 Curran Rd near the harbour and just past the camp site, charges £40 a double, while *Kilwaughter House* (☎ 01574-272591) at 61 Shanes Hill Rd charges £34. *Magheramorne House Hotel* (☎ 01574-279444), 59 Shore Rd, is a classy Victorian establishment on the A2 south of Larne, at £66 for a double. On Donaghy's Lane, 1½ km from town, the *Highways Hotel* (☎ 01574-272272) has doubles for £40.

Places to Eat

Main Street runs through the centre of town, with the inexpensive places at the harbour end. *Carriages* at No 105 does reasonable pizzas, kebabs and steaks and is open from noon to 11 pm Monday to Saturday. Two doors down the *Baile Bar* does reasonably priced bar meals and much pricier dinners. The *Lotus Flower* Chinese takeaway, popular with taxi drivers, is next door. More typically Irish meals – meat-dependent and substantial – are available at any of the four hotels. *Kiln* (☎ 01574-260924) is on the Old Glenarm Rd and has a decent reputation; it's in the £10 to £15 bracket. The *Captain's Kitchen* in the ferry terminal makes a good fallback for hot and cold food at odd hours.

Getting There & Away

Ferry P&O and Stena Sealink share Larne's smart ferry terminal, right beside a train station and bus stop and with car hire and foreign exchange facilities inside. P&O handles the route from Larne to Cairnryan and Stena Sealink the route from Larne to Stranraer, both in Scotland; crossings take just over two hours. The standard return is £40 for foot passengers (cycles free), with 50% discounts for students. Both companies offer return fares to cover a car and up to five passengers, with prices ranging from about £230 to £310, depending on the season and departure time; short-stay returns are often cheaper. For full details of P&O's six daily sailings contact the P&O Travel Centre, Pas-

senger Terminal, Larne Harbour, Larne, County Antrim BT40 1AQ (☎ 01574-274321) or Cairnryan, Stranraer, Wigtownshire DG9 8RF, Scotland (☎ 01581-200276). For Stena Sealink details contact the Sealink Travel Centre, Passenger Terminal, Larne Harbour BT40 1AW (☎ 0574-273616) or Sealink Travel Centre, Sea Terminal, Stranraer DG9 8EL (☎ 01776-702262). Note that the ferries get very busy over public holidays, when advance booking is advisable.

Bus See the introduction to this chapter for information on the summertime Monday to Saturday Antrim Coaster bus services along the coast. Bus No 156 is the regular service to and from Belfast. The earliest bus leaves the bus station, without calling at the harbour, at 7.15 am and the last one goes at 7.20 pm. It takes just over an hour and there are only three buses on a Sunday. Bus No 162 runs up and down the coast, calling at Glenarm, Carnlough, Waterfoot, Cushendall and Cushendun. It operates from the bus station and not the harbour.

Train Larne has two stations: Larne Town for the town centre and Larne Harbour (the end of the line) for the ferries. The journey from Belfast Central takes about 50 minutes.

ISLANDMAGEE

A day trip to Islandmagee (also known as Island Magee) makes a pleasant excursion. The name is deceptive in that this is an 11 by 3 km peninsula and not an island, but you get there by ferry. Close to the ferry landing point the Ballylumford Dolmen is domestically situated in the front garden of a private home. Also at this north end of the peninsula is Browns Bay, which has a sandy beach. Taking the more picturesque east coast road brings you to the Gobbins: over a mile of basalt cliffs with a path cut into the rock. During the 1641 rebellion, the garrison at Carrickfergus, seeking to revenge their fellow Protestants, massacred the Catholic inhabitants of the peninsula, throwing live and dead bodies over the cliffs.

Getting There & Away

The first Islandmagee ferries leave Larne at 7.30, 8 and 8.30 am, then hourly on the hour until 3 pm, and then every half hour until 5.30 pm; contact Larne Harbour Office (☎ 01574-279221) for more details.

CARRICKFERGUS

Carrickfergus (*Carraig Fhearghais*) is a commuter suburb just north of Belfast, noted for its wonderfully situated castle, overlooking the harbour where William III landed on 14 June 1690; there's a commemorative blue plaque on the site and a statue of the king on the seaward side of the castle. The town centre has some attractive 18th-century houses, and you can still trace a good part of the 17th-century city walls. Touches of kitsch abound; look out for the painted depiction of medieval life on a gable wall opposite the Town Hall at the end of High St.

Orientation & Information

The train station is at the end of North St. From there turn left outside the station and pass under North Gate; the castle is five minutes' walk downhill to the seafront. Ulsterbuses stop on Joymount Parade behind the town hall on the seafront.

The tourist information office (☎ 019603-366455) is inside the Heritage Plaza housing the new Knight Ride (see below); it's open April to September Monday to Saturday 10 am to 6 pm and Sunday noon to 6 pm; at other times of year it's open Monday to Friday 9 am to 5 pm.

Carrickfergus Castle

Theatrically sited on a rocky promontory, commanding the entrance to Belfast Lough, this fine castle was built by John de Courcy soon after his 1177 invasion of Ulster. Besieged by King John in 1210 and Edward Bruce in 1315, and briefly captured by the French in 1760, the castle also witnessed the attack on a British vessel in 1778 by the American John Paul Jones in the *Ranger* (the Americans won). The oldest part of the castle, going back to its Anglo-Norman origins, is the inner ward which is enclosed by a high wall. The keep houses a museum telling the castle's history, and the site

is dotted with life-size figures illustrating the castle's history and adding colour to what is undoubtedly Ireland's finest Norman castle.

The castle is open April to September from 10 am to 6 pm Monday to Saturday and from 2 to 6 pm Sunday; in winter it closes at 4 pm. Entry is £2.70/1.35, but joint tickets covering the Knight Ride as well cost £4.85/2.40.

Knight Ride

Inside the glistening, glassy Heritage Plaza in Antrim St is a Jorvik-style smells-and-all ride through Carrickfergus's past. Seated in a giant knight's helmet you swing out over the atrium and then run back in time, catching quick glimpses of Mary Dunbar's haunted house and the hanging corpses of members of the 18th-century O'Haughan gang. There's also more serious stuff about the castle narrated from the point of view of a child and his grandfather. Afterwards, you can recap the details on descriptive charts and examine a model of Carrickfergus in 1690 on the way out.

The Knight Ride is open April to September Monday to Saturday 10 am to 6 pm, and Sunday noon to 6 pm; the rest of the year it closes at 5 pm. Admission costs £2.60/1.35; or £4.85/2.40 for a combined ticket for the castle too.

St Nicholas' Church

The pillars in the nave date back to the church's establishment immediately after de Courcy's invasion of Ulster. Most of the rest dates to 17th-century restoration work, and a particularly fine example of such an addition is the Chichester memorial in the transept known as the Donegal aisle, probably the work of an English master mason who was influenced by the Renaissance style of northern Europe. Stained glass in the south side and the nave's west end is 16th-century Irish work. Sadly, you'll be lucky to find the church unlocked.

Andrew Jackson Centre

The parents of the US president left Carrickfergus in the second half of the 18th century, hence the Andrew Jackson Centre, a reconstructed dwelling of that era complete with fireside crane and earthen floor.

In summer the centre is open from 10 am to 1 pm and 2 to 6 pm Monday to Friday, 2 to 6 pm Saturday and Sunday, but opening time is changeable so ring ☎ 01960-366455 to check before setting out. The centre is in Boneybefore, three km north of Carrickfergus; there is a signposted right turn to the centre in Donaldson's Ave. The actual site of the ancestral home is indicated by a blue plaque just down the road from the centre. On weekdays you can get a bus to Downshire Rd whence it's a short walk; on a Sunday a taxi would cost £4 return from Carrickfergus town hall.

Places to Stay
The *Marine House* at 47-49 Irish Quarter South (☎ 019603-364055) does B&B for £17.50 a head, while the *Langsgarden* at 70-72 Scottish Quarter (☎ 019603-366369) charges £15. *Dobbins Inn Hotel* (☎ 019603-51905) at 6-8 High St has been around for over three centuries and has a priest's hole and 16th-century fireplace to prove it; it charges £60 for two. The least expensive B&B at £20 a double is *Marathon House* (☎ 01232-862475) in the satellite settlement of Greeniswood at 3 Upper Station Rd.

Places to Eat
The restaurant at the *Dobbins Inn Hotel* serves steak and bar meals as well as a set lunch. An evening meal is £10 at least. For just snacks and coffee, *Number 10* along the pedestrianised West St is OK, or try *Old Tech Griddle* farther up from the Dobbins Inn. At 38 Scotch Quarter the *Courtyard Coffee House* does light lunches as well, Monday to Saturday; it has a smaller branch inside Carrickfergus Castle. The *Gallery Restaurant* inside the Heritage Plaza also offers reasonably priced hot and cold food; on a Sunday it'll be your best, if not your only, option.

Getting There & Away
Ulsterbus No 165 takes 15 minutes to hop to Belfast (Oxford Bus Station), and bus No 163 takes 30 minutes. There are also regular daily trains from Belfast Central/Botanic stations.

ANTRIM TOWN
Antrim Town is no more interesting than the rest of inland County Antrim. In 1649 the town was burnt by General Monro, and in 1798 it resisted an attack by the United Irishmen. Modern Antrim Town is dominated by its shopping centre, but there are a few older buildings, including the fine courthouse which dates back to 1762. A heritage trail is available free from the tourist office (see below).

Information
The helpful tourist office (☎ 01849-428331) is at Pogue's Entry in Church St. It's open May to September from 10 am to 6 pm Monday to Saturday. Tentative plans exist for year-round opening. Until then the city council may be able to provide assistance in winter (☎ 01849-463113). Belfast Airport is handy, only six km to the south.

Round Tower
This 10th-century tower, 27 metres high, is all that remains of a monastery that once stood on the site. The walls are over a metre thick and the 10th-century dating is strong evidence for linking this and other towers with the Viking raids. The Antrim tower is in Steeple Park, about one mile north out of town; follow the signs for Steeple Industrial Estate and then for the Antrim Borough Council offices.

Pogue's Entry
In a narrow alley at the end of the main street a blue plaque marks the tiny, mud-floored home of Alexander Irvine (1863-1941), missionary and writer. His *My Lady of the Chimney Corner* tells the story of his mother's brave struggle to rear nine children in grinding poverty:

> Here amid these drab surroundings lived
> A lowly cobbler's wife
> All the darker shades of living
> Woven in her web of life.

Antrim Castle Grounds
Antrim Castle burnt down many years ago but the grounds are open as a public park,

tucked away behind the courthouse, along-side the river. The original gardens were laid out in the 17th century as a water garden and although some parts are pretty neglected this would be a good place for a summer picnic.

Places to Stay

It is best to avoid having to stay a night in Antrim if possible. There is only one hotel, *Deerpark Hotel* (☎ 01849-462480), on Dublin Rd, with doubles for £60. The camp site, *Sixmilewater Caravan Park* (☎ 01849-463113), is near the Antrim Forum just to the south-west of town. Washing facilities are a long walk away at the Forum but will be locked outside office hours. The camp site itself is only an open field and there is no attempt at any kind of security.

There are a few B&Bs in town, which include *Springhill* (☎ 01849-469117) at 37 Thornhill Rd with singles for £13 and doubles for £25. Down the road at No 23 (☎ 01849-462964) *Mrs Dennison* has rooms for the same prices. More B&Bs can be found in nearby Crumlin which is conve-nient for early morning flight departures. The tourist office has a complete list.

Places to Eat

Antrim is hardly filled with gourmet restau-rants but for a light lunch you could try *Lisa's Kitchen* in Church St, near the tourist office. The *Old Rogue* pub near the courthouse would do nicely for a drink afterwards.

Entertainment

Clotworthy Arts Centre (☎ 01849-428111) in the grounds of Antrim Castle has a small theatre and hosts changing exhibitions. The gallery is open from 9.30 am to 4.30 pm Monday to Friday and from 9.30 am to 1 pm Saturday, admission free. To find out what's on at the theatre without calling in you could try the tourist office or the local paper.

Getting There & Away

Ulsterbus No 20 from Ballymena to Belfast makes a stop in Antrim. There is also bus No 109 between Antrim and Belfast via Lisburn.

AROUND ANTRIM TOWN
Lough Neagh

The largest lake in Britain and Ireland covers 400 sq km, and legend has it that the giant Finn McCool created it by scooping out a lump of earth and throwing it into the Irish Sea, thus also creating the Isle of Man (which does bear a resemblance in shape and size to the lough). Of Northern Ireland's six coun-ties, only County Fermanagh doesn't border the lake. The *Maid of Antrim* cruises the lough but the schedule varies according to demand and it is best to check with the tourist office for the times. One-hour trips cost £2.50/1.50 and often leave at noon. A party can hire the entire boat for £80 per cruising hour, with another £35 per hour waiting time. The boat leaves from the marina just past the Antrim Forum.

Shane's Castle

The castle is on the western outskirts of Antrim on the A6 but at the time of writing the narrow-gauge railway was no longer running and it was unclear whether or in what form Shane's Castle would reopen to the public.

Patterson's Spade Mill

The National Trust now owns Ireland's last surviving water-driven mill for making spades and has opened it to the public, with continuous demonstrations of the processes involved in spade manufacture and a chance to buy your own spade should you have a spare £25 or so. The mill is open daily except Tuesday from June to August from 2 to 6 pm. In April, May and September it opens on weekend afternoons only. Admission is £2.50/1.25. To get there follow the A6 through Templepatrick towards Belfast and it's three km along on the left.

Randalstown

Six km west of Antrim the River Main flows under a crumbling aqueduct through Randalstown. The town has a Presbyterian church that's worth a second look – a mag-nificent oval building, put up in 1790, with an octagonal porch. As ever in Northern

Ireland, you won't be able to get inside it except during services.

BALLYMENA & AROUND

As you enter Ballymena (*An Baile Meánach*), a large sign proclaims it the 'City of the Seven Towers'. The story goes that one Sir Alexander Shafto Adair, owner of the Ballymena Estate, was standing on raised ground looking at the town when it occurred to him that you could see the towers of the old and new Episcopalian churches, the First Ballymena Presbyterian church, the Roman Catholic church, the town hall, the Braidwater spinning mill and the castle. The castle has since been demolished and the mill only ever had a chimney, not a tower, but you can pick up a tower trail for £1 in Morrow's Shop Museum (see below).

To get to Ballymena from Belfast, take the A26, a journey of 18 km.

This is the home town of Ian Paisley, founder leader of the Free Presbyterian Church and the stridently anti-Catholic Democratic Unionist Party. The town council was the first in the North to fall under control of the Democratic Unionist Party in 1977 and voted unanimously to remove all mention of Darwin's theory of evolution from religious education in Ballymena's schools, for, as the mayor explained, 'if you believe you come from a monkey you'll act like a monkey'. For those for whom politics is a closed book, it's also the birthplace of actor Liam Neeson of *Schindler's List* and *Rob Roy* fame.

While Ballymena's a pleasant enough small town, there's not much to linger for. The tourist office (☎ 01266-653663) at 13-15 Bridge St is open May to October from 10.30 am to 5 pm Monday to Friday and from 10 am to 4 pm Saturday. At other times of year contact Ballymena Borough Council (☎ 01266-44111) for information.

Morrow's Shop Museum

Right next door to the tourist office and open from 10 am to 1 pm and from 2 to 5 pm on weekdays (mornings only on Saturday) there's a small and not very inspiring exhibition of historical bits and bobs in Morrow's Shop Museum.

Arthur Cottage

The ancestors of Chester Alan Arthur, the 21st President of the United States, lived in a simple cottage about six km north-west of Ballymena, near the village of Cullybackey. It is open to visitors May to September from 10.30 am to 5 pm Monday to Friday, closing at 4 pm on Saturday. Interpreters in traditional costume demonstrate baking and crafts throughout June, July and August; call the Antrim tourist office for dates and times. Admission is £1/50p.

Gracehill

In the mid-18th century many Moravians fled their homeland to escape religious persecution and some of them settled in Gracehill where they became part of the larger Protestant community persecuting the Catholics. The Georgian architecture of their elegant village square includes a church (on the right as you enter the square) with separate entrances for men and women worshippers. If you'd like to see inside, visitors are welcome to Sunday services at 11 am and 6 pm. Even the graveyard at the back of the church is laid out for men on the left and women on the right, with the numbered tombstones lying flat either side of the walkway! Man and woman alike, they're rapidly vanishing beneath a coating of moss and grass.

To get to Gracehill from Ballymena, 2 km to the east, take the A42, which is the road that passes the bus and rail station in Ballymena. Look for a brown sign with a church marked on it and take the turning to the left.

Places to Eat

If you're passing through and just want somewhere for lunch the *Rendezvous Coffee Shop* in Balleymoney St near the car park does good soup-style lunches, or there's *Desperate Dan's* sandwich bar farther down the road. Alternatively, try the *Fern Room* in McKillen's department store in Church St.

LISBURN

The small town of Lisburn is just over half an hour's bus ride south-west of Belfast. In the early 1600s the Crown gave the Conways a lease to settle Lisburn. In 1627 they were also given permission to hold a Tuesday market which continues to this day (beside the bus terminal), making Tuesday the best day for a visit. A disastrous fire in 1707 destroyed much of Lisburn but the 17th-century Market House survived to become an assembly hall in the 18th century.

In the 18th and 19th centuries Lisburn grew rich on the proceeds of the linen industry; the modern post office in Linenhall St stands on the site of the old Brown Linen Hall where unbleached linen used to be sold. In the 18th century John Wesley came here several times, preaching in 1789 at Lisburn's first Methodist church in Market St. Nowadays the main reason to come here is to see the fine Linen Heritage Centre, a visit to which is included in Irish Linen Tours (see the Information section under Banbridge, County Down).

Information
The helpful tourist office (01846-663377) is housed in the same building as the Lisburn Museum and is open April to September Monday to Saturday from 9.30 am to 5.30 pm and Sunday 2 to 5.30 pm, closing half an hour earlier in winter. It has a bureau de change and can book accommodation.

Lisburn Museum & Linen Heritage Centre
The brand-new Linen Heritage Centre is housed beside Lisburn Museum, itself housed in the fine old Market House where brown linen was sold in the 18th century. The Heritage Centre is inside what was once a drapery shop. Visits start off on the ground floor where there are models of 18th-century linen traders in action. Upstairs there are temporary exhibits in what were the old Assembly Rooms, and then you proceed through a series of rooms which explain how linen is created and how it is used, with hand-loom damask weavers on hand to illustrate their trade. There are plenty of audiovisuals and hands-on exhibits to keep everyone amused. Finally you descend to the basement to see an audiovisual presentation about life in the 19th-century linen factories. Back on the ground floor there's an excellent café and gift shop.

The Lisburn Museum & Heritage Centre is open the same hours as the tourist office (see above) and admission is £2.50/1.50.

Castle Gardens Park
The park is immediately opposite a fine 19th-century building in Castle St which has had Lisburn College tacked onto it. There's a monument to Sir Richard Wallace, a large cannon, some odd pieces of city wall and fountains springing from stone birds.

Ballance House
With a car you could visit Ballance House (☎ 01846-648492) at 118A Lisburn Rd, Glenavy, 8.5 km north-west of Lisburn. It's the birthplace of New Zealand Prime Minister John Ballance (1839-1893). The farmhouse has been restored to its assumed appearance in 1850 and is open April to September.

Places to Stay & Eat
Lisburn is easily visited from Belfast but if you do want to stay, *Strathearn House* (☎ 01846-601661) at 19 Antrim Rd has rooms for £18/30 a single/double. *Overdale House* (☎ 01846-672275) at 150 Belsize Rd charges similar prices. Probably the best place to eat is *Café Crommelin* in the Heritage Centre which does soup and a roll for £1.50 or a wonderful selection of filled pastries. *Toffs* at 6 Railway St is owned by the same people and does curries, lasagnes and delicious cakes. *Montgomerys* at 26 Castle St does fish & chips; its ice cream with butterscotch sauce also receives rave reports. Provided it's before 11.30 am you can get breakfast for 99p at *Andrews Home Bakery/Restaurant* opposite the museum entrance.

Getting There & Away
Bus No 38 from Belfast leaves frequently from the Europa Bus Station. From Lisburn you can catch onward buses to Hillsborough, Banbridge and Newry. For more information phone ☎ 01846-662091.

Counties Tyrone & Fermanagh

Tyrone is the larger of the two counties but Fermanagh has most visitors with its lakes, rivers and medieval sites. In Tyrone the Sperrin Mountains are still relatively unspoiled and good hiking country. No trains operate in this part of Ireland, but Ulsterbus has services to most towns and larger villages.

County Tyrone

The attractions of County Tyrone are disparate ones – historical and forest parks, prehistoric sites, the lonely Sperrin Mountains – spread out between less-than-interesting towns in a way that makes it difficult for the visitor to get a feel for the county as a whole. But it's worth the effort of trying to get to know the place, for Tyrone has an illustrious history and its unspoiled countryside is perfect for anyone wanting to 'get away from it all'.

For centuries County Tyrone was the territory of the O'Neills, until the day when Hugh O'Neill, earl of Tyrone, finally submitted to the English at Mellifont in 1603. This marked the end of Gaelic Ireland. The English and Scottish planters moved in, introducing linen in the 18th century. Many local people subsequently migrated to America, and there are still links with the USA today. The huge Ulster-American Folk Park, sufficient reason in itself for visiting Tyrone, tells the story.

OMAGH

The county town of Tyrone, Omagh (*An Omaigh*) is pleasantly situated at the confluence of the rivers Camowen and Drumragh, which join to form the Strule. From the river the main street heads up to the classical 19th-century courthouse and divides in front of it. Although there are no special attractions in the town itself, it serves as a useful

Highlights
- Ulster-American Folk Park, eight km north of Omagh, one of the best museums in Ireland
- The lonely Sperrin Mountains, 64 km from east to west, which straddle the border with Derry
- Fishing and relaxing cruises on Upper and Lower Lough Erne, which stretches for 80 km from the North to the South
- Visiting the islands of Lough Erne, which contains many Celtic and early Christian archaeological sites
- The Janus Figure on Boa Island, one of the oldest stone statues in Ireland
- The round tower on Devenish Island, one of the best in the country

base for the surrounding area, and there are plenty of restaurants and shops. It's also a useful start or finish to a trip to the Sperrin Mountains or a local 16-km section of the Ulster Way. Decent places to eat are few and far between outside Omagh.

Information
The central tourist office (☎ 01662-247831), in the Sperrin Centre on the corner of Market St, is open from 9 am to 1 pm and 2 to 5 pm Monday to Friday, and also on Saturday during July and August. The post office is at 7 High St.

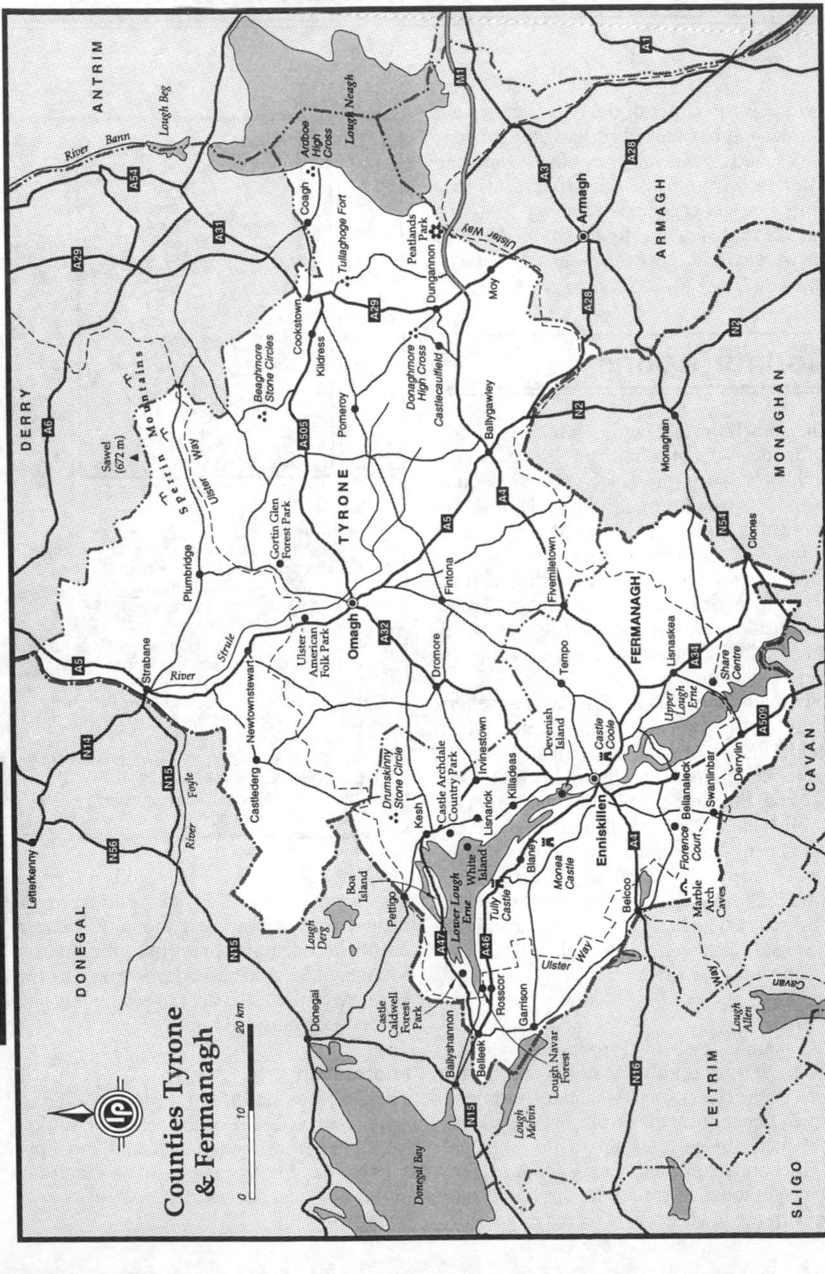

Counties Tyrone & Fermanagh

TYRONE & FERMANAGH

Places to Stay

There's little accommodation in the centre of Omagh. For details of the nearest camp site see the later Around Omagh section.

Hostel The YHANI *Glenhordial Hostel* (☎ 01662-241973), 9A Waterworks Rd, is three km north-east on the B48 Omagh to Gortin road. From the bus station take Mountjoy Rd; turn right at Killybrack Rd and follow the signs. It has 20 beds (three of which are adapted for wheelchair users) and free hot shower, rents bikes, charges £6 for a bed and is open all year. If you ring from the station they'll come and pick you up.

B&Bs A standard B&B close to the centre and charging £15 per person, is *Ardmore* (☎ 01662-243381), 12 Tamlaght Rd. Go up High St from the tourist office, heading for the courthouse at the top of the street and take the left turn in front of the church into Church St. Follow the road down and Tamlaght Rd is the second turning on the right. *Mrs Devine* (☎ 01662-241719), 1 Arleston Park off the Cookstown road, has two rooms at £13 per person.

Hotels The oldest hotel (dating from 1787) in Omagh is the *Royal Arms Hotel* (☎ 01662-243262), 51-53 High St just up from the tourist office, with singles/doubles at £35/65 for B&B. The *Silverbirch Hotel* (☎ 01662-242520), 5 Gortin Rd, has 29 rooms, all with bathroom, and charges £29/53 for B&B.

Places to Eat

The *Memory Lane Lounge* in the Royal Arms Hotel has pub lunches for around £3 to £4 and dinners for a couple of pounds more. The *Hunting Lodge*, also in the hotel, is a coffee lounge with tempting home-made snacks and sandwiches. Finally, there's the *Village Gossip Restaurant* in the hotel at which dinner for two costs around £20.

Opposite the hotel the *Shoppers' Restaurant* does lunches and salads, while the *Pink Elephant*, back on the hotel side up toward the courthouse, serves breakfast and lunches for £3. Close by, the *Carlton* does excellent pastries and breads and has a coffee shop at the back. Next to the courthouse at 2 High St, *Dragon Castle* is a Chinese restaurant also serving European food, with main dishes between £4 and £5. *Mister G*, down an alleyway opposite the tourist office, is in a quiet spot and does pizzas and snacks.

Down Bridge St toward the bus station *Old McDonald's* is suitable for fast-food fans and nearby the *Bridge* has breakfasts for £2.

Out of town, on the A5 road to Newtownstewart about 1.5 km from the Ulster-American Folk Park, is the *Mellon Country Inn*. It serves good food with buffet meals from £4 to £5.

Getting There & Away

Ulsterbus services connect Omagh with a number of towns in the North and the Republic. Bus No 273 runs nine times daily to Belfast (1¾ hours) and Derry (1¼ hours); and bus No 274 runs six times daily from Omagh to Dublin (3½ hours) via Monaghan (50 minutes). A number of other buses leave Omagh for Enniskillen, Donegal, Killybegs and Glenties. Bus No 296 leaves Omagh for Cork (9¼ hours) once a day Monday to Saturday, with connections to Athlone, Galway, Limerick and Waterford.

The bus station (☎ 01662-242711), 3 Mountjoy Rd, is a short walk from the town centre, down Bridge St and across the river.

Getting Around

Bicycles can be hired from Conway Cycles (☎ 016627-246195), 1 Old Market Place, for £7/30 a day/week. Apart from the Glenhordial Hostel, there are no hire places nearer to the Sperrin Mountains.

AROUND OMAGH
Ulster-American Folk Park

This is one of the best museums (☎ 01662-243292) in Ireland and well worth a visit. Thousands of Ulster people left their country to forge a new life across the Atlantic: 200,000 in the 18th century alone. The American Declaration of Independence was signed by five Ulster men, and the Exhibition

Hall is able to offer many more instances of this transatlantic link.

The real appeal of the folk park, though, is the outdoor museum. The number of life-size exhibits is impressive: a forge, weaver's cottage, Presbyterian meeting house, schoolhouse, log cabins, a 19th-century Ulster street, an early American street, and a ship and dockside gallery with reconstructed parts of an emigration ship. Costumed guides and craftspeople are on hand to chat and explain the art of cooking, spinning, weaving, candle making and so on. There is almost too much to absorb in one visit and at least half a day is needed to do it justice.

Admission is £3.50/1.70 (family £10). It is open Easter to early September from 11 am to 6.30 pm Monday to Saturday and to 7 pm Sunday. The rest of the year it's open from 10.30 am to 5 pm Monday to Friday.

The park is eight km north of Omagh on the A5 to Newtownstewart. Bus No 97 to Strabane and Derry stops outside the park. In July and August only on Tuesday and Thursday, bus No 213, the Sperrin Sprinter, leaves Omagh at 1.45 pm and stops at the park 20 minutes later, but you'd need to catch bus No 97 back.

Ulster History Park

The theme of this park is the story of settlements in Ireland from the Stone Age to the plantation. Full-scale models are on show of a Mesolithic encampment, Neolithic houses, a late Bronze Age crannóg, a 12th-century church settlement complete with stone round tower, and a Norman motte-and-bailey. There is also a reception building with a cafeteria, shop and audiovisual theatre and a model plantation settlement. The park is over-reliant on models and reconstructions, giving it a rather phoney feel.

It's open April to September from 11 am to 6 pm Monday to Friday, to 7 pm Saturday and from 1 to 7 pm Sunday. From October to March the hours are 11 am to 5 pm. Admission is £3/1.50.

The park is about 10 km north-east of Omagh off the B48 road to Gortin. Bus No 92 between Omagh and Gortin stops outside (there's no Sunday service).

Gortin Glen Forest Park

Over 400 hectares of the Gortin Glen Forest form the forest park, mostly planted with conifers, and containing a herd of Japanese Sika deer as well as other animals and birds. It's a park suited to cars and motorbikes, an eight-km tarmac drive being the main way to get around. Near the main car park there are some wildlife enclosures, an indoor exhibit, a small nature trail and a café. An entry ticket costs £2 for a car (£1.50 for a motorbike) from the ranger on duty or from the ticket machine.

There's a manageable day's walk from Gortin Forest Park to the Ulster-American Folk Park, along a section of the Ulster Way. The 16-km trip is mostly over small roads, forest roads and tracks, and from the folk park bus No 97 could be caught back to Omagh. The last bus leaves the folk park at 7.30 pm. A £1.50 leaflet, entitled The Ulster Way, North-West Section, covers this section with a map and should be available from the Omagh tourist office or by post from the Sports Council for Northern Ireland (☎ 01232-381222), House of Sport, Upper Malone Rd, Belfast BT9 5LA.

Fishing

There is fishing along stretches of the three rivers around Omagh – mainly for brown and sea trout, and salmon during the season from 1 April to mid-October. Permits, advice and information are available in Omagh from: C A Anderson (☎ 01662-242311), 64 Market St, or Chism Fishing Tackle (☎ 01662-244932), 2 Bridge St.

Places to Stay

Camping The nearest camp site is at Gortin Glen Caravan Park (☎ 016626-48108), 10 km north of Omagh on the B48 Omagh to Gortin road. Sites for tents are £4 to £7. Bus Nos 92 and 213 (summer only) will stop nearby. The camp site is a few minutes from the Ulster Way, and campers get a discount at the Omagh Leisure Centre.

The same distance to the north-east of Omagh is *Harrigan Caravan Park* (☎ 016626-61560) in Newtownstewart on the A5 past the Ulster-American Folk Park. There's only room for half a dozen pitches and you have to arrive before 5 pm, but it costs just £1.50 per person and it's open all year.

B&Bs If you wanted to make a day of it visiting the two museums, *Camphill Farm* (☎ 01662-245400) is very close to the Ulster-American Folk Park at 5 Mellon Rd, Mountjoy, and costs £14 per person. Another, less-expensive place close to the folk park is *Daleview* (☎ 01662-241182) at 96 Beltany Rd on the A5 just past the folk park, with rooms for £12.50 per person.

SPERRIN MOUNTAINS

In the north-east of the county the gentle contours of the Sperrin Mountains, 64 km from east to west, straddle the border with Derry. The blanket bog and heather of the open moorland in the upper reaches contrast with the farmland and wooded valleys on the lower slopes. Wildlife is plentiful and fishing for trout is common.

The mountains reach their highest point at Mt Sawel (672 metres) just behind the **Sperrin Heritage Centre** (☎ 0126626-48142). In the Heritage Centre, computer presentations and other displays are devoted to the historical, social and ecological aspects of the region. Gold has been found in the mountains and part of the exhibition is devoted to it. Barry McGuigan, the Irish world champion boxer, had his first gold medal made from the local gold.

The centre has a café and is open April to September from 11 am to 6 pm Monday to Friday, 11.30 am to 6 pm Saturday and 2 to 7 pm Sunday; admission is £1.80/80p. For 65/35p extra you can try your luck at prospecting for gold in a nearby stream.

The centre is on the B47. To get there from Omagh you go through Gortin to Plumbridge on the B48 and then it's about 13 km east. It can also be reached from the Dungiven or Cookstown side. Buses from Omagh go only as far as Plumbridge.

If you are thinking of **walking** up Mt Sawel, enquire at the centre as to the best route to take. The climb is easy, but some farmers are more accommodating than others. The Ulster Way comes in this direction, and it could be joined at Leagh's Bridge six km away. This point is roughly half way along the 55-km Dungiven to Gortin section of the Ulster Way. Another outdoor trip through the Sperrins would be on **horseback**. The Edergole Riding Centre (☎ 016487-62924), 70 Moneymore Rd, Cookstown BT80 8PY, is a horse-riding school that organises three-day trekking trips through the mountains, or hourly hire for £7 (see also Places to Stay in the Cookstown section).

COOKSTOWN

Until recently Cookstown (*An Chorr Chríochach*) represented Northern Ireland at its most forbidding. The town, founded in 1609 by planter Alan Cooke, has a 2.5-km-long, wide main street, with Catholics living at one end and Protestants at the other. The town has seen its share of sectarian violence, but since the ceasefire and the start of the peace process, local people are hopeful that the relatively normal way of life that has resumed can be maintained.

The two heavily guarded army checkpoints, nicknamed the 'daleks', that once stood at both approaches to the main street, have been removed. The army base is still there next to the Catholic school and you can't ignore the heavily barricaded courthouse, but the most visible human manifestation of authority out on the streets is the traffic warden.

Information

The tourist office (☎ 016487-66727), 48 Molesworth St, is open April to September from 9 am to 5 pm Monday to Friday, and to 1 pm Saturday. Molesworth St, which runs west off the main street, is the beginning of the B73 road to Coagh on the Derry border.

TYRONE & FERMANAGH

Places to Stay

The nearest camp site is *Drum Manor Forest Park*; see Around Cookstown later for details. The least expensive B&B is the *Central Inn* (☎ 016487-62255), 27 William St, at £12.50 per person. *Edergole* (☎ 016487-62924), 70 Moneymore Rd, costs £16 per person and has a horse-riding school. Both B&Bs are open all year.

Hotels in town are *Glenavon House Hotel* (☎ 016487-64949), 52 Drum Rd (the road to Omagh), at £40/60 a single/double for B&B; the nearby and cheaper *Greenvale Hotel* (☎ 016487-62243), at No 57, with rooms for £25/45; and the *Royal Hotel* (☎ 016487-62224), 68 Coagh St, with rates at £23/46.

Places to Eat

For takeaways and café cuisine try *Jo Mac's Diner* on Molesworth St. Inexpensive Chinese and European food is available at several Chinese restaurants; try *Dragon Palace*, at the southern approach to town, or *Gourmet Chinese*, at the other end and on the opposite side of the street. *Rossiter's*, also on the main street, is good for cheap standard meals (£2 to £3) during the day.

Lunch and dinner are available at the three hotels; the *Greenvale* is the most expensive at around £14 for dinner, while the *Glenavon House Hotel* charges about £10.

Getting There & Away

Bus No 210 connects Cookstown four times daily with Belfast (1¾ hours) Monday to Friday (once daily at weekends). The No 278 service runs to Dungannon (20 minutes), Armagh (50 minutes) and Monaghan (1¾ hours), from where you can catch Bus Éireann buses to Dublin. Bus No 80 shuttles regularly between Cookstown and Dungannon, where you can connect with bus No 273 to Belfast, Omagh or Derry.

The Ulsterbus station (☎ 016487-66440) is on Molesworth St near the tourist office.

AROUND COOKSTOWN

No public transport goes directly to the following sights though buses do pass close by. For bus numbers, times and fares check with the Ulsterbus station (☎ 016487-66440) in Cookstown.

Wellbrook Beetling Mill

Beetling is the final stage in the making of linen where the cloth is beaten with wooden hammers, or beetles, to give it a smooth sheen. There were once six mills at Wellbrook. The hammers were driven by water; one of them has been well maintained by the National Trust, and can be seen at work – it was literally deafening for those employed in these mills.

TYRONE & FERMANAGH

Bernadette Devlin

In 1947, Bernadette Devlin was born at the Catholic end of Cookstown. As a student she became involved in the Civil Rights movement, and was elected to Westminster in 1969 as the youngest-ever MP.

She was imprisoned for her part in the 1969 Bogside battle in Derry, and after Bloody Sunday in 1972 her notoriety reached its height when she physically attacked the British Home Secretary in the House of Commons.

Since withdrawing from parliamentary politics, she has been working on issues of human rights and social justice. She has fought campaigns on prisoners' issues, against discrimination in employment, and against sectarianism and repression. Her commitment to justice and democracy has brought its price. She was lucky to survive a Protestant assassination squad that attacked her home and family while they lay sleeping in 1981 and left her badly wounded. She remains physically disabled from the injuries she received, but continues to work against social injustice.

Bernadette McAliskey, as she is now known, and her family live in a small council flat near Cookstown. ■

The mill is open daily over Easter. In July and August it is open from 2 to 6 pm Wednesday to Monday, while from April to June and in September it is only open on Saturday, Sunday and bank holidays from 2 to 6 pm. Admission is £1.40/70p. Take the A505 Omagh road five km west to Kildress and turn right at the church; it's about a km from there.

Cregganconroe Chambered Cairn

This cairn, like most, is ancient but not spectacular. The lintel stone has collapsed onto the two portal stones that led into the burial gallery, and the huge capstone has also slipped. The site has not been excavated. To get there, take the A505 west from Cookstown and after a few km look for the signpost for Cregganconroe on the left. From there it is 10 km to the site.

Beaghmore Stone Circles

On the fringe of the Sperrin Mountains set on desolate moorland near Davagh Forest Park, this series of Bronze Age (2000 to 1200 BC) circles, cairns and stone alignments pose a mystery for archaeologists and visitors alike. Preserved in peat, these prehistorical monuments were only discovered in the mid-1950s. Especially intriguing is the 'Dragon's Teeth', one of the larger of the seven circles. It is filled with closely set stones that jut out of the ground in an apparently random manner. Various explanations have been suggested for these monuments – religious, astronomical and social – but the plain fact is that no-one knows for sure.

The circles, 14 km north-west of Cookstown, are signposted off the A505 road to Omagh.

Tullaghoge Fort

Unusually, something is known about the inhabitants of this hill fort. It was the burial ground of the O'Hagans and the inauguration place of the O'Neills as the kings of Ulster in the 11th century. A 1601 map marks the spot, on the hillside to the south-east, where the stone inauguration chair stood. The following year the chair was destroyed by Mountjoy while in pursuit of Hugh O'Neill, the last of the clan to be inaugurated.

To get there, leave town on the A29 Dungannon road south then turn left onto the B520; the fort is four km south-east of Cookstown. From the car park a path leads to the site.

Ardboe High Cross

The 10th-century Ardboe (the 'd' is not pronounced) high cross stands 5.5 metres high in front of a 6th-century monastery site, now housing the ruins of a 17th-century church – and with Lough Neagh in the background it ought to be more dramatic than it is. However, the cross is one of the best preserved in Ulster, with the east side showing Old Testament scenes and the west side New Testament ones. On the east side try making out Adam and Eve, the sacrifice of Isaac, Daniel and the Lions, the Burning Fiery Furnace, a bishop with people around, and Christ in glory. The New Testament side has the Magi, the Miracle at Cana, the Miracle of the Loaves and Fishes, the entry into Jerusalem, the arrest of Christ and the Crucifixion. Easier to decipher are some of the 18th-century tombstones in the churchyard.

Ardboe (*Ard Bo*) is 16 km east of Cookstown on the shore of Lough Neagh. To get there take the B73 through Coagh to just before Newtown Trench where you turn right (south).

Places to Stay

Drum Manor Forest Park (☎ 01868-759664), four km west of Cookstown on the A505 road to Omagh, has a small camping area costing £6 a night. It's a pleasant enough park, with a couple of lakes, a butterfly farm and arboretum, but there is no hot water or showers. You're likely to have the place to yourself, and a small barbecue could easily be set up. If you have a car be sure to arrive before 4 pm when a barrier goes down, and collect a key if you're intending to leave early in the morning.

DUNGANNON

Until 1602, when the castle and town were burnt to prevent them falling into the hands of the English, Dungannon was one of the chief seats of the O'Neill family. Plantation of English and Scottish settlers took place in the 17th and 18th centuries. In 1969 the town entered contemporary history books when the Civil Rights Association, formed a year earlier to protest against the rampant social and political inequalities suffered by Catholics, organised its first march from Coalisland to Dungannon. The crowd of 4000 was met by a police cordon outside the town, and although there was no serious violence, it was the beginning of a new era.

Information
Tourist information is available from the council offices (☎ 01868-725311), in Circular Rd, from 9 am to 1 pm and 2 to 5 pm, Monday to Friday. To get there follow the signs for the leisure centre; the council offices are next door to it.

The Control Zone in the town centre is enforced, which is why parked cars have at least one person inside; if you're driving, leave your car farther out or use the car park close to the square, which will cost a lot less than the £20 fine for leaving a vehicle unattended.

Tyrone Crystal
At Tyrone Crystal's (☎ 01868-725335) premises, just outside town, tours of the factory cover the different stages in the production of the crystal, starting with a visit to the furnace where the molten glass is prepared and then hand-blown. The glass pieces are then checked for faults, bevelled, marked, cut and polished.

The showroom contains examples of all the crystal, including slightly imperfect pieces that do not bear the Tyrone Crystal insignia but cost about 25% less. Tyrone Crystal may not have the illustrious reputation of Waterford glass, but it makes a splendid gift or souvenir. Prices range from £13 for a tumbler to £100 and more for vases and bowls.

The tour is £2, which you get back if you buy something. The factory is open from 9.30 am to 3.30 pm Monday to Thursday and

Saturday, but mornings only on Friday. To get there take the A45 north-east from town – it is clearly signposted – or else catch bus No 80.

Places to Stay
Camping The local council's *Killymaddy Tourist Centre* (☎ 01868-767259/725311), on Ballygawley Rd (the A4), has full facilities and costs £4. *Dungannon Park* (☎ 01868-727327), about 1.5 km south of town on Moy Rd signposted off the A29, is in a quiet location, has good facilities and also costs £4.

B&B & Hotels *Town House* (☎ 01868-723597), 32 Northland Row, is one of the least expensive B&Bs at £12 per person. The *Glengannon Hotel* (☎ 01868-727311), at Drumgormal on the A4 Ballygawley Rd, charges £30 per room for B&B, while the *Inn on the Park* (☎ 01868-725151), on Moy Rd, charges £37.50/55 a single/double.

Places to Eat
There's not a lot of choice. In the town square the *Dunowen Inn* serves pub food and set meals, as does *The Fort*, on Scotch St down from the square. The restaurant at the *Inn on the Park* serves decent steaks and fish for around £10.

For something fancy in the £20-a-head range, try the *Grange Lodge* (☎ 01868-784212) near Moy. This award-winning restaurant specialises in locally reared duckling. To get there, take the A29 south towards Armagh for 2.5 km and turn left at the signpost.

Getting There & Away
Bus No 80 shuttles regularly between Dungannon and Cookstown (20 minutes) to the north. The No 278 service runs south to Armagh (30 minutes) and Monaghan (1¼ hours) from where you can catch Bus Éireann buses to Dublin. The journey between Dungannon and Belfast (50 minutes, £4.10 one way) is possible on bus Nos 261, 262 and 273. These and other services, many direct, connect with most big

towns in Ulster, as well as routes to Donegal and the rest of the Republic.

The Ulsterbus station (☎ 01868-722251) is at the bottom of Scotch St, over the bridge and to the left.

AROUND DUNGANNON
Peatlands Park

The visitors' centre has an informative display about peat, aimed at a young audience. The bog garden is worth a visit if only to familiarise yourself with the sundew, one of Ireland's two carnivorous plants. It is a tiny plant, easily missed. Pitcher plants also thrive in the garden, but these were introduced into Ireland over a century ago from Canada. Also in the park are two lakes, a small forest and an orchard.

The open-top narrow-gauge railway, once used for transporting peat, does a 15-minute circuit of the park for children. From Easter to the end of September the trains run from 2 to 6 pm Saturday and Sunday (daily during July and August) for 70/30p. The visitors' centre has the same hours.

To get to this park, which is at the Birches 13 km east of Dungannon, take Exit 13 off the M1 motorway.

Donaghmore High Cross

The cross is a hybrid, being made of the base and shaft of one cross and the head and part shaft of another with the join clearly visible. The decorated biblical scenes are similar to those on the Ardboe Cross. On the east side are the Angel and the Shepherds, the Adoration of the Magi, the Miracle at Cana, the Miracle of the Loaves and Fishes and the arrest of Christ and the Crucifixion. On the west side are Adam and Eve, Cain and Abel and Abraham and Isaac.

The cross is eight km north-west of Dungannon on the B43 road to Pomeroy, easily spotted at a road junction.

Castlecaulfield

Not a castle as such, but the remains of what was once a substantial Jacobean house, Castlecaulfield was built in the early 17th century by Sir Toby Caulfield on the site of

an earlier Gaelic fort belonging to the O'Donnellys. Over the gatehouse the Caulfield coat of arms can be made out, and this survived the O'Donnellys' act of revenge in 1641 when the house was burned down. It was rebuilt; and hosted a church service by John Wesley, the founder of Methodism, in 1767.

To get there, take the A4 west out of Dungannon and after about six km a small road is signposted to the right.

Parkanaur Forest Park

About 1.5 km from Castlecaulfield, an oak forest is being developed on what was once the Burgess family estate, the Victorian dwelling now being a centre for the disabled. The old farm buildings display farm and forest machinery and there are some short nature trails. The park has five short walking trails.

The white fallow deer in the park are descended from the oldest deer herd in Ireland, going back to 1595 when a doe and hart, a gift from Elizabeth I to her goddaughter, were raised at Mallow Castle. Parkanaur Forest Park brought five deer from Mallow in 1978 and there are now about 20.

The park has a *camp site* (☎ 018687-58256) for £4 a night plus a deposit for the barrier key, but there's no hot water or showers. An entry ticket to the park costs £2 for cars (£1.50 for motorbikes) from the ranger on duty. The park entrance is 11 km west of Dungannon on the A4.

Ulysses S Grant Ancestral Homestead

Ulysses S Grant led Union forces to victory in the American Civil War and later became the 18th US president from 1869-77. The home of his mother's family has been restored in the style of a typical 19th-century Irish small farm. The furniture is not authentic, but the original field plan of this four-hectare farm is still there, together with various old farming implements.

The visitors' centre has an exhibition and café and is open May to September from noon to 5 pm Monday to Saturday and from

12.30 to 4.30 pm Sunday. The rest of the year it is open from 10.30 am to 4.30 pm Monday to Friday. Admission is £1/50p. The site is 18 km west of Dungannon. Take the A4 west and turn left at the sign just before the village of Ballygawley.

The Argory

This neoclassical house dates from 1824 and the National Trust advertise it as a 'time capsule' due to its complete turn-of-the-century furnishings. There is no electricity; the central stove and the oxyacetylene gas plant help to define the late-Victorian and Edwardian character of the house. Tours of the building and grounds take in the drawing room, with its rosewood Steinway piano, the study and billiard room and dining room. The courtyards house further displays as well as a shop and tearoom.

The Argory is open April to June, and also September, from 2 to 6 pm Saturday and Sunday, while during July, August and the Easter period it is open from 2 to 6 pm daily except Tuesday; admission is £2.20/1.10 plus £1 for the car park.

It's on Derrycaw Rd in Moy, nine km south-east of Dungannon: take the A29 south, then turn left onto the B106 and right onto the B34.

County Fermanagh

The River Erne wanders through County Fermanagh – one of the smallest counties in Ireland – into a lake which is 80 km long. Where Lough Erne constricts in the middle sits the town of Enniskillen, at the centre of Fermanagh and the obvious base for any exploration of the county. The town's tourist office serves the whole county and its literature includes a useful free booklet that gives comprehensive details of all types of accommodation in Fermanagh.

Lower Lough Erne attracts people for varying reasons: the fishing is superb, there are good facilities for water sports outside Enniskillen, and the islands of Devenish and White have remarkable ecclesiastical remains. A third island, Boa, has a cemetery with a unique stone statue dating back around 2000 years.

Early Christian missionaries came and settled in Fermanagh, but Christianity only slowly penetrated the local pagan culture; Viking and Norman invaders couldn't subdue the region and even the Tudors were unable to do so until after 1600, when Enniskillen finally fell to the English. Planters then moved in and quickly established a series of castles around Lough Erne. The town of Enniskillen was transformed into a centre of colonial power and its strategic importance to the British led to its unparalleled boast of possessing two royal regiments.

At the time of Partition, Fermanagh, despite the majority of its people being Catholic, was reluctantly drawn into Northern Ireland, but there is little evidence of its nationalist spirit diminishing. The British parliament does not like to be reminded that one of its members was allowed to starve himself to death in an effort to establish political recognition for IRA prisoners. Bobby Sands was elected as MP for Fermanagh and South Tyrone in the spring of 1981, and he died 66 days after beginning his fast, without ever taking up his seat in Westminster.

ENNISKILLEN

The small town of Enniskillen (*Inis Ceithleann*) is a handy centre for activities on Upper and Lower Lough Erne and the antiquities around them. Oscar Wilde and Samuel Beckett were both pupils at the Portora Royal School. The town is Catholic, close to the border, and lacks the dourness of some of the North's other towns.

In 1987 an IRA bomb exploded at a Remembrance Day service in Enniskillen and 13 innocent people lost their lives.

Orientation & Information

The town centre is on an island in the waterway connecting the upper and lower loughs. The main street changes name frequently, but the clocktower marks the centre. The other principal thoroughfare through town is Wellington Rd, which runs south of and parallel to the main street. Vehicles should not be left unattended in the town centre, but there are plenty of nearby car parks.

The well-run Fermanagh tourist office (☎ 01365-323110/325050), in the Lakeland Visitor Centre, just south of Wellington Rd, is open April and May from 9 am to 5 pm Monday to Friday, and from 10 am to 6 pm Saturday; June and September from 9 am to 5.30 pm Monday to Friday and from 10 am to 6 pm Saturday; and July and August from 9 am to 6.30 pm Monday to Friday, 10 am to 5 pm on Saturday and 11 am to 5 pm Sunday. The rest of the year it is open from 9 am to 5 pm Monday to Friday, except between 1 and 2 pm.

The post office, on East Bridge St, is open from 9.30 am to 5.30 pm Monday to Friday and from 9.30 am to 12.30 pm Saturday. The Halifax Bank, 20 High St, is open from 9 am to noon Saturday. As well as at the banks, you can change money at the post office, tourist office and the Crowe's Nest pub in High St.

Enniskillen Castle & Museums

The Fermanagh Heritage Centre and the Regimental Museum of the Royal Inniskilling Fusiliers (☎ 01365-323142) are both inside the castle. From land the castle looks unimpressive, but the turreted building known as **Watergate** looks good from the water.

The heritage centre occupies the central keep and contains artefacts on local farming and manufacturing, but it is not particularly interesting. The regimental museum has been extensively refurbished and is crammed full of medals, guns and uniforms of both the fusiliers and the dragoon guards, Enniskillen's other regiment. The centre and the museum are open from 10 am to 5 pm Tuesday to Friday and 2 to 5 pm Saturday to Monday; admission is £1.50/75p (students £1).

Cole's Monument

The monument, in Forthill Park at the eastern end of town, was named after the first earl of Enniskillen's son, Galbraith Lowry Cole (1772-1842), one of Wellington's generals. The 108 steps inside this Doric column can be climbed for rewarding views of the surrounding area. Mid-May to mid-September it is open from 11 am to 1 pm and 2 to 5 pm Monday to Friday, while at weekends it's open from 2 to 6 pm; admission is 50/30p.

Activities

The best place for hiring equipment for **water sports** is at the Lakeland Canoe Centre (☎ 01365-32450) on Castle Island in Enniskillen. Free ferries depart from the Lakeland Forum Leisure Centre just behind the Fermanagh tourist office. Canoes, sailboards, sailing boats and jet skis are all available for hire.

Erne Tours (☎ 01365-322882) run 1¾-hour **cruises** of Lough Erne aboard the MV *Kestrel* with a stop at Devenish Island. The boat leaves from the Round 'O' pier at Brook Park and the cruise costs £4/2.

Places to Stay

Camping & Hostel There is hostel-style accommodation and a camp site at the *Lakeland Canoe Centre* (☎ 01365-324250/ 322411) on Castle Island, which is reached by ferry (free) from the Lakeland Forum Leisure Centre. It costs £4 to camp, or £9 in the hostel.

B&Bs B&Bs can be found on the outskirts of town west along the A4 Sligo road. *Carraig Aonrai* (☎ 01365-324889), at No 19, is the least expensive at £10.50/20 a single/double. *Rossole House* (☎ 01365-323462), at No 85, is £14/28. A little farther out *Ashwood Guest House* (☎ 01365-323019) costs £18 per person and is well appointed and spacious.

At the other side of town B&Bs can be found along the B80 road to Tempo. *Lackaboy Farm House* (☎ 01365-322488), one km from the centre, has rooms for £15/28. *Drumcoo House* (☎ 01365-326672) is at 32 Cherryville, Cornagrade Rd, by the roundabout on the road north to Castle

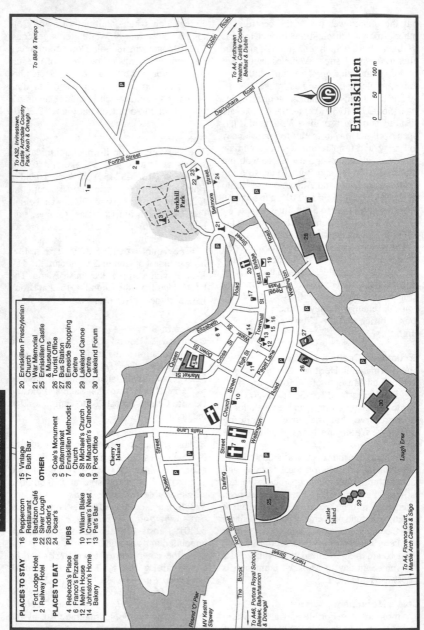

Enniskillen

0   50   100 m

PLACES TO STAY
1 Fort Lodge Hotel
2 Railway Hotel

PLACES TO EAT
4 Rebecca's Place
6 Franco's Pizzeria
12 Melvin House
14 Johnston's Home
    Bakery

16 Peppercorn
    Restaurant
18 Barbizon Café
22 Silver Lough
23 Saddler's
24 Oscar's

PUBS
10 William Blake
11 Crowe's Nest
13 Pat's Bar

15 Vintage
17 Bush Bar

OTHER
3 Cole's Monument
5 Buttermarket
7 Enniskillen Methodist
   Church
8 St Michael's Church
9 St Macartin's Cathedral
19 Post Office

20 Enniskillen Presbyterian
    Church
21 War Memorial
25 Enniskillen Castle
    & Museums
26 Tourist Office
27 Bus Station
28 Emeside Shopping
    Centre
29 Lakeland Canoe
    Centre
30 Lakeland Forum

Archdale and Omagh. Rooms are £16/32 and all have a bathroom.

Hotels The *Railway Hotel* (☎ 01365-322084), 34 Forthill St, at the eastern side of town on the road out to Omagh, has rooms from £23 per person for B&B. Nearby at No 72 is the *Fort Lodge Hotel* (☎ 01365-323275), where the rates are £25. More expensive, at £33 per person for B&B, the *Killyhevlin* (☎ 01365-323481) is on the Dublin road.

Rental Accommodation The average price for weekly accommodation in a double room is over £200. One place that offers good value at £140 is the *Belmore Court Hotel* (☎ 01365-326633), on the B80 road to Tempo, with facilities including TV, phone, kitchen and central heating.

Places to Eat
For snacks and coffee try *Rebecca's Place* in the Buttermarket; soup and a roll is £1.30. The popular *Franco's Pizzeria*, on Queen Elizabeth Rd on the north side of town, is adventurous: what other restaurant in Ireland dares to announce on the menu: 'we serve no chips'? Pizzas are £4.45 to £5.95, pasta dishes £5.95, and there's much more on offer, including a seafood bar. It's closed on Sunday.

Along the main East Bridge St the *Barbizon Café* is OK for snacks and a set lunch but closes at 6 pm. *Johnston's Home Bakery*, on Townhall St just east of the clocktower in the centre, has good sandwiches and pies. The *Crowe's Nest* pub, in High St, is aimed at the tourist, with menus in French and German.

Back along Townhall St the *Peppercorn Restaurant* is pleasant, serving breakfast and meals for under £5. Just a few doors away the restaurant upstairs at *Melvin House* has lunch specials for around £4; it closes at 6 pm Monday to Thursday, and at 9.30 pm Friday and Saturday. By the roundabout at the end of Belmore St, *Saddler's* is a steakhouse (£10) and is open daily. Exotic fare is on offer nearby at *Oscar's*, with vindaloo curry for £7.50; and the *Silver Lough*, across

the road, has Chinese and English menus including a vegetarian selection; most dishes are £4 to £5 and it's open until midnight every day.

Entertainment
The main street through town has a number of popular pubs. These include the resolutely Victorian *William Blake* on Church St, the *Crowe's Nest* on High St with good food and music in the evenings, the *Vintage* on Townhall St, the *Bush Bar* on East Bridge St, with traditional Irish music sessions, and *Pat's Bar*, next to Melvin House, which occasionally has music at night.

During the course of the year just about every kind of performance art takes place at the *Ardhowen Theatre* (☎ 01365-325440), about two km south of the town centre on Dublin Rd, the A4. The programme includes concerts, local amateur and professional drama and musical productions, pantomime and films.

Things to Buy
Small shops along Enniskillen's long main street sell Belleek pottery, but the showroom at the village of Belleek has the complete range. In town itself the best place for shopping is the Buttermarket, off Queen Elizabeth Rd. The refurbished buildings of the old market place house a variety of craft shops making and selling their wares – at US-tour-group prices. Ceramics and jewellery are the best buys. More mundane shopping is available at the Erneside Centre, a modern complex of shops, cafés and supermarket on the Shore Rd near the tourist office.

Getting There & Away
Ulsterbus No 261 runs up to 10 times daily via Dungannon to Belfast (two hours, £5.70) Monday to Saturday, though less frequently on Sunday. Bus No 296 runs between Derry (3¼ hours) and Cork (11¼ hours) via Omagh (one hour). From Omagh express buses also connect with Dublin. The No 262 service runs to Sligo (1½ hours), Ballina (1¼ hours) and Westport (4½ hours). There

is also a service from Enniskillen to Bundoran via Belleek.

The bus station (☎ 01365-322633) is conveniently located across from the tourist office on Shore Rd.

Getting Around

Bicycles can be hired at the Lakeland Canoe Centre (☎ 01365-32450) on Castle Island for £10 a day; from Erne Tours (☎ 01365-322882) for £7/35 a day/week; or from Spokes & Sports (☎ 01365-325321), on Church St, for £6/25.

AROUND ENNISKILLEN
Castle Coole

Towards the end of the 18th century, designers influenced by Greek and Roman models promoted the neoclassical style, and Castle Coole ranks as probably the purest expression of this school of architecture in Ireland. The house was completed in 1798. Over the following two centuries the Portland stone exterior absorbed water to the point at which the walls started to crumble.

The National Trust embarked on an expensive rebuilding of the outside walls and an extensive redecoration of the interior. (The present earl still lives on the 500-hectare estate.) The result is that now the house displays the pristine elegance of its original conception. The austerity of the design borders on sterility; the obsession with symmetry is almost neurotic; and the guided tour takes in many examples of form triumphing over substance: fake doors balancing real ones, hollow columns painted to resemble marble ones, a lavish state bedroom that was never used, keyhole covers on doors which have no keyholes.

The tour first visits the male sanctuary of the library where, as the guide points out, the doors, once locked, could only be opened from the inside, so who knows what they got up to. Most of the furniture is original, and the curtain rail is typical of the extravagance of the second earl of Belmore, who decorated the house. The first earl spent so much money having the place built that he had nothing left for decorations.

The castle is in a 600-hectare demesne and its lake is home to a colony of greylag geese.

The castle is open June to August daily from 1 to 6 pm Friday to Wednesday. April to May and September it is open from 1 to 6 pm Saturday, Sunday and public holidays, while over Easter it also opens daily; admission is £2.50 (children £1.25, but free in July and August). Castle Coole is on Dublin Rd (the A4), 2.5 km south-east of Enniskillen.

Florence Court

This Palladian mansion is named after the wife of John Cole, who settled in the area in the early 18th century. His son built the present central block and the wings were added by *his* son, although the architect is unknown. The house was acquired by the National Trust in the 1950s and partly rebuilt after a fire in 1955. It is said that every Irish yew tree has its origin from one in the garden of Florence Court!

Unlike Castle Coole, Florence Court has a lived-in character, and despite the fire much of the original rococo plasterwork remains – the staircase is the best example of it.

In the grounds there is a walled garden and a forest park which has a number of walking trails; one of the trails leads to the top of Cuilcagh Mountain (665 metres).

June to August it's open from 1 to 6 pm Wednesday to Monday, while April, May and September it's open from 1 to 6 pm weekends and public holidays only. It's also open from 1 to 6 pm during Easter. Admission is £2.50 (children £1.25, but free in July and August). The house is almost 13 km south-west of Enniskillen; take the A4 Sligo road and turn left (south) onto the A32 Swanlinbar road.

Marble Arch Caves

The extensive Marble Arch Caves (☎ 0136582-8855) are very commercialised and very popular; it's wise to phone ahead and book on the 1¼-hour tour. The caves are open April to September from 11 am daily, with the last tour at 5 pm. The cost is £4/2 (students £3.50, family £12) and starts with a boat trip on the river which runs through the caves.

During the summer there are occasional free guided walks through the surrounding limestone hills conducted by the Department of the Environment. Enquire at the tourist office in Enniskillen or contact the Nature Reserve Office (☎ 01365-621588) at Castle Archdale Country Park, Lisnarick.

The caves are 16 km south-west of Enniskillen near the border via the A4 Sligo road and the A32 Swanlibar road. It is well signposted.

LOUGH ERNE

Stretching for 80 km, Lough Erne is made up of two loughs, Upper in the south and Lower in the north, which are connected by the River Erne; the river begins its journey in County Cavan and flows out to Donegal Bay west of Ballyshannon. The lakes have numerous islands, many containing Celtic and early Christian archaeological sites (see Around Lough Erne). Coarse and game fish are plentiful, and birdlife, especially on Upper Lough Erne, is widespread.

Fishing

The lakes of Fermanagh are renowned for coarse fishing, but trout are found in the northern part of Lough Erne, close to Boa Island and Kesh Bay. Lough Melvin, near the town of Garrison, is home to the Gillaroo trout. The Lough Erne trout fishing season is from the beginning of March to the end of September. Salmon fishing begins in June and also continues to the end of September. The mayfly season usually lasts a month from the second week in May. There is no closed season for bream, eel, pike, perch, roach or rudd.

A coarse fishing licence or permit is required for Lough Erne and a game permit or licence for fishing in Lower Lough Erne other than from the shore. These can be purchased from Castle Marine (☎ 013656-28118) at Castle Archdale County Park, which also hires day boats. An eight-day joint licence and permit is £9.40 for coarse and £21.45 for game fishing. Most of the

rivers in Fermanagh are privately owned, and information on those rivers where permission need not be sought is available from the tourist office in Enniskillen.

Cruising Lough Erne

The MV *Kestrel* (☎ 01365-322882) is a 56-seater waterbus that cruises the lough for 1¾ hours, calling at Devenish Island along the way. It departs from the Round 'O' pier at Brook Park, a short distance out of Enniskillen on the A46 to Belleek. During May and June it departs at 2.30 pm Sunday and public holidays only; in July and August it departs at 10.30 am, 2.15 and 4.15 pm daily and at 7.15 pm Tuesday, Thursday and Sunday; and in September it departs at 2.30 pm on Tuesday, Saturday and Sunday. The cost is £4/2, with a 50p discount if you take the morning cruise.

There is also a Viking Cruise (☎ 013657-22122) from the Share Centre on the Derrylin road about 6.5 km from Lisnaskea. The replica of a Viking longboat does 90-minute cruises on Upper Lough Erne in May and June at 3 pm Friday, Saturday and Sunday; in July and August at 3 pm Wednesday to Monday and 11 am Saturday; and September at 11 am Saturday and 3 pm Sunday. The cost is £4/3.

There are about half a dozen companies in Fermanagh that hire out cruisers on a weekly basis. The rates vary from £390 for a four-berth in the low season to nearly £1000 for an eight-berth in the high season. Details are available from the Enniskillen tourist office, which has a full list of the companies and costs.

Erne Boat Services (☎ 01365-34828), at the Moorings in Bellanaleck, hires out electric boats at £30 per half day or £50 for the whole day. They also have diesel boats for day hire, which are less expensive. Bellanaleck is on the A509 road to Derrylin.

AROUND LOUGH ERNE

There are a number of ancient religious sites and other antiquities around Lough Erne. In early Christian times the lough was an important highway providing a route from the Donegal coast to inland Leitrim. Churches and monasteries acted as staging posts and in medieval times there was an important pilgrim route to Station Island in Donegal that went via the lough.

The village of Belleek, famous for its china, is just inside the border and easily reached from either side of the lough.

The places below are set out in an anti-clockwise tour from Enniskillen.

Devenish Island

The most extensive of the ancient sites is Devenish Island. This monastery, founded by St Molaise in the 6th century, was sacked by Vikings in 837 AD in just one incident in its colourful history. There are church and abbey ruins, some fascinating old grave-stones, an unusual high cross, an excellent small museum and one of the best round towers in Ireland; this 25-metre tower is in perfect condition and you can climb to the top.

A ferry runs across to the site from Trory Point landing, about six km north of Enniskillen. To get there, take the A32 to Irvinestown out of town and after five km look for the sign on the left. It is just after a Burmah service station and before the junction where the road forks left to Kesh and right to Omagh. The ferry runs April to September from 10 am to 7 pm Tuesday to Saturday and from 2 pm Sunday. The return fare is £2.25/1.20 and the crossing takes 10 minutes.

Killadeas Churchyard

Tucked away in a small graveyard stands the **Bishop's Stone**, a remarkable stone carving that encapsulates the transition from Celtic paganism to Christianity. The face that stares out from the front seems quite at odds with the side engraving of a bishop with bell and crozier.

Just after the turn off for Devenish Island on the A32 take the B82 along the shoreline toward Kesh and look for the sign to the Manor House Hotel. Continue past this sign for 1.1 km and look for the small church on

the left side of the road, opposite a house and Killadeas post office.

White Island

White Island, close to the eastern shore of the lough, has the remains of a small 12th-century **church** containing a line of eight statues thought to date from around the 6th century. Nothing remains of the earlier monastic settlement except the boundary bank which may still be discerned on the far side of the church. The most impressive sur-viving part of the church is the Romanesque door.

The eight **stone figures** are intriguing. The first bears much resemblance to a sheila-na-gig, while the next is of someone reading a book or holding some object. Number three is obviously ecclesiastical, and while the next one has been identified as the Boy David, the meaning of his hand pointing to his mouth has been lost. Number five is a curly-haired figure holding the necks of two gryphon-like birds. Number six has a mili-tary appearance, number seven is unfinished and the last one is a single frowning face that resembles a death mask.

The sheila-na-gig figure on White Island

Sheila-Na-Gig

The term sheila-na-gig is probably an anglicisation of *Síle na gcíoch* (Sheila of the paps). It refers to carvings of women displaying exaggerated genitalia. One theory traces their origin back to male and female exhibitionist figures found in French Romanesque churches. These were used to illustrate the ungodly powers which threaten men, and may well reflect the fear of women among a male clergy.

Another theory is that they are representations of Celtic war goddesses. Early Irish sagas like the epic *Táin Bó Cúailnge* refer to women using overt genital display as a weapon to subdue Cúchulainn. This may have encouraged the belief that the 'sheilas' could ward off evil and hence explain their incorporation into the architecture of early Christian churches. According to this interpretation, the figure on White Island would be related to the stone figure in the chapter house of Armagh Cathedral. The weakness of this theory is that female exhibitionist figures are not found in Ireland before the 9th or 10th centuries.

Another theory is that they may have been connected with some sort of fertility cult. ■

Places to Stay There's a good hostel at the *Castle Archdale Country Park* (☎ 013656-28118). A bed is £6.30, and as at all the YHANI hostels, family rooms are available. The park also has a *camp site* (☎ 013656-21333), which is huge and dominated by on-site caravans, but has good facilities. A site for a two-person tent is £5. Ulsterbus No 194 from Enniskillen to Pettigo will stop outside the park, from where the hostel is a 15-minute walk.

Getting There & Around During the summer a ferry runs across to the island from the marina in Castle Archdale Country Park, which is 16 km north of Enniskillen on the Kesh road. The ferry operates the same hours and for the same fare as the Devenish Island ferry.

If you want to cycle round the island, bikes can be hired from Cycle-Ops (☎ 013656-31850) at the marina in Castle Archdale Country Park.

Drumskinny Stone Circle & Alignment
This circle is made up of 39 stones with a small cairn and an alignment of 24 stones and has been dated to the Bronze Age. The circle is seven km north of Kesh and signposted just beyond the junction with the road to Boa Island.

Boa Island
At the north end of the lough is Boa Island, which is connected at both ends by bridges to the shore. The **Janus figure** in Caldragh graveyard could be 2000 years old, one of the oldest stone statues in Ireland and quite unparalleled. Another, more recent stone figure stands near it.

There's just a small sign to the cemetery, about a km from the bridge at the west end of the island, six km from the east end bridge. It is well worth the trip to see the figure, which exudes a kind of pagan strength.

The Janus figure on Boa Island in Lough Erne

TYRONE & FERMANAGH

Castle Caldwell Forest Park

At the entrance to the park, the **Fiddler's Stone** is a memorial to a fiddler who in 1770 fell off a boat in a drunken stupor and drowned. The castle itself was built in 1610 and 1619, but all that now remains is a ruin that is not safe to explore. It is a few minutes walk from the café and small visitors' centre. The park area is also a nature reserve full of birdlife and the main breeding ground of the common scoter duck.

The park is about five km west of Boa Island along the A47.

Belleek

The only reason for stopping at this border village is to visit the world-famous Belleek pottery works (☎ 013656-58501). Production of this pottery has provided work for the village since 1857. A lot of the china is marked with a design of shamrocks, disconcertingly similar to the cheap souvenirs found in tourist shops.

There are regular 30-minute tours from 9.30 am Monday to Friday, the last tour beginning at 4.15 pm (closed for lunch 12.15 to 2.15 pm) except on Friday, when the last tour is at 3.15 pm. The tour costs £1. The small museum, showroom and café are open March through June, and also September, from 9 am to 6 pm Monday to Friday, 10 am to 6 pm Saturday, and 2 to 6 pm Sunday; July and August from 9 am to 8 pm Monday to Friday, 10 am to 6 pm Saturday and 11 am to 8 pm Sunday; October from 9 am to 5.30 pm Monday to Friday and 10 am to 5.30 pm Saturday; and November through February from 9 am to 5.30 pm Monday to Friday.

Lough Navar Forest

In this conifer forest, on the western shore of Lough Erne, an 11-km scenic road leads up to a viewing point overlooking the lough and the mountains to the north. A section of the Ulster Way passes through the forest.

Tully Castle

A signposted left turn off the A46 some 16 km south-east of Belleek leads to Tully Castle. The castle was built in the early 17th century as a fortified home for a planter's family from Scotland, but it was captured, burned and abandoned in 1641. The bawn has four corner towers and retains a lot of the original paving. The vaulted ground floor has a large fireplace with an equally large staircase leading to the 2nd floor and attics above that.

The castle is open April to September from 10 am to 7 pm Monday to Saturday and 2 to 7 pm Sunday; admission is £1.

Monea Castle

Continuing south on the A46 to Enniskillen there is a signposted turn to the right for Monea Castle. This was built as the best of Fermanagh's plantation castles around the same time as Tully Castle. It too was captured in the 1641 rising but remained in use until the mid-18th century when it was gutted by fire. The main entrance has two imposing circular towers topped with built-out squares in a style that can be found in contemporary Scottish castles. There is no charge for viewing the remains. A crannóg sits in the nearby lake.

Places to Stay

Camping At Blaney, 13 km from town on the A46 to Belleek, behind the Blaney service station, *Blaney Caravan Park* (☎ 01365-41634) has tent sites for £5. On the other side of the lough outside Kesh, the *Lakeland Caravan Park* (☎ 013656-31578) also has camping. South of Enniskillen and about two km north-west of Lisnaskea near Upper Lough Erne, camping is possible at the *Mullynascarthy Caravan Park* (☎ 013657-21040) for £4.50 and the *Share Holiday Village* (☎ 013657-22122) in Shanaghy for £5.

B&Bs There are plenty of B&Bs along the roads that skirt either side of Lough Erne. *Lakeview Farm House* (☎ 013656-41263) is on the A46 at Blaney, 16 km north-west of Enniskillen, with singles/doubles for £16/29, and on the other side of the lough at Killadeas, the *Beeches* (☎ 013656-21557) has rooms for £16/28 and boats for hire.

Manville House (☎ 013656-31668), at Letter, 13 km from Kesh on the road to Belleek, is well situated for the angler, with boat hire available and four rooms at £15/29. In Belleek on the Donegal border *Moohan's Fiddlestone* (☎ 013656-58008), 15-17 Main St, is a friendly place with singles/doubles at £15/30 and a bar downstairs.

Hotels The grandly situated *Manor House Hotel* (☎ 013656-21561) is about 11 km from Enniskillen in Killadeas on the B82 to Kesh and has rooms from £35 per person for B&B. At *Mahon's Hotel* (☎ 013656-21656), in the centre of Irvinestown, rates are £29.50, and the bar is packed with locals at weekends. *Drumshane Hotel* (☎ 013656-21146), in Lisnarick between Irvinestown and Kesh, is a good hotel with a restaurant, a grand piano in the bar and rooms from £27.50. On the main street in Lisnaskea the *Ortine Hotel* (☎ 013657-21206) has rooms for £22.

Places to Eat

Open daily, the restaurant at the *Manor House Hotel*, on the B82 to Kesh, overlooks Lough Erne and has a set dinner as well as à la carte at around £18 per person. Music, traditional and country, is organised at weekends in summer.

In Irvinestown, 13 km north of Enniskillen, there is the *Hollander Restaurant* (☎ 013656-21231) in the main street. This family-run restaurant and pub has a deserved reputation for good food at reasonable prices. Reservations are recommended, vegetarian meals are always featured and you should count on £10 to £15 per person.

The restaurant opens at 5.30 pm. There's also bar food and the pub has some interesting photographs of the Catalina and Sunderland flying boats that operated from the nearby base at Castle Archduke. There is even a model of the plane that left here and spotted the *Bismarck*.

Across the road from the Hollander, the *Central Bar* serves food during the day and was a popular drinking hole for US pilots; only the TV sets and security monitor detract from the 1940s style of the place.

North-west of Kesh on Boa Island, reservations are recommended for the *Drumrush Lodge* (☎ 013656-31578) or *Mullynaval Lodge* (☎ 013656-31995). Pub food is available at the *May Fly* on the main street of Kesh or *Cleary's Corner Bar* in Belleek, which has traditional Irish music on Friday nights. Opposite, the *Carlton Inn* serves meals daily for £5 to £10.

Getting There & Away

From Enniskillen, Ulsterbus No 64 runs daily to Belleek (1¼ hours) via Garrison on the western side of Lower Lough Erne; bus No 99 also goes to Belleek, following the western shoreline through Blaney (15 minutes) past Tully Castle and Lough Navar Forest; on the eastern side bus No 194 goes to Irvinestown (35 minutes), Lisnarick (50 minutes) and Kesh (one hour).

Getting Around

Cycle-Ops (☎ 013656-31850), Mantlin Rd in Kesh, hires bikes for £7 a day; it has tandems, and child seats are available.

TYRONE & FERMANAGH

Glossary

An Óige – Irish youth hostel association.
Anglo-Norman – Norman, English and Welsh peoples who invaded Ireland in the 12th century.
Ard – Irish place name, meaning 'high'.

bailey – the space enclosed by castle walls.
bawn – enclosure surrounded by walls outside the main castle, acting as a defence as well as a place to keep cattle in time of trouble.
beehive hut – circular stone building, shaped like an old-fashioned beehive.
Black & Tans – British recruits to the Royal Irish Constabulary shortly after WW I, noted for their brutality.
Blarney Stone – bending over backwards to kiss this sacred rock in Blarney Castle, County Cork, is said to bestow the gift of the gab or allow you to 'gain the privilege of telling lies for seven years'.
bodhrán – (pronounced 'bore-run') hand-held goatskin drum.
Bord Fáilte – Irish Tourist Board.
botharin or **boreen** – a small lane or roadway.
Bronze Age – the earliest metal-using period, around 2000 BC to 500 BC in Ireland, after the Stone Age and before the Iron Age.
B-specials – Northern Irish auxiliary police force, disbanded in 1971.
bullaun – stone with a depression, probably used as a mortar for grinding medicine or food and often found on monastic sites.

cairn – a mound of stones heaped over a prehistoric grave.
caher – a stone-walled enclosed circular area.
cashel – stone-walled circular fort; see *rath*.
Cath – Irish place name, meaning battle.
ceilí or **ceilidh** – a session of traditional music and dancing.
Celts – Iron Age warrior tribes which arrived in Ireland around 300 BC and controlled the country for 1000 years.
chancel – the east end of a church where the altar is situated, reserved for the clergy and choir.
Cill or **Kill** – Irish place name, meaning church.
Claddagh ring – the wedding ring used throughout much of Connaught from the mid-18th century with a crowned heart nestling between two hands; if the heart points towards the hand then the wearer is taken or married, towards the fingertip means he or she is looking for a mate.
clochan – dry-stone beehive hut from the early Christian period.
control zone – area of a town centre, usually the main street, where parked cars must have at least one person inside.
craic or **crack** – conversation, gossip, fun, good times.
crannóg – an artificial island, made in a lake to provide habitation in a good defensive position.
creel – basket.
crios – a multicoloured woven woollen belt traditionally worn in the Aran Islands.
cromlech – see *dolmen*.
currach – rowing boat made of framework of laths covered with tarred canvas.

Dáil – lower house of the Irish parliament.
dairthech – an oratory, a small room set aside for private prayer.
demesne – landed property close to a house or castle.
diamond – town square.
dolmen – tomb chamber or portal tomb made of vertical stones topped by a huge capstone. From around 2000 BC.
drumlin – rounded hill formed by retreating glacier.
dun – a fort, usually constructed of stone.
DUP – Democratic Unionist Party, hard-line Northern Irish Protestant loyalist party founded by Ian Paisley.

Eire – Irish name for the Republic of Ireland.
esker – gravel ridge.

Fianna – a mythical band of warriors who feature in many tales of ancient Ireland.
Fianna Fáil – 'Warriors of Ireland', major political party in the Republic of Ireland, originating from the Sinn Féin faction opposed to the 1921 treaty with Britain.
Fine Gael – 'Tribe of the Gael', the other major political party, originating from the Sinn Féin faction which favoured the 1921 treaty with Britain. Formed the first government of independent Ireland but has subsequently only gained power as part of a coalition.
fir – man, sign on men's toilets.
fulachta fiadh – Bronze Age cooking place.

Gaeltacht – Irish-speaking area.
gardaí – Irish Republic police.
ghillie – a fishing or hunting guide.
Gort – Irish place name, meaning field.
Gothic – style of architecture characterised by pointed arches, from the 12th to the 16th centuries AD.

halla rónáin – dance hall.
Hibernia – the Roman name for Ireland and meaning 'the land of winter' (the Romans had confused Ireland with Iceland).
hill fort – usually dating from the Iron Age, hill forts are formed by a ditch that follows the contour of the hill to surround and fortify the summit.

INLA – Irish National Liberation Army, extremist IRA splinter group.
IRA – Irish Republican Army, dedicated to the removal of British troops from the North and the reunification of Ireland.
IRB – Irish Republican Brotherhood, a secret society also called the Fenians, believed in independence through violence if necessary; originally founded in 1858 and revived in the early 20th century; precursor to IRA.
Iron Age – in Ireland the Iron Age lasted from around the end of the Bronze Age in 500 BC to the arrival of Christianity in the 5th century.

jaunting car – Killarney's traditional horse-drawn transport.
jarvey – the driver of a jaunting car.

keep – the main tower of a castle.

Lambeg drum – a very large drum associated with Protestant loyalist marches.
leprechaun – a mischievous elf or sprite from Irish folklore.
lough – Irish word for lake, or a long narrow bay or arm of the sea.
Loyalist – person, usually a Northern Irish Protestant, insisting on the continuation of Northern Ireland's links with Britain.

Mesolithic – Middle Stone Age, the time of the first human settlers in Ireland.
mná – women, sign on women's toilets.
motte (or mott) – early Norman fortification consisting of a raised, flattened mound with a keep on top. When attached to a bailey it is known as a motte-and-bailey, many of which were built in Ireland until the early 13th century.

naomh – saint.
Nationalists – proponents of a united Ireland.
Neolithic – also known as the New Stone Age, a period characterised by a settled agriculture and lasting until around 2000 BC in Ireland.
North, The – the term refers to the political entity of Northern Ireland, not the northernmost geographic part of Ireland (not Donegal, for example).

Ogham stones – Ogham (pronounced 'o-am') was the earliest form of writing in Ireland, using a variety of notched strokes placed above, below or across a keyline, usually on stone.
OPW – Office of Public Works, a government department in charge of parks, monuments and gardens in the Republic.
Orange Order – loyalist Protestant organisation in Northern Ireland which takes its name from William of Orange, the Protestant victor of the Battle of the Boyne.

Members of the Orange Order are known as Orangemen and they meet in Orange Lodges.

OUP – Official Unionist Party, the principal Northern Irish Protestant political party.

Palladian – a style of architecture developed by Andrea Palladio (1508-80), based on ancient Roman architecture.

Partition – the division of Ireland in 1921.

passage grave – Celtic tomb with chamber reached by a narrow passage, typically buried in a mound.

penal laws – laws passed in the 18th century forbidding Catholics to buy land, hold public office etc.

plantation – the settlement of Protestant migrants in Ireland in the 17th century.

poteen – (pronounced 'potcheen'), illegally brewed potato-based firewater.

Prod – slang for Northern Irish Protestant.

Provisionals – the Provisional IRA, formed after a break with the Official IRA who are now largely inconsequential. Until the 1994 ceasefire, the Provisionals, named after the provisional government declared in 1916, were the main force combating the British army in the North.

rath – ring fort with earth banks around a circular timber wall, see *cashel*.

Republic of Ireland – twenty-six counties of the South.

Republican – supporter of a united Ireland.

ring fort – used from the Bronze Age right through to the Middle Ages, particularly in the early Christian period. Basically a circular habitation area surrounded by banks and ditches.

Romanesque – a style of architecture which dominated Europe until the arrival of Gothic in the 12th century. Characterised by rounded arches and vaulting.

round tower – tall circular tower from around the 9th to 11th century, built as a lookout and as a sanctuary during the period when monasteries were frequently subject to Viking raids.

RUC – Royal Ulster Constabulary, armed Northern Irish police force.

seisúns – a session.

shamrock – clover, a plant with three leaves said to have been used by St Patrick to illustrate the Holy Trinity.

SDLP – Social Democratic Labour Party of Northern Ireland. The party represents predominantly liberal, middle-class opinion opposed to violence. Mostly Catholic.

shebeens – drinking places.

sheila-na-gig – a female figure with exaggerated genitalia, carved in stone on the exteriors of some churches and castles. Various explanations have been offered for the iconography, ranging from male clerics warning against the perils of sex to the idea that they represent Celtic war goddesses.

shillelagh – a stout club or cudgel, especially one made of oak or blackthorn.

Sinn Féin – 'We Ourselves', political wing of the IRA.

Six Counties – the six out of nine counties of the old province of Ulster which form Northern Ireland.

snug – partitioned-off drinking area in a pub.

souterrain – an underground chamber usually associated with ring forts and hill forts. The purpose may have been to provide a hiding place or an escape route in times of trouble and/or a storage place for goods.

standing stone – upright stone set in the ground. Such stones are common across Ireland and date from a variety of periods. Usually the purpose is obscure, though some are burial markers.

Taoiseach – Irish prime minister.

TD – teachta Dála, member of the Irish parliament.

teampall – church.

Tholsel – city hall.

Tinkers – term used to describe Irish gypsies, itinerant communities that roam the country; see *Travellers*.

Travellers – today's more commonly used term to denote Ireland's itinerant communities.

Treaty – the Anglo-Irish Treaty of 1921, which divided Ireland and gave relative independence to the South. Cause of the Civil War of 1922-23.

Tricolour – green, white and orange Irish flag. It was designed to symbolise the hoped-for union of the green Catholic southern Irish with the orange Protestant northern Irish.

turloughs – small lakes which often disappear in dry summers.

Twenty-Six Counties – the Republic of Ireland, the South.

UDA – Ulster Defence Organisation, legal Northern Irish paramilitary organisation.

UDF – Ulster Defence Force, illegal Northern Irish paramilitary organisation.

UFF – Ulster Freedom Fighters, another illegal Northern Irish paramilitary organisation.

Ulster – one of the four ancient provinces of Ireland sometimes used to describe the six counties of the North, but also including Cavan, Monaghan and Donegal in the Republic.

Unionists – Northern Irish who want to retain the links with Britain.

United Irishmen – organisation founded in 1791 aiming to reduce British power in Ireland, which led a series of unsuccessful risings and invasions.

UVF – Ulster Volunteer Force, and yet another illegal Northern Irish paramilitary organisation.

Volunteers – an offshoot of the IRB that came to be known as the IRA.

way – a long-distance trail.

YHANI – Youth Hostel Association of Northern Ireland.

Appendix – Place Names

Place	Irish Name	County
Adare	Áth Dara	Limerick
Antrim	Aontroim	Antrim
Aran Islands	Oileáin Árainn	Galway
Ardboe	Ard Bo	Tyrone
Ardee	Baile Átha Fhirdhia	Louth
Ardfert	Ard Fhearta	Kerry
Ardglass	Ard Ghlais	Down
Ardmore	Ard Mór	Waterford
Arklow	An tInbhear Mór	Wicklow
Arlow	Eatharlach	Tipperary
Armagh	Ard Mhacha	Armagh
Arranmore	Árainn Mhór	Donegal
Athlone	Baile Átha Luain	Westmeath
Athy	Áth Í	Kildare
Avoca	Abhóca	Wicklow
Ballina	Béal an Átha	Mayo
Ballinasloe	Béal Átha na Sluaighe	Galway
Ballinspittle	Béal Átha an Spidéil	Cork
Ballintober	Bail an Tobair	Roscommon
Ballybunion	Baile an Bhuinneánaigh	Kerry
Ballymena	An Baile Meánach	Antrim
Ballyshannon	Béal Átha Seanaidh	Donegal
Bangor	Beannchar	Down
Bantry	Beanntrai	Cork
Belfast	Beál Feirste	Belfast
Birr	Biorra	Offaly
Blarney	An Bhlarna	Cork
Boyle	Mainistir na Búille	Roscommon
Bunbeg	An Bun Beag	Donegal
Bunratty	Bun Raite	Clare
Burren, The	Boireann	Clare
Cahir	An Cathair	Tipperary
Carlingford	Cairlinn	Louth
Carlow	Ceatharlach	Carlow
Carraroe	An Cheathgrú Rua	Galway
Carrickfergus	Carraig Fhearghais	Antrim
Carrick-on-Shannon	Cora Droma Rúisc	Leitrim
Cashel	Caiseal Mumhan	Tipperary
Cavan	An Cabhán	Cavan
Castlebar	Caislean an Bharraigh	Mayo

Place	Irish Name	County
Charleville	Rath Luirc	Cork
Clonmacnois	Cluain Mhic Nóis	Offaly
Clonmel	Cluain Meala	Tipperary
Clontarf	Cluain Tarbh	Dublin
Cobh	An Cobh	Cork
Cong	Conga	Mayo
Connemara	Conamara	Galway
Cookstown	An Chorr Chríochach	Tyrone
Cork	Corcaigh	Cork
Creeslough	An Craoslach	Donegal
Crossmaglen	Crois Mhic Lionnáin	Armagh
Dalkey	Deilginis	Dublin
Derry/Londonderry	Doire	Derry
Derrybeg	Doirí Beaga	Donegal
Dingle	An Daingean	Kerry
Donegal	Dún na nGall	Donegal
Downpatrick	Dún Pádraig	Down
Drogheda	Droichead Átha	Louth
Dublin	Baile Átha Cliath	Dublin
Dunfanaghy	Dún Fionnachaidh	Donegal
Dungarvan	Dún Garbhán	Waterford
Dungloc/Dunglow	Dúngleo	Donegal
Dunlewy	Dún Lúiche	Donegal
Ennis	Inis	Clare
Enniscorthy	Inis Coirthaidh	Wexford
Enniskillen	Inis Ceithleann	Fermanagh
Falcarragh	An Fal Carrach	Donegal
Galway	Gaillimh	Galway
Giant's Causeway, The	Clochán an Aifir	Antrim
Glendalough	Gleann dá Loch	Wicklow
Glengarriff	An Gleann Garbh	Cork
Glenveagh	Ghleann Bheatha	Donegal
Gweedore	Gaoth Dobhar	Donegal
Howth	Binn Éadair	Dublin
Inishmore/Inishmór	Árainn Mór	Galway
Inishmaan	Inis Meáin	Galway
Inishowen	Inis Eoghain	Donegal
Innisfree	Inis Fraoigh	Sligo
Kells	Ceanannas Mór	Meath
Kildare	Cill Dara	Kildare
Kilkenny	Cill Chainnigh	Kilkenny

Place	Irish Name	County
Killaloe	Cill Dalue	Clare
Killarney	Cill Airne	Kerry
Kilmainham	Cill Mhaigneann	Dublin
Kilmallock	Cill Mocheallóg	Limerick
Kilronan	Cill Ronáin	Galway
Kinsale	Cionn tSáile	Cork
Knowth	Cnóbha	Meath
Larne	Lutharna	Antrim
Leitrim	Liatroim	Leitrim
Letterkenny	Leitir Ceanainn	Donegal
Limerick	Luimneach	Limerick
Lisdoonvarna	Lios Dúin Bhearna	Clare
Lismore	Lios Mór	Waterford
Longford	An Longfort	Longord
Loughrea	Baile Locha Riach	Galway
Maam Cross	Crois Mám	Galway
Mallow	Mala	Cork
Maynooth	Maigh Nuad	Kildare
Mayo	Maigh Eo	Mayo
Monaghan	Muineachán	Monaghan
Monasterboice	Mainistir Bhuithe	Louth
Monasterevin	Mainistir Eimhín	Kildare
Mullingar	An Muileann gCearr	Westmeath
Naas	An Nás	Kildare
Navan	An Uaimh	Meath
Nenagh	An tAonach	Tipperary
Newbridge	Droichead Nua	Kildare
New Ross	Rhos Mhic Triúin	Wexford
Newry	An tIúr	Down
Omagh	An Omaigh	Tyrone
Portarlington	Cúil an tSúdaire	Laois
Portlaoise	Port Laoise	Laois
Rathfarnham	Ráth Fearnáin	Dublin
Rathlin Island	Reachlainn	Antrim
Roscommon	Ros Comáin	Roscommon
Roscrea	Ros Cré	Tipperary
Rosslare	Ros Láir	Wexford
Roundstone	Cloch na Rón	Galway
Scattery Island	Inis Cathaigh	Clare

Place	Irish Name	County
Skellig Islands	Oileáin na Scealaga	Kerry
Sligo	Sligeach	Sligo
Spiddal	An Spidéal	Galway
Strabane	An Srath Bán	Tyrone
Tara	Teamhair	Meath
Thurles	Durlas	Tipperary
Tipperary	Tiobraid Árann	Tipperary
Tory Island	Oileán Tóraigh	Donegal
Tralee	Trá Lí	Kerry
Trim	Baile Átha Troim	Meath
Tuam	Tuaim	Galway
Tullamore	Tulach Mór	Offaly
Waterford	Port Láirge	Waterford
Westport	Cathair na Mart	Mayo
Wexford	Loch Garman	Wexford
Wicklow	Cill Mhantáin	Wicklow
Youghal	Eochaill	Cork

Index

ABBREVIATIONS

MAPS

Thanks

Thanks to all the following travellers and others (apologies if we've mispelt your name) who took time to write to us about their experiences of Ireland. To those whose names have been omitted through oversight, your time and efforts are appreciated.

DL & DC Baker (UK), Carlo Bazzo (I), Fionnuala Behal (Irl), Brenda Berck (C), C R Berry (UK), Michael Birnhack (Isr), Phil Booth (UK), Penny Bowler (UK), Joanne Bowring (Irl), Denise Burke (Irl), Joyce Byrne (UK), Carol Clancy (Irl), Peter Convery (Aus), Peter Cornelissen (Nl), Mr & Mrs Coyne (Irl), C M Cox (UK), Tom Craig (USA), David Crerar (C), Magnus Dahlbring (S), Tony Daly (Irl), M Dayle (Irl), Ann De Schryver (B), M Devlin (Aus), Alison Diver (USA), Bob Doerr (USA), Katinka Dorhout (Nl), Jacqueline Douglas (Irl), Deborah Dowey (Irl), Patricia Dunworth (Irl), James Earl (Irl), Lisa Egen (NZ), Maria Ekerhag (S), Susan Erridge (Irl), Sylvia Fieres (B), D Fooney (Irl), Brian Foreman (UK), Ronda Foust (USA), Mrs Shiela Francis (UK), Mark French (Irl), Brett & Mandy Galt-Smith (Aus), Miss J L Gatty (UK), Martin Giblin (UK), Eira Gill (UK), Juliet Gill (USA), Danielle Glosser (USA), Ann Marie Gunn-Smith (UK), W V Harned (USA), Hans & Marja Henchak (Nl), Shaun Hennelly (Irl), Alain Herman (Fr), Tomas Homann (D), Urs Honegger (CH), Lawrence Hourahane (UK), Wendy Hughes (UK), Lorna Hyde (Irl), Uta Jester (D), Kees & Hanneke Jozee (Nl), Rachel Kemsley (UK), B & P Kennedy (USA), Constance Kerwin (USA), John Kissane (Irl), Eileen Landy (Irl), Marion Liebson (USA), Michael Lintner (USA), John Maher (UK), Liam Maher (UK), Stan Malcolm (Aus), Gary & Jane Martin (UK), Janie Matrisciano (USA), Gary Mayne (Irl), Marc Meindersma (Nl), Breda Monnin (Irl), Ursula Mueller (USA), George Von der Muhll (USA), Alan & Cathie Murdey (UK), Karen MacDonald (UK), Joanne McClenaghan (Irl), Siobhan McGee (Irl), Anne McGovern (Irl), Seamus McMenamin (Irl), Seanys & Kay McMenamin (Irl), Shona Nairn (UK), Lucia Nevai (USA), Brian & Jen Nuttall (Irl), Marisol Oliva (Sp), Chris Olsen (UK), Marco F Origgi (I), Eileen O'Brien (Aus), Seamus O'Brien (Irl), Ciaran O'Driscoll (Irl), Padraig O'Feeinneadha (Irl), Padraig O'Feinneadha (Irl), Padriac O'Struthian (Irl), Janwillem Paimans (Nl), Peter & Sue Parrington (Aus), John Peters (USA), Martin Phelan (Irl), Padraig Phelan (Irl), Margaret Powell (UK), Maryann Quinn (USA), Eric Rakowski (USA), Andrea Rathbone (USA), Cathy Roche (Irl), P Brian Rowan (Irl), Tobi Sanger (USA), Oliver Schmidt (D), J Siemelink (Nl), Pat Silver (UK), RJ Sims (UK), Elizabeth Smith (UK), Emma Smith (NZ), Cath Stallwood (Aus), Janice & Robin Tausig (UK), Maria Christina Tulisso (I), K S & I Tupper (Aus), Marie-Anne Ward (C), Mrs Brenda Weir (Irl), Mary White (Aus), M Wilson (UK), Robert Wilson (UK), Stephen Wilson (UK), H Williams (UK), C Winterton (UK)

Aus - Australia, B - Belgium, C - Canada, CH - Switzerland, D - Germany, Fr - France, Irl - Ireland, Isr - Israel, I - Italy, Nl - The Netherlands, NZ - New Zealand, Sp - Spain, UK - United Kingdom, USA - United States of America

LONELY PLANET PHRASEBOOKS

Building bridges,
Breaking barriers,
Beyond babble-on

Listen for the gems

Speak your own words

Ask your own
questions

Master of
your
own
image

- handy pocket-sized books
- easy to understand Pronunciation chapter
- clear and comprehensive Grammar chapter
- romanisation alongside script to allow ease of pronunciation
- script throughout so users can point to phrases
- extensive vocabulary sections, words and phrases for every situations
- full of cultural information and tips for the traveller

'...vital for a real DIY spirit and attitude in language learning' – Backpacker

'the phrasebooks have good cultural backgrounders and offer solid advice for challenging situations in remote locations' – San Francisco Examiner

'...they are unbeatable for their coverage of the world's more obscure languages' – The Geographical Magazine

---

Arabic (Egyptian)
Arabic (Moroccan)
Australia
  Australian English, Aboriginal and Torres Strait languages
Baltic States
  Estonian, Latvian, Lithuanian
Bengali
Burmese
Brazilian
Cantonese
Central Europe
  Czech, French, German, Hungarian, Italian and Slovak
Eastern Europe
  Bulgarian, Czech, Hungarian, Polish, Romanian and Slovak
Egyptian Arabic
Ethiopian (Amharic)
Fijian
Greek
Hindi/Urdu

Indonesian
Japanese
Korean
Lao
Latin American Spanish
Malay
Mandarin
Mediterranean Europe
  Albanian, Croatian, Greek, Italian, Macedonian, Maltese, Serbian, Slovene
Mongolian
Moroccan Arabic
Nepali
Papua New Guinea
Pilipino (Tagalog)
Quechua
Russian
Scandinavian Europe
  Danish, Finnish, Icelandic, Norwegian and Swedish

South-East Asia
  Burmese, Indonesian, Khmer, Lao, Malay, Tagalog (Pilipino), Thai and Vietnamese
Sri Lanka
Swahili
Thai
Thai Hill Tribes
Tibetan
Turkish
Ukrainian
USA
  US English, Vernacular Talk, Native American languages and Hawaiian
Vietnamese
Western Europe
  Basque, Catalan, Dutch, French, German, Irish, Italian, Portuguese, Scottish Gaelic, Spanish (Castilian) and Welsh

---

LONELY PLANET JOURNEYS

JOURNEYS is a unique collection of travel writing – published by the company that understands travel better than anyone else. It is a series for anyone who has ever experienced – or dreamed of – the magical moment when they encountered a strange culture or saw a place for the first time. They are tales to read while you're planning a trip, while you're on the road or while you're in an armchair, in front of a fire.

JOURNEYS books catch the spirit of a place, illuminate a culture, recount a crazy adventure, or introduce a fascinating way of life. They always entertain, and always enrich the experience of travel.

THE GATES OF DAMASCUS
Lieve Joris
Translated by Sam Garrett

This best-selling book is a beautifully drawn portrait of day-to-day life in modern Syria. Through her intimate contact with local people, Lieve Joris draws us into the fascinating world that lies behind the gates of Damascus. Hala's husband is a political prisoner, jailed for his opposition to the Assad regime; through the author's friendship with Hala we see how Syrian politics impacts on the lives of ordinary people.

Lieve Joris, who was born in Belgium, is one of Europe's leading travel writers. In addition to an award-winning book on Hungary, she has published widely acclaimed accounts of her journeys to the Middle East and Africa. *The Gates of Damascus* is her fifth book.

'*Expands the boundaries of travel writing*' – Times Literary Supplement

---

KINGDOM OF THE FILM STARS
Journey into Jordan
Annie Caulfield

Kingdom of the Film Stars is a travel book and a love story. With honesty and humour, Annie Caulfield writes of travelling in Jordan and falling in love with a Bedouin. Her book offers fascinating insights into the country – from the traditional tent life of nomadic tribes to the first woman MP's battle with fundamentalist colleagues. *Kingdom of the Film Stars* unpicks some of the tight-woven Western myths about the Arab world, presenting cultural and political issues within the intimate framework of a compelling love story.

Annie Caulfield, who was born in Ireland and currently lives in London, is an award-winning playwright and journalist. She has travelled widely in the Middle East.

'*Annie Caulfield is a remarkable traveller. Her story is fresh, courageous, moving, witty and sexy!*' – Dawn French

LONELY PLANET TRAVEL ATLASES

Lonely Planet has long been famous for the number and quality of its guidebook maps. Now we've gone one step further and in conjunction with Steinhart Katzir Publishers produced a handy companion series: Lonely Planet travel atlases – maps of a country produced in book form.

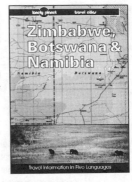

Unlike other maps, which look good but lead travellers astray, our travel atlases have been researched on the road by Lonely Planet's experienced team of writers. All details are carefully checked to ensure the atlas corresponds with the equivalent Lonely Planet guidebook.

The handy atlas format means no holes, wrinkles, torn sections or constant folding and unfolding. These atlases can survive long periods on the road, unlike cumbersome fold-out maps. The comprehensive index ensures easy reference.

- full-colour throughout
- maps researched and checked by Lonely Planet authors
- place names correspond with Lonely Planet guidebooks
  – no confusing spelling differences
- legend and travelling information in English, French, German, Japanese and Spanish
- size: 230 x 160 mm

Available now:
Chile & Easter Island • Egypt • India & Bangladesh • Israel & the Palestinian Territories •Jordan, Syria & Lebanon • Kenya • Laos • Portugal • South Africa, Lesotho & Swaziland • Thailand • Vietnam • Zimbabwe, Botswana & Namibia

---

LONELY PLANET TV SERIES & VIDEOS

Lonely Planet travel guides have been brought to life on television screens around the world. Like our guides, the programmes are based on the joy of independent travel, and look honestly at some of the most exciting, picturesque and frustrating places in the world. Each show is presented by one of three travellers from Australia, England or the USA and combines an innovative mixture of video, Super-8 film, atmospheric soundscapes and original music.

Videos of each episode – containing additional footage not shown on television – are available from good book and video shops, but the availability of individual videos varies with regional screening schedules.

Video destinations include: Alaska • American Rockies • Australia – The South-East • Baja California & the Copper Canyon • Brazil • Central Asia • Chile & Easter Island • Corsica, Sicily & Sardinia – The Mediterranean Islands • East Africa (Tanzania & Zanzibar) • Ecuador & the Galapagos Islands • Greenland & Iceland • Indonesia • Israel & the Sinai Desert • Jamaica • Japan • La Ruta Maya • Morocco • New York • North India • Pacific Islands (Fiji, Solomon Islands & Vanuatu) • South India • South West China • Turkey • Vietnam • West Africa • Zimbabwe, Botswana & Namibia

The Lonely Planet TV series is produced by:
Pilot Productions
Duke of Sussex Studios
44 Uxbridge St
London W8 7TG UK

Lonely Planet videos are distributed by:
IVN Communications Inc
2246 Camino Ramon
California 94583, USA

107 Power Road, Chiswick
London W4 5PL UK

Music from the TV series is available on CD & cassette.
For video availability and ordering information contact your nearest Lonely Planet office.

PLANET TALK

Lonely Planet's FREE quarterly newsletter

We love hearing from you and think you'd like to hear from us.

When...is the right time to see reindeer in Finland?
Where...can you hear the best palm-wine music in Ghana?
How...do you get from Asunción to Areguá by steam train?
What...is the best way to see India?

For the answer to these and many other questions read PLANET TALK.

Every issue is packed with up-to-date travel news and advice including:

* a letter from Lonely Planet co-founders Tony and Maureen Wheeler
* go behind the scenes on the road with a Lonely Planet author
* feature article on an important and topical travel issue
* a selection of recent letters from travellers
* details on forthcoming Lonely Planet promotions
* complete list of Lonely Planet products

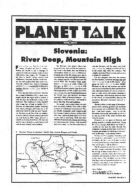

To join our mailing list contact any Lonely Planet office.

Also available: Lonely Planet T-shirts. 100% heavyweight cotton.

LONELY PLANET ONLINE

Get the latest travel information before you leave or while you're on the road

Whether you've just begun planning your next trip, or you're chasing down specific info on currency regulations or visa requirements, check out Lonely Planet Online for up-to-the minute travel information.

As well as travel profiles of your favourite destinations (including maps and photos), you'll find current reports from our researchers and other travellers, updates on health and visas, travel advisories, and discussion of the ecological and political issues you need to be aware of as you travel.

There's also an online travellers' forum where you can share your experience of life on the road, meet travel companions and ask other travellers for their recommendations and advice. We also have plenty of links to other online sites useful to independent travellers.

And of course we have a complete and up-to-date list of all Lonely Planet travel products including guides, phrasebooks, atlases, Journeys and videos and a simple online ordering facility if you can't find the book you want elsewhere.

www.lonelyplanet.com
or
AOL keyword: lp

LONELY PLANET PRODUCTS

Lonely Planet is known worldwide for publishing practical, reliable and no-nonsense travel information in our guides and on our web site. The Lonely Planet list covers just about every accessible part of the world. Currently there are eight series: *travel guides*, *shoestring guides*, *walking guides*, *city guides*, *phrasebooks*, *audio packs*, *travel atlases* and *Journeys* – a unique collection of travel writing.

EUROPE

Amsterdam • Austria • Baltic States & Kaliningrad • Baltic States phrasebook • Britain • Central Europe on a shoestring • Central Europe phrasebook • Czech & Slovak Republics • Denmark • Dublin • Eastern Europe on a shoestring • Eastern Europe phrasebook • Finland • France • Greece • Greek phrasebook • Hungary • Iceland, Greenland & the Faroe Islands • Ireland • Italy • Mediterranean Europe on a shoestring • Mediterranean Europe phrasebook • Paris • Poland • Portugal • Portugal travel atlas • Prague • Russia, Ukraine & Belarus • Russian phrasebook • Scandinavian & Baltic Europe on a shoestring • Scandinavian Europe phrasebook • Slovenia • Spain • St Petersburg • Switzerland • Trekking in Greece • Trekking in Spain • Ukrainian phrasebook • Vienna • Walking in Britain • Walking in Switzerland • Western Europe on a shoestring • Western Europe phrasebook

NORTH AMERICA

Alaska • Backpacking in Alaska • Baja California • California & Nevada • Canada • Florida • Hawaii • Honolulu • Los Angeles • Mexico • Miami • New England • New Orleans • New York, New Jersey & Pennsylvania • Pacific Northwest USA • Rocky Mountain States • San Francisco • Southwest USA • USA phrasebook • Washington, DC & the Capital Region

CENTRAL AMERICA & THE CARIBBEAN

Bermuda • Central America on a shoestring • Costa Rica • Cuba • Eastern Caribbean • Guatemala, Belize & Yucatán: La Ruta Maya • Jamaica

SOUTH AMERICA

Argentina, Uruguay & Paraguay • Bolivia • Brazil • Brazilian phrasebook • Buenos Aires • Chile & Easter Island • Chile & Easter Island travel atlas • Colombia • Ecuador & the Galápagos Islands • Latin American Spanish phrasebook • Peru • Quechua phrasebook • Rio de Janeiro • South America on a shoestring • Trekking in the Patagonian Andes • Venezuela

Travel Literature: Full Circle: A South American Journey

ANTARCTICA

Antarctica

ISLANDS OF THE INDIAN OCEAN

Madagascar & Comoros • Maldives & Islands of the East Indian Ocean • Mauritius, Réunion & Seychelles

AFRICA

Arabic (Moroccan) phrasebook • Africa on a shoestring • Cape Town • Central Africa • East Africa • Egypt • Egypt travel atlas • Ethiopian (Amharic) phrasebook • Kenya • Kenya travel atlas • Morocco • North Africa • South Africa, Lesotho & Swaziland • South Africa, Lesotho & Swaziland travel atlas • Swahili phrasebook • Trekking in East Africa • West Africa • Zimbabwe, Botswana & Namibia • Zimbabwe, Botswana & Namibia travel atlas

Travel Literature: The Rainbird: A Central African Journey • Songs to an African Sunset: A Zimbabwean Story

MAIL ORDER

nely Planet products are distributed worldwide. They are also available by mail order from Lonely
.net, so if you have difficulty finding a title please write to us. North American and South American
idents should write to Embarcadero West, 155 Filbert St, Suite 251, Oakland CA 94607, USA;
ropean and African residents should write to 10 Barley Mow Passage, Chiswick, London W4 4PH;
d residents of other countries to PO Box 617, Hawthorn, Victoria 3122, Australia.

RTH-EAST ASIA

jing • Cantonese phrasebook • China • Hong Kong,
cau & Guangzhou • Hong Kong • Japan • Japanese
asebook • Japanese audio pack • Korea • Korean
asebook • Mandarin phrasebook • Mongolia • Mon-
ian phrasebook • North-East Asia on a shoestring •
oul • Taiwan • Tibet • Tibet phrasebook • Tokyo

vel Literature: Lost Japan

DDLE EAST & CENTRAL ASIA

ib Gulf States • Arabic (Egyptian) phrasebook • Central
a • Iran • Israel & the Palestinian Territories • Israel &
Palestinian Territories travel atlas • Istanbul •
usalem • Jordan & Syria • Jordan, Syria & Lebanon
vel atlas • Middle East • Turkey • Turkish phrasebook •
men

avel Literature: The Gates of Damascus • Kingdom of

SO AVAILABLE:

avel with Children • Traveller's Tales

INDIAN SUBCONTINENT

Bangladesh • Bengali phrasebook • Delhi • Hindi/Urdu
phrasebook • India • India & Bangladesh travel atlas •
Indian Himalaya • Karakoram Highway • Nepal • Nepali
phrasebook • Pakistan • Rajasthan • Sri Lanka • Sri Lanka
phrasebook • Trekking in the Indian Himalaya • Trekking
in the Karakoram & Hindukush • Trekking in the Nepal
Himalaya

Travel Literature: In Rajasthan • Shopping for Buddhas

SOUTH-EAST ASIA

Bali & Lombok • Bangkok • Burmese phrasebook • Cam-
bodia • Ho Chi Minh City • Indonesia • Indonesian
phrasebook • Indonesian audio pack • Jakarta • Java •
Laos • Lao phrasebook • Laos travel atlas • Malay
phrasebook • Malaysia, Singapore & Brunei • Myanmar
(Burma) • Philippines • Pilipino phrasebook • Singapore •
South-East Asia on a shoestring • South-East Asia
phrasebook • Thailand • Thailand travel atlas • Thai
phrasebook • Thai audio pack • Thai Hill Tribes
phrasebook • Vietnam • Vietnamese phrasebook • Vietnam travel atlas

AUSTRALIA & THE PACIFIC

Australia • Australian phrasebook • Bushwalking in
Australia • Bushwalking in Papua New Guinea • Fiji •
Fijian phrasebook • Islands of Australia's Great Barrier
Reef • Melbourne • Micronesia • New Caledonia • New
South Wales & the ACT • New Zealand • Northern Ter-
ritory • Outback Australia • Papua New Guinea • Papua
New Guinea phrasebook • Queensland • Rarotonga & the
Cook Islands • Samoa • Solomon Islands • South Australia
• Sydney • Tahiti & French Polynesia • Tasmania • Tonga
• Tramping in New Zealand • Vanuatu • Victoria • Western
Australia

Travel Literature: Islands in the Clouds • Sean & David's
Long Drive

THE LONELY PLANET STORY

Lonely Planet published its first book in 1973 in response to the numerous 'How did you do it?' questions Maureen a Tony Wheeler were asked after driving, bussing, hitching, sailing and railing their way from England to Australia.

Written at a kitchen table and hand collated, trimmed and stapled, *Across Asia on the Cheap* became an instant loc bestseller, inspiring thoughts of another book.

Eighteen months in South-East Asia resulted in their second guide, *South-East Asia on a shoestring*, which they put togeth in a backstreet Chinese hotel in Singapore in 1975. The 'yellow bible', as it quickly became known to backpackers arou the world, soon became *the* guide to the region. It has sold well over half a million copies and is now in its 8th edition, s retaining its familiar yellow cover.

Today there are over 180 titles, including travel guides, walking guides, language kits & phrasebooks, travel atlases and tra literature. The company is one of the largest travel publishers in the world. Although Lonely Planet initially specialised in guid to Asia, we now cover most regions of the world, including the Pacific, North America, South America, Africa, the Middle East ar Europe.

The emphasis continues to be on travel for independent travellers. Tony and Maureen still travel for several months of ead year and play an active part in the writing, updating and quality control of Lonely Planet's guides.

They have been joined by over 70 authors and 170 staff at our offices in Melbourne (Australia), Oakland (USA), Londc (UK) and Paris (France). Travellers themselves also make a valuable contribution to the guides through the feedback w receive in thousands of letters each year.

The people at Lonely Planet strongly believe that travellers can make a positive contribution to the countries they visit, bo through their appreciation of the countries' culture, wildlife and natural features, and through the money they spend. addition, the company makes a direct contribution to the countries and regions it covers. Since 1986 a percentage of th income from each book has been donated to ventures such as famine relief in Africa; aid projects in India; agricultur projects in Central America; Greenpeace's efforts to halt French nuclear testing in the Pacific; and Amnesty Internationa

'I hope we send the people out with the right attitude about travel. You realise when you travel that there are s many different perspectives about the world, so we hope these books will make people more interested in wh they see. These are guidebooks, but you can't really guide people. All you can do is point them in the right directior
– Tony Wheele

LONELY PLANET PUBLICATIONS

Australia
PO Box 617, Hawthorn 3122, Victoria
tel: (03) 9819 1877 fax: (03) 9819 6459
e-mail: talk2us@lonelyplanet.com.au

USA
Embarcadero West, 155 Filbert St, Suite 251,
Oakland, CA 94607
tel: (510) 893 8555 TOLL FREE: 800 275-8555
fax: (510) 893 8563
e-mail: info@lonelyplanet.com

UK
10 Barley Mow Passage, Chiswick,
London W4 4PH
tel: (0181) 742 3161 fax: (0181) 742 2772
e-mail: 100413.3551@compuserve.com

France:
71 bis rue du Cardinal Lemoine, 75005 Paris
tel: 1 44 32 06 20 fax: 1 46 34 72 55
e-mail: 100560.415@compuserve.com

World Wide Web: http://www.lonelyplanet.com